International Encyclopedia of the
Social Sciences, 2nd edition

International Encyclopedia of the Social Sciences, 2nd edition

VOLUME 2
COHABITATION–ETHICS IN EXPERIMENTATION

William A. Darity Jr.
EDITOR IN CHIEF

MACMILLAN REFERENCE USA
A part of Gale, Cengage Learning

GALE
CENGAGE Learning

Detroit • New York • San Francisco • New Haven, Conn • Waterville, Maine • London

International Encyclopedia of the Social Sciences, 2nd edition

William A. Darity Jr., Editor in Chief

LIBRARY OF CONGRESS CATALOGING-IN-PUBLICATION DATA

International encyclopedia of the social sciences / William A. Darity, Jr., editor in chief.—2nd ed. v. cm. Rev. ed. of: International encyclopedia of the social sciences / David L. Sills, editor. c1968–c1991.
   Includes bibliographical references and index.
   ISBN 978-0-02-865965-7 (set hardcover : alk. paper)—ISBN 978-0-02-865966-4 (v. 1 hardcover : alk. paper)—ISBN 978-0-02-865967-1 (v. 2 hardcover : alk. paper)—ISBN 978-0-02-865968-8 (v. 3 hardcover : alk. paper)—ISBN 978-0-02-865969-5 (v. 4 hardcover : alk. paper)—ISBN 978-0-02-865970-1 (v. 5 hardcover : alk. paper)—ISBN 978-0-02-865971-8 (v. 6 hardcover : alk. paper)—ISBN 978-0-02-865972-5 (v. 7 hardcover : alk. paper)—ISBN 978-0-02-865973-2 (v. 8 hardcover : alk. paper)—ISBN 978-0-02-866141-4 (v. 9 hardcover : alk. paper)—ISBN 978-0-02-866117-9 (ebook : alk. paper)
   1. Social sciences—Dictionaries. 2. Social sciences—Encyclopedias. I. Darity, William A., 1953– II. Title: Encyclopedia of the social sciences.
   H40.A2I5 2008
   300.3–dc22

2007031829

0-02-865965-1 (set)
0-02-865966-X (v. 1)
0-02-865967-8 (v. 2)
0-02-865968-6 (v. 3)
0-02-865969-4 (v. 4)
0-02-865970-8 (v. 5)
0-02-865971-6 (v. 6)
0-02-865972-4 (v. 7)
0-02-865973-2 (v. 8)
0-02-866141-9 (v. 9)

This title is also available as an e-book.
ISBN 978-0-02-866117-9; 0-02-866117-6
Contact your Gale representative for ordering information.

Printed in the United States of America
3 4 5 6 7 8 14 13 12 11 10 09 08

Editorial Board

Contents

Contents

C

COGNITIVE DISTORTIONS

SEE *Psychotherapy.*

COGNITIVE MATRIX

SEE *Rituals.*

COHABITATION

Cohabitation is defined as a situation in which opposite-sex couples live together outside of marriage. Much of the literature on cohabitation is derived from research findings by sociologists and psychologists, which places this literature in a central position within the social sciences. This entry provides a brief discussion of who cohabits, why people choose to cohabit, and the consequences of cohabitation for couples, children, and society.

Cohabitation has become increasingly popular since the 1960s, with the majority of young adults in the United States experiencing cohabitation. For most couples, this is a relatively short-term experience, with only one-third of American couples cohabiting for at least two years and only 10 percent doing so for at least five years. About 60 percent of these unions eventually result in marriage. In 2007 nearly five million opposite-sex couples in the United States were living together outside of marriage, largely without legal protections, which is particularly

problematic for female cohabitants. This compares to 500,000 cohabiting couples in 1970.

This growing popularity of cohabitation has resulted in a concern among some observers that the practice presents a challenge to marriage as a method of coupling. They argue that marriage is being redefined as one of several choices. The literature suggests that for older cohabitants and for African American couples this lifestyle choice does represent an alternative to marriage. For most Americans, however, marriage remains the primary choice for coupling. Cohabitation is increasingly viewed as a transitional stage between single life and marriage, rather than as an alternative to marriage. Unlike in the United States, however, cohabitation is a significant alternative to marriage for young Scandinavian couples. In addition, increasing economic inequality in the United States is decreasing the opportunities for marriage among less-affluent Americans.

The most commonly cited reasons for moving in together are romance, convenience, the need for housing, and the chance to save money. How well do cohabitants get along with each other? Recent research has found that cohabiting couples are significantly less satisfied in their unions than those who are legally married. This is due, in part, to the fact that cohabiting couples often have more precarious economic circumstances than do married couples. In addition, the presence of children, which reduces satisfaction levels for both married and cohabiting couples, has a more profound effect on nonmarital unions. This is significant in that children are present for 40 percent of cohabiting couples. Further, it is widely assumed that the outcomes are worse for children raised by cohabiting couples, as opposed to children raised by married parents.

Lastly, does living with one's partner prior to marriage increase the likelihood of success after marriage? Couples who move in together before marriage have up to two times the odds of divorce compared to those couples who do not live together prior to marriage (Blackwell and Lichter 2000). Some argue that living together creates social pressure to get married, which can contribute to poor mate selection.

SEE ALSO *Family; Marriage*

BIBLIOGRAPHY

Blackwell, Debra L., and Daniel T. Lichter. 2000. Mate Selection among Married and Cohabiting Couples. *Journal of Family Issues* 21 (3): 275–302.

Willetts, Marion C. 2006. Union Quality Comparisons Between Long-Term Heterosexual Cohabitation and Legal Marriage. *Journal of Family Issues* 27 (1): 110–127.

Paul R. Newcomb

COHORT EFFECTS
SEE *Period Effects.*

COINCIDENT INDICATORS
SEE *Lagging, Leading, and Coincident Indicators.*

COINTEGRATION

Time-series data consist of multiple observations of firms, households, persons, or other entities over several time periods. Many economic time series have empirical distributions that are nonconstant over time, with changing means and variances, making these series nonstationary. Stochastic trends occur when there are persistent long-term movements in time series data; and such trends represent a major source of nonstationarity, causing variables to drift over time. Series with stochastic trends are thus called "integrated" or "unit-root" processes.

In 1982, Charles Nelson and Charles Plosser showed that, empirically, many macroeconomic time series appear to be integrated of order one [denoted I(1)]. Growth rates of these series do not tend to drift, which is consistent with the growth rates being nonintegrated, I.E., integrated of order zero [denoted I(0)]. Moreover, efficient-market theories in economics and finance suggest that asset and commodity prices follow a random walk, which is the simplest I(1) process.

Cointegration occurs when a relationship ties together nonstationary economic time series such that a combination of those time series is I(0). The concepts of integration and cointegration are intrinsically statistical in nature. Cointegration formalizes, in statistical terms, the property of a long-run relation between integrated economic variables.

SOME ECONOMIC IMPLICATIONS OF COINTEGRATION

While cointegration is a statistical concept, it has economic implications. For example, it plays important roles in five aspects of economics: (1) long-run relations, (2) agent optimization, (3) the problem of nonsense regressions, (4) equilibrium correction (or error correction) models (ECMs), and (5) economic forecasting.

First, cointegration embeds the economic notion of a long-run relationship between economic variables in a statistical model of those variables. If a long-run relation exists, then the variables are cointegrated.

Second, market forces or optimizing behavior often provide an economic rationale for cointegration. For instance, consumers' expenditure and income may be cointegrated because of economic agents' budget constraints or because of intertemporal optimization plans for lifetime saving.

Third, the statistical theory of unit-root processes aids inference about the empirical existence of cointegration. Econometric theory historically relied on the assumption of stationary data even though many observed economic time series were trending and nonstationary. Cointegration explicitly allows for nonstationarity, thus providing a sounder basis for empirical inference. Cointegration also clarifies the problem of nonsense regressions, in which intrinsically unrelated nonstationary time series are highly correlated with each other.

Fourth, cointegration implies, and is implied by, the existence of an equilibrium correction representation of the relevant variables. Cointegration thus solidifies the statistical and economic bases for the empirically successful class of equilibrium correction models, in which past disequilibria in levels have an effect on current changes in the variables. Through ECMs, cointegration provides a systematic framework for jointly analyzing short-run (e.g., cyclical) and long-run properties. This framework also resolves the debate on whether to model data in levels or in differences, with classical econometric models and George Box and Gwilym Jenkins's time-series models both being special cases of ECMs.

Fifth, optimal forecasts of cointegrated variables are themselves cointegrated. Hence, the existence of cointegration may improve the long-term forecasting of economic time series.

HISTORY

The history of cointegration was examined by David Hendry in "The Nobel Memorial Prize for Clive W. J. Granger" (2004). Hendry and Mary Morgan, in *The Foundations of Econometric Analysis* (1995), highlight the following events in that history. In 1901, R. H. Hooker illustrated and analyzed the difficulties attendant to nonstationarity, which he viewed as "common trends." In 1926, G. Udny Yule showed that I(1) and I(2) observations would generate "nonsense correlations"; for example, high correlations lacking causal explanation, such as between church marriages and mortality rates. In 1974, Clive Granger and Paul Newbold reemphasized the dangers of nonsense correlations, and Peter Phillips presented a formal analysis in 1986, which he updated in 1998. Klein's great ratios of economics (e.g., of consumption to income) suggested that variables' levels can be closely related. J. Denis Sargan established the link between static-equilibrium economic theory and ECMs in 1964. In the 1980s, Granger and Robert Engle developed cointegration analysis as such.

MODEL SPECIFICATION

In 1987, Engle and Granger established an isomorphism between cointegration and ECMs. Cointegration entails, and is entailed by, an ECM, which explicitly embeds a steady-state solution for its variables, while also allowing them to deviate from that steady state in the short run. In a nonstochastic steady state, an equilibrium relation would typically be motivated by economic theory. Hence, economic hypotheses are testable in a cointegration framework. In empirical work, conditional ECMs have been popular and may be interpretable as agents' contingent plans. Applications include wages and prices, consumers' expenditure, and money demand.

TESTING FOR INTEGRATION AND COINTEGRATION

Cointegration makes the economic concept of equilibrium operational; that is, data allow tests of whether a long-run relation holds. With suitable tests, asymptotically correct inferences can be obtained. In addition, spurious regressions can be detected and avoided, as can

unbalanced regressions involving variables of different orders of integration.

Economic theory rarely specifies orders of integration for variables, so a practitioner must analyze the data for both integration and cointegration. While the presence of unit roots complicates inference because some associated limiting distributions are nonstandard, critical values have been tabulated for many common cases. David Dickey and Wayne Fuller calculated critical values of tests for unit roots in univariate processes, and many robust unit-root tests have subsequently been developed.

Numerous cointegration tests have also been designed. In 1987, Engle and Granger proposed a single-equation approach that is intuitive and easy to implement, though it includes nuisance parameters in inference and may lack power (see Hendry 1986). A test of cointegration is also feasible in the corresponding ECM (see Neil Ericsson and James MacKinnon 2002).

Søren Johansen has provided a system-based approach in which cointegration relations are estimated via maximum likelihood in a vector autoregression (VAR). Johansen's test statistics for cointegration generalize the Dickey-Fuller statistic to the multivariate context. Several authors have tabulated critical values, which are also embodied in software such as Cats for Rats and PcGive. In Johansen's framework, hypotheses about cointegration properties are also testable. For instance, testing the long-run homogeneity of money with respect to prices is equivalent to testing whether the logs of money and prices are cointegrated with a unit coefficient. Other hypotheses, such as weak exogeneity, can be tested in Johansen's framework as well. Weak exogeneity is satisfied if the cointegrating vector entering the conditional model does not appear in the marginal model of the conditioning variables. Under weak exogeneity, inference on those parameters from the conditional model alone is without loss of information relative to inference in the complete system.

In summary, cointegration and equilibrium correction help us understand short-run and long-run properties of economic data, and they provide a framework for testing economic hypotheses about growth and fluctuations. At the outset of an empirical investigation, economic time series should be analyzed for integration and cointegration, and tests are readily available to do so. Such analyses can aid in the interpretation of subsequent results and may suggest possible modeling strategies and specifications that are consistent with the data, while also reducing the risk of spurious regressions.

BIBLIOGRAPHY

Banerjee, Anindya, Juan J. Dolado, John W. Galbraith, and David F. Hendry. 1993. *Co-integration, Error Correction, and the Econometric Analysis of Nonstationary Data.* Oxford: Oxford University Press.

Davidson, James E. H., David F. Hendry, Frank Srba, and Stephen Yeo. 1978. Econometric Modelling of the Aggregate Time-Series Relationship Between Consumers' Expenditure and Income in the United Kingdom. *Economic Journal* 88 (352): 661–692.

Dickey, David A., and Wayne A. Fuller. 1979. Distribution of the Estimators for Autoregressive Time Series with a Unit Root. *Journal of the American Statistical Association* 74 (366): 427–431.

Dickey, David A., and Wayne A. Fuller. 1981. Likelihood Ratio Statistics for Autoregressive Time Series with a Unit Root. *Econometrica* 49 (4): 1057–1072.

Engle, Robert F., and Clive W. J. Granger. 1987. Co-integration and Error Correction: Representation, Estimation, and Testing. *Econometrica* 55 (2): 251–276.

Ericsson, Neil R. 1992. Cointegration, Exogeneity, and Policy Analysis: An Overview. *Journal of Policy Modeling* 14 (3): 251–280.

Ericsson, Neil R., and James G. MacKinnon, 2002. Distributions of Error Correction Tests for Cointegration. *Econometrics Journal* 5 (2): 285–318.

Granger, Clive W. J. 1981. Some Properties of Time Series Data and Their Use in Econometric Model Specification. *Journal of Econometrics* 16 (1): 121–130.

Granger, Clive W. J. 1986. Developments in the Study of Cointegrated Economic Variables. *Oxford Bulletin of Economics and Statistics* 48 (3): 213–228.

Granger, Clive W. J., and Paul Newbold. 1974. Spurious Regressions in Econometrics. *Journal of Econometrics* 2 (2): 111–120.

Hendry, David F. 1986. Econometric Modelling with Cointegrated Variables: An Overview. *Oxford Bulletin of Economics and Statistics* 48 (3) 201–212.

Hendry, David F. 1995. *Dynamic Econometrics.* Oxford: Oxford University Press.

Hendry, David F. 2004. The Nobel Memorial Prize for Clive W. J. Granger. *Scandinavian Journal of Economics* 106 (2): 187–213.

Hendry, David F., and Katarina Juselius. 2001. Explaining Cointegration Analysis: Part II. *Energy Journal* 22 (1): 75–120.

Hendry, David F., and Mary S. Morgan, eds. 1995. *The Foundations of Econometric Analysis.* Cambridge, UK: Cambridge University Press.

Hooker, R. H. 1901. Correlation of the Marriage-Rate with Trade. *Journal of the Royal Statistical Society* 64 (3): 485–492.

Johansen, Søren. 1988. Statistical Analysis of Cointegration Vectors. *Journal of Economic Dynamics and Control* 12 (2/3): 231–254.

Johansen, Søren. 1995. *Likelihood-Based Inference in Cointegrated Vector Autoregressive Models.* Oxford: Oxford University Press.

Klein, Lawrence R. 1953. *A Textbook of Econometrics.* Evanston, IL: Row, Peterson.

Nelson, Charles R., and Charles I. Plosser. 1982. Trends and Random Walks in Macroeconomic Time Series: Some

Evidence and Implications. *Journal of Monetary Economics* 10 (2): 139–162.

Phillips, Peter C. B. 1986. Understanding Spurious Regressions in Econometrics. *Journal of Econometrics* 33 (3): 311–340.

Phillips, Peter C. B. 1991. Optimal Inference in Cointegrated Systems. *Econometrica* 59 (2): 283–306.

Phillips, Peter C. B. 1998. New Tools for Understanding Spurious Regressions. *Econometrica* 66 (6): 1299–1325.

Sargan, J. Denis. 1964. Wages and Prices in the United Kingdom: A Study in Econometric Methodology. In *Econometric Analysis for National Economic Planning*, Vol. 16 of Colston Papers, eds. P. E. Hart, G. Mills, and J. K. Whitaker, 25–54, with discussion. London: Butterworths.

Yule, G. Udny. 1926. Why Do We Sometimes Get Nonsense Correlations Between Time Series?—A Study in Sampling and the Nature of Time Series. *Journal of the Royal Statistical Society* 89 (1): 1–64.

Neil R. Ericsson
David F. Hendry

COLD WAR

The term *cold war* generally refers to the post–World War II global geostrategic, economic, and ideological competition between the East, led by the Soviet Union, and the West, led by the United States. Although there is no real agreement on the beginning of the cold war, its onset is often associated with the Yalta Conference in February 1945, when the United States, the United Kingdom, and the Soviet Union (led by Franklin D. Roosevelt, Winston Churchill, and Joseph Stalin, respectively) met to discuss the war in the Pacific and the postwar division of Germany. The term itself denotes the absence of direct armed conflict, but this period was characterized by mutual perceptions of hostile intentions between the U.S. and Soviet military-political alliances. The competition between East and West, which lasted from 1947 until 1991, vacillated between confrontation and cooperation. Stalin's refusal to honor an agreement to support democratic elections in Eastern Europe ultimately became a critical factor in East-West relations (see Schlesinger 1971). The end of World War II ushered in a bipolar, global balance of power, which rendered the once dominant powers of Europe militarily, economically, and psychologically dependent of the United States. This was due, in part, to the perceived menacing presence of the Soviet Union. The policy of containment, then, became the cornerstone of U.S. national security during the cold war years.

The dissolution of the European colonial empires provided the arena in which the two superpowers played upon each other's fears and competed for influence.

Competing across an ideological divide symbolized by the "Iron Curtain," they sought allies, trading partners, military bases, strategic minerals, and investment opportunities in Asian, African, Middle Eastern, and Latin American countries. Diplomatic maneuvering, economic pressure, selective aid, intimidation, propaganda, assassinations, low-intensity military operations, and full-scale proxy wars were used as instruments of influence and control from about 1947 until the decline of the Warsaw Pact (the Communist bloc of nations, led by the Soviet Union) in the late 1980s.

There are also variations in the intensity of the cold war relations that can be tied to changes in U.S. and Soviet political leadership. A slight weakening of hostilities following Stalin's death in 1953 was followed by escalating tensions following the Soviet launch of the Sputnik satellite in 1957, the erection of the Berlin Wall and the failed U.S. Bay of Pigs Invasion in 1961, and the Cuban Missile Crisis of 1962. Tension eased a bit with signing of the Nuclear Test-Ban Treaty in 1963, but Leonid Brezhnev's consolidation of power in the Soviet Union contributed to growing hostilities, which waned again in the 1970s during the era of détente and the Strategic Arms Limitation Talks (SALT I) Agreement.

The cold war also witnessed the largest arms race in history, leading to widespread global fears of a potential nuclear war (see Clausen 1993). The nuclear arms race, which began after the Korean War, was influenced by the actions and perceptions of both U.S. president John F. Kennedy and Soviet premier Nikita Khrushchev. Although the arms race made the policy of deterrence credible, it was very costly for both sides. In fact, the theory of mutual assured destruction (MAD) led to the militarization of both the United States and Soviet Union. Mikhail Gorbachev's ascension to power in the 1980s, however, paved the way for future reductions in nuclear weapons and improved U.S.-Soviet relations.

SEE ALSO *Arms Control and Arms Race; Bay of Pigs; Berlin Wall; Communism; Cuban Missile Crisis; Deterrence; Deterrence, Mutual; Gorbachev, Mikhail; Iron Curtain; Proliferation, Nuclear; Reagan, Ronald; Stalin, Joseph; Warsaw Pact; World War II*

BIBLIOGRAPHY

Clausen, Peter A. 1993. *Nonproliferation and the National Interest: America's Response to the Spread of Nuclear Weapons.* New York: HarperCollins.

Kegley, Charles, Jr., and Eugene R. Wittkopf. 1996. *American Foreign Policy: Pattern and Process*, 5th ed. New York: St. Martin's.

Parenti, Michael. 1989. *The Sword and the Dollar: Imperialism, Revolution, and the Arms Race.* New York: St. Martin's.

Patterson, Thomas G. 1992. *On Every Front: The Making and Unmaking of the Cold War*, rev. ed. New York: W.W. Norton.

Rourke, John T. 1993. Evolution of the World Political System. In *International Politics on the World Stage*, 4th ed., ed. John T. Rourke, 32–55. Guilford, CT: Dushkin Publishing Group, 1993.

Rubinstein, Alvin Z. 1992. *Soviet Foreign Policy since World War II: Imperial and Global*, 4th ed. New York: HarperCollins.

Schlesinger, Arthur. 1971. Origins of the Cold War. In *The Conduct of Soviet Foreign Policy*, ed. Erik P. Hoffman and Frederick J. Fleron Jr., 228–254. Chicago: Aldine.

Kathie Stromile Golden

COLEMAN, JAMES

SEE *Education, Unequal.*

COLLECTIVE ACTION

The logic of collective action (Olson 1965), which has proved to be applicable to a broad range of social and economic situations, assumes that cooperation must be explained by the individual's cost-benefit calculus rather than that of the group because the group as a whole is not rational but can only consist of rational individuals. Groups often seek public goods that are available, once they have been generated, to everyone, including those who did not contribute to producing them. Because individuals potentially can receive the benefits of public goods without having contributed to their production, they have an incentive to let others pay for them.

In classic examples of collective action problems, such as preserving the environment, sharing a natural resource, participating in national defense, voting in mass elections, and engaging in social protests, group members gain when all individuals do their share, but for any individual the marginal benefit of contributing exceeds the cost. If each individual follows his or her self-interest, the outcome—total defection—is worse for everyone than if all had cooperated in supplying the public good. Studies of collective action using game theory, laboratory experiments, and historical cases have been used to identify the conditions under which rational actors are likely to cooperate when they have a strong incentive to be free riders.

Many groups alter cost-benefit calculations by offering selective incentives in the form of material rewards to cooperators and punishments to free riders. Shame, praise, honor, and ostracism can be viewed in this regard as nonmaterial social selective incentives. The administration of a system of selective incentives by a central authority or by group members, however, usually entails a separate collective action problem that requires further explanation because individuals have an incentive not to contribute to the maintenance of such a system.

Another potential selective incentive is the psychological or expressive benefit inherent in the activity. In this case the motivation for cooperation is not the outcome sought through collective action but the process or experience of participation. For some people, political and organizational activity builds self-esteem and feelings of political efficacy, symbolizes political citizenship, reinforces moral convictions, and constitutes an enthralling experience.

Aside from changing individual incentives, cooperation in groups can be fostered by repeated social interactions that introduce long-term calculations. In iterated social interaction, a person can try to influence the behavior of others by making his or her choices contingent on their earlier choices. Cooperation is therefore possible among self-interested individuals if they care sufficiently about future payoffs to modify their current behavior.

Conditional cooperation is less likely to solve the collective action problem as group size increases because defection is harder to identify and deter when many people are involved. Intuitively the members of small groups are likely to have closer personal bonds, individual contributions will have a greater impact on the likelihood of collective success, and individual defections can be observed more readily. For this reason contingent cooperation in large-scale ventures is facilitated when collective action entails a federated network of community groups and organizations.

There is no reason to suppose that successful collective action can be driven by a single motivation, either coercive or voluntary. Self-interested calculations that are based on selective material incentives and ongoing social exchange often have to be supplemented by moral and psychological considerations and coordinated by political leadership to motivate people to contribute to collective goods. Also it is not necessary to assume that all contributors to collective action will employ the same cost-benefit calculus. Collective action frequently relies on the initiative and sacrifice of committed leaders who supply information, resources, and monitoring and lay the foundation for subsequent conditional cooperation among more narrowly self-interested actors.

SEE ALSO *Cooperation; Cost-Benefit Analysis; Free Rider; Groups; Interest Groups and Interests; Mobilization; Public Goods; Rational Choice Theory; Tragedy of the Commons; Transaction Cost*

BIBLIOGRAPHY

Chong, Dennis. 1991. *Collective Action and the Civil Rights Movement.* Chicago: University of Chicago Press.

Hardin, Russell. 1982. *Collective Action.* Baltimore, MD: Johns Hopkins University Press.

Olson, Mancur. 1965. *The Logic of Collective Action: Public Goods and the Theory of Groups.* Cambridge, MA: Harvard University Press.

Taylor, Michael. 1987. *The Possibility of Cooperation.* New York: Cambridge University Press.

Dennis Chong

COLLECTIVE ACTION GAMES

A collective action problem arises when two or more individuals have the potential to jointly coordinate on some mutually beneficial action, but do not face the right incentives to act in this manner. Such situations are ubiquitous in economic and social life, and arise in the context of political mobilization, electoral turnout, pollution abatement, common property resource use, and the private provision of public goods such as irrigation systems, parks, and national defense.

Collective action problems are often modeled using the theory of games. A simple example is the *public goods game*, which has the following structure. Consider a group of n individuals, each of whom can either "contribute" or "not contribute" to the provision of a "public good." The private cost of contributing is c. Each individual's contribution results in a benefit b to *each* member of the group, including those who do not contribute. The aggregate benefits resulting from a contribution are therefore equal to nb. If $b < c < nb$, then the benefit to the group of a contribution exceeds the cost, but the benefits that accrue to the contributor are less than the cost. In this case, individuals who are unconcerned with the effects of their actions on others will fail to contribute, and if the entire group is composed of such individuals, no contributions will be observed. This is a worse outcome from the perspective of each individual than would arise if all were forced to contribute. Each member of the group can therefore benefit if, instead of being allowed to freely make their own choices, they were all subject to "mutual coercion, mutually agreed upon" (Hardin 1968, p. 1247).

When some individuals behave in a manner that is beneficial to the group while others choose in accordance with their private interests alone, the latter are sometimes referred to as *free riders*. There are several ways in which collective action problems may be mitigated through the punishment of free-riding behavior. If the group is sufficiently small and stable, and interactions among its members are repeated over a long horizon, actions that benefit the group can be sustained by the fear that an individual deviation will trigger deviations by others, resulting in the complete collapse of prosocial behavior. Alternatively, even if interactions are not repeated, collective action can be sustained if individuals have the ability and the inclination to impose direct punishments on each other for free riding. Experimental evidence suggests that many individuals do indeed have such preferences for "altruistic punishment," and that such propensities have played a key role historically in the sustainable management of common property resources.

The most common solution to collective action problems is through the intervention of a centralized authority that can set rules for behavior and impose sanctions on those who fail to comply. Sometimes these sanctions take the form of monetary fines, as in the case of tax evasion or the failure to meet pollution standards. In many instances, however, punishments can take the form of ostracism or expulsion, as in the case of clubs, trade unions, or political parties.

SEE ALSO *Common Knowledge Rationality Games; Evolutionary Games; Game Theory; Noncooperative Games; Screening and Signaling Theory Games; Strategic Games*

BIBLIOGRAPHY

Bergstrom, Ted C., Larry Blume, and Hal Varian. 1986. On the Private Provision of Public Goods. *Journal of Public Economics* 29: 25–49.

Fehr, Ernst, and Simon Gächter. 2000. Cooperation and Punishment in Public Goods Experiments. *American Economic Review* 90: 980–994.

Hardin, Garret. 1968. The Tragedy of the Commons. *Science* 162: 1243–1248.

Marwell, Gerald, and Ruth E. Ames. 1981. Economists Free Ride, Does Anyone Else? *Journal of Public Economics* 15: 295–310.

Olson, Mancur. 1965. *The Logic of Collective Action: Public Goods and the Theory of Groups.* Cambridge, MA: Harvard University Press.

Ostrom, Elinor. 1990. *Governing the Commons: The Evolution of Institutions for Collective Action.* Cambridge, MA: Cambridge University Press.

Sethi, Rajiv, and E. Somanathan. 1996. The Evolution of Social Norms in Common Property Resource Use. *American Economic Review* 86: 766–788.

Rajiv Sethi

COLLECTIVE MEMORY

Contemporary usage of the term *collective memory* is largely traceable to Émile Durkheim (1858–1917), who wrote extensively in *The Elementary Forms of the Religious Life* (1912) about commemorative rituals, and to his student, Maurice Halbwachs (1877–1945), who published a landmark study on *The Social Frameworks of Memory* in 1925. For Halbwachs, who accepted Durkheim's sociological critique of philosophy, studying memory is not a matter of reflecting on the properties of the subjective mind; rather, memory is a matter of how minds work together in society, how their operations are structured by social arrangements: "It is in society that people normally acquire their memories. It is also in society that they recall, recognize, and localize their memories" (Halbwachs 1992, p. 38). Halbwachs thus argued that it is impossible for individuals to remember in any coherent and persistent fashion outside of their group contexts. Group memberships provide the materials for memory and prod the individual into recalling particular events and into forgetting others. Groups can even produce memories in individuals of events that they never experienced in any direct sense. Halbwachs thus resisted the more extreme intuitionist subjectivism of philosopher Henri Bergson (1859–1941) (whose work had nevertheless led Halbwachs to his interest in memory), as well as the commonsense view of remembering as a purely—perhaps even quintessentially—individual affair.

In contrast to Halbwachs's discussion in *The Social Frameworks of Memory*, however—in which he argues that what individuals remember is determined by their group memberships but still takes place in their own minds—in *The Legendary Topography of the Holy Land* (1941) and elsewhere Halbwachs focused on publicly available commemorative symbols, rituals, and representations. This more Durkheimian discussion in turn undergirded Halbwachs's contrast between "history" and "collective memory" not as one between public and private but as one based on the relevance of the past to the present: Both history and collective memory are publicly available social facts—the former "dead," the latter "living." Halbwachs alternately referred to *autobiographical memory, historical memory, history,* and *collective memory.* Autobiographical memory is memory of those events that we ourselves experience (though those experiences are shaped by group memberships), while historical memory is memory that reaches us only through historical records. History is the remembered past to which we no longer have an "organic" relation—the past that is no longer an important part of our lives—while collective memory is the active past that forms our identities.

While rightly credited with establishing "collective memory" both as a concept and as a subject for sociological research, Halbwachs is far from the only scholar to have thought systematically about the (changing) relationship between the past and the present. Before Halbwachs, the German philosopher G. W. F. Hegel (1770–1831) had distinguished among original history (eyewitnessing and chronicling), reflective history (scientific), and philosophical history (teleological). Friedrich Nietzsche (1844–1900) in turn distinguished among antiquarian, monumental, and critical uses of the past.

In contemporary scholarship, the so-called history of mentalities has pursued a "collective psychology" approach to cultural history, seeing images of the past as part of "the whole complex of ideas, aspirations, and feelings which links together the members of a social group" (Goldmann 1964, p. 17), and thus forms an important topic for historical investigation. In Germany, many historians and social scientists have revived an older, philosophical concept of "historical consciousness" (*Geschichtsbewusstsein*) to guide analysis, linking it to concerns about "the politics of history" (*Geschichtspolitik*), which indicates both the role of history in politics and the role of politics in history. Yet another camp has employed the awkward yet insightful term *mnemohistory*, which "unlike history proper … is concerned not with the past as such, but only with the past as it is remembered" (Assmann 1997, p. 9). Mnemohistory thus calls for a theory of cultural transmission that helps us understand history not simply as one thing after another nor as a series of objective stages, but as an active process of meaning-making through time, "the ongoing work of reconstructive imagination" (Assmann 1997, p. 9). Yet another similar argument comes out of the hermeneutic tradition, particularly as articulated by German philosopher Hans-Georg Gadamer (1900–2002), in which the meaning of life can be found in our ongoing making and remaking of self-consciousness through interpretation without end.

No matter what the specific conceptualization, what may be called *social memory studies* (Olick and Robbins 1998) has become a prominent feature of scholarly discourse in recent decades, when Western societies in particular have been experiencing a sort of "memory boom" (Winter 2006). Indeed, explaining this boom has been an important topic for social memory studies. Scholars have variously sought to explain the rise of interest in the past, memory, commemoration, nostalgia, and history in contexts ranging from consumer promotions, popular culture, interior and exterior design, and public space, as well as the rise of reparations, apologies, and other forms of redress in domestic and international politics. Answers have included the decline of the nation-state as a carrier of identity, the end of faith in progress, the rise of multiculturalism, and postmodernity more generally. Most famously, and most generally, the French historian and editor Pierre Nora has claimed that we spend so much time thinking about the past because there is so little of it left: Where we earlier lived lives suffused with pastness—the continuities of habit and custom—we now live disconnected from our pasts, seeing ourselves as radically different than our forebears. In Nora's terms, where once we were immersed in *milieux de mémoire* (worlds of memory), we moderns now consciously cultivate *lieux de mémoire* (places of memory) because memory is now a special topic. In a related manner, the Marxist historian Eric Hobsbawm has distinguished between worlds of custom and worlds of "invented tradition." Since the late nineteenth century, not only have nation-states sought to shore up declining legitimacy by propagating fictional pasts and a sense of their institutions' ancientness, people have invented the very category of tradition (as opposed to custom): the idea of self-conscious adherence to past ways of acting (whether genuine or spurious) is itself a product of our distance from the past, which has come to be seen as "a foreign country" (Lowenthal 1985).

SEE ALSO *History, Social; Identity; Memory*

BIBLIOGRAPHY

Assmann, Jan. 1997. *Moses the Egyptian: The Memory of Egypt in Western Monotheism.* Cambridge, MA: Harvard University Press.

Gadamer, Hans-Georg, 1989. *Truth and Method.* 2nd ed. Trans. Joel Weinsheimer and Donald G. Marshall. New York: Crossroad.

Goldman, Lucien. 1964. *The Hidden God: Study of Tragic Vision in the Pensées of Pascal and the Tragedies of Ra.* Trans. Philip Thody. London: Routledge and Kegan Paul, and New York: Routledge.

Halbwachs, Maurice. 1992. *On Collective Memory.* Trans. and ed. Lewis A. Coser. Chicago: University of Chicago Press.

Hobsbawm, Eric, and Terence Ranger, eds. 1992. *The Invention of Tradition.* Cambridge, U.K. and New York: Cambridge University Press.

Lowenthal, David, 1985. *The Past is a Foreign Country.* Cambridge, U.K. and New York: Cambridge University Press.

Nora, Pierre. 1989. Between Memory and History: Les Lieux de Mémoire. *Representations* 26 (Spring): 7–25.

Olick, Jeffrey K., and Joyce Robbins. 1998. Social Memory Studies: From Collective Memory to the Historical Sociology of Mnemonic Practices. *Annual Review of Sociology* 24: 105–140.

Winter, Jay. 2006. *Remembering War: The Great War between Memory and History in the Twentieth Century.* New Haven, CT: Yale University Press.

Jeffrey K. Olick

COLLECTIVE WISDOM

The term *collective wisdom* refers to the notion that the totality of knowledge, experience, and skills possessed by the members of a group, whether large or small, typically exceeds that of any individual in the group, and that the members acting in concert are thus capable of judgments, problem-solving, and decision-making that will lead to better outcomes than one could expect of any one of them acting alone. Such a belief, in part, lies at the base of democratically organized groups, as well as larger, more complex social entities. It is also reflected in such popular expressions as, "Two heads are better than one."

The above presumptions have been objects of skepticism historically, as James Surowiecki (2004) has aptly illustrated in citing the less than charitable views of such notable figures as Henry David Thoreau, Thomas Carlyle, Gustave Le Bon, and Friedrich Nietzsche, all of whom took a dim view of the virtues of collective judgment and action. Surowiecki credits Carlyle, for example, with the observation, "I do not believe in the collective wisdom of individual ignorance" (p. xvi). The derogatory phrase "pooling of ignorance," which one frequently hears critics ascribe to group decision-making and problem-solving, clearly resonates with Carlyle's cynicism, as well as that of others.

Underlying the skepticism, unfortunately, is a misrepresentation of the concept. The notion of collective wisdom does not entail the presumption that informed thought, judicious choice, and effective action result in some magical, inexplicable way from the combination of individuals who are not singly capable of these things. Rather, it assumes that the knowledge, experience, and skills of those acting as an entity are often complementary, as well as compensatory. As a result, the entity enlarges its potential for effective judgment, choice, and action. The potential of the group, however, does not exceed the limits of its members. Hence, a group whose members, for instance, lack relevant task-related expertise and ability is not one we would expect to surpass the performance of a single individual who does, let alone a group whose members are all in possession of such expertise and ability. Indeed, evidence supports this presumption (see Beach and Connolly 2005; Shaw 1981).

Collective wisdom was the focus of a good deal of scholarly interest early in the history of social psychology and the concept has continued to attract attention. From the 1920s to well into the 1960s, much attention was paid to questions concerning the relative superiority/inferiority of individuals versus groups in respect to judgment (e.g., Jenness 1932), problem-solving (e.g., Davis and Restle 1963), and learning (e.g., Yuker 1955). Comparative inquiries provided reasonably substantial evidence in support of the presumptions associated with the concept of collective wisdom, as in many cases groups were revealed to make better judgments, show greater effectiveness in problem-solving, and experience larger gains in learning than individuals with whom they were compared. Other later evidence from research on brainstorming further indicated that groups are capable of generating more ideas, as well as a higher proportion of high-quality and novel ideas, than individuals acting alone. Such findings by no means have been unequivocal, however, especially in respect to brainstorming (see Beach and Connolly 2005, Frey 1997; Shaw 1981).

Determining reasons for the discrepancy between the potential collective wisdom affords and the observed performance of groups in particular has been a focus of at least three different areas of scholarly inquiry: diversity of membership, the influence of social variables, and, most recently, collective information-sampling bias. Each offers a different understanding of and insight into the reasons for the inconsistency.

The oldest of the areas of inquiry mentioned is that relating to diversity. Early research had as a focus similarities and differences among the members of groups, initially in respect to abilities and demographic characteristics and later on the basis of personality profiles. On the whole, heterogeneous groups have been found to outperform homogeneous groups (Frey 1997; Shaw 1981). One explanation for why groups do not consistently outperform individuals, then, is suggested by such outcomes. Specifically, groups whose members are too similar to one another have little potential for displaying collective wisdom that exceeds the abilities of any given individual member. Conversely, diversity, while often an asset to a group, can also be a source of disruption that impairs relationships among members and thereby impedes performance (Porter and Samovar 2003).

Social variables can also limit the potential for collective wisdom to operate consistently. This has been demonstrated by Irving Janis's studies (1972, 1982, 1989) of groupthink, its sources (such as pressure for uniformity, the desire to maintain a harmonious climate, and the undue influence of those in positions of authority), and the heuristics, or mental shortcuts, to which the members of groups often resort when under groupthink's influence. If the interaction among the members of such groups does not function to overcome the constraints that contribute to the abandonment of rational forms of judgment and choice, one cannot expect to see groups perform more effectively than individuals (Gouran and Hirokawa 1996, 2003). In fact, one would have reason to predict that such bodies might well perform less effectively.

Finally, and most recently, some scholars have begun to focus on an interesting phenomenon in group interaction that has further explanatory value in accounting for the inconsistently demonstrable superiority of groups as compared to individuals: collective information-processing bias (see Beach and Connolly 2005; Propp 1999; Stasser and Titus 1985). There has been much evidence of a tendency for the members of groups to focus in decision-making and problem-solving discussions on the information they all have in common rather than information they as individuals uniquely possess. Under these circumstances, there is no reason to expect that a group would be more likely to arrive at better decisions and more effective solutions to problems than the most knowledgeable, experienced, and able individual member.

In conclusion, scholarship has established through empirical evidence that collective wisdom is a property of groups. It is not, however, a property that universally enables a group to surpass the performance or exceed the wisdom of its most competent member. How well it functions to assist groups in maximizing their performance depends on the amount they possess, as well as the extent to which other counteracting variables become intrusive.

SEE ALSO *Attitudes; Attitudes, Political; Conformity; Decision-making; Democracy; Elitism; Groupthink; Knowledge; Nietzsche, Friedrich; Rational Choice Theory; Rationality; Social Judgment Theory; Social Psychology; Thoreau, Henry David*

BIBLIOGRAPHY

Beach, Lee Roy, and Terry Connolly. 2005. *The Psychology of Decision Making: People in Organizations.* 2nd ed. Thousand Oaks, CA: Sage.

Davis, James H., and Frank Restle. 1963. The Analysis of Problems and Prediction of Group Problem Solving. *Journal of Abnormal and Social Psychology* 66 (February): 103–116.

Frey, Lawrence R. 1997. Individuals in Groups. In *Managing Group Life: Communicating in Decision-Making Groups*, eds. Lawrence R. Frey and J. Kevin Barge, 52–79. Boston: Houghton Mifflin.

Gouran, Dennis S., and Randy Y. Hirokawa. 1996. Functional Theory and Communication in Decision-Making and Problem-Solving Groups: An Expanded View. In *Communication and Group Decision Making*, 2nd ed., eds. Randy Y. Hirokawa and Marshall Scott Poole, 55–80. Thousand Oaks, CA: Sage.

Gouran, Dennis S., and Randy Y. Hirokawa. 2003. Effective Decision Making and Problem Solving in Groups: A Functional Perspective. In *Small Group Communication Theory and Research: An Anthology*, 8th ed., eds. Randy Y. Hirokawa, Robert S. Cathcart, Larry A. Samovar, and Linda D. Henman, 27–38. Los Angeles: Roxbury.

Janis, Irving L. 1982. *Groupthink: Psychological Studies of Policy Decisions and Fiascoes.* 2nd rev. ed. Boston: Houghton Mifflin. Originally published as *Victims of Groupthink: A Psychological Study of Foreign Policy Decisions and Fiascoes* (Boston: Houghton Mifflin, 1972).

Janis, Irving L. 1989. *Crucial Decisions: Leadership in Policymaking and Crisis Management.* New York: Free Press.

Jenness, Arthur. 1932. The Role of Discussion in Changing Opinions Regarding a Matter of Fact. *Journal of Abnormal and Social Psychology* 27: 279–296.

Porter, Richard E., and Larry A. Samovar. 2003. Communication in the Multicultural Group. In *Small Group Communication Theory and Research: An Anthology*, 8th ed., eds. Randy Y. Hirokawa, Robert S. Cathcart, Larry A. Samovar, and Linda D. Henman, 230–238. Los Angeles: Roxbury.

Propp, Kathleen M. 1999. Collective Information Processing in Groups. In *The Handbook of Group Communication Theory and Research*, eds. Lawrence R. Frey, Dennis S. Gouran, and Marshall Scott Poole, 225–250. Thousand Oaks, CA: Sage.

Shaw, Marvin E. 1981. *Group Dynamics: The Psychology of Small Group Behavior.* 3rd ed. New York: McGraw-Hill.

Stasser, Garold, and William Titus. 1985. Pooling of Unshared Information in Group Decision Making: Biased Information Sampling during Discussion. *Journal of Personality and Social Psychology* 48 (6): 1467–1478.

Surowiecki, James. 2004. *The Wisdom of Crowds: Why the Many Are Smarter Than the Few and How Collective Wisdom Shapes Business, Economies, Societies, and Nations.* New York: Doubleday.

Yuker, Harold E. 1955. Group Atmosphere and Memory. *Journal of Abnormal and Social Psychology* 51 (1): 17–23.

Dennis S. Gouran

COLLECTIVISM

Collectivism is a term used to describe various social, political, and economic relations that stress the primacy of the collective, which may be a group of individuals, a society, a state, a nation, race, or social class, over that of the individual. Collectivists subscribe to the belief that the group's societal or communal "will" takes precedence over that of the individual, who must then sacrifice self-interest for the good of the whole. Thus the group is the fundamental unit of social, political, and economic concern.

From a social perspective, collectivism maintains that humans are interdependent and closely linked to one or more groups. This doctrine views group harmony and solidarity as more important than personal desires and goals. In this case, the group might take the form of a family, race, social class, or religious denomination. Thus, respectfulness, cooperation, and conformity to group norms are expected. Competition and conflict are devalued within the group but viewed as acceptable intergroup behaviors.

Politically, collectivism might be viewed as a doctrine that maintains that the "will" of the people supersedes that of the individual, who must subordinate personal interests to those of the majority. Thus society as a whole is the standard of moral value. An early example of this kind of collectivism has been associated with Jean-Jacques Rosseau's social contract. In this work, Rousseau posits that human society is organized along the lines of an implicit contract between members of society, with the terms of the contract, such governmental powers, citizens' rights and responsibilities, defined by the "general will." This notion of collectivism is often equated with democracy.

As an economic doctrine, collectivism holds that material resources should be owned by the group and used for the benefit of all rather than being owned by individuals. Although this view of collectivism advocates public over private ownership of property, the state is not necessarily the manager or overseer of collective property, as has been the case with most modern day manifestations of communism. It should also be noted that the principle of collective ownership of property might refer to the means of production or to all commodities that are valued.

While there are many examples of societies characterized as collectivist, few, if any, are entirely collectivist. Moreover, one can find characteristics of collectivism in most societies. Perhaps the best-known practical applications of collectivism are those associated with the agriculture sector of societies. Many of these attempts, however, have resulted in some well-documented failures. For example, the Soviet state's experiment with agricultural collectivization in the 1920s and 1930s was abandoned owing to negative economic consequences. Similarly, Operation Dodoma, which refers to Julius Nyerere's 1974 program of forced collectivization of farming in Tanzania, was largely unsuccessful as a means of increasing benefits perceived to accrue from collective farming. China's 1958 attempt at collectivization of agricultural production, though somewhat more successful than that of the Soviet Union and Tanzania, also failed to yield perceived economic benefits.

SEE ALSO *Agricultural Industry; Communalism; Communism; Democracy; Rousseau, Jean-Jacques; Social Contract; Socialism; Socialism, African; Stalin, Joseph; Union of Soviet Socialist Republics*

BIBLIOGRAPHY

Ayittey, George B. 1991. *Africa Betrayed.* New York: St. Martin's Press.

Gregory, Paul R., and Robert C. Stuart. 1981. *Soviet Economic Structure and Performance.* 2nd ed. New York: Harper and Row.

Inkeles, Alex. 1971. *Social Change in Soviet Russia.* New York: Simon and Schuster.

Spence, Jonathan. 1990. *The Search for Modern China.* New York: Norton.

Triandis, Harry C. 1995. *Individualism and Collectivism.* Boulder, CO: Westview.

Kathie Stromile Golden

COLLECTIVIZATION
SEE *Collectivism.*

COLLUSION
SEE *Competition, Imperfect.*

COLONIALISM
The matrix of structures, ideologies, and actions that have formed both historical and contemporary patterns of colonialism have shaped the world-system in irreversible and deeply influential ways. Serious consideration of colonialism recognizes that no matter where the starting point for analyzing colonialism is set, the process, structure, and lingering effects of such a geohistorical phenomenon cannot be grasped in a simplistic or one-dimensional way by either academics or those who continue to live colonized lives, for the implications of such naïveté are too severe. Numerous critical scholars—such as Edward Said, Gayatri Spivak, Ania Loomba, Samir Amin, Immanuel Wallerstein, and Wole Soyinka—have devoted their academic careers (which are often rooted in their lived experience within colonial rule and systemic colonial endeavors) to understanding the social, cultural, and political project that is colonialism. While the terms *colonialism, empire, imperialism,* and even *globalization* have been employed to describe analogous processes, the realities behind colonialism are complex and systematically, structurally, and culturally catastrophic for the colonized. Colonialism can be critically discussed through three primary lenses: (1) the colonialism project as a structure of domination subjugating one group of people to another across political entities; (2) internal or domestic colonialism as a similar structure occurring within a given nation-state, typically against socially marked groups; and (3) the colonialism of the mind, wherein the colonized are institutionally, pedagogically, linguistically, and cognitively conquered by the colonizer.

Most common definitions of colonialism describe a general process in which a nation-state expands its territory as well as its social, cultural, and political structures into extant territories beyond its own national boundaries. Most standard definitions also describe a process in which one power exerts and maintains control over what ultimately becomes a dependent area or people. Yet such definitions are deeply insufficient for critical scholars of history, sociology, literary theory, anthropology, and other areas of study. Indeed, colonialism is a geopolitical, sociocultural, linguistic, and hegemonic project of domination and oppression rooted in the racialized and gendered contracts emerging out of Europe in the fifteenth and sixteenth centuries (see Mills 1997; Pateman 1988). As a project of the European Enlightenment, colonialism is critically seen not as aberration but as a purposeful design intended to spread a hegemonic structure whereby one people ("whites") benefit from the exploitation and subjugation of another people ("nonwhites"). Colonialism is a form of systemic oppression and domination. The basic, descriptive form of colonization existed before the emergence a distinctly European, racist, hegemonic project (e.g., in the ancient empires of Egypt, Persia, Macedonia, Mongolia, China, and Central and South America). But while the processes of colonialism were of a radically different form, the consequences for those who were colonized in ancient times were as thorough and deep as they were for those colonized in Africa, India, Latin America, and other areas by Europeans in the eighteenth and nineteenth centuries. In the contemporary world, neocolonialism and imperialism often mirror earlier colonization efforts through complex and ultimately exploitative economic, military, political, social, and cultural processes. Many see such processes at work in various episodes of foreign intervention by the United States either directly (Grenada, Panama, Iraq) or indirectly (Chile, Cuba, Indonesia).

Understanding the oppressive and exploitative nature of colonialism in the world-system is crucial. However, solely attending to such processes across sociopolitical boundaries can divert critical awareness away from similar ideologies and structures of colonization within a given context. Indeed, similar processes and exploitative "contracts" have emerged within countries since the fifteenth century. In the U.S. context, several critical scholars (e.g., Andre Gunder Frank, Robert Blauner, Immanuel Wallerstein, Maulana Karenga, and Vine Deloria Jr.) have raised the question about whether groups such as African Americans and Native Americans represent internal colonies within the United States.

Questions surrounding internal or domestic colonization focus on the fulfillment of several social structural components, highlighting the internal relationships of colonialism between oppressor and oppressed. First, if a particular group is politically disenfranchised within their own country (e.g., through electoral structure or limited access to discourse or positions), then that group may be an oppressed internal colony. Second, if the group in question is economically disadvantaged and exploited within the society it calls home, then the group represents the possibility of domestic colonization. Third, when members of a group are occupationally subordinated through segregation, impeded structural access to opportunities, or de facto discrimination and racism (e.g., African Americans or Native Americans), they are internally colonized within a matrix of colonialism. Fourth, when individuals in an ethnic or minority group are sociopsychologically humiliated through media misrepresentation, decentering (objects of history, rather than subjects) in education, and interactional isolation, they are part of an internal colony. Finally, minority groups often become culturally manipulated and commodified within their own societies through the market, the media, and campaigns of fear and consumption, and this can lead to domestic colonization. States often utilize the tools of colonialism against people within their own borders to effectively create internal colonies.

As the social landscape is also reflected and embedded within our mental and cognitive landscapes, existence within a structure of colonialism can affect individual and collective repertoires of action, thought, belief, and behavior. Thus, another lens through which one can view colonialism is that of the colonization of cultural, ideological, and cognitive terrains. The political philosopher Frantz Fanon, who was born in the French colony of Martinique, illuminated such a form of colonialism through his critical, structural, and psychoanalytic analysis of colonization. Fanon and others identified a "colonization of the mind," an internalization of inferiority that persists long after colonial powers have physically left. While some authors have discussed the kind of moral and epistemological psychology needed for oppressors to engage in colonialism, writers from the Brazilian educator Paulo Freire to Fanon recognize that, in a system of colonialism, the oppressor, buttressed by the system and enjoying systemic privilege, maps systemic forms of domination within the minds of the oppressed that fundamentally alter strategies of resistance, protest, political opposition, and notions of individual and collective identities.

Colonialism, in the almost 600 years of its world-system domination, is a systemic, hegemonic, and totalizing form of oppression stemming from the project of European Enlightenment, and as such it has structured the world-system in favor of the West. While direct colonialism, through colonial rule, may eventually wither away through anticolonial movements and processes of "decolonization," the effects of such a system linger in the international relations, internal structures, and mental cartography of the colonized. Such a structure has proved not only catastrophic for the colonized, but also, as Freire would argue, for the colonizer as well.

SEE ALSO *Anticolonial Movements; Decolonization; Empire; Imperialism; Neocolonialism; Postcolonialism*

BIBLIOGRAPHY

Amin, Samir. 1973. *Neo-Colonialism in West Africa.* Trans. Francis McDonagh. New York: Monthly Review Press.

Blauner, Robert. 1972. *Racial Oppression in America.* New York: Harper and Row.

Chaterjee, Partha. 1993. *The Nation and Its Fragments: Colonial and Postcolonial Histories.* Princeton, NJ: Princeton University Press.

Chinweizu. 1983. *Toward the Decolonization of African Literature.* Washington, DC: Howard University Press.

Deloria, Vine, Jr. 1969. *Custer Died for Your Sins: An Indian Manifesto.* New York: Macmillan.

Fanon, Frantz. 1965. *The Wretched of the Earth.* Trans. Constance Farrington. New York: Grove Press.

Frank, Andre Gunder. 1975. *On Capitalist Underdevelopment.* New York: Oxford University Press.

Freire, Paolo. 1970. *Pedagogy of the Oppressed.* Trans. Myra Bergman Ramos. New York: Herder and Herder.

Karenga, Maulana. 1993. *Introduction to Black Studies.* 2nd. ed. Los Angeles: University of Sankore Press.

Loomba, Ania. 2005. *Colonialism/Postcolonialism.* 2nd ed. London: Routledge.

Mamdani, Mahmood. 1983. *Imperialism and Fascism in Uganda.* Nairobi: Heinemann Educational Books.

Mills, Charles. 1997. *The Racial Contract.* Ithaca, NY: Cornell University Press.

Nandy, Ashis. 1983. *The Intimate Enemy: Loss and Recovery of Self Under Colonialism.* Delhi, India: Oxford University Press.

Pateman, Carole. 1988. *The Sexual Contract.* Stanford, CA: Stanford University Press.

Prakash, Gyan, ed. 1995. *After Colonialism: Imperial Histories and Postcolonial Displacements.* Princeton, NJ: Princeton University Press.

Rodney, Walter. 1981. *How Europe Underdeveloped Africa.* Washington, DC: Howard University Press.

Said, Edward. 1978. *Orientalism.* New York: Pantheon Books.

Soyinka, Wole. 1976. *Myth, Literature, and the African World.* Cambridge, U.K.: Cambridge University Press.

Spivak, Gayatri Chakravorty. 1999. *A Critique of Postcolonial Reason: Toward a History of the Vanishing Present.* Cambridge, MA: Harvard University Press.

Wallerstein, Immanuel. 1974–1989. *The Modern World System.* 3 vols. New York: Academic Press.

Zerubavel, Eviatar. 2003. *Time Maps: Collective Memory and the Social Shape of the Past.* Chicago: University of Chicago Press.

David L. Brunsma

COLONY, INTERNAL

During the 1960s in the United States there arose, in response to the militancy of the urban black masses, and secondarily because of the black power movement, a bur-geoning, if unevenly sophisticated literature that defined the situation of the African population within U.S. borders as colonial. In *Black Power: The Politics of Liberation in America* (1967), Stokely Carmichael and Charles Hamilton argued that the black condition in the United States is essentially colonial, even if not perfectly analogous to classic colonialism in the sense that there is not a separation of territory and no exploitation of raw materials. Such distinctions, however, were merely technicalities, they asserted, because politically, economically, and socially the black community is directly controlled by predominantly white institutions, even if these institutions also make use of indirect rule. For Carmichael and Hamilton the key role for black people in the United States is as a source of cheap and unskilled labor. Captive black communities also provide merchants, creditors, real estate interests, and so on with a market for cheap and shoddy goods.

Another important exponent of the "internal colonialism" notion was Robert Allen, who argued that "Black America is an oppressed nation, a semi-colony of the United States" (Allen 1970, p. 1), and that the black freedom struggle should thus take the form of a national liberation movement. Unlike Carmichael and Hamilton, who considered the comparison with colonialism inexact, Allen sought to avoid the "lack of perfect fit" by aligning himself with the position taken by Jack O'Dell (1967). O'Dell argued that "it is the role of the institutional mechanisms of colonial domination which … [is] decisive. Territory is merely the stage upon which these historically developed mechanisms of super-exploitation are organized into a system of oppression" (p. 8). And thus for Allen, colonialism was the "direct and overall subordination of one people, nation, or country to another with state power in the hands of the dominating power" (Allen 1970, p. 8). Allen and others have argued that in the United States the urban rebellions of the 1960s gave rise to a more neocolonial form of control, utilizing indirect rule. Under this system, black power became black capitalism, and a black middle class, militant rhetoric and all, was allowed to get a larger piece of the pie for themselves.

Bob Blauner's theory of internal colonialism (1972) added additional elements that had not been clearly argued previously. Blauner contended that while the conditions of black people do not really fit the traditional criteria of colonialism, which imply the establishment of domination over a "geographically external political unit, most often inhabited by people of a different race and culture" (p. 83), a common *process* of social oppression characterizes race relations in both classical and internal colonialism, because both developed out of similar technological, cultural, and power relations. According to Blauner, colonial systems—including black internal colonialism—are defined by certain processes and characteristics:

1. the colonized's mode of entry into the dominant society, or into a relationship with the dominant society, is forced, not voluntary;

2. the indigenous values, orientations, and ways of life of the colonized are destroyed;

3. the colonized have a special relationship to the governing or legal order in which they view themselves as being managed and manipulated by outsiders;

4. the colonized are characterized as inferior on the basis of alleged biological characteristics, as part of a process of social domination by which they are exploited, controlled, and oppressed socially and psychically; and

5. a separation in labor status occurs between the colonized and the colonizers.

A less widely known, but nonetheless influential examination of internal colonialism, Harold Cruse's article "Revolutionary Nationalism and the Afro-American," was published in *Studies on the Left* in 1962. Cruse placed internal colonialism in a broader historical context than most of the more popular exponents of the theory. He argued that the black domestic colony should be seen as a part of the worldwide colonial empire established by Pan-European capitalism. While the United States did not establish a colonial empire in Africa, it brought African colonial subjects home and installed them within the Southern states. From that time, blacks have existed in a condition of domestic colonialism everywhere within the United States. Cruse views the colonial revolution against capitalism, rather than the Western workers movement, as the leading edge of the revolutionary struggle. Some early 1960s black radicals, such as the Revolutionary Action Movement, took up Cruse's position and circulated his article widely among other black radicals.

While most exponents of the internal colony theory have been political activists, the issue has also been taken up by some economists. William Tabb (1970) argued that there are two key relationships that must exist before the colonial analogy can be accepted: (1) economic control and exploitation, and (2) political dependence and subjugation. The maintenance of such relationships requires social separation and inferior status (p. 23). Tabb agreed with black radicals who argued that the spatial separation of colony from colonizer was secondary to the actuality of control from the outside. Bennett Harrison (1974) viewed the internal colony as a social entity similar to a " 'less developed country' with a severe 'balance of payments' deficit and with 'foreign' control of the most important

local political and economic institutions" (p. 4). While he rejected the internal colonialism model, Harrison nonetheless saw striking similarities between the structural dualism pervading so many of the least developed countries and the segmentation of the American economy into a growing "core" and ghetto "periphery" (p. 6). Barry Bluestone (1969) expressed a more nuanced view of the ghetto economy. Like W. E. B. Du Bois in the 1930s, he argued that through developing the inner city economy the black community could gain the strength to win concessions from the government and corporate elites.

Ron Bailey (1973) stressed the racial dimension of internal colonialism. Bailey held that "race has always been a significant and relatively independent force in shaping material reality in capitalist society" (p. 162). He is critical of conventional Marxist analysis, which has not accorded race its proper significance, and has overlooked the centrality of "internal colonialism as the domestic face of world imperialism and the racist conquest and exploitation of people of color by Europeans" (p. 162). Bailey traces the black internal colony to the enslavement of Africans in the Americas as part of a global capitalist world-system. For Bailey, the black internal colony is a reservoir of superexploited labor, relegated to the lowest-paid and least-desirable jobs, and also supplies a large pool of unemployed workers that facilitates the exploitation of noncolonized workers. It is a zone of dependent development locked in the logic of spiraling impoverishment, and an expendable buffer zone used to cushion the antagonism-producing operations of the American capitalist economy.

Bailey argued that relations of monopoly and dependency were at the heart of the economic domination of the black internal colony. The black internal colony is a zone of white control both internally and externally. Whites control and monopolize the mechanisms of production, exchange, and distribution, in addition to mechanisms of economic diversification (banks, credit, technology). This dependent position of the black internal colony is a by-product of capitalist growth *outside* of the colony. The enclave structure of the black community generates employment outside the black community while black labor goes unemployed (Bailey 1973, p. 175).

For Bailey, dependency theory offered a set of organizing ideas that clarified how the black internal colony is a consequence of a set of historical forces and structures that consign it to underdevelopment and dependence (Bailey 1973, p. 176). Bailey concluded that the essential role of the black internal colony is to insure the smooth functioning of the relations of production and exploitation and that to guarantee the continued existence of this system, tokenism is used to pacify the black bourgeoisie.

Writing with Guillermo Flores (1973), Bailey argued that despite the affluence and power of the United States, "racial minorities remain unconquered by policies of forced assimilation, acculturation, and cultural extermination" (p. 158). Colonized minorities within U.S. borders are distinct from their people of origin, but also from white society within the United States, where they are rejected by the society that they helped build. For Bailey and Flores, the "national liberation struggles of racial minorities within the U.S. are important negations of U.S. capitalist domination inside its borders and converge with and strengthen the national liberation struggles of other third world peoples" (Bailey and Flores 1973, p. 158).

During the 1960s many in the United States came to equate the "colonial question" with the "social question." This equation had been the basis of past coalitions, but there had also been controversy over which of the two was primary. The old Left had consistently argued for the leading role of the working class, but that position was forcefully challenged by the concept of internal colonialism during the concept's heyday. By the 1980s one rarely found authors who supported the concept. Both Robert Allen and Robert Blauner recanted and adopted more pragmatic positions, in line with a change in the relations of force in favor of the dominant strata within the United States and on a world scale. In 2005, however, Allen published a reassessment in which he reasserted many of his earlier views.

SEE ALSO *Black Middle Class; Black Power; Colonialism; Du Bois, W. E. B.; Slave Mode of Production; Slavery*

BIBLIOGRAPHY

Allen, Robert L. 1970. *Black Awakening in Capitalist America: An Analytic History.* Garden City, NY: Anchor Books.

Allen, Robert L. 1976. Racism and the Black Nation Thesis. *Socialist Revolution* 6 (1): 145–150.

Allen, Robert L. 2005. Reassessing the Internal (Neo) Colonialism Theory. *Black Scholar* 35 (1): 2–11.

Bailey, Ronald. 1973. Economic Aspects of the Black Internal Colony. In *Structures of Dependency*, eds. Frank Bonilla and Robert Henriques Girling, 161–188. Nairobi [East Palo Alto], CA: distributed by Nairobi Bookstore.

Bailey, Ronald, and Guillermo Flores. 1973. Internal Colonialism and Racial Minorities in the U.S.: An Overview. In *Structures of Dependency*, eds. Frank Bonilla and Robert Henriques Girling, 149–159. Nairobi [East Palo Alto], CA: distributed by Nairobi Bookstore.

Blauner, Bob. 1972. *Racial Oppression in America.* New York: Harper and Row.

Blauner, Bob. 1989. *Black Lives, White Lives: Three Decades of Race Relations in America.* Berkeley: University of California Press.

Blauner, Bob, Harold Cruse, Stephen Steinberg, et al. 1990. Race and Class: A Discussion. *New Politics* 2 (4): 12–58.

Bluestone, Barry. 1969. Black Capitalism: The Path to Black Liberation? *Review of Radical Political Economics* 1: 36–55.

Burawoy, Michael. 1974. Race, Class, and Colonialism. *Social and Economic Studies* 23 (4): 521–550.

Carmichael, Stokely, and Charles V. Hamilton. 1967. *Black Power: The Politics of Liberation in America.* New York: Random House.

Cruse, Harold. 1962. Revolutionary Nationalism and the Afro-American. *Studies on the Left* 2 (3): 12–25.

Harrison, Bennett. 1974. Ghetto Economic Development: A Survey. *Journal of Economic Literature* 12 (1): 1–37.

Hind, Robert J. 1984. The Internal Colonialism Concept. *Comparative Studies in Society and History* 26 (3): 543–568.

O'Dell, J. H. 1966. Colonialism and the Negro American Experience. *Freedomways* 6 (4): 296–308.

O'Dell, J. H. 1967. A Special Variety of Colonialism. *Freedomways* 7 (1): 7–15.

Tabb, William K. 1970. *The Political Economy of the Black Ghetto.* New York: W. W. Norton.

Roderick Bush

COLOREDS (SOUTH AFRICA)

Contrary to international usage, in South Africa the term *Colored* does not refer to black people in general. It instead alludes to a phenotypically varied social group of highly diverse cultural and geographic origins. The Colored people are descended largely from Cape slaves, the indigenous Khoisan population, and other black people who had been assimilated into Cape colonial society by the late nineteenth century. Because they are also partly descended from European settlers, Coloreds are popularly regarded as being of "mixed race" and have held an intermediate status in the South African racial hierarchy, distinct from the historically dominant white minority and the numerically preponderant African population.

There are approximately four million Colored people in South Africa today. Constituting no more than 9 percent of the population throughout the twentieth century and lacking significant political or economic power, Colored people have always formed a marginal group. There has, moreover, been a marked regional concentration of Colored people. Approximately 90 percent live within the western third of the country, more than two-thirds in the Western Cape, and over 40 percent in the greater Cape Town area.

ORIGINS OF COLORED IDENTITY

In the decades after the emancipation of the Khoisan in 1828 and of slaves in 1838 the heterogeneous black laboring class in the Cape Colony started developing an incipient shared identity based on a common socioeconomic status and a shared culture derived from their incorporation into the lower ranks of Cape colonial society. The emergence of a full-fledged Colored identity was precipitated in the late nineteenth century by the sweeping social changes that came in the wake of the mineral revolution that altered the social and economic landscape of the subcontinent. Significant numbers of Bantu-speaking Africans started going to the western Cape from the 1870s onward. Also, assimilated colonial blacks and a wide variety of Bantu-speaking African people who had recently been incorporated into the capitalist economy were thrust together in the highly competitive environment of the newly established mining towns. These developments drove acculturated colonial blacks to assert a separate identity as Colored people in order to claim a position of relative privilege in relation to Bantu-speaking Africans, on the basis of their assimilation into Western culture and their being partly descended from European colonists.

RACIAL DISCRIMINATION AGAINST COLOREDS

The most consistent feature of Colored political history until the latter phases of apartheid was the continual erosion of the civil rights first bestowed nonracially in the Cape Colony by the British administration in the mid-nineteenth century. The attrition started in the late nineteenth century with franchise restrictions aimed at black voters. In the first decade of the twentieth century Colored people were excluded from the franchise in the former Boer republics after the Anglo-Boer War and were denied the right to be elected to parliament with the creation of the South African state in 1910. In the 1920s and 1930s, the economic advancement of the Colored community was undermined by the government's "civilized labor" policy of hiring white workers at high wages in the public sector, as well as by laws designed to favor whites over blacks in the competition for employment in the private sector. Furthermore, in 1930 the influence of the Colored vote was more than halved when white women were enfranchised, and Colored and black women were not.

It was during the apartheid era, however, that Colored people suffered the most severe discrimination. Their forced classification under the Population Registration Act of 1950, which categorized all South Africans according to race, made the implementation of rigid segregation possible. The Prohibition of Mixed Marriages Act of 1949 and the Immorality Amendment Act of 1950 outlawed marriage and sex across the color line, respectively. Under the Group Areas Act of 1950, over half a million Colored people were forcibly relocated to racially exclusive residential areas on the periphery of cities and towns, and in 1953 the Separate Amenities Act segregated all public facilities, creating deep resentment. In 1956, moreover, after a protracted legal and constitutional battle, the National Party succeeded in removing Colored people from the common voter's roll.

COLORED POLITICAL ORGANIZATION

Although the earliest Colored political organizations date back to the 1880s, the first substantive Colored political body, the African Political Organization (APO), was established in Cape Town in 1902. Under the leadership of the charismatic Abdullah Abdurahman, who served as president from 1905 until his death in 1940, the APO dominated Colored protest politics for nearly four decades. Until its demise in the mid-1940s, it was the main vehicle for expressing this community's assimilationist aspirations as well as its fears at the rising tide of segregationism. The failure of the APO's moderate approach contributed to the emergence of a radical movement within the better-educated, urbanized sector of the Colored community during the 1930s. Prone to fissure and unable to bridge the racial divisions within South African society, the radical movement failed in its quest to unite blacks in the struggle against segregation. Organized opposition to apartheid from within the Colored community was quelled by state repression following the Sharpeville shooting of March 1960, which initiated a harsh crackdown on the extraparliamentary opposition by the apartheid state. Organized Colored resistance only reemerged in the wake of the Soweto uprising of 1976.

RECENT DEVELOPMENTS

From the latter half of the 1970s, with the popularization of black-consciousness ideology within the Colored community, the nature of Colored identity became contentious as growing numbers of politicized people who had been classified "Colored" rejected the classification. The Soweto revolt of 1976 greatly accelerated this trend because it fomented a climate of open resistance to apartheid and fostered a sense of black solidarity. Coloredness increasingly came to be viewed as an artificial categorization imposed on the society by the ruling minority as part of its divide-and-rule strategies. The burgeoning of the nonracial democratic movement in the 1980s under the leadership of the United Democratic Front fed Colored rejectionism.

In spite of this, the salience of Colored identity has endured. During the four-year transition to democratic rule under President de Klerk, political parties across the ideological spectrum sought support by making ever more strident appeals to Colored identity and postapartheid South Africa has witnessed a resurgence of Colored assertiveness. This has been due partly to a desire to project a positive self-image in the face of the pervasive negative racial stereotyping of Colored people and partly to attempts at ethnic mobilization to take advantage of the newly democratic political environment. It has also been motivated by a fear of African majority rule and the perception that, as in the old order, Coloreds were once again being marginalized. Though far from allayed, these anxieties have, in recent years, been alleviated by the fading influence of "black peril" tactics in South African politics and by the acclimatization of people to the new political order.

SEE ALSO *Apartheid; Inequality, Racial; Miscegenation; Mulattos; Sex, Interracial*

BIBLIOGRAPHY

Adhikari, Mohamed. 2005. *Not White Enough, Not Black Enough: Racial Identity in the South African Coloured Community.* Athens: Ohio University Press.

Erasmus, Zimitri. 2001. *Coloured by History, Shaped by Place: New Perspectives on Colored Identities in Cape Town.* Cape Town: Kwela Books.

Goldin, Ian. 1987. *Making Race: The Politics and Economics of Coloured Identity in South Africa.* Cape Town: Maskew Miller Longman.

Lewis, Gavin. 1987. *Between the Wire and the Wall: A History of South African "Coloured" Politics.* Cape Town: David Philip.

Van der Ross, Richard E. 1986. *The Rise and Decline of Apartheid: A Study of Political Movements among the Coloured People of South Africa, 1880–1985.* Cape Town: Tafelberg Publishers.

Mohamed Adhikari

COLORISM

Colorism is the allocation of privilege and disadvantage according to the lightness or darkness of one's skin. The practices of colorism tend to favor lighter skin over darker skin, although in rare cases the opposite practice also occurs. Colorism is present both within and among racial groups, a testament to its role as something related to but different than race. Colorism is enacted among racial groups in various contexts, from preferences in classroom settings and hiring decisions to patterns in sentencing. For example, it has been shown that lighter-skinned minorities, particularly blacks and Latinos, attain a higher educational level and a higher workforce status than darker-skinned minorities. According to research by Arthur Goldsmith, Darrick Hamilton, and William Darity (2006), employers tend to prefer light-skinned black employees over dark-skinned black employees.

Further, their research indicates that there is a much greater discriminatory wage penalty for darker-skinned African American men compared to their lighter-skinned counterparts. That is, lighter-skinned African American men tend to earn higher wages compared to darker-skinned African American men.

Studies by Verna Keith and Cedric Herring (1991) as well as those by Margaret Hunter (2002) suggest that the effect of skin tone remains even when other socioeconomic factors such as parental income and educational statues are controlled. Further, a study by Trina Jones (2000) demonstrates that darker-skinned blacks receive longer sentences than lighter-skinned blacks for crimes against whites, despite similarities in criminal records. Similarly, research by Jennifer Eberhardt, Paul Davies, Valerie Purdie-Vaughns, and Sheri Lynn Johnson (2006) demonstrates that "blacker-looking" African American males are more likely to receive the death penalty compared to their lighter-skinned counterparts for comparable capital crimes. Their findings remain significant even after controlling for defendant attractiveness and other nonracial factors that are typically known to influence sentencing, such as murder severity or victim's socioeconomic status. Most social scientific studies of the effects of colorism have shown that there has been little improvement in this form of discrimination since the civil rights movement in the 1960s.

However, previous research on colorism tended to focus on color-based discrimination within racial groups, as evidenced by the historical existence of such groups as the Blue Vein Society, a black-created social club that excluded dark-skinned blacks. Studies show that nonwhites tend to embrace the beauty standards prevalent in most societies, which grant a higher desirability to lighter skin than to darker skin. This has been shown to affect not only the self-worth of nonwhites but also mate selection. Light skin attains a higher socioeconomic status in its own right, through greater access to education and workforce mobility; lighter-skinned nonwhites also disproportionately attract spouses with higher socioeconomic statuses. Most studies have found that gender interacts with the effect of skin tone, making lighter skin a form of social capital for both black women and Latinas, again having an impact that cannot be explained by generational privileges alone. Famously explored in Wallace Thurman's novel *The Blacker the Berry …* (1929) and Toni Morrison's *The Bluest Eye* (1970) but rarely discussed openly, colorism is a continuing line of discrimination among and within racial groups worldwide. Although frequently collapsed into discussions of racism, colorism often occurs independently of racism, thus meriting independent analysis.

Racism and colorism share some commonalities, despite being independent practices. Fundamentally, both ideas of race and perceptions of skin color are social constructions, created in historically specific contexts and used to justify various practices of power. Although racial boundary drawing often involves perceptions of skin color, skin color alone rarely has been the sole determinant of racial categorization. At the same time, within racial categories there exists a wide range of skin coloration and various other physical attributes that are given social meaning in the process of allocating power and status. Thus conflating racism and colorism misses a distinct mode of stratification. With colorism, discrimination is not based on racial categorization but rather on assumptions about the meaning associated with one's skin color. In this way, we can distinguish racism as the social meaning associated with one's racial group and colorism as the social meaning associated with one's pigmentation.

Although colorism is frequently found in societies whose histories include a significant era of European colonialism, colorism has also been noted in Japan, a nation whose history does not involve a Euro-colonial past. This has allowed some scholars to explore the symbolic dimensions associated with colorism's typical privileging of lightness over darkness. In many differing cultural contexts, whiteness or lightness often has been associated with purity, cleanliness, beauty, intelligence, morality, and civilization, whereas in deliberate contrast, blackness or darkness has been associated with sin, filth, ugliness, stupidity, deviance, and backwardness. Anthropologists estimate that out of 312 cultures worldwide, 51 use skin color as a determinant of beauty. Among them, only four contain a preference for dark skin over light.

Such symbolic associations have in many cases justified the political and economic strains of colonialism, which play a central role in the origins of colorism. In Brazil, for example, the Portuguese invasion in the sixteenth century created a color hierarchy that persists in the early twenty-first century. Although roughly 80 percent of Brazilians are of African or indigenous descent, whites still are privileged politically and economically. A similar correlation of color and privilege is found throughout much of Latin America. In India traces of colorism favoring light skin are known to have existed before British colonial rule. Under the caste system, skin color and caste shared a similar gradient of privilege, and even in the early twenty-first century color-based tensions pervade Indian society.

In the United States the arrival of Europeans initially fostered race mixing, although with increased entrenchment of power among European descendents, particularly after the beginnings of slavery, an effort was made to draw clear (albeit biologically arbitrary) boundaries among the races. Antimiscegenation laws, such as the "one-drop rule" or "hypo-descent rule" that proclaimed that any amount of African ancestry was enough to constitute legal or social black status and that classified people racially as the subordinate group, were first created in response to moral questions over slavery for mixed-race individuals. For instance, throughout most of U.S. history and in some regions in the U.S. in the early twenty-first century any person with a trace of African ancestry has been considered black. In the Deep South during the era of slavery, although children of white plantation owners and their slave mistresses often were treated harshly and faced conditions similar to other slaves, these children in some instances were given coveted indoor jobs. In a few instances they also were given freedom, property, and even their own slaves. The social status associated with such freedom and ownership was a privilege for many mixed-race individuals, who after emancipation worked to self-segregate from darker-skinned blacks via elite social clubs and various churches, colleges, and other social institutions that were open to light-skinned blacks only, perpetuating a color-based gradient of privilege that persists in the early twenty-first century.

Although there have been substantial challenges to the practice of colorism, ranging from Marcus Garvey's criticism of W. E. B. DuBois to Spike Lee's challenging film *School Daze*, colorism is still widely practiced within and among racial groups. As long as lighter skin allocates disparate practices in housing, education, employment, sentencing, and perceptions of beauty, it remains a significant line of stratification.

SEE ALSO *Attitudes, Racial; Colonialism; Du Bois, W. E. B.; Garvey, Marcus; Miscegenation; Phenotype; Prejudice; Race Mixing; Racism; Stratification*

BIBLIOGRAPHY

Eberhardt, Jennifer L., Paul G. Davies, Valerie J. Purdie-Vaughns, and Sheri Lynn Johnson. 2006. Looking Deathworthy: Perceived Stereotypicality of Black Defendants Predicts Capital-Sentencing Outcomes. *Psychological Science* 17: 383–386.

Goldsmith, Arthur H., Darrick Hamilton, and William A. Darity Jr. 2006. Shades of Discrimination: Skin Tone and Wages. *American Economic Review* 96 (2): 242–245.

Hill, Mark E. 2000. Color Differences in the Socioeconomic Status of African American Men: Results of a Longitudinal Study. *Social Forces* 78 (4): 1437–1460.

Hunter, Margaret L. 2002. "If You're Light You're Alright": Light Skin Color as Social Capital for Women of Color. *Gender and Society* 16 (2): 175–193.

Jones, Trina. 2000. Shades of Brown: The Law of Skin Color. *Duke Law Journal* 49 (6): 1487–1557.

Keith, Verna M., and Cedric Herring. 1991. Skin Tone and Stratification in the Black Community. *American Journal of Sociology* 97 (3): 760–778.

Russel, Kathy, Midge Wilson, and Ronald Hall. 1992. *The Color Complex: The Politics of Skin Color among African Americans.* New York: Harcourt, Brace, Jovanovich.

Udry, J. Richard, Karl E. Bauman, and Charles Chase. 1971. Skin Color, Status, and Mate Selection. *American Journal of Sociology* 76 (4): 722–733.

Meghan A. Burke
David G. Embrick

COLUMBUS, CHRISTOPHER
c. 1451–1506

School children across the United States immediately recognize the name Christopher Columbus. He has assumed iconic status as the instigator of European imperialism in the Americas. Much of the historical Columbus, though, became obscured by eighteenth- and nineteenth-century mythology that valorized the sailor.

Christopher Columbus (Cristóbal Colón in Spanish, Cristoforo Colombo in Italian) first approached the king of Portugal in 1484 with a bold plan to reach Asia by crossing the Atlantic Ocean. The king's advisors, however, scorned Columbus's ideas. Contrary to folklore, most educated Portuguese conceptualized the earth as a sphere by 1484. Skeptics of Columbus's plans, in other words, did not believe that Columbus would sail off the edge of a flat world. Rather, Columbus's dubious calculations about the size of the earth troubled many in the Portuguese court. Columbus proposed that only three thousand nautical miles separated Europe and Asia, a distance that ships of the day could easily traverse. Portuguese authorities did not know about the existence of North and South America, but they understood, based on their own calculations, that Columbus had seriously underestimated the globe's size. Indeed, reaching Asia via the Atlantic would mean traveling a distance of 10,600 nautical miles, more than three times the distance Columbus predicted. Portuguese scientists conjectured that Columbus and his crew would starve before reaching Asia, and they likely would have had they not happened upon the Western Hemisphere. Rather than adopting Columbus's westward plan, Portugal banked on reaching Asia by voyaging around Africa.

Rejected by Europe's major naval power, Columbus looked to Portugal's emerging rivals, Spain's Queen Isabella (1451–1504) of Castile and King Ferdinand (1452–1516) of Aragon. When Isabella and Ferdinand married, they united Spain's two largest kingdoms and ruled jointly. Isabella initially rejected Columbus's propos-

als as fantastical and expensive. Columbus persisted for seven years, however, eventually winning Isabella's approval on his third official proposal. Ferdinand later claimed credit for convincing Isabella to set aside her misgivings about Columbus. The Catholic sovereigns financed Columbus, offered him the title of governor for the lands that he claimed for Spain, and provided him with a modest fleet of three ships: the *Niña* and *Pinta*, two caravels, and the *Santa Maria*, a square-rigged vessel.

Columbus's ships crossed the Atlantic in twenty-nine days. The crew aboard the *Pinta* first spotted land on October 7, 1492, and made landfall three days later. Columbus encountered the indigenous Taíno (or Arawak) on Guanahani island, which he renamed San Salvador. During his first voyage, Columbus scouted various other islands throughout the Caribbean, including Hispaniola (now Haiti and the Dominican Republic) and Cuba.

Columbus did not understand or accept that he had arrived on lands unknown to contemporary Europeans. Instead, he steadfastly claimed to have reached Asia. The inexperienced navigator believed Cuba's mountains to be India's Himalayas, and he thus dubbed the indigenous people *Indians*.

Having lost the *Santa Maria* off the coast of Cuba, Columbus set sail with the *Niña* and *Pinta* for Spain on January 4, 1493. Encountering wicked storms and bad luck, he did not return to Castile until March.

Columbus found much glory when he entered the royal court. Spaniards marveled at the many unknown items he displayed from his first voyage, including a tobacco plant, a turkey, and a pineapple. He also showed several kidnapped natives, whom Columbus suggested would not interfere in Spain's colonization efforts.

Columbus's second voyage to the Western Hemisphere, which lasted from 1493 to 1496, showed the brutality and limits of European imperialism. Columbus had seventeen ships and 1,200 men to colonize the Taíno and Arawak territory. He created an elaborate design for the colonial capital, which he named Isabella. The town and expedition, however, largely failed.

Columbus navigated and charted islands in the Caribbean, including Puerto Rico. He also advocated enslaving the indigenous populations. Though Isabella and Ferdinand shunned the idea of outright enslavement, Columbus ultimately took 1,600 Arawaks into bondage. He dispatched around 550 of these Arawaks to Spain, but almost half died during the journey. Those who did survive spent a lengthy time imprisoned as Spain's legal system decided their fate. Ultimately, Spain ordered that they be shipped back to their native lands.

Columbus continued to petition the monarchy to consider their new colonies as a source for slaves. They, however, consistently refused. The monarchs' refusals over unconditional slavery, however, did not mean that they did not expect the indigenous to labor on their behalf as repayment for their conversion to Christianity.

Perhaps the greatest brutality during the second voyage resulted from the Spaniards' search for gold. Though they found some precious metals, Columbus's men could not locate the massive reserves that he had imagined existed. On the island of Haiti, Columbus imposed an unrealistic quota system on the indigenous population. The governor ordered the hands chopped off of any adult over the age of fourteen who failed to reach his quota in the gold mines. Even with this viciousness, Columbus failed to collect much gold during his second journey. He left behind, however, several permanent colonies for Spain.

Columbus's third journey to the Americas was notable for two reasons. First, a young Bartolomé de las Casas (1474–1566) traveled onboard one of the six ships. Las Casas would later gain fame for chronicling the abuse of indigenous people at the hands of Spain's colonists. Second, royal authorities arrested Columbus on August 23, 1500. Many of the colonists had grown angry with Columbus and his unfulfilled promises of wealth. Spain's monarchs eventually released Columbus, but stripped him of his title of governor.

Columbus's final trip to the Western Hemisphere lasted from 1502 to 1504. During this voyage, Columbus continued to hunt for gold and other material treasures. He made landfall in Central America, probably along the coasts of the modern-day nations of Honduras, Nicaragua, and Costa Rica. Bad weather, though, ultimately resulted in Columbus spending most of his final year in Jamaica. He returned to Spain on November 7, 1504, and never returned to the Americas again.

Columbus spent the last few years of his life fighting court battles in Spain. The seafarer sued the Spanish Crown, demanding it honor its original contract with him, which guaranteed 10 percent of the profits from his explorations. The court battles ultimately extended across five decades, with Columbus's heirs losing the fight.

COLUMBUS'S LEGACY

Columbus's entry into the Western Hemisphere radically changed the direction of Europe, Africa, and the Americas. Ideas about imperial expansion had already become part of Europe's most powerful kingdoms. European society quickly recognized that they could use their existing technology to colonize lands previously unknown to them.

In 1494 Spain and Portugal almost went to war over control of the world. Spain argued that the route and lands encountered by Columbus belonged to them. Portugal countered that Columbus could not have succeeded without Portuguese technology. Pope Alexander VI (1431–1503) negotiated a settlement, the Treaty of Tordesillas (1494), that pleased both Spain and Portugal. Essentially, the pontiff divided the globe on a line located 270 leagues west of the Azores. Any lands west of that line went to Spain, any lands to the east went to Portugal. Europeans had little idea of the size or shape of the Americas, but the line resulted in Portugal's claims to Brazil and Spain's initial dominance in North America. Alexander VI and the Iberian powers ignored whatever concerns the indigenous inhabitants might have had about this arrangement.

Most historians argue that Iberian subjugation of the Canary Islands became the model for the initial settlement of Europeans in the Western Hemisphere. Establishing colonies in the Canary Islands created imperial apparatuses for controlling lands and populations thousands of miles away from the center of government. Ostensibly a mission of religious conversion, Christian invaders interpreted resistance as a divine sanction for their colonial enterprise. Moreover, authorities rarely recognized the rights of baptized Canarians. Within a short period, Iberians sold tens of thousands of Canarians into slavery and confiscated their lands.

Columbus's immediate legacy, therefore, involved Spain importing these brutal methods to take control of indigenous lands in the Americas. By 1512 as many as ten thousand Spaniards lived in Hispaniola, supported by the forced labor of the original inhabitants. Puerto Rico, Cuba, and all the lesser islands soon fell to Spain's conquistadors. The Arawaks and Caribs faced exploitation under the guise of religious conversion.

Starting around 1515, Spaniards began to construct sugar mills, importing both technicians and African slaves to replace the indigenous people dying from disease and mistreatment. In 1519 Hernando Cortés (c. 1484–1547) entered to the core of the Aztec Empire in the center of modern-day Mexico. By 1600 Spain's imperial authority extended from the Río Grande del Norte to the Río de la Plata in southern Peru. Other European powers soon followed, including Portugal, Britain, France, and the Netherlands.

European invasion of the Americas brought profound suffering and death to indigenous groups. Overwork and lack of adequate provisions compounded the spread of disease as epidemics ravaged the Americas. The Mesoamerican population dropped from more than twenty million to as little as two million during the first century of contact. Populations on the Greater Antilles almost entirely disappeared.

Many historians frame Columbus's legacy around notions of exchange. As already suggested, the most profound exchange that occurred involved the transmission of diseases. Europeans brought typhus, measles, strains of influenza, and smallpox to the Americas for the first time. Some debate exists about whether syphilis originated in the Americas and, therefore, had been previously unknown in the Eastern Hemisphere. Recent studies, however, suggest that Europeans already had experiences with syphilis before Columbus set sail.

Outside of disease, the exchange of different plants, animals, and cultural practices radically altered the landscape and diets of Europeans, Africans, and Native Americans. Native Americans had never seen pigs, sheep, sugar, or domestic cattle. Arguably the most important addition, however, was the horse. Horses had not roamed the Americas since the last Ice Age. Native Americans quickly adapted the horse to their needs, using them for hunting, transportation, and warfare.

American crops, likewise, transformed European and African life and nutrition. Columbus brought back nutrient-packed maze (corn) on his first trip. During the next century, American beans, squash, potatoes, peppers, and tomatoes all became European staples. Tobacco became a prized commodity in Europe by the seventeenth century.

Columbus's voyage also had tremendous significance for Europe's minority populations, particularly the Jewish community. On March 30, 1492, less than a month before Columbus signed his crown contract, Isabella and Ferdinand issued a decree expelling Jews from Spain. Those Jews who did not convert to Christianity by August 2 forfeited their property to the royal couple and had to leave their kingdom.

Jews had already faced centuries of persecution throughout Europe. A sizable group opted to convert to Christianity, some out of religious faith, others for expediency. Their Christian neighbors, however, continued to disdain these *conversos* (converts), despairingly naming them *marannos* (literally, swine). Many conversos, often referred to as *crypto-Jews*, secretly maintained their Jewish faith and practices. This community, however, faced dire consequences if discovered. Under the Catholic Church's Inquisition, these conversos came under intense scrutiny. Church authorities executed any conversos who showed signs of practicing Judaism.

Columbus benefited from both the Jewish community and also their persecution. While in Lisbon, Columbus consulted with prominent Jewish and converso scientists like Joseph Veinho and Martin Behaim (1459–1507). Columbus also received substantial funding for his expedition from a converso in Ferdinand's royal court. Moreover, he employed numerous conversos in his crew, some just barely out of the Inquisition's clutches. Many recently baptized Christians even held key positions in his first fleet, including Rodrigo Sanchez, the comptroller; Alfonso de la Calle, the second mate; Maestro Bernal, the physician; and Luis de Torres, Columbus's interpreter.

The purge of Jews from Spain, though, also provided part of the royal funding for Columbus's various voyages. Seizure of Jewish property provided an immense budget for the second voyage, in particular. Much of the money for that expedition derived directly from the confiscation of Jewish lands and valuables, including some priceless synagogue artifacts.

Spain's expansion into the Americas, though, also provided unexpected opportunities for conversos and crypto-Jews. Colonization's first century offered a literal escape from Europe's Inquisition. Though officially forbidden from settling in Spain's new colonies, conversos often found the royal court more than willing to sell exemptions. If one could not obtain royal sanction, captains in the imperial navy also showed themselves ready to provide transport for the right price. By the 1630s, conversos could be found in almost every town in Spain's empire. Frontier locations, such as New Mexico or Florida, attracted a disproportionate number because of their remoteness from the Inquisitors' grasps.

THE HISTORICAL COLUMBUS AND THE COLUMBUS LEGENDS

Though widely known today, Columbus's name had almost been forgotten even before his death in 1506. In December 1500, Amerigo Vespucci (1454–1512) published a sensational account of his travels across the Atlantic. Vespucci claimed credit for finally establishing that Europeans had encountered previously unknown continents in the Western Hemisphere. When an authoritative German cartographer printed the first major world map in 1507, he gave the continents the name *America*, a feminine version of Vespucci's first name.

During the eighteenth century, however, Columbus's fame experienced a resurgence thanks, in part, to the tensions between North American colonists and the British government. As early as 1700, British colonists used *Columbia* as another name for the Americas. After U.S. independence, the historical Columbus and the feminine coinage Columbia became symbols for distinguishing the fledgling republic from its European counterparts. King's College in New York, for instance, found a new start as Columbia College. In 1791 the seat of government became known as the District of Columbia. Though 1692 passed with little fanfare, the leaders of the newly created United States made 1792 a year of fetes. Celebrating three centuries since his first journey, U.S. leaders declared Columbus the first "American" hero.

Columbus gained even greater notoriety with the publication of Washington Irving's (1783–1859) three-volume biography in 1828. Publishers have issued over

175 different editions of Irving's hefty study. In 1844 federal authorities commissioned a statute of the sailor for the U.S. Capitol building. His popularity continued to serge in the United States through the second half of the nineteenth century. Between 1830 and 1860, the U.S. Catholic population grew from three hundred thousand to over three million. These foreign-born immigrants faced intense hostility by nativist Protestants who believed Catholicism irreconcilable with U.S. nationalism. In response, the Catholic Church used Columbus as a symbol of Catholic legitimacy in the nation. A renewed mythology developed around the explorer as a man who brought Christianity to the Americas. A prominent Catholic fraternal group, for instance, assumed the name the Knights of Columbus in 1882. The immigration of Italians, which added roughly another four million Catholics to the United States between 1880 and 1920, increased the worship of Columbus. Because of Columbus's connection to Genoa, Italians felt a special claim to him. The increased fervor around the explorer resulted in spectacular celebrations in 1892 to mark the four hundredth anniversary of his sailing.

Through the twentieth century, scholars and activists became more critical of Columbus and his legacy. By 1992 almost equal attention was being given to the devastating consequences that befell indigenous and African populations following Columbus's journey five hundred years earlier. Though he became an iconic hero, conjecture abounds about Columbus's ancestry. Around the turn of the twentieth century, the Spanish historian Celso Garcia de la Riega speculated that a fifteenth-century Galcian family named Colón might have been Columbus's progenitor. Moreover, de la Riega suggested that the Galcian Colóns had married into a seemingly Jewish family, leading the historian to propose that Columbus had been a Jew or a "New Christian." Scholars have also pointed to Columbus's frequent references to the Hebrew Bible in his logs and letters. Moreover, he used the Jewish calendar for his personal records. His private letters also tantalize modern historians with their frequent references to such Hebrew Bible figures as King David and Moses.

Other theories developed that questioned the traditional story that Columbus hailed from Genoa, Italy. Among these propositions were theories that Columbus was Greek, Basque, and Portuguese. The most astounding and least plausible story proposed that Columbus was really Native American, had been blown by a storm to Europe, and proposed his naval venture as a means to return home.

Though this type of wild speculation continues, few new historical documents related to Columbus actually surfaced during the twentieth century. In early 2006, an international team of genetic researchers launched an ambitious DNA research project. Composed of scientists from Spain, the United States, Italy, and Germany, this team hopes to use the known remains of Columbus's brother and son to end the controversy about Columbus's origins.

SEE ALSO *Christianity; Colonialism; Exploitation*

BIBLIOGRAPHY

Cohen, J. M., ed. and trans. 1969. *The Four Voyages of Christopher Columbus: Being His Own Log-Book, Letters and Dispatches with Connecting Narrative Drawn from the Life of the Admiral by His Son Hernando Colon and Other Contemporary Historians.* Hammondsworth, U.K.: Penguin.

Crosby, Alfred. 1972. *The Columbian Exchange: Biological and Cultural Consequences of 1492.* Westport, CT: Greenwood Press.

Phillips, William D., Jr. and Carla Rahn Phillips. 1993. *The Worlds of Christopher Columbus.* Cambridge, U.K. and New York: Cambridge University Press.

Provost, Foster. 1991. *Columbus: An Annotated Guide to the Scholarship on His Life and Writings, 1750 to 1988.* Detroit, MI: Omnigraphics for the John Carter Brown Library.

Sale, Kirkpatrick. 1990. *Conquest of Paradise: Christopher Columbus and the Colombian Legacy.* New York: Alfred A. Knopf.

Schlereth, Thomas J. 1992. Columbia, Columbus, and Columbianism. *Journal of American History* (Discovering America: A Special Issue) 79 (3): 937–968.

Anthony Mora

COMBAHEE RIVER COLLECTIVE
SEE *Intersectionality.*

COMEDY

The social sciences have led the way in the scholarship on humor, looking to social dynamics to explain what people find funny, and why they find it funny. This enquiry began with *Le Rire: Essai sur la signification du comique* (1899), in which the French philosopher Henri Bergson, thinking as a social scientist might, explored how comedy depends upon the rupture of socialized standards of group behavior. A few years later, Sigmund Freud, in *Der Witz und sein Beziehung zum Unbewussten* (*Jokes and Their Relation to the Unconscious*, 1905), posited that it was the violation of social constructs (functions of the ego and superego) that makes people laugh.

Bergson would go on to cite "the worthless act" as a central component to laughter in the modern and mechanized world, explaining in "Laughter: An Essay on the Meaning of the Comic" (1911) that humor allows one to distance oneself from the dehumanizing effects of modern, civilized life. Modern scholarship might be said to begin an extension of this logic, looking not only to the essence of humor but also to its social functions. The Czech sociologist Antonin Obrdlik's "Gallows Humor, a Sociological Phenomenon," which first appeared in the March 1942 edition of the *American Journal of Sociology*, argued that "gallows humor" served as relief from the devaluation of human life at the hands of the Nazis.

Since World War II, the social sciences have continued to explore the social functions of humor, often contextualizing these functions by way of well-established theoretical models. In his introductory textbook *Humor and Society* (1988), Marvin R. Koller addresses the work of Obrdlik directly, examining gallows humor as an example of "relief theory." Koller then contextualizes relief theory as one of four "macrotheories of humor," the others being "ambivalence theory" (an embracing of a social construct while simultaneously holding it at arm's length), "superiority theory" (excluding other social groups from human commerce by way of pronouncing one's own their "betters"), and "incongruity theory" (reminding us of the perils in thinking we have codified our world more definitively than we have). As any seasoned sociologist will recognize, these theories are familiar approaches drawn from elsewhere in the discipline. Nonetheless, they are profitable means of categorizing and appreciating how humor is more than simply "funny."

A second contribution to humor scholarship has come from the willingness of the social sciences to look at how what people find funny can be determined by the groups of which they are a part. The social sciences in general, and sociology in particular, have explored the nature of humor by gender, by medium (e.g., print, television, motion pictures), by region, by professional group, and by race. Surely the most impressive scholarship in this regard has explored the relationship between humor and ethnicity. The early work in this area often employed "conflict-aggression" interpretations of ethnic humor, depicting ethnic humor as a means of ranking ethnic groups in a social hierarchy. More recent work though has found the phenomena to be flexible, even fluid. Christopher Davies, in *The Mirth of Nations* (2002), suggests that Polish jokes, for instance, ebb when definable tensions between Poles and other groups are most pronounced. Conversely, Polish jokes flourish when tensions are lowest.

The reach of scholarship in the social sciences is at once broad and deep. The work is yet to be fully synthesized however. Initially spread across psychology, sociol-

ogy, and anthropology, it is now also found in related fields such as philosophy, communications, folklore, and media studies. Hence, the most exciting scholarship is more often discovered in articles in interdisciplinary journals than in full-length books devoted to a particular social-science discipline.

BIBLIOGRAPHY

Bechtold, Robert Heilman. 1978. *The Ways of the World: Comedy and Society*. Seattle: University of Washington Press.

Davies, Christie. 1998. *Jokes and Their Relation to Society*. New York: Mouton de Gruyter.

Davies, Christie. 2002. *Mirth of Nations*. New Brunswick, NJ: Transaction Publishers.

Koller, Marvin R. 1988. *Humor and Society: Explorations in the Sociology of Humor*. Houston, TX: Cap and Gown Press.

Jay Boyer

COMIC BOOKS

Comics have a long history, especially in Europe, Japan, and the United States. The Arab states, China, India, Mexico, and South America also contribute to this history. U.S. comic books have played an important role in the entertainment industry, attracting varying degrees of academic attention since regular publication began in the late 1920s. The earliest U.S. comic book was Rodolphe Töppfer's *The Adventures of Obadiah Oldbuck*, published in September 1842. In 1896 Richard Outcault's *The Yellow Kid* became the first syndicated newspaper comic strip published in color. Dates for early comics vary depending on new discoveries and evolving definitions; Scott McCloud's *Understanding Comics* (1993) is considered a classic in defining comics.

Early U.S. comic books were compilations of Sunday newspaper comics. The importance of twentieth-century comics has been partially mapped out in Ian Gordon's *Comic Strips and Consumer Culture, 1890–1945* (1998) and Thomas Inge's *Comics as Culture* (1990); both analyze how comics sold newspapers, generated a vast array of merchandising, and influenced U.S. culture and language.

In 1938 Superman appeared in *Action Comics* number 1. The growth of comic book publishing expanded until the 1950s. The height of the comics industry occurred from 1950 to 1954. Americans spent close to $1 billion on comics and there were comics readers in more than 40 percent of U.S. households. A variety of genres existed, comprising over 600 titles. During the 1950s public opinion turned against comic books, due in part to Fredric Wertham's *Seduction of the Innocent* (1954).

Although the medium was perceived by most as children's literature, publishers were adapting to an aging readership who wanted more violence, sex, satire, and political/adult themes. The protests, spurred in part by Wertham's book, general public outcry, and a congressional hearing, resulted in the industry's self-censoring comics code, a sanitizing of comics, and a major drop in sales. Among the long list of dos and don'ts, the code regulated acceptable versus unacceptable titles (e.g., titles could not contain the words "horror," "fear," or "terror"), established a modest dress code for female characters, ensured that good would always win over evil (criminals were always caught), and reduced violent scenes (e.g., blood, decapitation, and torture were not allowed). The code also regulated language use, not allowing swear words or language alluding to sexual situations.

The 1960s saw two important developments. First, in mainstream comics, Marvel Comics slowly became DC Comics's major competitor by creating a new line of superheroes marketed to an emerging and economically important youth culture. These new superheroes were young, and some were teenagers themselves. Most of them acquired their powers through some type of accident or experiment related to radiation, and the story lines centered around the superhero's personal problems and struggles to understand and use the newfound powers. These new comics also made reference to current social issues such as drug use, the counterculture, the different social movements, and racism. The heroes of these comics included Spiderman, the Incredible Hulk, X-Men, and the Fantastic Four. The Black Panther and Luke Cage, the first African American superheroes, were an important addition, even though their earliest appearances followed a trend toward "blaxploitation" as opposed to a serious look at race issues. In the 1970s superheroes became more socially relevant and serious. Marvel revamped or modernized many earlier superheroes such as Captain America and Flash in a further effort to make their comics more relevant in terms of the youth culture and society at large. Marvel and DC Comics remained the dominant comics publishers, becoming almost indistinguishable in content until the 1980s, when DC Comics released their Vertigo line for more mature readers.

The second important development during the 1960s was the birth of underground "comix," which reflected counterculture sensibilities and rebelled against the comics code and social taboos. Important cartoonists from this period include Robert Crumb, Justin Green, Richard "Grass[hopper]" Green, Michele Brand, and Roberta Gregory. The undergrounds were especially important in terms of their influence on a future generation of comics creators and the types of innovative comics that emerged during the late 1980s and continued through the first half-decade of the 2000s.

After comics' silver age in the 1970s, significant developments began in the 1980s. The code weakened, many comics publishers ceased carrying the code's seal, or in addition to coded books, they carried a "mature" line which did not carry the seal. Groundbreaking works appeared, including Alan Moore's *Watchmen*, Frank Miller's *The Dark Knight Returns*, Art Spiegelman's *Maus*, and the Hernandez brothers' *Love and Rockets*. Independent and alternative publishers such as Dark Horse Comics, Fantagraphics, and Image lessened DC Comics's and Marvel Comics's control of the market. Self-publishing (e.g., Dave Sims's *Cerebus*) further expanded comics' potential as a diverse art form.

The term *graphic novel* became popular beginning in the late 1970s. Initially, the term was used to distinguish artistic or novelistic comics from mainstream, superhero comics. Some early examples include *Contract with God* by Will Eisner, *First Kingdom* by Jack Katz, and *Sabre* by Don McGregor and Paul Gulacy. Later, the term was used exclusively as a marketing tool and applied to hardback or paperback "drawn novels," collected superhero story-arcs, longer book-length comics, and anthologized comic strips (for example, *The Far Side* and *Calvin and Hobbes*).

Importation of European and Japanese comics (*manga*) saw a marked increase in the 1980s (and the importance of *manga* in the U.S. market continued through 2006). Finally, the 1989 film release of Tim Burton's *Batman* spawned other comics-related films and video and computer games. These trends grew exponentially during the first half-decade into the 2000s. Superhero stories accounted for most of the films' adaptations, but there were also adaptations of novelistic and slice-of-life comics (e.g., *American Splendor, Ghost World,* and *Road to Perdition*). Major book publishers such as Random House began publishing "drawn novels," and more book-length comics appeared without prior serialization; examples include Marjane Satrapi's *Persepolis,* Craig Thompson's *Blankets,* and Chris Ware's *Jimmy Corrigan: The Smartest Kid on Earth*.

Academic attention to comics increased substantially in the 1990s and continued through the first half-decade of the 2000s. Scholarly analysis focuses on comics history, fandom, the inner workings of the comics publishing and distribution industry, defining comics by applying formalist or structuralist theories, applying literary theory or semiotics for interpretation and analysis, and analyzing comics' cultural impact.

BIBLIOGRAPHY

Gordon, Ian. 1998. *Comic Strips and Consumer Culture, 1890–1945*. Washington, DC: Smithsonian Institution Press.

Inge, Thomas M. 1990. *Comics as Culture*. Jackson: University Press of Mississippi.

McCloud, Scott. 1993. *Understanding Comics: The Invisible Art.* New York: HarperCollins.

McGrath, Charles. 2004. Not Funnies. *New York Times,* July 11.

Sabin, Roger. 1993. *Adult Comics: An Introduction.* London: Routledge.

Wright, Bradford W. 2001. *Comic Book Nation.* Baltimore, MD: Johns Hopkins University Press.

Jeff Williams

COMMON CAUSE

SEE *Public Interest Advocacy.*

COMMON GOOD, THE

The common good refers to activities or policies that benefit the community. It is concerned with the well-being of the group as opposed to simply the interests of a particular individual or subgroup. What this well-being actually involves, however, is not self-evident. There is no generally accepted method for identifying the common good. Nonetheless, scholars have offered a number of theoretical approaches, which can typically be categorized as either liberal or communitarian.

A fundamental distinction between these two theoretical orientations is how they conceptualize the relationship between the individual and community. The liberal perspective tends to understand the community in terms of its individual members. The whole is considered the sum of its parts. Consequently, the common good is based on the interests of the individual members. The communitarian view, in contrast, conceives of the community as having ontological priority over its individual constituents; that is, the community has an existence that goes beyond its membership. The whole, therefore, is seen as greater than the sum of its parts. In this case, the community provides the standard for determining the common good.

Liberal theories share the general notion that the common good should be based on individual preferences and interests, which are all weighed equally. Examples of liberal procedures include utilitarian, deontological, and deliberative. Utilitarianism generally associates the common good with maximizing social welfare. Its basic goal is to produce the greatest overall utility for the greatest number of individuals. Utility, however, may be defined differently depending on the version of utilitarian theory being considered. Deontological approaches connect the common good to the maintenance of individual rights. These rights are considered inalienable; they cannot be taken away. Deontological theories identify sets of opportunities and resources that should be enjoyed equally by all individuals. Deliberative methods attempt to identify the common good through democratic discourse. Ideally, individual members of the community deliberate together and reach a consensus about what the common good entails. The outcomes of public deliberation are considered legitimate if the procedure meets certain requirements such as fairness, rationality, and reciprocity.

Communitarian theories assume communities have distinct ways of life shaped by custom and tradition. The common good, in this situation, involves advancing and maintaining the community's particular way of life. It identifies communal ends that are to be collectively embraced and pursued. Individual interests and preferences are seen as subordinate to the common good, which reflects the transcendent good of the community. Communitarian theories do not necessarily neglect the desires and needs of individuals; members, however, are expected to prioritize and share in their community's way of life. The common good, therefore, requires that individuals put aside their personal concerns in favor of communal goals.

In practice, liberal and communitarian attempts to achieve the common good reflect their respective emphases on the individual and community. The liberal approach often advocates the extension of social welfare for individuals and the protection of individual rights. The communitarian approach typically uses public institutions to inculcate civic virtues, facilitate social solidarity, and take care of the public welfare. The former advances the interests of individuals, while the latter promotes the well-being of the community.

SEE ALSO *Aristotle; Bentham, Jeremy; Communalism; Mill, John Stuart; Public Welfare; Social Welfare System; Utilitarianism*

BIBLIOGRAPHY

Kymlicka, Will. 1990. *Contemporary Political Philosophy: An Introduction.* New York: Oxford University Press.

Mulhall, Stephen, and Adam Swift. 1992. *Liberals and Communitarians.* Cambridge, MA: Blackwell.

Johnny Goldfinger

COMMON KNOWLEDGE RATIONALITY GAMES

When two or more agents knowingly interact in the sense that each knows how the outcomes for them depend not just on their own actions (strategies) but also on the actions of the others, they are playing a game. Each is rational when acting instrumentally to maximize his or her subjectively expected utility associated with the outcomes, and the game is a *common knowledge of rationality* (CKR) game when, in addition, (1) each knows that each is rational, and (2) each knows that each knows that each is rational, and so on in an infinite chain of recursively built knowledge.

The purpose of CKR is to place each agent, so to speak, in the mind of others with the result that no one will behave in a manner that surprises. In particular, CKR licenses the iterative deletion of dominated strategies. Strategies are dominated when they yield a worse outcome in every eventuality than some other available strategy (for example, the cooperative strategy in a prisoners' dilemma game).

Thus in a two-person game, when *A* knows that *B* is rational, he or she knows that *B* will not play a strategy that is dominated (so any such strategy can be effectively deleted). *B*, knowing this, also knows that *A* will not select a dominated strategy in terms of the payoffs that remain once *B*'s dominated strategies have been removed, and any such strategy of *A* can now also be ignored and so on. The strategies that remain are now referred to as *rationalizable* (Pearce 1984; Bernheim 1984); and in some, but far from all, games the result is a single strategy for each player (i.e., a unique prediction for rational agents will do).

It was sometimes thought that CKR delivered something potentially stronger: the Nash equilibrium solution concept, which identifies rational action with strategies that are best responses to each other. It is now typically accepted that in general the Nash equilibrium solution concept has to be motivated not only by CKR but also an assumption of common priors whereby rational agents hold a common view as to how a game will be played rationally. If there is such a unique, albeit possibly probabilistic, way in which each rational agent will play the game, then it will be apparent that, with CKR, rational actions must be best replies to each other (otherwise at least one agent would not be acting rationally).

CKR is sometimes modified so that agents only engage in some fixed level of reasoning of this sort. Thus first-order CKR refers to the case where *A* knows that *B* is rational and vice versa. Second-order CKR has in addition that *A* knows that *B* knows that *A* is rational and so on. Given the brain's limited processing capacity, this is often more appealing than full-blown CKR; and in experiments, it seems that most people rarely engage in more than second-order CKR (see Camerer 2003).

SEE ALSO *Collective Action Games; Dynamic Games; Evolutionary Games; Game Theory; Nash Equilibrium; Noncooperative Games; Prisoner's Dilemma (Economics); Screening and Signaling Theory Games; Strategic Games*

BIBLIOGRAPHY

Bernheim, B. Douglas. 1984. Rationalizable Strategic Behavior. *Econometrica* 52: 1007–1028.

Camerer, Colin. 2003. *Behavioral Game Theory: Experiments in Strategic Interaction.* Princeton, NJ: Princeton University Press.

Pearce, David G. 1984. Rationalizable Strategic Behavior and the Problem of Perfection. *Econometrica* 52: 1029–1050.

Shaun P. Hargreaves Heap

COMMON LAND

Common ownership of land, or a *commons*, is one of the most enduring social systems for owning and managing natural resources. Common land is controlled and managed by a defined group of people—tribes, peasants, and civic associations—for the collective benefit of its members.

This social regime of land management was the norm in prehistoric and medieval times, and it persists in the twenty-first century around the world, especially in developing countries. Even developed countries such as the United States have modern variants of common land, including land trusts, neighborhood-managed parks, and community-supported agriculture.

Common land stands in contrast to land owned as private property, in which individuals may possess the land and exclude others. It is also distinct from public land, in which government determines who may use the land and how, and from open access land, in which there are no property rights and no restrictions on how land may be used.

Collectively managed land has been a familiar socioeconomic institution in Latin America, Africa, Asia, India, and many developing nations for millennia. In societies with limited wealth and civil infrastructure, a commons provides an environmentally sustainable way to manage and allocate farmland, forests, water, wild game, and other natural resources. It also provides a certain measure of social equity in access and use of such resources. Community norms and sanctions tend to prevent anyone from abusing the land or appropriating more than his due share.

Since in a commons everyone is personally rooted to the land, there are keen incentives for responsible stewardship of resources. For this reason, common land systems tend to promote long-term sustainability over short-term productivity.

Since the 1990s a branch of political science and economics has studied the dynamics of "common-pool resources," or CPRs. Much of the case literature focuses on the specific ways in which communities in developing nations manage shared natural resources. Professor Elinor Ostrom of Indiana University is widely credited with pioneering research into common-pool resources in the early 1990s. Much work in the field is associated with the Workshop on Political Theory and Policy Analysis at Indiana University and the International Association for the Study of Common Property. The Digital Library of the Commons is a major online repository of academic monographs and bibliographies about a wide variety of commons.

THE FEUDAL COMMONS

In Western societies, the classic embodiment of a common land regime is the commons of feudal England and Europe. In this system, a medieval baron or lord was involved in a dense web of reciprocal economic and social relationships with peasants. In return for giving military service, a portion of crops, and personal loyalty to the manor, peasants shared usage rights to the manor's arable farmlands, pasture, and "waste" (forests, ponds, wetlands). Commoners might till their own individual strips of land, but no one had exclusive possession of the land or unrestricted freedom of use. Everyone's usage of the land was dependent upon the needs of the rest of the community.

Although this medieval system of commons was quite stable and sustainable, it required plentiful supplies of labor, and was not especially efficient or open to innovation. The system began to experience serious pressures, therefore, when the Black Death of the fourteenth century killed millions of people, and in the fifteenth and sixteenth centuries, when peasants often left the manor for towns in order to become tradesmen and entrepreneurs.

Further pressures on the commons arose when the landed gentry of England saw the money-making potential of wool production and trade with Europe. Especially in the seventeenth and eighteenth centuries, the nobility persuaded Parliament to override the common law and authorize it to "enclose," or privatize, the commons. This expropriation of common land cleared the way for a more efficient market use of common lands, and inaugurated the modern system of private property rights in land.

But the enclosures also caused enormous social disruptions and hardship as commoners were left to fend for themselves as landless, unskilled laborers. People whose lives were once nestled in stable, hierarchical communities that assured access to life-sustaining food, fuel, and household resources were thrust into a churning market order of shifting social roles and uncertain employment.

THE TRAGEDY OF OPEN ACCESS

In response to the triumph of capitalism and the decline of the commons, many modern economists and policy experts have come to believe that land cannot be managed effectively as a shared resource. Perhaps the most notable statement to this effect was an acclaimed 1968 essay, "The Tragedy of the Commons," by biologist Garrett Hardin. Hardin argued that people who share land as a commons will inevitably overexploit it. He cited the archetype of a common pasture to which anyone may add more livestock for grazing without restriction. In such circumstances, when individual farmers can reap private benefits from the commons without regard for its overall "carrying capacity," a shared resource will be overexploited and fall into ruin, said Hardin. Hence, the "tragedy of the commons."

The only solution to this tragedy, according to many economists, is to assign private property rights in land. Unlike commoners or government, it is argued, private landowners have the necessary incentives to take care of the land and make worthwhile investments in it. To support this general conclusion, neoclassical economists often cite "prisoner's dilemma" game experiments that demonstrate the difficulties of getting individuals to cooperate to solve shared problems. In his influential book, *The Logic of Collective Action* (1965), economist Mancur Olson argued that "rational, self-interested individuals will not act to achieve their common or group interests" (p. 2). Drawing upon such analyses, a generation of economists and policy experts has denigrated common ownership of land as impractical.

Many critics, however, have challenged the tragedy of the commons narrative and prisoner's dilemma experiments as unrealistic representations of real-world circumstances. They point out that social trust and communication are usually present in actual communities, and that these capacities can help groups overcome barriers to organizing collective-action solutions.

It has also been pointed out that the tragedy scenario that Hardin described is not, in fact, a commons, but rather a regime of unregulated open access. The land is "nonproperty" in the sense that no one has a recognized right to possess the land. There are no resource boundaries or governance rules, and anyone can appropriate whatever he or she wishes.

A commons, by contrast, is a system of governance and shared property rights for controlling access to and use of a resource. Successful commons generally have well defined boundaries, for example, and rules that are well understood by identifiable participants in the commons.

The governance rules may be informal and implicit, and embodied in social traditions and norms, or they may be explicit and formally codified in law. In either case, there is a shared social understanding about who has rights to use the land's resources and under what terms.

A commons regime depends critically upon socially enforced cooperation and the exclusion of outsiders. It also requires the ability to identify and punish "free riders" who try to use more than their allotted share of the land's resources. With sufficient transparency in the commons, participants are able to prevent cheaters from taking more of the resource than they are entitled to under the social compact.

Collective management of land can have environmental advantages because it is more likely to treat the land as an organic ecosystem rather than a fungible commodity. A system of private property might divide the land into a collection of parcels, for example, perhaps resulting in the over-harvesting of timber in one plot of land that then leads to soil erosion or habitat destruction in an adjacent plot. But when commoners manage land holistically as an intact ecosystem, any abuse or overexploitation by individual users is likely to be identified and controlled.

Especially in poorer communities, collective management of lands can offer economic advantages. Villages and regional governments may find it expensive to maintain a system of courts, land titles, and private attorneys to manage individual property rights, and even fencing may be prohibitively expensive. Social rules and norms can serve as less expensive substitutes.

Others argue, however, that the lack of clear property rights in land is precisely what prevents poor people in developing countries from improving their economic lot. If peasants were more able to obtain clear and enforceable title in their land, for example, they would be able to use their land as collateral and participate more effectively in the market economy. Hernando de Soto makes this argument in his book *The Mysteries of Capital* (2000).

It is a mistake to regard systems of common land and private property as totally distinct and mutually exclusive. Private landowners are frequently restricted in the use of their lands by zoning ordinances, access easements, environmental laws, and other expressions of public needs and values. Conversely, unless a piece of land is managed communally, even commons can accommodate a certain measure of individual autonomy.

Ultimately, however, there is a fundamental, unbridgeable difference between a commons and a system of private property rights. In the latter, a person may sell and transfer individual ownership rights for cash. In a commons, by contrast, one cannot own the land as an individual nor alienate usage rights for commercial purposes. Usage rights are wrapped up in a web of particular social relationships, and cannot be bought and sold.

SEE ALSO *Primitive Accumulation*

BIBLIOGRAPHY

De Soto, Hernando, 2000. *The Mysteries of Capital: Why Capitalism Triumphs in the West and Fails Everywhere Else.* New York: Basic Books.

Digital Library of the Commons. http://dlc.dlib.indiana.edu.

Freyfogle, Eric T. 2003. *The Land We Share: Private Property and the Common Good.* Washington, DC: Island Press.

National Research Council. 2002. *The Drama of the Commons: Committee on the Human Dimensions of Global Change.* Ed. Elinor Ostrom et al. Washington, DC: National Academy Press.

Olson, Mancur. 1965. *The Logic of Collective Action: Public Goods and the Theory of Groups.* Cambridge, MA: Harvard University Press.

Ostrom, Elinor. 1990. *Governing the Commons: The Evolution of Institutions for Collective Action.* Cambridge, U.K.: Cambridge University Press.

Rose, Carol M. 1994. *Property and Persuasion: Essays on the History, Theory, and Rhetoric of Ownership.* Boulder, CO: Westview Press.

Stevenson, Glenn G. 1991. *Common Property Economics: General Theory and Land Use Applications.* Cambridge, U.K.: Cambridge University Press.

David Bollier

COMMON MARKET, THE

The term *common market* has multiple connotations in the European Union (EU). It is a term that was once used as a synonym for the European Economic Community (EEC), one of the organizations that evolved into the European Union. It is also a term that refers to the market integration of the participating states within the EU. In this respect the terms *single market*, *internal market*, or *single European market* are now more widely used.

Following the end of World War II a central goal of politicians in Western Europe was the maintenance of peace, and particularly the desire to ensure that Germany would no longer threaten this peace. Of critical importance here were the views of Jean Monnet, a French civil servant. Monnet believed that the best way to secure lasting peace between France and Germany was by institutionalizing cooperation between the states. This plan led to the creation of an organization that linked the coal and steel industries and markets of France, West Germany, Italy, the Netherlands, Belgium, and Luxembourg.

Monnet also believed that integration between France and Germany, and other states that were willing to participate, would not stop at coal and steel but would spill over into other sectors. This proved to be the case when the original six member states signed the Treaty of Rome in 1957 and created the EEC.

A central element of the Treaty of Rome was the common market, which remains one of the major components of the EU. The common market aimed to link the economies of the participating states by creating a customs union (that is, removing internal tariff barriers and creating a common external tariff for goods coming from outside the common market), by approximating economic policies, and by allowing the free movement of people, goods, services, and capital inside the participating states.

The customs union was put in place by 1968 but the other elements of the common market have proved to be more contentious and slower in developing. The members of the EU made a renewed commitment to the creation of a common market in 1986 when they signed the Single European Act (SEA). The centerpiece of the SEA was a commitment to remove all barriers to the free movement of people, goods, services, and capital by the target date of December 31, 1992. As in the case of the earlier Treaty of Rome, this target was not met and indeed considerable gaps remain in the common market. People cannot, for example, move freely around all of the twenty-seven EU member states in search of work. There has, nevertheless, been remarkable progress toward the completion of the common market, especially when compared to the situation in 1950. In the 2000s, the European Union has a highly integrated economic market that contains more than 450 million consumers. It is a powerful trading bloc and many non-European businesses adjust their products or working patterns in order to comply with economic regulations established within the EU.

SEE ALSO *Euro, The; European Union; Tariffs; Unions*

BIBLIOGRAPHY

Monnet, Jean. 1976. *Memoirs.* London: Collins.

Young, Alasdair R. 2005. The Single Market: A New Approach to Policy. In *Policy-Making in the European Union*, eds. Helen Wallace, William Wallace, and Mark A. Pollack, 93–112. 5th ed. Oxford: Oxford University Press.

John B. Sutcliffe

COMMONS, THE

SEE *Tragedy of the Commons.*

COMMONWEALTH, THE

Commonwealth is a term (in Latin, *res publica*) with a rich and varied usage. It literally means the wealth or well-being of a public or whole body of people and sometimes implies a specific form of government. In the English language it was much used from the sixteenth century onwards, by Shakespeare for example. In the seventeenth century it was the name for England's government, from the overthrow of King Charles I in 1649 until the abdication of Richard Cromwell in 1659. It is also part of the official names for a few U.S. states and, since 1901, for Australia. The term also is used sometimes for a community or organization with shared interests, as in the phrase "the commonwealth of learning."

The principal and best-known contemporary use of the term is in relation to the more than fifty states that are members of what is today known simply as "the Commonwealth," which evolved out of what was earlier known as "the British Commonwealth." This Commonwealth as it is today emerged over decades out of the erstwhile British Empire and showed a considerable ability to modify, adapt, and reinvent itself. Britain initially ran the Commonwealth in tandem with the so-called *dominions* of Canada, Australia, New Zealand, South Africa, and, from 1921 to 1949, Ireland. Although it is a diplomatic ensemble, the Commonwealth has never been a clear cut economic or trade unit. While there was considerable overlap, the sterling area of the 1930s to the 1970s, made up of countries that used the pound sterling or pegged their currency to it, was never exactly coterminous with the Commonwealth.

By joining the Commonwealth in the late 1990s, India, Pakistan, and Ceylon (from 1972 Sri Lanka) turned membership from a white man's club into a postimperial multiracial association. In the late twentieth century, decolonization and anticolonial movements, including opposition to South Africa's apartheid policies, provided dynamism and led to expanding membership. In 1949 there were eight members; by 1965 when the Commonwealth Secretariat was launched (as a servicing bureaucracy for the whole Commonwealth), there were twenty-one members; by 2006 there were fifty-three members, of whom over half were small states with populations of less than 1.5 million each (many had much smaller populations, numbered merely in tens of thousands).

Today, the Commonwealth has an extensive range of special associations amounting to over one hundred nongovernmental organizations. Its two most publicized activities are the biennial Heads of Government Meetings (colloquially known by the acronym CHOGM) and the Commonwealth's Games held every fourth year. Over the past century there has been a very extensive literature of books, journals, and pamphlets devoted to the Commonwealth's characteristics, achievements, and shortcomings.

In addition to the commonwealth discussed above, there is another that attracts little publicity: the Commonwealth of Independent States (CIS). The CIS was founded on December 8, 1991, in Vistuli, capital for the Belarussian government, as a community of independent states that proclaimed itself the successor to the Union of Soviet Socialist Republics in some aspects of international law and affairs. The member states are the founders, Russia, Belarus, and Ukraine, plus nine subsequent adherents: Armenia, Azerbaijan, Georgia, Kazakhstan, Kyrgyzstan, Moldova, Tajikistan, Turkmenistan, and Uzbekistan.

BIBLIOGRAPHY

McIntyre, W. David. 2001. *A Guide to the Contemporary Commonwealth*. London: Palgrave.

Srinivasan, Krishnan. 2005. *The Rise, Decline, and Future of the British Commonwealth*. London: Palgrave.

Peter Lyon

COMMUNALISM

Communalism is the name for sets of social movements and theories (religious, social, and political). People usually live in communities, the exceptions being a few hermits, more slaves, and many more city dwellers (in the Roman Empire and in modern advanced societies). The city dwellers who live in society but not in community require the distinction between community and society. In parallel to this, Georg F. W. Hegel (1770–1831) and more explicitly Ferdinand Tönnies (1855–1936) offered the distinction between culture and civilization, observing that (the older) community lives by local custom and (the newer) society obeys the law of the land that Hegel sneered at, calling the equality that it supports "merely formal." Hegel and Tönnies tacitly advocated the return to communal life, alleging that strife and alienation are lesser there and culture is more integrated; the basis of culture is religion, whereas the basis of civilization is (scientific) technology.

The original communalist movement was Talmudic Judaism. It underwent deep reform after the abortive Bar Kokhba revolt (132–135 CE). Unable to endorse or reject the Roman cruel peace (*Pax Romana*), the Talmudic sages decided to sit it out and act, meanwhile, as the bearers of morals and enlightenment. To that end they geared Jewish law to utterly decentralized communal living rooted in education and family life, with each community politically, morally, and religiously autonomous; each rabbi is a supreme doctrinal authority functioning as a teacher of the community. This traditional description misses the major specific characteristic of Jewish communal theory and practice, which is that the diverse autonomous communities were linked in a powerful informal grassroots cultural network (called "Knesset Israel," in allusion to its role as a surrogate parliament).

Hardly noticed, this decentralized network was emulated in great variations in medieval Europe, with communities controlled by the church and fused under secular rulers, and in traditional Islam of the caliphate (with the caliph as both religious and lay ruler) run as a network. For centuries it was the social institution nearest to democracy, making the traditional West distinctive and amenable to its later, spectacular changes. The lesser authority of the Protestant minister—as compared to that of the Catholic priest—strengthened communal networks; these have survived and in the early twenty-first century are misnamed "family values" and promoted by some neoconservatives and by religious communalist philosophers, including Alastair MacIntyre and Charles Taylor, both Catholics. Most contemporary communalists, however, deem them obsolete.

Modernity began with the individualism of the Enlightenment movement that found its expression chiefly in the advocacy of individual reasoning and thus of science as superior to faith, as well as in the view that the free choice of citizens is the only possible legitimate source for the right of governments to rule. (This is the doctrine of the social contract.) The Enlightenment movement ignored the community as unproblematic and outmoded. The Romantic reaction to it preferred the community over the polity, and custom over law. In efforts to compromise between the two movements, utopian communities were repeatedly founded. Their standards were intolerably high and so they failed, although always while raising the standards of their societies, thereby making significant contributions to the modern lifestyle. They gave way to the new welfare state and the newer communalist efforts to bring society and community together. Only neoconservatives advocate the return of welfare services to the community, and even they admit implicitly that this return cannot be total.

Philosophically, as the Enlightenment movement anchored everything social in the individual, its problem was: How does society emerge out of a cluster of individuals? This question is unanswerable, said the Romantic philosophers, because the pre-social individual is fictional. They, on the contrary, considered society an organism and the individual a limb with no independent existence. This is empirically more tenable but not enough, and it is morally useless. A search began for an alternative, a *via media* and a *modus vivendi*. Georg Simmel (1858–1918) and Karl Popper (1902–1994) assumed the existence of both individual and society. Gustav Landauer (1870-1919) and Martin Buber (1878–1965) deviated less from traditional philosophy. Buber declared that both individual and society owe their existence to the individual's essential disposition for interpersonal relations; this disposition is (theoretically) prior to both.

This centrality of the disposition for interpersonal relations led to communalism as a new view of society that is more visionary than explanatory. Buber viewed the community as a network of individuals tied in a more-or-less face-to-face relation and the nation (more specifically, the culture) as a network of such communities. He played down the difference between society and community as he envisioned (in his 1946 book, *Paths in Utopia*) an urban society comprising a conglomerate of cooperative communes. He did not view all communities as communes or all communes as living in kibbutz style, but unlike the older utopians he did not elaborate. He considered the alienation of the modern urban individual a serious challenge, and communalism as its answer. The question is, where does politics enter the picture? Buber suggested that this question is less important than another question: How can politics be tamed so as to prevent it from destroying communal life. He found this question more practical than theoretical (unlike Popper who developed democratic theory around it). So he invested in communalist political activity.

The new communalists, with Amitai Etzioni (b. 1929) as their leader, aim at filling this theoretical gap. Etzioni founded the George Washington University Institute for Communitarian Policy Studies (and continues to serve as its director) as well as the Communitarian Network (1990). His communitarian principle is meant to be applicable to national and even international politics. To a large extent it is simply the applications of (updated) agreeable liberal attitudes to diverse political problems with an accent on individual responsibility. To the extent that there is a new principle here, it is this: Both society and community are essential for a quality life, and so political concerns should include attention to communal concerns and *vice versa*. This is not a proposal to unite community and polity but to increase their cooperation. The recent development of nongovernmental organizations (NGOs) and their contributions to both community and polity alike is a remarkable example.

The expected development of former colonies into liberal nation-states was halted because colonialists had encouraged community life as a poor substitute for national independence. As after independence different communities within one country struggle to maintain their relative independence there, the overall result is inter-communal strife and thus damage to national liberty. The proper move should be towards western-style pluralist nations with a heightened sense of community. This is easier said than done.

SEE ALSO *African Americans; Civilization; Communitarianism; Culture; Ethnic Fractionalization; Ethnicity; Family; Groups; Hegel, Georg Wilhelm Friedrich; Identity; Individualism; Jews; Marx, Karl; Marxism, Black; Nationalism and Nationality; Politics, Identity; Popper, Karl; Race*

BIBLIOGRAPHY

Buber, Martin. [1946] 1986. *Paths in Utopia*. New York: Colliers.

Gellner, Ernest. 1998. *Language and Solitude: Wittgenstein, Malinowski and the Habsburg Dilemma*, ed. David Gellner. Cambridge, U.K.: Cambridge University Press

MacIver, Robert Morrison. [1917] 1971. *Community, A Sociological Study; Being an Attempt to Set out the Nature and Fundamental Laws of Social Life*. New York: B. Blom.

Mair, L. 1984. *Anthropology and Development*. London: Macmillan.

Popper, Karl R. [1945] 1966. *The Open Society and Its Enemies*. London: Routledge.

Joseph Agassi

COMMUNICATION

Communication is inseparable from social and behavioral activities; as a consequence it has become an integral part of research and discussion in the social sciences. Mass media and rhetoric thus closely relate to political science, while semantics and rhetoric enrich the study of law. Perception, the tool used to make sense of messages, generates much discussion in psychology and psychiatry and both areas benefit from careful communication. As the psychotherapist Carl Rogers noted in *On Becoming a Person* (1961), "The whole task of psychotherapy is the task of dealing with a failure in communication" (p. 330). Sociology, in part the study of human interactions, benefits greatly from an understanding of communication's roles in those interactions.

Sociology focuses on groups while psychology focuses mainly on the individual. However, they blend in social psychology, and probably the greatest social science focus on communication has been in social psychology. This blended discipline studies the psychological basis of people's relationships with one another. Social psychologists posit that people have few if any solely individual attributes.

In the study of interaction patterns among people and methods of influencing people, much of the work done by these scholars naturally relates to communication. In seeking to determine these patterns, social psychologists follow the work of Erving Goffman as they speak of the self, a collection of attributes, social identity, self-concept, and appearance. Interpersonal communication is affected by where a person is in the social structure as well as by the influence of others.

Relative to communication, pioneering social psychologists like Robert Bales (1950) explored interactions in small groups, while Solomon Asch (1955) detailed the impact social factors have on perception. Michael Argyle looked at patterns of social relationships across social class, while more recently Deborah Tannen (1990) examined the social characteristics of gender and gender's effects on interactions.

Social psychological research in communication owes a heavy debt to scholars like Paul Ekman, W. V. Friesen, and Raymond Birdwhistell who focused on the complex patterns nonverbal communication takes. Their research has also explored possible commonalities in meaning of nonverbal signals within and across cultures.

While people engage in communication almost unconsciously, it remains a complex subject which defies simple explanations and calls for continued research. Overall, the insights into human interaction developed following social psychology research have led to numerous practical applications, especially in the business world.

COMMUNICATION DEFINED

In its simplest form, the term *communication* refers to the process by which one person transmits information (new knowledge) to another person (or persons). A number of communication models exist, but common elements delineated by Claude Shannon and Warren Weaver (1949) link them: a sender, a receiver, a channel, the message itself, and some effect or impact resulting from the message exchange (including feedback).

Feedback, a crucial part of the communication process, represents the response to a received message (not necessarily to the message intended to be sent, but to its interpretation). While an element in the overall process, feedback's transmission duplicates the communication process it responds to, and thus involves sending and receiving, as well as media, and it can be impacted by communication barriers. Feedback, in turn, may lead to a response. Mechanistic approaches like the classic Shannon-Weaver model are appealing in their simplicity in explaining the communication process, but they do not reflect communication's complexity, especially in terms of

perception (which reflects the application of past events as well as the context in which the message is being received). Perception, in fact, accounts for much of the complexity of the communication process.

PERCEPTION

The sender (often) and the receiver always use perception to make sense of the message passing in the communication interchange. The perceiver processes the message's signs, its tangible factors, to determine the meaning (intended or not intended). These signs include what is seen, heard, felt, tasted, or smelled. The receiver then uses the mental filters of past experience to sort the signs and apply the meanings gained from similar past sensory experiences. Meaning derives from that past experience as one makes sense of the present through that experience.

The sender of a message may intend one meaning for what is sent, but the experiences the sender draws on in assigning that intended meaning may be only partly shared with the receiver. The meaning derived is thus imperfectly shared between the parties if at all. Few (if any) messages represent a pure transfer of identical meaning. While spoken communication is usually interpreted by the receiver almost immediately and often in a close spatial context (mass media and telephonic messages are obvious spatial exceptions), written communication is likely to be received and interpreted after some time lag and at a spatial distance. The context in which it is received will most likely have changed through time, and these changes may affect the perception of the message. Additionally, in any communication interchange, the very experience of receiving the message alters the receiver's perception and will affect the next message that comes through. Perception is a dynamic, ongoing process, as communication theorist C. Glenn Pearce noted, and the sender and receiver's own perceptual filters change constantly as a result of the interaction.

COMMUNICATION AND INTENT

Even when unintentional, communication can still occur. A hapless job interviewee might make a poor first impression with unpolished shoes, a weak handshake, or slouching posture (elements of nonverbal communication). The interviewee likely intends to signal competence, but the outcome differs from that intended. Of course, much communication is intentional. The more effective sender learns skills to help achieve the intended results, but perception is still a major factor. Yet, if what one applies to interpret a message varies widely from the sender's intent, common meaning may not be achieved, especially in communication between cultures.

COMMUNICATION BARRIERS

Communication barriers, elements external to the message, also complicate the process. Barriers can be as simple as physical noise or can derive from intrapersonal, interpersonal and even organizational sources. These barriers are inevitable and communicators (senders and receivers) need to work to overcome them (where possible) to enhance communication effectiveness. Steven Golen's (1990) research into communication barriers has revealed their myriad sources and the challenges communicators face in overcoming them.

Some barriers are easier to overcome. Physical noise, for example, can be overcome by isolation or simple muting. However, the intrapersonal barrier of defensiveness is more challenging in calling for one's self-awareness and empathy. An organizational barrier like the serial transmission effect (the tendency for messages to change in passing through an organization's levels) calls for objective message management skills.

The goal of a message is to transmit information, knowledge the receiver does not already know. Shannon noted that the entropy rate, the amount of information the sender wishes to transmit, cannot exceed the channel capacity without creating uncorrectable transmission errors. Keeping the sender's entropy rate below channel capacity greatly reduces errors and enhances information transfer and helps combat communication barriers. Redundancy is another useful element in communication.

REDUNDANCY

Communication systems naturally utilize redundancy to help combat problems with communication barriers and perceptual differences. Redundancy, predictability built into the message to help insure comprehension, backs up the message. While redundancy can seem to be mechanical, senders use it naturally without even thinking. It derives largely from repetition, exemplification, orthography, grammar, syntax, and format. David Gibson and Barbara Mendleson (1984) explored the dynamics of redundancy and showed the linking of information and probability theories to semantics.

Messages sharing a common grammar, syntax, and orthography are likely to be more redundant and thus help ensure the receiver shares much of the sender's intended meaning. When redundancy is minimal, additional communication barriers can arise. Redundancy can be overused, of course, particularly in terms of exemplification or repetition.

NONVERBAL COMMUNICATION

Another source of information in communication exchanges is nonverbal communication. Although less precise than formal language, it is a very significant source of information in most interpersonal exchanges and often contains more information than in the spoken element of the message. A message's nonverbal elements include all the sources of information apart from the words themselves. Gestures, posture, tone, pitch, message duration, and intensity all add nuances to the message, and complexity. This latter is particularly the case in those cases where the nonverbals contradict the other signals. Social psychologists, notably Ekman and Friesen (1974), have closely studied nonverbal communication not just as a source of information in a message, but as a source of nonverbal leakage of deception as well.

The sender controls many nonverbal elements, of course, but other elements over which the sender has little or no control can be sources of meaning in communication. Thus one's age, race, gender, height, hair color, and even physical attractiveness can represent encoded signals for the receiver to interpret. Here intent is lacking, but the nonverbal signals still play an important role.

Whatever the source of the signs giving messages meaning, communication is a relevant part of the social sciences. While communication seems deceptively simple at first glance, its underlying complexity richly repays careful study both in terms of more effectively preparing (and understanding messages) and in terms of understanding and improving the human interactions in which communication takes place.

SEE ALSO *Contempt; Culture; Fanon, Frantz; Gaze, The; Goffman, Erving; Linguistic Turn; Nonverbal Communication; Recognition; Representation; Sartre, Jean-Paul; Stare, The*

BIBLIOGRAPHY

Asch, Solomon E. 1955. Opinions and Social Pressure. *Scientific American* 193 (November): 31–35.

Bales, Robert F. 1950. *Interaction Process Analysis.* Cambridge, MA: Addison-Wesley.

Birdwhistell, Ray L. 1970. *Kinesics and Context: Essays on Body Motion Communication.* Philadelphia: University of Pennsylvania Press.

Ekman, Paul. 1972. Universals and Cultural Differences in Facial Expressions of Emotion. In *Nebraska Symposium on Motivation 1971*, ed. J. K. Cole, 207–283. Lincoln: University of Nebraska Press.

Ekman, Paul, and W. V. Friesen. 1974. Detecting Deception from the Body or Face. *Journal of Personality and Social Psychology* 29: 288–289.

Gibson, David V., and Barbara E. Mendleson. 1984. Redundancy. *Journal of Business Communication* 1 (21): 43–61.

Goffman, Erving. 1956. *The Presentation of Self in Everyday Life.* Edinburgh: University of Edinburgh Social Sciences Research Centre.

Goffman, Erving. 1967. *Interaction Ritual: Essays on Face-to Face Behavior*. New York: Anchor Books.

Golen, Steven. 1990. A Factor Analysis of Barriers to Effective Listening. *Journal of Business Communication* 1 (27): 25–36.

Hall, Edward T. 1966. *The Hidden Dimension*. Garden City, NY: Doubleday.

Pearce, C. Glenn, Ross Figgins, and Steven Golen. 1984. *Principles of Business Communication: A Comprehensive Approach*. New York: Wiley.

Rogers, Carl. 1961. *On Becoming a Person*. Boston: Houghton Mifflin.

Rogers, Carl, and F. J. Roethlisberger. 1952. Barriers and Gateways to Communication. *Harvard Business Review* (July–August): 28–34.

Shannon, Claude, and Warren Weaver. 1949. *The Mathematical Theory of Communication*. Urbana: University of Illinois Press.

Tannen, Deborah. 1990. *You Just Don't Understand: Women and Men in Conversation*. New York: Ballantine Books.

Waltman, John L. 1984. Entropy and Business Communication. *Journal of Business Communication* 21: 63–80.

Wood, Julia T. 2001. *Gendered Lives: Communication, Gender, and Culture*. 4th ed. Belmont, CA: Wadsworth Publishing.

John L. Waltman

COMMUNISM

Communism, simply put, is a socioeconomic political doctrine that advocates a classless and stateless society wherein there is collective ownership and control of property and all means of production. The term *communism*, however, means different things to differently situated people and as such might be a function of time and place. Some people associate the term with liberation from colonialism or other forms of oppression and a defense of lower-class working-class interests, while others equate it with an idealized state, a political movement, or a way of life. Still others regard it as a rejection of traditional European and North American sociopolitical values. Despite such variations in meaning, embedded in each is the notion of change. Change, however, is not always organic but is, instead, often orchestrated by those overseeing societal transformation.

A core aspect of the practical application of communism, then, has been a strong centralization of decision-making and state planning, especially in the economic sector. State planning, as practiced in the Soviet Union, Eastern Europe, and the Third World, coupled with the need to effectively silence opposition to the imposition of the Communist political and economic order, has often hinged on the effective use of authoritarian practices and single-party rule. This does not mean, however, that authoritarianism is a necessary and sufficient condition for the flourishing of Communist practices. Moreover all political systems encompass a certain degree of authoritarianism and centralization.

DEVELOPMENT OF THE THEORY OF COMMUNISM

The notion of communism dates back to ancient Greece, where it was associated with a myth concerning the golden age of humanity, when society lived in full harmony. Plato (in *The Republic*) and other ancient political theorists advocated a kind of communal living, which is viewed as a form of communism. It is Karl Marx, however, with the assistance of Friedrich Engels, who is most often credited with providing the most popularized expression of communism. As expressed in the *Communist Manifesto* (1848), their theory of communism is underpinned by antecedent philosophical arguments about the history of humankind that include the dialectical and historical materialism of Georg Hegel and Ludwig Feuerbach and others who expressed views on socialism and communism prior to and during the beginning of the European socialist movements of the 1840s. Marx's view of communism was influenced by a long and established tradition of "utopian" socialists, but he embraced a "scientific" approach that added a new twist to existing thought. Moreover Marx and Engels referred to communism as *scientific socialism*.

Socialism, as a political theory, developed during the European working-class rebellions, when the predicament of workers was viewed against the backdrop of the prevailing liberal logic of the day. Its point of departure, according to the political scientist Alfred Meyer, was the assertion that the ideals associated with the American and French Revolutions—namely liberty, equality, fraternity, and the right to a human existence—had been aborted. Thus the promise of these revolutions could be fulfilled only when political rights were consonant with social and economic equality, which necessitated wiping out the differences between rich and poor. Drawing from this and earlier philosophical arguments and movements, Marx and Engels embarked on an attempt to further develop the theory.

Marx viewed communism as the highest stage of socialism and the history of humankind as imbued with struggles between the capitalist class (the owners of capital) and the working class (proletariats). His theory, as articulated in the *Communist Manifesto*, viewed the movement of society toward communism as a scientific fact. This view holds that inherent contradictions of capitalism paved the road to revolution, which would be fueled in part by class consciousness. According to Marx, a socialist society, ruled by the working class, would emerge out of this revolution. Eventually the socialist society would evolve into communism—a classless society free of exploitation, poverty, and government coercion. Although Marx continued to view economic classes as engines for moving society to higher stages of historical development, his later works encompassed more detailed and refined arguments, including an emphasis on the polarization of the impoverished working class. The emergence of the Communist society envisioned by Marx has never come into fruition, and this failure has facilitated the rise of other schools of communism. Nevertheless, the terms *communism, socialism, Marxism,* and *Marxism-Leninism* are often used interchangeably.

The school of communism associated with Vladimir Lenin, like that associated with Marx, is informed by precursor philosophies and is grounded in the Russian reality of the 1900s. Lenin's theoretical interpretations and practical application of doctrines espoused by Marx also contributed to the development of communism. Whereas Marx predicted that the proletarian revolution would occur in capitalist society, Lenin believed that revolution could occur in precapitalist colonial societies, no matter how primitive. His theory also holds that imperialism is the highest stage of monopoly capitalism, which results from the contradictions of capitalism that fuel the search for foreign outlets for surplus capital and production. The "dictatorship of the proletariat" would be implemented by a small, dedicated elite of the Communist Party, who would lead the revolution.

Lenin's interpretation of Marxist doctrines was shaped by events associated with the Russian Revolution of 1917, which convinced him that a successful revolution in Russia could not occur as a spontaneous popular uprising. He concluded that the revolution would have to be the work of a well-organized group of professional revolutionaries. Thus he pulled together a group comprised of discontented intellectuals, workers, and peasants of different nationalities who happened to be in the right place at the right time to seize the levers of state control in Russia.

RISE OF COMMUNIST STATES

Although Marxist communism was implemented in other areas of the world outside the Soviet Union, its expansion did not occur until after World War II (1939–1945). Prior to that time many Communist parties existed in various countries, though none held the reins of governmental power. Communism, as developed by Lenin, facilitated the spread of Communist states in Eastern Europe and other parts of the world. In fact underdeveloped societies facing a crisis of modernization implemented Marxism or Marxism-Leninism at a greater rate than did capitalist societies. Thus it can be argued that Marxism-Leninism

had a greater impact on the world than any other modern philosophy during the twentieth century.

According to Meyer, Third World Marxism originated in Asia in the early 1920s and gradually spread to Africa, Latin America, and other areas that were fighting traces of colonialism. This form of Marxism had the Leninist theory of imperialism as its base. The majority of states, however, were brought into the Communist sphere after World War II, fueled by the cold war rivalry between the United States and the Soviet Union. Soviet communism was appealing because of its focus on expunging imperialist exploitation and domination from Third World states. And though the Communist Party of the Soviet Union had developed into an exportable model of success, communism, as practiced in the third world, took on a variety of forms. The Soviet model, like earlier concepts of Marxism, was altered by its application in other countries. Third world (non-Western) communism took on characteristic features of the Chinese brand of communism rather than that of the Soviet Union.

There were also conscious attempts to break free of the Soviet model of communism in Eastern Europe. The first successful attempt occurred in Yugoslavia, where the leader of the Communist Party, Josef Broz Tito, did not owe his position to Josef Stalin. James Ozinga, in *Communism: The Story of the Idea and Its Implementation* (1991), notes that Yugoslavia became a middle ground between Soviet communism and the West, owing to Tito's abandonment of rural collectivization and implementation of free enterprise and real elections, among other non-Soviet practices. The second major attempt to loosen Soviet control occurred in Hungary in 1956, followed by Poland. A third attempt surfaced twelve years later in Czechoslovakia. Efforts to remove tight Soviet control began with these nations' Communist parties and represented an expressed desire for greater liberty and a more national approach to the socialist goal (see Lerner 1993).

Communism officially came to power throughout China in 1949, following the defeat of the Nationalist (Kuomintang) forces by the Red Army. The early Chinese Communist ideology was heavily influenced by the thoughts of Mao Zedong, but Marxism-Leninism provided the theoretical foundation for the Chinese Communist ideology and served as the guiding principle for the party and state. Mao's thoughts provided the principles for practical application.

Chinese communism, as articulated by Mao Zedong, viewed the peasantry as the class that had to be mobilized for the revolution. Unlike Lenin's enlightened leadership elite, Mao advocated use of the peasantry as a major rather than a secondary force in the revolution. This meant a reliance on a rural-based group, rather than an urban proletariat, to bring about a socialist transformation. Suzanne

Ogden, a Northeastern University professor who has written often on China, notes that an orthodox Marxist-led revolution against urban capitalism made no sense in China because few workers had been exploited by the capitalist class. Mao also believed that putting revolutionary theory into practice was critically significant in guiding expected social contradictions in the right direction. Thus dialectical confrontation did not end with the triumph of the political revolution but continued into socialism and communism, according to Mao's theory. Jiwei Ci argues in *Dialectic of the Chinese Revolution* (1994) that the establishment of the Communist regime in 1949 marked the successful acquisition of Marxism as cultural self-identity, and China's possession of it became monopolistic after its ideological break with the Soviet Union in 1960.

Similarly in Cuba traditional Communist doctrine (Soviet communism) was revised to reflect Cuba's historical reality. During Fidel Castro's 26th of July movement, the Communist Party played a secondary role. José Martí, not Marx, symbolized Cuban independence from Spain and inspired dramatic change. It was his ideas that were embraced by Castro. Thus the movement began with Castro and a group of dedicated nationalists. After the movement crushed the government forces, the new regime immediately committed to Marxism-Leninism and to Soviet patronage. This patronage was born more out of economic necessity than ideological congruence. By 1963 Castro realized that orthodox Communists were a threat to Cuba's contact with regional revolutionary regimes, which compelled him to reinvigorate the revolutionary will. Thus his Communist Party exercised doctrinal independence and was charismatic rather than bureaucratic.

A cursory historical examination of Communist states, both in Eastern Europe and in the developing world, reveals a wide range of differences in ideologies and approaches to the practical application of communism. It is clear that the revolution, as envisioned by Marx, never swept Communists into power in any country. Historical evidence indicates that internal conflicts between the petit bourgeois and the ruling class, external relations, and other intervening variables had as much if not more relevance for the implementation and the nature of the Communist rule in Africa, Asia, and Latin America than did working-class consciousness and commitments to the Marxist-Leninist philosophy per se.

Many of the Communist states that developed in tandem with the cold war politics of the United States and the Soviet Union took on the character of the individuals who came to power rather than strict adherence to the Soviet model. The "revolutionaries" turned Communist state leaders understood the nature of their societies and knew exactly when to infuse their articulation of Communist doctrine with interpretations that were more relevant to national realities. One must then consider the intersection of historical events and personality as important variables in explaining variations in Communist states. Obviously different interpretations make it almost impossible to speak in terms of the "theory of communism."

THE COLLAPSE OF COMMUNIST STATES

Mikhail Gorbachev's rise to power, which precipitated the collapse of the Soviet Union in 1991, contributed to the demise of Communist Party rule in Eastern Europe and other parts of the world. Gorbachev believed that a Soviet foreign policy based on military might was a luxury that could no longer be afforded. Thus he reversed the Brezhnev Doctrine, which for years had protected unpopular Communist regimes from their population. His message was simple: the Soviet Union would no longer intervene to save faltering Communist regimes. This, coupled with events in 1989 and 1990, signaled changes that were about to occur in the Soviet bloc. In the Soviet Union the constitutional monopoly of the Communist Party was repealed, and power gradually shifted to new, mostly elected institutions of government, while opposition parties in Eastern Europe defeated Communist candidates in many local and national elections in 1990.

By the early 1990s the only states in which communism was firmly entrenched were in East Asia and a few other regions, notably China and Cuba. The collapse of the Soviet Union in 1991 rendered the United States the sole superpower, which had enormous implications for the collapse of Communist regimes in other parts of the world. By the mid- to late 1990s more and more Third World Marxist-Leninist regimes were replaced by regimes willing to play to the U.S. global political and economic agenda. This by no means resulted in the complete demise of Communist regimes, however, but it did motivate a substantial number of old-guard Communist leaders to present themselves as reformed or rehabilitated advocates for a different kind of democratic rule and free enterprise. In 2007, in parts of the former Soviet Union, Eastern Europe, and other regions of the world, post-Communist states are led by former Communists who are authoritarian, dictatorial, and cloaked in corruption. This could create an environment conducive to the return of the Communist state.

SEE ALSO *Castro, Fidel; Cold War; Gorbachev, Mikhail; Iron Curtain; Lenin, Vladimir Ilitch; Mao Zedong; Marx, Karl; Stalin, Joseph; Union of Soviet Socialist Republics*

BIBLIOGRAPHY

Adams, Gordon. 1984. Cuba and Africa. In *How the World Works: A Critical Introduction to International Relations*, ed. Gary L. Olsen, 264–284. Glenview, IL: Scott, Foresman.

Arthur, C. J. 1970. Introduction. In *The German Ideology*, by Karl Marx and Frederick Engles, ed. C. J. Arthur, trans. W. Lough, C. Dutt, and C. P. Magill, 4–34. New York: International Publishers.

Ci, Jiwei. 1994. *Dialectic of the Chinese Revolution: From Utopianism to Hedonism*. Stanford, CA: Stanford University Press.

Gati, Charles. 1990. *The Bloc That Failed: Soviet-East European Relations in Transition*. Bloomington: Indiana University Press.

Horowitz, Irving L. 1972. *Cuban Communism*. 2nd ed. New Brunswick, NJ: Transaction Books.

Lerner, Warren. 1993. *A History of Socialism and Communism in Modern Times: Theorists, Activists, and Humanists*. 2nd ed. Englewood Cliffs, NJ: Prentice Hall.

Kittrie, Nicholas, and Ivan Volgyes, eds. 1988. *The Uncertain Future: Gorbachev's Eastern Bloc*. New York: Paragon House.

Marx, Karl, and Frederick Engels. [1848] 1964. *The Communist Manifesto*. Trans. Samuel Moore, ed. Joseph Katz. New York: Washington Square.

Moise, Edwin. 1994. *Modern China: A History*. 2nd ed. New York: Longman.

Meyer, Alfred G. 1984. *Communism*. 4th ed. New York: Random House.

Ogden, Suzanne. 1995. *China's Unresolved Issues*. 3rd ed. Englewood Cliffs, NJ: Prentice Hall.

Ozinga, James R. 1991. *Communism: The Story of the Idea and Its Implementation*. 2nd ed. Englewood Cliffs, NJ: Prentice Hall.

Valkenier, Elizabeth Kridl. 1983. *The Soviet Union and the Third World: An Economic Bind*. New York: Praeger.

Wang, James C. F. 1995. *Contemporary Chinese Politics*. 5th ed. Englewood Cliffs, NJ: Prentice Hall.

Wesson, Robert. 1980. *The Aging of Communism*. New York: Praeger.

Kathie Stromile Golden

COMMUNISM, PRIMITIVE

Primitive communism is the earliest mode of production in Marxist thought. Karl Marx proposed that Asiatic, ancient, feudal, and bourgeois modes of production are epochs that mark the transitions of societies. Also, the changes in the mode of production from primitive communism through slavery, feudalism, capitalism, and socialism to communism are due to the method of dialectic, and the theory of materialism. The dialectic method involves the meeting of extreme forces that merge into synthesis. At the early state of primitive communism, primitive forms of hunting gave way to primitive forms of agriculture and cattle rearing. Also, dialectic changes of the matriarchate to the patriarchate types were recognized. In the matriarchate form, women played a dominant role in production under primitive agriculture, while the men roamed the forest after game. In the patriarchate form, men played the dominant role in the hunting and cattle-rearing stages because they were efficient with a bow, arrows, spears, and lasso. The actual process of analyzing the changes of modes of production follows a materialistic theory. Through evolution, human beings developed a consciousness that became sensitized to material change. In primitive societies, production was in the simple form of adapting to nature. Land was cultivated before it was divided, and the consciousness was communal. As production processes changed, envisaging private ownership, people's consciousness changed in that direction.

One purpose of studying primitive communism is to understand how the three major classes—wage-laborers, capitalists, and landlords—have developed under capitalism. During primitive communism property belonged to the community and labor owned all the product of its labor in the absence of capital- and land-owning classes. If one tribe was conquered by another, the conquered tribe became propertyless, as was the case with slavery and serfdom. A tribe and its property formed a sort of unity that originated from the mode of production where individuals related to one another and to nature. The object of production was to reproduce the producer. For Marx, production is not possible without capital. In primitive communism capital could be just the hands of a hunter-gatherer. Strictly speaking, capital is specific to the bourgeois mode of production. Tools are not capital outside of capitalism. And production is not possible without human labor, not tools, which are a product of human labor and natural resources.

Marx wrote, "In early communal societies in which primitive communism prevailed, and even in the ancient communal town, it was this communal society itself with its conditions which appeared as the basis of production, and its reproduction appeared as its ultimate purpose" (Marx 1967b, p. 831). Primitive communism dissolved when the mode of production changed.

In specific forms of primitive communism, one finds two major forms of unity between labor and production conditions. This unity was observed in Asiatic communal systems and in small-scale agriculture (Rosdolsky 1977, p. 273). Marx appraised the small and ancient Indian community as possessing common ownership of land, blending agriculture and handicraft, and possessing an invariable form of division of labor. As the market was unchanging, the division of labor could not evolve to, for instance, the manufacturing level.

If population increases, a new community is formed on vacant land. Production is governed by tradition, rather than by command or markets. According to Marx, "this simplicity supplies the key to the secret of the unchangeableness of Asiatic societies" (Marx [1867] 1967a, pp. 357–358).

For Marx, logical methods based on observation and deduction can lead one to "primary equations" that point to the history of capitalism (Marx [1894] 1967b, pp. 460–461). It starts "… from simple relations, such as labor, division of labor, need, exchange value, to the level of the state, exchange between nations and the world market" (Marx [1857] 1973, pp. 100–101). These simple relations explain how production, distribution, and consumption are conducted within all societies. These activities are in turn subsumed under relations of production and forces of production. A fact of primitive communism is that although "the categories of bourgeois economies possess a truth for all other forms of society…. They contain them in a developed, or stunted, or caricatured form, etc., but always with an essential difference" (Marx [1857] 1973, p. 106).

Marx's writings on primitive communism occupied his mind all his life. The 1880–1882 *Ethnological Notebooks* containing his study of the ethnologists Lewis H. Morgan (1818–1881), John Phear, Henry Maine, and John Lubbock remain his last view on the subject. Morgan sourced property rights in primitive societies to personal relationships and Maine to impersonal forces, but to Marx the source is from the collective. Marx basically accepted Morgan's view on the ethnology of primitive peoples. He studied primitive groups for the origin of civil society and the state and he traced the production mode from these primitive groups to modern society.

Further exposition of primitive communism was taken up by Friedrich Engels (1820–1895), based on the works of Morgan, whose materialistic conception of history was similar to Marx's. Morgan discovered a kinship system among the Iroquois Indians that was common to all the aboriginal inhabitants of the United States. He found that the system was common to Asia, and to some extent to Africa and Australia. Morgan introduced the concepts of the matriarchate and patriarchate to characterize primitive communes. The order of primitive communes originated with the production of food, or subsistence needs. The human race has progressed from lower to higher forms to modern civilization as lower forms of savagery and barbarism have progressed to higher forms. The arts of subsistence advanced as inventions and instruments evolved. Property, government, and family progressed in this natural process. For instance, evolution

bequeathed group marriage for savages, pairing marriage for primitive communes, and monogamy for civil societies. Morgan's process paralleled Marx's ideas expressed some forty years earlier.

SEE ALSO *Asiatic Mode of Production; Communism; Division of Labor; Egalitarianism; Ethnography; Ethnology and Folklore; Marx, Karl; Marxism; Materialism; Mode of Production*

BIBLIOGRAPHY

Engels, Friedrich. [1884] 1942. *The Origin of the Family, Private Property, and the State.* New York: International Publishers.

Marx, Karl. [1857] 1973. *Grundrisse.* Trans. Martin Nicolaus. New York: Vintage.

Marx, Karl. [1859] 1965. *Pre-Capitalist Economic Formations*, ed. Eric J. Hobsbawm, trans. Jack Cohen. New York: International Publishers.

Marx, Karl. [1867] 1967a. *Capital, Volume I.* New York: International Publishers.

Marx, Karl. [1880–1882] 1972. *The Ethnological Notebooks of Karl Marx: Studies of Morgan, Phear, Maine, Lubbock*, ed. Lawrence Krader. Assen, Netherlands: Gorcum & Company.

Marx, Karl. [1894] 1967b. *Capital, Volume III.* New York: International Publishers.

Morgan, Lewis H. 1877. *Ancient Society, or Researches in the Lines of Human Progress from Savagery, through Barbarism, to Civilization.* London: Macmillan.

Rosdolsky, Roman. 1977. *The Making of Marx's 'Capital'.* Trans. Pete Burgess. London: Pluto Press.

Lall Ramrattan
Michael Szenberg

COMMUNITARIANISM

Communitarianism is a political philosophy that often stands in opposition to the principles of liberalism. Communitarians theorize that the community is the most important element of a society or culture. As such, the stability of the community must be enhanced and protected. Within the public sphere, communitarians explicitly argue against individualistic and pragmatic liberalism, citing a loss of moral and civic orientation. Communitarians posit that true ideals in a democracy cannot survive without a cohering center. Some communitarians, such as Robert Spaemann and Alan Bloom, consider that individualistic legacies of Enlightenment thinking have led to the decline of community as a way of life by harming the ability of the moral imagination to find solutions to community problems such as poverty or discrimination. Communitarians such as Markate Daly advance the notion that community is a part of life. As such, every individual is a member of a community and through this membership develops identities, relationships, and attachments with others; the members of a community express their values through their institutions and social needs. Those such as Amitai Etzioni criticize values of autonomy, natural rights, neutrality, universality, and individual interests in favor of values that emphasize traditions, common good, character, solidarity, social practices, and social responsibility. Communitarian goals bring about changes in habits, public policies, and morality that allow a community to work toward a future based on strong community goals and values.

Communitarians also posit that not all communities are moral. Communities that seek to destroy or diminish human life and property would not be allowed within the communitarian rubric. Rather, a true communitarian seeks stability and a community that flourishes. Democracy is seen as communitarian in that it joins community interests and institutions to bring about the will of the people.

Another common tenet of communitarianism is that loyalty is given to the community and group for the greater good of the community. As a political philosophy, resources for moral judgment and action are located in the established mores of the family, the workplace, and the like rather than within the individual; as such, the point and purpose of individual lives is to serve institutional needs and goals rather than vice versa. This system needs persons who can commit themselves to collective behaviors.

Some communitarians theorize that community views should not be challenged. It is more important that community leadership reinforce and strengthen the status quo. For example, the communitarian journalist should reinforce information necessary to maintain community values.

Additionally, communitarian leadership focuses on attaining ideals and keeping the group together, thereby maintaining a hard-earned position in the social structure. The group provides a presentation of a united front possessing power or the illusion of power. Individual members gain self-confidence from merely belonging but also will lose some individual identity. The system is more basic than the rights of individual members, so concepts of justice or fairness are sometimes ignored in favor of preservation of the group. Further, to some communitarians, loyalty to the group transcends the cause of truth.

Within the political realm, the community is usually advancing a cause, thereby seeking strength in numbers. Often the group is formed because of misuse of individual rights in a particular area, creating an attitude of "us versus them." Often the community remains together even after the goals for forming it are met. Additionally, the group has the ability to banish members who do not follow the rules of the community and individualist members who find a cause or a truth the group would rather not explore. Rules are set by the community, and often examination of the rules is not necessary. Because of a reluctance to examine rules, members are slow to develop their own moral reasoning and rely on the morality of the group.

Noted contemporary communitarians such as Alasdair MacIntyre find that the individualistic legacies of Enlightenment thinking have been "historically implicated in developments that have led to the decline of community as a way of life" (1984, p. 52). Amitai Etzioni celebrates these individuals who are committed to the community rather than to individual rights by stating that "communitarians are dedicated to working with our fellow citizens to bring about the changes in values, habits, and public policies that will allow us to do for society what the environmental movements seeks to do for nature: to safeguard and enhance our future" (1993, p. 3).

Philosopher Markate Daly (1994) believes it is essential that communitarianism become a way of life. In communitarian theory, philosophers assume that community is part of life; as such, every individual is a member of a community and through this develops identities, relationships, and attachments with others. The members of a community express their values through their institutions and social needs, tempered by kindness. She contrasts communitarian with liberal notions as, "instead of such values as individual interests, autonomy, universality, natural rights and neutrality, communitarian philosophy is framed in terms of the common good, social practices and traditions, character, solidarity and social responsibility" (Daly 1994, p. 17).

Jürgen Habermas (1990), a prominent continental philosopher, uses a system of communitarian philosophy in proposing a dialectic that must be open to the community. Within his system, all decisions, particularly problematic decisions, can be made by the collective. Each member who is competent to speak to the subject is given equal time and input into the decision process.

Wendell Berry (1990) reminds that not all communities are moral, and those communities set to destroy or diminish human life and property should not be considered communities. Clifford Christians, John P. Ferre, and P. Mark Fackler confirm Berry's sentiments, stating that "because a moral community is a condition for personhood, a group is not ipso facto good, and no community can excuse inhumane behavior" (1993, p. 69). Berry and Christians are examples of communitarian thinkers who realize the need for a conception of individual good to balance the supreme good of community stability.

Communalism is a distinct political theory and political practice. It differs from communitarianism in many ways. It generally involves a group of individuals committed to communal living and common ownership. This commitment involves loyalty to the interests of the communal minority or ethnic group rather than to society as a whole. Some forms of communalism work toward abolishing the state, not seizing power but doing away with power and the particular power attached to the business model of capitalism. Often, religion is a driving force in communal living.

A commune is described as the basic living habitat for the communal organization. Most are serious about being self-sustaining in both consumption and production. This means that the group should own enough land to feed itself and have a specialized means of commerce. Examples of successful communal groups are the Hutterites, who were financially successful craftsmen and agriculturalists. Oneida, Amana, and in the twentieth century the Brüderhof are also examples of successful communes.

In practice, Friedrich Engels and Karl Marx wrote extensively about the ideals of communist living in general but sometimes specifically about the ideals of communal life. *Socialism: Utopian and Scientific*, a pamphlet originally published in 1880 by Engels (2006), delineates the notions of communalism and contrasts it with socialism. Their plan calls for a new society founded on quality of life rather than slavish work. However, it does not give a plan for the ideal community.

Often the term *utopia* is used in conjunction with communalism, moving the commune to a visionary or an ideally perfect state of society. Sir Thomas More's *Utopia* ([1516] 2003) describes an imaginary island with the ideal social, legal, and political system. Humans can strive to create this within a community or globally in an effort to live more civilly. Sometimes *utopian* is used in a negative way to discredit ideas seen as impossible to realize.

SEE ALSO *Communalism; Democracy; Ethics; Leadership; Liberalism; Morality; Philosophy, Political; Utopianism*

BIBLIOGRAPHY

Barney, Ralph D. 1994. A Dangerous Drift? The Sirens' Call to Collectivism. Unpublished paper presented at the Association for Practical and Professional Ethics, Cleveland, OH, February 26, 1994.

Bohler, Dietrich. 1990. Transcendental Pragmatics and Critical Morality. In *The Communicative Ethics Controversy*, eds. Seyla Benhabib and Fred Dallmayr, 131. Cambridge, MA: MIT Press.

Christians, Clifford G. 1977. Fifty Years of Scholarship in Media Ethics. *Journal of Communication* 27 (autumn): 19–29.

Christians, Clifford G., John P. Ferre, and Mark Fackler. 1993. *Good News Social Ethics and the Press*. New York: Oxford University Press.

Daly, Markate, ed. 1994. *Communitarianism, A New Public Ethics*. Belmont, CA: Wadsworth.

Engels, Frederick (Friedrich). 2006. *Socialism: Utopian and Scientific*, ed. Andrew Moore. Mondial Press. Originally published May 1, 1880 as "Socialism: Utopian and Scientific," in *Revue Socialiste*.

Etzioni, Amitai. 1993. *The Spirit of Community: Rights, Responsibilities and the Communitarian Agenda*. New York: Crown.

Habermas, Jürgen. 1989. *The Structural Transformation of the Public Sphere: An Inquiry into a Category of Bourgeois Society*. Trans. Thomas Burger with Frederick Lawrence. Cambridge, MA: MIT Press.

Habermas, Jürgen. 1990. Discourse Ethics: Notes on Philosophical Justification. In *The Communicative Ethics Controversy*, eds. Seyla Benhabib and Fred Dallmayr. Cambridge, MA: MIT Press.

MacIntyre, Alasdair. 1984. *After Virtue*, 2nd ed. Notre Dame, IN: University of Notre Dame Press.

More, Thomas. 2003. *Utopia*, ed. Paul Turner. New York: Penguin Classics.

Mulhall, Stephen, and Adam Swift. 1996. *Liberals and Communitarians*, 2nd ed. Oxford: Blackwell.

Rawls, John. 1971. *A Theory of Justice*. Cambridge, MA: Harvard University Press.

Elaine E. Englehardt

COMMUNITY ACTION

SEE *War on Poverty.*

COMMUNITY ECONOMIC DEVELOPMENT

Community economic development is a term for the processes of change generated through place-based economic activities that are controlled by, or at least oriented toward, local residents for their betterment (Gordon Nembhard 1999, p. 297). Community economic development strategies encompass a variety of community empowerment and business development approaches, such as political advocacy, constituency group organizing, entrepreneurship development, education, job training, and labor development (University of Illinois at Chicago Center for Urban Economic Development 1987). Economic activities include job creation, entrepreneurship and business development, housing development, the provision of financial services, and the development of capital markets.

Local economic development practices can be categorized into five general chronological and overlapping phases: state industrial recruitment (starting in the 1930s); political critiques, advocacy planning, and community focus (1960s); export orientation, labor market research and development, and equity strategies (1970s and 1980s); environmental sustainability and social justice (1980s); and privatization and regional integration (1990s) (see Fitzgerald and Leigh 2002, pp. 9–26). Scholars and practitioners, particularly starting in the 1960s, have honed the term *community economic development* to focus on grassroots activity that is local and indigenous. Such efforts are centered on people and a variety of stakeholders (residents, workers, business owners, policymakers, civic and political organizations, etc.). Community control and economic stability, independence, and prosperity are the goals.

Economic development models range from traditional private business/corporation-centered models to alternative community-based, cooperative, and employee-owned models (see Gordon Nembhard 1999). The corporate model uses strategies to retain or attract businesses to the community, as well as strategies to make the residents "good" employees for those businesses. Municipalities attract the businesses with tax incentives and abatements, subsidies, below-market loans, favorable zoning changes, utility cost reductions, infrastructure improvements, the establishment of commercial districts, and the designation of industrial parks and business incubators. Using traditional strategies, municipalities will also try to ensure corporations a relatively cheap and dependable labor force, even though many of these businesses hire few local residents.

Community-based and community-initiated development, in contrast, combines public, private, and nonprofit economic activities to increase residents' and workers' human, social, and cultural capital; to facilitate organizational, managerial, and microenterprise experiences in establishing and maintaining small local businesses that are owned and operated by residents (and tend to hire more residents); and to maintain affordable housing. These kinds of enterprises include consumer, producer, worker, and housing cooperatives; credit unions; democratic ESOPs (employee stock ownership plans) and other employee-owned businesses; community land trusts; community development financial institutions; community development corporations; nonprofit businesses (social entrepreneurship); and municipally owned companies (Gordon Nembhard 1999; Democracy Collaborative 2005). Debates about contending strategies often revolve around false tradeoffs between pollution and jobs, education and recreation, livable wages versus subminimum wages, unionization and corporate growth,

cooperative ownership and private property, and affordable housing and prosperous real-estate markets.

Community economic development focuses on the neighborhood and municipality level, as separate from regional, state, federal, and international economic activity. Interactions are thus more intimate and intertwined, and the range of activities are more oriented toward and affected by place. A focus on community economic development often elevates microlevel activity and small-scale community-initiated projects as strategies to reach marginal and underserved populations. However, the effectiveness can be limited. Sometimes solutions to economic problems require broader participation and enhanced or increased resources pooled at the regional, state, or federal levels. On the other hand, higher-level policies can also undermine progressive local policies, such as national or international trade rules that do not recognize, or actually invalidate, local environmental or labor standards and tax laws. Corporate globalization increasingly undermines many aspects of community economic development by removing resources and control from local communities (Blakely and Bradshaw 2002; Gordon Nembhard 1999). Local strategies, particularly asset-based strategies that help residents develop and own a variety of wealth-producing assets, have become increasingly popular in the face of persistent poverty and globalization. Community economic development strategies anchor capital and keep the benefits circulating among those who produce it, service it, and need it.

BIBLIOGRAPHY

Blakely, Edward J., and Ted K. Bradshaw. 2002. *Planning Local Economic Development: Theory and Practice*. 3rd ed. Thousand Oaks, CA: Sage.

Democracy Collaborative. 2005. *Building Wealth: The New Asset-Based Approach to Solving Social and Economic Problems*. Washington, DC: Aspen Institute.

Fitzgerald, Joan, and Nancey Green Leigh. 2002. *Economic Revitalization: Cases and Strategies for City and Suburb*. Thousand Oaks, CA: Sage.

Gordon Nembhard, Jessica. 1999. Community Economic Development: Alternative Visions for the 21st Century. In *Readings in Black Political Economy*, eds. John Whitehead and Cobie Kwasi Harris, 295–304. Dubuque. IA: Kendall/Hunt.

Handy, John W. 1993. Community Economic Development: Some Critical Issues. *Review of Black Political Economy* 21: 41–64.

Kretzmann, John P., and John L. McKnight. 1993. *Building Communities from the Inside Out: A Path toward Finding and Mobilizing a Community's Assets*. Chicago: ACTA.

Sherbrooke Declaration. 1998. *The Proceedings of the Global Meetings on Community Economic Development*. Montreal, Quebec: Institut de formation en développement économique communautaire (IFDEC).

University of Illinois at Chicago Center for Urban Economic Development. 1987. *Community Economic Development Strategies: A Manual for Local Action.* Chicago: Author.

Whitehead, John, David Landes, and Jessica Gordon Nembhard. 2005. Inner-City Economic Development and Revitalization: A Community-Building Approach. In *African Americans in the U.S. Economy*, eds. Cecilia A. Conrad, John Whitehead, Patrick Mason, and James Stewart, 341–356. Lanham, MD: Rowman & Littlefield.

Jessica Gordon Nembhard

COMMUNITY POWER STUDIES

Power is a contested concept, with little agreement about what exactly to study or how to go about it. It is also a concept that belongs to many disciplines—political science, sociology, and psychology all accord it special importance. Furthermore, disciplinary differences overlap ideological ones.

One of the most intensely debated applications of power is in the study of local communities. Although concerned most directly with local politics, community power is linked to issues about the basic nature of democracy in modern society. The work that drew attention to power was Floyd Hunter's 1953 book on Atlanta, *Community Power Structure: A Study of Decision Makers.* Earlier community studies dealt with power only incidentally. Hunter made it central. Coming from a background in sociology and social work, Hunter nonetheless focused on politics and on how the system of representative government worked in practice. In response a pluralist school of thought headed by Robert Dahl (2005) challenged Hunter's finding that the business sector with its rich supply of economic and organizational resources could determine a locality's policy agenda. Instead, this school argued that governing is autonomous and that popular elections are the guiding force that keeps policy choices in line with citizen sentiments.

In its formative stage the community power debate set forth sharp alternatives. Are local communities dominated by the local business class like the pre–World War II "Middletown" studied by Robert S. Lynd and Helen M. Lynd (1929, 1937), or are they governed by shifting coalitions, with public officials often in the key role, like Dahl's postwar New Haven, Connecticut? With different cities at different times yielding different findings, grounds for amicable coexistence among researchers proved hard to establish. Hunter's *Community Power Structure* thus triggered a cross-disciplinary, ideologically infused controversy that lasted for a quarter of a century or longer. Each

side elaborated a case for its argument and against the opposing argument, largely neglecting alternative possibilities. With the research task framed narrowly, pluralists could demonstrate that, as in New Haven, a small elite is not in control. However, their critics could also show that less-privileged segments of the population are left out and have little voice in governance. Contending sides consistently talked past one another, a pattern that has much to do with the nature of power and an initial focus on power as control.

Besides power as the ability of one actor to dominate another, some scholars see power as a shared activity in which people come together to do something that individually they could not do. The two forms can be thought of as *power over* and *power to.* The first refers to conflict where the preferences of one clash directly with the preferences of another. The second refers to circumstances in which the capacity to act comes through a combined effort, preferences are not firmly fixed, and conflicts are largely indirect and inferred. While the two forms of power may seem to have little to do with each other, in a community setting there are ample instances of both, and oftentimes they overlap. In conflict scenarios efforts to dominate often generate resistance, thus running up the cost of control. Attempted domination may give way to tacit bargaining over the degree of control and can even evolve into a form of exchange in which each party decides to give up something to receive something. This form of bargaining can shade into instances of power to.

As bodies of people with shared concerns, whether it be to maintain public safety or provide a medical facility, communities have a need to act collectively. To the extent that they have this capacity, they can be self-governing; but that capacity does not come free of complications involving both forms of power. In complex societies the governing function takes a distinct form, seemingly differentiated from other functions, and thereby becomes somewhat separated from the people as a whole. Under such a separation some elements may come together in support of their particular version of how to meet community needs. In this way they give strength to a capacity to act, that is, give shape to a form of power to. However, if others find themselves left out, then those left out may experience power as a form of being dominated. A capacity by one set of actors to shape a priority agenda potentially leaves others in a marginal position in the governance of the community.

In principle representative government is a check against one element of society ignoring the concerns of others. Essentially, then, the community power debate is over how the representative process functions in practice, with wide disagreement about the degree to which formally democratic systems operate in line with the ideals of representative government. In a classic form set forth by Dahl, the pluralist school of thought sees politics as basically open and inclusive. No group is consigned to a marginal political standing. Pluralism, however, has been subject to a variety of critiques, including the charge that it is a legitimating ideology rather than an evidence-based explanation of how democratic politics actually works (Merelman 2003; see also Kariel 1966). Some antipluralists maintain that the central facts of local political life are about how some segments of society are well positioned to act on their concerns and to protect their interests while others suffer an unending disadvantage.

APPROACHES AND UNDERLYING ASSUMPTIONS

Pluralists and their critics (the latter variously called stratificationists, elitists, neo-elitists, or, the term used here, antipluralists) differ sharply in the assumptions they make about the political world to be studied. Although scholars do not divide into two highly unified camps, there are distinctly different schools of thought. Contrasting their assumptions is illuminating.

Pluralist

1. The authority of government is an important base of action, and in representative government competitive elections have a potential to make officials responsive to the citizenry. Although social and economic inequalities are consequential, universal suffrage can serve as a check against the accumulation of power in the hands of a few.

2. Society shapes politics in the following way: Over time deference to persons of high family status and wealth yields to instrumental understandings of authority. With increasingly differentiated roles and associated calculations of self-interest, conflicts are issue-specific and changeable. In this setting the exercise of control is costly and power inherently centrifugal.

3. Power is manifest in conflicting preferences and is evident in the observable actions of individuals.

Antipluralist

1. Because governing involves more than formal institutions of government, elected public officials have limited autonomy. They often seek support and cooperation from highly useful, even essential nongovernmental sources. Therefore, elections are not the pivot around which actual governance turns. Although there are rituals celebrating democracy and popular participation, they may disguise rather than reveal political reality. In a society in which investment capital is privately owned and various elements of society differ in capacity to mobilize, public officials are easily drawn to those who control abundant and attractive resources.

2. The functional usefulness of a governing capacity and the strategic advantages of positions within a governing arrangement serve to make resistance to those arrangements difficult. Although Robert Michels's (1959) law of oligarchy is less than ironclad, it is a factor because the leadership function is to varying degrees not subject to popular control. Therefore, even in a complex society, power is not inherently centrifugal.

3. Highly visible policy actions are insufficient evidence for understanding power. The flow of decisions and nondecisions is potentially more telling than specific controversies. Hence, agenda control is more fundamental than outcomes in particular issues. Asymmetrical dependencies, reputations for power, issue suppression, and manipulated rules and procedures are aspects of power important to study.

FINDINGS AND THEIR INTERPRETATION

Pluralist

1. In the continuing debate over community power, Dahl and other pluralists favor the term *dispersed inequalities*. It is contrasted with *traditional inequality*, in which a small group of notables enjoy the combined advantages of status, wealth, and political office. The claim of dispersion rests on two dynamics. One is that, with electoral popularity differentiated from historical forms of deference, numbers can counterbalance wealth and social standing. If any high-status group aims for an expanded scope of influence, then its members must contend for popular support rather than pursue control on their own terms. The other dispersing force comes from the distribution of immediate interests. Everyone cares intensely about only a few matters of special concern. Because complex society produces highly differentiated concerns, intensities fragment to coincide with highly particular interests. Thus, interest group rather than class is the most useful term of analysis.

2. Because contenders for electoral office have incentives to be responsive to those most concerned about any given issue, the intensely concerned are influential in their special area of interest. And because the overall pattern is one of fragmentation,

those who are influential on one narrow issue carry little weight on many other issues. The narrowness of issues means that over time many different groups can be satisfied to some degree, although few groups get all they want. Politics is fluid, and the central political factor is the electoral connection between vote-seeking politicians and a citizenry capable of mobilizing against any threat to its particular but varied interests. While most citizens are politically passive most of the time, elite competition keeps the system open.

Antipluralist

1. Although antipluralists come in various guises, their shared position is that social and economic inequalities have deep roots with profound consequences for political mobilization. For example, Rodney E. Hero (1992) finds what he labels two-tiered pluralism, which has a surface layer in which lesser issues correspond to pluralism and a deeper layer of issues about race and ethnicity that formal equalities in suffrage and legal standing are ineffective in addressing.

2. Political arrangements have limited pliability. Conflicts compete with one another and any established arrangement constitutes a mobilization of bias that is not easily overturned. When applied to local governance, one body of issues may crowd others out and elections may be captive to historic or other loyalties, thereby reducing their potential for exacting accountability.

ALTERNATIVE PERSPECTIVES

Despite decades of debate and criticism, there remains a tendency for pluralism to be defined operationally as the absence of control by a small, cohesive elite. However, meeting this loose definition is not the same as the claim that politics is open and widely inclusive. For critics of pluralism the puzzle is how, beyond such specific factors as the mobility of capital, to account for the ongoing political weakness of the less privileged. After its peak in the 1960s and 1970s, the pluralist-antipluralist debate receded in salience, in part because both sides cast their argument in terms too narrow to address the full picture of local governance. Still, the community power concept is appealing in part because in principle it addresses the whole of the local political order and not just the actions of officeholders.

The whole of the local political order should not, however, be equated with a self-contained form of rule. European scholars have long cautioned against such an assumption and have called attention to national context

(e.g., see Dunleavy 1980). They explain that the structure of intergovernmental relations may impinge greatly, and, depending on the circumstances that vary from country to country and from time period to time period, the business sector may not have a strong incentive to involve itself in local politics.

In the 1980s the aim of addressing the whole of the local political order regained footing through the idea of an urban regime. This concept shifts emphasis from who governs to questions about how governance takes place—which concerns have priority and why, what various participants in the process contribute, and how efforts come to be coordinated around some issues but not others. How key actors understand their situation is important, and this includes matters they take as a given. As a concept, urban regime provides a way of acknowledging that governance involves much more than operating the levers of the formal machinery of government. A regime consists of "the informal arrangements by which public bodies and private interests function together in order to be able to make and carry out governing decisions" (Stone 1989, p. 6). Arrangements, of course, do not just happen. They are created and maintained as a way of pursuing a set of aims, perhaps seeking to loosen some constraints while accommodating others. Because different agendas call for different kinds of arrangements, regimes in some sense indirectly compete. Any established arrangement for governing may hold a preemptive edge. While that edge may be surmountable, it takes a considerable combination of resources and effort to bring a new governing arrangement into being.

However, as with community power itself, it is important to remember that localities have only a constrained freedom to maneuver. Local governing arrangements mediate but do not control external forces. Thus, urban regimes are not autonomous, free-forming entities. Every regime is shaped by context, by the distribution of policy-relevant resources, by the mix of ideas at work, and by the ease with which various policy efforts can yield results. The internal dynamics of regime formation thus do not provide a sufficient basis for understanding how agendas take shape. Local agendas and the political arrangements that support them are, for example, greatly influenced by the position of a locality within a metropolitan region. Economic competition, the extent of revenue equalization through the intergovernmental system, and the ways in which local boundaries divide the metropolitan region socioeconomically all have a bearing on how agendas take shape and on what form political mobilization assumes. As a result, a full analysis of a local political order must pay close attention to context, both what part of the local context key players respond to actively and what part they take as a given.

The analysis of urban regimes calls for seeing power in a broader framework than power over. A useful step is to move away from the notion that actors are simply intentional agents pursuing self-defining interests. Such an understanding puts undue emphasis on who prevails in conflicts or who is positioned to suppress potential issues. It neglects the processes of attraction between potential coalition partners and how these processes affect policy aspirations.

If the world is seen as thoroughly relational in the sense that aims take shape in relations among actors who inform one another through deeds and words about opportunities and constraints, then it is understandable why socioeconomic inequalities are not easily overridden politically. Those inequalities are part of the building material out of which governing arrangements are constructed. There is deep tension between the ideal of political equality and the reality of socioeconomic inequality. Still, community power is about politics, and politics is about choosing. Political agency is the means for adjusting the terms on which socioeconomic inequalities and the equality of citizenship are accommodated to one another. Hence, the research task involves identifying creative ways to alter conditions and build new capacities. Some steps can make governing arrangements more open and inclusive, others less so. For that reason the study of community power remains timely even as the debates of the formative period have become less compelling.

POWER AND CONSTRAINED POLITICAL AGENCY

Since the publication of Dahl's classic work in 1961, debate has often centered on the adequacy of the pluralist conception of politics. For example, Patrick Dunleavy charges that pluralists simply assume that conventional "input processes" determine political and policy outcomes (1980, p. 13). Historically, this assumption reduced Hunter's concern with leadership in a broad community context to Dahl's question of who governs. Moreover, by highlighting particular leaders, Hunter's work also contributed to a preoccupation with who are the key policymakers. Subsequent work has only gradually returned to Hunter's original insight that power is embedded in relationships, in networks of how people are related to one another in perceiving and responding to a community's problems. The evolving intellectual challenge is to understand how human agents act within structured relationships, relationships that contain inconsistencies and are often in tension with one another. For example, one person/one vote is at odds with what Charles E. Lindblom terms the *privileged position of business* (1977). Because structures impinge on one another, they reach accommodations of varying depth and duration. For researchers,

charting these accommodations is no easy mater, and the question of how deeply economic relationships affect others continues as a matter of debate.

While human agents have a creative capacity, they are constrained to act collectively, not as asocial individuals, but as actors within an array of economic, social, and political relationships in place. Although change is feasible, working through well-established relationships is easier than bringing about fundamental change in relationships. However, because altering relationships is possible, one must look at varying capacities to reconstruct governing arrangements. This dimension of power is not evident on the surface in much political activity, because it works within and does not challenge most relationships. Standing alone, power over does not capture this deeper level. This deeper level involves the degree of difficulty encountered in reshaping power to. In short, some realignments are easier to bring about than others, but the complexity of that process defies being expressed in any succinct formula.

Consider the two aspects of power to. It has an output side—what human agents can produce together—and an input side—the factors that bring people together in a form of cooperation. Just as there are features that enable one actor to dominate or resist another, so there are features that make cooperation between actors more attractive or less so. To the extent that alignments for cooperation compete for governing space, competition may be indirect and lack overt expression. For example, some alignments may preemptively displace other possible alignments. Power at this level is hard to observe except through its expression in a long flow of events and their counterfactuals.

If analysts assume that politics is a kind of zero-sum game of openly clashing policy preferences, then they will not engage this underlying dimension of power. Players in the political game compete, but a different understanding of power emerges in realizing that they also have varying degrees of attraction to one another. As they come together, one constellation of attractions may foreclose others. Attraction stems partly from the objectives that players can achieve by combining efforts, but other considerations come into play as well.

The study of community power is ultimately about understanding how competition and attraction toward cooperation interact. Competition is easier to observe through the immediate actions of individuals. In contrast, attraction toward cooperation is embedded in and reinforced through relationships, some of which may simply be taken as a given. Political creativity is partly about altering relationships by developing new channels of awareness and thereby posing new possibilities.

That power has an intentional aspect should not lead to the conclusion that it operates only in an intentional manner. Discovery of the possible is part of the power process, and discovery may precede fully developed intention. However, discovery is constrained by the greater difficulty of altering some relationships over others. That is why power to is a necessary complement to power over. Because constructing some versions of power to is easier than others, a full understanding of community power has to include both power over and power to—both have a bearing on how the politics of democratic representation operates in practice.

The future prospects of a democratic way of life rest on an ongoing exercise of political creativity, but that creativity is itself constrained by the multiple networks of relationships within which it is exercised. Community power is a concept that treats power as relational and relations as structured by the ways in which multiple facets of life intersect. Questions about community power have not disappeared, but instead, since the formative period of debate, have evolved to take into account an expanded appreciation of the complexity of the local setting.

SEE ALSO *Dahl, Robert Alan*

BIBLIOGRAPHY

Bachrach, Peter, and Morton S. Baratz. 1970. *Power and Poverty: Theory and Practice.* New York: Oxford University Press.

Crenson, Matthew A. 1971. *The Un-politics of Air Pollution: A Study of Non-decisionmaking in the Cities.* Baltimore, MD: Johns Hopkins University Press.

Dahl, Robert. 2005. *Who Governs? Democracy and Power in an American City.* 2nd ed. New Haven, CT: Yale University Press.

Dowding, Keith M. 1996. *Power.* Minneapolis: University of Minnesota Press.

Dunleavy, Patrick. 1980. *Urban Political Analysis: The Politics of Collective Consumption.* London: Macmillan.

Elkin, Stephen L. 1987. *City and Regime in the American Republic.* Chicago: University of Chicago Press.

Flyvbjerg, Bent. 1998. *Rationality and Power: Democracy in Practice.* Trans. Steven Sampson. Chicago: University of Chicago Press.

Gaventa, John. 1980. *Power and Powerlessness: Quiescence and Rebellion in an Appalachian Valley.* Urbana: University of Illinois Press.

Harding, Alan. 1995. Elite Theory and Growth Machines. In *Theories of Urban Politics,* ed. David Judge, Gerry Stoker, and Harold Wolman. London: Sage.

Hayward, Clarissa Rile. 2000. *De-facing Power.* New York: Cambridge University Press.

Hero, Rodney E. 1992. *Latinos and the U.S. Political System: Two-Tiered Pluralism.* Philadelphia: Temple University Press.

Hunter, Floyd. 1953. *Community Power Structure: A Study of Decision Makers.* Chapel Hill: University of North Carolina Press.

Jones, Bryan D., and Lynn W. Bachelor. 1993. *The Sustaining Hand: Community Leadership and Corporate Power.* 2nd ed. Lawrence: University Press of Kansas.

Kariel, Henry S. 1966. *The Promise of Politics.* Englewood Cliffs, NJ: Prentice-Hall.

Lindblom, Charles E. 1977. *Politics and Markets: The World's Political Economic Systems.* New York: Basic Books.

Lukes, Steven. 2004. *Power: A Radical View.* 2nd ed. New York: Palgrave Macmillan.

Lynd, Robert S., and Helen M. Lynd. 1929. *Middletown: A Study in Contemporary American Culture.* New York: Harcourt, Brace.

Lynd, Robert S., and Helen M. Lynd. 1937. *Middletown in Transition.* New York: Harcourt, Brace.

Merelman, Richard M. 2003. *Pluralism at Yale: The Culture of Political Science in American.* Madison: University of Wisconsin Press.

Michels, Robert. 1959. *Political Parties: A Sociological Study of the Oligarchical Tendencies of Modern Democracy.* Trans. Eden Paul and Cedar Paul. New York: Dover.

Mollenkopf, John Hull. 1992. *A Phoenix in the Ashes: The Rise and Fall of the Koch Coalition in New York City Politics.* Princeton, NJ: Princeton University Press.

Newton, Kenneth. 1976. *Second City Politics: Democratic Processes and Decision-Making in Birmingham.* Oxford, U.K.: Clarendon Press.

Peterson, Paul E. 1981. *City Limits.* Chicago: University of Chicago Press.

Polsby, Nelson W. 1980. *Community Power and Political Theory: A Further Look at Problems of Evidence and Inference.* 2nd ed. New Haven, CT: Yale University Press.

Reed, Adolph, Jr. 1999. *Stirrings in the Jug: Black Politics in the Post-Segregation Era.* Minneapolis: University of Minnesota Press.

Rhyne, Edwin H. 1958. Political Parties and Decision Making in Three Southern Counties. *American Political Science Review* 52 (4) (December): 1091–1107.

Saunders, Peter. 1979. *Urban Politics: A Sociological Interpretation.* London: Hutchinson.

Schattschneider, E. E. 1960. *The Semisovereign People: A Realist's View of Democracy in America.* New York: Holt, Rinehart, and Winston.

Stacey, Margaret, et al. 1975. *Power, Persistence, and Change: A Second Study of Banbury.* London: Routledge and Kegan Paul.

Stoker, Gerry. 1995. Regime Theory and Urban Politics. In *Theories of Urban Politics,* ed. David Judge, Gerry Stoker, and Harold Wolman. London: Sage.

Stone, Clarence N. 1980. Systemic Power in Community Decision Making: A Restatement of Stratification Theory. *American Political Science Review* 74 (4) (December): 978–990.

Stone, Clarence N. 1989. *Regime Politics: Governing Atlanta, 1946–1988.* Lawrence: University Press of Kansas.

Stone, Clarence N. 2005. Looking Back to Look Forward: Reflections on Urban Regime Analysis. *Urban Affairs Review* 40 (3) (January): 309–341.

Walker, Jack L. 1966. A Critique of the Elitist Theory of Democracy. *American Political Science Review* 60 (2) (June): 285–295.

Clarence N. Stone

COMMUNITY STANDARDS

SEE *Censorship; Obscenity.*

COMPARATIVE DYNAMICS

Comparative dynamics does for dynamics what comparative statics does for statics. The difference lies in the fact that comparative dynamics is concerned with the effects of changes in the data (parameters, exogenous variables, initial conditions) on the whole motion over time of a dynamic economic model. This motion will usually be some sort of dynamic equilibrium path, such as, for example, a steady-state growth path where all variables grow at constant rates, or an optimal path deriving from a dynamic optimization problem.

The method of comparative dynamics can be summarized as follows. We have a set of dynamic functional equations, whose solution gives the time path of the economic system. In this solution, parameters, exogenous variables, and initial conditions also appear. Therefore, a different solution (time path) corresponds to a different set of data. It is then possible to ascertain the effect on the solution of a change in any one of the data.

Comparative dynamics, as such, does not say anything about the transition from one equilibrium growth path to another: The study of this transition belongs to stability analysis. Additionally, the conditions of stability of the equilibrium path may be useful in obtaining information on comparative dynamics: This can be regarded as the dynamic analogue of Paul Samuelson's *correspondence principle* in comparative statics, with *dynamic equilibrium path* replacing *static equilibrium point*.

This is about as far as one can go with intuition. Formally, take the case of steady-state growth and consider a differential equation system

$$\frac{dx(t)}{dt} = f[x(t), \omega(t), \theta], \qquad (1)$$

where x is a vector of endogenous variables, f is a vector of functions, ω is a vector of exogenous variables (given functions of time, also called forcing functions), and θ is a vector of parameters. We are interested in a particular solution of this system that serves as the reference path for comparative dynamics. If we assume that all the exogenous variables grow at a constant proportional rate (which may be equal or different across variables), we have

$$\omega_i(t) = \omega_i(0)e^{\gamma it}, \ i = 1, 2, \cdots, n, \qquad (2)$$

where $\omega_i(0)$ and γ_i are given. A steady-state (or balanced-growth) path is a particular solution to system (1) having the form

$$x_i(t) = x_i(0)e^{\rho it}, \qquad (3)$$

where the initial values $x_i(0)$ and the growth rates ρ_i are to be determined. This particular solution is usually obtained by the method of undetermined coefficients: equations (2) and (3) are substituted into system (1) and the values of $x_i(0)$ and ρ_i are determined so that the system is identically satisfied. This will give rise to a set of equations in the unknowns $x_i(0)$ and ρ_i. Typically, the ρ_i are obtained by solving the equations derived from equating to zero the coefficients of the terms containing t, whereas the $x_i(0)$ are obtained by solving the equations derived from equating to zero all the other terms not containing t.

The solution will express the unknowns in terms of the data; usually we shall obtain

$$\rho_i = h_i(\gamma, \vartheta), \qquad (4)$$

$$x_j(0) = \phi_j(\omega(0), \gamma, \theta), \qquad (5)$$

where $\vartheta \subset \theta$, that is, ϑ is a vector containing just a few parameters of the full set of the model's parameters. The functions h_i are typically fairly simple, while the functions φ_i are often very complicated. All results from comparative dynamics are obtained calculating the partial derivatives of the functions h_i and φ_i with respect to the element we are interested in.

SEE ALSO *Comparative Statics; Eigen-Values and Eigen-Vectors, Perron-Frobenius Theorem: Economic Applications; Phase Diagrams; Stability in Economics; Steady State*

BIBLIOGRAPHY

Gandolfo, Giancarlo. 1996. *Economic Dynamics* (chap. 20). 3rd ed. Berlin and New York: Springer.

Kamien, Morton I., and Nancy L. Schwartz. 1991. *Dynamic Optimization: The Calculus of Variations and Optimal Control in Economics and Management* (pt. 2, sect. 8). 2nd ed. Amsterdam: North-Holland.

Samuelson, Paul A. 1947. *Foundations of Economic Analysis* (chap. 12). Cambridge, MA: Harvard University Press.

Giancarlo Gandolfo

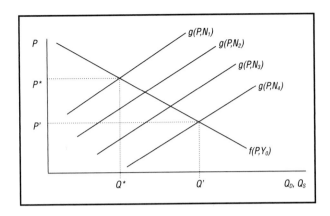

COMPARATIVE STATICS

Comparative statics is a methodological concept of economic theory and is related to *economic models*. An economic model consists of a set of relations among economic variables. These relations may be definitional, behavioral, or technological in nature. For instance, in the model of a competitive market there are three relations. The first two are behavioral relations describing how the buyers and sellers behave in the market. The behavior of the buyers is summarized in a demand relation in which the quantity of a good demanded in the market depends on its price and the total income of the buyers. The supply relation states that the quantity of the good supplied in the market depends on its price and the number of sellers supplying the good. The third relation of the model defines equilibrium as a situation in which the quantity demanded is equal to the quantity supplied. The market model involving these three relations is designed to explain the values of three *endogenous* variables: quantity demanded, quantity supplied, and the price of the good. Under certain conditions the model can be solved to get the values of endogenous variables in a static equilibrium. But there are two *exogenous* variables in the model—the total income of the buyers and the number of sellers—and the model is not designed to explain the values of these variables. A static equilibrium may be disturbed when there is a change in number of sellers, for instance. An increase in the number of sellers may occur if new firms enter the market where the existing firms are earning economic profits. In this case, a new static equilibrium will emerge. The methodology of comparative statics allows the theorist to compare these two static equilibria.

Comparative statics was introduced by the British economist Alfred Marshall (1842–1924) in his book *Principles of Economics* (1890), in which he discussed the effect of entry or exit of firms on market equilibrium. Later, Paul Samuelson developed the concept of comparative statics systematically in his book *Foundations of Economic Analysis* (1947), along with the related concept of comparative dynamics. Comparative static methodology is used in all branches of economic theory because it enables the theorist to derive a set of hypotheses that can be empirically tested. Theoretical econometrics and applied econometrics owe their existence largely to the development of comparative static methodology, and the contribution of these two allied fields of economics to economic policy analysis is tremendous.

To illustrate comparative statics in a market model let us state the demand and supply relations as:

1. $Q_D = f(P, Y)$

2. $Q_S = g(P, N)$

3. $Q_D = Q_S$

The endogenous variables in this three-equation market model are Q_D (quantity demanded), Q_S (quantity supplied) and P (price). The exogenous variables are Y (income) and N (number of sellers).

The figure above shows an inverse relationship between price and quantity demanded for a given level of income, Y_0. The relationship between price and quantity supplied is a positive one, and the diagram shows four supply curves for the number of sellers ranging between N_1 and N_4. The price quantity combination (P^*, Q^*) is one static equilibrium when the number of suppliers is N_1. Another static equilibrium is represented by the price quantity combination (P', Q') when the number of suppliers increases to N_4.

It is possible to derive a testable hypothesis by using comparative static methodology, provided that certain conditions are satisfied. First, the two static equilibria that we are comparing must exist and be stable. If the demand and supply curves do not intersect at all or if they do not intersect in the positive orthant, market equilibrium does not exist. Second, we must have an established theory connecting the number of firms that is exogenous to the model with the quantity supplied that is endogenous. Because the theory of supply predicts a positive relationship between the quantity supplied and the number of firms, the testable hypothesis that emerges is: as the number of firms increases in the industry, price falls and more quantity of the good is bought and sold in the market.

Comparative static methodology is also used in optimization models, where the conditions under which it works are somewhat different. In economic theory, consumers maximize utility subject to their budget constraint, or the producers maximize profits subject to technological constraints. These models also have a set of endogenous and exogenous variables. If we take the case of a competitive firm, the quantity of output produced or the quantities of inputs used in production are endogenous variables, but the prices of goods produced or the prices of inputs are exogenous variables. In the consumer model, the quantities of goods purchased are endogenous variables, but prices paid for these goods as well as amount of money spent are exogenous variables. A typical testable hypothesis is the law of demand that says that if the price of a good decreases, the consumer tends to purchase more quantities of that good. This hypothesis can be analytically derived by the use of comparative static methodology, provided that a *maximum* of the consumer's utility exists subject to the budget constraint. Similarly, for deriving any hypothesis related to the behavior of producers it is necessary that the profit function have a maximum. Thus, the comparative static methodology fails in the competitive model if there are increasing returns to scale, because profit function does not have a maximum. Under increasing returns to scale, the firm can always reduce unit cost by expanding the scale of output that can be sold at a fixed price.

Many economic variables such as quantity demanded or supplied are nonobservable. Econometricians can estimate both demand and supply functions only under certain conditions. In the figure above, demand is stable, but supply curve shifts as the number of firms changes. In this case, the demand curve can be estimated from data on price and quantity, but the supply curve cannot. Empirical estimation is crucial for predicting the effects of a tax or subsidy on welfare.

SEE ALSO *Comparative Dynamics*

BIBLIOGRAPHY

Kogiku, Kiichiro C. 1971. *Microeconomic Models.* New York: Harper.

Kuska, Edward A. 1973. *Maxima, Minima, and Comparative Statics.* London: Weidenfeld and Nicolson.

Marshall, Alfred. [1890] 1997. *Principles of Economics.* Amherst, NY: Prometheus.

Samuelson, Paul A. 1947. *Foundations of Economic Analysis.* Cambridge, MA: Harvard University Press.

Monica Das

COMPASSIONATE CONSERVATISM

SEE *Benign Neglect.*

COMPENSATING VARIATION

SEE *Wages, Compensating.*

COMPENSATION, UNEMPLOYMENT

Unemployment compensation (or benefit) consists of an insurance payment, generally financed by payroll contributions, that is paid to workers entering unemployment. This public insurance payment allows workers to smooth their consumption patterns when facing adverse employment outcomes in the presence of financial market imperfections and incompleteness that make it impossible or too costly for private, for-profit insurance firms to cover workers against such risks. The compensation is usually available for a limited amount of time, during which unemployed workers are supposed to search for a new job.

The first unemployment insurance system was introduced in 1789 in Basel, Switzerland, by a local trade union. More comprehensive schemes, managed by local authorities, were set up in France, Belgium, and Switzerland in the late nineteenth century. The first national program was established in the United Kingdom in 1911. Germany and the United States followed with, respectively, the Job Placement and Unemployment Insurance Act of 1927 and the Social Security Act of 1935 in response to the Great Depression. Nowadays unemployment compensation schemes are widespread under alternative enforcement rules and regulations in many Organization for Economic Cooperation and Development (OECD) countries.

One way of measuring the generosity of the unemployment compensation program adopted in a country is by calculating the amount of the average compensation as a ratio of the average wage. This indicator is known in the economic literature as "replacement ratio." Another important characteristic of unemployment compensation schemes is the duration of the benefit, which can range from a few months to indefinitely. A further important element of unemployment compensation programs is the strictness of the enforcement rules governing the reception of the benefit. For example, sometimes unemployment compensation is conditional on the recipient's actively searching for a new job or on accepting any job offered. These rules may be enforced with different degrees of strictness, depending on the formal and informal rules prevailing in each country. In the United States unemployment benefits are paid only to workers who lose their jobs as a result of dismissals; employees who voluntarily quit their jobs and new entrants to the labor market are not eligible. Federal law provides general guidance for administering unemployment compensation schemes, and each state has its own regulations and eligibility criteria.

Despite helping the unemployed in hard times, unemployment compensation schemes may also have perverse effects. Economic theory predicts that generous unemployment benefits tend to increase reservation wages. As a result, if the compensation is provided for an indefinite period, unemployment could increase as workers have less incentive to enter employment. In turn this could increase the average length of unemployment spells, triggering a rise in long-term unemployment. With this in mind, many countries have constructed unemployment compensation schemes that are limited in duration and contingent on active job search.

SEE ALSO *Duration Models; Psychological Capital; Recession; Unemployment; Welfare; Welfare State*

BIBLIOGRAPHY

Bertola, Giuseppe. 1999. Microeconomic Perspectives on Aggregate Labor Market. In *Handbook of Labor Economics*, vol. 3c, eds. Orley Ashenfelter and David Card, 2985–3028. Amsterdam: North-Holland.

Cahuc, Pierre, and André Zylberberg. 2004. *Labor Economics.* Cambridge, MA: MIT Press.

Layard, P. Richard G., Steven J. Nickell, and Richard Jackman. 1994. *The Unemployment Crisis.* Oxford and New York: Oxford University Press.

Luca Nunziata

COMPETITION

In neoclassical economic theory, the highest state of competition is called *perfect competition* in which there are a large number of small-sized firms each of which is assumed to be a passive price taker. With perfect information flows and mobility, inter-industrial competition ensures equalized profit rates across all sectors. Finally, intra-industrial competition ensures identical technologies thereby leading to equalized profit rates between firms within each industry. At equilibrium there is full capacity utilization.

Various models of *imperfect competition,* in which firms are price setters, are seen as the opposite of perfect competition. Under *monopolistic competition* there are a large number of firms. With free entry and exit, each firm's downward-sloping demand curve intersects the average total cost to the left of its minimum point on its average total cost curve. At the resultant equilibrium, there is excess capacity with higher-than-minimum cost and price.

Under *oligopolistic competition,* game theory is used to model strategically competitive behavior among a relatively small number of firms whose market power allows them to erect barriers to entry. Game theory, in which each firm is assumed to have the information to be able to anticipate precisely the actions of rival firms, generates a payoff matrix and devises the most optimal competitive strategy. At equilibrium, each firm maintains excess capacity to deter competition (Dockner et al. 2000, p. 253). As discussed below, this situation is likely to be unsustainable under Keynesian uncertainty when each firm strives to cut costs and prices.

The problem with all the above models is that none includes price- and cost-cutting behavior, an odd failing given the reality of outsourcing to low-wage regions of the world. The remaining part of this essay deals with three different theoretical schools that have rejected the neoclassical theory of competition. We first deal with the classical Marxian perspective (Clifton 1983; Shaikh 1980, 1982; Semmler 1984; Botwinick 1993). The central argument in this literature is that the quantity and size of firms is immaterial with regard to pricing: *all* firms are aggressive price setters. The pursuit of surplus value leads to increased levels of mechanization. Thus a larger scale of investment forces firms to increase their market shares in order to make such large investments profitable. Price- and cost-cutting constitute the main methods by which each firm "makes room for itself" in the market. Furthermore, this literature rejects the notion that large-sized firms have market power and therefore erect barriers to entry, since in recessions such firms can face *barriers to exit.* The presence of large amounts of sunk costs makes it difficult for such firms to disinvest, thereby making them subject to potentially heavy losses.

Indeed, it is the presence of varying levels of fixed capital that makes capital mobility across industries a relatively slow process. Quite simply, it takes time to invest and disinvest. Thus profit rates are likely to be different from one another at any given moment. Profit rate equalization happens only as an *approximate* process over what Karl Marx (1818–1883) called "the cycle of lean and fat years" (Marx 1894, p. 208).

Finally, technological change and fixed capital imply the existence within an industry of different technology vintages, each with its own unit production costs. With roughly equal selling prices, this implies the coexistence of different profit rates. The issue of monopoly power is irrelevant to both intraindustrial and interindustrial competition.

Based on the prewar survey work done by the Oxford Economists' Research Group (Andrews 1949), Roy Forbes Harrod (1900–1978) radically revised the conventional model of imperfect competition. As in the classical Marxian perspective, price- and cost-cutting are at the core of Harrod's critique (1952).

Harrod's critique begins with the standard assumptions of monopolistic competition: price-setting behavior, free entry and exit, and a downward-sloping demand curve faced by each firm. Harrod argues that the standard equilibrium in which there is excess capacity with above-minimum costs and prices is not sustainable since each firm faces a penalty for not minimizing costs and prices. The threat from potential low-cost rivals in a world of Keynesian uncertainty makes every firm defensively lower its costs and prices in an attempt to safeguard its market share. In the event of excess capacity, each firm will cut back investment, thereby reducing its capacity. In the aggregate, the reduction of investment will also reduce aggregate demand and thus output. With overutilization of capacity, the increase in investment will raise both aggregate capacity and output (demand). In either case, a solution to the knife-edge problem (Shaikh 1989) will ensure that output and capacity are approximately equal to each other around the minimum point of each firm's cost curve.

Finally, the Austrian school contends that static equilibrium and perfect information preclude the real-world rivalrous competitive behavior that entrepreneurs engage in under capitalism (Kirzner 1997). Austrian authors emphasize the fact that competition actually takes place under conditions of fundamental uncertainty that are not subject to probabilistic calculations. This in turn implies that price and quantity setting by firms may propel the system away from equilibrium for considerable periods, although there could also be tendencies toward equilibration. Competition is, in effect, a dynamic process.

SEE ALSO *Competition, Managed; Competition, Perfect*

BIBLIOGRAPHY

Andrews, P. W. S. 1949. *Manufacturing Business*. London: Macmillan.

Botwinick, Howard. 1993. *Persistent Inequalities: Wage Disparity under Capitalist Competition*. Princeton, NJ: Princeton University Press.

Clifton, James. 1983. Administered Pricing in the Context of Capitalist Development. *Contributions to Political Economy* 2: 23–38.

Dockner, Engelbert J., Steffen Jorgensen, Ngo Van Long, and Gerhard Sorger. 2000. *Differential Games in Economics and Management Science*. Cambridge, U.K.: Cambridge University Press.

Harrod, Roy Forbes. 1952. *Economic Essays*. New York: Harcourt.

Kirzner, Israel. 1997. Entrepreneurial Discovery and the Competitive Process: An Austrian Approach. *Journal of Economic Literature* 35 (1): 60–85.

Marx, Karl. [1894] 1967. *Capital*. Vol. 3. Reprint, New York: International.

Semmler, Willi. 1984. *Competition, Monopoly, and Differential Profit Rates: On the Relevance of the Classical and Marxian Theories of Production Prices for Modern Industrial and Corporate Pricing*. New York: Columbia University Press.

Shaikh, Anwar M. 1980. Marxian Competition versus Perfect Competition: Further Comments on the So-Called Choice of Technique. *Cambridge Journal of Economics* 4: 75–83.

Shaikh, Anwar M. 1982. Neo-Ricardian Economics: A Wealth of Algebra, a Poverty of Theory. *Review of Radical Political Economics* 14 (2): 67–83.

Shaikh Anwar M. 1989. Accumulation, Finance, and Effective Demand in Marx, Keynes, and Kalecki. In *Financial Dynamics and Business Cycles: New Perspectives*, ed. Willi Semmler, 63–86. Armonk, NY: Sharpe.

Jamee K. Moudud

COMPETITION, CLASSICAL

SEE *Long Period Analysis.*

COMPETITION, IMPERFECT

Imperfect competition exists in markets that are not perfectly competitive—that is, markets in which some buyer(s) or seller(s) have market power. That market power may derive from a limited number of buyers or sellers or from differentiation between each firm's products. Although almost every one of the world's markets falls into this category, we often study the simpler case of perfect competition first, then study monopoly, and follow those benchmarks with more detailed models of imperfect competition.

Perfect competition—that is, identical products sold to many buyers and available from many sellers who may easily enter and exit—may be one of the most unrealistic of market assumptions. Because there are many buyers and sellers, no single market participant can have a significant effect on the market price. As a result both buyers and sellers take the market price as fixed and use it to determine their levels of consumption and production. The market for wheat is an example of perfect competition. There are many buyers, many sellers, and little differentiation among each farmer's product. Although the theory of perfect competition appears unrealistic, many of its results are similar under other market structures. As Milton Friedman (1953) emphasizes, the usefulness of a theory lies not in its realism but in its ability to predict outcomes. Perfect competition does this well, and we should judge models of imperfect competition not on their realism but on their ability to make useful predictions and provide improved insights into the functioning of markets.

MONOPOLY AND MONOPSONY

Monopoly falls under the category of limited competition because it assumes that a single producer sells a product with no close substitutes to many buyers and benefits from barriers to entry by other firms. It is the simplest model of limited competition and lies at the opposite end of the spectrum from perfect competition. An example of monopoly in the early twenty-first century is Microsoft Corporation's operating system Windows (*U.S. v. Microsoft*, Civil Action No. 98–1232 [2000]). When a seller has market power, the price may remain higher than a competitive market would otherwise.

As in perfect competition, there are few markets that actually satisfy our assumptions, but this simple model of monopoly allows us to understand the basic features of market power. But even in the case of Microsoft, market share does not reach 100 percent.

The market power held by a monopolist can be measured in several ways. The Lerner Index (Lerner 1934) considers the price markup over marginal cost as a fraction of price: $(P - MC)/P$. It can be shown that this also equals the inverse of the own-price elasticity of demand (technically, its absolute value). Thus the more willing buyers are to do without the monopolist's product, the smaller the monopolist's profit-maximizing markup. Measuring marginal cost is difficult in practice (Fisher 1987) because economic cost (rather than accounting cost) is required. Typically neither policymakers nor the courts have good measures of the firm's true costs; if any measure is available, it is usually average cost rather than marginal cost. Elasticity is easier to measure than marginal cost. In antitrust proceedings, both the own-price elasticity (the reaction of a product's demand to changes in its own price) and various cross-price elasticities (the reaction of one product's demand to changes in other products' prices) are estimated to determine the extent of an alleged monopolist's market power. The legal definition of monopoly is 80 percent market share of the relevant market, where the markets are often defined using estimates of cross-price elasticities. It is important to note that monopolies are not illegal under U.S. law, but any firm found to have monopoly power is subject to more stringent laws concerning potential abuse of that firm's market power.

Monopsony is also a model of limited competition that lies at the opposite end of the spectrum from perfect competition; its simplicity is that a single buyer purchases from many sellers. For example, the steel mill in a town without other steel employers can be modeled as a monopsony, and so can the National Football League. In this case, the buyer has market power and may keep the price lower than a competitive market would otherwise. In our two examples, the "price" that is depressed due to market power is workers' salaries.

One economic cost to monopoly and monopsony (and to market power in general) is due to "allocative inefficiency," an outcome where marginal benefit (the marginal buyer's willingness to pay) is not equal to marginal cost (the marginal seller's willingness to sell). In the case of monopoly, this is because marginal cost is greater than the price charged, whereas in the case of monopsony, marginal benefit is less than the price paid. In both cases, market power causes too few goods to be traded—fewer goods, that is, than would be allocated by a competitive market.

If the number of buyers or sellers is small, they may "collude" to limit competition. This is referred to as a buyer or seller "cartel." Such behavior is illegal in the United States, but cartels such as the Organization of Petroleum Exporting Countries may operate internationally. Because the largest reward that any single seller or group of sellers can receive from participation in a market is the monopoly profit, we can consider a producers' cartel to be acting to maximize the members' joint profits. It is likely that any cartel will have difficulty policing its members' behavior. Each individual firm has an incentive to deviate from the seller cartel-maximizing price (by selling at a slightly lower price) or quantity (by selling slightly more quantity). A buyer cartel likewise has the incentive to deviate by offering a slightly higher price and buying more quantity than the buyer cartel's joint-maximizing price and quantity.

MONOPOLISTIC COMPETITION

With these simpler models described, we now consider firms with market power acting noncooperatively. As mentioned above, product differentiation is one reason market power may arise. This is the model of "monopolistic competition" (Robinson 1934; Chamberlin 1933) or "differentiated products" (Hotelling 1929; Salop 1979; Eaton and Lipsey 1989). Here, as in perfect competition, there are no barriers to entry, and as a result firms receive zero economic profits in the long run. Yet because differentiated products face a downward-sloping demand curve, price is still above marginal cost, and the market is not allocatively efficient. This does not tell us the entire story, however; we cannot ask firms to charge a lower price, as we might imagine asking the monopolist to do. The monopolistically competitive firms expect zero economic profits in the long run already. Instead, we focus on the incentive for firms to enter the market, to find products that differ in some aspect from existing products. This behavior results in "excessive product differentiation" and "excess capacity." Production costs are higher than they might otherwise be. Due to the many different products produced, firms do not minimize their average costs as perfectly competitive firms would. Just as many "realistic" markets are made up of many firms with differentiated products, this prediction of the models rings true as well. Do we really need so many different kinds of shoes, bicycles, and mystery novels to choose from? Of course in these cases it is also difficult to justify regulation that would lead to an improved outcome. One case in which we may observe market participants' bargaining to improve the outcome is in the health care industry. For example, Preferred Provider Organizations limit patients' choices in return for lower fees and physicians' lower average costs (*Arizona v. Maricopa County Medical Society* 457 U.S. 332, 334 [1982]; Lynk 1988).

OLIGOPOLY AND OLIGOPSONY

Market power may not only arise from differentiated products; it may also be due to the existence of only a few sellers in the market (oligopoly) or only a few buyers (oligopsony). Oligopolies' market power can be measured by an average of the firms' Lerner indices as well as through the firms' market shares. An industry's n-firm "concentration ratio" (CRn) is the market share held by the largest n firms. The Department of Justice and the Federal Trade Commission typically use the 4-firm concentration ratio, although in the early twenty-first century cellular phone market 2-firm concentration ratios are reported (because CR4 is often 100 percent), and in other markets the antitrust authorities may report 8-firm concentration ratios. Alternatively market power can be measured by the Herfindahl-Hirschman Index (HHI), which equals the sum of the squared market shares of all firms in the industry. Thus the HHI can vary from a limiting value of zero under perfect competition to $(100)^2 = 10,000$ under monopoly. Most cross-country industry studies measure similar variation for the HHI and CR4.

The study of oligopoly and oligopsony requires the mathematics of game theory because each firm takes into account its rivals' reactions to and anticipation of its own actions. Such behavior can lead to strategic decisions that are intended solely to constrain the choices of current and potential rivals. For example, an incumbent firm may choose to increase its productive capacity to deter other firms' future entry (Dixit 1979).

INTERNATIONAL TRADE

Market power can also explain the level of trade between nations (Helpman and Krugman 1985; Helpman 1988; Baldwin 1992). Two examples illustrate the effect of both sources of market power—product differentiation and few domestic producers—on international trade. Under perfect competition, it is hard to justify why two countries would trade the same product—wheat or potatoes, for example. Each country should focus on the good in which it has a comparative advantage. But when consumers value variety, as in the case of differentiated products such as computers or cars, then two countries can produce more varieties of the good than one country can. Rather than limiting consumers' choices to the varieties their own country produces, a wider market—an international market—can exist for both countries' varieties. Market power can even explain the prevalence of cross-border trade with identical products produced in each country if each firm has monopoly power (or equivalently, a cartel) in its domestic market. In this case, each country's monopolist has an incentive to compete with the other country's monopolist, as long as transportation costs are not too high, precisely because domestic prices are above marginal cost. Although consumers in both countries benefit because of the effect this international competition has on prices, the fact that both firms incur transportation costs to export from their home country means that the outcome is less efficient than if each firm had just increased its own domestic production.

SEE ALSO *Competition; Competition, Managed; Competition, Marxist; Competition, Monopolistic; Competition, Perfect; Consumer Surplus; Discrimination, Price; Game Theory; Monopoly; Monopsony; Producer Surplus; Robinson, Joan*

BIBLIOGRAPHY

Baldwin, Robert E. 1992. Are Economists' Traditional Trade Policy Views Still Valid? *Journal of Economic Literature* 30 (2): 804–829.

Chamberlin, Edward. 1933. *The Theory of Monopolistic Competition.* Cambridge, MA: Harvard University Press.

Dixit, Avinash. 1979. A Model of Duopoly Suggesting a Theory of Entry Barriers. *Bell Journal of Economics* 10 (1): 20–32.

Eaton, B. Curtis, and Richard G. Lipsey. 1989. Product Differentiation. In *The Handbook of Industrial Organization,* ed. Richard Schmalensee and Robert Willig, 723–768. Amsterdam: North-Holland.

Fisher, Franklin M. 1987. On the Misuse of the Profit-Sales Ratio to Infer Monopoly Power. *Rand Journal of Economics* 18 (Autumn): 384–396.

Friedman, Milton. 1953. The Methodology of Positive Economics. In *Essays in Positive Economics*, 3–43. Chicago: University of Chicago Press.

Helpman, Elhanan. 1988. Imperfect Competition and International Trade: Evidence from Fourteen Countries. In *International Competitiveness*, ed. A. Michael Spence and Heather Hazard, 197–220. Cambridge, MA: Ballinger.

Helpman, Elhanan, and Paul Krugman. 1985. *Market Structure and Foreign Trade: Increasing Returns, Imperfect Competition, and the International Economy.* Cambridge, MA: MIT Press.

Hotelling, Harold. 1929. Stability in Competition. *Economic Journal* 39 (153): 41–57.

Lerner, Abba P. 1934. The Concept of Monopoly and the Measurement of Monopoly Power. *Review of Economic Studies* 1 (June): 157–175.

Lynk, William J. 1988. Physician Price Fixing under the Sherman Act: An Indirect Test of the Maricopa Issues. *Journal of Health Economics* 7 (2): 95–109.

Robinson, Joan. 1934. What Is Perfect Competition? *Quarterly Journal of Economics* 49 (1): 104–120.

Salop, Steven C. 1979. Monopolistic Competition with Outside Goods. *Bell Journal of Economics* 10 (1): 141–156.

Christopher S. Ruebeck

COMPETITION, MANAGED

This idea for the reform of health-care finances was conceived by Alain C. Enthoven of Stanford University and fostered by a think tank of health-care professionals in Jackson Hole, Wyoming. Managed competition formed the basis of the proposed health-care reforms of the Bill Clinton administration. The plan required the creation of large health-insurance purchasing cooperatives, which were designed to have the leverage to enforce competition among different health-care plans. Managed competition aims to maintain quality of service and protect universal criteria of provision while also containing costs.

This strategy of financial management for health-care organizations has emerged since the mid-1970s in a context of mounting costs resulting from the increasing demand for services, especially in societies where aging populations and the decline of the family have put greater strain on existing services and institutions. Managed competition can be technically defined as a purchasing strategy to maximize value for both consumers and employers by adopting principles from microeconomics. A sponsor, whether in the private or the public sector, acting in the interests of a large number of subscribers, regulates the market to avoid attempts by insurers to suppress price competition. Through this strategy, the sponsor attempts to create price-elastic demand and reduce market risks. This type of financial management has been attractive for employers and insurers in the U.S. health sector because, while controlling prices, it offers pluralism in services and maintains individual choice for consumers, but it also approximates universal coverage.

In *The Logic of Health-Care Reform* (1994) the sociologist Paul Starr outlined several elements that are necessary for this strategy to achieve its objectives: There must be standard benefits that can guarantee a minimum level of coverage (such as hospitalization), thereby making comparisons in quality between plans possible; services should be accessible in principle to all customers regardless of any preexisting health condition (such as diabetes), and the premiums should not be unfairly influenced (for example, by age or gender); and the competition should force plans to provide detailed cost information to both consumers and employers.

Managed competition should be distinguished from *managed care* in health delivery. In managed care, networks of hospitals, physicians, and care providers offer accessible and economical care—for example, through preferred provider organizations (PPOs) that have contracted with insurers or employers for a discounted fee. However, such fee-discounting arrangements cannot in the long run monitor quality of service.

The aim of Enthoven's scheme was in fact to ensure that customers rather than employers would make health-care choices on the basis of cost. The difficulty facing most forms of health care is how to achieve equity in care between the chronically sick and the relatively healthy while also controlling costs. In the Enthoven scheme, one strategy to address this situation is through the creation of regional centers of medical technology to share technical costs with a range of groups.

Although managed competition as an idea has been around since the 1970s, it is generally agreed that the U.S. health-care system is failing in terms of cost control, quality, and provision of services across society. The employer-based system does not offer coverage to individuals whose employer does not offer health insurance or to those who are self-employed or who are unemployed but not poor. In the early twenty-first-century situation, there is little incentive for improving efficiency on the part of providers. In short, there is no market mechanism to create incentives for delivery systems to reduce the costs of care.

The health-care systems of all advanced societies are exposed to similar problems of price inflation, administrative inefficiencies, and mounting costs resulting from dependence on advanced medical technology, the health-care needs of aging populations with chronic illness, and the rising expectations of customers for better services. These difficulties face societies such as the United Kingdom and Sweden, which have had, at least since the end of World War II (1939–1945), state-supported, universal health care with free provision of services at the point of delivery. In these societies, however, there has been growing privatization of health care through greater provision of private medical insurance. In the United Kingdom both Conservative and Labour governments encouraged the creation of quasi-markets inside the National Health Service (NHS) to promote price controls through competitive tendering and outsourcing for services. Despite these reforms, there are many problems with the NHS, such as significant regional inequalities in provision—the so-called postcode lottery—and difficulties in recruiting adequately trained staff. Despite claims that managed competition has been successful (e.g., in Florida and Indianapolis) in cutting costs, it is not clear that any of these reforms have successfully sustained equality in services and cost-effectiveness in delivery.

SEE ALSO *Competition; Competition, Perfect; Medicine; Medicine, Socialized; Microeconomics; National Health Insurance; Public Health; Welfare State*

BIBLIOGRAPHY

Enthoven, Alain C. 1988. *Theory and Practice of Managed Competition in Health Care Finance.* Amsterdam: North Holland.

Enthoven, Alain C. 1991. Internal Market Reform in the British NHS. *Health Affairs* 10 (3): 60–70.

Rodwin, Victor G. 1984. *The Health Planning Predicament: France, Québec, England, and the United States.* Berkeley: University of California Press.

Starr, Paul. 1994. *The Logic of Health-Care Reform: Why and How the President's Plan Will Work.* Rev. ed. New York: Penguin.

Bryan S. Turner

COMPETITION, MARXIST

The treatment of competition captures the methodological difference between the neoclassical and materialist (Marxist) approach to social and economic relations. In the former, competition is the interaction of individual economic agents through exchange in pursuit of self interest, be they consumers, workers, or owners of capital. The principle conditions necessary for competition are many buyers and sellers, and free entry to and exit from the market. Thus, competition is a question of numbers. Competition declines as the number of producers declines; monopoly is the absence of competition. In this analysis competition is an equilibrating force that brings efficiency to markets. The restriction of competition by government action undermines this efficiency. Private sector barriers to competition, such as collusion among producers, represent market failure.

Marx criticized this approach as an "absurdity of regarding [competition] as the ... existence of free individuality in the sphere of consumption and exchange. Nothing can be more mistaken" (Marx [1858] 1973, p. 649). Briefly stated, Marx argued as follows: Capitalist production arises historically from the separation of labor from the means of production; in order to produce and live, workers must be employed by capital ("free wage labor"). This labor relation gives capital its mobility, both geographically and across sectors of production. Competition among producers (or "capitals," Marx's term) results from the conceptually prior competition between capital and labor: "Free competition ... is first the free movement of capital and nothing else" (Marx 1973, p. 651). A producer may temporarily monopolize the production and sale of a particular commodity, but cannot monopolize the market for labor services (labor power).

From this analysis it follows that as the number of competitors in a sector of industry declines, competition intensifies:

> In practical life we find not only competition, monopoly, and the antagonism between them, but also the synthesis of the two.... Monopoly produces competition, competition produces monopoly.... The synthesis is such that monopoly can only maintain itself by continually entering into the struggle of competition. (Marx and Engels 1976, p. 197)

By this line of argument, competition is not an equilibrating force, but a destabilizing conflict among capitalist enterprises, leading to imperialism and wars between capitalist powers (this is explained in Weeks 1981, Chapter 6). While this approach may seem strange to the point of bizarre to twenty-first-century economists, in the mid-twentieth century it was very much part of the mainstream. In 1947, K. W. Rothschild linked competition to conflict in an article in the *Economic Journal*, the most prestigious publication in the profession at the time. His argument is quite consistent with Marx's analysis:

> [A] theory of markets can be complete and relevant only if its framework includes all the main aspects of the struggle [by corporations] for security and position. Like price wars, open imperial-

ist conflicts will not be the daily routine of the oligopolistic market. But, like price wars, their possibility and the preparation for them will be a constantly existing background ... and the imperialistic aspects of modern wars or armed interventions must be seen as part of a dynamic market theory just as the more traditional "economic" activities like cut-throat pricing ... for there is no fundamental difference between the two. (Rothschild 1947, p. 319)

In light of the international tensions, conflicts, and wars since the end of the cold war, in some cases involving access to resources, it is perhaps worth revisiting Marx's analytical approach to capitalist competition.

BIBLIOGRAPHY

Marx, Karl. [1858] 1973. *Grundrisse. Foundations of the Critique of Political Economy.* Trans. Martin Nicolaus. New York: Vintage.

Marx, Karl, and Frederick Engels. 1976. *Collected Works.* New York: International Publishers.

Rothschild, K. W. 1947. Price Theory and Oligopoly. *Economic Journal* 57: (227): 229–320.

Weeks, John. 1981. *Capital and Exploitation.* Princeton, NJ: Princeton University Press.

John Weeks

COMPETITION, MONOPOLISTIC

Economists have a spectrum of models with which to analyze how competing firms interact. The simplest of these involve situations in which firms can choose quantities and other variables (product quality, and advertising), without having to consider the reaction their choices might generate from other firms. Obviously, when there is a single firm in a market (a monopolist), this occurs by definition, as there are no other firms to do the reacting. However, it is also the key assumption underlying perfect competition, where firms are assumed to take prevailing prices as given. Specifically, firms believe that if they charge a higher price than the market price, they will lose all of their customers. The problem with perfect competition is that, in reality, competing firms have some discretion over the price, and they can therefore raise them without losing all of their sales. In this situation, however, firms might be "small," and so it might be reasonable to presume that they can be modeled independently of other firms' potential reactions.

Monopolistic competition is the term given to this "middle ground." An industry is defined as monopolistically competitive if: (a) there are many producers and consumers in the industry; (b) consumers have preferences that may cause them to favor one specific firm over another; and (c) there are no barriers to entry or exit. Conditions a and c are also features of perfect competition, so the critical distinction comes from condition b, whereby the products sold by firms are not homogeneous (i.e., perfectly substitutable) in the eyes of consumers. Consumers may favor one firm over another because of location, branding issues, knowledge of quality, advertising and marketing appeal, or individual product characteristics.

In many respects, the outcomes from monopolistic competition are similar to those from perfect competition. First, in long-term equilibrium with identical firms, profits are dissipated by competition, and entry occurs at the point where the marginal firm is earning enough to cover fixed or sunk-market entry costs. Second, prices reflect average production costs. However, because the firms have some pricing discretion, they will charge a mark-up over their marginal costs (even in the long-run) and conceptually will be able to recover fixed costs associated with, say, product development. This also means that, compared with perfect competition, prices will be higher and quantity lower in monopolistic competition, leading to a debate as to whether this sacrifice is made up for by product variety.

It is this latter implication that has perhaps proved most significant in giving monopolistic competition greater prominence in economic analysis. Monopolistic competition was independently developed by Edward Chamberlin and Joan Robinson in the early 1930s. Each was motivated by a problem with perfect competition identified by Piero Sraffa, who noted in 1926 that if firms had fixed production costs and falling average costs (i.e., economies of scale), then perfect competition imposed no limit to firm size. This could not be reconciled with the reality of smaller firms even where economies of scale appeared to be present. Chamberlin and Robinson saw the reconciliation of this problem in the notion that competing firms might have downward sloping individual demand curves. Chamberlin assigned this trend to the existence of product differentiation, while Robinson found that it came about because of an imperfect adjustment response from other firms (today termed "residual demand"). This meant that individual firms would be limited in their ability to realize scale economies because of entry by others who could pick up some consumers by supplying a differentiated product.

The marrying of economies of scale and competitive pressures led to important developments in other areas of economics. In 1977, Avinash Dixit and Joseph Stiglitz developed a tractable model of monopolistic competition that allowed for a convenient analysis of product variety (and showed that too few products would be produced relative to the social optimum). This model formed the basis for new trade theory (Krugman 1979), new growth theory (Romer 1987), and new economic geography (Krugman 1991), each of which required a model that enabled firms to have economies of scale, yet also be limited by competitive pressure.

SEE ALSO *Competition; Competition, Imperfect; Discrimination, Price; Monopoly; Price Setting and Price Taking; Robinson, Joan*

BIBLIOGRAPHY

Chamberlin, Edward H. 1933. *The Theory of Monopolistic Competition.* Cambridge, MA: Harvard University Press.

Dixit, Avinash K., and Joseph E. Stiglitz. 1977. Monopolistic Competition and Optimal Product Diversity. *American Economic Review* 67 (3): 297–308.

Hotelling, H. 1929. Stability in Competition. *Economic Journal* 39: 41–57.

Krugman, Paul R. 1979. Increasing Returns, Monopolistic Competition, and International Trade. *Journal of International Economics.* 9 (4): 469–479.

Krugman, Paul R. 1991. Increasing Returns and Economic Geography. *Journal of Political Economy* 99 (3): 483–499.

Lancaster, Kelvin J. 1979. *Variety, Equity, and Efficiency: Product Variety in an Industrial Society.* New York: Columbia University Press.

Robinson, Joan. 1933. *The Economics of Imperfect Competition.* London: Macmillan.

Romer, Paul M. 1987. Growth Based on Increasing Returns Due to Specialization. *American Economic Review* 77 (2): 56–62.

Sraffa, Piero. 1926. The Law of Returns under Competitive Conditions. *Economic Journal* 36 (144): 535–560.

Joshua Gans

COMPETITION, NEOCLASSICAL

SEE *Competition, Perfect.*

COMPETITION, PERFECT

The concept of perfect competition is an idealization of friction-free, smoothly functioning, anonymous markets that, at best, serves as a benchmark to the markets that exist. Perfect competition is an abstraction based on underlying assumptions concerning: (1) the number of competitors; (2) the homogeneity of the product being sold; (3) the ease of entry into the market; (4) the level of knowledge and competence of competitors; and (5) the independence of competitors' behavior.

Heuristically, these five conditions are satisfied when: (1) both the number of buyers and the number of sellers are sufficiently large that it is virtually costless to switch trading partners; (2) the goods being traded by various sellers are more or less perfect substitutes for each other; (3) the entry and exit by buyers and sellers are more or less cost free and swift; (4) all agents are more or less aware of the previous market prices, and they are close together; and (5) the agents do not form coalitions in trading, and they act independently and more or less anonymously.

These conditions are easy to grasp in nontechnical terms, but making them mathematically precise is both worthwhile and difficult. Historically, the work in the economics of oligopoly of A. A. Cournot (1836) and Edward Chamberlin (1933) provides the basic examples for competition with homogeneous and differentiated goods. In the first instance, perfect substitutes are traded; in the second, the product of each individual differs from the others. The difference between oligopoly and perfect competition is that in the latter, numbers are assumed to be so great that it is not worthwhile for individuals to attempt to consider the detailed actions of other individuals. They thus view price and the market as an aggregate.

In perfect competition, the conditions for entry into the market amount to the proposition that there are no high barriers, such as hard-to-obtain licenses, social pressures, or extremely high set-up costs, to prevent potential new entrants from going into business. The condition that is possibly the most difficult to make precise is that on information. In the dynamics of the market, it is extremely difficult to determine who knows what from minute to minute. If there is a formal trading mechanism that forms price, such as a simultaneous sealed bid, the conditions can be described precisely. In an open-cry market, however, with bidders milling around the floor, description at best is only of aggregates.

In markets that meet frequently with established traders, it is feasible that over time implicit or explicit collaboration or collusion could evolve, even with numbers such as ten or twenty. This is ruled out by assumption in a competitive market; but it raises the question of how many competitors are necessary before collusion can be ruled out.

The formal methods of the theory of games have been utilized since the 1960s to make these intuitively simple concepts precise (see Shubik 1984). Even today, however, in highly practical problems, such as information leaks and insider trading in the stock market, an understanding of how to guarantee the appropriate conditions on information has not been reached.

Perfect competition is a useful ideal if it is not followed too slavishly. Possibly the closest approximation to it is provided by the New York Stock Exchange, where a reasonably close level of approximation to competition has been achieved through the building up of an enormous body of laws and regulations required to level the playing field in an actual market.

SEE ALSO *Competition; Competition, Imperfect; Competition, Managed; Price Setting and Price Taking*

BIBLIOGRAPHY

Chamberlin, Edward. 1933. *The Theory of Monopolistic Competition*. Cambridge, MA: Harvard University Press.

Cournot, A. A. [1838] 1897. *Researches into the Mathematical Principles of the Theory of Wealth*. Trans. Nathaniel T. Bacon. New York: Macmillan.

Shubik, Martin. 1984. *A Game Theoretic Approach to Political Economy*. Cambridge, MA: MIT Press.

Martin Shubik

COMPETITION, PURE

SEE *Competition, Perfect.*

COMPLEMENTARY/ ATTRACTION THEORY

SEE *Similarity/Attraction Theory.*

COMPLEXITY THEORY

SEE *System Analysis.*

COMPREHENSIVE SYSTEM

SEE *Rorschach Test.*

COMPULSORY VOTING

In order to be termed democratic, a regime must have certain characteristics. Even though political theorists debate the scope and depth of the characteristics of a democracy, there is a common understanding that certain minimum requirements comprise a democratic regime. In *Democracy and Its Critics* (1989), Robert A. Dahl identifies seven characteristics that should typically exist in a democracy. These are elected officials, free and fair elections, inclusive suffrage, right to run for office, freedom of expression, alternative information, and associational autonomy. The practices of these and similar characteristics vary from country to country. Inclusive suffrage in most representative democracies is understood as a requirement, allowing citizens the opportunity to influence their government through voting, and universal suffrage is seen as a sufficient condition. In some regimes, however, inclusive suffrage has been made mandatory by the introduction of compulsory voting.

There are different levels of compulsory voting. In its simplest form, there are legal regulations according to which voting is compulsory. The regulations can be stated through a common law or they can be coded in the constitution of the country. Moreover, this legal obligation can either be sanctioned or remain a mere moral proclamation. Further, sanctions can either consist of economic penalties in the form of a fine or there can be other legal consequences. The legal consequences vary, from the voter providing a legitimate reason for his or her abstention to disenfranchisement to imprisonment, the most severe consequence. Although imprisonment is not generally enforced as a penalty, in theory a court of justice can impose imprisonment if the nonvoter has failed to pay the fine. In any case, compulsory voting should not be seen as a discrete variable, but rather as an ordinal scale with different levels of compulsion.

Regulations on compulsory voting are not very common. According to an estimate by *International Idea* (Gratschew 2002), only some thirty countries have regulations on compulsory voting and of these only eight enforce it strictly. These countries are Australia, Belgium, Cyprus, Fiji, Luxembourg, Nauru, Singapore, and Uruguay. Also in the canton of Schaffhausen in Switzerland compulsory voting is strictly enforced, whereas voting in the other Swiss cantons is voluntary. In any case, less than one-fifth of the world's countries have any regulation on compulsory voting. Further, strictly enforced compulsory voting is a rarity; in less than 5 percent of all countries, compulsory voting is strictly enforced.

Compulsory voting has documented effects on voting behavior, particularly turnout. Strictly enforced compulsory voting boosts turnout, but also weakly enforced voting tends to increase turnout. However, merely a moral compulsion does not seem to affect turnout. Based on data from the Comparative Study of Electoral Systems,

Module 1, Pippa Norris in her book *Electoral Engineering* (2004) demonstrated that countries in which compulsory voting is strictly enforced have an average of 20 percentage points higher turnout than countries where voting is optional or where compulsory voting is not sanctioned in any way. Countries with weakly enforced compulsory voting systems fall in between, with an average turnout of 84 percent.

Compulsory voting tends to increase the number of invalid votes. Voters who do not have clear preferences but are still forced to the polls protest by voting blank or casting an invalid vote. According to David Farrell in his *Electoral Systems* (2001), the highest share of invalid votes in the 1990s was cast in Brazil, where the share was 19 percent. In Brazil, compulsory voting is weakly enforced.

Compulsory voting does not seem to contribute to a politically literate electorate. According to Kimmo Grönlund and Henry Milner in their article "The Determinants of Political Knowledge in Comparative Perspective" (2006), Belgium, a European country with a proportional electoral system and a multiparty system in combination with strictly enforced compulsory voting, deviates from its relevant European family in the dispersion of political knowledge. Political knowledge is highly dependent on the level of formal school education in Belgium, a pattern that is more typical for newly developed and developing countries, and not typical for European old democracies with proportional electoral systems.

Compulsory voting interferes with the logic of rational voting and abstaining. Since educated voting always involves personal effort, such as acquiring information and comparing parties' policies, it is rational that many people do not want to vote. In his book *Economic Theory of Democracy* (1957), Anthony Downs deduced that if voting were costless only people with preferences would vote and people with no preferences would abstain. In a system with compulsory voting the odds that a single vote is decisive are less than in a system where voting is optional and some people always abstain. The incentives to form an informed electoral opinion in order to cast a vote are therefore low in systems with strictly enforced compulsory voting. Contrary to policymakers' efforts to engage citizens politically by introducing compulsory voting, the system is more likely to increase the probability of uninformed and randomly assigned voting than to educate citizens. In the mid-2000s, however, there are no reliable comparative data on the effects of compulsory voting on political knowledge and informed voting.

SEE ALSO *Elections; Electoral Systems; Voting; Voting Patterns; Voting Schemes*

BIBLIOGRAPHY

Dahl, Robert A. 1989. *Democracy and Its Critics.* New Haven, CT: Yale University Press.

Downs, Anthony. 1957. *An Economic Theory of Democracy.* New York: Harper & Row.

Farrell, David M. 2001. *Electoral Systems: A Comparative Introduction.* Basingstoke and New York: Palgrave.

Franklin, Mark N. 2004. *Voter Turnout and the Dynamics of Electoral Competition in Established Democracies since 1945.* Cambridge, U.K.: Cambridge University Press.

Freedom House. Freedom in the World. http://www.freedomhouse.org/.

Gratschew, Maria. 2002. Compulsory Voting. In *Voter Turnout Since 1945. A Global Report*, 105–110. Stockholm: International IDEA.

Grönlund, Kimmo, and Henry Milner. 2006. The Determinants of Political Knowledge in Comparative Perspective. *Scandinavian Political Studies* 29 (4), 386–406.

IDEA. 2005. *Electoral System Design: The New International IDEA Handbook.* Stockholm: International IDEA.

Norris, Pippa. 2004. *Electoral Engineering: Voting Rules and Political Behavior.* Cambridge, U.K.: Cambridge University Press.

Powell, Bingham G. 2000. *Elections as Instruments of Democracy: Majoritarian and Proportional Visions.* New Haven, CT: Yale University Press.

Kimmo Grönlund

COMPUTER SIMULATION

SEE *Computers: Science and Society.*

COMPUTERS: SCIENCE AND SOCIETY

For decades, pundits with scholarly credentials have been predicting that computer and information technology would radically transform both science and society. Ultimately, they may be right, but the apparent changes to date have been limited and often contradictory.

SOCIETAL IMPACT OF COMPUTING

It is often said that rationalization, mechanization, and computerization of work contribute to the degradation of skills and thus the demotion of the workforce. Yet the research has shown varying effects: In 1987 William Form reported that technology sometimes led to the loss of skills but at other times required increased skills. Surveying a different large body of research, Jeffrey Liker, Carol Haddad, and Jennifer Karlin reported in 1999 that the consequences for work organization of new technologies are highly variable and contingent on a number of factors, including labor-management relations and the specific social process through which the technology was developed and introduced. Information technology has long been considered a tool that large corporations use to control their workers and governments use to monitor their citizens. This is true both in the United States, where much of the information technology has been developed, and in countries into which such technologies have been introduced, despite their very different social conditions. In 1977 Philip Kraft argued that corporate desires for control over employees led to routinization and fragmentation even of the profession of computer programming itself, with a consequent loss of innovativeness.

Perhaps ironically, 1977 was also the year in which the first really successful personal computer, the Apple II, was introduced, created by a tiny company started by two friends in a garage. Since that time computer innovation has resulted in a remarkable scenario: Visionary individuals develop a prototype of an innovation and found a start-up company, which either becomes a major corporation overnight or is purchased for millions of dollars by an existing major corporation. In many cases, such as Google and the first Web browsers, the innovators were graduate students who received government support from grants to their professors who were working on something only indirectly related.

In 1973 the sociologist Daniel Bell proclaimed "the coming of post-industrial society," a new form of information-intensive society that would be marked by five primary features:

1. Economic sector: the change from a goods-producing to a service economy.

2. Occupational distribution: the preeminence of the professional and technical class.

3. Axial principle: the centrality of theoretical knowledge as the source of innovation and of policy formulation for the society.

4. Future orientation: the control of technology and technological assessment.

5. Decision making: the creation of a new "intellectual technology."

In such a postindustrial society, social scientists and information scientists might have been expected to enjoy great prestige and their profession to have achieved a position of dominance. Yet in the United States, where modern information technology largely arose, almost the opposite has occurred. Since 1982, when the Reagan administration sought to eradicate social science from the National Science Foundation and did succeed in cutting budgets to 40 percent of their prior levels (and cutting all budgets for social scientists; Larsen 1992), the influence of social scientists (other than economists and, rarely, demographers) on American policies has been insignificant. During the Clinton administration of the 1990s, there was a brief government flirtation with social science as applied to the Internet, before the second Bush administration ended it.

The so-called digital divide was the subject of much discussion in the mid- to late 1990s. The term refers to the tendency of disadvantaged groups to have less access to the Internet, and thus to information in general, than other more privileged groups. When numerous studies found this digital divide in schools as well as in the adult world, some voiced concerns that computers, though they might have the potential to reduce socioeconomic inequality, were actually increasing it. By this logic, government should invest in Internet-related technologies as a fundamental solution for social problems stemming from poverty and lack of opportunities for education. Once most middle-class households hooked up to the Internet on home computers, the novelty of the issue faded, and unequal access to information came to be taken for granted.

Internet and other modern computer technologies raised ethical issues that were mostly updated versions of old ones—for example, product liability, with software manufacturers forcing customers to agree to licenses in which the producers promised nothing. Some of these ethical issues may be more acute in the information context, notably those concerning privacy and intellectual property rights, but they are not unprecedented. An extended debate has raged over whether computers degrade social relationships in society, enhance them, or merely provide a new environment in which they may take place. As Leah Lievrouw (2003) has observed, the Internet has become contested territory on which individuals and small groups assert their autonomy, major corporations monopolize attention and attempt to criminalize activities that threaten profits, and activists launch counterattacks against corporate tyranny. This is seen not only with respect to file sharing of music, but also blogs revealing government or corporate secrets, posting of programs called "mods" (modifications) that alter commercial software, and coopting commercial chatrooms to organize radical cultural, political, sexual, and economic networks.

Ray Kurzweil, among the most influential computer entrepreneurs and visionaries, argues in his 2005 book that technology is driving humanity toward a *singularity*, utterly transforming human life during the present century. He raises the possibility that humans may no longer be limited to biological bodies but dwell within robots or computers, and that artificial intelligences will surpass human intelligence. Whatever one thinks of this extreme possibility, Kurzweil suggests an interesting principle that puts all such prognostications in context: People tend to overestimate the near-term impact of a technological revolution and to underestimate the long-term impact. Social scientists have tended to stumble along these lines, asserting that the computer revolution has arrived but not contemplating where and when its greatest impacts will be felt.

IMPLICATIONS FOR SOCIAL SCIENCE

Arguably, the computer revolution began for social science at the beginning of the twentieth century, when Hermann Hollerith developed programmable, punch-card counting machines to analyze data from the 1900 U.S. census and founded what later became the IBM corporation. Thus social-science computing is a mature field, yet many promising computer methods are underused in the social sciences.

After decades of development, computer simulation still has only a marginal position in most of the social sciences. In 1974 Donella Meadows and colleagues published a dire and influential warning about the human future, called *The Limits to Human Growth*, based on computer simulations of the global socioeconomic system; but three decades later social scientists were still debating whether the approach has merit. A number of social scientists with classical training have taken up computer simulation as a methodology for developing theory and testing its logical consistency. For example, William Bainbridge (2006) used a system of 44,100 artificial intelligent agents to model the way that religious cognitions and social influences interact in a community the size of a small city. But much of the simulation work on human societies ignores traditional work on the same topics, thereby failing to integrate the simulation community with the rest of social science. A striking but not unusual example is the otherwise excellent textbook, *Simulation for the Social Scientist* (2005), by Nigel Gilbert and Klaus Troitzsch, which cites in its extensive bibliography almost none of the simulation studies published in mainstream social science journals.

The general field of human-centered computing (HCC), including the subfields called human-computer interaction (HCI) and computer-supported cooperative work (CSCW), has become major research territory, although a large fraction of the scientists come from outside the classical social sciences, and very little of this work is published in mainstream social science journals. The goal of these HCC researchers is generally to develop or evaluate hardware or software systems, rather than test

general theories, and their methodologies rarely meet social science standards of rigor. This "wild west phase" in the history of HCI and CSCW may be coming to an end, as evidenced by the papers presented at the international Communities and Technologies conferences that tend to cite a good mixture of traditional social science along with computer science work on Internet-based communication networks.

Although every social scientist today uses Internet search engines, few seem to realize that they are versatile tools for social analysis, and that other potentially useful tools can be found on commercial Web sites. A Web search engine needs not only to find Web sites that contain a particular word, but also to arrange the Web sites in descending order of probable value to the user, on the basis of *natural language processing* (NLP) and analysis of the network of links connecting Web sites. These methods could be used by social scientists to map the culture and society that produced all the Web sites. Business sites, such as Amazon and Netflix, include *recommender systems* (or *collaborative filtering* systems) that create advertisements personally tailored for the individual user, based on the buying patterns and expressed preferences of previous customers. Applied, for example, to books about politics, these methods could tell political scientists much about how citizens view leaders and issues. Even as social scientists study the impact of information technology on the rest of society, they should contemplate how it might transform their own disciplines, for good or ill.

SEE ALSO *Digital Divide; Internet; Internet, Impact on Politics; Knowledge Society; Limits of Growth; Managerial Class; New Class, The; Reagan, Ronald; Social Science; Society; Technological Progress, Economic Growth; Telecommunications Industry*

BIBLIOGRAPHY

Attewell, Paul. 2001. The First and Second Digital Divides. *Sociology of Education* 74 (3): 252–259.

Bainbridge, William Sims, ed. 2004. *Berkshire Encyclopedia of Human-Computer Interaction*. Great Barrington, MA: Berkshire.

Bainbridge, William Sims. 2006. *God from the Machine: Artificial Intelligence Models of Religious Cognition*. Lanham, MD: AltaMira.

Bell, Daniel. 1973. *The Coming of Post-Industrial Society: A Venture in Social Forecasting*. New York: Basic Books.

DiMaggio, Paul, Eszter Hargittai, W. Russell Neuman, and John P. Robinson. 2001. Social Implications of the Internet. *Annual Review of Sociology* 27: 307–336.

Form, William. 1987. On the Degradation of Skills. *Annual Review of Sociology* 13: 29–47.

Freiberger, Paul, and Michael Swaine. 1999. *Fire in the Valley: The Inside Story of Silicon Valley's Computer Pioneers*. Foster City, CA: IDG Books.

Gilbert, Nigel, and Klaus G. Troitzsch. 2005. *Simulation for the Social Scientist*. Buckingham, U.K.: Open University Press.

Kizza, Joseph Migga, ed. 1996. *Social and Ethical Effects of the Computer Revolution*. Jefferson, NC: McFarland.

Kurzweil, Ray. 2005. *The Singularity Is Near: When Humans Transcend Biology*. New York: Viking.

Larsen, Otto N. 1992. *Milestones and Millstones: Social Science at the National Science Foundation, 1945-1991*. New Brunswick, NJ: Transaction.

Lievrouw, Leah A. 2003. When Users Push Back: Oppositional New Media and Community. In *Communities and Technologies*, eds. Marleen Huysman, Etienne Wenger, and Volker Wulf, 391–406. Dordrecht, Netherlands: Kluwer.

Liker, Jeffrey K., Carol J. Haddad, and Jennifer Karlin. 1999. Perspectives on Technology and Work Organization. *Annual Review of Sociology* 25: 575–596.

Meadows, Donella H., et al. 1974. *The Limits to Growth*. 2nd ed. New York: Universe Books.

Van Den Besselaar, Peter, et al., eds. 2005. *Communities and Technologies 2005*. Dordrecht, Netherlands: Springer.

Wellman, Barry, et al. 1996. Computer Networks as Social Networks: Collaborative Work, Telework, and Virtual Community. *Annual Review of Sociology* 22: 213–238.

William Sims Bainbridge

COMTE, AUGUSTE
1798–1857

Auguste Comte was a French philosopher best known for founding the field of sociology and the philosophical school of positivism. Born into a Catholic and monarchial family in Montpellier on January 17, 1798, he rejected Catholicism and royalism at the age of thirteen and entered the progressive École Polytechnique in Paris three years later. He soon began a close association with the French social reformer Claude Henri de Rouvroy Saint-Simon (1760–1825) and served as his secretary for several years. After breaking with Saint-Simon and then suffering a mental collapse in 1827, Comte recovered and published the six volumes of his seminal *Course of Positive Philosophy* between 1830 and 1842. He also served as a tutor and examiner at the École Polytechnique beginning in 1832, but was dismissed in 1842 as a result of a dispute with its directors. He had gained a considerable following by this point, and for much of the remainder of his life his admirers and disciples supported him financially. In the early 1850s he began formulating his own humanitarian and non-theistic religion, the Religion of Humanity. His second and final major work, the four-volume *System of Positive Polity*, was published from 1851 to 1854. Soon afterward Comte's perennially poor health deteriorated even further, and he died of stomach cancer on September 5, 1857.

Comte is perhaps most famous for his "law of three stages," according to which intellectual and social development progresses through three chronological steps: the theological stage, in which events are attributed to the actions of gods and supernatural forces; the metaphysical stage, in which the world is explained through abstract concepts such as "nature" and "final causes"; and the final, positive stage, which is characterized by a willingness to simply observe the world without searching for a metaphysical cause or final principle that governs it. Comte believed that the "positive" method that had triumphed in mathematics, astronomy, and physics would eventually prevail in other fields such as economics and politics; this belief system made him an important forerunner of positivistic social science as it emerged in the mid-twentieth century, which held that mixing "facts" and "values" would entail a betrayal of scientific thinking. According to Comte, the positive method would culminate in a new science, sociology, the goal and achievement of which would be nothing less than the synthesis of all human knowledge and the resolution of the crisis of the modern world through the reorganization of society.

Comte maintained that nearly all social problems could be solved by organizing society into an all-embracing hierarchical system in which an intellectual elite helps to regulate education and public morality, an outlook which the English biologist Thomas H. Huxley (1825–1895) described as "Catholicism minus Christianity" (Pickering 1993, p. 17). The English philosopher John Stuart Mill may have overstated the case in arguing that Comte aimed at establishing "a despotism of society over the individual, surpassing anything contemplated in the political ideal of the most rigid disciplinarian among the ancient philosophers" (Comte 1975, p. xxviii), but it is difficult to deny that Comte's emphasis on hierarchy and obedience put him sharply at odds with liberalism and democracy.

SEE ALSO *Mill, John Stuart; Positivism; Sociology*

BIBLIOGRAPHY

Aron, Raymond. 1965. *Montesquieu, Comte, Marx, Tocqueville, the Sociologists and the Revolution of 1848*. Vol. 1 of *Main Currents in Sociological Thought*. New York: Basic Books.

Comte, Auguste. 1975. *Auguste Comte and Positivism: The Essential Writings*. Ed. Gertrud Lenzer. New York: Harper and Row.

Pickering, Mary. 1993. *Auguste Comte: An Intellectual Biography*. Cambridge, U.K.: Cambridge University Press.

Dennis C. Rasmussen

CONCENTRATION CAMPS

The concentration camp has become a paradigmatic symbol for oppression of the racial or ethnic "other." The *Oxford Dictionary* defines a concentration camp as "a camp where non-combatants of a district are accommodated." While this definition captures the basic description it does not articulate that concentration camps have become synonymous with starvation, rape, torture, violence, and mass extermination. Some camps also involve forced labor in addition to the other forms of inhumane treatment. Many states—Western and non-Western, democratic and undemocratic—have used concentration camps as tools to target civilian populations and hated ethnic groups. The justification for camps has generally been to cleanse the society of perceived internal threats to security and order. In most cases a distinct ethnic group or class of people is determined to be a threat and subject to internment by state decree in order to guarantee stability and prevent insurgency. Thus the development of concentration camps is driven in its earliest form as a counter-insurgency technique against anticolonial struggles.

The first use of concentration camps was by the British during the Boer war (1899–1902). Boers and black Africans were placed in camps so that they would be unable to aid Boer guerrillas. It is reported that more than 27,000 Boers and 14,000 Africans died in the camps from disease and starvation. Most of the dead were children, clearly noncombatants in the conflict. The British also employed the use of concentration camps in Namibia, the Isle of Man, Cyprus, Kenya, Channel Islands, and Northern Ireland. In Kenya during the Mau-Mau rebellion the British placed 1.5 million Kikuyu rebels in concentration camps. More than 300,000 Kenyans died as a result of these policies. These cases make it clear that even when concentration camps are not explicitly designed to exterminate large portions of the enemy population they are no less deadly in their effect.

Camps have almost always been justified by and surrounded conflicts whether civil or international. Some of the most notable examples have surrounded multinational conflicts like World Wars I (1914–1918) and II (1939–1945). During World War I, Austria-Hungary placed Serbs and Ukranians in concentration camps during the war. However, the most prominent examples emerge from the experience of World War II.

The experience of Nazi Germany in World War II stands as the paradigmatic example of concentration camps. The Nazi government led by Adolf Hitler and an ideology of cleansing the German nation and controlled territories of Non-Aryans, developed camps for mass extermination and forced labor. The primary groups targeted by Germans were Jews from Germany and territories occupied by Germany during World War II like the Netherlands, France, and Poland. However, while the Nazi camps are known for their extermination of Jews they were not the only populations placed in camps. Nazis also placed the Roma (Gypsies), Africans, homosexuals, and communists in camps for forced labor and extermination.

The Nazi camps first began in 1933 largely for internment but were converted to the cause of extermination in 1941. Evidence shows that more than six million Jews and some unknown others perished in the Nazi camps of Treblinka, Belzec, Auschwitz-Birkenau, and Sobibor. Methods of extermination included starvation, gas chambers, disease, and firing squads. According to some sources groups of individuals were used at times as target practice for German soldiers.

The Nazi concentration camp spawned immense creativity and social scientific work. Psychologist Viktor Frankl developed his psychological perspective called *logotherapy* based upon his experiences in Auschwitz and Dachau. Italian theorist Giorgio Agamben has developed theories around the *state of exception* and the *bare life* to see the concentration camp as a product of modern state sovereignty rather than as an aberration. Italians also placed Jews and communists into camps during World War II and camps also existed in the Netherlands and France.

However, Germany and Italy were not the only nations to use internment during World War II. The United States put ethnic Japanese, many of who were American citizens, into what were called internment camps beginning in 1942. This action was undertaken by the Roosevelt administration under executive order 9066 following the bombing of Pearl Harbor by Japan in December of 1941. More than 120,000 Japanese Americans and some German Americans, two-thirds of whom were U.S. citizens, were placed in internment camps. Lt. General J. L. DeWitt wrote in a letter to the Chief of Staff, U.S. Army, June 5, 1943, that, "The security of the Pacific Coast continues to require the exclusion of Japanese from the area now prohibited to them and will so continue as long as that military necessity exists" (p. vii).

Many Japanese died or suffered poor health and neglect in the camps. In order to leave the camps young men had to swear allegiance to the United States and agree to enter the U.S. military. Many refused and were punished, and their stories are captured in the novel *The No, No Boys* (1978)[MS1] referring to their decline of swearing allegiance to the U.S. and their decline of military conscription. In 1988 the U.S. Congress formally apologized to Japanese American victims of internment camps and granted reparations to the group according to the Japanese-American Reparation Act.

Japanese internment is not the only instance in the United States of the perceived use of what many identify as concentration camps. The practice of placing Native Americans on Indian reservations that had few services and little or no economic opportunities has been likened to the practice of concentration camps. The Native American experience begins with the Indian Removal Act of 1838, which relocated Southern tribes east of the Mississippi River and set the stage for moving them to reservations. Others like Stanley Elkins in his work on slavery compared slave plantations to concentration camps.

In the twenty-first century the detention and torture of terror suspects and so-called illegal combatants outside of the Geneva conventions at "Camp X-Ray" in Guantanamo Bay, Cuba, has been likened to concentration camps. Detainees have been subjected to a range of forms of extralegal torture that do not conform to the Geneva Conventions or other international law.

Latin America has not been free from the experience of concentration camps. The military junta in Argentina used camps to torture and kill more than 30,000 disappeared dissidents between 1976 and 1983 during what is called the "Dirty War." The military regime of Augusto Pinochet (1915–2006) in Chile also used similar camps to deal with dissidents during its reign following the coup against democratically elected leftist President Salvador Allende (1908–1973).

Between 1895 and 1898 the Spanish in Cuba employed camps to combat the insurgents fighting for Cuban independence. The atrocities in the camps, the bombing of the *Maine*, as well as the imperialist designs of the United States are cited as reasons the United States invaded Cuba in the Spanish-American War (1898). The Spanish also used camps in the Philippines in 1901 to quell descent against colonial rule.

Other uses of the concentration camp have involved the Khmer Rouge regime headed by Pol Pot (1925–1998) in Cambodia, North Korea, and the Peoples Republic of China reform and labor camps. The camps in Cambodia caused the deaths of 1.7 million enemies of the Khmer Rouge (1975–1979); the camps in North Korea held 1.6 million enemies of the state (1948–1994); and countless millions in the camps in China developed during the Great Leap Forward and the Cultural Revolution (1958–1961 and 1966–1969). In each case, these were communist regimes that used camps to "reform" political dissidents or those who were perceived to be ideological or ethnic enemies of the regime. In each case, thousands died in camps from starvation or from overwork or were executed. Soviet leader Joseph Stalin (1878–1953) used concentration camps called *gulags* to address political dissenters, Jews, and other ethnic groups in Russia. These camps included Trotskeyite political foes, and ethnic Ukranians, Chechens, Inguish, Crimean Tartars, Tajiks, Bashkirs, and Kazaks.

One of the more recent experiences with concentration camps was the Balkan War, following the break-up of Yugoslavia. In Bosnia and Herzegovina between 1992 and 1995 more than 200,000 Croats, Serbs, and Muslim were killed in camps and by acts of ethnic cleansing.

The widespread use of concentration camps for social scientists demonstrates the willingness of various kinds of states in different contexts to engage in this harsh form of population regulation. The camps themselves demonstrate the extensive power of modern states to regulate all aspects of everyday life for citizens and other populations contained within national, colonial, or imperial boundaries. Camps have also provided opportunities to understand the psychology of the oppressors and the oppressed. The concept of authoritarian personality was developed in part to understand the participation of regular Nazi soldiers in the extermination of Jews. Further, the works of Stanley Elkins, Avery Gordon, Agamben, and Frankl, among others, examine the effects of camps on individuals and groups. Beyond psychology, notions of collective memory and haunting have also been developed to analyze the way the experience of concentration camps structures the lives and memories of generations beyond the initial victims. Concentration camps are a devastating product of modern nation states and civil and international military conflicts. At the same time, they are a rich but disturbing area of study for those who seek to understand the role of the state and the psychology of violence and oppression.

SEE ALSO *Colonialism; Contempt; Genocide; Hitler, Adolf; Holocaust, The; Imperialism; Imprisonment; Incarceration, Japanese American; Jews; Nazism; Personality, Authoritarian; Reparations*

BIBLIOGRAPHY

Agamben, Giorgio. 1998. *Homo Sacer: Sovereign Power and Bare Life.* Palo Alto, CA: Stanford University Press.

Agamben, Giorgio. 2005. *State of Exception.* Chicago: University of Chicago Press.

Elkins, Stanley. 1968. *Slavery.* Chicago: University of Chicago Press.

Frankl, Viktor. 1997. *Man's Search for Meaning: An Introduction to Logotherapy.* New York: Touchstone.

Gordon, Avery. 1997. *Ghostly Matters: Haunting and the Sociological Imagination.* Minneapolis: University of Minnesota Press.

Lt. Gen. J. L. DeWitt to the Chief of Staff, U.S. Army, June 5, 1943. 1943. In *Final Report; Japanese Evacuation from the*

West Coast 1942. pp. vii–x. Washington DC: Government Printing Office.

Mark Sawyer

CONDITIONALITY

Conditionality is the practice used by international financial institutions (e.g., the International Monetary Fund and the World Bank) and bilateral donors to link their provision of financial support to developing and middle-income countries to the implementation of prespecified policy reforms.

Conditionality has its origins in the Articles of Agreement of the International Monetary Fund (IMF), adopted at the United Nations Monetary and Financial Conference in Bretton Woods, New Hampshire, in 1944, and amended several times since. The Articles of Agreement state that one of the purposes of the IMF is to provide temporary balance-of-payment support to countries that need it under "adequate safeguards" that the loans will be repaid (Article I(v) of the IMF Articles of Agreement). Since the early 1950s, these safeguards have been achieved through the imposition of specific policy conditions, set out in the stand-by arrangements negotiated by the IMF with countries receiving its support. These conditions were designed to ensure that the recipient country adopted macroeconomic policies that would allow it to be in a position to repay the foreign exchange funds lent by the IMF in the foreseeable future. Conditionality therefore acted as a substitute for the collateral used to guarantee loans between private companies.

The nature of conditionality has evolved since the early practice of the IMF. Initially, conditionality only included macroeconomic policy reforms aimed at addressing the external disequilibrium experienced by the recipient countries (e.g., reduction in domestic absorption, policies to promote exports). In the 1970s and 1980s conditionality became more extensive, and included structural conditions too (e.g., privatization of state-owned entities), in order to address larger balance-of-payments crises. Moreover, donors other than the IMF (most notably the World Bank) started to impose conditionality too, to ensure that their project lending would take place in a sound policy environment. Conditionality is still being used by the IMF in its support of middle countries experiencing significant currency crises (e.g., several East Asian countries in the late 1990s and Argentina from 2000 to 2002) and by all donors that lend money or give grants to developing countries. Conditionality applies to a wide variety of policy areas (including governance), even though donors are seeking to streamline its use.

Conditionality has been frequently criticized for its lack of effectiveness. One area of criticism relates to the type of orthodox economic policies (e.g., sharp reductions in expenditures and tight monetary policies) typically demanded by donors through conditionality. Critics have seen these policies as ineffective in stimulating growth and reducing the social costs from adjustment.

The second reason why conditionality has been seen as not effective is because of its lack of credibility. Countries receiving donor support can often anticipate that even if they do not fully implement the policy reforms demanded under conditionality, they will still receive support from the donors. This is because donors may have an interest in providing support even if conditionality is not adhered to, due to, for example, geopolitical considerations, pressure to spend aid budgets, and the need to ensure the repayments of past loans. This undermines the effectiveness of conditionality, leading only to partial implementation of the policy reforms demanded by donors in return for financial support.

SEE ALSO *International Monetary Fund; World Bank*

BIBLIOGRAPHY

Articles of Agreement of the International Monetary Fund. http://www.imf.org/external/pubs/ft/aa/index.htm.

Collier, Paul. 1997. Policy Essay No. 22: The Failure of Conditionality. In *Perspectives on Aid and Development*, ed. Catherine Gwin and Joan Nelson, 51–78. Washington, DC: Overseas Development Council.

Guitian, Manuel. 1995. Conditionality: Past, Present, and Future. *IMF Staff Papers* 42 (4): 792–835.

World Bank. 1998. *Assessing Aid: What Works, What Doesn't, and Why.* New York: Oxford University Press.

Giulio Federico

CONDORCET, MARQUIS DE
1743–1794

Marie Jean Antoine de Caritat, Marquis de Condorcet, a descendant of the ancient family of Caritat, was born on September 17, 1743, at Ribemont, Aisne, in France. His father died early, and Condorcet's devoutly Catholic mother ensured that he was educated at the Jesuit College of Rheims and at the College of Navarre in Paris. A talented young mathematician, he soon came to the attention of the mathematicians Jean le Rond d'Alembert (1717–1783) and Alexis Clairault (1713–1765). In 1765 Condorcet published a work on mathematics entitled

Essai sur le calcul intégral (Essay on Integral Calculus), and he was elected to the *Académie Royale des Sciences* four years later. After becoming acquainted with Anne Robert Jacques Turgot (1721–1781), who served as controller-general of finance under King Louis XV (1710–1774), Condorcet was appointed inspector general of the Monnaie de Paris (Paris Mint) in 1774. Condorcet later wrote a sympathetic *Life of Turgot* (1786), which supported Turgot's economic theories. In 1777 Condorcet was appointed secretary to the Académie des Sciences; in 1782 he became secretary of the Académie Française; and in 1789 he published his *Life of Voltaire*. Thomas Malthus's (1766–1834) *Essay on the Principle of Population* (1798) was published partly in response to the optimistic views on the perfectibility of society that Condorcet expressed in his writings.

Condorcet remains influential in the social sciences because he applied mathematical ideas to social and political problems. He became famous for what is now known as *Condorcet's paradox*, first presented in his *Essay on the Application of Analysis to the Probability of Majority Decisions* (1785), which describes the intransitivity of majority preferences in electoral politics. An election can occur even when there is no clear candidate whom the voters prefer to all other candidates. In such a situation, known as a *majority rule cycle* or *circular tie*, one majority prefers candidate *A* over *B*, another majority *B* over *C*, and a final majority *C* over *A*. To break such electoral circles, Condorcet invented a method in which voters rank candidates in order of preference; these electoral procedures are known as the *Condorcet method*, which is designed to secure a definite *Condorcet winner*.

Condorcet played a leading role in the French Revolution of 1789. In 1791 he was elected to represent Paris in the Legislative Assembly, where he presented plans for the creation of a state education system and drafted a new constitution for France. He also campaigned for the abolition of slavery and advocated female suffrage, publishing a pamphlet titled "On the Admission of Women to the Rights of Citizenship" in 1790. Although he was a revolutionary, he did not support the execution of the French king, and aligned himself with the more moderate Girondist Party. He opposed the so-called Montagnard Constitution, which he thought was too radical and far-reaching. As a result, he was regarded as a traitor and a warrant was issued for his arrest. While in hiding, Condorcet wrote his famous *Sketch for a Historical Picture of the Progress of the Human Mind*, which was published posthumously in 1795. This major text of the French Enlightenment describes the historical connection between the growth of science and the development of human rights.

In March 1794 Condorcet attempted to escape from Paris, but he was arrested and imprisoned, and was later found dead in his cell; the cause of his death has never been determined. Condorcet was interred in 1989 in the Panthéon in Paris in honor of the bicentennial of the French Revolution.

SEE ALSO *Human Rights; Majority Rule; Voting*

BIBLIOGRAPHY

McLean, Iain, and Fiona Hewitt, eds. and trans. 1994. *Condorcet: Foundations of Social Choice and Political Theory* Aldershot, U.K.: Edward Elgar.

Bryan S. Turner

CONFEDERATE STATES OF AMERICA

The Confederate States of America was officially founded in February 1861, after seven Southern states (South Carolina, Georgia, Florida, Alabama, Mississippi, Louisiana, and Texas) seceded from the United States. For years, Northern and Southern states had been debating the issue of slavery, especially in the territories, where it was not constitutionally protected. These debates had escalated during the 1850s, sometimes to the point of violence. When Abraham Lincoln, who represented a specifically antislavery party and wanted to end slavery in the territories, was elected president of the United States in 1860, these seven states declared they had had enough and left the Union.

They quickly went to work forming a provisional government. Shortly after announcing the new country, the Confederate Congress appointed Jefferson Davis president (he would be officially elected to office in November). It named Montgomery, Alabama, as the new nation's capital, and it adopted a constitution. This constitution was modeled largely on the United States Constitution (Confederates, like their Northern brothers, insisted they were the true heirs of the Founding Fathers) with several important exceptions. Where the federal Constitution had never used the words *slave* or *slavery*, but implicitly protected the peculiar institution, the Confederate document explicitly protected slavery—even deeming that Congress could pass no law that would impinge on "the right of property in negro slaves." Unlike the Americans, however, the Confederates immediately banned the international slave trade, except with states remaining in the Union. The president served a six-year term, and he could not be reelected. He also had the right to a line-item veto.

When fighting broke out with the Union in April, four more states (Virginia, Tennessee, North Carolina, and Arkansas) joined the Confederacy. In an acknowledgment of Virginia's importance, Confederate leaders quickly agreed to move the capital to the industrial and commercial city of Richmond. For the South in particular, this decision made Virginia the military focal point of the war. Because the Confederate leadership did not have the sense of urgency about the West that it did about Richmond, less able generals were often in command there, and the rebels suffered loss after loss.

War dominated the life of the Confederacy. Leaders at the state and national levels were constantly challenged with the problem of keeping the ranks filled and with feeding and clothing the army. The country had 5.5 million whites and about 3.5 million black slaves who would not be allowed to serve. By 1862 Confederates were so desperate for men that they resorted to a national draft. This was a deeply ironic development in a country that had embraced individual liberties and states' rights as being among its banner causes. Meanwhile, a successful Union blockade and the lack of internal infrastructure complicated efforts to procure and transport needed supplies. (The same issues made it exceedingly difficult for Southerners to export their main commodity, cotton.) Financing the war was another problem, one that Confederates never mastered. Relying principally on loans and the printing press to pay for the war, the government helped drive inflation through the roof. Congress passed a comprehensive tax measure in 1863, but the government did not effectively enforce it, and so it made little impact. Over the course of the war, prices increased by a factor of more than 90.

The stresses of war had profound effects at home. Rising prices, shrinking availability, speculation, and a drought in 1862 meant that civilians started to go hungry that year. By the following spring, bread riots were breaking out, including one on April 2, 1863, in Richmond that Davis personally broke up. Hoarding and price gouging only compounded matters, and concern for starving families led many Confederate soldiers to desert, especially in the last year of the war. Meanwhile, war itself forced many families into flight. The presence of federal armies also prompted many slaves to abandon their masters and run to the safety—and freedom—of Union lines.

A prickly micromanager, Davis was unable to lead the nation effectively. He had a running argument with more than one general (Robert E. Lee was the only general to whom he regularly deferred), and his cabinet was a revolving door (he had five secretaries of war, for instance). He never reached out to members of Congress or the press, and was barely on speaking terms with his own vice president, Alexander Stephens. Davis had repeated tussles with various governors, particularly Joseph Brown of Georgia and Zebulon Vance of North Carolina, both of whom resisted what they believed were Davis's encroachments on states' rights. In fairness, Davis's management troubles were not entirely of his own making. The one-term rule set out by the constitution rendered Davis a lame duck from the moment he stepped into office. Historians widely believe that the lack of political parties in the South, which blamed partisanship for many of its antebellum fights with Northerners, meant that criticism against Davis was not channeled and came at him from every angle. Without partisan machinery and the attendant patronage, Davis had no way to punish his enemies or reward his supporters.

By the end of the war, the Confederacy was a tangle of contradictions. In a nation founded partly on the principle of individual liberties, Davis suspended habeas corpus and declared martial law in some parts of the country, while Congress passed the first conscription measure in what had been the United States. In a country that was predicated on states' rights, the federal government had to consolidate power at the expense of the states in order to prosecute the war. And in the most striking irony, this state that had been founded to protect slavery decided in March 1865 to arm slaves in a last-ditch effort to hold off the Northern armies. The policy could not be implemented, however, before Lee surrendered to General Ulysses S. Grant on April 9, 1865. Although it took some time for news of the war's end to reach the far corners of the Confederacy, for all intents and purposes the Confederate States of America died with Lee's army.

In the 1870s, Southern white women in particular set out to venerate their fallen men and the Old South. In doing so, they created what has come to be known as the Lost Cause mythology, a moonlight-and-magnolias view of the slave-owning South and the Civil War. The central ideas behind the Lost Cause are that the Confederacy lost the Civil War because the North overwhelmed it with superior numbers, not better fighting, and that defeat ennobled the South rather than discredited it. This ideology is evident in various monuments, works of fiction, and film, with the most notable and culturally penetrating work being *Gone with the Wind.*

SEE ALSO *Civil War; Davis, Jefferson; Lee, Robert E.; U.S. Civil War*

BIBLIOGRAPHY

Davis, William C. 2002. *Look Away: A History of the Confederate States of America.* New York: Free Press.

Levine, Bruce. 2005. *Confederate Emancipation: Southern Plans to Free and Arm Slaves During the Civil War.* New York: Oxford University Press.

McPherson, James M. 2001. *Ordeal by Fire: The Civil War and Reconstruction.* 3rd ed. Boston: McGraw-Hill.

Potter, David M. 1968. *The South and the Sectional Conflict.* Baton Rouge: Louisiana State University Press.

Rable, George C. 1994. *The Confederate Republic: A Revolution Against Politics.* Chapel Hill: University of North Carolina Press.

Jennifer L. Weber

CONFEDERATIONS

A confederation is a voluntary association of sovereign, independent nation-states or political communities that manages, in limited ways, its members' common concerns, such as defense, foreign relations, trade, postal services, and a common currency. A confederation, therefore, ordinarily entails cooperative unity across a broader range of governmental functions than a customs union in which the member nations eliminate trade barriers among themselves and implement a common tariff policy toward nonunion nations.

The word *federal* comes from the Latin *foedus*, meaning "covenant," which signifies a partnership or marriage wherein individuals or groups consent voluntarily to unite for common purposes without surrendering their fundamental rights or identities. The verb *confederate* has traditionally meant to form an alliance to carry out the will of a coalition of interests, none of which relinquish sovereignty.

Commonly cited examples of confederations include the Aetolian (367–189 BCE) and Achaean leagues (280–146 BCE) of ancient Greece, the Iroquois Confederacy in North America (c. 1142–1794), the Swiss confederations (1291–1798 and 1814–1848), the Polish-Lithuanian Commonwealth (1569–1795), the Dutch Republic (1589–1795), the Articles of Confederation of the United States (1781–1789), the Germanic Confederation (1815–1866), and the southern Confederate States of America (1861–1865).

Before the framers of the U.S. Constitution invented modern federalism in 1787 the word *federal* referred to what is today called *confederal.* The U.S. founders transformed the historic concept of federalism as confederation into the modern concept of federation, thus generating today's widely held view that confederations are weak, even outmoded. Indeed, most modern confederations have been short-lived. Recent examples include the United Arab Republic (1958–1961), the West African union of Senegal and the Gambia (Senegambia, 1982–1989), and the State Union of Serbia and Montenegro (2003–2006) in southeastern Europe.

Confederations established before the 1700s sometimes lasted for several centuries, but confederations established since the 1700s have usually lasted less than a decade, in part because the modern nation-state and its attendant nationalism militate against merely confederal unity. Additionally, the complexity of modern governance strains the capabilities of confederations, while the availability of alternate means of functional cooperation, such as military alliances and trade agreements, render confederations less necessary. These problems are illustrated by the Commonwealth of Independent States (CIS), a quasi confederation established in 1991 by twelve successor states of the Union of Soviet Socialist Republics. Although the CIS still exists in form, it is weak, fractious, and pockmarked by separate alliances and agreements among subsets of its members.

A confederation is usually established by, and based on, a written document called *articles*, a *convention*, a *treaty*, or some other term. The document states the confederation's purposes, terms, structure, procedures, and specific powers. Attributes of sovereignty are not usually vested in a confederation; individuals retain citizenship in the separate member states; and member states can exit the confederation. Hence, a confederation usually possesses only limited, expressly delegated powers, and can exercise only those powers explicitly stated in the founding document. It cannot increase its powers through interpretation.

An important, common difference between a federation and a confederation is that a confederation usually cannot legislate for individuals. Consequently, the confederal government under the U.S. Articles of Confederation could not tax, fine, arrest, or regulate individuals, or conscript citizens of the constituent states into the confederal military. Ordinarily, a confederation can act only through its member states. Also, it possesses no independent sources of revenue to support its operations; instead, it must rely on contributions or dues payments by its member states.

All member states ordinarily have equal representation and one vote each in the confederation's decision-making council. The representatives are usually appointed and also paid by their member governments rather than being elected by the people of the member states and paid by the confederal government. Thus, the members of a confederal council are more like ambassadors than representatives. Frequently, majority voting is rejected in favor of supermajority and unanimous voting.

There is no precise, universal definition of *confederation* or exact distinction between confederation and federation because confederations, as well as federations, vary in their characteristics. Attributes of confederation and federation get mixed together in response to political circumstances. For example, Switzerland's constitution is titled the Federal Constitution of the Helvetic (or Swiss) Confederation. The European Union's (EU) core decision-making structure is confederal; yet, many of its operational features are federal. The EU is a hybrid—a confederal federation—that has endured because its confederal features guarantee the continuing authority and integrity of the member states, while its evolving federal features guarantee the operational viability of the union within its limited but gradually growing sphere of authority.

SEE ALSO *Confederate States of America; European Union; Pan-Arabism; Pan-Caribbeanism; Sovereignty; Union of Soviet Socialist Republics*

BIBLIOGRAPHY

Forsyth, Murray G. 1981. *Unions of States: The Theory and Practice of Confederation.* Leicester, U.K.: Leicester University Press.

Jensen, Merrill. 1948. *The Articles of Confederation: An Interpretation of the Social-Constitutional History of the American Revolution, 1774–1781.* Madison: University of Wisconsin Press.

Kincaid, John. 1999. Confederal Federalism and Citizen Representation in the European Union. *West European Politics* 22: 34–58.

Lister, Frederick K. 1996. *The European Union, the United Nations, and the Revival of Confederal Governance.* Westport, CT: Greenwood.

John Kincaid

CONFIDENCE INTERVALS

SEE *Statistics in the Social Sciences.*

CONFIDENCE LIMITS

SEE *Probability, Limits in.*

CONFISCATION

Legislation enabling courts to confiscate or remove illegal gain has grown rapidly in a wide range of both civil and common-law countries. The concept is not new: forfeiture was part of Roman law as early as 451 BCE and was also used by the ancient Greeks. In more recent times, confiscation has usually been introduced as a part of the fight against organized crime and drugs, either directly in drugs legislation or in a penal code and applicable to all kinds of crimes. In 1970 the U.S. Congress passed the first criminal forfeiture statutes in U.S. history. In the United Kingdom forfeiture was introduced in the Drug Trafficking Offences Act 1986 and has been subsequently strengthened and extended to other areas of crime via the Criminal Justice Act 1988 and 1993, the Drug Trafficking Act 1994, and the Proceeds of Crime Act 2002. In other countries the sanction of removing illegal gain has been introduced for a wide array of crimes, extending even to environmental statutes.

The power of courts to impose this sanction varies substantially across areas of the law and also across jurisdictions. In some countries, such as the United States, the proceeds of drug trafficking can be forfeited under civil powers, independent of any criminal proceedings. Although in the United States forfeiture is technically considered to be a civil sanction, the Supreme Court has recognized that forfeiture constitutes a significant punishment and is thus subject to constitutional limitations under the Eighth Amendment. In other countries, such as the United Kingdom, the confiscation of such assets is only possible as a subsidiary part of criminal proceedings.

The goal of removing illegal gain, according to legal doctrine, is to achieve *restitutio ad integrum*. This means that criminals should be put back in the situation in which they would have been had the crime not been committed. This corresponds to the general notion that crime should not pay. This restitutive goal may not be fully achieved with the imposition of other sanctions, such as fines or imprisonment: A fine may well be much lower than the profit from an offense, and imprisonment is no guarantee that the offender will be left without the profits of a crime. For offenses such as theft, the offender can be required to return stolen goods or to pay compensation to the victim of the crime. But for so-called "victimless crimes" such as environmental pollution or drug trafficking, the harm caused by crime is experienced by society at large rather than by identifiable victims, in which case the confiscation of illegal gain replaces individual compensation.

The goal of providing restitution through confiscation also has important consequences for legal character. Confiscation is not usually considered a criminal sanction, as is a fine or imprisonment, but a measure. (There are exceptions to this, however; in France confiscation may be a supplement to a penal sanction or, in some cases, even the primary sanction.) Measures are designed to be corrective or to provide restitution and aim either at protecting society or at restoring a loss. Therefore criminal sanctions are usually said to have a punitive goal, whereas this is not the case for measures.

Confiscation occurs after a crime has been committed and thus has little to add by way of deterrence, assuming the courts are applying efficient sanctions that already take illegal gain into account. But if the courts have been applying fines that exclude illegal gain, then a role for confiscation may emerge. Bowles, Faure, and Garoupa (2000, 2005) have argued that there are certain types of offense for which the removal of illegal gain provides a punishment superior to more traditional sanctions. Offenses committed sequentially and where the victims are unaware of offenses being committed may be very difficult (and costly) to detect. For example, a drug dealer may accumulate wealth from a large number of small illegal transactions, or a polluting firm may discharge illegal effluent over a prolonged interval. In such instances it is impracticable to prosecute each illegal action individually. Confiscation can be a way to tie sanctions more closely to an offender's cumulative ill-gotten gains and to increase the scale of sanctions. This can help compensate for weak deterrence in crimes such as illegal trading, where conviction probabilities are low and the fines imposed are low in relation to the potential gains.

SEE ALSO *Violence, Role in Resource Allocation*

BIBLIOGRAPHY

Bowles, Roger, Michael Faure, and Nuno Garoupa. 2000. Economic Analysis of the Removal of Illegal Gain. *International Review of Law and Economics* 20: 537–549.

Bowles, Roger, Michael Faure, and Nuno Garoupa. 2005. Forfeiture of Illegal Gain: An Economic Perspective. *Oxford Journal of Legal Studies* 25 (2): 275–295.

Roger Bowles
Michael Faure
Nuno Garoupa

CONFLICT

In general usage, a *conflict* is a disagreement or incompatibility of goals. In conflict resolution literature, however, *conflict* is distinguished from *dispute*, with the former being a long-term, deep-rooted problem, and the latter being a short-term, more superficial difference that can usually be resolved through simple negotiation. Conflicts, in this sense, are often caused by attacks on, or the absence of, basic human needs, especially identity, security, and a sense of self-worth. Most conflicts between ethnic groups, for example, are of this type. One group may threaten the legitimacy and value of another's identity, or it may attack or threaten them physically, psychologically, socially, economically, or politically, thereby causing a conflict.

Conflicts can also be caused by disagreements about fundamental moral values (e.g., definitions of right and wrong). In the United States, the conflicts over abortion rights, homosexual marriage, and the role of Christianity in public affairs are all examples of such value conflicts.

Finally, conflicts can involve disagreements about rights or denial of rights. These can include fundamental human rights, which are laid out in the Universal Declaration of Human Rights, or they can be more narrowly defined in national or state constitutions or laws, or in local ordinances. In all of these cases, the problem is not easily negotiable: people do not negotiate about their religious beliefs, nor do they compromise their basic rights. They fight for them.

Disputes, on the other hand, are often differences of interests: who is going to do what and when, how much someone will pay for something, or how a limited good will be distributed. Such disputes are usually negotiable, and a so-called win-win, or integrative, solution can often be found through which everyone is satisfied and the dispute is resolved.

Politics, being about the distribution and use of power, is inherently conflictual. It could be argued that all politics is conflict and conflict resolution, because it involves the processes used to determine who has power to make decisions and to prevail in disputes at the family, organizational, community, national, and international levels. At all of these levels, institutions have been developed to routinize the management of such disputes: families may use a consensus process or one of parental control; organizations have management policies and procedures; communities, nations, and even the international system have laws, legislatures, executive branches, and courts. All of these institutions are designed to resolve conflicts over who will do what, what rights people have, and even what moral codes will be followed (as, for instance, with abortion laws).

In general, these mechanisms work fairly well, and most conflicts are successfully prevented or resolved. Sometimes, however, established mechanisms break down and destructive and protracted conflicts develop. These may take the form of domestic violence or protracted family disputes between spouses or between parents and children. Also common are long-running conflicts within organizations over such topics as who will lead, what goals will be pursued, or how work is to be accomplished. When routinized conflict resolution mechanisms break down at the national or international level, insurgencies or overt war is often the result.

SEE ALSO *Government; Social Contract*

BIBLIOGRAPHY

Burgess, Heidi, and Guy M. Burgess. 1997. *Encyclopedia of Conflict Resolution.* Santa Barbara, CA: ABC-Clio.

Deutsch, Morton, and Peter Coleman, eds. 2000. *The Handbook of Conflict Resolution: Theory and Practice.* San Francisco: Jossey Bass.

Kriesberg, Louis. 2002. *Constructive Conflicts*, 2nd ed. Lanham, MD: Rowan & Littlefield.

Heidi Burgess

CONFLICT RESOLUTION

SEE *Conflict; Negotiation.*

CONFLICT THEORY

SEE *Sociology, Political.*

CONFORMITY

Ever since Émile Durkheim (1858–1917), considered one of the founders of sociology, conformity has often been discussed in sociology as a solution to the problem of social order. The basic norms and values in a society are internalized through the process of socialization. This process results in conformity, which contributes to keeping society together without resorting exclusively to external force or violence. These ideas were further developed by sociologists Talcott Parsons (1902–1979) and Robert K. Merton (1910–2003), among others, and became highly influential during the mid-twentieth century. For Merton two elements of the social and cultural structure of society are of particular importance: culturally defined goals, purposes and interests, which function as legitimate objectives that define what is "worth striving for"; and institutionalized norms that regulate "the acceptable modes of reaching out for these goals" (Merton 1957, pp. 132–133). Only insofar as an aggregate of people conforms to such values and norms may we call it a society, according to Merton; people who reject both the cultural goals and institutional means of a society are "strictly speaking in the society but not of it" (Merton 1957, p. 147). Non-conformers are

likely to be met by a variety of negative sanctions, formal as well as informal, which will put pressure on them to change their behavior, if not their beliefs.

INTERNAL AND EXTERNAL CONFORMITY

When discussing conformity it is important to bear in mind the distinction between conformity in beliefs or attitudes and conformity in behavior. People may conform behaviorally without giving up privately held deviant beliefs in order to escape negative sanctions or be rewarded economically or socially. The social psychologist Leon Festinger (1919–1989) emphasized this distinction by distinguishing between "internalization" (both belief conformity and behavioral conformity) and "compliance" (behavioral conformity but not belief conformity). Compliance is more likely to occur if a person is restricted from leaving a group or society and when there is a threat of punishment for non-compliance. The likelihood for internalization increases if the person is attracted to the group and wishes to remain a member.

During the 1950s, psychologist Solomon Asch conducted a series of social-psychological experiments that strongly influenced the scholarly discussion of conformity during the following decades. Individuals were asked to match the length of a line with other lines of different length. All but one of the individuals in the group was instructed to make a match that was obviously wrong. When the last, uninformed individual in each group was asked to make a match, one third of the participants yielded to the obviously erroneous judgment of the majority. Among the conforming subjects, a majority later said they conformed because they lacked confidence in their own judgement and concluded they must have been mistaken and the majority was correct. The second most common reason for the individuals were to believe that the majority was wrong, but to suppress this knowledge because of an unwillingness to deviate from the group. Asch showed that a majority of three persons was sufficient to have this effect.

Research in the 1990s by psychologist David A. Wilder has shown that people tend to conform more when the majority consists of ingroup-members, that is, people belonging to the same social category, while they conform less when it consists of outgroup-members, that is, people belonging to other social categories. As argued by psychologist John C. Turner, this fact indicates that group identity is a salient factor for understanding conformity. However, it is of crucial importance that the majority is unanimous; otherwise, conformity decreases dramatically. In a classic 1975 study by psychologist Vernon L. Allen, conformity decreased from about thirty-three to five percent when a single individual deviated from the group by giving the correct answer. Moreover, as demonstrated by psychologists Rod Bond and Peter B. Smith in 1996 in a meta-analysis of 133 studies from seventeen different countries, people conform more in collectivistic cultures than in individualistic ones.

Conformity is also more likely in cohesive groups and tends to decrease as groups or societies become more complex in terms of role differentiation. This fact indicates that conformity should decrease as societies become more modernized and individualized, a prediction that is supported by Bond and Smith's analysis.

WHY CONFORMITY OCCURS

Attempts to explain conformity can be grouped into explanations that focus on "normative influence" and those that focus on "informational influence." In normative influence, people conform in order to avoid negative sanctions or social ridicule. Such explanations have been common in sociology and in 1955 were put forward by Morton Deutsch and Harold Gerard in the field of social psychology. Informational influence is principally associated with Leon Festinger and proposes that processes of social comparison or social reality testing lead to increased belief conformity. In situations of subjective uncertainty in which people lack objective reference points for beliefs, people tend to compare their beliefs to those of significant others. The more their beliefs harmonize with those of significant others, the more valid they judge their beliefs. When people discover that their beliefs harmonize with the beliefs held by most others in the group, people tend to become confident in their rightness and seldom change their opinion. Situations in which people's beliefs harmonize poorly with those held by significant others, on the other hand, tend to aggravate the feeling of subjective uncertainty. To remedy this situation, people may either try to change the beliefs held by others in the group or change their own beliefs to better reflect those of the group, which is often far easier.

As sociologist Peter Hedström, among others, have argued, it is often a rational strategy to imitate others' behavior in situations of uncertainty, such as when one glances at other diners for information about which fork to use for the first course, or when the choice of restaurant is based on the number of other people already dining there. However, one risk associated with this strategy is that everyone may imitate the others, and that everyone may think that they alone are uncertain and confused or feel doubt about the rightness of the majority behavior. This phenomenon has been discussed in terms of "pluralistic ignorance." Pluralistic ignorance, especially when people experience strong normative and informational influence, may lead people to conform to a majority that actually does not exist. In other words, as in Hans

Christian Andersen's story *The Emperor's New Clothes*, the conformers may all come to believe that everyone else has understood something important of which they themselves are ignorant, and refrain from questioning the consensus because of fear of ridicule or ostracism. Pluralistic ignorance and conformity in general may thus undermine the potential for creativity and productiveness in a group or society.

Research by psychologist Irving Janis (1918–1990) on "groupthink" showed that compliance within cohesive groups may have disastrous consequences for decision making in crucial situations. The pressure on people to conform to the ingroup increases in polarized situations in which the cost of remaining a deviant or a passive bystander increases. As a result, moderates may suppress their true preferences, which give radical or fanatical elements disproportionate influence.

Conformity thus has a distinctly negative potential. This was demonstrated by research following the 1963 classic experiment by social psychologist Stanley Milgram (1933–1984). Milgram's experiment showed that many people would blindly follow authorities in situations of uncertainty. By combining these insights, many scholars have argued that conformity is an important prerequisite for military atrocities and fascist practices. As argued by psychologist Rupert Brown for instance, "the well-documented instances of group-instigated atrocities against civilians in Vietnam, former Yugoslavia and other war zones before and since suggest that social pressures to conform [can be] both prevalent in their frequency and tragic in their consequences" (Brown 2006, p. 131).

SEE ALSO *Asch, Solomon; Authority; Collectivism; Cults; Deviance; Durkheim, Émile; Experiments, Shock; Fascism; Festinger, Leon; Groupthink; Herd Behavior; Ignorance, Pluralistic; Merton, Robert K; Milgram, Stanley; Norms; Organization Man; Parsons, Talcott; Peer Influence; Social Psychology*

BIBLIOGRAPHY

Allen, Vernon L. 1975. Social Support for Nonconformity. In *Advances in Experimental Social Psychology*, ed. Leonard Berkowitz, 1–43. New York: Academic Press.

Asch, Solomon. 1956. Studies of Independence and Conformity: A Minority of One against a Unanimous Majority. *Psychological Monographs* 70.

Bond, Rod, and Peter B. Smith. 1996. Culture and Conformity: A Meta-Analysis of Studies Using Asch's Line Judgement Task. *Psychological Bulletin* 119: 111–137.

Brown, Rupert. 2006. *Group Processes. Dynamics Within and Between Groups.* Oxford: Blackwell.

Deutsch, Morton, and Harold B. Gerard. 1955. A Study of Normative and Informational Social Influence upon

Individual Judgement. *Journal of Abnormal and Social Psychology* 51: 629–636.

Festinger, Leon. 1950. Informal Social Communication. *Psychological Review* 57: 271–282.

Festinger, Leon. 1953. An Analysis of Compliant Behaviour. In *Group Relations at the Crossroads*, ed. Muzafer Sherif, and M. O. Wilson, 232–256. New York: Harper & Brothers.

Festinger, Leon. 1954. A theory of social comparison processes. *Human Relations* 7: 117–140.

Hedström, Peter. 1998. Rational Imitation. In *Social Mechanisms: An Analytical Approach to Social Theory*, eds. Peter Hedström, and Richard Swedberg, 306–327. Cambridge, U.K.: Cambridge University Press.

Janis, Irving L. 1972. *Victims of Groupthink*. Boston: Houghton Mifflin.

Merton, Robert K. 1957. Social Structure and Anomie. In *Social Theory and Social Structure*. New York: The Free Press.

Milgram, Stanley. 1963. Behavioral Study of Obedience. *Journal of Abnormal Social Psychology* 67: 371–378.

Turner, John C. 1991. *Social Influence*. Milton Keynes, U.K.: Open University Press.

Wilder, David A. 1990. Some Determinants of the Persuasive Power of Ingroups and Outgroups: Organization of Information and Attribution of Independence. *Journal of Personality and Social Psychology* 59: 1202–1213.

Jens Rydgren

CONGRESS, U.S.

The principal features of the U.S. Congress affecting its operation and outputs are the elements of its institutional structure, including its size, the manner in which its members are elected, its leadership offices, and the role of political parties. The outputs of Congress are significant because one of the main functions of Congress is to translate citizens' preferences and needs into government policies. Because Congress does not make decisions in isolation, its interactions with other branches of government also affect its functions.

INSTITUTIONAL STRUCTURE

Article 1, section 1 of the United States Constitution invests all legislative powers in a bicameral (two-house) Congress consisting of a House of Representatives and a Senate. The Constitution further provides that each state will have at least one member in the House of Representatives and two senators.

The House of Representatives contains 435 seats in accordance with federal legislation. Its size has not changed since the 1910 census reapportionment, the process by which the remaining 385 House seats are divided on the basis of state population after each state is allotted its constitutionally guaranteed representative. According to the Constitution, candidates for the House must be at least twenty-five years old, have been a citizen of the United States for seven years, and be a resident of the state (but not district) in which they seek election. House members are elected every two years in single-member (one member per district), plurality (first past the post) legislative districts in elections that must take place on the Tuesday after the first Monday in November in even-numbered years. As a result, every four years members of the House are elected on the day of a presidential election. House districts must be geographically compact and contiguous, have roughly equal population, and be racially fair.

The United States Senate is composed of 100 seats, with two senators elected from each of the fifty states regardless of state size or population. From 1789 to 1913 senators were elected by state legislatures. Senators currently are elected directly by citizens within states in accordance with the 17th Amendment of the U.S. Constitution. A senator must be at least thirty years old, have been a citizen of the United States for at least nine years, and be a resident of the state in which he or she is elected.

Congress uses a system of committees to organize itself. In the first Congresses, the body relied on ad hoc rather than standing committees, in which membership and policy jurisdiction are stable. In the early 1800s the failures of the ad hoc, or select, committee system resulted in a gradual expansion of the standing committee system, although its emergence was slower in the Senate than in the House. Major reductions of the number of committees in both chambers took place in the 1920s and 1940s. The majority party has usually held more seats than the minority on each standing committee. For more than a century, the parties have relied on a seniority rule to determine the chairs of committees.

In the early Congress, formal leadership of each chamber was minimal. There was frequent turnover of the House Speakership and only weak leadership in the Senate. During this period, first the floor and then the increasingly common standing committees often challenged party leaders for control. After the Civil War, polarization of the parties facilitated greater influence by their leaders. However, a lack of cohesion within the Democratic Party in particular, due to the distinctiveness of southern Democrats from the early 1900s to the 1960s, meant that committees, rather than party leaders, were used to organize authority in Congress. In the post-reform

Congress (1974 to the present), the parties have become more internally homogenous and differentiated, leading to greater assertiveness among party leaders such as Newt Gingrich, Speaker of the House from 1995 to 1999. The components of the parties' leadership structures include (if in the majority) the Speakership in the House and the president of the Senate, and for both parties the majority/minority leader and whip. Each party also maintains a caucus/conference committee, a policy committee, a committee to allocate committee seats, and a campaign committee charged to maximize the party's seats.

REPRESENTATION

A member of Congress's (MC) career is influenced by different goals, including crafting effective legislation and turning personal political preferences into public policy, maximizing his or her influence within the legislature, career ambition, and securing reelection. A week spent meeting with concerned lobbyists and raising campaign funds in Washington is usually followed by a weekend back home with one's constituents, listening to their specific needs and ensuring that the MC is not viewed as "out of touch."

The nature of congressional elections differs by chamber. House elections tend not to be competitive, with roughly 95 percent or more of incumbents who choose to stand for reelection retaining their office. In contrast, the Senate is more competitive, and Senate seats are much less likely to go unopposed. The cost of a congressional election is enormous and growing, with a majority of campaign expenditures used to purchase advertisements on television. Accordingly, MCs spend much of their time raising money for their next campaign from both political action committees and individual constituents, and potential challengers must prove they can raise the campaign funds necessary to be considered viable candidates. Much of federal campaign finance law is laid out in the Federal Election Campaign Act (FECA) of 1971. A Supreme Court decision, *Buckley v. Valeo* (1976), upheld FECA's contribution limits and reporting requirements but struck down restrictions on expenditures by candidates and independent political groups.

To be reelected, MCs must closely monitor their constituents' attitudes. They must also attempt to appeal both to their primary constituency, or the subset of constituents who will participate in their party's primary, and their geographic constituency, or the citizens eligible to vote in the general election. Representation of constituents' interests includes casework, bill sponsorship, committee selection and effort, making speeches on the floor, and roll-call voting. Empirical work has shown that MCs' roll-call votes tend to match closely the preferences of their district, and those MCs who deviate too far from their constituents receive fewer votes and are less likely to be reelected. In addition, MCs who represent competitive districts and homogenous districts tend to be more responsive to constituents. Senators are more responsive to constituents in the final two years of their six-year terms than in the first four years. Finally, retiring legislators appear to be somewhat less responsive to constituents' interests.

CONGRESS AND THE PRESIDENT

The relationship between Congress and the president is defined by constituencies and political parties. Each member of Congress must keep the interests of his or her district in mind when taking positions on legislation. The president's constituency, by contrast, encompasses the entire nation. The political and legislative priorities of the president are thus likely to be different from those of individual members of Congress, even those members within the president's own party.

Political parties also shape the relationship between the president and the Congress. If the president is affiliated with the majority party in Congress, in particular both of its chambers, the agendas of the president and congressional leadership are more likely to be similar, and opportunities for crafting and passing legislation are greater. If the president is affiliated with the minority party in Congress—a situation known as divided government—these opportunities may be fewer. However, the president may choose to bypass the legislative process in Congress through the use of direct action such as executive orders, which bear the force of law but are not approved by the Congress, or through the threatened or actual use of the presidential veto.

SEE ALSO *Checks and Balances; Consensus; Constitution, U.S.; Democracy, Representative and Participatory; Democratic Party, U.S.; Elections; Negotiation; Presidency, The; Republican Party; Roll Calls; Separation of Powers; U.S. Civil War; Voting Patterns*

BIBLIOGRAPHY

Fenno, Richard F., Jr. 1973. *Congressmen in Committees.* Boston: Little Brown.

Mayhew, David. 1974. *Congress: The Electoral Connection.* New Haven, CT: Yale University Press.

John D. Griffin
Anne Baker
Patrick Flavin
Michael Keane

CONGRESS OF RACIAL EQUALITY

The Congress of Racial Equality, or CORE, played a leading role in the civil rights movement of the 1960s. CORE is best known for organizing freedom rides to challenge segregation in interstate busing.

CORE was founded in Chicago in 1942 as "a permanent interracial group committed to the use of nonviolent direct action opposing discrimination" (Meier and Rudwick 1973, p. 8). The key components of CORE's ideology—interracialism and nonviolent direct action—stemmed from the teachings of Mahatma Gandhi (1869–1948). The charter members of CORE included both blacks and whites, many of whom were students at the University of Chicago. Several of CORE's founders had been jailed or interned as conscientious objectors to war.

CORE affiliates soon formed in cities across the country. The local affiliates organized sit-downs, or sit-ins as they later became known, to challenge racially segregated public accommodations. They also mounted campaigns to end discrimination in employment, housing, and schools.

In 1947 the national organization organized the Journey of Reconciliation, a two-week bus trip through the upper South to enforce a recent U.S. Supreme Court decision outlawing segregated seating on interstate buses and trains. The participants, who included eight black and eight white men, were arrested and jailed along the way, but most of the charges were later dropped. Although segregation in interstate travel persisted, CORE believed the publicity garnered by the journey made it a success. The Journey of Reconciliation provided the model for the freedom rides of the 1960s.

The student sit-in at a Greensboro, North Carolina, lunch counter in early 1960 gave new life to CORE's campaign to end segregation in public accommodations. Along with the National Association for the Advancement of Colored People (NAACP) and the Southern Christian Leadership Conference (SCLC), CORE helped to organize the sit-ins that spread throughout the South after Greensboro and resulted in the arrests of thousands of protesters. These organizations joined forces again in 1963 to launch a voter registration drive in the South.

James Farmer (1920–1999), who had been a founding member of CORE, was appointed national director in 1961. Farmer's leadership propelled the organization to the forefront of the civil rights movement. His first project was the Freedom Ride of 1961. The 1961 ride differed from the Journey of Reconciliation in a few respects—the riders included women, they traveled through the deep South, and they challenged segregated terminal facilities as well as seating. The severe violence encountered by the riders, including beatings and the firebombing of a bus, drew national attention to the cause. Other freedom rides followed.

The efforts of those involved in the civil rights movement came to fruition with the passage of the Civil Rights Act of 1964, banning racial discrimination in public accommodations, and the Voting Rights Act of 1965, enforcing the right to vote.

In the mid-1960s CORE's focus began to shift from direct action and voter registration to community organization and black identity. At the same time, the group's membership changed as well, from a balance between white and black members to a predominantly black makeup. At its 1966 national convention, CORE adopted "Black Power" as its slogan and renounced absolute nonviolence, and Floyd McKissick (1922–1991) was selected to succeed Farmer as national director. McKissick resigned in 1968 and was replaced by Roy Innis, who maintained the organization's emphasis on political and economic empowerment for blacks. At the end of the twentieth century, CORE had approximately 100,000 members.

SEE ALSO *Civil Rights; Civil Rights Movement, U.S.*

BIBLIOGRAPHY

Arsenault, Raymond. 2006. *Freedom Riders: 1961 and the Struggle for Racial Justice.* New York: Oxford University Press.

Meier, August, and Elliott Rudwick. 1973. *CORE: A Study in the Civil Rights Movement, 1942–1968.* New York: Oxford University Press.

Malia Reddick

CONGRESS PARTY, INDIA

The Indian National Congress (INC) has, since the beginning of modern electoral politics in India in the 1920s, been India's dominant political party. Its leader, Jawaharlal Nehru, became the country's first prime minister in 1947, the party's leaders framed the country's 1950 Constitution, and until 1989, except for a brief interlude from 1977 to 1979, the party always had a solid majority in the Indian parliament. Since 1989 the INC's position has weakened, with the emergence of a host of regional and caste-based parties that now account for around 40 percent of the seats in the Indian parliament, but the party has nonetheless retained its position as one of the two national parties capable of forming a coalition in New Delhi. Whether the INC or the Bharatiya Janata Party (BJP) wins power today is in large part a function of who makes the better preelection deals with these regional parties. In the 2004 elections, the INC played this game much better than the BJP: It won only 145 out of 543 seats outright, but its preelection deals gave the INC coalition as a whole 219 seats, unexpectedly enabling the INC to form the national government with the additional support of the Communists and a few smaller parties (Wilkinson 2005).

Unlike many of its rivals, the INC has always been a party of national breadth that has tried to incorporate members of all India's major religious, linguistic, regional, and caste groups. In contrast to the opposition BJP, the INC has supported a secular state in which minority rights are fully safeguarded, though at times—such as in their complicity in the anti-Sikh riots in Delhi after Indira Gandhi's assassination by her Sikh bodyguards in 1984—some members of the party have conspicuously failed to live up to the party's declared principles.

The INC was founded in 1885. In its first few decades it represented a relatively loose association of India's middle and upper middle classes, dedicated to improving Indians' political rights and employment opportunities within the context of British rule. In the 1920s and 1930s, however, under younger and more radical leadership, it was transformed into a mass party advocating for autonomy and then independence from Britain. Crucial to widening the party's appeal to the masses was the moral leadership of Mohandas K. Gandhi (1869–1948), who from his first noncooperation *satyagraha* in 1920 pioneered tactics of massive nonviolent resistance to colonial rule, tactics that would later be influential in civil rights movements in the United States and elsewhere. In the early 1920s, under Gandhi's influence, the INC forged a wide and deep party organization throughout the country. From 1923, when the INC first decided to compete in the new provincial legislatures set up by the British in 1919, until the late 1930s, the INC used this organization as well as mass campaigns of civil disobedience to establish itself as the country's dominant political party.

At its height, from the 1930s until the late 1960s, the INC was a strong, internally democratic party that used regular local, district, and national party elections to decide which leaders would receive "party tickets" for seats in the state and national assemblies. This *Congress system*—a term coined by Rajni Kothari (1963)—provided existing party leaders with an incentive to reach out to newly mobilized groups of voters from middle and lower castes in order to win party elections, and also gave leaders who won these party, state, and national elections

broad political support and legitimacy. This internal party democracy has been seen as a major factor in India's democratic success compared to Pakistan, where the Muslim League was highly centralized, and had no equivalent of the INC's local party organization, giving it a narrow leadership base that relied on state decrees (Weiner 1990). Unlike the Muslim League, which largely collapsed in Pakistan after the death of its two main leaders (Jinnah in 1948 and Liaquat Ali Khan in 1950), the INC had a solid cadre of democratically elected senior leaders that allowed it to overcome the untimely deaths of Mohandas K. Gandhi in 1948 and Home Minister Sardar Vallabhai Patel in 1950.

The INC's open membership was not always an unmixed blessing, however. The party's membership shot up from half a million to four and a half million in the two short years after the party's unexpected victory in five major provinces in the 1936 provincial elections, and Nehru complained to Gandhi in 1938 that many of these new members were more interested in the INC's patronage power than in the ideals of the party (Brown 2003, p. 131). Corruption and the abuse of patronage power at all levels of the party remain an issue for the INC, and have periodically helped increase support for various opposition parties, such as Swatantra in the 1960s and the BJP in the 1980s.

Several years after Nehru's death in 1964, a power struggle broke out in the party between his daughter, Indira Gandhi (prime minister 1967–1984, except for 1977–1979), and a "Syndicate" of INC party barons in the states. This struggle split the party in 1969, after which Mrs. Gandhi used her position as prime minister and her control of state resources to outflank her political opponents within and outside the party—for instance, through development programs that channeled money to her own supporters in the states and away from her opponents, and election finance reforms that effectively denied funding to the opposition Swatantra. In the 1971 national elections, Mrs. Gandhi campaigned as the victorious war leader who had just defeated Pakistan, and also on a platform of abolishing poverty. Her faction of the INC won more than two-thirds of the seats and over the next three years used its majority to push through large-scale nationalization of the financial sector, as well as large-scale nationally funded antipoverty and development programs. Both these programs served a dual purpose: fulfilling the party's ideological goals and providing large-scale patronage resources for INC leaders.

Under Mrs. Gandhi, however, the INC became more and more centralized—the visible symbol of which was the thousands of INC party hopefuls who traveled to New Delhi before national or state assembly elections to secure her family's nomination. In 1975 Mrs. Gandhi declared a national emergency to end growing opposition to her centralizing rule. Much of this opposition, ironically, was from INC members using the same nonviolent tactics they had used in earlier decades against the British. The emergency was deeply damaging to the party's reputation among lower castes and minorities, many of whom suffered disproportionately from slum clearances and sterilization projects directed by Mrs. Gandhi's son Sanjay. The emergency ended in 1977, when Mrs. Gandhi called national elections and then lost power to a hastily put together Janata coalition, which governed for two years before the INC won power back in 1980. The INC's crushing 1977 loss did not, however, lead to a fundamental reorganization and democratization of the party. No internal INC party elections have been held since the late 1960s, and the party has since the 1970s been run largely by members of the Nehru-Gandhi family and their allies: by Indira Gandhi (until her assassination in 1984), by her son Rajiv Gandhi (until his assassination in 1991), and then by Rajiv's Italian-born widow Sonia and her children Rahul and Priyanka.

Since the late 1980s the INC has been committed to reform of the "Permit Raj" regulation of much of industry and the economy instituted by the party under Nehru and Mrs. Gandhi. A balance of payments crisis in 1991 forced Prime Minister P. V. Narasimha Rao's INC coalition government to accelerate reforms, which have been largely continued and extended by subsequent BJP and INC governments. But because fundamental reforms would require large cuts in subsidies and a substantial scaling back of political patronage, both of which would threaten the INC's own "vote banks," the movement to reform is stop-start. In its attempts at reform, the INC government of Manmohan Singh (Rao's reforming finance minister in the early 1990s) has had to strike a balance between support from industrialists and opposition from many of its own voters and its coalition partners on the Left.

SEE ALSO *Ambedkar, B. R.; Caste; Coalition; Democracy; Gandhi, Indira; Gandhi, Mohandas K.; Indian National Army; Indian National Congress; Jinnah, Mohammed Ali; Minorities; Nehru, Jawaharlal; Parliaments and Parliamentary Systems; Politics*

BIBLIOGRAPHY

Brown, Judith M. 1984. *Modern India: The Origins of an Asian Democracy.* Oxford: Oxford University Press.

Brown, Judith M. 2003. *Nehru: A Political Life.* New Delhi: Oxford University Press.

Kothari, Rajni. 1964. The Congress "System" in India. *Asian Survey* 4 (12): 1161–1173.

Weiner, Myron. 1990. *The Indian Paradox: Essays in Indian Politics.* New Delhi: Sage Publications.

Wilkinson, Steven I. 2005. Elections in India: Behind the Congress Comeback. *Journal of Democracy* 16 (1): 153–167.

Steven I. Wilkinson

CONJUNCTURES, TRANSITIONAL

In Marxian theory, the term *transitional conjunctures* refers to a bounded geographical space over a discrete temporal interval within which a revolutionary transformation in class processes occurs. There is general agreement about five class processes based on the particular arrangement by which workers are organized to perform surplus labor: slave, feudal, capitalist, ancient (petty commodity production or self-employment), and communist. A capitalist society is one in which the capitalist class process prevails. A transitional conjuncture occurs when there is a switch of prevalence from one class process to another within a social formation. The holy grail of Marxian economic history has been the dynamics by which transitional conjunctures occurred in the period roughly from the fifteenth to the seventeenth centuries within the geographic space known as western Europe, resulting in a switch from the prevalence of feudal class processes to the prevalence of capitalist class processes.

One of the most influential hypotheses was that the transition from feudalism to capitalism was triggered by the rise of commodity production. Some Marxian theorists, such as Paul Sweezy (1976), assumed that monetized trade led inevitably to the dissolution of feudal relations of production and the rise of capitalist labor power markets. Maurice Dobb (1964) countered this argument by pointing out that serfs producing goods for a monetized market could still be bound in a feudal relationship. The lords could simply extract surplus value in money form, rather than in kind or in direct labor services. Dobb argued that the dissolution of feudal relations was, instead, the result of an economic and demographic crisis triggered by feudal appropriators extracting too large a surplus from the direct producers. The lords took so much surplus value that the serfs were unable to meet the subsistence needs of their families. These conditions resulted in a decline in population and a critical shortage of labor. According to Dobb, it was these conditions that triggered transitional conjunctures in most, if not all, European social formations.

Historian Perry Anderson argued that money exchange and commodity production did not signal a transition to capitalism, but were often precursors to more centralized versions of feudalism, under absolutist states. Another historian, Robert Brenner, analyzed the classic transitional conjuncture in England and argued that the lords implemented this transition as a profit-maximizing choice, not out of crisis. Based on historical evidence, Brenner reached an essentially postmodernist conclusion that transitional conjunctures varied among the societies of western Europe. Immanuel Wallerstein (1979), on the other hand, rejected the notion of multiple transitional conjunctures in favor of a singular world transition wherein hegemonic capitalism rose to incorporate all modes of production. Stephen Resnick and Richard Wolff (1979), returning to a Marxian class analytical framework grounded in the microeconomics of surplus labor performance and appropriation, argued that transitional conjunctures were not the result of a narrow subset of social factors, whether economic or political, but were, instead, the consequence of the entire matrix of social and environmental factors present in a social formation prior to the transition. For Resnick and Wolff, transitional conjunctures were the overdetermined result of the displacement of multiple conditions for the prevalence of one class process by multiple conditions in favor of the prevalence of an alternative class process.

SEE ALSO *Feudal Mode of Production; Feudalism*

BIBLIOGRAPHY

Anderson, Perry. 1977. *Passages from Antiquity to Feudalism.* London: NLB.

Anderson, Perry. 1979. *Lineages of the Absolutist State.* London: Verso.

Brenner, Robert. 1978. Dobb on the Transition from Feudalism to Capitalism. *Cambridge Journal of Economics* 1978 (2): 121–140.

Dobb, Maurice. 1964. *Studies in the Development of Capitalism.* Rev. ed. New York: International Publishers.

Resnick, Stephen, and Richard Wolff. 1979. The Theory of Transitional Conjunctures and the Transition from Feudalism to Capitalism. *Review of Radical Political Economy* 11: 3–22.

Sweezy, Paul, et al. 1976. *The Transition from Feudalism to Capitalism.* London: Verso.

Wallerstein, Immanuel. 1979. *The Capitalist World Economy: Essays.* New York: Cambridge University Press.

Satyananda J. Gabriel

CONNERLY, WARD

SEE *Race-Blind Policies.*

CONSCIENTIOUS OBJECTORS

SEE *Pacifism.*

CONSCIENTIOUS REFUSAL

SEE *Civil Disobedience.*

CONSCIOUSNESS

Consciousness is a multifaceted phenomenon, and many terms are used to describe its facets. *Consciousness, conscious, aware of, experience* (noun), and *experience* (verb)—all these words have different meanings in different contexts and for different people, so generalizations about their meaning will necessarily have limited validity. Considerable discrepancies also exist between the conceptual tools available in different languages for classifying consciousness and related phenomena. So, for example, the French *conscience* encompasses both "consciousness" and "conscience," as the latter words are used in English; in German the subtle difference between the meanings of the English words "consciousness" and "awareness" is lost when both these words have to be translated as *Bewusstsein*.

BASIC DEFINITIONS AND PHILOSOPHICAL ISSUES

Because of these linguistic and conceptual problems, every systematic treatment of consciousness has to start with a set of distinctions and definitions for the purpose at hand. The task of formulating these in a way that makes them useful for people with different mother tongues is far from simple. However, aspects of consciousness and related phenomena can be classified in three basic categories: cognitive consciousness, phenomenal consciousness, and control consciousness. All are the subject of ongoing philosophical debates.

Cognitive Consciousness Also referred to as *intentionality, consciousness-of, awareness-of,* and *transitive consciousness,* cognitive consciousness entails a mental relation to an object (not necessarily an existing one), and encompasses phenomena such as *thinking of* a dragon, *becoming aware of* the presence of another person, *attending to* a problem and *knowing* facts about a certain field. In English, *awareness* is often a more natural choice than *consciousness* when the cognitive aspect of consciousness is intended. However, the term "consciousness" is not seldom used in an exclusively cognitive sense—for example, the sociological and political terms *class consciousness, gender consciousness,* and *environmental consciousness.* Here consciousness stands for habitual attention to, and knowledge about, the issues in question.

The common denominator of all cognitive consciousness is its directedness toward an object, which may be concrete or abstract. It is an important conceptual fact that a person can properly be said to be cognitively conscious although she is in another sense (phenomenal consciousness, as discussed below) not conscious at all. For example, an environmentally conscious person is still environmentally conscious when sleeping dreamlessly. Similarly, since a person in dreamless sleep *knows* her mathematics, she is cognitively aware of mathematical facts while sleeping. On the other hand, there are forms of cognitive consciousness that cannot plausibly be ascribed to a dreamlessly sleeping subject, for example, *thinking of* or *presently attending to* the facts that she knows.

In this context it should also be mentioned that *self-consciousness,* which is not seldom given a fundamental role in conceptual schemes for handling matters of consciousness, can plausibly be argued to be a species of cognitive awareness (namely, of oneself). The same holds for *reflexive consciousness.*

Phenomenal Consciousness A good alternative term is *experiential consciousness*; *sentient consciousness* is often given a similar sense but can also have other connotations. A dreamless sleeper does not have any present experiences (or we may suppose so for the sake of this discussion), and is therefore not conscious in the phenomenal sense. An awake person, on the contrary, usually has sensory and perceptual experiences, feels emotions, and entertains mental imagery; all these belong to her phenomenal consciousness.

Two long-standing controversies in philosophy of mind primarily concern phenomenal consciousness: the *mind-body problem* and the *problem of other minds.* What is the relation between the brain and phenomenal consciousness? The philosopher David Chalmers (1996) has called this "the hard problem of consciousness." The problem of other minds is, can we ever know what another person's, or another animal's, experiences are like?

The relations between cognitive awareness and phenomenal consciousness have been the topic of many philosophical debates. One classic debate concerns whether cognition is necessarily rooted in phenomenal consciousness, or whether one could give an explanation of it in purely nonphenomenal (for example, physical) terms. Philosophers in the so-called phenomenological school argue for the first position, whereas most present-day analytical philosophers and cognitive scientists, not only those of a strictly materialist bent, defend the second.

Today this discussion is usually presented as an issue about the nature of mental representations. Another important controversy concerns whether phenomenal consciousness depends on cognition: Is a pain or a thought phenomenally conscious only by virtue of one's being conscious *of* it, or is phenomenal consciousness rather an intrinsic quality of experiences that can be possessed independently of any reflexive consciousness?

Control Consciousness The meaning of this term, for which there are no common synonyms, partly overlaps with that of what Ned Block (1994) calls *access consciousness.* In our commonsense understanding of ourselves and other people, as well as in many psychological, psychiatric, and neuroscientific theories, consciousness is given a role for initiating and/or controlling behavior. We talk about doing things with or without *conscious intention.* Psychologists and neurophysiologists speak about *automatic* versus *consciously controlled* behavior. A good example of the latter distinction is given by our ordinary, unconscious control of bodily posture versus conscious attempts not to fall when the automatic control fails for some internal or external reason. In some psychiatric theories, consciousness is even given the role of the superordinate controlling instance of mental life, and all mental disturbances are seen as results of more or less deepseated *disturbances of consciousness.*

A philosophically controversial issue here is: How can consciousness have a causal role to play in behavior, if all our behavior stems from processes in the brain (as neuroscience seems to say)? This problem is sometimes taken as a motive for a materialistically reductive analysis of control consciousness. Control consciousness is then explained in terms of physical or biological regulatory processes. However, such an approach also has to explain the fact that many paradigm cases of conscious control (e.g., consciously regaining posture) also have a phenomenal aspect.

HISTORICAL CONCEPTIONS OF CONSCIOUSNESS

The French philosopher and mathematician René Descartes (1596–1650) formulated a philosophical conception of consciousness in which the concept was differentiated from conscience, with which it was previously conflated. Descartes's dualism is well known, and already in the seventeenth century it posed an embarrassing philosophical issue, the body-mind problem. He regarded body and mind as two separate but interacting substances, body (or matter) being essentially characterized by spatial extension whereas mind is characterized by thinking. For Descartes the presence of conscious states was a mark of human beings, in contrast with animals, which he thought were mechanical automata.

Although a clear emphasis on cognitive consciousness can be discerned in Descartes's writings, the cognitive, phenomenal, and control dimensions of consciousness cannot really be disentangled in them. In seventeenth- and eighteenth-century British empiricist philosophy, phenomenally conscious processes and our consciousness of them are the main concerns. However, the problems of cognitive consciousness are still of central concern. For the British empiricists, *ideas* are experiential states that are accessible by means of introspection, but they are also themselves essentially *about* things.

John Locke (1632–1704) formulated the distinction between an outer sense—our experiential access to material objects—and an inner sense, reflecting on one's own experiences. His theory of inner sense can be regarded as the first systematic treatise of introspection. By consciousness Locke meant all ideas that passed in a man's own mind and his self-consciousness about them. Consciousness, not bodily continuity, was regarded as constitutive of personal identity.

The famous principle of *association of ideas* can be traced to Aristotle, but it was the British empiricists who made it the foundation of a whole new science. Locke's formulation of the principle became of utmost importance for the development of psychological ideas in later centuries. Our understanding of the world and of ourselves was seen as built up from associations between ideas that are similar or contrasting, or that just happen to be contiguous in our experience. Later schools of associationist philosophy and psychology (as exhibited in the work of David Hartley, David Hume, James Mill, John Stuart Mill, and Alexander Bain) took it for granted that conscious experience is built up from elements and processes that are discernible to the self-conscious mind. Simple ideas are copies of sensations, and complex ideas are construed from simple ideas according to the laws of association. Mental elements and the principles according to which conscious thoughts—or ideas—are built up and interact can be investigated by introspection.

In the late eighteenth century the German philosopher Immanuel Kant (1724–1804) questioned the program of the British associationist philosopher-psychologists. According to Kant, a science in the strict sense requires both mathematical measurement and experimental procedures. None of this is possible in the case of consciousness, as thoughts do not exist in a spatial continuum and as man cannot divide himself into one observing subject and one observed object.

THE BIRTH OF EXPERIMENTAL PSYCHOLOGY

Trying to overcome the obstacles put up by Kant, German philosophers in the nineteenth century formulated several programs for a science of psychology defined as the study of conscious processes. Based on the psychophysical methods the physicist Gustav Theodor Fechner (1801–1887) had devised in 1860, the German physiologist and philosopher Wilhelm Wundt (1832–1920) institutionalized the new science in Leipzig in 1879 as an experimental laboratory discipline. Wundt and his students defined psychology as the study of immediate experience. They held that it was a proper scientific discipline and that mental processes can be measured provided that one uses controlled experimental methods. Simple introspection was therefore replaced by experimental self-observation, a method that required a painstaking training before the subject could correctly describe the phenomena in his consciousness.

In his *Principles of Psychology* (1890), the American physician and philosopher William James (1842–1910) described psychology as "the science of mental life." He tried to give a holistic description of consciousness, stressing consciousness as personal, intentional, selective, shifting, and continuous. James's discussion of consciousness as "a stream of thought" is very similar to the understanding of consciousness in the theories of Franz Brentano, Carl Stumpf, and Edmund von Husserl. During the late nineteenth and early twentieth centuries, the latter philosophers developed what Husserl (1859–1938) in his 1900–1901 work named *phenomenology*. Phenomenology is a philosophy that emphasizes the intentionality of consciousness and the importance of investigating the detailed intentional structure of consciousness. This should be done by means of a certain method, which, although systematically related to introspection, is not identical to it.

In opposition to the British associationists, the phenomenologists stressed the fact that conscious ideas need not be similar to that which they are ideas of. In other words, it is not essential to ideas that they are *images* of their objects. At the beginning of the twentieth century, the psychologists of the so-called Würzburg school (Narziss Ach, Karl Bühler, Oswald Külpe, and others) took an interest in deeper descriptions of phenomena of consciousness. They found in the experimental subjects' introspective reports instances of "imageless" conscious phenomena (*Bewusstseinslagen*) that in their opinion questioned the traditional associationist psychology.

BIOLOGICAL, FUNCTIONALISTIC, AND BEHAVIORIST PERSPECTIVES

During the late nineteenth century there was widespread interest in the possibility of *unconscious* mental phenomena. Sigmund Freud (1856–1939) famously formulated a systematic theory, or rather several theories, about the unconscious mind. Such an enterprise requires a theory of consciousness. In a crucial paper written in 1915, Freud distinguishes between a "systematic" and a "descriptive" sense of "consciousness." The systematic sense is close to what is here called control consciousness. The descriptive sense has essentially to do with knowability, but Freud also speculates that a descriptively conscious mental state is conscious by virtue of its possessing a certain intrinsic quality. In Freud's later thinking, control consciousness is instead described in terms of the mental systems named *ego* and *super-ego*.

Within the American school of functionalism that William James was part of, the aim of studying consciousness was regarded with suspicion. In 1904 James even stated that consciousness did not exist, but he meant that it did not exist as an entity, only as a function. With the behaviorists of the early twentieth century, however, the interest radically shifted from consciousness (now often regarded as a metaphysical concept) to behavior. Humans should be understood through their actions and not their thoughts. The idea of finding the basic laws of mental elements using introspective methods was abandoned. The alternative, nonassociationist approaches, such as phenomenology and Gestalt psychology, were also relegated to a minor role in the psychological community. The behaviorists took diverse philosophical positions: Some took the strong metaphysical position that consciousness does not exist, whereas others only defended a moderate methodological statement to the effect that introspective methods should be abandoned as unscientific in favor of behavioral observation.

Behaviorism was to dominate the behavioral and social sciences from about 1920 to 1960. During this time the Gestalt psychologists, who thought in ways related to both phenomenology and the Würzburg school, kept up a keen interest in the study of perception and other forms of experience and did much valuable research on the structure of consciousness. In many respects the thrust of their work was biological, and they were much opposed to explanations of experience by means of *mental* laws. In Gestalt theory, immediate experience is a direct result of brain processes and cannot be explained by any association of mental elements.

Consciousness research continued throughout the behaviorist era in the fields of psychiatry and neurology. Karl Jaspers (1883–1969), a psychiatrist and philosopher in the phenomenological tradition, in 1913 created a clas-

sification scheme for pathological disturbances of consciousness that is still in use. During the whole of the twentieth century, the understanding of consciousness and its pathology was generally regarded as essential for the psychiatric understanding of patients. Around mid-century, the French psychiatrist Henri Ey (1900–1977)—who was also influenced by phenomenological thinking—formulated a new theory about consciousness, stressing its functional and controlling aspects. In most present-day psychiatric theories, however, consciousness is not given such a central explanatory role.

The Cognitive Revolution In the 1960s an important methodological and theoretical shift in the behavioral and social sciences occurred that is often referred to as the cognitive revolution. It was partly inspired by the possibilities offered by computer modeling of rational processes, and it is no coincidence that the main focus of cognitive psychology is memory and thinking. Consciousness was no longer a forbidden territory. Since the 1960s, cognitive psychologists have also shown a renewed interest in unconscious mental processes such as implicit memory, subliminal perception, and other forms of perception without phenomenal perceptual consciousness (e.g., blindsight).

Although consciousness and several different kinds of introspective procedures have once again been admitted into psychology, the terms introspection and consciousness are not used as frequently by psychologists as they were in the early twentieth century. This may not be of any importance in itself, but it reflects the more serious circumstance that there is a fundamental break of tradition between the old psychology and the new. This break also means that several philosophical and methodological issues, which were common knowledge in the psychological community in the early 1900s, seem to be little known by many behavioral and social scientists of the twenty-first century.

However, there are signs that this situation is changing. Since the 1990s a large amount of interdisciplinary work on consciousness has been accomplished, partly under the auspices of independent organizations such as ASSC (Association for the Scientific Study of Consciousness), but also within the academic programs of many universities around the world. Neuroscientists and philosophers, as well as behavioral and social scientists, participate in this effort. The body-mind problem occupies one focus under the name of a search for "the neural correlate of consciousness." The role of consciousness in perceptual and motor processes is another much researched and hotly debated topic. Finally, "mentalizing" (ascribing mental states to other people) is a third area of central concern for today's interdisciplinary study of consciousness.

SEE ALSO *Anthropology, Linguistic; Aristotle; Cognition; Epistemology; Freud, Sigmund; Gestalt Psychology; James, William; Kant, Immanuel; Knowledge; Locke, John; Mill, James; Mill, John Stuart; Phenomenology; Philosophy; Psycholinguistics; Psychology; Self-Consciousness, Private vs. Public; Theory of Mind*

BIBLIOGRAPHY

Block, Ned. 1994. Consciousness. In *A Companion to the Philosophy of Mind*, ed. Samual Guttenplan, 210–219. Oxford: Blackwell.

Chalmers, David J. 1996. *The Conscious Mind: In Search of a Fundamental Theory.* New York: Oxford University Press.

Ey, Henri. 1968. *La Conscience.* 2nd ed. Paris: Desclée De Brouwer.

Hassin, Ran R., James S. Uleman, and John A. Bargh, eds. 2005. *The New Unconscious.* Oxford: Oxford University Press.

Hilgard, Ernest R. 1980. Consciousness in Contemporary Psychology. *Annual Review of Psychology* 31: 1–26.

Hommel, Bernhard. 2007. Consciousness and Control: Not Identical Twins. *Journal of Consciousness Studies* 14 (1–2): 155–176.

Husserl, Edmund von. 1921. *Logische Untersuchungen.* Vols. 1 and 2. 2nd ed. Tübingen, Germany: Niemeyer.

James, William. 1890. *The Principles of Psychology.* Vols. 1 and 2. New York: Dover Publications, 1950.

Jaspers, Karl. 1913. *Allgemeine Psychopathologie.* Berlin: Springer.

Velman, Max, and Susan Schneider, eds. 2007. *The Blackwell Companion to Consciousness.* Malden, MA, and Oxford: Blackwell.

Helge Malmgren
Ingemar Nilsson

CONSCRIPTION, MILITARY

SEE *Napoléon Bonaparte; Selective Service.*

CONSENSUS

Consensus refers both to a state of common feeling or agreement in a group and to a decision rule by which a group or society determines legitimate political authority and coordinates political action. The term derives from the Latin *consens*, which is closely related to *consent*, and was first used in modern times to describe the relationship between different parts of a system in working toward the purpose of the whole. Characteristic of many nineteenth-century writers, Émile Durkheim posits the analogy of a "spontaneous consensus of parts" in the body social as a necessary condition for the preservation of order in increasingly differentiated societies (1984, p. 297). Contemporary theories of communitarianism, civic culture, and liberal pluralism follow Durkheim, to different degrees, in staking democratic order on a value consensus embedded in social norms, practices, and institutions.

Theorists of participatory and deliberative democracy often abandon the search for an empirical consensus underlying social order and instead hold consensus as a normative ideal of political decision making amid human conditions of difference and conflict. For Jean-Jacques Rousseau, legitimate political authority rests not on the consent of the majority—the domination of a part of society over the whole—but on a consensus that accounts for the interests of all members of society. Consensus thus seeks to preserve individual freedom and political equality. Indebted to Immanuel Kant's (1724–1804) theory of common sense, Jürgen Habermas (1990) locates the ideal of consensus in the fundamental practice of communication, which presupposes the possibility of shared understanding between speakers. The expectation of rational consensus inherent in speech establishes certain norms for political deliberation, most notably reason, inclusion, participation, and publicity. On many accounts, consensual politics requires both constitutionally protected public spaces and institutionalized procedures that incorporate the previous norms into decision-making processes.

Critics of consensualism worry that the ideal of consensus carries normalizing and repressive effects on groups and societies. Theorists of agonistic democracy, such as Iris Marion Young (2000) and William E. Connolly (1991), contend that commitment to a strong rational consensus privileges certain modes of expression and participation to the exclusion of others and often brackets difficult issues from public discussion altogether. Thus, consensual ideals of political engagement and outcome effectively silence some points of view. While agonistic democracy affirms the possibility of agreement on particular issues in particular circumstances, it recognizes the contingencies and exclusions that constitute any strong value consensus and emphasizes a care for difference and struggle as central elements of politics.

In practice, consensual politics have long embodied the ideals and tensions of these competing theoretical strains. While consensus was the aim, if not always the abiding practice, in the political assemblies of ancient Athens, classical writers from Thucydides (c. 460–c. 400 BCE) to Aristotle cautioned against the dangers of popular rhetoric in fomenting collective tyranny. The Iroquois

Confederacy explicitly protected dissenting views during consensual processes by establishing mechanisms for veto power and for the revisiting of contentious issues. The Religious Society of Friends and the peace and environmental movements of the late twentieth century are examples of groups that use consensus decision-making practices.

SEE ALSO *Conflict; Egalitarianism*

BIBLIOGRAPHY

Connolly, William E. 1991. *Identity/Difference: Democratic Negotiations of Political Paradox.* Ithaca, NY: Cornell University Press.

Durkheim, Émile. 1984. *Division of Labor in Society.* Translated by W. D. Halls. New York: The Free Press.

Habermas, Jürgen. 1990. *Moral Consciousness and Communicative Action.* Trans. Christian Lenhardt and Shierry Weber Nicholsen. Cambridge, MA: MIT Press.

Johanson, Bruce Elliott, and Barbara Alice Mann, eds. 2000. *Encyclopedia of the Haudenosaunee (Iroquois Confederacy).* Westport, CT: Greenwood Press.

Mansbridge, Jane J. 1980. *Beyond Adversary Democracy.* New York: Basic Books.

Ober, Josiah. 1998. *Political Dissent in Democratic Athens: Intellectual Critics of Popular Rule.* Princeton, NJ: Princeton University Press.

Pellow, David N. 1999. Framing Emerging Environmental Movement Tactics: Mobilizing Consensus, Demobilizing Conflict. *Sociological Forum* 14 (4): 659–683.

Rousseau, Jean-Jacques. 1987. *The Basic Political Writings.* Trans. and ed. by Donald A. Cress. Indianapolis, IN: Hackett Publishing.

Young, Iris Marion. 2000. *Inclusion and Democracy.* New York: Oxford University Press.

Laura Grattan

CONSERVATISM

The term *conservative* is derived from the word *conserve,* and in a political sense is often used to indicate a desire to preserve existing political and social arrangements, institutions, policies, or customs. This conception of conservative leaves as a critical defining question what it is that one is seeking to conserve.

Both European and American conservatism contain numerous strands, but share some points of commonality. To a significant extent, both developed as a response to revolutions from the Left, the violent revolution of the guillotine in France in the 1790s and the peaceful revolutions of New Deal economics and counterculture social mores in the United States in the 1930s and 1960s. Both

European and American conservatism have been imbued with a strong sense of anti-utopianism and a greater deference for religion, tradition, experience, and property than that found on the Left. On many other scores, however, the two versions of conservatism—or some of their constituent strands—are quite distinct. Those strands are defined by the question of whether they are a subset of liberal democratic politics or a reaction against it.

EUROPEAN CONSERVATISM

Representing one pole of European conservatism was Edmund Burke (1729–1797), the English parliamentarian who wrote *Reflections on the Revolution in France* in 1790. *Reflections* embodied not so much an ideology as an anti-ideology, a marked preference for experience, tradition, decentralization, and prudence over the abstract theorizing that drove the French Revolution and that, Burke predicted, would lead to a new and unconstrained form of despotism. Burke favored evolutionary, rather than revolutionary, change, though he supported the moderate American Revolution. He also favored a trustee model of representation consistent with his fear of mass democracy unchecked by moderating institutions. In essence, Burke advocated the conservation of liberal society though caution and prudence. Directly descended from Burke, nineteenth-century British conservatives like Benjamin Disraeli (1804–1881) called for "Tory democracy," reforms aimed at giving the lower classes a greater stake in the preservation of traditional English liberty. This conservatism retained, to some extent, an aristocratic and paternalistic cast.

The other pole of European conservatism was starkly reactionary, calling for a restoration of absolute monarchy and Catholic faith summed up in the slogan "throne and altar." Chief among these clerical monarchists were Count Joseph de Maistre (1753–1821) and Louis de Bonald (1754–1840). Where Burke extolled ordered liberty, Maistre and Bonald were content with order. In his *Essay on the Generative Principle of Political Constitutions* (1810), Maistre argued against rationalism in politics. He held with Burke that attempting to remake society on the basis of abstract conceptions through such devices as a declaration of rights or a written constitution was foolhardy (and often destructive). Human society was too complex to manipulate in that way. However, to Maistre, absolutism, tempered by religion—the combination of "Pope and executioner"—was the solution for social instability.

In nineteenth-century Germany, the antirationalist and clerical romantic school—heavily influenced by Maistre, but both political and literary in character—developed among thinkers like Adam Muller, K.L. von Haller, Joseph von Radowitz, and Karl von Vogelsang, idealizing the German Middle Ages. At the same time,

Joseph von Gorres, a former supporter of the French Revolution, swung around to embrace Maistre's theocratic vision. His Gorres circle of thinkers was important in German intellectual life at midcentury, and some argued that it contributed to subsequent German and Austrian authoritarianism.

Also clustered nearer to Maistre's pole than to Burke's, a strand of extreme nationalism appeared in the late nineteenth century, though its ultimate form arguably represented a repudiation of traditionalist conservatism rather than a completion of it. In France, Maurice Barres (1862–1923) and Charles Maurras (1868–1952) advocated nationalism as the sole source of social rootedness and authoritarianism as the means of expressing that nationalism. Maurras, unlike both Barres and traditional conservatives, embraced mass agitation and atheism and ultimately veered into fascism. More directly influencing national socialism, Heinrich von Treitschke (1834–1896), author of *German History in the Nineteenth Century* (1879–1894), advocated a blunt philosophy of racial nationalism, power, and militarism, themes at odds with the mainstay of European conservatism.

Clustered around Burke's pole were a variety of thinkers whose aim was not restoration of the Middle Ages but the ennobling and conservation of European liberty in one form or another. Like Burke, the Frenchman Alexis de Tocqueville (famous for writing *Democracy in America* in the 1830s and *Ancient Regime and the Revolution* twenty years later) was supportive of popular constitutional government and evolutionary change but cautioned against democracy's potential for excess. Indeed, it is an interesting conceptual question whether Tocqueville should be considered a liberal conservative or a conservative liberal. To the French revolutionaries, egalitarianism and liberty went hand in hand. To Tocqueville, the two values could easily conflict, as local liberty and individual difference might be sacrificed to a single-minded pursuit of equality. Tocqueville thus called for countervailing features like freedom of the press, independent courts, local government, a strong civil society, and Christian morality to preserve liberty.

Another school focused on economic liberty. From Adam Smith in the eighteenth century to the Austrian school of Ludwig von Mises and Friedrich Hayek in the twentieth, these thinkers shared an appreciation for private property, decentralization of power, and organic evolutionary change. While far removed from Maistre, they were compatible with Burke and Tocqueville. Hayek assaulted central planning in his 1944 book *The Road to Serfdom*, in which he argued that central planning invited both tyranny and economic inefficiency. Hayek preferred to call himself a liberal, but in the context of the rise of

both democratic and totalitarian socialism, must be (and usually was) counted a conservative.

In between the poles, Clemens von Metternich served as foreign minister of the Habsburg Empire from 1815 to 1848 and was a key figure in the Congress of Vienna, the 1815 diplomatic conference in which the kings of Europe agreed on a framework to keep the peace after the Napoleonic wars. That framework relied on the defense of monarchy and the suppression of radicalism. Although Metternich is widely criticized as a reactionary, he was also cosmopolitan and pacific and advised the Hapsburg emperor to grant more constitutional rights to Hungary and other outposts of the empire. He called his philosophy "conservative socialism": socialism defined as organic social unity in preference to atomistic individualism, a notion that defined much of European conservatism. Metternich's secretary Friedrich Gentz translated Burke's *Reflections* into German, wrote widely himself, and shared Metternich's cosmopolitanism.

In postwar, increasingly secular, Europe, both extreme nationalism and clericism withered; Maurras fell with Vichy France, and the last European outpost of Maistre was arguably Franco's Spain. Rather, the conservatism of the last half of the century was dominated by figures influenced most by the Burkean pole's paternalistic offshoot (the British statesman Winston Churchill [1874–1965], who sought to model himself after Disraeli), by its free-market offshoot (Britain's Margaret Thatcher or Italy's Silvio Berlusconi), or by Metternich's cosmopolitanism (Germany's Konrad Adenauer and Helmut Kohl and other European Christian Democrats).

In the nineteenth and twentieth centuries, a Latin American conservatism arose that largely paralleled its European counterpart. After independence, Maistre dominated, as conservatives promoted close church-state connections and centralized state authority. The twentieth century saw a divide between Maistre's conservatism, reflected in extreme form in the Argentinean junta among others, and a free-market, neoliberal conservatism more comfortable with Burke and Smith. (The Chilean military dictatorship incongruously melded Maistre's politics and Smith's economics.) In contrast to Europe, however, the Burkeans seemingly gained the upper hand only in the last fifth of the century.

AMERICAN CONSERVATISM

Historian Louis Hartz famously argued in 1955 that there were no true conservatives in America, only rival species of liberals. Nevertheless, American thinkers as disparate as the anti-federalists, Alexander Hamilton, John Adams, and John Calhoun have sometimes been labeled "conservative." Modern American conservatism, however, grew out of opposition to the New Deal and the rise of the welfare state. Its first mobilization took the form of the American Liberty League in the 1930s, consisting of an alliance between Republican businessmen and Jeffersonian Democrats. This nascent conservatism drew on a belief that the New Deal threatened constitutional principles by centralizing power, undermined the free enterprise system, and corrupted the civic virtue of Americans. If equality was the first value of the New Deal, the chief aim of these conservatives was the preservation of Lockean liberty. Like Hayek, President Herbert Hoover long argued that he was the real liberal, as he—not Franklin Roosevelt—had remained true to the tenets of limited government and free markets that defined classical liberalism. Senator Robert Taft (R-OH), though sometimes dubbed "Mr. Conservative" by contemporaries, fell in this category as well.

A number of other influential figures came to advance free-market economics and limited government. Among these was Nobel economist Milton Friedman, whose Chicago school advocated "monetarism"—an emphasis on free markets and control of the money supply—as an alternative to liberal Keynesianism. Though not as libertarian as the Austrian school of Hayek and von Mises, Friedman favored limits on government spending, taxing, and regulation, as well as school vouchers and a negative income tax as an alternative to welfare. In the 1970s, a school known as supply-side economics was advanced by economic thinkers like Arthur Laffer, Robert L. Bartley, and Jude Wanniski. The supply-siders emphasized improved incentives for work and investment. While differing on many specifics, the revived schools of free-market economics agreed that political liberty and economic liberty were intertwined.

A second strand of conservatism was skeptical of mass politics and abstractions like natural rights, and was concerned with the decline in importance of religion and traditional social forms and morals. The postwar traditionalists were anticipated in some respects by a school known as Southern Agrarianism (Richard Weaver, John Crowe Ransom, and others), whose unhappiness with industrialism and materialism was laid forth in their 1930 manifesto *I Take My Stand*. Traditionalism's most noteworthy spokesmen in the 1950s were Willmoore Kendall and Russell Kirk, the latter of whom argued his case for "the permanent things" in *The Conservative Mind from Burke to Eliot* (1953). Unlike many of the constitutionalists and the libertarian-leaning economists, these thinkers were not averse to the label "conservative." While these traditionalists may have been the most European strand of American conservatism, none were enamored of authoritarianism. Indeed, their fear was that tyranny would result from the collapse of virtue that they diagnosed. The traditionalists sought refuge for liberty in the Anglo-Saxon tradition of liberty rather than in natural rights, and what they sought to conserve above all was Western civilization.

A third strand of postwar conservatism consisted of a strong anticommunist movement. While Senator Joseph McCarthy (R-WI) is perhaps the best-known, and most notorious, anticommunist conservative of the era, anticommunism was widely shared by millions of Americans who were concerned by the totalitarian character of Leninist ideology, the international threat posed by the Soviet Union, and the penetration of domestic communism into American social and governmental institutions. Key intellectual figures in this movement were the former Trotskyite James Burnham and former communist Whittaker Chambers. Chambers testified against State Department official and Soviet spy Alger Hiss and wrote the widely read book *Witness* (1952) to chronicle his religious and political conversion. Anticommunism was an essential glue, appealing both to the religious scruples of the traditionalists and the limited government views of the economic conservatives.

While not part of the broad public resurgence of conservatism, other rightward intellectual currents of the time were represented by anti-utopian philosophers such as Leo Strauss (1899–1973) and Eric Voegelin (1901–1985). Strauss looked to classical Greek philosophy for guidance to the good life and best society. Voegelin fashioned a philosophy emphasizing experience and both the transcendence and limits of humans.

The conservative movement as a coherent force was forged in the mid-1950s when the three major strands of conservatism coalesced. A key moment in that effort was the founding by William F. Buckley of the conservative journal *National Review* in 1955. *National Review* advanced what became known as fusion, a conception of conservatism that balanced and wove together the three strands.

While the conservative movement was coming together at the intellectual level, it was also gaining at the grassroots level. Arizona Senator Barry Goldwater's 1964 Republican presidential campaign recruited tens of thousands of conservative volunteers into Republican politics and shifted the party to the right. Goldwater was the first major American political figure in the postwar era to embrace the label "conservative." In his 1960 book *Conscience of a Conservative*, Goldwater laid out a "fusionist" doctrine that was economically free-market, politically constitutionalist, vehemently anticommunist, and religiously grounded. It was also populist in the style of the English Whigs, the "country party" that regularly took the "court party" to task for its elitism, corruption, and autocratic tendencies. After Goldwater's landslide defeat against Lyndon Johnson in 1964, many commentators concluded that conservatism as a political force in America was finished.

However, developments in the 1960s and 1970s from stagflation to moral permissiveness to Soviet advances abroad made the conservative critique seem increasingly plausible. At the same time, three new ingredients were added to the stew of American conservatism. One was the growth of black intellectual conservatism represented by thinkers like economists Thomas Sowell and Walter Williams, social commentator Shelby Steele, and future Supreme Court Justice Clarence Thomas. Another was the development of neoconservatism in the form of figures such as Midge Decter, Nathan Glazer, Jeane Kirkpatrick, Irving Kristol, Norman Podhoretz, and Ben Wattenberg. Neoconservatives were typically once-liberal intellectuals who had shifted significantly to the right on the ideological spectrum owing to concerns about Soviet expansionism and cultural issues. While limited in number, the neoconservatives also added considerable intellectual heft to the conservative movement through organs such as *Commentary* and *The Public Interest*.

Finally, a new mass movement of social and religious conservatives arose to complement the traditionalist intellectuals. This movement was distressed by what it perceived as the moral breakdown of American society and the role of government policy in abetting that breakdown. Ultimately known as the "religious right" or the "Christian right," it was catalyzed by the Supreme Court's abortion, school prayer, and obscenity decisions, the fight over ratification of the Equal Rights Amendment, and rules proposed by the Internal Revenue Service during the Carter administration that threatened the tax-exempt status of many Christian schools. Mass organizations like the Moral Majority and, later, the Christian Coalition formed to promote socially conservative policies.

The growing strength of American conservatism helped lead to the 1980 and 1984 presidential victories of former California governor Ronald Reagan, by then the unquestioned standard-bearer of the conservative movement. Reagan, like Goldwater, promoted a populist blend of free market economics, cultural conservatism, and anticommunist nationalism, though without Goldwater's harder edges. Although falling short of many of his goals, Reagan achieved a significant rightward move in public policy and forged a strong Republican electoral coalition that contributed to the Republican takeover of Congress in 1994 and to Republican electoral successes in the early twenty-first century.

Nevertheless, when President Bill Clinton successfully stymied many of their policy departures after 1994, many conservatives searched for a new approach. In his 2000 campaign and subsequent presidency, George W. Bush offered what he called "compassionate conservatism," a reorientation of conservatism that would accommodate big government rather than trying to curtail it, and would institute reforms aimed at making it more accountable and more subject to citizen choice.

CONTRASTS AND TENSIONS

In Europe, a considerable distance separated Burke from Maistre, and a vast gulf divided Burke, Tocqueville, and even Metternich on one hand from the outliers Maurras and von Treitschke on the other. Even within the narrowed range of postwar European conservatism, divisions remained, for example between free-market Thatcherites and their more paternalistic and statist Tory compatriots in Britain. Arguably, not as much distance has divided American conservatives, who largely agreed that what they wanted to conserve was the synthesis between Lockeanism, biblical republicanism, and classical Western civilization that they held to be essential parts of the nation's heritage. Nevertheless, they have differed about what themes to emphasize, and have often differed over specific means. The more libertarian-leaning of the economic conservatives have an uneasy relationship with the social/cultural conservatives. Those traditionalists who eschew natural rights have clashed with other conservatives who defend the natural rights paradigm. Even the monetarists and the supply-siders have engaged in sometimes bitter disputes. When some post-Reagan conservatives argued for a conservatism grounded not in limited government but in promotion of "national greatness" or of a more accountable form of big government, this innovation brought vehement opposition from others. George W. Bush's compassionate conservatism was at the center of that debate.

American conservatism has been more populist and dynamic than its European counterpart, and less paternalistic, aristocratic, authoritarian, and clerical. There is no influential American counterpart to the tradition of Maistre, let alone Maurras. However, the gap between the continents has narrowed substantially as postwar European conservatism shifted decisively in favor of its Burkean pole. Reagan's kinship with Thatcher in the 1980s illuminated an increasing convergence in favor of a conservatism that seeks to preserve the (classical) liberal polity against more radical challenges at home and abroad.

SEE ALSO *Black Conservatism; Liberalism; Neoconservatism*

BIBLIOGRAPHY

Buckley, William F., Jr., and Charles R. Kesler, eds. 1988. *Keeping the Tablets: Modern American Conservative Thought.* New York: Harper & Row.

Burke, Edmund, and Isaac Kramnick. 1999. *The Portable Edmund Burke.* New York: Penguin.

Goldwater, Barry M. 1960. *The Conscience of a Conservative.* Shepherdsville, KY: Victor Publishing.

Hayek, Friedrich A. von. 1944. *The Road to Serfdom.* Chicago: University of Chicago Press.

Kirk, Russell, ed. 1982. *The Portable Conservative Reader.* New York: Viking Penguin.

Kirk, Russell. 1989. *The Conservative Mind from Burke to Eliot.* 7th ed. Chicago: Regnery.

Nash, George H. 1996. *The Conservative Intellectual Movement in America since 1945.* 2nd ed. Wilmington, DE: ISI Press.

Viereck, Peter. 1956. *Conservatism from John Adams to Churchill.* Princeton, NJ: D. Van Nostrand.

Andrew E. Busch

CONSERVATISM, BLACK

SEE *Black Conservatism.*

CONSERVATIVE PARTY (BRITAIN)

The British Conservative Party is one of the oldest and most successful democratic political parties in the world. The party originated in the late seventeenth century as the aristocratic "Tory" faction in parliament, with the name "Conservative" achieving currency only in the nineteenth century. In 1894 the party's official name became the "Conservative and Unionist Party" following a merger of the Conservatives and the Liberal Unionist Party. The merger was a result of a protracted conflict that split the Liberal Party into "home rule" and "unionist" groups, with the latter joining the Conservatives to maintain the union of Great Britain and Ireland. In the twentieth-century, the Liberals were replaced by the socialist Labour Party as the Conservatives' principal rivals for power following a further Liberal split during the First World War. The Liberals did not disappear, but they remained an ideologically centrist "third" party whose fortunes mostly waned, and occasionally waxed, over time.

There are three major components in Conservative thought. The first—often labeled "Tory" Conservatism—has roots in the ideas of the British philosopher-politician Edmund Burke (1729–1797). Burke argued that societies were organic, but not static, entities. Social change should be gradual and evolutionary, rather than abrupt and revolutionary. A principal task of the Conservative Party and its leaders was to guide change in ways that would preserve the essential elements of Britain's social fabric. For Burke, the maintenance of hierarchy, continuity, and an interlocking system of mutual social obligations were the ends of good government.

Burke's ideas were given renewed force in the late nineteenth century by Benjamin Disraeli (1804–1881). Leading his party and country when the Industrial Revolution was creating a new urban working class, Disraeli propounded the idea that Britain was "One Nation." Rather than arraying itself in a coalition with the middle and upper classes that was indifferent to working class concerns, Disraeli proposed that the Conservatives develop policies that would serve the interests of all classes.

Inspired by Disraeli's "One Nation" ideas, many subsequent Conservative politicians and political thinkers endorsed the broad panoply of social programs characteristic of the twentieth-century welfare state. Much of this was prompted by the Labour Party's victory in the general election of 1945 and the popular program of policy changes introduced by their government. By doing this, the Conservative Party was able to recover lost ground and capture power again in 1951. "One Nation" Conservatives also adopted assumptions of Keynesian economics, particularly the idea that substantial state intervention in the economy could control inflation and unemployment, while also promoting growth and innovation. By the late 1950s, Conservative and Labour policies had become rather similar, leading observers to coin the term *Butskellism*—an amalgam of the names of the leading Conservative politician "Rab" Butler and the Labour leader Hugh Gaitskell—to describe the convergence between the parties' platforms.

A third, "laissez-faire," component of Conservative thought rejects the interventionist thrust of the Disraeli-Butler tradition. This reflects the free-market ideas associated with Adam Smith that were originally embraced by the Liberal Party. Beginning in the late 1960s, Sir Keith Joseph and other advocates of free-market economics and smaller government became increasingly influential in the party. This neoliberal movement found a champion for its ideas in Margaret Thatcher, who succeeded Edward Heath as the party leader in 1975. In 1979, a combination of accelerating economic decline coupled with mounting social and political turmoil enabled Thatcher to lead her party to power. Thatcherism subsequently came to describe a mix of policies designed to promote free-market economics and lessen public reliance on what Mrs. Thatcher derisively termed the "nanny state." In foreign affairs, following Winston Churchill and other earlier Conservative leaders, Thatcher vigorously opposed communism and promoted strong ties with the United States.

Although initially unpopular, Thatcher's public standing improved markedly in 1982 as a result of

Britain's victory over Argentina in the Falklands War. After leading her party in two more successful general elections, her tenure as prime minister abruptly ended in November 1990 when she was ousted in an intra-party revolt. Her replacement was John Major, who achieved a very narrow and widely unexpected victory in the 1992 general election. Conservative support was then driven sharply downward by a relentless combination of recession and economic mismanagement, internecine conflict over relations with the European Union, and persistent allegations of "sleaze."

The party's vulnerability was enhanced by the resurgence of the Labour Party. Labour had lurched to the ideological left in the late 1970s, effectively making itself unelectable for nearly two decades. However, under the leadership of Neil Kinnock and John Smith, and then Tony Blair, Labour again became a serious contender for power. Chosen party leader in 1994, Blair argued that a Labour government should use the tools of capitalist economics to generate the resources needed to achieve egalitarian policy goals, specifically to fund cherished social programs cut by successive Thatcher-Major governments. In 1997, Blair's "New Labour" party won a landslide victory, reducing the Conservative vote to 30.7 percent, the lowest figure in over 100 years. In two ensuing general elections, that figure increased only marginally—to 31.7 percent in 2001, and to 32.4 percent in 2005.

In the early twenty-first century, the Conservatives are no longer the dominant force that prompted observers to lionize them as Britain's "natural governing party." Searching for new ideas with widespread appeal, subject to continuing intraparty conflict, and suffering much reduced local party membership, Conservatives have struggled to find a formula for renewal. Acting on the correct assumption that one part of a winning formula is leadership, the party has fielded four leaders—William Hague, Iain Duncan Smith, Michael Howard, and David Cameron—since their 1997 debacle. Two of these people (Hague and Howard) promptly led the party to electoral defeat, and one (Duncan Smith) was ousted before he had a chance to do so. However, Cameron may fare better. He is attempting to cast off the legacy of Thatcherism by moving his party back to the ideological center ground and casting himself as both competent and compassionate. His efforts to improve Conservative fortunes are being helped by widespread dissatisfaction among Labour supporters with Tony Blair, and by a series of misfortunes similar to those that beset the Conservatives in the 1990s. Whether this combination of strategy and circumstance will prove a winning one for the Conservative Party remains to be seen.

SEE ALSO *Labour Party (Britain); Liberal Party (Britain); Parliament, United Kingdom; Thatcher, Margaret*

BIBLIOGRAPHY

Boothroyd, David. 2001. *Politico's Guide to the History of British Political Parties.* London: Politico's Publishing.

Clarke, Harold D., David Sanders, Marianne C. Stewart, and Paul Whiteley. 2004. *Political Choice in Britain.* Oxford: Oxford University Press.

Norpoth, Helmut. 1992. *Confidence Regained: Economics, Mrs. Thatcher, and the British Voter.* Ann Arbor: University of Michigan Press.

Whiteley, Paul, Patrick Seyd, and Jeremy Richardson. 1994. *True Blues: The Politics of Conservative Party Membership.* Oxford: Oxford University Press.

Harold D. Clarke
Paul F. Whiteley

CONSISTENCY

SEE *Properties of Estimators (Asymptotic and Exact).*

CONSPICUOUS CONSUMPTION

The American economist Thorstein Veblen first introduced the term *conspicuous consumption* in his work *The Theory of the Leisure Class* (1899). The theoretical starting point for discussing the term is the evolution of hierarchical structures in societies, which produce more than is required for subsistence. An unproductive leisure class emerges that accumulates wealth and secures status that is not enjoyed by the laboring class. Conspicuous consumption is the vehicle by which members of the leisure class convey their position of wealth and status to other members of society. Veblen maintained it is not enough to be wealthy; to have status individuals must display their position of wealth via consumption.

In its most traditional guise, leisure is the main focus of conspicuous consumption. The old aristocracy spent much of the social calendar hunting, fishing, horse racing, and whatever else was of interest. As societies became more atomized, however, and capitalist enterprise became the main source of wealth, consumer goods became the main vehicle for social signaling.

Economists have used conspicuous consumption as an explanation of growth in consumer spending. For Veblen it was the main driving force behind the consumer boom that started in the 1890s. In 1982, the historians Neil McKendrick, John Brewer, and J. H. Plumb argued that it provided the birth of the consumer society itself at the time of the Industrial Revolution. This view has been contested by historians and scholars, who point out that most of the growth in consumption during the Industrial Revolution was in items such as domestic coal, for which there was no social cachet.

This separation between goods that confer status and goods that are more basic, or less visible, is usually employed in economics. Often a utility function that individuals maximize (the mathematical equation relating consumption to utility) is decomposed into two parts representing social and private utility. Under this neoclassical approach, an opportunity for welfare-improving taxation is afforded by individuals choosing wasteful conspicuous consumption. This approach has also been used to explain why indicators of happiness are stagnating in developed countries, since individuals are failing to achieve their status objectives.

Sociologists have emphasized the power of social structure on the consumption of all commodities. In his *Social Structures of the Economy* (2005), the leading theorist of consumption, Pierre Bourdieu, said, "While economics is about how people make choices, sociology is about how they don't have any choice to make" (p. 1). Instead of consciously choosing to engage in conspicuous consumption according to rational calculation, individuals are driven by cultural forces beyond their control. In the French housing market, for example, the desire to own a house takes on mythical proportions. People force themselves to go into large debt in order to meet a societal ideal.

Bourdieu's emphasis on the unconscious formation of social identities also offers a more subtle interpretation of conspicuous consumption than its usual crude association with overt displays of status. During the postwar period the rich have become less overt in distinguishing their consumption from the expenditure power of the rising middle classes. Bourdieu's work offers a framework in which the consumption patterns of the rich appear to be based on their cultural capital, made to appear natural as part of the unequal structure of power.

SEE ALSO *Class, Leisure; Consumption; Malthus, Thomas Robert; Relative Income Hypothesis; Veblen, Thorstein*

BIBLIOGRAPHY

Bourdieu, Pierre. 2005. *The Social Structures of the Economy.* Cambridge, U.K.: Polity.

McKendrick, Neil, John Brewer, and J. H. Plumb. 1982. *The Birth of Consumer Society: The Commercialization of Eighteenth-Century England.* London: Europa.

Veblen, Thorstein. 1994. The Theory of the Leisure Class. In *The Collected Works of Thorstein Veblen.* Vol. 1. London: Routledge. (Orig. pub. 1899).

Andrew B. Trigg

CONSTITUENCY

A *constituency* is the portion of a nation, state, or locality represented by a particular elected official or other political leader. The term can refer to a group of people (for instance, the constituency of a U.S. senator from Illinois includes all the people who live in Illinois) or a geographic area (the state itself). Political scientist Richard F. Fenno Jr. (1978) parses the term more finely, to incorporate four types of constituencies. A *geographic constituency* is defined by boundaries fixed by legislative or court action; it can be based on a district's size, its location, its industrial or business character, or the socioeconomic status, ethnicity, or other characteristics of its population. A *reelection constituency* consists of the people in a district whom a representative considers his or her supporters: that is, those likely to vote for the candidate's reelection. A *primary constituency* includes a representative's strongest supporters—his or her "base," often including activists for groups that ally themselves with the candidate. Finally, the term *personal constituency* refers to a representative's closest advisers and confidants, who may influence his or her decision-making. When a representative speaks of *constituency*, then, it is important for a social scientist to determine how the representative defines that term.

Research shows that a constituency can be represented in many ways (Eulau and Karps 1977). *Policy responsiveness* occurs when a representative advocates the preferred issues of the majority of his or her constituents. In the case of *service responsiveness*, the representative works to provide benefits for individual constituents or groups, ranging from tours of Congress to intervention with a government agency on a constituent's behalf. In the case of *allocation responsiveness*, the representative serves the constituency by "bringing home the bacon," including tangible, pork-barrel projects such as new highways. *Symbolic responsiveness* involves less tangible efforts by the representative to gain constituents' trust. A related notion is *mirror representation*, in which the representative shares salient characteristics with the constituency, such as race or gender. The value of mirror representation rests on the presumption that, for instance, an African American legislator can better understand and speak for the needs of African American constituents than a white legislator can (Pitkin 1967). This assumption helped lead to the creation of majority-minority legislative districts under the Voting Rights Act beginning in the 1980s.

The term *constituency* can also refer to the supporters of a public figure or the clientele of a business or interest. A prospective Senate candidate might direct his or her appeals to a national constituency of campaign contributors or to a specific group such as gun rights enthusiasts. Even an unelected public official, such as a bureaucrat working for the National Labor Relations Board, may well make decisions with the concerns of organized labor or small business owners in mind. Or a newspaper might change its format in order to expand its appeal to a local constituency of readers.

Democratic nations vary a great deal in constituency size and in the way constituencies are represented. For example, British Members of Parliament (MPs) have, on average, only one-seventh as many constituents as do American members of Congress, and MPs' constituencies tend to be much smaller geographically. However, constituency representation in the American Congress has traditionally focused more on service and allocation than is the case in Britain, despite the greater size of U.S. congressional constituencies, due to the American constitutional emphasis on separation of powers and federalism, which inhibits the development of stronger national political parties. Thus, members of Congress have greater independence from their parties, and consequently a greater need for a personal tie with constituents than do MPs. In recent years, however, personal ties have become more characteristic of the MP-constituent relationship (Cain, Ferejohn, and Fiorina 1987).

The power of a constituency to elect its representatives is central to the working of a democratic system, in that it offers the potential for popular control over government. The existence of that control in practice may be limited by several factors, however. Constituents have been found to gather relatively little information about public policies and the behavior of their representatives. Furthermore, the vote frequently fails to convey specific sets of instructions from constituents to their elected representatives as to what actions to take—especially in American elections, which are regularly scheduled and therefore do not necessarily occur at a time of special relevance for a particular issue. To communicate specific concerns, constituents can lobby their representatives through letters and e-mails, campaign contributions, protests, interest-group and party activism, media ads, visits to legislators, and testimony given to congressional committees—all costly to constituents in time, effort, and money.

Despite these very real limits on the ability of constituents to control their elected officials, the existence of a constituency with the power to select its representatives is nonetheless one of the most important checks on government power. Constituents also serve as the support for political parties and interest groups, two of the other primary restraints on government.

SEE ALSO *Authority; Campaigning; Democracy; Elections; Fenno, Richard F.; Gerrymandering; Interest Groups and Interests; Lobbying; Pitkin, Hanna; Political Parties; Political Science; Representation; Voting Patterns; Voting Rights Act*

BIBLIOGRAPHY

Cain, Bruce, John Ferejohn, and Morris Fiorina. 1987. *The Personal Vote: Constituency Service and Electoral Independence.* Cambridge, MA: Harvard University Press.

Eulau, Heinz, and Paul D. Karps. 1977. The Puzzle of Representation: Specifying Components of Responsiveness. *Legislative Studies Quarterly* 2 (3): 233–254.

Fenno, Richard F., Jr. 1978. *Home Style: House Members in Their Districts.* Boston: Little, Brown.

Pitkin, Hanna. 1967. *The Concept of Representation.* Berkeley: University of California Press.

Marjorie Randon Hershey

CONSTITUTION, U.S.

In 1787 delegations from twelve of the thirteen states of the fledgling United States (all but Rhode Island) descended on Philadelphia, Pennsylvania, to consider revising the Articles of Confederation, which had provided a roadmap for national government since their ratification in 1781. Over the course of four sweltering months, these delegations met under a cloak of secrecy to consider how best to keep the United States whole. The proposal that emerged in late September 1787 was not a revision of the Articles of Confederation but an entirely new document which, upon ratification, became the Constitution of the United States of America. That Constitution has survived, more or less intact, for more than 200 years.

In the years between the Revolutionary War and the Constitutional Convention, the United States operated pursuant to the Articles of Confederation. As the name implies, the Articles envisioned a confederation of autonomous states, with a limited national government to provide national defense and otherwise manage foreign affairs. The national government, however, could do little without the consent of at least nine of the thirteen states.

The Articles of Confederation proved unworkable. The national government had difficulty collecting funds from the states to pay the immense debts incurred during the war, and they could not even compensate the soldiers who had fought on behalf of independence. Moreover, as the states coined their own money, forgave debts of their citizens owed to citizens of other states, and erected trade barriers among themselves, the national economy floundered. Among the country's leaders, James Madison of Virginia and Alexander Hamilton of New York lobbied the loudest for reform. Shays' Rebellion, an armed insurgency by a band of impoverished Massachusetts farmers, lent a sense of urgency to their demands and the national Congress decided to convene a delegation of reform in Philadelphia.

The Philadelphia Convention brought together some of the most prominent political voices of the time. Some, such as James Madison, considered the convention an opportunity to create a strong national government. In a tactical coup, Madison and his delegation from Virginia arrived early, marshaled their arguments, and proffered a coherent plan for sweeping reform—the Virginia Plan—a mere four days after the convention was called to order.

Delegates who favored state sovereignty and limited national government proposed alternatives, most notably the New Jersey Plan. The Virginia delegation, however, had successfully framed the debate, and while the convention debate prompted considerable compromise, the proposal that emerged from the convention vastly increased the power of the national government relative to the states.

Specifically, the proposed constitution created a bicameral legislature, with representation based on population in one house and equal for every state in the other; a unitary executive; and a Supreme Court. Perhaps most importantly, the proposed constitution vested control over interstate and foreign commerce with the national government and gave the national government the power to levy taxes rather than rely upon the largesse of the states for funds. Overall, the proposed document gave the national government control over the nation's economy and foreign affairs; while states retained significant sovereign power, the document explicitly rendered that power inferior to that of the national government.

While the proposed constitution increased the power of the national government, it nevertheless reflected a deep skepticism of any unchecked power. The institutions of national government are each constrained by the others, forcing deliberation, compromise, and incremental policy making. Similarly, while the Congress and the president are ultimately accountable to electoral pressures, the Supreme Court is insulated from such forces by life tenure. In this way, the U.S. Constitution reflects the core concerns of classical liberal philosophy: a government guided by majority rule but providing protection for minority rights.

While the rhetoric surrounding the Revolutionary War and the framing of the Constitution emphasized equality and the inherent rights of man, the founders defined equality quite narrowly. Specifically, at the time of the founding, most states denied the right to vote and other privileges of citizenship to large classes of people, including women and citizens who did not own real property. Perhaps the most striking conflict between the ideals and the reality of the early United States was the institution of slavery.

The same citizens who were willing to fight and die for liberty during the Revolutionary War turned a blind eye to the institution of slavery or, in many cases, actually participated in it. While there were doubtless delegates who held personal moral objections to slavery, serious efforts to abolish slavery would have fragmented the foundling nation. The delegates to the Constitutional Convention discussed the issue of slavery, but the only serious concern was how slaves should be counted for purposes of taxation and representation. The ultimate compromise position—that each slave would count as three-fifths of a free person—remains an embarrassment to the nation.

The terms of the proposed constitution required ratification by nine of the thirteen states. Supporters of the new constitution, known as Federalists, appealed to middle-class merchants and creditors, exhorting the need for economic stability. Many state and local politicians, whose power was threatened by a strong national government, opposed the new constitution; these Anti-Federalists made emotional appeals about the burden of taxation the new government would create and raised the specter of Britain's tyranny over the colonies.

The Anti-Federalists spread their message through public rallies and through a series of essays published in newspapers across the country. These essays, written under pseudonyms such as "Cato" and "The Federal Farmer," later became known as the *Anti-Federalist Papers*. In response, Alexander Hamilton, John Jay, and James Madison collectively penned a series of 85 essays, dubbed the *Federalist Papers*, which sought to allay fears of government tyranny. These essays stand as perhaps the best defense of the United States' republican system of government.

Ultimately the Anti-Federalist forces lacked coordination and failed to offer a single, coherent alternative to the new constitution. By January 1788, five of the necessary nine states had ratified the new constitution. The Federalists ultimately attracted additional support by promising to recommend, as a first order of business for the new government, a series of amendments designed to protect individual liberty against the tyranny of the state; these amendments are known as the Bill of Rights. The

Constitution was ratified on June 21, 1788; almost two years later Rhode Island became the last of the original thirteen colonies to ratify the Constitution.

Since its ratification in 1788, the U.S. Constitution has endured remarkably well. Amending the U.S. Constitution is difficult, and this difficulty insulates the document from the most capricious tides of public sentiment, contributing to its stability. Amendments must first be proposed by two-thirds of both chambers of Congress or by a convention called by two-thirds of the state legislatures; ratification then requires approval from three-fourths of the states. Apart from the Bill of Rights, the United States has ratified only seventeen constitutional amendments. Most of the successful amendments have expanded the franchise or involved the administration of government; generally, efforts to amend the Constitution to implement social policy have failed. There are, however, two notable exceptions.

First, in the wake of the United States Civil War, the nation ratified three constitutional amendments related to the issues of race and slavery. The Thirteenth Amendment abolished slavery and involuntary servitude. The Fourteenth Amendment guaranteed citizens equal protection under the law and required the states to afford citizens due process. The Fifteenth Amendment required the states to extend the right to vote to all adult men, regardless of race or previous condition of servitude. Collectively, these amendments radically changed the social structure of the United States; while racial equality continued to evolve for the next century and, indeed, continues to elude the United States, these amendments have served as a moral compass pointing toward true equality.

The other successful attempt to regulate social policy through constitutional amendment was, frankly, only successful for a brief moment in time. In 1919 the United States ratified the Eighteenth Amendment, which prohibited the manufacture, sale, and trade of intoxicating liquors. For the next fourteen years, this policy—known as Prohibition—created a black market for alcohol and contributed to a dramatic increase in organized crime. In 1933 the Twenty-First Amendment, which repealed the Eighteenth, was ratified.

While the Constitution is stable, it is not rigid. Rather, interpretation of the Constitution has adapted to changing social and political circumstances, and thus insured its continued political viability. Specifically, the U.S. Supreme Court, through the mechanism of judicial review, interprets the U.S. Constitution, and fluidity in its interpretation has allowed the Constitution to bend to adapt to political demands.

For example, the equal protection and due process provisions of the Fourteenth Amendment—which were intended to protect racial minorities from mistreatment and discrimination—were construed by the Supreme Court to provide protection to large economic interests. Similarly, the Supreme Court has repeatedly recognized a "right to privacy" implicit in the protections of the First, Fourth, Fifth, and Fourteenth Amendments; the Supreme Court has determined that this right to privacy essentially protects most sexual and reproductive decisions from government interference.

Ultimately, the U.S. Constitution is a document born of necessity and compromise, but it has proven remarkably robust and resilient. As society and technology have evolved, the Constitution, too, has evolved. But its evolution has occurred, primarily, through changing interpretation of static language. As a result, the Constitution has adapted but its essential character—the basic principles of liberty, equality, and democracy reflected in its language—has endured.

SEE ALSO *American Revolution; Bill of Rights, U.S.; Civil Liberties; Civil Rights; Declaration of Independence, U.S.; Supreme Court, U.S.*

BIBLIOGRAPHY

Beard, Charles. 1986. *An Economic Interpretation of the Constitution of the United States.* New York: The Free Press. (Orig. pub. 1913).

Bowen, Catherine Drinker. 1966. *Miracle at Philadelphia: The Story of the Constitutional Convention, May–September, 1787.* Boston: Little, Brown.

Hamilton, Alexander, et al. 2003. *The Federalist Papers.* New York: New American Library.

Ketchum, Ralph. 2003. *The Anti-Federalist Papers and the Constitutional Convention Debates.* New York: New American Library.

Wendy L. Watson

CONSTITUTIONAL COURTS

Although Alexander Hamilton, one of the founders of the oldest constitutional court, promoted the judiciary as the "least dangerous" branch of government in 1788 (*The Federalist No. 78*), judicial practice has since proven that constitutional courts have considerable power potential and are less feeble than Hamilton suggested. Since the mid-twentieth century, constitutional courts have become particularly popular features in the constitutions of newly democratized states, specifically due to their potential to powerfully constrain the other governmental branches. In these states, constitutional courts carry the burden (though not always effectively) of safeguarding the democratic system.

Constitutional courts may have such political impact because they are specialized tribunals, charged (either exclusively or as the highest appellate court) with upholding the constitution and exercising judicial review by invalidating any legislative acts (or government actions) violating constitutional mandates. However, two schools of thought disagree whether this renders constitutional courts effective policymakers.

One school, known as the *dynamic court* view, holds that the exalted position of constitutional courts within the political system makes them more powerful than policymakers in other governmental institutions. However, this causes these courts to clash with other branches of government, producing what Alexander M. Bickel (1986) calls the *countermajoritarian difficulty*. Because they are not popularly elected, constitutional courts typically enjoy considerable independence from political pressures while wielding the power to invalidate acts of the popularly elected branches of government, frustrating the will of the (legislative) majority. Thus, their ability to shape public policies by setting constitutionally allowable parameters for legislation without being subject to traditional mechanisms of democratic accountability has prompted allegations of judicial activism.

In contrast, a second school of thought known as the *constrained court* view (Rosenberg 1991) argues that even the powerful U.S. Supreme Court is rarely able to effect social change because it is too constrained by the Constitution, by other institutions of government, and by its lack of policy-development tools. This school of thought is unconcerned about the countermajoritarian difficulty.

Notwithstanding this debate, constitutional courts are generally believed to have some (though not completely unrestrained) powers that may allow them to be effective guarantors of a democratic constitutional order. Scholars have begun to specify factors boosting a court's political power, including a store of political capital; the court's ability to pick from a wide range of cases (e.g., through generous standing rules, through the powers of both concrete and abstract review, as well as through a posteriori and a priori review), while being able to limit the docket; and the court's insulation from political pressures (e.g., through long terms of office). Neither centralized nor diffuse systems of judicial review appear to present power advantages to the court.

Interestingly, some constitutional courts established their power through their own rulings (c.f. the U.S. Supreme Court in *Marbury v. Madison* [1803], or the European Court of Justice in *Costa v. ENEL* [1964]), rather than through explicit constitutional empowerment

clauses. Some observers, such as C. Neal Tate and Torbjörn Vallinder, even detect a significant global trend toward the "judicialization of politics" (1995, p. 5) that increasingly puts constitutional (and ordinary) courts in the limelight of political conflict. Consequently, political analysis is no longer complete without a consideration of constitutional courts as political actors.

SEE ALSO *Judicial Review*

BIBLIOGRAPHY

Bickel, Alexander M. 1986. *The Least Dangerous Branch: The Supreme Court at the Bar of Politics*, 2nd ed. New Haven, CT: Yale University Press.

Hamilton, Alexander. 1778. *The Federalist No. 78—The Judiciary Department*. http://www.law.ou.edu/ushistory/federalist/.

Jacob, Herbert, et al. 1996. *Courts, Law, and Politics in Comparative Perspective*. New Haven, CT: Yale University Press.

Rosenberg, Gerald N. 1991. *The Hollow Hope: Can Courts Bring about Social Change?* Chicago: University of Chicago Press.

Shapiro, Martin M. 1981. *Courts: A Comparative and Political Analysis*. Chicago: University of Chicago Press.

Tate, C. Neal, and Torbjörn Vallinder, eds. 1995. *The Global Expansion of Judicial Power*. New York: New York University Press.

Anke Grosskopf

CONSTITUTIONALISM

Modern nation-states enact constitutions to bring society from its natural state of chaos to organization based on the rule of law. Unlike the war of all against all described by the English philosopher Thomas Hobbes (1588–1679), John Locke's (1632–1704) view of the state of nature recognized that humans have organized in family and cultural units throughout history. Though unnecessary for protection from outsiders, society could benefit from a *social contract*. Participants must agree to create structure (a legislature to make decisions), to designate an impartial judge, and to establish enforcement powers (an executive branch) in order to sustain a peaceful society. These entities, according to Locke, can only be created through the efforts of the members of a society to contract for continued institutional support.

The social contract is often embodied by a constitution, a set of principles by which a group of people agrees to govern and be governed. In order to operate as a constitution, these rules need not take the form of a written document. The social contract metaphor is limited in several ways, including, in most circumstances, the lack of third-party enforcement. It is more important that constitutional law represents the conventions accepted in a society, and that societal order is coordinated around these conventions. A "dualist" understanding views constitutions as frameworks within which other politics and institutions operate. They establish second-order rules that must be followed when making more specific laws.

By constraining rulers, constitutions aim to protect citizens' rights. When a constitution stipulates judicial review, citizens can petition courts to invalidate laws that violate constitutional principles. Although, as with the unwritten British constitution, not all provisions are judicially enforceable, they may nonetheless serve as focal points for legal interpretation and political debate, as well as indicators of which government interventions will be accepted by citizens.

A constitution serves, in some sense, to codify existing social relations. Constitutional design, therefore, is constrained by internal and external power dynamics. Resulting agreements reflect these relationships rather than pure legal ideals. As a result, underrepresented groups continue to be excluded, unless they gain influence by extraconstitutional means.

Russell Hardin (1999) sees constitutions more as models of mutual advantage than as binding contracts. It is usually in the best interest of all parties to uphold the rules that maintain order within their society. There are relatively few occasions when it would be more difficult to follow existing rules than to renegotiate the terms of a constitution.

Those rare circumstances on which recoordination is less costly for society are constitutional moments (Ackerman 1991). Changes in power alignments, in relation to internal politics or external influence, may necessitate a change in the substance of a constitution. These moments may involve major amendment to an existing constitution, as in the post–Civil War United States, or they may require a complete overhaul of the constitution, as in South Africa following the inclusion of the black population as full citizens in the 1990s. At these times, questions of legitimacy arise because the constitutional authors have not been elected by a process representing the new social contract, and may not represent the people who will be bound by the new document. If a new constitution is to remain a stable set of rules for the polity, it must represent a credible commitment by citizens and leaders who will not have an incentive to override or renegotiate it, or resort to violence. Such constitutional moments may arise in the context of postwar reconstruction, independence movements, domestic upheaval, or union of existing polities. In each situation, citizens encounter distributional gains and losses reflecting societal change.

SEE ALSO *Judicial Review; Locke, John*

BIBLIOGRAPHY

Ackerman, Bruce. 1991. *Foundations*. Vol. 1 of *We the People*. Cambridge, MA: Harvard University Press.

Hardin, Russell. 1999. *Liberalism, Constitutionalism, and Democracy*. New York: Oxford University Press.

Locke, John. [1690] 1988. *Two Treatises of Government*. Ed. Peter Laslett. New York: Cambridge University Press.

Mark Axelrod

CONSTITUTIONS

Constitutions can be defined as a set of rules that aim at regulating the channels of access to principal government positions, the allocation of powers among different branches of government, and the rights of citizens. Most constitutions also include rules establishing procedures for their own amendment and the conditions under which constitutional provisions can be suspended.

Nearly all countries in the contemporary world have written constitutions, often identified as the "fundamental law." Even for these countries, however, it would be misleading to restrict the constitution to a single document so named. Some of the rules that create the structures of government and delimit their authority are also contained in statute law (such as laws establishing the jurisdiction and powers of governmental departments or independent agencies) and in judicial decisions (such as the rulings of a constitutional court) that are not codified in a single document. In addition, there are always unwritten conventions that regulate the behavior of representatives and citizens, particularly in areas where written rules are silent or unclear. Moreover, most parts of a constitution can be composed of unwritten conventions, as is the case of the United Kingdom, New Zealand, and Israel.

Constitutions generally attempt to prevent the arbitrary use of state power. But there is a wide variation in the degree to which state authorities effectively abide by the constitution. Rulers are more likely to observe a constitution that emerged out of a democratically elected body representing a plurality of political forces. They are also likely to comply with the constitution when citizens agree on the authority of the constitution as a set of impartial procedures for the resolution of conflicts. This consensus, however, is often lacking when societies are divided by overlapping cleavages of an economic, religious, or ethnic nature.

Constitutions that are at least minimally enforced are essential for the existence and legitimacy of democratic regimes. Citizens would not be free to criticize the government and keep its decisions in check without basic constitutional rules guaranteeing freedom of expression and providing remedies against arbitrary state action. Truly competitive elections could not exist without constitutional rules guaranteeing freedom of assembly and organization.

There is great variation in the way constitutions organize a democratic regime. Constitutional democracies can be presidential, if the chief of government is elected by the people for a fixed term, or parliamentary, if he or she is elected by the assembly and responsible to the legislative majority. Legislative assemblies can be unicameral or bicameral. States can be unitary or federal. Most contemporary constitutions establish independent courts responsible for interpreting the constitution. Constitutional courts, however, vary in organization, composition, and powers. Finally, while the majority of constitutions include amendment rules that attempt to make constitutional reforms more difficult to pass than ordinary laws, these rules can be relatively flexible or extremely rigid.

In the twenty-first century constitutions are implicitly or explicitly central to some of the most important research fields in social sciences. Constitutions and their various designs are considered to have a crucial impact on the stability and quality of democracy, on economic policy and economic performance, and on the rate of policy change in political regimes.

SEE ALSO *Authority*

BIBLIOGRAPHY

Dahl, Robert. 1996. Thinking About Democratic Constitutions. In *Political Order: NOMOS XXXVIII*, ed. Ian Shapiro and Russell Hardin, 175–206. New York: New York University Press.

Elster, Jon, and Rune Slagstad. 1988. *Constitutionalism and Democracy*. Cambridge, U.K.: Cambridge University Press.

Ferejon, John, Jack Rakove, and Jonathan Riley, eds. 2001. *Constitutional Culture and Democratic Rule*. Cambridge, U.K.: Cambridge University Press.

Hardin, Russell. 1989. Why a Constitution? In *The Federalist Papers and the New Institutionalism*, ed. Bernard Grofman and Donald Wittman, 100–120. New York: Agathon Press.

Vogdanor, Vernon, ed. 1988. Introduction. In *Constitutions in Democratic Politics*, 1–13. Aldershot, U.K.: Gower Publishing Company.

Weingast, Barry R. 1997. The Political Foundations of Democracy and the Rule of Law. *American Political Science Review* 91 (2): 245–263.

Gabriel L. Negretto

CONSTRAINED CHOICE

Constrained choice occurs when an economic agent must determine the optimal combination of choice variables (given some relationship between combinations of those variables and payoffs) in the face of a constraint limiting the set of feasible combinations for those variables available to the agent. For instance, a consumer seeks to choose the combination within his or her means of consumption goods and services that maximizes welfare. More specifically, if C_1 and C_2 are the goods for which the consumer must choose the optimal combination, the consumer's problem is to maximize utility ($U(C_1, C_2)$) given a budget constraint: $p_1{}^*C_1 + p_2{}^*C_2 \leq M$, where p_1 and p_2 are the prices of the two goods and M is the consumer's overall income or purchasing power.

The concept of constrained choice has been extended both theoretically and empirically to more elaborate settings. It arises naturally when agents must make forward-looking decisions or when agents are uncertain. For instance, life cycle models of saving and consumption focus on the challenge presented to agents who must maximize discounted lifetime utility given the constraints imposed by current and future income, and prices and opportunities to save or borrow. Agents may face uncertainty in terms of future income and prices, as well as the returns to savings. The simple budget constraint posed must then be recast in intertemporal terms in a fashion that reflects the impact of per period saving or borrowing, as well as uncertainty regarding future income flows, returns to saving, and prices. A common way of approaching this is the value function method, which essentially reduces the rather complex intertemporal problem to a series of two-period problems.

The concept of constrained choice has also been extended to other behavioral settings, such as joint decision-making. For example, household bargaining models attempt to capture a household's members' efforts to maximize their personal utility from the consumption of goods and services, given a limit to overall household purchasing power. The household bargaining example also speaks to alternative approaches to choice. For instance, much of game theory studies interactive decision-making. This approach focuses on the constraints placed on an agent's decision-making by other agents' likely responses to his or her decisions. Thus the agent does not necessarily face a static, internal (to him- or herself) constraint as in the examples previously presented, but other agents' likely reactions to the agent's behavior, and their responses' implications for the agent's own payoff function, effectively constrain his or her behavior.

SEE ALSO *Choice in Economics*

BIBLIOGRAPHY

Mas-Colell, Andreu, Michael D. Whinston, and Jerry R. Green. 1995. *Microeconomic Theory.* New York: Oxford University Press.

Peter M. Lance

CONSTRUCTIVISM

Although the term *constructivism* is used as a label for an important movement in art history (as in Russian constructivism), *constructivism* in the social sciences refers to a distinctive approach to theory and research that is opposed to the dominant empiricist, naturalist, and realist frameworks of mainstream social thought. This general approach is also frequently designated by the terms *social constructivism* and *social constructionism.*

The constructivist outlook can be formulated based on three general claims: (1) the ontological thesis that what appears to be "natural" is in reality an effect of social processes and practices; (2) the epistemological thesis that knowledge of social phenomena is itself socially produced; and (3) the methodological thesis that the investigation of the social construction of reality must take priority over all other methodic procedures.

Historically, constructivist epistemologies have opposed both empiricist and realist philosophies of science. Empiricism is rejected for its passive view of mind and its assumption that beliefs and knowledge are formed through associative patterns of theory-neutral "sense data." Realism—the belief in independently existent objects—is criticized for ignoring the various interpretive and constructive processes through which cognition of objects is actually realized. Against these naïve epistemologies, constructivism commends something like a Copernican revolution in our taken-for-granted ways of conceptualizing knowledge and reality. For the constructivist, cognition is no longer viewed as an objective representation of the real, but is approached as an active construction of reality, shaped by particular interests, actions, representational media, and social practices. Human beings do not merely "adapt" to a preexisting world; rather, as active agents, they participate in the interpretive construction of reality.

One primary form of interpretation can be found in practical interaction mediated by everyday language and communicative forms. Thus, what might seem to be pregiven "natural" categories and relations are seen as products of particular social practices and interests. Moreover, such categories and relations are subject to historical change. Against empiricism and naturalism, constructivists argue that we should see every phenomenal order as the product of active processes of social interaction. The "real," in other words, is viewed as a construction of agents and productive activities. Whatever beliefs we hold about reality are contextually defined and culturally constructed. Orthodox epistemology and commonsense thinking influenced by it tend to be atomistic, monological, and representational, whereas constructivism is holistic, instrumentalist, and pragmatic.

This conflict between forms of realism and more pragmatic and praxis-oriented worldviews can be traced back to the scientific revolution of the seventeenth century and the thinking of the eighteenth-century Enlightenment. The constructivist spirit was symbolically expressed by a principle that was first proposed by the great Italian philosopher Giambattista Vico (1668–1744)—the *verum-factum principle*—according to which historians and social theorists can only truly know what has been made or shaped by human intention and design. For Vico, this idea opened the continent of history as a realm of contingent social constructions.

The other important philosophical source of constructivist themes is the antiempiricist critical epistemology formulated by Immanuel Kant (1724–1804) toward the end of the eighteenth century. Against the dominant empiricism of his day, Kant argued that cognition is not a passive reception of sensory data, but is, rather, the outcome of constructive processes of active cognition (involving a priori forms of intuition, categories of the understanding, and so on).

In keeping with the changing forms of empiricism and realism, the development of constructivism in the nineteenth and twentieth centuries took many forms. These include the historicist perspective of historical materialism (with Karl Marx's [1818–1883] elaboration of a more praxis-based "dialectical" realism); Émile Durkheim's (1858–1917) image of the social as a collective "social fact"; the *verstehende* or interpretive sociology defended by Wilhelm Dilthey (1833–1911), Georg Simmel (1858–1918), and Max Weber (1864–1920); Edmund Husserl's (1859–1938) transcendental phenomenology; the philosophical hermeneutics associated with the philosophers Hans-Georg Gadamer (1900–2002) and Paul Ricoeur (1913–2005); the social phenomenology of Alfred Schutz (1899–1959); the sociology of knowledge represented by Karl Mannheim (1893–1947); and a range of interpretive sociologies influenced by these thinkers. Perhaps the seminal text in post–World War II (1939–1945) American sociology was Peter Berger and Thomas Luckmann's *The Social Construction of Reality* (1966), which developed a sociology of knowledge synthesized from Marxist, Durkheimian, Meadian, and phenomenological traditions.

Constructivism became an influential current of thought in the 1960s and 1970s as it converged with new approaches to the understanding of the constitutive rules and regulatory processes that inform the framework of social life. This was particularly important in so-called labeling theories of deviance and the "new criminology"; in debates about the symbolic sources of social identity (in the symbolic interactionist tradition); in the study of stereotyping, prejudice, and authoritarianism in the field of ethnicity and race relations; in the renewed concern with the historical and political construction of sexuality and gender relations (associated, in particular, with feminist sociology); and in the emergence of more microsociological inquiries into the negotiated character of everyday social orders.

The constructivist outlook has had a major impact in shaping the landscape of contemporary intellectual life. Among the most important fields influenced by constructivism are: semiotics and structuralism, critical theory, general systems theory, structuration theory, postmodern theory, and gender theory.

In semiotics and structuralism, the structuralist movement explicitly embraces the constructive role of language and other cultural systems as reality-shaping forms of social production and reproduction (in terminology derived from Ferdinand de Saussure [1857–1913], language becomes a differential system of meaning construction). In psychology, Jean Piaget's (1896–1980) structuralism provided one of the first explicit constructivist conceptions of human cognition, learning, and socialization, and James Gibson's (1904–1979) theory of active *affordances* has led to constructivist research in perception and cognition (Gibson 1966).

In critical theory, the revision of historical materialism began with the Frankfurt School and continued under Jürgen Habermas and his students. Habermas's differentiation of knowledge into three basic interest-defined types—instrumental (knowledge constructed in relation to work and labor), interpretive-hermeneutic (knowledge concerned with practical understanding in social life), and emancipative (knowledge linked to social criticism and change)—is an example of constructivism in critical theory.

In general systems theory, societies actively construct their "environments" through cultural codes and representations. Structuration perspectives take as their theme the variable practices and differential processes of culturally mediated world construction. Examples of the latter are the "structuration" theories of society in the work of Pierre Bourdieu (1930–2002) and Anthony Giddens, and the closely related genealogical investigations of power/discourse formations associated with the work of Michel Foucault (1926–1984). Constructivism in postmodern theory is represented by the theory of language-games in

Jean-François Lyotard (1924–1998) and the theory of simulation and hyperreality formulated by Jean Baudrillard. Gender theory has become especially marked in accounts of the discourse-constructed character of gendered identities, sexual inequalities, and patriarchal power influenced by post-structuralist theories of language.

Constructivist approaches can be found in a wide range of perspectives in contemporary social thought. The first and most pervasive is the so-called linguistic turn within contemporary philosophy and, closely linked to this, the "cultural" turn across all the social sciences. This insight into the radically constitutive implications of cultural processes challenges naturalistic methodologies by demonstrating the way in which all social relations and spheres of society are culturally produced, organized, and reproduced (Burr 1995; Gergen 1999). One example is the influence of a type of discursive "genealogy" influenced by the writings of Foucault (in essence, Foucault's studies of disciplinary practices are inquiries into the discursive construction of "normal" schooling, penal practices, clinical medicine, and so on). In moving from a framework of individual construction (for example, the early work of Piaget) to theories of social construction, we emerge with a more radical sociology of the frameworks of knowledge viewed as cultural formations.

It is no exaggeration to say that a field such as ethnicity or "race" relations has been transformed by constructivist approaches to the discourses of "racial" differences and "racialized" inequalities and disadvantage. The history and sociology of racism has developed in ways that demonstrate how particular categories of ethnic difference have been constructed historically in order to sustain particular systems of domination. Viewing human groups in terms of "races" is a relatively recent example of the violence that can be inflicted upon populations and whole societies by social categories. Every ideology based upon a belief in the innate or culturally prescribed inferiority of one group defined by some physical attribute, characteristic, or trait is seen as an example of wider processes of socially mediated power and domination. Constructivism thus not only offers new avenues of research into the workings of racist discourse but also has led to a renewed sense of the ethical and political problems inherent in using "racial" terms and ethnic stereotypes. Divisions between groups and communities based upon such discourses are primary examples of socially constructed relations. The problem of institutionalized discrimination and how such inequalities are maintained by racialized discourse is seen as being central to the workings of power and domination in society (an insight that has led to renewed interest in the historical dynamics of colonial and postcolonial systems).

Another field in which constructivist approaches have been highly productive is the branch of microsociology inspired by the writings of Harold Garfinkel, Aaron Cicourel, David Sudnow, and Harvey Sacks. Their work has led to the emergence of a distinctive framework of research concerned with the sense-making activities of everyday discourse and conversation (usually referred to as *conversation analysis*). *Discourse perspectives* have also been influential in social psychology (as seen, for example, in the work of Jonathan Potter and Margaret Wetherell), including the explicitly social understandings of debates in experimental and physical science (Mulkay 1979; Knorr-Cetina 1981; Latour and Woolgar 1986), as well as the constructivist sociology of science associated with the Edinburgh School and approaches to the symbolic construction of organizations and organizational cultures (for example, in Karl Weick's *Sensemaking in Organizations* [1995]). Further analysis of the constructivist program would need to distinguish between the different varieties of sociological and phenomenological constructivism, symbolic interactionism (Plummer 2000), linguistic constructivism, moderate and radical constructivism, and more ideologically sensitive discourse-theoretical models of knowledge construction (Gadamer 1975; Edwards and Potter 1992; Gergen 1982 and 1999; Grint and Woolgar 1997; Potter 1996; Potter and Wetherell 1987).

Social constructivist approaches have actively transformed almost every subdisciplinary field within sociology and, more creatively, given rise to new research configurations and inquiries, most particularly associated with the sociology of the body, the self, cultural identity, and systems of difference. These approaches are most explicitly evident in the concept of embodiment regarded as a symbolically mediated process (Shotter 1993; Shotter and Gergen 1988); discursive psychology (Edwards and Potter 1992; Potter and Wetherell 1987); the symbolic dynamics of social identity and identity construction (Levine 1992; Bayer and Shotter 1998); the sociology of sex roles, sexuality, gender, and gender socialization (Burr 1998); critical investigations of ethnicity, racism, sexism, prejudice, and stereotyping (Billig 1991); the social construction of health and illness (White 2002); and more radical programs of reflexive social theory into the different forms of power and domination in everyday life and society (Sandywell 1996; Steier 1991). All of these approaches depend upon a more critical understanding of the historical dynamics of the construction of identity and difference in and as social relations. The challenge faced by contemporary constructivism is to open dialogues with these new problematics and to develop more reflexive frameworks that respect the constructive processes of social existence.

SEE ALSO *Realism; Structuralism*

BIBLIOGRAPHY

Bayer, Betty M., and John Shotter, eds. 1998. *Reconstructing the Psychological Subject: Bodies, Practices, and Technologies.* London and Thousand Oaks, CA: Sage.

Berger, Peter, and Thomas Luckmann. 1966. *The Social Construction of Reality: A Treatise in the Sociology of Knowledge.* New York: Doubleday.

Billig, Michael. 1991. *Ideologies and Opinions: Studies in Rhetorical Psychology.* London and Newbury Park, CA: Sage.

Burr, Vivian. 1995. *An Introduction to Social Constructionism.* New York and London: Routledge.

Burr, Vivian. 1998. *Gender and Social Psychology.* London: Routledge.

Edwards, Derek, and Jonathan Potter. 1992. *Discursive Psychology.* London and Newbury Park, CA: Sage.

Foucault, Michel. 1972. *The Archaeology of Knowledge.* Trans. A. M. Sheridan Smith. London: Tavistock.

Foucault, Michel. 1973. *The Birth of the Clinic: An Archaeology of Medical Perception.* Trans. A. M. Sheridan Smith. London: Tavistock.

Gadamer, Hans Georg. 1975. *Truth and Method.* New York: Seabury.

Garfinkel, Harold. 1967. *Studies in Ethnomethodology.* Englewood Cliffs, NJ: Prentice-Hall.

Gergen, Kenneth J. 1982. *Toward Transformation in Social Knowledge.* New York: Springer Verlag.

Gergen, Kenneth J. 1999. *An Invitation to Social Construction.* London and Thousand Oaks, CA: Sage.

Gibson, James Jerome. 1966. *The Senses Considered as Perceptual Systems.* Boston: Houghton Mifflin.

Grint, Keith, and Steve Woolgar. 1997. *The Machine at Work: Technology, Work, and Organization.* Cambridge, U.K.: Polity.

Knorr-Cetina, Karin. 1981. *The Manufacture of Knowledge: An Essay on the Constructivist and Contextual Nature of Science.* Oxford: Pergamon.

Latour, Bruno, and Steve Woolgar. 1986. *Laboratory Life: The Construction of Scientific Facts.* Princeton, NJ: Princeton University Press.

Levine, George, ed. 1992. *Constructions of the Self.* New Brunswick, NJ: Rutgers University Press.

Mulkay, Michael J. 1979. *Science and the Sociology of Knowledge.* London: Allen and Unwin.

Plummer, Ken. 2000. Symbolic Interactionism in the Twentieth Century. In *The Blackwell Companion to Social Theory*, 2nd ed., ed. Bryan S. Turner, 193–222. Oxford: Blackwell.

Potter, Jonathan. 1996. *Representing Reality: Discourse, Rhetoric, and Social Construction.* London: Sage.

Potter, Jonathan, and Margaret Wetherell. 1987. *Discourse and Social Psychology: Beyond Attitudes and Behaviour.* London: Sage.

Sandywell, Barry. 1996. *Logological Investigations.* 3 vols. London: Routledge.

Shotter, John. 1993. *Conversational Realities: Constructing Life Through Language.* London and Thousand Oaks, CA: Sage.

Shotter, John, and Kenneth J. Gergen, eds. 1988. *Texts of Identity.* London: Sage.

Steier, Frederick, ed. 1991. *Research and Reflexivity*. London: Sage.

Weick, Karl E. 1995. *Sensemaking in Organizations*. London and Thousand Oaks, CA: Sage.

White, Kevin. 2002. *An Introduction to the Sociology of Health and Illness*. London and Thousand Oaks, CA: Sage.

Barry Sandywell

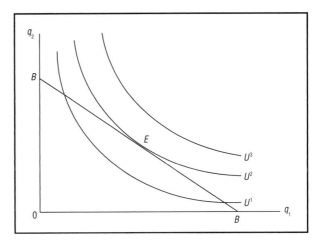

Figure 1

CONSUMER

The consumer plays a central role in mainstream economic analysis. This analysis explains economic behavior in terms of individual optimization, and the consumer, who buys and uses goods and services to maximize utility or seeks his or her highest level of satisfaction given the constraints he or she faces, is a central locus of decision making. Mainstream economics is often defined as the subject that examines how scarce resources are allocated to alternative uses to satisfy human wants, and these wants are embodied in the preferences of the consumer. Many of the key ideas of mainstream economics—such as the existence of general equilibrium in a market economy, and its property that this equilibrium is socially efficient—can be illustrated with economic models in which the only economic agents are consumers with given endowments of goods, interacting with others through market exchanges (without the producer, the other important agent in economics).

BASIC THEORY OF THE CONSUMER

The basic theory of the consumer examines an economic agent with a preference ordering over bundles of consumer goods. It is assumed that this ordering is complete (i.e., that the consumer can order all possible alternatives), reflexive, and transitive, and that more of any good is preferred to less (Barten and Bohm 1982). Under these assumptions the consumer's preferences can be represented by a utility function that assigns a real value to commodity bundles

$$U = U(q_1, q_2, \ldots, q_n)$$

where utility, U, increases with the quantity of each of N goods consumed, q_i. The consumer is also assumed to have a budget constraint given by $p_1q_1 + p_2q_2 + \cdots + p_nq_n \leq Y$,

where p_i denotes the (money) price of good i, exogenously given to the consumer, and Y is the (money) income of the consumer. The consumer is also assumed to maximize utility by choosing quantities of goods consumed, q_i. The solution of this maximization problem is usually shown

for the case of two goods ($N = 2$) with an indifference curve diagram as shown in the figure above, where the line BB is the consumer's budget line, which shows combinations of consumption bundles that satisfy the budget constraint with an equality (with the consumer spending his or her entire income) and the curves marked U are indifference curves, each one denoting a particular level of utility of satisfaction for the consumer, and drawn "smooth" and convex to the origin to show that consumers prefer "mixed" baskets to baskets containing a large amount of one good.

The consumer maximizes utility or reaches his or her highest level of satisfaction at the bundle E, which is the consumer's equilibrium. At equilibrium, the consumer equates the price ratio, p_1/p_2, the slope of the budget line, which shows the rate at which the consumer can substitute between the two goods at their prevailing prices, to the marginal rate of substitution between the two goods, the slope of the indifference curve, which shows the rate at which the consumer prefers to substitute between them to leave utility unchanged. In the general case with more than two goods, the consumer's equilibrium requires that the price ratio between any two goods is equated to the marginal rate of substitution between them.

This basic theory has a number of implications. First, given prices and preferences, an increase in income shifts the budget line outwards without changing its slope and increases the consumption of all goods if they are "normal" goods, and increases the consumer's utility. For some goods it may be that the quantity demand falls with income; these are called *inferior goods*. Second, other things remaining constant, a fall in the price of a good rotates the budget line outwards and increases the consumption of that good, provided it is a "normal" good. This increase occurs both because the relatively lower price of the good makes the consumer substitute away from the other good along an indifference curve (the "substitution effect"), and because the lower price in effect increases the real income of the consumer, inducing him or her to buy more of all goods (the "income effect"). This yields the consumer's demand function and curve showing the relation between the price and quantity consumed of a good. This, when aggregated over all individuals in the market, provides the market demand function and curve of the good. If the good is inferior, it is possible that the fall in the price of the good can lead to a fall in the quantity of the good consumed, with the consumer buying less of the good because he or she feels richer. Third, if the prices of all goods and the consumer's income change by the same proportion, the budget line will be unchanged, and the consumer will choose the same bundle. In other words, consumer demand is homogenous of degree zero in income and prices, which is known as the *homogeneity property*. Fourth, a shift in preferences favoring a good shifts the indifference curves towards the axis that measures the quantity of that good, and increases the consumption of that good.

ALTERNATIVE APPROACHES

This discussion has used utility and the level of satisfaction interchangeably. However, the early analysis of the consumer provided a hedonic interpretation of utility, identified it with pleasure, and took it to be cardinally measurable (Stigler 1950). It was assumed that utility increases with the level of consumption of a good, so that marginal utility—the change in utility due to the change in the quantity of a good consumed—is positive, but increases at a diminishing rate, so that marginal utility diminishes with increases in consumption. In this approach consumer equilibrium occurs when the marginal utility obtained from a commodity divided by its price is the same for all commodities. This equilibrium implies that an additional unit of money is allocated over different goods in such a way that it yields the same additional utility.

Concern with cardinal measurability led to the development of the ordinal utility theory of the consumer, with early contributions by Vilfredo Pareto (1909) and Eugene Slutsky (1915), and with later developments by John R. Hicks (1934) and Roy G. D. Allen (1934). In this theory, the concept of diminishing marginal utility is not meaningful, and is replaced by the assumption of the diminishing rate of marginal substitution (which states that the amount of a good that the consumer requires to stay at the same level of utility when he or she gives up a unit of another good increases as the consumer has more of the latter good), which is equivalent to indifference curves being convex to the origin. The implications of changes in income, prices, and preferences are the same with this approach as with the earlier one, without requiring the stronger assumption of cardinally measurable utility. The marginal rate of substitution between two goods is equivalent to the ratio of their marginal utilities.

The assumptions required for analyzing consumer behavior using Paul A. Samuelson's revealed preference approach (1938) are even less stringent, with no utility functions being assumed. Only the implications of observed behavior and the consistency of preferences are used to develop consumer theory.

Despite this trend towards requiring fewer assumptions, some analyses of consumer behavior, for example the examination of decision making in risky situations, and the evaluation of the well-being of the consumer, require stronger assumptions about the measurability of utility.

APPLICATIONS

The basic theory of the consumer has found many applications in economics (and even outside it) by suitable interpretations of "goods." The choice made by the consumer between consumption and leisure treats leisure as a good and takes into account the time constraint faced by the consumer that is allocated to work (which yields income) and leisure (which provides satisfaction but not income). This analysis is used to examine the labor-supply decision of the consumer. The choice made by the consumer between consumption in one period and consumption in the next (assuming a two-period life of the consumer, for simplicity) addresses the intertemporal dimension of the consumption-saving decision, with the relative price of consumption this period being determined by the interest that is yielded by savings. The additional amount of the good in the next period with which the consumer must be compensated (so that the consumer's level of utility does not change) for giving up a unit of the good this period is assumed to be greater than one by an amount that is called the *consumer's rate of time preference*, which measures the consumer's degree of impatience. In this theory, an increase in the interest rate reduces consumption in this period and increases saving through the substitution effect by making consumption this period more expensive, but it may reduce saving through the income effect of making the consumer increase consumption now. More generally, the consumer can be assumed to have a life-time horizon of longer than two periods. Sometimes the time horizon is taken to be infinitely long. The approach is used to examine choice when the consequence of choices is not certain. It is assumed that the outcome of a choice has a probability distribution, and the consumer maximizes expected utility, that is, the utility derived from each possible outcome weighted by its probability of occurrence. The approach is also used in the analysis of the portfolio choice among different assets for the asset-holding consumer. For example, if the consumer prefers higher returns to assets and lower risk, the consumer is taken to have a utility function over return and risk. Given the return and risk characteristics of different assets, the consumer can then choose the overall return and risk of his or her portfolio, and hence the allocation of wealth among different assets.

EMPIRICAL ISSUES

The empirical analysis of consumer behavior traditionally has been conducted using econometric methods, with the estimation of demand curves for particular products and systems of demand functions. This type of empirical work usually refers to an aggregate of consumers—for example, to all consumers in a country. Because the theoretical implications regarding individual consumers do not carry over to aggregates, additional theoretical assumptions, implying the existence of a representative consumer, are sometimes used to translate the theory regarding individual consumers to aggregate data. More recently, empirical estimation at the individual level has been conducted using survey and experimental data, as mentioned below.

The inverse relation between quantity demand of a product and its price has been repeatedly confirmed by the evidence. Charles Davenant's 1699 estimation of an inverse relation between the price of corn and the amount harvested is perhaps its earliest example. Subsequent attempts at estimating the demand functions for individual products and systems of demand functions yield the same result. Although the so-called "Giffen good," for which the quantity demand rises with the price, has been much discussed, no such empirical relationship has actually been documented.

This, however, should not be taken to imply that basic theory of consumer behavior is validated by empirical evidence. As mentioned earlier, the theory does not necessarily imply that quantity demanded falls with the price. Moreover, as shown by Gary Becker (1962), the inverse relation between price and quantity demanded can be explained in terms of individual behavior that is totally random (though restricted by the consumer's budget constraint) or determined by habit (as long as the consumer can afford to be governed by it), rather than by optimization, as assumed in consumer theory. Some other aspects of consumer theory do not seem to be consistent with empirical evidence. For instance, the homogeneity property is not usually confirmed. Survey evidence suggests that levels of utility as measured by self-reported indicators of happiness do not rise with the level of consumption and income, at least beyond a certain point. This casts doubt on the assumption that increases in consumption imply increases in utility. The usefulness of empirical

work on consumer behavior arguably lies not in testing the validity of consumer theory but in exploring empirical regularities such as the well-established Engel's law, which finds that people spend a smaller proportion of their budget on food as their income rises.

CRITICISMS AND DEVELOPMENTS

The theory of the consumer has been criticized from numerous angles, some of which have prompted its modification. Three may be briefly mentioned.

First, it is not clear who the consumer, the decision-making agent, really is. Given the preoccupation of mainstream economic theory with the optimizing agent, it is natural to interpret the consumer as an individual person. However, in studies of consumer behavior the consumer is often taken to be the household, or family, or even in some cases the family dynasty; this often leads to ignoring intrafamily differences. Even the idea of the individual as the consumer may be problematic if individuals are thought of as having multiple selves (Elster 1986).

Second, the notion that consumers can actually choose optimally over all possible consumption bundles has been criticized on the grounds that (1) they do not have easy access to all relevant information; (2) in uncertain environments they are unable to calculate realistic probabilities of outcomes; and (3) they do not have the information-processing capability of computing the optimal outcomes even if they had all the necessary information. Herbert A. Simon (1955) has argued that consumers and other economic agents are "satisficers" (a term he coined) rather than optimizers, in that they try to achieve satisfactory rather than optimal outcomes, and that they have, at best, bounded rationality. Because what is satisfactory is not as well defined as what is optimal, this approach has led to research on how consumers actually behave, using survey and experimental data. This research suggests that actual consumer behavior can deviate from what is considered optimizing behavior. For example, consumers give more weight to actual money costs than to opportunity costs (contrary to much of consumer theory), are more averse to gains than to losses, give greater weight to their own experiences and those of others that they know personally than to more objective data in making decisions in uncertain situations, and are myopic about the future.

Third, the notion that consumers have exogenously given preferences over commodity bundles flies in the face of evidence that people are affected by advertising, that they form habits that are difficult to break, and that they are affected by the behavior of other consumers. Many of these ideas can be incorporated into consumption theory by modifying it suitably. For example, it has been argued that a consumer's utility depends not only on the absolute level of consumption of the consumers, but also on what he or she consumes relative to other consumers (especially peers), and this may occur because of information issues, network externalities, and status. Although this modification can be made within the optimizing framework of consumer theory, it may have implications very different from it. For example, individual optimization may be inconsistent with social optimality (i.e., everyone could be better off if they consumed less and enjoyed more leisure, but they are prevented from achieving this outcome because they value their relative consumption level), and people may not be significantly (or even not at all) better off with significant increases in consumption (as mentioned earlier) when others consume more as well (Frank 1999).

SEE ALSO *Business; Consumption Function; Cooperatives; Firm; Labor Supply; Venture Capital*

BIBLIOGRAPHY

Allen, Roy G. D. 1934. A Reconsideration of the Theory of Value. *Economica* 1: 196–219.

Barten, Anton P., and Volker Böhm. 1982. Consumer Theory. In *Handbook of Mathematical Economics*, eds. Kenneth J. Arrow and Michael D. Intriligator, vol. 2, 381–429. Amsterdam: North-Holland.

Becker, Gary. 1962. Irrational Behavior and Economic Theory. *Journal of Political Economy* 70: 1–13.

Davenant, Charles. 1699. *An Essay Upon the Probable Methods of Making a People Gainers in the Balance of Trade.* London: J. Klapton. Reprinted in *The Political and Commercial Works of That Celebrated Writer Charles D'Avenant Relating to the Trade and Revenue of England.* New York: Gregg, 1967.

Elster, John, ed. 1986. *The Multiple Self.* Cambridge, U.K.: Cambridge University Press.

Frank, Robert. 1999. *Luxury Fever: Why Money Fails to Satisfy in an Era of Excess.* New York: Free Press.

Hicks, John R. 1934. A Reconsideration of the Theory of Value. *Economica* 1: 52–76.

Pareto, Vilfredo. [1909] 1971. *Manual of Political Economy.* Trans. A. S. Schwier. New York: Augustus M. Kelley.

Samuelson, Paul A. 1938. A Note on the Pure Theory of Consumer's Behavior. *Economica* 5: 61–71.

Simon, Herbert A. 1955. A Behavioral Model of Rational Choice. *Quarterly Journal of Economics* 69: 99–118.

Slutsky, Eugene E. [1915] 1952. On the Theory of the Budget of the Consumer. In *Readings in Price Theory*, eds. K. E. Boulding and George J. Stigler, 27–56. Chicago: Richard D. Irwin.

Stigler, George J. 1950. The Development of Utility Theory. *Journal of Political Economy* 58: 307–327, 373–396.

Amitava Krishna Dutt

CONSUMER PROTECTION

Typically, competition aligns the interests of producers with those of consumers. Consumers want higher quality and less costly products, and producers have an incentive to provide them because, if they do not, their rivals will. However, this alignment can break down in a variety of circumstances. For example, if consumers lack information about quality or price, they can end up purchasing products they would not have otherwise wanted. If there are enough uninformed consumers, producers may have the incentive to set prices that are too high or quality that is too low.

Consumer protection laws and regulations are designed to realign the incentives of producers with the goals of consumers by preventing certain kinds of firm behavior, like deceptive advertising, and by mandating others, like information disclosures. However, these regulations also raise costs, so assessing whether consumers are better off under these regulations requires careful benefit-cost analysis.

For example, in 2005 the European Commission required that airlines compensate passengers in the event of canceled flights, regardless of the cause. So when airlines sell tickets, they must bundle what amounts to trip insurance with the tickets. Consumers are better off if the price of airline tickets goes up by less than the value that consumers place on the trip insurance. But if some consumers value trip insurance while others do not, then unbundling tickets from insurance may be a better solution, as it allows those consumers who do not value the flight insurance to purchase tickets without it. Finally, there is the consideration of safety. If airlines were forced to pay more for canceled flights, one would expect to see more flights in bad weather, with a corresponding decrease in safety. Balancing all of these considerations is necessary to determine whether the regulation helps or hurts consumers.

Consumer protection agencies want to enforce regulations and laws where there is the biggest net benefit, and this has led them to focus most of their enforcement resources on prosecuting deception. If sellers misrepresent their products or services, mislead consumers about the terms of the bargain, or unilaterally try to change those terms postpurchase, then transactions can occur that reduce welfare. Such behavior is most likely where products are infrequently purchased, where claimed characteristics of the product are not verifiable by consumers or rival sellers at low cost, where seller reputations are unimportant for profitable sales, or where buyers are particularly vulnerable or gullible. Governments focus much of their consumer protection efforts on such markets. In this role, government can act as an efficient agent for the mass of consumers who might have suffered injury, but do not pursue individual legal remedies because of the cost. Governments attempt to obtain remedies that will correct the wrong, and also efficiently deter future violations by the offending firm (called specific deterrence) and others (called general deterrence).

Beyond simply deterring deception, consumer protection actions can sometimes improve market outcomes through the provision of information (e.g., health warnings by governments or by firms), by development of standard metrics that make consumer shopping and market competition more efficient (e.g., uniform interest rate calculations), or by regulating the conditions for sale of valuable, but potentially unsafe, products or services (e.g., minimum quality standards for drugs, or vehicle tires). Also, in instances of extreme consumer susceptibility, governments sometimes intervene to regulate the terms of implicit or explicit contracts (e.g., "at need" funeral purchases, unmonitored marketing to children, or mandatory waiting periods for finalizing mortgages).

Early-twenty-first-century changes in consumer protection laws and enforcement have been caused by the migration of advertising away from magazines and newspapers to broadcast radio and TV, cable, direct mail, telephones, and the Internet. Because the newer media span the globe and because retail marketing by distant sellers has become more common, consumer protection has become an international and multilingual endeavor, with cross-border partnerships being formed by regulators from different nations. Law revisions are designed to more efficiently deter deception, but some are aimed at ensuring consumer privacy. One of the most effective efforts is the 2003 Do Not Call rule that allowed U.S. consumers to choose to avoid a large portion of marketing calls. By 2005 more than 100 million Americans chose to have their phone number included on the list, allowing them to avoid unwanted telemarketing calls.

In the United States, consumer protection laws began in the early 1900s, by protecting competitors—not consumers—from damage resulting from rivals' deceptive claims. Over time, the law became more centered on harm to consumers, but the fear of monopoly power was often the only effect economists considered. Systematic thought about the economics of consumer issues began with George Stigler's 1961 paper inviting academics to think about how information and advertising might play a positive role in shaping market outcomes. At the same time, economist, social reformer, and U.S. Senator Paul H. Douglas (D-IL) drafted one of the first major consumer information rules—the Truth in Lending Act—that was enacted by Congress in 1968. A decade later, a small group of economists began working on consumer issues at the U.S. Federal Trade Commission.

SEE ALSO *Consumerism*

BIBLIOGRAPHY

Akerlof, George A. 1970. The Market for "Lemons": Quality Uncertainty and the Market Mechanism. *Quarterly Journal of Economics* 84: 488–500.

Beales, Howard, Richard Craswell, and Steven Salop. 1981. The Efficient Regulation of Consumer Information. *Journal of Law and Economics* 24: 491–539.

Becker, Gary S. 1968. Crime and Punishment: An Economic Approach. *Journal of Political Economy* 76: 169–217.

Butters, Gerard R. 1977. Equilibrium Distribution of Sales and Advertising Prices. *Review of Economic Studies* 44: 465–491.

Calfee, John E., and Janis K. Pappalardo. 1989. *How Should Health Claims for Foods Be Regulated? An Economic Perspective.* Washington, DC: Federal Trade Commission.

Darby, Michael A., and Edi Karni. 1973. Free Competition and the Optimal Amount of Fraud. *Journal of Law and Economics* 16: 67–88.

Ippolito, Pauline M. 1986. Consumer Protection Economics: A Selective Survey. In *Empirical Approaches to Consumer Protection Economics.* Ed. Pauline M. Ippolito and David T. Scheffman. Washington, DC: Federal Trade Commission.

Ippolito, Pauline M., and Alan D. Mathios. 1990. Information, Advertising, and Health Choices: A Study of the Cereals Market. *RAND Journal of Economics* 21 (3): 459–480.

Klein, Benjamin, and Keith B. Leffler. 1981. The Role of Market Forces in Assuring Contractual Performance. *Journal of Political Economy* 89: 615–641.

Nelson, Phillip. 1970. Information and Consumer Behavior. *Journal of Political Economy* 78: 311–329.

Peltzman, Sam. 1973. An Evaluation of Consumer Protection Legislation: The 1962 Drug Amendments. *Journal of Political Economy* 81: 1049–1091.

Polinsky, A. Mitchell, and William P. Rogerson. 1983. Products Liability, Consumer Misperceptions, and Market Power. *Bell Journal of Economics* 14: 581–589.

Posner, Richard A. 1973. *Regulation of Advertising by the FTC.* Washington, DC: American Enterprise Institute.

Posner, Richard A. 2003. *Economic Analysis of Law.* 6th ed. New York: Aspen Publishers.

Shavell, Steven. 1980. Strict Liability versus Negligence. *Journal of Legal Studies* 9: 1–25.

Stigler, George J. 1961. The Economics of Information. *Journal of Political Economy* 69: 213–225.

Luke M. Froeb
Paul A. Pautler

CONSUMER SOVEREIGNTY

SEE *Value, Subjective.*

CONSUMER SURPLUS

Consumer surplus, following the French economist and engineer Jules Dupuit (1804–1866) and the British economist Alfred Marshall (1842–1924), is a monetary measure of the benefits to consumers from being able to buy what they want at the going price. It is used to evaluate the gains from policy changes: cost-benefit analysis recognizes that much of the benefit may accrue in the form of surplus and so is not measured in actual market transactions. Consumer surplus is traditionally depicted as the area below the (ordinary, or Marshallian) demand curve and above the horizontal line representing price.

To illustrate, suppose that there are ten people whose individual reservation values (maximum willingness to pay) range from $10 down to $1 in one-dollar decrements. All consumers with reservation values above the market price buy, and each buyer enjoys a surplus equal to his or her reservation value minus the amount paid. So, if the market price is $6.50, four consumers buy, with surpluses ranging from $0.50 to $3.50, for a total (aggregate) consumer surplus of $8. This consumer surplus equals the gross benefit ($34 in the above example) minus consumer expenditures. A drop in price to $5.50 raises consumer surplus to $12.50: $1 extra accrues to each previous consumer directly from the price reduction, and one more consumer (who then enjoys $0.50 surplus) is induced to buy.

The same idea applies to a consumer buying several units of a good (or when many consumers each buy several units). Suppose the demand system described above represents the valuations of a single consumer for successive units purchased: the consumer will buy until the value of another unit falls below the price charged. At a price of $6.50, she buys four units and enjoys $8 in surplus. A price drop to $5.50 will induce her to buy more. Her surplus gain is $4.50 (more than the $4 saved on the previous four units). While the marginal unit purchased is valued at the price, all other (inframarginal) units provide surplus. Total consumer surplus aggregates these gains over all units purchased by all buyers.

The simple procedure described above gives the exact measure of the true benefit to consumers only under certain restrictive conditions. If there are "wealth effects," the consumer's willingness to pay for the marginal unit changes with the amount paid for the previous units. There is, thus, not just one measure of surplus change, but many. Most prominent are the *equivalent variation* (the additional money needed to make the consumer just as well off as the price change) and the *compensating variation* (the money that could be taken away after the price change to leave the consumer as well off as before). The consumer surplus change is bracketed between the equivalent and compensating variations. Fortunately, for small changes or when the good in question attracts a small frac-

tion of expenditure, it has been shown that these three measures give similar results.

Consumer surplus counts $1 in surplus the same irrespective of how deserving the recipient might be. Critics argue that it overemphasizes the preferences of the wealthy, insofar as they have greater willingness to pay. Defenders of consumer surplus argue that it is useful in measuring economic efficiency, while redistribution issues should be addressed separately.

SEE ALSO *Producer Surplus*

BIBLIOGRAPHY

Dupuit, Jules. On the Measurement of the Utility of Public Works. [1844] 1952. *International Economic Papers* 2: 83–110.

Marshall, Alfred. [1890] 1920. *Principles of Economics*. 8th ed. New York and London: Macmillan.

Willig, Robert D. Consumer's Surplus without Apology. 1976. *American Economic Review* 66: 589–597.

Simon P. Anderson
Maxim Engers

CONSUMERISM

Consumerism may be defined as a belief system that promotes high and rising levels of the personal consumption of material goods and services among a large segment of the population, ascribing to consumption a central role in promoting individual happiness. It is also associated with the view that the main goal of the economy should be to meet the (freely chosen) consumption decisions of people in the most efficient way.

It can be argued that economic development necessarily leads to consumerism. According to this view, the inherent competitiveness of people—which makes them try to stay ahead of, or at least to keep up with, the consumption of others—induces people to consume far beyond what is necessary for them, and to give consumption more importance in their lives when economic advancement makes this possible. This does not follow, however, since people need not increase their consumption significantly or attach much importance to consumption if they react to economic growth by increasing their leisure time (rather than to producing and consuming more) or to devoting more resources to nonrival consumption goods (like museums and public parks), or if they compete in spheres other than consumption. This appears to be confirmed by the fact that despite the wide reach of consumerism in the contemporary world, there are significant variations in its intensity (between, say, the

United States and Europe). Indeed, explanations of the emergence and growth of consumerism in the past have been sought in the weakening of traditional religious values and in the efforts of rising commercial and industrial interests to increase their profits by increasing the demand for their products. The spread of consumerism around the world, including to less-developed countries, can be explained in terms of globalization made possible in large part by technological changes that allow the easier spread of information (thereby strengthening what has been called the international demonstration effect) and by free market economic policies (such as free trade and fewer labor market regulations, which seek to allow consumers to obtain goods at lower prices).

Consumerism has been criticized by many, including religious leaders, moral philosophers, socialists, and environmentalists, for: diverting people's attention from arguably more noble goals, such as spiritual development; saving less and thereby slowing down economic growth that can benefit society; making people self-centered and willing to do less for others in society who are less fortunate than themselves; exacerbating inequality by inducing the poor to reduce saving and human capital formation, become more indebted, and accept an inequitable socioeconomic order; and harming the natural environment. However, it has also had its defenders. The critics have been dismissed as elitist in not recognizing the democratic appeal of the spread of consumerism and its ability to give pleasure, even of an artistic and spiritual kind, and of failing to show why some goods are necessities and others are luxuries. Consumerism has been applauded for providing people with incentives for hard work to improve their lives, for keeping profits up by causing a growth in the aggregate demand for goods and services, and for being the driving force for economic growth and for all the benefits it brings about.

While much of this debate has focused on the appropriate meaning of "the good life" and on the effects of consumerism on society, a recent literature, making use of self-reported happiness surveys, addresses directly whether higher levels of income and consumption actually make people happier by their own reckoning. This literature suggests that although the rich report higher levels of happiness than the poor in a given society, across countries increases in material well-being do not make people significantly happier beyond a certain threshold level of real income, and that in economically advanced countries increases in income and consumption do not significantly increase happiness. The finding that the growth of luxury consumption has not led to increases in happiness has been explained in a number of ways. Since people get habituated to higher levels of living and consumption norms, and because more goods and services are required to satisfy the same needs as average income increases (for instance people need better clothing to be socially acceptable), higher actual levels of consumption need not make them happier. To the extent that people consume more to obtain higher status by consuming more than others they expend more effort and experience more stress without improving their position because others do the same. The quest for more consumption leaves people less time to enjoy what they consume, less time for friends and family, and causes them to lose social connectedness, having an adverse effect on their happiness.

SEE ALSO *Conspicuous Consumption; Consumer; Consumer Protection; Consumption; Hidden Persuaders; Relative Income Hypothesis; Subliminal Suggestion; Want Creation*

BIBLIOGRAPHY

Crocker, David C., and Toby Linden, eds. 1998. *Ethics of Consumption: The Good Life, Justice and Global Stewardship.* Lanham, MD: Rowman and Littlefield.

Frank, Robert. 1999. *Luxury Fever: Why Money Fails to Satisfy in an Era of Excess.* New York: Free Press.

Scitovsky, Tibor. [1976] 1992. *The Joyless Economy: An Inquiry into Human Satisfaction and Consumer Dissatisfaction.* New York: Oxford University Press.

Stearns, Peter N. 2001. *Consumerism in World History: The Global Transformation of Desire.* London: Routledge.

Twitchell, James B. 2002. *Living It Up: America's Love Affair with Luxury.* New York: Columbia University Press.

Veblen, Thorstein. [1899] 1998. *The Theory of the Leisure Class: An Economic Study of Institutions.* Amherst, NY: Prometheus.

Amitava Krishna Dutt

CONSUMPTION

The study of consumption is important in many fields of social science, including anthropology, sociology, economics, and psychology. A key definition of *consumption* is one that reflects our use of the term in daily life. That is, consumption may be defined as the personal expenditure of individuals and families that involves the selection, usage, and disposal or reuse of goods and services. In this respect, we are all consumers, choosing and using goods and services, which we pay for with earnings, savings, or credit.

As late as the last century, the term was primarily linked to disease: *consumption* was another term used to describe pulmonary tuberculosis (TB). Because of this fact, as well as the conventional use of the term to designate wasting or destruction, *consumption* had a decidedly negative connotation until the middle to late twentieth century.

While there is a tendency to associate consumption of goods and services with modernity, where it has become central to the lives of individuals and the social and economic lives of communities and societies, consumption is part of any social order. In premodern societies, there was typically a closer relationship between the producer and consumer: for instance, the cows of a particular farmer produced milk, some of which he kept for his own use and some of which he may have traded to a neighbor in exchange for part of her crop of soybeans. Production and consumption were closely partnered and reflected an economic system constructed on subsistence production and precapitalist means of exchange, such as barter.

The capitalist economy is built on the relationship between production and consumption, and goods and services are exchanged for money and credit. In contrast to earlier economic forms, the distance between producer and consumer grows as the division of labor becomes more complex and fewer people grow their own food, make their own clothing, or receive education, protection, or other services from within their own family, clan, or other small group.

Classical economics, the product of eighteenth- and nineteenth-century thinkers like Adam Smith (1723–1790) and David Ricardo (1772–1823), theorized capitalist markets and argued for the power of the free market. Classical economics posited the notion of consumer rationality, assuming that consumers of goods and services are rational and spend money in ways that maximize satisfaction from purchases.

Another aspect of consumption theorized in economics is the phenomenon of underconsumption. In underconsumption theory, economic stagnation is fostered by an imbalance between consumer demand and the production of goods. Though underconsumption theory is not central in contemporary economics, it influenced both academic thinking and public policy in the early twentieth century. Beginning around this time, concerns about underconsumption spurred governmental intervention in the economy, particularly public-works spending, which was seen as central to putting disposable income into the hands of American consumers.

Economist John Kenneth Galbraith's (1908–2006) most widely recognized book, *The Affluent Society* (1958), offers a mid-twentieth-century perspective on economics and consumption. Galbraith proposed a corrective to the conventional theories of economics, which assumed a scarcity of resources. This scarcity, he suggested, justified increased private-sector production and limited government regulation and taxation. However, Galbraith believed the contemporary period on which he focused was characterized by an "affluent society" in which scarcity was not a central concern. As such, he posited that government economic practices were misguided and, in fact, fostered a paradoxical situation of private-sector affluence and public-sector squalor. That is, while private consumption grew, public spending on infrastructure projects, including parks and schools, diminished. Galbraith's support of public-sector spending has influenced liberal and neoliberal thinkers who followed him. Interestingly, the "affluent society" of which Galbraith wrote and about which he was concerned consumed far less than the consumer society of the late twentieth and early twenty-first centuries.

While Marxist economic theory is commonly associated with concerns about capitalism and production, Karl Marx (1818–1883) did not neglect to recognize the function of consumption in capitalist society. In the *Grundrisse*, he argued that a condition of production in capitalism is "the discovery, creation, and satisfaction of new needs arising from society itself.... [Capitalism involves] the developing of a constantly expanding and more comprehensive system of different kinds of labor, different kinds of production, to which a constantly enriched system of needs corresponds" (Marx [1857–1858] 1973, p. 409). While Marx highlighted production as a driving process of industrial capitalism, consumption, whether driven by need (associated with the proletariat) or materialist desires (associated with the bourgeoisie), was a critical partner.

Though the perspectives of classical economists (the "bourgeois economists," according to Marx) and Marxists differ in many respects, they share a similar perspective on the valuation of consumables (goods and services). The labor theory of value, embraced by classical economists through the middle of the nineteenth century and central to Marxist economic theory, holds that the exchange value of a good or service is derived from the amount of labor (including labor expended on gathering raw materials and producing machinery) required to produce it. Marxist economics, however, adds that the profit derived by capitalist owners of the means of production comes from value added by workers to the consumable good but not paid to them in wages. Capitalist production, thus, is exploitative, as workers produce goods and surplus value is appropriated by the owners.

The labor theory of value has been challenged by social scientists in, among others, the fields of economics and sociology. For instance, the theory of subjective value challenges the notion of intrinsic value that is present in that theory by suggesting that value derives from the power of an object (or service) to meet a need or a desire. The value of a consumable, thus, may derive from variables such as its utility, its scarcity, or its status. Among sociologists, nineteenth-century French scholar Gabriel Tarde (1843–1904) was among the first to locate the value of goods in the intensity of consumer desire rather than in the production process. Contemporary sociologists have elaborated the point more fully, highlighting the power of modern marketing in creating desire for goods and services.

Sociologist George Ritzer has written extensively on consumption (and overconsumption) as a sociological artifact of modern society. He argues that modern states are characterized far less by production than by consumption. That is, while in earlier decades, the economies of countries like the United States were focused on production of goods, today many modern states produce few tangible goods (though they continue to produce intangible goods like knowledge and information). Rather, consumption is central to the national economy.

In *Enchanting a Disenchanted World*, Ritzer suggests that, in understanding the nexus between consumption, capitalism, and modernity, social scientists need to attend to "the new means of consumption," which he defines as "those things that make it possible for people to acquire goods and services and for the same people to be controlled and exploited as consumers" (1999, p. 57). Examples of the new means of consumption are shopping malls, cruise ships, and Las Vegas–style casinos and resorts. All of these are places that offer the consumer ample buying opportunities but, at the same time, operate as instruments of consumer control, as consumers are convinced to buy what they do not need, to believe that they need what they only want, and to spend beyond their means in order to achieve a sought-after emotional state or status. Even the physical layout of buying venues like supermarkets and malls is constructed with the aim of maximizing spending by fostering impulse buying and forcing consumers to forge a path past a plethora of enticing products or shops before finding the products they need, or even the exit.

In his 1899 book, *The Theory of the Leisure Class*, iconoclastic economist Thorstein Veblen (1857–1929) argued that in well-off societies spending operates as a means by which individuals establish social position. He coined the term *conspicuous consumption*, which he suggested was common among the nouveau riche, a class that emerged from the new wealth generated in nineteenth-century America by the second Industrial Revolution. In this period, the rich flaunted their good fortune with the public consumption of luxury items. In this cultural context, Veblen suggested that ostentatious displays of wealth, rather than honest productivity, showed one's success to society. Of the culture on which he wrote, he commented that "labor comes to be associated in men's habits of thought with weakness and subjection to a master. It is

therefore a mark of inferiority" ([1899] 1994, p. 41). That is, it was participation in consumption rather than participation in production (the labor force) that defined one's status in society.

French sociologist Pierre Bourdieu (1930–2002) approached the issue of consumption from another angle. He argued in *Distinction* (1984) that "taste" can be understood as a "field" of contestation. Within this field, "taste" is contested and those with greater resources have the power to define what is in good taste and bad taste. Those in the upper classes, for instance, have the opportunity to both learn and define what is in good taste. By comparison, those in the working class lack the knowledge or the means to exhibit the distinctive ("good") tastes of the upper class and are disadvantaged by their lack of what Bourdieu calls "cultural capital." Bourdieu is not suggesting that these categories of culture are objectively real. Rather, he is arguing that taste is a field of play in which those with more power are able to both define and act out "good taste."

In terms of consumption, the "taste" for burgers or *foie gras*, commercial action films or foreign movies, and mass-produced beer or fine wine, and the classes we associate with those choices, are socially determined but, like many other social phenomena, take on the appearance of being "natural." Consequently, argues Bourdieu, taste is a field in which class inequalities are socially produced and reproduced.

One aspect of consumption that is endemic in the United States and other economically advanced countries like Japan and Australia is competitive consumption. In the middle of the twentieth century, Americans, particularly those in the rapidly expanding suburbs of post–World War II America, were concerned with "keeping up with the Joneses." Economist James Duesenberry (1949), writing in this period, focused on the phenomenon of competitive consumption. The demographic, economic, and technological boom years of the postwar era made acquisition of new consumer goods like dishwashers and color televisions possible, and competitive consumption made their acquisition probable.

Consumption is powerfully influenced by marketing. While this idea is axiomatic today, the power of advertising was not always so widely recognized. In the mid-twentieth century, Vance Packard (1914–1996) illuminated the tactics and techniques of the advertising industry in *The Hidden Persuaders* (1957). Packard described the marketing of goods through the use of motivational research, subliminal advertising, and other subtle but effective methods of persuasion based in scientific study. Packard linked the imperative to sell to a massive tide of production that followed World War II: marketers recognized the importance of creating an imperative to consume that could take advantage of the rising tide of affluence (also recognized by Galbraith). Packard took a position against consumer manipulation, arguing that it was a "moral question."

As Packard recognized, in contemporary America, competitive consumption is heavily driven by the influence of the media. While the reference groups of the past included neighbors who commonly inhabited the same socioeconomic status, the reference groups of the late twentieth and early twenty-first century include those whose earnings may far outpace those of the average consumer. Economist Juliet Schor's *The Overspent American* (1998) posits that while consumption in early postwar America revolved around keeping up with neighborhood norms, reference groups have "stretched" to include workplace colleagues. The movement of more women into the workplace may have been a catalyst in the transformation of reference groups, as working families may have less time to attend to the habits and acquisitions of neighbors (if they know them at all). Further, reference groups are now also composed of "friends" who inhabit the fantasy worlds of television and films (she gives the example of the popular American television program, *Friends*, on which stylishly dressed twentysomethings inhabited well-appointed apartments in New York City that few of their "real world" contemporaries could afford). Modern efforts to keep up with one's reference groups are thus more costly and more likely to drive one into debt.

Following close behind Schor's careful social scientific dissection of modern consumption is Robert H. Frank's *Luxury Fever* (1999). Frank argues that the "luxury fever" that has gripped modern America is characterized by the pursuit of grander, flashier, more costly goods, ranging from backyard grills (he discovers a top-of-the-line grill that retails for $5,000, not including shipping and handling) to automobiles to megahomes. This pursuit, he notes, is embraced not only by the very rich, but also by consumers with far less disposable income as well, leading to low rates of saving and growing rates of debt. Frank argues that an altered "spending environment," in which expectations regarding one's own consumption or even one's gifts to others, is the product of the profligate spending of those at the top of the economic pyramid and the availability of extravagantly priced products. He elaborates the example of the grill: "The real significance of offerings like the $5,000 Viking-Frontgate Professional Grill … is that their presence makes buying a $1,000 unit seem almost frugal. As more people buy these upmarket grills, the frame of reference that defines what the rest of us consider an acceptable outdoor grill will inevitably continue to shift" (1999, p. 11). To mitigate the effects of the country's febrile state, Frank prescribes tax exemption for savings and the institution of a progressive consumption tax, arguing, as did Galbraith, that there needs to be greater attention given to public infrastructure spending, which falls by the wayside in a society obsessed with private consumption.

The use of advertising to create a "relationship" between material products and people has been examined by Jean Kilbourne. In *Can't Buy My Love* (2000), Kilbourne argues that advertisers seek to spur consumption by disseminating the message that products fulfill human needs for things like love, relationships, and respect. Young people are particularly susceptible to messages that promise that product consumption will give them emotional fulfillment. The message has ample opportunities to reach its audience: according to Kilbourne, the average American is exposed to no fewer than 3,000 advertising messages each day.

Social pressures for status, relentless advertising, and easily accessible credit can bring about hyperconsumption. Psychology recognizes hyperconsumption as a disorder, and the term *oniomania* (which comes from the Greek term *onios,* "for sale") is a label used to designate people obsessed with shopping (conventionally called *shopaholics*). Because the profligate spending of money and the consumption of luxury goods is not only socially acceptable, but often appears desirable, a shopping addiction is less likely to be taken as seriously as other addictions, such as gambling or alcoholism.

Consumption, and arguably even overconsumption, is not only acceptable in the social arena of modern American society, but it is also embraced. Consumer spending accounts for fully two-thirds of all economic activity in the United States. As such, in spite of the substantial debt carried by Americans in contrast to the rest of the developed world, public policy is largely favorable to sustained and even increased consumption. In the wake of the terrorist attacks of September 11, 2001, some political commentators embraced the term *market patriotism* to describe the federal government's entreaties to continue buying and spending.

Modern market patriotism represents an interesting contrast to the wartime sacrifices asked of previous generations of Americans. For instance, during World War II, Americans were entreated to carefully control consumption. External controls like rationing were supplemented by appeals to patriotism, including the Consumer's Victory Pledge signed by millions of American housewives: "As a consumer, in the total defense of democracy, I will … buy carefully. I will take good care of things I have. I will waste nothing."

Internationally, the United States has a low rate of both national and household savings, far below that of Western European countries, Japan, or China. This reflects, in part, the priority given by different states and individuals in the global community to savings and consumption, as well as adversity to debt.

While the study and theorization of consumption in the social sciences has been in existence for a long time, it has evoked the greatest interest in the decades of the late twentieth and early twenty-first centuries. The growth in consumption, both nationally and globally, correlates with a rise in studies and publications on consumption, consumerism, overconsumption, and the transformation of modern societies from producers to consumers.

SEE ALSO *Absolute Income Hypothesis; Conspicuous Consumption; Consumption Tax; Economics; Macroeconomics; Microeconomics; Permanent Income Hypothesis; Relative Income Hypothesis; Underconsumption*

BIBLIOGRAPHY

Bourdieu, Pierre. 1984. *Distinction: A Social Critique of the Judgement of Taste.* Trans. Richard Nice. Cambridge, MA: Harvard University Press.

Douglas, Mary, and Baron Isherwood. 1979. *The World of Goods: Towards an Anthropology of Consumption.* New York: Basic Books. Rev. ed. 1996. London: Routledge.

Duesenberry, James S. 1949. *Income, Saving, and the Theory of Consumer Behavior.* Cambridge, MA: Harvard University Press.

Frank, Robert H. 1999. *Luxury Fever: Why Money Fails to Satisfy in an Era of Excess.* New York: Free Press.

Galbraith, John Kenneth. 1958. *The Affluent Society.* Boston: Houghton Mifflin.

Kilbourne, Jean. 2000. *Can't Buy My Love: How Advertising Changes the Way We Think and Feel.* New York: Free Press.

Marx, Karl. [1857–1858] 1973. *Grundrisse.* New York: Vintage.

Packard, Vance. 1957. *The Hidden Persuaders.* New York: McKay.

Ritzer, George. 1999. *Enchanting a Disenchanted World: Revolutionizing the Means of Consumption.* Thousand Oaks, CA: Pine Forge. 2nd ed. 2005.

Schor, Juliet. 1998. *The Overspent American: Why We Want What We Don't Need.* New York: HarperPerennial.

Smith, Adam. [1776] 1991. *The Wealth of Nations.* New York: Prometheus.

Veblen, Thorstein. [1899] 1994. *The Theory of the Leisure Class.* New York: Penguin.

Daina S. Eglitis

CONSUMPTION, CONSPICUOUS

SEE *Conspicuous Consumption.*

CONSUMPTION FUNCTION

The classical economists were concerned with the economic categories of *consumption, production,* and *exchange.* One description of the classical Say's Law is that it states that production and consumption are identical. From the perspective either of underconsumption or oversaving, one category is perceived as a limit of the other. In the hands of John Maynard Keynes, however, consumption became a function, relating aggregate consumption, C, mainly to aggregate disposable income, Y, defined as income less taxes and transfer payments. This equation has been called the *absolute income hypothesis* (AIH). Like a good gardener, Keynes weeded out many variables that could influence consumption, settling on disposable income as the most important one. Keynes wrote the implicit form of this relation as $C_w = \chi(Y_w)$. In another context, he held that $C = \varphi_1(W, Y)$, where the additional variable W represents the state of the news, a term that changes with long-term expectation.

The relation of consumption to income follows a psychological law stating that consumption increases with income but not by the same proportion. This law makes the consumption function a behavioral relationship that can be juxtaposed with data as opposed to a structural or identity equation. A testable linear form of the AIH is obtained by expanding the implicit relationship between consumption and income by the Taylor series, ignoring the nonlinear terms. The intercept, a, of the line captures *autonomous consumption*, that is, any consumption that is not induced by income. The slope of the line, $0 < dC/dY = b < 1$, is the *marginal propensity to consume* (MPC)—on average, the amount of an additional dollar that is consumed in a community. The Keynesian model uses the MPC to estimate a multiplier that predicts how a change in investment will boost GDP. By examining data for the United States, Keynes estimated the MPC to be between 60 and 70 percent.

The Keynesian consumption function sparked a new research program. For example, significant works by Milton Friedman on the permanent income hypothesis (PIH) and Franco Modigliani on the life cycle hypothesis (LCH) were in large part the catalysts for their Nobel Prizes in 1976 and 1985, respectively. The PIH-LCH models reconciled anomalies in the prediction of the AIH during the post–World War II period. The major anomaly was that the average propensity to consume was over 90 percent, whereas short-run MPC was between 60 and 70 percent. Modigliani and James Duesenberry reconciled the differences by postulating a previous peak income in the consumption function. Whereas Modigliani's work evolved into his LCH hypothesis, Duesenberry's relative income hypothesis (RIH) remained an example of external effects on consumption in line with Veblenesque norms; defined in terms such as *emulation, convention,* and *molding,* it holds that a person's consumption depends on the level and types of other people's consumption. RIH also holds that consumers would want to maintain a consumption pattern established by the highest income they had previously received. During a downswing phase of a business cycle, consumers experience a reduction in income but are hesitant to adjust their spending behavior away from what they had established during a previous peak period. Consumers prefer to draw down their savings or borrow in order to maintain their previous peak consumption. Only when they recover their previous peak level income will their consumption behavior change. The change is an unusual one, a sort of quantum leap or "ratchet" upward, perhaps due to pent-up demand during the downswing. This upward effect amounts to a reconciliation of the short- and long-run MPCs.

Robert Frank expanded and articulated the RIH paradigm in relation to the question of how current relative consumption will dominate future relative consumption. Parents who prefer to buy a house in a good school district now may be negatively affecting their future consumption after retirement. Conversely, spending now on a suit for a job interview may have a positive impact on future income. The experience of low relative consumption now may also set expectations for a low relative consumption in the future. Juliet Schor's "new consumerism" is also based on lifestyles and norms, and posits that consumers elevate their consumption to unsustainable levels that lead to mounting debts and bankruptcies, as well as longer working hours.

The LCH-PIH hypotheses advance consumption theory by introducing wealth or assets as well as income into the consumption function. In this scenario, consumers draw on their lifetime income and assets to smooth their consumption expenditures over their life cycle. We can speak of *permanent income*—changes in which have more significant effects on consumption than temporary or transitory changes in income. The two hypotheses have one major difference: Friedman made the income stream infinite, whereas Modigliani made the income stream finite. For instance, Modigliani estimated the consumption function as: $C = .766Y + .073A$. Here the short run MPC is 0.77, and if assets, A, are approximately five times income, while labor income is approximately 80 percent of income, then a long-run MPC of $0.98 = 0.8(.766Y) + 5(.073Y)$ is reached. Essentially, the presence of wealth in the AIH causes it to drift upward.

With the introduction of these hypotheses, the stage was set for a paradigmatic shift in the consumption function. Friedman estimated the PIH through a distributed lag model, which John Muth showed to be optimal under rational expectation assumptions. Because Friedman left the definition of income vague, Muth proceeded to measure permanent income by an exponentially moving average equal to the conditional expected value under rational expectations. Robert Lucas expanded the rational expectation concept by shifting the meaning of the consumption function from one relating consumption and income, to one relating permanent income and observed income. Robert Hall rescued the consumption function from that line of attack by postulating that only surprising events could be responsible for unexpected results. The model he specified maximizes the expected value of lifetime utility subject to an unchanging real interest rate. He presumed that consumers would make the ratios of marginal utilities for present and future consumption equal to the ratio of their prices. Hall tested his consumption function in the form $C_{t+1} = \lambda C_t + error_t$, a random walk model. Clive Granger referred to the consumption theory as "manna from heaven to macro-econometricians. It was easily stated and understood, and appears to be easy to test" (Granger 1999, pp. 42–43). In practical parlance, consumers will tend to adjust their individual consumption so that it will not differ from an expected level. This fact reinforces the underlying principle that consumers tend to smooth out spending over time, and that this practice relates to some uncertainty about income. Hall's model rendered the lagged income effect insignificant on consumption. If consumers have a quadratic utility function, then they will want to consume at the level where their future income will equal its mean value.

Marjorie Flavin, a student of Hall's, made two findings that furthered the development of the consumption function. One finding is that future consumption is sensitive to the previous level of consumption and can show a strong variation. Another finding is that the surprise element does not cause much variation in future consumption. John Campbell and Gregory Mankiw had the idea of combining these two findings in a convex way. This means that a proportion of the variation will be captured. Following Hall's model, the surprise element varies by a certain proportion and thus income will explain the less than proportional expected consumption. The combination of Hall's model with the LCH consumption equation resulted in a simple test of a change in consumption based on a change in disposable income. Since Hall's work, research on the consumption function has been escalating.

SEE ALSO *Absolute Income Hypothesis; Adaptive Expectations; Class, Leisure; Class, Rentier; Conspicuous Consumption; Consumerism; Consumption; Consumption Tax; Economics, Keynesian; Expectations, Rational; Life-Cycle Hypothesis; Macroeconomics; Permanent Income Hypothesis; Propensity to Consume, Marginal;*

Propensity to Save, Marginal; Relative Income Hypothesis; Underconsumption

BIBLIOGRAPHY

Campbell, John Y., and N. Gregory Mankiw. 1989. Consumption, Income, and Interest: Reinterpreting the Time Series Evidence. *NBER Macroeconomics Annual* 4: 185–216.

Duesenberry, James Stemble. 1949. *Income, Saving, and the Theory of Consumer Behavior.* Cambridge, MA: Harvard University Press.

Flavin, Marjorie A. 1981. The Adjustment of Consumption to Changing Expectation about Future Income. *Journal of Political Economy* 89 (5): 974–1009.

Frank, Robert H. 1999. *Luxury Fever: Why Money Fails to Satisfy in an Era of Excess.* New York: Free Press.

Frank, Robert H. 2005. Americans Save So Little, but What Can Be Done to Change That? *New York Times*, March 17.

Frank, Robert H. 2005. The Mysterious Disappearance of James Duesenberry. *New York Times*, June 9.

Friedman, Milton. 1957. *A Theory of the Consumption Function.* Trenton, NJ: Princeton University Press.

Granger, Clive W. J. 1999. *Empirical Modeling in Economics: Specification and Evaluation.* London: Cambridge University Press.

Hall, Robert E. 1978. Stochastic Implications of the Life Cycle-Permanent Income Hypothesis: Theory and Evidence. *Journal of Political Economy* 86 (6): 971–987.

Hall, Robert E. 1989. Consumption. In *Modern Business Cycle Theory*, ed. Robert J. Barro, 153–177. Cambridge, MA: Harvard University Press.

Keynes, John Maynard. 1936. *The General Theory of Employment, Interest, and Money.* London: Macmillan. Reprint, New York: St. Martin's Press, 1970.

Lucas, Robert E., Jr. 1976. Econometric Policy Evaluation: A Critique. In *Carnegie-Rochester Conference Series on Public Policy*, vol. 1, eds. Karl Brunner and Allan H. Meltzer, 19–46. Amsterdam: North-Holland.

Modigliani, Franco. [1949] 1980. Fluctuations in the Saving-Income Ratio: A Problem in Economic Forecasting. In *The Life Cycle Hypothesis of Saving*, vol. 2 of *The Collected Papers of Franco Modigliani*, eds. Andrew Abel and Simon Johnson, 4–40. Cambridge, MA: MIT Press.

Modigliani, Franco, and Richard Brumberg. [1954] 1980. Utility Analysis and the Consumption Function: An Interpretation of Cross-Section Data. In *The Life Cycle Hypothesis of Saving*, vol. 2 of *The Collected Papers of Franco Modigliani*, eds. Andrew Abel and Simon Johnson, 79–127. Cambridge, MA: MIT Press.

Muth, John F. 1960. Optimal Properties of Exponentially Weighted Forecasts. *Journal of the American Statistical Association* 55 (290): 299–306.

Romer, David. 1996. *Advanced Macroeconomics.* New York: McGraw-Hill.

Rymes, Thomas K. 1989. *Keynes' Lectures: 1932–35: Notes of a Representative Student.* Ann Arbor: University of Michigan Press.

Schor, Juliet B. 1998. *The Overspent American: Upscaling, Downshifting, and the New Consumer.* New York: Basic Books.

Lall Ramrattan
Michael Szenberg

CONTACT HYPOTHESIS

The contact hypothesis holds that contact between the members of different groups tends to reduce whatever negative intergroup attitudes may exist. The greater the contact, the less the antipathy. This idea is a crucial part of the broader theory that ethnic antagonism (as shown in prejudice, discrimination, and stereotyping) has psychological causes (misperception and projection) rather than social or economic causes (conflicts of interest).

The hypothesis can be traced far into the past, but it was given its contemporary form by Gordon W. Allport in *The Nature of Prejudice* (1954). He listed a large number of variables that could modify the effects of quantitative differences in contact. At the beginning of the twenty-first century, these are usually reduced to three or four key conditions for intergroup contact to reduce prejudice: equal status between the individuals having contact, common goals and cooperative interdependence in reaching them, and the support of social and institutional authorities for equal-status contact. In this qualified form, the hypothesis has figured prominently in discussions of racial desegregation in the United States.

As a conjecture about the effects of personal contact on individual attitudes, the hypothesis is easy to test, and the results of several hundred published studies are relatively easy to summarize. Regardless of whether the supposedly necessary conditions for favorable outcomes have been satisfied, greater contact is almost always associated, more or less strongly, with such outcomes (less prejudice and greater acceptance).

Difficulties arise when these results are extended from individuals to groups. It seems obvious that if an increase in contact improves the attitudes of individuals, it must do the same for the relations between groups, even if only a little. Nevertheless, both casual observation and careful studies suggest that there can be strong *positive* correlations at the group level between personal contact and negative attitudes. Comparisons of American states or counties on black-white contact and racial prejudice and discrimination provide the clearest illustrations of this relationship.

Allport's qualifications were meant to deal with this problem. If contact reduces prejudice, how could there be more of it in the South (at least in the 1950s) than in the

North or West? Under favorable conditions, he reasoned, more contact means less prejudice, but under unfavorable conditions (such as in the South), contact increases prejudice. As noted above, research at the individual level has not supported this view. Contact generally reduces prejudice, regardless of the situation.

An alternative approach starts from the assumption that different processes can prevail at the individual and group levels. As H. D. Forbes has shown in *Ethnic Conflict* (1997), the apparently contradictory correlations can be explained by a theory that distinguishes levels of analysis rather than situations or conditions of contact. When only individuals are compared, the standard correlation appears, but when all the individuals in an area are averaged and compared with all the individuals in another area of greater or less contact, generally speaking, the relationship is reversed. This approach is consistent with the contact hypothesis as a generalization about individuals, but it deprives it of much of its broader significance for social theory and public policy. It is not surprising, therefore, that recent reviews of the relevant literature still show a virtually undiminished allegiance to Allport's classic formulation, despite its empirical shortcomings.

SEE ALSO *Discrimination; Race; Racism; Segregation*

BIBLIOGRAPHY

Allport, Gordon W. 1954. *The Nature of Prejudice.* Reading, MA: Addison-Wesley.

Brewer, Marilynn B., and Samuel L. Gaertner. 2001. Toward Reduction of Prejudice: Intergroup Contact and Social Categorization. In *Blackwell Handbook of Social Psychology: Intergroup Processes*, ed. Rupert Brown and Samuel L. Gaertner. Oxford: Blackwell.

Forbes, H. D. 1997. *Ethnic Conflict: Commerce, Culture, and the Contact Hypothesis.* New Haven, CT: Yale University Press.

H. D. Forbes

CONTANGO

The term *contango* refers to a case where the futures price exceeds the expected future spot price of the underlying commodity. Futures prices are the prices of futures contracts for the commodity. Expected future spot prices are the prices of the commodity in the spot market that are expected to prevail in the future. Consequently, the futures price will fall to the spot price before the contract maturity date. This scenario is established under the expectation hypothesis, which suggests that futures prices are determined by market expectations. The opposite pattern, called *backwardation,* occurs when the futures price falls short of the expected future spot price. In this instance, the future rises toward the expected future spot price.

The relationship between the futures price and the expected future spot price depends on the net hedging position. Traders in the futures market can be classified into hedgers and speculators. Hedgers have a preexisting risk associated with a commodity and enter the market to reduce that risk, while speculators trade in the hope of profit. Hedgers, taken as a group, may be either long (i.e., they buy more than they sell) or short (i.e., they sell more than they buy). If hedgers are net short, speculators must be net long so that the market reaches equilibrium. To entice speculators, the futures price must be less than the expected future spot price and rise over time; hence the futures market exhibits backwardation. Conversely, if hedgers are net long, speculators must be net short. The futures price must lie above expected future spot price and fall over time to compensate the speculators, leading to contango.

An alternative definition relies upon the cost-of-carry arbitrage argument. Specifically, contango is referred to the case where the futures price exceeds the spot price. Moreover, the price of the futures contract with a distant maturity exceeds that with a nearby maturity. Conversely, backwardation refers to the situation in which futures price is less than the spot price; and the further away the contract maturity is, the smaller the futures price is.

In an efficient, frictionless market, to preclude arbitrage profits futures price must equal the spot price compounded at the risk-free rate, plus the cost of carry, which is future value of the storage costs minus the benefits (also called *convenience yield*) over the life of the contract. Because the cost of carry can be either positive or negative (depending upon the magnitude of the benefits), the futures price can be greater or less than the spot price. In reality, the principles of the cost-of-carry place at best a no-arbitrage bound on the futures prices. Within the bound, expectations are critical in establishing futures prices.

Generally, buyers prefer to receive the commodities right away, whereas sellers need time to produce. Consequently, the spot price tends to be larger than the futures price and backwardation is normally expected. Empirical investigations suggest that backwardation prevails in agricultural commodity and energy markets and contango occurs in currency markets. Nonetheless, the market may revert from backwardation to contango and vice versa from time to time. The financial loss of Metallgesellschaft Refining and Marketing (MGRM), Inc. in 1993 was partially due to contango that prevailed in unleaded gasoline and heating oil futures markets.

SEE ALSO *Hedging*

BIBLIOGRAPHY

Kolb, Robert W. 2000. *Futures, Options, and Swaps.* Malden, MA: Blackwell Publishers.

Smithson, Charles W. 1998. *Managing Financial Risk.* New York: McGraw-Hill.

Donald Lien
Mei Zhang

CONTEMPT

Contempt is a universal human emotion. While there are minor differences among emotion theorists and researchers, there is general consensus about the features of contempt. First, contempt is an interpersonal emotion; that is, it occurs in social situations, when people are interacting with or observing others. Second, it involves a negative evaluation of another person's behavior, which in and of itself signals one's sense of self-importance relative to others. Third, it involves feelings of moral superiority over the other person—that is, the feeling that the person is lower or unworthy. Fourth, it involves positive feelings about oneself.

Contempt is often confused with other emotions, particularly anger and disgust. Research, however, has demonstrated that contempt has its own unique facial expression—a unilateral curl and/or tightening of the lip corner, but only on one side of the face. This expression often occurs with a slight head raise and tilt, to give the appearance that one is "looking down one's nose" at the other, and/or turning away at the same time. Studies have also shown that individuals may not use the word "contempt" very frequently, and are generally not able to give a definition of it that includes the various components described above. Yet, most individuals certainly understand the situations in which it is elicited, and can reliably match the universal facial expression of contempt with those situations.

One of the functions of contempt is to create or maintain a social hierarchy. Being contemptuous of another person signifies one's judgment of the other person's social rank relative to one's own. Contempt prepares one to establish one's dominance in the hierarchy. Expressing that emotion through one's facial expressions, demeanor, or behaviors sends signals to others of one's intentions to establish hierarchical superiority. Recipients of those signals may either acquiesce, thereby conferring status to the contemptuous person, or they may prepare themselves for dominance struggles, which may set the stage for a new hierarchy.

Another function of the emotion of contempt is to validate one's self-worth. Although contempt is normally considered by many people to be a negative emotion, in reality contempt involves positive feelings about one's own self-worth. Thus, contempt may feel good, even though the situation that elicits it may be viewed as a negative one. Indeed, it may be important for all humans to validate their feelings of self-worth in this manner from time to time.

Although there is a class of emotions that humans share with other animals, there is some evidence to suggest that contempt may be an emotion that is unique to humans. This may be because contempt involves evaluations of one's moral superiority over others. Complex cognitive abilities are required in order for this evaluation to occur, particularly the ability to know that other people are intentional agents (i.e., they do things because they are motivated to do so), and the ability to evaluate the actions of others according to agreed-upon cultural norms and mores. These cognitive abilities exist in humans, but not other animals.

Contempt has unique interpersonal effects. Because contempt signals one's moral superiority over another person, it can lead to destructive outcomes in some social relationships. For example, research on distressed married couples has shown that if contempt is expressed by one member of the couple, especially the husband, when discussing areas of major disagreement, the couple is more likely to be in trouble, report greater marital dissatisfaction, report greater periods of marital separation, and experience greater health problems.

Contempt also has important intergroup effects. It serves to differentiate ingroups from outgroups, and helps individuals to depersonalize others. The depersonalization of others makes it easier for collective violence to occur, as it gives people permission to do unto others what they would normally be restrained from doing. Political leaders in the midst of war often describe the enemy with contempt-related words and phrases, suggesting that the enemy is "beneath" members of their culture, and somehow "unworthy." These feelings may be necessary to provoke humans to engage in collective violence against others. Thus, an analysis of contempt may play a major role in understanding intergroup conflict.

SEE ALSO *Genocide; Humiliation; Shame; Violence*

BIBLIOGRAPHY

Ekman, Paul, and Wallace V. Friesen. 1986. A New Pan-Cultural Facial Expression of Emotion. *Motivation and Emotion* 10 (2): 159–168.

Gottman, John M., Robert W. Levenson, and Erica Woodin. 2001. Facial Expressions during Marital Conflict. *Journal of Family Communication* 1 (1): 37–57.

Matsumoto, David, and Paul Ekman. 2004. The Relationship among Expressions, Labels, and Descriptions of Contempt. *Journal of Personality and Social Psychology* 87 (4): 529–540.

David Matsumoto

CONTENT VALIDITY

SEE *Validity, Statistical.*

CONTINGENCY THEORY

SEE *Organization Theory.*

CONTINUITY THEORIES

SEE *Stages of Development.*

CONTRACEPTION

The Fourth World Conference on Women, held in Beijing in 1995, reinforced that all human beings have the right to "decide freely and responsibly the number and spacing and timing of their children and to have the information and means to do so, and the right to attain the highest standard of sexual and reproductive health" (para. 95). A discussion of contraception provides us with an understanding of how access to comprehensive family planning services can improve the lives of women, men, and children around the world.

Contraception, or *birth control,* is the deliberate prevention of conception by hormones, devices, surgery, or avoiding intercourse during a woman's fertile time of the month. *Family planning* is the intentional decision on the number and spacing of children a couple will bear.

According to the World Health Organization (WHO), there are approximately 123 million women, mostly in developing countries, who are not using contraception. Some of the reasons include poor access to comprehensive services, inadequate information, male partner disapproval, and fears about side effects and safety. Religious beliefs and public policies also play an important role in methods that are available to couples in both developing and developed nations.

RELIGION AND PUBLIC POLICY

Humans have been using birth control from the earliest times. Ancient Islamic texts, Jewish writings, and Hindu sacred scriptures all mentioned that herbs could be used as temporary contraceptives. Modern religious stances vary according to their definition of the place of sex within marriage; for example, the Catholic Church prohibits any artificial means of birth control because it believes that the sole purpose of sexual intercourse is procreation. Some Christian fundamentalists, Evangelicals, and Anglicans share this view. Orthodox Judaism permits female contraceptives only for health reasons; while Conservative and Reform views leave the decision to the married couple, as does Christianity's Eastern Orthodox Church. The Islamic faith has wide variations on attitudes toward birth control, but despite this, procreation is emphasized as religious duty. There is no prohibition to birth control in Hinduism. As noted by Kathleen O'Grady in her 1999 article "Contraception and Religion, a Short History," the two common concerns of all major religions are fear of illicit sex and immorality, and destruction of the family. Particularly among non-Western religions, the worry is that liberal family planning policies could encourage Western modes of living, not only destroying the family, but family values as well. Some Christian fundamentalists in the United States agree with this stance. On the other hand, women's rights activists argue that prohibiting birth control is a fundamental way to control women and keep them dependent on men.

National and international public policy also plays a role with respect to sponsoring or funding reproductive health services, and policies are modified with changes in national leadership. In the United States, for example, President George W. Bush instituted a global "gag" rule regarding abortion in 2001. This means that foreign agencies, such as the WHO, no longer receive funding if they counsel women about abortion, consequently affecting family planning programs as well.

HISTORY OF CONTRACEPTION AND CURRENT METHODS

Despite religious decrees about contraception, there are many references that document three major methods that go as far back as ancient Greece: the use of herbal remedies as abortifacients, coitus interruptus (withdrawal of the penis from the vagina before ejaculation, hereafter referred to as *withdrawal*), and abstinence. Condoms were described as protection against sexually transmitted infections (STIs) in the early sixteenth century. Rubber condoms became available in the United States in the nineteenth century along with cervical caps, diaphragms, metal pessaries, and male and female sterilization. The birth control pill revolutionized contraception with its

Birth control methods

General Category	Method	Comments
Physiologic Methods (also called Natural Family Planning)	abstinence, withdrawal, fertility awareness, lactational amenorrhea	• Abstinence (not having penile-vaginal intercourse) is the only method that is 100% effective • Physiologic methods are not as effective as hormonal methods, but may fit a couple's cultural beliefs • Do not have systemic side effects.
Barrier Methods	male condom, female condom, diaphragm, Lea's Shield, cervical cap, vaginal sponge	• More effective than physiologic • Latex male condom is protective against STI/HIV
Sterilization	vasectomy; tubal ligation, tubal occlusion implants	• Permanent method • Highly effective
Hormonal methods	combined oral contraceptives (birth control pill), patch, vaginal ring, injectables, progestin only pills, implants, hormonal intrauterine device (IUD)	• Pills, patch, ring same effectiveness • Injectables more effective • IUD highly effective • Systemic side effects • Some contraindications
Other	copper intrauterine device	• Highly effective
Emergency contraception	Plan B	• Should be taken within 72 hours of sexual intercourse • Up to 89% effective in preventing pregnancy

Table 1

debut in 1959. There have been many advances in hormonal and non-hormonal contraceptive technologies for women in the last thirty years. Although research is being conducted on systemic methods for men, condoms, withdrawal, and sterilization remain the only contraceptive options for them. See Table 1 for current methods.

Male latex condoms, when used reliably and properly, are highly effective in preventing STIs and the human immunodeficiency virus (HIV). The female condom is the only female method that is effective in preventing pregnancy and STIs/HIV. People at risk for sexually transmitted infections (STIs) and/or HIV may be afforded dual protection against STI/HIV and pregnancy by using either male or female condoms. Using condoms and another form of birth control are even more effective measures of contraception.

INTERNATIONAL STRATEGIES

The World Health Organization has taken the lead on providing resources for international family planning since its inception in 1948. Paul Van Look, director of the WHO Department of Reproductive Health and Research, has stated that sexual and reproductive health are concerns for everyone at all stages of life and are fundamental to the economic and social development of nations, but also mirror basic inequalities such as wealth and gender. Women have been particularly harmed by lack of access to reproductive health services; research documents that the ability to space pregnancies impacts a woman's health and quality of life, as well as the health of her children. Family planning programs can also improve the economic and social situation of women's lives.

SEE ALSO *Abortion; AIDS; AIDS/HIV in Developing Countries, Impact of; Birth Control; Bush, George W.; Family Planning; Fundamentalism, Christian; Population Control; Population Studies; Reproduction; Sexuality; World Health Organization*

BIBLIOGRAPHY

Hatcher, Robert A. 2004. *Contraceptive Technology*, 18th ed. New York: Ardent Media.

O'Grady, Kathleen. 1999. Contraception and Religion, A Short History. In *The Encyclopedia of Women and World Religion*, ed. Serinity Young. New York: Macmillan Reference.

Potts, Malcolm, and Martha Campbell. 2002. History of Contraception. *Gynecology and Obstetrics* 6, ch. 8. http://big.berkeley.edu/ifplp.history.pdf.

United Nations Fourth World Conference on Women. 1995. *Action for Equality, Development and Peace*. Beijing: UN. http://www.un.org/womenwatch/daw/beijing/platform/health.htm#object1.

World Health Organization. 2006. *Medical Eligibility Criteria for Contraceptive Use*. Geneva: World Health Organization Press. http://www.who.int/reproductive-health.

Linda C. Andrist

CONTRACT CURVE

SEE *Welfare Economics.*

CONTRAS

SEE *Sandinistas.*

CONTROL CONSIOUSNESS

SEE *Consciousness.*

CONUNDRUM

Conundrums are problems of several types. They may be riddles with a pun for an answer. They may be puzzling problems that are complicated with intricate features. And they may be presented in the fashion of a rhetorical question, but with only conjecture for an answer.

Conundrums create paralyzing paradoxes or dilemmas. Psychologically, they are similar to approach-approach conflicts, such as a conflict known as Buridan's ass, which was posed by fourteenth-century philosopher Jean Buridan. An ass forced to choose between two equally luscious piles of hay that are equidistant starves to death. This is similar to the Malthusian dilemma, which states that helping the poor (humanitarian) may be increasing starvation (inhuman) when food supplies grow arithmetically while population grows geometrically.

The word conundrum is often used cynically to describe a puzzle that will probably never be solved because of a lack of data. The word conundrum is also used to describe a paradoxically difficult problem, such as the problem faced by economists in the second half of the twentieth century of how to achieve full employment without inflation.

Conundrums are puzzles that call for lateral thinking. In traditional logic puzzles an array chart can be used to sift through the possibilities in a systematic way. In lateral thinking, puzzles are not solved by a linear method but more in the fashion of brainstorming. Every possible piece of the riddle is identified and all solutions are posed as hypotheses with the mostly likely tested first.

Unlike traditional logic puzzles, conundrums use riddles with plays on words that seek to mystify or mislead, or a conundrum may pose a fanciful question that is answered with a pun. For example, the chicken conundrum: which came first, the chicken or the egg?

Conundrums pose problems that seem to defy solution because the problem is in the form of a dilemma wrapped in a riddle. Businesses, voluntary organizations, and other human enterprises often face problems that seem to be insolvable riddles. Should criminal wrongdoing be reported so that justice can be done, but also damage the institution by the exposure? What should be the treatment dilemmas for patients with complicated medical conditions when action "A" kills and inaction kills.

The structure of scientific revolutions has been one in which anomalies do not match the prevailing model. Eventually the anomalies defy the orthodox theory and create a conundrum. How is it possible for things to be both this and not this? What illumination travels like a wave and like a packet, but cannot be simultaneously both? Daylight dancing and waving until it delivers its quantum packets.

In the conundrums faced by political and economic decision-makers, the "play" aspect of conundrums suggests that game theories may help with solutions. Presumptions are abandoned and solutions are sought freely.

SEE ALSO *Economics; Kuhn, Thomas; Mystification; Paradigm; Revolutions, Scientific*

BIBLIOGRAPHY

Casati, Roberto, and Achille Varzi. 2004. *Insurmountable Simplicities: Thirty-Nine Philosophical Conundrums.* New York: Columbia University Press.

Katz, Leo. 1987. *Bad Acts and Guilty Minds: Conundrums of the Criminal Law.* Chicago: University of Chicago Press.

Kendzior, Lawrence J. 2004. *Conundrum: The Challenge of Execution in Middle-Market Companies.* New York: iUniverse, Inc.

Andrew J. Waskey

CONVENTIONS

SEE *Norms.*

CONVENTIONS, POLITICAL

SEE *Political Conventions.*

CONVERGENCE THEORY

As early as 1848 in the *Communist Manifesto* Karl Marx contended that human civilization developed in stages from pastoral to communist harmony, driven by an ineluctable historical dialectic. Capitalism from his perspective was an internally contradictory phase destined to be destroyed by a proletarian revolution ushering in a transitory socialist epoch before arriving at the end of history. Private property for Marx was the original sin that caused humanity's expulsion from the Garden of Eden. It provided a legal basis for concentrating community wealth in a few powerful hands, the emergence of market exploitation, the class struggle, and in Marx's view communism's inevitable triumph. Economies featuring private ownership of the means of production and markets consequently were intrinsically inferior (exploitive, inegalitarian, and unjust), and could not be blended with, or supersede, communism.

Vladimir Lenin and his Bolshevik successors accepted these concepts. Markets of various sorts could and did exist according to Soviet ideologists during the socialist interlude following the destruction of capitalism, but not in the final stage of historical dialectic.

However some Western liberals, like Francis Fukuyama, used similar historicist logic to reach the opposite conclusion. They argued that private ownership of the means of production was essential for individual utility maximization. Original sin for them was any power including the state that prevented people from achieving consumer sovereignty in the private sector, and democratic sovereignty over the provision of public goods. People's appreciation for the virtues of democratic free enterprise was weak before the eighteenth-century Scottish economist Adam Smith, but Fukuyama claimed that momentum is building and democratic capitalism will be the end of history (equated by many with globalization). As in the Marxist concept there is no room for blended solutions. Proletarian dictatorial democracy, and private propertyless capitalism are oxymorons. Capitalism and communism cannot converge, and socialism cannot be anything but transitory.

Consequently, Nobel Laureate Jan Tinbergen's assertion in the late 1950s and early 1960s that Soviet and Western market systems were immutably converging provoked a heated reaction from Marxists, democratic free enterprisers, and those who preferred various third ways. True believers of both Marxist and Fukuyamaist persuasions predictably rejected convergence out of hand, while those who supported cold war reconciliation without committing themselves to communism or democratic free enterprise welcomed Tinbergen's theory. Social democrats were especially pleased because Tinbergen's vision prefig-

ured the eventual triumph of the emerging European Union. The end of history would blend democracy, private ownership of the means of production, individual utility seeking, and markets with planning and state-supervised social justice. Of course, as the economist Ota Sik pointed out, the blending could go the other way, substituting authoritarianism for democracy, and Stalinist injustice for the welfare state, but supporters were confident that reason would preclude negative outcomes in the long run.

It is possible to dismiss Tinbergen's musing as partisan wishful thinking. Rationalist historicism is not physics. But convergence theory was predicated on a legitimate insight. Robert Dorfman, Paul Samuelson, and Robert Solow among others had used linear programming to demonstrate that there was a perfect duality between computopic (ideal, but unachievable computer based simulations of optimal market equilibria) planning and competitive market outcomes where planners' and consumers' preferences were identical. It followed that the gulf perceived by Marxist and democratic free enterprise theorists between communism and capitalism was only a matter of efficiency—the practical effectiveness of markets and plans—not a matter of technology or ideals. In an imperfect world where markets are sometimes exploitive and plans inefficient, neither communism nor perfect democratic free enterprise is attainable, and once this is appreciated, Tinbergen claimed democratic socialism would gradually become universally accepted as the pragmatic second best.

This conjecture—although seemingly supported in the 1960s by "converging" growth rates, institutional adaptation including European indicative planning, and the Soviets' partial introduction of profit-based managerial bonus incentives (Liberman reform)—however was not consistent with all the facts. The Soviets had not rescinded their criminalization of private ownership of the means of production, business, and entrepreneurship (Marxist national ownership of the means of production and state monopoly of business) as Tinbergen's theory required. European social democracy did not rely on physical systems management. And the ideal mixing of optimal planning and perfect markets never materialized.

Nor have subsequent developments been more confirming. Postcommunist reassessments of Soviet economic growth have shown that East-West growth convergence was an illusion. Indicative planning, central to Tinbergen's theory, has been largely abandoned by states, and the USSR never relinquished physical systems management, despite the economist John Kenneth Galbraith's predictions to the contrary. And most tellingly of all, the Soviet Union collapsed and Eastern Europe rejected communism in the early 1990s instead of converging. North Korea and

Laos have stayed the communist course rather than blend. And post-Soviet Russia and China failed to transition to social democracy despite adopting mixed economic arrangements. Other nations are resisting transition, and liberalization is altering social democracy as Tinbergen understood it. The evidence suggests that while rationalist historicism has widespread popular appeal convergence—like all end-of-history hypotheses—has little predictive value, a point lost on many theorists who continue to try to show using dubious official aggregate growth trends that alien systems are fundamentally alike, or are converging to a common high economic frontier.

SEE ALSO *Capitalism, State; Cold War; Decentralization; Democracy; Galbraith, John Kenneth; Liberalization, Trade; Marx, Karl; Russian Economics; Samuelson, Paul A.; Socialism; Socialism, Market; Solow, Robert M.; Tinbergen, Jan*

BIBLIOGRAPHY

Bernard, Andrew, and Charles Jones. 1996. Productivities across Industries and Countries: Time Series Theory and Evidence. *Review of Economics and Statistics* 78 (1): 135–146.

Dorfman, Robert, Paul Samuelson, and Robert Solow. 1958. *Linear Programming and Economic Analysis.* New York: McGraw-Hill.

Fukuyama, Francis. 1992. *The End of History and the Last Man.* New York: Free Press.

Galbraith, John Kenneth. 1967. *The New Industrial State.* Boston: Houghton Mifflin.

Islam, Nazrul. 2003. What Have We Learned from the Convergence Debate? *Journal of Economic Surveys* 17 (3): 309–362.

Maddison, Angus. 2003. *The World Economy: Historical Statistics.* Paris: OECD.

Rosefielde, Steven. 2007. *Russian Economics from Lenin to Putin.* Oxford, U.K.: Blackwell.

Sik, Ota. 1991. Socialism—Theory and Practice. In *Socialism Today? The Changing Meaning of Socialism,* ed. Ota Sik, 1–29. New York: Macmillan.

Tinbergen, Jan. 1959. *The Theory of the Optimum Regime.* Amsterdam: North Holland.

Tinbergen, Jan. 1960–61. Do Communist and Free Economies Show a Converging Pattern? *Soviet Studies* 12: 333–341.

Tinbergen, Jan. 1964. *Central Planning.* New Haven, CT: Yale University Press.

Steven Rosefielde

CONVERGENT VALIDITY

SEE *Validity, Statistical.*

CONVERSATIONAL ANALYSIS

Conversation Analysis (CA) was inspired by a convergence of Harold Garfinkel's ethnomethodology, Erving Goffman's interactionism, and sociolinguistics. Beginning with Harvey Sacks, Emanuel Schegloff, Gail Jefferson, and Anita Pomerantz in the 1960s, CA has become an international interdisciplinary enterprise. Since the mid-1970s there has been an explosion of interest in CA, which has been widely identified as a rigorous methodology. It has had significant impact on the fields of business (through studies of work and organizations), medicine (through analyses of doctor-patient interaction), legal studies (through examinations of deviance, policing, and courts), science, computer and information studies, robotics, gender studies, race and cross-cultural studies, as well as on sociology and social studies of language, linguistics, communication, and semiotics.

Inspired by Goffman and Garfinkel, largely through their mutual connection with Sacks, the first detailed analyses of conversation, articulated by Sacks, Schegloff, and Jefferson, combined a Goffman-inspired interest in the moral commitment involved in interaction with Garfinkel's interest in the details involved in the production of the fragile intelligibility that required that moral commitment.

The reputation of CA as a rigorous new approach to the study of language and social order was established through a foundational paper on "turntaking," "A Simplest Systematics for the Organization of Turntaking in Conversation," first published in 1974. Written jointly by Sacks, Schegloff, and Jefferson, the paper established an "economy of turns," and preferences related to turntaking orders, as basic organizing features of conversation. This article was augmented by Pomerantz's work on assessments and Alene Terasaki's work on "pre-sequences."

Sacks's lectures, given between 1964 and his death in 1975, were carefully transcribed by Jefferson, then circulated widely as photocopies for more than twenty years, before being published in 1996 in a volume edited and introduced by Schegloff. They had a huge impact on thinking not only about conversational orders, but also about orders of practice in many areas (including medicine, law, science, business, work, and information technology). Schegloff's work on repair and conversational sequencing and his sophisticated critiques of established linguistic and philosophical approaches to language were essential to establishing the CA enterprise. Jefferson also contributed essential work, especially on side-sequences and laughter. The spread of CA to various other disciplines was accomplished through the work of Schegloff, Jefferson, Pomerantz, Christian Heath, Doug Maynard, Don Zimmerman, Candace West, John Heritage, Paul

Drew, George Psathas, Jeff Coulter, and Paul Ten Have, among others.

The basic idea behind CA is that conversation is orderly in its details, that it is through detailed order that conversation has meaning, and that conversational details manifest themselves in specifiable forms. These include turn types, turn transitions, membership categorization devices, and forms of indexicality (words and sentence fragments with multiple possible meanings) that require constant attention to orderly production and ensure that participants maintain interactional reciprocity. The need to display attention to these preference orders solves the problem of how any speaker can know whether or not the listener has understood what was said and provides a way of explaining how the meaning of words are disambiguated in particular situations of use. It also introduces an inevitable moral dimension to interaction.

According to Sacks, the ability of any speaker to take a recognizably intelligible turn next, after a prior turn (given a sufficient degree of indexicality in the talk), displays understanding. Thus, speaking in indexical fragments, which linguistically would appear to be a problem, is a highly efficient device for ensuring mutual intelligibility. It ensures that all participants who take turns are fulfilling their listening and hearing requirements and either understand what has been said, or display their lack of understanding in their next turn. Even speaking last demonstrates attention to a long sequence of turns.

CA referred to this phenomenon as "recipient design," a process in which each speaker, at each next conversational point, designs a turn at talk with the "other," the recipient, and the last turn in the conversational sequence in view. The recipient, in turn, hears the talk as oriented specifically toward the current sequential ordering of turns, in the current interactional situation.

All conversational preference orders have direct implications for what can be done next in conversation and how immediately prior utterances can be heard to follow from those before. The general position on the problem of indexicality and social order was articulated by Garfinkel and Sacks in "On Formal Structures of Practical Actions" (1970). The importance of conversational sequencing was articulated in 1948 by Garfinkel (2006). Each interaction is a context for what occurs within it, but a context that is in essential ways independent of broader social contexts, except as a "context of accountability." This "context-free/context-sensitive" character of recipient design, as Sacks and Schegloff called it, is made possible by a move away from the symbolic content of words, to a focus on the enacted positioning of words in spoken sequences of turns.

Turntaking preferences are sensitive to both the sequential character of conversation, and the presenta-

tional selves of participants. There are thus elements of both "within-turn" and "between-turn" preference orders that transcend particular conversations. This view of the "context free/context sensitive" character of particular conversations is quite distinct from the more popular, but problematic idea of context as shared biographies, or shared cultural values—the view that characterizes conventional, postmodern, and interpretive sociologies.

Many social theorists have made superficially similar arguments, but none have been able to ground them in an approach to language and interactional practice that could provide for either the details of situated meaning or the moral commitments required. The tendency is to continue thinking in terms of associations (Bruno Latour) and the content of dialogue (Jürgen Habermas), instead of focusing on the situated and detailed sequential character of conversation.

The CA approach promises to explain not only how the mutual intelligibility of words is achieved in areas of practical, technical, and instrumental importance, but also why persons from different social "categories," including those associated with race, gender, culture and disability, experience conversational difficulties. "Membership-categorization" devices and small differences in the details of preference orders promise to unlock the key to many social issues.

The study of preference orders in medical settings has already made a significant contribution to studies of doctor-patient interaction, the study of diseases such as diabetes, and the delivery of what Maynard calls "bad news" in medical and other settings (see studies by Maynard, Pomerantz, Heritage, Halkowski, Clayman, Heath, and Mondada). Similar advances have occurred in the study of human-machine interaction (see studies by Heath, Greatbatch, Mondada, Orr, Hindmarsh, Button, Vinkhuyzen, and Whalen) Internet financial exchanges (Knorr-Cetina), business and technology (see studies by Heath, Vinkhuyzen, Boden, Hindmarsh, and Whalen), and technology and policing (see studies by Meehan, Zimmerman and Whalen, and Maynard). Paul Ten Have set up and maintained a CA Web site starting in the 1980s. There is also an ASA Section for Ethnomethodology and Conversation Analysis; an International Institute for Ethnomethodology and Conversational Analysis associated with Boston University and Manchester Metropolitan University; a work, *Interaction and Technology Research Group at Kings' College London*; and an Institute for Workplace Studies associated with faculty at Bentley College, all devoted equally to CA and ethnomethodology (EM).

With CA and EM, the sociological promise is transformed and rejuvenated. Instead of beginning with individuals, and aggregating their attachment to beliefs and symbols across large numbers of persons to reveal alleged underlying causal effects of institutions, CA and EM assume that institutions, where they exert an influence on daily life, will, and indeed must, manifest themselves in the sequential details of interaction. What is necessary is to discover those orders, which, when they are violated, render interaction unintelligible, and how such troubles are repaired. In this way the underlying social facts of social orders can be laid bare.

CA does not a study a *micro* order that accompanies a *macro* order, as some have claimed. Rather, the idea is that all social orders, including politics, race, class, inequality, and justice, must be enacted at the level of conversational and interactional orders, or they would cease to exist. This is not a reductionist argument, as many believe, and does not begin with the individual. The point of refusing to begin with so-called *macro structures* is not to deny that constraints exist beyond local orders of conversation. Rather, the argument is that the result of treating "macro" structures as independent entities that manifest themselves in the beliefs and values of individuals is to render invisible the effects of such constraints on persons engaged in producing living social orders.

Situated interaction itself, in situations of particular sorts, places requirements on what participants can and must do, and those must be understood by researchers. It is these situated requirements, in fact, that are the stuff and substance of EM and CA. Each situation requires persons to mobilize a set of resources in ways that will be recognizable to others in that situation. These orders are a basic feature of modernity—situations not grounded in shared belief—and their study offers a foundation for the discussion of politics and morality in a modern global context.

SEE ALSO *Anthropology, Linguistic; Discourse; Ethnomethodology; Goffman, Erving; Interactionism, Symbolic; Linguistic Turn; Modernity*

BIBLIOGRAPHY

Boden, Dierdre. 1994. *The Business of Talk: Organizations in Action*. London: Polity Press.

Boden, Dierdre, and Don H. Zimmerman, eds. 1991. *Talk and Social Structure: Studies in Ethnomethodology and Conversation Analysis*. Berkeley: University of California Press.

Button, Graham, and Wes Sharrock. 1994. Occasioned Practices in the Work of Software Engineers. In *Requirements in Engineering: Social and Technical Issues*, eds. M. Jirotka and J. A. Goguen, 217–240. London: Academic Press.

Clayman, Steven E., and Virginia T. Gill. 2004. Conversation Analysis. In *Handbook of Data Analysis*, eds. Alan Bryman and Melissa Hardy, 589–606. London and Thousand Oaks, CA: Sage.

Clayman, Steven E., John Heritage, Marc N. Elliott, and Laurie McDonald. 2007. When Does the Watchdog Bark?: Conditions of Aggressive Questioning in Presidential News Conferences. *American Sociological Review* 72: 23–41.

Coulter, Jeff. 1979. *The Social Construction of Mind: Studies in Ethnomethodology and Linguistic Philosophy*. London: Macmillan.

Drew, Paul, and John Heritage. 1992. *Talk at Work: Interaction in Institutional Settings*. Cambridge, U.K.: Cambridge University Press.

Garfinkel, Harold. 2006. *Seeing Sociologically*. Boulder, CO: Paradigm Publishers.

Garfinkel, Harold, and Harvey Sacks. 1970. On Formal Structures of Practical Actions. In *Theoretical Sociology: Perspectives and Developments*, eds. J. C. McKinney and E. A. Tiryakian, 338–366. New York: Appleton-Century-Crofts.

Goffman, Erving. 1959. *The Presentation of Self in Everyday Life*. Garden City, NY: Doubleday.

Greatbatch, David, Paul Luff, Christian Heath, and P. Campion. 1995. Conversation Analysis: Human-Computer Interaction and the General Practice Consultation. In *Perspectives on HCI: Diverse Approaches*, eds. A. Monk and G. N. Gilbert, 199–222. London: Academic Press.

Habermas, Jürgen. 1984–1987. *A Theory of Communicative Action*. Trans. Thomas McCarthy. Boston: Beacon Press.

Halkowski, Tim. 2006. Realizing the Illness: Patients' Narratives of Symptom Discovery. In *Communication in Medical Care: Interaction between Primary Care Physicians and Patients*, eds. John Heritage and Douglas Maynard. Cambridge, U.K.: Cambridge University Press.

Heath, Christian. 1982. *Talk and Recipiency: Sequential Organization in Speech and Body Movement*. Cambridge, U.K.: Cambridge University Press.

Heath, Christian, and Paul Luff, eds. 2000. *Technology in Action*. Cambridge, U.K.: Cambridge University Press.

Heritage, John, and Douglas W. Maynard. 2006. *Communication in Medical Care: Interaction between Primary Care Physicians and Patients*. Cambridge, U.K.: Cambridge University Press.

Hindmarsh, John, and Alison Pilnick. 2002. The Tacit Order of Teamwork: Collaboration and Embodied Conduct in Anaesthesia. *The Sociological Quarterly* 43 (2): 139–164.

Hindmarsh, John, Christian Heath, D. vom Lehn, and J. Cleverly. 2005. Creating Assemblies in Public Environments: Social Interaction, Interactive Exhibits and CSCW. *Computer Supported Cooperative Work* 14 (1): 1–41.

Jefferson, Gail. 1972. Side Sequences. In *Studies in Social Interaction*, comp. David N. Sudnow, 294–333. New York: Free Press.

Jefferson, Gail. 1973. A Case of Precision Timing in Ordinary Conversation: Overlapped Tag-positioned Address Terms in Closing Sequences. *Semiotica* 9 (1): 47–96.

Jefferson, Gail. 1974. Error Correction as an Interactional Resource. *Language in Society* 3 (2): 181–199.

Knorr-Cetina, Karin. 1999. *Epistemic Cultures: How the Sciences Make Knowledge*. Cambridge, MA: Harvard University Press.

Latour, Bruno, and Woolgar, Steve. 1979. *Laboratory Life: The Social Construction of Scientific Facts.* Beverly Hills, CA: Sage.

Maynard, Douglas W. 2003. *Bad News Good News: Conversational Order in Everyday Talk and Clinical Settings.* Chicago: University of Chicago Press.

Meehan, Albert J. 1990. Rule Recognition and Social Competence: The Case of Children's Games. *Sociological Studies of Child Development* 3: 245–262.

Meehan, Albert J. 1992. "I Don't Prevent Crime I Prevent Calls": Policing as Negotiated Order. *Symbolic Interaction* 15 (4): 455–480.

Mondada, Lorenza. 1994. *Verbalisation de l'espace et fabrication du savoir: approche linguistique de la construction des objets de discours [Entry of Charge of Space and Manufacture of the Knowledge: Linguistic Approach to the Construction of the Objects of Speech].* Lausanne: University of Lausanne.

Mondada, Lorenza. 1999. Forms of Sequentiality in the Emails and the Forums of Discussion. A Conversational Approach to Interaction on the Internet. *Apprentissage des Langues et Systems d'Information et de Communication* 2 (1): 3–25.

Orr, Julian E. 1996. *Talking About Machines: An Ethnography of a Modern Job.* Ithaca, NY: ILR Press.

Psathas, George. 1995. *Conversation Analysis: The Study of Talk-in-Interaction.* Thousand Oaks, CA: Sage.

Rawls, Anne Warfield. 1989. Language, Self and Social Order: A Re-evaluation of Goffman and Sacks. *Human Studies* 12 (1): 147–172.

Rawls, Anne Warfield, and Gary David. 2006. Accountably Other: Trust, Reciprocity and Exclusion in a Context of Situated Practice. *Human Studies* 28: 469–497.

Sacks, Harvey. 1926. *Lectures in Conversation*, Vols. 1 and 2. Cambridge, U.K.: Cambridge University Press.

Sacks, Harvey, Emanuel Schegloff, and Gail Jefferson. 1974. A Simplest Systematics for the Organization of Turntaking in Conversation. *Language* 50 (4; Part 1): 696–735.

Schegloff, Emanuel A. 1984. On Some Gestures' Relation to Talk. In *Structures of Social Action: Studies in Conversation Analysis*, ed. J. Maxwell Atkinson and John Heritage, 266–296. Cambridge, U.K.: Cambridge University Press.

Schegloff, Emanuel A., and Harvey Sacks. 1973. Opening up Closings. *Semiotica* 8: 289–327.

Schegloff, Emanuel A., Gail Jefferson, and Harvey Sacks. 1977. The Preference for Self-Correction in the Organization of Repair in Conversation. *Language* 50: 696–735.

Ten Have, Paul, and George Psathas. 1995. *Situated Order: Studies in the Social Organization of Talk and Embodied Activities.* Washington, DC: University Press of America

Vinkhuyzen, Eric, Margaret H. Szymanski, R. J. Moore, G. T. Raymond, Jack Whalen, and Marilyn Whalen. 2004. Would you like to do it yourself? Service Requests and Their Non-granting Responses. In *Applying Conversation Analysis*, eds. Paul Seedhouse and Keith Richards, 91–106. Basingstoke, U.K.: Palgrave Macmillan.

West, Candace. 1985. *Routine Complications: Tasks and Troubles on Medical Encounters.* Bloomington: Indiana University Press.

Whalen, Jack, and Eric Vinkhuyzen. 2000. Expert Systems in (Inter)action: Diagnosing Document Machine Problems over the Telephone. In *Workplace Studies: Recovering Work Practice and Informing System Design,* eds. Paul Luff, John Hindmarsh, and Christian Heath, 92–140. Cambridge, U.K.: Cambridge University Press.

Zimmerman, Don H., and Candace West. 1985. Gender, Language and Discourse. In *Handbook of Discourse Analysis,* Vol. 4, ed. Teun A. van Dijk, 103–124. London: Academic Press.

Zimmerman, Don H., and Marilyn Whalen. 1987. Sequential and Institutional Contexts in Calls for Help. *Social Psychology Quarterly* 50 (2): 172–185.

Anne Warfield Rawls

COOK, JAMES
1728–1779

James Cook became one of the most famous eighteenth-century British navigators and cartographers. Cook was born into a farming family in north Yorkshire. At age thirteen, Cook's father sent him to apprentice with a local shopkeeper. According to mythology, the young Cook spent most of his time staring out the shop's window at the sea. Whether true or not, the shopkeeper declared Cook ill-suited for that profession. He then became an apprentice in the merchant navy, where he learned navigation and astronomy.

As Britain prepared for war with France, Cook joined the Royal Navy in 1755. During the French and Indian War (1755–1763), the young sailor earned a reputation for his accuracy in cartography. In 1759 Cook surveyed and piloted the British fleet through the St. Lawrence River. During the critical battle over Quebec, the Plains of Abraham, the British commander depended on Cook's maps of the St. Lawrence River to devise his winning strategy.

After the war, Cook embarked on an often dangerous mission to map the jagged coastline of Newfoundland. The treacherous and unknown elements of the Newfoundland coast challenged both Cook's seamanship and charting abilities. By 1767, however, he produced a remarkably accurate map of Britain's newly acquired territory. The Newfoundland charting mission brought Cook to the attention of British Admiralty and the Royal Society for the Improvement of Natural Society.

Between 1768 and 1779, Cook conducted three extensive navigation missions through the Pacific Ocean. The British Admiralty expected the expedition to locate and chart the Australian continent. During his first voyage, Cook, commanding the HMS *Endeavor*, became the second known European to land on New Zealand and the first European to explore and chart Australia's eastern coastline. A group of Aborigine inhabitants attempted to prevent the intruders from landing as the British vessel dropped anchor in Botany Bay. The British sailors used their guns to force the warriors to retreat, making the first encounter between Europeans and Aborigines a hostile one. As Cook sailed further north along the coast, his ship struck the Great Barrier Reef. His crew needed to spend several weeks repairing the vessel. During this time, Cook established fairly cordial relations with the surrounding indigenous groups. After publishing the journals from his first journey (1768–1771), he gained a certain level of notoriety in Britain.

Only two months after his first mission, Cook departed for his second major journey (1772–1775). He piloted the HMS *Resolution* and circumnavigated the globe along a southern latitude. He charted South Georgia, Easter Island, Vanuatu, and numerous other islands. This journey resulted in more tense encounters with indigenous populations. Some of Cook's men lost their lives in skirmishes with New Zealand's Maori populations.

During Cook's last major expedition (1776–1779), he became the first European to visit the Hawaiian Islands. Cook initially named these Pacific islands the Sandwich Islands after his benefactor, the fourth Earl of Sandwich. The Polynesian inhabitants, who happened to be celebrating an important religious ritual, greeted Cook with great reverence during their first encounter. This goodwill, however, did not last. On Cook's second trip to Hawaii, his men engaged in a bloody battle after the local population stole one of their smaller boats. During the conflict, the inhabitants stabbed and bludgeoned Cook to death.

Cook's name still has great currency and one can find many monuments in his honor throughout the globe. He also has several universities and other educational facilities named in his honor.

SEE ALSO *Colonialism; Cultural Group Selection; Exploitation; Gaze, Colonial; Imperialism; Natives; Travel and Travel Writing*

BIBLIOGRAPHY

Beaglehole, J. C. 1974. *The Life of Captain James Cook*. Stanford, CA: Stanford University Press.

Obeyesekere, Gananath. 1997. *The Apotheosis of Captain Cook: European Mythmaking in the Pacific*. Princeton, NJ: Princeton University Press.

Smith, Bernard. 1992. *Imagining the Pacific: In the Wake of the Cook Voyages*. New Haven, CT: Yale University Press.

Anthony P. Mora

COOPERATION

Cooperation, wrote Karl Marx (1818–1883), occurs "when numerous workers work together side by side in accordance with a plan, whether in the same process, or in different but connected processes" ([1867] 1977, p. 443). What he describes in this passage about the economic realm is the superficial appearance of cooperation rather than the diverse cultural practices, social relations, and modes of production that underwrite it. He then proceeds to point out the diversity of those forms. Marx was acutely aware that people cooperate for other reasons besides the production of goods or the satisfaction of needs defined narrowly as economic rather than more broadly as intellectual development, aesthetic stimulation, play, or the fulfillment of social functions, to name only a few.

Authors with quite different ontological standpoints have written about cooperation. On the one hand, early theorists of liberalism, such as Thomas Hobbes (1588–1679) or John Locke (1632–1704), who presupposed that individuals existed before society, sought to explain the conditions under which innately competitive, natural men came together to constitute a society in order to pursue collectively life, liberty, and property. For intellectual descendants, like neoliberal policymakers or sociobiologists, the problem is to explain the development of cooperative (altruistic) behavior; their solution resides in exchange broadly written—the market for policymakers, the transmission of genes for sociobiologists. On the other hand, critics of liberal social theory—Georg F. W. Hegel (1770–1831), for example—presupposed the existence of sociality from the beginnings of humankind and sought to explain how the actual conditions of human existence have been transformed by the collective social activity of human beings. The problem from this perspective is to account for competition in a world that exhibits enormous amounts of cooperative activity.

Recent discussions of cooperation may be further obscured by six epistemological tendencies that are frequently encountered either explicitly or implicitly: (1) a philosophical reductionism which postulates that explanations framed in terms of lower-order molecular, neurobiological, or psychological structures (e.g., a universal human nature) are preferable to those couched in terms of emergent social and cultural phenomena; (2) a denial of sociohistorical change which postulates, for example, that the structures of meaning characteristic of the Roman Republic have persisted unchanged for millennia and are effectively the same ones that exist in the West today; (3) an assertion that cultural identities and logics of difference are forged largely in the unequal power relations and one-way discourse between colonizer and colonized; (4) a largely unexamined assumption that earlier writers in the anthropological tradition did not understand what they saw or were told, especially when their accounts differ from the social relations that exist in the same region today; (5) a related assumption that, since people find it difficult to think outside the analytical categories of their own intellectual tradition, it is also difficult for them to understand other intellectual or cultural traditions; and (6) a belief that all forms of cooperation are structurally equivalent to those of Western capitalism and hence can be adequately explained in terms of capitalist models. Such epistemological presumptions need to be examined carefully and justified, especially as they underpin discussions of cooperation.

Cooperation manifests itself in diverse ways and is buttressed by a variety of social forms. Let us consider briefly a few examples: (1) the factory described by Marx where a number of workers put into motion more or less elaborate technical divisions of labor to produce commodities for the owner; (2) the long-discussed and carefully planned hunting expeditions of San men of southern Africa, which are complete with details of how and with whom meat will be shared; (3) the annual, week-long fiestas in highland Andean communities that are constructed around cleaning and repairing local irrigation canals and terraces; (4) the rotating credit associations, pooling of resources, and almost continuous swapping of goods to defray the costs of everyday needs in rural settlements along the U.S.-Mexico border; (5) the Maasai women in eastern Africa who prepare food and drink for the age-set initiation ceremonies of their sons and husbands; and (6) the improvisations of jazz musicians in a jam session. Cooperation does not always mean that the interpersonal and social relations of the participants are harmonious; frequently, they are tense, and individuals may be cajoled or feel compelled to participate. Nevertheless, not cooperating may be unavoidable, unadvisable, or even unthinkable.

SEE ALSO *Altruism; Altruism and Prosocial Behavior*

BIBLIOGRAPHY

Leacock, Eleanor. 1872. Relations of Production in Band Society. In *Politics and History in Band Societies*, eds. Eleanor Leacock and Richard Lee, pp. 159–170. Cambridge, U.K.: Cambridge University Press.

Lee, Richard. 2005. Power and Property in Twenty-first Century Foragers: A Critical Examination. In *Property and Equality*, eds. Thomas Widlok and Wolde Gossa Tadesse, pp. 16–31. New York: Berghahn Books.

Marx, Karl. [1867] 1977. *Capital: A Critique of Political Economy*, Vol. 1. New York: Vintage.

Woodburn, James. 1998. Sharing is Not a Form of Exchange: An Analysis of Property-Sharing in Immediate-Return Hunter-Gatherer Societies. In *Property Relations: Renewing*

the Anthropological Tradition, ed. Chris Hann, pp. 48–63. Cambridge, U.K.: Cambridge University Press.

Thomas C. Patterson

COOPERATIVES

People in every society and throughout history have participated in cooperative arrangements, including joint decision-making; economic, social, and political collaboration; and collective ownership. There are a multitude of examples in every culture and era, starting with the early African nations, Aboriginal societies in Australia, the First Nations in the Americas, and Indian and Southeast Asian civilizations. Many grassroots cooperatives have operated throughout the world over the past two to three centuries. In modern history we refer to cooperatives as enterprises, usually businesses (for-profit and not-for-profit) that are jointly owned and governed by a collection of people for a specific economic and/or social purpose. Although these are found throughout the world, the most famous cooperatives have been located in Great Britain, Japan, Italy, Spain, and Canada. In 1752 Benjamin Franklin was one of the founders of the first formal cooperative recorded in history, a fire insurance company in the United States.

Cooperatives are companies owned by the people who use their services, those who formed the company for a particular purpose and are the members of the enterprise, i.e., member-owners. Cooperatives are created to satisfy a need—to provide a quality good or service at an affordable price (that the market is not adequately providing); or to create an economic structure to engage in needed production or facilitate more equal distribution to compensate for a market failure. The International Cooperative Alliance, a nongovernmental association founded in 1895 that represents and serves cooperatives worldwide, defines a cooperative as "an autonomous association of persons united voluntarily to meet their common economic, social, and cultural needs and aspirations through a jointly-owned and democratically-controlled enterprise.... Ranging from small-scale to multi-million dollar businesses across the globe, co-operatives employ more than 100 million women and men and have more than 800 million individual members" (International Cooperative Alliance [ICA] 2005).

Cooperatives are usually classified as consumer-owned, producer-owned, or worker-owned (or a hybrid of some combination of the stakeholders). For example, consumers come together and form a buying club or a cooperative grocery store in order to obtain the goods they need at an affordable price, particularly where fresh produce and natural and vegetarian foods are not supplied elsewhere or are very costly. In some places consumers also come together to buy electricity, environmentally friendly fuels, pharmaceuticals, child care, financial services (as in a credit union), or almost any good or service. Cooperative retail enterprises such as natural-food grocery stores and rural electric and energy cooperatives are some of the most numerous and successful examples. Cooperative financial institutions such as credit unions are some of the most widely used cooperatives. They make financial services and loans available in underserved communities, and keep financial resources circulating in the community. Producers also form cooperatives to jointly purchase supplies and equipment and/or to jointly process and market their goods, particularly in agriculture and arts and crafts. Workers form cooperatives to jointly own and manage a business themselves, to save a company that is being sold off, abandoned, or closed down, or to start a company that exemplifies workplace democracy and collective management. Worker-owned businesses offer economic security, income and wealth generation, and democratic economic participation to employees, as well as provide meaningful and decent jobs and environmental sustainability to communities (see Gordon Nembhard 2004b, 2002; Haynes and Gordon Nembhard 1999). Cooperative housing expands home or apartment ownership to more people, addressing both financing and maintenance issues, and often builds in long-term affordability. Cooperative ownership is growing in the provision of social services such as home health care, health care, drug rehabilitation, and child care; and in the area of fair trade.

DEMOCRATIC OWNERSHIP

Cooperatives, particularly worker-owned co-ops, are a form of democratically owned economic enterprises that allow members to control their own income and wealth, stimulate the local economy, address market failures, and be agents of change in their local sphere. Cooperatives are characterized by pooling of resources, joint ownership, democratic governance, and sharing risks and profits in the production, distribution, and/or acquisition of affordable high-quality goods and services. Cooperative businesses operate according to a set of agreed-upon values and principles or guidelines that have evolved over the past 150 years. The seven key principles are: voluntary and open membership; democratic control by members (based on "one member, one vote" rather than voting according to number of shares of stock owned); members' economic participation (returns based on use); autonomy and independence (self-help organizations controlled by members); continuous education, training, and information; cooperation among cooperatives; and concern for community (see International Co-operative Alliance 2005; Thordarson 1999). These seven modern coopera-

tive principles are based on the values and principles set forth by the Rochdale Equitable Pioneers Society, started in 1844, whose original members are considered to be "the founders of the Co-operative Movement" (ICA 2005; also Holyoake 1918 and Laurel House Co-op and Laurel Net Cooperative 1999.)

COOPERATIVE ECONOMICS, MARKET FAILURE, AND MULTIPLIERS

Cooperatives often develop and survive as a response to market failure and economic marginalization (see Fairbairn et al. 1991). Worker-owned cooperatives and other democratically owned businesses are some of the most innovative and empowering arrangements for bringing together labor and capital in an equitable and productive relationship. Cooperative economic development has been successful as an urban as well as rural economic development strategy to create jobs, increase incomes (and sometimes wealth), and reduce poverty around the world. Although cooperative models are not well known or well publicized, the United Nations and the International Labor Organization have recently recognized the potential of cooperative enterprises for economic development and poverty reduction (Birchall 2003; International Labour Conference 2002).

Some of the issues that cooperatives address are: local development in an increasingly globalizing world; community control in an age of transnational corporate concentration and expansion; social and community entrepreneurship, particularly when business development is increasingly complicated and especially risky; pooling of resources and profit-sharing in communities where capital is scarce and incomes low; and increased productivity, superior working conditions, and high worker satisfaction in industries where work conditions may be poor, and wages and benefits usually low. There is evidence to suggest that cooperatives lead to superior value creation. David Levine and Laura D'Andrea Tyson surveyed the research and found that "both participation and ownership have positive effects on productivity" (1990). Levine and Tyson also point out that many researchers note the superior working conditions in cooperatives:

> For example, the European worker co-ops, which have been the subject of extensive empirical inquiry, typically have managements committed to employee ownership and representation, job security, compressed status and compensation differentials, and guaranteed worker rights.... The results have been more consistently favorable in correlating worker ownership and management with lower turnover, absenteeism, and higher

worker satisfaction.... In almost no cases does participation make things worse. (Levine and Tyson 1990)

In a comparison of social and economic indicators in three towns in northern Italy with similar demographics but different levels of cooperative ownership, David Erdal (1999) found that citizens in Imola had a better quality of life than in the other two towns with fewer or no cooperative enterprises. Imola, with 25 percent of the workforce employed in cooperative businesses, is reputed to be the town with the largest number of cooperatives in Italy and Europe. In total, Imola scored highest (positively) on seventeen of the nineteen combined measures about quality of life. Experience of crime, police activity, cardiovascular mortality, and perception of gap between rich and poor, for example, were all lowest in Imola. Positives such as confidence in government, perceiving politicians to be on your side, posteducation training rates, and physical and emotional health, were all highest in Imola.

Cooperatives develop out of the wealth of cultural and social capital in communities, whose diverse residents often have strong social networks and few options but to work together. Cooperatives create social efficiencies derived from the democratic participation of all, self-help, self-management, and concern for community principles that guide them. Cooperatives encourage interaction, teamwork, intercooperation, and giving back to one's community. They also develop social ties among members and between members and the community—that is, social capital—so that networking and working together become the norm, and the skills to facilitate this are developed in all members. Gordon Nembhard and Blasingame (2002) find that co-op members and employee owners become used to the transparency and accountability in their own organizations (e.g., open-book policies, "one member, one vote," shared management, etc.). They come to expect transparency and accountability and help recreate this in civil society and political arenas. Many members become more active in their communities in general, taking on leadership roles both in their co-ops and in voluntary and community organizations (this was found especially with women members and in communities of color). In addition, citizen activism and advocacy often can be effective countervailing forces that increase democracy and participation.

PROMOTING RACIAL AND ETHNIC ECONOMIC INDEPENDENCE

Cooperative enterprises are a particularly effective and responsive way for subaltern populations to participate economically. Because subaltern peoples are discriminated against in mainstream labor, capital, and housing markets, they often have to rely on one another and work together.

Subaltern populations often have little personal wealth and are excluded from much of mainstream prosperity and economic stability: The market system does not often work for many members of subaltern groups.

Examples such as the Mondragon Cooperative Corporation (MCC) illustrate the economic power of the combination of ethnic solidarity, democratic ownership and participation, and interlocking economic activities. The Mondragon Cooperative Corporation is a complex of more than 150 industrial, financial, distributional, research, and educational cooperatives, mostly worker-owned, in northern Spain. The holding corporation is "rooted in grassroots networks of cooperative businesses owned by Basque nationalists" who chose cooperative enterprise development as a means to assert their economic independence (see Gordon Nembhard and Haynes 2002). The first cooperative was a worker-owned and worker-managed ceramic heater factory, started in 1956 by graduates of a community-run alternative "polytechnic" high school founded by a priest who taught cooperative economics and worker ownership. Additional cooperatives developed using the same model. Early members also established a credit union, Caja Laboral, that has continued to supply financing, technical assistance, and research and development for future cooperatives. Caja Laboral has become the seventh largest bank in Spain and is the MCC's engine of growth, supporting cooperative development as well as facilitating economic stability among the cooperatives in the system. Other schools and a university were established to support the growing worker-owned factories in the network. The complex of cooperatives also established its own social security system (Lagun-Aro) early on, when the government of Spain would not allow the member-owners to participate in the national system because they were considered to be self-employed. The association grew into a multibillion-dollar cooperative network of manufacturing, service, educational, financial, and distributive enterprises. Trends continue to show progressive growth in assets, sales, and workforce. In 2005, for example, total sales for all the cooperative's companies exceeded $11 billion euros (U.S. $15 billion); total assets were greater than $22 billion euros (U.S. $29 billion). The workforce reached 78,455 in 2005—81 percent of whom were member-owners (Mondragon Corporacion Cooperativa 2006). The fifty-year success of this cooperative holding company and its affiliated companies can be explained best and most fully when the panoply of economic, social, cultural, and political market and nonmarket forces involved are analyzed.

Freedom Quilting Bee in Alberta, Alabama, is another example of a successful cooperative organization that organized itself based on cultural and social solidarity as well as economic need and affinity (Rural Development Leadership Network 2002). In the mid-1960s a group of

African American women in sharecropping families in Alabama formed a craft cooperative to pool their resources to produce and market quilts to supplement their families' earnings. Sharecropping, a system of debt peonage, did not provide self-sufficiency for black farmers. In addition, during the civil rights era, white landowners were evicting black families from the land if they tried to register to vote or were involved in civil rights activity. The co-op helped the women buy sewing machines and other supplies, provided a place for them to quilt together, and marketed and distributed the quilts around the country, including through the Sears Roebuck catalog. The cooperative was so successful that it bought land, built a small sewing factory, started a day care center, and by 1991 was the largest employer in their town. In addition, the co-op was able to use its land to help sharecropping families relocate and eventually buy their own land, especially after they were denied access to their traditional farms because of their political activity. The income earned also was an important supplement to the meager income their families made from farming. In 1967 Freedom Quilting Bee was one of the founding members of the Federation of Southern Cooperatives—a predominantly African American cooperative development nonprofit organization with agencies in six southern states (Federation of Southern Cooperatives/Land Assistance Fund 1992, 2002).

BIBLIOGRAPHY

Birchall, Johnston. 2003. *Rediscovering the Cooperative Advantage: Poverty Reduction Through Self-help*. Geneva, Switzerland: Cooperative Branch, International Labour Office.

Cline, John. 1997. The Worker Co-operative: A Vehicle for Economic Development. Discussion paper, 1997 Atlantic Canada Economic Association Conference. http://www.geonewsletter.org/cline1.htm.

Curl, John. 2003. History of Worker Cooperation in America. http://www.red-coral.net/WorkCoops.html.

Du Bois, W. E. B. 1907. *Economic Cooperation Among Negro Americans*. Atlanta, GA: Atlanta University Press.

Elden, J. Maxwell. 1981. Political Efficacy at Work: The Connection Between More Autonomous Forms of Workplace Organization and a More Participatory Politics. *American Political Science Review* 75 (1): 43–58.

Erdal, David. 1999. The Psychology of Sharing: An Evolutionary Approach. PhD diss., University of St. Andrews, U.K.

Fairbairn, Brett, June Bold, Murray Fulton, et al. 1991. *Cooperatives and Community Development: Economics in Social Perspective*. Saskatoon: University of Saskatchewan Center for the Study of Cooperatives.

Federation of Southern Cooperatives/Land Assistance Fund. 1992. *25th Anniversary, Annual Report 1967–1992*. Atlanta, GA: Author.

Federation of Southern Cooperatives/Land Assistance Fund. 2002. *35th Anniversary—2002 Annual Report*. East Point, GA: Author.

Gordon Nembhard, Jessica. 2002. Cooperatives and Wealth Accumulation: Preliminary Analysis. *American Economic Review* 92 (2): 325–329.

Gordon Nembhard, Jessica. 2004a. Cooperative Ownership in the Struggle for African American Economic Empowerment. *Humanity and Society* 28 (3): 298–321.

Gordon Nembhard, Jessica. 2004b. Non-Traditional Analyses of Cooperative Economic Impacts: Preliminary Indicators and a Case Study. *Review of International Co-operation* 97 (1): 6–21.

Gordon Nembhard, Jessica, and Anthony A. Blasingame. 2002. Economic Dimensions of Civic Engagement and Political Efficacy. Working Paper of the Democracy Collaborative-Knight Foundation Civic Engagement Project, University of Maryland. College Park, MD.

Gordon Nembhard, Jessica, and Curtis Haynes Jr. 2002. Using Mondragon as a Model for African American Urban Redevelopment. In *From Community Economic Development and Ethnic Entrepreneurship to Economic Democracy: The Cooperative Alternative*, ed. Jonathan M. Feldman and Jessica Gordon Nembhard, 111-132. Ůmea, Sweden: Partnership for Multiethnic Inclusion, University of Ůmea.

Haynes, Curtis, Jr., and Jessica Gordon Nembhard. 1999. Cooperative Economics: A Community Revitalization Strategy. *Review of Black Political Economy* 27 (1): 47–71.

Holyoake, G. J. 1918. *The History of the Rochdale Pioneers*. 10th ed. New York: Scribner.

International Co-operative Alliance. 2005. What Is a Co-operative? http://www.ica.coop/coop.

International Co-operative Alliance and International Labor Office. No date (c. 2005). Cooperating out of Poverty: The Global Co-operative Campaign Against Poverty. Geneva, Switzerland. http://www.coop.org/outofpoverty/campaign.pdf.

International Labour Conference. 2002. Recommendation 193: Recommendation Concerning the Promotion of Cooperatives. http://www.ilo.org/coop.

Krimerman, Len, and Frank Lindenfeld, eds. 1992. *When Workers Decide: Workplace Democracy Takes Root in North America*. Philadelphia: New Society.

Laurel House Co-op and Laurel Net Cooperative. 1999. History of the Rochdale Cooperative. http://uts.cc.utexas.edu/~laurel/cooproots/history.html.

Levine, David, and Laura D'Andrea Tyson. 1990. Participation, Productivity, and the Firm's Environment. In *Paying for Productivity: A Look at the Evidence*, ed. Alan Blinder, 183–237. Washington, DC: Brookings Institute.

Logue, John, and Jacquelyn Yates. 2005. *Productivity in Cooperatives and Worker-Owned Enterprises: Ownership and Participation Make a Difference!* Geneva, Switzerland: International Labour Office.

MacLeod, Greg. 1997. *From Mondragon to America*. Sydney, Nova Scotia: University College of Cape Breton Press.

Mondragon Corporacion Cooperativa. 2006. The History of an
Experience; Economic Data: Most Relevant
Data.http://www.mcc.coop.

National Cooperative Business Association. 2005.
http://www.ncba.coop.

Pateman, Carol. 1970. *Participation and Democratic Theory.*
Cambridge, U.K.: Cambridge University Press.

Reynolds, Bruce J. 2001. A History of African-American Farmer
Cooperatives, 1938–2000. Presentation to the annual
meeting of the NCR-194, USDA/RBS/Cooperative Services.
Mimeo, U.S. Department of Agriculture.
http://www.agecon.ksu.edu/accc/ncr194/Events/2001meeting
/Reynolds01.pdf.

Rural Development Leadership Network. 2002. Freedom
Quilting Bee 2002.
http://www.ruraldevelopment.org/FQBhistory.html.

Spear, Roger. 1999. The Co-operative Advantage. Paper
presented at the International Co-operative Alliance Research
Conference. Quebec City, Canada, August 28–29.

Thomas, Karen. 2000. Lessons of Mondragon's Employee-
Owned Network. *Owners at Work* 12 (1): 5–9.

Thordarson, Bruce. 1999. Cooperative Legislation and the
Cooperative Identity Statement. *Journal of Co-operative
Studies* 32 (2): 87–93.

United States Department of Agriculture. 1995. What Are
Cooperatives? Cooperative Information Report 10.
Washington, DC: Author.

Weiss, Chris, and Christina Clamp. 1992. Women's
Cooperatives: Part of the Answer to Poverty? In *From the
Ground Up: Essays on "Grassroots and Workplace Democracy"*
by C. George Benello, ed. Len Krimerman, Frank Lindenfeld,
Carol Korty, and Julian Benello, 229–232. Boston: South
End Press.

Williams, Chancellor. 1961. The Economic Basis of African Life.
In *The Rebirth of African Civilization*, 151–181. Chicago:
Third World Press. Reprint 1993.

Jessica Gordon Nembhard

COORDINATION FAILURE

The notion of coordination failure can be understood by considering the simple coordination game in Table 1. In this game, Player 1 and Player 2 simultaneously and independently choose action A or B. The numbers in the table represent the payoffs associated with the different outcomes of interaction. If both players choose option A, both get a payoff of 1, if both choose B, they both get a payoff of 2, and if one player chooses A and the other B, the one who chose A gets 1, the other gets 0.

Coordination games, as outlined by Russell Cooper in his 1999 work, are characterized by multiple equilibria. In the following example, both players choosing A and

A coordination game

		Player 2 A	Player 2 B
Player 1 A		1, 1	1, 0
Player 1 B		0, 1	2, 2

Table 1

both players choosing B are equilibria (in addition, there is a mixed-strategy equilibrium in which both players choose A and B with a probability of ½). These equilibria are Pareto-ranked, meaning that both players are better off in one equilibrium than in the other. In the example, both players are better off if they coordinate on action B than if they coordinate on action A.

Coordination failure prevails if players coordinate on the inefficient equilibrium (here: both choose A). Coordination failure is an equilibrium phenomenon because given that one player chooses A, it is in the interest of the other player (i.e., it is a best reply) to also choose A. In colloquial language, the failure to coordinate on any equilibrium is sometimes also called *coordination failure*. It is more precise to talk about miscoordination in this case because a non-equilibrium phenomenon is concerned.

Coordination failure suggests an efficiency-enhancing role for policy intervention and collective action. If agents are in a Pareto-inferior equilibrium, individuals cannot move to the superior equilibrium by individual action (lock-in effect). In contrast, a coordinated move is necessary to reach a Pareto-superior equilibrium.

Coordination failure arises because of strategic uncertainty, not because a conflict of interest prevails. While choosing B is attractive because it possibly yields a higher payoff, it is also risky to choose B. If one player is uncertain that the other player will choose B, he might choose the safe option A. Therefore, confidence and expectations are important determinants of coordination failure.

Multiple equilibria arise in coordination games because of strategic complementarity, meaning that the optimal decision of one agent is positively dependent on the decisions of other players. Coordination games also exhibit positive spillovers in that the payoffs of one player increase as the action by the other player increases (assuming that action B represents a higher level of activity than action A).

EXAMPLES OF COORDINATION FAILURE

More elaborate versions of the coordination game in Table 1 with more than two players and two actions have been used to explain coordination failure in many contexts.

Teamwork Suppose two workers produce a joint output by providing costly effort and both are paid according to team output. Both workers are better off if both exert high effort (action B in the table) and coordination failure prevails if both provide low effort.

Education Acquiring education might be less profitable if others are not educated. If all agents expect others to acquire little education, investments in education might remain low.

Bank Runs If most creditors leave their savings in the bank, the bank is liquid and it is optimal to leave the savings in the bank. If all other creditors withdraw their savings, the bank becomes illiquid and it is best to also withdraw one's savings. A similar reasoning has been used to account for speculative currency attacks and decisions to refinance businesses on the verge of bankruptcy.

Search and Matching If few agents use a specific medium to search for a partner, the other players have little incentives to use this medium because of the low likeliness to find a good match in a "thin market." Coordination failure might therefore explain low intensity of search for employment. A similar reasoning has been used to explain failure to adopt superior technological standards or languages. Applications in development economics emphasize path-dependence and lock-in, suggesting that an economy might be stuck in a development trap today because agents failed to coordinate, possibly due to historical accident, on a Pareto-superior equilibrium in the past.

Macroeconomics Coordination failure has many applications in macroeconomics. A classic example refers to investments and expectations of future output. If most firms expect future aggregate demand to be low, they invest little today. This, in turn, induces low aggregate demand today, which might be interpreted as confirming low expectations. A recession might therefore result from self-fulfilling expectations. The literature on "sunspots" suggests that expectations might be coordinated by irrelevant events or information. For example, leading indicators of macroeconomic activity might be particularly accurate as long as economic agents believe they are good indicators.

The empirical relevance of these examples is contested in the literature because theories of coordination failure are difficult to test in the field. Economists have therefore sought to test the determinants of coordination failure in a broad range of coordination games in the experimental laboratory. Experimental economists have investigated elaborate versions of the game in Table 1, pure coordination games (in which equilibria are equally good, i.e., not Pareto-ranked), and asymmetric games (in which agents coordinate on different actions).

Coordination problems are related to but distinct from cooperation problems. The coordination game in Table 1 is transformed into a cooperation game (a prisoner's dilemma) if the payoffs in the lower left cell are changed to (0,3) and in the upper right cell to (3,0). Actions A and B are often called *defection* and *cooperation*. The resulting cooperation game has a unique and inefficient equilibrium [payoffs are (1,1)]. A rational and self-interested player chooses A (i.e., free-rides) irrespective of what the other player chooses in the cooperation game.

SEE ALSO *Multiple Equilibria; Nash Equilibrium; Prisoner's Dilemma (Psychology)*

BIBLIOGRAPHY

Camerer, Colin. 2003. *Behavioral Game Theory: Experiments in Strategic Interaction.* Princeton, NJ: Princeton University Press.

Cooper, Russell W. 1999. *Coordination Games: Complementarities and Macroeconomics.* Cambridge, U.K.: Cambridge University Press.

Fehr, Ernst, and Jean-Robert Tyran. 2007. Money Illusion and Coordination Failure. *Games and Economic Behavior* 58(2): 246–268.

Mankiw, N. Gregory, and David Romer, eds. 1991. *New Keynesian Economics: Coordination Failures and Real Rigidities.* Vol. 2. Cambridge, MA: MIT Press.

Jean-Robert Tyran

COPING

The stresses inherent in the daily challenges of life create a need for continuous monitoring and adjustment. *Coping* is the behavioral, cognitive, and emotional process of managing a stressful or threatening situation or circumstance. It is a nearly continuous process as people are frequently confronted with new and changing environmental demands that can lead to stress. Minimizing, mastering, or managing a situation in such a way as to render it less distressing is the goal of coping.

Richard Lazarus (1966) offered a three-process model of stress. *Primary appraisal* is the process of perceiving a threat to oneself. *Secondary appraisal* is the process of calling to mind a possible response to the threat. *Coping* is the execution of the response to the threat. The body has its own way of coping with stress. Any threat or challenge an individual perceives in the environment initiates a sequence of neuroendocrine events. These events are conceptualized as two separate responses: a *sympathetic/adrenal response*, in which catecholamines (epinephrine, norepinephrine) are secreted (i.e., the "fight or flight" response), and the *pituitary/adrenal response*, involving the secretion of corticosteroids, which act to restore the biological system to homeostasis (Frankenhauser 1986).

TYPES OF COPING

Lazarus and Susan Folkman (1984) were the first scholars to make the distinction between *problem-focused coping* and *emotion-focused coping*. Problem-focused coping seeks to ameliorate the stress being caused by a given situation by identifying and making efforts to deal with the source of the problem. It may involve taking action to remove a stressor or to evade a threatening stimulus. For example, changing trails to avoid a snake while on a nature walk would be an example of the problem-focused method of coping: By effectively removing oneself from the threatening situation, one lowers the stress it induces.

The goal of *emotion-focused coping* is to reduce the intensity of distressing emotions associated with stress—that is, the aim is to make oneself *feel* better about a real or perceived threat or stressor without addressing the source of the stress. Emotion-focused coping often occurs when problem-focused coping fails to reduce the stress in a situation or when the stressor is so great that problem-focused coping has no real likelihood of helping. It can also come into play when many aspects of a situation are out of one's control, such as when one is dealing with a terminal illness or the sudden death of a loved one.

Charles Carver and his colleagues (1989) developed an instrument to measure coping responses based on a number of conceptually distinct methods of responding to stressful life events. *Active coping* involves taking steps to remove oneself from a threatening situation. *Planning* involves generating strategies to cope with the stressor. Other strategies include *reinterpreting the stressor* as a positive or growth-oriented experience, *suppression of competing activities* (i.e., putting other concerns aside until the stressor sufficiently subsides), *restraint coping* (i.e., waiting for an opportunity to act effectively), *focusing on and venting of emotions* (i.e., expressing grief or "venting" anger), using *humor* to cope with the stressor, *mental* or *behavioral disengagement* (i.e., giving up on trying to solve a problem or reach a goal), *seeking social support*—either *instrumental support*, such as information or resources, or *emotional support*, such as sympathy and understanding—*turning to religion* (i.e., putting the problem in God's

hands), and *acceptance*, whereby the threat is accepted as unavoidable (as with, for example, terminal illness).

Sometimes the nature of a stressor is such that it overwhelms an individual's coping resources. When this occurs, rather than engaging in positive coping strategies, the person sometimes seeks to disengage from the stressful situation altogether. This emotion-focused strategy is called *avoidant coping*, and its goal is to escape or avoid feelings of distress. Denial of the existence of the stressor, for example, can be negative if it causes one to neglect to seek medical attention when symptoms of a possibly serious disease appear. Substance use (i.e., using alcohol and/or drugs) can aid in this disengagement from reality, but only for a time. People may also engage in "magical thinking" in an attempt to wish away a stressor. Unfortunately, in the end the stressor remains, and will inevitably resurface.

SOCIAL SUPPORT AND COPING

It is now widely accepted that receiving effective social support from one's social network can play a role in influencing health and well-being. The two main theories of how social support impacts stress and coping are the *main effect hypothesis*, which asserts that social support is beneficial whether or not one is experiencing increased stress, and the *stress buffering hypothesis*, which asserts that social support during time of elevated stress serves to protect an individual from a stressor's harmful effects (Cohen and Wills 1985).

Social support can take many forms. These include *instrumental support* (e.g., providing a family member with money to buy groceries), *informational support* (e.g., providing information about an illness), and *emotional support*—that is, providing care or comfort. For such support to be effective, however, it must be matched with the environmental demands causing the distress and be provided by the appropriate member of one's social network.

CONCLUSION

Often, the best coping strategies are a combination of problem-focused and emotion-focused strategies, which together engage the stressor in an effort to reduce both its force and the negative emotions it evokes. Seeking social support in times of elevated stress can also be an effective coping strategy. When one is faced with stress that greatly exceeds one's ability to cope, professional services may be helpful, both in strategizing ways to deal with the stressor and as a source of emotional support.

SEE ALSO *Emotion; Mental Health; Mental Illness; Neuroticism; Resiliency; Stress; Vulnerability*

BIBLIOGRAPHY

Carver, Charles S., Michael F. Scheier, and Jagdish Kumari Weintraub. 1989. Assessing Coping Strategies: A Theoretically Based Approach. *Journal of Personality and Social Psychology* 56 (2): 267–283.

Cohen, Sheldon, and Thomas A. Wills. 1985. Stress, Social Support, and the Buffering Hypothesis. *Psychological Bulletin* 98 (2): 310–357.

Frankenhauser, Marianne. 1986. A Psychobiological Framework for Research on Human Stress and Coping. In *Dynamic of Stress: Physiological, Psychological, and Social Perspectives*, eds. Mortimer H. Appley and Richard Trumbull, 101–116. New York: Plenum Press.

Lazarus, Richard S. 1966. *Psychological Stress and the Coping Process*. New York: McGraw-Hill.

Lazarus, Richard S., and Susan Folkman. 1984. *Stress, Appraisal, and Coping*. New York: Springer.

Scott Blum
Roxane Cohen Silver

COPPER INDUSTRY

The copper industry's growth and prosperity are based on the metal's inherent properties: an attractive appearance, high conductivity, good corrosion resistance, ability to alloy with other metals, and ease of working. While there are substitutes in specific uses, copper has entrenched and expanding markets in the electrical, electronic, and communications industries. Electrical and electronic products, including power cables, account for over one third of total usage, and construction, including wiring and water tubing, for a similar share. Transport industries use roughly one eighth of the total, industrial machinery and equipment nearly one tenth, and a wide range of consumer and other products the remainder. Global demand, which moves in step with capital expenditure, especially on construction and infrastructure, and with spending on automobiles and consumer durables, has increased from 3.7 million tonnes in 1960 to 6.8 million tonnes in 1970, 9 million tonnes in 1980, 10.9 million tonnes in 1990, 15.1 million tonnes in 2000, and 16.5 million tonnes in 2005. The annual average rate of growth is 3.1 percent, but with marked annual and geographical variations. The geographical center of demand has altered, with the most rapid increases in China, India, and the countries of the Asia-Pacific Rim. In 1980 the main markets were the countries of the European Union of 15 (30 percent), the United States (21 percent), the USSR (12 percent), and Japan (13 percent). By 2005 China had gained first place with 22 percent and the Asia-Pacific region had 14 percent. These increased shares were only partially offset by the collapse of demand in the former Soviet Union and its European satellites. In recent years demand has flattened out, or even fallen, in the United States (14 percent of the 2005 total), Japan (7 percent), and many of the European Union of 15 (20 percent) as their economic activity has become increasingly dependent on service industries and imported manufactures. Global turnover amounted to $21 billion in 2002 and $60 billion in 2005, with increased prices explaining most of the rise. World exports of refined copper metal accounted for 38 percent of production, worth almost $23 billion, in 2005.

Copper is priced on terminal markets, mainly the London Metal Exchange, and prices fluctuate with changes in the balance between supply and demand and with general economic and financial conditions. Whereas demand is cyclical, supply tends to be relatively inelastic as mines need to spread heavy fixed costs over as high an output as possible. The industry is a modest employer of labor, but is capital intensive at both the mining and refining stages. Volatile prices can be hedged in forward markets, but nonetheless create problems for producers and consumers alike. For example, the daily cash price fell from $3065/tonne on January 20, 1995, to a low of $1319/tonne on November 11, 2001, and rose to a high of $4650/tonne on December 28, 2005. The annual averages were $2934/tonne in 1995, $1560/tonne in 2002, and $3684/tonne in 2005. High prices both encourage substitution by other materials, and lead governments and labor to press for increased shares of profits. Weak prices inhibit exploration and new investment and may force the closure of higher cost mines.

The relatively strong growth of demand since the late 1980s has been facilitated by changes in the structure and nature of supply. Global mine production of copper was about 15 million tonnes in 2005, with the balance of demand for refined copper metal met from recycled materials. In many instances ores contain other payable products as well as copper, which can contribute considerably to mine profitability, and can influence production patterns. Because individual ore deposits are finite, continued spending on exploration and mine development is required merely to maintain output, let alone satisfy rising demand. Improved exploration techniques have partly offset the tendency for the average grade of copper ore to fall with the depletion of the richer and most accessible ore deposits. Also, technological improvements and rising mine size have tended to neutralize any impact of falling average grades on production costs. During the 1990s output became increasingly concentrated in large open-pit mines, where economies of scale more than offset the relatively low grades of contained metal in the ore. In 2004 the three largest mines produced about 2.5 million tonnes, or 15 percent of output. The annual copper output of the median mine grew from 75,000 tonnes in 1980 to 110,000 tonnes in 1990 and almost 200,000 tonnes in

2000. Larger mine sizes and falling average grades have greatly increased the local environmental impact of mining, as greatly increased volumes of waste and overburden have to be moved per tonne of recovered metal. Energy needs have also risen sharply. Most mines are located in relatively unpopulated areas, but social and community tensions can arise when they are developed near population centers, particularly where indigenous peoples are involved.

With the exhaustion of many small high-grade mines in Europe and parts of North America since the late 1980s, the geographical focus of output has shifted. That shift has been accompanied by changes in patterns of ownership. Whereas the shares of leading companies in total output have not altered significantly, the identity of those leading companies has changed markedly. During the 1950s, 1960s and early 1970s, many mines were wholly or partially nationalized, largely but not entirely in developing countries in accordance with the then-prevailing ethos of national ownership and control of mineral resources. In countries such as Chile, Zambia, and Zaire, foreign-owned mining companies had dominated, or even distorted, the local economy and exerted considerable political power, often fueling strong local resentment. Some nationalized U.S. companies, like Anaconda in Chile, blocked foreign aid and further investment in their former host countries in the 1970s. The greater part of U.S. mine output was acquired by oil companies during the 1970s. (For example, Anaconda Copper's Chilean assets were nationalized in the 1960s and early 1970s, and its remaining assets were acquired by Atlantic Richfield in the late 1970s.) Subsequent decades have witnessed the complete withdrawal of the oil companies from copper production, and the privatization of copper projects in many countries. As of 2007 only Chile retains a significant state holding, through Codelco, but the company now coexists with privately owned companies and accounts for only 35 percent of a greatly expanded Chilean output, compared with about 82 percent in the early 1980s. Elsewhere, state-owned producers generally failed to invest sufficiently to sustain their output and remain competitive. U.S. mine output collapsed from 1973's 1.6 million tonnes to 1 million tonnes in 1983, and it would have fallen further but for the oil companies' investment and the application of new technology. Until the late 1970s most copper ore was crushed, concentrated by a variety of means, and then smelted and refined. Not all ores are amenable to processing by such means and oxide ores were often left untreated. Acid leaching, followed by solvent extraction and electro-winning (SX-EW) enabled the treatment of such ores and waste dumps, often at low costs, and these hydrometallurgical processes were suitable for many deposits in the Southwestern United States. In consequence, U.S. mine output

expanded to 1.8 million tonnes in 1993 and 1.9 million tonnes in 1996, only to contract to 1.1 million tonnes by 2003, after prices had collapsed cyclically in the late 1990s.

Many South American copper ores are amenable to SX-EW processing and by 2004 the technique accounted for 18 percent of global mine output. One advantage is that the process produces saleable copper metal rather than intermediate products requiring further processing. Russian production fell with the collapse of the Soviet Union, and output fell during the 1980s and 1990s in Europe, Canada, Central Africa, and the Philippines. The number of producing countries has dwindled along with the number of mines. As of 2007 Chile accounts for 35 percent of global mine output, followed by the United States (8 percent), Indonesia (7 percent), Peru (7 percent), Australia (6 percent), and Russia (5.5 percent). The leading five copper mining companies supply 38 percent of global output, and the top ten 58 percent—similar shares to those of the mid 1970s. The five leading companies are Codelco (12.7 percent of 2004's output), BHPBilliton (7.3 percent), Phelps Dodge (7.1 percent), Grupo Mexico (6.1 percent), and Rio Tinto (5.1 percent).

There is large global trade in ores and concentrates (28 percent of total mine output, and 34 percent of the output of concentrates) as not all copper is smelted and refined at, or near, the mine site. Some smelters and refineries continued to produce from imported raw materials when local mines were depleted, and some countries, like Japan, Korea, and China, deliberately fostered metal production for strategic or developmental reasons. The main countries producing copper metal are Chile (17 percent), China (15 percent), European Union of 15 (11 percent), Japan (8 percent), and the United States (7 percent). The ownership of copper refineries is rather less concentrated than that of mines, with the ten leading companies having 50 percent of output, rather less than in the mid-1970s.

SEE ALSO *Allende, Salvador; Dependency; Mining Industry*

BIBLIOGRAPHY

Crowson, Phillip. 2003. Mine Size and the Structure of Costs. *Resources Policy* 29 (1–2): 15–36.

International Copper Study Group. *Copper Bulletin*. Lisbon, Portugal: ICSG. (Monthly.)

Prain, Ronald, Sir. 1975. *Copper: The Anatomy of an Industry*. London: Mining Journal Books.

Radetzki, Marian. 1985. *State Mineral Enterprises: An Investigation into Their Impact on International Mineral Markets*. Washington, DC: Resources for the Future.

U.S. Geological Survey. *Copper: Statistical Compendium*. Washington, DC: U.S. Geological Survey.

http://minerals.usgs.gov/minerals/pubs/commodity/copper/
stat.

U.S. Geological Survey. *Minerals Yearbook*. Washington, DC:
U.S. Geological Survey.
http://minerals.usgs.gov/minerals/pubs/commodity/copper.
(Annual; see chapters on copper.)

World Bureau of Metal Statistics. *World Metal Statistics*. Ware,
U.K.: WBMS. (Monthly.)

Phillip Crowson

COPTIC CHRISTIAN CHURCH

The identity of the Coptic (i.e., Egyptian) Orthodox Church is based on the foundation of the patriarchate of Alexandria by Mark the Evangelist. He is regarded as the first in an unbroken line of patriarchs represented in 2007 by Pope Shenuda III who, like the Greek Orthodox patriarch, is called the Pope of Alexandria and all Africa. The patriarchate is in Abbasiya, Cairo, in the complex of the Coptic Cathedral of Saint Mark, and there are roughly 8 million believers across the country.

Egyptian patriarchs of Alexandria wielded great influence at the various councils convened to reconcile disputes that plagued the early church. In 325, Alexander and his papal successor Athanasius subscribed to the Nicene Creed that God the Father and Christ the Son were full and equal participants in the Godhead; Arius, who presented that the Son was subordinate to the Father, was banished. When Constantinople gained the prestige that once belonged to Alexandria, Arius was recalled and Athanasius was driven into exile on five occasions, which coincided with the appointment of Arian bishops in Alexandria. The dispute was finally resolved in the Council of Constantinople in 381 when the Nicene Creed, defended for decades by Athanasius, was reaffirmed.

Egypt's refusal to endorse the decrees issued at the Council of Chalcedon in 451 was a nationalistic gesture of independence. Earlier, there existed no theological differences between the Church of Alexandria and the Churches of Rome, Constantinople, Antioch, and Jerusalem. The decisions that caused the divisions into "Chalcedonian" and "non-Chalcedonian" or "monophysite" churches were political rather than doctrinal because both claimed authority over the patriarchate of Alexandria. The Coptic Church is committed solely to the first three ecumenical councils: Nicea (325), Constantinople (381), and Ephesus (431), where Saint Cyril of Alexandria, champion of Christian orthodoxy, was honored for his defense against Nestorianism and for his definition of faith as expressed in the *Coptic Synaxarium*: "The Union of the Word of God with the flesh is as the union of the soul with the body, and as the union of fire with iron, which although they are of different natures, yet by their union they become one. Likewise, the Lord Christ is One Christ, One Lord, One Nature and One Will."

In the year 570, Copts appointed their own "pope and patriarch" residing at Wadi Natrun, west of the Delta. Egyptian Orthodox Christians henceforward ignored ecclesiastical representatives from Constantinople, adopted a Calendar of the Martyrs that begins its era on August 29, 284 in recollection of those who had died for their faith in the reign of Diocletion, translated the whole of the New Testament into Coptic, and followed the teachings of Saint Mark.

Periods of peace and persecution comprise the history of the Coptic Church. The Persian army destroyed churches and monasteries in 617. The religious life of the Copts suffered relatively little after the Arab invasion in 641, provided they paid a tax, but when repressive laws were later imposed, they drove the Copts to revolt on several occasions. The Church generally flourished under the Fatimids (969–1171), when there was a revival of Coptic identity, but this was followed by persecution under the Ayyubids (1171–1250). With the rise of the Mamelukes, churches and monasteries were plundered and destroyed, Copts became a small minority, and pressure continued under the Ottomans (1517–1808).

The position of the Coptic Church improved under the enlightened rule of Mohamed Ali's dynasty in the nineteenth and twentieth centuries. In the 1950s nationalization and "Arabization" policies under Egyptian president Gamal Abdel Nasser resulted in an exodus of a professional class abroad, including Copts. There are more than 80 Coptic Churches in the United States and Canada, 26 in Australia, and some 30 in Europe. A missionary movement has resulted in the establishment of six Coptic Orthodox Churches in Africa.

The tremendous cultural revival of the Coptic Church from the 1950s, mainly initiated under Pope Kyrollos and continued under Pope Shenuda, includes a surge of Sunday schools, Coptic institutions, orphanages, old age homes, hospitals, and social service centers.

Since the 1970s, Pope Shenuda has instigated theological discussions with the Roman Catholic Church, and the Greek and Oriental Orthodox Churches, with view to the Copts being fully accepted as Orthodox Christians by all members of the world community. In fact, ecumenical discussions at the Vatican in 1973 led to a general acceptance of the above-mentioned Christological formula of Saint Cyril of Alexandria.

SEE ALSO *Christianity; Church, The*

BIBLIOGRAPHY

Kamil, Jill. 2002. *Christianity in the Land of the Pharaohs: The Coptic Orthodox Church*. New York: Routledge.

Meinardus, Otto F. A. 1999. *Two Thousand Years of Coptic Christianity*. Cairo: American University in Cairo Press.

Jill Kamil

CORE

SEE *Congress of Racial Equality*.

CORE-PERIPHERY

SEE *Dependency Theory*.

CORN LAWS

The British repeal of the Corn Laws in 1846 is usually seen as the beginning of a unilateral move to free trade that served as the pivotal event in the spread of economic liberalization throughout western Europe. Historians have also seen the Repeal Act as reflecting Prime Minister Robert Peel's (1788–1850) personal devotion to free trade. It was a powerful symbol of his desire to minimize the role of vested interests and state power in the functioning of the economy, even at great political cost to his party (Howe 1997).

But more recent, revisionist work suggests that the transition to a free trade regime did not come as swiftly nor as smoothly as the conventional narrative presents. Nor was the Corn Law repeal as important for the spread of free trade in Europe. Many of the most onerous tariffs and import restrictions that had distorted British trade throughout the eighteenth century remained in place for decades.

Though often seen as symbolic of the various tariffs and quotes on imports denounced by Adam Smith (1723–1790) in his indictment of the mercantile system in *The Wealth of Nations* (1776), the Corn Laws themselves mostly came after Smith's great work. The Corn Laws referred to the various restrictions on both imports and exports of grain and related agricultural products put into place beginning in 1804, which were then followed by further restrictions culminating in the Corn Law of 1815. These laws, in turn, extended regulations in 1773 that had (1) prohibited exports of wheat when prices reached a preset level, and (2) imposed a sliding scale of duties on wheat that declined if market prices were high enough.

The intense attention paid to the political and ideological debates leading to the eventual repeal of these restrictions in the 1840s shows the danger of judging the economic importance of a legislative change by focusing on the political and cultural significance of that event. Whatever the symbolic meaning of the repeal for contemporaries, it is now clear that historical accounts of a lone free-trade Britain are inconsistent with an objective examination of the statistical record of British trade.

One of the reasons why the British tariff repeal has seemed so dramatic was the high level of British average tariffs in the 1820s (the *average tariff* is the value of all import duties as a fraction of the value of all imports). What matters is not how high the statutory level of tariffs was, but the level of tariffs for the goods that represented the bulk of British trade. (For a more technical analysis of the relative importance of British tariff restrictiveness based on a rigorous general equilibrium model, see Dakhlia and Nye [2004] and Nye [2007].) And British tariff levels were among the highest in Europe in the 1820s. Indeed, they were fully comparable to average tariffs for the United States, one of the most openly protectionist nations in the world. A comparison with Britain's traditional rival, France, shows how exaggerated the tale of unilateral British free trade has been. For the first three quarters of the nineteenth century, average tariffs in Britain were consistently higher than they were in France, a nation that was avowedly not a free trader. More refined calculations also indicate that British tariff policies imposed a greater burden on British welfare than did French tariffs on French trade. Part of this is due to the fact that history has exaggerated the extent to which French policy was protectionist.

But the important point is that after the abolition of the Corn Laws, most of the duties that Britain abolished were on manufactures or on items of minor importance to trade. Because Britain had an absolute and comparative advantage in the production of textiles and other manufactures, the effect of these liberalizations on British trade was muted. Though Britain in the 1850s had only a few tariffs, they were set at very high levels and were imposed on consumables such as wine, spirits, tea, coffee, and sugar that composed a large portion of British import trade.

Central to the system were the nearly prohibitive tariffs on wine and spirits—imposed after the War of Spanish Succession in the early 1700s—which were designed to spite Britain's enemy, France, and favor British allies such as Portugal. Britain had been especially concerned with its large trade deficit with France, and the war gave a pretext for crippling the French trade. Despite this, Britain ran a merchandise trade deficit for much of the eighteenth century and all of the nineteenth. The 1804 Methuen Treaty—cited as a prime example by Adam Smith of the old mercantilist system—established a permanent preferential tariff for Portuguese wines and spirits in exchange for continued British export access to Portuguese markets. Given that almost all Portuguese alcoholic exports went to only one nation, Britain, as a result of this preference, this gives the lie to David Ricardo's (1772–1823) famous example of trade between Britain and Portugal as illustrative of the virtues of comparative advantage.

High tariffs on imported wines and spirits, as well as on substitute beverages such as tea and coffee, had the effect of protecting domestic producers of beer, whiskey, and other spirits. Complicated preferential tariffs also favored colonial products such as rum.

The truly major change came about with the 1860 Anglo-French Treaty of Commerce brokered by Richard Cobden (1804–1865) and Michel Chevalier (1806–1879). Despite the correct claims of committed free traders that unilateral tariff reductions were first-best, the unwillingness of Britain to lower wine tariffs prior to 1860 did little to inspire other nations to move to free trade. However the 1860 treaty led to France removing all prohibitions on British textiles and lowering the overall level of tariffs in exchange for British concessions on wine and spirits. This event, not the repeal of the Corn Laws in the 1840s, was in fact the true start of European free trade. By 1870 almost all of the leading powers in Europe were to sign most-favored-nation trade treaties with Britain and France, thus leading to the rapid creation of a truly extensive and open trading network. Where mere exhortation had done little to induce other nations to liberalize commerce, the threat of being excluded from trade arrangements between the two great European powers was the critical incentive for a sustainable liberal trade regime.

The only major exception in the Western world was the United States. Whereas most nations in Europe were lowering tariffs in the 1860s, the United States began to raise tariffs significantly. To some extent, these restrictions were partially offset by the openness of world capital markets and by America's liberal immigration policy, which allowed free movement of labor.

Toward the end of the century, concerns about falling grain prices due to increased imports from the East caused France and Germany to raise tariffs and abandon the most-favored-nation system. But trade in Europe remained fairly open, and British tariffs were at an all-time low. This happy period of open European trade would only be destroyed with the coming of World War I (1914–1918).

SEE ALSO *Economics, Classical; Free Trade; Mercantilism; Ricardo, David; Tariffs*

BIBLIOGRAPHY

Dakhlia, Sami, and John V. C. Nye. 2004. Tax Britannica: Nineteenth Century Tariffs and British National Income. *Public Choice* 121 (3–4): 309–333.

Howe, Anthony. 1997. *Free Trade and Liberal England, 1846–1946.* Oxford: Clarendon.

Nye, John V. C. 2007. *War, Wine, and Taxes: The Political Economy of Anglo-French Trade, 1689–1900.* Princeton, NJ: Princeton University Press.

Schonhardt-Bailey, Cheryl. 2006. *From the Corn Laws to Free Trade: Interests, Ideas, and Institutions in Historical Perspective.* Cambridge, MA: MIT Press.

Smith, Adam. [1776] 1976. *An Inquiry into the Nature and Causes of the Wealth of Nations*, eds. R. H. Campbell and A. S. Skinner. Oxford: Clarendon.

John V. C. Nye

CORPORAL PUNISHMENT

Corporal punishment, including spanking, slapping, paddling, or the prolonged maintenance of a physically uncomfortable position, can be defined as the intentional infliction of physical pain in response to a child's misbehavior that has the goal (whether it is met or not) of correcting the misbehavior. A complicated and controversial issue, however, is where to draw the line between corporal punishment and physical abuse. Incidents of physical abuse often develop out of parents' disciplinary behaviors. For example, routine discipline may cross the line to become physically abusive if parents cannot control their anger, are unable to judge their own strength, or are unaware of children's physical vulnerabilities. Nonabusive parents are likely to tailor their punishments to children's misbehaviors, but abusive parents appear to use physical punishment indiscriminately. Moreover, physical abuse appears to be part of a constellation of parenting behaviors that also includes authoritarian control, anxiety induction, and a lack of expressed warmth toward the child.

One argument is that any form of corporal punishment constitutes physical abuse. Indeed, several countries have outlawed the use of corporal punishment. In 1979 Sweden became the first country to do so, adding a provision to the Parenthood and Guardianship Code stating, "Children are entitled to care, security and a good upbringing. Children are to be treated with respect for their person and individuality and may not be subjected to corporal punishment or any other humiliating treatment." Prior to the 1979 ban, more than half of the Swedish population believed that corporal punishment was necessary in child rearing; just two years after the ban, the rate was reduced by 50 percent, and by 1996, the rate was down to 11 percent. Decreases in rates of use of corporal punishment have accompanied changes in attitudes about its use (from nearly 100 percent before the ban to 40 percent by 2000). Several other countries, including Finland, Denmark, Norway, Austria, Cyprus, Latvia, and Croatia, have also outlawed the use of corporal punishment. Beginning in 1990 with the Convention on the Rights of the Child, the United Nations has placed the protection of children's rights at the forefront of issues before the international community. More recently, the United Nations has launched a global study of violence against children. In his interim report to the General Assembly in October 2005, independent investigator Paulo Pinheiro stated that the "objective of the study must be to ensure that children enjoy the same protection as adults. It will challenge social norms that condone any form of violence against children, including all corporal punishment, whether it occurs in the home, schools and other institutions."

Despite the banning of corporal punishment in several countries and the movement against its use in the international community, about 75 percent of American parents endorse the use of physical discipline, and over 90 percent of parents have used physical discipline with their children (Straus 1996). Individuals who argue that corporal punishment can be used effectively without constituting abuse suggest that corporal punishment should not be overly severe, that parents should be under control and not in danger of "losing it" from anger, that punishment should be motivated by concerns for the child rather than parent-oriented concerns, and that it should be used privately after a single warning with children ages two to six years and accompanied by reasoning (Larzelere 2000).

Across a wide range of countries, males are more likely to endorse the use of corporal punishment than are females, and parents are more likely to use corporal punishment with boys than with girls. Other demographic variables are also related to the likelihood of using corporal punishment. In particular, lower socioeconomic status, having more children, and being affiliated with a conservative Protestant religion are all related to using corporal punishment more frequently. African American parents have been found to use more corporal punishment than European American parents, even after controlling for socioeconomic status.

Cultural norms and parent-child relationships appear to affect how the experience of corporal punishment is related to children's adjustment. Certain family and cultural contexts may moderate the association between parents' behavior and children's adjustment to the extent that they influence children's construal of the parents' behav-

iors. Children who regard corporal punishment as a frightening experience in which their parents are out of control and acting in a way that is not accepted in their cultural context may interpret the experience as parental rejection (especially in the context of a parent-child relationship that is lacking in warmth) and may respond by escalating externalizing behaviors. On the other hand, children who regard spanking as a legitimate form of discipline that is normative in their cultural context may not interpret the experience of corporal punishment as their parents' rejection of them (especially if the parent-child relationship is generally characterized by warmth), and corporal punishment in this context may not be associated with elevated levels of behavior problems. Ethnic differences in the meaning that children attach to being corporally punished may explain why corporal punishment is related differently to their subsequent externalizing behavior. Among European Americans, parents' use of physical discipline has been related to higher levels of subsequent behavior problems in children, but this association is attenuated or reversed for African Americans. The finding has been replicated using different data sets and measures and controlling for potentially confounding variables. One purported explanation of these ethnic differences is that corporal punishment is more normative for African American than for European American families, which alters the meaning of corporal punishment to the child (Deater-Deckard and Dodge 1997). There is also some evidence that corporal punishment and children's adjustment can be unrelated, if one takes into account parental characteristics such as warmth and involvement, which may offset the potentially deleterious effects of corporal punishment. For example, Vonnie McLoyd and Julia Smith (2002), who examined data from the National Longitudinal Survey of Youth, found that only in the context of low levels of maternal support did spanking predict an increase over time in mother-reported internalizing and externalizing problems.

In a study that addressed the normativeness hypothesis directly, findings from six countries (China, India, Italy, Kenya, Philippines, and Thailand) revealed that countries differed in the reported use and normativeness of corporal punishment and in the way that corporal punishment was related to children's adjustment (Lansford et al. 2005). More frequent use of corporal punishment was less strongly associated with child aggression and anxiety when it was perceived as being more culturally accepted. In countries in which corporal punishment was more common and culturally accepted, children who experienced corporal punishment were less aggressive and less anxious than children who experienced corporal punishment in countries where corporal punishment was rarely used. In all countries, however, higher use of corporal punishment was associated with more child aggression and anxiety regardless of the level of acceptance.

A paradox is that although individual differences in corporal punishment do not strongly predict individual differences in child aggressive behavior within cultures for which corporal punishment is relatively normative, cultures in which corporal punishment is normative have higher levels of overall societal violence. Carol and Melvin Ember's 2005 analysis of ethnographies from 186 preindustrial societies found rates of corporal punishment use to be higher in societies that also had higher rates of homicide, assault, and war. Within the United States, corporal punishment is used more frequently in the South than in other regions, which is quite likely a reflection of the South's greater acceptance of a "culture of violence" that encompasses higher homicide rates as well as milder forms of violence.

SEE ALSO *Child Development; Children; Parenting Styles; Violence*

BIBLIOGRAPHY

Deater-Deckard, Kirby, and Kenneth A. Dodge. 1997. Externalizing Behavior Problems and Discipline Revisited: Nonlinear Effects and Variation by Culture, Context, and Gender. *Psychological Inquiry* 8 (3): 161–175.

Ember, Carol R., and Melvin Ember. 2005. Explaining Corporal Punishment of Children: A Cross-Cultural Study. *American Anthropologist* 107 (4): 609–619.

Lansford, Jennifer E., et al. 2005. Cultural Normativeness as a Moderator of the Link between Physical Discipline and Children's Adjustment: A Comparison of China, India, Italy, Kenya, Philippines, and Thailand. *Child Development* 76 (6): 1234–1246.

Larzelere, Robert E. 2000. Child Outcomes of Nonabusive and Customary Physical Punishment by Parents: An Updated Literature Review. *Clinical Child and Family Psychology Review* 3 (4): 199–221.

McLoyd, Vonnie C., and Julia Smith. 2002. Physical Discipline and Behavior Problems in African American, European American, and Latino Children: Emotional Support as a Moderator. *Journal of Marriage and the Family* 64 (1): 40–53.

Straus, Murray A. 1996. Spanking and the Making of a Violent Society. *Pediatrics* 98 (4S): 837–842.

Jennifer E. Lansford

CORPORATE ETHICS

SEE *Corporate Social Responsibility.*

CORPORATE GOVERNANCE

SEE *Capitalism, Managerial.*

CORPORATE SOCIAL RESPONSIBILITY

The term *corporate social responsibility* (CSR) refers to actions and activities undertaken by private profit-making enterprises with the ostensible objective of demonstrating that they are good citizens of the communities in which they operate and that they pursue objectives other than maximizing their profits. Firms engage in CSR activities in response to demand from the public that the firms be responsible to all stakeholders, not just the investors who are interested only in profits. A broadened definition of *stakeholders* can include employees, suppliers, customers, and the society at large. CSR requires firms to take actions and incur expenditures that are not required under the law. This demand from citizens and society, and sometimes even from customers and shareholders, comes at the same time as these firms are being asked to improve their internal management practices, and hence the performance as measured in terms of rates of returns, to reduce chances of fraud or mismanagement by those running the firm. In the post-ENRON world, CSR has become enmeshed with the concept of corporate governance; firms are being asked to be good citizens as well as earn large returns on their investments.

Demand for socially responsible behavior is largely an industrialized world phenomenon. It has come into vogue with the realization by many of the citizens that they are not sharing in the apparent prosperity of their economies. Income distributions within the richer countries appear to be worsening simultaneously with the rise of globalization. Corporations are held responsible for both these developments. They may shift jobs to countries where lax labor, human rights, and environmental standards allow them to escape some costs and restrictions imposed on them in the industrialized world. As capital has become mobile globally, returns for large investors as well as incomes of managers who facilitate the movement of capital have risen, sometimes dramatically, as more and more workers with lesser skills are pushed into minimum-wage jobs. Corporations are also seen as having acquired excessive control of, and manipulated, political and legislative processes for their own profits—processes that are supposed to represent all citizens. Although corporate influence on politics is nothing new, ever-growing segments within the richer societies are willing to question the supremacy of economic growth over all other goals of societies and hence demand that corporations modify their behavior.

WHAT DOES CSR IMPLY FOR CORPORATIONS?

Most corporations' responses to the demand for CSR fall somewhere between two extremes. At one end, demonstration of concern for socially responsible behavior—behavior for which the firm has to incur additional expenditures—can generate goodwill among customers in the long run. Resulting expansion of the firm's market actually makes the investment in CSR a profitable activity. In such cases investment in CSR is no different from investment in, say, an advertising campaign. It is judged on the basis of its effectiveness measured in terms of the firm's profits. At the other extreme, CSR expenditure becomes an exercise in damage control when it is unlikely to benefit the firm in terms of sales. In most of these cases CSR expenditures become necessary to prevent damage to the corporate brand names from other activities of the firm. This happens if the public takes offense at some corporate activities that, by themselves, may be legal. Past examples include oil companies that have extracted oil with scant regard for the environment or pharmaceutical companies that have tried to charge high prices for their patented medicines well beyond what may be required to justify their research expenditures. If such CSR expenditures were not undertaken, consumers might reject the firm's products or governments might impose stricter legislation that would become costly for the corporation in the long run.

There are many examples of firms that have combined social responsibility with profitable business. A frequently cited case is that of Body Shop. Its founder, Anita Roddick, expanded the firm from 1 outlet in 1976 to about 1,900 outlets in 50 countries by 2005 based on her philosophy of social and environmental responsibility while satisfying consumer needs with natural products. The first outlet was founded on these principles and it would be reasonable to conclude that the subsequent success of this firm was grounded on the philosophy of socially enlightened behavior.

Others have embraced CSR for its strategic value for the growth of the firm. Narayana Murthy, the founder of Infosys in India, is supposed to have created a multibillion-dollar information technology firm on the principles of social responsibility. Given his meager financial sacrifices for these activities, however, others have questioned whether the motivation for the public declarations of support for such behavior represents an enlightened attitude or merely an exploitation of the public's gullibility (Sinha 2005).

At the other extreme, firms have adopted a strategy of being socially responsible to prevent backlash from regulators or consumers. Comeco, a Canadian mining company, followed a policy of awarding service contracts to the native people of northern Saskatchewan to bring them onside to oppose the provincial government's attempts to impose strict regulations on uranium mining activities in that province. The higher cost of these service contracts with the natives was considered a good price to pay to avoid regulations and interference from nongovernmental organizations such as Greenpeace. It was later able to use the same strategy to avoid criticism in Kyrgyzstan after a potentially disastrous sodium cyanide spill in a village water supply.

Corporations appear to make a number of sequential decisions about their approaches to CSR activities. These decisions have to be made only for activities that are not required by law. Should they spend money on CSR activities when they do not have to? The answer would be yes if such activities would generate sufficient sales or would prevent loss of markets to competitors who are perceived as being more socially responsible. When not justified by economic profits, these activities will be undertaken when a costly backlash is expected from the consumers or the government.

RATIONALE FOR DEMANDS FOR CSR

To demand socially responsible behavior above and beyond what is legal is to recognize that ethical standards in a society should exceed the legal ones. Such a demand recognizes that the control of means of production of the society bestows strong powers on those who control them. With the control of means of production comes the temptation to control and manipulate the political and legal apparatus of the society.

From the point of view of the society, the essence of CSR is the clash between economic and noneconomic goals of the society. Pursuit of economic growth yields income that should result in higher welfare. However, what happens when, for example, the health insurance industry influences—legally—the political processes to ensure that the government does not provide health insurance to all citizens because such a move will reduce the number of people who buy insurance from firms within the industry?

How should this apparent conflict between economic and social goals be resolved? One approach would be to demand that those with economic power be held to ethical and moral standards that exceed what has been codified in the law. Mere adherence to the letter of the law would not be sufficient for those who control critical resources of the society. In this approach private enterprises will be judged not only on the products and services they provide but also on how they conduct themselves within the societies in which they operate. An opposite approach would be to recognize that the best strategy would be to completely separate economics and politics and ensure that economic interests are not allowed to influence the construction of the moral framework of the society. In this approach private enterprises will have to adhere strictly to the letter of the law but will not have to worry about being socially responsible.

SEE ALSO *Bribery; Corporations; Corruption; Crime and Criminology*

BIBLIOGRAPHY

Bhattacharya, C. B., and Sankar Sen. 2004. Doing Better at Doing Good: When, Why, and How Consumers Respond to Corporate Social Initiatives. *California Management Review* 47 (1): 9–24.

Reich, Robert. 1998. The New Meaning of Corporate Social Responsibility. *California Management Review* 40 (2): 8–17.

Sinha, Kamal. 2005. Narayana Murthy: Unofficial Biography (Story). Kamalsinha.com, April 3. http://www.kamalsinha.com/iit/people/narayana-murthy/.

Vogel, David. 2005. *The Market for Virtue: The Potential and Limits of Corporate Social Responsibility*. Washington, DC: Brookings Institution Press.

Arvind K. Jain

CORPORATE STRATEGIES

The groups of individuals that make up a *firm*, or *corporation*, are responsible for determining its actions. Those decisions are made in the context of the markets in which the firm participates as manufacturer, seller, buyer, and competitor. By defining and categorizing strategies, firms can better understand their options and opportunities. Social scientists and policymakers can also investigate the reasons for firms' success or failure and their contributions to society's welfare.

To understand the motivations behind corporate strategies, one can think in terms of the individual members of the firm who make decisions or in terms of the firm acting as a single entity. In economics, the starting point is to think of the firm as indivisible—essentially as an extension of the owner-entrepreneur whose goal is to maximize profit. Expanding that assumption to encompass long-run profits can account for a large variety of observed behavior. Thus the profit motive helps one understand decisions not only concerning pricing or production in the firm's current markets, but also investment to lower future costs and improve future quality, as well as

decisions to enter markets that promise large future profits and exit markets that provide inferior profit opportunities. In this way many of the changes that occur in products and market structure over time can be described. Many business decisions that are not immediately recognized as profit maximization can be understood in these terms—generating growth, creating and maintaining competitive advantages over other firms, and improving the inputs available to the firm. Because the firm wishes to maintain profits today and in the future, it will take actions that are not immediately profitable but provide the firm with greater future profits, so that the project's net present value of future profits exceeds the cost of implementation.

Milton Friedman's (1953) assertion that firms behave "as if" they were profit maximizers, by arguing that firms that do not maximize profits will not survive, was intended to justify behavior that does not immediately appear to maximize profit. Although the literature has found this evolutionary argument difficult to support, improvements in modeling firms' long-run goals have advanced understanding in the field.

Strategies can also be actions designed to make markets more amenable to the firm's success by changing the attractiveness of rivals' options (Bain 1956). For example, the firm can commit to large production by building additional manufacturing capacity or signing binding legal contracts. This in fact limits the firm's options, but as a result is a credible commitment to substantial future production. Potential competitors can then observe that their entry will be less profitable, and as a result the incumbent firm can deter entry. As another example, firms that sell durable goods can benefit from committing to limit future sales (Bulow 1982). This causes the future resale value of present goods to increase, and customers are then willing to pay more for the goods today.

Of course, firms are made up of individuals whose goals and incentives are likely to differ from those of the owners. Thus "the firm" may take actions that are not those of a single profit-maximizing entity. Departures from the owner-entrepreneurs' goals could be characterized as being caused by employees' pursuit of their own self-interest. The principal (the owner or upper-level manager, for example) takes this constraint into account by appropriately adjusting the incentives of the agents (those that report to the principal). These internally motivated dimensions to strategy may affect the firm's ability to pursue plans that would otherwise be optimal from the perspective of a single owner-entrepreneur.

As the firm interacts in markets, the description of its strategies can also be generalized with less precise foundations. In the business and management literatures, these generalized strategies serve as approximate heuristics for practicing managers. Corporate and business-level strategies may focus on growth (new or existing markets, new or existing products), portfolio analysis (each project's market share, market growth rate, and resulting cash flow), matches between industry opportunities and the firm's strengths and synergies, or fiscal properties such as the creation of shareholder value. These strategies are most successful when they are based on fundamentals from economics: the anticipation of costs, customers' trade-offs, and rivals' reactions. Michael Porter (1980) organizes the forces that affect the industry into these categories: buyers' market power, suppliers' market power, the threat of entry, linkages to substitutes and complements, and rivalry among firms in the industry. The implementation of these strategies in markets requires research in segmenting the market along demographic, geographic, or behavioral categories. Positioning products in chosen segments is particular to the firm's marketing group. These strategies are usually framed in terms of the 4 P's—product, price, promotion, and place (or distribution). An important ingredient for success is the recognition of linkages between these dimensions.

BIBLIOGRAPHY

Bain, Joe. 1956. *Barriers to New Competition: Their Character and Consequences in Manufacturing Industries.* Cambridge, MA: Harvard University Press.

Bulow, Jeremy. 1982. Durable Goods Monopolies. *Journal of Political Economy* 90: 314–332.

Friedman, Milton. 1953. *Essays in Positive Economics.* Chicago: University of Chicago Press.

Porter, Michael E. 1980. *Competitive Strategy: Techniques for Analyzing Industries and Competitors.* New York: Free Press.

Schmalensee, Richard, and Robert D. Willig, eds. 1989. *Handbook of Industrial Organization.* 2 vols. Amsterdam: North-Holland.

Christopher S. Ruebeck

CORPORATIONS

The rise of the corporation to its position of world preeminence has its roots in the corporate consolidation of finance and industry in the late nineteenth century, most especially in the United States. Competition for capital globally and within the confines of the United States played a central role in the rise of U.S. multinational firms, as revealed by an amendment to the New Jersey corporation law of 1889. Until this date, there were only a few large corporate combines of more than $10 million, except in railroads (Horwitz 1992, pp. 83–90; Roy 1997). The amended New Jersey corporation law, designed by William Nelson Cromwell (1854–1948) and his lawyers from the firm of Sullivan and Cromwell and acceded to by the New Jersey State Legislature as a way to attract capital to its domains, helped change all this. Businesses worth hundreds of millions of dollars fled from New York and other locations to set up shop in New Jersey. By the dawn of the twentieth century, roughly seven hundred corporations worth some $1 billion had incorporated in the state (Lisagor and Lipsius 1988, p. 27). With the expenses of New Jersey now paid from corporate fees, and with other regions losing business, rival states adopted similar laws to attract capital, thus largely curbing state regulation of corporations (Horwitz 1992, pp. 83–87).

Competition for capital, which the German sociologist and economist Max Weber (1864–1920) argued was key to corporate influence over states in the world system, thus displayed its power in the United States. Immediately after the New Jersey law's passage, from 1890 to 1893, the rise of Wall Street and the securitization of finance and equity—a major aspect of the financial expansion of the later twentieth century—began. Corporate stock in the new industrial firms became listed on the stock market and was traded by brokerage firms, being publicly offered for purchase on the stock exchange in 1897 as the U.S. merger movement gathered steam. Stock offerings rose from $57 million to $260 million between 1896 and 1907, and the corporate concentration of U.S. capitalism, warned against by such observers as the French writer Alexis de Tocqueville (1805–1859), was solidified (Horwitz 1992, p. 95).

From 1875 to 1904 approximately three thousand companies merged or consolidated as a full third of the country's largest firms evaporated through mergers and vertical integration. This is roughly the same percentage of Fortune 500 firms (the largest publicly held firms in the United States) eliminated during the merger wave and corporate restructuring of the late twentieth century as investment bankers and corporate lawyers once again ascended to the top of the corporate hierarchy (Sobel 1998, p. 24). Morton Horwitz argues that "if the private law of corporations—that is, the law regulating relations within the corporation as well as with private parties—had not changed after 1880, it is difficult to imagine how the enormous corporate consolidation of the next thirty years could have taken place" (1992, pp. 85–86).

Much the same can be said of the wave of state-corporate globalization occurring in the first decade of the twenty-first century. The proliferation of multinational corporations and related supranational institutions is directly related to this early adumbration of transnational firms freed from territorial regulation in the late nineteenth century, with its earlier roots in the Madisonian emphasis on property rights in the U.S. Constitution. The

American sociologist C. Wright Mills (1916–1962) and others dated the supremacy of corporate power in the United States to the elections of 1866 and the Supreme Court decision in *Santa Clara v. Southern Pacific Railroad Company* (1886), which declared the corporation a person under the Fourteenth Amendment. However, Horwitz argues: "More probably, the phenomenal migration of corporations to New Jersey after 1889 made legal thinkers finally see that, in fact as well as in theory, corporations could do virtually anything they wanted." (Horowitz 1992, p. 101). The subsequent replacement of the "artificial entity theory" of the corporation, which "represented a standing reminder of the social creation of property rights" by "the natural entity theory of the business corporation was to legitimate large-scale enterprise and to destroy any special basis for state regulation of the corporation that derived from its creation by the state" (Horwitz 1992, p. 104).

Corporations arose elsewhere, as exemplified by Japan's *zaibatsu*—the unparalleled family-controlled banking and industrial collaborations exemplified by Mitsui, Mitsubishi, Dai Ichi Kangyo, Sumitomo, Sanwa, and Fuyo—and Germany's heavy industrial corporations with links to universal banks. In the 2000s, of course, corporations extend their reach globally, with new corporate firms arising in such East Asian countries as China, Taiwan, and South Korea. With the growing power of corporate firms in the early twentieth century came increased attempts to regulate them, though in the United States antitrust legislation remained subordinate to the need to rely on corporations during wartime and in support of foreign policy. After the wave of nationalization that arose with the Russian, Chinese, and Cuban revolutions, U.S. corporations became increasingly contested and their relative freedom continued to be a mainstay of Western foreign policy.

In the aftermath of the Soviet Empire's collapse in the early 1990s, thousands of corporate firms and their foreign affiliates control about half of the value of all goods and services in the global economy, while the Fortune 500 is responsible for roughly half of all profits in the U.S. economy. Despite free market rhetoric, corporations are often heavily subsidized by their states; these subsidies include military spending, which is exempted from World Trade Organization bans against certain types of subsidies. Corporate exploitation of developing countries occurs through the use of resources and labor, often through subcontracting, a practice exemplified by one of the world's largest corporations, Wal-Mart. Meanwhile, foreign direct investment gives developed countries control over the economies of their junior partners. Simultaneously, limited liability serves to shelter shareholders and officers from corporate malfeasance, while the huge amount of money available for criminal defense often limits the severity of punishment for corporate crime, as evidenced in the wave of corporate accounting scandals involving such companies as Enron and Arthur Anderson in the early twenty-first century. Despite this, corporate advertising and public relations continue to be used to manipulate tastes for consumer goods and to put a positive public face on corporate business. In addition, lobbying associations such as the Business Roundtable in the United States represent the increased politicization of corporations as they use their immense power to influence legislation.

SEE ALSO *Capitalism; General Electric; General Motors; Lobbying; Transnationalism*

BIBLIOGRAPHY

Horwitz, Morton J. 1992. *The Transformation of American Law, 1870–1960.* New York: Oxford University Press.

Lisagor, Nancy, and Frank Lipsius. 1988. *A Law Unto Itself: The Untold Story of the Law Firm Sullivan & Cromwell.* New York: Morrow.

Roy, William G. 1997. *Socializing Capital: The Rise of the Large Industrial Corporation in America.* Princeton, NJ: Princeton University Press.

Sobel, Robert. 1998. Hubris Humbled: Merger Mania, Retribution, Reform—It's All Happened Before. *Barron's* 78 (15): 24–25.

Thomas Ehrlich Reifer

CORPORATISM

Corporatism is a system of interest intermediation in which vertically organized and functionally defined interest groups are granted official representation in the state policymaking apparatus. Corporatism is usefully contrasted with pluralism, a system in which interest groups openly compete with one another to gain access to the state. Under corporatist systems, groups such as labor and business are represented to the state by peak associations, which tend to be subsidized by the state. Other labor and business associations must thus work through these peak associations to gain access to the policymaking process. The major dilemma of corporatism is the balance between the autonomy and state control of interest groups.

Through the mid-twentieth century, corporatism was associated with the systems of interest intermediation found in Nazi Germany and fascist Italy. In the 1960s and 1970s, however, debate emerged over whether European industrial democracies were also characterized by corporatist arrangements. By the late 1970s, scholars had agreed that corporatism could indeed exist within democratic frameworks. They called this system *liberal* or *neocorpo-*

ratism, contrasting it with the *state corporatism* of earlier periods.

In the European democracies, corporatism was understood as either a response to or an accommodation of industrial capitalism. Neocorporatist systems allowed governments to facilitate consensus over economic policy by bringing together interest groups with significant stakes in the future of economic policy to negotiate with one another in a formal setting. In doing this, corporatist systems implicitly limited who would have the most influential voices in the economic policymaking process—and, as a result, helped shape the contours of the debate. For example, the Austrian Joint Commission on Prices and Wages—a corporatist arrangement that included the three largest agriculture, business, and labor associations in the country—was formed in 1957 to consider the future of Austrian economic policy. Sweden and Switzerland also developed particularly strong neocorporatist systems.

At the same time, scholars of the developing world generally—and Latin America particularly—were observing corporatist systems under nondemocratic regimes. In these nondemocratic polities, corporatism tended more toward a means of political control than a means of building consensus. That is, these corporatist arrangements were designed more to co-opt potentially disruptive political actors than to provide a forum for policy discussion and debate. In authoritarian Mexico, for example, labor and peasant groups engaged the state through peak associations that were heavily subsidized by the government. By creating this system of corporatist intermediation, the Mexican government could co-opt and control powerful social actors that had been influential in the early years of the Mexican Revolution. Brazil in the 1930s and Argentina in the 1940s also developed corporatist systems.

Though the early 1990s witnessed some debate over the possibility of new corporatist arrangements in the post-Soviet bloc, corporatism is no longer as frequently invoked as it was in earlier decades—due in large part to the current dominance of pluralist political and economic models of governance. Nonetheless, corporatism remains a viable alternative form of interest intermediation, should pluralist models of interest intermediation meet significant challenges.

SEE ALSO *Authoritarianism; Elites; Fascism; Interest Groups and Interests; Nazism; Politics; Power Elite*

BIBLIOGRAPHY

Collier, David. 1995. Trajectory of a Concept: "Corporatism" in the Study of Latin American Politics. In *Latin America in Comparative Perspective: New Approaches to Methods and Analysis*, ed. Peter H. Smith, 135–162. Boulder, CO: Westview.

Schmitter, Philippe C., and Gerhard Lehmbruch, eds. 1979. *Trends Toward Corporatist Intermediation.* Beverly Hills, CA: Sage.

William T. Barndt

CORRECTIONAL MENTAL HEALTH
SEE *Prison Psychology.*

CORRESPONDENCE PRINCIPLE
SEE *Comparative Dynamics; Comparative Statics.*

CORRESPONDENCE TESTS

Correspondence testing is a field-experimental technique used to investigate discrimination in hiring in the labor market.

THE EXPERIMENTAL PROCEDURE

Two carefully matched, fictitious applications are forwarded in response to advertised job vacancies. To avoid detection the applications cannot be identical, but the logic of the technique is to control strictly for all objective factors, such as education, qualifications, and experience, that influence job performance. Consequently, the only distinguishing feature of the two applications is the characteristic—such as race or sex—that is being tested for, with race or sex being identified by the name of the applicant. To safeguard against the possibility that letter style may influence employer response, the letters are regularly reversed and allocated equally between the candidates. In this way, the influence of race, or sex, on selection for interview is isolated.

HISTORY

The social scientists who innovated this technique were Roger Jowell and Patricia Prescott-Clarke. In a test of racial discrimination in England in 1969 they matched applicants with Anglo-Saxon names (John/Mary Robinson) against those with "West Indian" (Errol/Eva Gardiner) and Indian names (Santokh Singh and Ranwi Kaur). The test was at a time when most adult Indians and West Indians in Britain were first-generation immigrants, so that their race was also identified by their primary schooling having occurred in their country of origin, and by specification of their date of arrival in Britain. Applicants with an Anglo-Saxon name were found to be twice as likely to receive an invitation to interview as applicants with an Indian name. No significant discrimination was detected against applicants who were immigrants from the West Indies.

The first economists to use this technique to test for sexual discrimination were Peter Riach and Judith Rich, who applied the test to seven occupations in Melbourne in the 1980s. They found that men were invited to interview 13 percent more frequently than women in the occupation of computer analyst programmer, and 23 percent more frequently than women in the occupation of gardener. No significant discrimination was detected in the other five occupations. Riach and Rich also tested for racial discrimination in Melbourne in the 1980s, matching an Anglo-Celtic name (Baker) against a Greek name (Papadopoulos) and a Vietnamese name (Nguyen). They found that the Anglo-Celtic applicant was invited to interview 10 percent more frequently than the Greek applicant and 41 percent more frequently than the Vietnamese applicant.

Frank Bovenkerk investigated discrimination against Antilleans in France in the 1970s and found that an applicant with a French name was more than three times as likely to be invited to interview as an applicant with an Antillean name. In the 1990s Bovenkerk, in the Netherlands, found that applicants with Dutch names were 23 percent more likely to be invited to interview than those with Surinamese names and 17 percent more likely to be interviewed than those with Moroccan names.

Doris Weichselbaumer, in Austria, matched a man against a "feminine woman" and a "masculine woman," in two sex-integrated occupations, one female-dominated and one male-dominated occupation. She was able to do this because job applications in Austria include the applicant's photograph. She found that both types of women encountered some discrimination in the male-dominated occupation, that there was no significant difference in the treatment of the two female types, and that both types of women were more than twice as likely as men to be invited to interview in the female-dominated occupation of secretary.

E. Fry in 1986, and Pauline Graham, Antoinette Jordan, and Brian Lamb in a 1992 follow-up, tested discrimination against applicants with the disability of cerebral palsy, which confined them to a wheelchair. The occupation tested was secretary, and in both experiments the able-bodied applicant was approximately 60 percent more likely to receive an invitation to interview.

Full details of the above studies can be found in the critical survey article by Riach and Rich (2002).

TWENTY-FIRST CENTURY ACTIVITY

Marianne Bertrand and Sendhil Mullainathan (2004) made the first attempt to apply the technique to racial discrimination in the United States. They matched distinctive "African American" names, such as Aisha (female applicants) and Kareem (male applicants) against "white" names, such as Anne and Matthew. They tested four occupations in Boston and Chicago, and found that the white applicant was called back 60 percent more frequently than the African American applicant. Fictitious mailing addresses were used; consequently, any postal responses could not be recorded. Instead of sending carefully matched *pairs* of applications, which differed only in name, as in the other cited tests, their resumes were randomly generated from a bank of information and sometimes manipulated to match the advertised vacancy. A further problem has been identified by Roland Fryer and Steven Levitt (2004), who have challenged the control provided by the use of distinctive black names. They have demonstrated that since the 1970s distinctive black names have been highly related to lower socioeconomic background. This means that Bertrand and Mullainathan were recording the experience of a subset of African Americans, and employers could well have been responding to socioeconomic status rather than race. Their study is not a basis for generalizing about the labor market experience of African Americans; nevertheless, they did detect discriminatory hiring behavior. In view of the control established by the randomly generated resumes, employers are demonstrating either a statistical or animus-based discrimination purely in response to applicants' first names. An experiment identifying socioeconomic class by address or schooling would be one way of determining its impact relative to racial discrimination.

The correspondence technique is seriously challenged by racial groups whose mainstream members do not have names that clearly distinguish them from other racial groups. The name Patel identifies an Indian, Nguyen identifies a Vietnamese, and Papadopoulos identifies a Greek. They are all very common names, are not associated with any subset of those races and they are readily recognized by the inhabitants of the countries where they are present in substantial numbers. This is not the case with African Americans and Afro-Caribbeans, whose ancestors lost their original names when they were forcibly removed from Africa in the eighteenth century.

Riach and Rich (2006a) conducted the first experiment examining sexual discrimination in England. They found that in the male-dominated occupation of engineer, men had a 40 percent higher likelihood of invitation to interview; that in the female-dominated occupation of secretary, women were twice as likely to be invited to interview; and, without precedent, that women were preferred to men in two sex-integrated occupations: They were 67 percent more likely to be interviewed as computer analyst programmers and twice as likely to be interviewed as trainee chartered accountants. Riach and Rich also conducted the first correspondence test of age discrimination, matching two English women who had graduated simultaneously, but were different ages—one twenty-one, the other thirty-nine. The younger graduate was two-and-a-half times more likely to be interviewed than the woman of thirty-nine (Riach and Rich, 2006b).

ALTERNATIVES TO CORRESPONDENCE TESTS

One alternative approach is to train members of different racial groups to attend interviews and present themselves as having the same skills and level of motivation. British social scientists first used this approach in the 1960s and hired professional actors for their skill in role-playing. The Urban Institute in Washington subsequently adopted this approach, but eschewed the use of actors. A principal advantage of this personal attendance at interview is that it solves the problem of groups that are difficult to identify by name, such as Afro-Caribbeans and African Americans. A second advantage of this approach is that it tests discrimination at the point of job offer, rather than selection for interview. The disadvantage of this personal approach is that you do not have, and cannot demonstrate, the same strict control as exists with correspondence testing. Regardless of the level of training, it is always possible that candidates will present themselves in ways that highlight differences in personality and levels of motivation. This point was made by Robin Ward in the 1960s and again by James Heckman in the 1990s (full details are to be found in Riach and Rich 2002). Heckman has recommended that the candidates should be kept ignorant of the fact that they are operating in pairs and testing for employment discrimination. Ian Ayres did exactly this in a test of racial and sexual discrimination in car sales negotiations, but he also conducted equivalent tests in which the testers *were* aware that they were testing discrimination. He recorded similar results for both sets of tests (see Riach and Rich 2004 for full details).

Surveying employers about employment practices involves the possibility that there will be a discrepancy between what they report and what they actually practice; whereas correspondence testing unequivocally captures practice.

Inferring discrimination from racial or sexual wage differentials that are deemed inconsistent with productivity-determining variables, such as education and experience, begs the question of what the appropriate independent variables should be.

SEE ALSO *Discrimination; Racism*

BIBLIOGRAPHY

Bertrand, Marianne, and Sendhil Mullainathan. 2004. Are Emily and Greg More Employable Than Lakisha and Jamal? A Field Experiment on Labor Market Discrimination. *American Economic Review* 94 (4): 991–1013.

Fryer, Roland G., and Steven D. Levitt. 2004. The Causes and Consequences of Distinctively Black Names. *Quarterly Journal of Economics* 119 (3): 767–805.

Riach, P. A., and J. Rich. 2002. Field Experiments of Discrimination in the Market Place. *Economic Journal* 112 (483): F480–F518.

Riach, Peter A., and Judith Rich. 2004. Deceptive Field Experiments of Discrimination: Are They Ethical? *KYKLOS* 57 (3): 457–470.

Riach, Peter A., and Judith Rich. 2006a. An Experimental Investigation of Sexual Discrimination in Hiring in the English Labor Market. *Advances in Economic Analysis and Policy* 6 (2). http://www.bepress.com/bejeap/advances/vol6/iss2/art1.

Riach, Peter A., and Judith Rich. 2006b. How Age Discrimination Works. http://news.bbc.co.uk/2/hi/programmes/panorama/4879938.stm.

Peter A. Riach
Judith Rich

CORRESPONDENT INFERENCE THEORY

SEE *Jones, Edward Ellsworth.*

CORRUPTION

Corruption has been a part of human societies since the oldest of times. Corruption, fraud, embezzlement, theft, bribes, and kickbacks are all forms in which people try to increase their income at the cost of others. Beginning in the latter half of the 1990s, an increased recognition of these costs led to many international and nongovernmental organizations demanding that political and business leaders demonstrate high standards of honesty, ethics, and social responsibility. This in turn led to a concerted fight against corruption, money laundering, and black markets around the world as well as to the recognition of the importance of governance.

WHAT IS CORRUPTION?

Although disagreements abound, corruption is most frequently defined as the misuse of public power for personal gains. Corruption, unlike fraud and embezzlement, refers to decisions that politicians and public bureaucrats (public officials for ease of exposition) make based on authority delegated to them by the populace. When these decisions are motivated by personal gains rather than by the public's interest, other than politicians favoring segments of the population they represent, this is considered corruption. One of the difficulties of identifying corruption is that these self-serving decisions can often be disguised as good public policy.

Corruption exists in two broad forms—although there are many variations within these two categories and often the two will be intertwined with each other. Administrative, or petty, corruption refers to acts of bribery, kickbacks, or grease money, in which public officials extract a payment for implementing an existing decision. In its purest form this type of corruption is an attempt to redistribute rents or profits associated with a decision. When officials accept a bribe for favoring a particular contractor for a public construction project, they are asking the contractor to share profits associated with the contract with them. The main consequence of such an act of corruption is the redistribution of income that in turn will have some influence on resource allocation.

Political, or grand, corruption or "state capture" occurs when political leaders either allocate national budgets or introduce legislation to facilitate projects from which either they themselves or their close associates will benefit. In almost all cases of political corruption the public would not have made the same decision as the political elite if it were in a position to make that decision. The corrupt elite's profits come either in the form of bribes or from direct stakes in the projects that benefit from the decisions. Examples of corrupt politicians accepting bribes exist in almost every country—industrialized or developing. Also, examples of dictators who have managed to enrich themselves while impoverishing their countries abound: Haiti under François Duvalier (1907–1971), Philippines under Ferdinand Edralin Marcos (1917–1989), Zaire under Mobutu Sese Seko (1930–1997), Nigeria under Kwame Nkrumah (1909–1972), and Uganda under Idi Amin (c. 1925–2003) are just some of the examples. Political corruption leads to the misallocation of a country's economic resources while redistributing income within that country.

Corruption is difficult to measure, but it exists in all countries. In countries where corruption is not endemic, corrupt acts are carried out under secrecy. In countries where corruption is widespread, corrupt incomes take so many forms that measurement becomes meaningless. The most consistent attempt to measure corruption has been carried out by Transparency International (TI), a Berlin-based nongovernmental organization (NGO). Every year TI surveys business people and experts, and based on their perceptions it provides a rating between 10 (no corruption) and 1 (most corrupt). Of the 158 countries ranked in 2005, Iceland, Finland, and New Zealand were the least corrupt and Turkmenistan, Bangladesh, and Chad were the most corrupt.

WHY DOES CORRUPTION GROW, PERSIST, OR DECLINE?

To understand why corruption exists, it helps to examine why there is less corruption in some—usually industrialized—countries. One can start by recognizing that authority over public-sector budgets and regulatory frameworks comes with the potential for huge personal benefits. Assuming that only a small percentage of a population is pathologically honest, most public officials will be tempted to take advantage of their authority. Their gains, however, come at someone else's cost. Therefore, those who may lose from corruption want to control and check the powers of public officials. These checks come in the form of well-developed legal, political, and social institutions within the society. As such, the existence or absence of corruption depends on the balance between the powers of public officials against the strengths of institutions and control mechanisms that empower the public.

All countries have laws against corruption. Selection and retention of public officials, at least in democratic societies, will depend on the public officials demonstrating honest behavior. Democratic institutions that allow a fair and wide participation of the public in the selection of public officials create a barrier against the spread of corruption. Offending officials will be identified and punished by the judicial system or at least not reappointed to their positions. A free press accompanied by an independent and honest judiciary forms another barrier that prevents corruption. Institutions and a variety of organizations that represent specific interest groups in a given society will exert influence on public officials if corruption is likely to harm that society. In so far as politicians derive their authority and appointment from their constituencies, these institutions form another line of defense against corruption. Once in power, however, public officials will have means to render these control mechanisms less effective. A dictator usually succeeds in rendering them completely ineffective; hence, dictatorial regimes are often more corrupt than democratic ones. Democratic leaders are restricted by the strengths of the institutions in a society that constrains behavior of public officials.

Thus, institutions that play an important role in controlling corruption include a free press, an independent judiciary, and a free and democratic political system that gives full voice to the populace in the political process. Research clearly establishes that the absence of corruption within countries correlates with the level of development of these institutions. It is noteworthy that ideology does not seem to play a role in the extent of corruption. Daniel Kaufmann divided countries into "leftist" and "non leftist" regimes (1998, p. 140). The correlation between the extent of corruption and the type of regime was zero.

CONSEQUENCES OF CORRUPTION

Corruption—which is an important component of what is now called governance—is extremely inimical to economic growth and development (Jain 2001). It leads to misallocation of resources, distorts labor markets, discourages investments, and alters income distribution. The myth that corruption helps markets by "greasing the wheels of commerce" has been proven false. While it is true that a bribe may speed up one transaction, it creates incentives for more and higher bribes in previously bribe-free activities. In a remarkable study of bribery, Robert Wade (1985) shows that once bribes are introduced, bureaucracies redirect their attention from providing services to the public to maximizing bureaucrats' illicit incomes.

The most damaging consequence of corruption may be in how it inhibits investment in the economy. Research clearly establishes that countries with high corruption have lower levels of investment and economic growth (World Bank 2001). Corruption, which usually exists in an environment of poor overall governance, makes it difficult for entrepreneurs to invest by increasing the cost of starting a business venture. After investments have been made, corruption creates uncertainty for entrepreneurs because the public officials have an option to extract bribes from the venture should it prove profitable. This option increases entrepreneurs' risks and lowers their returns.

Corruption also distorts the selection of public-sector projects. Small maintenance projects are more effective in terms of their output, but corrupt officials do not like to spend money on smaller projects because they may be carried out by a larger number of contractors, making it more difficult to extract bribes. Thus, corruption biases investment expenditures from high-output to low-output projects. Construction of "roads that go nowhere," "bridges that no one crosses," and unused shells of school buildings that abound in the developing world may have been motivated by bribes, not the needs of the society. In addition, if measured by the extent of bribes as a percent of revenue of a firm, corruption affects small firms more than big ones. Because innovative activities in most economies tend to be taken up by small entrepreneurs, corruption stifles an important source of economic growth. Corruption also discriminates against foreign direct investment because dealing with corrupt officials requires familiarity, which is an advantage that domestic firms may possess.

Corruption affects the labor market by distorting returns for various activities. It distorts the allocation of talent between power-seeking activities and other productive activities in an economy. Furthermore, as noted earlier, corruption discourages the allocation of talent to entrepreneurial activities by lowering rewards and increasing risks.

Corruption does not affect all members of a society equally. The poor suffer relatively more from corruption in two ways. First, bribe payments may represent a higher percentage of their income than similar payments by the rich. In this sense, corruption acts as a regressive tax—lower-income households carry a larger burden than higher-income ones. Second, corruption causes the delivery of public services, for example, health care and education, to deteriorate. Such a deterioration affects the poor more than the rich first, because they may have to pay a bribe to receive the services and second, because they depend more on such services. Corruption may also allow the rich to pay fewer taxes than required by law. This lowers the revenues of the state, further deteriorating the ability of the state to provide services for the poor. Studies confirm that corruption causes income distribution to worsen.

FIGHTING CORRUPTION

Recognizing that corruption is a serious obstacle to fighting poverty, many international and nongovernmental organizations since the latter half of the 1990s have been leading the fight to reduce corruption around the world. This fight focuses on three areas: civil societies in which the public plays a key role, a top-down commitment from the political leadership to fight corruption, and a proactive private sector that accepts its social responsibility to operate in a corruption-free manner. Countries that belong to the Organization for Economic Cooperation and Development have accepted their responsibility in this fight by passing antibribery laws that prohibit their firms from paying bribes in other countries. These laws, however, are rarely strictly enforced.

It is difficult to assess the impact of global efforts to fight corruption. Stories of success tend to be anecdotal. If the ratings of TI are any indication, it will take several years before this fight has a significant impact on the extent of corruption around the world.

SEE ALSO *Accountability; Bribery; Capital Flight; Hot Money; Money Laundering; Transparency*

BIBLIOGRAPHY

Jain, Arvind K. 2001. Corruption: A Review. *Journal of Economic Surveys* 15 (1): 71–121.

Kaufmann, Daniel. 1998. Research on Corruption: Critical Empirical Issues. In *Economics of Corruption*. Ed. Arvind K. Jain. Boston: Kluwer Academic.

Transparency International. 2005. Corruption Perceptions Index 2005. Transparency International. http://www.transparency. org/policy_and_research/surveys_indices/cpi/2005.

Wade, Robert. 1985. The Market for Public Office: Why the Indian State Is Not Better at Development. *World Development* 13 (4): 467–497.

World Bank. 2001. Governance and Corruption. World Bank Group. http://www.worldbank.org/wbi/governance.

Arvind K. Jain

CORTÉS, HERNÁN
1485–1547

Hernán Cortés is best known as commander of the Spanish conquest of Mexico. His life reveals the human, political, and intellectual dimensions of Spain's American empire and the use of history in shaping an understanding of this collective enterprise.

CHILDHOOD, EDUCATION, AND EARLY EXPERIENCE

As commonly occurs in the biographies of self-made heroes, the few facts of Cortés's youth have been supplanted by speculation to invent the lineage, training, and experience that befit so-called singular men of the Renaissance.

Cortés was born in 1485 in Medellín, a small town beside the Guadiana River in Extremadura. His parents were poor *hidalgos* (members of the lower nobility), for whom biographers would claim illustrious ancestors, celebrated for heroism and learning. At fourteen, Cortés was sent to learn Latin with the husband of his father's half-sister in Salamanca. These preparatory studies have been misconstrued and, since 1875, when Bartolomé de las Casas's *History of the Indies* (c. 1560) was published, others have repeated his belief that Cortés held a bachelor's degree in law from the University of Salamanca. However, Cortés returned home after two years, for which the decisive event in his education was instead an apprenticeship with an *escribano* (notary) in Valladolid, from whom he learned the skills used in the Caribbean and later in his own letters, reports, edicts, and briefs.

Cortés departed Spain in 1504, landing in Hispaniola, the administrative center of Spain's colony and only permanent settlement until 1507. He received a small *encomienda* (grant of land with the right to native labor) from the governor Nicolás de Ovando and was made notary of the newly founded town of Azua, in the south of the island, an area subdued with his aid. Because an abscess in his thigh (perhaps syphilis) left Cortés unable to join the ill-fated 1509 expedition of Alonso de Hojeda and Diego de Nicuesa to Darién and Veragua, he remained in Azua until 1511, when he enrolled in the conquest of Cuba, serving its leader, Diego Velázquez, as secretary more than as soldier.

Cortés's years as notary had earned him allies and taught him the workings of the colony at a key juncture in its existence. In 1509, Christopher Columbus's son, Diego Colón, had replaced Ovando as governor, spurring the settlement of neighboring islands. Justifiably wary of Colón's ambitions, the royal treasurer Miguel de Pasamonte would recruit Cortés to report on the conquest of Cuba, a service that Cortés capably performed without alienating Velázquez. Despite such oversight, demands for exploration grew over the next years due to the influx of settlers and the precipitous decline of Hispaniola's native population. The conquests of Puerto Rico (1508), the Bahamas and Jamaica (1509), and Cuba (1511) only temporarily relieved this labor shortage, and did even less to satisfy the ambitions of colonists from Europe.

This state of affairs was further complicated by the protections ceded to the Amerindians under the Laws of Burgos of 1512, the recall of Colón to Spain in 1514, and the death in 1516 of Ferdinand II of Aragon, who had ruled Castile and its overseas possessions as regent after Isabel I died in 1504. Amid uncertainty and competing claims to legitimate and effective authority, the governor of Cuba, Diego Velázquez, sought to steal a march on potential rivals by organizing an expedition to the uncharted lands southwest of Cuba, about which there had been reports as early as 1506, and especially since the voyage of Vasco Núñez de Balboa in 1511. To this end, a small fleet embarked under Francisco Hernández de Córdoba in 1517 and, when this group reported finding a rich land (the Yucatán peninsula) with an advanced, urban population (the Maya), another flotilla was sent under Juan de Grijalva in 1518. Although this expedition met armed resistance, this was seen as a sign of social and political order, a conclusion reinforced by the artisanship of the items obtained in trade and by stories of a great land called México. Using this information, brought in advance of Grijalva's return by a ship bearing the most seriously wounded, Velázquez demanded formal consent to colonize from the Hieronymite friars representing the Crown in Hispaniola, and from the Crown itself in Spain. While awaiting an answer, Velázquez sought to advance his claim to the title of *adelantado* (military and civil governor of a frontier province) by launching a much larger mission, ostensibly to search for Grijalva who had in fact returned, and also "to investigate and learn the secret" of any new lands discovered (*Documentos cortesianos*, vol. 1, p. 55).

It is possible that Velázquez conspired to have this expedition defy his orders not to settle these new lands, in that Las Casas reported that he later reprimanded Grijalva "because he had not broken his instruction" in this regard (Las Casas 1965, vol. 3, p. 220). In any event, Velázquez did not anticipate the disobedience to be shown by Cortés, whom he made its captain. Velázquez's motives in naming Cortés remain unclear; for although Cortés had served Velázquez and was able to commit resources, he was an independent spirit; although liked and respected, he was not known as a soldier. The difficulty of hiding Grijalva's return and the uncertainty of Cortés's loyalties together explain the haste of the latter's departure, which occurred on February 18, 1519, with six hundred soldiers and sailors in total.

CORTÉS AND THE CONQUEST OF MEXICO

From the expedition's start, there were tensions between hidalgos with holdings in Cuba, loyal to Velázquez, and others hoping to improve their lot by backing Cortés. The voyage along the coast of the present-day states of Yucatán, Campeche, and Tabasco confirmed these lands' civilization and wealth, and provided an essential means for their eventual conquest: a shipwrecked Spaniard held captive by the Maya, Gerónimo de Aguilar, and a Nahuatl-speaking native woman enslaved in Tabasco, Malinche (Malintzin or Marina). Translating in tandem and later independently, they enabled the Spaniards to communicate and gather intelligence.

A key fact learned was that many of the peoples subject to the Mexica (Nahua or Aztecs) deeply resented the tribute imposed upon them, and that others such as the city-state of Tlaxcala were at war. Cortés would astutely exploit these ethnic and regional divisions, which persisted under Spanish rule, but first he needed to free himself and his troops of the commission received from Velázquez so they might lay claim to the profit of their endeavor. To this end, he arranged to found the settlement of Villa Rica de la Vera Cruz and had its *cabildo* (town council) review the legitimacy of Velázquez's orders. The report sent to Spain with an impressive cargo of booty on July 10, 1519, was signed by this cabildo, yet bears Cortés's imprimatur in its style and content. Depicting Velázquez as a self-serving tyrant, it states that the collective will of the Crown's subjects residing in the land was to assist their nation and faith by settling there, so they might lead its people from abhorrent rites to Christian religion. For this, the settlers would answer only to the Crown and had implored Cortés to be their captain. It would not suit Cortés to relate these actions, in which he

is said not to rebel but to acquiesce to the legitimate demands of his fellow subjects; it is unlikely that Cortés sent a letter of his own, as he and others have claimed.

Stripping and scuttling his ships so that no one could turn back and sailors might become soldiers, Cortés headed inland toward the Mexican capital of Tenochtitlán with approximately 15 horsemen, 400 foot soldiers, and more than 1,300 Totonac Indians. Claiming to be either an ally or foe of the Mexica in accordance with the loyalties of those encountered, Cortés made his way first to Tlaxcala, and then to Cholula, negotiating an alliance with the former after a series of skirmishes, and defeating the latter in part with intelligence obtained through Malinche, who warned that the Cholulans had prepared an ambush, despite protestations of friendship. Here as later, Cortés used exemplary punishment to make known the cost of treason, executing several thousand Cholulans as a warning to others. Though effective, this act was condemned in later years by political rivals and critics.

On November 8, 1519, the Spaniards were received by Montezuma II in the city of Tenochtitlán. Although impressed by the splendor of the city and Montezuma's control of such a vast and diverse empire, Cortés was concerned by what might happen to his forces, amassed on an island in a lake, should this control falter, as indeed came to pass. For when he left to meet the challenge posed to his authority by an armada sent by Velázquez, hostilities broke out, so that by Cortés's return on June 24, 1520, the fighting was such that Montezuma himself, held prisoner by the Spaniards, could not quell it. Accounts of these events and of Montezuma's death a few days later differ, with blame assigned either to the greed of the Spaniards, who allegedly ordered a celebration held in the main temple to slaughter the Mexican warriors, or to the treachery of the Mexica, who allegedly used this event to arm an attack. In any event, the Spaniards were obliged to flee Tenochtitlán during the night of June 30 (*la noche triste*), losing more than half their forces and nearly all the plunder. These losses fell heaviest on the troops newly recruited, with promises and threats, from among the men sent to arrest Cortés by Velázquez.

Escaping with further casualties to Tlaxcala—which would be accorded special privileges for its partly self-interested loyalty: tax exemptions, the right of its citizens to ride horses and use the honorific title *Don*—Cortés understood that retreat to the coast and on to Cuba or Hispaniola was impossible given the doubtful legality of his status as Captain General of the Spanish forces, which, although Cortés did not know it, Charles V had pointedly left unaddressed after receiving the cabildo's letter and delegates. Cortés therefore began plans to retake Tenochtitlán, rallied his allies and troops (which, after the rout suffered on *la noche triste*, included the most resolute and battle-hardened of those previously in his command), and wrote to the king on October 30, 1520, assuring success while blaming defeat on Velázquez's meddling, which, he said, had diverted his energies at a crucial moment, undermining his command over the Spaniards and his stature in the eyes of the Mexica.

This letter is key to an understanding of the conquest as a whole. Although it was designed to bolster Cortés's claim to leadership—for example, by recasting fortuitous events as evidence of his foresight and God's favor, or by narrating successful actions in the first-person singular—it also brings to light differences between the mainly political tactics of the first march to Tenochtitlán and the violent means ultimately used in its military conquest. The picture put forth in this letter of an enemy seemingly bewildered by technology (ships, firearms, and iron weapons), horses, psychological warfare, and Cortés's ability to anticipate Montezuma's every move and moreover use rhetoric and his own irrational beliefs against him—notably the idea that the Spaniards had been sent by the god Quetzalcoatl, an idea that would in fact become current only after conquest as justification for defeat—has led to the assumption of cultural superiority. Furthermore, it has prompted neglect of the difficulties encountered by the Spaniards after their initial entry into Tenochtitlán and especially after *la noche triste*. The introduction of diseases such as smallpox to which the Amerindians lacked immunity certainly affected the two sides equally.

The advantages cited by Cortés in his report to the king might have been decisive had the conquest been rapid; but, as it endured, the Mexica were able to devise countermeasures. Even as Cortés ordered thirteen brigantines built to ferry troops and attack Tenochtitlán from the water, where its defenses were most vulnerable, the Mexica were digging trenches armed with sharply pointed sticks and captured lances to kill or hobble the Spaniards' horses. So too would the Mexica make a display of sacrificing and cannibalizing the Spaniards taken in battle to terrorize their comrades as the latter had before used firearms, horses, and dogs to terrorize them. The resulting pursuit of captives for sacrifice would prove costly for the Mexica insofar as it allowed Cortés and others in his company to escape death on several occasions. For this and the far larger number of Mexican combatants—despite the welcome arrival of reinforcements while in Tlaxcala, Cortés reports that in the final assault on Tenochtitlán his forces comprised barely 700 infantry, 118 musketeers and crossbowmen, 86 horsemen, 3 canon, 15 field guns, and an unspecified number of native fighters and bearers, apparently fewer than had supported him on his previous entry—Cortés was obliged to abandon his intent to take the city without destruction.

Despite more than two months of siege, beginning on May 30, 1521, the Mexica, though visibly starving, refused to surrender, prompting the Spaniards to raze the city sector by sector to maximize the effect of canon and to deprive the Mexica of cover for attack. Dismayed by the devastation of these final days and their aftermath, during which little was or could be done to restrain the Tlaxcalan forces, Cortés would remark in his third letter to the Crown (May 15, 1522): "So loud was the wailing of the women and children that there was not one man amongst us whose heart did not bleed at the sound; and indeed we had more trouble in preventing our allies from killing with such cruelty than we had in fighting the enemy. For no race, however savage, has ever practiced such fierce and unnatural cruelty as the natives of these parts" (Cortés 1986, pp. 261–262). On August 13, 1521, Tenochtitlán and its new leader, Cuauhtémoc, surrendered.

CORTÉS'S LEGACY

Although Cortés reorganized and governed the conquered territory, renamed New Spain, until 1528, and led another, this time disastrous, expedition to Honduras (1524–1526), his final years, until his death in 1547, were spent in relative obscurity. His actions in exploring the Pacific coast northward in search of the legendary riches of Cíbola (1532–1536) and in support of Charles V in the unsuccessful assault on Algiers (1541) show a man broken in spirit. It is telling that writers of the sixteenth and seventeenth centuries celebrate Cortés's role, not as military commander, but as an instrument of God, delivering the New World from idolatry and extending the rule of Catholic faith in opposition to Martin Luther, who they wrongly said was born in the same year. Although this image has faded from modern accounts, replaced by that of Machiavelli's ruthless prince, the audacity of Cortés's exploits has not. For this and the power of his discourse, Cortés's letters to the Crown are required reading for scholars of Renaissance society.

BIBLIOGRAPHY

PRIMARY WORKS

Cortés, Hernán. [1519–1526] 1986. *Letters from Mexico.* Trans. and ed. Anthony Pagden. Introd. John H. Elliott. New Haven, CT: Yale University Press.

SECONDARY WORKS

Boruchoff, David A. 1991. Beyond Utopia and Paradise: Cortés, Bernal Díaz and the Rhetoric of Consecration. *MLN* 106: 330–369.

Casas, Bartolomé de las. [c. 1560] 1965. *Historia de las Indias.* Ed. Agustín Millares Carlo. 2nd ed. 3 vol. Mexico City: Universidad Nacional Autónoma de México.

Clendinnen, Inga. 1991. "Fierce and Unnatural Cruelty": Cortés and the Conquest of Mexico. *Representations* 33: 65–100.

Díaz del Castillo, Bernal. [1575] 1908–1916. *The True History of the Conquest of New Spain by Bernal Díaz del Castillo, One of Its Conquerors.* Trans. Alfred Percival Maudslay. 5 vols. London: The Hakluyt Society.

Documentos cortesianos. 1990–1992. Ed. José Luis Martínez. 4 vols. Mexico City: Universidad Nacional Autónoma de México and Fondo de Cultura Económica.

López de Gómara, Francisco. [1552] 1964. *Cortés: The Life of the Conqueror by His Secretary, Francisco López de Gómara.* Trans. Lesley Byrd Simpson. Berkeley: University of California Press.

Martínez, José Luis. 1990. *Hernán Cortés.* Mexico City: Universidad Nacional Autónoma de México and Fondo de Cultura Económica.

Ramos, Demetrio. 1992. *Hernán Cortés: Mentalidad y propósitos.* Madrid: Ediciones Rialp.

David A. Boruchoff

COSMOPOLITANISM

Cosmopolitanism is a term derived from the Greek word *kosmopolite* ("citizen of the world"). It emerged as a philosophical and ultimately cultural worldview during the Hellenistic period, when thinkers traced the conceptual evolution of the people's *mentalité* from that of the citizen of the city-state to that of the citizen of the entire *ecumene* (or extended Hellenic world). After a long eclipse, the concept reemerged in the writings of Kant, where the future evolution of the world into a cosmopolitan society was originally contemplated. Adam Smith should also receive credit, however, for his endorsement of free trade as a cosmopolitan stance. In the nineteenth century, the word gained a negative connotation through its juxtaposition with the popular idea of nationalism, a trend that reached its peak in the word's employment as a derogatory term by the Nazis.

Although cosmopolitanism reemerged as a potentially powerful concept in the late 1990s, it is important to note that the concept continues to lack a universally shared definition. It has been applied to philosophical and normative orientations as well as to political and cultural attributes, and its employment in the discourse of different disciplines is far from uniform. Moreover, cosmopolitanism has been related both to efforts to construct forms of transnational solidarity, and to the various urban cultures of past and present metropolitan centers. Perhaps the most important contributions to the literature on cosmopolitanism can be found in the writings of Ulrich Beck, and in work inquiring into the possibility of cosmopolitanism providing the foundation for a future European identity.

Generally speaking, contributors to the growing literature on cosmopolitanism interpret the term in a threefold manner. Some authors advocate "thin" cosmopolitanism, whereby cosmopolitanism is conceived as a form of detachment from local ties, whereas others argue in favor of "rooted" or context-specific or vernacular cosmopolitanism, whereby cosmopolitanism is conceived as congruent with locality. Finally, some suggest the existence of "glocalized" cosmopolitanism, whereby global detachment and local attachment coexist in a symbiotic relationship. Thus, depending upon the particular definition employed, specific groups of people can be conceived either as carriers of cosmopolitanism or as excluded from it altogether. For example, immigrant groups have been viewed as carriers of vernacular cosmopolitanism, but they are almost by definition excluded from some versions of "thin" cosmopolitanism.

In contrast to the growing body of theoretical work on cosmopolitanism, there is to date only a limited amount of empirical research in the literature. Ultimately, only empirical research will be in a position to determine which one of the different theoretical strands of cosmopolitanism might be the most promising one for sociology. Such work might also help to evaluate whether the world is indeed experiencing a trend toward cosmopolitanism, and might identify which attributes are observable among the public and the extent to which these are related to other trends—such as the growth of transnational connections or a revived sense of religiosity.

SEE ALSO *Cooperation; Globalization, Anthropological Aspects of; Globalization, Social and Economic Aspects of; Internationalism; Trade; Trust*

BIBLIOGRAPHY

Beck, Ulrich. 2005. *Cosmopolitan Vision.* Oxford, U.K.: Polity.

Cheah, Pheng, and Bruce Robbins, eds.1998. *Cosmopolitics: Thinking and Feeling beyond the Nation.* Minneapolis: University of Minnesota Press.

Robertson, Roland, and David Inglis. 2004. The Global *Animus:* In the Tracks of World Consciousness. *Globalizations* (1) 1: 38–49.

Roudometof, Victor. 2005. Transnationalism, Cosmopolitanism, and Glocalization. *Current Sociology* 53 (1): 113–135.

Rumford, Chris, ed. 2007. *Cosmopolitanism and Europe.* Liverpool, U.K.: Liverpool University Press.

Szerszynski, Bronislaw, and John Urry. 2002. Cultures of Cosmopolitanism. *Sociological Review* 50 (4): 461–481.

Theory, Culture, and Society 19 (1–2). 2002. (Special issue on cosmopolitanism.)

Vertovec, Steven, and Robin Cohen, eds. 2002. *Conceiving Cosmopolitanism: Theory, Context, and Practice.* Oxford, U.K.: Oxford University Press.

Victor Roudometof

COST-BENEFIT ANALYSIS

The process of cost-benefit analysis, or CBA, enables analysts to exploit a set of analytical economic and econometrics tools to evaluate project investments and policy options. It has been made a legal prerequisite for public policy decisions in most countries. In the United States, for example, Executive Order 12991, signed by President Ronald Reagan in 1981, codified CBA as a requirement for agencies when conducting risk assessments in health, safety, and environmental regulation.

There is a large body of literature available dealing with CBA, some of which dates back to the 1920s, when large-scale engineering projects in the United States required some type of project evaluation. Although CBA is not itself a self-contained field of economics—sitting somewhat uneasily between several scholarly discourses, including philosophy, psychology and politics—the central procedures of CBA have been predominantly defined by economists. The standard introductory textbook was written by an economist, Edward J. Mishan. Originally published in 1971, the fourth edition of Mishan's *Cost-Benefit Analysis* appeared in 1988. While the original purpose of CBA was to capture the costs and benefits accruing to a single enterprise, its scope was soon expanded to evaluate policy options applicable to the well-being of society as a whole, and most literature in the social sciences now refers to CBA in this context.

A cost-benefit analysis can be seen as proceeding through a number of stages. First, for any proposal under consideration, including the option of doing nothing, a qualitative statement of its expected costs and benefits is to be provided. Second, each cost and benefit should be rendered in quantitative form, usually as a monetary value. Third, the expected costs or benefits should be aggregated. Finally, a decision should be taken on the basis of which proposal produces the greatest sum of benefits over costs. The first stage seems essential to any rational decision-making process, but each further stage is highly contested on conceptual, economic, and philosophical grounds. Three issue areas in particular are worth pointing out: (1) monetary valuation, (2) aggregation, and (3) the subordination of other values.

MONETARY VALUATION

In order for CBA not to be arbitrary or fetishistic, some connection between the currency of the economic analysis and human well-being must be established. The monetary value of goods is usually chosen for this purpose, because it is said to reflect the strength of individuals' preferences for that good, which in turn is a measure of the well-being provided by it. Yet various objections have been raised regarding this approach. First, some goods and services—such as most ecosystem services—are not traded in markets at all, and therefore no monetary value can be ascertained. The social sciences have developed various surrogate methods to rectify this deficiency, and "contingent valuation" (CV) has been particularly influential. Through CV, economists seek to create hypothetical markets by eliciting people's "willingness to pay" (WTP) for the satisfaction of a preference if there was a market. However, WTP has been criticized as an inadequate proxy for market prices because of the ambiguity and limited reliability of the stated preferences used in CV (as opposed to those revealed in the market). There is also some doubt as to whether coherent preferences on policy issues are actually susceptible to valuation and extractable through interviews or questionnaires.

Second, preferences conceal well-known facts about human nature, and they are therefore not always a suitable basis for policy decisions. For example, individuals may adjust their aspirations to their perceptions of possibilities; preferences may be misinformed or malformed, and they may therefore cause individuals to inflict harm on themselves (e.g., the addict; the gambler) or on others (e.g., the murderer); and preference satisfaction fails to accord the proper moral status to those beings that are incapable of expressing a preference—whether human (e.g., children) or nonhuman (e.g., animals).

Finally, where monetary valuation in a market is possible, that value may not be a valid indicator of the well-being the good provides to society because of the conceptual difference between a good's monetary "exchange value" and its "use value." Gold, for example, has a high exchange value but a low value in actual use. The use value of the air we breathe, by contrast, is infinite (it being a physical necessity for our lives), while its exchange value is zero.

AGGREGATION

Once attributes of well-being have been valued, CBA requires that they be aggregated into a single standard. They need to be compared across lives, so that an increase in well-being for individual A in one dimension can be weighed against the foregone improvement individual B would have experienced in another. This is no easy task. It may be possible to make comparisons of well-being in an ordinal sense—in the case of, say, health care, one person may be able to stipulate that he or she feels better than someone who is in great physical pain—but not in a cardinal sense. That is to say, a person cannot know exactly how much better he or she is. Cardinality presupposes two characteristics of the currency used: (1) a number must be attached to the outcome that represents the strength of the preference relative to others, so that a health state of, say,

0.6 is three times better than one of 0.2; and (2) the scale must have an equal interval property where equal differences at different points along the scale are equally meaningful, so that boosting a patient from, say, 0.1 to 0.2 on that scale is of equal benefit to raising someone from 0.8 to 0.9. Despite various methodological advancements, these requirements are still not met for all CBAs.

THE SUBORDINATION OF OTHER VALUES

Finally, CBA imposes a unitary standard on the valuation and comparison of goods, and it thus subordinates other values to the new standard of monetary exchange value. In environmental CBAs, for example, the existence value of nonhuman species, the survival of which is deemed to be worth protecting, may be overridden by CBA calculations. Their value cannot be priced in real or hypothetical markets because the expected benefit of their survival does not accrue to those who might be asked to reveal or state a WTP for their preference.

As far as human beings are concerned, similar predicaments present themselves: is it permissible to kill one person because his organs could save the lives of four patients whose names are on a donor waiting list? Most of us would consider this option to be objectionable, but given the rationale of CBA it is justifiable, if not mandatory, to proceed that way. The problem encountered here is that with CBA every individual counts as one, and can thus be added up to, or traded against, someone else. In so doing, CBA will override the intrinsic value of human life, a term that denotes our interest in our own continued existence according to which we cannot be used solely as a means for other individuals' ends. Yet, this is what CBA would recommend us to do. Intrinsic values are nonrelational; that is, they are not defined relative to some other human being, species, or object, nor to the benefit it might provide to them.

The objections presented here are not a reason to reject CBA per se, for it does provide relevant information. Yet they are a reminder that economic evaluations such as CBA should be understood as an input into, rather than a substitute for, political deliberation and judgment.

SEE ALSO *Coordination Failure; Prisoner's Dilemma (Psychology); Public Goods; Public Policy; Rational Choice Theory; Tragedy of the Commons; Transaction Cost*

BIBLIOGRAPHY

Adler, M. D., and E. A. Posner, eds. 2001. *Cost Benefit Analysis: Legal, Economic, and Philosophical Perspectives.* Chicago: Chicago University Press.

Layard, R., and S. Glaister, eds. 1994. *Cost-Benefit Analysis.* 2nd ed. Cambridge University Press.

Mishan, E. J. 1988. *Cost-Benefit Analysis.* 4th ed. London: Unwin Hyman.

Dirk Haubrich

COST, CARRYING

SEE *Carrying Cost.*

COTTON INDUSTRY

Gossypium—the scientific term referring to the genus of cotton plants—belongs to the small tribe of *Gossypieae*, which, in turn, is part of the *Malvaceae* family. Four separate species of cotton—two in Asia-Africa (*G. arboreum* and *G. herbaceum*) and two in the Americas (*G. barbadense* and *G. hirsutum*)—have been domesticated independently, a process that is unusual among crop plants. While the geographical point of origin of *G. arboreum* is not known, the origin of *G. herbaceum* is the Arabian peninsula or Africa. The exact time and place of domestication of the Old World cottons is not clear but archeological remains recovered from sites in India and Pakistan indicate that domestication of *G. arboreum* took place about 4,300 years ago. Furthermore, because *G. arboreum* is agronomically superior to *G. herbaceum*, it was widely dispersed throughout northern Africa, Arabia, Iraq, and western India. With respect to the New World cottons, the earlier archeological remains of *G. barbadense* have been located in the coastal areas of Peru and Ecuador, dating 5,000 to 5,500 years ago. The primary route of dispersal appears to have been through the Andes into northeastern South America and later to Central America, the Caribbean, and the Pacific.

The oldest archeological remains of *G. hirsutum* have been located in the Tehuacan Valley of Mexico, dated from 4,000 to 5,000 years ago. The vast majority of cotton varieties used for lint production in the 2000s come either from *G. hirsutum* (referred to as upland cotton in the United States and middling elsewhere, accounting for 90% of global production) or from *G. barbadense* (referred to as long-staple cotton or Pima in the United States and Giza in Egypt, accounting for 10% of global production). The Asian-African species produce low-quality lint with low yields and have been mostly (but not entirely) abandoned. The oldest archeological record of cotton textiles was found in Pakistan and dates back to 3000 BCE. Cotton specimens have been located in northern Peru, dating as far back as 2500 BCE.

Trade of cotton goods was taking place between India and Persia as early as the fifth century BCE. Cotton was brought to southern Europe (Greece, Sicily, and Spain) on a large scale by Arab traders during the ninth and tenth centuries CE while it was imported to North Europe during the thirteenth century. The known history of cotton in the New World begins with the arrival of Spanish explorer Christopher Columbus (1451–1506) in the Bahamas Islands in the autumn of 1492 (see John Baffes's article "The History of Cotton Trade: From Origin to the Nineteenth Century" [2005] for a comprehensive history of the cotton trade).

Considerable growth in cotton production and trade took place toward the end of the eighteenth century. Several factors contributed to such growth. First, advances in industrial revolution lowered the costs of manufacturing textile products. For example, between 1786 and 1882, the labor and capital cost of producing one pound of yarn went from thirty-four shillings to one shilling. Second, the use of cheap slave labor in the United States lowered the costs of cotton picking (cotton along with sugar and tobacco are often referred to as the slave commodities). Prior to the U.S. Civil War, about one-third of U.S. slaves were employed in cotton fields. (In 1897 Mathew Hammond reported that of the 3.5 million slaves in 1840, at least 1.2 million were engaged in the U.S. cotton industry). Third, the invention of the saw gin by Eli Whitney in 1793, which changed the separation of lint and seed from a laborious to a simple mechanical process, freed labor that eventually became involved in cotton production (seed cotton consists of about one-third lint and two-thirds seed; the two byproducts of seed are cotton oil for human consumption and cotton meal for animal consumption).

Cotton trade was further enhanced with the arrival of the first steamer in New York in 1838, which effectively halved the time to cross the Atlantic. Because the steamers would bring information on the U.S. cotton market conditions to England in half the time compared to the actual delivery of cotton, cotton traders in Liverpool, England's dominant cotton trading center at the time, began to trade forward contracts, thus giving rise to speculation. Furthermore, the successful installation of the first transatlantic cable in 1865 would transform cotton trade in a permanent way. For the first time in history, information on market conditions in the U.S. was transmitted instantaneously to England and vice-versa. By the end of the 1880s, five cotton futures exchanges (New York, New Orleans, Liverpool, Le Havre, and Alexandria) spanning three continents were trading cotton futures contracts and were connected by cable.

The global cotton industry was also affected by the U.S. Civil War, which caused exports from the United States to decline to a few thousand tons, from half a million prior to the war. Cotton prices experienced the most dramatic rise in the history of the commodity to cause what was coined later the "cotton famine." England, whose textile industry would collapse without U.S. cotton supplies, sought supplies from elsewhere including Turkey, India, Central Asia, and sub-Saharan Africa. While the United States regained its dominance as the world's key cotton supplier after the war, the other cotton-producing countries also held their position. The structure of cotton production has remained the same in the twenty-first century. However, throughout the twentieth century, especially the second half, cotton consumption moved from Europe to Asia where the most of the textile industry is located and where most of the synthetic fiber production takes place.

THE MODERN COTTON INDUSTRY

Global cotton production at the beginning of the twenty-first century averaged about 25 million tons, worth about $30 billion. About one-third is internationally traded, representing about 0.1 percent of global merchandize trade. Despite its low share in global trade, cotton trade is very important to many poor countries, especially in sub-Saharan Africa where an estimated 2 million rural poor households depend on the commodity.

Since the 1960s cotton production grew at 1.8 percent annually to reach 24 million tons in 2005 from 10.2 million tons in 1960. Most of this growth came from China and India and to a lesser extent from Australia, Greece, Pakistan, Turkey, and Francophone Africa. As of 2005 more than one-quarter of the area allocated to cotton was under genetically modified (GM) varieties, accounting for almost 40 percent of world production. GM cotton in the United States—where it was first introduced in 1996—currently accounts for about 80 percent of the area allocated to cotton. Other major GM cotton producers are Argentina, Australia, China, Colombia, India, Mexico, and South Africa.

China, the leading textile producer, consumes more than one-third of cotton output. Other major textile producers are India, Pakistan, Turkey, and the United States, which together with China account for more than three-quarters of global consumption. Several East Asian countries have emerged as important cotton consumers. For example, Indonesia, Korea, Taiwan, and Thailand, which together consumed 130,000 tons in 1960 (1.2% of world consumption), absorbed more than 1.5 million tons in 2005 (6.5% of world consumption).

Between 1960 and 2005, cotton demand has grown at the same rate as population (about 1.8% per annum) implying that per capita cotton consumption has remained relatively unchanged at about 7.7 pounds. By contrast, consumption of man-made fibers, which compete closely with cotton, has increased consistently since the mid-twentieth century by 2.2 percent per annum, causing cotton's share in total fiber consumption to decline from 60 percent in 1960 to 40 percent in 2002. Apart from the substantial reduction in their costs of production, the increasing share of chemical fibers reflects new uses, quality improvements which made their properties very similar to those of cotton, increased use for clothing suitable to extreme weather conditions (e.g. rain, cold) and other uses such as sportswear.

The three dominant exporters—the United States, Central Asia, and Francophone Africa—account for more than two-thirds of global trade. In the mid-2000s the ten largest importers account for more than 70 percent of global trade. Three major producers—China, Turkey, and Pakistan—also import cotton to supply their textile industries. The four East Asian textile producers—Indonesia, Thailand, Taiwan, and Korea—accounted for 22 percent of world cotton imports in 2002, compared to just 3 percent in 1960.

Real cotton prices have been declining since the nineteenth century, although with temporary spikes. The reasons for such decline are similar to those characterizing most primary commodities: on the supply side reduced production costs due to technological improvements and on the demand side stagnant per capita consumption and competition from manmade fibers. Between 1960 and 1964 and between 1999 and 2003 real cotton prices fell by 55 percent, remarkably similar to the 50 percent decline in the broad agriculture price index. Reductions in the costs of production have been associated primarily with yields increases (from 270 pounds per acre in 1960 to 625 pounds per acre in 2005). The phenomenal growth in yield has been aided by the introduction of improved cotton varieties, expansion of irrigation and use of chemicals and fertilizers. Technological improvements have also taken place in the textile industry, so that the same quality of fabric can now be produced with lower quality cotton, a trend that has taken place in many other industries whose main input is a primary commodity.

World cotton trade is carried out by a large number of cotton trading companies—the so-called cotton merchants. A survey conducted in 2005 by the International Cotton Advisory Committee (ICAC) found that 21 large companies (either private or state-owned) traded cotton during 2004 with volumes greater than 200,000 tons. Another 48 companies traded cotton with volumes between 50,000 and 200,000 tons, followed by 43 firms with volumes between 20,000 and 50,000 tons and another 362 smaller companies with volumes less than 20,000 tons.

There are two widely used price indicators in the cotton market: the Cotlook A Index and the New York Board of Trade (NYBOT) futures price. The A Index—compiled daily by Cotlook Ltd., a private company located in Liverpool, United Kingdom—is the average of the five lowest quotations of nineteen types of cotton traded in the ports of East Asia. Quotations of NYBOT futures are readily available continuously from the NYBOT. Apart from NYBOT, whose contract exhibits high liquidity, Brazil, India, and China operate cotton futures exchanges.

COTTON POLICIES

Cotton has been subject to various marketing and trade interventions; typically taxation in low income countries, especially sub-Saharan Africa and Central Asia, and subsidization by rich countries, especially the United States and the European Union (EU). The ICAC, which monitors cotton subsidies on a regular basis, reported that in 2001—the year in which support was highest—government assistance to U.S. cotton producers reached $3.9 billion, China's totaled $1.2 billion, and the EU received almost $1 billion. The high level of cotton subsidies also coincided with cotton prices reaching their lowest level ever, causing two noteworthy reactions, the Brazil/U.S. cotton dispute brought to the World Trade Organization (WTO) in 2002 and the Francophone Africa cotton initiative submitted also to the WTO in 2003.

On September 27, 2002, Brazil requested consultation with the United States regarding U.S. subsidies to cotton producers. On March 18, 2003, the Dispute Settlement Body of the WTO established a panel to examine the issues, and on April 26, 2004, the WTO issued an interim ruling in favor of Brazil. The final ruling (issued on September 8, 2004) concluded that the United States is under the obligation to take appropriate steps to remove the adverse effects or withdraw the subsidy. While the United States removed a small share of its subsidies in July 2006, it appears that more must be done in order to fully comply with WTO's ruling.

On May 16, 2003, four West African cotton-producing countries (Benin, Burkina Faso, Chad, and Mali) submitted a joint proposal to the WTO demanding removal of support to the cotton sector by the United States, China, and the European Union and compensation for damages until full removal of support. The West African countries were aided in this move, often referred to as the "cotton initiative," by IDEAS, a Geneva-based nongovernmental organization funded by the Swiss government. It is believed that the inability to successfully deal with the cotton initiative played a role in the WTO's collapse of the Fifth WTO Ministerial in Cancun (September 10–13, 2004). The cotton initiative also figured prominently in the Sixth WTO Ministerial in Hong Kong (December 13–18, 2005).

THE OUTLOOK

The future of the global cotton industry is likely to follow a similar path as other primary commodities. Prices are likely to decline even further, mainly a reflection of technological improvements. Consumption, which has been growing at the same rate as population growth, will, most likely, continue to grow in a similar fashion. If twenty-first-century trends continue, GM cotton will most likely dominate the global cotton market. Organic cotton, on the other hand, despite concerted efforts has not made much progress. The key reason behind the GM and organic cotton trends is that, because it is not a food crop, there is not much consumer resistance. Finally, the competition from synthetic fibers will continue, although there is evidence that consumers' preferences have changed toward consuming more cotton.

SEE ALSO *Agricultural Industry; Slave Trade; Slavery; Textile Industry; U.S. Civil War*

BIBLIOGRAPHY

Baffes, John. 2005. The Cotton Problem. *World Bank Research Observer* 20 (1): 109–144.

Baffes, John. 2005. The History of Cotton Trade: From Origin to the Nineteenth Century. In *Cotton Trading Manual*, ed. Secretariat of the International Cotton Advisory Committee. Cambridge, U.K.: Woodhead Publishing Limited.

Baffes, John, and Ioannis Kaltsas. 2004. Cotton Futures Exchanges: Their Past, Their Present, and Their Future. *Quarterly Journal of International Agriculture* 43: 153–176.

Brubaker, C. L., F. M. Bourland, and J. F. Wendel. 1999. The Origin and Domestication of Cotton. In *Cotton: Origin, History, Technology, and Production*, eds. C. Wayne Smith and J. Tom Cothren. New York: John Wiley and Sons.

Hammond, Mathew Brown. 1897. *An Essay in American Economic History*. New York: Johnson Reprint Co.

International Cotton Advisory Committee. 2003. *Production and Trade Policies Affecting the Cotton Industry*. Washington, D.C.: Author.

International Cotton Advisory Committee. 2005. The Structure of World Trade. *Cotton: Review of the World Situation* 58 (January–February): 11–15.

John Baffes

COUNCIL OF EUROPE

SEE *Civil Liberties.*

COUNCIL ON ENVIRONMENTAL QUALITY

SEE *Environmental Impact Assessment.*

COUNTERTERRORISM

Many different programs and activities, at all levels of government and in the private sector, help to save lives and property from terrorism and are properly considered aspects of counterterrorism. The activities that are most commonly and explicitly labeled as counterterrorism are offensive efforts by security services to uncover and erode the capabilities of terrorist groups to conduct attacks. Another major element of counterterrorism—although it sometimes bears the label *antiterrorism*—is creating defensive security measures to protect possible targets from terrorist attack. Still another is the development of capabilities to respond quickly to terrorist attacks in a way that will mitigate their damaging effects. Less commonly described as counterterrorism are activities that affect the motivations of groups to use terrorism or of individuals to join terrorist groups in the first place, although this last element can have as great an effect as the others on the incidence of terrorism.

OFFENSIVE AND DEFENSIVE TOOLS

Offensive counterterrorism is aimed chiefly at disrupting or destroying the leadership, planning, finances, and organizational structure of terrorist groups. Common techniques include raids to break up terrorist cells, seizure of documents and materials, arrests of key individuals, and rendition of suspected terrorists to countries where they are wanted for interrogation or prosecution. Intelligence, diplomacy, criminal justice, financial controls, and military force are the principal tools that national governments use to weaken the capabilities of terrorist groups. Each tool has its limitations as well as its strengths, and effective counterterrorist programs use all of them in combination.

Intelligence tends to be the most heavily relied upon counterterrorist tool, particularly because of the hope that it will uncover enough specific information about impending terrorist attacks to preempt the attacks. The inherent difficulties in obtaining highly specific information about closely held terrorist plots, however, means some plots will inevitably escape such exposure. Intelligence makes larger contributions to the disruption of terrorist infrastructures and to the strategic assessment of threats from particular terrorist groups or in particular countries or regions.

Because terrorism always involves the commission of crimes, criminal justice systems play a major counterterrorist role, both in the investigation of past or possible future terrorist attacks and in the prosecution and incarceration of individual terrorists. Limitations of criminal justice systems include the frequent difficulty in obtaining strong enough evidence for a successful prosecution. Closely associated with intelligence and law enforcement work are efforts, usually centered in finance ministries, to seize or freeze financial assets belonging to terrorist groups. A limitation of financial efforts is difficulty in tracking terrorist money that moves through informal channels outside any banking system.

Diplomacy supports the other offensive tools through, for example, demarches to foreign governments to enlist their cooperation in arresting suspected terrorists or in providing information to facilitate counterterrorist investigations. Counterterrorist diplomacy has also assumed more of a multilateral role, particularly since the 1990s. The negotiation of more than a dozen international conventions on terrorism has provided a framework for cooperation on such matters as the handling of hijacking incidents and the tagging of explosives (insertion of a distinctive chemical during manufacture of explosives, permitting investigators to trace the origin of any one batch of explosives).

Military force has been used relatively sparingly for counterterrorist purposes, and mostly by the United States. Its principal role formerly was to retaliate for terrorist acts already committed, as with U.S. retaliatory strikes against Libya in 1986 and Iraq in 1993. The U.S. intervention in Afghanistan in 2001 marked an expanded use of military force in that it served not only to retaliate for Al Qaeda's attack against the United States in September of that year but also to roust the group from its base of operations and to drive from power its close ally, the Afghan Taliban regime.

Defensive security measures are used to protect individual sites that are potentially attractive to terrorists (e.g., prominent government buildings), systems critical to public safety or the economy (e.g., civil aviation or electric power grids), and national borders. All these areas were included in major efforts, following Al Qaeda's attack in September 2001, to bolster defenses against terrorism within the United States, efforts that collectively come under the title *homeland security*. A major challenge is in finding ways to safeguard inherently open, and thus vulnerable, public facilities and systems such as ports and transit lines without resorting to measures that are economically damaging or that unduly impair civil liberties. Another challenge is that terrorists have the offensive side's advantage of choosing which out of many possible targets to strike.

Incident response capabilities are designed both to limit the physical damage of terrorist attacks and to reassure the public that authorities have emergency situations under control. Counterterrorist response capabilities have focused particularly on the possibility of attacks using chemical, biological, radiological, or nuclear means. With some of these unconventional attack methods, a quick and well-planned response is critical in limiting the effects. An attack using an infectious biological agent, for example, would be less effective insofar as the response included early identification of the agent, isolation of infected persons, and inoculation of other persons in danger of becoming infected.

ORGANIZATIONAL ROLES

Offensive counterterrorist responsibilities exist mainly at the level of national governments, although organizational structures vary. In most developed countries important counterterrorist organizations are domestic security services such as MI-5 in the United Kingdom or the Public Security Investigation Agency in Japan. The United States has no such service; the Federal Bureau of Investigation performs both this role and its criminal law enforcement functions. Intelligence agencies, militaries, and coordinating bodies such as the National Security Council in the United States also play major roles.

Responding to terrorist incidents is more the responsibility of local authorities, with municipal fire or police departments necessarily performing the role of first responders. National resources will often provide augmentation, however, in the event of major terrorist incidents.

Homeland security functions are spread among different levels of government. The biggest organizational innovation was the creation in the United States in 2002 of a Department of Homeland Security, which assumed primary responsibility for border security and the protection of assets such as the civil aviation system. Protection of many individual sites is still at least as much a local responsibility. Moreover, the security of many potential terrorist targets, from power plants to the electronic infrastructure used by financial markets, depends in large part on measures by the private sector.

BIBLIOGRAPHY

Cronin, Audrey Kurth, and James M. Ludes, eds. 2004. *Attacking Terrorism: Elements of a Grand Strategy*. Washington, DC: Georgetown University Press.

Hoge, James F., Jr., and Gideon Rose, eds. 2005. *Understanding the War on Terror*. Washington, DC: Foreign Affairs.

Pillar, Paul R. 2003. *Terrorism and U.S. Foreign Policy*, 2nd ed. Washington, DC: Brookings Institution Press.

Wilkinson, Paul. 2000. *Terrorism versus Democracy: The Liberal State Response*. London: Frank Cass.

Paul R. Pillar

COUNTRY AND WESTERN MUSIC

SEE *Music.*

COUP D'ETAT

Coup d'etat is an important, often violent type of political leadership change. Coups involve a small group of conspirators plotting to seize state power and then doing so on their own or with the support of others. Coup attempts are swift, lasting hours or a few days. Often attempts fail, but if state power is taken and held, the event is a coup d'etat. Both failed and successful coups may involve many deaths as a result of fighting between the coup participants and loyal armed forces, or they may be bloodless coups in which no one dies. Historically most coups have been military coups involving elements from the state's own military and police because their firepower is needed to crush any possible opposition. When coups overthrow constitutionally elected governments, they are forceful, illegal means of political change. When coups are against dictatorships they are sudden, unexpected, and irregular means of political change.

The term *coup d'etat* ("blow against the state") comes from Napoléon Bonaparte's use of his troops on the 18th Brumaire (November 9, 1799) to overthrow the constitution of the First French Republic and ultimately to place himself in power as emperor. After independence in the early nineteenth century, most Latin American states experienced repeated coups (*Los Golpes Militares*) led by innumerable *caudillos* (dictators), a phenomenon lasting until the 1980s. After decolonization, coups d'etat occurred in many new states of North Africa, the Middle East, Asia, and Africa. The 48 states of sub-Saharan Africa have seen the most coups, with 40 states experiencing 83 successful and 112 failed coups between 1956 and 2004. While rare in developed countries, coups have occurred in Europe, in Greece in 1967 and in Portugal in 1974. On some occasions coups have brought to power men who tried to better their countries, but generally coups have produced poor political leadership, further impoverishing their countries.

Coup leaders often proclaim themselves "revolutionaries," but coups are not revolutions. Revolutions involve armed conflict; some coups do not. Revolutions last for months or years, coups last mere hours or days. Revolutions are mass political events involving much of the population; coups are made by a few coup-makers who are often political or military elites. Revolutionaries seek fundamental social, economic, and political change; coup-makers may seek this, but they may act to prevent change or merely to gain the rewards of political office. Revolutions produce profound societal change; coups produce changes in political leadership and often little else.

When countries have weak political institutions—political parties, legislatures, courts, and bureaucracies—they may suffer frequent military interventions into politics. Harvard political scientist Samuel P. Huntington has called such countries *praetorian polities*. The type of coups they experience and the style of the resulting military rule depend upon the degree of political participation among the population: (1) when participation is low, only among elites, *oligarchical coups* and rule occur as in Paraguay under Alfredo Stroessner (1954–1989); (2) when participation is moderate, including both elites and the middle classes, *radical coups* and rule happen as in Egypt under Gamal Abdel Nasser (1956–1970); and (3) when participation is high, including all social classes, the results are *mass coups* and rule as in Argentina under Juan Domingo Perón (1946–1955). Huntington's variables, the strength of political institutions, and the level of political participation are key to understanding why and where coups d'etat happen.

BIBLIOGRAPHY

Finer, Samuel Edward. 1988. *The Man on Horseback: The Role of the Military in Politics*. 2nd ed. Boulder, CO: Westview Press.

Huntington, Samuel P. 1968. *Political Order in Changing Societies*. New Haven, CT: Yale University Press.

Patrick J. McGowan

COURTS, CONSTITUTIONAL

SEE *Constitutional Courts.*

COVARIANCE

The covariance is a measure of the magnitude of association between the scores of cases on two variables that have been measured at the interval or ratio level. It describes both the direction and the strength of the association. In

$$COV(X,Y) = \frac{\sum_{i=1}^{N}(x_i - \overline{X})(y_i - \overline{Y})}{N}$$

Figure 1

the social sciences, the covariance is most commonly used in structural equation modeling of systems of linear equations of measured and unmeasured variables.

Formally, the covariance between the scores of c cases (*i* through *N*) on the variables *X* and *Y* is:

$$COV(X,Y) = \frac{\sum_{i=1}^{N}(x_i - \overline{X})(y_i - \overline{Y})}{N}.$$

That is: subtract the first case's score on *X* from the mean of *X*; subtract the first case's score on *Y* from the mean of *Y*; multiply these "deviations." Repeat this process for all of the cases, and sum the results. Divide this product by the population size (*N*).

When the relationship between *X* and *Y* is being examined in a random sample of cases drawn from the population, *N* − 1 is usually substituted in the denominator. Most statistical software uses *N* − 1.

The covariance of a variable with itself (e.g., COV (*X, X*)) is the variance. (For a more in-depth formal treatment of the covariance, see Snedecor and Cochran 1980).

If there is a tendency for higher scores on *X* to co-occur with higher scores on *Y*, the covariance will have a positive value; if there is a tendency for higher scores on *X* to co-occur with lower scores on *Y*, the covariance will be negative. If the scores on two variables are not associated, the covariance will equal zero. The units of measurement of the covariance are *XY*; for example, if *X* was measured in dollars, and *Y* was measured in years, the magnitude of the covariance would be dollar-years. When we are working with multiple variables, the variances and covariances among all the variables are arrayed in a symmetric "variance-covariance" matrix.

Consider the relationship shown in the scatter-plot, between the level of urbanization (*X*) and female life expectancy (*Y*) in nineteen African countries in the mid-1990s. Inspection suggests that the scores positively co-vary: on the average (but not in all cases), the higher the urbanization, the higher the life expectancy.

The covariance for this relationship is 57.538. The positive value indicates a positive relationship. The strength of the relationship is difficult to assess because the unit of measurement of the covariance is percent-years. Because of this peculiar metric, the covariance is

rarely used as a simple description. The Pearson correlation (which is .47 in this example) is preferred.

The covariance is the most commonly used measure of association when research involves predicting *Y* from *X* using structural equation modeling. In predictive modeling, there is often the desire to describe the relationship between *Y* and *X* in the original scales of the variables: How much *Y* do we get for each unit of *X*?

Some warnings: Restricted variation in either variable, non-linearity in the relationship, and non-normality in the joint distribution of *X* and *Y* can limit the validity of the covariance as an index of the strength and direction of the relationship.

SEE ALSO *Standard Deviation*

BIBLIOGRAPHY

Snedecor, George W., and William Gemmell Cochran. 1980. *Statistical Methods.* 7th ed. Ames: Iowa State Press.

Robert Hanneman

COX, OLIVER C.
1901–1974

Oliver Cromwell Cox was a Caribbean-born sociologist who challenged the social sciences by pointing out problems with scholarly theories that attempted to explain race relations and the social and economic organization of race. Cox's life itself paralleled the state of race relations during the twentieth century in that his work was for many years overlooked, and he was marginalized both by black and white students of race relations. Yet he made a lasting contribution to the scientific understanding of cultural and sexual relations, as well as the sometimes violent social disorder that develops in the context of race. Unlike earlier scholars, Cox analyzed black-white relations in the United States in terms of race rather than caste, and he criticized what were then the dominant theories for explaining the impact of capitalism on the social system.

Cox was born on August 24, 1901, in Port of Spain, Trinidad. He received his primary school education at the Saint Thomas Boys' School, where he studied algebra, English literature, French, geometry, Greek, history, and Latin—the normal subjects that young boys were required to study in colonial Trinidad. Growing up in Trinidad, Cox also had to contend with colonial society's strict adherence to the social norms of decorum and respectability that were associated with colonial bourgeois pretensions. Obsession with skin color was embedded in Trinidadian culture during Cox's early life. For most black Trinidadians, light-colored skin was thought to be more attractive and worthy of greater social esteem, an idea that had been introduced into the culture by European colonists. Cox later explored this color line in *Caste, Class, and Race: A Study in Social Dynamics* (1948), in which he argued that such an obsession with skin color prevented social cohesion among blacks, who would otherwise have shared a similar interest in opposing social oppression.

In 1919 Cox moved to the United States and settled in Chicago. The summer of that year became known as "Red Summer" after racial tensions in Chicago erupted into major riots and fighting between whites and blacks, resulting in deaths as well as numerous injuries and arrests. Cox, however, was not particularly concerned with social problems at that time; he was primarily focused on gaining a college education. His schooling in Trinidad was not deemed equivalent to a high school education in the United States, and Cox had to return to high school. He graduated in 1923, and went on to earn a two-year college degree in 1925, and a bachelor of science degree from Northwestern University in 1928. The following year Cox was incapacitated by polio, and he was confined to a wheelchair for the remainder of his life. However, by that time he had decided to become an academic, and he entered the University of Chicago, where he earned a PhD in sociology in 1938 with a thesis on the "Factors Affecting the Marital Status of Negroes in the United States." Cox subsequently held academic appointments at Wiley College in Marshall, Texas (1938–1944), the Tuskegee Institute in Alabama (1944–1949), and Lincoln University in Jefferson City, Missouri (1949–1974).

During his academic career, Cox developed the unique theory that ideology was responsible for producing a social system in which black people were considered inferior to whites. Cox observed that race antagonism developed in the fifteenth century with the rise of capitalism and nationalism, and that race conflict was not a natural or universal phenomenon but a specific ideology that had become embedded in social theory. For Cox, the purpose of this ideology was one group's domination of another. In earlier societies, mechanisms and ideologies other than race, such as religion and culture, were used to subjugate entire groups of people. Cox argued that the ideology of white supremacy is inextricable from the political economy. Ideologies supporting control by whites are not designed to demonstrate that whites are superior to other human beings; rather, they are designed to proclaim that whites must be in control, and violence serves to enforce this arrangement. Racism, then, is not merely a system of beliefs; it is a relationship of power that is coordinated by an assembly of social institutions that work together to marginalize blacks. Cox identified seven "situations of race relations" that account for the varying demographics and organizations that develop in the assembling of social institutions.

At the center of these social institutions is the state. Cox's major work, *Caste, Class, and Race*, demonstrated that a political class that espoused a race ideology had emerged in the United States, as well as in other nations, such as Nazi Germany. In such states, commitment to the state-sanctioned racial ideology leads to a citizen's inclusion into the political class, whose primary goal is to control the state. The political class is organized to promote its heritage, an idea that Cox explored in *The Foundations of Capitalism* (1959) and *Capitalism as a System* (1962). The heritage of a capitalist state is that it emerges from and survives on the exploitation of lesser capitalist or non-capitalist territories and nations. Therefore, capitalism is not a unique development in the United States. Rather, the leading position of the United States in relation to other capitalist states, such as Great Britain, resulted because capitalism was inherited, embedded, and refined in the United States. Cox developed this theory in *Capitalism and American Leadership* (1962).

Cox's views stood in opposition to the caste school of race relations that was led by the social psychologist John Dollard (1900–1980) and the social anthropologist W. Lloyd Warner (1898–1970). These scholars applied the concept of caste to understand the separation between blacks and whites in the United States. Cox argued that caste divisions in India were a coherent system based on the rule of inequality. In such a system, a man's child by a woman of a lower caste, for example, might become accepted into the father's higher caste. In contrast, the U.S. color line contradicted an American creed of equality for all people, and a technique of "passing" developed to conceal the "lower" racial status of a "mixed-blood" person. However, if the mixed blood of a passing individual were ever discovered, it could trigger severe consequences.

In *Caste, Class, and Race*, Cox disputed the twentieth century's major sociological theories examining race relations. In addition to his critique of the caste school, Cox demonstrated the weaknesses in analyses by other major scholars, including the cultural anthropologist Ruth Benedict (1887–1948), the sociologist Robert E. Park (1864–1944), and the sociologist Gunnar Myrdal (1898–1987). Benedict promoted a rhetorical explanation of "racism," while Park saw race relations as cycles starting with contact and ending in assimilation of subordinate groups, and Myrdal argued that racial segregation was a moral problem of the "white" race. In opposing these views, Cox stressed the inextricable relationship between capital and racial antagonism. He argued that capitalism could not have developed out of feudalism, and had to be viewed as a form of social organization in which a capitalist nation is inconceivable without a capitalist world system. Cox concluded that three social forces were essential—an economic order, a national and territorial government, and a religious structure—before a racial organization could be produced and sustained.

SEE ALSO *Capitalism; Caste; Class; Race*

BIBLIOGRAPHY

Cox, Oliver. 1948. *Caste, Class, and Race: A Study in Social Dynamics.* New York: Monthly Review Press.

Hare, Nathan. 2000. Cox's Critique of the 'Black Bourgeoisie' School. In *The Sociology of Oliver C. Cox: New Perspectives,* ed. Herbert M. Hunter, 41–53. Stamford, CT: JAI Press.

Hunter, Herbert M., and Sameer Y. Abarham. 1987. *Race, Class, and the World System: The Sociology of Oliver C. Cox.* New York: Monthly Review Press.

Lemelle, Anthony J. 2001. Oliver Cromwell Cox: Toward a Pan-Africanist Epistemology for Community Action. *Journal of Black Studies* 31 (3): 325–347.

Vera, Hernán. 2000. The Liberation Sociology of Oliver Cromwell Cox. In *The Sociology of Oliver C. Cox: New Perspectives,* ed. Herbert M. Hunter, 237–250. Stamford, CT: JAI Press.

Anthony J. Lemelle Jr.

CRAFT UNIONS
SEE *Unions.*

CRAMER'S RULE
SEE *Determinants.*

CRAZY HORSE
c. 1842–1877

Crazy Horse (a translation of his Lakotan name, Tasunke Witko) achieved notoriety while he was alive for his skill as a military leader and his defiant attempt to resist Westernizing influences. Since his death, his actions have taken on further meaning, and he is highly regarded as a symbol of Lakota resistance, oftentimes considered *wakan* (spiritually powerful), and he continues to be emblematic of a traditional past.

Crazy Horse was born in 1841 or 1842 near the Black Hills (South Dakota). He apparently had yellow-brown hair and was initially called Light Hair and Curly. His father was a medicine man; but less is known about his mother, who died young; his father later remarried. He was reportedly good with horses, and this garnered him

the name His Horses Looking. His interest in a married woman, Black Buffalo Woman, led to a shooting that left Crazy Horse with a scar. Later, he married Black Shawl and they had a daughter, They Are Afraid of Her, who died at age 2. In 1877 he also married Nellie Laravie, an 18-year-old mixed-blood woman.

His father and grandfather both were named Crazy Horse, and he himself finally earned this name in his teen years. Around this time, Crazy Horse had a vision that involved a horseman who is plainly dressed and riding untouched through a storm. Crazy Horse himself began to dress plainly, with a red-tailed hawk feather, and it was assumed that he and his horse were invulnerable. There are also reports that he would throw dust over his horse before battle and that he wore a small stone, or *wotawe* (sacred charm), for protection. He was a quiet and intro-spective man who seldom joined in public events.

In an effort to resolve the conflicts following from Western expansion, Red Cloud and Spotted Tail agreed to settle at agencies, camps associated with government Indian agents that later became reservations, with the sign-ing of the 1868 Fort Laramie treaty. Crazy Horse alone resolved to stay on his own lands in the Black Hills, until several events led to his surrender. Gold was discovered in the Black Hills and battles commenced against those who resisted the order to reservation land. Crazy Horse fought his best in the last two great battles, Rosebud and Little Bighorn. On June 17, 1876, assaults forced Brigadier General George Crook's troops to retreat at the Battle of the Rosebud. Days later (June 25), Crazy Horse and oth-ers led the victory against Lieutenant Colonel George Armstrong Custer at the Battle of Little Bighorn.

These victories led to increased military pressure and famine. Supplies and morale diminished at Crazy Horse's camp with the dwindling of buffalo, restricted trade, and a cold winter. Given the promise of an agency in the northern country, Crazy Horse led 889 followers to Fort Robinson in May 1877, but the promised agency fell through, and Crazy Horse was given a campsite near Red Cloud's agency close to the White River (Nebraska). There was concern on the part of those trying to maintain stable relations—both Indian agents and Lakota leaders—that Crazy Horse would continue to hunt, given his refusal of rations, and that he would weaken the elders' efforts to maintain peace at the agency. Also, there might have been concern from the Lakota leaders of Red Cloud's and Spotted Tail's agencies that Crazy Horse was gaining too much favor from the Indian agents and unsettling the status of existing agencies.

After four months in the camps, General Crook issued an order for Crazy Horse's arrest. Crazy Horse at first assumed he was going to a council meeting, but resisted when he realized he might be imprisoned. It seems that his ally Little Big Man restrained him, either to placate him, in order to protect himself from Crazy Horse's knife, or to serve questionable political interests. A low-ranking cavalry soldier named William Gentiles is credited with stabbing Crazy Horse with a bayonet, intentionally or not. Crazy Horse died September 5, 1877, at Fort Robinson, and his father buried his son at an undisclosed site with the agreement of those in attendance that they smoke a pipe and pledge not to reveal its location.

BIBLIOGRAPHY

Kadlecek, Edward, and Mabell Kadlecek. 1981. *To Kill an Eagle: Indian Views on the Last Days of Crazy Horse*. Boulder, CO: Johnson Books.

Marshall, Joseph M. 2004. *The Journey of Crazy Horse: A Lakota History*. New York: Viking.

McMurtry, Larry. 1999. *Crazy Horse: A Penguin Life*. New York: Viking.

Larissa Petrillo

CREAMING

Creaming (creaming off, or skimming) is the practice of serving a select client base in order to improve the efficiency or efficacy of a treatment. Creaming generally occurs in a response to incentives. For example, when hospitals receive a fixed reimbursement payment for treating a given ailment, they have an incentive to seek out the most healthy patients among those afflicted with that condition; this improves the apparent efficiency of their care because the most healthy can typically be treated at lower cost. Similarly, job training programs that are evaluated based on the success of their clients obtaining subsequent employment have an incentive to recruit clients who are most likely to succeed following the completion of their training; in doing so the programs appear highly effective. Scholars continue to debate whether specialized schools such as magnet or charter schools practice creaming by attracting the strongest students from within the larger pool of students who are eligible to attend.

The practice of creaming has both social and statistical consequences. When clients (patients, trainees, or students, for example) who are already relatively advantaged obtain the most favorable treatment, inequality of opportunity is exacerbated. In some cases, that may be a goal of the program, such as when the aim is to maximize the number of program completers who are able to perform a specific role following training. More often, however, creaming produces results that are considered undesirable because it allocates resources unequally in favor of those who are already privileged. As an example, school choice programs that allow greater access to specialized schools to children from more educated families tend to increase rather than reduce segregation and inequality.

The statistical consequence of creaming is that it tends to distort efforts to assess program impact. Viewed narrowly as intended for a select population, creaming may limit generalizability; that is, if the program is intended for a particular subgroup, its effects may be properly assessed on that subgroup, but the effects may not generalize to the larger population. This pattern may be uncovered through examination of disaggregated data to identify the relevant subgroups. Generally, however, creaming produces biased estimates of program effects when the estimates fail to take into account the selectivity of the population undergoing the favored treatment in contrast to those without such access. Anderson, Burkhauser, and Raymond showed in a 1993 study that the remarkable performance of the Job Training Partnership Act of 1982 (a federal employment program in the United States) in preparing unemployed persons for work reflected in part the selection of those trainees who were most likely to obtain employment irrespective of their training opportunities. However, the bias was not as large as the critics had supposed. Responses to bias caused by creaming include statistical adjustments, such as instrumental variables analyses and propensity score models, and design-based solutions, such as randomized controlled trials with random assignment of participants to treatment and control groups.

SEE ALSO *Heckman Selection Correction Procedure; Inequality, Political; Instrumental Variables Regression; Sampling; Selection Bias; Statistics*

BIBLIOGRAPHY

Anderson, Katryn H., Richard Burkhauser, and Jennie E. Raymond. 1993. The Effect of Creaming on Placement Rates under the Job Training Partnership Act. *Industrial and Labor Relations Review* 46: 613–624.

Bell, Stephen H., and Larry Orr. 2002. Screening (and Creaming?) Applicants to Job Training Programs: The AFDC Homemaker-Home Health Aide Demonstration. *Labour Economics* 9: 279–301.

Ellis, Randall P. 1998. Creaming, Skimping, and Dumping: Provider Competition on the Intensive and Extensive Margins. *Journal of Health Economics*, 17: 537–555.

Hanushek, Eric A., and Dale Jorgenson, eds. 1996. *Improving America's Schools: The Role of Incentives*. Washington, DC: National Academies Press.

Lacireno-Paquet, Natalie, Thomas T. Holyoke, M. Moser, and Jeffrey R. Henig. 2002. Creaming Versus Cropping: Charter School Enrollment Practices in Response to Market

Incentives. *Educational Evaluation and Policy Analysis*, 24: 145–158.

Smrekar, Claire, and Ellen Goldring. 1999. *School Choice in Urban America: Magnet Schools and the Pursuit of Equity.* New York: Teachers College Press.

Adam Gamoran

CREAMY LAYER, THE

The affirmative action program in India (the reservation, or quota, system) has shown substantial redistributive effects, in that access to education and jobs is spread wider in the spectrum of Scheduled Castes and Scheduled Tribes (SCs and STs) than it had been previously. This redistribution is not spread evenly throughout the beneficiary groups, however. There is evidence of clustering, and the benefits of the program appear to be confined to a narrow, privileged section of the SCs and STs. This elite section is referred to, in popular discourse, as the "creamy layer." The existence of this layer is one of the arguments used to oppose the affirmative action program. However, this tendency toward clustering is not unique to this program, and it probably reflects structural factors, for the better-off sections enjoy a disproportionate share of benefits in every government program in India.

One of the critiques of the reservation system argues that the vast majority of Dalits are rural and poor. *Dalit*, literally "the oppressed," is a term of pride referring to the SCs and STs, the latter a product of official terminology. Because the reservation of jobs and seats in institutions of higher education is meaningful mainly in urban areas, the benefits are cornered by the "creamy layer," leaving the vast majority of Dalits untouched. However, even the limited reservation of jobs has brought a many-fold increase in the number of families liberated from subservient roles. In addition, the reservation of jobs, even if confined to urban areas, offers a potential avenue of employment that even rural Dalits can aspire to.

One of the concerns about the quota system is that, in the short run, beneficiaries might get singled out and experience social rejection in offices, college hostels, and other places where they are introduced through affirmative action. (There is no explicit affirmative action in college hostels, however, and affirmative action in colleges leads to the entry of SC/ST students into college hostels.) In the long run, however, education and jobs weaken the stigmatizing association of Dalits with ignorance and incompetence. Thus, the existence of the "creamy layer" can perhaps play a positive role, for successful members of the Dalit community demonstrate that, when given equal opportunity over a few generations, they can be just as successful as non-Dalits and are not intrinsically "inferior."

The existence of the creamy layer or the Dalit middle class has kept the beneficiary groups and their problems visible to the educated public. Thus, it is no longer possible for any political party to publicly oppose affirmative action. However, given the pro-upper-caste and anti-affirmative-action bias of the political and social elite, this has not translated into motivated widespread concern for the inclusion of Dalits beyond what is mandated by government policy.

One of the objectives of the affirmative action program is to achieve upward social mobility of the Dalits. However, while this mobility is limited and ought to be viewed positively, it is pejoratively described as a "creamy layer" within the Dalit community. Concerns about intra-group inequality are not invalid, but estimates indicate that intra-group inequality is much more significant among the non-Dalits than among the Dalits. Thus, contrary to conventional wisdom, if groups need to worry about their own creamy layer, the concern should be far greater for the non-Dalits than for the Dalits.

SEE ALSO *Affirmative Action; Caste; Dalits*

BIBLIOGRAPHY

Deshpande, Ashwini. 2004. Decomposing Inequality: Significance of Caste. In *The Dalit Question: Reforms and Social Justice*, ed. Bibek Debroy and D. Shyam Babu, 33–52. New Delhi: Globus Books.

Galanter, Marc. 1984. *Competing Equalities: Law and the Backward Classes in India.* New Delhi: Oxford University Press.

Ashwini Deshpande

CREATIONISM

Creationism is an idiosyncratic form of Protestant biblical literalism that developed in the United States in the nineteenth century. Creationism comes in two forms, one that accepts that the earth is probably very old but that insists that there was an intervention of a creative kind at the beginning to populate the world with organisms, and the other—known as *young earth creationism*—that claims that the earth is about six thousand years old (based on the genealogies of the Bible). Creationism should not be confused with the belief by Christians (and others in the Abrahamic tradition) that God created the earth from nothing, nor should it be confused with traditional Christian thinking about the veracity of the Bible. From at least the time of Saint Augustine (354–430 CE), it has been the position of Christians—Catholics and (later) Protestants—that God often spoke in simplified or metaphorical terms, and that the Bible should not be used as a work of science. In an oft-quoted phrase, the Bible tells human beings where they are going, not where they came from. It should also be noted that although traditional Christianity has always had a place for natural theology, proving God and his attributes through reason, it has never been the case that natural theology has taken the primary role. For Christians, faith is what counts. Hence when skeptics criticize proofs—for instance, pointing out that if one claims that God is the first cause, then who caused God?—believers are not worried. They argue that God is the cause of himself and this is something that is beyond rational proof.

The nineteenth century saw major divisions in the United States, particularly between North and South, exploding into the violent Civil War (1861–1865), something that to this day still marks social and cultural fractures in the country. People in the North, particularly Protestants from older denominations (Episcopalians, Presbyterians, Unitarians), moved steadily in tune with the major movements from Europe, especially the movement to interpret the Bible as a work written by humans (so-called *higher criticism*), and advances in science, especially Charles Darwin's (1809–1882) theory of evolution as expressed in his *On the Origin of Species* (1859).

In the South, and increasingly (as the country moved West) in the central states, Protestants in the more evangelical religions (Baptists and Methodists) turned to the Bible read literally for comfort and understanding. Holy scripture was used to justify slavery and, after the Civil War, many took heart in the ways in which God often punishes or makes life hard for those who have a special place in his heart. The Old Testament story of the Israelites in captivity in Babylon was taken to be a cameo for the way in which, after the war, the South was seen as a society in captivity to the North. New doctrines were added to Christianity, particularly the belief in *dispensations*, or historical periods ended by violent conflagration, the first of which terminated in Noah's flood and the last of which will end with Armageddon and the return of Jesus. Often added to this was a belief in the *Rapture*, according to which the saved will go straight to heaven before the end times, and also the significance of Israel with the return and conversion of the Jews.

This literalism, known in the first part of the twentieth century as *fundamentalism*, was as much a social as a religious movement. The emphasis was on returning to God and working toward personal purity, rather than trying to effect wholesale changes in society for the overall good. This underlying theology was exhibited clearly by the famous Scopes trial of 1925 in Dayton, Tennessee,

when a young school teacher was put on trial for teaching evolution to his class. Prosecuted by three-time presidential candidate and ardent evangelical Christian William Jennings Bryan (1860–1925) and defended by noted agnostic Clarence Darrow (1857–1938), the trial was less about gaps in the fossil record and more about the new modes of education and learning that people in the South felt were being imposed on them by northerners.

Many laughed at the literalists of Tennessee, and fundamentalism withdrew from the public gaze. Then, in the early 1960s, the divide was again exposed and deepened, thanks to a book penned by biblical scholar John C. Whitcomb and hydraulics engineer Henry M. Morris (1918–2006). *The Genesis Flood* (1961), much influenced by Seventh-day Adventist views about the very short (less than 10,000-year) span of the earth, argued that all of geology can be traced to the worldwide deluge through which Noah and his family sailed for forty days. Deeply committed to dispensationalism—the belief that the world's history is divided into phases (seven is a popular number), each ending with a disaster—Whitcomb and Morris were determined to show that there had been such an upheaval, and they warned of one to come. Before *The Genesis Flood*, the general belief had been in a long-history earth; now public opinion followed these authors in opting for young earth creationism.

As before, the main message was less one of science and more one of social prescription, with dire warnings about a nation lax on sexual and other morals. Because *The Genesis Flood* was clearly religious in nature and because of the constitutional separation of church and state in the United States, creationists (as they were now called) began to present a supposedly science-based version of their views—*creation science*—and a law mandating its treatment in state-supported schools was enacted in Arkansas in 1981. A federal judge ruled the law unconstitutional, and a similar bill in Louisiana met a similar fate later in the decade. But creationism was evolving and since 1990 has presented itself in a new guise, *intelligent design* theory. Sparked by law professor Phillip E. Johnson, author of *Darwin on Trial* (1991), its supporters claim that the organic world is so complex that it could not have been produced by blind law. Publicly, it is denied that this intelligent designer necessarily has anything to do with the God of the Bible. Privately, both supporters and opponents agree that intelligent design theory is a form of creationism-lite designed to slip through the barriers between church and state.

Legally, intelligent design theory has been no more successful than creation science. In 2005 a federal judge in Dover, Pennsylvania, ruled that it is not science and hence cannot be taught in state schools. But the battle is not yet over, especially given that polls constantly show more than

50 percent of Americans believe that the earth was created in six days less than ten thousand years ago.

Creationism remains a threat to biology, and also to the rest of science. Geological theories about plate tectonics are ruled out, physical theories about big bangs are ruled out, and in the social sciences, at the very least, anthropology and archeology as understood today are made impossible. This point should be emphasized, for often people think that creationism affects only the biological sciences. If one takes a literal biblical view, then it is hard to see how one can have any approach to humankind that argues (for instance) that social factors were supreme in ordering human behavior. The same is true of biological factors with the same effects—for instance, the purported discovery by geneticist Dean Hamer (2004) that there is a gene for belief in God's existence. All of these things—for instance, the suggestion that sexual orientation might not be a function of someone's free will—will be anathematized. So far, science is holding fast, but the battle has not ended.

SEE ALSO *Fundamentalism, Christian; Scopes Trial*

BIBLIOGRAPHY

Hamer, Dean. 2004. *The God Gene: How Faith is Hardwired into Our Genes.* New York: Doubleday.

Johnson, Phillip E. 1993. *Darwin on Trial*. 2nd ed. Downer's Grove, IL: InterVarsity.

Larson, Edward J. 1997. *Summer for the Gods: The Scopes Trial and America's Continuing Debate over Science and Religion.* New York: Basic Books.

Numbers, Ronald L. 1992. *The Creationists: The Evolution of Scientific Creationism.* New York: Knopf.

Ruse, Michael. 2005. *The Evolution-Creation Struggle.* Cambridge, MA: Harvard University Press.

Whitcomb, John C., Jr., and Henry M. Morris. 1961. *The Genesis Flood: The Biblical Record and its Scientific Implications.* Philadelphia: Presbyterian and Reformed Publishing.

Michael Ruse

CREATIVE DESTRUCTION

The phrase *creative destruction* was introduced by the economist Joseph Schumpeter (1883–1950) in 1942 to describe the process by which innovation occurs in capitalist societies. A "process of industrial mutation" occurs as markets are opened up, revolutionizing "the economic structure from within, incessantly destroying the old one, incessantly creating a new one." Schumpeter called this process "creative destruction," and he held that it was the "essential fact about capitalism" (1962, p. 83).

For Schumpeter, the competitive process that characterized capitalism was not the timid elements of cost reduction but instead the creation of new products, new technology, or new markets, all of which threatened the lives of currently existing products or firms (1962, p. 84). It was such innovation that, for Schumpeter, generated overall economic growth and development, even while it often destroyed the value of sustained companies and monopoly rents. Successful innovation created new monopoly rents, but the process continued with waves of successive innovation. Schumpeter's theory of creative destruction provides an explanation for dynamic industrial change.

The "Schumpeterian hypothesis" that temporary monopoly power is associated with economic growth has engaged generations of empirical workers who struggle with the requirement to make precise what is understood by "temporary" and "innovation" and what must be treated as exogenous to make such tests. There seems to be evidence for a positive association between research and development productivity and firm size, but it is not clear that this is sufficient for the hypothesis itself. Recent work on endogenous growth theory has attempted to operationalize Schumpeter's notion of creative destruction by which one innovation destroys another.

The creative energy for innovation was supplied, Schumpeter argued, by the entrepreneur. It was the entrepreneur who found the means to put new inventions into place. Like Karl Marx (1818–1883), Schumpeter was persuaded that capitalism was destined to pass away: "Can capitalism survive?" Schumpeter asks in *Capitalism, Socialism, and Democracy* (1942), "No. I do not think it can" (1962, p. 61). But unlike Marx, Schumpeter saw the threat to capitalism coming from its very success, from an overreliance on rationality that he associated with capitalism. And unlike Marx, Schumpeter offered a prediction, not a prescription.

Schumpeter's is a "tory" worldview (Stolper 1994, p. 30), not a sedate caricature of the feudal past but instead something akin to that expressed in Scottish essayist and historian Thomas Carlyle's (1795–1881) description of the captains of industry as the heroes for a new age. Markus C. Becker and Thorbjørn Knudsen's 2002 translation of omitted material from Schumpeter's *Theory of Economic Development* (1911) makes clear the parallel between Schumpeter's entrepreneur and Carlyle's hero. Creative destruction is capitalism in the age of the hero, where the entrepreneur provides the creative energy for innovation and the destruction that it entails. What will destroy capitalism is the rationality that kills the heroic (Schumpeter 1962, p. 160).

Without the heroic ethic, which regards risk-taking as an obligation, the capitalist could not defend himself against those who wished to arrest the gales of creative destruction. In notes to Schumpeter's "Can Capitalism Survive?" the editor reports this fascinating floor discussion:

> Schumpeter was now asked why the feudal class in its days of glory was so much more capable of defending itself than the bourgeoisie is today. According to Schumpeter the answer was very simple. The knights of the feudal times were trained to fight and in battle they were superior to everyone else. The only way of defending itself that the bourgeoisie, however, has, is to take up the telephone and telephone Senator X and say, "Good God! Good God! Can't you help us?" (Schumpeter 1991, p. 315)

This would not have been the response from an older capitalism manned by those bound to spouse and children, for whom "navigare necesse est, vivere non necesse est" (Seafaring is necessary, living is not), as noted in an inscription on an old house in Bremen, Germany (Schumpeter 1962, p. 160).

On the face of it, Schumpeter's analysis suggests a role for policy in the promotion of growth through patent laws or subsidized research and development. But if Schumpeter's capitalist can call up government assistance with a telephone call, then government policy with regard to technology should be considered endogenous. Once policy related to technological change is endogenous, it may benefit the existing few instead of the uncreated many of the future.

SEE ALSO *Capitalism; Schumpeter, Joseph*

BIBLIOGRAPHY

Schumpeter, Joseph A. [1942] 1962. *Capitalism, Socialism, and Democracy.* 3rd ed. New York: Harper and Row.

Schumpeter, Joseph A. 1991. *The Economics and Sociology of Capitalism.* Ed. Richard Swedberg. Princeton, NJ: Princeton University Press.

Schumpeter, Joseph A. 2002. New Translations from *Theorie der wirtschaftlichen Entwicklung.* Trans. Markus C. Becker and Thorbjørn Knudsen. *American Journal of Economics and Sociology* 61 (2): 405–437.

Stolper, Wolfgang F. 1994. *Joseph Alois Schumpeter: The Public Life of a Private Man.* Princeton, NJ: Princeton University Press.

Sandra J. Peart
David M. Levy

CREATIVITY

Since the mid-nineteenth century creativity has become increasingly recognized as an extremely valuable natural resource. It plays a role in cultural evolution, innovation, and virtually all societal change. It also plays a significant role on an individual level, contributing to psychological health, learning, and adaptability, as well as to artistic and scientific endeavors. Creativity is not easy to define, in part because it plays such diverse roles.

DEFINING CREATIVITY

When defining creativity most people agree that originality is necessary but not sufficient for creativity. Yet creative things are more than merely original; they must also be fitting, solve a problem, or have some sort of value or aesthetic appeal. This is especially easy to see when creativity is put to use solving problems, for then the creative solution is an original one that also solves the problem. Yet many creative activities and behaviors do not depend on problem solving. Sometimes, creativity is self-expression.

Creativity may also be distinguished from problem solving by defining it to include problem finding, which must occur before a solution is attempted. Problem finding may involve problem identification (recognizing that there is a problem at hand) or problem definition and redefinition (changing a problem such that it can be solved). The German physicist Albert Einstein (1879–1955) and many other unambiguously creative individuals have pointed to problem finding as more important to creative achievement than problem solving.

Definitions of creativity are sometimes debated because it can be difficult to separate self-expression from problem solving. This ambiguity is apparent in the arts, where self-expression is artistic performance; yet artists may be solving problems of technique or solving problems in the sense of finding the best way to express themselves. It may even be that there are preconscious processes at work and the artist is dealing with a problem, even if the artist him- or herself is unaware of the origin or exact nature of the problem. Engaging in artwork can sometimes be an attempt to clarify one's thinking and feelings.

PERSONALITY CHARACTERISTICS

Researchers agree that creativity is tied to motivation. Studies of eminent individuals, as well as investigations that recognize the wider distribution of creative potential, confirm that creativity does not just occur. People work at it, are interested in it, and intentionally nurture or utilize it. Although some creative achievements have been extrinsically motivated, and the creator interested in fame, money, or some sort of reward, it appears as if the vast majority of creative actions are motivated by intrinsic interests. In fact, when an individual is intrinsically interested to perform in a creative fashion, extrinsic incentives can undermine and lower the eventual creative output. Intrinsic interest is also tied to the creative process in the sense that individuals may be more capable of considering a broad range of options and more capable of finding original insights when extrinsic pressures do not distract them.

Personality studies often include intrinsic motivation as one of the core characteristics of creativity. Other relevant personality characteristics include a wide range of interests, autonomy, openness to experience, and nonconformity. Frequently humor and introversion are tied to creativity, but there is much more variation with these two character traits. Some creative domains, such as the performing arts, preclude introversion. The most widely recognized domains that include creativity are linguistic, mathematical, musical, and scientific, though some theories also pinpoint bodily-kinesthetic, interpersonal, and intrapersonal domains. Contemporary research has supported an everyday domain, which includes original and adaptive behaviors used in daily life (e.g., when driving, cooking, and conversing).

It is not uncommon for social scientists to also include seemingly unhealthy characteristics in the list of personality traits that are related to creativity. Nonconformity can be considered one such trait, in the sense that an individual can have excess nonconformity and thereby be alienated from social activities. Another common example of a potentially unhealthful tendency involves affect, and in particular mood disorders. These are frequently observed in eminent creative individuals, and there are reasons to believe that mood swings can facilitate the creative process. Mood disorders contribute to the long-standing and widely recognized stereotype of the mad genius or the highly eccentric creative person.

Another characteristic that may contribute to the creative process involves the capacity to tap one's unconscious. The Swiss psychologist Carl Jung (1875–1961) emphasized the creative individual's capacity to utilize unconscious material in an effective manner, saying that "the ability to reach a rich vein of such material [from the unconscious] and to translate it effectively into philosophy, literature, music, or scientific discovery is one of the hallmarks of what we call genius" (1964, p. 25). He also concluded that "completely new thoughts and creative ideas can also present themselves from the unconscious—thoughts and ideas that have never been conscious before. They grow up from the dark depths of the mind like a lotus and form a most important part of the subliminal psyche" (p. 25).

For Jung, material from the unconscious often takes a symbolic form. Some symbols are widely shared, as is implied by Jung's theory of the collective unconscious.

Jung's view of creativity and the unconscious is entirely consistent with late-twentieth-century views of incubation and its role in creative thought. Biographies of famous creators often describe how good ideas and insights depend on this kind of incubation and only become conscious through sudden insight, often described as the "a-ha!" moment. On the other hand, in 1988 the psychologist Howard Gruber demonstrated that sudden insights are not all that sudden; instead they are protracted and require time and energy. The appearance of the insight is sudden, but the thinking that led up to it is not. However, because insight is an unconscious process, one is not necessarily aware of the work involved in bringing it about.

PROGRAMS AND TECHNIQUES TO ENHANCE CREATIVITY

Many programs and techniques have been designed to encourage and enhance creative potential. Some techniques focus on very specific tactics that can help the individual break mental sets, question assumptions, become more flexible and original, shift perspectives, and produce original insights. Other programs are formal educational efforts and parts of programs for gifted and talented children, which depend heavily on tests of creativity. The most common test utilizes the concept of divergent thinking, which involves performing open-ended tasks that produce a large number of ideas or answers, many of which are divergent or remote. Divergent thinking tasks are statistically independent from convergent thinking tasks (which yield one correct or conventional answer), meaning that children who produce many original ideas may not be the ones who have high intelligence quotients (IQs), and vice versa. Divergent thinking is only moderately predictive of real-world achievement, however, probably because many other factors play a role in the creative process. Intrinsic motivation is an example of one of these other influences on creative work. An individual needs more than the capacity to produce ideas and think in an original fashion; he or she also needs to be interested in doing just that, and perhaps also have the temperament to be unique and unconventional.

Educational programs targeting creativity assume that creativity is widely distributed in the human population. Because creativity is a multifaceted personality trait, existing educational programs and existing tests of creative potential may not fully capture the range of possible creative expressions, nor even the multidimensional nature of the creative process.

BIBLIOGRAPHY

Gruber, Howard E. 1988. The Evolving Systems Approach to Creative Work. *Creativity Research Journal* 1: 27–51.

Jung, Carl G. 1964. *Man and His Symbols.* New York: Dell.

Runco, Mark A. 2004. Creativity. *Annual Review of Psychology* 55: 657–687.

Runco, Mark A. 2006. *Creativity: Theories, Themes, and Issues* San Diego, CA: Academic Press.

Mark A. Runco

CREDENTIALISM

Credentialism, as a social phenomenon, refers to reliance upon formal credentials conferred by educational institutions, professional organizations, and other associations as a principal means to determine the qualifications of individuals to perform a range of particular occupational tasks or to make authoritative statements as "experts" in specific subject areas. As an ideology, it reflects the ostensibly meritocratic idea that positions within the occupational structure ought to be filled by those who have obtained their qualifications through institutional mechanisms (e.g., training and education within certified schools; successful completion of formal examinations) culminating in the attainment of degrees, diplomas, or certificates. As a social-scientific concept, it is closely associated with the discourses of the sociologies of education and work.

Historically, the concept of credentialism emerged as part of the critique of professionalism and in the service of the "deschooling movement" of the 1960s and 1970s. Radical critics of professional education, such as Ivan Ilich (1971), proceeded from the assumption that most if not all of the skills needed to competently perform the work tasks carried out by many professionals could be acquired through practical experience and with much less in the way of formal schooling than is usually needed to obtain the "required" credentials. From this perspective, the disguised purpose of much formal schooling (its "hidden curriculum") is to impart a particular disciplinary paradigm, ideological orientation, or set of values to those seeking formal credentials to work in prestigious or "high-status" fields such as medicine, law, and education. Furthermore, the credential systems developed in a number of occupational areas are part of the "collective mobility projects" of practitioners to achieve a "professional status" that brings with it greater material and symbolic rewards. Thus credentialism is closely associated with strategies of "social closure" (to use Max Weber's expression) that permit social groups to maximize rewards "by restricting access to resources and opportunities to a limited circle of eligibles" (Parkin 1979, p. 44).

The pursuit of credentials through bureaucratized, institutional channels constitutes a kind of "rite of passage" for those who aspire to socially privileged positions while also allowing established professional or occupational groups to control the supply of practitioners, to regulate their activities, and to maintain a monopoly of legitimacy in the provision of particular services. The credential system also legitimates the establishment of legal restrictions by the state in concert with professional, occupational, or skilled trades associations concerning who is deemed qualified to perform particular tasks or provide specific services. One example has been the legal barriers that have been put into place in many jurisdictions to prevent midwives from providing birthing services to expectant mothers, thereby ensuring that such services will remain the exclusive preserve of medical doctors.

The "credential inflation" that occurred over the last third of the twentieth century was a product of the tremendous expansion in postsecondary education that occurred in many of the more developed industrial or "postindustrial" societies in the post–World War II (1939–1945) era. Jobs previously filled by people possessing only high-school diplomas (for example, insurance salespeople) were increasingly filled by those with college diplomas or undergraduate university degrees. The proliferation of employment opportunities in the "service sector" combined with the contraction of the manufacturing labor force increased labor market competition for "white-collar" jobs requiring reasonably high levels of literacy or numeracy. However, many if not most of these jobs did not require as many specific skill sets as the blue-collar jobs that they displaced. It is therefore arguable whether the shift from a predominantly manufacturing to a "service" or even "knowledge-based" economy has brought with it the imperative of higher levels of formal educational attainment for the mass of the labor force. Even so, the members of this labor force have felt compelled to pursue higher levels of education (as symbolized by college diplomas and university degrees) to avoid relegation to employment in the vast array of poorly paid and menial jobs that characterize the so-called "postindustrial" economy. In this context, a college diploma or undergraduate university degree is not so much a ticket to "success" as a safeguard against migration into the most undesirable regions of the labor market. The corollary to this phenomenon is that many workers regard themselves as overqualified for the jobs they perform and experience workplace dissatisfaction stemming from the perception that many of the intellectual skills they attained through "higher education" are being underutilized or even wasted.

With the advent of globalization and the increased mobility of professionals and workers of all kinds across national boundaries, the problem of recognizing "credentials" obtained in other countries has come to the fore. On the one hand, professional organizations and other occupational associations are concerned that the influx of such credentialed individuals may weaken their control over the supply of "qualified" labor; on the other hand, governments are under pressure to recognize such "foreign credentials" by a public that is anxious to alleviate a real or perceived scarcity of professional service providers in such areas as medicine and law.

For most of its critics, credentialism is fundamentally a set of practices and an ideology associated with the reproduction of structures of social inequality and the intergenerational perpetuation of class and status distinctions. For its defenders, it is an inevitable concomitant of a rationalized occupational division of labor, necessary to maintaining optimal levels of productivity and performance. There are clearly elements of truth in both positions, but their satisfactory articulation requires recognition of the ways in which class, race, gender, and citizenship shape both occupational and opportunity structures in contemporary societies and of how credentialism conceals and obscures this reality behind a rationale of technical necessity.

SEE ALSO *Division of Labor; Education, USA; Globalization, Social and Economic Aspects of; Hierarchy; Human Capital; Knowledge Society; Managerial Class; Merit; Meritocracy; Productivity; Professionalization; Stratification; University, The*

BIBLIOGRAPHY

Collins, Randall. 1979. *The Credential Society.* New York: Academic.

Derber, Charles, William A. Schwartz, and Yale Magrass. 1990. *Power in the Highest Degree: Professionals and the Rise of a New Mandarin Order.* Oxford: Oxford University Press.

Illich, Ivan. 1971. *Deschooling Society.* New York: Harper and Row.

Parkin, Frank. 1979. *The Marxist Theory of Class: A Bourgeois Critique.* London: Tavistock.

Murray Smith

CREDIBILITY LIMITS

SEE *Probability, Limits in.*

CREDIT

SEE *Finance; Loans.*

CRENSHAW, KIMBERLÉ

SEE *Critical Race Theory.*

CREOLE

The English term *creole* derives from the Portuguese antecedent *crioulo*, which was adopted by the Spanish as *criollo* ("person native to a locality") and the French as *créole*. The Portuguese word *crioulo* is a diminutive of *cria*, meaning a person raised in the house, usually a servant. The derivation is from the verb *criar*, "to bring up or raise as children," from the Latin *crere*, "to beget." Thus, from very early on the term has indicated novel creation, usually of a lower-status person, and has implied that this novelty is "irregular," or out of place. The term gained currency during the initial growth of European colonial power in the sixteenth century. As European powers established colonies in the Americas, Africa, Asia, and Oceania, new populations were created out of unions between the colonizers, local inhabitants, and immigrants (initially slaves or laborers) transported by Europeans. Initially, the term *creole* was assigned to people born in the colonies, to distinguish them from the upper-class, European-born immigrants. The application of the term has varied from place to place and era to era in important ways, and has also been used to designate languages that have evolved from historical experiences of cultural contact.

CREOLE LANGUAGE

In general, a Creole language is a defined and stable language that arises from long-standing contact between two or more distinct languages. Prior to "creolization," a rudimentary contact language is known as a *pidgin*. Typically, with Creole languages there are many distinctive features that do not derive from any of the parent tongues. In cases where a Creole person was simply a European born in the New World, there was usually no distinction between the language spoken by foreign colonials and their local, white, counterparts. However, as the notion of a Creole came to include anyone born in the New World, the term came to encompass hybrid linguistic forms, some of whose antecedents were not European languages. Generally, Creole populations occupied a low status in the eyes of European colonial administrators, thus Creole languages were regarded as "impoverished dialects" of the colonial languages, and eventually the term was used in opposition to the term *language*, rather than as a type of language. For example, one might say a French Creole as opposed to a Creole language based on French and Fon (a language of West Africa). However, in contemporary linguistics such distinctions are not made, and Creole languages are treated equally alongside other types of language. Furthermore, the term *creole* and its cognates in other languages—such as *crioulo*, *criollo*, and so on—are now applied to distinct languages and ethnic groups in many countries and from a variety of eras, and the terms all have rather different meanings.

CREOLE GROUPS

The Portuguese term *crioulo* can be traced to the fifteenth century, when it gained currency in the trading and military outposts established by Portugal in West Africa and Cape Verde. Initially it simply meant a Portuguese person born and raised in the colony. (The word then came into use, in translation, by other colonial powers.) In the Portuguese colonies the *crioulo* population eventually came to comprise people of mixed Portuguese and African ancestry; especially as the growing numbers of people of mixed heritage dwarfed the population of local whites. In time, *crioulos* of mixed Portuguese and African descent produced important ethnic groups in Africa, especially in Cape Verde, Angola, Mozambique, Guinea-Bissau, São Tomé e Príncipe, and Ziguinchor. These groups have come to think of themselves as culturally distinct from their neighbors. In Brazil, a Portuguese colony from the sixteenth century to 1822, the word came to mean a person with especially dark skin, indicating a strong African heritage. African slaves were imported into Brazil from the seventeenth century until the first half of the nineteenth century. The presence of large numbers of Africans from ethnically diverse origins led to a substantial mixed population as Africans and Europeans began to have children. Mixing was encouraged by many nationalist Brazilian intellectuals as a way of "whitening" the population thereby creating a unique, New World Brazilian identity separate from a Portuguese or European one. As a result, *crioulo* came to be a purely phenotypic label, with harsh, negative connotations.

As in the Portuguese colonies, the Spanish term *criollo* initially meant a person of unmixed Spanish ancestry born in the New World. Locally born Europeans were prohibited from holding offices of high rank and were often shunned socially by the ruling *peninsulares*, or Spaniards born on the Iberian Peninsula.

Eventually the exclusion of the *criollos* by the foreign-born Spanish led to widespread rebellion and the development of a nativist movement. By the 1830s these Creole-based nationalist wars of independence had spread throughout Spanish-speaking Latin America in the form of the Mexican War of Independence (1810–1821) and the South American Wars of Independence (1810–1825).

In other parts of the Spanish Empire the term *criollo* did not enjoy the same currency. Inhabitants of the Spanish colony of the Philippines, for example, generally referred to the locally born Spanish as *Filipinos* or *insulares* ("from the islands"). (*Peninsulare* was still the common

name for those born in the Iberian Peninsula.) Today the term *Filipino* means quite the opposite, indicating a locally born, often ethnically mixed inhabitant of the Philippines. This transformation came about as a result of the Filipino nationalist movements of the late nineteenth century.

In the United States the word *creole* has a complex cluster of meanings and is often misunderstood. In general, a Creole is a person of any race or racial mixture descended from the original European settlers of French Louisiana prior to its incorporation into the United States via the Louisiana Purchase in 1803. It is quite common for Americans in other parts of the country to assume that a Creole is a person of mixed African and European ancestry in Louisiana, but this is not the way the term has historically been used locally. Creoles encompass a wide variety of people of many ethnicities and races who share a French or even Spanish background. Most commonly, a Creole person can lay claim to a francophone heritage from either France or a French-speaking Caribbean island such as Haiti (Saint Domingue prior to 1804), Martinique, or Guadeloupe. White and "colored" migrants from these regions brought their French-speaking, predominantly African slaves with them, thereby establishing a racially heterogeneous Creole population of Louisianans. The Louisiana French, who trace their ancestry to the Acadians of French Canada, usually identify themselves as Cajun. The distinction is sometimes made for local cuisine as well, with a distinction being made between Creole food, which has many African elements, and Cajun cooking, which derives from the culinary practices of mostly white, often rural Cajun-French speakers in Louisiana.

Although in the Americas Creoles were initially Europeans born in the New World, the idea of a mixed population being a "Creole" population has gained wide currency. Indeed, *creolization* has come to mean the blending of one or more cultural identities into a new, hybrid identity. Toward that end, people of mixed native Alaskan and Russian ancestry are frequently called "Alaskan Creoles." In the late eighteenth century Russian adventurers, hunters, and traders known as *promyshleniki* came into contact with and married or formed unions with native Alaskan women, giving rise to a people who assumed a prominent position in the economy of fur trading in the northern Pacific. For example, by 1880, the U.S. census documented fifty-three "Creoles" (people of Russian-Sugpiaq ancestry) living in Ninilchik, a village located on the west coast of the Kenai Peninsula in Alaska. There also exist varieties of Russian–native Alaskan languages—either pidgins or Creoles—throughout the region, such as Copper Island Aleut, a mixed Aleut-Russian language spoken on Mednyy, or Copper Island.

In the English-speaking Caribbean a Creole was originally a European born in the New World, but the term is most commonly used to describe anyone, regardless of race or ethnicity, who was born and raised in the region. It is also in the English-speaking, formerly British colonial Caribbean that the term has come to indicate the syncretism or blending of the various cultural forms or institutions: African, French, British, and Spanish, among others. *Creolization* in this context can mean anything from syncretized religious forms such as Vodou, Santeria, and Orisha, to culinary practices, to musical forms such as calypso, reggae, mambo, zouk, merengue, and many others. Yet the term also may have a variety of local meanings. In Trinidad, for instance, Creole culture generally refers to the practices of local African-Trinidadians as opposed to local whites (often known as French Creoles) and Indo-Trinidadians (the descendants of Indian indentured laborers brought to the island from 1845 to 1917).

In Réunion island and Mauritius, in the Indian Ocean, Creoles fall generally into two categories: (Malagasy) Creoles and Creole-Mazambe. The former were brought in as slaves to work the plantations of Mauritius (as well as Réunion and Seychelles). These laborers were mostly Malagasy (natives of Madagascar), but other African minorities, from Mozambique, Malawi, Tanzania, and Zambia, also were enslaved. In present-day Mauritius Creoles of all kinds are outnumbered by the Indo-Mauritians; however, they still form the majority in Réunion and the Seychelles. Although English is the official language of Mauritius, a French-based Creole language is widely used by all ethnic groups.

BIBLIOGRAPHY

Black, Lydia T. 2004. *Russians in Alaska, 1732–1867.* Fairbanks: University of Alaska Press.

Boswell, Rosabelle. 2005. *Slavery, Blackness, and Hybridity: Mauritius and the Malaise Creole.* London: Kegan Paul.

Brading, David A. 1993. *The First America: The Spanish Monarchy, Creole Patriots, and the Liberal State, 1492–1866.* Cambridge, U.K.: Cambridge University Press.

Garraway, Doris. 2005. *The Libertine Colony: Creolization in the Early French Caribbean.* Durham, NC: Duke University Press.

Holm, John. 2000. *An Introduction to Pidgins and Creoles.* Cambridge, U.K.: Cambridge University Press.

Kein, Sybil, ed. 2000. *Creole: The History and Legacy of Louisiana's Free People of Color.* Baton Rouge: Louisiana State University Press.

Lambert, David. 2005. *White Creole Culture, Politics, and Identity During the Age of Abolition.* Cambridge, U.K.: Cambridge University Press.

Sansone, Livio. 2003. *Blackness without Ethnicity: Constructing Race in Brazil.* London: Palgrave Macmillan.

Philip W. Scher

CREOLIZATION

Creolization, in its most general meaning, is a process of cultural change, the origins of which lie in encounters between Africans and Europeans, initially in a context of slavery and colonialism. This process produces new "creole" cultures and societies. Creolization is characteristic of the Caribbean, Louisiana, and much of Latin America, where *creole* refers to people, languages, music, and things that are created in the "New World" but are not of indigenous ancestry. The term may also refer to the cultures of Liberia, Sierra Leone, and Mauritius. More specific meanings are demographic, where *creolization* refers to an increasing proportion of the population being locally born of African, European, or mixed descent, as distinct from both indigenous people and immigrants; and linguistic, where it means the development of a new language, such as Haitian or Jamaican Creole, which normally coexists with, but is distinct from, a particular European language.

Creole people, languages, and products resulted from interactions between external influences and local conditions, where power was a pervasive factor. When slave owners, missionaries, and colonial administrators tried to suppress African cultures and impose aspects of European cultures, they were often ignored or resisted. In many Caribbean societies during the period of slavery, most people were enslaved Africans who came from many different cultures, while power was exercised by a minority of Europeans and white Creoles. Africans tried to maintain their traditions, and the process of creolization was an adaptation to the physical environments and social constraints in which they lived. A creole culture is generally not homogeneous, but may be conceived as a continuum between its Afro-creole and Euro-creole variants.

Édouard Glissant, a poet, playwright, novelist, and cultural theorist from Martinique, views creolization as the central cultural process that defines the Caribbean. He emphasizes that creole cultures, like the ceaselessly changing creole languages, are characterized by diverse origins, fragmentation and adaptation, fluidity and openness. Glissant posits that the creolization process, unlike assimilation or acculturation, is creative, accepts difference, and remains open, because people may adopt aspects of "other" cultures without relinquishing their own.

The concept of creolization has ideological and political implications. Creole people and culture are evaluated negatively by those who consider them inferior because they are not "pure" European, but positively by those who view them as being authentic and appropriate to the places where they developed. The positive evaluation of creole culture and identity became an important aspect of cultural nationalism because it emphasizes the local and unifying nature of the creole way of life, but people and cultures that are defined as "noncreole" may be excluded from full participation in nations that are defined as creole. In Trinidad and Tobago, for example, the Afro-creole culture that includes carnival, calypso, and steel bands is promoted as the center of national culture, so many Trinidadians of Indian descent feel marginalized.

Acculturation, hybridization, and transculturation are related concepts that are more general in application than creolization. Acculturation emphasizes the process in which an ethnic group acquires another culture in a largely one-way process of cultural change, and hybridization implies a process of miscegenation, or biological mixing. Transculturation, a concept coined by the Cuban scholar Fernando Ortiz (1881–1969) in 1940, refers to the multiple interactions and creation of new cultures, not limited to creole cultures in the Caribbean. Creolization, despite its ideological implications, is a useful concept because it focuses on creative aspects of cultural change, without assuming the unlimited power and success of the Europeans, but it is limited by its specific association with cultures that originated from encounters between Africans and Europeans.

BIBLIOGRAPHY

Burton, Richard D. E. 1997. *Afro-Creole: Power, Opposition, and Play in the Caribbean*. Ithaca, NY: Cornell University Press.

Shepherd, Verene A., and Glen L. Richards, eds. 2002. *Questioning Creole: Creolisation Discourses in Caribbean Culture*. Kingston, Jamaica: Ian Randle.

O. Nigel Bolland

CRIME, ORGANIZED

SEE *Crime and Criminology*.

CRIME, WHITE COLLAR

SEE *Crime and Criminology*.

CRIME AND CRIMINOLOGY

Criminology is the study of crime, criminal behavior, and the criminal justice system. While this captures the essence of the discipline, there has been considerable debate about what constitutes criminal behavior and how it differs from other behaviors widely held to be socially deviant. This debate has produced five types of definitions of criminality: natural law explanations, moralistic expla-

nations, labeling explanations, social harm explanations, and legalistic explanations.

Natural law explanations of criminality are perhaps the oldest of the five. They are influenced by natural law theory, which suggests that some behaviors must be universally prohibited because by their nature they are so morally repugnant or detrimental to the normal functioning of society. Like natural law definitions, moralistic definitions suggest that crime, as defined by statutes and codes, is a direct reflection of society's moral consensus. When the majority of people living in any given society finds a particular action morally reprehensible, their will, often expressed through representative legislators, becomes law.

In contrast to natural law and moralistic definitions of crime, labeling or critical definitions suggest that no behavior is intrinsically criminal, nor is the will of the majority of society members necessarily relevant to the designation of a behavior as criminal. Rather, crimes are behaviors that are defined as such by those in positions of power. In support of these claims, labeling theorists point out that affluent and powerful people are far more likely than the poor and powerless to escape criminal prosecution. In addition, when the affluent *are* subjected to criminal prosecution, because of their social status (which they have in common with those in positions to make law) they tend to escape being labeled as "criminal," a designation typically reserved for the poor and minorities. Other definitions of crime have rested on more pragmatic considerations, such as social harm. Harms-based definitions suggest that crime is any behavior that infringes upon basic human rights or otherwise produces individual or social harm.

Each of these theories has influenced how crime has been defined in different eras, but the definition that most of today's criminologists rely upon to distinguish criminal behavior from other types of social deviance is the legalistic definition. This definition suggests that a crime is any behavior that is legislatively prohibited and committed without defense or justification. When these three elements converge—an act or behavior, a statement by a legislature that these behaviors are unacceptable, and the absence of a legally valid reason for committing the act—then regardless of social harm, moral judgments, or relative power, a person has committed a crime.

One important caveat in any discussion of crime is that virtually everything people do in modern industrial and postindustrial societies is regulated by law, and most of it has nothing to do with the criminal law or crime. Contracts we enter into, nutrition labels on foods, levels of vehicle emissions, the amount of taxes we are required to pay, the methods we use in voting, the height of the buildings in which we work, and nearly everything else we do and experience in our day-to-day lives are regulated by a complex web of laws that have nothing to do with *criminal* law. Nonetheless, because of the personal nature of many crimes, the criminal law tends to be the most visible category of law in modern societies.

TYPES OF CRIME

For the purposes of data collection and comparison, crime data is usually divided into two broad categories: personal crimes and property crimes. Personal crimes include crimes of violence such as murder and robbery as well as any other criminal offenses that involve direct contact between a perpetrator and a victim, such as rape, aggravated assault, and battery. Property crimes are those in which personal property is the object of the offense and there is no force or threat of force used against the person to whom the property rightfully belongs. Examples of property crimes include larceny-theft, burglary, motor-vehicle theft, and arson. Property crimes occur with far greater frequency than personal crimes, making up between 85 and 90 percent of all crimes reported to U.S. law-enforcement agencies. Expressed differently, according to official data, every 23.1 seconds in the United States a crime of violence is committed, and every 3.1 seconds a property crime is committed.

Beyond the distinction between personal and property crimes, other more detailed differentiations among criminal behaviors exist. Some of the more common crime types include violent crime, white collar and corporate crime, organized crime, and "victimless" crime. Other types not discussed in this article include hate crime, environmental crime, technological crime, and political crime.

Violent Crime There are four major violent crimes tracked by both the Federal Bureau of Investigation and most international policing agencies: murder, rape, robbery, and aggravated assault. Murder/nonnegligent manslaughter involves the willful killing of one human being by another without excuse or justification. In most cases, accomplices are equally as culpable in the victim's death as the person who directly causes the victim's death. Forcible rape involves unlawful sexual intercourse committed against the victim's will. In the United States the trend has been to view both force by the accused and the victim's substantial impairment of power to appraise or control conduct as bases for prosecution for rape. Many countries also recognize statutory rape—sexual intercourse with a person (usually female) under the legal age of consent (which varies from country to country). Robbery involves taking personal property from the possession of another against his or her will by the use or threat of force. The threat of violence is what distinguishes robbery from the lesser offense of theft. Aggravated assault

refers to an unlawful attack by one person on another for the purpose of inflicting severe bodily injury.

Among Western industrialized nations, the United States long has been considered a particularly violent and crime-ridden society. However, according to the International Crime Victimization Survey, U.S. victimization rates for many personal and property crimes may not be much different from other nations (Mayhew and van Dijk 1997). This survey notwithstanding, the United States continues to have rates of murder and other serious violent crimes that vastly exceed those of other high-income nations.

White Collar and Corporate Crime The greatest economic costs to society from crime come not from those acts commonly referred to as "street crimes"—that is, the personal and property crimes that receive most of the public's attention—but from white-collar and corporate crime. The term *white-collar crime* was coined by Edwin Sutherland, former president of the American Sociological Association. In his 1939 presidential address Sutherland discussed persons of the upper socioeconomic class whose criminal behavior is dealt with much less severely than that of the lower socioeconomic classes (Sutherland 1940). He defined white-collar crime as "crimes committed by a person of high respectability and high social status in the course of his occupation" (Rosoff et al. 2003, p. 2), distinguishing it from crime committed by persons of a lower occupational status ("blue-collar").

Contemporary criminologists have expanded Sutherland's definition to include other types of crimes committed in the course of someone's legitimate occupation. These more recent definitions of white-collar crime usually contain some or all of the following elements: an illegal act, committed by nonphysical means, with concealment or guile, to obtain money or property, or to obtain a business or personal advantage. Criminologists have also begun to recognize corporate crime as a distinct form of white-collar crime, in which the immediate benefits of the criminal behavior go to a corporation rather than to any particular individual.

In the United States conservative estimates place the material costs of white-collar at more than $300 billion annually. In comparison, losses from property theft/damages, cash losses, medical expenses, and lost pay due to injuries suffered or other activities related to other types of crime cost Americans an estimated $15 to $20 billion per year (Rosoff et al. 2003). Similarly, about 16,000 people are murdered each year in the United States, but far more people die as the result of white-collar criminal activities. For example, more than 100,000 people die each year in the United States because of neglect of worker-safety requirements, on-the-job accidents, and exposure to hazardous materials in the workplace (Reiman 2003).

Organized Crime Organized crime refers to criminal enterprises that specialize in vice crimes such as gambling, prostitution, drug operations, and other correlated illegal activities, including money laundering and racketeering. The origin of organized crime in the United States is often traced to national Prohibition in the 1920s (Brown et al. 2004). The controversial federal ban on alcoholic beverages brought about by the passage of the Eighteenth Amendment to the Constitution and the Volstead Act created opportunities for criminal syndicates to flourish by illegally supplying liquor; later they were able to expand their enterprises into vice and other illicit activities. Today, in spite of international efforts to control organized crime, various sources estimate that international organized crime syndicates draw about $1 trillion in profits each year (Federal Bureau of Investigation 2006).

Victimless Crime Victimless crime refers to illicit behaviors in which the participants do not recognize that anyone involved in the illegal transaction is directly victimized by the deed. These crimes are often referred to as "complainantless" because nobody directly involved is likely to initiate enforcement by complaining to the police. Examples of victimless crimes include prostitution, pornography, illegal gambling, and drug use. *Victimless crime* is a contentious label because, while none of the parties sees themselves as victims, many people argue that society itself is harmed by the prohibited behaviors. For example, it is argued that illegal drug use drives up healthcare costs for everyone, destabilizes families and communities, drains worker productivity, and leads to a number of additional social problems. Further, a meta-analysis of North American studies on prostitution found that prostitutes are very likely to become victims of violence during the course of their work (Farley and Kelley 2000).

In contrast, other theorists argue that victimless crimes should not be considered crimes at all. Rather, they are private behaviors that, when criminalized, represent an overreach of the state's authority. In support of these latter claims, they highlight the variations in prohibitions from state to state and country to country, and societal ambivalence toward many of the prohibited activities. Toward this last point, in 2004 an estimated 19.1 million Americans aged 12 or older were current illicit drug users, spending around $100 billion on illegal drugs. Critics of the criminalization of these behaviors also refer to substances such as alcohol and tobacco that are legally available but cause greater social harm than illicit substances.

THE SOCIAL PRODUCTION OF CRIME

Perhaps the most understudied area of criminology is the role society plays in fostering certain types of crime, such as domestic abuse, hate crime, and sexual assault. Over the past century most societies have changed for the better with regard to recognizing all people as equals irrespective of characteristics such as race, gender, sexual orientation, and religion. However, the extensive histories of inequality and violence have undoubtedly shaped how crimes are defined, and have also played a role in the types of crimes prevalent in any given society. For example, many theorists have argued that the relatively high rates of serious violent crime in the United States can be traced to the culture of violence produced during its particularly hostile settlement: African slavery, Native American genocide, and warfare related to Manifest Destiny all set the stage for a future mired by violence.

Rape presents another example of the social production of crime. For much of world history, patriarchy has been a primary principle around which societies have been structured. Many theorists have argued that this history of socially constructed male supremacy is strongly correlated with rates of male-on-female sexual assault and has shaped how sexual assault has been defined over time. Only in the latter part of the twentieth century did U.S. lawmakers pass laws against marital rape—that is, a rape committed by a husband upon his lawful wife. Before then, the legal standard in the United States was largely consistent with that expressed by Sir Matthew Hale, a chief justice in seventeenth-century England, who wrote "the husband cannot be guilty of a rape committed by himself upon his lawful wife, for by their mutual matrimonial consent and contract, the wife hath given herself in kind unto the husband which she cannot retract" (European Court of Human Rights 1995).

Tolerance for rape in marriage, as well as rape laws that historically have protected the property interests of men over the personal safety of women, may partially explain why rape is so prevalent: each year in the United States nearly 100,000 forcible rapes are reported to police. This figure does not reflect the estimated 100,000 unreported forcible rapes committed against women each year in the United States, nor does it capture lesser-degree sexual assaults that do not meet the reporting criteria required for a charge of forcible rape.

PREDICTORS OF CRIMINAL BEHAVIOR

Contrary to the efforts of hard-line positivist criminologists who seek to identify biological traits that predispose people to criminal behavior, and rational-choice theorists who suggest people commit crimes of their own free will, the consensus among most criminologists is that sociological factors play a significant role in producing criminal behavior. Criminological research has shown that there is no one socioeconomic factor that has proved an accurate predictor of criminal behavior. However, there are some variables that seem to affect the likelihood, volume, and type of crimes that occur in particular countries, regions, and communities. For traditional street crimes, socioeconomic variables such as median income, educational attainment and access to education, religion, family conditions (e.g., divorce and overall family cohesion), and job availability have been correlated with criminal behavior. Population density and the degree of urbanization, the concentration of youth in a community, community stability (e.g., population turnover rates and commuting patterns), alcohol and drug use, the strength of law enforcement agencies in a particular area, community attitudes toward law enforcement, and even climate and weather have all been shown to affect the number of and types of crime that occur.

Of all of these links, the correlation between alcohol and drug use and crime receives the greatest attention from both academicians and policymakers. According to the Bureau of Justice Statistics, 35 to 40 percent of all convicted offenders under the jurisdiction of U.S. corrections agencies were estimated to have been under the influence of alcohol when they offended. Alcohol use is widespread among those convicted of public-order crimes, the most common type of offense among those in jail or on probation. Among violent offenders, about 40 percent of probationers, local jail inmates, and state prisoners, as well as 20 percent of federal prison inmates, were estimated to have been drinking when they committed the crime for which they were sentenced. Comparatively, in a recent survey of jail inmates nearly 30 percent reported drug use at the time they committed their offense, and an estimated 16 percent of convicted jail inmates committed their offenses to get money for drugs. According to the National Survey on Drug Use and Health, about 40 percent of adults who were on parole, probation, or some other form of supervised release from jail were classified as drug dependents or drug abusers, compared to 9 percent of the general U.S. population (U.S. Department of Health and Human Services 2005).

In the United States, if recent incarceration rates remain unchanged, an estimated one of every fifteen persons will serve time in a prison during his or her lifetime. However, the lifetime chances of a person being sentenced to a prison term differ based on race, ethnicity, and gender. Men stand an 11.3 percent chance of going to prison, compared to a 1.8 percent chance for women. This dramatic difference remains in spite of the significant increases in rates of female criminality since the 1970s. Of even greater concern to criminologists are the differences

that exist along racial and ethnic lines. In 2001, approximately 65 percent of U.S. state prison inmates belong to a racial or ethnic minority. African Americans have an 18.6 percent chance of going to prison, Hispanics have a 10 percent chance, and whites have a 3.4 percent of serving time in a prison. Based on current rates of first incarceration, an estimated 32 percent of black males will enter state or federal prison during their lifetime, compared to 17 percent of Hispanic males and 5.9 percent of white males (Bureau of Justice Statistics).

INADEQUACIES OF THE U.S. CRIMINAL JUSTICE SYSTEM

It comes as no surprise to most criminologists that the U.S. criminal justice system is not an effective tool in preventing crime. One reason for this lies in the uncoordinated structure of the system itself. As Barkan and Bryjak note in *Fundamentals of Criminal Justice*, "the U.S. criminal justice system is only partly a 'system' as usually defined. 'System' implies a coordinated and unified plan of procedure. Criminal justice in the United States is only partly coordinated and unified . . . the U.S. criminal justice system is really thousands of systems" (p. 7). Another reason the criminal justice system is largely incapable of preventing crime is that law enforcement, courts, and corrections are reactive institutions; they respond to crimes already committed rather than addressing the root causes of criminal behavior before they fester into crime. This is not a condemnation of the efforts of law enforcement or corrections officers: the criminal justice system simply does not have the resources, expertise, or capabilities to deal with most predictors of criminal behavior.

Politicians and the public present another obstacle in effectively addressing crime. For many reasons, including sensationalized accounts of crime in news and entertainment media, the inability of academics to package criminological research in a publicly palatable fashion, fear promoted by opportunistic political figures, and the unwillingness or inability of the public to inform themselves on crime and justice issues, the public has a distorted image of the crime problem in the United States (Reiman 2003). This distorted image leads to ill-advised, impractical, and ineffective criminal justice policies such as "three-strikes" laws (laws requiring prison terms of 25 years or more for offenders convicted of their third felony or serious crime), mandatory minimum sentencing, and the mandatory charging of juveniles as adults for certain offenses. These policies appeal to politicians because it allows them to appear to be "tough on crime" and makes the public think that the justice system is working. However, these policies represent knee-jerk responses to complex problems of crime; they divert resources from other approaches that carry a greater likelihood of success, and they take discretion away from sentencing judges and other criminal justice practitioners who have a more accurate sense of the crime problem. Ultimately, the onus falls upon members of the academic community to debunk crime myths, dispel stereotypes regarding deviant groups, and promote responsible criminal justice policy.

SEE ALSO *Deviance; Justice, Social; Labeling Theory; Norms*

BIBLIOGRAPHY

Barkan, Steven E., and George Bryjak. 2004. *Fundamentals of Criminal Justice.* Boston, MA: Allyn and Bacon.

Brown, Stephen E., Finn-Aage Esbensen, and Gilbert Geis. 2004. *Criminology: Explaining Crime and Its Context.* 5th ed. Dayton, OH: Anderson Publishing.

Bureau of Justice Statistics. U.S. Department of Justice, Office of Justice Programs. http://www.ojp.usdoj.gov/bjs/welcome.html.

Catalano, Shannan M. 2005. Criminal Victimization 2004. Washington, DC: U.S. Department of Justice, Office of Justice Programs.

European Court of Human Rights. 1995. *S.W. v. The United Kingdom* –20166/92 [1995] ECHR 52 (22 November 1995). http://www.worldlii.org/eu/cases/ECHR/1995/52.html.

Farley, Melissa, and Vanessa Kelly. 2000. Prostitution: A Critical Review of the Medical and Social Sciences Literature. *Women and Criminal Justice* 11: 29–63.

Federal Bureau of Investigation. About Organized Crime. http://www.fbi.gov/hq/cid/orgcrime/ocshome.htm.

Federal Bureau of Investigation. 2005. Crime in the United States 2004. http://www.fbi.gov/ucr/cius_04/.

Mayhew, Pat, and Jan J. M. van Dijk. 1997. Criminal Victimisation in Eleven Industrialised Countries: Key Findings from the 1996 International Crime Victims Survey. The Hague, Netherlands: Ministry of Justice. http://ruljis.leidenuniv.nl/group/jfcr/www/icvs/data/i_VIC.HTM.

Office of National Drug Control Policy. 2000. What America's Users Spend on Illegal Drugs, 1988–1998. http://www.whitehousedrugpolicy.gov/publications/pdf/american_users_spend_2002.pdf#search=%22%22what%20america's%20users%20spend%20on%20illegal%20drugs%22%22.

Reiman, Jeffrey. 2003. *The Rich Get Richer and the Poor Get Prison: Ideology, Class, and Criminal Justice.* 7th ed. Boston, MA: Allyn and Bacon.

Rosoff, Stephen M., Henry N. Pontell, and Robert H. Tillman. 2003. *Profit Without Honor: White Collar Crime and the Looting of America.* 3rd ed. Upper Saddle River, NJ: Prentice Hall.

Sutherland, Edwin H. 1940. White Collar Criminality. *American Sociological Review* 5: 1–12.

Sutherland, Edwin H. 1949. *White Collar Crime.* New York: Dreyden Press.

U.S. Department of Health and Human Services. 2005. National Survey on Drug Use and Health, 2004.

Washington, DC. http://oas.samhsa.gov/nsduh/2k4nsduh/2k4results/2k4results.htm.

A. Rafik Mohamed

CRIMES AGAINST HUMANITY
SEE *Genocide.*

CRISES, ECONOMIC
SEE *Economic Crises.*

CRISIS, THE
SEE *Du Bois, W. E. B.; National Association for the Advancement of Colored People (NAACP).*

CRITICAL LEGAL STUDIES
SEE *Critical Race Theory.*

CRITICAL RACE THEORY

Critical race theory is an intellectual and political movement within legal studies to transform the legal academy in terms of its analysis of racial inequalities and use the law to transform society in markedly antiracist directions. The intellectual breadth of critical race theory presages a much larger contribution to the social sciences aimed at understanding race relations in more interdisciplinary manners. Arising from the critical legal studies movement, critical race theory is identified in terms of two separate origins stories. Kimberlé Crenshaw (Crenshaw et al. 1995, 2002) identifies its origins in the work of Derrick Bell and the Harvard Law School. Sumi Cho and Robert Westley (2002) identify the development of critical race theory on the West Coast and the law school of the University of California Berkeley, Boalt Hall, and the free speech and Third World student movements that gripped college campuses in the 1960s.

Crenshaw, Richard Delgado, and Angela Harris identify the official beginning of critical race theory (CRT) in

1989, with the first workshop on the topic held in Madison, Wisconsin. Many of the scholars associated with critical race theory attended this and subsequent workshops. The impetus for a gathering of law faculty and students of color was their shared frustration over the colorblind veneer of critical legal studies.

Critical legal studies and critical race theory share a commitment to understanding the role that law plays in shaping social relations. Challenging the centrist model of jurisprudence that assumes law to be a self-contained, objective, rational entity designed to make maximally efficient decisions under the rule of law, critical legal studies scholars argue that law often structures social inequalities. Law operates like a bureaucratic iron cage that limits equal access and shapes economic and political hierarchies in society.

Focusing specifically on racial inequalities, critical race theory scholars share a commitment to viewing the law as exacerbating inequalities while maximizing its transformative potential. The foremost scholar in critical race theory is Derrick Bell, whose legal storytelling method has shifted scholarly boundaries between fiction and nonfiction, autobiography and legal analysis, legal and social science scholarship, and law and society. Bell's *And We Are Not Saved* (1987) and *Faces at the Bottom of the Well* (1992) feature the fictional character Geneva Crenshaw, a civil rights lawyer who enters into a dialogue with Bell the law professor on the role that race continues to play in a post–civil rights era. Similar dialogues have been composed by Richard Delgado and his fictional student Rodrigo in *The Rodrigo Chronicles* (1995) and *The Coming Race War?* (1996).

For Crenshaw, the origins of the 1989 critical race theory workshop rest in the Harvard Law School and Bell's decision to leave Harvard over the law school's unwillingness to tenure a woman of color. The Alternative Course was a course on civil rights, race and law designed to continue Bell's intellectual legacy and push to diversify a homogenously white, male faculty. Harvard law students of color fought hard through the 1980s to study race from a critical perspective and diversify the law school's students, faculty, and curriculum.

Other legal scholars, particularly Cho and Westley, identify the origins of critical race theory in the Free Speech and Third World consciousness-raising student movements of the 1960s. Particularly on the West Coast, university students from a plurality of minority communities came together to challenge the white, male patterns of privilege and reproduction. Harvard was not the only law school where students challenged the patterns of racial exclusion. The Boalt Coalition for a Diversified Faculty orchestrated the Nationwide Law Student Strike on April 6, 1989, to publicize the dearth of faculty of color at the nation's law schools (30 percent had never hired a faculty member of color, and 34 percent had made only a token or single hire as of 1981).

Today, many of the most influential law professors identify with critical race theory or its progenies. Derrick Bell, Sumi Cho, Kimberlé Crenshaw, Jerome Culp, Richard Delgado, Neil Gotanda, Lani Guinier, Ian Haney Lopez, Angela Harris, Kevin Johnson, Charles Lawrence, Mari Matsuda, Margaret Montoya, Michael Olivas, Robert Westley, Alfreda Robinson, Dorothy Roberts, Mary Romero, Jean Stefancic, Francisco Valdes, Patricia Williams, Robert Williams, and Eric Yamamoto are widely recognized scholars associated with critical race theory. This list is clearly not exhaustive but simply illustrative of a few of the many names associated with the intellectual movement.

Critical race theory finds its most influential, current expression in the New York University Press's Critical America Series, edited by Delgado and Stefancic. Critical race theory is also cultivating offshoots that are blossoming into their own research programs. Current offshoots include: LatCrit, addressing Latinos, law, and identity; OutCrit, addressing the legal predicaments of lesbian, gay, bisexual, and transgender communities; critical race feminism, which takes an intersectional approach to law, race, and gender; NatCrit, addressing Native Americans and law; ClassCrit, addressing social class and law; critical white studies, challenging white privileges inscribed in law; and mixed-race crit, addressing law from biracial and multiracial identities.

The topics of inquiry in critical race theory vary but include hate speech, hate crimes, reparations, diversity in higher education and the legal academy, racial categorizations and law, identities theorized in relation to anti-essentialisms and multi-positionalities, corporate social responsibility, immigration enforcement, racial profiling, civil rights legislation, race-based backlash, and retrenchment. Many CRT scholars were instrumental in the successful reparations claim on the part of Japanese American internees. Reparations for African Americans (based on slavery and Jim Crow institutions), Native Americans (artifacts, land, and treaties), Mexican Americans (for mass repatriation during the Great Depression and the temporary worker or Bracero Program from 1942 to 1964), and Jewish Holocaust survivors represent critical race theory movements where law and politics intersect to advocate for social change.

The contributions to the social sciences include new approaches to narrative inquiry, the legal storytelling tradition, identities, and politics. The narrative storytelling tradition and its validation in the academy serve as major contributions not only to legal studies but to most fields of the humanities and social sciences. The fundamental epistemological claims of whose knowledge is deemed valid, how we come to "know truth," and the privileged position of outsiders in understanding power relations are revolutionary contributions to an alternative philosophy of science that informs the social sciences.

Finally, fields such as education and interdisciplinary studies in law and society have incorporated critical race theory into their analytical frameworks. University of Wisconsin educators Gloria Ladson-Billings and William Tate's 1995 call for the application of critical race theory to the fundamental issues of race in education has been answered by scholars such as Sofia Villenas, Tara Yosso, and Daniel Solorzano.

SEE ALSO *Bracero Program; Critical Theory; Holocaust, The; Jim Crow; Narratives; Politics; Race; Racism; Slavery; Social Constructs; Social Science; Storytelling; Whiteness*

BIBLIOGRAPHY

Crenshaw, Kimberlé, Neil Gotanda, Gary Peller, and Kendall Thomas, eds. 1995. *Critical Race Theory: The Key Writings that Formed the Movement*. New York: New Press.

Delgado, Richard, and Jean Stefancic. 2001. *Critical Race Theory: An Introduction*. New York: New York University Press.

Hernández-Truyol, Berta, Angela Harris, and Francisco Valdes. 2005. LatCrit X Afterword, Beyond the First Decade: A Forward-Looking History of LatCrit Theory, Community, and Praxis. LatCrit.Org. http://www.arts.cornell.edu/latcrit/welcome/history/latcritxafterword_v_21.pdf.

Ladson-Billings, Gloria, and William F. Tate, IV. 1995. Toward a Critical Race Theory of Education. *Teachers College Record* 97 (1): 47–68.

Valdes, Francisco Valdes, Jerome McCristal Culp, and Angela P. Harris, eds. 2002. *Crossroads, Directions, and a New Critical Race Theory*. Philadelphia: Temple University Press.

Ronald L. Mize Jr.

CRITICAL THEORY

The Frankfurt school of critical theory is one of the major schools of neo-Marxist social theory, best known for its analysis of advanced capitalism. Opposed to the determinism and scientism of Soviet Marxism, critical theory challenged the philosophical foundations of Marxist theory, and formulated an original analysis and diagnosis of the major changes in social structure that took place in the twentieth century.

The philosopher and social theorist Max Horkheimer (1895–1973) was appointed director of the Institute for Social Research in 1930, and shifted its emphasis from historical research to a project of interdisciplinary social research with an empirical intent. Horkheimer wanted to know why the working class supported the Nazi regime when it was not in their interest to do so. He rejected the deterministic view that consciousness was a product of class position, and looked to integrate psychology, more specifically Sigmund Freud's (1856–1939) psychoanalysis, into a critical theory of society. To carry out his research program, Horkheimer brought into the institute Erich Fromm (1900–1980), a trained psychoanalyst, who fused psychoanalysis with social theory. Horkheimer further expanded the focus of research to include Leo Löwenthal (1900–1993), Herbert Marcuse (1898–1979), later Theodor Adorno (1903–1969), and the lesser-known figures Frederich Pollock (1894–1970), Franz L. Neumann (1900–1954), and Otto Kirchheimer (1905–1965).

The psychological dynamics of rising authoritarian attitudes were the focus of the institute's early empirical research. A larger project that included the study of working-class attitudes toward authority remained uncompleted when the institute fled Germany to avoid the Nazis and went first to Switzerland and then was relocated at Columbia University in New York.

The term *critical theory* is often thought of as a code word to avoid the association of the institute's research with Marxism. *Critical theory*, however, also drew upon German idealism from Immanuel Kant (1724–1804) onward. Kant saw critique as a theory of the scope and limits of understanding that combated dogmatic conceptions of absolute knowledge. The Hegelian tradition came to see critique as a reflective self-consciousness that encompassed both self and social formation in one grasp. Both were crisis-ridden processes of struggle in which humans won their freedom through freedom from necessity and social domination.

Horkheimer rejected the idealism of G. W. F. Hegel's (1770–1831) conception, but saw critical theory as a philosophy of engaged theorizing. Traditional theory took an objective observer perspective. It saw the ideal of theory construction as the achievement of a deductive system of propositions that are systematic and logical. In contrast, critical theory has an interest in freedom from unnecessary constraint and the improvement of practical life. It is a partisan in the struggle for a better life. Theory is tied to emancipation and freedom. Marcuse especially emphasized the Hegelian elements found in Karl Marx's (1818–1883) early manuscripts (then just discovered) and their link to problems of alienation and reification.

The second phase of critical theory, which began at the end of the 1930s, was concerned with the great transformations in economic structure that were occurring in advanced capitalist and socialist societies, such as the rise of state capitalism. Critical theory linked the increasing concentration of economic power by large corporations and government to the need for state administrative activity to support a crisis-ridden economy. Governments were not watchman states. They had to intervene directly in the economy to assure the conditions of successful economic accumulation.

The Frankfurt school analysis of late capitalism, however, went beyond economic analysis to depict state intervention in socialization processes. Intervention in social processes like schooling and social welfare became necessary in order to effectively manage state capitalism. The school also analyzed the emergence of mass media, which developed sophisticated modes of persuasion and manipulation in order to create a more compliant and agreeable citizenry. The Frankfurt school developed a pessimistic diagnosis of the power of advanced capitalism to control the populace and limit the possibilities of constructive social transformation.

The culmination of this stage was the publication of Horkheimer and Adorno's *Dialectic of Enlightenment* (1944). Here, critical theory becomes a critique of instrumental reason. For Horkheimer and Adorno, reason (and science) no longer retained its link to human freedom, and had, in becoming instrumentalized, transformed into a force for domination and oppression. Marx's thought itself, and not merely its orthodox deformations, were sometimes guilty of a technological determinism. Horkheimer and Adorno, however, unlike some poststructuralists, never fully rejected reason, or looked to a realm of the ineffable or irrational, but were keenly aware of the paradoxes and contradictions of modern instrumental rationality.

Horkheimer and Adorno looked to other dimensions of reason that were resistant to the forces of instrumental rationalization, notably to art, to find potentials for freedom. A somewhat different and more positive evaluation of the role of mass culture and art was developed by Walter Benjamin (1892–1940), a literary theorist who, though marginal in the institute, came to exert a strong influence on Adorno's aesthetic theory.

Adorno's work eclipsed Horkheimer after their return to Germany in 1950. In *Negative Dialectics* (1966) and *Aesthetic Theory* (1970), Adorno formulated a critique of reason using the power of the negative. The latter equated rationalization with reification. Positive reason, which always has a residue of instrumentality, is contrasted with a dimension of reason that can never be fully specified but holds truth content.

In the United States, Marcuse made some significant contributions to critical theory in the 1950s and 1960s. Marcuse's *Eros and Civilization* (1955) was perhaps the school's most successful fusion of Marx and Freud.

Marcuse developed a dialectic of civilization that linked labor and economic scarcity with social and psychic repression. Marcuse's acceptance of the death instinct, however, was controversial. His *One-Dimensional Man* (1964) and *An Essay on Liberation* (1969) continued the Frankfurt school's critique of the pathology of technological reason. One-dimensional reason represented a global project of instrumental reason that suppressed the aesthetic aspects of sensibility and feelings. Marcuse's more politically charged version of the dialectic of enlightenment struck a chord with the New Left in the United States and Europe.

Jürgen Habermas is the preeminent figure in the second generation of critical theory. Habermas modified key aspects of critical theory, especially the critique of instrumental reason, and made significant contributions to a critical theory of democracy, a task neglected by earlier theorists. Habermas's first book, *Structural Transformation of the Public Sphere* (1962), took issue with the first-generation reading of the freedom-creating potentials of liberalism. Habermas depicted the rise of a sphere of civil society in early modern Europe as a public sphere of free discussion of political affairs. While Habermas concurred in broad terms with the critique of instrumental reason, he did not equate rationalization with reification. Habermas argued that instrumental reason had a legitimate role and was not inherently repressive. Reliance on technical expertise leaves out the elements of public debate and discussion.

In *Knowledge and Human Interests* (1968), Habermas reformulated Horkheimer's idea of emancipatory social theory. Habermas developed three distinct cognitive interests—instrumental, communicative, and emancipatory—and rejected the idea that critical reason is found in negation alone. Returning to a more Hegelian-perspective critique requires an intersubjective process of understanding that emphasizes critical reflection on the formative processes of self and society. The emancipatory interest is a form of reflection on coequal processes of social formation (instrumental and communicative) that frees action from domination.

Theory of Communicative Action (1981) was the first systematic statement of Habermas's mature theory of society. The cognitive interests were replaced by a broadly interpretive social theory that distinguishes two basic forms of social action: instrumental and communicative. The first is action oriented toward success. The second is action oriented toward mutual understanding.

Habermas's revision of Marx centers on the conflict between intersubjective forms of understanding and the impingement of system imperatives on social life. In complex modern societies, some functions, such as the economy, have become detached from moral and political regulation in order to efficiently carry out social reproduction. However, in capitalism this rationalization process is one-sided. It replaces realms of communicative action that are constitutive of human subjectivity and intersubjectivity with system imperatives. Habermas coined the phrase "colonization of the life world" to indicate the way in which these communicative spheres are controlled and reified by instrumental and functional imperatives. Reification involves threats to the integrity of communicative subjectivity in the contradictions between democracy and capitalism in modern society.

Most of Habermas's later work has focused on the formation of a cosmopolitan legal, moral, and political theory. This emphasis maintains a tenuous link to emancipatory theory and social crisis. Habermas's discourse ethics revises the Kantian principle of universalization in light of intersubjective aspects of communicative rationality. Kant's categorical imperative applies to the individual who reflects by himself or herself. It asks us to "act only according to a maxim by which you can at the same time will that it shall become a general law" (Kant, 39). In contrast, Habermas's discourse ethics requires a social, intersubjective perspective. Participants have to reflect on the consequences for all those potentially affected by a norm: "for a norm to be valid, the consequences and side effects of its general observation for the satisfaction each person's interests must be acceptable to all" (Lenhardt and Nicholson, 197). The only norms that can be valid are those which can be accepted by all participants in discourse.

In *Between Facts and Norms* (1992), Habermas extends the communicative basis of discourse theory to democratic constitutionalism. Communicative freedom in Habermas's view incorporates aspects of liberal democracy and republican theory. It stresses the self-determination emphasized by liberal theory and the self-realization of republican theories.

Many critics also see Habermas's moral and political theory as a return to a Kantian moral theory. It can, however, also be viewed as an attempt to fuse Kantian insights into Hegelian notions of concrete intersubjectivity. In addition, post-structuralists reject the idea of an inclusive intersubjective foundation for ethics, politics, and law. For Jacques Derrida (1930–2004), for example, law is a closed system instituted through violence. Genuine intersubjectivity is rooted, in contrast, in care and compassion for the other, which is always beyond law and justice. On this reading, Habermas replays the earlier notion of a unified social subject. Habermas's use of systems theory in *Theory of Communicative Action* has also been criticized by interpretive social theorists who believe that Habermas's theory of society is inconsistent with his general commitment to interpretive and critical social science.

SEE ALSO *Alienation; Critical Race Theory; Cultural Capital; Culture; Derrida, Jacques; Discourse; Ethics; Frankfurt School; Freedom; Freud, Sigmund; Habermas, Jürgen; Hegelians; Ideology; Kant, Immanuel; Law; Liberalism; Marcuse, Herbert; Marx, Karl; Marxism; Neumann, Franz; Psychoanalytic Theory; Psychology; Social Psychology; Working Class*

BIBLIOGRAPHY

Adorno, Theodor. [1966] 1973. *Negative Dialectics*. Trans. E. B. Ashton. New York: Seabury.

Adorno, Theodor. [1970] 1984. *Aesthetic Theory*. Trans. Christian Lenhardt. New York: Routledge and Kegan Paul.

Benhabib, Seyla. 1986. *Critique Norm and Utopia: A Study of the Foundations of Critical Theory*. New York: Columbia University Press.

Benjamin, Walter. [1961] 1968. *Illuminations*. Trans. Harry Zohn. New York: Harcourt.

Buck-Morss, Susan. 1977. *The Origin of Negative Dialectics: Theodor W. Adorno, Walter Benjamin, and the Frankfurt Institute*. New York: Free Press.

Dubiel, Helmut. 1986. *Theory and Politics: Studies in the Development of Critical Theory*. Trans. Benjamin Gregg. Cambridge, MA: MIT Press.

Habermas, Jürgen. [1962] 1991. *Structural Transformation of the Public Sphere: An Inquiry into a Category of Bourgeois Society*. Trans. Thomas Burger and Frederick Lawrence. Cambridge, MA: MIT Press.

Habermas, Jürgen. [1968] 1971. *Knowledge and Human Interests*. Trans. Jeremy J. Shapiro. Boston: Beacon.

Habermas, Jürgen. [1981] 1984–1987. *Theory of Communicative Action*. 2 vol. Trans. Thomas McCarthy. Boston: Beacon.

Habermas, Jürgen. 1990. Morality and Ethical Life: Does Hegel's Critique of Kant Apply to Discourse Ethics? in *Moral Consciousness and Communicative Action*. Trans. Christian Lenhardt and Shierry Weber Nicholsen. Cambridge, MA: MIT Press.

Habermas, Jürgen. [1992] 1996. *Between Facts and Norms: Contributions to a Discourse Theory of Law and Democracy*. Trans. William Rehg. Cambridge, MA: MIT Press.

Held, David. 1980. *Introduction to Critical Theory: Horkheimer to Habermas*. Berkeley: University of California Press.

Horkheimer, Max. 1993. *Between Philosophy and Social Science: Selected Early Writings*. Trans. G. Frederick Hunter, Matthew S. Kramer, and John Torpey. Cambridge, MA: MIT Press.

Horkheimer, Max, and Theodor Adorno. [1944] 2002. *The Dialectic of Enlightenment: Philosophical Fragments*, ed. Gunzelin Schmid Noerr; trans. Edmund Jephcott. Stanford, CA: Stanford University Press.

Jay, Martin. 1996. *The Dialectical Imagination: A History of the Frankfurt School and the Institute for Social Research, 1923–1950*. 2nd ed. Berkeley: University of California Press.

Kant, Immanuel. 1959. *Foundations of Metaphysics of Morals*. Trans. Lewis White Beck. Indianapolis: Bobbs Merrill.

Kellner, Douglas. 1989. *Critical Theory Marxism and Modernity*. Baltimore, MD: Johns Hopkins University Press.

Marcuse, Herbert. 1955. *Eros and Civilization: A Philosophical Inquiry into Freud.* Boston: Beacon.

Marcuse, Herbert. 1964. *One-Dimensional Man: Studies in the Ideology of Advanced Industrial Society.* Boston: Beacon.

Wiggershaus, Rolf. 1994. *The Frankfurt School: Its History, Theories, and Political Significance.* Trans. Michael Robertson. Cambridge, MA: MIT Press.

Brian J. Caterino

CRITICAL WHITE STUDIES

SEE *Critical Race Theory; Whiteness.*

CROATS

Croats are a Slavic people, but theories of their origins are widely disputed. The most widely accepted "Slavic" theory of the origin of the Croats traces their migration starting in the seventh century from the area north of the Carpathian Mountains into the western Dinaric Alps. Croats are predominantly Roman Catholic. The name Hrvat (Croat) was recorded for the first time on the Adriatic coast in 852.

The earliest Croatian state was the Principality of Dalmatia. In 925 the Croatian duke of Dalmatia, Tomislav of Trpimir, united all Croats. He organized a state by annexing the Principality of Pannonia. Throughout history, Croats were subjected to forced Magyarization as well as Germanization. After World War I, most Croats united within the Kingdom of Slovenes, Croats, and Serbs. The state was transformed into the Kingdom of Yugoslavia in 1929, and the Croats became part of a new nation called the Yugoslavs or South Slavs. In 1939 the Croats attained a high degree of autonomy when the Banovina of Croatia was created, which united almost all ethnic Croatian territories within the kingdom. During World War II, the Axis created a puppet state—the State of Croatia, led by fascists whose goal was an ethnically clean Croatian state. At the same time, many Croats joined the antifascist partisan movement led by the Communist Party of Yugoslavia.

Croats have maintained a strong culture and sense of national identity, and the Roman Catholic Church has contributed to this significantly. The most distinctive features of Croatian folklore include *klapas* of Dalmatia (*klapa*, meaning "company" or "ensemble," refers to folksinging groups) and the orchestras of Slavonia. Folk arts are performed at special events and festivals.

In the early twenty-first century, in addition to their homeland, where about 4 million Croats live, 600,000 Croats live in Bosnia and Herzegovina, while 100,000 to 200,000 live in other states of the former Yugoslavia. The largest immigrant groups live in western Europe, primarily Germany, Italy, and Sweden. Outside Europe, Croats live in the United States and Canada as well as in Argentina, Chile, Peru, and Bolivia. The earliest Croatian settlement in America is dated to 1573, when a peasant uprising was crushed in Croatia and many of them left. There are also large Croatian communities in Australia, New Zealand, and South Africa.

The Croatian national identity, which was suppressed in the name of the preservation of an overarching Yugoslav national identity during the cold war, experienced a new resurgence and played a crucial role in Croatia's involvement in the Yugoslav war in the 1990s. This resurgence of Croatian nationalism and the desire for the creation of a nation-state caused the rebirth of historical ethnic tensions with the neighboring Serbs. Part of the reemergence of the national identity was the Croat campaign to distinguish Croatian as a language separate from the previously united Serbo-Croatian language.

SEE ALSO *Ethnic Conflict; Identity; Nationalism and Nationality; Roman Catholic Church; Serbs*

BIBLIOGRAPHY

Eterovich, Francis H., and Christopher Spalatin, eds. 1970. *Croatia: Land, People, Culture.* Toronto: University of Toronto Press.

Dagmar Radin

CROCKETT, DAVY

SEE *Mexican-American War.*

CRONBACH'S ALPHA

SEE *Validity, Statistical.*

CRONBACH'S COEFFICIENT

SEE *Psychometrics.*

CRONY CAPITALISM

The term *crony capitalism* refers to forms of capitalism in which leading businessmen enjoy close personal relationships with key politicians. Crony capitalism is often associated with corruption and many commentators have seen it as a major obstacle to Third World development. Commentators often contrast crony capitalism with highly idealized neoclassical models of capitalism. In actuality, however, significant linkages between political elites and business classes can be found in almost all capitalist regimes, past and present, and the real task is to identify the variety of ways in which such linkages either facilitate or hinder economic development.

In many underdeveloped countries crony capitalism may be perceived both as corrupt and as antinational. Crony capitalists often belong to ethnic minority groups whose activities have been historically concentrated within the business or financial sector and who in some cases had enjoyed protection under earlier colonial regimes. As in the cases of the Lebanese in Sierra Leone, Indians in Kenya, and the Chinese throughout Southeast Asia, perceived government favoritism toward entrepreneurial minorities may lead to fierce ethnic conflicts and the shattering of polities.

Crony capitalism may result in corruption. But corruption's effects on economic development need not necessarily be lethal and corruption is certainly not unique to modern Third World nations. While the World Bank and the U.S. government have intervened to make aid conditional on struggles against corruption, relatively little attention has been given to historical studies of the effects of corruption on economic development. American civic life in the era of the Second Industrial Revolution between 1870 and 1914 was immensely corrupt, though the effect of this corruption on U.S. economic growth remains largely unexplored. In *The Shame of the Cities* (1902) the social reformer Lincoln Steffens documented many cases of corrupt ties between businessmen and politicians during the era of the so-called Robber Barons. Steffens condemned the "shamelessness" of municipal politics in St. Louis, a politics characterized by "government of the people, by the rogues and for the rich." Recent examples of cronyism show that the spirit of the Robber Barons continues: In 2001 the Enron case revealed collusion between politicians and corporate executives, while 2006 saw the conviction of the lobbyist Jack Abramoff, who had served as an intermediary between businessmen and key congressmen.

Some sociologists and political scientists have even maintained that some forms of crony capitalism may be indispensable for capitalist development, particularly when those forms of cronyism help prevent untrammeled corruption. As modern China shows, personal political networks tying central government leaders to regional industrialists may be invaluable in combating entrepreneurial corruption. China's increased movement away from state-owned enterprise has greatly increased opportunities for corruption at the higher ranks of society. Interestingly, however, the emerging Chinese culture of corruption so far seems mainly limited to regional levels, as the political elite that rules China at the national level has resisted absorption into this culture. Much of the success of the current Chinese economy may be due to the combination of local businessmen adept at adapting laws to local conditions and an uncorrupted political elite with ties to regional economic leaders that imposes limits on regional corruption and maintains a legal framework on which local and foreign businessmen can rely.

Cronyism has been an important element of capitalism everywhere, but the relationship between cronyism, business, and politics and cronyism's effect on development vary greatly from nation to nation.

SEE ALSO *Capitalism; Networks*

BIBLIOGRAPHY

Chua, Amy. 2003. *World on Fire: How Exporting Free Market Democracy Breeds Ethnic Hatred and Global Instability.* New York: Doubleday.

Domhoff, G. William. 1970. *The Higher Circles: The Governing Class in America.* New York: Vintage.

Lambsdorff, Johann Graf, Markus Taube, and Matthias Schramm, eds. 2005. *The New Institutional Economics of Corruption.* New York: Routledge.

Sun, Yan. 2005. Corruption, Growth, and Reform: The Chinese Enigma. *Current History* 104 (683): 257–263.

Michael Hanagan

CROSS OF GOLD

In a passionate speech to the Democratic national convention on July 9, 1896, William Jennings Bryan (1860–1925) used the "cross of gold" metaphor to attack the U.S. gold standard and defend the "free coinage of silver." Bryan's nomination as the presidential candidate of the Democratic Party made the national currency the central issue of the fall election. Bryan's defeat in the landmark 1896 election ushered in a new political era in American politics.

The federal government had begun to restrict the supply of money in the United States after the Civil War (1861–1865). In 1879 the U.S. government effectively adopted the gold standard, pegging the value of the dollar to a fixed amount of gold. In a nation with a growing population and an expanding economy, this restrictive monetary policy helped force prices downward. Prices for agricultural commodities fell dramatically from the late 1860s to the late 1890s. Falling prices created hardship for many farmers, especially in the South and West. Indebted farmers in these areas resented the flow of capital to creditors in northeastern cities. Naturally, these farmers blamed the gold standard as the reason for their problems. They demanded that the government circulate more currency to alleviate these pressures. At first, they urged the government to support "greenback" (paper) dollars. By the 1870s, they were insisting on the "free coinage" of silver, that is, the circulation of silver and silver-backed currency, valued at a sixteen to one ratio to gold-backed currency. Their resentment of the gold standard fueled the growth of the populist movement in the late 1880s and the 1890s.

The economic depression of 1893 discredited gold supporters in the Democratic Party because it occurred during the presidency of Democrat Grover Cleveland (1837–1908), a staunch defender of the gold standard. The successes of the silver-supporting People's Party in the 1892 election strengthened the influence of Democrats who supported silver in 1896. During a crucial convention debate over the currency plank at the 1896 Democratic national convention, thirty-six-year-old Bryan, a silver supporter and former U.S. representative from Nebraska, gave an electrifying speech for silver. Bryan insisted to gold supporters that "you shall not press down upon the brow of labor this crown of thorns, you shall not crucify mankind upon a cross of gold." Nominated for president on the fifth ballot, Bryan ran a campaign of unprecedented energy, traveling eighteen thousand miles and making over six hundred speeches. Gold standard supporters dominated the 1896 Republican convention and nominated Ohio governor William McKinley (1843–1901) for president, thus making currency the central issue of the election. Bryan lost the popular vote by 4 percent and the electoral college 271 votes to 176. Though Bryan won a wide swath of southern and western states, McKinley carried the more densely populated states of the Midwest and Northeast. The 1896 election revitalized and realigned the American party system, creating a "fourth party system," in which Republicans dominated most national elections. During McKinley's presidency, the U.S. formally adopted the gold standard.

BIBLIOGRAPHY

Bensel, Richard Franklin. 2000. *The Political Economy of American Industrialization, 1877–1900.* Cambridge, U.K., and New York: Cambridge University Press.

Durden, Robert F. 1965. *The Climax of Populism: The Election of 1896.* Lexington: University of Kentucky Press.

Ritter, Gretchen. 1997. *Goldbugs and Greenbacks: The Antimonopoly Tradition and the Politics of Finance in America, 1865–1896.* Cambridge, U.K., and New York: Cambridge University Press.

David Brian Robertson

CROWDING HYPOTHESIS

Societies have been stratified on the basis of income since ancient times. One of the main axes of stratification is the occupational hierarchy. Evidence of the nonrandom distribution of social groups among occupations is apparent in labor markets around the world (e.g., secretaries are disproportionately female). Social groups that are restricted from access to the range of occupations tend to concentrate in those occupations with the lowest economic rewards. For example in *Black Metropolis: A Study of Negro Life in a Northern City* (1993), St. Clair Drake and Horace R. Cayton noted that in 1930, 56 percent of black females in Chicago were servants of some kind.

The *crowding hypothesis* originated in the United States during the women's union movement of 1890 to 1925. In 1922 British economist F. Y. Edgeworth (1845–1926) argued that women's lower pay was explained by the fact that women crowded into a small number of occupations. Unions had excluded women from "men's work," causing an oversupply of female workers and reducing the price (wage) for their labor. Thus crowding was caused by institutional barriers that artificially distorted the operation of the labor market, resulting in lower wages for some groups and higher wages for others. The crowding hypothesis received little attention until 1971 when economist Barbara R. Bergmann published a pathbreaking paper called "The Effect on White Incomes of Discrimination in Employment." She estimated that the integration of black male blue-collar workers into white occupations would have a negative effect on white male incomes. In 1974 Bergmann analyzed crowding among female workers and since then economists have considered occupational segregation by sex to be a major determinant of the gender disparity in wages.

The empirical evidence is clear that crowding benefits some groups by reducing competition for the most desirable occupations. This helps to explain why occupational segregation is so universal. The crowding hypothesis is simple yet very powerful because it employs the fundamental laws of economics, supply and demand, to explain intergroup wage disparity. Sir William Arthur Lewis

(1915–1991), a Nobel-prize winning economist, stated in *Racial Conflict and Economic Development* (1985) that "The essence of discrimination is its measures to restrict relative numbers in higher paid occupations. Race is not a necessary factor; such measures are found even in homogenous societies" (Lewis 1985, p. 43). Discrimination occurs when devices such as unions and credentialing processes restrict entry; it becomes imbedded in the system and is not necessarily intentional. Lewis theorized that restrictions on access to preferred occupations can render groups noncompeting, making it easier to deny discrimination.

A critique of the crowding hypothesis is that crowding could arise from factors other than discrimination. Women may prefer jobs considered "women's work," such as the nurturing occupations of nursing and childcare. Human capital factors such as education and skill level may also influence crowding. Another critique is that market competition should eliminate crowding as profit-seeking employers replace high-wage workers with low-wage workers from crowded occupations. In "The Crowding Hypothesis" (2005) Timothy Bates and Daniel Fusfield reported little evidence of this. They consider racial crowding self-perpetuating because it traps workers in occupations requiring little skill and with high unemployment rates. Workers have little incentive to acquire skills and racial hostility is mutually reinforced—thus crowding is both the cause *and* effect of "racial antagonisms and the lack of human capital on the part of blacks and other minority groups" (Bates and Fusfield 2005, p. 109). The crowding hypothesis offers a most useful way to think about the problems of urban labor market structures (e.g., low wages, little training, and job insecurity) impacting low-income communities of color. Crowding plays an important role in the black unemployment rate, which has been double the white rate since the mid-1950s.

There is ample empirical evidence linking occupational crowding and lower wages, though most studies concern sex segregation. Estimates are that 12 to 37 percent of the U.S. gender wage gap is attributable to crowding. Analytical techniques for measuring this relationship have become more sophisticated to control for worker characteristics and adjust to data limitations, statistical bias, and other problems. Evidence from detailed, matched employer-employee datasets with sex, occupation, industry, and work establishment data supports the crowding hypothesis. Beginning in the 1970s women's opportunities in white-collar and service employment widened. While black male and female occupational patterns (and wages) have improved as well, especially in public sector employment, white males still dominate high-skill blue collar occupations (e.g., carpenter). Blacks have made less progress in white-collar managerial and executive positions. In "Male Interracial Wage Differentials: Competing Explanations" (1999) Patrick L. Mason showed that wage discrimination accounts for 21 percent of the black male/white male wage differential and 17 percent of the Latino/non-Hispanic white male wage differential. However once the differences in the race-gender employment densities of the occupations are accounted for, the black male/white male unexplained wage differential declines to 7 percent, while the Latino/non-Hispanic white male unexplained wage differential declines to 11 percent. Hence crowding accounts for 14 percent of the black/white male wage differential and 6 percent of the Latino/white male differential. Further for all groups individual wages rise with white employment density, though white males receive the largest boost to individual wages.

Affirmative action policies have widened occupational choice for women and racial minorities. Continued occupational crowding, however, reveals the need for more rigorous enforcement of equal employment law. The notion of comparable worth (equal pay for different work) derives from the crowding hypothesis, but policies to achieve it are complicated and face stiff resistance. Some view economic growth as the most effective remedy, however this too has limits. Crowding is increasingly important as an impediment to equality and efficiency in a globalized economy.

SEE ALSO *Affirmative Action; Credentialism; Discrimination; Drake, St. Clair; Economics, Stratification; Hierarchy; Human Capital; Inequality, Gender; Inequality, Racial; Lewis, W. Arthur; Occupational Status; Segregation; Stratification; Unemployment; Unions; Work and Women*

BIBLIOGRAPHY

Bates, Timothy, and Daniel Fusfield. 2005. The Crowding Hypothesis. In *African Americans in the U. S. Economy*, eds. Cecilia A. Conrad, John Whitehead, Patrick Mason, and James Stewart, 101–109. Lanham, MD: Rowman and Littlefield.

Bergmann, Barbara R. 1971. The Effect on White Incomes of Discrimination in Employment. *Journal of Political Economy* 79 (2): 294–313.

Bergmann, Barbara R. 1974. Occupational Segregation, Wages and Profits When Employers Discriminate by Race or Sex. *Eastern Economic Journal* 1 (2): 103–110.

Blau, Francine D., Patricia Simpson, and Deborah Anderson. 1998. Continuing Progress? Trends in Occupational Segregation in the United States over the 1970s and 1980s. *Feminist Economics* 4 (3): 29–71.

Drake, St. Clair, and Horace R. Cayton. 1993. *Black Metropolis: A Study of Negro Life in a Northern City*. Rev. and enl. ed. Chicago: University of Chicago Press.

Edgeworth, Francis Y. 1922. Equal Pay to Men and Women for Equal Work. *Economic Journal* 32 (128): 431–457.

Lewis, W. Arthur. 1985. *Racial Conflict and Economic Development*. Cambridge, MA: Harvard University Press.

Mason, Patrick L. 1999. Male Interracial Wage Differentials: Competing Explanations. *Cambridge Journal of Economics* 23 (3): 261–299.

Karen J. Gibson

CROWLEY, ALEISTER

SEE *Magic*.

CRUSADES

SEE *Church, The*.

CUBAN MISSILE CRISIS

Perhaps no single event in the history of the cold war presented as great a challenge to world peace and the continued existence of humankind as the thirteen days of the Cuban Missile Crisis in October 1962. The outcome of the crisis has been linked to the development of a direct Teletype "hotline" between Moscow and Washington, D.C., the initial stages of superpower détente, and the ratification of a bilateral atmospheric testing ban on nuclear weapons.

LEADING UP TO OCTOBER 1962

Despite the failed U.S. effort to overthrow Cuban dictator Fidel Castro during the Bay of Pigs invasion in April 1961, President John F. Kennedy continued to make Castro's removal a primary goal. In November 1961, Kennedy initiated Operation Mongoose, a covert operations plan designed to incite dissident Cubans against Castro. Perhaps as a result, Castro, who enjoyed the Soviet Union's political and military backing, began receiving regular covert shipments of Soviet arms, ostensibly for defensive purposes only.

SOVIET NUCLEAR MISSILES IN CUBA

On October 14, 1962, a U2 spy plane, flying a routine Strategic Air Command mission over Cuba, snapped a series of photographs that became the first direct evidence of Soviet medium-range ballistic nuclear missiles in Cuba. These missiles clearly constituted an offensive weapons buildup on the island.

On the morning of October 16, National Security Adviser McGeorge Bundy presented a detailed analysis of the photographic evidence to Kennedy at an Oval Office briefing. Just before noon, Kennedy convened the first meeting of fourteen administration officials and advisers. The group became known as the Executive Committee of the National Security Council, or ExComm.

Time was of the essence. ExComm members received estimates that the Soviet missiles could be at full operation within fourteen days, with individual missiles readied within eighteen hours under a crash program. Most missiles were determined to be SS-4s, with a range of approximately 1,100 nautical miles (1,266 statute miles). This placed major American cities, including Dallas and Washington, D.C., within range of a strike. Later, photographic evidence concluded that several SS-5s, with a range of 2,200 nautical miles, were also included in the Soviet arms shipments.

For the next seven days, ExComm debated the merits of three general approaches to the developing crisis, all while keeping a tight public lid on the Cuban discovery. The first was a surgical airstrike targeting as many missile sites as possible. The second was an air strike followed by a U.S. military invasion of Cuba. The third was a blockade of Soviet ships thought to be carrying additional materials in support of the offensive weapons program.

In an attempt to allow diplomatic approaches an opportunity to work, Kennedy opted for the blockade, which was termed a quarantine so as to avoid warlike denotations.

THE QUARANTINE

On October 22, in anticipation of a Cuban and/or Soviet reaction to the quarantine, the joint chiefs of staff placed U.S. military forces worldwide on DEFCON 3 alert. At five that afternoon, Kennedy met with seventeen congressional leaders from both major parties to discuss the situation. The president received some support for the quarantine, but notable exceptions included Senators J. William Fulbright and Richard B. Russell, both of whom believed that the strategy would not compel the Soviets to abandon their missiles.

By six that evening, Secretary of State Dean Rusk met with the Soviet ambassador to the United States, Anatoly Dobrynin, and presented the ambassador with an advanced copy of Kennedy's address. At seven, Kennedy addressed the American public in a seventeen-minute speech. His major objective, in addition to calling public attention to the Soviet missiles in Cuba, was to outline the U.S. response—the quarantine of all offensive military equipment under shipment to Cuba.

Soviet premier Nikita Khrushchev's reply to Kennedy's speech arrived on the morning of October 23.

Premier Khrushchev's letter insisted that the Soviet missiles in Cuba were defensive in nature, and that the proposed U.S. response constituted a grave threat to world peace.

Kennedy was concerned that Berlin, which was divided into segments of East and West at the end of World War II, would become a focal point for Soviet retaliation. As such, he directed the Central Intelligence Agency (CIA) to develop plans for protecting Berlin in the event the Soviets mounted a quarantine around the city.

By the evening of October 23, Kennedy and ExComm had new worries much closer to home. Earlier in the day, the CIA began tracking several Soviet submarines unexpectedly moving toward Cuba. This made the Navy's job of conducting the quarantine more complicated, as it now had to track the changing position of the Soviet subs in order to ensure the safety of its own vessels.

The quarantine, which received the unanimous backing of the Organization of American States, went into effect at 10:00 a.m. on October 24.

Early morning intelligence on that day suggested that sixteen of the nineteen Soviet cargo ships identified as Cuban bound were reversing course. The remaining three, however, were nearing the quarantine line, including the *Gagarin* and *Komiles*. Naval intelligence reported that one of the Soviet subs had taken a position between the two ships. Kennedy, though wishing to avoid conflict with the sub, authorized the aircraft carrier USS *Essex* to take whatever defensive measures were necessary against the submarine. This was perhaps the most dangerous moment of the cold war, as both superpowers were armed and mere moments from turning the war hot. Just prior to any armed hostilities, however, both Soviet ships stopped dead in the water, and eventually reversed course.

Realizing that a diplomatic resolution to the crisis was imperative, Kennedy and senior ExComm advisers began to consider offering the Soviets a missile trade. Specifically, if Khrushchev pulled his missiles out of Cuba, the United States would dismantle and remove its Jupiter missiles in Turkey.

RAISING THE STAKES

October 25 found the U.S. ambassador to the United Nations, Adlai Stevenson, publicly confronting the Soviet ambassador, Valerian Zorin, in front of the United Nations Security Council. The Soviet Union had, until this date, denied that offensive Soviet missiles were in Cuba. At this point, Stevenson showed the council, and the world, several reconnaissance photographs of the Cuban missiles.

This triumph was short-lived. By five that evening, CIA director John McCone reported to ExComm that some of the Cuban missiles were now operational.

By the morning of October 26, Kennedy was convinced that only an invasion of Cuba could succeed in removing the missiles. ExComm initiated preliminary civil defense measures for the American Southeast, while the State Department began to devise plans for establishing a new civil government in the wake of Castro's deposing. By that afternoon, the U.S. military was poised to conduct a land invasion. Secretary of Defense Robert McNamara advised Kennedy to expect heavy American casualties in the campaign.

At six that evening, the State Department received a letter from Khruschev proposing that the U.S. declare it would not invade Cuba in exchange for the Soviets dismantling the missiles. Later that evening, Attorney General Robert F. Kennedy, the president's closest adviser and brother, held another in a series of private meetings with Dobrynin. It was at this meeting that Kennedy, with the president's approval, began to specifically discuss the option of a Turkey-for-Cuba missile trade.

Any positive momentum from this meeting stalled on the morning of October 27. A second letter from Khruschev arrived at the State Department around eleven. This letter replaced the noninvasion pledge with the requirement of a complete removal of U.S. missiles in Turkey. This raised the stakes for the Kennedy administration, as any public agreement on the Jupiter missiles would appear as a quid pro quo, with the U.S. forced to develop its security and foreign policies under severe threat.

The situation deteriorated even further when a U2, piloted by Major Rudolf Anderson, was shot down over Cuba around noon. Sensing that he was losing control of the crisis, Kennedy decided not to retaliate against the anti-aircraft site that fired on Anderson, much to the consternation of his military leaders.

At an ExComm meeting later that evening, the idea of responding only to the offer in Khrushchev's first letter—the noninvasion pledge—while ignoring the terms of the second letter, was debated. President Kennedy eventually came to adopt the proposal. Robert Kennedy was sent to discuss the terms with Dobrynin, which included an agreement not to publicly disclose the Turkey-for-Cuba missile trade, so as to avoid the appearance of a quid pro quo.

MAXIMUM DANGER AVERTED

President Kennedy, while hopeful that a deal would be reached, activated twenty-four Air Force units in preparation for a Cuban invasion to occur no later than October 29.

A CIA update in the early morning of October 28 claimed that all MRBM sites in Cuba were now operational. At nine that morning, Radio Moscow broadcast

Khrushchev's reply to the terms outlined to Dobrynin the night before. In it, Khruschev stated that all Soviet missiles in Cuba would be dismantled and crated. No public mention of the missile trade deal was made. The Cuban Missile Crisis was over, and a world war with nuclear weapons had most likely been averted.

Many historians generally view President Kennedy's performance in the crisis as exemplary, and worthy of emulation by all chief executives. However, some revisionary scholars have criticized Kennedy's interpretation of the threat posed by the Cuban missiles as an overreaction not warranted by a sober assessment of Soviet intentions and strategic goals.

UNDERSTANDING THE CRISIS

Of the many scholarly works devoted to understanding the dynamics of the missile crisis, and its effects on policymakers on both sides of the Atlantic, is Graham T. Allison and Philip Zelikow's *Essence of Decision* (1999). This volume has perhaps the greatest continuing impact for scholars and other interested persons alike. Allison analyzes the crisis through three distinct models. Model One assesses foreign policy from the rational actor approach, which considers each state as an individual or person, and attempts to understand actor behavior according to specified risks and payoffs. Model Two examines the crisis from the vantage point of the individual agencies involved, while Model Three attempts to capture the individual interests and proclivities of the major players involved.

Allison and Zelikow use the unique exigencies presented by the crisis to suggest that the models are incompatible in understanding the strategic calculus between states. Yet their description leaves the models open to the argument that they are not able to account for the novel and immediate adaptations that events, such as the Cuban Missile Crisis, require of government actors. At the same time, it is not clear that there is much true difference between the models, especially two and three, as all three are steeped in the rational choice tradition. Thus, while the examination does help to shed some light on the internal dynamics inherent in government decision-making processes, the uniqueness of the Cuban Missile Crisis and the relative inability of the three models to capture the dynamics at work in both Washington and Moscow serve as a reminder of how critical, and potentially catastrophic, a period the thirteen days in October 1962 truly were.

SEE ALSO *Castro, Fidel; Cold War; Communism; Democracy; Kennedy, John F.; Khrushchev, Nikita; Union of Soviet Socialist Republics*

BIBLIOGRAPHY

Allison, Graham, and Philip Zelikow. 1999. *Essence of Decision: Explaining the Cuban Missile Crisis.* 2nd ed. New York: Longman.

Brune, Lester H. 1985. *The Missile Crisis of October 1962: A Review of Issues and References.* Claremont, CA: Regina Books.

Hilsman, Roger. 1967. *To Move a Nation: The Politics of Foreign Policy in the Administration of John F. Kennedy.* Garden City, NY: Doubleday.

Medland, William J. 1990. The Cuban Missile Crisis: Evolving Historical Perspectives. *The History Teacher* 23: 433–447.

Rostow, Walt W. 1972. *The Diffusion of Power: An Essay in Recent History.* New York: Macmillan.

Sorensen, Theodore C. 1965. *Kennedy.* New York: Harper and Row.

Brian Robert Calfano

CUBAN REVOLUTION

The Cuban revolution headed by Fidel Castro (b. 1926) began on January 1, 1959, after Cuban military dictator Fulgencio Batista (1901–1973) fled the country. Since that time Cuba has been headed by a nationalist, revolutionary government. The prime mover of the revolutionary process has been Fidel Castro himself, although his brother Raúl Castro took over in August 2006 when the 80-year-old president underwent major abdominal surgery.

THE SEEDS OF REVOLUTION

To understand the Cuban revolutionary process, it is necessary to appreciate the philosophy of Cuban patriot and writer José Martí (1853–1895), whose radical anti-imperialist thought was adopted by the Castro government several decades after Martí's death. Martí was the leader of the movement for Cuban independence from Spain and was killed in battle in 1895. It is also crucially important to bear in mind the United States's role in Cuba. After Martí was killed fighting against Spanish forces, the war for Cuban independence dragged on for three more years. Under U.S. president William McKinley (1843–1901), and following the destruction of the USS *Maine* in Havana harbor, U.S. troops intervened, and three months later Spanish forces surrendered. This liberation war (1868–1878, and 1895–1898) is often referred to as the "Spanish American War," an act of historical oversight, since the name ignores the Cuban role in the struggle for independence and the death of over 200,000 Cubans.

From 1899 to 1902 the U.S. military ran the country, under the leadership of two American generals. U.S. investment grew quickly in agriculture, banking, mining, transportation, and utilities, and by 1911 U.S. investment had reached about $200 million. U.S. military intervention also occurred on several occasions, to shore up governments friendly to Washington. The end result was a profound frustration among many Cubans with U.S. domination of the political and economic systems. This combination of the radical thought of José Martí and a sense of frustrated nationhood brought about the overthrow of Cuban dictator Gerardo Machado (1871–1939) in 1933, and it would later result in the downfall of Batista in 1958.

Fidel Castro was already well known in Cuba before 1959. He had been a candidate for political office in 1952, though those elections never took place since Batista mounted a military coup. Afterwards the young Castro decided to use arms as a means of taking power and attacked the second largest military garrison in Santiago, Cuba, on July 26, 1953. Castro was arrested, but his prison sentence was commuted in an amnesty given by Batista, a costly mistake for the dictator. Castro laid out many of his basic tenets in his defense speech at trial (later published as *History Will Absolve Me*). After his trial Castro left for Mexico where he trained approximately eighty men (including Argentine physician and revolutionary leader Ernesto "Che" Guevara [1928–1967] and his brother Raúl Castro), and on December 2, 1956, they arrived in Cuba in a small yacht called the *Granma*. Castro and his followers took to the mountains where they fought a relentless guerrilla campaign until December 31, 1958, when Batista fled Cuba.

CASTRO SEIZES POWER

There has been much debate as to the nature of the political thought of Fidel Castro when he took over as leader of Cuba in 1959. For some he was a committed Marxist, determined to install a Communist dictatorship in Cuba. Others saw him as a nationalist radical, intent on bringing social justice to Cuba after another mammoth struggle in which an estimated 30,000 were killed—many as the result of acts of barbarism by Batista's forces.

There were several stages in the revolutionary process. The initial years witnessed a political radicalization, with massive social divisions appearing. The revolutionary government brought in sweeping legislation to protect the weakest sectors of society—reforms that were introduced at the expense of the middle class. Of the population of almost six million in 1958, approximately 10 percent formed a powerful middle class, who came second only to Venezuela in terms of per capita income and lifestyle.

Meanwhile, while Havana boasted that in 1954 it sold more Cadillacs per capita than any city in the world, rural Cuba suffered. Some 25 percent of the total labor force worked only 100 days annually (mainly in the sugar industry) and lacked many basic amenities. The urban-rural division was a major factor for many Cubans in supporting the revolution: rural illiteracy, for example, was four times that found in cities, while only 9 percent of rural homes—compared with 87 percent in the cities—had electricity.

The period from 1959 to 1961 was accompanied by social, economic, and political reforms—mainly realized at the expense of the wealthy middle-class sectors. The nationalization of many businesses, a sweeping land reform, an urban reform law, legislation protecting the rights of Afro-Cubans, closure of private schools, and criticism of the influential Catholic Church and opposition media, all resulted in a broad social polarization. Many U.S. businesses were expropriated, and Washington responded by breaking diplomatic relations with Cuba in January 1961.

THE GOLDEN YEARS

After this rupture the revolutionary process appeared in dire straits. Cuba's major export product, sugar, went to one major client—the United States. It appeared only a matter of time before the revolution crumbled. But the cold war with the Soviet Union and the United States was about to warm up considerably, with Moscow arranging to buy all of Cuba's sugar, and to provide arms, industrial training, technology, investment, and aid to Cuba. This arrangement of increasingly close Cuban-Soviet cooperation continued until the implosion of the Soviet Union in 1989–1990.

In many ways the cooperation with the Soviet Union and other socialist countries constituted the golden years for the Cuban revolution. Generous subsidies (approximately $4 billion per year) flowed in, Soviet technology was installed, and military protection was effectively guaranteed. This was seen as being particularly important after the U.S.-sponsored invasion of Cuba by Cuban exiles in April 1961 (known as the Bay of Pigs) and the October 1962 Cuban Missile Crisis, when Soviet nuclear weapons in Cuba were dismantled after enormous international tension brought the world to the brink of nuclear war.

At this time Cuba was largely isolated in international circles, being suspended from the Organization of American States, and ignored by most members of NATO. Gradually, however, Havana was able to make alliances with nations in the developing world, many of whom respected the cooperation that the Castro government provided. In 2006 Cuba reached the zenith of this international support, with its motion condemning the U.S. embargo of Cuba winning the support of 183 countries (with 4 voting against, and 1 abstention). Also in that year Cuba took over as the elected leader of the Non-Aligned Movement (representing countries with 60 percent of the world's population). Moreover, with the exceptions of Costa Rica and El Salvador, Cuba now has excellent diplomatic relations with all countries in Latin America and the Caribbean. Cuban medical assistance is particularly noteworthy, with 30,000 doctors working in 68 countries in 2006.

Until 1990 Cuba was dependent on the Soviet Union for its technology, market, supplies (particularly its oil supply of which 95 percent came from the Soviets), and industrial inputs. In terms of foreign policy, however, it mainly pursued an independent line. Its role in Angola starting in 1975 (when an initial 36,000 Cuban troops were sent to support the MPLA government, otherwise known as the Popular Movement for the Liberation of Angola) illustrates this well, and it is clear that Moscow was not pleased with Cuban military expeditions to Africa and Latin America.

There were several periods of crisis during this period. In 1980, for example, an estimated 125,000 Cubans left for the United States from the port of Mariel in a large flotilla of boats. In all about 10 percent of the Cuban population has left Cuba, and most have settled in southern Florida, where their presence has revitalized the city of Miami. There have been several periods when an attempt has been made to improve relations between Havana and Washington—most notably during the presidency of Jimmy Carter in the late 1970s—but these efforts have largely been fruitless. Intransigence has been the order of the day for almost five decades, with President George W. Bush being the tenth U.S. president in a row seeking "regime change" in Cuba.

CUBA TODAY

Following the demise of the Soviet Union, the Cuban revolution faced major challenges. Again Cuba had to find new markets for its goods, but also it now had to retool its industries, find suppliers for its factories, secure fuel—and it had to do so in a harsh international capitalist market. After some five extremely difficult years, the economy bottomed out, but it has grown annually since 1994. In no small measure this is due to a series of economic reforms, including the legalization of hard currency, the promotion of joint ventures with foreign capital, and the development of the tourism industry. An exchange program with Venezuela—which provides 90,000 barrels of oil per day in return for the medical services of 20,000 Cubans—has also proved beneficial.

The radical thought of José Martí in the late nineteenth century, the resentment of U.S. control, and the subsequent profoundly rooted nationalism, all came together to produce a leader who has held center stage in Cuban politics for five centuries. Despised by a vocal minority (most of whom have voted with their feet and

are living in exile), Fidel Castro has acted as a lightning rod for social change in Cuba, a process that has brought about a revolutionary socialist society and which to the present has survived against all odds.

SEE ALSO *Anticolonial Movements; Authoritarianism; Bush, George W.; Carter, Jimmy; Castro, Fidel; Cold War; Cuban Missile Crisis; Justice, Social; Nationalism and Nationality; Protest; Revolution; Socialism; Sugar Industry; Union of Soviet Socialist Republics; Urbanization*

BIBLIOGRAPHY

Azicri, Max. 2000. *Cuba Today and Tomorrow: Reinventing Socialism.* Gainesville: University Press of Florida.

Bardach, Ann Louise. 2002. *Cuba Confidential: Love and Vengeance in Miami and Havana.* New York: Random House.

Castro, Fidel. 1975. *History Will Absolve Me.* Havana: Editorial Ciencias Sociales.

Chomsky, Aviva, Barry Carr, and Pamela Maria Smorkaloff, eds. 2003. *The Cuba Reader: History, Culture, Politics.* Durham, NC: Duke University Press.

Domínguez, Jorge I. 1978. *Cuba: Order and Revolution.* Cambridge, MA: Belknap Press of Harvard University.

Erisman, H. Michael. 1985. *Cuba's International Relations: The Anatomy of a Nationalistic Foreign Policy.* Boulder, CO: Westview Press.

Pérez, Louis A. 2006. *Cuba: Between Reform and Revolution.* 3rd ed. New York: Oxford University Press.

John M. Kirk

CUE COMPETITION
SEE *Reinforcement Theories.*

CUES
SEE *Priming.*

CULTS

The term *cult* is derived from a Latin root meaning "to break ground," particularly in preparing (cultivating) a field for domesticated crops. The same root is seen in *culture*, in both a specialized scientific sense (a bacteria *culture*) and in a broader social sense (human *culture*). By extension, it was originally used in a religious sense, meaning behavior glorifying a deity or saint (the "cult" of Saint James). By the nineteenth century, the word came to be used pejoratively about those who were excessively devoted to popular authors (the "cult" of Wordsworth), worshiping them as modern "saints." Around 1900, this pejorative use influenced anthropologists to use *cult* to refer to ancient or allegedly primitive religious practices (as in "cult" objects or "cargo cults").

The popularity of this negative sense makes the term difficult to define objectively, since a "cult" in an outsider's eyes may well be a "new religion" to someone inside the group. Both the positive and negative uses of the term, however, agree that a cult is a small religious group that exists in tension with a predominant religion. In particular, such groups are highly cohesive in structure and are headed by a dominant leader who influences members' behavior in dramatic ways. They pursue a transcendent goal, claiming that the truths they preserve will transform all of society, and encourage direct religious experience through participation in rituals intended to foster ecstatic or supernatural phenomena. Often (though not always) they are apocalyptic in nature, holding that contemporary society is hopelessly corrupt and will soon be destroyed or transformed through the direct intervention of supernatural forces.

Cult behavior in the ordinary sense needs to be differentiated from the popular image of dangerous cults, drawn from the most extreme cases. In the popular imagination, cult leaders prey on impressionable youth and use mind control, brainwashing, hypnosis, and physical and sexual abuse to entrap and hold them against their will. "Cult" activity, in the most sensationalized images, includes ritualized sex abuse, self-mutilation, and, in some unconfirmed accounts, animal and human blood sacrifice. Often the agenda of such groups is thought to be to overturn organized religion or to promote the political agenda of evil others. Contributing to such pejorative images is the faux-etymology of *cult* as derived from *occult*, although this term, originally meaning "hidden" or "concealed," has a distinct history. Few of these claims have ever held up to skeptical inquiry; nevertheless, popular accounts frequently assume that sociopathic behavior is integral to these cults' activities.

Most cults in the historical record have been short-lived, but some persist to become the nuclei of important religious movements. Cults in both senses have been commonplace in European history from ancient times. Mystery cults, common in the Greek and Roman world, clearly were seen as charismatic movements that presented challenges to mainstream religions. Such groups, particularly the Bacchanalia, were frequently accused of being cults in the negative, sociopathic sense. Similarly, the persecution of the early Christian church by Roman authorities was based on persistent rumors that it was a dangerous cult that abducted and cannibalized babies.

During medieval times, Christianity itself fostered the growth of locally based movements devoted to the veneration of a local saint. Many of these developed into cultlike groups, and, while most were limited to a town or region in their influence, some, like the followers of Saint Francis of Assisi (c. 1181–1226), became important institutions (the Franciscan monks) in their own right. In early modern times, a number of breakaway factions of Protestant Christianity similarly began as small, strongly differentiated cults, and then grew into persistent religious movements. Some of these groups, like the Shakers, eventually declined, while others, like the Amish and Mormons (Church of Latter-day Saints) developed into stable institutions.

During the late twentieth century, rumors of cult activities in the United States especially developed around the development of new religious movements. Rumors that such cults engaged in blood sacrifices, orgiastic sex rituals, or child abuse became especially prevalent in the second half of the twentieth century. The Process, an allegedly "satanic" organization active in Great Britain and the United States during the 1960s, was repeatedly targeted as a "cult" in this negative sense, but a detailed sociological study of the group by William Bainbridge (1978) showed that the popular image was misleading.

Yet some cults did engage in violent and abusive acts, giving warrant to these fears. Two notorious examples were the People's Temple, founded by James Warren Jones (1931–1978) in Indianapolis during the 1950s, and the Heaven's Gate movement, begun by Marshall Herff Applewhite (1931–1997) in the Pacific Northwest during the 1970s. Both cults ended their existence in spectacular acts of group suicide, the first in 1978, the second in 1997. Both have been extensively studied, and while both groups came to the same tragic end, the factors leading up to their self-destruction varied considerably. Both can be seen as extreme examples of cult behavior caused by each group's isolation from outside culture and the growing mental instability of their leaders.

Both cults drew much of their ideology from the doomsday worldview prevalent among charismatic groups, which have become an important factor in both Catholic and Protestant Christianity. This ideology emphasizes controlling one's personal and social behavior strictly in preparation for an imminent, violent apocalyptic struggle against demonic forces. This mindset makes such groups potentially dangerous when contacted unwisely by outsiders. The notorious 1857 Mountain Meadows massacre, carried out in part by members of the early Mormon Church, and the bloody counterattacks taken by the Branch Davidian enclave (near Waco, Texas) against federal agents in 1993 illustrate two additional cases in which embattled cults turned to violent acts against outsiders.

Such extreme cases should not, however, distract scholars from studying objectively the many cults that continue to arise within mainstream religions and as alternatives to them. However, many more such groups remain diffuse enough that their members' involvement in these religious groups does not separate them from their everyday work and social worlds. Such cults have been and will continue to be positive factors in the development of new religions and the modification of mainstream sects in response to the cults' challenge. In addition to cults composed of charismatic Christians, many more such groups have become devoted to reviving neo-pagan rituals and investigating paranormal phenomena such as UFOs. According to the 2001 American Religious Identification Survey, the numbers of self-proclaimed Wiccans increased nearly seventeen-fold from 8000 to 138,000 during the previous ten years, with an additional 200,000 now belonging to a "pagan" or "new age" (Kosmin and Mayer 2001). Such new movements continue to provide individuals with creative means for pursuing religious experience.

SEE ALSO *Christianity; Conformity; Groupthink; Mysticism; Religion; Social Dominance Orientation; Suicide; Unidentified Flying Objects*

BIBLIOGRAPHY

Bainbridge, William Sims. 1978. *Satan's Power: A Deviant Psychotherapy Cult.* Berkeley: University of California Press.

Brown, Peter. 1981. *The Cult of the Saints: Its Rise and Function in Latin Christianity.* Chicago: University of Chicago Press.

Burkert, Walter. 1987. *Ancient Mystery Cults.* Cambridge, MA: Harvard University Press.

Denzler, Brenda. 2001. *The Lure of the Edge: Scientific Passions, Religious Beliefs, and the Pursuit of UFOs.* Berkeley: University of California Press.

Ellis, Bill. 2000. *Raising the Devil: Satanism, New Religions, and the Media.* Lexington: University of Kentucky Press.

Galanter, Marc. 1999. *Cults: Faith, Healing, and Coercion.* 2nd ed. New York: Oxford University Press.

Kosmin, Barry A., and Egon Mayer. 2001. American Religious Identification Survey. The Graduate Center, CUNY. http://www.gc.cuny.edu/faculty/research_briefs/aris/aris_index.htm.

Quarantelli, E. L., and Dennis Wenger. 1973. A Voice from the Thirteenth Century: The Characteristics and Conditions for the Emergence of a Ouija Board Cult. *Urban Life and Culture* 1: 379–400.

Wojcik, Daniel. 1997. *The End of the World as We Know It: Faith, Fatalism, and Apocalypse in America.* New York: New York University Press.

Bill Ellis

CULTURAL CAPITAL

The concept of "cultural capital" posits that the way of life of a community constitutes a dynamic structure, including a number of services, that enhances the livelihood of the people. It also forms the basis of power relations and class. The origins of the concept stem mainly from the work of the French sociologist Pierre Bourdieu (1930–2002), who argued that it represents one of the many forms of capital that people can draw on to enhance their lives. The other forms include social capital, human capital, durable fixed capital, ecological capital, and even bodily capital. The notion of cultural capital is part of the "multiple capital paradigm" (O'Hara 2001), and one must link various capitals to comprehend macro-sociological processes such as inequality, stratification, and conflict.

DIMENSIONS OF CULTURAL CAPITAL

There are three main types of cultural capital: cultural artifacts, institutions, and embodied capital. Cultural artifacts include reproductions of the cultural creations of society. These may be materials in museums, art galleries, and libraries; modes of dress; symbolic commodities; or modes of architecture. These artifacts can be seen as a form of embodied cultural labor, provided they truly form part of the historical or contemporaneous life process of the community. These artifacts may be critical in the study of previous cultures, particularly if there is little or no written record of cultural habits and practices. For contemporary market capitalist economies, artifacts sold for money provide a source of knowledge about the relationship between cultural and economic capitals.

Institutions provide insights into the way of life of the community. For instance, the institutions of nationalism provide insights into the way in which people bond together as a nation-state, while the institutions of education help comprehend the reproduction of knowledge and class in society. The family, as an institution, enables insights into critical forms of gender relations, kinship linkages, and networks of privilege and association. Market institutions, meanwhile, enable one to recognize how symbols, status, and financial advantage are interrelated and reproduced through historical time.

The third form of cultural capital, embodied capital, is a personal form of intergenerational transfer of networks and relations. Families, for instance, provide a series of lifestyle habits and relationships through networks, which become a sort of "advance" to the next generation of children. There is a tendency for these family linkages to shape people's behavior and values from generation to generation. This relates to practices such as manners, connections, qualifications and habits of life and livelihood.

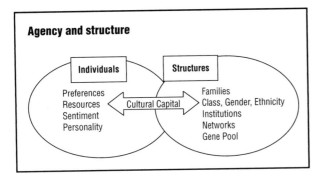

Figure 1

Such linkages are critical to the generation of class differences between people.

AGENCY AND STRUCTURE

Bourdieu's analysis of cultural capital has been quite successful in linking agency and structure in the determination of class, habit, and space. Class relationships are reproduced in a subtle manner through association, upbringing, emotional ties, education, and access to material resources. Individuals are as important as institutions in the generation of privilege and power.

Individuals and structures are linked through cultural capital, as shown in Figure 1. Individuals and structures interact through time in the determination of socioeconomic processes. Individuals have certain preferences, resources, sentiments, and personalities that impact on their quality of life and contribution to society. Structures—in the form of families, classes, gender, ethnicity, institutions, networks, and the gene pool—also impact on individuals. Agency and structure are linked through cultural capital, particularly through the activation of habits in particular cultural spaces.

Bourdieu's notion of "habitus" refers to the acquired habits of dress, manners, modes of perception, ways of speaking, personal hygiene, and other traits of everyday life. Many of these habits have commonalities among certain groups, classes, and nations, and they help to bind people together in networks and institutions.

The notion of "cultural space" or "field" is also important here, for people's everyday behavior is acted out in various relatively autonomous arenas. There are a multiplicity of such spaces, which are interrelated yet become activated through their own logic of operation and motion (see Emirbayer et al. 2005). These include the fields of legal space, economic space, social space, bureaucratic space, familial space, and so on. These can be delimited further—social space, for example, includes further microcosms of fashion, media, literature, art, and academia. The habits of individuals acted out in various cultural spaces demonstrate how people interact as social individuals, thus linking agency and structure.

Evidence shows that, in many contemporary societies, there are distinct differences in the way parents bring up their children, inculcating them with certain habits in familial space. Middle-class parents tend to inculcate a degree of debate and exploration in their children. They also tend to stimulate fairly wide social networks and nurture a degree of independence of thought. Working-class parents, on the other hand, tend to be more specific in their directions and discussions; have stronger family, rather than social, networks; and have children who are more dependent upon them emotionally and physically (see Egerton 1997). These variable forms of cultural capital are critical to the reproduction of privilege, advantage, and power.

POWER, CULTURE, AND POLICY

Cultural capital also illuminates the role of power in society. Power is not simply a product of economic and political relationships. It also emanates more broadly from cultural associations. Power resides in the ability of people to form and maintain dynamic social networks, with reciprocity and friendships being an important part of the process. Power is enhanced by cultural capital through the building and maintaining of relationships and habits of advantage. These advantages take many forms, including material and monetary wealth, political influence, friendships and relationships, health, and safety within the society.

Those individuals and groups seeking power and authority thus either need to be ideally suited (or adapted to) the dominant modes of interplay of habitus and space, or they must try and condition people's habitus through these cultural spaces. They can try and change the very rules through which people act out their social life, but it must be done subtly and with a thorough knowledge of the cultural way of life of the community. Similarly, policymakers must put their measures into practice within the framework of this nexus of individual-social habits and cultural space. Social capital is important in the provision of trust and sociality required to divert resources and assets in the prescribed direction.

Cultural capital is thus part of the multiple capital paradigm, which by linking agency and structure interprets relations of class, power, ethnicity, and social position. Some questions remain in areas such as class, gender, and ethnicity, with a need for more complexity and historical specificity, and for more empirical and theoretical development. Overall, though, cultural capital is a powerful mode of interpretation of structures of diversity, cooperation, and power in the contemporary world.

SEE ALSO *Capital; Human Capital; Physical Capital; Skill; Social Capital; Soft Skills*

BIBLIOGRAPHY

Bourdieu, Pierre. 1993. *The Field of Cultural Production.* New York: Columbia University Press.

Bourdieu, Pierre. 1997. The Forms of Capital. In *Education: Culture, Economy, and Society,* eds. A.H. Halsey et al. Oxford: Oxford University Press.

Egerton, Muriel. 1997. Occupational Inheritance: The Role of Cultural Capital and Gender. *Employment and Society* 11 (2): 263–282.

Emirbayer, Mustafa, and Eva M. Williams. 2005. Bourdieu and Social Work. *Social Service Review* 79 (4): 689–724.

Gunn, Simon. 2005. Translating Bourdieu: Cultural Capital and the English Middle Class in Historical Perspective. *British Journal of Sociology* 56 (1): 49–64.

Lee, Jung-Sook, and Natasha K. Bowen. 2006. Parent Involvement, Cultural Capital, and the Achievement Gap Among Elementary School Children. *American Educational Research Journal* 43 (2): 193–218.

O'Hara, Phillip Anthony. 2001. Wealth Distribution and Global Inequality in the Multiple Capital Paradigm. *International Journal of Human Development* 1 (2): 121–140.

Phillip Anthony O'Hara

CULTURAL DETERMINISM

SEE *Culture; Determinism.*

CULTURAL EQUIVALENCE MODEL

SEE *Parent-Child Relationships.*

CULTURAL GROUP SELECTION

The concept of group selection is controversial in both the natural and social sciences. In contrast to the standard social science assumption of methodological individualism and the biological assumption of the gene as the relevant unit of selection, group selection posits that distinct evolutionary and selection pressures may operate at the level of the group rather than the individual level. As a result, group selection argues that it may be possible for social rules and biological traits to evolve and persist that cause individuals to act *altruistically,* that is, in ways that are good for others or the group as a whole, but detrimental to particular individuals within the group. In group selection models, the relevant level of selection for some questions is thus at the level of the group (family, firm, cultural group, nation) rather than among the constituent individuals that compose those groups.

The concept of group selection gained some intellectual currency in the 1960s and its leading modern advocate in the social sciences was F. A. Hayek. These early naïve group selection models were swept aside by the rise of "selfish gene" theory as the dominant paradigm in evolutionary biology. Selfish gene theory argues that altruism is not an evolutionary stable strategy as an *a priori* matter because selfish individuals will have the incentive and opportunity to free ride by accepting the benefits of others' altruism without bearing the costs. Those with selfish genes will prey on the altruists in the population, thereby rendering the altruistic tendencies unfit for survival and replication. Critics of cultural group selection have similarly argued that those models are similarly suspect because cultural rules and practices are similarly subject to erosion by free riding by selfish individuals who comparatively benefit from refusing to abide by socially beneficial rules (such as prohibitions on fraud or theft) followed by others. Both critiques thus conclude that group selection models lack appropriate microfoundations that ground group level selection in the incentives and interest of the individuals that compose the group and thus should be selected against in the population.

Subsequent analysis, however, has concluded that the plausibility of group selection models is an empirical question, not a priori question. Group selection rests on a tension between two competing forces that push in opposite directions—intragroup selection, that is, competition among different individuals within a given group, versus intergroup selection, or competition between different groups. Intragroup selection promotes individual selfishness and free riding in seeking to appropriate a disproportionate share of the social surplus. Intergroup selection, by contrast, promotes altruism within a given group because it benefits the group as a whole in competition with other groups (and thereby indirectly benefits each member of the group), even though altruistic individuals contribute more to the group than they personally receive in exchange.

In reconciling these competing pressures, the plausibility of a group selection model thus rests on three basic operative conditions. First, the genetic trait or cultural rule must promise sufficient benefits to the group that the members of the group will benefit from adopting it when compared with groups that do not adopt the rule or practice, that is, a social surplus is generated. These rules may be invented consciously or may simply arise by accident.

Second, there must be some mechanism for between-group competition to occur, that is, for groups with superior traits or practices to displace others. This competition and displacement may occur through warfare and conquest by the more successful group, migration from the less-successful group to the more successful, or imitation of the more successful by the less successful.

Third, the group must be able to restrain free riders that will dissipate the social surplus generated by the beneficial trait or rule. It is not necessary to completely eradicate free riding (which will be virtually impossible given the individual incentives to free ride), but simply to reduce it to the point where the overall benefits to the group are sufficiently large such that the benefits of retaining the trait or practice are large enough to offset the costs imposed by free riders. Social norms against antisocial behavior, legal and political institutions such as police forces that prevent theft, and constitutional institutions that encourage positive-sum wealth creation activities rather than zero-sum redistributive activities (or negative-sum rent-seeking activities), can all be viewed as mechanisms to limit the ability of free riders to dissipate the social surplus.

SEE ALSO *Altruism; Collective Action; Cooperation; Determinism, Biological; Determinism, Genetic; Hayek, Friedrich August von; Microfoundations; Natural Selection; Norms; Sociobiology*

BIBLIOGRAPHY

Dawkins, Richard. 1989. *The Selfish Gene*. New York: Oxford University Press.

Hayek, F. A. 1973. *Rules and Order*. Vol. 1 of *Law, Legislation, and Liberty*. Chicago: University of Chicago Press.

Hayek, F. A. 1984. The Origins and Effects of Our Morals: A Problem for Science. In *The Essence of Hayek*, eds. Chiaki Nishiyama and Kurt R. Leube, 318–330. Stanford, CA: Hoover Institution Press.

Hayek, F. A. 1988. The Fatal Conceit: The Errors of Socialism. In *The Collected Works of F. A. Hayek*, ed. W. W. Bartley III. Chicago: University of Chicago Press.

Koppl, Roger, ed. 2005. *Evolutionary Psychology and Economic Theory. Advances in Austrian Economics*, Vol. 7. Oxford: Elsevier JAI Press.

Sober, Elliott, and David Sloan Wilson. 1988. *Unto Others: The Evolution and Psychology of Unselfish Behavior*. Cambridge, MA: Harvard University Press.

Vanberg, V. 1986. Spontaneous Market Order and Social Rules: A Critique of F. A. Hayek's Theory of Cultural Evolution. *Economics and Philosophy* 2: 75–100.

Wilson, David Sloan. 2003. *Darwin's Cathedral: Evolution, Religion, and the Nature of Society*. Chicago: University of Chicago Press.

Zywicki, Todd J. 2000. Was Hayek Right about Group Selection after All? Review Essay of *Unto Others: The Evolution and Psychology of Unselfish Behavior*, by Elliot Sober and David Sloan Wilson. *Review of Austrian Economics* 13: 81–95.

Zywicki, Todd J. 2005. Reconciling Group Selection and Methodological Individualism. *Advances in Austrian Economics* 7: 267–278.

Todd J. Zywicki

CULTURAL LANDSCAPE

Landscape is a word introduced into the English language during the late sixteenth century as a technical term used by painters. The word derived from the Dutch *landschap* and was known in English for some time as *landskip*. This painterly source of the landscape notion is significant. Landscape was recognized as such because it reminded the viewer of a painted landscape—a piece of inland scenery (Thomas 1984, p. 265; Groth and Wilson 2003, pp. 2–3).

Landscape became a prominent, if contested, concept in mid-twentieth-century geography through the work of Carl Sauer (1889–1975)(see Livingstone 1992). His ideas about landscape were influenced by the debates between the German geographer Friedrich Ratzel (1844–1904) and the French sociologist Émile Durkheim (1858–1917), debates that focused on the *society-milieu* relationship (Buttimer 1971). Sauer argued that culture shaped the natural landscape to produce a "cultural landscape" (Sauer 1963, p. 343). He sought to avoid the environmental determinism of Ratzel, but acknowledged that it was not possible to devise an objective procedure for the study and comparison of landscape: a subjective, aesthetic, or meaningful element always remained (see Cosgrove 1984; Cosgrove and Daniels 1988).

Independent of this tradition of thought, the cultural and literary critic Raymond Williams (1921–1988) argued in *The Country and the City* (1973) that it is "outsiders"—estate owners, improvers, industrialists, artists—who have recourse to the notion of landscape, not those who live and work "in" the landscape. His influential work introduced the key element of politics and power to the way landscapes—cultural landscapes—are understood (see Bender 1993). Williams's sharp distinction between "insider" and "outsider," though, is difficult to sustain in any particular context and suggests that only some people make use of this concept.

Recent research and writing in anthropology, history, and related disciplines argue that peoples around the world shape and view their surroundings in ways not dissimilar to that captured by the Western concept of landscape and that the distinction between a "natural" and "cultural" landscape is fraught with problems (see Ingold 2000). Consider the case of the Amazonian rainforest. It is often viewed as a pristine "natural" environment in which separate "cultures" live and draw upon its resources. However, historical ecology has shown that the current form of this environment is the outcome of extensive human manipulation over substantial time periods—creating grasslands, forests, and savannas (see Balée 1998). In a comparable manner the forest-savanna transition zone of Guinea in West Africa has been viewed by environmental policymakers for many decades as a relic of a once-extensive natural forest now destroyed by local farming and fire-setting. By contrast, anthropological research demonstrates that the landscape had been "misread": local peoples explicitly create "forest islands" in which to live, and these are viewed as an index of prosperity and are aesthetically valued (Fairhead and Leach 1996). The historian William Cronon (1983, 1991) has documented analogous transformations in colonial New England and with respect to the rise of Chicago and the West: landscapes—whether prairie or forest—were reformed to enable the production and expansion of property ownership and commodity capitalism. In short, all landscapes are inherently "natural" and "cultural" (see Schama 1995). Landscapes are thus a *process* where people seek to realize, in diverse ways, the possibilities of their culture by simultaneously creating themselves and their environments or natures (see Hirsch 1995, 2004).

SEE ALSO *Culture; Human Ecology; Phenomenology*

BIBLIOGRAPHY

Balée, William. 1998. Historical Ecology: Premises and Postulates. In *Advances in Historical Ecology*, ed. William Balée, 13–29. New York: Columbia University Press.

Bender, Barbara, ed. 1993. *Landscape: Politics and Perspectives.* Oxford: Berg.

Buttimer, Anne. 1971. *Society and Milieu in the French Geographic Tradition.* Chicago: Association of American Geographers.

Cosgrove, Denis. 1984. *Social Formation and Symbolic Landscape.* London: Croom Helm.

Cosgrove, Denis, and Stephen Daniels, eds. 1988. *The Iconography of Landscape: Essays on the Symbolic Representation, Design, and Use of Past Environments.* Cambridge, U.K.: Cambridge University Press.

Cronon, William. 1983. *Changes in the Land: Indians, Colonists, and the Ecology of New England.* New York: Hill and Wang.

Cronon, William. 1991. *Nature's Metropolis: Chicago and the Great West.* New York: Norton.

Fairhead, James, and Melissa Leach 1996. *Misreading the African Landscape: Society and Ecology in a Forest-Savanna Mosaic.* Cambridge, MA: Cambridge University Press.

Groth, Paul, and Chris Wilson. 2003. The Polyphony of Cultural Landscape Study: An Introduction. In *Everyday America: Cultural Landscape Studies after J. B. Jackson*, eds. Paul Groth and Chris Wilson, 1–22. Berkeley: University of California Press.

Hirsch, Eric. 1995. Introduction: Landscape—Between Place and Space. In *The Anthropology of Landscape: Perspectives on Place and Space*, eds. Eric Hirsch and Michael O'Hanlon, 1–30. Oxford: Clarendon.

Hirsch, Eric. 2004. Environment and Economy: Mutual Connections and Diverse Perspectives. *Anthropological Theory* 4: 435–453.

Ingold, Tim. 2000. *The Perception of the Environment: Essays on Livelihood, Dwelling, and Skill.* London: Routledge.

Livingstone, David. 1992. *The Geographical Tradition: Episodes in the History of a Contested Enterprise.* Oxford: Blackwell.

Sauer, Carl. 1963. *Land and Life: A Selection from the Writings of Carl Ortwin Sauer*, ed. John Leighly. Berkeley: University of California Press.

Schama, Simon. 1995. *Landscape and Memory.* London: HarperCollins.

Thomas, Keith. 1984. *Man and the Natural World: Changing Attitudes in England, 1500–1800.* Harmondsworth, U.K.: Penguin.

Williams, Raymond. 1973. *The Country and the City.* London: Chatto & Windus.

Eric Hirsch

CULTURAL RELATIVISM

More than a century of ethnographic research profoundly supports the theory of *cultural relativity*, the theory that culture shapes beliefs, provides concepts, organizes value systems, and informs and orients human behavior. Anthropologists find it obvious that human behavior is culturally informed and culturally specific, and best approached as a series of "practices" with specific cultural orientations and entailments. Anthropologists are comfortable with cultural relativity as a matter of fact. While other disciplines have struggled to accommodate the realities of cultural relativity, in recent decades anthropologists have debated the social organization of cultural differences in complex societies under modern conditions. Cultural relativism, the paradoxical extension of the facts of cultural difference into an epistemology and moral philosophy doubtful of all absolutes, troubles other kinds of social scientists far more than it does anthropologists, who are, by and large, still confident of their capacity to critically understand matters of fact and questions of value under conditions of cultural variety and complexity. While other disciplines debate the perils of relativism, anthropologists debate the fate of cultural differences in a globalizing world.

Anthropologists are comfortable with facts of cultural difference because such differences are the very stuff of their research. Ongoing successes in the description and analysis of cultural differences are degrees of proof, after all, against strong forms of cultural relativism. Insofar as ethnographers—researchers into particular cultures—can successfully understand and explain unanticipated cultural differences, then regardless of the extremity of differences, cultures are not truly incommunicably and ungraspably variant. To this degree they are not "incommensurable," to use a term from Romanticist philology made popular (by Thomas Kuhn) in twentieth century philosophy of science. However, in other social science disciplines, facts of cultural difference have often seemed to threaten the quality of data rather than integrating it. In some disciplines, acknowledging fundamental cultural differences has seemed tantamount to succumbing to a knowledge-defeating relativism. In psychology and in linguistics, cultural relativism is rendered into an extreme, fascinating, but partly dubious theory of perception; for economics, political science, and sociology it is a challenge to the generalizability of research findings; for philosophy it is a contemptible threat to the certainty and even adequacy of any and all concepts and conclusions. Ironically, thus, cultural relativism means different things in different contexts. What it means and the depth of its threat to knowledge varies significantly according to the premises, needs, and purposes of the various disciplines. The public, like academic disciplines, can also take different stances toward different cultural relativisms; the same person can be a fascinated cosmopolitan when trying new clothing or food, an appalled observer watching a news broadcast, an angry voter, and a generous neighbor. Cultural relativities and cultural relativism can be unevenly acknowledged within a single discipline or person.

Debates about cultural relativism and cultural relativity predate the beginnings of the modern social sciences, and play an important role in their foundation. At one key juncture in the history of ideas, the philosopher Immanuel Kant was challenged by his one-time student, Johannes Gottfried Herder, over the origin and nature of concepts. Herder inspired research in the disciplines of geography, ethnology, and above all philology—the study of the history of words—when he doubted his teacher's theory of pure reason. In a dispute that was simultaneously theological, political, and scientific, Herder argued that human beings observably relied upon signs to gain their concepts, and that their ideas neither came from nor moved toward any ethereal realm but began with words handed down within human communities. Human communities each thereby had their own kinds of knowledge, understanding, and meaning, not passively imbibed but actively fashioned and changed, with each person and each society its own blooming, self-fashioned work of art. Kant's vision was of humanity gaining enlightenment slowly, reaching closer to a single, ultimate, God-given potential, and progressing most when political control was wisest and most absolute. In Herder's view, humans had to rely on signs that were "arbitrary," and highly variant from place to place and time to time, as part of God's divine plan: The unending need to critically assess and change their signs and concepts gave humanity creativity and free will.

As philological research led to nineteenth-century efforts to found a science of language in general, one of the pioneers of this transition, F. Max Müller, coined one of the most extreme expressions of a language-sign-based cultural relativity: "No reason without thought; no thought without language." By this formulation, reason and truth would be entirely dependent on language. Müller debated with Charles Darwin over the origins of language and thought; Müller thought he had found a perfect synthesis of Kant, Herder, and all religion in a theory that posited humanity's active corruption of originally perfect God-given signs and symbols. Darwin argued for a material origin in natural history for thoughts, concepts, and language, and was joined by William Dwight Whitney, another of the founders of linguistics, who reconfigured Herder's conception of the arbitrary nature of signs into a theory of the material, natural origins of words and concepts. Whitney led linguistics to seek an evolutionary theory of language without recourse to divine reason or invention.

By the twentieth century, especially in U.S. anthropology under the leadership of Franz Boas and his students, the debates moved from language to culture, and scholars resorted to theological arguments much more rarely. Perhaps the most famous explorer of linguistic relativity and its significance was anthropological linguist Benjamin Lee Whorf. Whorf proposed that Hopi habitual thought and behavior was organized by ontological premises also present in Hopi language grammar; he claimed especially that the Hopi thought about time differently than Europeans, and organized their way of life, including ritual, politics, and economics, around premises about repetition and duration that were readily understandable from study of their language grammar.

Whorf's arguments have been misunderstood, largely because psychologists had great need for a different argument, suitable for laboratory testing. What became known in psychology as the *Whorf hypothesis* or the *Sapir-Whorf hypothesis* (Edward Sapir being another leading Boasian linguist) was the idea that language shaped human perception of things. This argument could have and probably should have been attributed to Müller, who made it, rather than to Whorf, who did not. (Whorf argued that Hopi perceived space the same way Europeans did, the focusing system of their eyes generating the same figure-ground gestalt perception of something foregrounded in a larger visual field.) Regardless of the misnomer, much laboratory and field research attempted to operationalize this hypothesis into tests of the relationship of language categories and grammatical structures to perceptions. The results, ironically, were very close to what Whorf would have expected. Human perception is not infinitely plastic, not capable of being rendered wholly unseeing or unhearing of things without name or existence within the logic of language. However, systems of discrimination of types of things are highly sensitive to paradigms, norms, distinctions, and examples provided by language and culture. Training can overcome the difficulties a person has making fine distinctions between sounds or colors to which he or she has never before attended, up to limits provided by the actual range and acuity of sensory systems. But it is not easy to reorient extremely complex and highly developed systems for the perception of very specific things in the world.

Psychologists have been most interested, for obvious reasons, in the significance of variations in language and culture for apparatuses of cognitive function, and in particular the relations of systems of perception and cognition. They find increasingly precise and complex means to identify what is variant and invariant in the structure and organization of human perception and cognition. The situation is different for other social sciences (and for some branches of psychology as well, including social psychology and abnormal psychology, and the emerging field of biosociality). When research focuses not on processes happening within mind and body, but rather on larger social fields of interaction between people, then the issues connected to cultural relativity challenge scholarship differently.

The Boasians also opened up the questions in this area. Ruth Benedict, a student of Franz Boas, wrote extensively in the 1930s and 1940s about social and political implications of cultural relativity. Some credit her with coining the concept. In *Patterns of Culture* (1934) and *The Chrysanthemum and the Sword* (1946) she wrote directly to the U.S. reading public, on a mission to demonstrate the reality and significance of cultural differences. On a "shrinking planet," she argued, with societies increasingly interconnected and interdependent, the hard work of mutual understanding was increasingly vital to achieving peace, health, and prosperity. Americans still strongly tended to imagine that their most cherished values came straight from God, and while few social scientists took that route many still hoped to directly observe behaviors generated by an unmediated human nature, and were disappointed to discover that culture mediated even passions and pleasures, and expectations of risk and reward. At the end of World War II, Benedict was greatly concerned about an American society that mistook for human nature the fundamental tenets of its own political culture, such as the individual's right to the pursuit of happiness, which Americans gave a near sacred status. Benedict argued for culture-consciousness in mature political debate. She exemplified the fact that consciousness of cultural relativity need not lead to relativism in morality and politics. She allied herself with skepticism, not relativism, in philosophy, and had no trouble aligning her science with specific politics, as in her anti-Nazi, pro–civil rights treatise against prejudice in the assessment of race differences, *Race: Science, and Politics* (1940), which disputed allegations of difference in racial capacities, and traced the connection of such allegations to other forms of prejudice.

In the division of labor in the social sciences, anthropologists continue as students of cultural difference and skeptics of claims about human universals, while other disciplines accommodate facts of cultural difference while pursuing more general truths. The tensions here are productive. Anthropologists have also, for decades now, studied the creative conflicts that result when people, societies, and cultures productively and destructively interact. While some political commentators at the end of the twentieth century were convinced that globalization and democratization had brought on "the end of history," few anthropologists agreed. Reflections on the extremities of twentieth-century political violence make moral relativism unsustainable—not only for what it would allow, but also for what it would license us to forget or ignore. But in between moral relativism and universalistic insistence on one best final outcome for all political, social, and cultural questions there are, still, the positions pioneered by the Boasians—scientific skepticism with recognition of cultural relativity, and perhaps room even for a version of the philosophical plenitism pioneered by Herder. If scientists are, by method, skeptical of final claims, it does not make them relativist. The science of culture, even in the most cosmopolitan zones and most self-conscious reflections on selves and others, still produces a plenitude of evaluations—the point is not that "anything goes," but that many things continue and new things come along, and that all things might be improvable with reflective recognition of cultural specificities and differences.

Culture is the condition of possibility of meaning, and in both small scale and large, it thrives and grows with human success in making the world meaningful. It is an irreducible part of the environment, a built environment, an environment that makes human intelligence useable and increasingly useful. Some seek to move beyond cultural relativity, and try to think beyond culture, and seek truths independent of culture or constant across all cultures. Ironically, recurrent and persistent renewal of this quest is a hallmark of the culture of the European enlightenment, especially in the dreams of freedom and independence that it shares with its own countercurrent,

Romanticism. Neither this Enlightenment tradition, nor many other value systems, are likely to submerge easily into a homogenous and unitary global culture, no matter how much our global civil society intertwines.

SEE ALSO *Anthropology; Benedict, Ruth; Boas, Franz; Cultural Studies; Darwin, Charles; Enlightenment; Linguistic Turn; Mead, Margaret; Morality; Paradigm; Prejudice; Racism; Relativism; Science*

BIBLIOGRAPHY

Asad, Talal. 1986. The Concept of Cultural Translation in British Social Anthropology. In *Writing Culture: The Poetics and Politics of Ethnography*, eds. James Clifford and George E. Marcus, 141–164. Berkeley: University of California Press.

Benedict, Ruth. 1934. *Patterns of Culture*. New York: New American Library.

Benedict, Ruth. 1940. *Race: Science and Politics*. New York: Modern Age Books.

Benedict, Ruth. 1946. *The Chrysanthemum and the Sword: Patterns of Japanese Culture*. Boston: Houghton Mifflin Company.

Boon, James A. 1999. *Verging on Extra-Vagance: Anthropology, History, Religion, Literature, Arts, ... Showbiz*. Princeton, NJ: Princeton University Press, 1999.

Evans-Pritchard, E. E. 1937. *Witchcraft, Oracles, and Magic among the Azande*. Oxford: Clarendon Press.

Fukuyama, Francis. 1992. *The End of History and the Last Man*. New York: Free Press.

Geertz, Clifford. 1984. Anti Anti-Relativism. *American Anthropologist*, n.s., 86 (2): 263–278.

Gellner, Ernest. 1970. Concepts and Society. In *Rationality*, ed. Bryan R. Wilson, 18–49. Oxford: Basil Blackwell.

Kuhn, Thomas S. 1970. *The Structure of Scientific Revolutions*. 2nd rev. ed. Chicago: University of Chicago Press.

Latour, Bruno. 1988. Irreductions. In his *The Pasteurization of France*, trans. Alan Sheridan and John Law, 151–236. Cambridge, MA: Harvard University Press.

Latour, Bruno. 1999. *Pandora's Hope: Essays on the Reality of Science Studies*. Cambridge, MA: Harvard University Press.

Lucy, John A. 1992. *Language Diversity and Thought: A Reformulation of the Linguistic Relativity Hypothesis*. Cambridge, U.K.: Cambridge University Press.

Postel, Danny. 2006. "The 'End of History' Revisited: Francis Fukuyama and His Critics." OpenDemocracy Website. http://www.opendemocracy.net/democracy-fukuyama/intro_3493.jsp.

Whorf, Benjamin Lee. 1956. *Language, Thought, and Reality*. Cambridge, MA: MIT Press.

John Kelly

CULTURAL RESOURCE MANAGEMENT

Mostly used in North America, the term *cultural resources* refers to important sites, objects, and places that have some form of legal protection. The term has its origins in the late 1960s as part of an effort to gain the same level of legal protection for places of cultural and historic importance as had been achieved by endangered natural resources. The term *cultural resource management* (CRM) can be defined as the practice of managing cultural resources in response to some legal or policy mandate. The terms *heritage resources* and *heritage management* are common synonyms for cultural resources and CRM, respectively.

Cultural resources include a vast range of properties whose importance derives from their aesthetic, historic, religious, or scientific value. A cultural resource may be a traditional plant-gathering area or an example of high Victorian architecture. The term covers places and objects both glorious and modest: archaeological sites from the most ancient of prehistoric sites of all eras to the remains of 1930s labor camps; buildings ranging from St. Paul's Cathedral in London to a vernacular cabin; structures, including canals and bridges; and places that are important to living cultures, from historic battlefields to sites of religious or traditional significance to indigenous groups.

Despite their diversity of forms, all cultural resources have two characteristics in common: they are regarded as important by a segment of contemporary society (be it a group of neighbors, an Aboriginal clan, or professional archaeologists); and they are considered worthy of some form of protection because of this value.

The goal of CRM is to manage important cultural properties for the public benefit. This is achieved by the application of law and public policy. Since every nation has its own unique and important history and cultures, most have developed their own statutes on national, regional, and even local levels that govern how cultural resources should be treated. In the United States, for example, the National Environmental Policy Act (NEPA), the National Historic Preservation Act, and dozens of state laws, such as the California Environmental Quality Act, require analysis of potential impacts on cultural resources. This process has a general counterpart in the United Kingdom in the requirements of "Planning Policy Guidance 16," in New Zealand in the Historic Places Act (1993), and in Australia in the Environmental Protection and Biodiversity Conservation Act (1999). Like nonfederal governments worldwide, the Australian state of Victoria has enacted its own law—the Heritage Act (1995). This statute offers more protection than is provided by federal legislation, which is principally concerned with nationally significant resources.

The looting of historic shipwrecks located in international waters is a matter of continuing discussion between nations and the International Congress on Monuments and Sites (ICOMOS), an influential nongovernmental organization. While many national governments have taken measures to protect wrecks from looting within their own waters—such as the United Kingdom's National Heritage Act (2002)—few restrictions apply to the open seas. ICOMOS's Charter on the Protection and Management of Underwater Cultural Heritage (1996) is an attempt to fill this gap; it is, however, still to be ratified by many nations.

As a practical matter, the CRM process is usually set in motion when an activity is proposed and the potential impacts are reviewed by a public agency to comply with an environmental protection law. Building a dam and reservoir, for example, may lead to the inundation of an indigenous group's traditional plant gathering site—a type of cultural resource. Construction projects often involve three phases of CRM: identifying resources by means of an on-the-ground inventory, evaluating their importance, and deciding how impacts to significant examples should be managed.

CRM is not synonymous with preservation. Since it assures a process, not a result, the only guaranteed outcome of CRM is that the values contained in cultural resources are weighed in relation to other social benefits. Thus, a government agency might allow the destruction of an important archaeological site in the interest of improving a dangerous road. In this case, the project proponent may be required to scientifically excavate the site to retrieve important information it contains before the data are destroyed by construction. This commonly imposed mitigation measure is termed *preservation by record* or *data recovery* in the United Kingdom and United States, respectively.

As a profession, CRM is practiced by anthropologists, architectural historians, geographers, environmental planners, historians, and archaeologists, among others. It has been estimated that CRM accounts for over 90 percent of archaeological projects carried out in the United States.

BIBLIOGRAPHY

Hunter, John, and Ian Ralston, eds. 1993. *Archaeological Resource Management in the UK: An Introduction.* Dover, NH: Allen Sutton.

King, Thomas F. 2002. *Thinking about Cultural Resource Management: Essays from the Edge.* Walnut Creek, CA: AltaMira Press.

Trapeznik, Alexander, ed. 2000. *Common Ground? Heritage and Public Places in New Zealand.* Dunedin, New Zealand: University of Otago Press.

Adrian Praetzellis

CULTURAL RIGHTS

The term *cultural rights* refers to a claimed entitlement on the part of identity groups—typically based on religion, ethnicity, language, or nationality—to be able to express and maintain their traditions or practices. Such an entitlement usually implies some form of political or legal recognition. Cultural rights have developed as a distinct set of rights claims particularly since the 1960s, and then largely in light of the experience of cultural minorities—such as indigenous peoples, substate nationalities, and immigrant groups—living in a state or society that is characterized by a dominant culture. "Cultural rights" thus figure prominently in discussions of national minority rights and multiculturalism. Nevertheless, cultural rights are commonly understood as a universal human right, one that recognizes the fundamental importance of a sense of cultural identity, membership, and shared values to human well-being and flourishing.

The political and legal recognition associated with cultural rights may take various forms. Such recognition may be symbolic, as when a state includes the symbols of one or more of its minorities in the national flag or observes a minority holiday as a public holiday. It may involve accommodation of specific minority cultural practices, such as granting exemptions from generally applicable dress codes to members of religious minorities who wish to wear their special clothing. It may concern the public subsidization of cultural groups—through direct grants or tax relief—so that they might better preserve their cultural heritage and community life. It may encompass intellectual-cum-cultural property rights that compensate groups for the use of their artifacts, land, or participation. Recognition may also include allowing citizens to hold dual or multiple citizenships, admitting cultural defense in criminal proceedings, or granting cultural or linguistic autonomy to particular groups to run their own educational and cultural institutions in their own languages. Finally, cultural recognition may be overtly political in the sense of granting special political representation or even political autonomy or self-government to particular cultural groups.

As these examples suggest, cultural rights should be distinguished from rights to nondiscrimination and affirmative action policies, which also relate to group membership. Where antidiscrimination legislation seeks to preclude, and affirmative action seeks to redress, the prejudicial denial of offices and opportunities to individuals on the basis of their background group characteristics, cultural rights are concerned with enabling cultural groups or their members to express and maintain their cultural attachments. Nevertheless, an important historical and conceptual connection between antidiscrimination legislation and cultural rights has been the growing recognition among human rights bodies and governments since the 1970s that generally applicable laws can adversely affect members of cultural minorities unintentionally. So some antidiscrimination provisions implicitly recognize the right to cultural liberty by seeking to remove unintended obstacles to cultural observance.

Cultural rights remain controversial in political theory and practice. A major reservation historically has been that cultural rights undermine the cultural unity of the nation-state and threaten its political integration. In fact, very few nation-states are culturally homogeneous, and *not* recognizing cultural minorities often promotes political conflict and instability. Another widespread concern is that cultural rights sanction cultural relativism or the notion that all cultural practices are equally valuable or legitimate. A related worry is that cultural rights compromise the individual rights of the cultural group's members, especially those most vulnerable, such as women and children. Such criticisms have force where cultural rights are asserted or recognized in the name of preserving cultural identity. However, cultural rights also have been formulated as human rights on the basis of liberal principles of individual liberty and equality and, in this case, oppose cultural relativism. For example, an individual right to the free exercise of culture does not sanction cultural practices such as female genital mutilation that seriously harm particular members, or that are imposed on members against their will, as in the case of coercive or even arranged marriages. In any case, cultural rights claims are subject to the laws and governing public values of the state, as adjudicated by state authorities. In the case of liberal democracies, this qualification typically means that the fundamental rights of the individual are protected over the claims of the group.

Cultural rights have been recognized in various international protocols and legal instruments. The 1948 Universal Declaration of Human Rights states that "everyone, as a member of society" is entitled to "cultural rights indispensable for his dignity and the free development of his personality" (Article 22). Article 15 of the International Covenant on Economic, Social, and Cultural Rights (1966) recognizes the right to "take part in cultural life," and Article 27 of the International Covenant on Civil and Political Rights (1966) asserts the right of "persons belonging" to "ethnic, religious, or linguistic minorities" to "enjoy their own culture, to profess and practice their own religion, or to use their own language." The Declaration on the Rights of Persons Belonging to National or Ethnic, Religious, and Linguistic Minorities (1992) stipulates further that such persons have the right to enjoy their own culture "in private and in public," and that states "shall take measures to create favourable conditions to enable" individuals to exercise their cultural rights (Articles 2 and 4). Although not binding, a major United Nations research report, *The Human Development Report 2004: Cultural Liberty in Today's Diverse World*, helpfully addresses the major issues and concerns surrounding cultural rights by incorporating them into a broader human development framework.

SEE ALSO *Human Rights; Relativism, Cultural*

BIBLIOGRAPHY

Kymlicka, Will, ed. 1995. *The Rights of Minority Cultures.* Oxford, U.K.: Oxford University Press.

Shweder, Richard, Martha Minow, and Hazel Rose, eds. 2002. *Engaging Cultural Differences: The Multicultural Challenge in Liberal Democracies.* New York: Russell Sage Foundation.

United Nations. 1948. Universal Declaration of Human Rights. www.un.org/Overview/rights.html.

United Nations. 1992. Office of the High Commissioner for Human Rights. Declaration on the Rights of Persons Belonging to National or Ethnic, Religious, and Linguistic Minorities. http://www.ohchr.org/english/law/minorities.htm.

United Nations Development Programme. 2004. *The Human Development Report 2004: Cultural Liberty in Today's Diverse World.* New York: Author.

United Nations Treaty Body Data Base. http://www.unhchr.ch/tbs/doc.nsf.

Geoffrey Brahm Levey

CULTURAL STUDIES

Anyone attempting a definition of *cultural studies* is confronted at the outset by a paradox. On the one hand, the emergence of cultural studies as a recognized discipline or field of study, particularly from the 1970s onward, can be clearly seen in the proliferation of academic departments, degree programs, academic journals, and scholars who proclaim themselves to be producing work in "cultural studies." On the other hand, what precisely "cultural studies" takes as its object or area of study, its definitive theoretical, epistemological, or methodological approach, is less clearly identifiable—indeed, some scholars have claimed it is this very breadth and eclecticism that is the definition of *cultural studies* (Barker 2003; During 1999, 2005). Colin Sparks has thus described cultural studies as "a veritable rag-bag of ideas, methods, and concerns" (1996, p. 14).

At a basic level, cultural studies is, as the term suggests, the study of "culture." It takes as its focus the ways in which people live, think, and express themselves in everyday practices and contexts. Raymond Williams (1921–1988), one of the founding figures of cultural studies, famously described culture as "a particular way of life, whether of a people, a period, or a group" (1976, p.

90)—a definition that has close links to the anthropological idea of culture. However, the focus for cultural studies has been primarily on Western, modern, and contemporary cultures, on understanding the seemingly ordinary practices, objects, and images that surround us and that make up our sense of who we are—from music and media to education, inner-city subcultures, pubs, and shopping malls. Its focus stretches from the microstudy of local identities, such as gangs, to the global movement of cultural commodities, such as hip-hop or Bollywood films. To this end, cultural studies has been resolutely inter-, multi-, or even antidisciplinary in its approach, drawing from disciplines such as sociology, anthropology, history, and English literature. Similarly, cultural studies utilizes a range of research methods, from in-depth ethnographic fieldwork to textual and visual analysis.

STARTING POINTS: THE BRITISH CONTEXT AND THE CCCS

Cultural studies is now a global phenomenon, but it is generally agreed that the discipline began locally, at the Centre for Contemporary Cultural Studies (CCCS) in Birmingham, England, in the 1960s. Most scholars trace the emergence of cultural studies to the interventions of three men and three seminal texts: Richard Hoggart's *The Uses of Literacy* (1957), Raymond Williams's *Culture and Society* (1958), and E. P. Thompson's *The Making of the English Working Class* (1963). Hoggart, indeed, was the founder and first director of the CCCS, which was established as a postgraduate research center attached to the University of Birmingham in 1964.

What these three texts shared, albeit in very different ways, was a concern with "popular culture" that sought to challenge traditional elitist notions of culture as art and aesthetics—what Matthew Arnold (1822–1888) referred to as "the best that has been thought and said in the world" ([1869] 1960, p. 6)—or as "civilization" (Jenks 2004). In its place, they celebrated culture as ubiquitous, as everyday, and as made by ordinary people—"the study of relationships between elements in a whole way of life" (Williams [1961] 1965, p. 63). There are two key arguments that characterize these texts: firstly, that culture expresses meanings (i.e., it reflects our understanding of the world around us); and secondly, that culture flows from the experiences of ordinary people (hence, Williams's assertion that "culture is ordinary") (Procter 2004). Furthermore, this experience comes out of the historical and social location of individuals and groups—specifically, their class location. In particular, the authors claimed a sense of legitimacy and agency for working-class and popular cultures as valid and valuable sources of cultural expression and meaning making (Hall 1996).

THE STRUGGLE FOR CULTURE

Stuart Hall took over the directorship of the CCCS in 1968, marking a change in the way cultural studies was both thought and done. In particular, Hall brought the center's engagement with Marxism into creative tension with *structuralist* theory, as exemplified in the works of French theorists Claude Lévi-Strauss, Roland Barthes (1915–1980), and Louis Althusser (1918–1990) (Hall 1992a, 1996; Procter 2004). Put simply, structuralism contests the assumed connection between culture and meaning. Rather than seeing culture as simply *reflecting* meaning (as Williams had done), structuralism sees this relationship as *constructed* and arbitrary (Hall 1997). This means that culture is not simply an embodiment of a real experience, but creates that experience and shapes its meaning for us.

Hall sought to bring these two paradigms—*culturalist* and *structuralist*—together through the work of Italian Marxist Antonio Gramsci (1891–1937) and his theory of *hegemony*. This refers to the ways in which a dominant group maintains its control over other groups not through coercion, but through winning and shaping assent "so that its ascendency commands widespread consent and appears natural and inevitable" (Hall 1997b, p. 259). This is achieved in the realm of "culture"—through shaping how people think of and experience their world. However, because our societies are marked by forms of social division and inequality, subordinate groups enter into conflict with the dominant group to contest these meanings. Culture thus becomes the site where social divisions (class, gender, race and ethnicity, sexuality, disability, etc.) are both established and resisted.

Culture, in the traditional cultural studies paradigm, is thus highly contested and politicized. Firstly, it rejects the distinction of high and low culture, and celebrates popular and mass cultures as legitimate forms of expression. Secondly, it sees culture as always changing and dynamic—as a process rather than a possession. Thirdly, it sees cultures as challenging and transforming meanings, images, and understandings (Hall 1997a; Jenks 2004). Fourthly, it has taken as its primary focus of study subordinated and marginalized cultural forms and expressions—particularly around working-class and youth (sub)cultures.

This classic cultural studies approach was challenged in the 1980s and 1990s through the emergence of postmodern and post-structural theories. Although part of a much broader intellectual movement, postmodernism rejects the idea of coherent or stable cultural identities and meanings, and insists instead on the fragmentary and transitory nature of culture. Stuart Hall thus writes of "the breakdown of *all* strong cultural identities . . . producing that fragmentation of cultural codes, that multiplicity of styles, emphasis on the ephemeral, the fleeting, the impermanent, and on difference and cultural pluralism" (1992b, p. 302). This view of culture is linked closely to the increased globalization and commodification of culture. Individuals become *bricoleurs*, creating their own styles and inhabiting a multiplicity of identities, and opening up a range of cultural options, meanings, and political possibilities (Barker 2003; During 2005).

CULTURAL STUDIES GOES GLOBAL

Through the 1990s, cultural studies has grown both in terms of scope and of content, traversing disciplines and diversifying its subject matter and theoretical and methodological approaches. In particular, as researchers have engaged with the increasingly globalized nature of cultural forms and connections, cultural studies can also be said to have gone global—at once exploring the ways in which culture travels and how it is shaped within particular local or national contexts (During 2005). "Cultural studies" as an academic discipline is now well established in the Anglophone world, particularly in Australia, Canada, and the United States, and is increasingly linked to the arts and media practitioners. Interest in the field is also growing in Asia, Africa, and Latin America, though in all these places it takes on different forms and emphases. In the United States, for example, where "cultural studies" as both a discipline and set of institutions has exploded, cultural studies traces its historical development from postwar American studies and from African American writers, scholars, and activists (During 2005) and is closely linked contemporarily with the study of minorities, postcoloniality, multiculturalism, and race. This is in sharp contrast to the United Kingdom (and Australia), which has traditionally marginalized issues of race and ethnicity—as well as gender—in cultural studies (Hall 1992a).

CULTURAL STUDIES IN CRISIS?

Cultural studies is not without its critics, both from outside and within the field. Indeed, as cultural studies has expanded and transformed, it has been argued that it has lost its original engagement with politics and power, with the lived experiences of "the everyday," and has instead become overly fascinated with cultural commodification, consumption, and production. Focusing on music, film, literature, and the media, cultural studies has, it is argued, privileged texts and discourse over people, and cultural practices and pleasures over the structures of power and material contexts within which these practices and pleasures take shape (Hall 1992a; McRobbie 1992). Still others have argued that the neo-Marxist underpinnings of the cultural studies project have been thrown "into crisis" by its encounter with postmodernism and post-structural-

ism, which have fractured ideas of power and meaning, and the relationship between them, and have privileged an individualistic and overcelebratory version of cultural expression (Storey 1996; During 2005). The lack of engagement of some strands and traditions of cultural studies with race and gender has already been commented upon. The growth and institutionalization of cultural studies have led some to fear for a loss of focus—that cultural studies could mean anything—and others to fear for a regulation of its critical and political edge in favor of a marketable pedagogy (Hall 1992a).

Clearly, what cultural studies is, or may become, is open to debate, contestation, and transformation. However, as Hall has stated, the study of culture is "a deadly serious matter . . . a practice which always thinks about its intervention in a world in which it would make some difference" (1992a, p. 286).

SEE ALSO *Althusser, Louis; Anthropology, U.S.; Hall, Stuart; Marxism; Structuralism*

BIBLIOGRAPHY

Arnold, Matthew. [1869] 1960. *Culture and Anarchy.* Cambridge, U.K.: Cambridge University Press.

Barker, Chris. 2003. *Cultural Studies: Theory and Practice.* 2nd ed. London and Thousand Oaks, CA: Sage.

During, Simon, ed. 1999. *The Cultural Studies Reader.* 2nd ed. London and New York: Routledge.

During, Simon. 2005. *Cultural Studies: A Critical Introduction.* London and New York: Routledge.

Hall, Stuart. 1992a. Cultural Studies and Its Theoretical Legacies. In *Cultural Studies*, eds. Lawrence Grossberg, Cary Nelson, and Paula Treichler, 277–294. London and New York: Routledge.

Hall, Stuart. 1992b. The Question of Cultural Identity. In *Modernity and Its Futures*, eds. Stuart Hall, David Held, and Tony McGrew, 273–326. Cambridge, U.K.: Polity.

Hall, Stuart. 1996. Cultural Studies: Two Paradigms. In *What Is Cultural Studies? A Reader*, ed. John Storey, 31–48. London and New York: Arnold Press.

Hall, Stuart. 1997a. The Work of Representation. In *Representation: Cultural Representations and Signifying Practices*, ed. Stuart Hall, 13–74. London: Sage.

Hall, Stuart. 1997b. The Spectacle of the Other. In *Representation: Cultural Representations and Signifying Practices*, ed. Stuart Hall, 223–290. London: Sage.

Hoggart, Richard. 1957. *The Uses of Literacy: Aspects of Working-Class Life with Special References to Publications and Entertainments.* London: Chatto and Windus.

Jenks, Chris. 2004. *Culture.* 2nd ed. London and New York: Routledge.

McRobbie, Angela. 1992. Post-Marxism and Cultural Studies: A Post-Script. In *Cultural Studies*, ed. Lawrence Grossberg, Cary Nelson, and Paula Treichler, 719–730. London and New York: Routledge.

Procter, James. 2004. *Stuart Hall.* London and New York: Routledge.

Sparks, Colin. 1996. The Evolution of Cultural Studies.… In *What Is Cultural Studies? A Reader*, ed. John Storey, 14–30. London and New York: Arnold Press.

Storey, John, ed. 1996. *What Is Cultural Studies? A Reader.* London and New York: Arnold Press.

Storey, John. 1996. Cultural Studies: An Introduction. In *What Is Cultural Studies?: A Reader*, ed. John Storey, 1–13. London and New York: Arnold Press.

Thompson, E. P. 1963. *The Making of the English Working Class.* London: V. Gollancz.

Williams, Raymond. 1958. *Culture and Society, 1780–1950.* London: Chatto and Windus.

Williams, Raymond. [1961] 1965. *The Long Revolution.* London: Penguin.

Williams, Raymond. 1976. *Keywords: A Vocabulary of Culture and Society.* London: Fontana.

Claire Alexander

CULTURAL TOURISM

Cultural tourism is a type of special interest tourism involving leisure travel for the purpose of viewing or experiencing the distinctive character of a place, its peoples, and its products or productions. A wide range of destinations and cultural activities fall under the umbrella heading of cultural tourism: visits to UNESCO World Heritage Sites (e.g. China's Great Wall, Chichén-Itzá); tours of historic cities, architectural sites, cathedrals, and battlefields; excursions to museums; trips to sample typical regional foods; tours of ethnic neighborhoods; travel to local music festivals and cultural performances; visits to indigenous villages or distinctive cultural landscapes (e.g. observing farming practices in Asian rice fields). Although cultural tourists' motives vary, some common themes include the desire to experience an "authentic" cultural landscape, interest in other cultures, and an interest in scenery that fosters an engagement with the past.

Since anthropologists and sociologists first turned their attention to tourism in the 1970s, there have been a variety of attempts to classify particular types of tourism. Some scholars, such as Valene Smith (1989), have proposed more refined subdivisions to the broader category of cultural tourism, including ethnic tourism (to see indigenous peoples), historical tourism (focused on the glories of the past, museums, monuments, and ruins), and, in a separate category, cultural tourism, which she defines as travels to see "vestiges of a vanishing lifestyle that lies within human memory" and involves "rustic inns, folklore performances, [and] costumed wine festivals" (Smith 1989, pp. 4–5). While some scholars embrace these taxonomic distinctions, others simply utilize the broader umbrella term cultural tourism. Recognizing that most tourists engage in a variety of activities on any given trip (ranging from sampling local delicacies to touring picturesque villages), more social scientific attention has been directed away from refining taxonomies and toward better understanding the sociocultural transformations that are part and parcel of cultural tourism.

A number of scholars have chronicled how the advent of tourism has transformed local peoples' conceptions of their own identities and cultural products. Tourism literature tends to project fixed and alluring images of destinations, despite the fact that these destinations are undergoing transformations in tandem with the broader dynamics of globalization, including tourism development. In some locales, the promotion of cultural or ethnic tourism has prompted residents to become experts in marketing their own authenticity, playing the native and drawing on and manipulating the cultural symbols spotlighted in the tourist literature for economic gain or to enhance their cultural standing *vis-à-vis* other ethnic groups, as Timothy Oakes (1998) has illustrated in his analysis of ethnic villages in China. As Pierre van den Berghe (1994) and Nelson Graburn (1976) observe, the focus of ethnic tourists' gazes are often Fourth World peoples, members of disempowered communities on the fringes of larger nations. For such peoples, while tourism can potentially bring new sources of revenue, it can also attract outside entrepreneurs who may substantially divert the flow of income.

Likewise, cultural tourism can fuel the commoditization of ethnic arts, dances, and rituals. Although commoditization does not necessarily bring loss of meaning, as Graburn notes, the significance may be transformed. For example, Michel Picard (1990) observes that tourism and tourist productions have become so intrinsic in Bali that they have contributed to shaping contemporary Balinese ethnic identity. Other scholars find that cultural tourism can be a factor in reconfiguring aspects of local gender relations. For instance, Elayne Zorn (2004) documents how the new tourist market for textiles woven by Taquilean women has enabled these Andean women to take on more visible roles in public life. Elsewhere, cultural tourism may contribute to the eroding of local rank hierarchies and to newfound ethnic self-consciousness and cultural pride, as Kathleen Adams (2006) has chronicled among the Sa'dan Toraja of Indonesia.

Cultural tourism can be highly political. As Michel Picard and Robert Wood illustrate, states are deeply involved in structuring cultural tourism and in "shaping the visible contours of ethnicity" (1997, p. 5). In some cases, such as the Mexican government's promotion of Aztec pyramids as national symbols, tourist sites associated with the heritage of indigenous minorities are used to legitimate the nation. In other cases, such as the bombing of Egyptian pyramids by militant Muslims, cultural tourism is so enmeshed with international politics that destinations frequented by tourists from Western nations become targets.

In some places cultural tourism has led to the transformation of physical settings, environmental degradation, soaring land prices, and reduced access to the land for indigenous peoples. Cultural tourism can also create conflict between tourists, tourism promoters, and locals over the meaning and use of sites. Australia's Ayers Rock is one such setting, where tourists scaling the peak violate indigenous views of it as a sacred site. In some settings, locals have developed strategies to reduce the intrusive aspects of tourism, formally or informally delineating front-stage areas for tourists and back stage areas for local life beyond the tourist gaze (MacCannell 1989).

SEE ALSO *Anthropology; Distinctions, Social and Cultural; Gaze, Colonial; Gaze, The; Going Native; Liverpool Slave Trade; National Geographic; Natives; Other, The; Primitivism; Reflexivity; Sociology; Stare, The; Tourism; Tourism Industry; Tribe; Vacations*

BIBLIOGRAPHY

Adams, Kathleen M. 2006. *Art as Politics: Re-crafting Identities, Tourism, and Power in Tana Toraja, Indonesia.* Honolulu: University of Hawaii Press.

Bruner, Edward M. 2005. *Culture on Tour: Ethnographies of Travel.* Chicago: University of Chicago Press.

Crick, Malcolm. 1989. Representations of International Tourism in the Social Sciences: Sun, Sex, Sights, Savings, and Servility. *Annual Review of Anthropology* 18: 307–344.

Graburn, Nelson H., ed. 1976. *Ethnic and Tourist Arts: Cultural Expressions from the Fourth World.* Berkeley: University of California Press.

MacCannell, Dean. [1976] 1989. *The Tourist: A New Theory of the Leisure Class.* New York: Schocken Books.

Oakes, Timothy. 1998. *Tourism and Modernity in China.* New York: Routledge.

Picard, Michel. 1990. "Cultural Tourism" in Bali: Cultural Performances as Tourist Attraction. *Indonesia* 49: 37–74.

Picard, Michel and Robert E. Wood, eds. 1997. *Tourism, Ethnicity, and the State in Asian and Pacific Societies.* Honolulu: University of Hawaii Press.

Smith, Valene L., ed. [1977] 1989. *Hosts and Guests: The Anthropology of Tourism.* 2nd ed. Philadelphia: University of Pennsylvania Press.

Stronza, Amanda. 2001. Anthropology of Tourism: Forging New Ground for Ecotourism and Other Alternatives. *Annual Review of Anthropology* 30: 261–283.

Van den Berghe, Pierre. 1980. Tourism as Ethnic Relations: A Case Study of Cuzco, Peru. *Ethnic and Racial Studies* 3 (6): 345–391.

Van den Berghe, Pierre. 1994. *The Quest for the Other: Ethnic Tourism in San Cristobal, Mexico.* Seattle: University of Washington Press.

Zorn, Elayne. 2004. *Weaving a Future: Tourism, Cloth, and Culture on an Andean Island.* Iowa City: University of Iowa Press.

Kathleen M. Adams

CULTURE

Culture is notoriously one of the most difficult terms to define. The cultural historian Raymond Williams (1921–1988) notes that the difficulty in defining the word is located on its "intricate historical development" in European languages and on the fact that despite its long history the term is relatively new in the English language (Williams 1983, p. 87). The word derives from the Latin *cultura*, which in turn comes from the Latin verb *colere*, which had a wide range of meanings that corresponded to different domains in life: agricultural (to cultivate), domestic (to inhabit), religious (to honor a deity through worship), social (to protect). Williams pointed to the eventual divergences of these original meanings, such as the derivation of the term *colony*, from the meaning of *cultura* "to inhabit," or *cult*, from the meaning "to honor through worship." The primary meaning of cultivation, in *cultura*, has nevertheless been retained within the integrity of the word. Hence *culture* and *cultura* still echo the original main meaning of cultivation. The poet and critic T. S. Eliot (1885–1965), in his 1949 book *Notes Towards the Definition of Culture*, observed that the term "cultivation" applies as much to "the work of the bacteriologist or the *agri*culturalist" as "to the improvement of the human mind and spirit," (p. 19) although he concludes that the primary location of culture is religion.

By the mid-eighteenth century the term appears in both French and English in its proto-modern form, and in German it appears as a borrowing from the French first as *Cultur* (in the eighteenth century) and then as *Kultur* (in the nineteenth century) as almost synonymous with "civilization." The German philosopher Johann Gottfried von Herder (1744–1803) observed that the slippery nature of the two terms denoted the slippery understanding of "culture" and "civilization" and the frequent conflation of the two. Herder separated the notion of "civilization" from the notion of "culture" and developed the theory of "cultures" in the plural, refuting the universalist theories of a unified development of humanity. The anthropological development of the theory of culture rests precisely on this notion of "culture-in-the-plural," the acknowledgment that specific cultures existed in different times and places, and that even within specific nations there existed a number of different cultures (Herder [1784] 1968).

The English anthropologist Edward Tylor (1832–1917) in 1871 proposed a definition of culture that conflated "culture" with "civilization" and informed early anthropological definitions of the term: "Culture, or civilization … is that complex whole which includes knowledge, belief, art, law, morals, custom, and any other capabilities and habits acquired by man as a member of society" (Tylor 1871, p. 1). Franz Boas (1858–1942), one of the key figures in modern anthropology, especially in the history of U.S. anthropology, comes from the intellectual tradition begun by Herder and furthered by Tylor; Boas developed a theory of culture from which he derived a theory of racism. He noted that cultures cannot be judged according to an a priori value system. Rather, each culture has its own integrity, and all cultures are equal to each other and ought to be gauged according to their own system of values. This relativist approach to culture underlined Herder's original idea that one ought not be thinking about *a* culture to which all the rest would be held accountable but about *cultures* as they appear in different formulations and places over time. Boas wrote: "Culture may be defined as the totality of mental and physical reactions and activities that characterize the behavior of the individuals composing a social group" (Boas 1938, p. 159)—a definition strangely constricted from the one he had produced only eight years earlier: "[C]ulture embraces all the manifestations of social habits of a community, the reactions of the individual as affected by the habits of the group in which he lives, and the products of human activities as determined by these habits" (Boas 1930, p. 79). Leslie White expanded the definition of culture provided by Boas by including in its definition not only the traits that characterize it but also "the traits that do not characterize it" including, thus, within the definition of culture as comprising the characteristic traits of a group those traits which could be considered as marginal, resistant, or, even, abjected (White and Dillingham 1973, p. 32).

The anthropological definitions of culture were in part a reaction to the exclusionary definitions put forth in 1869, two years before Tylor's, by the British poet and critic Matthew Arnold (1822–1888). Against the Herderian opening of culture and civilization to all human societies, Arnold erected the discourse of *a priori* perfection: "I have been trying to show that Culture is, ought to be, the study and pursuit of perfection," Arnold wrote, "and that of perfection as pursued by culture, beauty and intelligence, or, in other words, sweetness and light, are the main characters" (Arnold 1869, p. 11). Arnold thus articulated the difference between what is called "high" culture (sublime, light, sweet, beautiful) and "low" culture (what later came to be called popular culture).

In a critique of this sublimity of culture as presented by Arnold, the literary theorist Edward Said (1935–2003) argued that high culture was complicit with the project of imperialism. In his 1979 book *Orientalism*, Said showed the ways in which the constructed distinctions made between the Orient and Occident as fabricated geographical ideas were mainly located in the internalization of the idea of high culture as intrinsic to Europe set against "cultures" that needed to be translated into the European intellectual idiom.

The Frankfurt School philosophers Max Horkheimer (1875–1973) and Theodor Adorno (1903–1969), in their *Dialectic of Enlightenment*, apply a rigorous critique to popular culture (especially what they call "the culture industry" of Hollywood and jazz music). They argue that popular culture destroys the careful distinctions between the object of high culture (the elevation of the individual as an autonomous subject) and that of popular culture (the degradation of the subject into the position of the nonthinking object). Popular culture as a means of production of a compliant body politic is at the core of the theory of hegemony as developed by the Italian theorist Antonio Gramsci (1891–1937). In a gentle critique of Marx's theory of revolution, Gramsci explains that the reason why the industrial workers of the large capitalist countries did not become a revolutionary force was that capitalism makes enough minor cultural concessions to them (primarily minor commodities) to assure their acquiescence. For Gramsci, keeping the cultural programs of the Italian Fascist state in mind, the process of producing a compliant body politic, what he calls *hegemony*, is mapped onto the process of participation in popular culture. In a tone more celebratory of popular culture, the German critic and philosopher Walter Benjamin (1892–1940) notes how the availability of mechanical reproduction of art problematized the notions (in his view outdated) of genius and creativity. Benjamin proposed that proletarian art might thus be able to participate in the production of a form of culture that would neutralize the distinction between high and low.

The French cultural theorist Jean Baudrillard (1929–2007) in *Symbolic Exchange and Death* attempts to provide a radically different theory of culture. He first presents his theory of the *simulacrum* as the delineation of the relationship between reality and its artistic reproduction. For example, Disneyland is the result of simulation of the reality of southern California in the 1930s and 1940s as it had been represented in the comic cartoons of Mickey Mouse, which, in its turn, has been simulated as its actualization in the United States of the 1950s. In this sense the comic cartoons simulated southern Californian realities in the 1930s and 1940s, which southern California simulated in the 1950s and then Disneyland represented in the 1960s. Baudrillard then substitutes the notion of symbolic exchange for the classic Marxist notion of exchange value, claiming that symbolic exchange (e.g., the living providing prayers for the salvation of the dead in exchange for the intercession of the dead with God on behalf of the living) dislocates utility from the center of the exchange system and replaces it with a cultural value that rests on a symbolic rather than a monetary value system.

SEE ALSO *Anthropology; Anthropology, British; Anthropology, U.S.; Boas, Franz; Civilization; Cultural Capital; Cultural Relativism; Culture of Poverty; Culture, Low and High; Determinism, Cultural; Disney, Walt; Frankfurt School; Gramsci, Antonio; Hegemony; Marx, Karl; Said, Edward; Symbols*

BIBLIOGRAPHY

Arnold, Matthew. 1869. *Culture and Anarchy. An Essay in Political and Social Criticism.* London: Smith, Eler and Co.

Baudrillard, Jean. [1976] 1993. *Symbolic Exchange and Death.* Trans. Iain Hamilton Grant. London and Thousand Oaks, CA: Sage.

Benjamin, Walter. 1969. *Illuminations: Essays and Reflections.* Trans. Harry Zohn. New York: Harcourt Brace.

Boas, Franz. 1930. Anthropology. In *The Encyclopedia of the Social Sciences*, Vol. 2. New York: Macmillan.

Boas, Franz. 1938. *The Mind of Primitive Man.* Rev ed. New York: Macmillan.

Eliot, T. S. 1949. *Notes Towards the Definition of Culture.* New York: Harcourt, Brace.

Gramsci, Antonio. 1971. *Selections from the Prison Notebooks of Antonio Gramsci*, ed. and trans. Quintin Hoare and Geoffrey Nowell Smith. London: Lawrence and Wishart.

Herder, Johann Gottfried. [1784] 1968. *Reflections on the Philosophy of the History of Mankind.* Abridged and intro. Frank E. Manual. Trans. T. O. Churchill, 1800. Chicago: University of Chicago Press.

Horkheimer, Max, and Theodor W. Adorno. 1972. *Dialectic of Enlightenment: Philosophical Fragments.* Trans. John Cumming. New York: Seabury Press.

Kroeber, A. L., and Clyde Kluckhohn. 1953. *Culture: A Critical Review of Concepts and Definitions.* New York: Vintage.

Said, Edward. 1979. *Orientalism.* New York: Vintage Books.

Tylor, Edward B. 1871. *Primitive Culture: Researches into the Development of Mythology, Philosophy, Religion, Art, and Custom*, Vol. 1. London: J. Murray.

White, Leslie A., and Beth Dillingham. 1973. *The Concept of Culture.* Minneapolis, MN: Burgess Publishing.

Williams, Raymond. 1983. *Keywords.* Rev. ed. London: Fontana.

Neni Panourgiá

CULTURE, LOW AND HIGH

Discussions and analyses of culture are common in the social sciences. Sociologists, anthropologists, and other social scientists are often interested in similarities and differences between groups and societies. An important component of social scientific research on culture revolves around the question of stratification. In other words, are some cultures more valued than others?

According to sociologist Herbert Gans, cultures can be divided according to various tastes. In his article *American Popular Culture and High Culture in a Changing Class Structure* (1986), Gans argues that "taste cultures" are the "array of arts, and forms of entertainment and information, as well as consumer goods available to different taste publics" (pp. 17–18). Taste cultures fall into at least five categories, each differing by preferences in literature, art, consumption patterns, hobbies, and other leisure activities. According to the author, the categories are different, but not implicitly unequal.

However, empirical evidence suggests that not all cultures are equally valued. A stratification system exists in which some cultures are considered "high" cultures while others are considered "low." According to Tia DeNora (1991), the differential valuation of cultures has been present throughout history in a variety of nations and is maintained through an array of institutional practices.

The difference between high culture and low culture is somewhat arbitrary. Both types of culture involve tastes in music, art, literature, and various material goods, for example, so the distinction generally revolves around specific types of tastes within those categories. High culture, in general, involves an interest in classical music or opera, fine art, gourmet foods, and so forth. Low culture tastes, in contrast, fall outside of these particular preferences.

Because high culture is valued more highly than other forms, several advantages are bestowed upon those who participate in high cultural activities. According to Pierre Bourdieu (1977), participation or interest in high culture leads to a form of capital that can be used to produce various types of "profits." For example, several scholars have argued that children who possess cultural capital are advantaged in the school system because teachers may "communicate more easily with students who participate in elite status cultures, give them more attention and special assistance, and perceive them as more intelligent or gifted than students who lack cultural capital" (DiMaggio 1982, p. 190). Numerous empirical studies have supported this claim. Students with higher degrees of cultural capital tend to have higher grades, higher educational attainment, and higher educational expectations.

Theoretically, the opportunity to obtain cultural capital is open to all members of a society. However, there is a strong correlation between cultural capital and socioeconomic status. Since cultural capital is likely to be obtained through socialization, family background strongly influences whether or not individuals will have access to opportunities that could increase their levels of capital. According to Gans, "it takes money to buy culture" (1986, pp. 18–19). Those with low incomes may be unable to afford to participate in high culture activities. Other factors that can affect the accumulation of cultural capital include educational attainment and occupational status. To be able to understand and appreciate high culture, one may need to have a particular level of education. Because information about cultural events is likely to be transmitted through social networks, occupation status becomes important. Because the poor have lower incomes, lower levels of education, and fall into the lower levels of the occupational hierarchy, they may be excluded from opportunities to participate in high culture activities, which will limit the amount of cultural capital they, and their children, possess.

Members of racial and ethnic minority groups may also be excluded from opportunities to obtain cultural capital, partially due to those factors that exclude the poor in general. Members of minority groups are disproportionately represented in the lower classes of society, have lower levels of educational attainment, and are underrepresented in professional occupations. Therefore, like poor whites, they may lack opportunities to participate in high culture activities. However, minority groups may face further exclusion based on various unique circumstances they face as a result of racial or ethnic group status.

As high culture, to a great extent, is synonymous with Euro-American culture, those who are not Euro-American may be particularly disadvantaged with regard to access to cultural capital. According to Paul DiMaggio and Francie Ostrower (1990), historical practices involving overt discrimination excluded African Americans from fully participating in high culture activities. For example, various museums either denied or limited access to blacks, black artists and white artists were segregated, and audiences were often separated by race. Discrimination in education, the economy, and other institutions also played a role in limiting cultural opportunities.

Although opportunities for blacks have expanded since the 1960s, both past and present discrimination may continue to limit access. As noted earlier, race continues to affect socioeconomic status. Due to high degrees of educational and occupational segregation, blacks may lack access to important forms of economic and social capital that could contribute positively to participation in high culture activities. According to DiMaggio and Ostrower,

blacks may also participate less in high culture because the benefits of doing so vary by race. For example, attendance at high culture events may be uncomfortable for blacks, as they may be less familiar with these environments, or may be subjected to "'social slurs, unpleasant incidents,' and discrimination" (DiMaggio and Ostrower 1990, p. 758). Therefore, the cost of attendance may outweigh the benefits.

Another important factor to consider is that of taste. DiMaggio and Ostrower find that blacks, for example, are more likely to attend or participate in events that involve jazz, soul, rhythm-and-blues, and other forms of music. Because these tastes are historically associated with African American culture rather than Euro-American culture, they tend to be valued less. Since these tastes are not considered to be as valuable or prestigious, blacks may be excluded from the rewards they might otherwise have received by conforming to dominant cultural tastes.

In conclusion, cultures are not only different but also unequal. Since participation in high culture activities is dependent upon factors such as socioeconomic status, equal opportunity, and taste preferences, poor and minority group members may be excluded from participation, and may therefore also be excluded from the benefits that accompany involvement.

SEE ALSO *Bourdieu, Pierre; Class; Class, Leisure; Culture; Distinctions, Social and Cultural; Gans, Herbert J.; Lewis, Oscar; Lifestyles; Popular Culture; Street Culture; Tastes; Veblen, Thorstein*

BIBLIOGRAPHY

Bourdieu, Pierre. 1977. Cultural Reproduction and Social Reproduction. In *Power and Ideology in Education*, ed. Jerome Karabel and A. H. Halsey, 487–511. New York: Oxford University Press.

DeNora, Tia. 1991. Musical Patronage and Social Change in Beethoven's Vienna. *American Journal of Sociology* 97 (2): 310–346.

DiMaggio, Paul. 1982. Cultural Capital and School Success: The Impact of Status Culture Participation on the Grades of U.S. High School Students. *American Sociological Review* 47: 189–201.

DiMaggio, Paul, and Francie Ostrower. 1990. Participation in the Arts by Black and White Americans. *Social Forces* 68: 753–778.

Gans, Herbert. 1986. American Popular Culture and High Culture in a Changing Class Structure. In *Prospects: An Annual of American Cultural Studies*, Vol. 10, 17–38. New York: Cambridge University Press.

Amy J. Orr

CULTURE, STREET
SEE *Street Culture.*

CULTURE, YOUTH
SEE *Youth Culture.*

CULTURE OF POVERTY

The theory of a "culture of poverty" was created by the anthropologist Oscar Lewis in his 1959 book, *Five Families: Mexican Case Studies in the Culture of Poverty.* The culture of poverty theory states that living in conditions of pervasive poverty will lead to the development of a culture or subculture adapted to those conditions. This culture is characterized by pervasive feelings of helplessness, dependency, marginality, and powerlessness. Furthermore, Lewis described individuals living within a culture of poverty as having little or no sense of history and therefore lacking the knowledge to alleviate their own conditions through collective action, instead focusing solely on their own troubles. Thus, for Lewis, the imposition of poverty on a population was the structural cause of the development of a culture of poverty, which then becomes autonomous, as behaviors and attitudes developed within a culture of poverty get passed down to subsequent generations through socialization processes.

Critics of the culture of poverty theory have pointed out several flaws within both the theory itself and the ways in which it has been interpreted and applied to society. The culture of poverty assumes that culture itself is relatively fixed and unchanging—that once a population exists within the culture of poverty, no amount of intervention in terms of the alleviation of poverty will change the cultural attitudes and behaviors held by members of that population. Thus public assistance to the poor, in the form of welfare or other direct assistance, cannot eliminate poverty, since poverty is inherent in the culture of the poor. Following this reasoning, the culture of poverty theory shifts the blame for poverty from social and economic conditions to the poor themselves. The theory acknowledges past factors that led to the initial condition of poverty, such as substandard housing and education, lack of sufficient social services, lack of job opportunities, and persistent racial segregation and discrimination, but focuses on the cause of present poverty as the behaviors and attitudes of the poor.

Much of the evidence presented in support of the culture of poverty suffers from methodological fallacies, particularly a reliance on the assumption that behavior derives solely from preferred cultural values. That is, evidence of poverty itself, including rates of unemployment, crime, school dropout rates, and drug use, are assumed to be the result of behavior preferred by individuals living within conditions of poverty. The culture of poverty theory presumes the development of a set of deviant norms, whereby behaviors like drug use and gang participation are viewed as the standard (normative) and even desired behaviors of those living in the ghetto. An alternative explanation is that individuals behave in ways that are nominally illegal, like participation in the underground economy or participation in gangs, not because they wish to do so or are following cultural norms, but because they have no choice, given the lack of educational and job opportunities available in their neighborhoods. In other words, individuals living in the ghetto may see themselves as forced to turn to illegal methods of getting money, for example by selling drugs, simply to survive within the conditions of poverty. Thus so-called "ghetto behaviors" are adaptive, not normative, and given sufficient opportunities, individuals within the ghetto would eagerly turn to conventional means of earning a living.

The culture of poverty theory has had a tremendous impact on U.S. public policy, forming the basis for public policy toward the poor since the early to mid-1960s and strongly influencing President Lyndon Johnson's War on Poverty. In 1965 Senator Daniel Patrick Moynihan authored a report entitled "The Negro Family: The Case for National Action." In the report Moynihan stated that poor blacks in the United States were caught in a "tangle of pathology," the core reason for which was the breakdown of the black family—specifically the decline of the traditional male-headed household, resulting in a deviant matriarchal family structure. In Moynihan's conception, this family breakdown was responsible for the failure of black males to succeed, both in school and later in jobs, and that this failure was transmitted down generations. Moynihan argued that the origins of this deviant family structure lay in slavery, where the destruction of the "traditional" family "broke the will of the Negro people," particularly black males. This sense of powerlessness led to, in essence, a culture of dependency.

The related notions of a culture of poverty and a culture of dependency have become the foundations for antipoverty legislation, such as Temporary Assistance for Needy Families, enacted in 1997 and reauthorized in 2005 as a part of welfare reform. This and other programs rely on the assumption that behavior generates poverty, citing the need to end the dependence of the poor on government benefits and promote work and marriage as social norms. Among scholars, sociologists in the field, and government policy makers, the debate as to whether poverty stems from social, political, and economic conditions or from entrenched behaviors on the part of the poor themselves, continues.

SEE ALSO *Benign Neglect; Culture; Culture, Low and High; Determinism, Cultural; Deviance; Lewis, Oscar; Moynihan Report; Moynihan, Daniel Patrick; Pathology, Social; Poverty; Public Assistance; Street Culture; Structuralism; Welfare State*

BIBLIOGRAPHY

Leacock, Eleanor Burke. 1971. *The Culture of Poverty: A Critique.* New York: Simon and Schuster.

Lewis, Oscar. 1959. *Five Families: Mexican Case Studies in the Culture of Poverty.* New York: Basic Books.

Moynihan, Daniel Patrick. 1965. *The Negro Family: The Case for National Action.* Washington, DC: U.S. Department of Labor, Office of Policy Planning and Research.

O'Connor, Alice. 2001. *Poverty Knowledge: Social Science, Social Policy, and the Poor in Twentieth-Century U.S. History.* Princeton, NJ: Princeton University Press.

Ryan, William. 1976. *Blaming the Victim.* New York: Vintage Books.

David Dietrich

CULTURE OF THE POOR

SEE *Culture of Poverty.*

CUMULATIVE CAUSATION

Cumulative causation refers to a self-reinforcing process during which an impulse to a system triggers further changes in the same direction as the original impulse, thus taking the system further away from its initial position in virtuous or vicious circles of change that may result in a continuing increase in advantages (to some people or activities) and disadvantages (to others).

The term *cumulative causation* was coined by the Swedish economist Gunnar Myrdal (1898–1987), even though the basic hypothesis first appeared in American economist Allyn Young's (1876–1929) analysis of economic progress ("Increasing Returns and Economic Progress," 1928). In *An American Dilemma* (1944), Myrdal used the concept of cumulative causation to explain race relations in the United States. In a vicious circle of social determination, the prejudice of the white populations and the low living standards of the black populations could reinforce each other in a downward spiral: a decline in black living conditions could worsen white prejudice and trigger institutional discriminatory processes, further deteriorating black Americans' standards of living.

In Myrdal's analysis, the circular interdependence between social, economic, and political forces, by hindering identification of the "primary" factors (e.g., economic) behind social issues, challenges traditional scholastic boundaries among the social sciences. Fundamentally, Myrdal's notion of cumulative causation conflicts with the concept of "stable equilibrium" (central to most social sciences, particularly to economics)—that is, the self-stabilization properties of the social system, whereby a disturbance to it will trigger a reaction directed toward restoring a new state of balance between forces. In *Economic Theory and Under-Developed Regions* (1957), Myrdal addressed the failure of neoclassical economic theory to account for the persistence and widening of spatial differences in economic development within and between countries. He ascribes these differences to cumulative processes, whereby regions or nations that gain an initial advantage maintain and expand it as they attract migration, capital, and trade to the detriment of development elsewhere, an idea that permeates the voluminous "nonformal" literature on "uneven development" of the 1960s and 1970s.

As discussed in the valuable surveys by Amitava Dutt (1989) and William Darity and Lewis Davis (2005), in the 1970s and 1980s cumulative causation was incorporated into formal models of "North-South" trade and growth and into models of the "structuralist" tradition that explicitly recognized structural and institutional asymmetries between industrial ("Northern") and developing ("Southern") countries. These models challenged the static neoclassical framework and captured explicitly, by means of dynamic analyses based on differential equations and phase diagrams, the role of history in the evolution of economic processes, resulting in unorthodox effects of trade and in cumulative processes of diverging growth and incomes between countries.

Cumulative causation is also central to the view of economic growth as a "learning process" (resulting from virtuous circles of specialization and technical progress) that emerged in the 1960s and 1970s (e.g., Arrow 1962). However, its assimilation into mainstream economic theory was hampered by the difficulty of modeling "increasing returns," on which it inherently relies. Inspired by Adam Smith (1723–1790) and Alfred Marshall (1842–1924), Young (1928) emphasized how increasing returns stem primarily from the process of the division of labor and specialization in production. In Young's virtuous circle, an expansion of the market deepens the division of labor, ensuing in cumulative increases in production efficiency and in market size. Nicholas Kaldor (1966) formalized this idea in his four-stage model of industrial development. In Paul Krugman's model (1981), increasing returns in manufacturing effect, via virtuous circles of capital accumulation and cost reductions, uneven patterns of industrialization. Increasing returns are crucial to the self-reinforcing cumulative nature of economic processes and became central to most of the "endogenous" growth literature (whereby growth is generated within the economy), pioneered by Paul Romer (1987), which accounts for persistent international inequality.

The "new" economic geography literature that emerged in the 1990s formalizes cumulative causation mechanisms that account for the uneven geographical distribution of economic activity. Regions or countries with similar underlying structures are shown to endogenously differentiate into a rich "core" and a poor "periphery," as production of manufactures concentrates where the market is larger, which in turn will occur where the concentration of manufactures is higher. In Krugman's seminal paper (1991), the tendency for firms and workers to cluster together as economic integration increases is driven by the interaction of labor migration across regions with increasing returns and transport costs. Larger markets attract more firms, which in turn attract more workers. The larger population eases competition in the labor market and thus attracts more firms.

In Anthony Venables's (1996) model, agglomeration of industry occurs via cumulative processes triggered by input-output linkages between "upstream" intermediate producers and "downstream" final-good firms. With increasing returns to scale, upstream firms have an incentive to concentrate where there is a large downstream industry to produce at a more efficient scale. This in turn will make it attractive to downstream firms to locate where there is a large upstream industry, as the cost of the intermediate goods will be lower there. These models, in which the market output depends on the initial conditions, offer a neat formalization of Myrdal's idea and capture the role of history in determining spatial differences in development, acknowledging how minor changes in the socioeconomic environment may result in large and self-perpetuating asymmetric geographical configurations.

SEE ALSO *American Dilemma; Backwash Effects; Differential Equations; Long Run; Myrdal, Gunnar; Phase Diagrams; Stockholm School; Taylor, Lance*

BIBLIOGRAPHY

Arrow, Kenneth J. 1962. The Economic Implications of Learning-by-Doing. *Review of Economic Studies* 29: 155–173.

Darity, William, and Lewis S. Davis. 2005. Growth, Trade, and Uneven Development. *Cambridge Journal of Economics* 29: 141–170.

Dutt, Amitava K. 1989. Uneven Development in Alternative Models of North-South Trade. *Eastern Economic Journal* 15: 91–106.

Kaldor, Nicholas. 1966. *Causes of the Slow Rate of Economic Growth of the United Kingdom: An Inaugural Lecture.* Cambridge, U.K.: Cambridge University Press.

Krugman, Paul. 1981. Trade, Accumulation, and Uneven Development. *Journal of Development Economics* 8: 149–61.

Krugman, Paul. 1991. Increasing Returns and Economic Geography. *Journal of Political Economy* 99: 484–499.

Myrdal, Gunnar. 1944. *An American Dilemma: The Negro Problem and Modern Democracy.* New York: Harper & Row.

Myrdal, Gunnar. 1957. *Economic Theory and Under-Developed Regions.* London: Gerald Duckworth.

Romer, Paul. 1987. Growth Based on Increasing Returns Due to Specialization. *American Economic Review Papers and Proceedings* 77: 56–72.

Venables, Anthony J. 1996. Equilibrium Locations of Vertically Linked Industries. *International Economic Review* 37: 341–359.

Young, Allyn. 1928. Increasing Returns and Economic Progress. *Economic Journal* 38: 527–542.

Catia Montagna

CUMULATIVE PROBABILITY DISTRIBUTION FUNCTION

SEE *Probability Distributions.*

CURRENCY

In economics and finance, *currency* refers to paper money and coins that represent the monetary base of a country. Currency is a form of money, which is used primarily as a medium of exchange. In international economics, the word *currency* is used mostly as a reference to foreign currency, the monetary unit of a foreign country.

Currency developed because of the need for a unit of exchange that would be portable, nonperishable, and easily divisible. It appeared with a shift from commodity money to coins made out of precious metals. Currency further developed into *fiat money*, money that carries no intrinsic value, such as coins made out of nonprecious metals and banknotes, the paper money that is used in most countries today. In the form of fiat money, currency's value is based on the universal acceptance of the currency for payments. For a given level of a country's output, the more currency that is in circulation, the higher would be the level of prices in the country.

Many countries have their own national currency, such as the dollar in the United States. There are some countries, however, that do not have their own currency. Economists separate the latter into two groups: those that belong to a common currency area, and those that simply use foreign currency for transactions in their countries. An example of a common currency area is the European Monetary Union. The members of the European Monetary Union all use the same currency, the euro. Countries and regions that use foreign currency are Panama, Ecuador, and El Salvador, which use the U.S. dollar; Kosovo and Montenegro, which use the euro; and small countries and island nations that use the currencies of their closest neighbors or the country that had formerly governed them as a protectorate. Such economies are referred to as *dollarized*, even if the currency they use is not called "the dollar."

The amount of currency in circulation is determined by the monetary authority of the country and represents one of the instruments of the country's monetary policy. In the United States, the monetary authority is the Federal Reserve System. In the European Monetary Union, the European Central Bank, which includes representatives from all the member countries, determines the amount of currency in circulation. Dollarized countries cannot influence the amount of currency in circulation and therefore do not have an independent monetary policy.

Should each country have its own currency? This question, first analyzed in modern economics literature by Robert Mundell (1961), has been the subject of heated debate ever since. Mundell's theory suggests that two countries should have a common currency if monetary efficiency gain outweighs economic stability loss from having a common currency. This will more likely be the case if the two countries are closely integrated through trade, capital, and labor mobility. Many economists believe that the European Monetary Union is not an optimum currency area because the economies that represent it are too diverse and are not sufficiently integrated. On the other hand, most economists agree that the United States is an optimum currency area, and that it would be costly for each state to use its own currency. Some believe that the world can benefit from the introduction of the single global currency, but most economists think it is not a good idea because independent monetary policy is important to stabilize both real goods and asset markets in conjunction with fiscal policy.

SEE ALSO *Euro, The; Money; Quantity Theory of Money*

BIBLIOGRAPHY

Mundell, Robert. 1961. A Theory of Optimum Currency Area. *The American Economic Review* 51 (4): 657–665.

Single Global Currency Association. http://www.singleglobalcurrency.org/.

Galina Hale

CURRENCY APPRECIATION AND DEPRECIATION

In economics, the terms *currency appreciation* and *currency depreciation* describe the movements of the exchange rate induced by market fluctuations. If a country is fixing the exchange rate, official adjustments to the fixed exchange rate are called currency *revaluation* and *devaluation*. Currency appreciates when its value increases with respect to the value of another currency or a "basket" of other currencies. Currency depreciates when its value falls with respect to the value of another currency or a basket of other currencies.

These special terms have to be used because exchange rates can be expressed in different ways, so that using the words "rise" and "fall," or "increase" and "decrease," for changes in the exchange rate can be confusing. For example, if the exchange rate between the U.S. dollar and the euro is expressed in dollars per euro (e.g., 1.20 dollars per euro), an increase in the exchange rate (e.g., to 1.25 dollars per euro) means that the dollar depreciates with respect to the euro and the euro appreciates with respect to the dollar. In other words, the dollar becomes less valuable and the euro becomes more valuable. The same exchange rate can be expressed in euros per dollar (e.g., 0.83 euros per dollar). In this case, an increase in the exchange rate (e.g., to 0.9 euros per dollar) means that the dollar appreciates with respect to the euro and the euro depreciates with respect to the dollar.

In the short run, currency appreciations and depreciations are driven by changes in demand and supply for a currency in the foreign exchange market. The demand and supply of currency depend on a country's imports and exports, international financial transactions, speculations on the foreign exchange market, and, under "dirty float," government interventions in the foreign exchange market. In the long run, currency appreciations and depreciations are determined by the inflation rate and economic growth of the country.

Forecasting currency appreciations and depreciations turns out to be a big challenge for economic theorists. In a 1983 paper titled "Empirical Exchange Rate Models of the Seventies: Do They Fit Out of Sample?" Richard Meese and Kenneth Rogoff demonstrated that a simple statistical model of the random walk—which states that the best forecast of the exchange rate tomorrow is the exchange rate today—does a better job at forecasting the exchange rate than any of the economic models available at that time. In addition, economic researchers have shown that the exchange rate tends to be "disconnected" from the fundamentals, or the factors that usually affect the exchange rate in economic models. These findings are known as the Meese-Rogoff puzzle and the "exchange rate disconnect" puzzle, respectively. In a 2005 paper, "Exchange Rates and Fundamentals," Charles Engel and Kenneth West demonstrated that given the statistical properties of the fundamentals and the discount factor of the individuals (the weight they place on future consumption relative to today's consumption), it should be expected that exchange rate behavior is similar to a random walk.

In a 2002 paper, "Order Flow and Exchange Rate Dynamics," Charles Evans and Richard Lyons took another approach. They showed that using information on the demand and supply of foreign currency (the order flows by the banks participating in the foreign exchange market), it is possible to forecast currency appreciation and depreciation in the short run better than using the random walk.

Currency appreciation and depreciation affect all the international transactions of a country because they affect international relative prices. In international trade, currency appreciation makes a country's exports more expensive for the residents of other countries if exporters in that country can increase the prices at which they sell their goods to foreign customers. If the exporters cannot increase their sale prices due to competition, their profits fall because the cost of production, which is denominated in their domestic currency, rises relative to their revenues, which are denominated in the foreign currency. If the profits decline a lot, some firms will stop exporting, so that the volume of exports from a country experiencing currency appreciation will decline. The reverse is also true: Currency depreciation will make a country's exports more competitive, increase exporters' profits, and increase the volume of country's exports.

Similar mechanisms link currency appreciation and depreciation to a country's imports. If a currency appreciates, the country's residents will find imported goods inexpensive relative to goods produced domestically, and the volume of imports will increase. Likewise, if a currency depreciates, the country's residents will find that imported goods are very expensive, and they will prefer to switch to buying goods produced domestically, thus lowering the volume of imports. Such changes in trade pattern occur in response to the long-run changes in the exchange rate, and they develop slowly over time because international trade contracts are written well in advance.

Currency appreciation and depreciation also affect international asset trade and the value of the holdings of foreign assets. If a domestic currency depreciates, the value of that country's residents' foreign currency asset holdings increases (because foreign currencies become relatively more valuable), while the value of foreigners' holdings of that country's assets declines. These changes can be described as capital losses and gains due to changes in the exchange rate. In the beginning of the 2000s, the U.S. dollar experienced substantial depreciation. While the United States continued to borrow abroad, its total debt to foreigners did not increase, because dollar depreciation meant capital gains for the U.S. residents and capital losses for the foreigners, which offset new borrowing by U.S. residents. This effect is known in economic literature as a *valuation effect* of exchange rate changes. Cédric Tille, in his 2003 paper "The Impact of Exchange Rate Movements on U.S. Foreign Debt," calculated the exact contribution of the valuation effect to the international financial position of the United States.

When a country accumulates a large amount of foreign currency debt, a sharp depreciation of its currency can be very harmful. If firms' revenues or assets are denominated in their own currency while their debts or liabilities are denominated in foreign currency, the currency depreciation will lower the value of firms' assets relative to liabilities, sometimes so much that firms become bankrupt. Such an effect is known in the economic literature as the *balance sheet effect*. During the financial crises of the late 1990s, the negative balance sheet effects of currency depreciations outweighed their positive effects on exporters' profits. This experience exposed the importance of matching the currency composition of assets and liabilities.

SEE ALSO *Balance of Payments; Central Banks; Currency Depreciation; Currency Devaluation and Revaluation; Dirty Float; Exchange Rates; Greenspan, Alan; Hedging; Macroeconomics; Money; Mundell-Fleming Model; Purchasing Power Parity; Reserves, Foreign; Trade Surplus*

BIBLIOGRAPHY

Engel, Charles, and Kenneth D. West. 2005. Exchange Rates and Fundamentals. *Journal of Political Economy* 113: 485–517.

Evans, Martin D., and Richard K. Lyons. 2002. Order Flow and Exchange Rate Dynamics. *Journal of Political Economy* 110 (1): 170–180.

Meese, Richard, and Kenneth Rogoff. 1983. Empirical Exchange Rate Models of the Seventies: Do They Fit Out of Sample? *Journal of International Economics* 14: 3–24.

Tille, Cédric. 2003. The Impact of Exchange Rate Movements on U.S. Foreign Debt. *Current Issues in Economics and Finance* 9 (1): 1–7.

Galina Hale

CURRENCY DEVALUATION AND REVALUATION

In economics, the terms *currency devaluation* and *currency revaluation* refer to large changes in the value of a country's currency relative to other currencies under a fixed exchange rate regime. These changes are made by the country's government or monetary authority. If a country has a floating exchange rate regime, or if the changes in the exchange rate under a fixed exchange rate regime are small (within the boundaries allowed by the government), the changes in the exchange rate induced by market fluctuations are referred to as currency *depreciation* and *appreciation*.

When a government conducts a devaluation, or devalues its currency, it changes the fixed exchange rate in a way that makes its currency worth less. When a government conducts a revaluation, or revalues its currency, it changes the fixed exchange rate in a way that makes its currency worth more. Since the exchange rates are usually bilateral, an increase in the value of one currency corresponds to a decline in the value of another currency. The convention is to use the term that describes the origin of the policy change. For example, during the period when the Bretton Woods system of currencies was in use (from 1944 to 1973, when many currencies were fixed to the U.S. dollar and the U.S. dollar was fixed to gold), there were cases of devaluations and revaluations. Figure 1 shows how, in November 1967, the British pound was devalued with respect to the U.S. dollar from 2.8 dollars per pound to 2.4 dollars per pound. The pound thus became less valuable with respect to the U.S. dollar, while the dollar became more valuable with respect to the pound. Such an episode is referred to as pound devaluation, rather than a dollar revaluation, because it was originated by the British government.

Before World War II (1939–1945), many countries were fixing their currency to gold. In order to improve the competitiveness of their exporters, the countries engaged in competitive "beggar-thy-neighbor" devaluations, meaning that one country would devalue its currency (with respect to gold and therefore with respect to all other currencies that were pegged to gold) and another would devalue in response. Such competitive devaluations were harmful for the international financial system overall. One reason behind the establishment of the Bretton Woods system and the International Monetary Fund (IMF) in July 1944 was to avoid such competitive depreciations in the future. The charter of the IMF directs policymakers to avoid "manipulating the exchange rates … to gain an unfair competitive advantage over other members."

Governments usually fix the exchange rates to allow for stable conditions in foreign trade or to fight high levels of inflation driven by high inflationary expectations. In the fixed exchange rate regime, the exchange rate is not determined by the markets. It can therefore deviate from the equilibrium exchange rate, creating disequilibrium in international prices. Thus, countries that fix their currency frequently find themselves in a situation in which their currency is either overvalued (is worth more than in equilibrium) or undervalued (is worth less than in equilibrium). In the case of overvalued currency, the government has to keep selling foreign exchange reserves in exchange

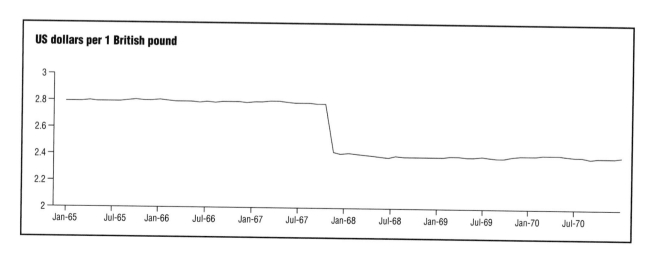

for domestic currency in order to maintain the value of domestic currency above equilibrium. When the reserves run out (or, as Paul Krugman showed in his 1979 article "A Model of Balance-of-Payments Crises," even before the reserves run out), the country has to either devalue the currency or let it float and depreciate while adjusting to its equilibrium exchange rate. Most countries with fixed exchange rate regimes either devalued their currency or switched to a floating exchange rate regime within less than five years after the initiation of the peg (Rose 2006).

The situation is different when the currency is undervalued. In order to keep the value of domestic currency below equilibrium, the government has to keep selling domestic currency in exchange for foreign currency. In this case, the government accumulates foreign exchange reserves and can always print more domestic currency. Thus, there is no well-defined limit on such foreign exchange interventions. Because the cases of undervalued currency are less common, they are less studied in economic literature than cases of overvalued currency.

The most discussed case of undervalued currency is the Chinese renminbi. China was fixing its exchange rate to be equal to 8.3 yuan (a unit of renminbi) per one U.S. dollar between January 1994 and July 2005, when China revalued the renminbi to 8.11 yuan per one U.S. dollar. After July 2005, the renminbi experienced a small controlled appreciation of about 3 percent per year. At the end of 2006, many economists believed that the renminbi remained undervalued, which explains an increasing amount of export from China (because, for the rest of the world, the goods produced in China seem inexpensive). However, since the equilibrium value of the currency is not observed in the fixed exchange rate regime, there was a disagreement as to how much revaluation would be needed to restore the equilibrium. At one extreme, Barry Eichengreen suggested that China allow its currency to float freely and adjust to its equilibrium level. At the other extreme, Michael Dooley and Peter Garber argued that there was no need for renminbi readjustment at all. There was a whole range of opinions in the middle as well, such as suggesting that China revalue its currency by 10 percent right away and let it float some time later, or that China allow a controlled appreciation of the currency.

As outlined by Andrew Rose in a 2006 discussion paper, most economies that are now open to international capital flows let their currencies float freely, meaning that devaluations and revaluations are slowly becoming a phenomenon of the past.

SEE ALSO *Central Banks; Currency; Currency Appreciation and Depreciation; Exchange Rates; International Monetary Fund; Money*

BIBLIOGRAPHY

Dooley, Michael, and Peter Garber. 2005. Is It 1958 or 1968? Three Notes on the Longevity of the Revived Bretton Woods System. *Brookings Papers on Economics Activity* 1: 147–187.

Eichengreen, Barry. 2005. Chinese Currency Controversies. *CEPR Discussion Paper 4375.* London: Centre for Economic Policy Research.

Krugman, Paul R. 1979. A Model of Balance-of-Payments Crises. *Journal of Money, Credit, and Banking.* 11 (3): 311–325.

Rose, Andrew K. 2006. A Stable International Monetary System Emerges: Bretton Woods, Reversed. *CEPR Discussion Paper 5854.* London: Centre for Economic Policy Research.

Galina Hale

CURRENT ACCOUNT

SEE *Balance of Trade; Trade Deficit; Trade Surplus.*

CURRENT POPULATION SURVEY

The Current Population Survey (CPS) is a survey of fifty thousand to sixty thousand households in the United States that has been conducted monthly since 1940 by the U.S. Census Bureau for the Bureau of Labor Statistics. The CPS has been used extensively by social science researchers to address a wide variety of questions, and it is the source used to compile numerous official statistics for the U.S. government.

The CPS emerged from a survey implemented in 1937, the Enumerative Check Census, that attempted to measure unemployment nationwide. One of the largest and most important changes to the survey occurred in 1954 when the number of primary sampling units increased more than threefold. In 1994, due to technological advances in computing, a redesign of the survey was instituted to obtain more accurate and comprehensive information.

THE STRUCTURE OF THE CPS

The CPS is administered to a sample representing the civilian noninstitutional population of the United States living in housing units. (For more on the material in this section, see U.S. Department of Labor 2002.) Each housing unit is in the sample for a total of eight months over a sixteen-month time horizon—four months in, eight months out, and four months in. This rotation cycle ensures that 75 percent of the sample overlaps from month to month and

50 percent overlaps from year to year. (These need not be the same households, since the CPS is a housing unit–based sample rather than a household-based sample.) The survey is administered mostly by phone interviews with occasional site visits. The information is available at the individual, family, and household level.

The core portion of the CPS contains numerous variables portraying the employment status of all members of the households over the age of sixteen, including items such as their status in the paid labor force, occupation, number of hours worked, and reasons for not working. In addition, information on such subjects as age, sex, race, ethnicity, and education is collected. The CPS also collects supplemental data from additional questions besides the core content of the survey. Areas of supplemental data include length of time spent in the same occupation, reasons for changing occupations, use of unemployment benefits or health insurance benefits, migration, citizenship status, birth history, childcare, school enrollment, food insecurity, and food expenditures. Of particular note is the March Supplement of the CPS, where extensive information on income and its sources is garnered along with other relevant demographic variables, including participation in assistance programs.

RESEARCH USES OF THE CPS

CPS data is used by researchers across a wide variety of research topics, including the following four areas. First, researchers and government policymakers use the CPS to assess the nation's economic situation and to obtain unemployment data and information regarding participation rates in the paid workforce. Specific areas examined include wage gaps among different races across different occupations, recent trends in economic status across races, and the hiring and firing experiences of different groups of people. Along the same lines, general income data is generated that is used to address such issues as income distribution among occupations, stability of earnings of males and females in marital relationships, and the relationship between stock market performance and retirement behavior.

Second, data from the CPS is used to study the well-being of families and children. The CPS aids in understanding the prevalence and severity of poverty, the determinants that lead to poverty, and the determinants of participation in government programs, such as the Food Stamp Program (e.g., Gundersen and Offutt 2005). One of the more visible reports is the annual report on income, poverty, and health insurance coverage in the United States (DeNavas-Walt et al. 2004, 2005).

Third, health issues and insurance coverage have been examined utilizing CPS data. Workplace policies to reduce smoking prevalence among workers have been investigated along with job attainment and the number of hours worked among ill individuals. Researchers have also studied the effect of Medicaid care provided by clinics and hospitals on insurance coverage, as well as gaps in health insurance coverage between different races and between men and women.

Fourth, CPS data has been used to explore issues in education. Such topics include the gap in early education between children of different income groups, the influence of maternal age on children's disability status and school progress, and factors influencing educational attainment of immigrant children, adolescents, and adults. Additionally, researchers have explored the relationship between access to home computers and improved educational outcomes.

SEE ALSO *National Family Health Surveys; National Longitudinal Survey of Youth; Panel Study of Income Dynamics; Surveys, Sample*

BIBLIOGRAPHY

DeNavas-Walt, Carmen, Bernadette D. Proctor, and Cheryl Hill Lee. 2005. *Income, Poverty, and Health Insurance Coverage in the United States: 2004*. U.S. Census Bureau Publication, P60-229. http://www.census.gov/prod/2005pubs/p60-229.pdf.

DeNavas-Walt, Carmen, Bernadette D. Proctor, and Robert J. Mills. 2004. *Income, Poverty, and Health Insurance Coverage in the United States: 2003*. U.S. Census Bureau Publication, P60-226. http://www.census.gov/prod/2004pubs/p60-226.pdf.

Gundersen, Craig, and Susan Offutt. 2005. Farm Poverty and Safety Nets. *American Journal of Agricultural Economics* 87 (4): 885–899.

U.S. Department of Labor, Bureau of Labor Statistics, and U.S Department of Commerce, U.S. Census Bureau. 2002. *Current Population Survey: Design and Methodology*. Technical Paper 63RV. http://www.bls.census.gov/cps/tp/tp63.htm.

Brandie M. Ward
Craig Gundersen

CURRICULUM

Curriculum theory, research, and reform have long been informed by a question posed by Herbert Spencer in 1861: "What knowledge is of most worth?" This question has continued to be examined and revised through significant educational and curricular reform movements. As a result, the competing interests of teachers, administrators, academicians, politicians, parents, and other stakeholders have led to a struggle for control of the American curriculum.

There are four major U.S. curricular initiatives that can be identified in the history of curriculum development and reform: (1) academic rationalism, (2) the social efficiency model, (3) progressive education, and 4) social reconstructionism. While each of these movements experienced varying degrees of support and criticism throughout the twentieth century, they more often overlapped in terms of development. For example, the academic rationalist orientation, with its roots during the Enlightenment, focused on the "Great Books" as the foundation of the Western cultural tradition. The goal of this approach, which was very popular at the turn of the century, was to develop the student's mind to tackle life's ultimate purpose, which was seen as a quest for truth, beauty, goodness, and liberty. Academic rationalism, however, continued to have strong support throughout the century. Beginning in the 1920s and continuing into the 1960s with the space revolution, the social efficiency model emphasized the efficient nature of the curriculum through operationally designed skills and knowledge. John Dewey's progressive education movement was especially popular during the first two decades of the twentieth century, and advocated a child-centered approach that allowed the curriculum to accommodate children's natural interests, and thus grow directly from the interests of the child. Lastly, the 1930s saw the advent of the social reconstructionist conception which posits that the curriculum should stress the needs of society over the needs of the individual, redress social injustice, and serve as an agent for social change (Schubert, 1986).

Although each curricular orientation has been vital in the formation of American schooling, the most recent, and most controversial, has been social reconstructionism. One of the most prominent proponents of social reconstructionism was the Brazilian scholar Paulo Freire (1921–1997). In his seminal work *Pedagogy of the Oppressed* (1970), Freire argued that only through "conscientization" can people liberate themselves from political and economic oppression. According to Freire, conscientization is the process by which the individual achieves a deep awareness of the social and cultural reality that shapes his or her life, and of the individual's ability to transform that reality (Freire 1970b).

A product of Freire's work is the concept of critical pedagogy, which emphasizes that education be viewed as a political, social, and cultural enterprise. In order to appreciate the contribution of critical pedagogy to curricular reform, it is imperative to understand the undeniable relationship between curriculum theory, the power of capital, and the state. For example, in light of the focus on the global marketplace that developed in the late twentieth century, capitalist ideology continuously encourages the consumption of commodities as a mechanism to continue the cycle of accumulation. Within educational settings, this is evident in the push toward integrating corporate management pedagogies within the classroom. As a result, academic success is almost exclusively defined in terms of "capital accumulation and the logic of the marketplace" (McLaren 2002, p. 34). Looking at this phenomenon through a Marxist lens, capitalism diminishes the individual to a commodity that can be bought and sold in the name of profit.

Western society, through the school curriculum, teaches that success can only be achieved through intelligence, hard work, and creativity. This type of pedagogical approach affects teachers, middle-class students, and working-class students. Reforms were initiated in the late twentieth century to provide "teacher-proof state-mandated curricula," which some see as reducing the role of the teacher to nothing more than a "semi-skilled, low-paid clerk" (McLaren 2002, p. 187). From this perspective, students who possess the dominant cultural assets (e.g., particular ways of talking, acting, and socializing) are rewarded, while those possessing cultural assets of the oppressed are devalued. As a result, the curriculum perpetuates the unjust system of inequality based on cultural capital. As Freire points out, however, this practice is not perpetuated by force (McNeil 1996). Instead, the dominant culture is able to exercise power over subordinate classes through hegemony. Thus, this domination is maintained through consensual social practices, social forms, and social structures.

Critical pedagogy also advocates an analysis of the "hidden curriculum," or the unintended outcomes of schooling that transmit messages to students through the "total physical and instructional environment" (McLaren 2002, p. 212). The curriculum is inextricably linked to the issue of power not only by culture but also by gender. For example, teachers often allow boys to dominate classroom conversations and offer them more academic praise than girls. While few teachers would admit to intentional sexist ideology, such interactions perpetuate sexist behavior. As a result, girls are often more hesitant to contribute to class discussions. Research also shows that girls are less likely to view themselves as competent in mathematics and science, and by the time they reach high school they are far less likely than boys to enroll in advanced math and science courses (McLaren 2002). Furthermore, girls are more likely to attribute failure to personal factors such as competence and ability.

As a consequence, men and women continue to be affected by the sexist nature of the hidden curriculum well into adulthood. For example, men tend to speak more often than women and frequently interrupt them in both professional and personal settings. It is also more difficult for women to be regarded as experts in their chosen occupations, and they are far less likely to obtain positions of power and authority.

Curriculum, from a critical theorist's standpoint, encourages teachers and students to foster democratic principles in order to question how the curriculum creates inequities between dominant and oppressed groups. Thus, the curriculum could help a society come to terms with its history, helping students understand the inequitable distribution of power and resources common to many nations. Encouraging students to value and articulate their own experiences of injustice are the first steps in creating a new social order.

To date, however, curricular reform in the U.S. that addresses inequity and injustice has been controversial and, at times, considered "dangerous" territory. However, to ignore these issues is to deny students a voice as active, reflective citizens. Just as the current educational system was "made," it can be "unmade" and "made over" (McLaren 2002). The first and most important step is to remove the fear of questioning the unquestionable and realize the role that the curriculum plays in political, social, and cultural life.

SEE ALSO *Education, USA; Pedagogy; Schooling in the USA*

BIBLIOGRAPHY

Aronowitz, Stanley, and Giroux, Henry. 1991. *Postmodern Education: Politics, Culture, and Social Criticism.* Minneapolis: University of Minnesota Press.

Counts, George S. 1978. *Dare the School Build a New Social Order?* Carbondale: Southern Illinois University Press (Orig. pub. 1932).

Freire, Paolo. 1970a. *Pedagogy of the Oppressed.* Trans. Myra Bergman Ramos. New York: Herder and Herder.

Freire, Paolo. 1970b. Cultural Action and Conscientization. *Harvard Educational Review.* 40 (3): 452–477.

Illich, Ivan. 1971. *Deschooling Society.* New York: Harper & Row.

Kliebard, Herbert. 1995. *The Struggle for the American Curriculum 1893–1958.* 2nd ed. New York: Routledge.

McLaren, Peter. 2002. *Life in Schools: An Introduction to Critical Pedagogy in the Foundations of Education.* 4th ed. Boston: Allyn & Bacon.

McNeil, John. 1996. *Curriculum: A Comprehensive Introduction.* 5th ed. New York: HarperCollins.

Pinar, William, William Reynolds, Patrick Slattery, and Peter Taubman. 1995. *Understanding Curriculum: An Introduction to the Study of Historical and Contemporary Curriculum Discourses.* New York: Peter Lang.

Schubert, William. 1986. *Curriculum: Perspective, Paradigm, and Possibility.* New York: Macmillan.

Spencer, Herbert. 1861. What Knowledge is of Most Worth? In *Education: Intellectual, Moral, and Physical.* New York: Appleton.

Shelby Gilbert

CURTIN, PHILIP
SEE *Slave Trade.*

CUSTER'S LAST STAND
SEE *Battle of the Little Big Horn.*

CUSTOMS
SEE *Tradition.*

CUSTOMS UNION

Economic integration is the process designed to eliminate discrimination among economic units located within different political boundaries. The traditional categories include Free Trade Area (FTA), Customs Union (CU), Common Market (CM), Economic Community (EC), and Complete Economic Integration (CEI). The various categories delineate the degree to which barriers to economic interaction are formally removed. In an FTA participating countries agree to remove barriers to trade among each other. In a CU the member countries agree not only to remove barriers to trade but also to set common levels of protection against all nonmember countries. Examples of a CU include the 1940s Benelux countries agreement (among Belgium, the Netherlands, and Luxembourg) and the Southern African Customs Union, signed in 1969 and still in existence. The CM agreement goes a step further than a CU agreement by removing barriers to movements of factors (essentially labor and capital) among members in addition to the CU components. An EC represents an additional step toward complete economic integration in that there is some degree of harmonization of national policies where community policies and institutions take precedence over national policies. An example of the latter is the Common Agricultural Policy of the European Economic Community.

A formal definition of a CU was provided by the General Agreement on Tariffs on Trade (GATT) in 1952:

> A customs union shall be understood to mean the substitution of a single customs territory for two or more customs territories, so that (i) duties and other restrictive regulations of commerce are eliminated with respect to substantially all the trade between the constituent territories of the union … and (ii) substantially the same duties and other regulations of commerce are applied by each of

the members of the union to the trade of territories not included in the union.

The implementation of a CU represents a reduction in protection between member countries, but it keeps in place discriminatory policies against nonmember countries. Although the former represents a clear movement toward less restricted trade and increased world welfare, the discrimination against nonmembers represents a potential loss in world trade and welfare. Thus whether a CU represents an overall movement toward less restricted trade and increased world welfare depends on the relative strength of these two forces, which are typically discussed as the static effects of economic integration under the categories of Trade Creation and Trade Diversion.

Trade Creation refers to the shift from higher-cost domestic producers to lower-cost partner producers. It is thus a shift from less efficient to more efficient production and is trade expanding. It also reflects a gain in country welfare. Trade Diversion refers to the shift from lower-cost nonmember suppliers to higher-cost partner suppliers, which takes place because of the tariff faced by nonmember products. It thus represents a loss in efficiency and a decrease in welfare. There are also accompanying consumption effects as consumers switch from domestic products to the now cheaper import products. Whether or not the CU represents a movement toward less restricted trade and enhanced welfare in the static sense depends on the relative size of these two effects. Whether the overall effect is positive or negative depends on a number of considerations, including the complementarity or competitiveness of the individual economies, the size of transportation costs between member countries, the height of tariffs before and after integration, the economic size of the member countries, and the elasticities of supply and demand within the member countries. Empirical estimates of the static effects of economic integration have generally been a net, though small, positive.

Economists tend to agree that the major benefits of economic integration occur because of the dynamic effects associated with increased economic interaction between member countries. These dynamic considerations include the benefits associated with a more competitive economic environment, which reduces the degree of monopoly power that possibly existed in the preintegration environment. In addition, access to larger markets within the integrated area may result in economies of scale in the expanding export sector as a result of both internal and external economies of scale. The growing and more profitable economic environment may also generate greater investment from both internal and external sources. Finally, there may also be dynamic benefits resulting from increased economic interaction with other countries in terms of increased access to technology, foreign institutions, and cultural factors.

SEE ALSO *Common Market, The; Economics, International; European Union; Free Trade; General Agreement on Tariffs and Trade; North American Free Trade Agreement; Quotas, Trade; Tariffs; Trade*

BIBLIOGRAPHY

Appleyard, Dennis R., Alfred J. Field Jr., and Steven L. Cobb. 2006. *International Economics.* 5th ed. New York: McGraw-Hill Irwin.

Balassa, Bela. 1961. *The Theory of Economic Integration.* Homewood, IL: R. D. Irwin.

Balassa, Bela. 1974. Trade Creation and Trade Diversion in the European Common Market: An Appraisal of the Evidence. *Manchester School of Economic and Social Studies* 42 (2): 93–135.

General Agreement on Tariffs and Trade. 1952. *Basic Instruments and Selected Documents.* Vol. 1, part 3, article 24, section 8(a). Geneva: World Trade Organization.

Meade, J. E. 1955. *The Theory of Customs Unions.* Amsterdam: North-Holland Publishing. Repr., Westport, CT: Greenwood, 1980.

Viner, Jacob. 1950. *The Customs Union Issue.* New York: Carnegie Endowment for International Peace. Repr., New York: Garland, 1983.

Alfred J. Field Jr.

CYBERSPACE

The term *cyberspace*, was originally a creation of late twentieth-century science fiction, and it has come to have two extended uses. In technical training contexts, it has become a useful handle for the notional "space" a person (or "user") enters when logging on to a computer. In a social science context, the term refers to new social spaces fostered by computer-enabled automated information and communication technologies (AICTs). Often, those using cyberspace in this way confer on it important, and even transformative, impacts on "real life" social relations. However, a tendency to assume transformation without demonstrating it means descriptions of cyberspace should be approached with caution.

The term was first used by William Gibson in his 1984 novel *Neuromancer.* By making an electronic connection, or "jacking in," to networked computers, a character in the novel entered into "cyberspace," an alternative and rather dark social universe whose interaction with real life drove the novel's plot. Shedding negative connotations, "navigating in cyberspace" became a helpful metaphor for the experiences of getting around a computer's virtual "desktop," navigating in and out of open software "windows," or projecting a personal "avatar" in an online virtual game or business communications environment.

As computers appeared in more and more human activities, technology talk was similarly cyberspaced. This use paralleled the late twentieth-century, popular use of the term *technology*, which was often equated linguistically with advanced technological forms and innovations. Thus, the realm of technology became coterminous with cyberspace.

It is now common in social science to critique such uses of technology, and thus to be suspicious of cybertalk. Since all cultures are substantially mediated by technologies of one sort or another, to equate the technological with cyberspace is ethnocentric. In the field of STS (science and technology studies), *technology* is used analytically to refer to any complex of artifacts, actors, and practices. Still, social scientists interested in the relationship between technology and social change (e.g., Hakken 1999) have found interactions between cyberspace and real life to be a convenient point at which to start analyzing the dynamics of hybrid (computered and noncomputered) social spaces.

The term *information technology* (IT) also became widely used in this period; it was used to refer to any system of practices involving devices for automatically storing and manipulating digitized information (e.g., computers). IT shifts the focus away from a particular computing machine to the broadening range of more general systems in which it becomes embedded. Particularly with the rise of the Internet and similar technologies of communication with embedded IT, scholars began to talk more about information and communication technologies (ICTs). What is distinctive about computer-mediated ICTs, and thus of cyberspace, is the extent to which information storage, manipulation, and communication take place according to protocols built into hardware and software.

Like other labels, such as *Information Age* or *Knowledge Society*, cyberspace tends to be equated with epochal social change. AICTs are presumed to play a seminal, causal role in globalization (see Friedman 2005). Such presumptions fit neatly into long traditions of theorizing, from Leninist Marxisms to postmodernisms, that privilege technologies as engines of social change. In the long, especially American version of technological determinism, the impact of any other social dynamics on technologies is largely ignored.

Ironically, the social correlates of automated ICTs, and the dynamics of cyberspace, become both more pronounced and harder to see. The attribution of transformational changes in social relations to the adoption of AICTs

is reinforced by, and reinforces, popular perceptions of massive, technology-induced social change. That AICTs automate processes (make them more rapid, more far-reaching, etc.) is what gives them their potential to transform. Yet in carrying out interactions among data, information, and knowledge "behind our backs," AICTs also make these social processes more opaque. The political and social theorist Langdon Winner points to a dazzled, computing-induced "technological somnambulism" that has made the age of cyberspace an era of "mythinformation" (Winner 1984).

Thus, there is a belief that cyberspace colonizes real life, that the new social relations engendered by computing first influence and then come to dominate what went before. Its popularity explains why social science attends to cybertalk, but to many observers it should do so as hypothesis, not as presumption. Social scientists need to explore the ways in which the social dynamics of computer-mediated spaces are influenced by, as well as influence, other social dynamics. Some, such as Frank Webster, have studied cyberspace in this even-handed empirical manner, and those with long ethnographic involvement in cyberspace tend to document social continuities between cyberspace and other social dynamics. Yet even this work too often complexifies its own interpretation, performing transformationalist rhetoric irrespective of—and often in contradiction to—its own empirical results.

In practice, university courses on the social impacts of computing outnumber those on the impacts of social processes on computing. The pervasive sense that transformative social change is inevitable, and therefore not worth thinking about too much, may follow functionally from the actions of powerful social forces that have an interest in promoting this view. For all these reasons, social research on cyberspace, like most popular musings on technology, needs to be approached with skepticism.

SEE ALSO *Technology; Technology, Adoption of*

BIBLIOGRAPHY

Bell, Daniel. 1973. *The Coming of Post-Industrial Society: A Venture in Social Forecasting.* New York: Basic Books.

Gibson, William. 1984. *Neuromancer.* New York: Ace Books.

Hakken David. 1999. *Cyborgs@Cyberspace?: An Ethnographer Looks to the Future.* New York: Routledge.

Webster, Frank. 2002. *Theories of the Information Society.* 2nd ed. London: Taylor & Francis.

Winner, Langdon. 1984. Mythinformation in the High Tech Era. *IEEE Spectrum* 21 (6): 90–96.

David Hakken

D

DAHL, ROBERT ALAN
1915–

Robert Dahl, Sterling Professor of Political Science, Emeritus, Yale University, and past president of the American Political Science Association (1967), is most widely known as the leading theorist of pluralist theory, the dominant theory in the study of U.S. politics for about ten years after the publication of his *Who Governs?* in 1961. Dahl was the chief originator of this pluralist theory of political power, which needs to be distinguished from other uses of the term *pluralism* in the social science literature. Three of these are: pluralism as the doctrine opposed to the emphasis of the idea of sovereignty of the state; pluralism as the description of societal ethnic diversity; and pluralism as a value preference for furthering ethnic and gender diversity in state policy. Dahl's pluralist theory of political power often has been mistakenly identified with pluralism as group theory, the idea that political groups are the chief explanatory variable in politics, often carrying the connotation that all groups in the United States are equally free to organize. Dahl explicitly denied this use of pluralism (1961, p. 4; 1982, pp. 207–209).

Dahl's pluralist theory of political power was developed in distinction to power elite theory, as put forth by C. Wright Mills and by Floyd Hunter. Dahl argued that a sufficient research design for the study of political power should incorporate the following elements: (1) the concept of power as gaining one's way through changing the behavior of others, and that *power* should not be equated with the resources used to gain power, such as money or prestige; (2) that power should be observed through con-struction of case studies of political action; (3) that there are different domains of political action, and power in one is not necessarily the same as power in another; (4) that one should define *power* in terms of the goals of the actors themselves, not in terms of some theoretical construct not understood by the actors.

In *Who Governs?* Dahl found that political power in the city of New Haven, Connecticut, was plural; that is, power in each of the different sectors of action was held by different people, except for the mayor, who was powerful in more than one area, but who was accountable to the voters through regular competitive elections. This pluralist theory of political power stated a general model for studying and interpreting political power, and as such, was readily applied in numerous studies of power in cities and towns, in legislatures, in federalist interactions, and even within the executive branches of various governments. Normally, pluralist studies of power in the United States found that power was dispersed within the institution studied.

Although it provided the dominant political science theory in the study of U.S. politics during the 1960s, Dahl's pluralist theory was soon challenged by a number of arguments. Peter Bachrach and Morton Baratz argued that Dahl provided no method for the study of power over the determination of the agenda for political issues. Theodore J. Lowi Jr. argued that the fragmentation of power in pluralist theory often amounted to the finding of "islands of power," in which unrepresentative coalitions of interest groups, administrative decision makers, and legislative committees controlled an area of public policy without countervailing power from the legislature as a whole. Mancur Olson Jr. propounded *The Logic of*

Collective Action (1965), which indicated that such dominance of particular public policy areas by unrepresentative coalitions is based on a fundamental logic of group formation. Carole Pateman (1970) and other political philosophers criticized *Who Governs?* as based on a constricted view of political participation, omitting the classical viewpoint of participation as public discussion of issues affecting the entire community.

Foreshadowing postmodernist theory, Henry Kariel (1969) argued that political participation sometimes involves the creation of new forms of political reality, an idea precluded by Dahl's empirical studies of individual action in the policy process. Others criticized Dahl for finding interest group domination of politics, leaving little role for policy initiatives organized by government, but this criticism confused Dahl's pluralism with group theory. In addition, Dahl and pluralist theorists were frequently criticized as expressing a favorable view of the political status quo, although in writings after 1970 Dahl clearly indicated he had no such intention. In the final analysis, Dahl's pluralist theory of political power made a major and lasting contribution to the study of power, in that many in succeeding generations of political scientists used most of Dahl's basic methods in the study of power, although they often interpreted research results differently, as exemplified by Lowi's theory of "interest-group liberalism"—the unaccountable "islands of power." After 1980 much political science work in the study of power in public policymaking, in urban politics, and in interest group activity can be described as *neopluralist*, as much of Dahl's outlook has been retained but methodological and interpretive corrections have been made for the problems found in Dahl's pluralism (for instance, allowing for concern for the political agenda and recognition that islands of power exist). These neopluralist researchers include John W. Kingdon (1984), Jack L. Walker Jr. (1991), Frank R. Baumgartner and Bryan D. Jones (1993), Jeffrey M. Berry (1999), and Virginia Gray and David Lowery (2004).

In his studies of democracy, after 1970 Dahl turned from the pluralist theory approach to other approaches based upon comparative political studies and his own egalitarian philosophy. Dahl sometimes used the term *polyarchy*, rule by the many, rather than the controversial *democracy*. At first he stressed the usefulness of comparative indicators of democracy, emphasizing stable electoral competition among political elites (*Polyarchy*, 1971). Realizing that democracy is based on more than regular competitive elections, Dahl broadened his approach to include diversity of political communications, economic development level of society, tolerance of political oppositions, and institutional legitimacy as an antidote to military coups. In addition, Dahl explored issues concerning the extent of political participation and the control of the political agenda, advances beyond his initial pluralist theory. Moreover, Dahl exhibited an egalitarian impulse by exploring contradictions between unequal distribution of wealth and democracy, and he examined possibilities for wider participation in business decision making as a means for controlling corporate power. Dahl's comparative indices of democracy contributed to the theory of democratic peace, the finding that democracies almost never in the last century engaged in war with one another. Comparative indices of democracy are now widely used as a basis for the evaluation of political regimes by political and economic-development decision makers. The conclusions of Dahl's thirty years of writing in the comparative and philosophical vein are summarized in nontechnical language in his *On Democracy* (1998).

Dahl is also known for exploring the links between the logical bases of U.S. governmental and political institutions and political outcomes. At first, in *Preface to Democratic Theory* (1956), Dahl argued that the logic of majority voting did not pose a critical threat to civil liberties and democracy, but later, in *How Democratic Is the American Constitution?* (2003), he became concerned about the effects of equal state representation in the Senate and of imbalanced campaign contributions on representative democracy.

SEE ALSO *Community Power Studies; Democracy; Pluralism; Political Science*

BIBLIOGRAPHY

Bachrach, Peter, and Morton Baratz. 1962. Two Faces of Power. *American Political Science Review* 56 (December): 947–952.

Baumgartner, Frank R., and Bryan D. Jones. 1993. *Agendas and Instability in American Politics*. Chicago: University of Chicago Press.

Berry, Jeffrey M. 1999. *The New Liberalism: The Rising Power of Citizen Groups*. Washington, DC: Brookings Institution.

Dahl, Robert A. 1956. *Preface to Democratic Theory*. Chicago: University of Chicago Press.

Dahl, Robert A. 1961. *Who Governs?* New Haven, CT: Yale University Press.

Dahl, Robert A. 1971. *Polyarchy*. New Haven, CT: Yale University Press.

Dahl, Robert A. 1982. *Dilemmas of Pluralist Democracy*. New Haven, CT: Yale University Press.

Dahl, Robert A. 1998. *On Democracy*. New Haven, CT: Yale University Press.

Dahl, Robert A. 2003. *How Democratic Is the American Constitution?* New Haven, CT: Yale University Press.

Gray, Virginia, and David Lowery. 2004. A Neopluralist Perspective on Research on Organized Interests. *Political Research Quarterly* 57: 163–175.

Hunter, Floyd. 1953. *Community Power Structure*. Chapel Hill: University of North Carolina Press.

Kariel, Henry S. 1969. *Open Systems: Arenas for Political Action.* Itasca, IL: F. E. Peacock.

Kingdon, John W. 1984. *Agendas, Alternatives, and Public Policies.* Boston: Little, Brown.

Lowi, Theodore J., Jr. 1979. *The End of Liberalism.* Rev. ed. New York: W. W. Norton.

McFarland, Andrew S. 2004. *Neopluralism.* Lawrence: University Press of Kansas.

Mills, C. Wright. 1956. *The Power Elite.* New York: Oxford University Press.

Olson, Mancur, Jr. 1965. *The Logic of Collective Action.* Cambridge, MA: Harvard University Press.

Pateman, Carole. 1970. *Participation and Democratic Theory.* Cambridge, U.K.: Cambridge University Press.

Walker, Jack L., Jr. 1991. *Mobilizing Interest Groups in America.* Ann Arbor: University of Michigan Press.

Andrew McFarland

DALITS

Historically, Hindu society in India has been characterized by a high degree of social stratification and institutional inequality governed by the caste system. The caste system as a societal order of social, economic, and religious governance for Hindus is based on the principle of inequality and unequal rights. The *dalits* or the *untouchables* (known as *scheduled castes* in government parlance) stand at the bottom of the caste hierarchy, and were historically denied equal rights to property, education, and business, as well as civil, cultural, and religious rights. They were also considered to be polluting, and they suffered from social and physical segregation and isolation. The result was a high level of deprivation and poverty.

SOCIAL MOVEMENTS

Past religious and cultural movements, such as Buddhism, opposed Brahmanic Hinduism and attempted to construct Indian society on principles of equality and fraternity. The dalits themselves initiated social movements against the denial of equal rights and oppression in the latter half of the nineteenth century and the first half of the twentieth century, notably the social-political movement of the Indian reformer and politician Bhimrao Ramji Ambedkar (1891–1956). During the 1970s and the 1980s, collective action emerged among the dalits in the form of the Dalit Panther movement in Maharashtra State and the Dalit Sangarsh Samiti in Karnataka, and the rise of such political parties as the Bahujan Samaj Party in the north, and similar efforts throughout the country. A strong nongovernmental organization movement also emerged, particularly in south India. In 1998 these groups

formed a coalition of civil society organizations and activists: the National Campaign on Dalit Human Rights. This coalition facilitated the establishment of an International Dalit Solidarity Network in Europe and the United States.

By 2006, dalit assertion has transcended national boundaries with the dalit diaspora organizing itself into the Ambedkar Mission Society, the Federation of Ambedkarite and Buddhist Organization, the Voice of Dalit International in the United Kingdom, Volunteers in Service to India's Oppressed and Neglected in the United States, and similar organizations in Canada. These organizations generate and disseminate literature about problems of the dalits, undertake advocacy, and use modern information and communication tools to generate discussion and build solidarity.

CONSTITUTIONAL PROVISIONS AND STRATEGIES OF SCHEDULE CASTE EMPOWERMENT

The constitution of India (1950) guarantees equality before the law (Article 14); prohibits discrimination on the basis of religion, race, caste, sex, or place of birth (Article 15); and abolished untouchability (Article 17). It further assigned responsibility to the state for the promotion of the educational and economic interests of the dalits (Article 46). On this basis, legal safeguards have been provided, including the Anti-Untouchability Act of 1955, and affirmative action policies in public employment, educational institutions, and the legislature, and other measures for the general economic empowerment of the dalit community. Government policies thus aim to overcome the multiple deprivations that dalits have inherited from exclusion in the past, and provide protection against exclusion and discrimination in the present.

Affirmative action policies are confined to the public sector. In the absence of such policies for the private sector, the state has developed programs for the economic, educational, and social empowerment of the dalits with a focus on improving the private ownership of fixed capital assets, human resource capabilities, and access to basic civil amenities, among other things.

CHANGE AND THE STATUS OF DALITS IN THE TWENTY-FIRST CENTURY

Government policies from 1950 to 2000 indicate both positive change and continuity in deprivation. There has indeed been some improvement. In 2000 about 17 percent of dalits cultivated land, and about 12 percent of dalits in rural areas and 28 percent in urban areas owned small businesses. Literacy rates among dalits have risen from 10.27 percent in 1960 to 54.69 percent in 2001.

The unemployment rate in rural areas has been reduced from 6.77 percent in 1978 to 5 percent in 2000, and from 7.37 percent to 5.20 percent in urban areas for the same periods. Lingering limitations in access to assets are the residue of a similar denial in the past.

Affirmative action policies have seen limited, yet positive, gains. The number of dalits employed in central government jobs increased in 2002, along with the number of dalit employees in public sector undertakings. The number of dalits employed in government banks also rose in 2004. In education, about a third of dalit students enrolled in universities and colleges were pursuing higher education in desirable programs because of reservation policies. As a consequence of such positive changes, poverty among dalits declined from 58 percent in 1984 to 37 percent in 2000 in rural areas, and from 56 percent in 1983 to 38 percent in 2000 in urban areas. Furthermore, caste discrimination against dalits in civil, cultural, and religious spheres has been reduced in some public spheres, although more so in urban than in rural areas.

Notwithstanding these gains, India's dalits continue to suffer in terms of absolute levels of deprivation and indicators of human development. About 70 percent of dalits inhabit rural areas; in 2000 about two-thirds of dalit rural households were landless or near landless (the figure is one-third for nondalits). Less than one-third of the dalit population had access to capital assets (40% for nondalits); 60 percent of dalits were dependent upon wage labor (25% for nondalits); and the dalit unemployment and literacy rate was 5.5 percent and 54.69 percent respectively, compared to 3 percent and 58 percent for nondalits. In addition, the prevalence of anemia among dalit women and mortality among children was high.

Various studies indicate that dalits continue to face discrimination in market and nonmarket transactions, in social services (education, health, and housing), and in political participation. Thus, there remains a long way to go before India's dalits can imagine a reasonable degree of dignity in their lives and livelihoods.

POLICY INITIATIVES

In 1992 the Indian government withdrew from some public spheres under an overall policy of liberalization. This development weakened the possibility of public sector employment for dalits. The government has made efforts to establish affirmative action policies that apply to the private sector; these efforts have seen response from India's corporate sector in 2006, but they have not yet taken any shape in terms of policy. However, other initiatives include reserved spots for dalits in private educational institutions, as well as scholarships for research and technical education. In addition, in 2005 India passed the Employment Guarantee Act, which ensures minimum employment for rural laborers. Such initiatives are likely to enhance the status of the dalits.

During 2006, the Indian government has taken new initiative by extending reservation to Other Backward Castes in public educational institutions and proposed to extend the same to private educational institutions. The reservation in private education institutions would also benefit the Schedule Castes. The progressive extensions of reservation to Other Backward Castes has widened and strengthened the safeguards against the hierarchal discrimination faced by different sections of lower castes. This has encouraged solidarity among Scheduled Castes and Other Backward Castes.

SEE ALSO *Ambedkar, B. R.*

BIBLIOGRAPHY

Bailey, F. G. 1957. *Caste and the Economic Frontier: A Village in Highland Orissa.*. Manchester, U.K.: Manchester University Press.

Dumont, Louis. 1970. *Homo Hierarchicus: The Caste System and its Implications.* Trans. Mark Sainsbury. London: Weidenfeld & Nicolson. Rev. English ed. 1980. Trans. Mark Sainsbury, Louis Dumont, and Basia Gulati. Chicago: University of Chicago Press.

Ghurye, G. S. 1969. *Caste and Race in India.* 5th ed. Bombay: Popular Prakashan.

Kothari, Rajni, ed. 1970. *Caste in Indian Politics.* New Delhi: Orient Longman; New York: Gordon and Breach.

Omvedt, Gail. 2003. *Buddhism in India: Challenging Brahmanism and Caste.* Thousand Oaks, CA: Sage.

Shah, Ghanshyam, ed. 2001. *Dalit Identity and Politics.* Thousand Oaks, CA: Sage.

Shah, Ghanshyam, ed. 2002. *Social Movements and the State.* Thousand Oaks, CA: Sage.

Srinivas, M. N., ed. 1996. *Caste: Its Twentieth Century Avatar.* New Delhi and New York: Penguin.

Thorat, Sukhadeo. 1996. Policy and Economic Change: Emerging Situation of Scheduled Castes. In *Fourth World: Ideological Perspective and Developmental Prognoses*, ed. R. K. Nayak, 202–215. New Delhi: Manohar.

Thorat, Sukhadeo. 2004. Situation of Dalits Since Independence: Some Reflections. In *The Dalit Question: Reforms and Social Justice*, eds. Bibek Debroy and D. Shyam Babu, 5–15. New Delhi: Globus.

Thorat, Sukhadeo, with R. S. Deshpande. 1999. Caste and Labour Market Discrimination. *Indian Journal of Labour Economics* (conference issue) 42 (4): 25–35.

Thorat, Sukhadeo, Aryama, and Prashant Negi, eds. 2005. *Reservation and Private Sector: Quest for Equal Opportunity and Growth.* Jaipur, India: Rawat.

Sukhadeo Thorat

DANCE

Dance, or the human body making rhythmic patterns in time and space for a purpose transcending utility, has been approached by anthropologists as one aspect of human behavior inextricably bound up with all those aspects that constitute what we call culture. Early ethnographers attended to dance as an adjunct to ritual or as an accompaniment to leisure social activities. Contemporary scholars examine it as belonging to the more general category of embodied knowledge. Their scope extends to classical performance traditions, modern popular forms, and communally embedded traditional dance.

Throughout human history, dance has always elicited powerful responses—on one hand, it has been banned, feared, seen as a corrupting influence, criticized for its sexual nature, and anathema to those who privilege the mind; on the other, dance has been praised for its ability to entertain, viewed as the essential element in rituals of healing, transformation from one state to another, and thanksgiving, and as ordered movement, a symbol of a cosmic "great chain of being." Through its performance by the human body and its ability to elicit a kinesthetic response in performer and viewer alike, it becomes elemental. Its universality across cultures is equaled by the strength of human responses to it, in which there appears to be no neutral position. Anthropologist Maurice Bloch, in his influential 1974 article, argues for the language of song, dance, and music as a special form of assertion toward which no argument is possible. Whatever meanings are encoded in these forms, the listener or viewer may only agree or disagree. There is no dialogue possible.

The medium of dance, composed by individuals and embodied by other individuals, creates meanings that are polysemous and multivocalic. The choreographer of a piece or a ritual may have one message to convey, the performers other interpretations, and the audience yet other understandings. This quality compounds the difficulties faced by scholars who wish to understand how and why dance occupies the position it does in society. Dance can be viewed for its formal aspects, its meanings or content, or for the relationships it has to its larger social context. In the history of American anthropology, the last approach has been the most popular. The reasons for this have to do with an implicit hierarchy of ethnographic areas of inquiry with the arts being relegated to the least central to understanding society. Even within the arts, visual arts have always been favored, perhaps because they are easier to document, unlike performing arts, whose "products" are ephemeral. Secondly, dance is notoriously hard to observe, record, and analyze. A focus on who participates in dance and how it functions within society made dance seem like other social categories. Early descriptions paid minimal attention to form, preferring the safer ground of functional analysis.

Ironically, French anthropologist Marcel Mauss (1872–1950) had no such hesitation in exploring the body in motion. In his article "Body Techniques" (1934), he examined body actions in ordinary life, relating them to expectations about gender, about practice, and about habits of the body. His definition of techniques of the body—highly developed body actions that embody aspects of a given culture—was the foundation for Pierre Bourdieu's (1930–2002) *habitus,* a notion that has influenced much of contemporary social science.

American anthropologist Franz Boas (1858–1942) acknowledged dance as a universal human phenomenon and, in the case of the Kwakiutl of the northwest coast of North America, as an essential part of their culture, but he found the form of dance more difficult to describe than visual arts, house types, music, or kinship systems. He was one of the first, however, to use film to record dance. Although the first system for notating was published in 1588 (*Orchesographie* by Thoinot Arbeau), it would not be until the 1930s, when Hungarian dancer Rudolf von Laban (1879–1958) created a dance and movement notation based on universal and arbitrary symbols, that it was possible to make an adequate record of dance that might be a basis for formal analysis. Laban's system, *labanotation,* and its offshoot, *effort-shape notation,* revolutionized the way in which dance is described and preserved. While most dance ethnographers prefer their own shorthand systems, supplemented by film, for field research, these two notation systems prove invaluable for both structural analyses of dance as well as for permanent records. European folklorists and ethnomusicologists were much quicker than their American counterparts to document such formal aspects of dance as steps, choreography, movement patterns, and floor plans. They were also quicker to use labanotation and effort-shape in their work (Royce 1977).

Attention to the formal aspects of dance did not occur in the United States until dancers trained as anthropologists entered the field. Katherine Dunham (1909–2006), who worked in Haiti and the Caribbean, and Pearl Primus (1919–1994), who examined West African dance and its American forms, approached their subject as dancers and as anthropologists. As dancers, they were comfortable with the dance itself, settling it in their own bodies. As anthropologists, they documented its purpose in those societies they studied. Both women ultimately focused on theatrical performance as a way of bringing the richness of African diasporic cultures to the widest possible audience. Regarded as performers rather than as scholars, their important work was largely ignored.

Gertrude P. Kurath (1903–1992), a dancer with degrees in music, drama, and art history, was initially more successful. Invited by anthropologist Sol Tax (1907–1995) to write an article on dance ethnology for the first issue of *Current Anthropology,* Kurath defined and laid out the shape of research on dance within American anthropology. Sound research on dance, she wrote, could only be done by "dancers who have achieved the insight and point of view of the ethnologist, or by musicians and ethnologists with dance training" (Kurath 1960, p. 247). This, indeed, has been the pattern, with dance-trained anthropologists forming the majority of dance scholars. Kurath herself documented dance in cultures as widely separated as the American Southwest, Mexico, eastern and southern Europe, and ancient Mesoamerica, as well as Iroquois dance. Her most long-lasting contributions to the anthropology of dance have been her meticulous ethnographic description, and her development and use of a notation system easily learned and easily understood by readers. Kurath's superb monograph, *Music and Dance of the Tewa Pueblos* (written with Antonio Garcia, 1970) provided ethnographer Jill Sweet a foundation on which to trace the trajectory of Tewa dance. Sweet, with forty years of involvement with the Tewa, published a second edition of her book *Dances of the Tewa Pueblo Indians* in 2004. Most significantly, she included the voices of Tewa themselves, who reflect on the continuities and disjunctures of their dance.

In the late 1960s and 1970s, a small group of anthropologists elaborated different approaches to dance within anthropology. Adrienne Kaeppler used linguistic analysis to explore the structure of Tongan dance. Drid Williams argued for a linguistic approach based on transformational grammar. Judith Lynne Hanna, working initially with West African and African diasporic dance, employed communications theory as a way to examine dance. Joann Kealiinohomoku took the work of Boas and Melville Herskovits (1895–1963) in new directions, looking at dance holistically as performed by the biological, language-using, social, culturally embedded human being. Anya Peterson Royce weighed the merits of historic, comparative, symbolic, and structural approaches to dance as an aspect of human society. The early contributions of these scholars to the emergence of the anthropology of dance as a scientific field of inquiry is the subject of a 2005 volume, *Anthropologie de la Danse* (Anthropology of Dance). Its editors, Andrée Grau and Georgiana Wierre-Gore, included important European scholars whose work is both fundamental and provocative. These include Rodryk Lange, John Blacking, György Martin, Ernô Pesovár, Anca Giurchescu, and Egil Bakka.

Since the 1980s, dance scholars have kept pace with the discourse of anthropology as it has dealt with issues such as borders and boundaries, postcolonial societies,

exile and appropriation, gender, power and agency, the articulation of us and them, and not least, an embodied anthropology of the senses. The tango and the samba provided a multivocalic point of entry into matters of exile, identity, agency, and embodied memory and action for three anthropologists and their work: Barbara Browning's *Samba: Resistance in Motion* (1995), Marta Savigliano's *Tango and the Political Economy of Passion* (1995), and Julie Taylor's *Paper Tangos* (1998). All three authors capture what it means to be embodied in the dance, and communicate it in their writing. Browning writes of the way in which the dancing body communicates as a complex speaking of the body. Savigliano, an Argentine herself, describes the tango from the inside out in words that allow the reader not only to "see" the dance but also to "feel" it. Taylor, who lived in Argentina for more than twenty years, takes us beyond the observable steps into the meanings deep in the dancers' bodies, and does so in language that situates the reader in the tango itself. Taylor and Savigliano speak eloquently and powerfully to the issues of exile and appropriation, the recombination of old stereotypes with new territories, and introspection and memory in the face of political terror. These key themes in contemporary anthropology gain new significance from their embodied treatment.

Browning's important contribution is to speak of the agency in the body, especially the danced body. She writes, "the insistence of Brazilians to keep dancing is not a means of forgetting but rather a perseverance, an unrelenting attempt to intellectualize, theorize, understand a history and a present of social injustice" (Browning 1995, p. 167). The active, creative, and creating body in dance is the subject of studies by Susan Leigh Foster in her perceptive commentaries on theory, by Cynthia Novack (1947–1996), who examined contact improvisation and American culture, and by Kazuko Yamazaki, who describes changing Japanese notions about the gendered body and its implications for innovation in dance.

The nuanced complexities of cultural perceptions and the social manipulations of dance and embodied movement have been the focus of several recent studies. Two of those are Jennifer Nevile's *The Eloquent Body: Dance and Humanist Culture in Fifteenth-Century Italy* (2004) and Anne Décoret-Ahiha's *Les Danses Exotiques en France, 1880–1940* (2004). Nevile discusses the moral divide between the noble dances of the Italian court and the graceless dances of the peasants. Dancing masters, and the court humanists who were the arbiters of intellectual and moral engagement, molded their pupils' bodies into the ordered, virtuous symbols of nobility. The peasantry, in contrast, were divorced from any philosophical foundations of morality, their dances therefore reflecting that lack in their sensual formlessness (Nevile 2004, pp. 2–3).

Décoret-Ahiha contrasts nineteenth-century French popular dance with popular dance between 1900 and 1940. Both periods were fascinated with the "exotic," but how exotic was defined differed. Nineteenth-century exoticism in the form of world's fairs and ethnological exhibits found a welcome audience of people who flocked to see these "primitive" and strange peoples and customs. At the beginning of the twentieth century, exotic dance dominated the music hall scene and drawing rooms. This shifted as artists and companies from all over the world made their way to Paris. Sergei Diaghilev's (1872–1929) Ballets Russes, with its lush ballets on Oriental themes and works that evoked the Russian soul, was one such company. The author's interest lies in the discourses produced by these periods of fascination with the exotic and their impact on society and on the dance itself. Hers is a richly textured commentary that enriches our notion of the "exotic other."

Anthropology of dance has expanded its scope to include studies of form as well as meaning, Western and non-Western dance, historic and contemporary phenomena, classical forms as well as popular or traditional dance, comparative and cross-genre performance traditions, and such issues as aesthetics, virtuosity, and the relationship between creator, performer, and audience. These topics have allowed scholars to move beyond ethnographic description and surface meaning to the kind of theory-building that contributes to all those fields concerned with human thought and behavior. It builds, interestingly enough, upon the generalizations, comparisons, and theories about style and structure that Boas and Claude Lévi-Strauss developed in the visual arts and oral genres. The shifts within anthropology toward process rather than structure, and performance rather than competence, have led scholars to an acknowledgment of the body, embodiment, and embodied knowledge as essential ways of being and of knowing (Royce 2004).

The field has not only grown since Kurath's 1960 statement of its potential. One has only to compare Kaeppler's 1978 review of the field with Susan Reed's 1998 review. Since 1998, dance scholarship has expanded still further. Most importantly, the field has established itself within anthropology as a focus and method that contributes to general theories of culture and society. Whatever issues anthropologists define as worthy of examination, they must pay attention to their embodiment in the repertoire of individual actors and societies. Anthropologists will not be successful in that endeavor unless they acknowledge and practice embodied ways of knowing. They have recognized that dance and performance provide unique and subtle entryways to artistic expression. They have now begun to see the value of that lens for examining cultural understanding as a whole.

SEE ALSO *Anthropology; Boas, Franz; Culture; Entertainment Industry; Ethnography; Ethnology and Folklore; Ethnomusicology; Exoticism; Levi-Strauss, Claude*

BIBLIOGRAPHY

Bloch, Maurice. 1989. Symbols, Song, Dance, and Features of Articulation: Is Religion an Extreme Form of Traditional Authority? (1974). In *Ritual History and Power: Selected Papers in Anthropology*. 19-45 London: Athlone.

Browning, Barbara. 1995. *Samba: Resistance in Motion*. Bloomington: Indiana University Press.

Décoret-Ahiha, Anne. 2004. *Les Danses Exotiques en France, 1880–1940*. Pantin, France: Centre National de la Danse.

Grau, Andrée, and Georgiana Wierre-Gore, eds. 2005. *Anthropologie de la Danse: Genèse et Construction d'une Discipline*. Pantin, France: Centre National de la Danse.

Kaeppler, Adrienne. 1978. Dance in Anthropological Perspective. *Annual Review of Anthropology* 7: 31–49.

Kurath, Gertrude P. 1960. Panorama of Dance Ethnology. *Current Anthropology* 1 (3): 233–254.

Kurath, Gertrude P., and Antonio Garcia. 1970. *Music and Dance of the Tewa Pueblos*. Santa Fe: Museum of New Mexico Press.

Mauss, Marcel. 1979. Body Techniques (1934). In *Sociology and Psychology: Essays*, trans. Ben Brewster: 95-123. London: Routledge and Kegan Paul.

Nevile, Jennifer. 2004. *The Eloquent Body: Dance and Humanist Culture in Fifteenth-Century Italy*. Bloomington: Indiana University Press.

Reed, Susan A. 1998. The Politics and Poetics of Dance. *Annual Review of Anthropology* 57 (1): 503–532.

Royce, Anya Peterson. 1977. *The Anthropology of Dance*. Bloomington: Indiana University Press.

Royce, Anya Peterson. 2004. *Anthropology of the Performing Arts: Artistry, Virtuosity, and Interpretation in a Cross-Cultural Perspective*. Walnut Creek, CA: AltaMira Press.

Savigliano, Marta E. 1995. *Tango and the Political Economy of Passion*. Boulder, CO: Westview.

Sweet, Jill D. 2004. *Dances of the Tewa Pueblo Indians: Expressions of New Life*. 2nd ed. Santa Fe, NM: School of American Research Press.

Taylor, Julie 1998. *Paper Tangos*. Durham, NC: Duke University Press.

Anya Peterson Royce

DANTE ALIGHIERI

SEE *Purgatory.*

DARFUR

Darfur is the westernmost province of Sudan. A remote region whose concerns were long eclipsed by the civil war in South Sudan, Darfur became a center of international concern when a new civil war emerged there in 2003. The war was fought between nominally "black" ethnic groups and Arab militias called *Janjaweed* who, with support from the Sudanese government, killed and displaced hundreds of thousands of people. The violence had roots in economic underdevelopment and long-standing conflicts over land, but became far more destructive as external political influences grew and as conceptions of ethnic identity changed.

EVOLUTION OF THE CONFLICT

The name *Darfur* is Arabic, meaning "home of the Fur," one of the territory's largest tribes, but the province is home to at least three dozen distinct ethnic groups and many more subgroups. Today, nearly the entire population of Darfur is Muslim, owing to a policy of Islamization carried out in the fourteenth and fifteenth centuries when Darfur was an independent sultanate.

The terms *Arab* and *black* (or, alternatively, *African*) are broad categories used to identify the general affiliation of smaller tribes. The terms do not necessarily relate to physical appearance, and they have not always been decisive in determining political alignments. Arab groups are generally herders, whereas most (but not all) of the black tribes are sedentary farmers. These differing types of agriculture can produce disputes over land use, which in some cases leads to violence between tribes. Until the end of the twentieth century such conflicts in Darfur were generally contained and limited; although intergroup conflict has long been a feature of Darfur's history, it existed alongside considerable constructive economic and social relationships. Intermarriage was common between Arab and African tribes. Cattle herders and sedentary farmers traded for agricultural products such as grains and milk, as well as for grazing rights from farmers. Prosperous sedentary farmers sometimes invested in cattle, further blurring the distinctions between the groups.

Darfur contains rich agricultural land, but the entire region has been threatened by desertification since the 1970s. It experienced a famine in 1984. Dwindling fertile land combined with the lack of alternative economic development increased the potential for conflict at a time when forces from outside began to intervene. Also in the 1970s the Sudanese government began to dismantle the Native Administration system that had been set up by British colonial authorities, by which tribal chiefs were granted considerable autonomy and were often able to mediate intergroup conflict. In the late 1970s and early 1980s Chad's civil war increased the flow of arms in the region, and increased the interests of both Chadian and Libyan governments in the politics of Darfur. In the mid-1980s the Sudanese government began arming militias of Arab tribes in Darfur, fearing that the civil war in the south might spread. These external influences encouraged groups in Darfur to identify themselves as Arab or black and to make this the defining distinction in determining their political affiliation. Along with the influx of weapons from outside, this shift in ethnic identity helped to broaden conflicts that might otherwise have remained isolated.

From 1987 to 1989 a dispute over grazing land erupted between the Fur and some cattle-herding tribes in northern Darfur. The conflict quickly escalated. A new organization called the Arab Gathering emerged, organizing twenty-seven smaller tribes and asserting a platform of Arab supremacy. The Fur conflict also marked the first prominent appearance of Janjaweed fighters, bands of armed men riding horses and camels who attacked Fur villages. By its end, the Fur-Arab conflict killed around 3,000 people and destroyed hundreds of villages.

In the mid-1990s the Sudanese government split Darfur into separate administrative regions, a policy that effectively transferred control of much land to Arab-oriented tribes. In 1996 violence erupted again, this time between Arab militias and the non-Arab Masalit tribe. Masalit villages were burned by Janjaweed attacks, and more than 100,000 Masalit fled into Chad and other neighboring countries.

In the late 1990s Masalit exiles based in Egypt began publishing some of the first international warnings about accelerating ethnic cleansing in Darfur, alleging that attacks on the Masalit and other black groups were planned by Sudanese military leaders. These allegations were initially disregarded by western governments and major human rights organizations, who cast the Darfur conflict as local tribal violence or did not report on events there at all. The United Nations refugee agency refused protection to many asylum seekers from Darfur, arguing that either they were not credible or were not sufficiently at risk.

2003: DARFUR ERUPTS

After 2000 two major opposition organizations emerged among the black population. The first was the Justice and Equality Movement (JEM), which had an Islamist ideological orientation and maintained links with religious leaders who had split from the Sudanese government in the 1990s. Another group, the Sudanese Liberation Movement/Army (SLA) modeled itself on the southern Sudanese Peoples Liberation Movement/Army (SPLA), and offered a secular platform. In February 2003 the JEM and SLA launched successful military assaults on government targets in Darfur.

With the outbreak of full-fledged civil war, the government adopted what the International Crisis Group called a "scorched-earth" strategy to defeat the rebels. This relied heavily on the Janjaweed to attack the civilian populations that might support the rebellion, backed up by government air strikes. The Janjaweed attacks included mass killings, rapes, whippings, cattle theft, and the burning of hundreds of villages. A small force of 7,000 African Union soldiers entered Darfur in August 2004, but failed to stop the violence. Survivors fled, especially to Chad, and by late 2005 fighting began to cross the border. By the beginning of 2006 up to 2 million people were displaced from their homes and at least 180,000 were dead, most of them members of non-Arab/black tribes.

After 2003 debate grew about whether the Sudanese government and the Arab militias were guilty of genocide, a label that would increase the pressure for strong international intervention. But the complex origins of the violence and the fact that the worst abuses were committed by diffuse Janjaweed bands rather than by government troops fed the dispute about how the atrocities should be described.

On July 23, 2004, the U.S. Congress passed a resolution calling the Darfur conflict a genocide, a position later adopted by the Bush administration. On January 25, 2005 a UN Commission of Inquiry confirmed that "government forces and militias" may be guilty of crimes against humanity in waging a violent campaign to defeat the rebellion. But the commission concluded that the violence could not be labeled genocide because the government's intent was not to destroy any particular ethnic or racial group, the essential legal criteria for applying the genocide label.

On March 29, 2005, the UN Security Council asked the International Criminal Court to investigate the Darfur atrocities. In May 2006 the government of Sudan signed a peace accord with the SLA, but the JEM rejected the agreement, as did splinter factions of the SLA. The UN reported that violence in Darfur actually increased in the months after the accord; divisions among the rebels coupled with the difficulty in disarming Janjaweed militias posed major challenges to restoring order.

SEE ALSO *Civil Wars; Ethnic Conflict; Ethnicity; Genocide; Organization of African Unity (OAU); United Nations*

BIBLIOGRAPHY

Flint, Julie, and Alex De Waal. 2005. *Darfur: A Short History of a Long War*. London: Zed Books.

International Commission of Inquiry on Darfur. 2005. *Report of the International Commission of Inquiry on Darfur to the United Nations Secretary-General Pursuant to Security Council Resolution 1564 of 18 September 2004*. Geneva: United Nations.

International Crisis Group. 2004. *Darfur Rising: Sudan's New Crisis*. Nairobi and Brussels: Author.

Prunier, Gerard. 2005. *Darfur: The Ambiguous Genocide*. Ithaca, NY: Cornell University Press.

Salih, Dawud I., Muhammad A. Yahya, Abdul Hafiz O. Sharief, and Osman Abbakorah. 1999. The Hidden Slaughter and Ethnic Cleansing in Western Sudan: An Open Letter to the International Community. Cairo: Representatives of the Massaleit Community in Exile. http://www.damanga.org/1999hiddenslaughter.html.

Michael Kagan

DARROW, CLARENCE

SEE *Scopes Trial.*

DARWIN, CHARLES
1809–1882

Charles Robert Darwin is regarded as one of the greatest scientists who ever lived. He was the son of a wealthy provincial British doctor and entered into the study of medicine at Edinburgh University, but did not like it. He was then expected by his family to become a clergyman and graduated from Cambridge University. However, he was unenthused about pursuing a career in the church.

Fortunately for him, as well as the world of the biological sciences, he was offered an unpaid position assisting the captain of the British survey ship *Beagle*. From this little ship, Darwin spent the next five years exploring the natural world. His observations fostered a deep interest in biology and geology and motivated him to pursue the sciences as a career and eventually develop the theory of natural selection.

Charles Darwin's theory of evolution by natural selection is the only scientific explanation for the nature and variety of life on our planet. Moreover, if life in other parts of our galaxy is governed by the same natural laws that govern it here, then Darwin's logic also explains the verities of life in distant parts of our galaxy. However, it does not explain the origin of life itself. Darwin's theory leaves the very beginning of life—the formation of the first primitive organic molecules—to chemists, physicists, and maybe even theologians. This entry focuses on the logic of how natural selection shapes the tools that enable organisms to survive the challenges of their environment, on some misconceptions about the theory of evolution, and on how evolutionary theory can help us understand human behavior. Finally, it briefly mentions some of the scientific and political controversies associated with current evolutionary thinking. Those interested in the vast evidence for Darwin's theory should consult Mark Pagel's *Encyclopedia of Evolution* (2002).

DARWIN'S FINCHES AND THE LOGIC OF NATURAL SELECTION

The Galapagos Archipelago is a group of islands off the coast of Peru. Eons ago, a single species of finch landed on one of the islands. Because resources for survival and reproduction were limited, the finches began competing for them. Some finches migrated to other islands. Since the environments of the islands differed, various biological tools, such as the shape of the birds' beaks, differed in their effectiveness for dealing with these environments. Over time, fourteen species of finches evolved in the archipelago. Although the species vary in many ways, such as in size and coloration, differences in their beaks are particularly salient. The study of how the beaks of Galapagos finches contribute to survival and reproduction in the environments of the different islands has contributed greatly to the development of evolutionary theory (Weiner 1994).

Biological tools that contribute to an individual's survival and reproduction are called *adaptations*. An adaptation is a trait—an anatomical structure, physiological process, or behavior pattern—that contributes more to an individual's ability to survive, grow, or reproduce in comparison with alternate traits in the population. The large, powerful beak of the *Geospiza magnirostris* finch, useful for cracking large seeds, and the small, delicate beak of *Certhidea olivacea*, useful for extracting insects from the bark of trees, provide examples. *Natural selection* is the differential contribution of offspring to the next generation by genetically different members of a population, that is, the number of progeny of finches with genes for different beaks. The logic of natural selection can be explained in terms of assumptions and inferences that follow from the assumptions (Crawford 1998).

Assumption 1: The number of descendents of organisms in a population can grow exponentially.

Assumption 2: Resources enabling individuals in a population to exist can expand only arithmetically.

Assumption 3: The size of a population of individuals remains relatively stable across time.

Inference A: Competition for survival and reproduction ensues between individuals in a population.

Assumption 4: Individuals differ on traits that enable them to survive and reproduce.

Assumption 5: Some of the variation in these traits is genetic in origin.

Inference B: There is "differential contribution of offspring to the next generation by genetically different members of a population" (natural selection, by definition).

Inference C: Over many generations, "anatomical structures, physiological processes or behavior patterns that contribute more to individuals' ability to survive, grow and reproduce in comparison with alternate traits in the population" (adaptations, by definition) are created.

In summary, some feature of the environment—for example, the arrival of a new predator or a change in climate—poses a problem for organisms in a population. A solution (e.g., longer legs, thicker fur) aids survival and reproduction. The above assumptions and inferences explain how natural selection provides the solution. Preexisting adaptations, sometimes called *preadaptations*, provide both stepping stones and limits to the solutions natural selection can provide (Pagel 2002).

SOME MISCONCEPTIONS ABOUT DARWIN'S THEORY

Assumptions 1, 2, and 3 do not require nature to be "red in tooth and claw," as the poet Alfred Tennyson described it in *In Memoriam* (1850). A variety of subtle, and not so subtle, adaptations help individuals survive and reproduce. For example, animals in herds, such as wildebeests, may minimize the relative risk of predation by maneuvering to place other animals between themselves and predators (Hamilton 1971). Many types of camouflage coloration have evolved to protect organisms from their predators (Pagel 2002).

Although genes are involved in the development of all adaptations, assumptions 4 and 5 do not require that differences between individuals in evolved traits are genetically preprogrammed. Traits whose development is influenced by environmental factors are called *facultative traits*. Although male white-crowned sparrows, for example, cannot learn the song of another species, when they are nestlings they must hear an adult male of their own species sing and then themselves sing as juveniles if they are to sing a full song as adults (Konishi 1965).

Organisms do not evolve to act for the good of their species or the groups with which they live (Williams 1966). Since an organism's time and energy are limited, an organism that helped a member of its species or group would pay a reproductive cost (i.e., have fewer offspring) to do the helping. Hence, one of its competitors who did not help would leave more offspring, and its kind would spread through the group or species at the expense of the helpers. However, modern Darwinists have two methods of explaining the widespread helping behavior seen in nature. The first is the evolution of cooperation, in which both parties increase their reproductive success by helping the other (Trivers 1971). The second is through helping genetic kin (Hamilton 1964). Genetic kin, such as brothers and sisters, have copies of genes that are identical to those of common ancestors. If a brother inherited a gene from his mother that predisposes him to help his sister produce offspring, that helping gene can spread through the sister's offspring (his nieces and nephews) even though it reduces the brother's own reproductive success. The reason is that the sister has a fifty-fifty chance of inheriting the same helping gene from their mother and passing it on to her children, her brother's nieces and nephews.

Finally, natural selection does not have a goal. It is a purely mechanical process: traits that contribute more to survival and reproduction spread at the expense of traits that contribute less to survival and reproduction. Humans may evolve to be godlike creatures in the distant future. However, if this happens it will not be because natural selection had the goal of producing such beings.

EVOLUTIONARY PSYCHOLOGY

Evolutionary psychology uses the principles of natural selection to understand the origin and functioning of the cognitive and emotional adaptations that helped us deal with problems in our ancestral environment, known as the *environment of evolutionary adaptedness*, and how those mechanisms function now (Crawford and Anderson 1989).

Mating of close genetic relatives, for example, can be detrimental to reproduction and survival because it brings together deleterious recessive alleles, such as those causing some genetic diseases, in the offspring of such mates. Some Darwinists have argued that intimate rearing of brothers and sisters during their first few years, which reduces or eliminates adult sexual attraction between them, may reflect one mechanism humans evolved to avoid this problem (Westermarck 1891). This argument is supported by evidence from: (1) boys and girls reared in the same children's houses in Israeli kibbutzim, who rarely find each other sexually attractive as adults (Shepher 1983); (2) the reduced success of Chinese *shim pau* marriages, in which a genetically unrelated baby girl is

adopted into a family at birth with the expectation that she will marry a son of the family at their sexual maturity (Wolf 1995); and (3) sexual attraction between adult genetic siblings who were separated at birth (Bevc and Silverman 2000).

In the upper panel of Figure 1, the assumption is that brothers and sisters with genes enabling them to develop psychological mechanisms to avoid incest had greater lifetime reproductive success across evolutionary time than those who did not. The result is the ancestral genotype for the avoidance mental mechanism. The ancestral developmental environment—intimate rearing with genetic siblings—produced the genetically organized ancestral cognitive and emotional mechanism(s) (the ancestral phenotype) that reduced sexual attraction between adult childhood intimates. The ancestral immediate environment refers to encounters between sexually mature, ancestral, opposite-sex individuals. Finally, natural selection favored the genes that enabled the development of the avoidance mental mechanisms.

The bottom panel represents an infinitesimal segment of evolutionary time—a few years in an Israeli kibbutz or a Chinese *sim pau* marriage or the meeting of an adult brother and sister who were reared apart from birth. In all cases, the putative adaptation functions as it evolved to function with respect to childhood intimates. However, because it functions in novel environments, its decision processes produce consequences that do not serve its evolutionary purpose. That is, it does nothing to prevent the mating of the genetic siblings, while reducing the likelihood of the success of the kibbutz and *shim pau* marriages.

Finally, evolutionary psychology is concerned with: (1) the problems that our hominid and primate ancestors encountered in their daily lives; (2) the psychological adaptations that natural selection shaped to help deal with those problems; and (3) the way the resulting evolved adaptations function in current environments (Crawford and Anderson, 1989).

CONTROVERSIES ABOUT DARWINISM AND HUMAN BEHAVIOR

Because of the great explanatory potential of Darwin's theory of evolution, it engenders continuing scientific, religious, political, and social controversy. For example, if biologically based race, gender, and social class differences in anatomy, physiology, or behavior exist, then evolutionary theory helps explain their origin and significance (Degler 1991; Pagel 2002). However, the most salient issue—the one that underlies most controversies—is the degree of genetic specialization of evolved cognitive and emotional behavior–producing mechanisms. If natural selection produced primarily general-purpose psychologi-

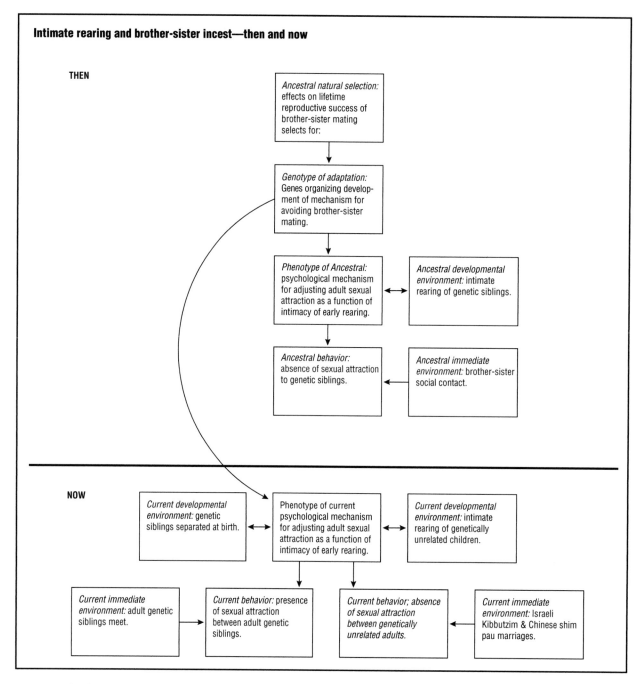

Intimate rearing and brother-sister incest—then and now

THEN

Ancestral natural selection: effects on lifetime reproductive success of brother-sister mating selects for:

Genotype of adaptation: Genes organizing development of mechanism for avoiding brother-sister mating.

Phenotype of Ancestral: psychological mechanism for adjusting adult sexual attraction as a function of intimacy of early rearing.

Ancestral developmental environment: intimate rearing of genetic siblings.

Ancestral behavior: absence of sexual attraction to genetic siblings.

Ancestral immediate environment: brother-sister social contact.

NOW

Current developmental environment: genetic siblings separated at birth.

Phenotype of current psychological mechanism for adjusting adult sexual attraction as a function of intimacy of early rearing.

Current developmental environment: intimate rearing of genetically unrelated children.

Current immediate environment: adult genetic siblings meet.

Current behavior: presence of sexual attraction between adult genetic siblings.

Current behavior; absence of sexual attraction between genetically unrelated adults.

Current immediate environment: Israeli Kibbutzim & Chinese shim pau marriages.

Figure 1: *This figure illustrates the evolutionary psychologist's perspective on how an evolved genotype in conjunction with the developmental and immediate environments can produce different behaviors in ancestral and current environments. Note that the genotype that prevented brother-sister incest in ancestral environments can produce either sexual attraction between genetic siblings or absence of sexual attraction between genetically unrelated individuals, depending on the conditions of rearing in the current environment. Because there is a clear distinction between ancestral and current environments, and between ancestral and current phenotypes (although not between ancestral and current genotypes), ancestral and current behavior may differ considerably. Although ancestral behavior contributed to ancestral fitness and, hence, to the evolution of the genotype, current behavior need not contribute to current fitness (modified from Figure 1 in Crawford and Salmon [2004], p.40).*

cal mechanisms, as many social anthropologists and social activists argue, then evolutionary theory is of limited use in understanding human behavior. However, if it pro-

duced genetically highly-specialized psychological mechanisms, as most evolutionary psychologists argue (Barkow et al. 1992), then it is invaluable for understanding

Outcomes of the debate about the role of ancestrally evolved innate genetic factors in the development of psychological mechanisms

Scientific Theories about the Degree of Innate Genetic Involvement in the Development of Specialized Psychological Mechanisms	Possible States of Nature: Degree of Genetic Involvement in Development of Specialized Behavior Producing Psychological Mechanisms	
	Low: Few Limitations on Social options	High: Many Limitations on Social Options
Small role for genetic involvement in development • The social science model of culture (Durkheim,1895/1982) • Tabula rasa – mind as a blank slate • Classic behaviorism • Cultural determinism • Post modernism • Social constructions • Cultural anthropology	**Valid Outcome: Implementation realizable** • Interchangeability of sex roles • Eliminating homosexuality through "education" works • Walden Two (Skinner, 1948/1976) is a harmonious society • Effective laws for regulating sexual/reproductive behavior • Russian communism workable • Gene therapy of no use • *Homosexuality considered abnormal/normal* • *State supported education* • *Socialized medicine*	**Invalid Outcome: implementation difficult – Social Constructionists' Risks** • Attempts to equalize sex roles fails • Eliminating homosexuality through "education" fails • Walden Two (Skinner,1948/1976) produces oppressive society • Ineffective laws for regulating sexual/reproductive behaviour • Russian communism fails • Gene therapy not tried • *Homosexuality considered abnormal/normal* • *State supported education* • *Socialized medicine*
Large role for genetic involvement in development • The evolutionary approach to culture (Barkow *et al.*,1992) • Classic ethology • Behavior genetics • Evolutionary psychology • Sociobiology • Human behavioral ecology • Evolutionary anthropology	**Invalid Outcome: Implementation difficult – Evolutionary Psychologists' Risks** • Inappropriate special schools for males/females/classes/races • Ineffective laws for regulating sexual/reproductive behavior • Communism not tried • American dream not tried • Gene/drug/physical therapy not tried • *Homosexual marriage accepted/rejected* • *State supported education* • *Social class exploitation* • *Socialized medicine*	**Valid Outcome: Implementation realizable** • Appropriate special schools for males/females/classes/races • Effective laws for regulating sexual/reproductive behavior • Communism leads to corruption • American dream for all fails • Gene/drug/physical psychotherapy useful • *Homosexual marriage accepted/rejected* • *State supported education* • *Social class exploitation* • *Socialized medicine*

Modified from p. 10 Crawford, C. B. (2004). Public Policy and Personal Decisions: The Evolutionary Context. Chapter One of Crawford, C. B. & Salmon, C. (Eds.). Evolutionary psychology, public policy, and personal decisions.

Table 1

human mind and behavior and in developing solutions to social problems.

Table 1 shows the consequences for social policy of these two perspectives. The assumption underlying the table is that although specialized peripheral, information-processing mechanisms produce behavior, these specialized mechanisms can be assumed to develop from either a low or a high degree of innate genetic specialization of development. The columns under "Possible States of Nature" describe the possible states of the ancestral genotype shown in Figure 1. The rows indicate the two approaches to developing scientific explanations. Note that several different scientific approaches are listed in each row. The four cells in the table enumerate the outcomes of pairs of possibilities, that is, of pairing a high degree of genetic specialization with the scientific belief in a low degree of genetic specialization. Two cells describe valid outcomes. The two cells labeled "Evolutionary Psychologists' Risk" and "Social Constructionists' Risk" describe invalid outcomes. Many social activists, such as feminists and social constructionists, assume that the consequences of either making an evolutionary psychologist's error or living in a society where ancestral evolved adaptations have an impact on current life, liberty, and happiness are so grave that they reject the possibility of the scientific explanations in the bottom row of the table.

Evolutionary psychologists reject this view. First, they worry about the suffering that could be caused by the social constructionist errors shown in Table 1. Second, they claim that accurate scientific knowledge about the human mind is crucial for developing more caring and harmonious societies. Third, they claim that natural selection has given the human species many evolved cognitive and emotional mechanisms, such as those underlying reciprocity and kinship, which if their functioning is understood can help us produce a better world. Fourth, they claim that evolutionary psychology is in fact an environmentalist discipline (Crawford and Anderson 1989)—the specialized psychological mechanisms that produce behavior, described in Figure 1, evolved to help humans deal with problems and stresses in their environments. Hence, understanding how these evolved cognitive and emotional mechanisms work can help us create better places to pursue life, liberty, and happiness.

SEE ALSO *Darwinism, Social; Natural Selection*

BIBLIOGRAPHY

Barkow, Jerome, Leda Cosmides, and John Tooby. 1992. *The Adapted Mind: Evolutionary Psychology and the Generation of Culture.* New York: Oxford University Press.

Bevc, Irene, and Irwin Silverman. 2000. Early Separation and Sibling Incest: A Test of the Revised Westermarck Theory. *Evolution and Human Behavior* 21: 151–161.

Crawford, Charles. 1998. The Theory of Evolution in the Study of Human Behavior: An Introduction and Overview. In *Handbook of Evolutionary Psychology: Ideas, Issues, and Applications*, eds. Charles Crawford and Dennis Krebs, 3-42. Mahwah, NJ: Erlbaum.

Crawford, Charles, and Catherine Salmon. 2004. The Essence of Evolutionary Psychology: An Introduction. In *Evolutionary Psychology, Public Policy, and Personal Decisions*, eds. Charles Crawford and Catherine Salmon, 23–50. Mahwah, NJ: Erlbaum.

Crawford, Charles, and Judith Anderson. 1989. Sociobiology: An Environmentalist Discipline? *American Psychologist* 44: 1449–1459.

Degler, Carl. 1991. *In Search of Human Nature: The Decline and Revival of Darwinism in American Social Thought.* New York: Oxford University Press.

Hamilton, William D. 1964. The Genetical Evolution of Social Behavior, I and II. *Journal of Theoretical Biology* 7: 1–52.

Hamilton, William D. 1971. Geometry of the Selfish Herd. *Journal of Theoretical Biology* 31: 295–311.

Konishi, M. 1965. The Role of Auditory Feedback in the Control of Vocalization in the White-Crowned Sparrow. *Zeitschrift für Tierpsychologie* 22: 770–783.

Pagel, Mark. 2002. *Encyclopedia of Evolution.* Oxford: Oxford University Press.

Shepher, Joseph. 1983. *Incest: A Biosocial View.* New York: Academic Press.

Trivers, Robert L. 1971. The Evolution of Reciprocal Altruism. *The Quarterly Review of Biology* 46: 35–57.

Weiner, Jonathan. 1994. *The Beak of the Finch: A Story of Evolution in our Time.* New York: Knopf.

Westermarck, Edward A. 1891. *The History of Human Marriage.* New York: Macmillan.

Williams, George C. 1966. *Adaptation and Natural Selection: A Critique of Some Current Evolutionary Thought.* Princeton, NJ: Princeton University Press.

Wolf, Arthur P. 1995. *Sexual Attraction and Childhood Association: A Chinese Brief for Edward Westermarck.* Stanford, CA: Stanford University Press.

Charles Crawford

DARWINISM, SOCIAL

Social Darwinism is a philosophical, economic, social, and scientific movement that claims that the way society functions is, and ought to be, a reflection of the methods and movements of biological evolution. The term is generally applied to thinkers from around 1850 to the end of the nineteenth century, although the term itself was not popularized until the publication of Richard Hofstadter's *Social Darwinism in American Thought* in 1944. Despite the title's reference to Charles Darwin (1809–1882), most scholars think that his fellow English evolutionist Herbert Spencer (1820–1903) was a far more influential figure in Britain and America.

Postulated links between society and biology are as old as evolutionary thinking. In the early eighteenth century, evolutionists such as Denis Diderot (1713–1784) saw biological evolution—the natural rise of organisms from primitive beginnings to sophisticated life-forms, including humans—reflected in the rise of societies. European evolutionists believed societies evolved in the same way organisms did, rising from the savages of Africa and other barbaric (i.e. non-European) parts of the world to the supremely civilized peoples of western Europe. At the end of the eighteenth century, later evolutionists, including Charles Darwin's grandfather Erasmus, likewise saw society as a mirror of what happens in the world of organisms, and like everyone else they happily conflated the way things are with the way things ought to be. Progress was the backbone of evolutionary thinking—from the simple to the complex, from the less desirable to the more desirable, from the monad to the man (in the language of the day)—and the way that things had been was taken as a guide to the way that things ought to be, then and in the future.

THE NINETEENTH CENTURY

In the middle of the nineteenth century, Herbert Spencer began his dizzying rise to fame and influence, casting a spell over Victorian Britain and much of the rest of the world that lasted until Queen Victoria died in 1901. Spencer was explicit in his belief that the patterns of society were reflected in the ways of biological development; indeed for him they were all part of one world-encompassing process, a process that was perpetually pushing upward, until the human species emerged at the top. Spencer was a liberal in the old-fashioned sense of disliking state interference and (particularly in his early years) he endorsed a strong program of laissez-faire, believing that the government should stay out of everything: the economy, education, welfare, even the provision of lighthouses to guide ships to harbor. This was, in Spencer's view, the only way to guarantee progress.

Superficially Spencer's worldview seemed like a logical application of Charles Darwin's theory of evolution, presented in his *On the Origin of Species* in 1859. There Darwin argued that an ongoing, bloody struggle for existence leads to natural selection, the motive force behind organic change, what Darwin called "descent with modification." Social Darwinism sees a direct corollary between struggle in the biological world and struggle in the social world, with winners moving upward to success and losers eliminated: losing organisms fail to reproduce, losing firms go bust, losing people starve.

In reality, things are a bit more complex. Darwin himself was reluctant to draw a parallel between biological and social evolution. He certainly did believe that certain peoples were superior to others: typically Victorian, he believed the English were superior to other Europeans, and Europeans were superior to everyone else; but he also approved strongly of moves to ameliorate the woes of the less successful. Spencer himself held views far more complex than his legend gives him credit for. In many respects, he saw struggle between peoples as stupid and not at all conducive to progress. He was strongly against militarism and presciently believed the end-of-the-century arms race between Britain and Germany, as each country built everbigger battle ships, to be absolute madness.

Spencer's followers were equally complex, especially those in America. Some, like sociologist William Graham Sumner (1840–1910), seem at times to be outdoing the master in prescribing brutal socioeconomic systems, but most held more sophisticated views. The great Scottishborn industrialist Andrew Carnegie (1835–1919) was an ardent Spencerian, but his understanding focused (perhaps unsurprisingly) more on celebrating the worth of the successful than the inadequacy of the unsuccessful. To this end, he became a major philanthropist, funding public libraries in America and elsewhere in the world. His hope was that these institutions would be places where the poor-but-gifted could, through reading and education, rise up in the social scale.

Victorian thinkers took a variety of different routes in the name of evolution. Darwin's fellow evolutionist Alfred Russel Wallace (1823–1913) was a lifelong socialist. Taking the opposite tack from Spencer, he used biology to justify a state welfare system. In his view the evolutionary struggle was between groups, not individuals; therefore people within the same society should band together and help each other. Russian prince and anarchist Pyotr Kropotkin (1842–1921) came from a tradition which saw a struggle less between people as individuals than between organisms and their environment. He therefore believed that biologically all organisms have a sense of caring, an urge to mutual aid, directed toward members of their own species; politically he translated this into anarchism.

THE TWENTIETH CENTURY

Social Darwinism fell out of fashion by the beginning of the twentieth century. A belief in progress, fundamental to the idea that biology was mirrored in the social world, had declined. It became apparent that despite advances in science and industry the world's ills—poverty, disease, violence—persisted. The First World War made the optimism of the nineteenth century seem almost obscene. Coupled with this, more and more people saw something fallacious about equating evolution with behavior. Thomas Henry Huxley (1825–1895), an English biologist and advocate of Darwin's theories, was eloquent on this subject, pointing out that what is moral often requires us to deny our animal heritage and go in a direction contrary to our evolved inclinations.

Nevertheless the ideas of Social Darwinian persisted, if not by that or any other name, transformed to suit the biology and social demands of the twentieth century. Julian Huxley (1887–1975), Thomas Henry's grandson (and the older brother of Aldous, the novelist) believed that biology provides a guide to life showing that progress is a rule that runs through the world, from the living to the social and cultural. He had faith in the power of science and technology; arguing that true progress comes only when the state harnesses its energies and intelligence and uses them for the common good. He considered the Tennessee Valley Authority, which had brought power to millions of people, a paradigmatic example of progress in action.

There was a darker side to Social Darwinism. It has been implicated in the rise of National Socialism, and some think that evolutionary ideas, particularly as promoted by Darwin's great German champion Ernst Haeckel (1834–1919), were significant. There may be truth in this last claim. Certainly, passages in Hitler's *Mein Kampf* (1925) seem to be taken directly from popular accounts of Darwinism as applied to society in *On the Origin of Species*. But the history of German anti-

Semitism is too complex for a straight causal connection to be made. Apart from anything else, the Nazis hated the evolutionary idea that all humans are descended from monkeys and that biologically Aryans and Jews are not much different.

THE TWENTY-FIRST CENTURY

In the twenty-first century, Social Darwinism continues to influence public debate. Harvard entomologist and sociobiologist Edward O. Wilson has been a leader in arguing that biology must inform social policies. He believes that humans have evolved in a symbiotic relationship with other organisms, and that humans must cherish and promote biodiversity or die as a species. Linking Wilson strongly to the nineteenth century is a belief in progress, in both biology and society. For Wilson, the moral imperative to promote biodiversity flows from a belief that if humans become extinct, the highest life form on the planet will have vanished. He sees this in itself as a bad thing and a reason for action.

Throughout the centuries since its inception, Social Darwinism has meant different things to different people. Was it a good thing or a bad thing? As with most philosophies, that question has no simple answer. In the hands of some, Social Darwinism was a force for good, in other hands much less so. We can say that it was important as a social influence, and its underlying ideas persist today, although they often go by other names.

SEE ALSO *Aryans; Darwin, Charles; Hitler, Adolf; Nazism; Sociobiology; Spencer, Herbert*

BIBLIOGRAPHY

Bannister, Robert C. 1979. *Social Darwinism: Science and Myth in Anglo-American Social Thought.* Philadelphia: Temple University Press.

Hofstadter, Richard. 1944. *Social Darwinism in American Thought.* Philadelphia: University of Pennsylvania Press.

Richards, Robert J. 1987. *Darwin and the Emergence of Evolutionary Theories of Mind and Behavior.* Chicago: University of Chicago Press.

Ruse, Michael. 1996. *Monad to Man: The Concept of Progress in Evolutionary Biology.* Cambridge, MA: Harvard University Press.

Michael Ruse

DATA

The word *data* (singular, *datum*) is originally Latin for "things given or granted." Because of its humble and generic meaning, the term enjoys considerable latitude both in technical and common usage, for almost anything can be referred to as a "thing given or granted" (Cherry 1978). With reasonable approximation, four principal interpretations may be identified in the literature. The first three capture part of the nature of the concept and are discussed in the next section. The fourth is the most fundamental and satisfactory, so it is discussed separately in the subsequent section. Further clarifications about the nature of data are also introduced. A reminder about the social, legal, and ethical issues raised by the use of data concludes this entry.

THREE INTERPRETATIONS OF THE CONCEPT OF DATA

According to the *epistemic* (i.e., knowledge-oriented) interpretation, data are collections of *facts*. In this sense, data provide the basis for further reasoning—as when one speaks of data as the *givens* of a mathematical problem—or represent the basic *assumptions* or empirical *evidence* on which further evaluations can be based, as in a legal context. The limits of this interpretation are mainly two. First, it is overly restrictive in that it fails to explain, for example, processes such as *data compression* (any encoding of data that reduces the number of data units to represent some unencoded data; see Sayood [2006] for an introduction) or *data cryptography* (any procedure used to transform available data into data accessible only by their intended recipient; see Singh [1999] for an introduction), which may apply to facts only in a loosely metaphorical sense. Second, it trades one difficult concept (data) for an equally difficult one (facts), when actually facts are more easily understood as the outcome of data processing. For example, census data may establish a number of facts about the composition of a population.

According to the *informational* interpretation, data are *information*. In this sense, for example, *personal data* are equivalent to information about the corresponding individual. This interpretation is useful in order to make sense of expressions such as *data mining* (information gathering; see Han and Kamber [2001] for an introduction) or *data warehouse* (information repository). However, two major shortcomings show its partial inadequacy. First, although it is important to stress how information depends on data, it is common to understand the former in terms of the latter, not vice versa: information is meaningful and truthful data—for example, "paper is inflammable" (Floridi 2003). So one is left with the problem of understanding what data are in themselves. Second, not all data are informational in the ordinary sense in which information is equivalent to some content (e.g., a railway timetable) about a referent (the schedule of trains from Oxford to London). A music CD may contain gigabytes of data, but no information about anything (Floridi 2005).

According to the *computational* interpretation, data are collections (sets, strings, classes, clusters, etc.) of *binary elements* (digits, symbols, electrical signals, magnetic patterns, etc.) processed and transmitted electronically by technologies such as computers and cellular phones. This interpretation has several advantages. It explains why pictures, music files, or videos are also constituted by data. It is profitably related both to the informational and to the epistemic interpretation, since a binary format is increasingly often the only one in which experimental observations or raw facts may be available and further manipulated (collected, stored, processed, etc.) to generate information, for example, in the course of scientific investigations (von Baeyer 2003). Finally, it highlights the malleable nature of data and hence the possibility of their automatic processing (Pierce 1980). The main limit of this interpretation lies in the confusion between data and the format in which data may be encoded. Data need not be discrete (digital); data can also be analog (continuous). A CD and a vinyl record both contain music data. Binary digits are only the most recent and common incarnation of data.

Given these interpretations, it seems wise to exercise some flexibility and tolerance when using the concept of data in different contexts. On the other hand, it is interesting to note that the aforementioned interpretations all presuppose a more fundamental definition of data, to which we now turn.

THE DIAPHORIC INTERPRETATION OF DATA

A good way to uncover the most fundamental nature of data is by trying to understand what it means to erase, damage, or lose data. Imagine the page of a book encrypted or written in a language unknown to us. We have all the data, but we do not know the meaning, hence we have no information, facts, or evidence. Suppose the data are continuous pictograms. We still have all the data, but no binary bits. Let us now erase half of the pictograms. We may say that we have halved the data as well. If we continue in this process, when we are left with only one pictogram we might be tempted to say that data require, or may be identical with, some sort of representation. But now let us erase that last pictogram too. We are left with a white page, yet not without data. For the presence of a white page is still a datum, as long as there is a difference between the white page and the page on which something is written. Compare this to the common phenomenon of "silent assent": silence, or the lack of perceivable data, is as much a datum as the presence of some rumor, exactly like the zeros of a binary system. We shall

return to this point presently, but at the moment it is sufficient to grasp that a genuine, complete erasure of all data can be achieved only by the elimination of all possible differences. This clarifies why a datum is ultimately reducible to a lack of uniformity.

More formally, according to the *diaphoric interpretation* (*diaphora* is the Greek word for "difference"), the general definition of a datum is: (D) datum = x being distinct from y, where x and y are two uninterpreted variables and the domain is left open to further interpretation.

This definition can be applied at three levels: (1) Data as diaphora *de re*, that is, as a lack of uniformity in the world (Seife 2006). There is no specific name for such "data in the wild." A possible suggestion is to refer to such data as *dedomena* ("data" in Greek; note that the word *data* comes from the Latin translation of a work by Euclid entitled *Dedomena*). Dedomena are not to be confused with environmental data. Dedomena are pure data or proto-epistemic data—that is, data before they are interpreted. Dedomena can be posited as an external anchor of information, for dedomena are never accessed or elaborated independently of a level of abstraction. They can be reconstructed as requirements for any further analysis: they are not experienced but their presence is empirically inferred from (and required by) experience. Of course, no example can be provided, but data as dedomena are whatever lack of uniformity in the world is the source of (what looks to information systems like us as) data—for example, a red light against a dark background.

(2) Data as diaphora *de signo*, that is, as a lack of uniformity between (the perception of) at least two physical states of a system, such as a higher or lower charge in a battery, a variable electrical signal in a telephone conversation, or the dot and the dash in the Morse alphabet.

(3) Data as diaphora *de dicto*, that is, as a lack of uniformity between two symbols of a code—for example, the letters A and B in the Latin alphabet.

Depending on one's interpretation, dedomena in (1) may be either identical with, or what make possible, signals in (2), and signals in (2) are what make possible the coding of symbols in (3).

The dependence of information on the occurrence of well-structured data, and of data on the occurrence of differences (dedomena) variously implementable physically, explains why information can so easily be decoupled from its support. The actual *format, medium,* and *language* in which data (and hence information) are encoded are often irrelevant and hence disregardable. In particular, the same data may be analog or digital, printed on paper or viewed on a screen, in English or in some other language, expressed in words or pictures, or quantitative or qualitative.

Interpretations of the support-independence of data can vary radically, for the definition (D) above leaves underdetermined:

- the classification of the relata (taxonomic neutrality);
- the logical type to which the relata belong (typological neutrality);
- the dependence of their semantics on a producer (genetic neutrality).

We shall now look at each form of neutrality in turn.

Taxonomic Neutrality A datum is usually classified as the entity exhibiting the anomaly, often because the latter is perceptually more conspicuous or less redundant than the background conditions. However, the relation of inequality is binary and symmetric. A white sheet of paper is not just the necessary background condition for the occurrence of a black dot as a datum; it is a constitutive part of the (black-dot-on-white-sheet) datum itself, together with the fundamental relation of inequality that couples it with the dot. Nothing is a datum in itself. Rather, being a datum is an external property. This view is summarized by the principle of taxonomic neutrality (TaN): a datum is a relational entity.

The slogan is "data are relata," but the definition of data as differences is neutral with respect to the identification of data with *specific* relata. In our example, one may refrain from identifying either the red light or the white background as the datum.

Typological Neutrality Five classifications of different types of data as relata are common. They are not mutually exclusive, and the same data may fit different classifications depending on the circumstances, the type of analysis conducted, and the level of abstraction adopted.

Primary data are the principal data stored in, for example, a database. Such data may be a simple array of numbers. They are the data an information-management system is generally designed to convey (in the form of information) to the end user. Normally, when speaking of data one implicitly assumes that *primary* data are what is in question. So, by default, the flashing red light of the low-battery indicator is assumed to be an instance of primary data conveying primary information.

Secondary data are the converse of primary data, constituted by their absence. Clearly, silence may be very informative. This is a peculiarity of data: their absence may also be informative.

Metadata are indications about the nature of some other (usually primary) data. Metadata describe properties such as location, format, updating, availability, usage restrictions, and so forth. Correspondingly, *metainformation* is information about the nature of information. The statement "'Rome is the capital of Italy' is encoded in English" is a simple example.

Operational data are data regarding the operations of the entire data system and the system's performance. Correspondingly, *operational information* is information about the dynamics of an information system. Suppose a car has a yellow light that, when flashing, indicates that the car-checking system is malfunctioning. The fact that the light is on may indicate that the low-battery indicator is not working properly, thus undermining the hypothesis that the battery is flat.

Derivative data can be extracted whenever data are used as indirect sources in a search for patterns, clues, or inferential evidence about something other than that directly addressed by the data themselves, as in comparative and quantitative analyses. Derivative data are used, for example, when one infers a person's whereabouts at a given time from her credit card data and the purchase of gasoline at a certain gas station.

Let us now return to the question of whether or not there can be dataless information. The definition of data given above (D) does not specify which types of relata are in question, only that data are a matter of a relation of difference. This typological neutrality is justified by the fact that, when the apparent absence of data is not reducible to the occurrence of negative primary data, what becomes available and qualifies as information is some further non-primary information *x* about *y* constituted by some non-primary data *z*. For example, if a database query provides an answer, it will provide at least a *negative* answer—for example, "no documents found." This datum conveys primary negative information. However, if the database provides no answer, either it fails to provide any data at all, in which case no specific information is available (so the rule "no information without data" still applies) or it can provide some data to establish, for example, that it is running in a loop. Likewise, silence, this time as a reply to a question, could represent negative primary information such as implicit assent or denial, or it could carry nonprimary information—for example, about whether the person heard the question or about the level of noise in the room.

Genetic Neutrality Finally, let us consider the semantic nature of the data. How data can come to have an assigned meaning and function in a semiotic system in the first place is one of the hardest problems in semantics. Luckily, the question is not *how* but *whether* data constituting information as semantic content can be meaningful *independently* of an informee. The *genetic neutrality* (GeN) principle states that: GeN data can have a semantics *independently* of any informee.

Before the discovery of the Rosetta stone in 1799, ancient Egyptian hieroglyphics were already regarded as information, even if their semantics was beyond the comprehension of any interpreter. The discovery of an interface between Greek and Egyptian did not affect the semantics of the hieroglyphics, but only its accessibility. This is the weak sense in which meaningful data may be embedded in information-carriers informee-independently. GeN supports the possibility of *information without an informed subject*, and it is to be distinguished from the stronger, realist thesis (supported, for example, by Dretske [1981]), according to which data could also have their own semantics independently of an intelligent *producer/informer*.

CONCLUSION

Much social research involves the study of logical relationships between sets of attributes (variables). Some of these variables are dependent; they represent the facts that a theory seeks to explain. Other variables are independent; they are the data on which the theory is developed. Thus, data are treated as factual elements that provide the foundation for any further theorizing. It follows that data observation, collection, and analysis are fundamental processes to elaborate a theory, and computational social science (high-performance computing, very large data storage systems, and software for fast and efficient data collection and analysis) has become an indispensable tool for the social scientist. This poses several challenges. Some are technical. For example, data may result from a variety of disparate sources (especially when collected through the Internet) whose reliability needs to be checked; data may be obtainable only through sophisticated processes of data mining and analysis whose accurate functioning needs to be under constant control; or the scale, complexity, and heterogeneous nature of the dataset may pose daunting difficulties, computationally, conceptually, and financially. Other challenges are intellectual, ethical, political, or indeed social. Some of the main issues that determine the initial possibility and final value of social research include quality control (e.g., timely, updated, and reliable data); availability (e.g., which and whose data are archived, and using what tools); accessibility (e.g., privacy issues and old codification systems or expensive fees that can make data practically inaccessible); centralization (e.g., economy of scale, potential synergies, the increased value of large databases); and political control (e.g., who exercises what power over which available datasets and their dissemination).

Data are the sap of any information system and any social research that relies on it. Their corruption, wanton destruction, unjustified concealment, or illegal or unethical use may easily undermine the basic processes on which not only scientific research but also the life of individuals and their complex societies depend (Brown and Duguid 2000). In light of the importance of data, their entire life cycle—from collection or generation through storage and manipulation to usage and possible erasure—is often protected, at different stages, by legal systems in various ways and in many different contexts. Examples include copyright and ownership legislation, patent systems, privacy-protection laws, fair-use agreements, regulations about the availability and accessibility of sensitive data, and so forth. The more societies develop into databased societies, the more concerned and careful they need to become about their very foundation. Unsurprisingly, since the 1980s, a new area of applied ethics, known as *information ethics* (Floridi 1999), has begun to address the challenging ethical issues raised by the new databased environment in which advanced societies grow.

SEE ALSO *Data, Pseudopanel; Methods, Qualitative; Methods, Quantitative*

BIBLIOGRAPHY

Brown, John S., and Paul Duguid. 2000. *The Social Life of Information*. Boston: Harvard Business School Press.

Cherry, Colin. 1978. *On Human Communication: A Review, a Survey, and a Criticism*. 3rd ed. Cambridge, MA: MIT Press.

Dretske, Fred I. 1981. *Knowledge and the Flow of Information*. Oxford, U.K.: Blackwell.

Floridi, Luciano. 1999. Information Ethics: On the Philosophical Foundations of Computer Ethics. *Ethics and Information Technology* 1 (1): 37–56.

Floridi, Luciano. 2003. Information. In *The Blackwell Guide to the Philosophy of Computing and Information*, ed. Luciano Floridi, 40–61. Oxford, U.K., and Malden, MA: Blackwell.

Floridi, Luciano. 2005. Is Information Meaningful Data? *Philosophy and Phenomenological Research* 70 (2): 351–370.

Han, Jiawei, and Micheline Kamber. 2001. *Data Mining: Concepts and Techniques*. San Francisco: Morgan Kaufmann.

Pierce, John R. 1980. *An Introduction to Information Theory: Symbols, Signals, & Noise*. 2nd ed. New York: Dover.

Sayood, Khalid. 2006. *Introduction to Data Compression*. 3rd ed. Amsterdam and London: Elsevier.

Seife, Charles. 2006. *Decoding the Universe: How the New Science of Information Is Explaining Everything in the Cosmos, from Our Brains to Black Holes*. New York: Viking.

Singh, Simon. 1999. *The Code Book: The Science of Secrecy from Ancient Egypt to Quantum Cryptography*. London: Fourth Estate.

Von Baeyer, Hans Christian. 2003. *Information: The New Language of Science*. London: Weidenfeld and Nicolson.

Luciano Floridi

DATA, LONGITUDINAL

To understand the characteristics and uses of *longitudinal data*, it is first important to understand what *cross-sectional data* are. Social science researchers have used cross-sectional data, which are drawn from surveys of samples of individuals or groups (aggregate data), to investigate the differences or differentiations among the individuals or groups. Unlike longitudinal data, cross-sectional data collect information only one time. As with cross-sectional data, longitudinal data may be used to understand differences among individuals. If repeated, the cross-sectional data could be considered a subset of longitudinal data. However, the major purpose of gathering longitudinal data is to investigate the changes within the samples over a period of time, from a few months to several decades (life-course studies). Researchers explore many different aspects of longitudinal data, including the distribution of values, temporal trends, anomalies, and the relationship between multiple responses and covariates in relation to time.

Researchers who make use of longitudinal data are often most interested in the changes within individuals while considering the changes of other relevant variables, such as ecological changes, situational factors, changes of social interaction over time, and/or developmental life stages. For example, in 1997 the Panel Study of Income Dynamics that updated the sample combinations (representative data for the current population in the United States) was intended to collect detailed information about economic and social disparities in child development on a national scale. A follow-up wave of the same subjects was conducted in 2002. As presented by Robert Mare and Margot Jackson in their 2004 article, researchers used these data to investigate how residential mobility and neighborhood change contribute to the overall socioeconomic variation in children's neighborhoods.

Criminologists use longitudinal data to survey trends in substance use (or other deviant behaviors) within a cohort or individual substance use (or other deviant behaviors) over time. Sociologists have used the National Longitudinal Youth Survey, a longitudinal study that presents self-reports of deviant and illegal behavior from the initial wave of 1976 to the 2003 wave (with data collection ongoing); it also presents other variables relevant to families, schools, and peer association, aiding sociologists in their investigation of the life cycles of families, immigration mobility, and their consequences. The political scientists Michael Delli Carpini and Scott Keeler (1991) used the U.S. censuses over a period of decades to determine whether contemporary U.S. citizens were better or more poorly informed about politics than were citizens of earlier generations. These studies are also referred to as *pseudopanel studies* because they try to investigate the changes over time in a certain population, while subjects are chosen independently each time. In other words, such studies are not the same as the narrowly defined *longitudinal studies*. Nevertheless, some researchers may view them as such. The social psychologists Howard Kaplan and Cheng-Hsien Lin (2000) investigated whether the link between mental health and deviance is reciprocal or unidirectional by repeatedly surveying the same subjects and, more important, whether both variables covariate over time. This study especially took advantage of the causal implications indicated by longitudinal data to resolve confusion over causal direction suggested by theories.

ADVANTAGES AND DISADVANTAGES

Longitudinal datasets provide several advantages over cross-sectional data. First, such datasets can track the changes among subjects over a short or a long period of time. Social scientists use such data to explore the potential trends underlying social mobility and unexpected trends in a society. Second, longitudinal datasets indicate the nature of covariates among variables over time to clarify their relations. In other words, controlling the previous measures of these variables helps social scientists determine the strength of relations among them. Third, the causal relations between variables can be verified through a clear time sequence of these variables. Researchers can examine many factors, such as deviant peer association and deviant behavior, with regard to their theoretical reciprocal relations only by using longitudinal data analysis. Finally, longitudinal data can indicate developmental (life stages) and historical trends; cross-sectional data can only partially indicate or describe developmental trends because the influences of confounding effects of historical trends cannot be taken into account in the analysis.

Nevertheless, longitudinal data are collected at high cost. First, because they require at least two waves, the cost of their collection is much higher than that of cross-sectional data in terms of both labor required and economic demands. Second, if the initial wave of a dataset was biased for any reason, the follow-ups will amplify the bias because of the repeated survey of the sampled subjects. Third, repeat respondents may develop a pattern of response attitudes to make every follow-up interview easier, which may lead to invalid responses (an effect known as panel conditioning). The developing pattern of interactions between an interviewer and an interviewee may also result in invalid responses. For example, an interviewer may learn that subjects would like to avoid certain sensitive questions, so, to avoid unpleasant confrontations, the interviewer may assume that the subject would give the same or a similar reply as in the earlier sessions of the interview.

Finally, if researchers use a type of longitudinal data collection known as panel study design, panel attrition because of death and/or withdrawal of some participants may bring unexpected bias to the data analyses. For example, studies that collect data about delinquent behavior among juveniles may lose some of the more serious delinquents in the first wave if they in fact become criminals, are arrested and imprisoned, or die from their criminal activities. Such first-wave respondents are less likely to hold a long-term job and thus will be difficult to locate for future interviews. It is not surprising that these subjects are quite different from the rest of the samples. Conclusions to be drawn from analyses of the longitudinal data are thus at risk.

TYPES OF LONGITUDINAL STUDIES

Longitudinal data have different forms. Trend studies use the same measurements to investigate samples of a society at intervals to see if the society has held certain attitudes or values over time. Such studies survey different sampled groups in every wave of data collection and then compare the changes. Research on political preferences in different decades often makes use of trend data. A potential problem in trend studies is the possibility of incomparable samples collected in different waves. For example, a common problem is that the sample interviewed in an early wave is less educated than the second wave because educational attainment tends to increase in subsequent generations. Since educational attainment is often closely related to other social and individual factors, the discrepancy in educational attainment between generations may make the data suggesting changing trends of certain social attitudes and values less credible.

Cohort data tighten the selection of samples by focusing on a cohort or a subpopulation in a society. Although it may sample different groups out of the whole population, every sampled group shares a common feature. They might have been born within a certain span of years or raised during a particular societal event, such as World War II or the civil rights movement. The analyses of cohort data provide information about how a generation's attitudes may change over time. It avoids the problem of generational differences that are compounded by trend studies.

Panel data collect information from the same group of subjects over time and are intended to examine the changes within individuals specifically. Whereas in general trend data and cohort data indicate overall changes in the society or a studied subgroup, panel studies attempt to examine how each subject's attitudes and behaviors changed individually over the studied years. The most serious problem in collecting panel data is sample attri-

tion, but this method provides the most comprehensive data on change. Researchers must be aware of the risk when drawing conclusions based on their studies.

Longitudinal data have grown in popularity among social scientists since the 1970s, becoming the mainstream in the 1990s. New, convenient statistical programs dealing with time-series analysis, latent growth curve models, hierarchical linear models, event history analysis, and structural equation models have greatly aided researchers using panel studies in clarifying relations among psychological and behavioral variables. Most likely, the scientific benefits of longitudinal data will make them the dominant data form.

SEE ALSO *Data; Data, Pseudopanel; Deviance; Methods, Quantitative; Methods, Survey; National Education Longitudinal Study; National Longitudinal Study of Adolescent Health; National Longitudinal Survey of Youth; Panel Studies; Panel Study of Income Dynamics; Research, Cross-Sectional; Research, Longitudinal; Survey; Surveys, Sample*

BIBLIOGRAPHY

Delli Carpini, Michael X., and Scott Keeter. 1991. Stability and Change in the U.S. Public's Knowledge of Politics. *Public Opinion Quarterly* 55 (4): 583–612.

Hofferth, Sandra, et al. 1997. *The Child Development Supplement to the Panel Study of Income Dynamics: 1997 User's Guide.* Panel Study of Income Dynamics, Institute for Social Research, University of Michigan, Ann Arbor. http://psidonline.isr.umich.edu/CDS/usergd.html.

Kaplan, Howard B., and Cheng-Hsien Lin. 2000. Deviant Identity as a Moderator of the Relation between Negative Self-Feelings and Deviant Behavior. *Journal of Early Adolescence* 20 (2): 150–177.

Mare, Robert, and Margot Jackson. 2004. Cross-sectional and Longitudinal Measurements of Neighborhood Experience and Their Effects on Children. California Center for Population Research. On-Line Working Paper Series. Paper CCPR-029-04. http://repositories.cdlib.org/ccpr/olwp/CCPR-029-04.

Menard, Scott, and Delbert S. Elliott. 1990. Longitudinal and Cross-sectional Data Collection and Analysis in the Study of Crime and Delinquency. *Justice Quarterly* 7 (1): 11–55.

Cheng-Hsien Lin

DATA, PSEUDOPANEL

Among all sociological research designs, longitudinal studies are the best choice if the purpose of research is to examine changes over time. Cross-sectional studies observe a phenomenon at only one point in time, and causal relationships between independent and dependent variables in cross-sectional studies are unclear because the time sequences cannot be established. There are three special types of longitudinal studies usually adopted by researchers: trend studies, cohort studies, and panel studies. Of them, panel studies are the most difficult for researchers who are collecting data because they have to interview the same sample of subjects repeatedly. Trend studies and cohort studies can provide changes of attitudes or behaviors of a population, but they cannot detect changes in a subject, only overall changes of the studied samples.

Panel studies can eliminate such a problem by examining the same subjects over time; typically researchers find that overall changes remain stable (the number of subjects who change their responses from A to B is balanced by those who change their responses from B to A). Although this is a great advantage of panel studies, it has its shortcomings. Panel studies are costly in both time and money (due to the high number of interviewers and the expenses associated with interviews and traveling), especially in a large-scale survey across several regions or states. Moreover panel studies often have a common problem: sample attrition. Researchers must revisit these subjects for a long-term research project, and subjects may fall out of contact. In order to retain most of the advantages and avoid the disadvantages of panel studies as well as the limitations researchers sometimes encounter in obtaining sufficient supports for panel studies, pseudopanel studies may be the second-best choice.

Pseudopanel studies may take different formats. In one a researcher asks respondents about past and current attitudes or behaviors and then treats the data as if they represented different time points. Another format uses simple logic to infer the time order of two or more variables. For example, it is more likely that people have tried cigarettes before cocaine because smoking is more socially acceptable than using cocaine; criminological studies have supported this conclusion. Researchers use established causal relationships from prior studies to assume similar relationships in their current studies when adopting cross-sectional study design.

Although the pseudopanel study avoids some of the problems or difficulties of the panel study, it is not recommended unless a panel study design is not accessible. Pseudopanel study is vulnerable to its own problems. For one, people's faulty memories are hard to detect and not uncommon for many reasons. Subjects may sincerely forget things that occurred in their pasts due to poor memory, or they may lie about their pasts for various reasons. In addition the use of logical inferences depends on the researchers' knowledge of the research topic. An expert might have a strong knowledgeable background to make

robust inferences, but still that might not rule out the potential errors of pseudopanel study design.

SEE ALSO *Census; Data, Longitudinal; Integrated Public Use Microdata Series; Methodology; Methods, Quantitative; Panel Studies; Research, Longitudinal*

BIBLIOGRAPHY

Babbie, Earl R. 2007. *The Practice of Social Research.* 11th ed. Belmont, CA: Wadsworth.

Hsiao, Cheng, Andrew Chesher, and Matthew Jackson. 2002. *Analysis of Panel Data.* 2nd ed. New York: Cambridge University Press.

Cheng-Hsien Lin

DATA ENVELOPMENT ANALYSIS

Data Envelopment Analysis (DEA) is a technique relying on mathematical programming methods for estimating various types of efficiency in production. First applied by Michael Farrell in 1957, the technique was popularized and named by Abraham Charnes, William W. Cooper, and Eduardo Rhodes in the late 1970s. As of 2004, more than 1,800 articles using DEA had been published (see Gattoufi et al. 2004).

Standard microeconomic theory of the firm describes a production set containing all feasible combinations of input quantities and output quantities for a given industry. Firms operating on the upper boundary of this set are technically efficient, while firms operating below the upper boundary are technically inefficient. Technically efficient firms may be allocatively inefficient if they do not use the optimal mix of inputs (determined by input prices) to produce the optimal mix of outputs (determined by output prices). Technically inefficient firms can feasibly reduce the quantities of inputs used without reducing output quantities, increase output quantities without increasing input quantities, or simultaneously reduce input quantities while increasing output quantities.

Various measures of efficiency have been defined, and, in each case, efficiency depends on the firm's location within the production set. Given observations on pairs of input and output quantities, DEA estimates the unknown production set using a convex set determined by the data. As a practical matter, DEA efficiency estimates are usually computed by solving a linear program.

The usefulness of DEA lies in its ability to estimate efficiency when multiple inputs are used to produce multiple outputs, without the need to specify distributions or functional forms. DEA is a fully nonparametric estimation method. For estimating technical efficiency, DEA does not require information about prices, making it especially useful in many public-policy applications, where economically meaningful prices often do not exist. These features contrast with parametric approaches, where distributions for random variables reflecting noise and inefficiency, as well as a functional form (e.g., translog) for the response function, must be specified. The nonparametric nature of DEA means that it is very flexible and can potentially be used to describe a wide variety of situations.

Unlike parametric approaches, however, DEA makes no allowance for noise or measurement error, which can severely distort DEA efficiency estimates. A number of outlier-detection techniques have been developed for use with DEA estimators (e.g., Wilson 1993; Simar 2003; Porembski et al. 2005). In addition, researchers have recently introduced new estimators that retain the nonparametric feature of DEA but are resistant to the effects of outliers and related problems.

Until recently, the statistical properties of DEA estimators remained unknown, and methods for making inferences about efficiency using DEA estimators were unavailable. In 2000, Léopold Simar and Paul Wilson provided a survey of new developments. In particular, the convergence rates of DEA estimators depend on the numbers of inputs and outputs, or the dimensionality of the production set. These rates worsen with increasing dimensionality. Consequently, to retain the same order of magnitude in estimation error, sample sizes must increase exponentially as dimensionality increases. Computationally intensive bootstrap methods provide the only practical approach to inference with DEA estimators. Due to the boundary of the production set, standard bootstrap methods must be modified by smoothing procedures to yield consistent inference.

SEE ALSO *Bootstrap Method; Production Frontier; Productivity*

BIBLIOGRAPHY

Charnes, Abraham, William W. Cooper, and Eduardo Rhodes. 1978. Measuring the Efficiency of Decision Making Units. *European Journal of Operational Research* 2: 429–444.

Charnes, Abraham, William W. Cooper, and Eduardo Rhodes. 1981. Evaluating Program and Managerial Efficiency: An Application of Data Envelopment Analysis to Program Follow Through. *Management Science* 27: 668–697.

Farrell, Michael J. 1957. The Measurement of Productive Efficiency. *Journal of the Royal Statistical Society* 120 (A): 253–281.

Gattoufi, Said, Muhittin Oral, and Arnold Reisman. 2004. Data Envelopment Analysis Literature: A Bibliography Update (1951–2001). *Socio-Economic Planning Sciences* 38: 159–229.

Porembski, Marcus, Kristina Breitenstein, and Paul Alpar. 2005. Visualizing Efficiency and Reference Relations in Data Envelopment Analysis with an Application to the Branches of a German Bank. *Journal of Productivity Analysis* 23: 203–221.

Simar, Léopold. 2003. Detecting Outliers in Frontier Models: A Simple Approach. *Journal of Productivity Analysis* 20 (3): 391–424.

Simar, Léopold, and Paul W. Wilson. 1998. Sensitivity Analysis of Efficiency Scores: How to Bootstrap in Nonparametric Frontier Models. *Management Science* 44 (1): 49–61.

Simar, Léopold, and Paul W. Wilson. 2000a. A General Methodology for Bootstrapping in Non-parametric Frontier Models. *Journal of Applied Statistics* 27 (6): 779–802.

Simar, Léopold, and Paul W. Wilson. 2000b. Statistical Inference in Nonparametric Frontier Models: The State of the Art. *Journal of Productivity Analysis* 13 (1): 49–78.

Wilson, Paul W. 1993. Detecting Outliers in Deterministic Nonparametric Frontier Models with Multiple Outputs. *Journal of Business and Economic Statistics* 11 (3): 319–323.

Paul W. Wilson

DAUGHTERS OF THE AMERICAN REVOLUTION

The Daughters of the American Revolution (DAR) is generally known as the oldest and largest women's lineal descent-based patriotic organization in the United States. Although the DAR, often regarded as an innocuous social club, has not attracted much attention from scholars until recently, it played a significant role in the formation of modern U.S. nationalism and national identity, particularly during the first half of the twentieth century.

The DAR was established in October 1890 by a group of upper- and middle-class women in Washington, D.C., after their failed bid to join in the founding of a similar ancestral organization, the Sons of the American Revolution (SAR), in the previous year. Although the DAR's membership was originally restricted to adult female (and white) descendents of those who had served in one capacity or another for the cause of American Independence, the group was quick to seek nationwide recognition and membership. The origins of this ancestral, patriotic organization are multifarious. During the late nineteenth century, increased immigration from South and East Europe, labor and agrarian conflicts, and American expansion overseas caused many people in the United States to question who they were. More broadly, the United States was at the time emerging as a modern nation state whose people were beginning to share a sense of American identity. The formation of national identity was facilitated by improvements in mass communication and transportation, the growth of a national market and public schooling, and the increasing power of the state over people's daily lives. It was against this backdrop that the DAR, despite its traditional hereditary exclusiveness, was simultaneously able to promote among the general public a rather modern, abstract vision of loyalty to the nation.

The constitution of the DAR mentioned three main objectives of the society: (1) to perpetuate the memory and spirit of the men and women who achieved American Independence; (2) to promote institutions of learning so that the young and old can develop the largest capacity for performing the duties of American Citizens; and (3) to cherish, maintain, and extend the institutions of American freedom and to foster true patriotism and love of country. Based on these ideals, the DAR engaged in various activities such as sponsoring historical restoration projects, distributing pamphlets to immigrants on how to become good American citizens, and publishing patriotic materials for schoolchildren.

The organizational motto of the DAR, "God, Home, and Country," represented its proven political conservatism on issues like Christianity, gender and family relations, and communism. Yet a closer analysis of the DAR and its activities reveals some seeming contradictions, such as tolerance toward immigrants (who were seen as objects of Americanization) coupled with (until recently) exclusivist policies on many racial matters. Thus the DAR is best seen not just as a typical conservative organization but as a mirror reflecting the differentiating and hierarchical nature of modern nationalism.

SEE ALSO *American Revolution; Americanism; Conservatism; Immigration; Inequality, Gender; Nationalism and Nationality; Nation-State; Patriotism; Racism; Symbols*

BIBLIOGRAPHY

Hunter, Ann Arnold. 1991. *A Century of Service: The Story of the DAR.* Washington, DC: National Society of the Daughters of the American Revolution.

McConnell, Stuart. 1996. Reading the Flag: A Reconsideration of the Patriotic Cults of the 1890s. In *Bonds of Affection: Americans Define Their Patriotism*, ed. John Bodnar. Princeton, NJ: Princeton University Press.

Medlicott, Carol. 2004. "Autograph of a Nation": The Daughters of the American Revolution and the National Old Trails Road, 1910–1927. *National Identities* 6 (3) 233–260.

Morgan, Francesca Constance. 1998. "Home and Country": Women, Nation, and the Daughters of the American Revolution, 1890–1939. PhD diss., New York: Columbia University.

Ken Chujo

DAVIS, ANGELA
1944–

Angela Davis established an early reputation as a scholar who linked race, class, and gender with activism. She became nationally known in 1970 when, after she was indicted for owning guns used in a courtroom shootout in California, she went underground. After a two-month search, the FBI arrested her in New York City. In those politically turbulent years, Davis became a highly visible prisoner, a symbol as an African American woman fighting for justice in prisons, and her imprisonment was protested across the nation and elsewhere in the world. She was acquitted of all charges in 1972.

Angela Davis was born in Birmingham, Alabama, on January 24, 1944; her father was a gas station owner, her mother a schoolteacher. Birmingham was a deeply racist city, referred to as Bombingham in the 1960s because of the many bombings of African American homes, businesses, and churches, but nevertheless even in the 1950s her mother and grandmother took her to protests. She attended segregated schools until high school, when she received a scholarship that allowed her to attend a private school in New York City. That experience provided further support for her developing political views, as she joined a socialist club and interacted with teachers with radical views. After high school she went to Brandeis University and attended the Sorbonne in Paris, where she developed a deeper understanding of political oppression in Algeria, which was under French control at the time, and began a political dialogue with Algerian students protesting French colonialism. While at Brandeis she studied with Herbert Marcuse, a radical philosopher. She graduated with honors from Brandeis with a major in French and then went to West Germany to study philosophy with Theodor Adorno, another radical intellectual. She went to Los Angeles in 1967 and began working with the Student Nonviolent Coordinating Committee, the Black Panther Party, and the Communist Party of the United States. She earned her master's degree in philosophy in 1969 after completing all requirements for her doctorate except the dissertation and began teaching philosophy at the University of California at Los Angeles (UCLA).

In 1970, UCLA fired Davis because of her membership in the Communist Party, but she succeeded in convincing the courts to reinstate her. Soon thereafter she began work on the "Soledad Brothers" cause on behalf of inmates at California's Soledad prison, which led to her indictment for gun ownership, her decision to go underground, and the FBI labeling her as a most wanted criminal. She returned to Germany to earn her doctorate at the Humboldt University of Berlin, and she taught at Stanford University, the Claremont Colleges, the

California College of Arts and Crafts, the San Francisco Art Institute, and eventually at San Francisco State University from 1979 to 1991. In 1980 and 1984 she ran for vice president for the Communist Party USA. In 1991 she became a faculty member at the University of California at Santa Cruz, and from 1995 to 1997, she held the prestigious appointment of University of California Presidential Chair. She continues to be a tenured full professor in the History of Consciousness program at the university.

Her contributions to political philosophy result from her persistent identification of resistance among groups too commonly assumed to be compliant with authority, such as African American women. She uses the work of Michel Foucault to analyze the intricacies of race and punishment in the United States and how incarceration has colonized many groups such as Native Americans forced onto reservations, acts that reaffirm white norms of not only behavior but also such apparent ideals as freedom. She argues that we should imagine and act toward a social order without prisons and de-incarceration, rather than having a social order that forces large numbers of people, including groups suffering from racism, to spend time in prison. She also argues that privatization of prisons is directly linked to racial, gender, and class oppression, providing profit for corporations while reifying the identity of people of color and the lower classes as problematic.

In her work both as a professor and as a political activist, Angela Davis has articulated the complex relationships among race, class, and gender that result in what she sees as pervasive elements of oppression. Her experience as a political prisoner, which captured international attention, combines with her scholarly work to create an intersection of personal commitment and scholarship, evidencing forms of feminism intertwined with race, ethnicity, and class in an international context. She continues her deep interest in the prison system and the difficult lives of inmates in increasingly privatized prisons in the United States.

SEE ALSO *Black Panthers; Communism; Imprisonment; Marcuse, Herbert; Marxism, Black; Philosophy, Political; Prisons; Protest; Radicalism; Revolution; Student Nonviolent Coordinating Committee*

BIBLIOGRAPHY

Aptheker, Bettina. 1999. *The Morning Breaks: The Trial of Angela Davis.* Ithaca, NY: Cornell University Press.

Davis, Angela Y. 1974. *Angela Davis: An Autobiography.* New York: Random House.

Davis, Angela Y. 2005. *Abolition Democracy: Beyond Empire, Prisons, and Torture, Interviews with Angela Y. Davis.* New York: Seven Stories Press.

Philo A. Hutcheson

DAVIS, JEFFERSON
1808–1889

Jefferson Davis will always be associated with the Confederate States of America. There is a certain irony in this association. Although he was president of the Confederacy, Davis was not the "fire-eater" that South Carolina secessionist Rhett Barnwell Butler was. He did not favor immediate secession upon Abraham Lincoln's election to the presidency and in fact served on the Committee of Thirteen that fashioned the Crittenden Compromise select committee that attempted to compromise the Union back together again during the lame-duck congressional session of 1860–1861. He was not known for his public defenses of slavery or states rights, as another reluctant secessionist, James Henry Hammond, was. Davis's major contribution to those debates was post hoc. He wrote *The Rise and Fall of the Confederate Government* (1881) well after the Civil War ended. As a prominent Mississippi planter, Davis had always supported slavery and states rights, but his association with those causes was forged during the war, not prior to it.

Prior to the war, Davis had a notable military and political career. He graduated from West Point in 1828 at the age of twenty. He served as an army officer until 1835, when he resigned his commission to marry his first wife and develop a plantation on land that his older brother had provided him. He also became active in Democratic politics. By the time he was elected to the House of Representatives in 1845, Davis was a wealthy cotton grower and slaveholder. At the outbreak of the Mexican War, he left Congress to serve as an officer in the Mississippi militia. Davis and his unit served with distinction at the Battle of Buena Vista. Upon his return to Mississippi in 1847, he was appointed and then elected to the United States Senate. In 1851 he resigned to unsuccessfully run for governor of Mississippi but he soon returned to Washington, D.C., as Franklin Pierce's secretary of war. After the Pierce administration left office, Davis was again elected to the Senate. His final Senate term ended in January 1861, when Mississippi seceded from the union.

Davis was the first and only president of the Confederate States of America. As president of the Confederacy, Davis faced a number of military and political crises. The opinions of historians vary as to how successfully he met those crises but they almost invariably compare him unfavorably to his Union counterpart. Yet there are a number of parallels. Both Lincoln and Davis oversaw the creation of strong states that heavily taxed and conscripted their male citizens to pursue their war efforts. Both Lincoln and Davis involved themselves in day-to-day military decisions and seemed plagued by inept generals. Both Lincoln and Davis ultimately decided to recruit African-American soldiers, though, in Davis's case, the war ended before the policy could be implemented.

At the conclusion of the war, Davis was among a number of Confederate leaders and generals who were imprisoned for treason. President Andrew Johnson eventually ordered all of them released except for Davis, whose case became entangled in impeachment politics. After Davis had been in military custody for two years, he finally appeared in civil court and was granted bail. The federal government eventually decided not to prosecute him. During the last twenty years of his life, Davis experienced financial difficulties and continuing ill health but his popularity in the former Confederate states never waned. By the time of his death, he had come to personify the South's "lost cause."

SEE ALSO *Confederate States of America; Cotton Industry; Lee, Robert E.; Lincoln, Abraham; Mexican-American War; Plantation; Selective Service; Slavery; Slavery Industry; U.S. Civil War*

BIBLIOGRAPHY

Cooper, William, Jr. 2000. *Jefferson Davis, American.* New York: Knopf.

Davis, Jefferson. [1881] 1971. *The Rise and Fall of the Confederate Government.* Gloucester, MA: Peter Smith.

David F. Ericson

DAVIS, KINGSLEY

SEE *Demographic Transition.*

DAWES, ROBYN
1936–

Robyn Mason Dawes is the Charles J. Queenan Professor and former chair at the department of Social and Decision Sciences at Carnegie Mellon University. He received his PhD in mathematical psychology from the University of Michigan in 1963. Dawes's work on human judgment and decision-making has influenced theory, research, and practice in diverse areas of psychology, including cognition, social behavior, and clinical assessment.

Inspired by Paul Meehl's demonstration that simple statistical models outperform clinical judgment, Dawes showed that improper (i.e., unit-weight or even random-weight) regression models perform better than individual clinicians do as long as each predictor variable has some validity. Application of a linear combination formula yields reliable predictions, assuming the model's user "knows how to add." In contrast, intuitive judgments remain vulnerable to random errors and systematic biases. Although statistical prediction models promise to make judgments about people easy, efficient, and accountable, many practitioners continue to reject them, a resistance that has led Dawes to explore human irrationality more broadly.

Dawes's analysis of human (ir)rationality is informed by Daniel Kahneman and Amos Tversky's work on heuristics and biases. Although judgmental heuristics often yield correct predictions, they guarantee that some contradictions will also occur. One such contradiction involves a structural availability bias that seduces people to make frequency judgments about events they could not have observed. For example, clinical psychologists sometimes claim that certain problem behaviors never stop on their own without therapy, when they have no information about behavior outside of the therapeutic context.

Dawes's focus on internal consistency as a criterion of rationality is narrower, but also more precise than competing definitions of rationality in terms of evolutionary or ecological adaptiveness. Dawes identifies the failure to make appropriate comparative judgments as a hallmark of irrationality. Often, people seek to understand surprising or distressing events retrospectively. For example, an airplane crash tends to stimulate reviews of other crashes in hopes that a cause can be found. To reach a valid conclusion, however, flights ending in crashes need to be compared with successful flights. The former analysis can only reveal what the flights of interest have in common, but it obscures crucial information about whether the rate of these common features is actually higher (or perhaps lower) than their rate in uneventful flights.

In Bayesian statistics, comparisons are expressed as likelihood ratios. For example, the probability of a plane crash given fog in the landing area is divided by the probability of a crash given the absence of fog. When multiplied with an event's base rate, the likelihood ratio yields coherent predictions. Although base rate neglect is also a facet of irrationality, Dawes is mainly concerned with the human tendency to neglect the ratio's denominator.

Nonetheless, Dawes is optimistic about people's capacity to think rationally. His analogy is learning how to swim. Novices try to keep their heads above water at all times, which makes drowning more likely. Once they learn to keep their faces in the water, and to come up for air only intermittently, they "get it."

Coherent judgments reduce the number of prediction errors, but they do not guarantee that outcomes will be desirable. Evil can be rational and banal, as a reading of the autobiography of Rudolf Höss, commandant at Auschwitz, suggests. If the premises are loathsome, rational deductions are sure to be loathsome too. After rejecting the classic view that irrationality stems necessarily from the intrusion of emotions, Dawes concludes, like Bertrand Russell had done before him, that sensitivity to affect can benefit social judgment.

The inability of pure rationality to provide socially desirable outcomes is most evident in social dilemmas. Here, freedom-from-contradiction rationality dictates that each individual defect from the group (e.g., by choosing to pollute) because no matter what others do, the individual is better off. Garrett Hardin famously derided appeals to conscience as a way of increasing social cooperation. Dawes and colleagues, however, showed that allowing people to form a sense of a shared group identity makes them more likely to exchange and honor promises of cooperation. However, identity-based cooperation is still irrational. In a group of promise-makers, an individual who believes that others will be true to their word may be even more tempted to defect.

Dawes's rigorous analyses have some surprising implications. He argues, for example, that when proper comparisons cannot be made, the only rational conclusion is to conclude nothing. In research, randomized trials provide the only rational basis for causal conclusions, which means that causal inferences from post-hoc statistical controls have no defensible basis, and that it would therefore be better not to conduct such studies. Like researchers, ordinary individuals must find out when to give up. People who fail to acknowledge uncertainties that cannot be overcome, end up overpredicting their future and persisting in costly behaviors that have no demonstrable benefits.

The impact of Dawes's work within psychology and across disciplinary boundaries is noteworthy because Dawes did not establish an academic school of thought. His legacy is a firm rejection of academic tribalism and grand theorizing. Instead, he champions rigorous research, careful analysis, and acceptance of the limits of that which can be known.

SEE ALSO *Bayesian Statistics; Cognition; Rationality; Social Cognition; Social Cognitive Map; Social Psychology*

BIBLIOGRAPHY

Dawes, Robyn. 1988. *Rational Choice in an Uncertain World: The Psychology of Judgment and Decision Making.* San Diego, CA: Harcourt, Brace, Jovanovich.

Dawes, Robyn. 1994. *House of Cards: Psychology and Psychotherapy Based on Myth.* New York: Free Press.

Dawes, Robyn. 2001. *Everyday Irrationality: How Pseudo-Scientists, Lunatics, and the Rest of Us Systematically Fail to Think Rationally.* Boulder, CO: Westview.

Dawes, Robyn, with Clyde H. Coombs and Amos Tversky. 1970. *Mathematical Psychology: An Elementary Introduction.* Englewood Cliffs, NJ: Prentice Hall.

Joachim I. Krueger

DAY CARE

Day care is a term that is commonly used in English-speaking North America. It refers to the care of young children by persons other than parents, guardians, or other close relatives (grandparents, for example) during a period when the children's parents are not able to provide care. Typically, day care is associated with care for a child while the parent(s) are employed or participating in an educational program away from the home. (Programs such as preschools, nurseries, and kindergartens are typically part-time and less commonly associated with employment-related care.)

Day care takes a wide variety of forms, from what are termed "informal" arrangements (such as care in the home of a neighbor or friend, with no regulation by government), to more "formal" arrangements (such as care in a purpose-built facility with licensing by one or more levels of government). In most parts of North America informal care is more common than formal care. The numbers of children in care settings, the ages of those children, the number of adults present, the nature of activities provided in these settings, and the training of care providers vary significantly.

The care of children while their parents are employed outside the home has a lengthy history in Europe and North America. One of the very first programs to develop as a specific response to parental employment was the Infant Schools established in New Lanark, Scotland, in 1816. Robert Owen's "Institution for the Formation of Character" was envisioned as much more than caregiving—it was an experiment in individual and broader societal development (Owen 1816). Infant schools moved beyond Scotland, and by the late 1820s similar programs could be found in North America, from Prince Edward Island to the Carolinas. However, by the late 1830s the infant school movement had died out in North America, an early victim of a complex interplay of ideologies, labor-force dynamics, class structures, immigration, social movements, and political positions that persist to the present. The public face of this dynamic was that "the mother's place is in the home with her children"—an argument heard from the pulpit in the 1830s and a continuing force in day care debates today (Pence 1989).

As the labor force expanded in the late twentieth century to include an ever higher proportion of women, including mothers, pressure mounted for governments, at both federal and state or provincial levels, to address the very significant and growing need for day care services through the establishment of funded and regulated systems of care. Adding to pressure felt by a changing labor force has been the strategic use of research on early childhood, including research on early brain development (Carnegie Task Force 1994; Shonkoff and Phillips 2000), to make a case for "high quality" care. These forces, augmented most recently by comparative studies of child care in other industrialized countries (OECD 2001, 2004), tipped the scales in Canada in early 2005, and the Liberal-led federal government committed $5 billion over five years toward the development of "high-quality developmental early learning and child care in collaboration with provinces and territories" (Governments of Canada and Manitoba 2005). When the Liberal government was defeated later that year, the new Conservative-led government withdrew support for the program. The sociopolitical dynamics of day care that arose in the early nineteenth century are still evident in the twenty-first century.

SEE ALSO *Child Development; Children*

BIBLIOGRAPHY

Carnegie Task Force on Meeting the Needs of Young Children. 1994. *Starting Points: Meeting the Needs of Our Youngest Children.* New York: Author.

Governments of Canada and Manitoba. 2005. Moving Forward: Governments of Canada and Manitoba Sign an Agreement on Early Learning and Child Care. http://www.gov.mb.ca/chc/press/top/2005/04/2005-04-29-07.

Organization for Economic Cooperation and Development. 2001. *Starting Strong: Early Childhood Education and Care.* Paris: Author.

Organization for Economic Cooperation and Development. 2004. The Country Note for Canada: Early Childhood Education and Care Policy. Paris: Author. http://www.oecd.org/dataoecd/42/34/33850725.pdf.

Owen, Robert. 1816. *A New View of Society.* London: J. M. Dent.

Pence, Alan R. 1989. In the Shadow of Mother-Care: Contexts for an Understanding of Child Day Care. *Canadian Psychology* 30 (2): 140–147.

Shonkoff, Jack P., and Phillips, Deborah. 2000. *From Neurons to Neighborhoods: The Science of Early Childhood Development.* Washington, DC: National Academies Press.

Alan R. Pence

DEALIGNMENT

The term *party dealignment* refers to the erosion of party loyalties in an electorate. In theory, dealignment can occur in any electoral system, but the term is applied mostly to American politics. As used, here, it refers to the decrease in the percentage of American adults that identify either as Democrats or Republicans, and the corresponding increase in the percentage that identify as independents.

PARTY IDENTIFICATION AND ITS MEASUREMENT

Party identification is an individual's psychological attachment to one or another of the major political parties. Those who identify as Democrats or Republicans are referred to as *party identifiers*, while those who decline to declare themselves either Democrats or Republicans are referred to as *independents*. Pollsters generally use a seven-point scale to measure party identification. The American National Election Studies (ANES) asks survey respondents, "Generally speaking, do you think of yourself as a Republican, Democrat, an independent, or what?" Next, Republican or Democratic identifiers are asked whether they identify strongly or not so strongly with their party, while independents are asked whether they lean toward one party or the other. Based on responses, pollsters then place respondents along a 7-point scale (1: Strong Democrat; 2: Weak Democrat; 3: Independent Democrat; 4: Independent Independent; 5: Independent Republican 6: Weak Republican; 7: Strong Republican).

DEALIGNMENT AND ITS CONSEQUENCES

In the American electorate, dealignment occurred primarily between the 1960s and 1990s. The political scientist Marjorie R. Hershey describes the process as follows:

> In the 1950s and early 1960s, many more Americans called themselves Democrats than independents or Republicans. The Democratic edge began to erode after 1964, but Republicans were not immediately able to capitalize on the Democrats' losses. In fact, the proportion of Republican identifiers declined from 1964 through the 1970s, even when a Republican president, Richard Nixon, was elected in 1968 and re-elected by a landslide in 1972. Democrats retained control of Congress, split-ticket voting was fairly common, the proportion of "pure independent" identifiers increased, and there was a steady stream of independent and third-party candidates. These changes in partisanship struck many scholars as resembling a *dealignment*, or decline in party loyalties. (2006, p. 133)

Party identification data indicate the trend well. The share of Americans identifying as either pure independents or independent "leaners" increased from 23 percent in 1952 to around 33 percent during the 1980s, to 40 percent in 2000, and remained nearly steady at 39 percent in 2004 (Hershey 2006, p. 325). However, further examination of the data also suggests that the share of Americans identifying as "pure" independents has decreased since the 1990s, while the share identifying as strong partisans, independent Democrats, and independent Republicans has also increased. Some political scientists argue that this indicates a renewed partisan polarization in the American electorate.

The consequences of dealignment include an increase in split-ticket voting (voting for different parties' candidates for different offices) and lower voter turnout. Party identification is the single most important influence on voting, and as fewer Americans identify with a major party, straight-ticket voting (for candidates of only one party) becomes less attractive and Americans are more likely to support different parties' candidates for different offices. Similarly, party identification simplifies voting decisions. But as more Americans identify as independents, they lose the easy voting cues that identification with a major party provides. Thus, more Americans must invest time and energy in researching and forming impressions of individual candidates, office by office. For some, the costs of this are too high, and voter turnout is likely to decline as a result.

DEALIGNMENT VERSUS REALIGNMENT

Party dealignment is a distinct concept from realignment. While *dealignment* means an erosion of party loyalties, *realignment* refers to an enduring shift in loyalty from one major party to the other among large numbers of voters. Further, this usually occurs in large enough numbers to create a new and lasting partisan majority. Thus, the 1896 election marked a partisan realignment that created a Republican majority in American politics that lasted until 1932. That year, perceived Republican inadequacies in addressing the Great Depression forged a Democratic majority in national politics that lasted until 1968.

In 1968, controversies over race relations, the Vietnam War, and the increasing importance of cultural issues contributed to partisan dealignment. During the 1970s and 1980s, that dealignment eroded Democratic dominance, but the number of independents increased much more than the number of Republicans did. More recently, other factors, including the realignment of white southerners toward the Republican Party and the renewed focus on national security issues after the September 11, 2001, attacks, contributed to Republican gains in party identification. In 2004 the share of Americans identifying as Democrats and Republicans was identical (at 33 percent) for the first time since the advent of modern polling.

SEE ALSO *Dixiecrats; Elections; New Deal, The; Party Systems, Competitive; Political Parties; Voting; Voting Patterns*

BIBLIOGRAPHY

American National Election Studies (ANES). Party Identification 7-Point Scale 1952–2004. Ann Arbor, MI: ANES. http://www.electionstudies.org/nesguide/toptable/tab2a_1.htm.

Campbell, Angus, Philip Converse, Warren Miller, and Donald Stokes. 1960. *The American Vote.* Chicago: University of Chicago Press.

Hershey, Marjorie R. 2006. *Party Politics in America.* 12th ed. New York: Pearson Longman.

Keefe, William J., and Marc J. Hetherington. 2003. *Parties, Politics, and Public Policy in America.* 9th ed. Washington, DC: CQ Press.

Sundquist, James L. 1983. *Dynamics of the Party System: Alignment and Realignment of Political Parties in the United States.* Rev. ed. Washington, DC: Brookings Institution.

Fred Slocum

DEATH AND DYING

Death is as much a cultural reality as it is a biological one. The only creature known to be aware of its inevitable demise, humans have dealt with their unique insight with considerable creative ritual and belief. Many have argued that religion, philosophy, consumerism, and even civilization itself were all created as antidotes to this terrifying insight (Becker 1973). Mythologist Joseph Campbell (1904–1987) hypothesized that mythmaking began with the first awareness of mortality, forcing early humans to seek purpose, to rationalize the irrational, and to deny death's finality. Perhaps it should thus be of no surprise that much of what we know of past cultures is based on funerary artifacts—their attempts at death transcendence.

A culture's death system, or death ethos, determines such widely ranging phenomena as a people's militancy and suicide rate; their preferences for bullfights, gladiator battles, or horror movies; their fears of or hopes for reincarnation and resurrection; their willingness to perform organ transplants or purchase life insurance; their decisions to bury, cremate, or eat their dead; and their attitudes toward capital punishment, abortion, and what constitutes a "good death."

Cultures have been classified in terms of their death systems, shedding light on the meanings they give to life. Historian Arnold Toynbee (1889–1975), for example, categorized cultures by whether they are death-accepting or death-denying, hold a hedonistic or pessimistic view toward life, perceive death to be the end of existence or a transition to some personal or collective form of immortality, view corpses as sacred or profane objects, and whether or not the dead are believed to play an active role in the affairs of the living (and whether in a positive or negative way). In the death-defying West, for instance, strategies for salvation have historically featured activism and asceticism, whereas in the East they have often been more contemplative and mystical. In the West, postdeath conceptions typically involve the integrity and continuity of one's personal self; in the East, the ultimate goal is often an undifferentiated and impersonal oneness with the universe.

Changes in social solidarities (i.e., urbanization, religious pluralism), in selfhood (i.e., the shift from collectivist to individualistic identities), and in who dies and why, have historically produced several recognized epochs in the West, each featuring distinctive conceptions of death and funerary ritual. For most of human history, when life was short and "death in the midst of life" was a literal and not a figurative notion, cultural rituals and social systems were oriented to this fact. People were constantly reminded about time's invariable passage and their inevitable mortal fate. Ancient Egyptians would have skeletons brought to their feasts; colonial Americans would daily walk past their church cemeteries, whose tombstones were adorned with skulls and crossbones. Death was "tame," according to social historian Philippe Ariès (1914–1984). Deathbeds were community gathering places; public meeting spaces were often adjacent to mass graves whose contents were often partially visible. In early colonial America, realizing that two or three of their children would not survive until age ten, Puritan parents would send their offspring to family and friends as apprentices to avoid excessive attachments with them and the grief their deaths would cause (Stannard 1977).

According to Ariès, the contemporary era in the West features death denials and "invisible death," fueling the illusion of immortality with institutions that conceal the dying (over 70 percent of Americans currently die within institutionalized settings) and that make the dead appear lifelike for funerary services. Those most likely to die are the old (nearly eight in ten deaths in the United States are those sixty and older), who are largely disengaged from many of their roles and physically segregated from other age groups in retirement communities and long-term care facilities. Gerontophobia, or fear of aging, has become interwoven with cultural thanatophobia, the fear of death.

So great is the power of an ethos, this construction of meaning thrown up against the terror of death, that social agencies invariably seek to harness its energy as a means of social control—and to enhance the social status of their members. For instance, consider religion's traditional threats of agonizing hells or bad reincarnations as a means for keeping the living in line. The power and status of the medical establishment increased dramatically during the last century with its growing ability to postpone death. Because of scientific breakthroughs, modern medicine has largely eliminated many traditional causes of premature death, especially infectious disease, and the medical establishment competes with religion's traditional control over the dying process. Accordingly, death is shifting from being a moral rite of passage to a technological one. Traditional fears of postmortem judgment are morphing into fears of dying; those most likely to die, the old, fear being institutionalized within nursing homes more than they fear death.

With most premature death now the result of manmade and hence theoretically avoidable causes (e.g., accidents, homicides, and suicides), its occurrence has become increasingly tragic and highly politicized. Political rulers have long enforced their control through death squads, pogroms, war, capital punishment, and campaigns of fear. Disdaining such strategies, modern regimes instead establish legitimacy and citizen loyalty by thwarting (or at least predicting) the death threats of enemies with the country's military forces, of lethal microbes with health care systems, of violent storms with weather satellites, of possible earthquakes or volcanic eruptions with seismic monitoring stations, and of potential asteroid or meteor collisions with telescope arrays.

Some of the most contentious moral debates in the contemporary United States center on the right to end life (e.g., capital punishment, physician-assisted suicide, and civilian casualties in military campaigns) and precisely where the line between life and death occurs, as in the controversies over abortion and euthanasia.

Materialism, individualism, secularism, and the distractions of consumer and popular cultures have not eliminated individuals' fears of death nor their desires to transcend it. The proportion of Americans believing in an afterlife has generally increased over recent decades, with more than seven in ten confident that their existence does not conclude with death. At a minimum, cultural death systems promise at least symbolic immortality (Lifton 1979), such as being remembered through one's progeny or works of art, or surviving through the preservation of political or natural orders. Thus we witness the proliferation of such projects as halls of fame, the Social Security Administration's online database of deceased Americans, and *Forbes* magazine's annual ranking of top-earning deceased celebrities.

SEE ALSO *Euthanasia and Assisted Suicide; Funerals; Suicide*

BIBLIOGRAPHY

Ariès, Philippe. 1981. *The Hour of Our Death*. Trans. Helen Weaver. New York: Knopf.

Becker, Ernest. 1973. *The Denial of Death*. New York: Free Press.

Campbell, Joseph. 1974. *The Mythic Image*. Princeton, NJ: Princeton University Press.

Lifton, Robert. 1979. *The Broken Connection: On Death and the Continuity of Life*. New York: Simon and Schuster.

Stannard, David. 1977. *The Puritan Way of Death: A Study in Religion, Culture, and Social Change*. New York: Oxford University Press.

Toynbee, Arnold. 1980. Various Ways in Which Human Beings Have Sought to Reconcile Themselves to the Fact of Death. In *Death: Current Perspectives*, ed. Edwin Shneidman, 11–34. 2nd ed. Palo Alto, CA: Mayfield.

Michael C. Kearl

DE BEAUVOIR, SIMONE

SEE *Feminism*.

DEBREU, GERARD
1921–2005

Gerard Debreu, a French-born American mathematical economist and 1983 Nobel laureate, was a major force in the advancement of the theory of general equilibrium. His early influence came from the 1988 French Nobel laureate, Maurice Allais, who introduced him to the writings of Leon Walras (1834–1910), the founder of the mathematical theory of general equilibrium analysis.

In 1949 Debreu visited several premier universities, including Harvard and the University of California, Berkeley, on a Rockefeller fellowship. Following the fellowship, he spent a decade with the Cowles Commission, then attached to the University of Chicago, working on Pareto optima, the existence of a general economics equilibrium, and utility theory. Subsequently, after one year at Stanford, he moved to Berkeley in 1962 where he remained until his retirement in 1991. Besides mathematics, Debreu was so taken by the U.S. rule of law during the Watergate scandal that he became an American citizen in 1975.

Debreu's research interest was general equilibrium analysis, in line with Walras, whose method was to equate equations and unknowns. The essential idea is to show how prices gravitate from disequilibrium to their natural or equilibrium levels. Debreu liberated the analysis by opting for fixed-point and convex tools for general equilibrium analysis.

Convexity requires that the production and consumption sets be bowl-shaped. Debreu would "slip a hyperplane," as he would say, through the tangent of those convex sets. He first revealed a proof at the 1950 meeting of the Econometric Society at Harvard that did not use the convexity solution. Many optimal solutions of the Pareto type and some possible competitive solutions resulted where prices are given and agents maximize their affairs. In 1954, in collaboration with Kenneth Arrow and using topological methods, which Debreu had used previously, he proved the existence of general equilibrium in an "epoch-making" paper, "Existence of an Equilibrium for a Competitive Economy."

Debreu's early book, *The Theory of Value* (1959), produced the hard-core ideas of his lifetime research program. He expressed the economy as $\xi_i\left(p, \left(p \cdot \omega_i + \sum_{j=1}^{n} \theta_{ij} \pi\, j(p)\right)\right)$, where each consumer, $i = 1....m$, has an initial endowment, ω_i, a share of jth producer's profit, $\theta_{i,j}$, and an underlying utility function for his or her preferences. Each producer, $j = 1....n$, takes the prices that are announced, and maximizes profits, π_j. The inner-bracketed terms represent the consumer budget from the initial endowment and shares of profits. Consumers will maximize their utility subject to their budget constraints, yielding demand functions. Excess demand functions are now possible by summing all the demand functions less endowment. Thus we can derive the equilibrium prices from the excess demand functions, which in two dimensions are usually the zeros or solutions of a quadratic equation.

Debreu built his theories on axioms, where a primitive such as a commodity becomes a mathematical object with spatiotemporal and physical characteristics. He urged his students to be concise, mentioning that John Nash demonstrated the equilibrium for finite games on only one page. During his lectures his eyes would light up when he demonstrated the superiority of mathematical reasoning. He used to say that mathematical economists have the best of two worlds—mathematical discoveries when they are young and economic discoveries when they are old.

SEE ALSO *Arrow-Debreu Model; General Equilibrium; Pareto Optimum; Tatonnement*

BIBLIOGRAPHY

Arrow, Kenneth J., and Gerard Debreu. 1954. Existence of an Equilibrium for a Competitive Economy. *Econometrica* 22: 265–290.

Arrow, Kenneth J., and Michael D. Intriligator. 1982. Existence of Competitive Equilibrium. In *Handbook of Mathematical*

Economics, eds. Kenneth J. Arrow and Michael D. Intriligator,Vol. 2: *Mathematical Approaches to Microeconomic Theory*, 677–743. Amsterdam, NY: Elsevier North-Holland.

Debreu, Gerard. 1959. Separation Theorem for Convex Set. *SIAM Review* 1: 95–98.

Debreu, Gerard. 1959. *The Theory of Value: An Axiomatic Analysis of Economic Equilibrium.* New York: Wiley.

Debreu, Gerard. 1983. *Mathematical Economics: Twenty Papers of Gerard Debreu.* New York and Cambridge, U.K.: Cambridge University Press.

Debreu, Gerard. 1993. Random Walk and Life Philosophy. In *Eminent Economists, Their Life Philosophies*, ed. Michael Szenberg, 107–114. New York and Cambridge, U.K.: Cambridge University Press.

Ramrattan, Lall, and Michael Szenberg. 2005. Gerard Debreu: The General Equilibrium Model (1921–2005). *The American Economist* 49 (1): 3–14.

Lall Ramrattan
Michael Szenberg

DEBT CRISIS

SEE *Herd Behavior; Loan Pushing.*

DEBT PEONAGE

SEE *Servitude.*

DECENTRALIZATION

Decentralization is the transfer or sharing of decision-making power from a central authority toward lower-level units or the end users. Decentralization signifies the disbursement of power from the top down within any type of organizational hierarchy, such as political, educational, or economic systems. The literature on political economy suggests that a greater degree of decentralization leads to higher levels of efficiency in the distribution of public resources and is associated with the use of locals' own resources to address local needs and issues.

There are various types of governmental decentralization, depending on the constitutionality granted to lower-level units of government. Federalism is an arrangement in which different levels of the government enjoy constitutionally designated power and functions. The central authority in a federal system exists when lower-level units decide to enable the national government to have overseeing powers. In the United States, authority at the national government does not preclude the political rights that reside at the state level. The fifty states exercise their own taxing and spending authority and maintain primary control over their own affairs (such as public education). The national government does play an important role in federalism. It can allocate its centrally collected resources to address regional disparity and to provide services that benefit several subnational units, such as environmental protection.

Unitary governments, whose lower-level units may not enjoy constitutional guarantees of autonomy, can reallocate their power within the administrative and territorial system. In Great Britain, for example, regional autonomy exists in Northern Ireland, Wales, and Scotland, and the national government grants municipal autonomy to London. Although it can be repealed by the British Parliament and the monarchy, the complex system of elected local governments constitutes an integral part of the British political system. In other unitary systems, territorial decentralization is constitutionally provided for, and the powers of locally chosen officials are prescribed. The Japanese constitution, for example, specifies certain autonomous functions to be carried out by local administrative authorities.

Another governance arrangement may involve a hybrid of central supervision and local control. A good example is France. Until March 1982, when a law on decentralization was enacted, the French administrative system was constructed around departments, each directed by a prefect, and subdivided departments, each directed by an underprefect. The prefects and the underprefects were appointed by the national government in Paris to act as agents of the central government and also as the directors of the regional governments, which included locally elected officials. That system combined central supervision of local affairs through appointed officials with territorial representation through locally elected governmental bodies.

The degree of decentralization, to be sure, involves trade-offs in governmental functions and political power. A decentralized system of governance is likely to implement fiscal policy based on the "benefits-received" principle, where local taxpayers receive locally funded services. This practice may lead to intercommunity competition for private capital and productive workers, as they form the basis of a sound local economy.

A race to the bottom can occur as power is decentralized to municipalities. To enhance their competitiveness, local governmental units tend to reduce locally funded social welfare services and to relax labor and environmental regulations as much as possible to lure economic investment. In developing economies, for example, communities that offer the least costly workforce tend to attract foreign capital. In putting into practice the notion of cost-reducing scale economies, companies prefer lower overhead costs with lower local taxes and greater discretion over wages.

At the same time, a centralized system may make allocative decisions that do not necessarily reflect local and regional needs to the extent that the system functions at a suboptimal level. In other words, a mix of decentralized decision-making and centralized coordination is necessary to promote efficiency and fairness.

SEE ALSO *Authority; Autonomy; Bureaucracy; Constitutions; Decision-making; Federalism; Government; Government, Federal; Government, Unitary; Organizations; Policy, Fiscal*

BIBLIOGRAPHY

Abromeit, H. 1998. *Democracy in Europe: Legitimising Politics in a Non-State Polity.* New York: Berghahn Books.

Besley, T., and S. Coate. 1999. Centralized Versus Decentralized Provision of Local Public Goods: A Political Economy Analysis. NBER Working Paper no. 7084.

Fabbrini, S. 1999. American Democracy from a European Perspective. *Annual Review of Political Science* 37 (1): 3–14.

Fisman, R., and R. Gatti. 2002. Decentralization and Corruption: Evidence Across Countries. *Journal of Public Economics* 83 (3): 325–345.

Mendoza, R., and C. Bahadur. 2002. Towards Free and Fair Trade: A Global Public Good Perspective. *Challenge* 45 (5): 21–62.

Oates, W. 1972. *Fiscal Federalism.* New York: Harcourt Brace Jovanovich.

Peterson, P. E. 1981. *City Limits.* Chicago: University of Chicago Press.

Tiebout, C. 1956. A Pure Theory of Local Expenditures. *Journal of Political Economy* 64 (5): 416–424.

Kenneth K. Wong
Ted Socha

DECEPTION

SEE *Lying.*

DECISION-MAKING

Standard models of decision-making hold that rational agents maximize expected utility. These models presuppose a notion of rationality that is substantive (i.e., that involves making choices that have certain substantive outcomes, such as maximizing expected utility) and forward-looking (i.e., that is solely a function of future costs and benefits). Despite the fact that this notion of "utility" is notoriously vague, utility maximization theories have a formal clarity and precision. Unfortunately, they also make highly idealized assumptions about decision-makers—namely that they are superhuman probability calculators whose preferences are precisely and stably ordered.

Since the 1950s, economists and psychologists have moved away from forward-looking, substantive theories of rationality, and toward procedural theories of rationality. Procedural theories take rationality to involve making choices in accordance with certain rules or processes, and these rules or processes are typically grounded in psychologically realistic accounts of decision-making. This focus has led to an explosion of research into decision-making in business, government, and the marketplace. Much of the groundbreaking work in this area was done by Amos Tversky and Daniel Kahneman (Kahneman won the Nobel Prize for Economics in 2002 for his research on the economics of choice).

AUTOMATIC VS. DELIBERATIVE PROCESSES

While the paradigm case of decision-making is voluntary and deliberative (e.g., selecting a new car or a retirement plan), many cognitive processes are involuntary and automatic. Some automatic decision-making seems to occur in a perception-like system. These "System 1" processes are fast, automatic, parallel, effortless, associative, and emotional. "System 2" processes, on the other hand, are slow (in the deliberative sense), serial, controlled, effortful, rule-governed, flexible and emotionally neutral. Reasoning is a characteristic System 2 process. Which system is being used can be determined by an effort diagnostic: System 2 processes are easily interfered with by a simultaneous activity.

System 1 processes include impression formation, one-on-one communication, and much group behavior. John Bargh's work shows that much of our social behavior (e.g., nose-scratching) is imitative, triggered automatically by an activation of the motor cortex. Consumer choice, memory for events, mathematical skills, and hostility for others are regulated by automatic processes that people are largely unaware of, and which can be triggered by environmental features to which people pay no explicit attention. For example, music in a store can reduce the shopper's blink rate from the normal average of thirty-two times a minute to a hypnotic (and suggestible) fourteen blinks a minute (Smith and Curnow 1966).

FRAMING EFFECTS

Framing effects occur when messages carrying the same statistical information cast in different ways prompt different behavior. If someone who tests positive for HIV or breast cancer has a 70 percent chance of living beyond seven years, then that person has a 30 percent chance of dying within seven years. But these messages have different impacts. In 2001, Tamera Schneider and colleagues created gain-framed videos that explained the positive effects of healthful behavior and regular breast exams, as well as loss-framed videos that attempted to frighten viewers with the potential negative consequences of not seeing a doctor. Subjects in the gain-framed message condition were significantly more likely to arrange mammograms. In a 2003 paper, Anne Marie Apanovitch, Danielle McCarthy, and Peter Salovey showed that message framing also motivates subjects to get tested for HIV.

THE FUNDAMENTAL ATTRIBUTION ERROR

When observing the behavior of others, people tend to overattribute behavior to dispositional factors, such as motives, capacities, and personality traits. They also tend to underestimate the causal influence of situational factors, such as whether the subject is pressed for time or is in an uncomfortably warm room. This "fundamental attribution error" (FAE) has proved both stable and resistant to correction. Interestingly, however, Incheol Choi and Richard Nisbett found in 1998 that Koreans are significantly less susceptible to the FAE than Americans.

The FAE leads to the actor-observer effect, where people tend to explain their own behavior in terms of situational factors, while other people's behavior is explained in terms of dispositional factors. A noteworthy consequence of the actor-observer effect is that people tend to explain other people's economic successes or difficulties in terms of behavioral and dispositional factors. They tend to explain wealth in terms of hard work and wise decisions, but rather than explain poverty in terms of the situations of those suffering, it is often explained with derogatory attributions. In other words, it is often believed that people are poor because they are lazy, stupid or ignorant. Situational factors are, however, thought to exert a potent influence on social behavior.

AFFECTIVE FORECASTING

A number of studies that allow subjects to predict how some event will affect their life or the lives of others have confirmed that people are not good at tracking the impact and duration that events will have on our lives. There is a wide gulf between what people believe makes them happy and what actually does make them happy. Events that are predicted to be devastating, such as getting denied tenure, and those thought to make one happy, such as gaining tenure or winning the lottery, often have no lasting impact on human happiness (see Gilbert, et al. 1998; Brickman et al. 1978). It may be difficult for people to admit, but

affective forecasting—the psychological process of predicting how one will react to life events—cannot be trusted (see Wilson and Gilbert 2003). As Kahneman et al. put it, "People are unable to produce an accurate and unbiased evaluation of experiences that extend over time" (2004, p. 430). When it comes to what makes one happy, people have a mixture of true beliefs (having a satisfying occupation; having a number of caring, emotionally intimate relationships; sound health; or the feeling of security from personal threat) and false beliefs (having more money [if they are middle class or above], a fast car, or a vacation home).

DISCOUNTING THE FUTURE

People tend to discount the future. If given a choice between taking ten dollars now or in ten years, it is undoubtedly more rational to take the money now. Certainly inflation will make it less valuable in ten years, and the future is uncertain. But the problem is that people tend to discount the future far too steeply. This is evident in the very low contribution rates many people make to their retirement plans. People take their money now, even when the payoff at retirement is high and the probability of an interfering event is low. In so doing, people end up making choices that are inconsistent with their life plans.

But perhaps the impulse for immediate satisfaction should be forgiven. When people lying in a magnetic resonance imaging (MRI) machine are asked to choose between two options—an item now and a more valuable one in the future—the prefrontal cortex busily calculates the various payoffs over time, lighting up the image with blood flow activity (McClure et al. 2004). But when a person chooses the present pleasure, the limbic system—which governs the emotions and spontaneous responses—also flashes brilliantly. Thus, people are biologically programmed to respond more strongly to present pleasures, and while they might find it difficult to eliminate their biases, some biases can be used to cancel out others. Richard Thaler and Shlomo Benartzi's Save More Tomorrow Plan (SMT) is a fine example of this sort of psychological ju jitsu.

SMT uses one set of biases (the tendency toward decision-making inertia and procrastination) to counteract another bias (the failure to properly discount the future). The plan application asks prospective participants if they would like to start saving three months from now, and it commits them to doing so at the time of enrollment. The time lag allows people to experience whatever they find attractive about procrastination, but once enrolled in the plan, inertia takes over and people tend not to opt out. Thaler and Benartzi also curb a powerful psychological factor—loss aversion—that would lead people to decline to participate in the plan. People tend to weigh losses far more heavily than gains, and so tend to work hard to avoid sure losses. Loss aversion tends to prevent people from enrolling in a program in which they will witness a decrease in their paycheck. So SMT takes the increased contribution out of the employee's pay raise, so that it is not experienced as a loss. For those involved in this plan, saving rates more than tripled, from 3.5 percent to 11.6 percent, over 28 months.

Contemporary research into decision-making focuses on describing the processes employed by decision-makers. By discovering processes that consistently lead to decisions that are in some sense non-optimal, researchers can offer psychologically tractable proposals for improving decision-making. This research has produced, and will continue to produce, important practical and theoretical results for economics, organizational behavior, investment performance, organ donation planning, insurance, traffic theory, criminal corrections, medical diagnosis, and many other areas that are significant to people's lives.

SEE ALSO *Choice in Economics; Choice in Psychology*

BIBLIOGRAPHY

Apanovitch, Anne Marie, Danielle McCarthy, and Peter Salovey. 2003. Using Message Framing to Motivate HIV Testing Among Low-Income, Ethnic Minority Women. *Health Psychology* 22 (1): 60–67.

Bargh, John. 1996. Automaticity and Social Psychology. In *Social Psychology: Handbook of Basic Principles*, ed. E. Tory Higgins and Arie Kruglanski, 169–183. New York: Guilford.

Brickman, Philip, Dan Coates, and Ronnie J. Janoff-Bulman. 1978. Lottery Winners and Accident Victims: Is Happiness Relative? *Journal of Personality and Social Psychology* 36: 917–927.

Choi, Incheol, and Richard. E. Nisbett. 1998. Situational Salience and Cultural Differences in the Correspondence Bias and Actor-Observer Differences. *Personality and Social Psychology Bulletin* 24 (9): 949–960.

Gilbert, Daniel, et al. 1998. Immune Neglect: A Source of Durability Bias in Affective Forecasting. *Journal of Personality and Social Psychology* 75 (3): 617–638.

Gilovich, Thomas, Dale Griffin, and Daniel Kahneman, eds. 2002. *Heuristics and Biases: The Psychology of Intuitive Judgment*. New York: Cambridge University Press.

Kahneman, Daniel, et al. 2004. Toward National Well-Being Accounts. *American Economic Review* 94 (2): 429–434.

Kahneman, Daniel, Paul Slovic, and Amos Tversky, eds. 1982. *Judgment Under Uncertainty: Heuristics and Biases*. New York: Cambridge University Press.

McClure, Samuel M., et al. 2004. Separate Neural Systems Value Immediate and Delayed Monetary Rewards. *Science* 306 (5695): 503–507.

Plous, Scott. 1993. *The Psychology of Judgment and Decision Making*. New York: McGraw-Hill.

Ross, Lee. 1977. The Intuitive Psychologist and His Shortcomings: Distortions in the Attribution Process. In *Advances in Experimental Social Psychology*, ed. L. Berkowitz, Vol. 10, 173–220. New York: Academic Press.

Schneider, Tamera R., et al. 2001. The Effects of Message Framing and Ethnic Targeting on Mammography Use Among Low-Income Women. *Health Psychology* 20 (4): 256–266.

Simon, Herbert A. 1976. From Substantive to Procedural Rationality. In *Method and Appraisal in Economics*, ed. S. J. Latsis, 129–148. New York: Cambridge University Press.

Simon, Herbert A. 1986. Rationality in Psychology and Economics. *The Journal of Business* 59 (4) pt. 2: S209–S224.

Smith, P., and R. Curnow. 1966. 'Arousal Hypothesis' and the Effects of Music on Purchasing Behavior. *Journal of Applied Psychology* 50 (3): 255–256.

Thaler, Richard H., and Shlomo Benartzi. 2004. Save More Tomorrow™: Using Behavioral Economics to Increase Employee Savings. *Journal of Political Economy* 112 (1): 164–187.

Trout, J. D. 2007. The Psychology of Discounting: A Policy of Balancing Biases. *Public Affairs Quarterly* 21.

Wilson, Tim D., and Daniel T. Gilbert. 2003. Affective Forecasting. *Advances in Experimental Social Psychology* 35: 345–411.

Michael A Bishop
J. D. Trout

DECISIVE EVENTS

An event with persistent consequences that influences the economic activity in significant regions of the world, and that marks a shift in structural conditions for investment, trade, relative prices, or central state policy, is termed a *decisive event*. Because economic reasoning is concerned with an explanatory-factor approach to empirical regularities, decisive events often appear as abrupt and depth breaks of these regularities. For this reason, the initial occurrence that unleashes the full sequence of changes is perceived as the fundamental turning-point moment, and is often used like a marker to outline time periods and differentiate chronologies. The idea that once a turning point is reached, a cascade of irreversible consequences will follow, is akin to the representation of thermodynamic systems that are no longer in a state of equilibrium. In reality, decisive events in economic terms are equated in the short run as moments of system disequilibrium.

Within this framework, what matters is not so much the intensity, breadth, and pace of the turning-point event, but rather how the system responds to changes in the environment. In historical terms, this entails the distinction between train and explosion, between the narrative of singular occurrences and the mechanisms that generate one particular outcome: When the stock market fell almost exactly the same amount on almost exactly the same dates in 1929 and in 1987, why did the first collapse lead to a world crisis, but the second have only limited consequences? The answer is that a stock-market crash is not enough to trigger a depression. There must be some causal mechanisms at work that contribute to spreading a single initial occurrence in a sequence of events across sectors of activity and across nations. The primary propagation channel of the 1929 crash could have been the banking panics, the postwar system of the gold standard that spread the shock by indicating that deflation policies were the appropriate remedy for the ills of the 1930s, or both. The important point to note is that decisive events join together a turning-point occurrence and a powerful propagation mechanism.

World Wars I (1914–1918) and II (1939–1945), the stock-market crash of 1929, the oil shock of 1974, and the fall of the Berlin Wall in 1989 constituted the most decisive events of the twentieth century, from an economic point of view. Each of these episodes was meaningful to historical actors before they became meaningful as objects of research. Narrative memory and intrinsic plot formation therefore established preliminary grounds and agendas in which the analysts developed their work. To most contemporary observers, the abrupt shifts were felt with some uncertainty and distress, provoked by the dense concentration of facts in short periods, and by the need for personal adjustment to a changing world. Hence, the thick time of decisive events appears cognitively and emotionally as an overload of data and occurrences that disturbs the degrees of rational belief. Under these conditions, it becomes increasingly difficult to estimate some hypotheses, given the evidence, or to forecast possible tendencies of the future.

SEE ALSO *Berlin Wall; Deflation; Depression, Economic; Economic Crises; Inflation; Organization of Petroleum Exporting Countries (OPEC); Stock Exchanges; Uncertainty; World War I; World War II*

BIBLIOGRAPHY

Griffin, Larry J. 1999. Temporality, Events, and Explanation in Historical Sociology. *Sociological Methods and Research* 20 (4): 403–427.

Temin, Peter. 1996. *Lessons From the Great Depression.* 2nd ed. Cambridge, MA: MIT Press.

Nuno Luís Madureira

DECLARATION OF INDEPENDENCE, U.S.

The Declaration of Independence, written in 1776, marked the birth of a new nation, the United States of America. Drafted mainly by Thomas Jefferson, edited by a committee consisting of Jefferson, John Adams, Benjamin Franklin, Roger Sherman, and Robert R. Livingston, and then by the Second Continental Congress that had appointed the committee, the Declaration set forth not only the causes that led Americans to sever their political ties with England but also a moral and political vision that speaks to the ages. In a few brief lines, penned at the beginning of America's struggle for independence, the founders distilled their philosophy of government: individual liberty, defined by rights to life, liberty, and the pursuit of happiness, secured by a government instituted for that purpose, its powers grounded in the consent of the governed.

At the time, these were revolutionary ideas, because no people had instituted them as Americans would eventually do, first with the Constitution of 1787, then with the Bill of Rights, ratified in 1791, and finally with the amendments that followed the Civil War (1861–1865). Yet the ideas themselves grew from a history stretching back to antiquity. Two influences were seminal, however: the five-hundred-year evolution of judge-made common law in England, which fleshed out the rights individuals had against one another and, in time, against government itself; and John Locke's *Second Treatise of Government* (1690), which drew upon that tradition to fashion a theory of legitimate government, grounded in natural rights. Thus, by the time Jefferson sat down to draft the Declaration, these ideas were commonplace in the colonies, even if it remained to institute them securely.

The document itself has three main parts. Invoking "the Laws of Nature and of Nature's God," it begins by stating the need, out of "a decent Respect to the Opinions of Mankind," to declare the causes of the separation, then sets forth the famous lines about liberty and limited government—the moral foundation that justifies those causes. There follow next the causes themselves, the "long Train of Abuses and Usurpations" the king of England had visited upon the colonies. Finally, appealing "to the Supreme Judge of the World for the Rectitude of [their] Intentions," the founders declare "That these United Colonies are, and of Right ought to be, Free and Independent States."

So important are the Declaration's famous lines setting forth the founders' moral and political vision that they bear statement and closer examination: "WE hold these Truths to be self-evident, that all Men are created equal, that they are endowed by their Creator with certain unalienable Rights, that among these are Life, Liberty, and the Pursuit of Happiness—That to secure these Rights, Governments are instituted among Men, deriving their just Powers from the Consent of the Governed." Note first that these truths are said to be "self-evident"—truths of reason. To be sure, the founders were men of faith, and of various faiths; but they were mindful also that they were setting forth universal truths, truths for all people, whatever their beliefs. Thus, they appeal to reason, not to faith or mere will. Second, notice that they set forth the moral order first, then the political and legal order it entails. Following Locke, they begin the business of justification by determining first, through reason, what rights and obligations individuals have respecting one another. They can then determine how legitimate government might arise through the exercise of those rights.

Turning to the truths themselves, the founders begin with a simple premise, that all men are created equal, then define that equality as a matter of rights to life, liberty, and the pursuit of happiness. Three fundamental points emerge here. First, men are all equal only in having equal natural rights, not in any other sense. But that point is crucial because it means that no one has natural rights superior to those of anyone else; and yet it allows for the inequality that invariably arises when people exercise their liberties as they wish and may. Second, by grounding their vision in rights rather than values, virtues, or other moral notions, the founders paved the way for liberty through law. Rights define the acts that are permitted, prohibited, or required, whether or not those acts are valuable or virtuous. Finally, as a corollary, people are free to pursue happiness as they wish, by their own lights, provided only that they respect the equal rights of others in the process. Others are free to criticize these pursuits, but not to restrict them. People are free to be virtuous, however defined, but not compelled to be. That is the very essence of a free society.

To secure that freedom, however, government is the natural instrument. But one must be careful, because government itself can be tyrannical. Thus, when the founders turn at last in this passage to government, it is twice limited: by its ends—securing individual rights; and by its means—to be just, the governed must consent to its powers. Reason and consent, the two traditional sources of political legitimacy, are there joined for "a candid World" to see.

The Declaration's principles have never been fully realized, of course. When the Constitution was drafted eleven years later it drew heavily on these principles; to ensure the union, however, it recognized slavery, albeit obliquely. The framers wrestled with the issue, hoping the institution would wither away over time. It did not. It took a civil war to end slavery, and the passage of the Civil War amendments to incorporate in the Constitution at last the grand principles of the Declaration. And in other ways too—not least, the growth of modern government—Americans have strayed from the Declaration's vision of liberty through limited government. Nevertheless, that vision—the right of every individual to chart a course through life, free from the interference of others or of government—continues to inspire millions around the world who see in the Declaration of Independence the principles under which they themselves aspire to live.

SEE ALSO *American Revolution; Congress, U.S.; Franklin, Benjamin; Jefferson, Thomas; Locke, John; Natural Rights*

BIBLIOGRAPHY

Bailyn, Bernard. 1967. *The Ideological Origins of the American Revolution.* Cambridge, MA: Harvard University Press, Belknap Press.

Becker, Carl L. 1942. *The Declaration of Independence: A Study in the History of Political Ideas.* New York: Knopf.

Maier, Pauline. 1997. *American Scripture: Making the Declaration of Independence.* New York: Knopf.

Pilon, Roger. 1999. The Purpose and Limits of Government. In *Limiting Leviathan*, eds. Donald P. Racheter and Richard E. Wagner, 13–37. Northampton, MA: Edward Elgar. Reprinted as *The Purpose and Limits of Government.* Cato's Letter #13 (Washington, DC: Cato Institute, 1999).

Reinstein, Robert J. 1993. Completing the Constitution: The Declaration of Independence, Bill of Rights, and Fourteenth Amendment. *Temple Law Review* 66 (2): 361–418.

Roger Pilon

DECOLONIZATION

Decolonization has shaped modern world history, and continues to do so. In the eighteenth century the American Revolution (1776–1783) laid the foundations for the United States' regional, then world influence. In the early nineteenth century Latin and Central American territories freed themselves from Spanish and Portuguese control (e.g., Paraguay in 1811 and Brazil in 1822). The European settler populations there, and in Canada, Australia, and other areas, used European styles of organization and, if necessary, warfare, to pressure imperial powers, and the result was full independence or more limited self-government, depending on the flexibility of the imperial power. But the most dramatic wave of decolonization was concentrated in the period from 1918 to the 1960s, when more than fifty countries and more than 800 million people gained independence from European rule. More recently, since the 1990s, the breakup of the Soviet Union's "empire" of satellite states has dramatically changed European and wider international relations, leaving the United States as the only global superpower.

As late as 1914, however, it seemed likely that most Asian and African countries would have to wait generations for internal self-government, let alone full independence. Their populations were limited to traditional forms of resistance, often involving royal elites and their retainers and levies, or to localized peasant revolts against harsh rule, high taxes, and alien customs. For Asians and Africans, decolonization's roots lay with the development of new local elites trained in modern disciplines—law, medicine, civil service—and their establishment of national-level political and, later, military organizations. These organizations had a dual significance: They could bridge tribal and regional differences to provide a "nation" in whose name sovereignty could be demanded, and they could organize state-wide resistance, ranging from peaceful civil disobedience to sustained guerilla warfare.

In analyzing these trends, scholars have identified three types of cause of decolonization: metrocentric, peripheral, and international. In short, these involve causes in the imperial power, in the colonized territory, and in the wider world. Some argue that one or another cause has the greatest influence: for example, that the cold war (an international cause) made postwar European empires expensive, as communist ideology blamed western capitalism and imperialism for indigenous poverty, and communist countries encouraged and aided revolts. In truth, such world or systemic tensions are not deterministic. They do exert pressure, but ultimately imperial powers may choose to maintain their empires if they are willing to accept increased costs.

The influence of metrocentric agency becomes obvious when we examine cases of empires that persisted during the cold war. One such case is the informal empire of the Soviet Union, which dominated satellite states in eastern and central Europe. When any of these states attempted to relax adherence to Soviet military and ideological norms, as Hungary did in 1956, they quickly discovered that Soviet tanks blocked their way. When Soviet "decolonization" did gather pace in the 1980s to 1990s it was not so much a result of pressures from the periphery as from Soviet President Mikhail Gorbachev's decision that openness and reform were necessary for central economic rejuvenation. Likewise, Portugal, which by the time of the cold war had one of the smallest European empires, tolerated guerilla warfare until the fall of its dictatorship in 1975 brought to power a left-wing government averse to the cost, and authoritarianism, of empire. After 1975 Portugal more or less scuttled its empire, leaving Angola, Mozambique, Guinea-Bissau, and East Timor to their own devices. Portugal's empire thus proved more durable than Britain's and France's, most of which was gone by 1971. In short, just as metrocentric concerns—centered in a metropolis or dominating central state—sometimes drive expansion, they sometimes accelerate or delay decolonization too.

Even in the case of Portugal, however, where metrocentric changes triggered the end of an overall imperial system, peripheral pressures did exist, with rebellion having started in Angola as early as 1961. Peripheral approaches also help explain individual examples of decolonization, and details such as the timing and nature of events. The demonstration effect of success in one colony can also create a domino effect, as in the Spanish colonies in the early nineteenth century, and in Soviet satellites in the 1990s, thus helping to explain the end of entire empires. In addition, in some cases only the peripheral explanation can explain how imperial powers were forced to disgorge territories they desperately clung on to. Key examples include Indochina (Vietnam), where the determination of first France (1946–1954) and then the United States (1965–1975) was ground down by Marxist-inspired nationalist guerilla forces. Likewise, in Algeria, France reluctantly ceded independence in 1961 despite initially claiming the territory as an overseas department and integral part of the French state.

Although peripheral causes can help to explain the pressures on an imperial power, and metrocentric approaches can help explain how each empire responds, neither is adequate to explain the pulses or waves of decolonization outlined above, when several empires simultaneously decolonized. International pressures and events are also indispensable in explaining how some imperial powers crashed from glory to dissolution in the space of just a few short years.

Portugal's grip on Brazil and Spain's on its colonies, for example, were at first loosened by the Napoleonic Wars, which brought virtual autonomy to Brazil. Britain's inability to quell revolt in its American colonies was as much due to France broadening the conflict as the colonists' determination. More dramatically, defeats in war allowed enemies to quickly deconstruct the Austro-Hungarian Empire after 1918, and the Japanese Empire after 1945. Clearly, changes in the international environment, for example Woodrow Wilson's championing of "self-determination" as a fundamental principle in international affairs in 1917, and the United Nations' support for decolonization after 1945, also raised the costs and lowered the benefits of empire.

The above discussion adheres to a classic idea of decolonization as constitutional and legal liberation. This is decolonization as the formal handover of sovereignty, the lowering of the old flag and the raising of the new. Some people argue that decolonization is precisely that, others that it is much more, and does not always end at the point where formal independence starts. At one level, formal independence does not preclude metropolitan companies' controlling much of the economy, and metropolitan scheming in local politics, even up to encouraging the removal of elected local rulers. After 1961 French culture continued to have an effect on elites in formally independent French-speaking Africa, and military and economic agreements ensured ongoing influence. This raises the question of how far decolonization goes to remove the ongoing political and economic hegemony of a former colonial power.

If decolonization is the removal of domination by nonindigenous forces, this could include the colonizer's legacies in other areas, such as race and culture. One might think of full decolonization in terms of three Ms: the mass, the mind, and the metropole. Traditional approaches concentrate only on the mass, or the colonial territory itself and its main political, security, and financial institutions. Newer approaches also emphasize decolonizing the mind (i.e., freeing postcolonial culture and thought from tutelage to western ideas) and the metropole (i.e., freeing the metropole from its own tendency to inferiorize and dominate other peoples and territories). In this latter sense, postcolonialism (as a process of contesting the impact of colonialism after formal independence) and decolonization (as a process of removing control of indigenous peoples by other groups) overlap. The object of decolonization is not just government, but also other areas such as economics and its effect on the culture, ideas, and institutions of imperial domination.

The two approaches can be seen operating together through individuals such as Martinique's Frantz Fanon (1925–1961), for whom imperialism was not so much a formal process as a mental hegemony, a domination of how people think. French imperialism aimed to absorb indigenous elites as francophone, and Fanon came from a family in Martinique—a French overseas department—which initially thought in these terms. But his experiences of discrimination in the Free French Forces, as a doctor in France, and of imperial violence in Algeria, where as a psychiatrist he treated victims of torture, convinced him that domination was exercised by a social system and experienced as a mental state not dissimilar to a mental illness. He later concluded that violent struggle was a powerful antidote to the condition. For him the violence was in itself empowering and liberating. He later supported the Algerian resistance, and his books *Black Skin, White Masks* (1952) and *The Wretched of the Earth* (1961)—the latter calling for peasant revolution to ensure real transfer of economic power, rather than mere accommodation—influenced other revolutionary leaders such as Che Guevara (1928–1967) and Steve Biko (1946–1977). Fanon's own ideas, such as his conception of imperialism as an affliction affecting both the colonized and the colonizer, are important as an example of a general trend toward highlighting the cultural and aspects of decolonization and postcolonialism.

Decolonization remains a very real issue. It is an issue in terms of whether existing groups under outside domination, such as Tibet and Muslim Xinjiang under China's hand, will one day assert nationhood, perhaps using force to demand independence. It is an issue in terms of whether the United States has inherited Britain's mantle as an "informal empire," asserting supposedly universal liberal and democratic values by "gunboat imperialism." It is an issue in terms of how far "first peoples" such as Canada's Inuit and Australia's Aborginals will demand, and receive, further compensation and assistance to counter past repression and past appropriation of their lands. And finally it is an issue in terms of ex-imperial powers reexamining the domestic vestiges of imperialism in their populations, their prejudices, and their cultures.

SEE ALSO *Colonialism; Nkrumah, Kwame; Third World; Williams, Eric*

BIBLIOGRAPHY

Betts, Raymond. 1997. *Decolonization.* London: Routledge.

Darwin, John. 1991. *The End of the British Empire: The Historical Debate.* London: Macmillan.

Dawisha, Karen, and Bruce Parrott, eds. 1997. *The End of Empire? The Transformation of the USSR in Comparative Perspective.* London: M. E. Sharpe.

Ferro, Marc. 1997. *Colonization: A Global History.* London: Routledge.

Loomba, Ania. 1998. *Colonialism/Postcolonialism.* London: Routledge.

Karl A. Hack

DECONSTRUCTION

SEE *Derrida, Jacques; Postmodernism.*

DEFECTIVES

SEE *Sterilization, Human.*

DEFENSE

Defense, in the social sciences, traditionally focuses on how states jockey for premier position in the global system. Periodically, it also examines preparations by different societies for countering internal and external threats.

Self-defense, in the dominant realist school of international relations, stands alone as the raison d'être of the state. Other functions proposed by liberal philosophers, including providing the laws and infrastructure for commerce or protecting individual freedom of citizens, presumptively come second to survival. This does not mean, however, that the demands of defense, even for the realist, are met at any price. In fact, defense policy may be understood as the art of balancing the combined risks of destruction from war or dissolution from rebellion against the benefits of preserving cherished principles of the state.

ORIGINS OF DEFENSE

These founding principles reside in the provisions of a so-called social contract between citizens and their governing institutions. Beyond the explicit articles of written constitutions, the social contract as a concept captures the pattern of expectations concerning rights and obligations for individuals living under protection of the state. When states are under extreme circumstances, when internal or external disintegrating forces are high, Thomas Hobbes in his classic work *Leviathan* ([1651] 1985) argued people would and should accept sharp curtailment of their liberty to fortify the state.

As a counterweight to this prescription for centralization of power in the state, most Enlightenment liberals stressed the importance of preserving individual freedoms and maintaining ultimate accountability of the government to its people, even in the face of grave security threats. Historically, through the evolution of the international system of states during the nineteenth century, the advent of nuclear weapons in the twentieth century, and the rise of nonstate security actors in the twenty-first century, states have had to reconcile the imperatives of self-preservation with the implicit call of their social contract to provide for a better life at home.

DEFENSE POLICY PROCESS

The responsibility for striking this balance lies primarily with the executive and legislative powers of the state, though in cases where there is an independent judiciary defense decisions may be countermanded according to legal codes. In keeping with Hobbes's line of argument, the more defense measures hinge on emergency maneuvers and closely held intelligence, the more power tends to be concentrated in the executive, even in otherwise liberal societies. Defense, however, involves a mixture of long-term reflective planning and time-critical choices. In practice, there is often feedback between various stages of defense policy, but as a point of departure Peter L. Hays, Brenda J. Vallance, and Alan R. Van Tassel (1997) provide a linear guide to the process as follows.

Responsible officials assess the threat environment. Of common concern to all states are challenges to territo-

rial integrity. Assessing these challenges involves geopolitical calculations based on resource capacity and the geographical position of potential rivals. In addition, national defense must account for intentions, essentially the risk that foreign capability will actually be organized and directed against the state. For most states in the international system, high-probability threats to existence are rare. Consequently, political leaders usually have the luxury of determining many of their defense priorities not just according to the necessity for survival but also through the lens of national values. The ethnic composition of a foreign state, its respect for human rights, or the quality of its democracy may affect the level of cooperation it enjoys from external actors in its own defense.

Grand strategy is the art of matching finite national capabilities against interests so as to reduce vulnerabilities and maximize opportunities in the international environment. The means for grand strategy are conventionally categorized according to economic, military, and diplomatic instruments of power. While national security depends on all the available instruments, defense analysis normally focuses on the role of the military instrument in the development and implementation of grand strategy.

States trade off between expanding their total resources for defense through alliances and increasing their autonomy through arms buildup. During the cold war, U.S. diplomatic efforts to nurture the North Atlantic Treaty Organization (NATO) were part of a grand strategy of containment, which relied on external balancing to prevent a Soviet invasion of Western Europe. The U.S.-Soviet rivalry also featured internal balancing as both sides spent vast sums to greatly expand the number and variety of nuclear weapons under their control.

Both external and internal balancing during the cold war supported containment, largely based on deterrence, or defense through the credible threat of imposing unacceptable costs on an enemy to dissuade it from attack. Still, even in the era of the superpower nuclear standoff, defense strategists in some cases lowered the threshold for taking the military offensive. Israel famously ordered a preemptive strike on massed Egyptian air power to clear the way to victory in the Six-Day War of 1967. Both the United States and the Soviet Union employed preventive uses of force in buffer zones such as Eastern Europe and the Caribbean to cover vulnerabilities in their respective spheres of influence. With the relaxation of tensions between the largest nuclear powers and the rise of terrorist organizations demonstrating their potential to make strategic use of weapons of mass destruction, the defense pendulum swung farther from deterrence toward preemptive and preventive grand strategies.

DEFENSE CHALLENGES

In *Taming the Sovereigns: Institutional Change in International Politics* (2004), Kalevi J. Holsti marks a turning point as well in the relationship between defense policy and the normal workings of the international system. Through the nineteenth and most of the twentieth century, states—as opposed to feudal structures, tribal groups, or warlords—reigned as the supreme institutions for harnessing people and technology in defense of their interests. Especially after the Industrial Revolution and the rise of nationalism, highly capitalized technology came to dominate the equation for national capability. So much so, that during the nuclear arms race there arose the question of whether or not the most powerful states, with no recourse to international governing authority, possessed the political acumen to save themselves from arsenals that promised "mutual assured destruction."

While the likelihood of a great power launching thousands of nuclear warheads in the name of defense declined after the end of the cold war, the September 11, 2001, terrorist attacks demonstrated in dramatic fashion a shift in the nature of the deadliest challenges confronting civilization among nations. Though military technologies for both mass destruction and precision strike continue to evolve, the greater danger may now lie with the rise of new types of organizations that defy the state monopoly on force.

Above the state, international organizations such as the United Nations confer legitimacy and broker burden-sharing agreements as modern great powers wheel about to secure globalized interests. With the value of their security functions rising, international organizations gain voice and impose new constraints on defense calculations for even the most powerful sovereigns.

Constrained states, as John Arquilla and David Ronfeldt discuss in *In Athena's Camp: Preparing for Conflict in the Information Age* (1997), also perceive growing threats from below. Ethnic paramilitaries, warlords, criminal gangs, and Al-Qaeda–inspired terrorist cells, all draw sustenance from hard-to-kill transnational networks and exploit vulnerabilities in economically developed, highly interdependent societies. In the post–September 11 environment, violent nonstate actors challenge weak or failing states for control of territory and population seemingly without need of supplies from governments bound by an ultimate interest in continuation of the interstate system. Faced with a millennial challenge not simply against particular regimes but also to the primacy of the nation-state in international governance, both developed and developing countries have adapted by delegating more of their core function—providing national defense—to intergovernmental organizations such as NATO or to substate actors such as private security companies.

SEE ALSO *Arms Race; Cold War; Defense, National; Preemptive Strike; Weaponry, Nuclear; Weapons of Mass Destruction*

BIBLIOGRAPHY

Arquilla, John, and David Ronfeldt. 1997. *In Athena's Camp: Preparing for Conflict in the Information Age.* Santa Monica, CA: RAND.

Hays, Peter L., Brenda J. Vallance, and Alan R. Van Tassel. 1997. What Is American Defense Policy? In *American Defense Policy,* 7th ed. Ed. Peter L. Hays, Brenda J. Vallance, and Alan R. Van Tassel. Baltimore, MD: Johns Hopkins University Press.

Hobbes, Thomas. 1651 [1985]. *Leviathan.* Ed. with an introduction by C. B. Macpherson. London: Penguin.

Holsti, Kalevi J. 2004. *Taming the Sovereigns: Institutional Change in International Politics.* New York: Cambridge University Press.

Damon Coletta
This academic work does not represent official policy of the United States Air Force or the United States Government.

DEFENSE, NATIONAL

National security would seem to be a simple concept to define. Joseph Nye Jr., who served as assistant secretary of defense for international security affairs (1994–1995) during President Bill Clinton's first term, observed that security is like oxygen—it is essential to all other governmental activity. Without it, a government is likely to become paralyzed and incapable of action, and may ultimately risk collapse. Not surprisingly, states generally regard national security as their primary responsibility. In common American parlance, the term *national security* has almost become a cliché and refers to the government's efforts to defend the state from threats, mainly military threats but perhaps internal subversion as well. In other words, "security" seemingly equates to "defense." However, while defense is an integral aspect of security, military defense does not exhaust the range of functions that governments must perform to ensure security, nor does it reflect the institutional affiliations of the people who work to provide security.

The term *national defense* evokes an era when the nation and the state, especially in northwest Europe and the United States, were thought to be one and the same—hence the term *nation-state.* Defense of the state meant defense of the nation, and security was largely defined in ways that reinforced this equation. In fact, virtually every modern state is multinational or multiethnic, even multiconfessional. Frequently, this diversity of religion directly relates to diversity of nationalities in the state, and many states are driven by conflicts among these diverse religions and nationalities. Therefore, a state, to be secure, must act in ways that forestall the emergence of crippling interethnic or interreligious confrontations. Such internal divisions frequently invite foreign intervention. In these contexts, security extends beyond defense against external invaders to include the prevention of civil war. Such a situation developed, for example, in Iraq, where contending Islamic groups became divided on the basis of religion and ethnicity (Shia and Sunni) and nationality (Sunni, Shia, and Kurd), and where foreigners intervened on every side.

Such internal divisions also developed in conflicts in Africa and the former Yugoslavia in the late twentieth and early twenty-first centuries. Many such conflicts, particularly in the third world, exemplify the fact that security pertains as much to the assurance of continuing internal order as it does to defense of the realm. Many third world countries simultaneously face the exigencies of state-building—that is, assuring internal security and defense against external threats—without sufficient time or resources to compete successfully with other more established states. Not surprisingly, the primary concern of the government becomes internal security and its continuation in power, leading to a proliferation of military, intelligence, and police forces. Indeed, for these states, and arguably even for transitional states like Russia during the 1990s and early 2000s, internal police forces are granted greater state resources than regular armies, this being a key indicator of the primacy of internal security as part of national security. Nevertheless, if states cannot defend themselves militarily against threats that have arisen due to a previous failure to provide security, the states themselves may fail.

Because of the breadth of domestic or foreign threats to the security of a society or a state in the modern world, national security can no longer be limited to defense against military attacks or internal unrest. Governments in the twenty-first century must defend against a multitude of threats to the health, viability, and integrity of society. Such threats extend beyond the canonical threat of war with another state or domestic unrest that culminates in revolution or civil war. The potential threats to state security include terrorism, large-scale criminality, narcotics trafficking, uncontrolled immigration, natural disasters, epidemics, and chemical and biological warfare. The threats facing states may also include major international economic crises, such as the Asian financial crisis of 1997 to 1998. These threats also tend increasingly to spill over national borders, often uniting the transnational purveyors of the threat (e.g., terrorist movements, crime syndicates). The range of potential threats blurs the distinction between military and police missions. Often, both institutions act together to promote security, as

exemplified by the participation of the U.S. military in antidrug activities, homeland security, and the response to natural disasters. Thus, in the wake of hurricanes Katrina and Rita in 2005, calls multiplied in the United States for revising legal codes to permit greater scope for domestic military action during natural disasters.

Homeland security was proclaimed as the U.S. military's main mission after the terrorist attacks of September 11, 2001, leading to a dramatic expansion of its domestic role. This change has reopened the debate over the legitimate role of the armed forces in domestic security, and has stimulated the Department of Defense, the armed services, and intelligence agencies such as the FBI and CIA to advocate substantial enhancement of their domestic powers. Thus the erosion of distinctions between security and defense, or between power projection abroad and homeland defense, creates difficult and persisting issues of possible encroachments on the domestic civil rights of Americans. These matters ultimately must be decided by the courts and legislatures. But their reemergence indicates that a fundamental component of national security remains the internal balance of power between civilian and democratic authorities and the armed forces that are supposed to be subordinate to them. These issues also raise the equally perennial question of the legal limits of state power in wartime, when it becomes too easy to argue that defense of the state overrides previously granted rights that are enjoyed without question (or seemingly so) in peacetime.

The same issues have arisen in other countries. The war that began in 1991 in the republic of Chechnya in southeastern Russia served as the primary justification for the curtailment of Russian federalism and of innumerable civil rights for the population and the media. In Great Britain, the government's reaction to the terrorist bombings in July 2005 occasioned a lively debate over the civil rights of Muslim immigrants to Great Britain and of British citizens in general. Thus the contemporary threat environment, punctuated by the global fear of and war against terrorism, is a manifestation of global trends and issues. This overall similarity of trends and agendas relates in important ways to the universal and transnational nature of twenty-first-century threats. And because contemporary threats to security are transnational, they must often be dealt with in international forums or through multilateral cooperation. The erosion of distinctions between security and defense, along with the globalization of threats, has generated global counterresponses.

Nonetheless, if states cannot defend against any or some combination, let alone all, of these threats, their security immediately becomes at risk as societal cohesion comes under threat. Indonesia's regime collapsed in 1998 for failing to cope with the Asian financial crisis. The governments of China, Russia, and the countries of Central Asia also believe that their internal cohesion and thus security are under threat from the ideologies of democracy, allegedly supported by foreign nongovernmental organizations and by states who use these organizations, as well as the tools of the media and information technology, to undermine their regimes. These regimes' leaders frequently charge that the United States is orchestrating a campaign to promote democracy, and even that democracy threatens their security and sovereignty.

Thus the term *national security* must encompass societal or state security against the entire range of threats described above, including traditional war, insurgency, and revolution. National security reaches beyond the defense of the state to encompass the goal of achieving and sustaining a broader societal cohesion, resilience, and integrity that can withstand numerous shocks or threats. Since the contemporary environment makes ensuring state security in this broad sense government's most fundamental responsibility, with defense being the main component of the provision of security, the burden of state spending on security and defense is huge. Similarly, many state organizations beyond defense ministries are involved in providing security, and their missions are steadily expanding.

Strategic threats to a society or state, threats that can overwhelm a state's ability to overcome or even effectively respond to them, have become multidimensional, and may originate from and be targeted at the land, the seas and other bodies of water, the air, space, and the ether (cyberspace). Consequently, threats, as well as the response to them, are no longer exclusively determined by geography. Any actor anywhere in the world, be it an individual or an institution, with the means to carry out an attack, can target anyone or any object in any of these dimensions. Moreover, the originator of these threats need not launch an attack from his or her point of origin. All an enemy need do is set an attack in motion, as the Saudi-born terrorist Osama bin Laden did in 2001 when he initiated attacks on New York City and the Washington, D.C., area from Afghanistan. Those actually carrying out the mission can identify the appropriate medium and locales wherein they can launch an attack. This backdrop also greatly multiplies the possibilities for shadowy relationships between sponsoring states and transnational terrorist organizations like Al-Qaeda. In America's "war on terror," for example, the enemy has no geographical center.

As a result, the number of possible strategic targets is greatly expanded. Any place on earth can become a target or a launching site for major attacks. Since no state can preplan sufficiently to ensure global and multidimensional readiness, governments everywhere face so variegated a repertoire of threats that they must devise new methods of responding or they must greatly transform existing institutions to meet the variety of threats. Many more issues than before now come under the rubric of national security, as do many more state organs and policies. Since providing for security has become even more of a challenge to a state's capability and resources, often stretching the state beyond the breaking point, expanded multilateral forms of security cooperation among states have developed. This cooperation may involve agencies responsible for the military, police, intelligence, public health, the treasury, immigration, and so on. This expanded burden upon states adds substantially to the pressures upon states who face major challenges of state building (e.g., Afghanistan, and Pakistan) and helps explain why so many regimes are on the verge of failure.

The centrality of security as the state's preeminent responsibility emerges clearly from comparisons of different states' approaches to the task of providing security. This is not just because of the priority accorded in the United States to homeland defense since 2001. In the war on terrorism, security is no longer the sole province of the regular armed forces, whereas in the United States as well as in other nations, defense remains very much a military prerogative. Security, on the other hand, can be provided by the police forces, intelligence agencies, bank inspectors, public health services, and airport security personnel. Indeed, it is universally agreed that all providers of security, wherever they may function, ideally should be coordinated so that efforts and information flow freely between different agencies, and that effective responses to threats may be coordinated either among the various components of national bureaucracies or among transnational institutions.

In Afghanistan since 2001, for example, the North Atlantic Treaty Organization (NATO) provides defense in support of the U.S. military mission there. In fact, both NATO and the U.S. armed forces became engaged in the overall reconstruction of the state after the deposing of the Taliban government in late 2001. The situation was similar in Iraq after U.S. forces invaded the country in 2003. Such international cooperation is necessary, given the nature of the contemporary threat environment and the rise of what scholars discern as new paradigms of war. In one new paradigm, warfare takes place among the people and entails more than just providing defense. In such a war, it becomes necessary to provide security and to enable the revival of a functioning state.

This is by no means an exclusively American view. French defense minister Michèle Alliot-Marie wrote that "to respond to such testing situations, solutions must be developed which if not purely military, must be military above all" (2005, p. 15). In other words, the expanded threat environment of the twenty-first century imposes security and defense missions on the armed forces that extend far beyond previous concepts of security and defense, or the simple notion of operational victory over opposing armed forces. This environment necessarily brings into the picture both greater transnational threats and greater cooperation against them, as well as expanded roles in the provision of security for a much broader range of state agencies.

At the same time, it is not the case that all states view the expanded range of threats in the same light. Whereas the U.S. government sees terrorism primarily in terms of a military threat, Germany (at least under the administration [1998–2005] of Chancellor Gerhard Schroeder) sees terrorism mainly as a criminal phenomenon that must be confronted by police and nonmilitary measures. Italy, on the other hand, provides for a much greater range of military involvement under the rubric of national and civil defense. However, many states and analysts of international security affairs warn that despite the enlistment of the armed forces in antiterrorist operations, antiterrorism must not supplant the traditional defense missions of the regular armed forces.

Security, therefore, is broader than defense and encompasses efforts to maintain the well-being and integrity of society as a whole. Defense, in contrast, relates to ensuring that the state itself and its citizens, armed forces, and vital interests are not attacked, or if they are attacked, that the attacker is defeated. Undoubtedly, security encompasses defense, but not vice versa. Moreover, there is no universal agreement on the nature of the threat posed by terrorists, as the German example illustrates. Neither is it possible to assume that the provision of security in this broad comprehensive sense will eclipse the need for armies to defend against major attacks on a state's vital interests and resources, human or material. The September 11, 2001, attacks were an act of war carried out against the United States on a global scale and should be seen as such, even if the entire range of instruments of power available to the U.S. government must be brought into play across a broad agenda that encompasses such realms as financial monitoring, antiproliferation, public health, and emergency management.

National security does not refer merely to national defense, as it did during the cold war. But, at the same time, it cannot mean less than national defense. War remains the ultimate argument of states, and defense, even more than security in the broad sense, remains their primary responsibility. While it is true that failure to provide adequate security, in the comprehensive definition of the term given here, places a state's future at risk, failure to defend the state against violent threats transforms that risk into the certainty of defeat. While security encompasses defense, defense is the most critical aspect of security and is likely to remain so.

SEE ALSO *Arms Control and Arms Race; Arms Race; Deterrence; Military*

BIBLIOGRAPHY

Alliot-Marie, Michèle. 2005. Security Could Be Europe's Great Rallying Point. *Financial Times* December 5: 15.

Cabigiosu, Carlo. 2005. The Role of Italy's Military in Supporting the Civil Authorities. *Connections: The Quarterly Journal* 4 (3): 59–70.

Klose, Gerhard J. 2005. The Weight of History: Germany's Military and Domestic Security. *Connections: The Quarterly Journal* 4 (3): 53–55.

Smith, Rupert. 2005. *The Utility of Force: The Art of War in the Modern World.* London: Allen Lane.

Stephen Blank
The views expressed here do not represent those of the U.S. Army, the U.S. Department of Defense, or the U.S. government.

DEFENSE MECHANISMS
SEE *Psychoanalytic Theory.*

DEFLATION
SEE *Inflation.*

DEFORESTATION

Deforestation can be defined as the conversion of forested areas to something that is different. Net deforestation accounts for afforestation (the establishment of forests on land that has not been recently forested), reforestation (the reestablishment of forests on land that was recently forested), and the natural expansion of forests. While the calculation of net deforestation is comparatively easy on a small scale, it is difficult on a global scale, despite modern technology such as extensive satellite surveillance. There are several reasons for this difficulty.

First, there is no universally agreed-upon definition of *forest.* The first *Global Biodiversity Outlook* (2001) defines forests as "ecosystems in which trees are the predominant life forms" but it also notes that a more precise definition is "surprisingly elusive" (p. 91). The Food and Agricultural Organization of the United Nations (FAO) has a more liberal definition, classing forests as "ecosystems dominated by trees (defined as perennial woody plants taller than 5 meters at maturity), where the tree crown cover exceeds 10% and the area is larger than 0.5 hectares" (a half of a hectare is about 1.2 acres) (FAO 2001, p. 365). This definition thus embraces areas that some investigators think too lightly wooded to be considered a forest.

The FAO definition of *forest* also includes tree plantations established for the production of timber or pulpwood (used for paper) while excluding orchards. Critics point out that the inclusion of biodiversity-poor plantations in the definition of forests understates the loss of qualities that many people associate with the word "forest." These qualities are found in woodland areas that retain a significant "natural" element and provide habitat for varied species, including trees of different species and ages. More controversially, the FAO includes in its definition forests that are "temporarily unstocked," such as areas that have been cleared and burned. Because the duration of clearance and the certainty of restocking are unclear, inclusion of such temporarily cleared land complicates estimates of the extent and trend of current deforestation.

Other problems arise in determining the extent and trend of global deforestation. The aggregate data on which the FAO relies is supplied by its member states (as is the case with all global data used by the UN). The survey and statistical resources in many poor countries are weak, and often declining. The greatest disagreement over the extent of deforestation concerns the biodiversity-rich tropical forests. Yet such areas are disproportionately concentrated in countries where statistical resources are weak. Remote sensing methods have been increasingly used to try to compensate for these deficiencies. However, data obtained by these methods are also imperfect, for reasons such as persistent cloud cover and the problem of ground-truthing on a global basis (comparing satellite data with data observed on the ground).

THE EXTENT OF DEFORESTATION

About 8,000 years ago, forests are estimated to have covered about 15 billion acres, almost half of the earth's land surface. Since then human populations and fire have had a significant impact on these forests. This impact is roughly proportional to the increase in human population and its environmental impact. In the near future there is a risk that these effects may be multiplied by climate change.

A review by the Millennium Ecosystem Assessment—the most authoritative assessment of the causes, composition, and consequences of global deforestation—concluded that the world's global forest area has shrunk by over 40 percent in recent centuries. The area of global forest in 2000 is thought to include from 9.6 to 10.9 billion acres.

The pattern of current deforestation shows two trends. At higher latitudes the boreal and temperate forest areas have either stabilized or are now expanding in size (by about 7.4 million acres per annum, of which about 2.5 million acres are plantations). However, in tropical regions, forests continue to decline in both area and quality (by about 30 million acres per annum).

Compared to the decade 1980–1990, net deforestation slowed in the following decade, from minus 30 million acres to minus 20 million acres per year. According to the *Global Biodiversity Outlook 2* (2006), this trend in reduction in forest clearance has continued since 2000, with a loss of about 18 million acres per year in the five years to 2005. This decrease is mostly the result of expansion in plantations (including almost 5 million acres per annum in tropical regions). Thus, despite this slowing, the rate of loss of natural ("primary") forests in the last two decades is thought to have remained about the same. Many forests are also declining in quality. Forest fragmentation, most commonly by the incursion of roads and agricultural settlements, leaves forests vulnerable to further disturbance, including drying, fires, and the invasion of exotic species.

TROPICAL DEFORESTATION

Tropical rainforest is the most extensive forest type in the world, constituting 26 percent of global forest area. Almost 60 percent of existing tropical forests are rain forest; the remainder are mostly sparse forests in dryland areas and degraded forests. In tropical forests, biodiversity, including of trees, is very high, with often more than 100 tree species per hectare. Tropical forests (both moist and dry) harbor from 50 percent to 90 percent of the earth's terrestrial species.

Most tropical forests are mainly in South America (1.4 billion acres), Africa (670 million acres), and Asia (490 million acres). From 1980 to 1990 about 25 million acres of tropical forest was cleared, of which about 15 million acres were of moist forests. In the following decade, total tropical forest clearance is thought to have increased to about 37 million acres per annum (about 1.2 percent of the global tropical forest total). While some of this loss is compensated for by tropical forest plantations, plantations are much lower in biodiversity.

CONTROLLING DEFORESTATION

Deforestation has largely occurred because of the expansion of agricultural land. Increasing populations and increasing demand for products that can be grown on land that is currently forested land (such as palm oil, a source of biofuel) will drive ongoing tropical deforestation. Climate change may worsen this, though it may also allow the expansion of some high-latitude forests, even if warmer winters allow increased populations of insect pests.

While there is considerable discussion of sustainable forest management, this is not yet having a significant mitigative effect. Until population growth substantially abates, the loss of quantity and especially of quality of forests in the tropics is likely to continue. And, because of climate change, tropical deforestation could continue even after population peaks.

SEE ALSO *Agricultural Industry; Boserup, Ester; Fertility, Human; Human Ecology; Population Growth; Resource Economics; Resources*

BIBLIOGRAPHY

Achard, Frédéric, Hugh D. Eva, Hans-Jürgen Stibig, et al. 2002. Determination of Deforestation Rates of the World's Humid Tropical Forests. *Science* 297 (August 9): 999–1002.

Cox, Peter M, Richard A Betts, Chris D. Jones, et al. 2000. Acceleration of Global Warming Due to Carbon-Cycle Feedbacks in a Coupled Climate Model. *Nature* 408 (November 9): 184–187.

Food and Agricultural Organization of the United Nations. 2001. Global Forest Resources Assessment 2000—Main Report. FAO Foresty Paper 140. http://www.fao.org/forestry/site/fra2000report/en/.

Hoare, A. 2005. Irrational Numbers: Why the FAO's Forest Assessments Are Misleading. London: Rainforest Foundation. http://www.rainforestfoundationuk.org/files/RF_Irrational%20numbers.pdf.

Secretariat of the Convention on Biological Diversity. 2001. *Global Biodiversity Outlook*. Montreal, Canada.

Secretariat of the Convention on Biological Diversity. 2006. *Global Biodiversity Outlook 2*. Montreal, Canada. http://www.cbd.int/doc/gbo2/cbd-gbo2.pdf.

Shvidenko, Anatoly, Charles Victor Barber, Reidar Persson, et al. 2005. Forest and Woodland Systems. In *Ecosystems and Human Well-Being: Current State and Trends*, Vol 1, eds. Rashid Hassan, Robert Scholes, and Neville Ash, 585–621. Washington, DC: Island Press.

Colin Butler

DE GAULLE, CHARLES
1890–1970

Charles de Gaulle was the leading French statesman of the twentieth century. His military career spanned both world wars and his political career, interrupted by a temporary retreat from public affairs in the 1950s, occurred during the hardships of the 1940s and then a number of serious challenges to political stability in the 1960s. As a military commander, he advocated an aggressive, tactical approach to warfare; as a politician, he was often careful in internal matters but more outspoken in international affairs.

De Gaulle was raised in a Roman Catholic family, and at an early age he showed an interest in military affairs. He entered the Military Academy of Saint-Cyr at the age of nineteen and then joined the military in 1913, commissioned as a lieutenant. He fought in World War I (1914–1918), including at the famous 1916 battle at Verdun, and he spent almost three years as a prisoner of war. After the war, he taught at his alma mater and also attended the École Supérieure de Guerre (a war college). In 1925 Marshal Philippe Pétain (1856–1951) promoted him to the staff of the Supreme Defense Council. Two years later de Gaulle began serving as a major in the occupation army for the Rhineland, an experience that illustrated the German potential for military action. Although the French prided themselves on what they saw as the impenetrable Maginot Line, in 1933 de Gaulle wrote an article arguing for a professionalized and armored French army.

When World War II (1939–1945) began, de Gaulle was commander of a tank brigade. In 1940 he was promoted to brigadier general, a position he held until his death. In the same year, he became the French undersecretary of state for defense and war, but he left the government almost immediately when Pétain became head of the government and indicated that he wanted an armistice with the Germans. De Gaulle went to England, where he began to encourage the French to continue fighting the Germans. In August 1940 he was sentenced to death by a French military court for treason. Although de Gaulle had no political base, he was deeply committed to a free France. He formed a shadow government, eventually known as the Free French Forces, although his military background was not attractive to French liberals and his condemnation of the Pétain government meant that French conservatives held little regard for him. He also had problems with the Allies, often because of his strong commitment to a free France. De Gaulle maintained contact with French resistance groups, and he broadcast radio appeals to his fellow citizens, creating increased national recognition of his leadership.

In 1943 he moved to Algiers, Algeria, where he formed the French Committee of National Liberation. He served as co-president of the committee with Henri Giraud (1879–1949), but successfully moved Giraud out of the role, signaling his political abilities. In August 1944 de Gaulle returned to Paris with the victorious Allied armed forces; he refused to meet with the envoy Pétain sent to establish peace, and de Gaulle became head of the new French government.

De Gaulle resigned, however, in 1946 because of his dissatisfaction with the power of the various political parties that formed a new Fourth French Republic. For twelve years de Gaulle argued against the republic because he saw it as too similar to the Third French Republic, which he thought had been unable to govern effectively. He organized a loose party, the Rally of the French People, which became powerful enough to win a sizable number of seats in the French National Assembly, but he left the group in 1953. His political activity ended temporarily in 1955, when he began to work on his memoirs, but in 1958 he returned to public life.

By the end of the 1950s, France was embroiled in a military and political conflict in one of its colonies, Algeria. De Gaulle presented himself as a candidate for prime minister in 1958, and the National Assembly authorized him to change the French constitution; in December 1958 de Gaulle was elected president of France. His changes to the nation's constitution strengthened the position of the presidency, including giving the president ruling powers during emergencies. Despite that centralization of power, de Gaulle supported the democratic principles of the government; he also made sure he was a highly visible and even personable president, spending a great deal of time giving addresses and speaking with individual citizens. De Gaulle's ministers were often friends from World War II, and they assisted him in maintaining a strong presidency.

Algeria presented a very difficult set of problems when de Gaulle became president, a situation that deeply split French liberals and conservatives. The former argued for Algerian independence, while the latter advocated that Algeria ought to remain a colony. The Algerian insurrectionists wanted only freedom, and de Gaulle recognized that he had to free the country. French military leaders in Algeria, however, moved against de Gaulle, forming the Secret Army Organization and taking control of Algeria in 1961. This organization indicated that it was ready to actually attack France, but de Gaulle used his presidential powers to thwart them; French citizens and the French military sided with de Gaulle. Although the Secret Army Organization continued to fight de Gaulle, using bombings and assassinations, de Gaulle's broad support resulted in his ability to establish Algeria's independence in 1962.

Once the Algerian situation was settled, de Gaulle moved to other national issues, including reinvigorating the economy, developing France's own atomic bomb, and instituting constitutional changes to establish independence for France's other colonies. Nevertheless, the position that he held upon his election in 1958 was no longer as secure because he had solved the Algerian problem. He again turned to constitutional changes as a means to strengthen his position. Previously, an electoral college consisting of local politicians elected the president; in 1962 French citizens chose between de Gaulle's resignation and a constitutional amendment that allowed direct election of the president. The referendum was a decisive victory for de Gaulle, and his party gained control of the National

Assembly later that year. As a result, de Gaulle was able to further his plans to develop France into an international power, focusing on independent actions. For example, the year after his reelection as president in 1965, he withdrew France from the military branch of the North Atlantic Treaty Organization (NATO), although France remained part of the Atlantic Alliance, a political association.

In international affairs, de Gaulle sought to convince nations that neutrality was preferable to aggression, but that approach meant he was seen as opposing the United States because he wanted the United States to withdraw from Vietnam. He also encouraged stronger relations with the Soviet Union, Eastern European countries under Soviet rule, and the People's Republic of China. De Gaulle argued that Europe had the potential to disengage from the influence of the United States. Internal strife, however, resulted in a serious weakening of de Gaulle's position; in May 1968 university students and left-wing unionists in France nearly toppled the government, and de Gaulle had to return from an international trip to initiate a state of emergency. Although the coalition of leftist resistance quickly fragmented because the French Communist Party did not view the students as genuine radicals, de Gaulle did not emerge as a victor. French citizens opposed the rebellion and supported de Gaulle, but when in 1969 he again proposed a constitutional change, this time to reorganize the Senate, the voters rejected the proposal. De Gaulle resigned from the presidency, and Georges Pompidou (1911–1974), who had served as France's prime minister from 1962 to 1968, became president. De Gaulle retired, planning to finish his memoirs; he died of a heart attack in 1970.

Charles de Gaulle's stature, in France and internationally, seems to be readily apparent and yet resists interpretation. He was able to form a liberation army and government during World War II, and he brought France through the bloody war for independence in Algeria. Although he was at the center of so much military and political activity, he resisted personification of his work, asking his supporters not to use his name as a party identification; nevertheless, they were indeed known as Gaullists. His attempts to create an internationally independent France attracted a great deal of attention, but did not necessarily result in political influence.

SEE ALSO *Battle of Algiers, The; Decolonization; Liberation; Nazism; Neutral States; Vietnam War; Weaponry, Nuclear; World War I; World War II*

BIBLIOGRAPHY

Cogan, Charles. 1996. *Charles de Gaulle: A Brief Biography with Documents.* Boston: Bedford.

De Gaulle, Charles. 1971. *Memoirs of Hope: Renewal and Endeavor.* Trans. Terence Kilmartin. New York: Simon and Schuster.

Lacouture, Jean. 1990–1992. *De Gaulle.* 2 vols. Trans. Patrick O'Brian and Alan Sheridan. New York: Norton.

Peyrefitte, Alain. 1994–2000. *C'était de Gaulle.* 3 vols. Paris: Editions de Fallois, Fayard.

Williams, Charles. 1993. *The Last Great Frenchman: A Life of General de Gaulle.* London: Little, Brown.

Philo A. Hutcheson

DEGREES OF FREEDOM

There are several ways to talk about degrees of freedom, usually shortened to *df* in text. A one-sentence definition for a set of data is: *The number of degrees of freedom of a set of data is the dimension of the smallest space in which the data lie.* From this (perhaps rather puzzling) sentence, all other descriptions of *df* emerge after suitable connections are established.

Consider the following set of data: $(y_1, y_2, y_3, y_4, y_5, y_6, y_7)$ = (26, 32, 35, 41, 43, 51, 52) are 7 values of the output variable of a simple process that has been set to 7 different sets of conditions, not obtained in the indicated order but rearranged for convenience. If all these responses were separately and independently generated, we would say that these numbers have (or possess, or carry) seven degrees of freedom. If plotted in a seven-dimensional space, they would define a single, unambiguous point. (If the entire experiment were repeated, another single point, elsewhere in this space, would be defined, and so on.)

Suppose we want to estimate the true mean μ of the distribution of possible *y*-values using this sample of values. The mean (or average) of the data is $\bar{y} = 40$. The deviations from this average are of the form $y_i - \bar{y} = -14, -8, -5, 1, 3, 11, 12$, respectively. These seven numbers also define the coordinates of a point in the seven-dimensional space, but *the point cannot lie anywhere in the space.* It is constrained by the fact that these seven numbers are now *deviations from the mean* and so must sum to zero. Thus the point defined by deviations from this estimated mean lies in a subspace of 6 dimensions defined by $\Sigma(y_i - \bar{y}) = 0$ and contained within the original 7-dimensional space. We can talk about this in the following manner: We have used the original seven data values to estimate one parameter, the mean μ. This estimated mean "carries" or "has" or "uses up" or "takes up" one degree of freedom. Consequently the 7 deviations *from* that mean, the so-called residuals, $y_i - \bar{y}$ for $i = 1, 2, ..., 7$, must carry the remaining 6 *df*. Suppose now that obtaining data from our

simple process above required the setting and resetting of an input variable x and that the *x*s associated with the *y*-data above were, in the same respective order, $(x_1, x_2, ..., x_7)$ = (8, 9, 10, 11, 12, 13, 14). We might wish to check if there were a linear relationship between the *y*s and the *x*s. This could be done by fitting a straight line, namely a *first order linear regression equation* of the form

$$y_i = \beta_0 + \beta_1 x_i + \epsilon_i, \qquad (1)$$

where β_0 and β_1 are parameters (to be estimated by the method of least squares) and ε_i, $i = 1, 2, ..., n$ (where $n = 7$ for our example) represent random errors. The *least squares estimates*, b_0 and b_1 of β_0 and β_1 respectively, are given by $b_0 = -8.714$, $b_1 = 4.429$ so that the *fitted equation* (or *fitted model)* is

$$\hat{y} = -8.714 + 4.429x \qquad (2)$$

The residuals from this regression calculation, namely the $y_i - \hat{y}_i$ values using predictions obtained by substituting the 7 values of x individually into (2), are, in order, –0.714, 0.857, –0.571, 1.000, –1.429, 2.143, –1.286. These residuals, like the ones above, also sum to zero. However, because of the mathematical calculations involved in the least squares process, the sum of the cross products $\Sigma x_i(y_i - \hat{y}_i) = 8(-0.714) + 9(0.857) + ... + 14(-1.286) = 0$ also. So the estimation of the 2 parameters β_0 and β_1 has now "taken up" 2 of the original 7 *df*, leaving the 7 residuals carrying only $7 - 2 = 5$ *df*.

Suppose at this stage we wish to estimate the variance σ^2 of the *y*-distribution. The appropriate estimate would be $s^2 = \Sigma(y_i - \hat{y}_i)^2/(n-2)$ using the $\hat{y}_i$ values of equation (2) and where n is the original total number of *df*s. The numerical value of this estimate is $\{(-0.714)^2 + (0.857)^2 + (-0.571)^2 + (1.000)^2 + (-1.429)^2 + (2.143)^2 + (-1.286)^2\}/(7 - 2) = 10.8586/5 = 2.172$. Notice that the divisor $7 - 2 = 5$ is the appropriate residual df left over after fitting the 2-parameter straight line model. If additional parameters were added to the model, the reduction in *df* would have to be adjusted suitably. For more examples and details, see Norman R. Draper and Harry Smith's *Applied Regression Analysis* (1998).

More generally, all sums of squares involving response values in statistical work can be written in the form $y'My$, where $y' = (y_1, y_2, ..., y_n)$ and its transpose y are, respectively, a row and a column vector of observations and where M is a specific $n \times n$ symmetric matrix whose diagonal elements are the coefficients of y_i^2 and whose off-diagonal entries are one-half the coefficients of the $y_i y_j$ in the sum of squares. The *df* attached to such a sum of squares is always the rank of the matrix M. This rank can best be discovered numerically by asking a computer to produce the eigenvalues of M and counting how many of these eigenvalues are nonzero.

We can carry out various statistical tests on data like the above. These tests are not discussed here. However, all such tests involve a test statistic, which is compared to a selected percentage point of an appropriate statistical distribution. When the n statistical errors ε_i can be assumed to be normally distributed, tests on regression parameters typically involve either a $t(v)$ distribution or an $F(v_1, v_2)$ distribution, where the vs represent appropriate numbers of degrees of freedom determined by the df of quantities occurring in the tests. Tables of the percentage points of t and F distributions appear in most statistical textbooks, tabulated by their degrees of freedom.

Another area where degrees of freedom need to be calculated is *contingency tables*, in which discrete (noncontinuous) data arise in categories such as the number of piston-ring failures in four compressors, each of which has three sections, the North, the Center, and the South. This particular example leads to a 4×3 2-way table with 12 entries. The test statistic in this type of problem is distributed approximately as a $\chi^2(v)$ variable where, for our example, $v = (4 - 1)(3 - 1) = 6$. Again, percentage points of χ^2 distributions appear in most statistical textbooks. A lucid account of this and similar examples is in Owen L. Davies and Peter L. Goldsmith's *Statistical Methods in Research and Production* (1986, pp. 317–334).

There exists, in the area of nonparametric regression, the similar concept of *equivalent degrees of freedom*. For this, see P. J. Green and B. W. Silverman's *Nonparametric Regression and Generalized Linear Models* (1994, p. 37).

SEE ALSO *Econometric Decomposition; Eigen-Values and Eigen-Vectors, Perron-Frobenius Theorem: Economic Applications; Frequency Distributions; Hypothesis and Hypothesis Testing; Least Squares, Ordinary; Nonparametric Estimation; Nonparametric Regression; Regression; Regression Analysis; Statistics*

BIBLIOGRAPHY

Davies, Owen L., and Peter L. Goldsmith, eds. 1986. *Statistical Methods in Research and Production.* 4th ed. New York: Longman.

Draper, Norman R., and Harry Smith. 1998. *Applied Regression Analysis.* 3rd ed. New York: Wiley.

Green, P. J., and B. W. Silverman. 1994. *Nonparametric Regression and Generalized Linear Models.* New York: Chapman and Hall.

Norman R. Draper

DEINDUSTRIALI-ZATION

SEE *Neighborhood Effects.*

DEININGER AND SQUIRE WORLD BANK INEQUALITY DATABASE

Measurements of income distribution are widely used in studies of social and economic inequality. Although the distribution of income is not the only factor that determines social stratification in a particular country or region, it is one of the most important factors. Economists have been especially interested in the presumed link between income distribution and economic growth. Some researchers have used income distribution as a dependent variable (i.e., a variable influenced by economic growth), whereas others have treated income inequality as an independent variable that affects the prospects for economic growth. Researchers who posit that income distribution and economic growth are reciprocally connected have tested this hypothesis by conducting least-squares regressions of simultaneous equations models.

Despite the frequent use of income distribution as a variable in econometric studies, researchers have long encountered problems in finding reliable statistics. The database entries for a time series of income distribution are fully valid only if they are derived from nationally representative household surveys. Moreover, the entries must be uniform in three respects: First, they must refer to the same type of income (wages, wages plus non-wage income, etc.); second, they must measure income at the same stage (before or after taxes); and third, they must designate the same unit as a recipient of income (households, families, individuals, wage-earners, etc.). A time series that does not include uniform data will not yield meaningful results when analyzed. The collection of uniform data, however, is difficult and expensive, especially for international comparisons of income distribution over many years. Statistical agencies in different countries vary in the way they measure income distribution (if they measure it at all), and many of them fail to provide adequate information about their measurement techniques. In some cases they have altered their methods without announcing it and without adjusting earlier data, thus causing temporal inconsistencies. Some international organizations that compile income distribution data for countries in specific regions, such as the European Bank for Reconstruction and Development and the Asian Development Bank, also have not disclosed enough information about their means of tabulation. Hence, panel datasets with long time series of income distribution covering dozens of countries around the world are rare.

The greatest success in producing comprehensive panel datasets of income distribution has been achieved by the World Bank and by the United Nations World Institute for Development Economics Research (WIDER). The first major advance along these lines was the effort in the mid-1990s by two World Bank economists, Klaus Deininger and Lyn Squire, to put together what they described in a 1996 article as a "new data set on inequality" that would "represent a significant expansion in coverage and a substantial improvement in quality" as "compared with earlier data sets" (Deininger and Squire 1996, p. 566). They noted that "although a large number of earlier studies on inequality have amassed substantial data on inequality, the information included is often of dubious quality," and they indicated that their own compilation was "based on household surveys, on comprehensive coverage of the population, and on comprehensive coverage of income sources" (p. 567). Deininger and Squire explained why they used two types of distributional indicators—the Gini coefficient (an aggregate measure covering the full population) and the population-quintile shares (a disaggregated index permitting comparisons of population groups)—and highlighted the advantages and limitations of the new dataset. In particular, they explained how to distinguish "high-quality data" from entries that are less reliable and emphasized the advantages of using the new dataset for time-series analysis. The full Deininger-Squire dataset was made available to other researchers and became a standard resource for social scientists.

The Deininger-Squire dataset covers 138 countries in total, though the density of the coverage varies a good deal. For some countries dozens of observations are available, whereas for other countries the number of observations is much smaller. The coverage extends from 1890 to 1996, though the bulk of the information is from the 1960s to the early 1990s, after which the coverage is spotty despite periodic updates. As a result, researchers interested in studying patterns of income distribution since the early 1990s, particularly those who want to examine how income distribution has been affected by the economic and political transformations of the former communist countries in East-Central Europe, have relied on other sources of data that in some cases are of lower quality.

After Deininger and Squire presented their initial dataset, a few other large research institutes sought to compile new panel datasets that would fill in some of the gaps and bolster the quality of the data. Most of these undertakings were designed to build on the Deininger-Squire dataset, though a few were intended to supplant the Deininger-Squire project by relying on different distributional indicators and alternative sources of information. The most successful effort to put together a new dataset—one that built on but went well beyond the Deininger-Squire project—was WIDER's compilation of its World Income Inequality Database (WIID), which increased the coverage to 152 countries, extended the timeframe to 2003, augmented the number of distributional indicators (including decile as well as quintile shares and the use of

an *adjusted* Gini coefficient to supplement the *reported* Gini numbers), and expanded the number of data observations to provide for higher quality. The first version of WIID was compiled from 1997 to 1999 and made available in September 2000, and a second, substantially improved version was released in June 2005. WIDER has continued to update the WIID since 2005, allowing further improvements in the quality of data, the extent of international coverage, and the length of the time series.

Despite these advances, the Deininger-Squire project will remain important as the first systematic attempt to compile high-quality data for comparisons of income distribution in dozens of countries over several decades. The Deininger-Squire effort provided a crucial foundation for subsequent compilations of high-quality data on income distribution.

SEE ALSO *Gini Coefficient; Income Distribution; Inequality, Income; Inequality, Wealth; Kuznets Hypothesis; Theil Index; University of Texas Inequality Project*

BIBLIOGRAPHY

Atkinson, Anthony B., and François Bourguignon, eds. 2000. *Handbook of Income Distribution.* Amsterdam and New York: Elsevier.

Babones, Salvatore J., and María José Alvarez-Rivadulla. 2007. Standardized Income Inequality Data for Use in Cross-National Research. *Sociological Inquiry* 77 (1): 3–22.

Deininger, Klaus, and Lyn Squire. 1996. A New Data Set Measuring Income Inequality. *The World Bank Economic Review* 10 (3): 565–591.

Deininger, Klaus, and Lyn Squire. 1998. New Ways of Looking at Old Issues: Inequality and Growth. *Journal of Development Economics* 57 (2): 259–287.

United Nations University, World Institute for Development Economics Research. 2005. *World Income Inequality Database: User Guide and Data Sources.* Vol. 2.0a (June). Helsinki: UNU/WIDER.

Mark Kramer

DELAYED GRATIFICATION

SEE *Time Orientation.*

DEMAND

In economics, demand theory examines the purchasing behavior of an individual, or of a group of individuals, in terms of its responses to changes in purchasing constraints or other institutional factors. In the most basic setting, an individual chooses a bundle of commodities, considering both their prices and a maximum income that he or she can spend. It is assumed that the individual compares bundles of commodities according to his or her own preferences, and that he or she chooses to purchase the best bundle that is affordable; in economics, this type of behavior is called "rational" or "preference maximizing." The first systematic analysis of this problem was done by Leon Walras in 1874. In 1886 Giovanni Antonelli studied the problem of constructing preferences that can explain a given demand function, and in 1915 Eugene Slutsky obtained a full set of implications of preference maximization on demand behavior. In the mid-twentieth century, the economist Paul Samuelson called for a revision of the theory, whereby observable behavior, rather than unobservable preferences, would constitute the foundation of demand theory. This proposal led to the development of *revealed-preference analysis*, an exhaustive series of conditions that must be satisfied by demand behavior, if it is consistent with preference maximization.

The standard problem of demand theory is that of an individual who chooses a bundle of L commodities, ranking different bundles according to his or her preferences. The individual faces prices $p = (p_1, \ldots, p_L)$ and can spend up to a nominal income of m. Consumption bundles are denoted by $x = (x_1, \ldots, x_L)$. A rational individual chooses a bundle $\hat{x}$ that is:

1. feasible: $p \cdot \hat{x} = p_1 \hat{x}_1 + \ldots + p_L \hat{x}_L \leq m$; and

2. optimal: there does not exist an alternative bundle that the consumer can afford and prefers to $\hat{x}$.

Under well-known assumptions on the preferences of the individual, one such $\hat{x}$ is guaranteed to exist, and is uniquely defined. Then, $x(p, m) = \hat{x}$ is known as the *Marshallian demand* of the individual, and constitutes the central element of demand theory: It says how much of each commodity the consumer demands, as a function of the prices he or she encounters in the market and of the income he or she has.

Function x is homogeneous of degree zero: multiplying all prices and income by the same positive number does not change demand. When a consumer prefers more to less consumption of at least one commodity, Marshallian demand satisfies Walras's law: the consumer will spend all his or her income, so $p \cdot x(p, m) = m$. When Marshallian demand is differentiable, these properties impose restrictions on the derivatives of the demand with respect to prices and income, which can be used to restrict empirical estimations of demand. More importantly, the substitution matrix, S, defined by $S(p, m) = D_p x(p, m) + D_m x(p, m) x(p, m)'$, and which isolates the effects of changes in relative prices, is a symmetric, negative-semi-

definite matrix of rank $L - 1$. Suppose that the preferences of the consumer are represented by a utility function u. Then, the indirect utility function, v, defined by $v(p, m) = u(x(p, m))$, and which measures the utility that the consumer obtains when he or she faces income m and prices p, is homogeneous of degree zero and, remarkably, satisfies Roy's identity: the negative of the ratio of the derivative of the indirect utility with respect to the price of a commodity to the marginal utility of income equals the Marshallian demand for that commodity; formally, $-(D_m v(p, m))^{-1} D_p v(p, m) = x(p, m)'$.

Representability of preferences—via utility functions that assigned higher utility levels to more preferred bundles than to less preferred bundles—allows for an auxiliary problem: fixing a benchmark utility level $\bar{u}$, and given prices p, determine a bundle $\hat{x}$ that:

1. gives at least that level of utility: $u(\hat{x}) \geq \bar{u}$; and

2. minimizes expenditure: every other bundle that gives utility of at least $\bar{u}$ costs at least $p \cdot \hat{x}$.

The solution to this problem defines the Hicksian demand function, $h(p, \bar{u}) = \hat{x}$, whose cost defines the expenditure function, $e(p, \bar{u}) = p \cdot h(p, \bar{u})$. Functions $h(p, \bar{u})$ and $e(p, \bar{u})$ are, respectively, homogeneous of degrees zero and one in prices. When small changes of consumption only induce small changes of utility (a condition known as "continuity of preferences"), the utility level given by the expenditure-minimizing bundle is exactly the required level: $u(h(p, \bar{u})) = \bar{u}$. Function e is strictly increasing in $\bar{u}$ and nondecreasing and concave in p, while Hicksian demand satisfies the "compensated law of demand" (this is not true for Marshallian demand), in a sense that Hicksian demands are nonincreasing in prices: $(p - p') \cdot (h(p, \bar{u}) - h(p', \bar{u}))$. Under differentiability, Hicksian demand satisfies Shephard's lemma: the derivative of the expenditure function with respect to the price of a commodity equals the Hicksian demand for that commodity, $D_p e(p, \bar{u}) = h(p, \bar{u})$.

Duality theory establishes, with minor qualifications, that Marshallian and Hicksian demands mirror each other: (1) the solution of the expenditure minimization problem also solves the preference maximization problem at income equal to the minimized expenditure: $x(p, e(p, \bar{u})) = h(p, \bar{u})$; (2) the solution of the utility maximization problem also solves the expenditure minimization problem at benchmark utility equal to the maximized utility: $h(p, v(p, m)) = x(p, m)$; (3) the maximal utility achievable with income equal to the minimized expenditure is the benchmark utility, $v(p, e(p, \bar{u})) = \bar{u}$; and (4) with lower income, it is impossible to obtain at least the maximized utility level, $e(p, v(p, m)) = m$. Shephard's lemma shows that the first equality yields the Slutsky decomposition: $D_p h(p, \bar{u}) = S(p, e(p, \bar{u}))$, which allows for empirical estimations of Hicksian demand. A commodity is said to be inferior if its demand decreases when the consumer has more income, and "Giffen" if it increases when the price of the commodity increases. It follows from Slutsky decomposition and the compensated law of demand (for Hicksian demands) that Giffen commodities are inferior.

Samuelson's program looked for conditions on demand data that were equivalent to the existence of the unobservable preferences: Given a series $(p_t, m_t, x_t)_{t=1}^T$ of observations of prices, incomes, and demanded bundles, do there exist preferences such that, at every observation, the observed demand is rational according to those preferences $(x(p_t, m_t) = x_t)$? A necessary condition for the existence of such preferences is the *Weak Axiom of Revealed Preference*, or WARP: If $p_{t'} \cdot x_t \leq m_{t'}$ and $x_t \neq x_{t'}$, then $p_{t'} \cdot x_{t'} > m_t$; that is, if the bundle purchased at observation t', $x_{t'}$, could have been purchased at t (since it was affordable) but bundle x_t was purchased instead, then it must be that the consumer prefers bundle x_t to bundle $x_{t'}$. Then, at observation t', when the consumer actually purchased bundle $x_{t'}$, it must be that the more preferred bundle, x_t, was not affordable. WARP is not, however, a sufficient condition. It compares only pairs of bundles, whereas rationality requires comparisons of sequences of bundles, since it implies that preference is a transitive relation. A transitive chain of reasonings—like the ones posed by WARP, known as the *Strong Axiom of Revealed Preference*—is a necessary and sufficient condition for rationality.

Antonelli's "integrability" result shows that homogeneity of degree zero, symmetry and negative semi-definiteness of the substitution matrix, and Walras's law exhaust the necessary conditions of a rational Marshallian demand. Using the solution to the system of differential equations implied by S, one can construct an expenditure function whose variation with respect to prices can be used to preferences that, when maximized, would yield the observed demand behavior.

The separability problem, first considered by John Hicks, studies how a group of commodities whose prices are kept in fixed proportions can be treated as a single, composite commodity whose price is constructed through the aggregation of the individual prices. This analysis provides the basis for the construction of price indices. A related problem assumes that preferences satisfy the following separability property: a group of commodities exists whose variation is ranked by the individual independently of the level of consumption of all other commodities. In this case, there is a "subutility" function, defined for the group in question, and the overall utility depends on the consumption of the group only via the subutility level. When preferences satisfy this separability condition, demand can be determined in a two-stage process: first, the individual decides how much to spend in the group, and then the individual decides how to allocate expenditures across commodities in the group.

Suppose that there is a set of consumers $\{1, ..., i, ..., I\}$, with individual variables indexed by i. The aggregate demand function is $x(p, m^1, ..., m^I) = x^1(p, m^1) + ... + x^I(p, m^I)$. The aggregation (or representative consumer) problem asks whether one can find an individual demand function $\bar{x}$ such that $x(p, m^1, ..., m^I) = \bar{x}(p, m^1 + ... + m^I)$. The answer to this question is, in general, no, for it requires that all individuals have parallel wealth-expansion paths (the trajectories defined by changing individual incomes at given prices). Also, even under aggregation, individual satisfaction of WARP does not imply its satisfaction in the aggregate. WARP, in the aggregate, is obtained whenever individual Marshallian demands satisfy the law of demand, a condition that does not generally occur. (The definition of aggregate demand given here should not be confused with Hicks's aggregate demand, which is used in macroeconomic models and in national accounts.)

In the standard setting, commodities can be interpreted to accommodate intertemporal problems. If there is only one commodity in each time period, relative prices represent interest rates, and an impatient consumer will anticipate consumption unless interest rates compensate for his or her impatience. In general, if intertemporal preferences are convex, an individual prefers a consumption plan that smooths consumption, in the sense that it avoids high levels of consumption in some periods and low levels in other periods. A canonical case for consumption smoothing is the life-cycle model originally proposed by Franco Modigliani, who divided life into three periods: (1) youth, when income is low; (2) adulthood, when income is high; and (3) retirement, when income is once again low. A consumer without restrictions will choose a smooth consumption plan that includes accruing debt during youth, repaying this debt and saving during adulthood, and spending savings during retirement. Consumption is determined by lifetime (discounted) income, while temporary deviations from this "permanent" income are accommodated by savings. A more general version of this model, involving different individuals at different stages in life, is known as the *overlapping generations model*. This model constitutes the basic tool for the economics of Social Security.

When the interpretation of commodities includes different states of nature, the model permits the study of uncertainty. In this case, convexity of preferences means that the individual dislikes risk and will avoid large consumption in some states if it implies low consumption in other states, unless prices compensate for this effect. This effect means that, if available, the individual will use insurance opportunities, or, alternatively, that groups of individuals will prefer risk-sharing schemes that disseminate risks.

Applied work usually imposes particular functional forms useful for estimation. An important, flexible functional form is the *Almost Ideal Demand System* (AIDS), which imposes an expenditure function of the form $e(p, \bar{u}) = \alpha(p) + \beta(p)\bar{u}$, where $\alpha(p) = \alpha_0 + \sum_l \alpha_l \log(p_l) + \sum_{l,j} \alpha_{l,j} \log(p_l) \log(p_j)$, $\beta(p) = \beta_0 \Pi_l p_l \beta_l$, and some conditions on the parameters of these two functions are imposed. Applied work also uses "hedonic" models to impose additional structure on demand systems. It is assumed that individuals do not directly care about the commodities, but only about their attributes (physical features), which are, normally, objectively observable.

SEE ALSO *Aggregate Demand; Aggregate Supply; Equilibrium in Economics; Excess Demand; Hedonic Prices; Markets; Rationality; Samuelson, Paul A.; Supply; Utility Function*

BIBLIOGRAPHY

Ando, Albert, and Franco Modigliani. 1963. The "Life-Cycle" Hypothesis of Savings: Aggregate Implications and Tests. *American Economic Review* 53 (1): 55–84.

Deaton, Angus, and John Muelbauer. 1980. *Economics and Consumer Behavior*. Cambridge, U.K.: Cambridge University Press.

Hildenbrand, Werner. 1994. *Market Demand*. Princeton, NJ: Princeton University Press.

Samuelson, Paul. 1938. A Note on the Pure Theory of Consumer's Behaviour. *Economica* 5: 61–71.

Andrés Carvajal

DEMENTIA

Although there is growing understanding of dementia, it remains a poorly understood condition that continues to be associated with negative attitudes and stigmas. *Dementia* is not a disease but a clinical syndrome, meaning a set of symptoms relating to the breakdown of intellectual (cognitive) functions. Operational diagnostic criteria for dementia stipulate (1) an impairment in memory; (2) an impairment in at least one other cognitive domain (e.g., language, visuospatial, knowledge and understanding, executive functions, control over social and emotional behaviors); (3) that the impairment represents a decline from the person's previous levels of ability; and (4) that the impairments are severe enough to interfere with the person's everyday life.

The main risk factor for the development of dementia is age. Prevalence rises from 1 in 1,000 for those aged 45 to 65; to 1 in 5 for those aged 80 to 90; to 1 in 3 among those over age 90. Until the late twentieth century, dementia in an elderly person (defined to be someone over 65 years of age) was commonly diagnosed as "senility" or "senile dementia." These terms, however, are no longer recommended because they have been used with a lack of diagnostic rigor and there is a lack of scientific evidence to justify the diagnostic distinction between "presenile dementia" (dementia in someone under age 65) and "senile dementia" (identical symptoms in someone age 65 or more). Furthermore, the term senility carries negative connotations and implies that the dementia syndrome is an inevitability of old age. This implication is not supported by the evidence and leads to poor recognition of dementia syndrome. The symptoms of dementia in elderly people often get dismissed on the basis that these are just signs of old age, although dementia in middle-aged people is commonly misdiagnosed as a functional psychiatric disorder.

Most causes of dementia are slowly progressing neurodegenerative diseases with Alzheimer's disease being the most common cause, accounting for 50 to 60 percent of all cases. Dementia is typically thought of as progressing from a mild stage, characterized by slips of the memory and confusion in complex situations, through a moderate stage, during which the degree of cognitive impairment intensifies to affect an increasing number of activities of daily living (e.g., use of language, ability to recognize friends and relatives, ability to make sense of the visual world, ability to use household objects or appliances effectively and safely, ability to dress and attend to personal hygiene). The severe stage of dementia is characterized by serious disability in which the person is likely to have limited language and understanding and to be totally dependent upon others for all their physical needs (eating, drinking, toileting).

However, typical schemes of dementia symptoms and progression need to be treated with extreme caution. The precise symptoms a person experiences will depend upon the particular cause of that person's dementia and the parts of the brain that were damaged. Also, the symptoms of dementia must be understood as complex interplay between neurological damage and psychological and social variables, such as the person's life history, personality, and quality of the care environment. These considerations are particularly important when assessing the non-cognitive symptoms of dementia, such as apathy, anxiety, wandering, or aggression. Such behaviors may reflect the individual's personality or coping style, or they may be a valid response to an environment in which the person's needs and personhood are being overlooked or neglected.

With over two hundred possible causes of dementia there is still a lot to be learned about how specific causes manifest. The stages of dementia outlined are strongly influenced by the specific characteristics of Alzheimer's disease. Other forms of dementia are known to have different characteristics and growing knowledge of these differences is stimulating a move away from the generic criteria for dementia toward operational criteria for specific diagnoses (e.g., dementia of the Alzheimer type, vascular dementia). In particular, early memory loss is often cited as the key feature of dementia but this symptom has a specific link with Alzheimer's disease and there are forms of dementia in which memory loss is not a central feature (e.g., frontotemporal and Lewy body dementia).

After Alzheimer's disease, vascular dementia is the next most common form of primary dementia, accounting for 20 percent of all dementias. The blood supply to the brain can become fragile in old age and the term vascular dementia covers all forms of dementia that result from cerebrovascular pathologies. Lewy body disease, frontotemporal atrophy, alcohol abuse, and the AIDS complex are also significant causes of dementia. Some dementias are due to reversible causes (e.g., depression, hypothyroidism, vitamin B deficiency) and are called "secondary dementias." It is important that the diagnostic procedure fully investigates secondary causes for dementia before diagnosing a primary (irreversible) cause.

Pharmacological treatments for primary dementias are limited. A number of anti-cholinesterases are available that aim to alleviate some of the cognitive and functional symptoms of dementia by boosting levels of the neurotransmitter acetylcholine. These drugs were designed to specifically target the Alzheimer's disease process, although there is evidence that they may be beneficial in other forms of dementia, particularly vascular dementia and Lewy body dementia. Memantine is an alternative drug that aims to protect undamaged nerve cells from the toxic effects of high levels of the neurotransmitter glutamate, which is released in excessive amounts when cells are damaged. Both types of drug are aimed at damage limitation; neither can stop the underlying disease processes themselves. The evidence suggests anti-cholinesterases and memantine provide some benefit, but it is modest.

It is also important to support drug interventions with non-pharmacological interventions (e.g., reminiscence therapies, sensory therapies, support and discussion groups). These interventions will also not cure the problem but will protect well-being and ensure that the symptoms of dementia are not exacerbated through poor care, inappropriate expectations, and lack of support. The person with dementia's well-being is critically dependent upon that of their care giver. When care givers are not properly supported there is a high risk that their own mental and physical health will be affected, leading to a poor outcome for both the care giver and patient.

In terms of prevention, control of vascular risk, particularly cholesterol levels and hypertension, is emerging as the main preventative strategy for both vascular dementia and Alzheimer's disease. People can control their vascular risk either through diet or pharmaceuticals. An increased risk for dementia has also been associated with low education or intelligence, socioeconomic disadvantage, stress, and dietary factors (particularly the B vitamins) but untangling the direction of causation among this complex set of factors remains a significant challenge. For example, the well-established correlation between low intelligence and risk for dementia has been interpreted in terms of compensation, such that the effects of pathology are masked by higher ability, but some recent prospective studies, most notably the nun studies organized by David Snowden, suggest that low intelligence in early life may be directly involved in the pathogenesis of Alzheimer's disease. Similarly, low intake of vitamin B12 and folate are associated with elevated levels of homocysteine, another vascular risk factor which has been associated with risk for Alzheimer's disease. However, it is less clear whether increasing the dietary intake of vitamin B12 and folate has any protective effect.

SEE ALSO *Alzheimer's Disease; Gerontology; Madness; Medicine; Memory in Psychology; Mental Illness; Neuroscience; Psychopathology; Psychotherapy; Stigma*

BIBLIOGRAPHY

Burns, Alistair, John O'Brien, and David Ames. 2005. *Dementia.* 3rd ed. London: Hodder Arnold.

Kitwood, Tom. 1997. *Dementia Reconsidered.* Buckingham, U.K.: Open University Press.

Sabat, Steven R. 2001. *The Experience of Alzheimer's Disease: Life Through a Tangled Veil.* Oxford: Blackwell.

Snowden, David. 2001 *Aging with Grace: The Nun Study and the Science of Old Age.* London: Fourth Estate.

Elizabeth J. Anderson

DEMOCRACY

Democracy is a concept that means different things to different people. For some it is a political system that ensures political equality and self-rule. To others, it is a system that allows the presence of equal opportunities and rights. The two different conceptualizations of democracy are based on the experiences of the two major democratic experiments that the world has seen so far: democracies in classical Greece and modern nation-states. The classical model of democracy draws its inspiration from the democratic experiments of ancient Greek city-states. In such an arrangement, citizens were both the rulers and the ruled; political sovereignty and power rested with the people. Each individual citizen had a right and an obligation to serve in administrative duties. Citizens were politically active. Women, slaves, and immigrants were, however, excluded from political participation. The small size of the cities allowed citizens to meet face to face and make direct deliberations and decisions on various issues.

There are at least two problems with the classical democratic arrangement: first, it is applicable more to small city-states than to modern nation-states. Face-to-face political participation and deliberations are easier to conduct in small communities. Modern democracies are established in much larger nation-states, making a representative form of government a necessity. Second, the conditions under which political equality is possible are not spelled out; it is simply asserted as a self-evident truth. There is no strong consensus among citizens and scholars in such an assertion. Indeed, some argue that individual liberty, which is promoted in modern democracies, makes some form of inequality inevitable.

Although there is no consensus, many scholars would agree that democracy in modern nation-states means the presence of political rights and civil liberties. Political rights include the right to vote, the right to run for office, and the presence of fair and free electoral competition; civil liberties include the presence of due process, freedom of speech and assembly, and equality before the law. Democracy, however, even as a procedural concept, is much more than the mere occurrence of elections and liberties. For instance, the presence of a majoritarian decision-making or voting mechanism, often overlooked and taken for granted, is an essential procedure in the democratic process. Elected and, in some cases, appointed representatives and officials utilize the simple majority rule as a minimum requirement for the passage of laws, judicial decisions, and administrative policies; a majority voting system is commonly used to resolve major issues, including difficult and divisive ones, by legislation or judicial interpretation. Thus, democracy may be defined as the presence of fair and free elections, civil liberties, and a majoritarian decision-making procedure. Nevertheless, not all scholars would agree with such a procedural definition. For instance, it does not fully account for the variation in the distribution of political power or influence among citizens. In other words, why is it that some citizens can exert more influence on political leaders than do others? Why do some individuals have a better chance of becoming a president or a member of parliament than others do?

TRANSITION TO DEMOCRACY

Compared to other older forms of political systems, such as autocracy, modern democracy is a relatively new phenomenon. James Bryce (1921) noted that in the early nineteenth century only Switzerland had a working democracy in Europe. Great Britain had greater freedom than any other nation on the European continent, but its government was still oligarchic. By 1921, however, Bryce observed that almost all the monarchies of Europe had become democracies. He counted twenty new democratic countries in the Western Hemisphere, and five more among the British colonies. The political evolution toward a free society heralded "the universal acceptance of democracy as the normal and natural form of government" (p. 4). Outside Europe, the United States, which is considered as the oldest democracy, had ratified its constitution in 1789. Thus, it is fair to assume that modern democracy is perhaps a consequence of the modern period, mainly of the Industrial Revolution and the Enlightenment.

The initial quality of democracy in countries such as Great Britain, Sweden, and the United States was, however, low by today's standards. More often than not, those who had property voted. Mass democracy was possible only after the spread of mass literacy and the spread of wealth to a significant number of individuals. In other words, the conditions under which democracy has arisen would, among other things, seem to be an increased level of education and economic development. Seymour M. Lipset (1959), following Aristotle, argues that socioeconomic development leads to educated citizenry and a large middle class. An educated citizenry and a large middle class seem to be the social foundations of modern democracy. Despite the presence of counterfindings, empirical studies support Lipset's argument. Socioeconomic development, however, may not be the only factor that accounts for the presence of democracy. The political process, particularly political leadership, and external factors are two other possible variables.

In the latter part of the eighteenth century the United States was not, for instance, a developed country. In the absence of a developed economy the framers of the U.S. Constitution were able to establish a political system that would become one of the most stable democracies in the world. To be sure, the architects of the U.S. Constitution, such as James Madison, were themselves influenced by the evolution of European political thought and by the level of education they had received. Still, not all leaders in all countries attempted to establish a freer system of governance at the time. This was a choice made by the framers. Thus, it is fair to contend that the framers of the U.S. Constitution have contributed to the emergence and development of democracy in the United States.

Democracy, once emerged in countries such as the United States, has found its way to other parts of the world. For instance, one of the legacies of European colonialism was the spread of modern democratic institutions in some of the former colonies. Former British colonies like India, Botswana, Mauritius, and Trinidad and Tobago have maintained democratic rule since independence. Given that not all former British colonies have maintained democracy, however, it was perhaps a mixture of this legacy and a democratically predisposed indigenous leadership that have helped maintain democratic rule in these countries. Leaders like Seretse Khama (1921–1980) of Botswana and Jawaharlal Nehru (1889–1964) of India were predisposed to democracy.

ALTERNATIVES TO AND VARIANTS OF DEMOCRACY

Democracy is a complex political system. It requires give-and-take compromises when issues are debated and decisions are made. Political leaders and their constituents must consistently, and often painfully, compromise their political and economic interests with others. A decision by one branch of government is often checked and balanced by the others. Officials' private and public lives are often scrutinized by the media. Despite the foregoing inconveniences, democracy is perhaps the only known political system that can provide individuals with the right to be treated equally before the law, the right to vote, and the right to own personal property. Other autocratic systems, such as monarchy, theocracy, and communism, have not adequately done so in the past and are not logically expected to do so in the future.

Democracy has, however, its variants, the most important ones being liberal democracy and social democracy. Although these variants adhere to the fundamental principles of democracy, including the presence of fair and free elections and civil liberties, they seem to have distinct socioeconomic principles. While liberal democracy stresses the importance of individuals as the deciding force of their own economic opportunities, social democracy seems to emphasize the role of the public in promoting social equity. More specifically, liberal democracy is grounded on the principle that individuals must, with little or no societal and government encroachments, be free to possess personal property and pursue their own economic interests. While such a system may bring affluence to most of the people, some individuals will probably become less successful or remain poor. By contrast, social democracy assumes that the market economic system cannot by itself evenly promote the economic interests of every individual; hence, society and government are expected to contribute to the socioeconomic well-being and advancement of the poor. The United States and

Sweden may be considered as examples of the former and the latter, respectively. Such differences in economic policy cannot be exaggerated, however. In practice, even liberal democracies attempt to support the poorer segment of society and the variation in the level of such a support between the two variants seems to be only a matter of degree. Indeed, global economic competition and electoral politics seem to have tempered the different approach that the two variants of democracy have followed. Relatively higher taxation policies, as seen in social democracies, will quite likely hamper the competitiveness of corporations. Similarly, liberal democracies may have to increase their support to the poor because not doing so will probably not be favored by most people. A convergence of the two variants is apt to be inevitable.

DEMOCRATIC DEVELOPMENT AFTER TRANSITION

Once countries transition to democratic rule, the next logical step is to stabilize such a system. Again, the stability of the new democracies seems to rest, among other things, on continuous socioeconomic development. The case of African countries right after independence suggests that poor or "immature" democracies are likely to be unstable and will probably revert to authoritarian systems. Nevertheless, the cases of India and Botswana suggest that poor democracies can become stable if they have good leadership and promote socioeconomic development. While continuous socioeconomic development may promote social mobility and affluence, good leadership tends to serve as an arbitrator for the presence of fair distribution of societal interests. By far, the most important role of democratic governments for promoting democracy has been public expenditures and investments in education, particularly in the education of impoverished children. Thus, the political process, including good political leadership and interest group politics, and continuous economic development continue to be two of the most important factors for the consolidation of democracy. But is the democratic process static or dynamic?

One can consider the cases of Sweden and Mali, for instance. While the former has been democratic since the early twentieth century, the latter has been so only since the 1990s. Can one logically assume that these two countries have an equal level of democracy? According to major democracy indices such as the Freedom House and Polity IV, the answer is, more or less, yes. Still, older democracies, particularly those in industrial countries, tend to have a higher quality of democracy than younger ones. While the basic attributes of democracy, such as fair and free electoral competition, civil liberties, and a majoritarian decision-making procedure, may be more or less present in both cases, the distribution of power among citizens in the two societies is quite different. Citizens in the older industrial democracies are more affluent and highly educated; as a result, they may have a greater chance of running for and winning elections for public offices and influencing public policies. Income and education resources would lead to political influence. If the income among citizens is unequal, how can they be politically equal? And because higher levels of affluence and educational achievement are a function of time, it follows that the diffusion of power or a higher level of democracy is likely to be dynamic.

Thus, the effect of socioeconomic development (and good leadership) after the transition to democracy may not merely be to maintain democracy but also to keep it evolving. Nevertheless, some scholars consider political systems as autonomous and static; that is, political systems are either autocracies or democracies. Others contend that political systems may be defined as trichotomous. These latter scholars can see at least a classification of political systems as autocracies, semi- or transitional democracies, and established democracies. A third group of scholars posit that democracy is a continuous concept. When scholars argue that democracy is continuous, they usually and mainly refer to the political process that occurs between autocratic rule and democratic transition. Dahl (1971) suggests that democratic development could go beyond the autocracy-democratic transition continuum and argues that current democracies or polyarchies are only an approximation of the ideal democracy. The main reason that no perfect democracy exists, according to Dahl, is the presence of income inequality. Thus, to speed up the establishment of a more equal democratic system, Dahl (1985) prescribes for the replacement of the current private enterprise economy by a system that allows employee-ownership of firms. He seems to imply that some form of political agreement and action would bring about political equality. Dahl's position, however, seems to clash with individuals' right to own private property. Indeed, the failures of ancient Greek democracies and twentieth-century communism can be partly explained by the absence of, or impediment to, economic liberty in these systems. The two forms of political systems maintained that "true democracy" could be achieved by forceful redistribution of property. What followed in these systems was political instability and economic inefficiency, leading to the demise of both political experiments. If democracy ensures economic and political freedoms and if such a process is also dynamic, it follows that the concept of democracy has to be defined accordingly.

Gizachew Tiruneh (2004) posits that the distribution of power among individuals must be considered when one rates or defines democracies. He contends that the procedural attributes of democracy, such as electoral competition, civil liberties, and a majoritarian decision-making procedure, are fundamental but once achieved they cannot be adequately used to differentiate the level of democracy among democracies. Power differences, according to Tiruneh, stem from differences in the level of income and rationality among individuals. And because individual achievement and competition are protected rights in democracies, some individuals are likely to become more successful than others. The more income an individual has, the more influence or political power he or she will possess. Assuming that the distribution of income itself is dynamic (being propelled by socioeconomic development), the diffusion of power or the level of democracy will quite likely increase over time. However, because not all individuals will have the same level of income and rationality, perfect political equality may not necessarily be achieved.

Thus, perfect political equality may, similar to the perfect competition argument in economics, be considered as a political ideal on which modern democracies may be judged. Rather than considering democracy as two separate phenomena, a political ideal and a political system, one may consider it as a single, open-ended (perhaps an infinite) process. A more achievable and optimal level of democracy, according to Tiruneh, occurs when the distribution of power, including income and rationality, among citizens takes the shape of a normal or bell curve. Modern industrial democracies have, in contrast, a skewed distribution of power (and income and rationality), where the mean or average citizen lies to right of center. In other words, the distribution of power, income, and rationality in modern democracies are skewed toward the upper classes. As the level of democracy increases over time, however, the mean citizen would gravitate to the center of the normal curve (where the preponderant majority or the middle class is located), and it would have the most decisive voice and power in democratic politics. Whereas those individuals to the right of the mean will in theory have more power than those to the left of the mean, and it is likely that most leaders may come out of the former group, the political agendas and policies of leaders will probably be dictated by the preferences of the mean citizen. The normal or bell-curve distribution of power would represent a democratic system the quality or degree of which is apt to be optimal. In sum, Tiruneh defines democracy as "a political procedure that allows the presence of political rights, civil liberties, and a majoritarian decision-making or voting mechanism, and which permits the continuous achievement of a more equal distribution of political power" (2004, p. 473). He terms such a state of political evolution as *normal democracy.*

However, some scholars disagree with some aspects of Tiruneh's theory of democracy. For instance, they may contend that democracies, after transition, will remain stabilized; that is, democracies after transition will not continuously evolve. Others may, on philosophical or moral grounds, contend that, regardless of levels of income and rationality, citizens ought to possess an equal distribution of power. It is not clear, however, whether such possible contentions will successfully undermine Tiruneh's thesis. What is clear is that until most or all scholars agree on a more acceptable definition of democracy, an understanding of the concept will remain incomplete.

SEE ALSO *Authority; Citizenship; Democracy, Christian; Democracy, Consociational; Democracy, Indices of; Democracy, Racial; Democracy, Representative and Participatory; Elections; Parties, Political; Voting Patterns*

BIBLIOGRAPHY

Almond, Gabriel A., and Sydney Verba. 1963. *The Civic Culture: Political Attitudes and Democracy in Five Nations.* Princeton, NJ: Princeton University Press.

Bryce, James. 1921. *Modern Democracies.* New York: Macmillan.

Collier, David, and Robert Adcock. 1999. Democracy and Dichotomies: A Pragmatic Approach to Choices about Concepts. *Annual Review of Political Science* 2: 537–565.

Dahl, Robert A. 1971. *Polyarchy: Participation and Opposition.* New Haven, CT: Yale University Press.

Dahl, Robert A. 1985. *A Preface to Economic Democracy.* Berkeley: University of California Press.

Friedman, Milton. 1962. *Capitalism and Freedom.* Chicago: University of Chicago Press.

Gastil, Raymond D. 1991. The Comparative Survey of Freedom: Experiences and Suggestions. In *On Measuring Democracy: Its Consequences and Concomitants,* ed. Alex Inkeles. New Brunswick, NJ: Transaction Publishers.

Lipset, Seymour M. 1959. Some Social Requisites of Democracy. *American Political Science Review* 53 (1): 69–105.

Przeworski, Adam, and Fernando Limongi. 1997. Modernization: Theories and Facts. *World Politics* 49 (2): 155–183.

Sartori, Giovanni. 1968. Democracy. In *International Encyclopedia of the Social Sciences,* Vol. 4. Ed. David L. Sills. New York: Macmillan.

Schumpeter, Joseph A. 1976. *Capitalism, Socialism, and Democracy,* 5th ed. London: Allen and Unwin.

Tiruneh, Gizachew. 2004. Towards Normal Democracy: Theory and Prediction with Special Reference to the Developing Countries. *Journal of Social, Political and Economic Studies* 29 (4): 469–489.

Gizachew Tiruneh

DEMOCRACY, CHRISTIAN

Christian Democracy can be described as a political ideology that has largely been shaped by the social teaching of the Roman Catholic Church, which has given rise to polit-ical parties representing the middle of the political spectrum, between liberalism and socialism. Although many Christian Democratic political parties became less associated with the Catholic Church over time, such parties have had the greatest electoral success in European and Latin American countries that have significant Catholic populations, such as Austria, Belgium, the Netherlands, Italy, Germany, Chile, Costa Rica, El Salvador, and Venezuela. While Christian Democratic ideology and political parties had a significant impact on state and society during the second half of the twentieth century, the end of the cold war and the demise of left-oriented social movements and political parties significantly weakened Christian Democratic parties by the end of the twentieth century. The rise of the Left during the first decade of the twenty-first century in certain Latin American countries raises interesting questions about the possibility of a rebirth of Christian Democracy and a reinvigoration of Christian Democratic parties.

As a political ideology, Christian Democracy originated in response to the rise of liberalism in Europe and Latin America during the nineteenth century. It was subsequently shaped by the spread of socialism in these regions during the twentieth century. Although there is evidence that many Europeans and Latin Americans sympathized with liberals, who argued for an end to monarchies and to the privileges enjoyed by the church vis-à-vis the state, it also became clear that, unlike the radical liberals, most Europeans and Latin Americans believed that religious faith and values deserved a privileged place in society. In European countries such as Austria, Belgium, Italy, Germany, and Prussia, liberals suffered stunning electoral defeats during the late nineteenth century, largely thanks to the mobilizing power of religion.

After it became clear that religion was capable of mobilizing voters, what came to be called or categorized as Christian Democratic political parties were founded by laypersons and some clergy. Contrary to what one might assume, Catholic bishops and the Catholic Church's hierarchy tried to prevent the formation of these political parties. During the middle of the nineteenth century, Catholic bishops feared that the formation of Catholic political parties would imply that the Catholic Church endorsed democratic political systems that might not give rise to governments respectful of what the bishops considered to be the rightful place of the church in society. By the late nineteenth century and early twentieth century, the Catholic hierarchy refused to fully endorse what came to be called Christian Democratic parties, fearing that if these parties lost elections the church would forfeit the few privileges it might otherwise manage to maintain under democratic systems.

Although they officially kept their distance from Christian Democratic parties, church leaders came to recognize the value of, and to provide ideological guidance to, organized Catholic political activity. In 1891, Pope Leo XIII issued an encyclical letter titled *Rerum Novarum*, which criticized liberalism and socialism. It reaffirmed the right to private property (subject to the good of society), promoted a living wage, defended the rights of workers to organize in order to achieve a living wage, and encouraged the formation of civil society. Essentially, *Rerum Novarum* reflected and reinforced the principles already promoted by Catholic political parties in Belgium, the Netherlands, Germany, and Austria. After *Rerum Novarum*, Pope Pius XI's encyclical *Quadregesimo Anno* (1931) had the greatest impact on the development of Christian Democratic ideology. *Quadregesimo Anno* reaffirmed the teachings of *Rerum Novarum*, but it placed an even greater emphasis on the importance of subsidiarity and the rightful role of civil society. According to the principle of subsidiarity, decisions should be made, to the extent possible, by the people whose lives would be affected by the decisions. Thus, while rejecting unfettered free-market systems, it rejected the idea of an all-powerful state and centralized economic planning. *Quadregesimo Anno* promoted a corporatist framework, according to which there would be institutionalized collaboration between labor and capital within the state in order to prevent class conflict and promote the common good.

The official recognition and guidance offered by Leo XIII and Pius XI spawned further development of the Christian Democratic ideological orientation by Catholic intellectuals. Foremost among them was the French philosopher Jacques Maritain, who, in his book *Integral Humanism* (1936), argued that a society in which there is political democracy, social pluralism, and religious freedom is the most Christian society.

While Christian Democratic parties have varied greatly in terms of ideological emphasis, they had a significant impact in several European and some Latin American countries during the second half of the twentieth century, particularly Italy, Germany, and Chile. However, most of these parties had become very weak by the close of the twentieth century. In large part, the decline of Christian Democratic political parties may be the result of the end of the cold war and the demise of the radical Left. Christian Democrats have typically attracted people who were wary of polar ideological extremes. With the demise of radical socialism at the end of the twentieth century, Christian Democrats found themselves searching for new ideological positions and new ways to distinguish themselves from political conservatives and social liberals.

The rise of left-oriented and centralizing political leaders during the first decade of the twenty-first century in certain Latin American countries, especially Bolivia and Venezuela, raises interesting questions about the rebirth of Christian Democracy. It is possible that Christian Democratic movements will be born or reinvigorated wherever and whenever the extreme Left or extreme Right gains popularity and power. However, there are many other factors that may affect the feasibility of Christian Democracy, such as poverty, inequality, the vitality of the Catholic Church, the extent to which the church cuts across class, and the extent to which it has been involved in education and the development of intellectuals and politicians. Of course, it is also possible that a new version of Christian Democracy will develop that will be influenced less by Catholic Christianity than by Evangelical Christianity, which has been growing in much of Latin America. For those interested in religion and politics, and more specifically in the feasibility of Christian Democracy, the twenty-first century promises to be an interesting period.

SEE ALSO *Decentralization; Socialism, Christian; Vatican, The*

BIBLIOGRAPHY

Fogarty, Michael P. 1957. *Christian Democracy in Western Europe, 1820–1953*. London: Routledge and Kegan Paul.

Kalyvas, Stathis. 1996. *The Rise of Christian Democracy in Europe*. Ithaca, NY: Cornell University Press.

Mainwaring, Scott, and Timothy R. Scully. 2003. The Diversity of Christian Democracy in Latin America. In *Christian Democracy in Latin America: Electoral Competition and Regime Conflicts*, ed. Scott Mainwaring and Timothy R. Scully. Stanford, CA: Stanford University Press.

Maritain, Jacques. 1936. *Integral Humanism*. Trans. Joseph W. Evans. New York: Scribner, 1968.

O'Brien, David J., and Thomas A. Shannon, eds. 1992. *Catholic Social Thought: The Documentary Heritage*. Maryknoll, NY: Orbis.

Sigmund, Paul. 2003. The Transformation of Christian Democratic Ideology: Transcending Left or Right or Whatever Happened to the Third Way? In *Christian Democracy in Latin America: Electoral Competition and Regime Conflicts*, ed. Scott Mainwaring and Timothy R. Scully. Stanford, CA: Stanford University Press.

Robert A. Dowd C.S.C.

DEMOCRACY, CONSOCIATIONAL

The etymology of *consociation* derives from the Latin for "with" and "society": *Consociatio* translates as "union" or "connection." Today, consociation describes a "society of societies." The concept has some similarities with federation, but is not a synonym; consociations can exist in non-federal states.

Consociation was first developed in political theory by the Protestant jurist and philosopher Johannes Althusius (1557–1638). In the twentieth century the Dutch political scientist Arend Lijphart revived the term to describe political systems in which parallel communities, differentiated by ethnicity, language, religion, or culture, share political power while retaining autonomy (Lijphart 1968, 1977). He recognized his ideas had antecedents in the writings of the Austro-Marxists, Karl Renner, and Otto Bauer, and the Nobel laureate Sir Arthur Lewis. Lijphart argued that consociation is frequently invented by politicians negotiating political settlements. Contemporary examples of functioning or attempted consociations exist in Belgium, Bosnia and Herzegovina, Canada, the Netherlands, Switzerland, Northern Ireland, Lebanon, and Macedonia.

Consociations have three necessary features: executive power sharing among representatives of specific communities; proportional representation and allocation in governmental posts and resources; and community self-government, especially in cultural domains, for example in schools with different languages of instruction (O'Leary 2005). Fully fledged consociations empower representatives with veto rights over constitutional or legal changes.

Consociations are promoted to prevent, manage, or resolve conflicts, especially between communities divided by nationality, ethnicity, race, religion, or language. Consociationalists and their critics differ radically over their merits, and also over how consociations are established, maintained, or break down (McGarry and O'Leary 2004).

CRITICISMS OF CONSOCIATIONS

Some critics condemn consociational ideas as futile, and claim that consociational institutions have no (or no long-run) impact on deeply rooted, identity-based conflicts. Others attack consociations as perverse, claiming that they achieve the opposite of their ostensible purposes by institutionalizing the sources of conflict: By allegedly freezing the relevant collective identities, they encourage a politics of gridlock. Critics suggest that consociationalists are primordial pessimists who take people as they are, and not as they might be. These opponents prefer integration, the creation of a common citizenship and public sphere, and the nonrecognition of cultural differences in the public domain. They also claim that consociation jeopardizes important liberal values, and that it leads to the irreversible formation of ethnic, communal, or sectarian parties. The use of quotas, affirmative action programs, and preferential policies

weaken the merit principle, creating new injustices and inefficiencies. Others claim that consociation is undemocratic because it allegedly excludes opposition and inhibits alternations in power. Some claim it is elitist (Brass 1991, p. 339; Jung and Shapiro 1995, p. 273). Another argument denies the existence of consociations, claiming that there is no place that fits the criteria.

DEFENSES OF CONSOCIATIONS

Proponents argue that consociations cannot simultaneously be perverse—that is, reinforce and re-entrench ethnic antagonisms—and jeopardize all key liberal, democratic, and international values, and, all the while, be futile. The futility thesis is evidently the weakest criticism. It scarcely explains the passionate (and logical) criticisms of consociational theory and practice in the last three decades.

Consociationalists understand themselves as realists and counselors of necessary political triage. They believe that certain collective identities, especially those based on nationality, ethnicity, language, and religion, are generally fairly durable once formed. That does not mean that they are primordial or immutable, or that they are intrinsically desirable. But such durable identities are often mobilized in a politics of antagonism, especially during the democratization of political systems, and cannot be easily transcended. Politicians, parties, and communities certainly interpret their histories and futures through narratives, myths, and symbols, but they may have realistic rather than merely prejudiced appraisals of past group antagonisms. Consociationalists maintain that it is their critics—"social constructionists" and certain liberals and socialists—who are too optimistic about the capacities of political regimes to dissolve, transform, or transcend inherited collective identities. Consociationalists question the cosmopolitan protestations of many anticonsociationalists, who may cloak a partisan endorsement of one community's identity and interests (into which others are to be encouraged to integrate or assimilate, in their own best interests).

The case for power sharing is advanced on grounds of necessity. Consociation provides good incentives for cooperation—a share in power. Consociationalists do not embrace cultural pluralism for its own sake. Sometimes the effective choice is between consociation and much worse alternatives: armed conflict, genocide and ethnic expulsion, imposed partition, or control by one group or coalition. The real choice in many deeply divided regions is therefore between consociational democracy and no (worthwhile) democracy—or breakup. The target of consociational criticism is integrationism and majoritarian democracy, which only work well, consociationalists argue, as political recipes in societies that are already homogeneous, or in immigrant states where immigrants are expected to integrate.

Consociationalists are skeptical about the current celebration of civil society as the (or even a) vehicle of transformation, peace making, and peace building. In divided places there is often more than one society, and their relations may be far from civil. Those who embrace a politics of deliberative democracy are reminded that deliberation takes place in languages, dialects, accents, and ethnically toned voices. Consociationalists respond to left-wing critics by observing that consociational ideas are present in the more thoughtful socialist traditions (Bauer 2000; Nimni 2004), and by observing how working-class and popular unity have been rendered hopeless by national, ethnic, religious, and communal divisions. Within consociational arrangements, trust may develop that may enable wider working-class or popular unity behind the welfare state or other forms of distributive politics.

Consociationalists therefore are friends of democracy, but critics of its palpably inappropriate versions in deeply divided places. They want majorities rather than the majority, or the plurality, to control government. Elite bargaining and adjustment should be designed to achieve widespread consensus—to prevent the possibility that democracy will degenerate into a war of communities. They endorse a politics of accommodation, of leaving each group to its own affairs where that is possible and widely sought—"good fences make good neighbors" (Esman 2000; Noel 1993, pp. 55–56). Consociations protect the basic natural rights of individuals and communities—especially the right to exist.

Consociationalists argue positively for consociation, not just by pointing to the horrors of the alternatives. Consociation provides autonomy for communities, and enables sensible shared intercommunity cooperation. It offers a more inclusive model of democracy—more than a plurality or a majority influence or control of the executive. More than a majority get effective "voice." Consociation does not eliminate democratic opposition, but enables such divisions and oppositions as exist to flourish in conditions of generalized security. Nothing need preclude democratic competition within communities, and turnover of political elites, and shifts of support between parties. In a liberal consociation nothing blocks the voluntary dissolution of historic identities if that is what voters want.

TYPES OF CONSOCIATIONS

It is a fallacy to suppose that consociation mandates that governments be wholly encompassing, grand coalitions of all communities (O'Leary 2005). One should distinguish among complete, concurrent, and "pluralitarian" consociational executives. In a complete consociation, all parties and all groups are included in the executive and enjoy popular support within their blocs. This is the rare case of

the grand coalition, which may indeed preclude effective opposition, and may be made necessary by wartime conditions or postconflict state-building. In concurrent executives, by contrast, the major parties, which enjoy majority support within their blocs, are included within the executive, but opposition groups exist in parliament and elsewhere. In "pluralitarian" executives, the major communities may be represented by their strongest parties in the executive, but one or more of these parties may enjoy just plurality support within its respective bloc. What matters, therefore, is not the wholesale inclusion of all, but meaningful, cross-community or joint decision making within the executive. This clarification resolves a recurrent misunderstanding that all consociational practices preclude opposition.

Consociational arrangements may facilitate greater justice. Groups govern themselves in agreed domains of autonomy. Distributions that follow proportional allocations may be very fair: to each according to their numbers. There is a correlation between numbers and potential power that makes such distributive justice likely to be stable and legitimate. Consociationalists need not endorse the view that justice is "each according to their threat-advantage," but in some cases proportional allocations of public posts and resources are regarded as fair distributions, and will be robust as a result.

Consociationalists observe that consociations occur without their urgings. They are reinvented by politicians as "natural" creative political responses to a politics of antagonism. Politicians, Lijphart observes, invented consociational institutions in the Netherlands in 1917, in Lebanon in 1943, in Malaysia in 1958, and in Northern Ireland in 1972 (Lijphart 1990, p. viii) and again in 1998 (McGarry and O'Leary 2004, 2007). They were reinvented by American diplomats to end the war in Bosnia and Herzegovina at Dayton in 1995; by Lebanese politicians with external promptings in 1989; and by European Union diplomats in promoting the Ohrid agreement between Macedonian Slavs and Macedonian Albanians. The United Nations and the European Union have been trying to mediate a consociational and federal settlement in Cyprus. Within academic political theory, many contemporary multiculturalists advance consociational agendas, including inclusivity (cross-community power sharing), quotas (proportionality), and group rights (autonomy and veto) (Kymlicka and Norman 2000).

The rival evaluations of consociation are unlikely to be resolved. They probably are not amenable to decisive falsification or verification. Anticonsociationalists fear consociation will bring back racism, fundamentalism, and patriarchy. Consociationalists fear integrationists will provoke avoidable wars and are biased toward dominant communities (McGarry and O'Leary 2004). The intensity with which this debate rages attests to the influence of consociational thought.

Exponents of consociation, when their case is put carefully, successfully rebut the wilder charges made against their positions. Consociations are difficult to love and celebrate—even if their makers often merit intellectual, moral, and political admiration. They are usually the product of cold bargains, even if they may be tempered by political imagination. As for the explanation of consociations, although significant preliminary work has been done, a comprehensive comparative historical analysis of consociational settlements and their outcomes remains to be completed.

SEE ALSO *Affirmative Action; Ethnic Conflict; Ethnic Fractionalization; Ethnicity; Majoritarianism; Majority Rule; Political Instability, Indices of; Politics, Identity; Quotas; Tyranny of the Majority; Vote, Alternative; Voting Schemes*

BIBLIOGRAPHY

Bauer, Otto. 2000. *The Question of Nationalities and Social Democracy*, ed. Ephraim Nimni, trans. Joseph O'Donnell. Minneapolis: University of Minnesota Press.

Brass, Paul R. 1991. Ethnic Conflict in Multiethnic Societies: The Consociational Solution and Its Critics. In *Ethnicity and Nationalism: Theory and Comparison*, 333–348. New Delhi: Sage.

Esman, Milton. 2000. Power Sharing and the Constructionist Fallacy. In *Democracy and Institutions: The Life Work of Arend Lijphart*, eds. Markus M. L. Crepaz, Thomas A. Koelbe, and David Wilsford, 91–113. Ann Arbor: University of Michigan Press.

Horowitz, Donald L. 2000. Constitutional Design: An Oxymoron? In *Designing Democratic Institutions*, eds. Ian Shapiro and Stephen Macedo, 253–284. New York: New York University Press.

Jung, Courtney, and Ian Shapiro. 1995. South Africa's Negotiated Transition: Democracy, Opposition, and the New Constitutional Order. *Politics and Society* 23 (3): 269–308.

Kymlicka, Will, and Wayne Norman, eds. 2000. *Citizenship in Diverse Societies*. Oxford: Oxford University Press.

Lijphart, Arend. 1968. *The Politics of Accommodation: Pluralism and Democracy in the Netherlands*. Berkeley: University of California Press.

Lijphart, Arend. 1977. *Democracy in Plural Societies: A Comparative Exploration*. New Haven, CT: Yale University Press.

Lijphart, Arend. 1990. Foreword: One Basic Problem, Many Theoretical Options—and a Practical Solution? In *The Future of Northern Ireland*, eds. John McGarry and Brendan O'Leary, vi–viii. Oxford: Clarendon Press.

Lustick, Ian S. 1997. Lijphart, Lakatos, and Consociationalism. *World Politics* 50 (October): 88–117.

McGarry, John, and Brendan O'Leary. 2004. Introduction: Consociational Theory and Northern Ireland. In *Essays on the Northern Ireland Conflict: Consociational Engagements*, 1–61. Oxford: Oxford University Press.

Nimni, Ephraim. 2004. *National-Cultural Autonomy and Its Contemporary Critics*. London: Routledge.

Noel, Sid J. R. 1993. Canadian Responses to Ethnic Conflict: Consociationalism, Federalism, and Control. In *The Politics of Ethnic Conflict-Regulation: Case Studies of Protracted Ethnic Conflicts*, eds. John McGarry and Brendan O'Leary, 41–61. London: Routledge.

O'Leary, Brendan. 2005. Debating Consociation: Normative and Explanatory Arguments. In *From Power-Sharing to Democracy: Post-Conflict Institutions in Ethnically Divided Societies*, ed. Sid J. R. Noel, 3–43. Toronto: McGill-Queens University Press.

O'Leary, Brendan, and John McGarry. 2008. *Understanding Northern Ireland: Colonialism, Control, and Consociation*. London: Routledge.

Brendan O'Leary

DEMOCRACY, DIRECT

SEE *Democracy, Representative and Participatory.*

DEMOCRACY, INDICES OF

In order to document democratic development, a number of indices of democracy have been developed. These indices are formulated in a variety of ways, yet most are basically oriented to political, liberal democracy—what the political scientist Robert Dahl has called "participation and contestation" (Dahl 1971). Relatively high statistical correlations on the aggregated level also point to a far-reaching unity of viewpoint among those designing the different indices. The correlation coefficient (r) tends to lie at the 0.75–0.95 level (0.00 representing no concordance; 1.00 complete concordance). At the same time, there are differences—both conceptual and methodological—that make it significant which index is chosen. Experience has shown, namely, that in certain cases the choice of index can influence the results (Elkins 2000; Casper and Tufis 2003).

As a rule, extreme differences among countries (e.g., between Australia and Saudi Arabia) will register in much the same way no matter what index is used. Where more modest differences are concerned, however, the coding becomes more arbitrary, especially at lower or medium levels of democracy. It is likely, therefore, that changes over time will be registered differently by different indices. When studying gradual changes in the level of democracy, the results could, to a substantial degree, reflect which index is used (Hadenius and Teorell 2005).

The choice of index, in other words, is not trivial. Hence, it is important to account for the way they are constructed. One difference concerns what prime aspects of democracy are actually measured. Some indices are based on a broad range of criteria, which are aggregated into a scale. Freedom House (FH), which is a frequently used index, is a typical example. It includes an extensive checklist of political rights (related to elections) and civil liberties, which are certainly relevant. However, it also includes certain criteria that could be seen as less relevant, such as free enterprise, property rights, and lack of corruption. The other leading index, Polity, has a more limited focus. It accounts for a number of electoral requisites, but pays no heed to political freedoms.

A few other indices deserve to be mentioned. Reich applies criteria that relate both to elections and political freedoms, whereas Vanhanen and Alvarez et al. are more constrained. Vanhanen looks at electoral participation (which is a strongly contested indicator) and the share of parliamentary seats for the governing party, while Alvarez et al. is concentrated on a fairly narrow set of electoral criteria.

One question that has occasioned controversy has to do with dichotomous versus continuous measures of democracy. The main argument in favor of the dichotomous approach (which distinguishes only between democracies and nondemocracies) is that this divide is the most essential one. The main counterargument is that this is too rough an assessment, and that it therefore misses more graded differences. Among the indices mentioned, only Alvarez et al. is dichotomous in character.

Indices also differ with respect to methodological qualities, such as how the operational measures have been chosen and what rules of coding and aggregation have been applied. It is important that the transformation of the data be openly displayed, so that the process can be replicated and made the subject of both testing and alternative coding and aggregation.

Polity, Vanhanen, and Alvarez et al. are generally held to meet high methodological standards, especially with respect to transparency. The construction of the Freedom House scale is a more concealed process, while Reich is even more problematic in this respect, for it provides almost no information about the operationalizations and the coding rules applied.

On balance—considering both conceptual and methodological aspects—Polity and Freedom House are the most useful indices. Comparing these indices for possible biases (which have been argued to exist), it turns out that they do not differ with respect to region, religion, or colonial background. But the type of regime does matter, at least in some respects. Freedom House treats traditional monarchies more favorably, while Polity is generally more "dichotomous" in character (most cases are located at the top or the bottom of the scale). Polity therefore applies greater rewards to democratic improvements. In addition, Freedom House is more concerned about political violence and repression, while Polity puts stronger emphasis on electoral performance.

It seems that in most instances in the 1970s and 1980s, Freedom House tended to overestimate the level of democracy, whereas Polity underestimated it. During the 1990s, however, it was the other way around: Freedom House made relatively strict assessments, to the effect that democracy tended to be underrated. The opposite held for Polity. An average score, therefore, based on the two indices, seems to give the most accurate assessment.

SEE ALSO *Democracy; Democratization*

BIBLIOGRAPHY

Alvarez, Mike, José Antonio Cheibub, Fernando Limongi, and Adam Przeworski. 1996. Classifying Political Regimes. *Studies in Comparative International Development* 31: 3–36.

Casper, Gretchen, and Claudiu Tufis. 2003. Correlation versus Interchangeability: The Limited Robustness of Empirical Findings Using Highly Correlated Data Sets. *Political Analysis* 11: 196–203.

Dahl, Robert. 1971. *Polyarchy: Participation and Opposition.* New Haven: Yale University Press.

Elkins, Zachary. 2000. Gradations of Democracy? Empirical Tests of Alternative Conceptualizations. *American Journal of Political Science* 44 (2): 287–294.

Freedom House. 1994. *Freedom in the World 1994.* New York: Freedom House.

Hadenius, Axel, and Jan Teorell. 2005. Assessing Alternative Indices of Democracy. *C&M Working Papers.* International Political Science Association. http://www.concepts-methods.org/working_papers/20050812_16_PC%206%20H adenius%20&%20Teorell.pdf.

Marshall, Monty, and Keith Jaggers (2002). Political Regime Characteristics and Transitions, 1800–2002: Dataset Users' Manual. Polity IV Project, University of Maryland. http://www.cidcm.umd.edu/inscr/polity.

Munck, Gerardo L., and Jay Verkuilen. 2002. Conceptualizing and Measuring Democracy: Evaluating Alternative Indices. *Comparative Political Studies* 35 (1): 5–34.

Reich, Garry. 2002. Categorizing Political Regimes: New Data for Old Problems. *Democratization* 9 (4): 1–24.

Vanhanen, Tatu. 2000. A New Dataset for Measuring Democracy, 1810–1998. *Journal of Peace Research* 37 (2): 251–265.

Axel Hadenius

DEMOCRACY, PARTICIPATORY

SEE *Democracy, Representative and Participatory.*

DEMOCRACY, RACIAL

The ideological construct referred to as the "Myth of Racial Democracy" continues to constitute the central framework for understanding the "racial commonsense" in Brazil, as well as in much of Latin America. The essence of this myth is contained within a traditional allegory addressing the origins of Brazil's population, the "fable of the three races" (Da Matta 1997, p. 71). This fable holds that the Brazilian nation originated from three formerly discrete racial entities, Europeans, Africans, and Indians. These "races" subsequently mixed, each contributing to the formation of a uniquely Brazilian population, culturally and biologically fused.

The scholar Gilberto Freyre is credited with popularizing the notion of racial democracy in Brazil in the 1930s in his work *New World in the Tropics: The Culture of Modern Brazil* (1959). Confronted with scientific racism beliefs in the superiority of a white "race" and that mixed blood created degeneracy, Freyre proposed instead that "cross-breeding" produced hybrid vigor in humans, thereby enabling a bright future for the otherwise condemned dark Brazilian nation. He emphasized, for example, an uncommon flexibility on the part of Portuguese colonizers that made possible extensive miscegenation and claimed that mixed Brazilians were giving birth to a new meta-race, constituting a new world in the tropics.

The result of the Brazilian racial fusion, according to Freyre, was an "ethnic democracy, the almost perfect equality for all men [sic] regardless of race or color" (p. 7). In reality, Brazil is stratified along color lines, and Freyre's academic musings reflect a romanticized view. His vision suggests a serious disjuncture between "ideal" versus "real" culture, between what Brazil is supposed to, or even said to, look like and how it actually is. Color or racial characteristics clearly correlate with lower socioeconomic status and disadvantaged life chances in general in Brazil. Individuals of varying degrees of African descent historically and in modern times occupy the lower rungs of the color hierarchy. The disparities along racial lines are produced and perpetuated by both historic and contemporary factors. Among the former is the early uneven industrialization among Brazilian states coupled with the concentration of non-whites in underdeveloped regions. Prominent among the contemporary factors is the continuation of negative black stereotyping that reverberates in countless areas, resulting in poorer educational experiences, police profiling and abuse, and discrimination in the labor market.

In this context marked by racial inequality, a majority of researchers view the racial democracy or miscegenation imagery as fostering a false conception of the reality of Brazilian racial dynamics, leading to the denial of racial discrimination. The myth has been described, for example, as an ideology of nondiscrimination and the prejudice of not having prejudice. This denial of racial discrimination on the part of both white and non-whites, then, is generally understood as the defining element of the myth.

In addition to masking racism, the Brazilianist literature further faults this construct for discouraging positive black racial identification and for neutralizing support for antiracism strategies. These two latter elements are believed to be highly correlated, as robust racial identities are generally considered a sine qua non of antiracist mobilization. In Brazil, racial subjectivity is diffuse, diluted in part by a traditional focus on ambiguous classification schemas. Furthermore, there has also been little history of the type of mass mobilizations against racial inequality that one might expect in such a context. Hence, participants in Brazil's modest but growing black movement struggle to foster black racial identity formation among the masses at the service of antiracism.

Some researchers, however, question this wholly negative stance towards the myth of racial democracy. Rather than viewed primarily as an empirical description of racial dynamics characterized as "colorblind," as elites have traditionally argued, the myth may instead constitute a moral high ground common to non-elite Brazilians that both recognizes and repudiates discrimination based on "race." In fact, some newer research demonstrates that not only is there a keen awareness of racial discrimination in Brazil on the part of whites and non-whites alike, but there is also substantial support for antiracism measures. Hence, researchers argue that this racial fusion myth may be harnessed in ways that promote subordinate populations; the myth endorses the utopian dream of a less discriminatory society and thus can act as a charter for social action. Viewed as a positive cultural value, Roberto Da Matta wrote that we should "... elevate the myth of racial democracy as a patrimony that is capable of helping Brazil in ... honoring its commitment to equalitarianism" (1997, p. 74).

In the end, myths are not necessarily untruths or statements of truth; rather, they are part of belief systems justifying specific cultural values and social rules. They can have a powerful impact on individuals because they communicate and reinforce particular commonsense understandings. The myth of racial democracy will continue to be scrutinized as long as Brazil is characterized by a disjuncture between "ideal" and "real" culture, between racial democracy and racial inequality. It is clear that higher rates of racial intermarriage do not in and of themselves ensure a society beyond the reach of racial discrimination.

BIBLIOGRAPHY

Bailey, Stanley R. 2004. Group Dominance and the Myth of Racial Democracy: Antiracism Attitudes in Brazil. *American Sociological Review* 69: 728–747.

Da Matta, Roberto. 1997. Notas Sobre o Racismo Á Brasileira. In *Multiculturalismo e Racismo: uma Comparação Brasil—Estados Unidos*, ed. J. Souza, 69–74. Brasilia, Brazil: Paralelo 15.

Freyre, Gilberto. 1959. *New World in the Tropics: The Culture of Modern Brazil.* New York: Knopf.

Sheriff, Robin. 2001. *Dreaming Equality: Color, Race, and Racism in Urban Brazil.* New Brunswick, NJ: Rutgers University Press.

Telles, Edward E. 2004. *Race in Another America: The Significance of Skin Color in Brazil.* Princeton, NJ: Princeton University Press.

Twine, France Winddance. 1998. *Racism in a Racial Democracy: The Maintenance of White Supremacy.* New Brunswick, NJ: Rutgers University Press.

Stanley R. Bailey

DEMOCRACY, REPRESENTATIVE AND PARTICIPATORY

Democracy was born in the Western world in the form of participatory democracy, making the term *participatory democracy* redundant. The word *participatory* discloses the core meaning of popular sovereignty as self-government. In the original ancient Greek meaning, *demo-kratia* ("rule of the demes," or "tribes" into which the Athenian people were divided) entailed engaged citizenship and regular participation. In modern times, however, when democracy has become associated more closely with representation, accountability, and a form of indirect government in which the people select the rulers rather than ruling themselves, participatory democracy has come to be seen as an alternative form of democracy. Consequently participatory, or direct or "strong," democracy and representative democracy have evolved into conceptual antonyms: two fundamentally distinctive forms of democracy rooted in contrary understandings of popular sovereignty as direct self-rule by the people and indirect rule by circulating elites chosen by the people, who otherwise remain outside government.

PARTICIPATORY DEMOCRACY AND REPRESENTATIVE DEMOCRACY

In principle all democracy is to a certain extent participatory. Every democratic system is rooted in an act of original consent through a popularly ratified social contract or constitution as well as ongoing popular input in the form of periodic elections. To this extent, to say that democracy is consensual is to say that it is participatory. In the modern era, however, participatory democracy implies much more than original consent or periodic elections. It denotes extensive and active engagement of citizens in the governing process, often through participatory devices such as initiatives and referenda, and emphasizes the role of the citizen as an active agent in self-legislation and a real stakeholder in governance.

This is in stark contrast to representative democracy, in which the citizen becomes a passive client of government, a watchdog to whom the government remains accountable but otherwise ignores, and a periodic elector responsible for selecting those who actually govern. Philosophers of participatory democracy such as Jean-Jacques Rousseau (1762) and Robert Michels (1911) have understood this "thin" representative construction of democracy as contrary to the core meaning of democracy. When there is representation, the democratic principle is nullified. In Michels's terms, under representative democracy liberty can be said to disappear along with the ballot when it is dropped into the box.

HISTORICAL GROWTH OF POLITIES

The transition from direct democracy to representative democracy was dictated at least in part by historical changes in the nature and scale of society. Democracy was born in and designed for small-scale societies: towns, poleis, principalities, and city-states of the kind found in ancient Greece, early modern Europe, and pre-Revolutionary America. In such settings active participation by citizens in governance could be seen as synonymous with democracy, both desirable and practicable. However, the transformation of city republics into larger states and empires (Rome, for example, as it moved from a town-based republic to a continental empire) created novel constraints and revealed how early direct democracy was bound by limiting conditions, such as simplicity of manners and interests, relative homogeneity of culture and religion, and a small demographic and geographic scale that allowed the citizenry to meet in common in a public place. The ideal population was perhaps five hundred to five thousand, and the maximum size was approximately twenty thousand citizens: the number of active residents engaged in politics in Athens during the Periclean Age in the mid-fifth century BCE. Aristotle had suggested that democracy could exist only on a territory a man could traverse on his way to join a democratic assembly in a single day.

The increase in scale that came with the evolution of towns into cities, then city-dominated provinces, and finally nation-states consisting of cities and provinces bound by nationalism mandated a reconsideration of democratic principles. If democracy entailed participation by all citizens in basic lawmaking, as Rousseau had insisted in the *Social Contract* (1762), the scale of capital cities such as Paris, Lisbon, and London ruled out effective participatory democratic rule and thus, for Rousseau, legitimate democracy. The American founders implicitly recognized that critique by arguing that a republic of potentially continental extent could be ruled only by a popular sovereign willing to be represented in the actual governing process. To Rousseau and his allies, that was an impossible compromise, for as Immanuel Kant had argued, autonomy demands self-legislation, and hence only those who govern themselves directly can be said to be free.

AMERICAN REPRESENTATIVE DEMOCRACY

In American representative democracy the tensions between direct popular government and indirect rule by chosen surrogates became evident, for the American representative principle was not merely a pragmatic way to preserve democracy in large-scale societies but also implied a critique of direct democracy. Direct popular rule risked enthroning not merely the popular sovereign but an incompetent and impassioned mass: a mob or, in French, a *foule*.

Representation had the virtue not only of facilitating popular sovereignty in large-scale settings but also of placing a filter between the masses and prudent or "good" government. Representatives had the obligation not only to represent the people's will but also, in Edmund Burke's terms, to filter it through and subordinate it to their own prudent judgment. Elected representatives could act in the name of the interests of the people as they understood those interests rather than being bound by the people's "mandate" based on their own often faulty understanding. Even the popular right to choose representatives might be delegated prudently to other wise electors, as was meant to happen with the Electoral College, through which, in the first years of the American Republic, both senators and a president were to be chosen.

Behind the Madisonian distrust of direct democracy lies distrust of all popular power. Even the ancients worried that, just as aristocracy could deteriorate into oligarchy, democracy could morph into ochlocracy, Aristotle's term for a people's tyranny. Although the spirit of modern representative democracy is not antidemocratic, its spirit is cautionary and skeptical about majority rule, mirroring the skepticism about representation that is inherent in direct democracy. If power is dangerous, popular power is more dangerous because it has a righteous legitimacy. Indirect rule thus becomes a check on popular power consistent with the rule of law and constitutional limits on absolute power, especially when that power is popular.

CIVIC EDUCATION

Participatory democrats are cognizant of the critique of popular government as a euphemism for the rule of the passions—the sovereignty of the mob over cool reason as embodied in laws—and for that reason have focused on citizen (civic) education. Historical arguments about direct democracy have been conducted as arguments about education. Plato's *Republic* is an argument on behalf of aristocratic education that denies that the majority has the capacity to govern. Rousseau's philosophical educational novel *Émile* is an essay on democratic education.

Later democrats from Thomas Jefferson to John Dewey rested their case for democratic participation on the efficacy of democratic education. Dewey's primary work on democracy is titled *Democracy and Education* (1954), and Jefferson was persuaded that in the absence of universal education for citizens, democracy could not work. Hence he deemed his work in establishing the University of Virginia (featured on the inscription he prepared for his tombstone) as more important in the long term than his presidency. The logic behind the Declaration of Independence and the Bill of Rights was tied closely to the logic of civic education. Rights belonged to everyone but could be exercised only by those schooled in citizenship. In 1840 Alexis de Tocqueville spoke of the "apprenticeship of liberty," the "most arduous" of all apprenticeships, as a precondition of prudent democratic government.

Classical participatory democrats agreed that popular passions had to be filtered if popular government was to succeed, but they believed that the filter should be within the heads of citizens, and that entailed intensive citizen education. For the participatory or strong democrat, democracy means the government of citizens rather than merely the government of the people. In this formulation citizens are as far from ordinary people as public-thinking and civic-minded communitarians are from self-absorbed, narcissistic consumers of government services.

It is here that participatory democracy can be associated closely with deliberative democracy. To act as a citizen is not merely to voice private interests; it is to interact and deliberate with others in search of common ground and public goods. The aim of participation is not merely to express interests but to foster deliberation and public-mindedness about interests. When Jefferson suggested that the remedy for the ills of democracy was more democracy, he intimated that democracy was deliberative and involved learning. Modern experiments in deliberative democracy such as those of James Fishkin (1991) have demonstrated that citizens can change their minds and become more open to public goods when exposed to deliberative procedures.

THE ROLE OF TECHNOLOGY

Fishkin's deliberative poll experiments utilized the new electronic technologies in ways that suggest that those technologies may help create conditions conducive to direct democracy, affording large-scale societies some of the democratic possibilities of small-scale townships. On the World Wide Web the world becomes a village, and physical communities that are ruled out by size or distance can be reestablished as digitally convened virtual communities. If democracy depends on association and communication, digital technologies that facilitate them become obvious tools of democracy. Presidential elections in the United States have offered opportunities for interaction among citizens, such as "meet-ups," that give a participatory dimension to classical representative electoral campaigns.

The history of democracy began with forms of engagement and participation that were dependent on small-scale township government. Over time systems of representation were tailored to changes in social scale and an increasing distrust of popular rule. As the scale of potential governance becomes global, new technologies have the potential to relegitimize forms of local self-rule that have been deemed outmoded, completing the paradoxical circle of the history of democracy.

SEE ALSO *Aristotle; Campaigning; Decentralization; Democracy; Direct Action; Elections; Federalism; Internet, Impact on Politics; Jefferson, Thomas; Madison, James; Party Systems, Competitive; Political Parties; Rousseau, Jean-Jacques; Self-Determination; Voting Patterns; Voting Schemes*

BIBLIOGRAPHY

Barber, Benjamin R. 1984. *Strong Democracy: Participatory Politics for a New Age.* Berkeley: University of California Press.

Dahl, Robert. 1956. *Preface to Democratic Theory.* Chicago: University of Chicago Press.

Dewey, John. 1954. *Democracy and Education.* New York: Free Press.

Dunn, John. 2005. *Democracy: A History.* New York: Atlantic Monthly.

Elster, Jon, ed. 1998. *Deliberative Democracy.* Cambridge, U.K., and New York: Cambridge University Press.

The Federalist Papers. 1791. Introduction, table of contents, and index of ideas by Clinton Rossiter. New York: New American Library, 1961.

Fishkin, James S. 1991. *Democracy and Deliberation: New Directions for Democratic Reform.* New Haven, CT: Yale University Press.

Michels, Robert. 1911. *Political Parties: A Sociological Study of the Oligarchical Tendencies of Modern Democracy.* Trans. Eden Paul and Cedar Paul. New York: Free Press, 1966.

Pateman, Carole. 1970. *Participation and Democratic Theory.* Cambridge, U.K.: Cambridge University Press.

Rousseau, Jean-Jacques. 1762. *The Social Contract.* In *On the Social Contract, with Geneva Manuscript and Political Economy,* ed. Roger D. Masters, trans. Judith R. Masters. New York: St. Martin's, 1978.

Tocqueville, Alexis de. 1840. *Democracy in America.* Trans. Phillips Bradley. New York: Knopf, 1994.

Benjamin R. Barber

DEMOCRATIC CENTRALISM

In the Marxist literature, *democratic centralism* refers to the organization of a Leninist party that allows members participation and voice, but compels them to follow the party line once a decision has been made. A more contemporary (and liberal) meaning of the term, which is the one discussed in this entry, refers to democratic countries that are organized along unitary lines or that are characterized by a high degree of fiscal, political, or administrative centralization.

Centralization is one of the distinguishing features of the modern state. While some European proto-states before the sixteenth century and the great empires of Asia successfully extended their rule over large territories, those political organizations were decentralized arrangements, characterized by a great deal of local autonomy in, for example, the financing of the state through tax farming or the exercise of political authority through satrapies, tributary provinces, and other accommodations of local rule. A fundamental shift occurred in Europe in the modern era, particularly during the eighteenth century, as nation-states were pressed to centralize authority in order to collect sufficient revenues to wage increasingly expensive wars. Alexis de Tocqueville (1805–1859) can be credited as the earliest theorist of democratic centralism. Perhaps the most important aspect of his analysis was to note that government capacity is endogenous to centralization: to the extent that administration becomes more centralized, local authorities become less empowered and more ineffective.

Early democratic experiences were both centralized, as in France and England, or highly decentralized, as in the United States and Switzerland. Hence there is no necessary link between centralization and democracy. Democratic centralism is often equated with a unitary, as opposed to a federal, form of government. However, William Riker (1964) noted that the survival of the United States as a political unit required the creation of a centralized federalism, which could enhance the territorial scope of the country while allowing it to confront external military threats. Thus, a link between centralization and the threat of war was present in the early history of the United States, as well as in the histories of the other federations in Europe and Latin America.

In both democratic and authoritarian countries, centralization (measured through the share of fiscal resources controlled by the national government, as compared to provincial or state and local governments) increased in the course of the nineteenth and twentieth centuries. However, between the 1930s and the peak of fiscal centralization observed around the world in the 1970s, local and intermediate levels of government in democratic regimes retained a larger share of revenue and expenditure authority than their authoritarian counterparts.

After the 1970s, a trend toward decentralization swept both advanced industrial democracies and developing countries. Decentralization has often been accompanied by the introduction of elections at the subnational levels of government, and the timing of decentralization has often coincided with democratization. This has led many observers to believe that centralism is incompatible with democratization. However, democratic countries show variations in fiscal, political, and administrative centralization through time, depending on the demands placed by citizens on various levels of government. Thus, there is no necessary link between decentralization and democracy.

SEE ALSO *Democracy; Leninism; Totalitarianism*

BIBLIOGRAPHY

Bonney, Richard. 1995. *Economic Systems and State Finance.* Oxford: Oxford University Press.

Panizza, Ugo. 1999. On the Determinants of Fiscal Centralization: Theory and Evidence. *Journal of Public Economics* 74: 97–139.

Riker, William. 1964. *Federalism: Origin, Operation, Significance.* Boston: Little, Brown.

Tilly, Charles. 1990. *Coercion, Capital, and European States, A.D. 990–1990.* Oxford: Oxford University Press.

Tocqueville, Alexis de. [1856] 1983. *The Old Regime and the Revolution.* New York: Anchor.

Alberto Diaz-Cayeros

DEMOCRATIC PARTY, U.S.

The Democratic Party is the oldest, continuously existing political party in the world. It is one of the two major political parties in the two-party system of the United States of America, and has nominated and helped to elect such internationally famous presidents as Thomas Jefferson, Woodrow Wilson, Franklin D. Roosevelt, and John F. Kennedy.

ORIGINS

The Democratic Party, previously named the Democratic-Republican Party, traces its origins to the Anti-Federalists. The Anti-Federalists initially opposed the ratification of the U.S. Constitution during the 1780s because of their concern that it would create an excessively powerful national government dominated by bankers and threaten states' rights. After the Constitution was ratified, the Anti-Federalists emphasized a strict interpretation of the Constitution so that states' rights and civil liberties would be protected from the new national government. Led by Thomas Jefferson and James Madison, the Anti-Federalists formally named and organized the Democratic-Republican Party in 1798. The Democratic-Republican Party often opposed the Federalist Party. Founded by Alexander Hamilton and John Adams, the Federalist Party favored a stronger national government, limited states' rights, a national bank, a pro-British foreign policy, a tight money supply, and high tariffs to encourage the development of American manufacturing. These Federalist policies dominated the presidencies of George Washington (1789–1797) and John Adams (1797–1801).

From the election of Jefferson as president in 1800 until the election of Abraham Lincoln, a Republican, in 1860, most presidents during this era were Democrats. The Democratic-Republican Party officially renamed itself the Democratic Party in 1844. The Democratic Party experienced a sharp increase in membership and electoral strength during and shortly after the presidency of Andrew Jackson (1829–1837). The so-called Jacksonian Democrats claimed that the Democratic Party was "the party of the common man." They asserted that their policies and ideas, such as less federal regulation of the economy, lower tariffs, stronger states' rights, opposition to the national bank, and stronger voting rights for poor white men, benefited the common man by increasing his political and economic power against the Whig Party and northern business interests.

Although the Democratic Party succeeded in attracting more voters who were Irish or German immigrants, urban laborers, and frontier settlers from 1828 until 1860, most of its voting strength remained in the South.

Consequently, the Democratic Party became severely divided and weakened by the issues of slavery and the South's secession from the United States in 1861. While most Southern Democrats favored secession and the creation of the Confederacy, most Northern Democrats either favored accommodation and compromise with the Confederacy or supported the Union war effort led by President Lincoln (1861–1865).

REPUBLICAN DOMINANCE: 1860–1932

Established during the late 1850s from remnants of the Federalist and Whig parties, the Republican Party emerged as the new, second major party in the United States. It elected all but two presidents, usually controlled Congress, and dominated American national politics and domestic and foreign policies from 1860 until 1932 when Franklin D. Roosevelt, a Democrat, was elected president. Even during brief periods when the Democratic Party elected presidents Grover Cleveland (1885–1889, 1893–1897) and Woodrow Wilson (1913–1921) and occasionally controlled Congress, it was often divided between its multiethnic, urban northern wing and its mostly rural, white, Protestant, southern wing. The party's southern wing dominated Democratic membership in Congress and decisions at Democratic national conventions.

In an effort to co-opt the anti–big business, agrarian economic protest movement known as Populism, the Democratic Party nominated William Jennings Bryan for president in 1896. Bryan was the Populist Party's presidential nominee in 1892. However, many conservative Democrats and northern laborers perceived Bryan as a dangerous rural, economic radical. Many of them voted Republican in 1896 resulting in a long-term Republican realignment within the two-party system.

THE WILSON PRESIDENCY AND THE 1920s

Although Woodrow Wilson was elected with only 45 percent of the popular vote in 1912, Wilson managed to unite most Democrats in Congress concerning his foreign policy in World War I and his domestic policies of improving child welfare and labor conditions, reforming the banking system, and supporting women's suffrage. During the 1920s, however, the Democratic Party became more divided over such cultural issues as the national prohibition of alcohol, restrictive immigration laws, the Ku Klux Klan, and the Catholic faith of Al Smith, the Democratic presidential nominee in 1928. Consequently, the Republicans easily won the presidential elections of 1920, 1924, and 1928.

The Great Depression, which began with the stock market crash of 1929, resulted in high unemployment, deflation, bank failures, and widespread economic suffering. The Democrats became more united on economic issues and blamed Republican policies for causing or worsening the Great Depression. Attracting the votes of many alienated Republicans and independents, the Democratic Party easily won control of the presidency and Congress with Franklin D. Roosevelt as its presidential nominee in 1932. Collectively known as the New Deal, Roosevelt's most popular economic and social welfare policies included the Works Progress Administration (WPA), the Social Security Act of 1935, legal rights for labor unions, agricultural price supports, rural electrification, and stricter federal regulations on banks and the stock market.

THE 1932–1936 DEMOCRATIC REALIGNMENT TO THE CIVIL RIGHTS ERA

In the 1936 federal elections, Roosevelt was reelected with 62 percent of the popular vote, carried all but two states in the Electoral College, and helped the Democratic Party to increase its majorities in Congress. For the first time since 1856, most voters were Democrats. The 1932 and 1936 elections were a realignment of the two-party system establishing a long-term Democratic majority among voters. This enabled the Democratic Party to win most presidential elections, usually control Congress, and dominate foreign and domestic policymaking until 1968.

President Harry S. Truman, Roosevelt's Democratic successor, won the 1948 presidential election despite the defection of some anti–civil rights southern Democrats led by Governor J. Strom Thurmond of South Carolina. Commonly known as the Dixiecrats, the States Rights Democratic Party nominated Thurmond for president in 1948. The Dixiecrats opposed Truman's civil rights bill, his desegregation of the military, and the increasing support of northern Democrats for federal civil rights policies that would protect African Americans from racial discrimination and end racial segregation.

For the next twenty years, the Democratic Party was increasingly divided over the issue of federal civil rights for African Americans. The narrowness of Democrat John F. Kennedy's victory in the 1960 presidential election was partially caused by the unpopularity of his pro–civil rights positions among southern Democrats. Likewise, despite his landslide victory in the 1964 election, Lyndon B. Johnson, Kennedy's successor and a southern Democrat, failed to carry most states in the Deep South because of his support for civil rights.

By the late 1960s, the Democratic Party was bitterly divided over civil rights, the anti-poverty programs of the Great Society, the Vietnam War, and the selection of its presidential nominee for the 1968 election. In 1968, events such as the assassination of presidential candidate Robert F. Kennedy, the violence and disunity of the Democratic National Convention in Chicago, and the unpopularity of Johnson and Vice President Hubert H. Humphrey among antiwar Democrats plagued the Democratic Party. Humphrey, the Democratic nominee, narrowly lost the 1968 presidential election to Republican nominee Richard M. Nixon as most white voters supported either Nixon or George C. Wallace, an anti–civil rights southern Democrat.

REPUBLICAN DOMINANCE:
1968–1992

From 1968 until 1992, the Republican Party won five of the six presidential elections and controlled the Senate from 1981 until 1987. Historians attribute the narrow Democratic victory of James E. Carter in the 1976 presidential election to economic problems and the damaging effects of the Watergate scandals on the Republican Party. During this period, many middle-class white voters negatively perceived the Democratic Party, especially in presidential elections, as favoring excessive welfare spending and high taxes, weak on crime control, and ineffective in cold war foreign and defense policies.

THE CLINTON ERA AND POST-2000

In 1992 William J. Clinton, a Democrat, was elected president with 43 percent of the popular vote after defeating Republican president George H. W. Bush and Ross Perot, an independent candidate. Clinton portrayed himself as a moderate who was tough on crime and welfare dependency and would reduce the high budget deficit. The end of the cold war and the Persian Gulf War in 1991 had reduced the Republican advantage on foreign and defense policy issues. In 1996 Clinton became the first Democratic president since Roosevelt to be reelected to a second term. With a Republican Congress, Clinton achieved moderate, compromised results in welfare reform and deficit reduction but unsuccessfully opposed his impeachment.

Al Gore, Clinton's vice president, received approximately 550,000 more votes than George W. Bush, his Republican opponent, in the 2000 presidential election. But Bush won this election when the Supreme Court ruled that he had legitimately received all of Florida's Electoral College votes. Despite growing public criticism of his policies in the Iraq War, Bush was reelected in 2004 after defeating John F. Kerry, the Democratic presidential nominee. Confronting a two-term Republican president and a Republican Congress, the Democratic Party began to discuss how to improve its voter appeal and reconsider its ideas and policy positions in order to win future presi-

dential and congressional elections. In 2006 Democrats regained control of Congress.

SEE ALSO *Civil Rights; Clinton, Bill; Dixiecrats; Great Society, The; Johnson, Lyndon B.; Kennedy, John F.; Populism; Roosevelt, Franklin D.*

BIBLIOGRAPHY

Goldman, Ralph M. 1979. *Search for Consensus: The Story of the Democratic Party.* Philadelphia: Temple University Press.

Parmet, Herbert S. 1977. *The Democrats: The Years after FDR.* New York: Oxford University Press.

Savage, Sean J. 2004. *JFK, LBJ, and the Democratic Party.* Albany: State University of New York Press.

Sean J. Savage

DEMOCRATIZATION

Democracy has widely become the norm within the international community. To promote democracy around the world is not only a key goal of international organizations such as the World Bank, but it is also on the foreign policy agenda of many European and North American countries. Nevertheless, democracy is a notoriously vague and encompassing term. It is often used as a synonym of whatever is desirable in a state, such as good governance and democratic values of elites and citizens. Illustrative of the lack of consensus about its meaning are the results of a survey finding that 150 different studies used more than 550 subtypes of democracy (Collier and Levitsky 1997).

CONCEPTS

Despite this lack of consensus, most political scientists and policy makers use the minimalist definition of democracy described in Robert A. Dahl's 1971 book, *Polyarchy.* According to this definition, democracy is a system of government in which citizens choose their political leaders during periodic free and fair elections, thereby giving those leaders the right to rule after the elections. There are two main theoretical dimensions of democratization: competition among political parties for the people's vote on the one hand, and inclusive suffrage and political participation on the other hand. South Africa's apartheid government (1948–1994) was competitive but not inclusive, because the vast (black) majority was excluded from the right to vote. Regimes in the People's Republic of China and North Korea are inclusive but not competitive, because one political party dominates political life completely. Only regimes with both competition and inclusive suffrage can be classified as a (minimal) democracy.

Democratization is the process whereby a country adopts a democratic regime. Dankwart A. Rustow (1970) distinguished four different phases. During the first phase national borders, national unity, and a coherent national identity must emerge, before democratization can occur. The second "preparatory" phase is characterized by political conflicts between old and new elites in which the new ones demand more influence in national politics. During the "decision phase," key actors, such as the political parties, must accept a fundamental set of democratic rules and practices. Finally, basic democratic institutions and the rules of the game are established in the "habituation phase." Each phase is the result of different causal processes. Given their different causes, it is useful to separate them.

Moreover, scholars often distinguish the phases of "transition" to and "consolidation" of democracy from each other. Transitions are defined as the interval between the dissolution of the old regime and the installation of a new regime, while the essence of consolidation is in defining and fixing the core rules of democratic competition. It should be noted, however, that there is a huge debate about the exact meaning of both terms in the democratization literature (Schedler 1998).

TRENDS OF DEMOCRATIZATION

Democratization is a relatively recent phenomenon. Although some Greek city-states had democratic characteristics, modern—or minimal—democracy dates only from the late nineteenth century. Since the publication of Samuel P. Huntington's influential 1991 study of democratization, *The Third Wave*, scholars have come to take for granted the notion that the spread of democracy has come in waves. A wave of democratization is defined as a group of transitions from nondemocratic to democratic regimes that occurs within a specified period and that significantly outnumbers transitions in the opposite direction.

During the so-called first wave of democratization between 1893 and 1924, New Zealand, Australia, the United States, and many countries in western Europe made a transition to democracy. The regime changes to authoritarianism during the second reverse wave after 1924 reflected the rise of the ideologies of communism and fascism. A second short wave began after World War II (1939–1945) and continued until approximately 1960. Allied occupation promoted the installation of democratic institutions in West Germany, Japan, and Finland. Costa Rica, Chile, and Uruguay were the Latin American states that adopted a democratic system during this period. There is no clear second reverse wave, but the 1960s and 1970s can better be described as an intermezzo, in which transitions to both nondemocratic and democratic regimes occurred (Doorenspleet 2000). In this period, for

example, Colombia and Venezuela became democratic. By contrast, the polarized Chilean democracy was overthrown by a military coup led in 1973 by General Augusto Pinochet (1915–2006). Military coups in Uruguay and Argentina ended democracy in these countries as well.

The third wave began in southern Europe in the 1970s in Portugal, Greece, and Spain. Then it spread to Latin America—to Ecuador, Peru, Bolivia, Argentina, El Salvador, Uruguay, Honduras, and Brazil. This wave of democratization also affected some Asian countries in the late 1980s, such as the Philippines and South Korea. The so-called fourth wave since 1989 was overwhelming and global. At the end of the 1980s, the wave swept through Eastern Europe. The 1990s saw widespread rapid collapse of nondemocratic regimes in Africa, and more than a dozen democracies emerged. The decade after the cold war was a fruitful period for democratization around the world.

EXPLANATIONS OF DEMOCRATIZATION

Nevertheless, many countries remained authoritarian. So, why do some countries democratize whereas others do not? According to modernization theories, which became dominant in the late 1950s, democratization is less likely in poor countries. If less-developed countries are not able to undergo this political modernization process, it is caused by a low level of socioeconomic development in the country. Each less-developed country would have to follow the same path already traversed by the now developed and democratic countries. After the publication of Seymour Martin Lipset's 1959 article, "Some Social Requisites of Democracy," many statistical studies showed that there was indeed a positive correlation between development and democracy. India, with its democratic regime and low economic development, is always brought up as an important exception to this general pattern, though. Moreover, studies of the 1990s show that modernization theory can explain democratic consolidation, but not transitions to democracy (Przeworski and Limongi 1997).

As a reaction and alternative to the modernization approach, the dependency and world-system theories emerged in the early 1970s in Latin America (Bollen 1983). The underdevelopment of Latin America was attributable to its reliance on the export of primary products to the industrial states of the capitalist system, and it was argued that Latin America had been turned into a satellite of the capitalist metropolises of Europe and North America. This approach states that a country's position in the world system, located in either the dominant rich core or impoverished subordinate periphery, is an important determinant of democracy. According to this approach, if a country is not able to become democratic, this is due to external factors—rather than internal domestic factors.

In addition to economic development and international dependency, cultural influences, ethnic divisions, the type of religion, and historical institutional arrangements have been mentioned by researchers as important structural explanations of democratization. According to actor-oriented theorists, however, regime transitions are not determined by structural factors, but are shaped by what principal political actors do as well as by when and how they do so. In their 1986 study *Transitions from Authoritarian Rule*, Guillermo O'Donnell, Philippe C. Schmitter, and Laurence Whitehead abandoned their earlier structuralist perspective and began to focus on the role of elites. They emphasized that elite dispositions, calculations, and pacts largely determine whether or not an opening to democracy will occur at all. Strategic interaction between elites from the state (political parties, the military, and political leaders) and elites from the society (social movements, civil society groups, and intellectuals) establishes the mode of transition and the type of regime that emerges afterward. In "transitions from below" mounting popular pressures and mass mobilization eventually lead to regime change, while in "transitions from above" political and military rulers respond to crises by introducing democratic reforms whose timing and substance they hope to control.

Since the early 1990s, democratization scholars emphasize that the described approaches complement rather than contradict each other, and suggest that a comprehensive theory of democratization should include not only structural but also actor-oriented factors.

DEMOCRATIZATION AND WAR

Democratization processes seldom follow an easy, smooth path. On the contrary, violent conflicts and wars often occur in democratizing states. Conflict can be prevented more easily in very nondemocratic regimes on the one end (because these regimes are willing and able to suppress dissent) and in democratic regimes on the other end (because these regimes recognize minority rights and try to conciliate, thereby reducing dissatisfaction and conflict). Democratizing countries, however, are situated in a dangerous phase in which conflict is very likely.

Not all democratic transitions are dangerous, but the chance of war rises especially in those transitional states that lack the strong political institutions that are needed to make democracy work, such as an effective state and organized political parties (Mansfield and Snyder 2005). The most important reason for this is that political leaders try to use nationalism or ethnic identity as an ideological motivator of collective action in the absence of effective political institutions. Then politicians have the

incentives to resort to violent nationalist or ethnic appeals, tarring their opponents as enemies of the nation or the ethnic group, in order to prevail in electoral competition. When political institutions are strong, though, war can be prevented. This is particularly crucial in ethnically divided countries. A stable democracy is impossible in a country without strong political institutions.

SEE ALSO *Democracy; Democracy, Indices of; Dependency; Elite Theory; Ethnocentrism; Huntington, Samuel P.; Nationalism and Nationality; War; World Bank, The; World-System*

BIBLIOGRAPHY

Bollen, Kenneth A. 1983. World System Position, Dependency, and Democracy: The Cross-National Evidence. *American Sociological Review* 48 (4): 468–479.

Collier, David, and Steven Levitsky. 1997. Democracy with Adjectives: Conceptual Innovation in Comparative Research. *World Politics* 49 (3): 430–451.

Dahl, Robert A. 1971. *Polyarchy: Participation and Opposition.* New Haven, CT: Yale University Press.

Doorenspleet, Renske. 2000. Reassessing the Three Waves of Democratization. *World Politics* 52 (3): 384–406.

Huntington, Samuel P. 1991. *The Third Wave: Democratization in the Late Twentieth Century.* Norman: University of Oklahoma Press.

Lipset, Seymour Martin. 1959. Some Social Requisites of Democracy: Economic Development and Political Legitimacy. *American Political Science Review* 53 (1): 69–105.

Mansfield, Edward D., and Jack Snyder. 2005. *Electing to Fight: Why Emerging Democracies Go to War.* Cambridge, MA: MIT Press.

O'Donnell, Guillermo, Philippe C. Schmitter, and Laurence Whitehead, eds. 1986. *Transitions from Authoritarian Rule: Prospects for Democracy.* Baltimore: Johns Hopkins University Press.

Przeworski, Adam, and Fernando Limongi. 1997. Modernization: Theories and Facts. *World Politics* 49 (2): 155–183.

Rustow, Dankwart A. 1970. Transitions to Democracy: Toward a Dynamic Model. *Comparative Politics* 2 (3): 337–363.

Schedler, Andreas. 1998. What Is Democratic Consolidation? *Journal of Democracy* 9 (2): 91–107.

Renske Doorenspleet

DEMOGRAPHIC TRANSITION

The term *demographic transition* originally described the major social shift that occurred in Western societies from the late nineteenth century to the 1930s. At that time,

European societies, and their settler offshoots overseas, moved with considerable speed from a high-mortality, high-fertility population regime to low fertility and low mortality, with major social consequences. This historic shift saw the decline of family size from approximately six children per family to fewer than two. The transition also provided the preconditions for women to move from the private sphere and constant childbearing to the public domain and the expanding industrial work force.

Explanations for this world-shaping change abounded, and a field known as *demographic transition theory* developed, which, while hotly contested, remains influential. Population trends, such as the post–World War II (1939–1945) "baby boom," have shaken the theory of continuing fertility decline, yet it has remained remarkably resilient. It is clear now that demographic transition is a global phenomenon, not just a Western trend, and that since 1960 much of the world is exhibiting declining fertility, with sub-Saharan Africa probably the last to change. Most now accept that a second demographic transition is occurring (van de Kaa 1987), dating from the 1960s, as even lower birthrates, well below replacement level, prevail in several European and Asian countries. While many demographers expected that birthrates would reach the replacement level, and then plateau, now there is concern that some countries' birthrates are so low that their societies will eventually shrink, possibly disappear.

The concern with demographic change has considerable implications for political and social decision making in relation to the family, the labor market, and immigration policy. Fertility decline has moved from being a preoccupation of demographers to a central concern for politicians and social commentators. It takes on a new urgency as low fertility leads to inevitable population ageing.

In the 1960s exponents of demographic transition theory in the West, fearful of a "population explosion," particularly in the developing world, and eager to gain political advantage in a cold war climate, sought to apply the theory, with varying results, in developing countries through agencies such as the World Bank and the United Nations Fund for Population Activities. The birth control pill, adopted so centrally in the West, was originally funded to provide contraception in the developing world on the understanding that knowledge of birth control was all that was needed for fertility decline. Later, more considered approaches are based on the broader finding of demographic transition theory—that socioeconomic change is more likely to lead to reduced fertility.

HISTORY OF THE THEORY

Demographic transition theory is curiously paradoxical. While there is no general agreement as to its explanatory frameworks, it is constantly invoked as if there were. This is due in part to demography's post–World War II desire to be a science and to establish a "grand theory" of population and fertility decline. Yet even in this quantitatively based discipline, wider intellectual currents have intruded: postmodernism and cultural and anthropological explanations have recently entered the field. Short-term theory is now the order of the day.

In 1937 Kingsley Davis (1908–1997), an early exponent of the theory, suggested that ultimately the reproduction of the species is incompatible with advanced industrial society. Thus he established the major framework of the theory, which held that socioeconomic development and modernization are major causal forces. It is this element of the theory that remains robust. In a 2006 volume titled *Demographic Transition Theory,* one of the most influential twentieth-century exponents, John C. Caldwell, argued that in industrial society the old values essential to agricultural societies—strong family, virginity, loyalty, legitimate births—are no longer necessary except as "social pacifiers." Industrial society and, even more, postindustrial knowledge economies, need mobile, educated individuals unencumbered with babies and family ties.

Within the overarching model of socioeconomic change, there is no common acceptance of particular determinants of transformation, as different societies take varying paths to declining birthrates. The onset and tempo of mortality and fertility decline vary widely. Must a falling off in mortality precede a fertility decline? Are modern technologies of birth control essential or indeed sufficient? Is decline more likely in conjugal families (those based on husband, wife, and children) rather than the joint (extended) families of much of Asia and Africa? How critical are gender regimes? It is now overwhelmingly clear that women's education is inversely related to fertility. The more highly educated women are, the fewer children they produce, with few exceptions. How critical is institutional change, such as government policy in relation to education, to welfare provision, and to legal frameworks (McDonald 2006)? What role does ideational change play—the decline of religious belief, the centrality of individuals and their entitlements, the significance of planning modern lives, women's reproductive rights, and notions of consumption and leisure? All of these elements have played a significant part in variants of demographic transition theory.

Some countries (Japan, Singapore, Taiwan, as well as much of central Europe and southern Europe) now exhibit very low fertility, defined as continuing fertility under 1.5 births per woman on average, sometimes referred to as a *birth strike.* Most commentators agree that this is largely due to women working and to the inability of states to make women's work and childbearing compatible. Does this low fertility foretell the future or is the experience of the United States, which since the late 1970s has exhibited a rise to replacement-level fertility, an opposing model? How significant is mode of production versus changing ideas and attitudes? Dirk van de Kaa, an influential demographer from the Netherlands, maintains that cohorts of young people with common, postmodern, individualistic ideas are implicated, whereas Caldwell insists that mode of production is primary and that neoliberalism and the accompanying insecurity it produces in the workplace play a significant role in inhibiting births.

Some theorists have predicted that the creation of a world economic system where children are of no immediate economic value to their parents will inevitably lead to lower world population—a goal much desired by environmentalists. Others point out that in much of Asia and Africa, patriarchy, a regime that puts children and lineage before women's rights, is still dominant and that fertility decline may not be inevitable. Prediction is always fraught, and an element that has been overlooked in much twentieth-century demography may well come back to haunt us. Secularization, the decline of traditional religious belief, is a key to changing Western fertility patterns. Yet any assumption that secularization will inevitably increase is risky in the light of resurgent fundamentalisms across all religious belief systems. Anthropological demography reminds us that we are not all rational actors, and that myth, superstition, and culture are all pervasive.

Between 1965 and 2000, the fertility (as measured by the total fertility rate) of both the developing world and the whole world nearly halved (Caldwell et al. 2006, p. 13). On the basis of the United Nations World Population Prospects (2004) and other findings, demographers have predicted that global population growth will almost come to a halt by 2050, "with the Earth having around 9 billion or fewer inhabitants" (Caldwell et al. 2006, p. 316). Higher and lower projections have been offered, the latter demonstrating population halving every two hundred years—surely an unacceptable outcome. With the rate of world population growth slowing, some are turning to issues of the composition of the population.

A third demographic transition has been proposed for Europe and the United States, one that sees the ancestry of some national populations being radically and permanently altered through high levels of immigration of people with distinctively different ethnic ancestry into countries with low fertility (Coleman 2006, p. 401). This is a radical departure from previous demographic transition theory in its focus on immigration. It demonstrates, however, the resilience of the theory. The demographic transition may well continue to surprise us.

SEE ALSO *Anthropology; Birth Control; Club of Rome; Demography; Development Economics; Development,* *Rural; Fertility, Human; Gender Gap; Health in Developing Countries; Immigration; Inequality, Gender; Malthusian Trap; Modernization; Overpopulation; Population Growth; Population Studies*

BIBLIOGRAPHY

Bulatao, R. A., and John Casterline, eds. 2001. *Global Fertility Transition.* A supplement to *Population and Development Review* 127.

Caldwell, John C., Bruce K. Caldwell, Pat Caldwell, et al. 2006. *Demographic Transition Theory.* Dordrecht, Netherlands: Springer.

Coleman, David. 2006. Immigration and Ethnic Change in Low-fertility Countries: A Third Demographic Transition. *Population and Development Review* 32 (3): 401–439.

Davis, Kingsley. 1937. Reproductive Institutions and the Pressure for Population. *Sociological Review* 29: 289–306. Reprinted as: Kingsley Davis on Reproductive Institutions and the Pressures for Population. 1997. *Population and Development Review* 23 (3): 611–624.

Jones, Gavin W., Robert Douglas, John Caldwell, and Rennie D'Souza, eds. 1997. *The Continuing Demographic Transition.* Oxford: Clarendon.

Kertzer, David, and Tom Fricke, eds. 1997. *Anthropological Demography: Toward a New Synthesis.* Chicago: University of Chicago Press.

McDonald, Peter. 2006. Low Fertility and the State: The Efficacy of Policy. *Population and Development Review* 32 (3): 485–510.

United Nations Department of Economic and Social Affairs: Population Division. World Population Prospects: The 2004 Revision. http://esa.un.org/unpp/.

Van de Kaa, Dirk. 1987. Europe's Second Demographic Transition. *Population Bulletin* 42 (1).

Alison Mackinnon

DEMOGRAPHY

Demography is the scientific study of the size, composition, and distribution of human populations, and their changes resulting from fertility, mortality, and migration. Demography is concerned with how large (or small) populations are, that is, their size; how the populations are composed according to age, sex, race, marital status, and other characteristics, that is, their composition; and how populations are distributed in physical space (e.g., how urban and rural they are), that is, their spatial distribution (Bogue 1969). Demography is also interested in the changes over time in the size, composition, and distribution of human populations, and how these result from the processes of fertility, mortality, and migration.

The term *demography* is from the Greek *demos* (population) and *graphia* (writing). It is believed to have first appeared in print in 1855 in the book *Elements of Human Statistics or Comparative Demography* by the Belgian statistician Achille Guillard (1799–1876) (Borrie 1973, p. 75; Rowland 2003, p. 16).

Some demographers argue that demography is best treated as a subdiscipline or specialization of sociology owing to its organizational relationship with sociology (Moore 1959, p. 833). However, the organizational affinity in universities between demography and sociology is not universal. In some Eastern European universities, demography is organizationally linked with economics, and in some Western European universities, with geography. In many countries (e.g., China), demography is taught in a separate university department.

The American sociologist Kingsley Davis (1908–1997), who served at different times as president of both the Population Association of America and the American Sociological Association, wrote in 1948 in his classic sociology textbook, *Human Society*, that "the science of population, sometimes called demography, represents a fundamental approach to the understanding of human society" (1948, p. 551). The relationship between sociology and demography is hence a fundamental one: "Society is both a necessary and sufficient cause of population trends" (1948, pp. 553–554).

There are only two ways to enter a population, by birth and by in-migration. There are two ways to leave a population, by death and by out-migration. Thus, a population is often defined by demographers according to the specific needs of the research and researcher. Samuel Preston and his colleagues have written that the "term 'population' refers to a collection of items, for example, balls in an urn. Demographers use the term in a similar way to denote a collection of persons alive at a specified point in time who meet certain criteria" (2001, p 1). For example, the population of interest may be that of students attending a specific university during a specific year. In this situation, the students are born (i.e., enter) into the population when they enroll, and they die (i.e., leave) when they graduate.

Generally, demographers use vital registration (birth and death) records to count births and deaths in a population to determine fertility and mortality rates. The more difficult demographic process to measure is migration because in most countries registration records are not maintained when persons migrate into or out of the population. Data gathered around the world from decennial census and sample surveys are also used by demographers to examine demographic and sociodemographic issues.

Demographic techniques allow for the calculation of population projections, which specify the future size of the population by utilizing specific assumptions about the parameters driving the future fertility, mortality, and migration of the population. Population projections for all the countries around the world are periodically calculated by demographers at the United Nations and other international organizations and are made publicly available. Such projections are often used by government agencies and private firms to plan the infrastructure of cities, such as the number of schools, hospitals, airports, and parks that would be needed in the future in order for the cities to be able to function properly.

Demography is concerned not only with the observation and description of the size, composition, and spatial distribution of human populations and the changes resulting from fertility, mortality, and migration. Demography is also concerned with developing explanations for why the demographic variables operate and change in the ways they do: That is, why do some populations increase in size and others decrease? Why do some become older and others become younger? Why are some more urban and others more rural?

One paradigm in demography, known as *formal demography*, uses only demographic variables, such as age and sex, as independent variables to answer the above questions. Another paradigm, known as *social demography*, uses such nondemographic variables as marital status, race, education, socioeconomic status, occupation, household size, and type of place of residence—variables drawn mainly from sociology, economics, psychology, geography, anthropology, biology, and other disciplines—to answer the questions.

To illustrate, formal demographers might address differences in populations in their birth rates and death rates by considering their differences in age composition or in sex composition. Younger populations typically have higher birth rates than older populations; and populations with more females than males will usually have lower death rates than populations with more males than females (Poston 2005). Social demographers might address the above differences in populations in their birth rates and death rates by examining differences among them in, say, their socioeconomic status. Usually, populations with high socioeconomic status will have lower birth rates and death rates than populations with low socioeconomic status.

Demographic data may be introduced to provide some perspective for distinguishing between these two approaches. Human populations have different levels of fertility. Countries thus differ with respect to their total fertility rates (roughly defined as the average number of children born to a woman during her childbearing years). In 2004 Poland and Romania had very low fertility rates of 1.2, among the lowest in the world. Conversely, Niger,

Guinea-Bissau, and Yemen had very high fertility rates of 8.0, 7.1, and 7.0, respectively—the highest in the world (Population Reference Bureau, 2004). Why do these fertility differences exist? Why do Niger, Guinea-Bissau, and Yemen have fertility rates that are so much higher than those of Poland and Romania? To answer this question, the social demographer would go beyond purely demographic issues of age and sex composition and would focus on the processes of industrialization and modernization.

Another example focuses on what demographers refer to as the percentage rate of natural increase/decrease, that is, the difference between the birth rate and the death rate. In 2004 both Russia and Bulgaria had a rate of -0.6 percent: that is, the difference between their crude birth and death rates was about -6/1000 or -0.6/100. In contrast, the rate in both Madagascar and Saudi Arabia was 3.0 percent. In these countries, the difference between their birth and death rates was 30/1000 or 3/100.

Why are these four countries growing at such drastically different rates? Why do Russia and Bulgaria have negative growth rates, and why do Madagascar and Saudi Arabia have positive rates? The formal demographer might develop an answer by considering the birth rates of these countries. The numbers of babies born per 1,000 population in 2004 in Russia, Bulgaria, Madagascar, and Saudi Arabia were 10, 10, 43, and 32, respectively. The latter two countries have higher rates of growth than the former two countries because their birth rates are so much higher. The social demographer would first consider the birth rate differentials, but would then go beyond this demographic consideration to an answer involving nondemographic factors that may be influencing the birth rates. Perhaps the economy has something to do with it (poorer countries have higher birth rates). Perhaps the level of industrialization of the country has an impact (the more industrialized countries generally have lower birth rates). Perhaps the role of women compared to men is having an effect (countries with more gender equity tend to have lower birth rates).

Whatever the reasons, the social demographer extends the answer beyond demographic reasons. Social demography is broader in scope and orientation than formal demography. Preston has noted, for example, that demography includes "research of any disciplinary stripe on the causes and consequences of population change" (1993, p. 593).

Given the impact of industrialization in the reduction of fertility and mortality and the international migration flows from less developed to more developed countries around the world, it is a common practice among demographers to observe separately the demographic processes in less developed countries from those in more developed countries. The issues that concern demographers often vary depending on the level of industrialization of each country. In less developed countries, high levels of fertility, high levels of infant mortality, a high prevalence of HIV/AIDS, and high levels of out-migration to more developed countries tend to be some of the main demographic concerns. In more developed countries, low fertility patterns, women having babies at later ages, populations with below replacement levels of fertility, and large numbers of migrants from less developed countries are some of the main issues being examined by demographers.

A frequent concern in demography is the extent to which changes in individual-level behavior have an effect on aggregate processes (Preston et al. 2001). For example, if it suddenly became normative for individuals in a population to become smokers once they reach a certain age, then the demographer would want to find out to what extent the life expectancy at age x would be affected, as well as the death rate for that population. Similarly, regarding fertility, if women in a certain country decided to have children at older ages, then the concern becomes to what extent such behavior can have an effect on the total fertility rate, on the growth rate, and on whether the population will be maintained at a replacement level of fertility (which in populations with low levels of mortality is around 2.1 children per woman).

Demographers also are often concerned with how social policy could impact the aggregate population processes. In China, for example, demographers have identified a relationship between the enforcement of fertility policies and increasing levels of social and economic development and the sex ratio at birth (Poston et al. 1997; Poston and Glover 2005). The sex ratio at birth is the number of males born per 100 females born and is around 105 in most societies. Since the 1980s in China it has been significantly above 105. In 2000 China's sex ratio at birth was near 120. The rapid reduction of fertility in China, along with the long-standing preference for sons, has led to the selective abortion of female fetuses, and a sex ratio at birth above normal levels. As a consequence, in China there will not be enough women in the population for the next few decades for Chinese men to marry. This is a major effect of societal modernization and fertility-control policies (Poston and Morrison 2005).

Demographers do not always agree about the boundaries and restrictions of their field. John Caldwell stated the problem succinctly: "What demography is and what demographers should be confined to doing remains a difficult area in terms not only of the scope of professional interests, but also of the coverage aimed at in the syllabuses for students and in what is acceptable for journals in the field" (1996, p. 305).

Other demographers argue for a broader approach, noting that demography is not a specialization of sociology, or of any discipline, but a discipline in its own right. Consider the definition of demography in the popular demography textbook *Population: An Introduction to Concepts and Issues* by John Weeks: Demography is "concerned with virtually everything that influences, or can be influenced by" population size, distribution, processes, structures, or characteristics (2005, p. 5).

It is no wonder that J. Mayone Stycos observed that "as a field with its own body of interrelated concepts, techniques, journals and professional associations, demography is clearly a discipline" (1987, p. 616). Caldwell also reached this conclusion, but more for methodological reasons: "Demography will remain a distinct discipline because of its approach: its demand that conclusions be in keeping with observable and testable data in the real world, that these data be used as shrewdly as possible to elicit their real meanings, and that the study should be representative of sizable or significant and definable populations" (1996, p. 333).

SEE ALSO *Fertility, Human; Malthus, Thomas Robert; Population Growth*

BIBLIOGRAPHY

Bogue, Donald J. 1969. *Principles of Demography*. New York: Wiley.

Borrie, W. D. 1973. The Place of Demography in the Development of the Social Sciences. In *International Population Conference, Liege, 1973*, 73–93. Liege, Belgium: International Union for the Scientific Study of Population.

Caldwell, John C. 1996. Demography and Social Science. *Population Studies* 50: 305–333.

Davis, Kingsley. 1948. *Human Society*. New York: Macmillan.

Hauser, Philip M., and Otis Dudley Duncan. 1959. The Nature of Demography. In *The Study of Population: An Inventory and Appraisal*, ed. Philip M. Hauser and Otis Dudley Duncan, 29–44. Chicago: University of Chicago Press.

McFalls, Joseph, Jr. 2003. Population: A Lively Introduction. 4th ed. *Population Bulletin* 58 (4). http://www.prb.org/pdf/PopulationLivelyIntro.pdf.

Micklin, Michael, and Dudley L. Poston Jr. 2005. Prologue: The Demographer's Ken: 50 Years of Growth and Change. In *Handbook of Population*, ed. Dudley L. Poston Jr. and Michael Micklin, 1–15. New York: Springer.

Moore, Wilbert E. 1959. Sociology and Demography. In *The Study of Population: An Inventory and Appraisal*, ed. Philip M. Hauser and Otis Dudley Duncan, 832–851. Chicago: University of Chicago Press.

Population Reference Bureau. 2004. *2004 World Population Data Sheet*. Washington, DC: Population Reference Bureau. http://www.prb.org/pdf04/04WorldDataSheet_Eng.pdf.

Population Reference Bureau. 2005. *2005 World Population Data Sheet*. Washington, DC: Population Reference Bureau. http://www.prb.org/pdf05/05WorldDataSheet_Eng.pdf.

Poston, Dudley L., Jr. 2005. Age and Sex. In *Handbook of Population*, ed. Dudley L. Poston Jr. and Michael Micklin, 19–58. New York: Springer.

Poston, Dudley L., Jr., and Karen S. Glover. 2005. Too Many Males: Marriage Market Implications of Gender Imbalances in China. *Genus* 61: 119–140.

Poston, Dudley L., Jr., Baochang Gu, Peihang Liu, and Terra McDaniel. 1997. Son Preference and the Sex Ratio at Birth in China: A Provincial Level Analysis. *Social Biology* 44: 55–76.

Poston, Dudley L., Jr., and Peter A. Morrison. 2005. China: Bachelor Bomb. *International Herald Tribune* (September 14): 10.

Pressat, Roland. 1985. *The Dictionary of Demography*. Oxford: Blackwell.

Preston, Samuel H. 1993. The Contours of Demography: Estimates and Projections. *Demography* 30: 593–606.

Preston, Samuel H., Patrick Heuveline, and Michel Guillot. 2001. *Demography: Measuring and Modeling Population Processes*. Oxford: Blackwell.

Rowland, Donald T. 2003. *Demographic Methods and Concepts*. New York: Oxford University Press.

Stycos, J. Mayone. 1987. Demography as an Interdiscipline. *Sociological Forum* 2: 615–628.

Weeks, John R. 2005. *Population: An Introduction to Concepts and Issues*. 9th ed. Belmont, CA: Wadsworth.

Dudley L. Poston Jr.
Nadia Y. Flores

DEMOGRAPHY, SOCIAL

The field of social demography uses demographic data and methods to describe, explain, and predict social phenomena. It also measures the effect of social forces on population distribution. Distinct from formal demography, which focuses more generally on population composition and distribution, social demography investigates the social-status composition and distribution of a population.

DEVELOPMENT OF SOCIAL DEMOGRAPHY

Social demography emerged as an academic discipline in the United States over the course of the last half of the twentieth century. Kingsley Davis coined the term *social demography* in a 1963 paper (Heer 2005). Previously, the term *population studies* was used to denote the study of social status using demographic techniques. In 1970, Thomas Ford and Gordon DeJong published a textbook titled *Social Demography*, which included research exemplars in the field. In 1975 the first conference on social demography was held at the University of Wisconsin.

Social demography developed in the United States as an outgrowth of regular census data, the development of demographic techniques, an interest in scientific investigation, and a general curiosity concerning social issues. Institutionalized by the U.S. Constitution, the U.S. Census has received increased funding and been accompanied by increased research activity and scientific rigor with each succeeding decennium. This continuous expansion has offered rich datasets to researchers. Thus, the application of modern statistical methods to demographic data collection and analysis has increased the validity and reliability of demography in general.

Corollary to the development of demographic techniques was a glorification of scientific solutions to modern problems. Social issues came to be viewed as problems that could be solved scientifically. Social demography emerged as a prime tool to isolate, explain, and predict factors influencing social issues such as residential segregation, unemployment, and income gaps between status groups.

Sociology and social demography developed in tandem over the course of the twentieth century. Early social theorists utilized demographic data as empirical evidence of their claims. W. E. B. Du Bois, for example, chronicled the experience of the African American population at the end of the nineteenth century through the use of census enumeration data, independent surveys, and cartography. Robert Park and Ernest Burgess, along with many others within the Chicago school of sociology, later extended the use of demographic data to support sociological claims of urban growth and population distribution by socioeconomic status. In the late 1950s, Philip Hauser and Otis Duncan codified the connection of sociology and demography in their work *Population Studies*.

Beginning in the 1960s, training in social demography became formalized into academia. Research and training in the discipline developed at university centers such as Chicago, Wisconsin, North Carolina, and Michigan. Also, population research centers at Princeton, Brown, and the University of Texas contributed scholars and research to social demography.

CURRENT TRENDS IN SOCIAL DEMOGRAPHY

Charles Hirschman and Stewart Tolnay (2005) identify three distinct areas within the current state of social demography: (1) data collection and descriptive interpretation; (2) theory development and model testing; and (3) contextual analysis.

Data collection is a staple of social demography. Modern democracies and consumer economies rely heavily on reliable data and descriptive analyses to fit policies and services to their respective constituents and con-

sumers. Indeed, demographic data and interpretation are ubiquitous in modern society. Politicians, business leaders, historians, and the media offer many, and often contradictory, interpretive reports based on social demographic data each day. Social indicators for income, labor, occupation, housing, immigration and migration, and family status are regularly collected, analyzed, and released to the public.

In addition to data collection and descriptive analysis, social demographers contribute to cumulative knowledge through theory development. Researchers use statistical models to isolate and compare the effects of variables on social phenomena. For example, the sociologist Otis Dudley Duncan was able to test and ultimately refute the "culture of poverty" hypothesis, which was a common theory of the economic disparity between African Americans and whites (1970). Using the demographic method of direct standardization, Duncan held constant the effects of occupation, education, parental status, mental ability, and many other factors affecting income. By varying only the race of the respondent, Duncan showed that black men earned 83 cents to every dollar earned by white men, even though no other significant differences between the groups existed. Race alone was responsible for the seventeen-cent differential, not culture-of-poverty variables such as "father's education" or "family type."

Finally, contextual analysis may be a promising area of development in the near future. Contextual analysis investigates the interaction of the individual and the demographic environment in which that individual is situated. The role of structural context on individual behavior is commonly accepted in sociology. For instance, research on "school effects" attempts to show the role of schools in the educational attainment of individual students. However, contextual-analysis reports in education reveal relatively small school effects once the individual's variables are controlled. Until recently, contextual analysis has been hindered by conceptual and methodological constraints. However, recent developments in statistical methods and software may yield much future research in this area.

LIMITATIONS FACING SOCIAL DEMOGRAPHY

Although social demography enjoys a high status within the social sciences, there are limitations to its applicability. Not all changes that occur within a society are a function of population composition. For example, the mid-twentieth century baby boom occurred across all educational, age, and racial groups. Therefore, the common approaches social demographers use cannot isolate the source of the variation in fertility. The source of the variation in the case of the baby boom was contextual: political and economic circumstances had changed greatly after World War II. The source of the variation in fertility did not, therefore, come from various segments of the U.S. population.

Another limitation for much social demographic research is that it is oriented towards disproving false hypotheses. False hypotheses are uncovered by statistically revealing the amount of variation caused in a dependent variable by exposure to an independent variable. But this technique cannot prove a hypothesis to be true, for there is always the possibility that the true causes of social change are not included in the model.

SEE ALSO *Demography*

BIBLIOGRAPHY

Duncan, Otis Dudley. 1970. Inheritance of Poverty or Inheritance of Race. In *On Understanding Poverty: Perspectives from the Social Sciences*, ed. D. P. Moynihan, 85–110. New York: Basic Books.

Ford, Thomas, and Gordon DeJong, eds. 1970. *Social Demography*. Englewood Cliffs, NJ: Prentice-Hall.

Hauser, Phillip, and Otis D. Duncan, eds. 1959. *The Study of Population*. Chicago: University of Chicago Press.

Heer, David M. 2005. *Kingsley Davis: A Biography and Selections from his Writings*. New Brunswick, NJ: Transaction Publishers.

Hirschman, Charles, and Stewart Tolnay. 2005. Social Demography. In *Handbook of Population*, eds. Dudley Poston and Michael Micklin, 419–449. New York: Kluwer Academic.

Warren Waren

DEONTOLOGY
SEE *Philosophy, Moral.*

DEPENDENCY

The term *dependency* is most commonly used to describe a situation wherein one person relies upon another for help, guidance, reassurance, protection, or emotional support. However, it is also possible for an individual to be dependent upon a substance rather than a person, as in chemical dependency. Other uses of the dependency concept in social science include economic dependency (i.e., one person's reliance on another for financial support), and functional dependency (i.e., one person's reliance on another for physical help, or for assistance in carrying out activities of daily living).

PERSONALITY TRAITS

Although different forms of dependency are of interest to economists, sociologists, gerontologists, and others, the dependency concept is most widely used in psychology. In addition to studying chemical dependency, psychologists have devoted considerable effort to understanding the causes and consequences of dependent personality traits. In this context, researchers distinguish interpersonal dependency from pathological dependency. Interpersonal dependency describes the normal help- and reassurance-seeking that most people exhibit in everyday life; individuals with high levels of interpersonal dependency show above-average rates of help- and reassurance-seeking. Pathological dependency—which when pronounced may warrant a diagnosis of dependent personality disorder—describes an extreme form of maladaptive, inflexible dependency characterized by fear of abandonment, feelings of powerlessness and ineffectiveness, and an inability to initiate tasks or make decisions without excessive advice and reassurance from others.

High levels of interpersonal dependency are associated with a predictable array of personality traits including conformity, compliance, suggestibility, introversion, insecurity, interpersonal yielding, and low self-esteem. Among the psychological disorders most commonly found in people with pathological dependency are depression, anxiety disorders (especially social phobia and agoraphobia), and eating disorders (i.e., anorexia and bulimia). Contrary to clinical lore, high levels of pathological dependency do not predispose people to chemical dependency. In fact, studies show that in most cases increases in dependent attitudes and behaviors follow, rather than precede, the onset of addiction.

Although about 30 percent of the variance in level of both interpersonal and pathological dependency is attributable to genetic factors (presumably inherited differences in infantile temperament), parenting plays a key role in the etiology of dependent personality traits. Two parenting styles are particularly important in this context. First, overprotective parenting is associated with high levels of dependency in offspring. In addition, authoritarian (i.e., rigid, inflexible) parenting leads to high levels of dependency later in life. Both parenting styles lead to increased dependency because overprotective and authoritarian parents inadvertently teach children to look to others for guidance, protection, and support, and accede to others' demands without question.

Most psychologists conceptualize dependent personality traits as consisting of four major components: (1) cognitive (a perception of oneself as vulnerable and weak, coupled with the belief that other people are comparatively powerful and potent); (2) motivational (a strong desire to obtain and maintain nurturant, supportive relationships); (3) emotional (fear of abandonment and fear of negative evaluation by others); and (4) behavioral (use of various self-presentation strategies to strengthen interpersonal ties). Among the self-presentation strategies most commonly associated with dependency in adults are supplication (appearing weak to elicit caregiving responses from others), and ingratiation (performing favors to create a sense of indebtedness in others). However, when these more common interpersonal strategies prove ineffective, people with pathological dependency may resort to intimidation (e.g., breakdown threats, suicide gestures) in a desperate attempt to preclude abandonment.

Although the cognitive, motivational, emotional, and behavioral features of dependency are relatively stable over time and across situation, dependency is expressed in different ways at different ages. During childhood dependency needs are directed primarily toward parents and other authority figures (e.g., teachers, coaches), but in adolescence the target of dependency strivings often shifts to the peer group. During early and middle adulthood dependency strivings are expressed most commonly around romantic partners, friends, supervisors, and colleagues at work; later in life dependency needs tend to be directed toward caregivers as well as romantic partners and peers.

CONSEQUENCES, FACTORS

Despite the fact that dependency in adults is usually regarded as a sign of weakness, dysfunction, and immaturity, dependent personality traits are actually associated with both positive and negative consequences. On the negative side, dependent people tend to overuse health and mental health services, react strongly to even minor relationship conflict, and have difficulty assuming leadership positions. On the positive side, however, dependent people delay less long than nondependent people in seeking medical help following symptom onset, are skilled at deciphering subtle verbal and nonverbal cues, and perform well in collaborative tasks when provided with adequate structure.

On questionnaire and interview measures of interpersonal and pathological dependency women tend to obtain higher scores than men do. These gender differences in self-reported dependency begin by mid-childhood and persist through late adulthood. A very different pattern is obtained when projective measures (e.g., the Rorschach Inkblot Test) are used to assess dependency: When these more subtle measures are administered women and men obtain comparable dependency scores. It appears that women and men have similar levels of underlying dependency needs (as reflected in comparable scores on projective dependency tests). However, men are less willing than women to acknowledge these needs in interviews and on questionnaires.

Like gender, culture affects the expression of interpersonal dependency, with individuals raised in sociocentric cultures (i.e., cultures that emphasize interrelatedness over individual achievement) showing higher self-reported dependency than individuals raised in individualistic cultures (which typically emphasize individuation and achievement over interpersonal connectedness). Studies further suggest that when individuals immigrate and gradually become acculturated to a new society, dependency levels tend to increase or decrease in accordance with the norms and values of that society.

BIBLIOGRAPHY

Baltes, Margaret M. 1996. *The Many Faces of Dependency in Old Age*. Cambridge, U.K.: Cambridge University Press.

Bornstein, Robert F. 1993. *The Dependent Personality*. New York: Guilford Press.

Bornstein, Robert F. 2005. *The Dependent Patient: A Practitioner's Guide*. Washington, DC: American Psychological Association.

Pincus, Aaron L., and Kelly R. Wilson. 2001. Interpersonal Variability in Dependent Personality. *Journal of Personality* 69 (2): 223–251.

Rusbult, Caryl E., and Paul A. M. Van Lange. 2003. Interdependence, Interaction, and Relationships. *Annual Review of Psychology* 54: 351–375.

Robert F. Bornstein

DEPENDENCY THEORY

In the early 1950s, a group of economists stationed at the United Nations Economic Commission for Latin America (ECLA) in Santiago, Chile, launched a rigorous research program around one pressing question: What accounts for the growing divergence in living standards and gross domestic product (GDP) between the wealthy countries of the industrialized North and the poorer developing countries of the South? In 1850, for example, Argentina was among the richest nations of the world and GDP per capita in Latin America was $245, compared to $239 in North America. A century later, Argentina was mired in debt and poverty, and GDP per capita in Canada and the United States had quickly outpaced that of Latin America as both had firmly joined the ranks of the developed-country bloc.

According to neoclassical economic theory, strong trade and investment linkages between North and South should lead to a positive-sum outcome for all participants. However, by the 1950s it was difficult to ignore the widening global cleavages between North and South, as well as the growing gap between rich and poor within the developing countries. This latter trend, characterized by an uneasy coexistence between a modern urbanized sector of the economy with strong global ties and a largely rural traditional sector where production modes sorely lagged, was increasingly referred to as *dualism*. Both dualism and the North-South divide became the focus of conceptual debates and practical policy prescriptions for a new generation of dependency school theorists that emerged during the 1960s and 1970s.

At heart, most dependency theorists saw the problem of underdevelopment as the inherently exploitive and contradictory nature of the capitalist system, which pitted capitalists and workers against each other as both sought to maximize their respective economic well-being. The North, with its capital abundance and accumulation of wealth, was the oppressor, while the South, with its ready supply of cheap labor and vastly rich land and natural resources, was the oppressed. It was the external sector that perpetuated underdevelopment, as well as the various private (multinational corporations) and public entities (the World Bank, the International Monetary Fund, and industrial-bloc governments) that represented it.

Whereas the earlier diagnoses of ECLA had generated proposals for restructuring the developing world's economic relationship with the northern industrial bloc, the dependency school advocated assertive state intervention to promote the economic and political independence of the developing world vis-à-vis the North. Along with endorsing ambitious programs of import-substitution industrialization, the dependency school expanded the ECLA critique to include the urgent need for the underdeveloped South to overcome its dependence on the developed North through any variety of means, state intervention being one of these.

A RICH DEBATE

An initial wave of dependency thinking was triggered by the work of the Argentine economist Raúl Prebisch (1901–1986), director of his country's first central bank from 1935 to 1943 and subsequently the executive secretary of ECLA between 1949 and 1963. In Prebisch's classic 1949 treatise, *The Economic Development of Latin America and Its Principal Problems*, he introduced the idea of an industrial, hegemonic center and an agrarian, dependent periphery as a framework for understanding the emerging international division of labor between North and South. Prebisch argued that the wealth of poor nations tended to decrease when that of rich nations increased due to an unequal exchange of industrial versus agricultural goods in the North-South trading relationship. For the early structuralists, industrialization was considered a necessary step toward rectifying this pattern of unequal exchange and thus the most important objective in a development program.

From here, dependency theory quickly divided into diverse strands. Most notably, André Gunder Frank (1929–2005) adapted it to Marxism, as did Paul Baran (1910–1964), arguing that imperialism and the colonial legacy had left Asia, Africa, and Latin America in a highly disadvantageous position. Like Karl Marx (1818–1883), these theorists argued that economics was the main determinant of politics, and that social class should be the prime unit of analysis. Frank identified a "comprador class" of local southern elites whose interests and profits from this system of exploitation had become closely intertwined with their counterparts in the developed or metropolitan countries. For both Baran and Frank, this third world bourgeoisie was parasitic in nature, leaving it to workers and peasants to break with imperialism and move a given nation toward progress. While acknowledging the debilitating nature of these dual economies, others such as Ernesto Laclau criticized the Marxists for overlooking important distinctions between capitalist and precapitalist modes of production in the South. Given the tenacity of the latter, Laclau argued, it made no sense for dependency analysts to focus solely on capitalist modes of production as the linchpin for change.

Another key debate within the dependency school concerned the weight that should be given to domestic or international factors. In contrast to the hard-line Marxian viewpoint, which held that southern development could only be grasped by placing this process within its proper global historical context, Fernando Henrique Cardoso and Enzo Faletto (1935–2003) argued that it is the internal dynamics of the nation-state and not its structural location in the international division of labor that determines a country's fate. Cardoso and Faletto emphasized that external factors had different impacts across the developing world due to the diverse internal conditions (history, factors of endowment, social structures) inherent in each country. In contrast to Frank or Baran, they regarded the national bourgeoisie within dependent peripheral societies as a potentially powerful force for social change and economic progress.

There were other points of consensus among dependency theorists. First, most saw the problem of underdevelopment as deeply rooted in the colonial experience and subsequently perpetuated by a sophisticated set of transnational class linkages composed of political and military elites, powerful economic interests, multinational corporations, and multilateral institutions like the International Monetary Fund. Second, and in light of this cumulative historical legacy, dependency theorists saw the world economy as a functionally integrated whole in which a huge underdeveloped periphery of poor states, and a semiperipheral group of partially industrialized developing countries, are dominated by the industrial-bloc countries that form the core. Third, the nature of economic interaction between these segmented markets is such that the peripheral and semiperipheral countries are stuck in a zero-sum game characterized by diminishing returns from trade and investment with the North.

Dependency theorists were most likely to part ways when it came to the practical political and economic policy prescriptions that flowed from this worldview. One main difference arose between those advocating that the development of the periphery could still be achieved by working within the confines of the capitalist system and those who saw the need for a complete rupture with the advanced capitalist powers and the pursuit of a state-planned socialist model. The former stance embraced a more dynamic and evolutionary view of economic development and the possibilities to achieve upward mobility within the capitalist framework; the latter saw the future of the underdeveloped periphery as locked into a static world economic system that had determined its fate since the sixteenth century and could only be rectified via outright revolution and the installation of a socialist economy.

EMPIRICAL CHALLENGES

Even as dependency theory flourished in Africa, Asia, and Latin America, the empirical validity for many of its presumptions was shaky at best. The more revolutionary brand of dependency thinking had been fueled by evidence of the region's robust growth during the first and second world wars, as demand boomed for the region's commodities. Although a unique set of historical circumstances, this wartime boom prompted some to call for a complete de-linking of North and South, the nationalization of major industries, and levels of protectionism akin to autarky. Chile and Peru proceeded along such lines in the early 1970s, but with fairly dismal results.

State planners and economic policymakers in Argentina, Brazil, and Mexico also subscribed to dependency thinking, but chose to work within the capitalist system. It was the track record in such countries that informed some of the main empirical hypotheses that underpinned the dependency model, for example the Prebisch-Singer hypothesis about the secular deterioration of the terms of trade and the Lewis-Nurkse hypothesis. These hypotheses refer to an international pattern of specialization that has the northern countries exporting manufactures among themselves while the southern countries send their primary products to the North, and thus suggest that a balanced growth strategy would be the ideal strategy for less-developed countries.

The dependency era was replete with ambitious state-led policies geared toward industrial modernization and the full exploitation of those endogenous endowment factors (land, labor, and rich natural resources) with which the developing countries had been blessed. Yet, by the end of this period, the international division of labor between North and South remained basically the same, as did the pattern of "unequal exchange" that that ECLA and dependency theorists alike had originally decried. That is, the South was still largely dependent on the import of increasingly expensive manufactured and technology-intensive goods from the North and the export of primary commodities plagued by volatile price trends in return.

Perhaps the biggest empirical challenge to dependency theory was the takeoff of the newly industrializing countries of East Asia in the 1970s. While Latin America seemed to be running in place with rising inflation, poverty, and debt, countries like Japan, Taiwan, and South Korea were proving that the seemingly hierarchical structure of the world economy was not structurally determined. Under a more pragmatic set of economic policies that combined state and market approaches, this smaller and much less-endowed group of Asian countries showed that it was possible to produce high growth with better income distribution and to do so by integrating more strategically into international markets for trade and investment. Strong leadership and sound economic institutions could, in fact, mitigate the external challenges inherent in the North-South divide.

A LASTING LEGACY

While few of the dependency school's theoretical assertions have stood the test of time, this perspective continues to offer a powerful description of the political and economic plight of the majority of countries that remain on the periphery of the world economy. A full understanding of the causal mechanisms and policy solutions for remedying underdevelopment may still be a long way off; however, the dependency school's specification of concrete problems like dualism, inequality, diminishing returns to trade, and the North-South divide have enriched debates about development and helped them to move forward.

SEE ALSO *Dual Economy; Harris-Todaro Model; North-South Models; Underdevelopment; Unequal Exchange*

BIBLIOGRAPHY

Amin, Samir. 1974. *Accumulation on a World Scale: A Critique of the Theory of Underdevelopment.* Trans. Brian Pearce. New York: Monthly Review Press.

Cardoso, Fernando Henrique, and Enzo Faletto. 1979. *Dependency and Development in Latin America.* Trans. Marjory Mattingly Urquidi. Berkeley: University of California Press.

Darity, William. 1981. On the Long-Run Outcome of the Lewis-Nurkse International Growth Process. *Journal of Development Economics* 10 (3): 271–278.

Love, Joseph. 2005. The Rise and Decline of Economic Structuralism in Latin America. *Latin American Research Review* 40 (3): 100–125.

Mamdani, Mahmood. 1996. *Citizen and Subject: Contemporary Africa and the Legacy of Late Colonialism.* Princeton, NJ: Princeton University Press.

Wallerstein, Immanuel. 1979. *The Capitalist World Economy: Essays.* New York: Cambridge University Press.

Carol Wise

DEPOPULATION

Depopulation, or population decline, has become an especially relevant topic given that depopulation is projected to occur in most countries of the world during the twenty-first century. Despite the vast amount of attention paid to the phenomenon of overpopulation since the late 1960s (see Ehrlich 1968; Meadows, Randers, and Meadows 2004; Friedman 2005), declines in population are expected to occur in around fifty or more countries by the year 2050, according to the Population Reference Bureau, and in even more countries thereafter. Although the overall population of the world is projected to continue to grow, reaching around 9.1 billion by 2050 (according to the United Nation's medium-variant projection), a slowing of the rate of population growth is already under way, and a decline in the size of the population of the world could begin as early the middle of the twenty-first century. The region of the world most significantly impacted by depopulation is Europe. Between 2000 and 2005 at least sixteen countries in Europe had already experienced a decline in population. The largest net loss in population has occurred in Russia, with a decline of almost 3.4 million persons in the five years between 2000 and 2005.

For most of the world's countries, the reason for the net loss in population is sustained low fertility. In order for a population to be stationary (neither grow nor decline), the total fertility rates (TFRs) need to be at replacement level (2.1 children per woman) for an extended period of time, and the cohorts in the childbearing ages cannot be larger than those in other age groups. If there are large numbers of people in the parental ages, replacement level fertility alone will not result in depopulation. This is due to the phenomenon of what demographers refer to as "population momentum," which is the lag between the decline in total fertility rates and the decline in crude birth rates. This occurs when there are large numbers of women still in their childbearing years

because of past high fertility. The United Nations reports that in the 2000–2005 period there were sixty-five countries with fertility rates below replacement levels. Fifteen of these had rates that were at extremely low levels (a TFR below 1.3). In 2006 the Population Reference Bureau reported that as many as seventy-three countries were experiencing total fertility rates below the replacement level (Population Reference Bureau 2006).

Many countries with relatively high TFRs experienced declines in their fertility in the late twentieth century. For example, the United Nations reports that of the thirty-five countries with a TFR of five or higher, twenty-two experienced declines in fertility between 1990 and 2005. These rates of fertility, which are lower than they were previously, coupled with low rates of mortality and immigration are responsible for population declines in the majority of countries projected to lose population. For a few countries, population decline is expected to occur even though their fertility rate is above replacement level. These countries, namely, Botswana, Lesotho, and Swaziland, are significantly impacted by the HIV/AIDS epidemic, leading to a net loss in population.

The depopulation of most of the countries in the developed world has significant economic impacts and implications. Major impacts will most likely be felt through population aging. As fertility declines, birth cohorts become progressively smaller. These smaller birth cohorts, coupled with increases in life expectancy, lead to an increasingly larger proportion of the population over the age of sixty-five and a smaller proportion of the population in the working age range. The United Nations reports that the period between 2005 and 2050 will see a doubling of the old-age dependency ratio (the ratio of the population aged 65 and over to the population aged 15 to 64, times 100) in developed countries, with this ratio growing from 22.6 to 44.4 (United Nations 2005). For many countries, health care and pension programs are ill-equipped to handle large increases in the numbers of elderly persons, who themselves will live longer than their predecessors.

The long-term effects of depopulation have prompted some countries to enact policies to encourage increases in fertility. These include financial remittances for each child born, liberal parental leave policies, and guaranteed child care and schooling for children. According to Michael Balter, writing in 2006, one of the most expansive and generous fertility policies has been enacted in Australia, where remittances per child have exceeded US$3,000. However, the effectiveness of these fertility incentives is hotly debated. Some argue that incentives are beneficial in easing the financial burdens caused by additional children, making families more willing to increase their childbearing. Others emphasize that any increases due to these policies will be small. While financial resources may make it easier for families to pay for the children they already want to have, they are unlikely to raise fertility to the level necessary to stave off population decline.

As an alternative to policies that encourage fertility increases, some demographers suggest that imbalances in population age structure can be corrected through increases in immigration. Ben Wattenberg notes in *Fewer: How the New Demography of Depopulation Will Shape Our Future* (2004) that since most developing countries are still experiencing high birthrates and population growth, immigration originating from these countries can supplement small working age cohorts in other countries. While international migration may be beneficial in the redistribution of national populations, immigration policies encouraging immigration from developing countries remain the least favored policies of countries experiencing population declines.

SEE ALSO *Demography; Fertility, Human; Migration; Morbidity and Mortality; Overpopulation; Population Control*

BIBLIOGRAPHY

Balter, Michael. 2006. The Baby Deficit. *Science* 312 (5782): 1894–1897.

Ehrlich, Paul. 1968. *The Population Bomb*. New York: Ballantine.

Friedman, Benjamin M. 2005. *The Moral Consequences of Economic Growth*. New York: Knopf.

Meadows, Donella, Jorgen Randers, and Dennis L. Meadows. 2004. *Limits to Growth: The Thirty-Year Update*. White River Junction, VT: Chelsea Green.

Population Reference Bureau. 2006. *2006 World Population Data Sheet*. Washington, DC: Population Reference Bureau. http://www.prb.org/.

United Nations. 2003. *Demographic Yearbook 2003*. New York: United Nations. http://unstats.un.org/unsd/demographic/products/dyb/dyb2.htm.

United Nations. 2005. *Analytical Report*. Vol. 3 of *World Population Prospects: The 2004 Revision*. New York: United Nations. http://esa.un.org/unpp/.

Wattenberg, Ben J. 2004. *Fewer: How the New Demography of Depopulation Will Shape Our Future*. Chicago: Ivan R. Dee.

Lindsay M. Howden
Dudley L. Poston Jr.

DEPRECIATION, CURRENCY

SEE *Currency Appreciation and Depreciation.*

DEPRESSION, ECONOMIC

There is an accepted statistical definition of a *recession*, developed by the National Bureau of Economic Research, as the period from the peak to the trough of a range of cyclical economic data including "real GDP, real income, employment, industrial production, and wholesale-retail sales" (Hall et al. 2003). On this formal definition, the United States experienced thirty-two recessions in the one and a half centuries from 1854 till 2001, or roughly one recession of about one and a half year's duration every five years. No such accepted statistical definition exists for the much more severe and infrequent phenomenon of a *depression*. At the minimum, depressions are recessions extended in either severity or duration; symptomatically, they are marked by financial crises and falling prices.

Figure 1 allows us to identify four periods since 1870 in which the United States has experienced the statistical symptoms of a depression: 1873–1878 (though real GDP rose slightly), 1892–1896, 1919–1921, and 1929–1938. In all four periods, output stagnated (and fell in per capita terms), prices fell, and money supply growth either ceased or became negative.

Similar events occurred roughly every two decades in the nineteenth century, with notable "financial panics" occurring in 1819, 1837, and 1857. A more recent instance of a depression in an advanced economy was Japan in the period from 1990 till 2005. The Great Depression was by far the most extreme such event, and most academic debate about the causes of depressions focuses upon it. However, debate about whether capitalism had an innate tendency toward either full employment or depression began at the dawn of economics.

The chief proponent of the full employment belief was Jean-Baptiste Say (1767–1832), whose proposition, which John Maynard Keynes (1883–1946) later paraphrased as "supply creates its own demand" (Keynes 1936, p. 18), became known as *Say's law*. Say argued that "every producer asks for money in exchange for his products, only for the purpose of employing that money again immediately in the purchase of another product" (Say [1821] 1967, p. 105). A supply of one good was thus simultaneously a demand for others of an equivalent total value, and in the aggregate, demand was identical to supply—though individual markets, including the labor market, could have deficient or excess demand, due to disequilibrium pricing. Where any individual market had more supply than demand, the solution was for the suppliers to lower their asking price. The solution to widespread unemployment was thus to reduce wages.

Despite the fact that Say's analysis proceeded from a subjective, utility-based theory of value, his macroeconomic arguments were accepted by David Ricardo

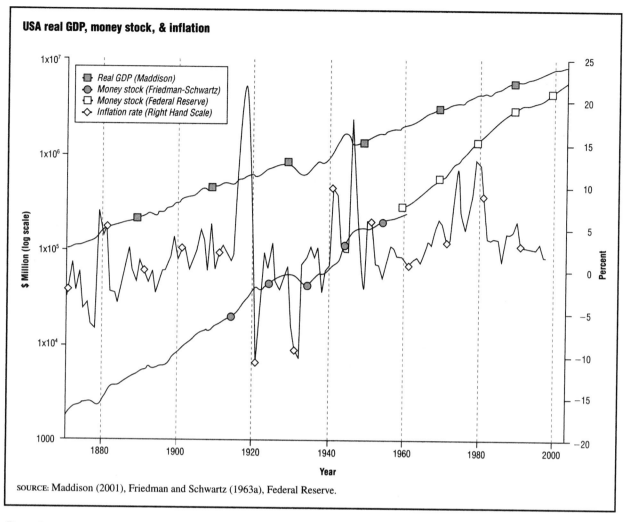

USA real GDP, money stock, & inflation

SOURCE: Maddison (2001), Friedman and Schwartz (1963a), Federal Reserve.

Figure 1

(1772–1823), who followed a classical theory of value. In contrast, Thomas Malthus (1766–1834) rejected Say's analysis, and, in modern terms, argued that either excessive investment due to overoptimistic expectations, or hoarding, could lead to a general slump.

The most systematic nineteenth-century argument for the possibility of a general slump was given by Karl Marx (1818–1883), who divided demand into two "circuits": the circuit of commodities C-M-C' and the circuit of capital M-C-M+. In the former, Say's law in general applied; but in the latter, the capitalist's aim "is not to equalize his supply and demand, but to make the inequality between them … as great as possible" (Marx 1885, pp. 120–121). Since aggregate demand was the sum of the two circuits, it was entirely possible for a "general glut"— or depression—to occur, if capitalist expectations of profit were depressed.

During the Great Depression itself, Keynes put forward an argument similar to Marx's (and in a 1933 draft of his 1936 *General Theory*, Keynes cited Marx directly [Dillard 1984, p. 424]). Dividing effective demand into consumption demand D_1 and investment demand D_2, he argued that the sum could be insufficient to employ "the supply of labour potentially available at the existing real wage" (Keynes 1936, p. 30).

Irving Fisher (1867–1947) introduced a financial interpretation of the tendency to depression in 1933. Though Fisher had earlier developed the equilibrium model of finance, the rejection of equilibrium analysis was pivotal to his "debt deflation theory of great depressions." It was, he argued, as absurd to assume that key economic variables were always at their equilibrium values as it was "to assume that the Atlantic Ocean can ever be without a wave" (Fisher 1933, p. 339).

Fisher argued that the Great Depression was caused by the confluence of two disequilibria: "over-indebtedness to start with and deflation following soon after" (Fisher 1933, p. 341). Excessive debt forced businesses to liquidate stock at distressed prices, leading to a fall in the price level that actually reduced the capacity to repay debt. This caused a "chain reaction" of further disturbances, including a decline in bank deposits, a fall in the velocity of circulation, unemployment, increased pessimism, an evaporation of investment, and "complicated disturbances in the rates of interest, in particular, a fall in the nominal, or money, rates and a rise in the real, or commodity, rates of interest" (Fisher 1933, p. 342).

The end product was *Fisher's paradox* that "the more the debtors pay, the more they owe" (Fisher 1933, p. 344): the real debt burden rose because of deflation, even though nominal debt had been reduced by debt repayment. Fisher asserted that private debt fell by 20 percent between 1929 and 1933, but real debt rose 40 percent because of the impact of four years of steeply falling prices. He argued that the only policy that could engineer an escape from a depression was reflation, and for that reason he strongly supported Franklin D. Roosevelt's New Deal.

The position that capitalism was innately stable, and that the Great Depression had been caused by government policy, was first put by Milton Friedman (1912–2006) and Anna Jacobson Schwartz. They claimed that the depression occurred because of deflationary policies pursued by the Federal Reserve that reduced the stock of money, and asserted that "the Federal Reserve at all times had power to prevent the decline in the money stock or to increase it to any desired degree, by providing enough high-powered money to satisfy the banks' desire for liquidity" (Friedman and Schwartz 1963a, p. 52).

Today, neoclassical analysis of depressions is dominated by real business cycle theory, which argues that any economic outcome is the result of the actions of rational agents in a stochastically uncertain environment. In this view, the Great Depression was either the result of optimal responses by rational agents to less-than-optimal government policies, or it was the product of a monetary or productivity shock (Prescott 1999). However, since real business cycle models presume that a market economy rapidly returns to equilibrium after a shock, the slow speed of recovery from the Great Depression needs an explanation. Most theorists argue that the downward inflexibility of money wages, combined with deflation, kept real wages above equilibrium for a substantial period.

The modern representative of the "innate tendency to depression" argument is the *financial instability hypothesis* (FIH) developed by Hyman Minsky (1919–1996). Fisher's debt-deflation hypothesis is one of its two pillars,

the other being Joseph Schumpeter's (1883–1950) vision of capitalism as innately cyclical. The FIH argues that capitalist economies have a cyclical tendency to accumulate excessive debt, and depressions are a runaway process in which interest on existing debt overwhelms the economy's capacity to service debt.

There are thus two modern perspectives on the causes of depressions—neoclassical real business theory and the FIH—with fundamentally opposed analyses and policy prescriptions. Deciding which is right is therefore important, given that what one says will cure a depression, the other says will make it worse.

An essential premise of the neoclassical perspective is that the government controls the money supply. This not only makes the government a cause of depressions, but also gives it an easy means to overcome one. In the words of Federal Reserve Chairman Ben Bernanke, "If we do fall into deflation, however, we can take comfort that … sufficient injections of money will ultimately always reverse a deflation" (Bernanke 2002).

The FIH, on the other hand, argues that money is largely endogenous, so that attempting to increase liquidity by "the logic of the printing press" (Bernanke 2002) is, in effect, "pushing on a string." Strictly, monetary attempts to reflate out of a depression will, in this theory's view, probably fail. However, this model concurs that the government should attempt to maintain liquidity during a depression.

Since the neoclassical model sees sticky wages as part of the problem, its solution is to remove labor market institutions that prevent wages from falling sufficiently quickly. The debt-deflation model puts the contrary position that falling money wages will only lead to further falls in prices, which will exacerbate the problem of deflation. It recommends the opposite policy: that money wages should be increased to cause inflation and thus reduce the real debt burden.

Though neoclassical real business cycle theory dominates academic economics today, many papers in this tradition are candid about the empirical weakness of their models, with implausibly large productivity shocks or monetary reaction functions being required to fit the data. The Japanese depression of 1990 until 2005 also challenges the belief that deflation can be easily reversed by increasing base money. Very large changes in M1—at rates of up to 32 percent per annum—had little discernible impact on either the overall money supply (M2) or price levels (see Figure 2).

On this measure at least, the evidence appears to support the FIH perspective. However, given the dominant position of neoclassical analysis within economics, there is little doubt that, should a depression recur, the policies followed in the first instance will be neoclassical in nature.

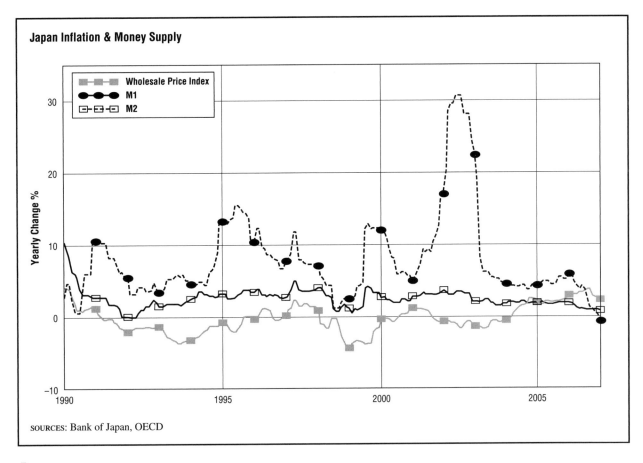

Japan Inflation & Money Supply

SOURCES: Bank of Japan, OECD

Figure 2

SEE ALSO *Business Cycles, Real; Business Cycles, Theories; Great Depression; Natural Rate of Unemployment; Recession; Say's Law; Stagflation; Stagnation*

BIBLIOGRAPHY

Bernanke, Ben S. 2002. Deflation: Making Sure "It" Doesn't Happen Here. Remarks by Governor Ben S. Bernanke before the National Economists Club, Washington, DC, November 21, 2002. http://www.federalreserve.gov/boarddocs/speeches/2002/default.htm.

Dillard, Dudley. 1984. Keynes and Marx: A Centenary Appraisal. *Journal of Post Keynesian Economics* 6: 421–432.

Fisher, Irving. 1933. The Debt-Deflation Theory of Great Depressions. *Econometrica* 1: 337–357.

Friedman, Milton, and Anna Jacobson Schwartz. 1963a. *A Monetary History of the United States, 1867–1960.* Princeton, NJ: Princeton University Press.

Friedman, Milton, and Anna Jacobson Schwartz. 1963b. Money and Business Cycles. *Review of Economic Statistics* 45: 64–95.

Hall, Robert, Martin Feldstein, Jeffrey Frankel, et al. 2003. National Bureau of Economic Research, Business Cycle Dating Committee: The NBER's Recession Dating Procedure. http://www.nber.org/cycles/recessions.html.

Keen, Steve. 1995. Finance and Economic Breakdown: Modeling Minsky's Financial Instability Hypothesis. *Journal of Post Keynesian Economics* 17: 607–635.

Keen, Steve. 2003. Nudge Nudge, Wink Wink, Say No More. In *Two Hundred Years of Say's Law: Essays on Economic Theory's Most Controversial Principle,* ed. Steven Kates, 199–209. Aldershot, U.K.: Elgar.

Keynes, John Maynard. 1936. *The General Theory of Employment, Interest, and Money.* London: Macmillan.

Maddison, Angus. 2001. *The World Economy: A Millennial Perspective.* Paris: OECD.

Malthus, Thomas Robert. [1820] 2001. *Principles of Political Economy.* New York: Adamant Media.

Mark, Karl, (1885 [1956]), *Capital.* Vol. II. Moscow: Progress Press Publishers.

Minsky, Hyman. 1982. *Can "It" Happen Again? Essays on Instability and Finance.* Armonk, NY: Sharpe.

Prescott, Edward C. 1999. Some Observations on the Great Depression. *Federal Reserve Bank of Minneapolis Quarterly Review* 23 (1): 25–31.

Ricardo, David. [1815] 2001. *Principles of Political Economy and Taxation.* New York: Adamant Media.

Say, Jean-Baptiste. [1821] 1967. *Letters to Mr. Malthus on Several Subjects of Political Economy and on the Cause of the*

Stagnation of Commerce, to which is Added a Catechism of Political Economy, or, Familiar Conversations on the Manner in which Wealth is Produced, Distributed, and Consumed in Society. Trans. John Richter. New York: Kelley.

Schumpeter, Joseph Alois. [1934] 1982. *The Theory of Economic Development: An Inquiry into Profits, Capital, Credit, Interest, and the Business Cycle.* New York: Transaction.

Steve Keen

DEPRESSION, PSYCHOLOGICAL

Depression is a common psychiatric disorder that places a great burden on society. Major depressive disorder (MDD) is defined by the American Psychiatric Association as characterized by dysphoric mood and/or loss of interest or pleasure in all or nearly all activities, plus at least four other symptoms (i.e., sleep problems, appetite disturbance, fatigue, psychomotor agitation or retardation, feelings of worthlessness or guilt, difficulty concentrating or making decisions, recurrent thoughts of death or suicide), that occur during most of the day, nearly every day, for at least two weeks and with significant impairment in social or occupational functioning. Dysthymic disorder (DD) lasts at least two years in adults (and at least one year in children and adolescents). It is defined by similar, although fewer, symptoms (i.e., depressed mood and at least two of the following: appetite problems, sleep disturbance, fatigue, low self-esteem, concentration difficulties, hopelessness).

Subtypes of MDD include atypical depression (characterized by weight gain and an increase in sleep and appetite), melancholic depression (characterized by pervasive loss of interest or pleasure, or lack of mood reactivity, and at least three of the following: distinct quality of mood, mood worse in the morning, terminal insomnia, psychomotor disturbance, significant appetite decrease or weight loss, excessive guilt) and cyclical depression (e.g., seasonal affective disorder).

Bipolar disorder is characterized by dramatic swings from depressive to manic episodes (e.g., elevated, expansive, or irritable mood) that last at least one week (four days for hypomania), or any duration if hospitalized, during which individuals experience at least three of the following symptoms (four, if mood is only irritable): inflated self-esteem, decreased need for sleep, pressured speech, racing thoughts, distractibility, increased goal-directed activity, or risky behaviors. These symptoms occur most of the day, nearly every day, with clinically significant impairment.

Depression also falls on a continuum of severity from sad mood to diagnosed depressive disorders. The subjective state of sadness by itself is not necessarily pathological, but when it occurs simultaneously with other symptoms it is referred to as a symptom complex or syndrome. A clinical syndrome is considered a distinct disorder when it has a specific course, outcome, etiology, and treatment response.

EPIDEMIOLOGY

In the United States, lifetime prevalence rates are 20.8 percent for any mood disorder; 16.6 percent for MDD; 2.5 percent for DD; and 3.9 percent for Bipolar. Lifetime prevalence rates of MDD differ by gender, with 21.3 percent reported for women and 12.7 percent for men; by age, with 0.3–2.5 percent reported for children, 15–20 percent for adolescents, and 10.6 percent for older adults; and by nation, with 1.5 percent reported in Nagasaki, Japan, and 27.3 percent in Santiago, Chile. In a given year in the United States, the incidence of MDD is 3.0 per 1,000 and the incidence of any mood disorder is 9.5 percent.

Depression is recurrent and often chronic. Median MDD durations range from 19 to 22 weeks in adults across multiple episodes, and mean durations range from 26 to 36 weeks in children and adolescents. Remission is defined as no longer meeting full criteria for a depressive episode. If another "episode" develops before two months pass with only minimal symptoms, it is considered a relapse (for predictors of relapse see Keller et al. 1983); if more than two months have elapsed, it is considered a recurrence (for predictors of recurrence see Keller and Bolland 1998).

ETIOLOGY

The etiology of depression involves the complex interplay of genetic, biological, personality, cognitive, interpersonal, and environmental factors. Kenneth Kendler's developmental model of MDD in women has identified an internalizing pathway (including neuroticism and early-onset anxiety disorders), an externalizing pathway (focusing on the role of conduct disorder and substance misuse), and an adversity pathway (e.g., disturbed family environment, childhood sexual abuse, parental loss), all of which might be anchored in genetic risk.

There is extensive evidence showing a link between stressful life events and the onset and maintenance of depression in both children and adults, although there is considerable variability in how different individuals respond to the same stressful event. Diathesis-stress theories focus on interactions among individual vulnerabilities and life stressors. Stress "activates a diathesis, transforming the potential of predisposition into the presence of psychopathology" (Monroe and Simons 1991, p. 406). A wide range of genetic and psychosocial vulnerability factors have been identified with regard to depression. Avshalom Caspi and colleagues (2003), and others, have shown one such gene-environment interaction: a functional polymorphism in the promoter region of the serotonin transporter gene that moderates the influence of stressful life events on depression.

It is not clear how much variance in depression can be attributed to genetic factors. Twin studies conducted by Patrick Sullivan, Michael Neale, and Kenneth Kendler in 2000 found that 31 to 42 percent of the variance in liability to depression was explained by additive genetic effects, 58 to 67 percent by individual specific environmental effects, and a negligible 0 to 5 percent by shared environmental effects. In contrast, adoption studies have typically reported negligible genetic effects and evidence of small but significant shared environment effects.

A number of biological processes have been implicated in depressive disorders. As outlined by Michael Thase, Ripu Jindal, and Robert Howland in 2002, depressed individuals show neuroendocrine dysregulation in the form of abnormal hypothalamic-pituitary-adrenal (HPA) axis response to stress, hyposecretion of growth hormone (GH) in response to pharmacologic challenge, and neurochemical dysregulation, particularly in the serotoninergic and dopaminergic systems. Studies have also found that abnormal functioning of the prefrontal cortex-limbic-striatal regions, reduced prefrontal volume, and hippocampal abnormalities are associated with depression (see Davidson et al. 2002).

Personality, defined as an individual's characteristic pattern of thinking, feeling, behaving, and relating to others, has long been linked with depression, and it may moderate the effect of stress on depression. The personality trait of negative emotionality (NE), defined as the propensity to experience negative emotions (e.g., anxiety, fear, sadness, anger), has been particularly associated with depression. Related constructs include negative affectivity and neuroticism.

Cognitive models of depression assert that individuals who have negative beliefs about themselves, the world, and their future, and who have a tendency to make global, stable, and internal attributions for negative events, are more likely to become depressed when confronted with stressors than are individuals without such negative beliefs. Evidence consistent with the cognitive-stress interaction has not been found prior to late childhood or early adolescence around the time when children are developing abstract reasoning and formal operational thought.

Interpersonal vulnerability to depression is characterized by impaired social skills, interpersonal dependency, and social inhibition. The relation between interpersonal difficulties and depression is most likely reciprocal and transactional. Some depressed individuals engage in excessive reassurance-seeking from others concerning their worth and lovability. This behavior may provoke frustration and irritation in others, thereby eroding social support and generating increased stress. The centrality of social ties in relation to depression has received considerable empirical support, and such ties may play a role in gender differences in the rates of depression that begin to emerge during adolescence.

INTERVENTION

Pharmacotherapy is the most common approach to the treatment of depressive disorders. Meta-analyses of randomized controlled studies indicate that serotonin and noradrenaline re-uptake inhibitors (SNRIs) demonstrate superior efficacy over selective serotonin re-uptake inhibitors (SSRIs), which in turn present with different side-effect profiles and superior general tolerability compared to tricyclic antidepressants (TCAs). In depressed youth, fluoxetine, an SSRI, has been found to perform significantly better than a placebo. Patients with bipolar disorder are frequently treated with mood stabilizers such as lithium, valproate (Depakote), or lamotrigine (Lamictal).

Cognitive-behavioral therapy (CBT) is one of the most effective psychosocial treatments for depression. In CBT, individuals are taught to modify negative thought patterns, realistically evaluate the accuracy of their beliefs, and develop problem-solving and coping skills (see Beck et al. 1979). In a 1999 mega-analysis of data from several treatment studies, Robert DeRubeis and colleagues found that cognitive therapy was as effective as medications in the treatment of more severely depressed adult patients. Although medications can be quite effective in reducing acute symptoms of depression, they do not reduce the risk of subsequent depressive episodes once their use is discontinued. In contrast, cognitive therapy has been shown to have an enduring effect following successful treatment. In adolescents, a large clinical trial yielded favorable results for CBT compared to supportive or family therapy (see Brent et al. 1997). The Treatment for Adolescents with Depression Study (TADS 2004) found that at the 12-week assessment CBT alone did not fare as well as medications (fluoxetine) alone or medications in combination with CBT. However, the difference between CBT and medications alone was no longer present by the 18-week assessment.

Interpersonal psychotherapy (IPT) for depression addresses problems associated with role transitions, grief, interpersonal deficits, and interpersonal disputes. In studies with depressed adults, IPT has performed better than treatment as usually provided in the clinic, or placebo, although not better than cognitive therapy or tricyclic antidepressant medications with and without IPT (see Shulberg et al. 1996). An adaptation of IPT for use with depressed adolescents has been found to be efficacious (see Mufson et al. 1999).

Studies aimed at preventing depression have shown positive, albeit modest, effects. Universal prevention programs, which target all members of a population, have not been found to be as effective as selective programs targeting individuals at risk or indicated programs targeting individuals who are already showing symptoms but do not have the full disorder. Although evidence is growing that depression can be prevented, the effects have tended to be relatively short-lived. Future research needs to develop and test interventions that have more enduring preventive effects. It is also important to identify who is most likely to benefit from which type of intervention, as well as the mechanisms through which such programs work.

BIBLIOGRAPHY

Beck, Aaron T., Augustus J. Rush, Brian F. Shaw, and Gary Emery. 1979. *Cognitive Therapy of Depression.* New York: Guilford.

Brent, D. A., et al. 1997. A Clinical Psychotherapy Trial for Adolescent Depression Comparing Cognitive, Family, and Supportive Treatments. *Archives of General Psychiatry* 54: 877–885.

Caspi, A., et al. 2003. Influence of Life Stress on Depression: Moderation by a Polymorphism in the 5-HTT Gene. *Science* 301: 386–389.

DeRubeis, R. J., L. A. Gelfand, T. Z. Tang, and A. D. Simons. 1999. Medication versus Cognitive Behavior Therapy for Severely Depressed Outpatients: Mega-Analysis of Four Randomized Comparisons. *American Journal of Psychiatry* 156: 1007–1013.

Keller, M. B., and R. J. Bolland. 1998. Implications of Failing to Achieve Successful Long-Term Maintenance Treatment of Recurrent Unipolar Major Depression. *Biological Psychiatry* 44 (5): 348–360.

Keller, M. B., P. W. Lavori, C. E. Lewis, and G. L. Klerman. 1983. Predictors of Relapse in Major Depressive Disorder. *Journal of the American Medical Association* 250 (24): 3299–3304.

Monroe, S. M., and A. D. Simons. 1991. Diathesis-Stress Theories in the Context of Life Stress Research: Implications for the Depressive Disorders. *Psychological Bulletin* 110 (3): 406–425.

Mufson, L., M. M. Weissman, D. Moreau, and R. Garfinkel. 1999. Efficacy of Interpersonal Psychotherapy for Depressed Adolescents. *Archives of General Psychiatry* 56 (6): 573–579.

Sullivan, Patrick, Michael Neale, and Kenneth Kendler. 2000. Genetic Epidemiology of Major Depression: Review and Meta-Analysis. *American Journal of Psychiatry* 157: 1552–1562.

Thase, Michael E., Ripu Jindal, and Robert. H. Howland. 2002. Biological Aspects of Depression. In *Handbook of Depression,* ed. Ian H. Gotlib and Constance L. Hammen, 192–218. New York: Guilford.

Treatment for Adolescents with Depression Study (TADS) Team. 2004. Fluoxetine, Cognitive-Behavioral Therapy, and Their Combination for Adolescents with Depression: Treatment for Adolescents with Depression Study (TADS) Randomized Controlled Trial. *Journal of the American Medical Association* 292 (7): 807–820.

Judy Garber
Matthew C. Morris

DEREGULATION

Throughout most of the twentieth century, advanced industrialized nations embraced a notion of the state as being an agency of the "common good," as overarching and mediating the sectional and competing interests of civil society. The material underpinning of this discourse was the failure of private corporations to maintain an adequate provision of public goods through the market as well as the general belief that firms, if left unfettered, might conduct their business at the expense of the "public interest." In order to protect citizens and consumers, therefore, the state undertook the direct administration and provision of certain public goods—such as defense, the rule of law, various aspects of education, health, water supply, and electricity—through the planning of investment and the allocation of resources. Markets for private goods, in turn, were subjected to regulations with regard to product quality, safety, and other attributes.

During the last two decades of the century, however, it became clear that the state was embedded in a global capitalist system, and that its autonomy to engage in regulation and provision had become constrained by the logic and dynamics of that system. State regulation and planning ultimately resulted in an increasingly severe fiscal crisis, with rising public expenditures and debts, persistently high levels of inflation, and weak balances of payment. Governments were forced to reassess their approach, and they started to embrace the emerging doctrine of neoliberal economic and social theory.

NEOLIBERAL THEORY

Neoliberal economics is premised upon a conception of the individual as a rational utility-maximizing consumer. Neoliberal proponents argue that when consumers spontaneously and impersonally interact in the market, the result is both individual liberty and economic efficiency. The market, which has no ends or purposes, allows individuals to incorporate their consumption into a personal plan that spontaneously produces the optimum allocation of social resources.

The resultant neoliberal restructuring of the state was an attempt to realign both the state and international capital by depoliticizing decisions about the allocation and provision of services. This has involved the privatization of some sectors of the economy, a redefinition of the concept of public services, and the gradual removal of restrictions on businesses. The stated rationale was that fewer regulations would lead to greater competitiveness, and therefore to higher productivity and efficiency, and to lower prices for consumers.

MARKET FAILURES AND RE-REGULATION

However, various high-profile failures of deregulation—such as the savings and loans crisis in the United States in the 1980s and the California electricity crisis at the end of the 1990s—brought home the point that consumers and citizens require protection from various forms of market failure, such as:

1. negative externalities, which occur when the socially optimal output diverges from the private optimum, as is the case with environmental pollution;

2. monopolies, which occur when an entity's market power prevents competition, and therefore allows higher prices to be charged at lower output than is feasible in a competitive market, producing a net economic welfare loss, allocative inefficiency, and a Pareto suboptimal equilibrium;

3. instances in which some public goods may not be provided by the free market at all because of their characteristics of nonexcludability and nonrivalry;

4. inequality, which occurs when differences in income and wealth restrict some members of society from accessing vital goods and services.

Strengthened regimes of re-regulation were developed as a result of these concerns. If regulation can reduce prices below monopoly levels and provide a remedy for other market failures without compromising new entry, competition, choice, innovation, and other long-term attributes of a competitive market, then the case for it is compelling, at least during the transition to a competitive market. Examples include pollution taxes to correct for externalities; taxation of monopoly profits (the "windfall tax"); regulation of oligopolies and cartel behavior; continued and direct provision of some public goods (e.g., defense; law and order); subsidies; product and safety regulations; the specification of output levels and quality; and price controls.

CRITICISMS

Regulation creates questions about the extent to which it actually works in the public interest. The specification of what the optimum regulatory solution should be is insufficient if not supplemented by a theory of the behavioral motivations underlying both regulators and those regulated. The "capture model," for example, argues that actors' respective self-interests will produce a regulation policy that maximizes their joint interest in stable and predictable outcomes, but that may also be skewed toward the monopoly solution that regulatory policy is seeking to prevent in the first place.

In addition, regulators may not have sufficiently precise information about the cost structure and consumer responsiveness to price changes to be able to properly set output and prices in a given industry. Regulators are therefore dependent upon those regulated to provide them with basic information, a situation that may create opportunistic behavior in the resultant interaction process. The challenge, then, is well known from other areas of the social sciences and is generally referred to as the principal-agent problem, namely how best to design a system of contracts that motivates the regulatees to act in the interest of the regulators—within the constraints of imprecision, lack of observability, bounded rationality, and asymmetric strategic moves.

SEE ALSO *Antitrust; Antitrust Regulation; Equality; Pareto Optimum; Privatization; Public Goods; Taxation*

BIBLIOGRAPHY

Francis, John. 1993. *The Politics of Regulation: A Comparative Perspective.* Oxford: Blackwell.

Lane, Jan-Erik. 2000. *The Public Sector: Concepts Models and Approaches,* 3rd ed. Thousand Oaks, CA: Sage.

Posner, Richard. 1974. Theories of Economic Regulation. *Bell Journal of Economics and Management Science* 5: 335–358.

Dirk Haubrich

DERRIDA, JACQUES
1931–2004

Jacques Derrida was one of the most original and influential French philosophers in the contemporary world. He was born in Algeria on July 15, 1931, to a Sephardic Jewish family. He moved to France in 1949 and studied in Paris at the École Normale Supérieure, where he wrote his dissertation on Edmund Husserl's genetic phenomenology (*Le Problème de la genèse dans la philosophie de Husserl*

[The Problem of Genesis in Husserl's Philosophy], 1953–1954). In the 1960s Derrida published major works concerned with the limitations of phenomenological and structuralist thought in the human sciences. Prior to his death, he was the director of studies at the École des Hautes Études en Sciences Sociales in Paris and professor of humanities at the University of California, Irvine. Derrida died on October 8, 2004.

Derrida is today universally recognized as the leading figure in the field of poststructuralist thought designated by the term *deconstruction*. He is typically referred to as the most prominent critic of Western metaphysics (understood as a universal discourse that is foundational, subject-oriented, and logocentric); he is also frequently described as an antihumanist, a postphenomenologist, and the founding father of the discipline of grammatology. His early writings are best represented by three key texts: *La Voix et le phénomène* (Speech and Phenomena), *De la Grammatologie* (Of Grammatology), and *L'Écriture et la différence* (Writing and Difference), all published in 1967. These works were the first to circulate the poststructuralist themes of the role of *différance*, textuality, and writing in all systems of meaning (and thereby to set into play wider currents of research in disciplines concerned with the dynamic characteristics of texts, writing, and cultural dissemination).

Derrida is particularly noted for questioning the unity, direction, and stability of traditional philosophical discourse. Yet thematically his major writings have all been concerned to advance careful readings and interpretations of the texts of major figures in both ancient and modern philosophy, including Plato (427–347 BCE), Immanuel Kant (1724–1804), Jean-Jacques Rousseau (1712–1778), G. W. F. Hegel (1770–1831), Edmund Husserl (1859–1938), Martin Heidegger (1889–1976), and Sigmund Freud (1856–1939). These writings are supplemented by analyses of such "nonphilosophers" as Samuel Beckett (1906–1989), Maurice Blanchot (1907–2003), George Bataille (1897–1962), and Jean Genet (1910–1986), among other important literary figures. Derrida reads all of these texts as complex intertextual "objects" saturated with indeterminate meanings, ambivalent oppositions, and "undecideable" interpretations.

For many readers in the analytic or Anglophone tradition of philosophical thought, Derrida is a subversive relativist, a nihilist word-player who has largely abandoned the pursuit of rational criticism to embrace a form of negative and playful experiment with words and their indefinite allusions and meanings. Derrida's pantextualism was notoriously symbolized by his claim "*Il n'y a pas de hors-texte*," usually translated as "There is nothing outside of the text," but perhaps more literally expressed as "There is nothing outside of text" (a declaration that

Derrida later reformulated to "*Il n'y a pas de hors contexte*," or "There is nothing outside of context"). On this reading, Derrida is frequently grouped with other "enemies of reason" as an irrationalist or even a nihilist. In this interpretation, the terms *deconstruction* and *deconstructionist* have been used as derogatory expressions designed to define deconstruction as a method of literary criticism rather than serious philosophy (an approach that remains oblivious to the fact that Derrida spent a lifetime of painstaking reading and commentary with the objective of questioning and deconstructing this type of binary opposition).

Despite such one-sided interpretations, what has come to be called *deconstructive studies* has had a major impact upon contemporary philosophy, literary theory and criticism, sociology, educational practices, media, and cultural studies. One of the first intellectual traditions to assimilate Derrida's work was the Yale school of literary criticism, struggling to elaborate forms of reading and interpretation richer than the available models of new criticism. In this context, we can mention the work of Paul de Man (1919–1983), Harold Bloom, Geoffrey Hartman, and J. Hillis Miller. Following Derrida's lead, these critics have radically questioned the nature of literary "meaning," "authorship," and "authorial intentionality" by uncovering the metaphysical presuppositions and binary oppositions that have structured the methods of traditional textual analysis and interpretation. In generalizing deconstruction from texts narrowly conceived in literary-critical terms to the "general text" of social life, we have come to see that all theory and research in the human sciences is inextricably involved in complex questions of language and interpretation.

In his later work, Derrida turned to a range of problems linked with contemporary social and political life. His writings became increasingly preoccupied with urgent ethical and political problems of European integration, immigration and the treatment of "asylum seekers," and questions of friendship and otherness in an increasingly borderless, cosmopolitan world order. His books *Of Hospitality* (2000), *On Cosmopolitanism and Forgiveness* (2001), and *The Work of Mourning* (2001) are indicative of these themes.

While Derrida's work has profoundly changed the practice of philosophical analysis, literary theory, and other textual sciences, perhaps his most long-lasting impact lies in the turn toward ethical and political issues that has transformed the intellectual landscape of what passes for the theory and practice of the human sciences, the arts, and philosophy.

SEE ALSO *Critical Theory; Ethics; Literature; Narratives; Philosophy; Postmodernism; Poststructuralism*

BIBLIOGRAPHY

PRIMARY WORKS

Derrida, Jacques. 1962. *L'Origine de la géométrie*. Paris: Presses Universitaires de France. English trans.: 1978. *Edmund Husserl's Origin of Geometry: An Introduction*. Trans. John P. Leavey. Pittsburgh, PA: Duquesne University Press.

Derrida, Jacques. 1967. *De la Grammatologie*. Paris: Minuit. English trans.: 1974. *Of Grammatology*. Trans. Gayatri Chakravorty Spivak. Baltimore, MD: Johns Hopkins University Press.

Derrida, Jacques. 1967. *La Voix et le phénomène: Introduction au problème du signe dans la phénoménologie de Husserl*. Paris: Presses Universitaires de France. English trans.: [1973] 1979. *Speech and Phenomena, and Other Essays on Husserl's Theory of Signs*. Trans. David B. Allinson and Newton Garver. Evanston, IL: Northwestern University Press.

Derrida, Jacques. 1967. *L'Écriture et la différence*. Paris: Seuil. English. trans.: 1978. *Writing and Difference*. Trans. Alan Bass. Chicago: University of Chicago Press.

Derrida, Jacques. 1969. *The Politics of Friendship*. Trans. George Collins. London: Verso.

Derrida, Jacques. [1972] 1982. *Marges de la philosophie*. Paris: Minuit. English trans.: 1982. *Margins of Philosophy*. Trans. Alan Bass. Chicago: University of Chicago Press; Brighton, U.K.: Harvester.

Derrida, Jacques. 1987. *The Post Card: From Socrates to Freud and Beyond*. Trans. Alan Bass. Chicago: University of Chicago Press.

Derrida, Jacques. 1987. *The Truth in Painting*. Trans. Geoff Bennington and Ian McLeod. Chicago: University of Chicago Press.

Derrida, Jacques. 1989. *Mémoires: For Paul de Man*. Trans. Eduardo Cadava, Jonathan Culler, and Cecile Lindsay. New York: Columbia University Press.

Derrida, Jacques. 1992. *Acts of Literature*, ed. Derek Attridge. New York: Routledge.

Derrida, Jacques. 1992. *The Other Heading: Reflections on Today's Europe*. Trans. Pascale-Anne Brault and Michael Naas. Bloomington: Indiana University Press.

Derrida, Jacques. 1994. *Specters of Marx: The State of the Debt, the Work of Mourning, and the New International*. Trans. Peggy Kamuf. New York: Routledge.

Derrida, Jacques. 1998. *Monolingualism of the Other, or, The Prosthesis of Origin*. Trans. Patrick Mensah. Stanford, CA: Stanford University Press.

Derrida, Jacques. 2000. *Of Hospitality: Anne Dufourmantelle Invites Jacques Derrida to Respond*. Trans. Rachel Bowlby. Stanford, CA: Stanford University Press.

Derrida, Jacques. 2001. *On Cosmopolitanism and Forgiveness*. Trans. Mark Dooley and Michael Hughes. New York: Routledge.

Derrida, Jacques. 2001. *The Work of Mourning*, ed. Pascale-Anne Brault and Michael Naas. Chicago: University of Chicago Press.

SECONDARY WORKS

Llewelyn, John. 1986. *Derrida on the Threshold of Sense*. London: Macmillan.

Norris, Christopher. 1987. *Derrida*. London: Fontana.

Sallis, John, ed. 1987. *Deconstruction and Philosophy: The Texts of Jacques Derrida*. Chicago and London: University of Chicago Press.

Wood, D., and R. Bernasconi, eds. 1988. *Derrida and Difference*. Evanston, Ill.: Northwestern University Press.

Barry Sandywell

DE SAUSSURE, FERDINAND

SEE *Anthropology, Linguistic; Semiotics.*

DESCRIPTIVE STATISTICS

Descriptive statistics, which are widely used in empirical research in the social sciences, summarize certain features of the data set in a study. The data set nearly always consists of lists of numbers that describe a population. Descriptive statistics are used to summarize the information in the data using simple measures. Thus, descriptive statistics can help to represent large data sets in a simple manner. However, an incautious use of descriptive statistics can lead to a distorted picture of the data by leaving out potentially important details.

THE HISTOGRAM

Descriptive statistics take as a starting point observations from a population. So suppose we have observed $n > 1$ draws from a population, and let $[x_1, \ldots, x_n]$ denote these observations. These observations could, for example, be a survey of income levels in n individual households, in which case x_1 would be the income level of the first household and so forth. One way of doing this is through the distribution of the data that gives a summary of the frequency of individual observations. The distribution is calculated by grouping the raw observations into categories according to ranges of values. As a simple example, Table 1 reports the distribution of a data set of income levels for 1,654 households in the United Kingdom. The data set has been grouped into five income categories. These categories represent income in U.S. dollars within the following ranges: $0–$700; $701–$1,400; $1,401–$2,100; $2,101–$2,800; and $2,801–$3,500. The second row in Table 1 shows the number of households in each income

Weekly salary ($)	0–700	701–1400	1401–2100	2101–2800	2801–3500
Distribution of weekly salaries					
Number of households	1160	429	41	17	7
Percentage of households (%)	70.13	25.94	2.48	1.03	0.42

SOURCE: UK Family Expenditure Survey, 1995.

Table 1

range. The corresponding frequencies are found by dividing each cell with the number of observations; these are given in the third row.

One can also present the frequencies as a graph. This type of graph is normally referred to as a *histogram*. The frequencies in Table 1 are depicted as a histogram in Figure 1.

SUMMARY STATISTICS

An even more parsimonious representation of the data set can be done through summary statistics. The most typical ones are measures of the center and dispersion of the data. Other standard summary statistics are *kurtosis* and *skewness*.

The three most popular measures of the center of the distribution are the *mean*, *median*, and *mode*. The mean, or average, is calculated by adding up all the observed values and dividing by the number of observations:

$$\bar{x} = \frac{x_1 + \dots + x_n}{n} = \frac{1}{n}\sum_{i=1}^{n} x_i.$$

The median represents the middle of the set of observations when these are ordered by value. Thus, 50 percent of the observations are smaller and 50 percent are greater than the median. Finally, the mode is calculated as the most frequently occurring value in the data set.

The dispersion of the data set tells how much the observations are spread around the central tendency. Three frequently used measures of this are the *variance* (and its associated standard deviation), *mean deviation*, and *range*. The variance (VAR) is calculated as the sum of squared deviations from the mean, divided by the number of observations:

$$VAR = \frac{1}{n}\sum_{i=1}^{n}(x_i - \bar{x})^2$$

The standard deviation (SD) is the square-root of the variance: $\sqrt{VAR}$. The mean deviation (MD) measures the average absolute deviation from the mean:

$$MD = \frac{1}{n}\sum_{i=1}^{n}|x_i - \bar{x}|$$

The range is calculated as the highest minus the lowest observed value. The range is very sensitive to extremely large or extremely small values, (or outliers), and it may, therefore, not always give an accurate picture of the data.

Skewness is a measure of the degree of asymmetry of the distribution relative to the center. Roughly speaking, a distribution has positive skew if most of the observations are situated to the right of the center, and a negative skew if most of the observations are situated to the left of the center. Skewness is calculated as:

$$SKEW = \frac{m_3}{SD^3}, \ m_3 = \frac{1}{n}\sum_{i=1}^{n}(x_i - \bar{x})^3$$

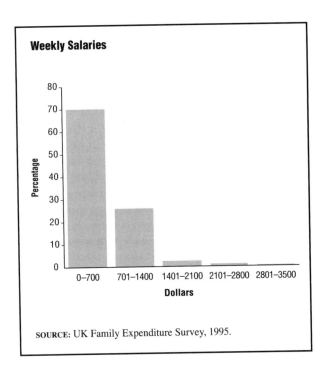

Weekly Salaries

SOURCE: UK Family Expenditure Survey, 1995.

Figure 1

Kurtosis measures the "peakedness" of the distribution. Higher kurtosis means more of the variance is due to infrequent extreme deviations. The kurtosis is calculated as:

$$KURT = \frac{m_4}{SD^4}, \; m_3 = \frac{1}{n} \sum_{i=1}^{n} (x_i - \bar{x})^4$$

SEE ALSO *Mean, The; Mode, The; Moment Generating Function; Random Samples; Standard Deviation*

BIBLIOGRAPHY

Anderson, David R., Dennis J. Sweeney, and Thomas A. Williams. 2001. *Statistics for Business and Economics*, 8th ed. Cincinnati, OH: South-Western Thomson Learning.

Freedman, David, Robert Pisani, and Roger Purves. 1998. *Statistics*, 3rd ed. New York: Norton.

Dennis Kristensen

DESEGREGATION

Segregation can be both voluntary and involuntary, forced and by mutual agreement. When segregation results in exclusion from public goods, rewards, and privileges, or when segregation results in stigmas, then a violation of the basic conditions of democracy is evident. When such segregation occurs along racial lines, it becomes racial segregation. When racial segregation is operant across major social institutions, it is considered institutional racism.

Efforts in the United States since the mid-twentieth century have been aimed at reversing racial segregation. These efforts, labeled *desegregation*, are political processes that make use of civil protest, litigation, and economic sanctions to eliminate racial segregation. Racial segregation, both de jure and de facto, has historically served to restrict access to education and training, economic and political institutions, occupational and social mobility, religious and social institutions, and neighborhoods and transportation facilities. Within the United States, most desegregation activity has focused on educational institutions, public accommodation, and the military.

While many cite the 1954 Supreme Court decision in *Brown v. Board of Education of Topeka* as the beginning of desegregation, in actuality desegregation reflects a process that continues into the twenty-first century. The *Brown* decision, by striking down legal segregation on the basis of race in public schools, reversed the Supreme Court's 1896 decision in *Plessy v. Ferguson*.

DESEGREGATION IN EDUCATIONAL INSTITUTIONS

Throughout history, one of the primary tactics of exploitative systems was control of access to education. Some of the first laws aimed at controlling Africans during the slavery era prohibited or restricted educational access. These laws, which carried harsh sanctions, denied educational access not only to slaves but to freed Africans as well. The same method was used to keep European women, Native Americans, Chinese, and others in subordinate positions. It is no wonder that one of the major features of the various civil rights movements has been directed at dismantling segregated or restricted access to educational institutions.

Although many thought the Civil War (1861–1865) and the associated constitutional amendments would resolve the issue of segregation in the United States, the *Plessy v. Ferguson* ruling actually mandated it. Within months after this historic ruling, seventeen southern states began to implement sets of laws—known as *Jim Crow* or *de jure segregation*—that formalized and legitimized racial segregation in most institutional spaces. Among these were laws that established "separate but equal" educational facilities. While often lacking specific legislation, the North accomplished the same effect through what has been termed *de facto segregation*.

The 1954 *Brown v. Board of Education* ruling, with its aim to end school segregation, struck at the heart of the system of racial entitlements in the United States. Nothing less then a revolution was envisioned. As pointed out by Gary Orfield and Susan Eaton (1996), integration did not represent a magical process in which simply situating whites and blacks in the same room would end centuries of discrimination. Rather, it recognized that white dominance had been engineered through exclusive control of select schools. Ending this dominance and making such schools available to all would serve to remove the racial stigma and victimization of blacks, provide black Americans access to other major institutions, and level the playing field, thereby assuring equality and freedom. The Supreme Court ruled that racially segregated schools did indeed perpetuate racial stigmas among blacks, and that such schools were therefore inherently unequal. Yet, in striking down *Plessy*, the Supreme Court decided ambiguously that integration should take place "with all deliberate speed."

"All deliberate speed" has been described as simultaneously placing the country's feet on both the accelerator and the brake. Throughout the South, a multitude of strategies were instituted to delay, divert, or otherwise circumvent the *Brown* ruling. In 1956 advocates of segregation were successful in convincing Virginia's governor and state assembly to pass laws blocking the funding of school integration. One of the most striking anti-integration efforts occurred in 1957 when Arkansas governor Orval Faubus (1910–1994) ordered the state's national guard to block the doors to Little Rock's Central High School, preventing nine black teenagers from entering. Only after President Dwight Eisenhower (1890–1969) sent federal troops to the site were the nine students allowed to attend the school. Other states were equally creative. Prince Edward County in Virginia decided to close all of its public schools rather than integrate them. Lawsuits filed on behalf of blacks throughout the South filled the courts. More definitive court rulings ensued, but the road to integration was fraught with many obstacles.

A decade after the *Brown* decision, southern schools remained 98 percent segregated. Continual agitation on the part of blacks led to the 1964 Civil Rights Act. Thereafter, courts prescribed more immediate and encompassing integration efforts. Starting in 1966 with *United States v. Jefferson County Board of Education*, the Fifth Circuit Court not only ordered integration but also remedies to redress historical segregation. In *Green v. County School Board of New Kent County* (1968), the U.S. Supreme Court ordered schools to provide immediate integration. Similar court rulings, aggressive enforcement by the federal government, and the vigilance of southern blacks eventually led to the racial transformation of schools in the South. By 1970, slightly more than 45 percent of black youths in the South attended integrated schools. Frustrated, however, with the slow pace of integration, in 1971 the Supreme Court ordered a massive urban desegregation plan in *Swann v. Charlotte-Meklenburg Board of Education*. In this plan, with the aid of busing, the first district-wide school desegregation order was provided. Busing, as it came to be known, became a very controversial tool to achieve integration.

Busing and forced integration generated considerable fear among many white Americans. This fear resulted in "white flight" (i.e., when whites leave typically urban areas to avoid living in proximity to blacks), and it fueled a conservative backlash against desegregation efforts. During the 1970s, some Republican politicians, such as Richard Nixon (1913–1994), would ride the waves of this backlash all the way to the White House and control of both houses of Congress. These conservative forces also oversaw the first set of reversals. By 1974 in *Milliken v. Bradley*, the Supreme Court blocked a Detroit area busing plan. In this and subsequent cases, the courts ruled that local decisions regarding school integration should be respected.

As segregation was challenged in the North, the Supreme Court would institute even more radical moves, inaugurating the era of busing, teacher integration, gradual integration, and magnet schools. Although partial success may be claimed, more than fifty years after *Brown*, little progress has been made toward the racial integration of America's school system. White flight, private schools, and the more recent voucher movement have all served to preserve racial segregation in schools.

DESEGREGATION IN PUBLIC ACCOMMODATIONS

Access to public space and private dwellings has long been disputed terrain in the United States. Property and the access to property has been the determinant not only of status, but also of political and social rights and privilege. In the United States, the rights to vote, hold political office, and seek legal recourse were all initially reserved for those who owned property. Thus, the first sets of laws aimed at controlling blacks included laws that not only declared them property but also restricted their ownership rights.

The battle to gain access to the totality of American liberties would be incomplete without access to public accommodations. Black Americans pinned their hopes of total freedom on the Thirteenth, Fourteenth, and Fifteenth Amendments to the U.S. Constitution, which together granted them full citizenship. In *Plessy v. Ferguson*, the Supreme Court declared that black Americans would retain the stigma of race and second-class citizenship, and be denied even basic access to public accommodations. This ruling, more than any other single action, led to the dissolution of good will, the dismantling of postwar Reconstruction, and the wholesale creation of the extensive apparatus of Jim Crow segregation under the misbegotten rubric of "separate but equal." It would take almost a half-century, several hundred lynchings, and countless court cases before *Plessy* would be overturned.

The 1964 Civil Rights Act put an end to segregated lunch counters, hotels, trains, buses, and theaters. This legislation owes its enactment to the courage and determination of many who became heroes of the modern civil rights movement. One such hero was Rosa Parks (1913–2005), who on December 1, 1955, challenged the whites-only Jim Crow laws of Montgomery, Alabama, by refusing to give her seat on a bus to a white patron. Her courageous action launched the modern civil rights movement.

On February 27, 1960, four black college students in Greensboro, North Carolina, defied the laws of segregation by sitting down at a whites-only Woolworth's lunch counter and requesting service. Although they were not served, their defiance sparked similar acts in over one hundred American cities throughout the 1960s. In 1961 civil rights activists known as "Freedom Riders" began to protest the whites-only policies in public bathrooms and buses. In May 1961 thirteen Freedom Riders, white and black, left Washington, D.C., in two buses heading south.

Riders on the first bus were attacked by pipe-toting men in Anniston and Birmingham, Alabama. The second bus was fire-bombed just outside of Anniston. Undaunted, sit-ins, freedom rides, and other forms of protests compelled a reluctant Congress and president to pass and sign into law the 1964 Civil Rights Act.

DESEGREGATION IN MILITARY INSTITUTIONS

Black Americans have consistently put their lives on the line in defense of their country. However, their service was for many years dismissed, isolated, and segregated. Notwithstanding the valor of such revolutionary-era heroes as Crispus Attucks, a patriot killed by British soldiers in Boston in 1770, General George Washington in 1775 officially barred blacks from serving in the Continental Army. This order, reflecting the legal view of many in the colonies, was followed by the 1792 Congressional Act, which barred blacks from serving in state militias. Congress also prohibited the Marine Corps from its inception in 1798 from recruiting blacks.

Ironically, the First Rhode Island Regiment, formed in 1778, was composed almost entirely of former black slaves. Furthermore, unlike the Continental Army, the Continental Navy recruited heavily among blacks, both free and slave. These sailors, sought for both their skills and to fill major gaps, served with distinction throughout the revolutionary period. Late in the Revolutionary War (1775–1783), in response to British recruitment among slaves, Washington reluctantly eased the ban on the recruitment of slaves. These blacks, however, served in segregated regiments under white officers.

Although blacks have served with distinction and honor throughout American history, their service was typically ignored and downplayed. The U.S. military remained segregated until shortly after World War II (1939–1945), when President Harry S Truman's (1884–1972) Executive Order 9981 (1948) called for the end of racial segregation in the armed forces. It was not until war broke out in Korea in 1950, however, and the United States faced heavy casualties that the military decided to act upon this order and create the first racially integrated units.

By 2006, with African Americans filling over seven thousand officer posts and composing 20 percent of all service personnel, the military represents the most desegregated institution in the United States. Finally, while blacks do serve in significant numbers at all levels in the military, their service tends to be restricted to noncombat and communications roles. For example, black service members make up less then 3 percent of the pilots, tank commanders, and special forces personnel. Thus, although the U.S. military is formally integrated, nominal segregation by training, specialty, and duty remains the rule.

DESEGREGATION OUTSIDE OF THE UNITED STATES

Segregation has developed wherever there have been racially based societies. What makes these societal situations different has to do with the relative permeability (perceived or real) of segregation. Thus, countries such as France and England exhibit relatively more racial flexibility than such countries as Australia or South Africa. In both France and England, with the decline in their colonial empires, there were deliberate attempts to integrate a greater number of nonwhite citizens into the cultural, political, and social life. In both France and England, noncolonial persons of color experienced a greater degree of social mobility than former colonial subjects. And while much progress has been made, racial unrest in both countries in the first decade of the twenty-first century indicates that more progress needs to be made.

In contrast, extremely rigid castelike structures of racial segregation have only fallen in the last few decades in such countries as Australia and South Africa. In both of these countries, indigenous persons of color experienced decades of exclusion from power, economic advancement, and education, and they were forced to live in enclaves, reservations, or specially designated communities. While these formal walls of racial discrimination have fallen, informal walls remain as "Coloreds" in South Africa and Aboriginals in Australia continue to seek an expansion of their political, economic, educational, and societal power.

SEE ALSO Brown v. Board of Education, *1954;* Brown v. Board of Education, *1955; Civil Rights Movement, U.S.; Desegregation, School; Resegregation of Schools; Segregation; Segregation, Residential; Segregation, School*

BIBLIOGRAPHY

Massey, Douglas S., and Nancy A. Denton. 1993. *American Apartheid: Segregation and the Making of the Underclass.* Cambridge, MA: Harvard University Press.

Orfield, Gary, and Susan E. Eaton. 1996. *Dismantling Desegregation: The Quiet Reversal of Brown v. Board of Education.* New York: New Press.

Winant, Howard. 2002. *The World Is a Ghetto: Race and Democracy since World War II.* New York: Basic Books.

Rodney D. Coates

DESEGREGATION, SCHOOL

In *Brown v. Board of Education of Topeka* (1954), the U.S. Supreme Court issued a rare unanimous opinion ruling that racially segregated public schools were inherently unequal and therefore in violation of the Fourteenth Amendment to the U.S. Constitution. As Peter Irons wrote of the *Brown* case and the opinion of newly appointed Chief Justice Earl Warren (1891–1974) in particular, "it was a promise to America's black children of an education 'available to all on equal terms' with that given to whites" (2002, p. xi). However, within a year of *Brown*, southern legislatures and school officials had already begun to defy the Court's firm but vague ruling that schools be desegregated with "all deliberate speed."

In 1956 this resistance to integration was epitomized by the state of Arkansas when the state legislature passed an amendment to the state constitution commanding the Arkansas General Assembly to oppose "in every Constitutional manner the Un-constitutional desegregation decisions" in *Brown*. In 1957, when the first nine black students attempted to enter Little Rock's Central High School in accordance with the court ordered desegregation plan, they were turned away by armed Arkansas National Guardsmen dispatched by Governor Orval Faubus (1910–1994). This defiance of federal law by state and local officials ultimately culminated in *Cooper v. Aaron* (1958), a Supreme Court case where the court reaffirmed the nation's commitment to racial equality articulated in *Brown*. In a rare opinion bearing the signature of all nine justices, the Court wrote, "The principles announced in [the *Brown*] decision and the obedience of the States to them, according to the command of the Constitution, are indispensable for the protection of the freedoms guaranteed by our fundamental charter for all of us. Our constitutional ideal of equal justice under the law is thus made a living truth."

The ruling in *Cooper* marked the end of the Court's patience with attempts to delay the integration of public schools. While southern states and school districts continued to challenge court-ordered school integration, the justices handed down decisions ordering schools to continue along the path toward racial equality under the law.

Some scholars argue that the federal government's shift from a prosegregation position to one in support of racial equality in the 1950s and 1960s stemmed more from foreign policy interests and a desire to reshape the cold war world in the image of the United States than from any earnest desire to bring an end to racial discrimination (Dudziak 1988–1989). This may explain why, beginning in the late 1970s and more rapidly since the early 1990s, school segregation is increasing rather than decreasing, yet the federal courts, legislature, and executive branch appear reluctant to intercede on behalf of integration efforts. Nonetheless, for nearly thirty-five years following the *Brown* decision, the law of the land was that race needed to be taken into consideration when assessing the quality and fairness of public education in the United States.

In the decades following *Brown*, federal support for desegregation appeared to be working, albeit slowly. For example, the percentage of black students attending majority white schools nationwide rose from slightly over 23 percent in the 1968–1969 school year to slightly more than 37 percent in the 1980–1981 school year. Similarly, over 64 percent of black children attended schools that were 90 percent or more minority in the 1968–1969 school year. However, this percentage decreased to fewer than 39 percent by the start of the 1974 school year, and was 32 percent by 1988 (Brown 2005).

THE POSTDESEGREGATION ERA

After decades of court orders and state and local laws mandating school integration efforts, as well as resistance to these efforts by primarily white citizens and citizen groups, by the middle of the 1980s, progress toward integration had been made. Yet, American schools in many areas remained starkly segregated, and those that had made strides toward greater integration were rapidly become resegregated by the end of the Ronald Reagan (1911–2004) era in 1989 (Frankenberg and Lee 2002). After touring schools across the nation in 1988, Jonathan Kozol observed in his classic *Savage Inequalities*, "What startled me the most . . . was the remarkable degree of racial segregation that persisted. . . . In no school that I saw anywhere in the United States were nonwhite children in large numbers truly intermingled with white children" (1991, pp. 2–3). The reasons observed by Kozol for this continued segregation include: white flight to suburbs, the establishment of private and parochial education for white children, continued housing discrimination against racial and ethnic minorities, some self-segregation by racial and ethnic minorities, and significant shifts in judicial interpretations of desegregation and antidiscrimination law.

WHITE FLIGHT, AND PAROCHIAL AND PRIVATE SCHOOLS

Throughout many parts of the United States, white children are conspicuously underrepresented in public education. According to the 2000 census, slightly over 68 percent of the under-eighteen U.S. population was non-Hispanic white. However, in the 2001–2002 school year, only about 60 percent of public school children were non-Hispanic white (Brown 2005). Los Angeles, California, provides an even more stark example of this dearth of white children. While approximately 47 percent of the city's population is white, fewer than 9 percent of students enrolled in Los Angeles Unified schools in the 2005–2006 school year were white. Among the reasons for this disparity are the exodus of white people from areas that are becoming increasingly minority and the proliferation of private and parochial schools as an alternative to desegregated public schools.

In the 1960s and 1970s, cities across the country saw radical changes in the demographic makeup and location of their populations. For example, in the 1960s, the white population of Detroit declined by 350,000 people, while the white population of the surrounding suburbs increased by 350,000. At the same time, Detroit's black population grew by approximately 170,000 people (Irons 2002). As Irons writes, "The phenomenon of 'white flight' had already begun in Detroit, as white families with school-age children either moved to the suburbs or sent their children to private or parochial schools" (2002, p. 237). In *The Agony of Education* (1996), Joe Feagin, Hernán Vera, and Nikitah Imani note that in U.S. society, whites are more likely to self-segregate even when opportunities exist to interact with minorities, blacks in particular. This separationist behavior is due, in part, to negative stereotypes that whites harbor about blacks.

The private school movement for whites was particularly evident in the South, where the rigid social customs prohibiting intermingling of the races allowed for blacks and whites to live closer to one another than in other parts of the country where de facto and de jure housing segregation kept the races apart. Thus, when desegregation of public schools was ordered, white people in the South found their children in precisely the same school district as black children. As a 2002 study at Duke University found, private schools have grown in the South since 1960 as a response to school desegregation and the region's rising affluence.

STEERING, REDLINING, AND OTHER FORMS OF HOUSING DISCRIMINATION

School districts are often based on "neighborhood" boundaries. Accordingly, de facto school segregation is often the result of segregation in housing. Prior to *Brown*, whites were protected from living among minorities through laws restricting where minorities could live. In places where these laws did not exist, white homeowners often banded together and agreed to racially restrictive housing covenants—private agreements that prevented minorities from owning property in particular neighborhoods. These covenants were effectively deemed illegal by the Supreme Court in 1948, however their intentions were kept intact by other social and business practices

such as discriminatory mortgage lending; intimidation of blacks and other minorities who sought housing in white areas; steering—the funneling of home buyers by realtors to racially specific areas; and redlining—the practice of a lending institution denying loans, manipulating loan terms, or restricting loans for certain areas of a community. In *The Ethnic Experience*, Grace Pena Delgado and Troy Johnson sum up these processes well: "In the United States, Blacks have been forced into segregated suburbs and channeled into segregated cities through institutionalized discrimination in the real estate and banking industries, racially biased public policies, and persistent White prejudice" (2005, p. 258).

While most of these discriminatory practices were outlawed in 1968 when Congress passed the Fair Housing Act, studies show that they are still practiced and their effects clearly linger. For example, as of 2000, on average in U.S. metropolitan areas nearly 65 percent of all African Americans would have to change residence in order for neighborhoods in these areas to achieve residential desegregation (Iceland et al. 2002).

To a lesser, but still significant extent, minority segregation in education can be attributed to self-segregation in housing by minorities. This is particularly true for recent immigrants who often find it easier to adjust to life in the United States when surrounded by people who are culturally similar. There is also some evidence that affluent black families often choose to live in expensive "all-black" suburbs rather than deal with potential prejudice in predominantly white suburbs.

CHANGES IN THE COURT

In *Milliken v. Bradley* (1974), the Supreme Court ruled against city-suburban desegregation and made real desegregation in education impossible in a growing number of cities experiencing an increase in their minority populations. In *UC Regents v. Bakke* (1978), a blow was struck to policies designed to increase minority representation in public higher education. However, it was not until the late 1980s and early 1990s that significant doctrinal shifts altered the way the Court would evaluate school desegregation. Between 1990 and 1995, the Supreme Court decided three cases in which the desegregation orders of lower-court judges were "terminated" and school officials were subsequently free to adopt "race neutral" school assignment policies and maintain segregated schools without fear of future judicial intervention (Irons 2002). The last of these cases involved a primarily black school district in Missouri in which the conditions were so deplorable that one school official "stated that he would not send his own child to that facility" (Irons 2002, p. ix). Over the 1990s as a whole, the Supreme Court increasingly looked unfavorably upon school desegregation decrees—court requirements that school districts aggressively pursue desegregation. As Kevin Brown writes, "Since school assignment policies are no longer motivated by a desire to maintain racial and ethnic integration, segregation inevitably increases" (Brown 2005, p. 7).

SCHOOL SEGREGATION IN THE TWENTY-FIRST CENTURY

One of the most striking developments in school segregation at the national level has resulted from a transformation in race and ethnicity in U.S. society. At the time of the *Brown* decision, the racial debate was most often cast in terms of black and white. This was the case, in significant part, because the legacy of slavery in the South and racial intolerance in the North had long been a biracial issue dealing primarily with the interactions between former slaves and white Americans of European ancestry. Also, throughout the twentieth century, black people comprised the largest racial minority in the country.

However, in the closing decades of the twentieth century, educational discrimination against Latinos began to draw more attention as two things happened. First, Latinos began migrating in greater numbers from the western United States, where they had always been a significant presence, to the Midwest, South, and East. Secondly, Latinos in the United States continued to grow in numbers over these decades, ultimately surpassing African Americans as the single largest minority group in the United States. While issues of school segregation had been of significance in western state courts long before *Brown* ever made its way to the Supreme Court (see *Alvarez v. Lemon Grove* [1931] and *Mendez v. Westminster* [1946]), because of the growing number of Latinos in the United States, the school desegregation debate has become black, white, and brown.

In the first decade of the twenty-first century, schools across the United States continue to be separated along racial, ethnic, and economic lines that are drawn primarily to the advantage of white Americans and to the disadvantage of African and Latino Americans. As Nanette Asimov writes, "Even though no board of education still has the power to exclude students based on ethnicity, the schools' racial barrier lives on in the segregated lives of the rich and the poor" (2004). In states like California, where changes in state policy have eroded the property tax base, one of the traditional mainstays of educational funding for all public schools, affluent communities have used their economic and political resources to ensure that the schools serving their children have adequate learning materials, technological resources, less overcrowding, and qualified teachers. In comparison, poor and minority school districts without these resources have found themselves left behind. Asimov continues, "Today's Linda Browns [the

lead petitioner in *Brown v. Board of Education*] are students whose parents cannot afford to supplement schools with computers, books, art classes and equipment as parents in wealthier communities do" (2004).

Even in situations where white and minority children attend the same school, studies have shown that they do not necessarily receive the same quality of education. For example, educational tracking—the placement of students into courses based on their performance in standardized achievement tests—has been criticized for effectively segregating white students, who are more commonly placed on high-achievement tracks, from students of color. Further, there is evidence of teachers being more helpful toward white students and of differential grading of students favoring white students over their minority peers (Feagin et al. 1996)

In the early twenty-first century, most African American and Latino children attended predominantly minority schools, and nearly 40 percent of these children attended schools that are at least 90 percent minority (Brown 2005). These resegregated schools exist in the former Jim Crow South as well as the "liberal" North and the progressive West. The end result of resegregated education in America is an "opportunity gap" that has significant consequences for the educational and life chances of poor students and students of color. As Judith Blau notes in *Race in the Schools* (2003), public schools operate to the detriment of all students because they are racial settings that reproduce white advantage, rather than equalizing forces in U.S. society.

A 2006 report from the the Civil Rights Project at Harvard University indicates the gap between whites and minorities in education only seems to be widening, and doing so with the tacit support of government officials and the courts (Orfield and Lee 2006). Kozol writes, "the dual society, at least in public education, seems in general to be unquestioned" (1991, p. 4). UCLA's Institute for Democracy, Education, and Access (2004) adds that this widespread resegregation not only fails the promise for equality made in *Brown*; these schools do not even live up to the pre-*Brown* doctrine of "separate but equal" set forth by the Court in *Plessy v. Ferguson* (1896).

SEE ALSO Brown v. Board of Education, *1954;* Brown v. Board of Education, *1955; Desegregation; Segregation*

BIBLIOGRAPHY

Asimov, Nanette. 2004. Brown vs. Board of Education: 50 Years Later. *San Francisco Chronicle.* May 16.

Blau, Judith R. 2003. *Race in the Schools: Perpetuating White Dominance?* Boulder, CO: Lynne Rienner.

Brown, Kevin. 2005. *Race, Law, and Education in the Post-Desegregation Era: Four Perspectives on Desegregation and Resegregation.* Durham, NC: Carolina Academic Press.

Clotfelter, Charles T. 2002. The Resegregation of Southern Schools? A Crucial Moment in the History (and the Future) of Public Schooling in America. Conference paper presented at the University of North Carolina, Chapel Hill, sponsored by the Center for Civil Rights at the UNC School of Law and the Civil Rights Project of Harvard University.

Clotfelter, Charles T., Helen F. Ladd, and Jacob L. Vigdor. 2003. Segregation and Resegregation in North Carolina's Public School Classrooms. *North Carolina Law Review* 81 (May 2003), 1463–1511.

Delgado, Grace Pena, and Troy R. Johnson. 2005. *The Ethnic Experience in the United States.* Dubuque, IA: Kendall/Hunt.

Dudziak, Mary L. 1988–1989. Desegregation as a Cold War Imperative. *Stanford Law Review* 4: 61–120.

Feagin, Joe R., Hernán Vera, and Nikitah Imani. 1996. *The Agony of Education: Black Students at White Colleges and Universities.* New York: Routledge.

Frankenberg, Erika, and Chungmei Lee. 2002. Race in American Public Schools: Rapidly Resegregating School Districts. The Civil Rights Project, Harvard University. http://www.civilrightsproject.harvard.edu/research/deseg/reseg_schools02.php.

Iceland, John, Daniel Weinberg, and Erika Steinmetz. 2002. Racial and Ethnic Residential Segregation in the United States: 1980–2000. http://www.census.gov/hhes/www/housing/housing_patterns/pdf/censr-3.pdf

Irons, Peter. 2002. *Jim Crow's Children: The Broken Promise of the Brown Decision.* New York: Viking.

Kozol, Jonathan. 1991. *Savage Inequalities: Children in America's Schools.* New York: Crown.

Kozol, Jonathan. 2005. *The Shame of the Nation: The Restoration of Apartheid Schooling in America.* New York: Crown.

Lewis, Amanda E. 2003. *Race in the Schoolyard: Negotiating the Color Line in Classrooms and Communities.* New Brunswick, NJ: Rutgers University Press.

Orfield, Gary, and Chungmei Lee. 2006. Racial Transformation and the Changing Nature of Segregation. The Civil Rights Project, Harvard University. http://www.civilrightsproject.harvard.edu/research/deseg/Racial_Transformation.pdf

UCLA Institute for Democracy, Education, and Access. 2004. Separate and Unequal 50 Years after Brown: California's Racial "Opportunity Gap." http://www.idea.gseis.ucla.edu/publications/idea/index.html.

A. Rafik Mohamed

DESIGN, MECHANISM
SEE *Mechanism Design.*

DESIGNER BABIES
SEE *Infertility Drugs, Psychosocial Issues; Mendel's Law; Eugenics.*

DESIS, THE
SEE *East Indian Diaspora.*

DE SOTO, HERNANDO
1941–

The Peruvian economist, Hernando de Soto, best known for his work on the informal economy and its negative effect on poverty amelioration, was born in 1941 in Arequipa. After his father left Peru in 1948 following a military coup, de Soto was educated in Switzerland and did not return to Peru until 1979. He founded the Institute for Liberty and Democracy (ILD) in Lima the next year and serves as it president.

De Soto has written two major books expounding his ideas: *The Other Path: The Economic Answer to Terrorism* (1986) and *The Mystery of Capital: Why Capitalism Triumphs in the West and Fails Everywhere Else* (2000). For both, the subtitles are as significant as the titles. Terrorism is a topic with which de Soto is familiar. He and the ILD have been attacked (physically, not just intellectually) by the Shining Path, a leftist revolutionary Peruvian movement.

De Soto discusses five mysteries of capital in *The Mystery of Capital.* The three most significant are missing capital, the lessons of U.S. history, and legal failure. The basic argument is that the problems of the poor—whether in Peru, Egypt, Haiti, the Philippines, or elsewhere—are not due to lack of possessions or assets but to lack of legally recognized property rights. His researchers have documented the problems that the poor face in major cities, where it takes too long for them to get a license for a legitimate business and their capital is *dead capital*, preventing them from benefiting from standardization, legal transferability of property, and the use of property as collateral. De Soto claims that over half the grievances of the poor in Peru concern difficulties of getting legal title to real estate: houses, offices, factories, and agricultural land. He claims that the changes in the developing world since the 1960s rival those of the Industrial Revolution since they have involved a massive migration of four billion people leaving their traditional way of life.

De Soto and the ILD have been involved in designing and implementing programs to empower the poor in many areas of the world: Africa, Asia, Hispanic America, the Middle East, and the former USSR. *The Other Path* (a title chosen as a deliberate antithesis to the Shining Path) argues that the real enemy of the poor is not capitalism or "feudalism" but mercantilism: the predominant system in Europe in the early modern pre–Adam Smith (1723–1790) era and a continuing socioeconomic system in postcolonial Hispanic America. It was in *The Other Path* that de Soto first developed the ideas behind the informal economy: "informal" because it is not formally recognized by the law but functions outside it. It includes informal housing, informal trade, and informal transport.

De Soto points out the hidden costs of informality and the significance of the law as a determinant of development, and he critiques the redistributive tradition, which he associates with the early mercantilist system. He contrasts the relatively peaceful resolution of socioeconomic problems in England (and the United States) with the much more violent revolutions in France, Spain, and Russia. The unlearned lesson of U.S. history was its implementation of widespread property rights in the late nineteenth century.

Numerous criticisms have been made of de Soto's theories and of attempts to implement them to empower the poor. He has been accused of favoring a "single bullet" approach, and the statistical basis of his data has been questioned. Some critics argue that it is difficult to establish who owns what in an informal economy and that some ILD reforms (such as those in Bogotá) have not improved conditions for the poor. Critics also argue that de Soto ignores the importance of culture and that, while he may be correct in his vision of property rights, the sequencing of reforms is just as important as the need to pay attention to local social context.

In response de Soto (as well as a prominent colleague of his, Madeleine Albright, former U.S. secretary of state) have countered that arguments for the importance of legally recognized property rights do not imply "a silver bullet" but a "missing link." De Soto argues that heads of state want his help in quantifying the informal sector and that ILD is the only organization doing such detailed research. Perhaps the best summary of de Soto's views would be that he has the correct diagnosis but an as yet imperfect prognosis; nevertheless, he has started the important process of documenting the (legally) unrecognized assets of the poor.

SEE ALSO *Capital; Development Economics; Informal Economy; Land Claims; Poverty; Property; Property Rights*

BIBLIOGRAPHY

PRIMARY WORKS

De Soto, Hernando. [1986] 2002. *The Other Path: The Economic Answer to Terrorism.* Trans. June Abbott. New York: Basic Books.

De Soto, Hernando. 2000. *The Mystery of Capital: Why Capitalism Triumphs in the West and Fails Everywhere Else.* New York: Basic Books.

De Soto, Hernando. 2003. The Economist versus the Terrorist. *Economist*, Feb. 1: 62.

De Soto, Hernando. 2003. Listening to the Barking Dogs: Property Law against Poverty in the Non-West. *Focaal: European Journal of Anthropology* 41: 179–185.

SECONDARY WORKS

Albright, Madeleine. 2007. The World in 2007: It's Time for Empowerment. *Economist*, 21st special yearly edition: 65.

Institute for Liberty and Democracy (ILD). http://www.ild.org.pe/home.htm.

The Mystery of Capital Deepens. 2006. *Economist*, August 24: 58.

Rossini, R. G., and J. J. Thomas. 1990. The Size of the Informal Sector in Peru: A Critical Comment on Hernando de Soto's *El Otro Sendero. World Development* 18 (1): 125–135.

Samuelson, Robert. 2001. The Spirit of Capitalism. *Foreign Affairs* 80 (1): 205–211.

Woodruff, Christopher. 2001. Review of de Soto's *The Mystery of Capitalism. Journal of Economic Literature* 39 (4): 1215–1223.

Calvin Hayes

DESTABILIZATION

The concept of destabilization implies that there is something that is destabilized. What, then, is this "something"? It should reasonably be an "order" of some kind. But what kind of "order"? The Polish sociologist Zygmunt Bauman argues that the current age is one of "floating modernity," meaning that flexibility and mobility now permeate societal and private life. Employment contracts are becoming increasingly short-term; uncertainty—in both positive and negative meanings—has become epidemic; and the belief of permanent happiness is being replaced by the belief of episodic enjoyment. Changing jobs, once looked down upon, is now seen as something positive and good for personal development. Temporary relationships have gained an increased legitimacy, with divorce becoming a part of everyday life. During early modernity, workers started their careers at one company and often ended them at the same place. In an era of floating modernity, however, where one starts one's career is no longer a guide to where it will end.

From a societal standpoint, destabilization thus means that power elites become less and less permanent, and that power becomes more difficult to define. This change in power relations means that individuals' identities vary more and more over time, and that the dominant norms place the temporary, not the permanent, in a primary position.

What are the causes of destabilization? The communications revolution has affected destabilization and individualization in a number of ways—by changing the significance of the territory, by improving the possibilities for network cooperation both within and outside of nation-state borders, and by increasing the significance of innovation and flexibility as a means of productivity and competition. The place of the individual in social, political, and economic networks determines the extent of power that the individual possesses or might exercise. Since the networks are dynamic (or instable), and since individuals can move in and out of these networks, there are no longer any stable power elites. Characteristics belonging to the individual, such as knowledge and education, thus become decisive for corporations and for the economy. Whether a specific individual fits into one of these networks is determined by the individual's personal characteristics, knowledge profile, originality, creativity, and entrepreneurial skills. Because innovation, creativity, and specialized knowledge form the basis of productivity, every supplier of knowledge becomes a unique carrier of surplus generating competencies. This creates power positions and self-interests, and it helps the information producers become global actors. In addition, shortsighted profits from the stock and currency markets become more important than long-term direct investments. Essentially, cultures are no longer created and shaped by people who share the same time and space, but by individuals who construct their own values on the basis of their own experiences in a world that is constantly being rearranged. In modern parlance, one "is" one's experiences, and these experiences give rise to the self.

It is fruitful to analyze destabilization in terms of three concepts: power, identity, and norms. Power elites have become changeable and difficult to define, and nation-states are being challenged by different groups of actors who create temporary alliances to further specific issues. Within nation-states, traditional power elites are being challenged by loosely organized networks, which also create temporary alliances.

In addition, the identities of individuals vary more and more over time. This is especially true for those groups of people who actively use the possibilities that the communicational revolution and network society creates. The norms emphasize the short term instead of the long term, impressions instead of experiences, and freedom of action instead of predictability or safety.

As with the concept of individualization, "power," "identity," and "norms" are not at the same analytical level. Changes in identity and norms must be considered as part of the destabilitzation process implying that power relations have become more diffuse and varying. Identity changes in pace with changes in power relations, and the modern emphasis on the short term, happenings, and freedom of action in societal norms is connected with the modern transience of power.

SEE ALSO *Civil War; Creativity; Elites; Identity; Norms; Political Instability, Indices of; Uncertainty*

BIBLIOGRAPHY

Bauman, Zygmunt. 2001. *The Individualized Society.* Malden, MA: Polity.

Florida, Richard. 2004. *The Rise of the Creative Class: And How It's Transforming Work, Leisure, Community, and Everyday Life.* New York: Basic Books.

Inglehart, Robert. 1997. *Modernization and Postmodernization: Cultural, Economic, and Political Change in 43 Societies.* Princeton, NJ: Princeton University Press.

Ulf Bjereld

DESTRUCTIVE OBEDIENCE
SEE *Obedience, Destructive.*

DETERMINANTS

As used in mathematics, the word *determinant* refers to a number associated with a square matrix, that is, an array of numerical quantities arranged in, say, n rows and n columns. Matrices of this sort typically arise as a means for representing the coefficients in a system of n linear equations in n unknowns.

Suppose the system of equations is

$$a_{11}x_1 + a_{12}x_2 + \cdots + a_{1n}x_n = b_1$$
$$a_{21}x_1 + a_{22}x_2 + \cdots + a_{2n}x_n = b_2$$
$$\vdots$$
$$a_{n1}x_1 + a_{n2}x_2 + \cdots + a_{nn}x_n = b_n$$

Then the matrix of detached coefficients

$$A = \begin{bmatrix} a_{11} & a_{12} & \cdots & a_{1n} \\ a_{21} & a_{22} & \cdots & a_{2n} \\ \vdots & \vdots & & \vdots \\ a_{n1} & a_{n2} & \cdots & a_{nn} \end{bmatrix}$$

is said to be *nonsingular* if and only if its *determinant* is nonzero. The existence and uniqueness of a solution to the system of equations are determined by the nonsingularity of A. If A lacks this property, it is said to be *singular*, and when this is the case, the system might have no solution (nonexistence) or infinitely many solutions (nonuniqueness).

The determinant of a square matrix A is the number

$$\det(A) = \sum_{j=1}^{n} (-1)^{i+j} a_{ij} \det(A(i|j))$$

where $A(i|j)$ denotes the submatrix obtained from A by deleting its ith row and jth column. This definition of the determinant uses what is called *expansion by a row*, in this case by row i. There is an analogous definition of $\det(A)$ in terms of *expansion by a column*, say j, which says

$$\det(A) = \sum_{i=1}^{n} (-1)^{i+j} a_{ij} \det(A(i|j)).$$

These formulas are associated with the name of the French mathematician Pierre-Simon Laplace (1749–1827). From either of them it is evident that the determinant of the identity matrix I is 1, and hence it is nonsingular.

The determinant of a square matrix A and that of its transpose A^T are always equal. Moreover, the determinant of the product of two square matrices is the product of their determinants. In symbols, if A and B are two $n \times n$ matrices, then

$$\det(AB) = \det(A)\,\det(B).$$

From this and the fact that the determinant of the identity matrix I is 1, it follows that when A is nonsingular,

$$\det(A^{-1}) = \frac{1}{\det(A)}.$$

Thus, the determinant of a nonsingular matrix and that of its inverse are reciprocals of each other.

As can readily be appreciated, the calculation of the determinant of a large matrix by means of a row or column expansion can entail a significant amount of work. Fortunately, there are matrices whose determinants are not difficult to compute. Among these are diagonal matrices (the identity matrix being an example) and, more generally, lower triangular matrices. The determinant of any such matrix is the product of its diagonal elements. (The same is true for all upper triangular matrices.) Finding a determinant is aided by procedures (such as Gaussian elimination) that transform the matrix to another whose structure permits relatively easy calculation of its determinant.

Cramer's Rule for solving the system $Ax = b$ proceeds from the assumption that A is nonsingular. In that case, the system has a unique solution: $x = A^{-1}b$. Cramer's rule gives formulae for the values for the components of this vector in terms of the data, specifically as ratios of determinants. The expression of these ratios requires the introduction of a notation for the matrix obtained from A and b by replacing the jth column of A by the vector b. Let this notation be $A_{-j}(b)$. Then Cramer's Rule says that for each $j = 1, \ldots, n$

$$x_j = \frac{\det(A_{-j}(b))}{\det(A)}$$

In the system

$$\begin{bmatrix} 4 & -1 & 3 \\ 2 & 0 & 1 \\ -3 & 1 & 5 \end{bmatrix} \begin{bmatrix} x_1 \\ x_2 \\ x_3 \end{bmatrix} = \begin{bmatrix} 2 \\ -1 \\ 0 \end{bmatrix}$$

the determinant of A is 15. The matrices $A_{-1}(b)$, $A_{-2}(b)$, $A_{-3}(b)$ are, respectively,

$$\begin{bmatrix} 2 & -1 & 3 \\ -1 & 0 & 1 \\ 0 & 1 & 5 \end{bmatrix}, \begin{bmatrix} 4 & 2 & 3 \\ 2 & -1 & 1 \\ -3 & 0 & 5 \end{bmatrix}, \text{ and } \begin{bmatrix} 4 & -1 & 2 \\ 2 & 0 & -1 \\ -3 & 1 & 0 \end{bmatrix}$$

To use Cramer's Rule in this case, one would compute

$$\det(A_1(b)) = -10, \det(A_2(b)) = -55, \text{ and } \det(A_3(b)) = 5.$$

Cramer's Rule then yields

$$x_1 = -\frac{10}{15}, \quad x_2 = -\frac{55}{15}, \text{ and } x_3 = -\frac{5}{15}.$$

Although Cramer's Rule is useful in numerically solving small systems of equations (those consisting of two equations in two unknowns, or three equations in three unknowns), it is not recommended for solving larger systems due to the difficulty in computing determinants of order larger than 3. This caution does not apply to situations in which the calculation is entirely symbolic. An example of the latter sort can be found in P. A. Samuelson's *Foundations of Economic Analysis* (Harvard University Press, Cambridge, 1963; see equation 7, p. 14).

The task of solving square systems of linear equations arises from least-squares problems which in turn arise in linear regression analysis. The square system is typically of the form $A^T A x = A^T b$. These are called the normal equations. The problem is to find x. The first question one faces is whether the matrix $A^T A$ is nonsingular. If it is not—that is, $\det(A^T A) = 0$—then Cramer's Rule is not applicable. If it is nonsingular, then in principle, the solution is $x = (A^T A)^{-1} A^T b$. When n, the number of variables $x_1, \ldots, x_n$, is quite small (and $\det[A^T A] \neq 0$), the use of Cramer's Rule for solving equations can be considered. But most practical problems of this nature are not small and need to be solved with computers. Since exact arithmetic is then lost, several numerical issues come to the fore. The extensive use of determinants is not advisable simply on computational efficiency grounds. Another consideration, the condition number of $A^T A$, enters the picture here. As stated by Gilbert Strang, "Forming A^TA can turn a healthy problem into a sick one, and it is much better (except for very small problems) to use either Gram-Schmidt or the singular value decomposition" (Strang 1976, p. 272).

SEE ALSO *Inverse Matrix; Matrix Algebra; Simultaneous Equation Bias*

BIBLIOGRAPHY

Aitken, A. C. 1964. *Determinants and Matrices.* Edinburgh: Oliver & Boyd.

Marcus, Marvin, and Henryk Minc. 1964. *A Survey of Matrix Theory and Matrix Inequalities.* Boston: Allyn & Bacon.

Strang, Gilbert. 1976. *Linear Algebra and Its Applications.* New York: Academic Press.

Richard W. Cottle

DETERMINISM

Any doctrine positing that one kind or order of phenomena is the necessary and sufficient condition of another kind or order of phenomena is a strongly deterministic doctrine. On the other hand, if a doctrine posits that some order of phenomena is only a necessary or a sufficient condition of another, it is considered to be only weakly deterministic. Since their inception, the social sciences have been home to many such doctrines.

From Arthur de Gobineau (1816–1882) in the nineteenth century to J. Philippe Rushton's work in the 1990s, racist accounts of variations in character or intelligence are among the least credible and most enduring of deterministic doctrines. Psychobiological accounts of the roots of war and violence have had nearly as long a hearing. Somewhat more credibly, contemporary evolutionary psychologists of diverse disciplinary provenance are reviving the pursuit of accounts of humanly universal behavior, as well as of racially marked or ethnically distinctive behavior, as positive adaptations to or resolutions of existential or situational problems (Buss 1999).

The environmental determinism of Johannes Gottfried von Herder (1744–1803), who treated variations of climate and physical environment as the chief source of variations of human character, was popular in the eighteenth and early nineteenth centuries. Herder's latter-day successors are more circumspect, typically treating particular conditions of climate and geography as imposing on the human populations who live with and under them a cap on the upward bounds of politico-economic complexity. A noteworthy case in point is the historian Fernand Braudel's 1949 thesis that the preindustrial societies occupying the borders of the Mediterranean Sea were effectively ecologically precluded from sustaining political organization beyond the level of the city-state.

Technology, however, changes everything, or such at least has been the opinion of a long line of determinists since the heyday of the Industrial Revolution. In the 1930s Braudel's elder colleague Marc Bloch traced the pivotal source of the social organization of French agriculture to the invention of the double-bladed plow. A half-century before, the cultural materialist Henry Louis Morgan had appealed more generally to technological innovation as the essential index of broader civilizational progress. The Victorian biologist and philosopher Herbert Spencer (1820–1903) saw in technological development—first military, then economic—the lynchpin of the advance of utilitarian happiness. Though not quite a utilitarian, Talcott Parsons (1902–1979) is among Spencer's recognizable evolutionist heirs. Less sanguine is the anthropologist Leslie White (1900–1975), who made the post–Hiroshima assessment that the increasing efficiency of the technologies of harvesting energy is the causal underpinning of collective evolution—for better and for worse. White's ambivalence grew darker in such seminal assessments of the harmful environmental consequences of industrial and atomic technologies as Rachel Carson's *Silent Spring* (1962) and Mark Harwell's *Nuclear Winter* (1984). In *The Condition of Postmodernity* (1990), David Harvey argues that the far-flung reach and unprecedented speed of communicative technologies is effecting a global compression of space and time that tends to unmoor human experience from its typically local bearings. Harvey articulates (with a dark ambivalence) a specifically digital determinism.

Cultural determinism of a less material and materialist sort has two prominent installments, both traceable to the early students of Franz Boas. Ruth Benedict (1887–1948) and Margaret Mead (1901–1978) were the early champions of the cultural determination of personality. Encouraging now-discredited distillations of "national character," their work also gave rise to sustained research into child rearing and other practices that remain the focus of the anthropology and sociology of childhood and education (Whiting and Child 1953; Christie 1999; Jones 1995). Edward Sapir (1884–1939) and Benjamin Whorf (1897–1941) were the eponymous champions of the speculative thesis—erroneously deemed a "hypothesis"—of the linguistic determination of what is presumed to be reality itself. The Sapir-Whorf hypothesis may have had its roots in the thought of such Romantic philosophers as Wilhelm von Humboldt. As an assertion of linguistic relativism or linguistic mediationism, it has many counterparts in semiotics and semiotically grounded theories of knowledge, past and present.

Émile Durkheim began *The Elementary Forms of the Religious Life* (1912) with the bold claim that social structure and organization determine the structure and organization of the basic categories of thought. His influence remains most obvious in the work of Mary Douglas. Institutionally more specific, and by far the most influential social determinist, was Karl Marx, especially when writing in collaboration with Friedrich Engels. Marx and Engels's transference of the presumptive human primacy of a finite set of material needs to that of the institution best disposed to satisfy them—the economy—was the initial step in their theorization of the means and mode of economic production as determinative of the form and content of every other institutional order. Marx's *Capital* (1867) and his and Engels's *German Ideology* (1932) were the benchmarks of leftist social and political thought from the turn of the twentieth century until the 1970s. The analysis of the commodity (and its fetishization) in the former treatise stimulated Georg Lukács's inquiries in the 1920s into the broader capitalist habit of "reification," the process of construing the related parts of systemic wholes as independent entities in their own right. It would later inspire Max Horkheimer and Theodor Adorno's critique of the mass-produced debasement of what they called "the culture industry." The problem of the relation between class interest and truth inherent in *The German Ideology* (1932) gave rise to a Marxist sociology of knowledge from Lenin through Antonio Gramsci and Karl Mannheim to Jürgen Habermas. Especially in its stronger expressions, Marxist determinism brings to an account of human action the same logical assets and liabilities as any other determinism. It is an attractively powerful device of intellectual focus and direction, but it runs two risks: (1) circularity, or taking for granted the very hypotheses that it is obliged to prove; and (2) a drift into the metaphysical, leaving behind any possibility of putting its hypotheses to the test at all.

SEE ALSO *Benedict, Ruth; Boas, Franz; Freud, Sigmund; Gobineau, Comte de; Gramsci, Antonio; Marx, Karl; Mead, Margaret; Parsons, Talcott; Racism*

BIBLIOGRAPHY

Benedict, Ruth. 1934. *Patterns of Culture*. Boston: Houghton Mifflin.

Bloch, Marc. 1966. *French Rural History: An Essay on Its Basic Characteristics*. Trans. Janet Sondheimer. Berkeley: University of California Press.

Braudel, Fernand. 1949. *The Mediterranean and the Mediterranean World in the Age of Philip II*. Trans. Siân Reynolds. London: Collins, 1972.

Buss, David M. 1999. *Evolutionary Psychology: The New Science of the Mind*. Boston: Allyn and Bacon.

Carson, Rachel. 1962. *Silent Spring*. Boston: Houghton Mifflin.

Cassirer, Ernst. 1923–1929. *The Philosophy of Symbolic Forms*. Trans. Ralph Mannheim. New Haven: Yale University Press, 1955–1957.

Christie, Frances, ed. 1999. *Pedagogy and the Shaping of Consciousness: Linguistic and Social Processes*. London: Cassell.

Derrida, Jacques. 1967. *Of Grammatology*. Trans. Gayatri Chakravorty Spivak. Baltimore, MD: Johns Hopkins University Press, 1976.

Douglas, Mary. 1970. *Natural Symbols: Explorations in Cosmology*. New York: Pantheon.

Douglas, Mary. 1986. *How Institutions Think*. Syracuse, NY: Syracuse University Press.

Durkheim, Émile. 1912. *The Elementary Forms of the Religious Life*. Trans. Karen E. Fields. New York: The Free Press, 1995.

Freud, Sigmund. 1930. *Civilization and Its Discontents*. Trans. James Strachey. New York: W. W. Norton, 1961.

Gobineau, Arthur, Comte de. 1853. *Essai sur l'inégalité des races humaines (Essay on the inequality of the Human Races)*. Présentation de Hubert Juin. Paris: P. Belfond, 1967.

Gramsci, Antonio. 1929–1935. *Selections from the Prison Notebooks of Antonio Gramsci*, eds. and trans. Quentin Hoare and Geoffrey Nowell Smith. New York: International Publishers, 1971.

Habermas, Jürgen. 1971. *Knowledge and Human Interests*. Trans. Jeremy J. Shapiro. Boston: Beacon Press.

Harvey, David. 1990. *The Condition of Postmodernity: An Enquiry into the Origins of Cultural Change*. Cambridge, MA: Blackwell.

Harwell, Mark, et al. 1984. *Nuclear Winter: The Human Consequences of Nuclear War*. New York: Springer-Verlag.

Herder, Johann G. 1784–1791. *Outlines of a Philosophy of the History of Man*. Trans. T. Churchill. New York: Bergman Publishers, 1966.

Horkheimer, Max, and Theodor Adorno. 1947. *The Dialectic of Enlightenment: Philosophical Fragments*, ed. Gunzelin Schmid Noerr; trans. Edward Jephcott. Stanford, CA: Stanford University Press, 2002.

Humboldt, Wilhelm, Frieherr von. 1836. *On Language: On the Diversity of Human Language Construction and Its Influence on the Mental Development of the Human Species*, ed. Michael Losonsky; trans. Peter Heath. New York: Cambridge University Press, 1999.

Jones, Raya A. 1995. *The Child-school Interface: Environment and Behavior*. New York: Cassell.

Lenin, Vladimir I. 1902. *What Is To Be Done?* Ed. Robert Service; trans. Joe Feinberg and George Hanna. New York: Penguin, 1988.

Lorenz, Konrad. 1966. *On Aggression*. Trans. Marjorie Kerr Wilson. New York: Harcourt, Brace & World.

Lucy, John A. 1992. *Language Diversity and Thought: A Reformulation of the Linguistic Relativity Hypothesis*. New York: Cambridge University Press.

Lukács, Georg. 1923. *History and Class Consciousness: Studies in Marxist Dialectics*. Trans. Rodney Livingstone. Cambridge, Mass.: MIT Press, 1971.

Mannheim, Karl. 1936. *Ideology and Utopia: An Introduction to the Sociology of Knowledge.* Trans. Louis Wirth and Edward Shils. New York: Harcourt, Brace, and World.

Marx, Karl. 1867. *Capital: A Critique of Political Economy.* Trans. Ben Fowkes. New York: Penguin, 1990.

Marx, Karl, and Friedrich Engels. 1932. *The German Ideology, Parts I and III,* ed. R. Pascal. New York: International Publishers, 1947.

Mead, Margaret. 1928. *Coming of Age in Samoa.* New York: William Morrow.

Mead, Margaret. 1930. *Growing Up in New Guinea.* New York: New American Library.

Morgan, Lewis Henry. 1877. *Ancient Society: Researches in the Lines of Progress from Savagery through Barbarism to Civilization.* London: Routledge/Thoemmes Press, 1998.

Parsons, Talcott. 1960. *Structure and Process in Modern Societies.* Glencoe, IL: The Free Press.

Penn, Julia. 1972. *Linguistic Relativity Versus Innate Ideas: The Origins of the Sapir-Whorf Hypothesis in German Thought.* The Hague: Mouton.

Rushton, J. Philippe. 1995. *Race, Evolution, and Behavior: A Life History Perspective.* New Brunswick, NJ: Transaction Publishers.

Spencer, Herbert. 1876–1896. *The Principles of Sociology,* abridged ed., ed. Stanislav Andreski. London: Macmillan, 1969.

White, Leslie. 1949. *The Science of Culture: A Study of Man and Civilization.* New York: Farrar, Strauss.

Whiting, John Wesley, and Irvin I. Child. 1953. *Child Training and Personality: A Cross-Cultural Study.* New York: Yale University Press.

Whorf, Benjamin Lee. *Language, Thought, and Reality: Selected Writings of Benjamin Lee Whorf,* ed. John B. Carroll. Cambridge, MA: MIT Press.

James D. Faubion

DETERMINISM, BIOLOGICAL

Biological determinism refers to the idea that all human behavior is innate, determined by genes, brain size, or other biological attributes. This theory stands in contrast to the notion that human behavior is determined by culture or other social forces. Inherent to biological determinism is the denial of free will: individuals have no internal control over their behavior and dispositions, and thus are devoid of responsibility for their actions. Often implicit in this line of reasoning is the idea that because humans lack responsibility for determining their own lives, they are rightfully subject to the control of persons biologically determined in more socially acceptable ways. While few biologists fully believe in the idea of biological determinism, the theory has had cultural and political currency both in the shaping of human racial history and in current debates over the relative importance of our genetic qualities (i.e., nature) versus our socialization process (i.e., nurture) in determining our individual physical and behavioral characteristics.

Although the first traces of biological determinism are suggested in Aristotle's (384–322 BCE) proclamation in *Politics* that "there are species in which a distinction is already marked, immediately at birth, between those of its members who are intended for being ruled and those who are intended to rule," (Baker, 1950, p. 14) it was Enlightenment thinking that ushered in the most robust and politically salient strains of this line of thinking. Using what would consistently prove to be a faulty scientific approach among racial determinists, Carolus Linnaeus (1707–1778) was the first to divide the human race into four categories (red, yellow, white, and black) in 1735. He also began what was to be a trend: racial determinism has never been a project of merely answering questions based in curiosity about human variety; it has always carried a belief in the characteristics associated with these racial categorizations. These beliefs, without fail, served to justify white supremacy in a political context.

Every method of determining a racial hierarchy within the human race has failed to stand up to scientific scrutiny. Nonetheless, such supposed justifications have included measurements of brain size, stature, hair texture, genetic analysis of heredity, and many other measurable attributes. Perhaps the most well-known analysis of this type was Samuel Morton's (1799–1851) *Crania Americana* (1839), a selective study of more than eight hundred skulls undertaken to try to prove the innate superiority of Caucasians. A similarly popular work, *Essay on the Inequality of Human Races* (1853) by Joseph-Arthur de Gobineau (1816–1882), makes an argument in regard to the inherent superiority of the same group, whom he identified as *Aryans*: "Everything great, noble, and fruitful in the works of man on this earth, in science, art and civilization, derives from a single starting-point, is the development of a single germ and the result of a single thought; it belongs to one family alone, the different branches of which have reigned in all the civilized countries of the universe" (Gobineau [1853] 1970, p. 113). In each examination of racial determinism undertaken by nineteenth-century and early twentieth-century scientists, it has been established that a racist bias at the outset had an impact on the scientist's findings. Indeed, the history of biological determinism is a prime example of how science is a deeply political practice, despite its claims to universal knowledge.

At the same time, some scientists' findings have been manipulated by interested parties in order to justify power relations. For example, even though Charles Darwin

(1809–1882) refers to "civilized" and "savage" races as different from one another in *On the Origin of Species* (1859), he does so as an aside to his major argument that a long process of natural selection has differentiated humans from animals. This claim, however, did not alter the racial determinism of his contemporaries. In fact, his theory became something of a metaphor for those who practiced racial determinism. Darwin's notion of struggle was generational, and depended on species' interrelationships rather than isolation. However, social Darwinist thinking developed in order to argue that this struggle was actually among races. Herbert Spencer (1820–1903), in particular, jumped on the idea of the "survival of the fittest" to argue not only for white racial superiority, but also for justification of segregationist policies and a lack of social support for nonwhites. For social Darwinists, science had provided a basis on which moral arguments could be made; to create any form of social support (be it charity or state support) for nonwhites would be to contradict the laws of nature. Many social Darwinists felt comfortable with the idea that the inequality of races was a pity, but something that would inevitably lead to the decline and disappearance of nonwhite, and implicitly inferior, races.

Eugenics policies were also based on the ideas of racial determinism. However, unlike the social Darwinists who wanted to allow nature to take its course, eugenicists were more active in their belief in white supremacy. Belief in certain human stock as superior to other human stock (in terms of intelligence, creativity, capacity for self rule, and many other areas) almost always took a racial or ethnic form. While the fascist policy of Nazi Germany is an obvious example of eugenicist thinking, the United States and many other nations have also enacted policies based on eugenics. In the United States, this has meant everything from sterilization of Jewish women upon immigration to the United States, antimiscegenation policies whose selective enforcement prevented white women from bearing children with black and Asian men, and sterilization policies affecting Puerto Rican women after Operation Bootstrap, among many other examples. Many race and gender scholars argue that current policies affecting reproductive rights for poor nonwhite women, while not overtly racist, carry implicit strains of eugenicist thinking.

Biological determinism, while proven to be scientifically invalid in terms of racial categorization and racial meaning, is still present in contemporary debates concerning sexual orientation, genetic research as part of the Human Genome Project, and various overt international policies, such as China's Maternal and Infant Health Care Law. In fact, an unexpected resurgence of biological determinism has taken place since the mid-1980s, most noticeably with the controversial publication of Richard J.

Herrnstein (1930–1994) and Charles Murray's *The Bell Curve* (1994). In their book, Herrnstein and Murray argue not only that intelligence is genetically heritable, but also that there are racial and ethnic differences that account for why whites are better off socioeconomically compared to blacks. More recently, Stephen J. Dubner and Steven D. Levitt argue in *Freakonomics* (2005) that there is a correlation between crime rates and access to abortion. More specifically, the authors argue that greater access to abortion has led to a decrease in the criminally predisposed population. Although a number of scholars, including a few economists, have disputed Dubner and Levitt's claims, the controversial argument has received national attention and even political notoriety. One example of such political incongruity, based on Dubner and Levitt's claims, can be witnessed by former Secretary of Education William Bennett's comment in 2005 on his radio show *Morning in America* that "if you wanted to reduce crime, you could—if that were your sole purpose, you could abort every black baby in this country, and your crime rate would go down."

While scientific research about hormones, genes, and other human biological characteristics warrants continuation, social scientists largely accept the idea that social rather than biological or genetic forces drive human choices, human diversity, and the various ways in which difference is both perceived and translates into issues of equality. Of the scholars whose work has stood in opposition to biological determinism, most notable are Ashley Montagu (1905–1999), a distinguished British anthropologist whose early writings in the 1940s and 1950s questioned the validity of race as a biological concept; Stephen Jay Gould (1941–2002), an American evolutionary biologist who refuted many of *The Bell Curve*'s claims in his 1996 book *The Mismeasure of Man*; and Joseph L. Graves Jr., an American biologist who argues that "the traditional concept of race as a biological fact is a myth" (Graves 2005, p. xxv).

SEE ALSO *Darwinism, Social; Determinism, Cultural; Determinism, Environmental; Determinism, Genetic; Eugenics; Nature vs. Nurture*

BIBLIOGRAPHY

Baker, Earnest. 1950. *The Politics of Aristotle.* London: Oxford University Press.

Darwin, Charles. 1859. *On the Origin of Species by Means of Natural Selection, or the Preservation of Favoured Races in the Struggle for Life.* London: John Murray.

Dubner, Stephen J., and Steven D. Levitt. 2005. *Freakonomics: A Rogue Economist Explores the Hidden Side of Everything.* New York: HarperCollins.

Gobineau, Joseph-Arthur de. [1853] 1970. Essay on the Inequality of Human Races. In *Father of Racist Ideology: The*

Social and Political Thought of Count Gobineau, ed. Michael D. Biddiss, p. 113. New York: Weybright and Talley.

Gould, Stephen Jay. 1996. *The Mismeasure of Man*. Rev. ed. New York: Norton.

Graves, Joseph L., Jr. 2005. *The Race Myth: Why We Pretend Race Exists in America*. New York: Plume.

Herrnstein, Richard J., and Charles Murray. 1994. *The Bell Curve: Intelligence and Class Structure in American Life*. New York: Free Press.

Montagu, Ashley, ed. 1964. *The Concept of Race*. London: Collier.

Tucker, William H. 1994. *The Science and Politics of Racial Research*. Urbana: University of Illinois Press.

Meghan A. Burke
David G. Embrick

DETERMINISM, ENVIRONMENTAL

Environmental determinism proposes that physical environmental features alone cause human social and cultural behaviors. These features and their changes over time include: climate and temperature; land and soil conditions; rainfall and other water resources; harvestable wildlife and other natural resources; and levels of competition and predation among species.

HISTORICAL OVERVIEW

Dating to the writings of the Greek philosopher and geographer Strabo (c. 64 BCE–23 CE), environmental determinism became prominent during the late 1800s of the Enlightenment period, when many scholars searched for explanations for and methods to study human behavior and societal organization. Its physical nature premise, which was one among many competing for theoretical hegemony, was based on the evolutionary biology of Jean-Baptiste de Lamarck (1790–1869) and Charles Darwin (1809–1882). Lamarck believed that characteristics acquired by habits and other behavioral adaptations to changes in the environment could be genetically transmitted to offspring. (This idea was the precursor of biological or genetic determinism.) Darwin was strongly influenced by Lamarckism, as well as by the population dynamics described in *An Essay on the Principle of Population* by Thomas Malthus (1766–1834), and by ideas regarding natural selection introduced by Alfred Russell Wallace (1823–1913). Darwin explained in his 1859 book *On the Origin of Species by Means of Natural Selection, or the Preservation of Favoured Races in the Struggle for Life* how biological evolution of a species occurred as a result of its population's environmental adaptation. In this adaptation process, traits that contribute to a species' competitive struggle for survival are naturally selected and reproductively transmitted to future generations.

These ideas and the development of scientific positivism had a profound impact on Enlightenment thinking. According to Richard Hofstadter, "Darwinism established a new approach to nature and gave fresh impetus to the conception of development; it impelled men to try to exploit its findings and methods through schemes of evolutionary development and organic analogies" (1955, p. 5). Among the social philosophers who saw immediate opportunities to apply Darwinian principles and scientific empiricism, Herbert Spencer (1820–1903) led the way to conceptualize society as an evolving social organism whose change from one stage to the next was the basis of social progress. Within this perspective, known as social Darwinism, Spencer reconciled the dualistic problem of natural and human processes by placing humankind within nature and subjecting it to the same natural laws of competition and survival of the fittest. Meanwhile, other scholars counter-argued for the distinctiveness of social phenomena, which they considered to be sui generis. They believed phenomena such as social behaviors, beliefs, norms, society, and culture are socially constructed products based on human rational choices and collective interaction.

During and after the 1880s, however, European naturalists and social scientists struggled to explain the causes of different levels of societal and cultural variation within and across different geographical spaces. Carl Ritter (1779–1859) incorporated social Darwinism to argue in his nineteen-volume *Die Erdkunde im Verhältniss zur Natur und zur Geschichte des Menschen* (The Science of the Earth in Relation to Nature and the History of Mankind) written from 1817 to 1859, that these differences were attributable to a nation's pursuit of *lebensraum* (living space) as a biological necessity for its growth. Frederick Ratzel (1844–1904) later expanded the concept's meaning to propose the idea of the "organic state," which included human cultural evolution and the diffusion of ideas that occurs as a growing nation acquires more territory and natural resources, greater societal complexity, and higher levels of culture and civilization to meet its needs. The imperialist histories of Great Britain and Germany were often the benchmarks in comparative historical studies. Environmental determinists justified national expansionism by suggesting that primitive societies culturally benefited from contact with more civilized nations. The racist implication of this hierarchical reasoning was that primitive societies, especially those located in the equatorial latitudes, were inferior and culturally lethargic compared to the Nordic races of highly industrialized Northern Europe.

Environmental determinism still had a following, albeit minority, during the early 1900s. Ellen Churchill Semple (1863–1932), a former student of Ratzel and a reluctant social Darwinist, introduced his theory into the mainstream of American geography, though she rejected his idea of the organic state and established her own course. Her most prominent books, *American History and Its Geographic Conditions* (1903) and *Influences of Geographic Environment* (1911), were widely acclaimed (Colby 1933). Throughout her work, which was best known for studies of rural Kentucky, she applied scientific methods to demonstrate that geographic factors worked directly to influence the expression of racial characteristics and indirectly to define a people's psychological, social, political, and cultural characteristics (Peet 1985, p. 319). This racial theme, or "scientific racism," was promoted during the next three decades particularly in the climatic determinism of Ellsworth Huntington (1876–1947) and in ethnographic studies conducted by Griffith Taylor (1880–1963) on Australia, Canada, and Antarctica. It even provided the Nazi regime with a convenient but distorted justification for its geopolitical and eugenic policies during the late 1930s and early 1940s. Although racist overtones were discarded in later decades, environmental determinism appears in a few contemporary studies by American geographers and other scholars (e.g., Frenkel 1992; Diamond 1999).

COUNTERARGUMENTS

Many geographers and social scientists either eschewed or eventually divorced themselves from both social Darwinism and environmental determinism. Others eased into less apologetic possibilistic and probabilistic perspectives that viewed environmental factors as one among many influences on human choices and on the probable development of particular cultural patterns, dependent on specific social and economic conditions (Lewthwaite 1966). They charged that such a singular deterministic explanation (environmental or otherwise) is insensitive to epistemic differences among cultural, social, and psychological phenomena and the variations in ecological conditions. The anthropologist Franz Boas (1858–1942) argued, for example, that all humans have the same intellectual capacity, all cultures are based on the same basic mental principles, and phenomena have meaning only in terms of their human perception or experience. He distinguished between the physical sciences, which seek to discover natural laws, and the historical sciences, which seek to achieve a comprehensive understanding of phenomena in their own contextual terms. For him and many other scholars, environmental determinism failed to offer a theory of human consciousness and purpose, as well as explanations of differences in and histories of societal organization and processes (Peet 1985, pp. 328–329).

SEE ALSO *Determinism; Determinism, Biological; Determinism, Cultural; Determinism, Technological*

BIBLIOGRAPHY

Boas, Franz, ed. 1938. *General Anthropology.* New York: D.C. Heath.

Carnoy, Martin. 1974. *Education as Cultural Imperialism.* New York: David McKay.

Colby, Charles C. 1933. Ellen Churchill Semple. *Annals of the Association of American Geographers* 23 (4): 229–240.

Darwin, Charles. [1859] 1979. *On the Origin of Species by Means of Natural Selection, or the Preservation of Favoured Races in the Struggle for Life.* New York: Gramercy Books.

Diamond, Jared. 1997. *Guns, Germs, and Steel: The Fate of Human Societies.* New York: W. W. Norton.

Frenkel, Stephen. 1992. Geography, Empire, and Environmental Determinism. *Geographical Review* 82 (2): 143–153.

Hofstadter, Richard. 1955. *Social Darwinism in American Thought.* Rev. ed. Boston: Beacon Press.

Huntington, Ellsworth. [1924] 2003. *Character of Races: Influenced by Physical Environment Natural Selection and Historical Development (Anti-movements in America).* Whitefish, MT: Kessinger Publishers.

Huntington, Ellsworth. 1924. *Mainsprings of Civilization.* New York: John Wiley and Sons.

Huntington, Ellsworth. 1934. *Principles of Human Geography.* 4th ed. New York: John Wiley and Sons.

Lewthwaite, Gordon. 1966. Environmentalism and Determinism: A Search for Clarification. *Annals of the Association of American Geographers* 56 (1): 1–23.

Peet, Richard. 1985. The Social Origins of Environmental Determinism. *Annals of the Association of American Geographers* 75 (3): 309–333.

Semple, Ellen Churchill. 1903. *American History and Its Geographic Conditions.* New York: H. Holt and Company.

Semple, Ellen Churchill. 1911. *Influences of Geographic Environment.* New York: Russell and Russell.

Taylor, Griffith. 1927. *Environment and Race: A Study of the Evolution, Migration, Settlement, and Status of the Races of Man.* London: Oxford University Press.

Taylor, Griffith. 1942. Environment, Village, and City: A Genetic Approach to Urban Geography with Some Reference to Possibilism. *Annals of the Association of the American Geographers* 32 (1): 1–67.

Wallace, Walter L. 1988. Toward a Disciplinary Matrix in Sociology. In *The Handbook of Sociology*, ed. Neil J. Smelser, 23–86. Beverly Hills, CA: Sage Publications.

John K. Thomas

DETERMINISM, GENETIC

Genetic determinism is the notion that an individual's genetic makeup equates to behavioral destiny. This definition is slightly different from one stating that all human beings have the same genetic blueprint. The classic textbook *Gray's Anatomy* illustrates and, indeed, medical scientists rely for treatment upon, a genetically determined, universal description of the human body. All normally developed humans have eyes for seeing, hearts for pumping blood, and so on, as specified by this genetic blueprint.

Behavioral genetic determinism is an extreme form of nativism that emphasizes the innateness of knowledge. Historically, nativism has been contrasted with empiricism, which emphasizes the environment as the source of knowledge, learning, and behavior. A modern doctrine of empiricism is found in British philosophy of the 1700s and 1800s, which argued that humans are born with no innate mental content, equating the mind to a blank slate for experience to write upon. Modern nativism did not emerge until Charles Darwin (1809–1882) proposed in 1859 that, through natural selection, humans are descended from other life forms. In the social sciences, initial support for nativism was provided by William James (1842–1910), who argued that humans have more instincts than animals, thus shattering the dichotomy between instinct and reason. At that time it was believed that animals were instinctive and unintelligent, whereas humans were rational and intelligent. The pendulum swung back to empiricism when behaviorism, a new paradigm in psychology, emerged and endorsed domain-general learning through simple conditioning procedures as the source of all knowledge. Psychology, anthropology, and sociology endorsed this position for much of the twentieth century.

Contrasting genetically determined versus environmentally determined explanations of behavior is analogous to the long-standing debate that incorrectly pits nature (genes, instincts, adaptations, biology) against nurture (environment, experience, general learning mechanisms, culture). Anthropologist Edward Hagen (2005) argues, however, that nature is a product of nurture, and that nurture is a product of nature. To illustrate this statement, one must examine evolution through natural selection. Hagen compares natural selection to a learning algorithm that uses information from the environment to select gene combinations that aid in reproduction. These gene combinations are stored in the genome as this learned information forms the basis of an adaptation. Because adaptations are the product of environmental influences, and are designed by natural selection over evolutionary history, it would be uninformed to discuss genes or adaptations without knowledge of the context in which they evolved. In this way, nature is a product of nurture.

At the same time, nurture is a product of nature. It is unlikely that a truly blank-slate version of the mind would be able to learn anything from the environment. This was the nativist argument advanced by anthropologist John Tooby and psychologist Leda Cosmides (1992) regarding the functional design of the mind. Tooby and Cosmides argued that learning and behavior depend on content-dependent information processing mechanisms and that once a specialized psychological architecture is in place, adaptive challenges can be met with ease. All humans have a universal, species-typical mind, in the same way that all humans have a universal, species-typical physical anatomy.

One way to illustrate this universal architecture is to examine fear. In an experiment designed by psychologist Susan Mineka and colleagues (1980), infant rhesus monkeys were exposed to one of two videotaped scenarios, one depicting a monkey reacting in terror to a snake, the other depicting a monkey reacting in terror to flowers. Monkeys that viewed the tape showing the reaction to a snake quickly acquired a fear of snakes, but monkeys that viewed the tape showing the same reaction to flowers did not acquire a fear of flowers. It appears that humans also are prepared to learn quickly which features in the environment are threatening and ignore those features that are not. Common phobias in humans include spiders, darkness, and snakes, all of which were adaptive threats in ancestral environments. Learning is not an explanation of behavior, but behavior requiring explanation. The explanation lies in an evolved psychology and the specific problems this psychology has been designed to solve.

Disgust also provides an example of the nature/nurture interaction. Psychologist Paul Ekman (1980) demonstrated that disgust is an emotion that is experienced universally, and the facial expression showing disgust is a reaction that is recognized universally by others. Paul Rozin and April Fallon (1987) hypothesized that disgust is a human adaptation designed to prevent parasites and disease from entering the body. Rotten meat is disgusting to all humans because if consumed it would probably lead to illness. Many species of flies, however, find rotten meat appealing because flies have different evolved mechanisms. Not all cues are as obvious to the human senses as rotten meat, however. With thousands of potentially edible fruits and plants, it would have been beneficial to use the reactions of others when deciding what to eat, rather than relying on a trial-and-error learning system. If a harmful substance is sensed, the body will expel and withdraw from the substance and the disgust face will be made. Other individuals will benefit from this disgust reaction only if they are equipped to pair the disgust face to the disgusting substance, and learn to avoid it. Again, learning is guided by a universal psychological architecture and explained according to the adaptive challenges it has been designed to solve.

If all humans have the same design of the mind, does that mean human behavior is genetically determined? Adaptations have a genetic basis. However, Hagen argues that because the mind contains many adaptations, all of which respond to cues in the environment, the mind could encompass an enormous number of states with an enormous number of behavioral outcomes. Because humans have an evolved fear of snakes does not mean that everyone is destined to fear all snakes in all situations. Many people have an affinity for snakes, even allowing them into their home as pets. Adaptations do not limit behavior, but instead enable behavior and create behavioral flexibility because a larger set of adaptations can respond with a greater array of behavioral outcomes. Insights from biology, cognitive science, ecology, anthropology, and psychology have been combined to examine genes from an adaptationist perspective in the emerging discipline of evolutionary psychology. Strict genetic determinism is rejected in favor of an account of human behavior that includes both genetic and environmental influences.

SEE ALSO *Determinism; Determinism, Reciprocal; Evolutionary Psychology; Nature vs. Nurture; Phenotype*

BIBLIOGRAPHY

Darwin, Charles. 1859. *On the Origin of Species.* London: Murray.

Ekman, Paul. 1980. *The Face of Man: Expressions of Universal Emotions in a New Guinea Village.* New York: Garland STPM.

Hagen, Edward. 2005. Controversial Issues in Evolutionary Psychology. In *The Handbook of Evolutionary Psychology*, ed. David Buss, 145–173. Hoboken, NJ: Wiley.

James, William. 1890. *The Principles of Psychology.* New York: Henry Holt.

Mineka, Susan, Richard Keir, and Veda Price. 1980. Fear of Snakes in Wild- and Laboratory-reared Rhesus Monkeys *(Macaca mulatta). Animal Learning and Behavior* 8: 653–663.

Rozin, Paul, and April E. Fallon. 1987. A Perspective on Disgust. *Psychological Review* 94: 23–41.

Tooby, John, and Leda Cosmides. 1992. The Psychological Foundations of Culture. In *The Adapted Mind: Evolutionary Psychology and the Generation of Culture*, ed. Jerome H. Barkow, Leda Cosmides, and John Tooby, 19–136. New York: Oxford University Press.

Lucas D. Schipper
Todd K. Shackelford

DETERMINISM, NONADDITIVE

The principle of *nonadditive determinism* derives from the literature on integrative, multilevel analyses, which extend across levels of organization (e.g., psychological, physiological, cellular) and analysis (e.g., behavioral, neurophysiological, molecular). The principle of nonadditive determinism specifies that properties of the whole are not always readily predictable from the properties of the parts (see Cacioppo and Berntson 1992). Some properties of crystals (e.g., table salt) cannot be predicted from the characteristics of the individual elements (sodium and chloride) in isolation. Those properties become known only when the elements are found in association or interaction with others. A behavioral example comes from the considerable individual differences that are apparent in the effects of drugs. Some individuals are more affected by, and at greater risk for addiction to, cocaine or other drugs of abuse. Similarly, studies with primates have shown that some monkeys work harder and self-administer more cocaine than others (Morgan et al. 2002). This is not mere random variation, but relates to the animal's social status—submissive animals show higher levels of cocaine self-administration than dominant animals. This is now understood to be attributable to reciprocal interactions between social dominance, brain dopamine function, and drug reward processes. The important point is that social status, which serves as the informative and organizing construct in this literature, could not be determined in the absence of behavioral measures in a social context.

Even if the properties of, for example, Beethoven's Ninth Symphony can be fully specified through reference to lower-level physical characteristics (i.e., time-varying frequencies), the composition's aesthetic features may be more readily apparent or appreciated through higher-level auditory perception. This presence of higher-level aesthetic processes defines a functional quality of the acoustic signals that might otherwise escape recognition. It also serves to focus attention on the important interactions among levels of organization and analysis that may ultimately contribute to the development of a science of aesthetics.

Reciprocal determinism is a related construct. Reciprocal determinism is the mutual back-and-forth interaction among distinct levels of organization (e.g., behavioral and cellular) that requires consideration of both levels for a comprehensive understanding of either. Hormones, for example, can have notable psychological effects, but it is also the case that psychological variables can powerfully impact hormone levels. It is this reciprocal back-and-forth interaction among levels that often underlies nonadditive determinism, in which the whole can seem to be more than the sum of its parts.

Nonadditive determinism is not inconsistent with genetic determinism. Drug administration is subject to potent *genetic determinants*, related to dopamine functions as well as a range of other heritable characteristics, including behavioral variables that contribute to dominance status. Rather, nonadditive determinism is orthogonal to genetic determinism—that is, the two operate independently but simultaneously, emphasizing the multiple levels of organization that interact in the manifestations of genetic (as well as environmental) determinants. Genetic determinism focuses on the gene and gene products, whereas nonadditive determinism emphasizes the structural and functional architectures through which genetic and environmental factors determine outcomes and behaviors.

SEE ALSO *Neuroscience, Social*

BIBLIOGRAPHY

Anderson, N. B. 1998. Levels of Analysis in Health Science: A Framework for Integrating Sociobehavioral and Biomedical Research. *Annals of the New York Academy of Science* 840 (1): 563–576.

Cacioppo, John T., and Gary G. Berntson. 1992. Social Psychological Contributions to the Decade of the Brain: Doctrine of Multilevel Analysis. *American Psychologist* 47 (8): 1019–1028.

Cacioppo, John T., Gary G. Berntson, John F. Sheridan, and Martha K. McClintock. 2000. Multi-Level Integrative Analyses of Human Behavior: The Complementing Nature of Social and Biological Approaches. *Psychological Bulletin* 126 (6): 829–843.

Morgan, Drake, et al. 2002. Social Dominance in Monkeys: Dopamine D2 Receptors and Cocaine Self-Administration. *Nature Neuroscience* 5 (2): 169–174.

Gary G. Berntson
John T. Cacioppo

DETERMINISM, RECIPROCAL

In 1986 the psychologist Albert Bandura put forth a social cognitive theory of human behavior in which human functioning is viewed as the product of a dynamic interplay between personal, behavioral, and environmental influences. This interplay is the foundation of reciprocal determinism, the view that (a) personal factors, such as habits of thinking, emotions, and biological characteristics, (b) human behavior, and (c) environmental forces influence each other reciprocally.

This reciprocal nature of the causes of human functioning makes it possible to direct attention at people's personal, environmental, or behavioral factors. In school, for example, teachers can foster the competence and confidence of the students in their care by improving their students' emotional states and by correcting their faulty self-beliefs and habits of thinking (personal factors), enhancing students' academic skills and self-regulatory practices (behavior), and altering the school and classroom structures that may work to undermine student success (the environment).

Social cognitive theory stands in contrast to views of human functioning that overemphasize the role that environmental factors play in the development of human behavior. Behaviorist theories, for example, show little interest in self-processes because theorists assume that human behavior is caused by external forces. Inner processes, which are viewed as transmitting rather than causing behavior, are dismissed as a redundant factor in the cause and effect workings of behavior. For Bandura, people make sense of their psychological processes by looking into their own conscious mind.

Similarly, social cognitive theory differs from views of human functioning that overemphasize the influence of biological factors. Although it acknowledges the influence of evolutionary factors in human adaptation, the theory rejects the type of evolutionism that views human behavior as the product of evolved biology. Instead, reciprocal determinism posits a bidirectional influence between evolutionary pressures and human development such that individuals create increasingly complex social and technological innovations that in turn create new selection pressures for adaptiveness. These new selection pressures result in the evolution of specialized biological systems for functional consciousness, thought, language, and symbolic communication. It is this bidirectional influence that is responsible for the remarkable intercultural and intracultural diversity evident on the planet.

Rooted within Bandura's conception of reciprocal determinism is the understanding that individuals are imbued with the personal factors that define what it is to be human. Primary among these are the capabilities to symbolize, plan alternative strategies (forethought), learn through vicarious experience, self-regulate, and self-reflect. These capabilities provide human beings with the cognitive means by which they are influential in determining their own destiny. The capability that is most distinctly human is that of self-reflection, for it is through self-reflection that people make sense of their experiences, explore their own cognitions and self-beliefs, engage in self-evaluation, and alter their thinking and behavior accordingly. Through self-reflection people also assess their own capabilities. These self-efficacy beliefs provide the foundation for human motivation, well-being, and personal accomplishment because unless people believe that their actions can produce the outcomes they desire, they have little incentive to act or to persevere in the face of difficulties.

SEE ALSO *Bandura, Albert; Self-Efficacy*

BIBLIOGRAPHY

Bandura, Albert. 1978. The Self System in Reciprocal Determinism. *American Psychologist* 33: 344–358.

Bandura, Albert. 1982. Temporal Dynamics and Decomposition of Reciprocal Determinism. *Psychological Review* 90: 166–170.

Bandura, Albert. 1985. Reciprocal Determinism. In *Advances in Social Learning Theory*, ed. S. Sukemune. Tokyo: Kaneko-shoho.

Bandura, Albert. 1986. *Social Foundations of Thought and Action: A Social Cognitive Theory.* Englewood Cliffs, NJ: Prentice-Hall.

Frank Pajares

DETERMINISM, TECHNOLOGICAL

From a social-science perspective, technological determinism can be an exasperating concept. Its underlying premise—that technological invention and development are independent causal factors driving change in human history—reduces individuals, society, and culture to mere epiphenomena of a basic, autonomous force. Although the concept suggests that history is overdetermined, at least in its extreme form, the simplicity, tangibility, and rhetorical power of the central argument explains its popular impact. Yet the academic debate also remains lively, as the concept addresses fundamental questions about modern society.

In *Does Technology Drive History?* (1994), a key text tackling the concept, Merritt Smith and Leo Marx place the various approaches to technological determinism along a spectrum between the extremes of hard and soft determinism. Hard determinists assign agency—the power to effect change autonomously—to technology itself, and to the institutions and structures built to facilitate it. Soft determinists still treat technology as a locus of historical agency—operating within a complex economic, political, and sociocultural matrix—but, crucially, not as an *autonomous* locus.

Merritt Smith also focuses on three individuals whose work, he argues, is central to the debate: Lewis Mumford, Jacques Ellul, and Langdon Winner. Of the three, Ellul's

position is perhaps the "hardest." His characterization of "technological society" is almost as totalizing as it is pessimistic. It sees individual personal liberty as nearly impossible in the face of a fundamentally organized, rationalized, and autonomous world of machines, technological devices, and interlocking institutions and organizations created around them. Mumford and Winner both map out broadly similar scenarios for the emerging technological order, though both take "softer" approaches, finding arguments for some sort of human or cultural agency (albeit limited) within the dominant structure provided by technology. Add in Robert Heilbroner's classic essay on technology's central role in society's historical development, "Do Machines Make History?" (1994), and Raymond Williams's more humanistic call for technology to be treated as a symptom, rather than a cause, of social change, *Television: Technology and Cultural Form* (1989), and the stage for the debate was set. And if participants rarely pushed their arguments to the extremes, they nevertheless have slugged it out over the extent to which technology determines, or is determined by, societal change.

The debate has flourished through works examining the role of technologies as varied as weaponry, agricultural implements, and industrial automation in effecting social change. A particularly fruitful topic of debate has been over the role of new information and communication technologies in society, which is closely related to economic studies of how post-Fordism and postindustrial changes have affected Western economies, particularly since the 1970s. The trend since the 1990s has been toward a harder approach to technological determinism under the guise of information theory. The rise of the Internet and satellite communication as a global force has brought back into vogue, both at the academic level and in the popular imagination, the writings of Marshall McLuhan, perhaps one of the most deterministic of all scholars. More recent academic expositions by Manuel Castells and others on the power of the Internet-driven, global network society have built on the ground laid by McLuhan, Daniel Bell, Alvin Toffler, Howard Rheingold, and even Jean Baudrillard, all of whom have enjoyed a significant popular following, as well as scholarly fame.

SEE ALSO *Change, Technological; Forces of Production*

BIBLIOGRAPHY

Heilbroner, Robert L. 1994. Do Machines Make History? In *Does Technology Drive History? The Dilemma of Technological Determinism*, ed. Merritt R. Smith and Leo Marx. Cambridge, MA: MIT Press.

Smith, Merritt R., and Leo Marx, eds. 1994. *Does Technology Drive History? The Dilemma of Technological Determinism.* Cambridge, MA: MIT Press.

Williams, Raymond. 1989. *Television: Technology and Cultural Form*. London: Routledge.

Douglas Bicket

DETERRENCE

Deterrence is a military strategy in which one actor attempts to prevent an action by another actor by means of threatening punishment if the action is undertaken. Deterrence is, in essence, a threat to use force in response to a specific behavior. While deterrence is an inherently defensive strategy, it does not involve defense; that is, the deterring party does not actively protect its assets or try to prevent its opponent from taking the action, but rather threatens the use of violence to convince the opponent not to act in the first place.

THEORETICAL UNDERPINNINGS

Deterrence can best be understood with reference to the "3 Cs": capability, communication, and credibility. Any deterrent threat must meet all three criteria to succeed. Capability refers to whether the actor issuing the deterrent threat is capable of carrying out the threat. Thus, the ability to successfully deter depends to some degree on the power of the deterring actor. Capability is, generally, the most straightforward category, as states typically match deterrent threats to their extant military capabilities. States can, however, dissemble by threatening actions requiring capabilities that they do not have, or by claiming capabilities that they do not possess, though subterfuge and secrecy tend to undermine the efficacy of a deterrent threat.

In order for deterrence to work, a state must communicate its threats. If a state does not know that an action is proscribed, it cannot be deterred from taking that action. Communication is therefore essential if states are to know what actions they are not supposed to take, as well as what will happen if the action is taken. Thus, good lines of communication are crucial. The "hot line" between the Soviet Union and the United States during the cold war served this function well. With deterrence, the goal is to avoid armed conflict and communication is vital to create boundaries and reveal expectations.

The final C, credibility, is perhaps the most difficult criterion to meet. Deterrence is, in a sense, a fundamentally irrational action, because the threat is carried out after the violation occurs. Once the forbidden action is taken, it does not necessarily make sense to carry out the threat that was intended to deter that action in the first place. This is similar to the economic theory of "sunk costs," in which costs that have already been incurred should not be included in decisions about future behaviors. States have to work very hard at establishing their credibility, especially in situations of extended deterrence (explained below), and they often try to "tie their hands" meaning the decision to carry out the deterrent threat is made automatically. During the cold war, the U.S. soldiers stationed in West Germany had no chance of repelling a Soviet invasion of Western Europe. Instead, the troops served as a "tripwire," ensuring Americans would be killed in any Soviet invasion and increasing the odds that the U.S. would come to the defense of Western Europe, making more credible the American deterrent threat.

TYPES OF DETERRENCE

There are two fundamental types of deterrence: central and extended. Central deterrence occurs when a state attempts to deter attacks against itself, its nationals, or other intrinsic assets. In extended deterrence, a state attempts to prevent attacks against an ally or another third party. Credibility is usually easier to establish with central deterrence, because the need to develop a reputation for protecting one's own assets is vital to the strength of a state. Credibility is much more difficult to build in extended deterrence, because it is harder for the deterring state to risk war to protect an ally.

Deterrence can also be broken down into two strategic categories: denial and punishment. In a denial strategy, also known as counterforce deterrence, the military deterrence is targeted at the enemy's military and political assets, such as military bases, command and control assets, and governmental facilities. The purpose of the deterrent is, therefore, to prevent the enemy from achieving whatever goal it seeks with the use of force. If the opponent correctly reads the deterrent threat as sufficiently reducing the likelihood of obtaining the desired outcome, then the action will not be taken and deterrence will succeed. Flexible response, discussed below, is an example of denial strategy.

In punishment, or countervalue, deterrence, the deterrent threat is targeted at the enemy's "soft" targets, such as population centers or industrial capabilities. The aim of punishment deterrence is to threaten such a high cost to the fabric of the opponent's society that the action in question will no longer be worth the cost. Both massive retaliation and mutual assured destruction are illustrations of punishment strategies.

DETERRENCE STRATEGIES

While deterrence can be based on both nuclear and conventional forces, deterrence strategy can best be demonstrated by examining the evolution of U.S. nuclear strategy over time. The first formulation of nuclear deterrence was "massive retaliation," a punishment strategy created by John Foster Dulles, the U.S. secretary of state under President Dwight Eisenhower. Here, the United States reserved the right to respond to any military provocation with nuclear weapons, and particularly with much greater force than the original attack. The United States was thus relying on its superior nuclear forces to deter the numerically superior Soviet Union from invading Western Europe. The main problem was the inability to deal with minor threats. As the Soviet nuclear arsenal became more capable of matching that of the United States, massive retaliation was replaced, under the Kennedy Administration, with "flexible response," a denial strategy that created a menu of responses that could be tailored to a specific action. The intent was to make the threatened use of nuclear weapons more credible. However, it was determined that any use of nuclear weapons could escalate into large-scale nuclear exchanges, and flexible response was discarded and replaced with "mutual assured destruction" or MAD. This was a punishment strategy that relied on the ability of both nations to completely destroy each other.

Deterrence is a critical part of the strategic arsenal of countries because all nations usually seek to avoid armed conflict and war. The need to maintain a strong deterrent posture can also inhibit states from achieving other political goals. For example, there was great resistance to the Israeli withdrawals from Lebanon in 2000 and from Gaza in 2005 because of fears that these actions would undermine Israeli deterrence capabilities. However, the years since 1950 have been something of a triumph for deterrence theory, and for nuclear deterrence in particular, as a conflict between the major powers has been avoided.

SEE ALSO *Deterrence, Mutual; Military; Violence*

BIBLIOGRAPHY

Freedman, Lawrence. 2004. *Deterrence*. Cambridge, U.K.: Polity Press.

Sagan, Scott, and Kenneth Waltz. 1995. *The Spread of Nuclear Weapons: A Debate*. New York: W.W. Norton.

Schelling, Thomas. 1966. *Arms and Influence*. New Haven, CT: Yale University Press.

Seth Weinberger

DETERRENCE, MUTUAL

The concept of deterrence implies that, through threats of raising potential costs through means such as attack or retaliation, a party to a dispute can dissuade an opponent from undertaking an undesired action, such as starting a war. It is difficult to know when an opponent is "deterred," since one must determine whether the party in question ever actually intended to act and also whether the adversary's threat dissuaded them. Under *mutual deterrence*, two or more parties simultaneously deter each other, a process even more complicated to verify.

Mutuality implies that both parties' threats raise such negative consequences that neither party takes action. Each party must possess both sufficient resolve and capabilities to make threats credible; costs must outweigh any advantages gained by aggressive action.

Deterrence theory stems from the longstanding international relations theory of the *balance of power*, a much-debated notion that nations try to negate each other's power advantages by strengthening their own forces and joining offsetting alliances. War supposedly can be averted through a balance of forces, though World War I (1914–1918) and other wars have broken out between powers supposedly engaged in such balances.

The post-1945 advent of mass destructive weapons and the cold war raised the possibility of a "balance of terror" between nuclear-armed alliances. Implicit was the threat that if one side struck with nuclear weapons, the other side would retaliate. Thus both sides would refrain from attack out of mutual fear of destruction. It is debatable whether nuclear standoff or more conventional power and interest calculations preserved the tense thirty-five-year peace between the United States and the Soviet Union.

Mutual deterrence thus took the form of a cold war doctrine of *mutually assured destruction*. In this remarkable and costly initiative, both Washington, D.C., and Moscow agreed to "harden" their retaliatory nuclear missile forces in impregnable underground silos and submarines at sea to assure that if one side launched a nuclear "first strike," the other side would surely be able and willing to respond, inflicting unacceptable damage on the initiator. *Stable deterrence* implied that neither side should do anything—for example, defend its cities—to upset the psychological assurance of effective retaliation.

Game theory became an integral part of the strategic thought accompanying these policies. Scenarios such as the prisoner's dilemma and chicken games denoted costs and benefits of either collaborating or "defecting" from peaceful strategies. Temptations to build up arms and attack would inspire similar behavior in the opponent; in seeking security through armament, both sides might become less rather than more secure (the so-called security dilemma).

Deterrence in today's post-cold war world is still premised on assumptions that nuclear-armed adversaries, such as India and Pakistan, are restrained from attack by the possibility of unacceptable damage in return. No such restraint supposedly applies where only one side is heavily armed. The logic or illogic of unilateral or mutual deterrence remains puzzling, for example, as big powers attempt to dissuade smaller powers and nonstate or "terrorist" organizations from initiating violence. As actors adopt unorthodox forms of violence (e.g., personnel bombings and sabotage), it is not clear when political and social costs inflicted by military reprisals or other means are sufficient to deter further violence.

SEE ALSO *Cold War; Deterrence; Weaponry, Nuclear; World War II*

BIBLIOGRAPHY

Cimbala, Stephen. 1998. *The Past and Future of Nuclear Deterrence.* Westport, CT: Praeger.

Jervis, Robert. 1978. *Deterrence Theory Revisited.* Los Angeles: University of California, Center for Arms Control and International Security.

Morgan, Patrick. 2003. *Deterrence Now.* Cambridge, U.K.: Cambridge University Press.

Zagare, Frank C. 1987. *The Dynamics of Deterrence.* Chicago: University of Chicago Press.

Frederic Pearson

DEVALUATION, CURRENCY

SEE *Currency Devaluation and Revaluation.*

DEVELOPING COUNTRIES

Developing countries—generally referring to the countries of Africa, Asia, and Latin America—is a term that was inspired by Walt Whitman Rostow's classic work, *The Stages of Economic Growth: A Non-Communist Manifesto* (1960). Rostow argued that all countries go through a series of stages of economic development from "underdeveloped" to "developed"; that the United States, Western Europe, and Japan had reached the "highest stage" or "developed-country" status; and that those countries that were not mature, developed capitalist countries were in the process of "developing" and moving through the required stages.

A variety of terms have been used to refer to these "developing" countries. These include *less-developed countries, underdeveloped countries, undeveloped countries, backward countries, Third World countries,* and *newly industrializing countries.* Except for *Third World,* which was advanced in the late 1960s and early 1970s to refer affirmatively to countries that were politically independent of the United States and the Soviet Union, these terms are more-or-less pejorative. *Newly industrializing* is more specific than the other terms, in that it refers to a limited number of countries that have begun industrializing since the 1970s.

Implicit in the term *developing countries* is the suggestion that things will improve over (some unforeseeable period of) time. However, this terminology has been used to hide the exploitation and oppression of people in the so-called developing countries—exploitation by corporations headquartered in the developed countries, by dictators installed or supported by the U.S. government or its allies, or by the governments and militaries of the developing countries themselves.

As hinted at by its subtitle, Rostow's work was designed to support the U.S. imperial project and aimed not only to bypass but to supersede the Communist concept of *imperialism.* To Rostow—and to the U.S. government, for which he later worked—the Communist challenge in Southeast Asia was a serious one, especially because the region was deemed of strategic importance. Rostow argued that the lot of poor, exploited, and mistreated peasants in the developing countries would get better over time, whereas the Communists maintained that things could not improve under capitalism—that is, that revolution, not acquiescence based on "hope," was the only path to a better life.

The upper echelon of the U.S. government saw its post–World War II (1939–1945) project to achieve political, economic, military, and cultural hegemony over the countries of the world—at least those outside of the Soviet Empire—as being threatened by various revolutionary struggles in the developing countries. In response, the United States designed a global strategy of counterinsurgency to undercut indigenous struggles to gain independence (Post 1990, pp. 1–41). Along with this went various forms of ideology and propaganda, a key component of which was the theory of *modernization,* of which Rostow was the primary proponent.

CRITICAL APPROACHES

One of the first critical thinkers to analyze the true situation of the developing countries was Raúl Prebisch of the Economic Commission for Latin America, who argued that the relationship between developed and developing countries was exploitive. This perspective was further developed by Andre Gunder Frank, who introduced the concept of *dependent development.* According to Frank, development strategies promoted by the wealthy countries were designed to ensure that the "developing" countries remained in a subordinate position.

A more systemic and historical perspective was proposed by Immanuel Wallerstein (1974, 1980, 1989). Wallerstein's *world-system theory* holds that beginning in the sixteenth century, capitalists backed by "strong states" spread outward from Western Europe to control the world, obtaining cheap labor and raw materials through trade relationships that benefited those in the European—and later U.S.—"core" countries. Wallerstein posits three levels of economic development represented by concentric "rings," moving from the advanced "core" countries to peripheral countries, with the "semi-periphery" located in between.

Despite having generated extensive research, Wallerstein's conceptualization has a critical weakness: While it is quite perceptive, it is a static model. Once a country gets "located" in one of the three "rings," world-system theory cannot explain how it can move from one ring to another. The case of South Korea is perhaps the most obvious example of a transition world-system theory cannot explain. Wallerstein's model has other problems as well. Historical evidence does not support the existence of a singular world-system—at least before 1989. In addition, Wallerstein's conception is overly economistic.

A much more interesting approach is that of Jan Nederveen Pieterse (1989). Nederveen Pieterse, who unfortunately did not have the "marketing" acumen of Wallerstein, never named his conceptualization. Yet his book *Empire and Emancipation: Power and Liberation on a World Scale* (1989) is the best explanation to date of relations between the European and, later, American nation-states and those referred to as *developing countries*. Nederveen Pieterse argues that to understand European global domination, one must begin by returning to the Crusades, out of which, he maintains, modern "Europe" developed. He carefully considers the processes of European development, taking a poststructural, processural approach instead of a static one. Nederveen Pieterse sees the domination of Europe and the United States as being imperialistic, but unlike Marxists, he does not give primacy to economics: He recognizes imperialism as (1) being a process of domination; (2) being characterized by interaction between economics and politics; and (3) always harming the people in the dominated countries. Interestingly, Nederveen Pieterse does not confine his understanding of imperialism to the nation-state level. Instead, he argues that imperialism is the domination of one political community over another, encompassing not only states, but also supra-states (e.g., the United Nations), subnational communities, and even organizations, such as the AFL-CIO.

Nederveen Pieterse is not satisfied, however, with focusing his analysis on domination alone; he argues that one must also analyze and theorize historical resistance to domination. Thus, he recognizes the Haitian Revolution and its key role in world history, the struggles of Native Americans against Euro-American settlers, and other efforts to resist domination.

NEOCOLONIALISM AND POSTCOLONIALISM

With only a few exceptions, such as Ethiopia, Iran, and Thailand (formerly Siam), most of the world's developing countries were formerly colonies. While formal colonization has largely ended, either through the granting of independence or through wars of liberation, many formerly colonized countries have continued their earlier political-economic relationships with their former colonial master. The reason for this is easy to understand: Colonization involved structuring the economy of the colonized country to serve the needs of the colonizing country and its corporations. Local administrators trained during the colonial period know little else, and therefore the old relationships have continued, only under new leadership (the color of the faces is usually all that has been apparently changed, but usually violence against formerly colonized peoples has been drastically reduced, if not ended). This continuation of earlier colonial political-economic relations is generally referred to as *neocolonialism*. Neocolonial relationships have been encouraged by both the International Monetary Fund (IMF) and the World Bank. Both have promoted neoliberal development programs. This neoliberal economic model has resulted in what Kim Scipes's study of the Philippines from 1962 to 1999 calls "detrimental development" (Scipes 1999).

Perhaps the most interesting phenomena of the late 1990s and early 2000s is the development of *postcolonial* states. These are states that have decided to develop their respective economies in ways that challenge the hegemony of the U.S.-controlled IMF and World Bank. Great progress has been made by several postcolonial countries, including South Korea, which went from the periphery to the core (using Wallerstein's terminology) in less than thirty years. Venezuela, a major oil-producer, is also currently showing success at developing its economy independently.

Postcolonial development models differ widely. South Korea's rapid industrialization, as impressive as it was, was in large part achieved through extreme exploitation of young women. Venezuela, on the other hand, has set a slower pace of development, and the government of President Hugo Chavez is trying to find ways to improve the lives of Venezuela's people through diverting some of the country's oil profits into social programs. How far

Venezuela can go in meeting the needs of the people, especially in light of U.S. intervention in its domestic affairs, remains to be seen. However, Venezuela's mobilization of large masses of the population to address their own problems—that is, development from "below," as opposed to the imposition of state "plans" from above—is an exciting process that holds out the promise of development without oppression.

SEE ALSO *Chavez, Hugo; Colonialism; Decolonization; Dependency; Development; Development Economics; Development in Sociology; Development, Institutional; Development, Rural; Economic Growth; Exploitation; Frank, Andre Gunder; Gender and Development; Globalization, Social and Economic Aspects of; Haitian Revolution; Health in Developing Countries; Imperialism; Industrialization; Inequality, Income; Inequality, Political; Inequality, Wealth; Labor Law; Migration, Rural to Urban; Modernization; North and South, The (Global); Poverty; Prebisch, Raúl; Privatization; Stages of Economic Growth; Third World; Wallerstein, Immanuel; Washington Consensus; World-System*

BIBLIOGRAPHY

Nederveen Pieterse, Jan P. 1989. *Empire and Emancipation: Power and Liberation on a World Scale.* New York: Praeger.

Post, Ken. 1990. *The Failure of Counter-Insurgency in the South.* Vol. 4 of *Revolution, Socialism, and Nationalism in Viet Nam.* Belmont, CA: Wadsworth Publishing Company.

Rostow, W. W. 1960. *The Stages of Economic Growth: A Non-Communist Manifesto.* Cambridge, U.K.: Cambridge University Press.

Scipes, Kim. 1999. Global Economic Crisis, Neoliberal Solutions, and the Philippines. *Monthly Review* 51 (7): 1–14.

Wallerstein, Immanuel. 1974, 1980, 1989. *The Modern World-System.* 3 vols. San Diego, CA: Academic Press.

Kim Scipes

DEVELOPMENT

Development theory is largely a product of post–World War II (1939–1945) thinking in the social sciences and international policy studies. The key intellectual challenges for development theory are these: What are the causes of economic transformation in human societies? What are some of the policies through which governments can stimulate the processes of economic growth? These questions have been the subject of inquiry within classical political economy for several centuries, and interest in the determinants of growth and modernization has

been part of economic theory since its beginnings. But modern development theory took its impulse from global developments following World War II—the needs of reconstruction of Europe and Japan following World War II; the creation of international monetary and trading regimes to facilitate international economic interaction; the circumstances that followed from the dissolution of European colonies in Asia, Africa, and Latin America; growing attention to the persistence of poverty in the developing world; and focus in the 1990s on the phenomena of globalization.

The concept of development has encompassed several separate ideas in the past sixty years: the idea of modernization of economic and social institutions, the idea of sustained economic growth within a national economy, the idea of the continuing improvement of the material well-being of the earth's human population, the idea of more extensive utilization of the world's resources, and the idea of the replacement of "traditional" institutions and values with "modern" successors. Some of the large questions that have guided development theory include these: What are the features of society that can be characterized as "modern"? What causes a society to undergo sustained "modernization" and sustained economic growth? What institutional features are important causes in economic development? What steps can governments or other major institutions take to stimulate development? What is the significance of the specific features of western European economic development since 1600? Are there alternative pathways through which "modernization," growth, and improvement of human well-being can occur? Are there cultural assumptions that are made in valorizing development, growth, and modernization over tradition, moderate consumption, and stable cultural practices? How can one best define the goals of development in terms of human well-being? How should considerations having to do with equality, equity, and justice be incorporated into analysis and policy of development?

Development theory has taken shape through efforts in several areas of the social sciences: economics (theories of efficient markets, trade, and income distribution); sociology (research on concrete processes of social change in different parts of the world); anthropology (research on the values and practices of a range of non-Western cultures); political science (research on the institutions and interests that drive international economic policy); history (research on the dynamic circumstances that created modern national and international economic institutions); and critical social science (focus on features of inequality, power, and exploitation that have often characterized international economic institutions). Each of these strands captures something important about the historical experience of parts of the modern world, and yet they fall short of a full and general approach to the topic of development. Development theory is an expansive, eclectic, and interdisciplinary field defined by a diverse set of questions and methods—not an exact subdiscipline within economics.

Decolonization and the aftermath of World War II stimulated a wave of academic and policy interest in the dynamics of economic growth and development. President Harry Truman highlighted the crucial importance of addressing global issues of poverty and hunger in his 1949 State of the Union address, an emphasis that stimulated new United States and international commitments in support of economic development in the decolonized world. The 1950s witnessed a surge of early development theory, in the hands of such authors as Simon Kuznets, W. Arthur Lewis, and Ben Hoflitz. A central thrust of these efforts was the formulation of economic theories of growth that, it was hoped, could help to guide policy in the economic transformations associated with decolonization. Postwar development theory also provided some of the intellectual foundations for the establishment of postwar international economic institutions such as the World Bank and the International Monetary Fund. Much of this work presupposed the idea that there were distinct stages of economic development, and it focused on the relationship between economic growth and savings as the basis for capital formation. The role of trade in economic development also played a central role in these theories. W. Arthur Lewis's theory of the "dual economy" was particularly prominent as a basis for attempting to understand the economies of the previously colonial world. This model postulates an economy consisting of a "traditional" sector (labor) and a "modern" sector (capital). Lewis postulated that firm owners in the modern sector were profit-maximizing, whereas those in the traditional sector were not, and that there was surplus labor in the traditional sector. So a strategy for growth is to induce a shift of economic activity from the traditional to the modern sector. This approach would increase savings and capital formation, leading to growth and rising incomes. Other economists such as Irma Adelman and Hollis Chenery cast doubt on the stage theory and further broadened the perspective by bringing distribution and welfare into the discussions.

There has been emphasis since the 1960s—sometimes waxing, sometimes waning—on the crucial importance of alleviating poverty in the developing world. Throughout much of its history the World Bank has expressed its adherence to the priority of poverty alleviation. The United Nations Millennium Goals for 2005 place poverty alleviation at the center of the development agenda for the coming fifty years. But even placing a sincere priority on poverty alleviation, there is a wide range of disagreement over the steps that should be taken to achieve this goal.

Several important frameworks of thought have been important in development theory thinking. Neoliberal development theory reflects the folk wisdom of neoclassical economic and political theory. Described as the "Washington Consensus," this approach to development postulates that modern economic development requires free markets, effective systems of law, and highly limited powers of government. The slogan of "Getting the Prices Right" was a rule of thumb for economic institutional reform in countries receiving advice and assistance from international institutions. This school of thought places great importance on free trade within the international economic system. Neoliberal structural adjustment reforms in the 1980s, enforced through International Monetary Fund and World Bank policies, pushed third-world governments toward harsh domestic reforms (currency devaluation, reduction of programs aimed at the poor, elimination of subsidies for rural development, liberalization of trade practices). Critics have argued that these structural adjustment policies have had the effect of further impoverishing the poorest of many developing societies.

Critical of the neoliberal consensus is an influential group of development theorists who emphasize the centrality of human well-being in development theorizing and the crucial role that public policies and expenditures play in successful efforts to improve the well-being of the poor in developing societies. Amartya Sen, Martha Nussbaum, and others argue for placing a nuanced theory of human development grounded in capabilities and functionings at the center of development policy. And they argue for the crucial role that public policy has in creating the human welfare infrastructure that is essential for the successful alleviation of destitution: public health, nutrition, free education, and democratic freedoms. On this view, the narrow conception of the role of the state associated with the neoliberal approach almost inevitably implies further degradation of the conditions of life of the least-well-off in the developing world. A concrete achievement of this approach is the creation and maintenance of the Human Development Index by the United Nations Development Program. This index is designed to provide a measure of economic development that goes beyond measuring growth of per-capita income, and instead focuses on measures that are correlated with quality of life: health, longevity, and educational attainment, for example. Another such measure is the Physical Quality of Life Index.

There have been critical voices within development theory throughout its history. Postwar theories of colonialism emphasize the extractive role that the system of colonial control represented, with a flow of natural resources from periphery to metropole. Dependency theory is the view that the world economy since 1945 has been constructed around a set of institutions that systematically disadvantage the South for the benefit of the North, by structuring production and trade in such a way as to limit economic growth in the third world. The South is integrated into the "modern world system," but on terms that systemically work to the disadvantage of the countries and peoples of the periphery. The Brandt Report (Independent Commission on International Development Issues, 1980) focused attention on the relations between the wealthy North and the impoverished South. This approach emphasizes structural inequalities, systemic institutional disadvantages, patterns of unequal exchange, and resulting uneven development. A different line of critical thought emerges from cultural critics of modernization. Arturo Escobar is a central voice in this body of criticism. This perspective offers a critique of the discourse and presuppositions of development thinking in the West: the presumed primacy of Western values, the unquestioned importance of consumerism, the teleology associated with the concept of "modernization," and other ways in which the values and assumptions of development theory reflect unquestioned ethnocentrism and universalism.

The concept of development incorporates several debatable assumptions. First, it has a tendency towards Eurocentrism. The paradigm of development incorporated in much development theorizing is the experience of western Europe during the Industrial Revolution. Non-European societies that undergo "development" (Japan, Taiwan, and Argentina) are frequently categorized in terms of a baseline comparison to the western European experience. Historical research conducted since the mid-1980s casts doubt on this single-track theory. Asian economic development in the seventeenth century and the twentieth century gives substantial evidence of the availability of alternative pathways of development, and there is considerable institutional variation within regions of western Europe itself.

Second, the concept of development is burdened with an implicit teleology. The word implies a progressive transformation from "less developed" to "more developed"; it implies the creation of more complex, sophisticated, and humanly adequate systems out of simpler and less adequate systems. (Rostow's concept of "stages of growth" captures this assumption precisely.) Historians have long since abandoned the idea that history has directionality, and have demonstrated the many false starts, wrong turns, reversals, and stalls that all societies have experienced.

Third, the concept of development brings with it an idealized set of assumptions in the background about what a "developed" society ought to include: consumerism, democracy, markets for everything, individualism, impersonal legal systems, large complex societies, and

a high material standard of living. This is a social ideal that is deeply embedded in development theory and that can be legitimately questioned. The values that are associated with western consumer culture represent one possible framework of human values—but only one such framework. In fact, it may be that the constraints of long-term environmental sustainability make this complex of values doubly questionable.

Finally, development theory has been forced to confront the contradictions between economic growth and environmental sustainability. Resource depletion, destruction of forests and wetlands, urban sprawl, air and water pollution, and global climate change resulting from carbon dioxide emissions all call into doubt the feasibility of permanent economic growth. Prudent multigenerational planning for the future of the planet will require more consistency between the needs of consumption and the needs of environmental sustainability.

SEE ALSO *Civilization; Colonialism; Third World*

BIBLIOGRAPHY

Adelman, Irma. 1978. *Redistribution Before Growth: A Strategy for Developing Countries.* The Hague: Martinus Nijhof.

Bates, Robert H. 1981. *Markets and States in Tropical Africa: The Political Basis of Agricultural Policies.* Berkeley: University of California Press.

Bhagwati, Jagdish N. 1969. *Trade, Tariffs and Growth: Essays in International Economics.* London: Weidenfeld & Nicolson.

Chenery, Hollis, et al. 1974. *Redistribution with Growth.* New York: Oxford University Press.

Drèze, Jean, and Amartya Kumar Sen. 1989. *Hunger and Public Action.* Oxford: Clarendon Press.

Escobar, Arturo. 1995. *Encountering Development: The Making and Unmaking of the Third World.* Princeton, NJ: Princeton University Press.

Frank, Andre Gunder. 1967. *Capitalism and Underdevelopment in Latin America: Historical Studies of Chile and Brazil.* New York: Monthly Review Press.

Independent Commission on International Development Issues. 1980. *North-South, a Program for Survival: Report of the Independent Commission on International Development Issues.* Cambridge, MA: MIT Press.

Lal, Deepak. 1985. *The Poverty of "Development Economics."* Cambridge, MA: Harvard University Press.

Lewis, W. Arthur. 1955. *The Theory of Economic Growth.* London: Allen & Unwin.

Morris, Morris David. 1979. *Measuring the Condition of the World's Poor: The Physical Quality of Life Index, Pergamon Policy Studies.* New York: Published for the Overseas Development Council by Pergamon Press.

Nussbaum, Martha Craven. 2000. *Women and Human Development: The Capabilities Approach.* Cambridge, U.K.: Cambridge University Press.

Rodrik, Dani. 1997. *Has Globalization Gone Too Far?* Washington, DC: Institute of International Economics.

Rostow, W. W. 1960. *The Stages of Economic Growth, a Non-Communist Manifesto.* Cambridge, U.K.: Cambridge University Press.

Sabel, Charles F., and Jonathan Zeitlin. 1997. *Worlds of Possibility: Flexibility and Mass Production in Western Industrialization.* Cambridge, U.K.: Cambridge University Press.

Sen, Amartya Kumar. 1999. *Development As Freedom.* New York: Knopf.

Stiglitz, Joseph E. 2002. *Globalization and Its Discontents.* New York: W. W. Norton.

Timmer, C. Peter. 1986. *Getting Prices Right: The Scope and Limits of Agricultural Price Policy.* Ithaca, NY: Cornell University Press.

United Nations Development Program. 2000. *Human Development Report 2000.* New York: Oxford University Press.

United Nations Environment Program. 2002. *Global Environmental Outlook 3.* Nairobi, Kenya: United Nations Environment Program.

UN Millennium Project 2005. 2005. *Investing in Development: A Practical Plan to Achieve the Millennium Development Goals. Overview.* New York: United Nations Development Program.

Wallerstein, Immanuel. 1974. *Capitalist Agriculture and the Origins of the European World-Economy in the Sixteenth Century.* New York: Academic Press.

Wong, R. Bin. 1997. *China Transformed: Historical Change and the Limits of European Experience.* Ithaca, NY: Cornell University Press.

World Bank. 1990. *World Development Report 1990: Poverty.* New York: Oxford University Press.

World Bank. 2001. *World Development Report 2000/2001: Attacking Poverty.* New York: Oxford University Press.

Daniel Little

DEVELOPMENT, GENDER AND

SEE *Gender and Development.*

DEVELOPMENT, INSTITUTIONAL

In the social sciences, organizational theory, and politics, the term *institutional development* is often used as a synonym for institutional and organizational change, implying that social transformation occurs in an organizational framework. Institutional development aims at establishing and improving an institutional structural unit and its capabilities, as well as the impact and effectiveness of organizations. This effort is understood as a long-term multiple-stakeholder process in which numerous factors and power relations influence the final outcomes and their everyday relevance. Institutional changes may also be influenced by previous policy practices, and development is shaped by a wide range of stakeholders, including staff capacity and capability, as well as equipment and infrastructure. It is thus increasingly recognized that institutional development must be seen in terms of a longer trajectory. By and large, the long-term process of institutional development must be established in the form of carefully designed projects. Institutional development projects hence address issues as organizational and technological management.

Development issues in the field of education include the setting up, upgrading, and enhancement of course design and curricula and of equipment infrastructure, the establishment of new policies, and the improvement of existing regulations within professional organizations. This process is often supported or even devised by consulting partners. In the field of development aid or, in more general terms, philanthropy, the process of institutional development as practiced, for example, by nongovernmental organizations can be seen as the improvement of an organization's responsiveness to the needs of its intended beneficiaries, the finer discrimination between different needs, and a quicker response to these needs.

The danger in both fields is that institutions meant to be intermediaries, and thereby a means to an end, are treated as ends in themselves. In the domain of education, this can easily lead to an over-decentralization of education due to different stakeholder interests, and consequently to a loss of societal control over contents or standards. In the case of institutional development in philanthropy, those whose welfare is of ultimate concern may recede into the background.

In evaluating institutions and their impact on outcomes in the field of development aid, high-quality standards have been identified as an important aspect. But institutions do not stand alone. They are embedded in local settings and are influenced by history and culture. So the impact of institutions on developmental progress is framed by particularities of local settings, stakeholder perspectives, time horizons, informal rules, social norms, customs, policies, and so forth, apart from the intention and will to reach a certain development goal. To incorporate these different factors into a specific institutional development project poses a considerable challenge that demands drawing on knowledge gained in the field of cross-cultural psychology and related disciplines.

The designs of institutional development projects vary considerably. Tools and approaches for institutional development include the process approach, total quality management, knowledge management, change management, monitoring and evaluation, and formative or summative approaches. Institutional development projects often lead to the conclusion that there are no "recipes" for changing institutions. In some cases, projects may develop guidelines describing tools to be used in practice. A large number of such guides can be found, written, and used by those who are involved in institutional development. All of these have strengths and weaknesses, and need to be adapted in the specific context of application. They reflect different theoretical backgrounds and are usually based on the practical experiences of those who used them while they were adopted. As exemplified in numerous project descriptions and evaluations, the first step to institutional development is always a serious analysis and diagnosis of the organization in its institutional context. Different stakeholder interests must be identified, goals of change or development have to be determined, and the process of change needs to be planned, implemented, and evaluated.

Nevertheless, measuring the success or effectiveness of institutional development remains difficult. Certain pitfalls that tend to occur in the process can be explained by the low standards of institutions initiating the change processes or by the conflicting interests of stakeholders. There are also cases of institutional "stickiness," where actors fail to respond to changes in the environment. Identifying factors driving institutional development is still a challenging research question. There is a need for a generalization of specific success factors in institutional development based on case studies and best-practice examples. Scientific literature on institutional development is quite dispersed, and no overall state-of-the-art volume is available.

SEE ALSO *Developing Countries; Economics, Institutional; Education, USA; Institutionalism; Neoinstitutionalism; Norms; Organizations; Stakeholders; Third World*

BIBLIOGRAPHY

Crouch, Colin, and Henry Farrell. 2002. *Breaking the Path of Institutional Development?: Alternatives to the New Determinism.* Cologne, Germany: MPIFG.

U.K. Department for International Development. 2003. *Conducting Institutional and Organisational Appraisal and Development: Guidelines for DFID and Sourcebook.* London: Author.

Dagmar Bergs-Winkels
Klaus Boehnke

DEVELOPMENT, RURAL

Rural development is the process by which sparsely populated areas improve their standing on socioeconomic measures. Political leaders try to hasten the pace of rural development through a wide array of policies. Concern about rural development arises because most rural areas lag behind metropolitan areas on basic indicators such as income, employment rates, and health outcomes. Rural development includes infrastructure, economic capacities, and the ability of local institutions to adapt to change in positive ways.

In the United States prior to the 1860s, action to foster rural development was focused on facilitating the westward movement of people. The emphasis shifted in 1862, when the Morrill Act granted land to states to create colleges with a mission to promote the liberal and practical education of the industrial classes. In 1887 the Hatch Act bolstered the capacities of these colleges, known as "land grants," to conduct research on improving agricultural practices. In 1914 the Smith-Lever Act established cooperative extension. The cooperative extension system is managed jointly by the land grants and the U.S. Department of Agriculture (USDA), and its mission is to teach the public how to apply land-grant research to improve their lives. Cooperative extension initially focused on agriculture and home economics, but evolved with the changing times and broadened its scope to include rural development functions such as leadership development, small-town development, management of human and natural resources, education of youth, and improving the competitiveness of rural manufacturing. The land grants and the USDA partner in supporting four regional rural development centers, based at land-grant institutions, each focusing on rural development issues in multistate regions.

President Franklin D. Roosevelt's New Deal policies established the Rural Electrification Administration (REA) in 1935, which brought electricity to most farms within fifteen years of its inception. Electrification greatly improved the quality of rural life and accelerated the industrialization of agriculture. As farming became more industrialized, rural labor was released, creating demands to create other kinds of rural enterprises to occupy the workforce. The New Deal also created the Farmer's Home Administration (FmHA) to provide loans for farms and rural infrastructure projects. In the mid-1990s the FmHA changed its name to USDA Rural Development to better reflect the full portfolio of its activities.

Although various rural development programs enjoyed some success in developing nonfarm jobs, they could not produce enough jobs to employ all the people leaving agriculture, and rural people began to move to cities. From the 1950s onward, major rural issues have been how to adjust to population decline in rural areas located far from metropolitan areas, and how to mitigate sprawl and the accompanying loss of the land base in metro-adjacent areas. These issues sparked activism and generated grants from organizations such as the W. K. Kellogg Foundation, the Farm Foundation, the Rural School and Community Trust, the American Farmland Trust, and the National Association of Towns and Townships. State and local governments also responded by supporting creation of local economic-development authorities and land-use planning authorities.

Although some concerns about the rural areas of the United States remain, the rural quality of life is far better in the United States than in many other areas of the world. Since the late 1940s there have been attempts to apply the lessons learned in the United States to less-developed countries. The movement began after World War II (1939–1945), when the successful reconstruction of war zones through the Marshall Plan convinced U.S. policy makers and others that foreign development assistance could be effective. At the same time, policy makers began to notice the impact that Norman Borlaug (with support from the Rockefeller Foundation) was having in reducing famine in Latin America and Asia through improved varieties of cereals, in what came to be known as the "Green Revolution." (Borlaug was awarded the Nobel Peace Prize in 1970 for his work.) The internationally funded World Bank, the United States Agency for International Development, and similar agencies from other wealthy countries began to fund agricultural and rural development projects in many low-income countries. The projects included long-term support for internationally distributed basic agricultural research through the fifteen centers of the Consultative Group on International Agricultural Research, and associated projects to mitigate the negative impacts of increased technology in agriculture, such as increased dependence on purchased inputs, a higher rate of social inequality due to faster adoption rates among wealthier households, and the environmental consequences of increased cropping areas and pesticide use.

The decolonization of countries in sub-Saharan Africa between 1960 and 1980 made many of them more open to multilateral trade and assistance, so international aid agencies, along with foundations such as the Ford Foundation, the Rockefeller Foundation, the W. K. Kellogg Foundation, and the Bill and Melinda Gates Foundation, responded with substantial investments. Rural development programs in Africa have not had the same level of success enjoyed in other parts of the world. The reasons for this are the focus of scholarly debate.

SEE ALSO *Agricultural Industry; Decolonization; Development Economics; Foundations, Charitable; Gender and Development; Green Revolution; Inequality, Wealth; Microfinance; Migration, Rural to Urban; New Deal, The; Peasantry; Poverty; Roosevelt, Franklin D.; Urbanization; World Bank, The*

BIBLIOGRAPHY

Byerlee, Derek, and Akmal Siddiq. 1994. Has the Green Revolution Been Sustained? The Quantitative Impact of the Seed Fertilizer Revolution in Pakistan Revisited. *World Development* 22 (9): 1345–1361.

Castle, Emery, ed. 1995. *The Changing American Countryside: Rural People and Places.* Lawrence: University Press of Kansas.

Eicher, Carl K., and John M. Staatz, eds. 1990. *Agricultural Development in the Third World.* 2nd ed. Baltimore: Johns Hopkins University Press.

Flora, Cornelia Butler, Jan L. Flora, with Susan Fey. 2004. *Rural Communities: Legacy and Change.* 2nd ed. Boulder, CO: Westview Press.

Scott Loveridge

DEVELOPMENT AND ETHNIC DIVERSITY

Societies that are developed afford their members a higher level of economic prosperity and political security. A key issue is whether ethnic diversity promotes or undermines the capacity to develop.

An ethnic group is a collectivity whose members believe they share a common ancestry. Many such groups speak a common language and come from a common place of origin. They tend to share a common history. The members of ethnic groups therefore often regard each other as kin, even when they cannot precisely trace the links that define their relationship. When a political entity, be it a nation or city, contains many such groups, it can be described as ethnically diverse.

In the process of development, the foundations of the economy shift from agriculture to industry. To become prosperous, individuals in developing societies therefore need to acquire new skills and to shift their place of employment. While still an active subject of investigation, research thus far suggests that ethnic groups contribute to the private welfare of individuals by assisting them in this transformation. It also suggests that at the onset of development, ethnic diversity may impede the development process, while at a later stage, it may promote it.

PRIVATE INVESTMENT

To improve the welfare of their people, ethnic groups fund schools and promote literacy. They also promote migration from country to town within a given nation and from poor countries to rich, and thus enable their members to get better jobs and to earn higher incomes. Some ethnic groups specialize in particular forms of economic activity, and therefore master skills that they then impart to kin.

By thus enhancing the prosperity of their members, ethnic groups contribute to the process of development.

ETHNIC DIVERSITY

There is some evidence that ethnic diversity enhances the impact of ethnic groups. People who live in culturally diverse cities in the United States pay higher rents, for example, suggesting that in such settings people can be more productive and thus both more willing and better able to dwell in such settings. One reason that diversity may enhance productivity may be competition among ethnic groups, which would lead to higher levels of investment in education and job skills; another may be that the special skills of one group enhance the productivity of the special skills of another. Because researchers, including Alberta Alesina and Eliana La Ferrara in 2005, report that the relationship between diversity and productivity is more pronounced in richer cities, the latter seems the more likely account.

Late-twentieth-century research has also focused on the impact of ethnic diversity on public policies, such as education, transportation, and health care. Some of these studies (Alesina et al. 1999) are based upon comparisons between urban centers in the United States; others (Miguel and Gugerty 2002), on small-scale communities in Africa. In both areas, scholars tend to find that the more ethnically diverse the political setting, the lower the quality of public services.

LEVELS OF DEVELOPMENT

That ethnic diversity inhibits the formation of public services may help to explain a major finding in this field: the negative relationship between ethnic diversity and economic growth in poor societies. First reported in William Easterly and Ross Levine's 1997 article for the *Quarterly Journal of Economics*, the finding has been replicated using cross-national data and data for urban areas in the United States. Since that time, however, researchers have noted that the relationship between ethnic diversity and growth is not straightforward. While negative in poor societies, it turns positive at higher levels of income, according to research by Alesina and La Ferrara (2005).

In the underdeveloped nations, economic growth may require better roads, schools, and other services, and ethnic diversity appears to make it difficult for people to cooperate in their provision. In richer economies, economic growth may be driven by the private sector, and ethnic diversity appears to enhance economic productivity.

VIOLENCE

Many argue that ethnic diversity threatens development by rendering violence more likely. This claim derives from studies of political conflicts, which often focus on the ethnic tensions that underlie them.

The claim can be challenged on several grounds. As stressed by James Fearon and David Latin (1996), the evidence is improperly drawn; societies at peace are often ethnically diverse as well. Moreover, ethnic diversity is related to poverty and poverty to political conflict; it is therefore difficult to isolate the independent contribution of ethnic diversity to political disorder. Students of Africa—the most ethnically diverse region in the world—report that it is not the diversity that promotes violence but rather concentration: when one group is big enough to capture the state, then others fear the possibility of political exclusion and political tensions therefore rise.

Ethnic groups thus energize the transformation of economies from agrarian to industrial and of societies from rural to urban; by so doing, they promote development. At low levels of income, ethnic diversity may impede development; at higher levels, it may promote it. The political dangers of ethnic diversity appear overdrawn.

SEE ALSO *Development Economics; Economic Growth; Ethnic Conflict; Ethnic Fractionalization; Ethnicity*

BIBLIOGRAPHY

Alesina, Alberto, Reza Baqir, and William Easterley. 1999. Public Goods and Ethnic Divisions. *Quarterly Journal of Economics* 114: 1243–1284.

Alesina, Alberto, and Eliana La Ferrara. 2005. Ethnic Diversity and Economic Performance. *Journal of Economic Literature* 43: 762–800.

Bates, Robert H., and Irene Yackolev. 2002. Ethnicity in Africa. In *The Role of Social Capital in Development*, ed. Christiaan Grootaert and Tiery van Bastelaer. New York: Cambridge University Press.

Collier, Paul. 1999. The Political Economy of Ethnicity. In *Proceedings of the Annual Bank Conference on Development Economics*, ed. Boris Pleskovic and Joseph Stigler. Washington, DC: The World Bank.

Easterly, William, and Ross Levine. 1997. Africa's Growth Tragedy: Policies and Ethnic Divisions. *Quarterly Journal of Economics* 112: 1203–1250.

Fearon, James D., and David D. Latin. 1996. Explaining Interethnic Cooperation. *American Political Science Review* 90: 715–735.

Miguel, Edward, and Mary K. Gugerty. 2005. Ethnic Diversity, Social Sanctions, and Public Goods in Kenya. *Journal of Public Economics* 89: 2325–2368.

Robert H. Bates

DEVELOPMENT ECONOMICS

Development economics is the field of study devoted to understanding the economic experience of less-developed countries. Development economics arose during the period of European decolonization that took place immediately before and after World War II (1939–1945), as national independence movements gave rise to a large number of newly independent countries in Asia, Africa, and Latin America. While highly diverse in terms of their history, culture, climate, population size, and natural resource endowments, these countries shared a common set of economic goals, including the desire to rapidly increase their per capita incomes and reduce often widespread poverty. These desires were often linked to the related goals of rapid urbanization and industrialization that were seen as part of a larger project of modernization, and thought to be integral to national political goals including economic independence and political power on the world stage. Development economics arose as an attempt to address the economic priorities and challenges faced by these countries.

To at least some degree, the advent of development economics was a response to the perceived inadequacies of traditional economic theory as a framework for addressing the challenges posed by economic development. Traditional economics was mostly concerned with the static issue of market efficiency. In contrast, in less-developed countries, the central question was a dynamic one: how to radically transform the economy through the interlocking processes of economic growth, industrialization, and urbanization. Moreover, traditional economic analysis presumed the existence of a system of relatively well-functioning markets that simply did not exist in many developing countries. A new set of theories would be needed to understand the causes of persistent underdevelopment and suggest ways in which government policy could overcome existing market failures to speed and direct the development process.

STRUCTURALISM, DUALISM, AND DEVELOPMENT

To early development economists, the flaws in traditional economics were obvious. Less-developed countries were poorly characterized by the highly flexible national markets that typified traditional economic theory. Markets were often local and fragmentary, and individuals appeared to be more concerned with tradition and family ties than efficiency or profit. A prominent alternative was structuralism, which argued that underdeveloped markets were highly inflexible. Prices were fixed or adjusted slowly, and economic agents responded slowly to changing prices. With markets functioning poorly, the government should play an active role in directing labor and capital to their best uses.

Developing economies often appear to be "dualistic," comprised of a modern industrial sector and a more traditional agricultural sector. The most influential model of dualistic development is due to Sir W. Arthur Lewis (1915–1991), who suggested that the traditional sector had a supply of underutilized workers who earned a *subsistence wage*. This *surplus labor* constituted a free resource that could be used for industrialization. Workers could be withdrawn from the traditional sector without reducing the total agricultural output. The main constraint on the rate of development was a country's ability to accumulate capital to expand the modern industrial sector.

Until it was exhausted, the surplus of labor would hold wages at a subsistence level. The gains from industrialization would go entirely to the owners of capital. Eventually, however, the expanding modern sector would exhaust the supply of surplus labor, and wages would begin to rise. Rising wages would cut into profits, slowing the rate of industrialization but also spreading its benefits to the population at large. At least initially, however, rising inequality might be an unavoidable byproduct of rapid development.

INDUSTRIALIZATION AND MARKET FAILURE

Lewis's thinking placed industrialization at the heart of economic development. Further analysis suggested that poorly functioning markets could undermine the two processes on which industrialization relied, capital accumulation and the transfer of labor from agriculture to industry. In practice, industrial development often was accompanied by unusually high and persistent urban unemployment. John Harris and Michael Todaro (1970) suggested that this was the result of inflexible labor markets that set the modern-sector wage too high. In its simplest formulation, the Harris-Todaro model suggests that if the modern-sector wage is two times the rural wage, then each new modern-sector job will attract two rural migrants. As a result, job creation programs will actually increase urban unemployment since each new job attracts more than one rural migrant.

Markets may also fail to induce the investments in physical capital—factories, tools, and machinery—at the heart of industrialization. Many investments are profitable only if other projects are undertaken at the same time, but no one investor has the resources to finance all the relevant investments. Unless the actions of many different investors can be coordinated, none of the investments will take place. This may be the case when different investment projects are closely linked—like factories that make car bodies, tires, and glass—but the link between investments may not be so obvious. If workers at the shoe factory use their wages to purchase bicycles, and vice versa, then the profitability of investing in bicycle and shoe production will be linked.

A second problem is that financial markets and institutions may function poorly. When functioning well, banks collect savings from those with extra income and make loans to households and firms with profitable investment opportunities. In less-developed countries, this may not occur because households are geographically isolated or because it is too costly to make or collect on small loans to the poor, who often have the best investment opportunities. State-run banks may waste scarce investment resources by favoring politically powerful borrowers. Finally, some countries limit the interest rate a bank may charge. If the inflation rate is higher than the allowable interest rate, banks automatically lose money on every loan they make, resulting in financial repression.

In spite of these problems, once industrialization begins it is often self-sustaining, with the profits from initial investments providing the savings to finance additional investment. Instead of experiencing this virtuous cycle, however, many less-developed countries appeared to be caught in a poverty trap with low levels of income, profit, investment, and savings. To get the virtuous cycle started, many development economists advocated a "big push" in which the government coordinated and funded a large number of investment projects. If an underdeveloped banking system resulted in low levels of private savings, the government could finance investment through tax revenues. International aid could be used to close the *financing gap* if a country was too poor to finance the necessary investments on its own.

INTERNATIONAL TRADE AND ECONOMIC DEVELOPMENT

Skepticism regarding the role of markets in economic development was most pronounced in attitudes toward international trade. During the colonial era, many developing countries had become specialized in the production of food, minerals, and other primary products, relying on international trade for many manufactured goods. Many development economists believed this pattern of trade would make industrialization more difficult. Furthermore, the technological advantages of developed industrial countries would make it impossible for less-developed countries to compete as exporters of manufactured goods.

A highly influential version of this idea was formulated by development economists Raúl Prebisch (1901–1986) and Hans Singer (1910–2006), who argued that the price of primary products tends to fall over time relative to the price of manufactured goods. According to

the Prebisch-Singer hypothesis, a developing country's ability to industrialize would be limited by that fact that, year after year, each ton of sugar or copper or coffee exported would purchase fewer machines. These ideas led to the development of North-South trade models that examined the conditions under which trade between an industrial "North" specialized in manufactured goods and a developing "South" specialized in primary goods could lead to uneven development in which southern income is stagnant or lags northern income indefinitely. More generally, the Prebisch-Singer hypothesis furthered the argument that markets were not up to the task of guiding a country's development.

The idea that guided developing countries' trade policy was import-substitution industrialization. A country would industrialize by gradually replacing manufactured imports with domestically produced counterparts. Led by the infant industry argument, many developing countries adopted import quotas and import tariffs to protect domestic manufacturers until they had matured enough to compete in international markets. In the early 1960s, a few East Asian countries rejected the inward-looking policies of import substitution in favor of export promotion. Successful exporters were rewarded with subsidies, easy credit, and other forms of support.

RADICAL PERSPECTIVES

Market skepticism also gave rise to more radical perspectives. According to André Gunder Frank (1929–2005), the father of dependency theory, the existence of a traditional sector was evidence not of capitalism's absence but of its fundamentally predatory nature. This is seen primarily in the tendency of capital to flow from underdeveloped rural regions to developed urban regions of a country. Center-periphery models addressed this dynamic in the international arena. Unequal exchange in international markets and the repatriation of profits by multinational firms would lead to the permanent concentration of capital in the hands of global economic elites, guaranteeing a persistent state of economic dependence for developing countries. The political domination of colonialism had been replaced by a neocolonial economic domination.

Radical economists believed that standard policy interventions were not enough to foster development. Successful development would require a fundamental restructuring of the international economic order and, often, the overthrow of the local political elite, who were viewed as the local representatives of global capital.

THE CONTINUING DEVELOPMENT OF DEVELOPMENT ECONOMICS

Development economics has continued to evolve since the mid-twentieth century. Development economics has re-embraced economic theory as it has become more adept at addressing the particularities of the markets of developing countries. More importantly, economists have learned from their accumulated experience with economic development. In practice, the emphasis on industrialization often led to an "urban bias" in development, resulting in tax and trade policies that reduced incomes in rural areas where poverty was already the most severe. Early theories may also have overemphasized the role of developing-country governments, which are themselves developing and limited in their capacity for administration and oversight. Many economists point to the development success of relatively market-oriented East Asian countries and recent work emphasizing the role of corruption in continued underdevelopment. While both governments and markets are prone to fail, in developing countries the perils of government failure may well be more important.

SEE ALSO *Demographic Transition; Economics; Export Promotion; Harris-Todaro Model; Import Substitution; Input-Output Matrix; Kuznets Hypothesis; Labor, Surplus: Marxist and Radical Economics; Lewis, W. Arthur; Structural Transformation*

BIBLIOGRAPHY

Harris, John, and Michael Todaro. 1970. Migration, Unemployment, and Development: A Two-Sector Analysis. *American Economic Review* 60 (1): 126–142.

Krueger, Anne O. 1997. Trade Policy and Economic Development: How We Learn. *American Economic Review* 87 (1): 1–22.

Krugman, Paul. 1995. The Fall and Rise of Development Economics. In *Rethinking the Development Experience: Essays Provoked by the Work of Alberto O. Hirschman*, eds. Lloyd Rodwin and Donald Schön, 39–58. Washington, DC: Brookings Institution.

Lewis, W. Arthur. 1954. Economic Development with Unlimited Supplies of Labor. *The Manchester School* 22: 139–191.

Myrdal, Gunnar. 1957. *Rich Lands and Poor: The Road to World Prosperity.* New York: Harper.

Rosenstein-Rodan, Paul N. 1943. Problems of Industrialization of Eastern and South-Eastern Europe. *Economic Journal* 53: 202–211.

Lewis S. Davis

DEVELOPMENT IN SOCIOLOGY

Development was a post–World War II concept used to describe and explain economic and social change throughout Africa, Asia, Latin America, and southeastern Europe.

President Harry Truman (1884–1972) launched "the era of development" in 1949 when he committed the United States to making scientific and industrial advances available to underdeveloped areas. Four major theoretical and policy perspectives regarding development have been proposed: modernity (roughly 1940s–1950s), dependency (1960s–1970s), world systems (1980s–2000s), and market reform (1980s–2000s). Institutional, feminist, and capability perspectives also have informed development discourse. In various contexts, development has signified economic growth, income disparity, or class conflict within and between nation-states and regions of the world, and it has incorporated economic, political, and social change as well as enhanced individual freedom.

MODERNITY

Modernity theorists focused on economic growth accompanied by political stability, not on social transformation itself. They assessed economic development primarily by gross domestic product, per capita income, or extent of poverty. Political stability implied preferable but not exclusive emphasis on the development of democratic institutions. Informing the modernity school were classical evolutionary theorists, including Auguste Comte (1798–1857), Émile Durkheim (1859–1917), Herbert Spencer (1820–1903), and Ferdinand Tönnies (1855–1936), and functionalist theorists such as Talcott Parsons (1902–1979) and Edward Shils (1911–1995).

The modernity school included economists, such as Walt W. Rostow, who stressed the importance of speeding up productive investments; political scientists, including Samuel Eisenstadt and Gabriel Almond, who highlighted the need to enhance the capacity of political systems; and sociologists, such as Marion Levy and Neil Smelser, who focused on changes in Parsons's pattern variables (a way of characterizing interactions between people) and social differentiation. Reflecting evolutionary theory, modernization was viewed as a phased process, exemplified by Rostow in *The Stages of Economic Growth* (1960), and as a lengthy homogenizing process, tending toward irreversible and progressive convergence among societies over long periods of time. Some have argued that modern societies had better capacity to handle national identity, legitimacy, participation, and distribution than those with traditional political systems. Reflecting functionalist theory, modernity was also treated as a systematic and pervasive process.

Early modernization theorists such as James Coleman, Rostow, and Parsons constructed ahistorical abstract typologies, viewed tradition as an obstacle to development, and neglected external factors and conflict as sources of change. In the 1980s modernity theorists such as Siu-Lun Wong, Winston Davis, and Samuel

Huntington treated tradition as an additive factor of development, conducted case studies, used historical analyses, posited multidirectional paths of development, and identified external factors and conflict as sources of development.

DEPENDENCY

Dependency theory arose in Latin America in the early 1960s, in part due to the economic stagnation associated with the United Nations Economic Commission for Latin America's policy of import substitution (producing food and raw materials for industrialized centers and, in return, receiving processed goods from these centers). Classical dependency theorists, such as Andre Gunder Frank (1929–2005), Theotonio Dos Santos (b. 1936), and Samir Amin (b. 1931), posited the bipolar theoretical construct of core (industrialized nations) versus periphery (underdeveloped nations) as an alternative to the modernists' modernity versus tradition. The historical heritage of colonialism and the perpetuation of an unequal division of international labor precluded the development of the periphery. The flow of economic surplus to European and North American developed countries kept countries in the Third World underdeveloped.

New dependency theorists and researchers of the 1970s and 1980s, such as Fernando H. Cardoso, Thomas B. Gold, Guillermo O'Donnell, and Peter Evans, viewed the nature of dependency in sociopolitical terms and as coexisting with development, rather than as mutually exclusive of it—that is, leading only to underdevelopment. They focused on historical-structural aspects of dependency, emphasizing internal aspects, class conflict, and the role of the state.

WORLD SYSTEMS

World-systems theorists, such as Andre Gunder Frank, Christopher Chase-Dunn, and Immanuel Wallerstein, made the unit of analysis the world system or, more generally, the "historical social system." They used historical explanations from the viewpoint of the world system—the functions and interactions of all societies—and examined large-scale changes over long periods of time. As the world system expanded or contracted in its totality, that is, in terms of overall economic growth, regions and countries changed at different rates and in different directions. To account for uneven development, Wallerstein characterized capitalist world economy as exhibiting a trimodal structure of core, semi-periphery, and periphery. The addition of the semi-periphery component enabled the examination of upward mobility (a peripheral region or country moving into the semi-periphery or a semi-peripheral region or country moving into the core) as well as downward mobility (a core region or country moving into the semi-periphery or a semi-peripheral regional or country moving into the periphery).

Alejandro Portes (1997) contends that postulating a single worldwide unit of analysis and the long-term view are major flaws of the world-systems theory. This is because most development problems, dilemmas, and decisions occur in the intermediary level of nations and communities seeking to cope with constraints in their immediate, particular situations. As a result, world-systems theorists remain outside policy debates, and their influence with sociology has been mitigated somewhat, although as So (1990) and Peet (1999) note, greater attention to microregions has much promise theoretically and practically.

MARKET REFORM

According to Portes (1997), market reform consists of seven basic steps:

1. unilateral opening to foreign trade;
2. extensive privatization of state enterprises;
3. deregulation of goods, services, and labor markets;
4. liberalization of the capital market with extensive privatization of pension funds;
5. fiscal adjustment based on a sharp reduction in public outlays;
6. downscaling state-supported social programs; and
7. an end to industrial policies and a concentration on macroeconomic management or monetary policy.

According to this model, development means success in the marketplace, with little or no attention paid to the distributive effects of aggregate economic gains either between or within countries.

Access to and integration in worldwide markets, however, is assessed by criteria that go well beyond the economic sphere. For example, the A.T. Kearney *Foreign Policy* globalization index, which measures the impact of globalization in sixty-two countries, comprises four dimensions of nation-state development:

1. economic integration (trade and foreign direct investment);
2. personal contact (telephone, travel, remittances, and personal transfers);
3. technological connectivity (Internet users, Internet hosts, secure servers); and
4. political engagement (international organizations, UN peacekeeping, treaties, and government transfers).

INSTITUTIONAL PERSPECTIVES

Institutional theorists, such as Nicole Woolsey Biggart and Mauro F. Guillén, propose that "development depends on successfully linking a country's historical patterns of social organization with opportunities made available by global markets" (Biggart and Guillén 1999, p. 723). In the *World Development Report 2002: Building Institutions for Markets*, published in 2001, the World Bank acknowledges the importance of institutions' mainstream approaches to development policy. The framework of Andrew Dorward et al. (2005) incorporates bottom-up, nonmarket organizations such as microfinance groups and community-property resource-management groups. Institutional change is explained in terms of the responses of powerful groups to changes in relative prices, transaction costs, and technologies. In addition to a government's regulatory capacity, much depends on how such actors perceive possible opportunities and threats posed to their interests by alternative paths of institutional change or stagnation and their political effectiveness in influencing the paths and pace of institutional change. Change can therefore be anti-development or pro-development, with much variation within and across nations and regions throughout the world.

The approach of Dorward et al. is consistent with that of Portes (1997), who argues for a sustained systematic analysis of differing outcomes. Specifically, the analysis should require a conceptual apparatus that goes beyond the assumptions of rational self-interest and unrestricted pursuit of gain that underlie neoliberal adjustment policies. The conceptual apparatus of economic sociology, which emphasizes the embeddedness of economic action in social structures, including political and demographic factors and the roles of class and networks in guiding collective strategies, is most suited for this task.

FEMINIST PERSPECTIVES

Women in development (WID) theorists (1970s–1990s) accepted prevailing modernity theory, stressing development as a linear process of economic growth. Confined to the noneconomic domestic sphere of society, women in developing nations had been left out of the development process, according to the WID theorists. Drawing from the dependency school, women and development (WAD) theorists (1980s–1990s) argued that women have always been part of the development process and that it was this link to modernization that had impoverished them. Women were used as cheap labor for multinational corporations in export-processing zones. Gender and development (GAD) theorists (1990s) rejected the sexual division of labor as the main ordering principle of social hierarchy. Instead, race, gender, and class mattered. Unlike WID and WAD theorists, GAD theorists (1990s–2000s) treated

the state as an important actor promoting women's emancipation.

Women, environment, and development (WED) theorists (1970s) made sustainable development a central issue: They linked ideas of equity between generations, the maintenance of a balance between environmental and economic needs to conserve nonrenewable resources, and the reduction of industrialization's waste and pollution. Postmodernism and development (PAD) theorists (1980s–2000s) did not reject theories of economic development per se, but rather favored an approach to development that accepted difference, incorporated power discourse, and fostered consultative dialogue to empower women to articulate their own needs and agenda.

CAPABILITIES

In *Development as Freedom* (1999), Amartya Sen conceptualizes development as a process of expanding freedoms that people enjoy. People's capabilities underlie valuable goals of development of which measures such as gross domestic product, per capita income, industrialization, and technological advances are only indirect indicators. The notion of capabilities suggests that quality-of-life conditions must enhance the substantive freedoms that people enjoy if they are to lead the kinds of lives they have reason to value.

In *Women and Human Development* (2000), Martha C. Nussbaum shows how the combination of gender inequality and poverty clarifies the need for attention to capabilities. Questions about how satisfied people are with their lives or about the resources they have at hand are less important than what they are actually able to do and to be. Capabilities include being able to have good health, including reproductive health; being able to form a conception of what is good and engage in critical reflection about planning one's life; being able to work; exercising practical reason; and entering into meaningful relationships of mutual recognition with other workers. A foremost goal of the capabilities approach is to maximize individual choice. Individuals should not be denied choice by cultures, religions, or families of which they are members, although these institutions might well provide the conditions under which individuals flourish. No institution, however, is sacred, and it is the responsibility of governments to protect individuals from any community that prohibits them from developing and exercising the basic human capacities.

SEE ALSO *Almond, Gabriel A.; Amin, Samir; Comte, Auguste; Decolonization; Dependency Theory; Developing Countries; Development and Ethnic Diversity; Development Economics; Durkheim, Émile; Feminism; Frank, Andre Gunder; Gender and Development; Globalization, Social and Economic*

Aspects of; Huntington, Samuel P.; Inequality, Gender; Institutionalism; Liberalization, Trade; Modernization; Neocolonialism; Neoimperialism; Parsons, Talcott; Postcolonialism; Sen, Amartya Kumar; Spencer, Herbert; Stages of Economic Growth; Wallerstein, Immanuel; World-System

BIBLIOGRAPHY

Biggart, Nicole Woolsey, and Mauro F. Guillén. 1999. Developing Difference: Social Organization and the Rise of the Auto Industries of South Korea, Taiwan, Spain, and Argentina. *American Sociological Review* 64 (5): 722–747.

Dorward, Andrew, Jonathan Kidd, Jamie Morrison, and Colin Poulton. 2005. Institutions, Markets, and Economic Coordination: Linking Development Policy to Theory and Praxis. *Development and Change* 36 (1): 1–25.

Edelman, Marc, and Angelique Haugerud, eds. 2005. *The Anthropology of Development and Globalization: From Classical Political Economy to Contemporary Neoliberalism.* Malden, MA: Blackwell.

Haggard, Stephan. 1990. *Pathways from the Periphery: The Politics of Growth in the Newly Industrializing Countries.* Ithaca, NY: Cornell University Press.

Leys, Colin. 1996. *The Rise and Fall of Development Theory.* Bloomington: Indiana University Press.

McMichael, Philip. 2004. *Development and Social Change: A Global Perspective.* 3rd ed. Thousand Oaks, CA: Pine Forge Press.

Nussbaum, Martha C. 2000. *Women and Human Development: The Capabilities Approach.* Cambridge, U.K.: Cambridge University Press.

Peet, Richard, with Elaine Hartwick. 1999. *Theories of Development.* New York: Guilford.

Portes, Alejandro. 1997. Neoliberalism and the Sociology of Development: Emerging Trends and Unanticipated Facts. *Population and Development Review* 23 (2): 229–259.

Roberts, J. Timmons, and Amy Hite, eds. 2000. *From Modernization to Globalization: Perspectives on Development and Social Change.* Malden, MA: Blackwell.

Rostow, W. W. 1960. *The Stages of Economic Growth: A Non-Communist Manifesto.* Cambridge, U.K.: Cambridge University Press.

Seligson, Mitchell A., and John T. Passé-Smith, eds. 2003. *Development and Underdevelopment: The Political Economy of Global Inequality.* 3rd ed. Boulder, CO: Lynne Rienner.

Sen, Amartya. 1999. *Development as Freedom.* New York: Knopf.

So, Alvin Y. 1990. *Social Change and Development: Modernization, Dependency, and World-Systems Theories.* Newbury Park, CA: Sage.

Walby, Sylvia. 2002. Feminism in a Global Era. *Economy and Society* 31 (4): 533–557.

World Bank. 2001. *World Development Report 2002: Building Institutions for Markets.* Washington, DC: World Bank.

Richard K. Caputo

DEVELOPMENTAL PSYCHOLOGY

Developmental psychology is the branch of psychology dedicated to identifying and explaining the continuities and changes that individuals display over their lifetimes. In particular developmental psychologists seek to understand the mechanisms or factors that are deemed responsible for the immense changes that occur in human thought, behavior, biology, and emotion from the very beginning of life through to the end—from "womb to tomb" (Shaffer, Wood, and Willoughby 2002).

Historically, early theories of development focused on trying to explain the development that occurs primarily during the first decade of life, with a focus on infancy and early child development. Scant attention was paid to the development that occurs during adolescence and on into adulthood. Societal changes that occurred during the 1950s and 1960s, however, led to a critical shift in theories and research in the field of developmental psychology. With respect to adolescence, for instance, the youth movements of the 1960s brought a new interest in understanding the teenage years and led to a marked theoretical alteration in the understanding of adolescence. Before then little attention had been paid to the empirical investigation of adolescents, and the extant theories of adolescence, primarily based on clinical experiences and anecdotal reports, portrayed the teen years as a time of "storm and stress"—a time during which individuals experience severe emotional turmoil and disturbance (e.g., Hall 1904). But data collected from adolescents themselves revealed that the teen years were not as tumultuous as previously assumed and that in fact the majority of adolescents (80%) reported traversing the teen years with little turmoil, relating well to their families and peers, and being comfortable with their social and cultural values (Offer and Schonert-Reichl 1992).

THEORETICAL FRAMEWORKS

Early twenty-first century views of development examine development across the life span: the prenatal period, infancy and toddlerhood, the preschool period, middle childhood, adolescence, young adulthood, middle adulthood, and late adulthood. A life span approach to development encompasses the scientific study of human growth, change, and stability (Feldman 2006). Researchers with this perspective seek to unravel universal principles of development, characteristics, and traits that differentiate people from one another, with a focus on physical, cognitive, personality, and social development. Demographic changes since the 1980s have spurred a new conception of development for the period identified as "emerging adulthood," which spans the ages eighteen to twenty-five (Arnett 2000).

In contrast to the life span development approach, another theoretical framework for understanding development over time is the life course perspective. Life course theory emerged in the 1960s from the need to understand how individual lives are socially patterned over time and to examine the processes by which lives are changed by changing environments in which time, context, and process are an explicit part of the analysis. More specifically, life course researchers take into account both stability and change in lives as they unfold across time and generations and in historical, social, and cultural contexts.

The life course approach is an increasingly influential paradigm in social scientific thinking. In the words of Anne Colby, this theoretical approach represents "one of the most important achievements of social science in the second half of the 20th century" (Colby 1998, p. viii). One of the pioneers in this field is Glen Elder Jr., who studied children of the Great Depression, emphasizing how individual lives are socially patterned over time and the processes by which lives are changed by changing environments (Elder and Shanahan 2006).

The science of developmental psychology lacks a comprehensive and widely accepted developmental theory that unifies the field (Cole, Cole, and Lightfoot 2005). Instead, many different theories have been proposed in the study of development, demonstrating how different theories lead to different explanations of behavior across the life span. The most influential and enduring theoretical frameworks have included the psychoanalytic, learning, cognitive-developmental, and ecological systems viewpoints. Sigmund Freud was among the first to emphasize the centrality of emotional life to the formation and function of personality development (Cole, Cole, and Lightfoot 2005). His psychoanalytic theory was rooted in the idea that development moves through a series of stages in which individuals confront conflicts between their biological drives and their social expectations. Freud envisioned the immense power of the unconscious as a determinant of behavior and argued that development is largely molded by experiences in the first years of life. Although psychoanalytic theory has profoundly influenced psychology, among other fields, it is subject to criticism. Even among his own circle of disciples, Freud's theories did not go unchallenged (Passer, Smith, Atkinson, et al. 2005). Although neoanalytic contemporaries of Freud, such as Alfred Adler, Karen Horney, Erik Erikson, and Carl Jung, agreed on the importance of both the unconscious and of childhood experiences, most argued that Freud did not give social and cultural factors sufficient importance in the role of development. Indeed because of the many criticisms leveled at Freud's theories in terms of generalizabilty and testability, few present-day developmentalists are strong supporters of Freud's theories (Shaffer, Wood, and Willoughby 2002).

In contrast to psychoanalytic theories, learning theories emphasize that development occurs as a result of behaviors learned through associations with different kinds of consequences. The most influential proponents of this perspective, John B. Watson and B. F. Skinner, argued that individuals tend to repeat behaviors that have resulted in rewards or that have allowed them to avoid unpleasant consequences. Social learning theorists such as Albert Bandura expanded upon traditional learning views to consider that a great deal of learning develops through the observation of others in the social context. Through a process known as modeling, children come to imitate behaviors they have seen others do, especially if they observe such behaviors to have positive consequences (DeHart, Sroufe, and Cooper 2004). Perhaps the greatest contribution of the learning viewpoint to understanding development has been the wealth of information gleaned through tightly controlled experiments. Learning theories are precise and testable and have helped developmentalists begin to understand why and how people form emotional attachments, adopt gender roles, make friends, and learn to abide by laws and rules (Shaffer, Wood, and Willoughby 2002). Nonetheless, the learning approach is a grossly oversimplified account of human development; it tends to overlook the contexts in which development occurs and often fails to recognize the cognitively active role that individuals play in their own development.

The cognitive-developmental perspective addresses some of these criticisms by focusing on the view that individuals actively construct a system for understanding the world rather than passively acquiring new information through simple learning mechanisms. Cognitive developmentalists seek to understand and explain the normative development of reasoning and thinking skills and argue that such skills progress through a universal sequence of invariant and qualitatively different stages. Jean Piaget is the most prominent developmental psychologist of the twentieth century, having contributed more to our understanding of cognitive development than any other scholar (Shaffer, Wood, and Willoughby 2002). Piaget's theories legitimized the study of children's thinking, linked moral development to cognitive development, and contributed to developmental research in social cognition—the kind of thinking that people display about the thoughts, feelings, motives, and behaviors of themselves and other people (Shaffer, Wood, and Willoughby 2002). Although critics have challenged the sequence of Piaget's stages and recognize that he underestimated the ages at which cognitive skills develop, it is almost impossible to exaggerate the impact that Piaget's thinking has had on developmental psychology (Beilin 1994).

A final theoretical framework is ecological systems theory, posited by Urie Bronfrennbrenner (1979). This perspective begins by assuming that natural environments are the major source of influence on developing persons (Shaffer, Wood, and Willoughby 2002). The ecological framework views individuals in the context of all the various settings they inhabit on a daily bases (microsystems). These settings are related to one another in a variety of ways (mesosystems), which are in turn linked to settings and social institutions where an individual is not immediately present but which have an important influence on his or her development (exosystems). All of these systems are organized in terms of the culture's dominant beliefs and ideologies (the macrosystem). Although the ecological systems perspective has gifted developmental psychology with an understanding of the complexities of the natural environment, the theory fails to explain how individuals process and learn from environmental information and is therefore not a complete account of how humans develop (Shaffer, Wood, and Willoughby 2002).

INVESTIGATIVE METHODS

Without a unified theory, how do developmental psychologists know anything about human development? Since the 1990s a variety of methods has been refined for gathering information about how development occurs (Cole, Cole, and Lightfoot 2005). Among the most widely used are naturalistic observations, survey research, and research experiments. However, no single method can answer every question about human development; each approach has its own strengths and limitations. Various approaches have a strategic role to play, dependent upon the topic under investigation and the answers being sought.

The most direct way to gather information about how development occurs is through naturalistic observation. By definition, naturalistic observation involves observing and recording behavior in naturally occurring situations without trying to manipulate the environment. Naturalistic observations allow developmentalists to observe how individuals behave in everyday life. However, such an approach is not without its limitations. For example, when people know they are being watched, they often behave differently than they normally would. In addition researchers often enter observational settings with expectations about what they are going to see and inevitably observe selectively in accordance with those expectations. Nonetheless, observational methods are a keystone of developmental research and a critical source of data about development (Cole, Cole, and Lightfoot 2005).

Researchers who opt for survey methods utilize structured questionnaire or interview techniques to ask participants questions related to such aspects of development as perceptions, feelings, or beliefs. Despite obvious shortcomings, such as attempts by respondents to present themselves in socially desirable ways, survey research is an excellent method for obtaining large amounts of informa-

tion, often from a large number of participants, in relatively short periods of time.

A final investigative approach is the psychology experiment. In a true experiment the researcher controls conditions and systematically manipulates one or more variables so as to rule out all other influences on development except the one being investigated. The clear strength of the experimental method is its unique ability to isolate causal factors. That is, by controlling extraneous variables that may be influencing development, researchers can be confident that the variable of interest does indeed have an effect. A major drawback to experimental research is that the findings are not always generalizable to everyday settings, given that people do not always respond in the laboratory the way they do in the natural environment. Thus, as with the myriad of theories utilized to explain development, there are numerous approaches for investigation in the field of developmental psychology.

SEE ALSO *Adolescent Psychology; Behaviorism; Child Development; Cognition; Erikson, Erik; Experiments; Freud, Sigmund; Gerontology; Jung, Carl; Maturation; Methodology; Piaget, Jean; Psychology; Skinner, B. F.; Stages of Development; Survey*

BIBLIOGRAPHY

Arnett, Jeffrey Jensen. 2000. Emerging Adulthood: A Theory of Development from the Late Teens through the Twenties. *American Psychologist* 55: 469–480.

Beilin, Harry. 1994. Jean Piaget's Enduring Contribution to Developmental Psychology. In *A Century of Developmental Psychology*, eds. Ross D. Parke, Peter A. Ornstein, John J. Reiser, and Carolyn Zahn-Waxler, 257–290. Washington, DC: American Psychological Association.

Bronfrennbrenner, Urie. 1979. *The Ecology of Human Development.* Cambridge, MA: Harvard University Press.

Colby, Anne. 1998. Forward: Crafting Life Course Studies. In *Methods of Life Course Research: Qualitative and Quantitative Approaches*, eds. Janet Z. Giele and Glen H. Elder Jr., viii. Thousand Oaks, CA: Sage.

Cole, Michael, Sheila R. Cole, and Cynthia Lightfoot. 2005. *The Development of Children.* 5th ed. New York: Worth.

DeHart, Gabie B., L. Alan Sroufe, and Robert G. Cooper. 2004. *Child Development: Its Nature and Course.* 5th ed. New York: McGraw Hill.

Elder, Glen H., Jr., and Michael J. Shanahan. 2006. The Life Course and Human Development. In *Theoretical Models of Human Development*, ed. Richard E. Lerner, 665–715. Vol. 1 of *The Handbook of Child Psychology.* 6th ed. New York: Wiley.

Feldman, Robert S. 2006. *Development across the Life Span.* 4th ed. Englewood Cliffs, NJ: Prentice Hall.

Hall, G. Stanley. 1904. *Adolescence: Its Psychology and Its Relation to Physiology, Anthropology, Sociology, Sex, Crime, Religion, and Education.* New York: D. Appleton.

Offer, Daniel, and Kimberly A. Schonert-Reichl. 1992. Debunking the Myths of Adolescence: Findings from Recent Research. *Journal of the American Academy of Child and Adolescent Psychiatry* 31: 1003–1014.

Passer, Michael W., Ronald E. Smith, Michael L. Atkinson, et al. 2005. *Psychology: Frontiers and Applications.* 2nd Canadian ed. Toronto: McGraw-Hill.

Shaffer, David R., Eileen Wood, and Teena Willoughby. 2002. *Developmental Psychology: Childhood and Adolescence.* 1st Canadian ed. Scarborough, ON: Thomson Nelson.

Cory L. Pedersen
Kimberly A. Schonert-Reichl

DEVIANCE

In *Deviant Behavior*, Erich Goode defined deviance as "behavior or characteristics that some people in a society find offensive or reprehensible and that generates—or would generate if discovered—in these people disapproval, punishment, condemnation of, or hostility toward, the actor or possessor" (1997, p. 26). While this definition of deviance is acceptable to much of the academic community, there is no consensus among academics or in the general public over what should and should not be considered deviant. Certainly, large groups of people may be able to agree on very general precepts of acceptable behavior. For example, most people in the world may agree that the killing of another person is unacceptable and therefore deviant. However, the heated debates that exist over capital punishment, abortion, stem cell research, or the permissibility of one country engaging in military action against another all highlight the difficulties in identifying something like the killing of another person as deviant. Beyond these sweeping generalities, a closer look at what is and is not permitted reveals that deviance is truly relative; what is considered deviant changes from society to society and over time within any given society, and often changes based on who carries out the particular behaviors. In academia, definitions of deviance tend to fall under one of four major categories: natural law definitions, normative definitions, labeling definitions, and critical definitions.

Perhaps the oldest conceptions of deviance, natural law or absolutist definitions, suggest that some norms, prohibitions, and codes of conduct are appropriate for all people in any social context at all times. These include taboos like incest and cannibalism, thought to be so morally repugnant that they are universally prohibited. But they also include codes of conduct governing other, less extreme, behaviors that are seen as necessary for a society to function properly. Contemporary sociologists tend to be critical of these definitions because they assume some degree of global consensus over what is right and wrong. These sociologists also criticize natural law approaches for denying the role that power inequalities play in shaping definitions of deviant behavior.

Prior to the 1960s, normative definitions of deviance were those to which most sociologists adhered. Proponents of these definitions suggest that deviance is rule-breaking behavior. All social groups have norms—authoritative standards of behavior—by which all group members are expected to abide. These norms range from less serious rules of social etiquette, such as not chewing food with your mouth open, to legal norms that prohibit behaviors like murder and terrorism that threaten the values that society holds up to be most important. Similar to the criticisms of natural law definitions of deviance, normative definitions are often criticized for their presumption of societal consensus over which rules will bind people together. Further, normative definitions are also criticized for not examining the role that power inequalities play in classifying behavior as deviant. Finally, these conceptions of deviance are criticized for the disjunctions that exist between what sociologists refer to as ideal culture (norms and values that a society holds up as paramount) and real culture (the behaviors that members of a society actually practice). For example, possession of marijuana is strictly prohibited by federal law in the United States, and thousands of people are incarcerated each year for violating these laws. However, over 40 percent of all adult Americans surveyed admit to using marijuana at least once in their lifetime (USDHHS 2005).

Often referred to as "social reaction" definitions, labeling definitions of deviance begin with the assumption that no act is inherently deviant. Every society has people who engage in norm-violating behavior. In fact, at some point in their lives, most people engage in deviant or criminal behavior. However, many of these rule breakers are able to avoid being formally labeled or identified as deviant because of their power or prestige, and other attributes like race or social class. Therefore, it is not the act itself that is deviant, it is how society reacts to the act that determines whether something or someone will be viewed as deviant. As Howard Becker wrote in *Outsiders*, "Deviance is not a quality of the act the person commits, but rather a consequence of the application by others of rules and sanctions to an 'offender.' The deviant is one to whom that label has successfully been applied; deviant behavior is behavior that people so label" (1973, p. 9).

Becker and other labeling theorists have been criticized for overstating the relativity of deviance and for failing to explain why some groups tend to be involved in more criminal and deviant behavior than others. Nonetheless, the labeling approach continues to be the dominant perspective in studies of deviance.

Many of the tenets of the labeling approach to deviance were adopted and built upon by supporters of the critical approach. Critical theorists argue that definitions of deviance intentionally favor those in positions of economic and political privilege. The political and economic elite use the law and other agencies of socialization under their control, such as the mass media, to simultaneously play up the threat of the deviant and criminal underclass while neutralizing their own law-violating and otherwise deviant behaviors. This neutralization allows the elite to profit and conduct themselves in ways that go against the best interests of society at the expense of the less powerful. Most criticisms of critical theories of deviance suggest that these theories are too vague and broad to have any practical import.

THE RELATIVITY OF DEVIANCE

The dominant belief among sociologists today is that, to a great extent, deviance is relative; what is acceptable in one place and at one time is not acceptable in a different place and time. Consistent with the labeling and critical theories, deviance is a matter of power relationships and personal and collective perspective. For example, in many contemporary societies, women who attempt to access political institutions are regarded as deviant and socially unacceptable. In all of these cases, it is men who control these institutions and therefore have the most to lose if women were to gain a political foothold. As was the case with the Taliban in Afghanistan, these men embrace norms and make rules designed to relegate women to inferior social-status positions. In contrast, formal barriers to female participation in politics are scoffed at by most people in the Western world. However, it was not until 1920 that women were guaranteed the right to vote in the United States. Only recently have surveys indicated support for a female president of the United States, and the United States still lags well behind many other nations when it comes to the number of women who hold elected government positions (Duggan 2005). Thus, while people in the United States may rightfully view Afghanistan under the Taliban as a sexist and deviant society, people in other nations where women are routinely elected to the highest political offices might think similarly of the United States.

Also, with regard to the relativity of deviance, formal distinctions between deviant and acceptable behaviors often have little to do with an objective analysis of harm or societal consensus. Rather, because of their appeal, perceived legitimacy as authorities, or control over political institutions and important resources like money and power, certain groups have a disproportionate influence over which behaviors are acceptable in a society. As sociologist John Curra writes, "Deviance, like beauty, is in the eye of the beholder, and it exists because some groups decide that other groups ought not to be doing what they are" (2000, p. 16).

Michel Foucault (1926–1984) was among the pioneers of this relativity perspective insisting that defining deviance requires the proper social perspective and an analysis of power relationships in society. In 1961 Foucault published *Madness and Civilization*, the results of his doctoral research—and his first major published work. In this book, Foucault examines the different ways that "madness" was perceived and addressed by those in power during the classical age (the late sixteenth century through the eighteenth century). Madness begins the era as an "undifferentiated experience," but over the course of the classical age, due to moral and economic factors, the mad are labeled as deviant, alienated from society, and subjected to various forms of confinement by those in positions of power.

Often, certain types of behaviors are defined as deviant, not because of the will of the majority or the interests of the power elite, but because of interest groups who wish to define these behaviors as deviant because they do not fit within their value systems. In many respects, the thirteen-year prohibition of alcohol in the early twentieth-century United States resulted from the pressure exerted upon lawmakers by these "moral entrepreneurs"—people on a personal or social crusade to change attitudes toward particular behaviors. While these "reformers" were successful in formally labeling alcohol consumption as deviant behavior, large numbers of people refused to accept this label. Subsequently, a black market for alcohol emerged, leading to deaths caused by the ingestion of toxic "bootlegged" alcohol. Of even greater social consequence, Prohibition created what many historians have pinpointed as the genesis of organized crime in the United States as crime syndicates were established to meet the public demand for illegal alcohol.

In the United States, there is an ongoing crusade by moral entrepreneurs to deny gay and lesbian couples many of the basic rights and privileges that heterosexual couples take for granted. Such issues as same-sex marriage, gay couples adopting orphaned children, rights of inheritance, and coverage for domestic partners under private insurance plans are all examples of these contested issues. There have been some symbolic victories for gay couples. For example, in *Lawrence v. Texas* (2003), the U.S. Supreme Court declared unconstitutional laws that singled out gay couples for criminal prosecution under state sodomy laws. However, the moral entrepreneurs have gained significant ground in their efforts; many states have adopted laws prohibiting same-sex marriages and banning adoption by gay couples. As with prohibition, only time will tell of any unintended consequences of these changes in formal conceptions of deviance.

THE DEVIANT OTHER

Traditionally, studies and theories of deviance and crime research have been primarily based on segments of the population without political and economic power, particularly racial and ethnic minorities and immigrants. Much of this research has reinforced the idea that deviance and criminality remain problems of the lower classes and people of color. Perhaps nowhere is this more evident than in deviance and drug research. While the sociological literature on drug use is extensive, the vast majority of this research explores the drug using and dealing habits of urban minorities, particularly African Americans. This is in spite of the fact that the data indicate that rates of drug use are fairly evenly distributed across race and social class, and that white people are more likely than either black people or Latinos to have used illegal drugs in their lifetime (USDHHS 2005).

A study by A. Rafik Mohamed and Erik D. Fritsvold (2006) exploring drug dealing among predominantly white college students uncovered a profitable drug network in which both the patrons and providers did not fit the stereotype of drug users and dealers. But, because of their relative affluence, race, access to costly legal counsel, and other factors related to their social status, when the illegal behaviors in this market were exposed, the dealers and users were not labeled as deviants. This study made clear that both researchers and the engineers of U.S. drug policy still do not gear drug research or drug law strategies toward people whom they resemble in social class and status. Instead, the war on drugs, like much of the research on deviant behavior in general, ignores the illicit enterprises of the affluent and continues to operate as a furtive attack against the poor and people of color.

SEE ALSO *Crime and Criminology; Justice, Social; Labeling Theory; Power*

BIBLIOGRAPHY

Becker, Howard S. 1973. *Outsiders: Studies in the Sociology of Deviance.* 2nd ed. New York: Free Press.

Bourdieu, Pierre. 1991. *Language and Symbolic Power.* Trans. Gino Raymond and Matthew Adamson. Cambridge, MA: Harvard University Press.

Chambliss, William J. 1973. The Saints and the Roughnecks. *Society* 11(1): 24–3.

Curra, John. 2000. *The Relativity of Deviance.* Thousand Oaks, CA: Sage.

DeKeseredy, Walter S., Desmond Ellis, and Shahid Alvi. 2005. *Deviance + Crime: Theory, Research, and Policy.* 3rd ed. Cincinnati, OH: Anderson.

Duggan, Erin. 2005. Most Americans Ready for Woman to Be President: Clinton Leads Group of Possible Female Candidates, Poll Finds. *Albany Times Union,* February 21.

Foucault, Michel. 1965. *Madness and Civilization: A History of Insanity in the Age of Reason.* Trans. Richard Howard. New York: Pantheon.

Goode, Erich. 1997. *Deviant Behavior.* 5th ed. Upper Saddle River, NJ: Prentice Hall. 7th ed., 2005.

Lawrence v. Texas (02-102) 539 U.S. 558. 2003. http://www.law.cornell.edu/supct/html/02-102.ZS.html.

Mohamed, A. Rafik, and Erik D. Fritsvold. 2006. Damn, It Feels Good to Be a Gangsta: The Social Organization of the Illicit Drug Trade Servicing a Private College Campus. *Deviant Behavior* 27: 97–125.

U.S. Department of Health and Human Services (USDHHS), Substance Abuse and Mental Health Services Administration, Office of Applied Statistics. 2005. *National Survey on Drug Use and Health, 2004.* http://oas.samhsa.gov/nsduh/2k4nsduh/2k4results/2k4results.htm.

A. Rafik Mohamed

DEVIANCY TRAINING

SEE *Deviance; Peer Effects.*

DIALECTICAL MATERIALISM

SEE *Communism, Primitive.*

DIAMOND INDUSTRY

The modern economic origin of the diamond industry is the outgrowth of the two depressions in 1893 and in 1929. In the aftermath of the 1893 market collapse, Cecil Rhodes succeeded in consolidating the majority of the South African diamond mines within DeBeers Mines and formed the London Diamond Syndicate.

The present-day successor to the original syndicate and the Central Selling Organization (CSO), which was reorganized by Ernest Oppenheimer in 1929, is the Diamond Trading Company (DTC). The DTC still has a substantial position in the distribution of the rough, controlling about 50 percent of the world output, down from 80 percent in the 1980s, through the exploitation of its own mines (these account for over 40 percent of world output) or through purchasing contracts with independent diamond producers. As new discoveries of diamond deposits and sales independent of CSO are expected, the monopoly power of DTC will continue to decline.

Stabilization of the supply of rough and thus of prices by the CSO is accomplished in three ways: allocation of production quotas for the mines with a guaranteed minimum quota sufficient to secure continuity of production, regardless of the state of the world market; 10 yearly offerings of rough, known as "sights" to about 150 cutters and dealers in the various diamond centers; and accumulation of stocks when demand cannot sustain the prices until the market improves. The sorted and graded diamonds are placed in boxes marked with the name of the purchaser and the price. For diamonds under 14.8 carats, prices set are not negotiable. Irregular purchases may lead to exclusion from the list.

To obtain 1 carat (200 milligrams) of rough, 20 tons of rock and gravel need to be mined. Industrial diamonds, used in cutting and grinding tools, which until General Electric's (GE) 1951 synthesis were mined as a by-product of gemstones, are no longer tied to the production of the latter. In the early twenty-first century GE and DeBeers each produced about 40 percent of industrial synthetic diamonds. Still, in some industrial cases, a preference exists for use of natural diamonds. Furthermore GE succeeded in developing synthetic gem diamonds, produced in the early twenty-first century by two companies, Gemesis and Apollo, in the United States. The industry insists that synthetic diamonds used in jewelry be promoted as such.

Diamonds show an enormous variety of shape, size, quality, and color; thus there are no set prices for diamonds, in contrast to precious metals. The industry operates then in an uninformed market in that buyers lack the knowledge of the nature of the goods they wish to purchase and therefore rely mainly on advertising as a guide, despite the existence of gemological associations that certify diamonds. DeBeers's advertising strategy with its "a diamond is forever" ad, romanticizing and glorifying the diamond as a cultural imperative, is considered the most successful marketing campaign in history to date.

In 2000 DeBeers decided to loosen its supply control model and increase retail demand by pressuring its sight holders to engage in creative marketing. Companies began branding and patenting designer diamonds. Also vertical integration of the diamond pipeline spread in that DeBeers and independent mines sold directly to polishers and partnered with luxury retail establishments, thereby excluding middlemen.

In 2004 over 50, 25, and 15 percent of rough of 162 million carats were mined in sub-Saharan Africa, Russia, and Canada, respectively. Twenty countries produced diamonds whose value reached over $12 billion, of which Africa's share was 60 percent. About 20 percent of the total volume was gems, and 45 percent were near gem quality. In terms of retail activity, the United States, Japan, and Europe accounted for 53, 13, and 12 percent, respectively.

The polishing of diamonds, which involves a 50 percent weight loss, constitutes an appreciable industry in several countries, of which India, with its 700,000 workers, dominates, followed by Russia, Israel, Belgium, China, and Thailand, each with thousands of employees only. The structure of the industry is highly competitive at both the polishing and the distribution levels. Concentration is much lower at the polishing end due to the prevalence of subcontracting and the absence of substantial economics of scale.

Maintenance of a distributive outlet for diamonds represents a substantial investment and requires the ability to offer a wide line of processed diamonds to potential customers. In general the greater the variety and range offered, the greater the chance of securing high margins, since the seller is able to follow changes in demand. Such higher profits can be accomplished only by large fabricators or large wholesalers who have the financial resources to stock gems whenever market conditions warrant. There is also a tendency to dispatch the polished diamonds on consignment—a practice requiring a substantial amount of working capital.

For the solely polishing centers, the volume of diamond exports should not, however, be taken as the measure of the industry's role in the earning of foreign exchange. The value of imported rough amounts to nearly 80 percent of the value of exports, and the industry in such countries is completely dependent upon imports for its rough. The foreign currency earning rate, defined as

(Export Value – Value Import Content)/Export Value

ranges between 12.1 and 24.1 percent.

Ironically, while officials of DeBeers inveighed against the brutality of the South African apartheid system and even supported the emergence of black labor unions in the 1970s, the miners, separated from their families, were housed in crowded compounds with little privacy. Following legislation enacted in 2004 of the "Broad Based Black Economic Empowerment Act" passed by the South African parliament, DeBeers is to transfer for "fair market value" 26 percent of its South African diamond interests to enhance black ownership within five to ten years. Also, the company must sell a portion of its rough to a government agency, which will help expand the polishing centers in the country.

The ease with which diamonds can be transported and laundered has fueled the most vicious civil wars in Africa and has heightened Al-Qaeda's terrorist strategies. As a result in 1998 the United Nations Security Council, governments, and the industry enacted, with a modicum of success, anti-laundering legislation and the Kimberly Process certification system, which certifies the legitimate shipment of rough. The 2006 movie *Blood Diamond* is generally a correct manifestation of the cruelty pervading the diamond trade in several African countries. It illustrates the factional greed of the leaders who usurp the wealth of resources of African countries.

Of special concern to human rights groups is the employment in some countries, such as the Republic of Congo and India, of children in the mining and polishing plants despite legislation prohibiting it. Of special concern to environmental groups is the impact that open pits diamond mining has on the environment because the population is displaced to facilitate mining exploration and chemicals leach into ground water.

SEE ALSO *Apartheid; Child Labor; Corruption; Industry; Mining Industry*

BIBLIOGRAPHY

Aronheim, W. 1943. The Development of the Diamond Industry and Trade in Peace and War. MA thesis, New School for Social Research.

Epstein, Edward J. 1982. *The Rise and Fall of Diamonds: The Shattering of a Brilliant Illusion.* New York: Simon and Schuster.

Frontline. 1994. The Diamond Empire. PBS, February 1, transcript, 1–33.

Government of the Northwest Territories, Canada. 2006. Diamond Facts. http://www.iti.gov.nt.ca/diamond/pdf/DiamondFactsCover2006.pdf.

Gregory, T. E. 1962. *Ernest Oppenheimer and the Economic Development of Southern Africa.* New York: Oxford University Press.

Innes, Duncan. 1984. *Anglo American and the Rise of Modern South Africa.* New York: Monthly Review.

Laan, H. L. van der. 1965. *The Sierra Leone Diamonds.* London: Oxford University Press.

Szenberg, Michael. 1973. *The Economics of the Israeli Diamond Industry.* Foreword by Milton Friedman. New York: Basic Books.

Tolansky, Samuel. 1962. *The History and Use of Diamond.* London: Methuen.

Weber, Lauren. 2001. The Diamond Game, Shedding Its Mystery. *New York Times,* April 8.

Zoellner, Tom. 2006. *The Heartless Stone.* New York: St. Martin's.

Lall Ramrattan
Michael Szenberg

DIASPORA

Diaspora takes its name from the ancient Greek *dispersion*, meaning "to scatter," and, in the past, has been most closely associated with "the settling of scattered colonies of Jews outside Palestine after the Babylonian exile" (*Merriam-Webster* 2004, p. 345). For historians and social scientists, the concept embodies an assumption of forced dispersal, but also a shared identity organized around a mythic homeland, and the belief in a massive return (Akenson 1995, pp. 378–379). The creation of Israel, a real nation, did little to diminish this association, and the conflicts surrounding Israel's expansion in the region still generate much discussion about the ongoing victimization of the Jewish people (Morehouse, pp. 7–8; Cohen 1997).

EXPANDING THE DIASPORA CONCEPT

The next significant groups associated with the diaspora concept are those that form the "African diaspora." Similar to ancient and modern-day Jews, the scattering of African-descended people owes its origins to the coercive systems of colonialism, slavery, and imperialism that resulted in the forced migration of thousands of Africans to the New World, and later involuntary migration. For newly Christianized African slaves and their descendants, the story of Jewish displacement held special appeal, especially the belief in the return home. Marcus Garvey (1887–1940), founder in 1917 of the United Negro Improvement Association and African Communities League (UNIA-ACL), seized upon the diaspora desire to return home. He spearheaded a "Back-to-Africa" movement that had strong financial support, although the Black Star Line he built was intended to promote commerce between African Americans and Africa rather than return people to the land of their origins.

With such a strong symbolic connection among Christian blacks to the injustices that Jews had endured across time and space and their belief in a mythic homeland, it is not surprising that black scholars would seize upon the diaspora concept in their work. According to Brent Hayes Edwards, this concept of "*diaspora* is taken up at a particular conjuncture in black scholarly discourse to do a particular kind of epistemological work" (2001, p. 46). That "work," as described by W. E. B. Du Bois (1868–1963), was an activist-scholarly agenda aimed at bringing "intellectual understanding and co-operation among all groups of Negro descent in order to bring about at the earliest possible time the industrial and spiritual emancipation of the Negro people" (1933, p. 247).

An interest in linking the scattered population of New World people to their African homeland is central to the ideas and planning that produced the 1900 Pan-

African Congress, organized by Henry Sylvester Williams (1869–1911), and the subsequent Pan-African congresses in 1919, 1921, 1923, 1927, 1945, and 1974 organized by Du Bois and others. But most scholars studying the history of the African diaspora credit George Shepperson with joining *African* to *diaspora* (Alpers 2001, p. 4) in his 1965 paper, "The African Abroad or the African Diaspora," for the International Congress of African Historians: Diaspora versus Migration. Seventeen years later, the organizer of the panel on which Shepperson presented his paper, Joseph Harris, would go on to edit one of the seminal texts on the topic, *Global Dimensions of the African Diaspora*. His classic definition would shape how generations of scholars interpreted the concept:

> The African diaspora concept subsumes the following: the global dispersion (voluntary and involuntary) of Africans throughout history; the emergence of a cultural identity abroad based on origin and social condition; and the psychological or physical return to the homeland, Africa. Thus viewed, the African diaspora assumes the character of a dynamic, continuous, and complex phenomenon stretching across time, geography, class and gender. (Harris [1982] 1993, pp. 3–4)

TO BE OR NOT TO BE A DIASPORA

While the use of *diaspora* "as social form," "as type of consciousness," "as mode of cultural production" (Vertovec 1997, p. 277–278), as paradigm (Hamilton 1990), or as interpretive framework (Drake 1991; Gilroy 1993; Hall 1990) has grown in popularity in cultural studies, history, and the social sciences, it has also generated much controversy. Some scholars, such as Donald Akenson, argue for "a degree of skepticism" when employing the concept. He asserts that its most pristine application is to modern Jews, and anything else leads to imprecision: "That is why, were we to be master of our vocabulary, 'diaspora' would be a term limited only to the ancient Hebrews and their descendents, the modern Jews. To use the word 'diaspora' even as a metaphor for other groups is to replace a precise connotation with a fuzzy one" (Akenson 1995, p. 379). Steven Vertovec agrees, and argues that "the current overuse and under-theorization of the notion of 'diaspora' among academics, transnational intellectuals and 'community leaders' alike—which sees the term become a loose reference conflating categories such as immigrants, guestworkers, ethnic and 'racial' minorities, refugees, expatriates and travelers—threatens the term's descriptive usefulness" (Vertovec 1997, p. 277).

Östen Wahlbeck counters by asserting that it is the new application of an old concept that produces new understandings of globalization and transnationalism:

> In the 1990s, migration researchers have used this old concept for a variety of new purposes. Instead of studying international migration, the focus is often on transnational diasporas…. I propose that the concept of diaspora, understood as transnational social organization relating both to the country of origin and the country of exile, can give a deeper understanding of the social reality in which refugees live. (Wahlbeck 2002, pp. 221–222)

Stuart Hall offers another notion of diaspora that challenges traditional views:

> Diaspora does not refer to those scattered tribes whose identity can only be secured in relation to some sacred homeland to which they must at all costs return…. The diaspora experience as I intend it here is defined, not by essence or purity, but by the recognition of a necessary heterogeneity, diversity; by a conception of 'identity' which lives with and through, not despite, difference; by hybridity. (Hall 1990, p. 235)

Despite these new ways of conceptualizing diaspora and the debates over the use of *diaspora* to account for so many diverse forms of movement by groups of people across time and space and for varied reasons, it remains a powerful and useful concept for history and the social sciences.

SEE ALSO *African Diaspora; Chinese Diaspora; Du Bois, W. E. B.; East Indian Diaspora; Ethnicity; Hall, Stuart; Jewish Diaspora; Migration; Nationalism and Nationality; Palestinian Diaspora; Pan-African Congresses; Pan-Africanism*

BIBLIOGRAPHY

Akenson, Donald Harman. 1995. The Historiography of English-Speaking Canada and the Concept of Diaspora: A Sceptical Appreciation. *Canadian Historical Review* 76 (3): 377–409.

Alpers, Edward. 2001. "Defining the African Diaspora." Paper presented to the Center for Comparative Social Analysis Workshop. October 21.

Cohen, Robin. 1997. *Global Diaspora: An Introduction*. Seattle: University of Washington Press.

Drake, St. Clair. 1991. *Black Folk Here and There: An Essay in History and Anthropology*. Berkeley: University of California Press.

Du Bois, W. E. B. 1933. Pan-Africa and New Racial Philosophy. *Crisis* 40: 247–262.

Edwards, Brent Hayes. 2001. The Uses of Diaspora. *Social Texts*–66 19 (1): 45–73.

Gilroy, Paul. 1993. *The Black Atlantic: Modernity and Double-Consciousness*. Cambridge, MA: Harvard University Press.

Hall, Stuart. 1990. Cultural Identity and Diaspora. In *Identity, Community, Culture, Difference*, ed. Jonathan Rutherford, 222–237. London: Lawrence and Wishart.

Hamilton, Ruth Simms. 1990. *Creating a Paradigm and Research Agenda for Comparative Studies of the Worldwide Dispersion of African Peoples*. East Lansing: African Diaspora Research Project, Michigan State University.

Harris, Joseph E., ed. [1982] 1993. *Global Dimensions of the African Diaspora*. 2nd ed. Washington, DC: Howard University Press.

Merriam-Webster, Inc. 2004. *Merriam-Webster's Collegiate Dictionary*. 11th ed. Springfield, MA: Author.

Miller, Ivor. 2004. Introduction. *Contours* 2 (3): 141–156.

Morehouse, Maggi M. nd. The African Diaspora: An Investigation of the Theories and Methods Employed when Categorizing and Identifying Transnational Communities. http://people.cohums.ohio-state.edu/avorgbedor1/diaspmo.pdf.

Vertovec, Stephen. 1997. Three Meanings of "Diaspora," Exemplified among South Asian Religions. *Diaspora: A Journal of Transnational Studies* 6 (3): 277–299.

Wahlbeck, Östen. 2002. The Concept of Diaspora as an Analytical Tool in the Study of Refugee Communities. *Journal of Ethnic and Migration Studies* 28 (2): 221–238.

Irma McClaurin

DIASPORIC CITIZENSHIP

SEE *Immigrants, Latin American.*

DIATHESIS-STRESS MODEL

The premise underlying the "diathesis-stress" model is that a person is more likely to suffer an illness if he or she has a particular *diathesis* (i.e., vulnerability or susceptibility) and is under a high level of stress. Diathesis factors that have been studied include family history of substance abuse or mental illness; individual psychological characteristics such as hostility or impulsivity; biological characteristics (e.g., cardiovascular reactivity, hypothalamic-pituitary-adrenal responsivity); and environmental characteristics such as childhood maltreatment or low socioeconomic status. Diathesis factors are generally assumed to be relatively stable but not necessarily permanent.

The term *stress* refers to events and experiences that may cause psychological distress. Stress can influence mechanisms that help to maintain the stability of an individual's cognition, physiology, and emotion. Although the notion that stress can influence the development of illness has been held since the mid-nineteenth century, it was not until theories of schizophrenia proposed during the 1960s that the concepts of stress and diathesis were combined. In studies of depression that found empirical support for the model, stress has most commonly been operationalized as having experienced major negative events within the past year.

An implication of the diathesis-stress model is that the greater the vulnerability an individual has, the less stress is required for that individual to become ill. It is necessary to consider both the presence of a diathesis and a person's level of stress in order to determine the degree of risk for the onset or reoccurrence of an illness. For example, a study of depression showed that among subjects with a diathesis in the form of genetic risk, 10 percent developed depression at low stress levels but 33 percent developed depression at high levels. For those without the diathesis, the figures were 10 percent and 17 percent, respectively.

Other health problems to which the diathesis-stress model has been widely applied include substance use, schizophrenia, and heart disease. Studies have investigated a broad range of both environmental and psychological vulnerabilities, as well as biological vulnerabilities, some of which involve genetic expression. Interest in the role of genetics in disease onset has also led to studies on gene-environment interaction, which suggest that elevation of disease risk by an environmental factor occurs primarily for individuals with a susceptible genotype.

Empirical support for the applicability of the diathesis-stress model is robust and has warranted preventive interventions targeting those at highest risk of developing negative health outcomes. For example, psychological interventions address the way a person with high vulnerability appraises and responds to stressful life events. Researchers seek to refine measures of vulnerability, provide suggestions for preventive strategies, and gather empirical evidence for the effectiveness of preventive interventions. Overall, the diathesis-stress model has provided researchers and clinicians with a framework in which knowledge about biological, environmental, and psychological processes can be used to decrease the likelihood that an illness will develop or reoccur.

SEE ALSO *Coping; Stress-Buffering Model*

BIBLIOGRAPHY

Caspi, Avshalom, Karen Sugden, Terrie E. Moffitt, Alan Taylor, et al. 2003. Influence of Life Stress on Depression: Moderation by a Polymorphism in the 5-HTT Gene. *Science* 301 (5631): 386–389.

Hankin, Benjamin L., and John R. Z. Abela, eds. 2005. *Development of Psychopathology: A Vulnerability-Stress Perspective.* Thousand Oaks, CA: Sage.

Monroe, Scott M., and Anne D. Simons. 1991. Diathesis-Stress Theories in the Context of Life Stress Research: Implications for the Depressive Disorders. *Psychological Bulletin* 110 (3): 406–425.

Scher, Christine D., Rick E. Ingram, and Zindel V. Segal. 2005. Cognitive Reactivity and Vulnerability: Empirical Evaluation of Construct Activation and Cognitive Diathesis in Unipolar Depression. *Clinical Psychology Review* 25: 487–510.

Michael G. Ainette
Thomas A. Wills

DICTATORSHIP

The concept of dictatorship originated in Rome; it was defined as rule by a leader who was selected by the Consul to govern during periods of emergency brought on by external war or internal rebellion. While legally endowed with broad powers to resolve crises, the dictator was required to step down within six months or before the end of the term of the Consul that appointed him. In addition, such exceptional power was to be used to restore the previous political order. Although dictatorial power was faithfully applied in most cases, Mark Antony (82 or 81–30 BCE) abolished the institution after both Lucius Cornelius Sulla (138–78 BCE) and Julius Caesar (100–44 BCE) used force to rule beyond their mandated terms.

The temporary nature of dictatorship was central to its conception, leading writers such as Niccolò Machiavelli (1469–1527) and Jean-Jacques Rousseau to defend its powers in responding to crises. Even rulers acknowledged the specific meaning of the term. After Napoleon Bonaparte (1769–1821) seized power extralegally, for example, he was known as "emperor," not as "dictator." The one exception seems to have been José Gaspar Rodríguez de Francia (1766–1840) in Paraguay, who labeled himself "the perpetual dictator"—an oxymoron by the standards of original meaning.

CONTEMPORARY UNDERSTANDING

The term *dictatorship* did not gain prominence again until the early twentieth century, when it reappeared in the guises of the self-proclaimed "dictatorship of the proletariat" in Russia and the fascist dictatorship in Italy. Both uses of the term were deviations from the original Roman conception. The fascists were never committed to any temporary notion of power. The dictatorship of the proletariat was to be temporary in nature; but as a fundamental step in the transformation from bourgeois to communist democracy, it would obviously not aim for restoration of the old order.

Attempting to retrieve the concept from communists, Carl Schmitt (1921) distinguished between commissarial and sovereign dictatorship. Commissarial dictatorship conforms to the Roman usage of the term, but is likely to give way to sovereign dictatorship that, in contrast, is unlimited and likely will establish a new order. In making such a distinction Schmitt sought to justify the extensive use of emergency powers to address social and economic crises in Weimar Germany. Still, his conception of sovereign dictatorship is important because it cements an important shift in the understanding of the term: Dictatorships need not be temporary nor restorative of the prior constitutional order.

As a consequence, the post–World War II conception of dictatorship is necessarily a broader one in which dictatorship encompasses all regimes that are not democratic. Dictatorships may be distinguished from democracies as regimes in which rulers are not governed by law (Kelsen 1945) or selected by elections (Schumpeter 1942). Still, such minimalist criteria mean that dictatorships demonstrate wide heterogeneity in their organization and bases for rule.

TYPES OF CONTEMPORARY DICTATORSHIPS

Dictatorships include both totalitarian and authoritarian regimes: The former deeply pervades society through ideological fervor, mobilization efforts, and intolerance of autonomous organization, while the latter is more pluralistic and predictable in nature (Friedrich and Brzezinski 1961, Linz 1970). Besides Nazi Germany and Joseph Stalin's Soviet Union, however, relatively few totalitarian regimes exist. As a result, most dictatorships are authoritarian regimes, and the two terms often are used synonymously.

The most prominent distinction among contemporary dictatorships is in the location of decision-making power, which determines their bases of institutional support and their constraints. While debates abound over the exact criteria for classification, the main categories consist of military, party, monarchical, and personalist regimes.

Military dictatorships emerge by coup d'état, an extralegal seizure of power. Paul Brooker (2000) notes that the military intervention in politics may stem from "national interest" in times of crises or corporate and self-interests in the quest for greater resources. Once in power, the military consolidates both executive and legislative powers within a junta, a small collective that typically is composed of high-ranking officers. The junta is responsible for major decisions, including those governing succession. In decision making the degree of power sharing among service branches varies and is a common source of friction among junta members. The tension between governing and maintaining military cohesion has often led to the demise of these regimes.

In party dictatorships, power is concentrated within a single regime party that dominates political life (Huntington and Moore 1970). Other political parties may exist, but they do not pose any serious competition. Major policy decisions and issues of succession are determined by an inner sanctum of the party. Still, the party's organizational reach is broad, pervading the armed forces and local institutions, down to the level of villages, firms, and schools. Because the party is a vehicle through which individuals may advance their careers and earn patronage, it serves as an important tool for the dictatorship in mobilizing support, collecting information, and supervising the behaviors of others. The party's infiltration of the military also ensures civilian control over the armed forces.

Monarchies are typically treated as distinct from other forms of tyrannical rule. However, the minimalist criteria distinguishing democratic and nondemocratic regimes clearly require classifying these regimes as dictatorships. In monarchies the institution at the center of power is the dynastic family that claims historical rights to rule and monopolizes succession. The king is the effective head of government, yet as Michael Herb (1999) observes, major policy decisions and the choice of successor from within the family is determined only with the consent of other family members. Kin networks are also used to maintain control over the military and to staff government positions, ensuring the dominance of the ruling family.

Personalist regimes are those in which dictators do not overtly rely on the armed forces, a regime party, or a dynastic family to maintain their rule. As a consequence, they seemingly monopolize decision-making and conform to stereotypical notions of dictatorships as "one-man rule." Personalist dictators may come to power via a coup or legitimate elections and are able to consolidate power by the skillful use of patronage and "charismatic authority" (following Max Weber's notion in *The Theory of Social and Economic Organization* [1947]) such that they are able to avoid dependence on a single institution and hence constraints on their decision-making power.

SEE ALSO *Authoritarianism; Autocracy; Totalitarianism*

BIBLIOGRAPHY

Brooker, Paul. 2000. *Non-democratic Regimes: Theory, Government, and Politics.* New York: St. Martin's Press.

Friedrich, Carl J., and Zbigniew K. Brzezinski. 1961. *Totalitarian Dictatorship and Autocracy.* New York: Praeger.

Herb, Michael. 1999. *All in the Family: Absolutism, Revolution, and Democracy in the Middle Eastern Monarchies.* Albany: State University of New York Press.

Huntington, Samuel P., and Clement H. Moore, eds. 1970. *Authoritarian Politics in Modern Society: The Dynamics of Established One-Party Systems.* New York: Basic Books.

Kelsen, Hans. 1945. *General Theory of Law and State.* Trans. Anders Wedberg. Cambridge, MA: Harvard University Press.

Linz, Juan. 1970. An Authoritarian Regime: Spain. In *Mass Politics: Studies in Political Sociology*, eds. Erik Allardt and Stein Rokkan. New York: The Free Press.

Schmitt, Carl. 1921. *Die Diktatur von den Anfängen des modernen Souveränitätsgedankens bis zum proletarischen Klassenkampf.* Munich, Germany: Duncker and Humblot.

Schumpeter, Joseph A. 1942. *Capitalism, Socialism, and Democracy.* New York: Harper and Row.

Weber, Max. 1947. *The Theory of Social and Economic Organization.* Trans. Alexander M. Henderson and Talcott Parsons. New York: Oxford University Press.

Jennifer Gandhi

DIET, THE

A legislature, which is the most essential political institution in modern democracies, is denoted by different terms in different countries. One such term, Diet, is the name of the national legislature of Japan. The Imperial Diet, established in 1890 by virtue of the Meiji Constitution, was the first legislature in Japan. Under the Meiji Constitution, the emperor's prerogative was extensive, whereas the Imperial Diet functioned simply as an advisory organ to the emperor in his conduct of state affairs. The Imperial Diet consisted of two houses, the House of Peers and the House of Representatives. The former was composed of members of the imperial family, individuals who paid high taxes, and others appointed by the emperor. Members of the House of Representatives were elected by a limited franchise.

After World War II, the Imperial Diet was replaced by the National Diet under a new constitution. The Diet is now the highest organ of state power and the sole lawmaking entity of the state. Under the new constitution, Japan has a parliamentary system, in which the prime minister is chosen from among the Diet members by a resolution of the Diet. The Cabinet is collectively responsible to the Diet in the exercise of executive power.

The National Diet is bicameral, composed of the House of Representatives and the House of Councillors. Similar to the U.S. Congress, but different from many European legislatures, members of both houses are elected by universal adult suffrage. The electoral system in the House of Representatives is a combination of single-member districts (300 in total) and proportional representation systems (180 in total). This system was adopted in 1994, replacing the multiple-member district system. Ninety-six members of the House of Councillors are elected on the basis of a proportional representation system, while the remaining 146 are elected by a multiple-member prefectural district system.

The constitution proclaims the superiority of the House of Representatives with respect to budget legislation, approval of treaties, nominations for prime minister, and other matters. If a bill is passed by the House of Representatives but rejected by the House of Councillors, the bill can still become law if two-thirds or more of members support the bill in the second deliberation in the House of Representatives.

One feature of the legislative process in the Diet is the committee system, which is similar to that of the U.S. Congress. When a bill is introduced in the House of Representatives, the speaker refers it to the committee under whose jurisdiction it falls. The deliberation in the committee is more detailed and likely to take more time than that in the plenary session.

Secondly, the method of interparty negotiation regarding the management of Diet affairs is peculiar to Japan. Each party represented in the Diet has its own Diet Affairs Committee or similarly named party apparatus, and the committee chairpersons of ruling and opposition parties hold a conference to find a negotiated solution to an interparty confrontation. These conferences, which are typically held behind closed doors, significantly influence the business of the Diet, although the Diet Affairs Committees are not formal organs of the Diet. This system for managing Diet affairs is considered to be one factor that makes deliberations in the Diet difficult to understand.

SEE ALSO *Bicameralism; Congress, U.S.; Democracy; Government; Knesset, The; Parliament, United Kingdom*

BIBLIOGRAPHY

House of Councillors of Japan.
http://www.sangiin.go.jp/eng/index.htm.

House of Representatives of Japan.
http://www.shugiin.go.jp/index.nsf/html/index_e.htm.

Mochizuki, Mike Masato. 1982. Managing and Influencing the Japanese Legislative Process: The Roles of Parties and the National Diet. PhD diss., Harvard University.

Noritada Matsuda

DIFFERENCE EQUATIONS

Difference equations or, rather, systems of these are mathematical models of some systems in the real world that are believed to change their states at discrete and equidistant points of time. An example of such a system is a university that accepts students twice a year. The state of such a university would be described in terms of student numbers—which are constant for half a year and change at two discrete points in the course of a year (based on the number of students that pass their exams and the number of students accepted). Continuous systems, on the other hand, change their states at any time. Systems in the real world can usually be described in terms of both continuous and discrete time. When, however, the most important state changes occur only within a very small part of a time span (such as within just a week per semester in a university), difference equations are the method of choice. The same preference applies when processes are modeled that are only measured at regular time intervals (once a year, once a month)—as is common, since most statistics are only published at discrete times (even though individual events such as births, deaths, or unemployment occur more or less continuously).

Difference equation models connect the future state of a system to the current state or even past states of the same system, in a way comparable to the manner in which differential equations allow the calculation of future states of a system from its current state. The application of difference equations supposes, however, that the processes within the modeled system are discrete in time, whereas in the case of differential equations processes are continuous in time.

For a number of real systems, the use of difference equations seems appropriate—for instance, in the case of populations of animals with non-overlapping generations. Here, one is only (or at least mainly) interested in the size x_{t+1} of a given population next year when x_t, the size of the population in a given year t, is known; x_{t+1} is then expected to be some function of x_t. More generally speaking, t is the parameter of a process $\{x_t, t \in T\}$ where T is an enumerable set, and the general form of a (first-order) difference equation is

$$x_{t+1} = f(x_t).$$

Difference equations of higher order are also possible; a second-order difference equation has the general form

$$x_{t+1} = f(x_t, x_{t-1})$$

and is often transformed into a system of difference equations, such that

$$x_{t+1} = f(x_t, y_t); \; y_{t+1} = x_t.$$

LOGISTIC GROWTH

One of the simplest cases of a difference equation in one variable—which also displays some interesting behavior—is the so-called logistic or Verhulst equation, which in its time-discrete version has the form

$$x_{t+1} = rx_t (1 - x_t/K).$$

One of the interpretations of this equation is that it describes a population in a habitat with carrying capacity K, whose size in the next generation is proportional to a growth constant (sometimes called the Malthusian parameter) r, to the current population size x_t and to the proportion of the habitat that, in some way, is so far unused $(1 - x_t/K)$. The equation has two stationary solutions, namely $x_{st0} = 0$ and $x_{st1} = K(r - 1)/r$. For $r \leq 1$, only $x_{st0} = 0$ is stable, and the population dies out, whereas for $1 < r < 3$, $x_{st1} = K(r - 1)/r$ is stable, and the population will stabilize at this size, and for $r \geq 3$, x_{st1} is again unstable, and the system displays some interesting chaotic or fractal behavior (Schuster 1984, pp. 31–46).

AGE STRUCTURE OF A POPULATION

Another example also comes from mathematical demography, and here a system of difference equations is used to project the age distribution in a given population characterized by age-dependent death rates (which may differ between males and females) and birth rates that depend on the age of the mother. If one writes, for instance, $m_a(t)$ and $f_a(t)$ for the number of males and females, respectively, in the a-th year of age, and δ_a^m and δ_a^f for the age-dependent death rates of males and females, then the death part of the system of difference equations is easily formulated:

$$m_a(t + 1) = m_a(t)(1 - \delta_a^m) \text{ and } f_a(t + 1) = f_a(t)(1 - \delta_a^f)$$

for all $a > 1$

and for $a = 1$ the difference equation is

$$m_1(t + 1) = \gamma \Sigma_{a=15}^{45} \beta_a f_a(t) \text{ and } f_1(t + 1) = (1 - \gamma) \Sigma_{a=15}^{45} \beta_a f_a(t)$$

where γ is the proportion of male births and β_a the age-dependent fertility rate. This system of difference equations yields a series of age pyramids.

ARMA MODEL OF TIME SERIES

Time series are also often modeled with the help of difference equations. The so-called ARMA model (Box and Jenkins 1970) is of this type, where the current value of a time series is modeled as a sum of autoregressive (AR) terms and a (weighted) moving average (MA) of random shocks:

$$x_t = \alpha_1 x_{t-1} + \alpha_2 x_{t-2} + \ldots + \alpha_p x_{t-p} + \varepsilon_t + \beta_1 \varepsilon_{t-1} + \beta_2 \varepsilon_{t-2} + \ldots + \beta_q \varepsilon_{t-q}.$$

BUSINESS CYCLES

Finally, differential equations with delay are a mixture of difference and differential equations. One major example is Michał Kalecki's model of business cycles, which can be formulated as follows:

$$K^\bullet(t) = \alpha/\tau K(t) - (\alpha/\tau + \delta)K(t - \tau)$$

where K and $K^\bullet$ represent capital and capital growth respectively, and τ is the delay between the decision to invest and the realization of this decision, while α and δ are two parameters that weight the influence of profit and of capital on the decision. Generally speaking, this model shows oscillating behavior for a wide range of values of α, δ, and τ, where these oscillations can be of constant amplitude, damped or negatively damped.

As in other cases, the Kalecki equation can be rewritten into a system of difference and differential equations:

$$K^\bullet(t) = \alpha/\tau K(t) - (\alpha/\tau + \delta)L(t)$$
$$L(t) = K(t - \tau)$$

where the first is a differential equation and the second is a difference equation. Kalecki's approach shows that with relatively simple assumptions about the investment behavior in an economy, business cycles can be modeled. The idea is that there is always a delay between an investment decision and the realization of the capital investment, and Kalecki's model relates business cycles to just this delay. K and $K^\bullet$ are aggregated variables that in principle can be measured at very short time intervals and thus can be modeled in terms of differential equations, whereas τ is a considerably longer period of time.

SEE ALSO *Comparative Dynamics; Differential Equations; Kalecki, Michał; System Analysis*

BIBLIOGRAPHY

Box, George E. P., and Gwilym M. Jenkins. 1970. *Time Series Analysis: Forecasting and Control.* San Francisco: Holden-Day.

Kalecki, Michał. 1935. A Macrodynamic Theory of Business Cycles. *Econometrica* 3 (3): 327–344.

Pressat, Roland. 1972. *Demographic Analysis. Methods, Results, Applications.* Trans. Judah Matras. New York: Aldine-Atherton.

Schuster, Heinz Georg. 1984. *Deterministic Chaos: An Introduction.* Weinheim, Germany: Physik-Verlag.

Verhulst, Pierre-François. 1847. Deuxième mémoire sur la loi d'accroissement de la population. *Nouveaux mémoires de l'Academie Royale des Sciences et Belles-Lettres de Bruxelles* 20: 1–32.

Klaus G. Troitzsch

DIFFERENCE PRINCIPLE

The difference principle is the second part of the second principle of John Rawls's theory of justice. The first principle requires that citizens enjoy equal basic liberties. The first part of the second principle requires fair equality of opportunity. These rules have priority over the difference principle; the difference principle cannot justify policies or institutions that abrogate them. The difference principle governs the distribution of income and wealth, positions of responsibility and power, and the social bases of self-respect. It holds that inequalities in the distribution of these goods are permissible only if they benefit the least well-off positions of society.

Rawls's argument for the principle is based on the premise that citizens have, as their highest interest, two moral powers. The first power is the ability to propose and act on principles of justice all can accept. The second power is the ability to hold, revise, and pursue a conception of the good. It follows that any principle of justice, including those that regulate social and economic inequalities, must be acceptable to all and help each citizen pursue his or her conception of the good.

Rawls argues that citizens concerned to protect and exercise their moral powers would agree on principles that guarantee equal basic liberties (his first principle of justice) and the resources to pursue their good. This rules out libertarianism, perfectionism, theocracy, and utilitarianism. Citizens would not choose a rule requiring absolute equality, for everyone could do better by allowing inequalities that spur economic production. Rules that allow more inequality than the difference principle ask the worst off to accept inequalities that do not benefit them; this violates reciprocity. Moreover, citizens must have self-respect if they are to pursue their good. Self-respect depends both on having the resources to pursue one's good and others' recognition of one's worth. The difference principle supports the self-respect of the worst off more than alternative principles because it maximizes their resources and expresses the commitment of the better off to share their fate. Last, Rawls argues that a principle allowing some citizens advantages that do not benefit the worst off implies that the latter are not equally worthy members of society. This endangers social stability by causing them to withdraw in sullen resentment from the public world.

Critics have charged that Rawls's argument ignores the principle that people with greater talents deserve greater rewards than others. Rawls responds that the point of any system of cooperation citizens construct is to enable them to exercise their moral powers and pursue their good. Because citizens are equal in their moral features, they have an equal claim to the benefits from the system of cooperation. The principle of desert implies the cooperative scheme ought to reward talent rather than to respond to the essential moral features of citizens. Rawls also argues that people do not deserve their talent or the character that allows them to develop it, for they have willed neither. Last, citizens have a variety of moral, reli-gious, and philosophical views about what constitutes desert and so could not agree on what to reward.

SEE ALSO *Equality; Justice, Distributive; Political Economy; Rawls, John; Wealth*

BIBLIOGRAPHY

Cohen, Joshua. 1989. Democratic Equality. *Ethics* 99 (July): 727–751.

Pogge, Thomas W. 1989. *Realizing Rawls*. Ithaca, NY: Cornell University Press.

Rawls, John. 1971. *A Theory of Justice*. Cambridge, MA: Belknap Press of Harvard University Press.

Rawls, John. 2001. *Justice as Fairness: A Restatement*. Ed. Erin Kelly. Cambridge, MA: Harvard University Press.

Van Parijs, Philippe. 2003. Difference Principles. In *The Cambridge Companion to Rawls*, ed. Samuel Freedman. New York: Cambridge University Press.

Alexander Moon

DIFFERENTIAL EQUATIONS

Differential equations are models of real systems that are believed to change their states continuously, or, to put it more precisely, at infinitesimally short intervals in time. Differential equations, or rather systems of differential equations, connect a change in the state of a system to its current state, or even the change in a change of the state of the same system, in a way that is comparable to the way *difference equations* allow the calculation of future states of a system from its current state. But unlike difference equations, the application of differential equations supposes that the processes within the system modeled by these equations are continuous in time, whereas with difference equations, processes are discrete in time.

For a number of real systems, the approach of differential equations seems appropriate, for instance in the case of the movement of an arrow through the air or of the local concentration of some pollutant in a lake. Here, one is only (or at least mainly) interested in the current value of some continuously measurable variable that is seen as varying continuously over time. More generally speaking, t is the parameter of a process $\{x_t, t \in T\}$ where T is a continuous set with the same cardinality as that of the set of real numbers; the general form of a (first-order ordinary) difference equation is

$$dx / dt = \dot{x} = f(x)$$

Here, in a more symbolic way, dx is the change that occurs to the state variable x of the system in question during the infinitesimally short time interval dt at any time t. Differential equations of higher order are also possible; a second-order differential equation has the general form

$$d^2x/dt^2 = \ddot{x} = f(x)$$

and is often transformed into a system of differential equations

$$\dot{y} = \ddot{x} = f(x) = g(y)$$
$$y = \dot{x} = h(x)$$

Strictly speaking, in the realm of the social and economic sciences, applications of differential equations and systems of them are only approximations, because the state variables of social and economic systems cannot undergo continuous changes. In demography, for example, we can only talk about the birth and death of an integer number of people, and in economics we can only calculate with a fixed number of products sold to the customer (not even with the exception of fluid, gaseous goods, or energy, which can be physically split down to molecules and energy quanta). In social psychology, it is still an open question whether attitudes change continuously (they are usually measured on four- or seven-point scales). And even if all these variables were continuous, the question remains whether these changes occur in a continuous manner: Children are born at a certain point in time, prices are paid at a certain point in time, and until the next payment arrives in one's bank account, the balance is constant.

On the other hand, with a large number of demographic events or financial transactions, one could argue that a differential equation is a sufficiently good approximation that is, in most cases, more easily treatable than the discrete event formalization of the real process (this even applies when the alternative is a deterministic difference equation). Differential equations can also treat probabilistic problems (then we have stochastic differential equations) and can describe processes in time and space, for instance in diffusion processes where the distribution of local concentrations or frequencies changes over time.

UNRESTRICTED GROWTH

Linear differential equations of the type $\dot{x} = \lambda x$ and systems of such equations can always be solved, that is, it is always possible to write down the time-dependent function that obeys the differential equation (which is the exponential function $x(t) = Ae^{\lambda t}$, where A and λ are two constants that depend on the initial condition and the proportionality constant between $\dot{x}$ and x, respectively). If the proportionality constant is positive, this results in an infinite growth, whereas with a negative proportionality ("the higher the value of x, the higher its decrease") the value of x approaches 0, though only in infinite time. This differential equation was first used in Thomas Malthus's (1766–1834) theories of demographic and economic growth.

ARMS RACE

A system of linear differential equations has a vector-valued exponential function as its solution. One of the earlier applications of a very simple system of linear differential equations was Lewis Fry Richardson's (1960) model of an arms race between two powers. The idea behind this model is that each block increases the armament budget both proportional to the current armament expenses of the other block and the budget available for other purposes. Thus, the change in the armament budget of block 1 is

$$\dot{x} = m(x_{max} - x) + ay = g + mx + ay \text{ with } g = mx_{max}$$

The same holds for the other block:

$$\dot{y} = bx + n(y_{max} - y) = h + bx + ny \text{ with } h = ny_{max}$$

The analytical solution for this system of two linear differential equations has the general form

$$q(t) = \theta_1 q_1 \, exp(\lambda_1 t) + \theta_2 q_2 \, exp(\lambda_2 t) + q_3$$

where q and $\dot{q}$ are vectors with elements x and y and elements $\dot{x}$ and $\dot{y}$ respectively, while θ_1, θ_2, λ_1, λ_2, q_1, q_2 and q_3 are constants that depend on a, b, g, h, m, and n. In a way, only λ_1 and λ_2 are of special interest, because they are—as multipliers in the arguments to the exponential functions in the analytical solution—responsible for the overall behavior of the system. They can be shown to be the eigen-values of the matrix formed of $-m$, a, b, and $-n$, and these eigen-values can be complex, which means that besides stationary solutions, periodic solutions are also possible, at least in principle (although not in this case, where m, a, b, and n are all positive). If both λ_1 and λ_2 are negative, $q(t)$ approaches q_3 as times goes by; if at least one of them is positive, $q(t)$ grows beyond all limits (which of course is impossible in the real world).

LOGISTIC GROWTH

One of the simplest cases of a differential equation in one variable—which also displays some interesting behavior—is the so-called logistic or Verhulst equation, which in its time-continuous version has the form

$$\dot{x} = rx(K - x)$$

One of the interpretations of this equation is that it describes a population in a habitat with carrying capacity K whose size changes continuously in such a way that the relative change ($\dot{x}/x$) is proportional both to the current size x and to the difference between the current size and the carrying capacity ($K - x$, this difference is the proportion of the habitat that, in a way, is so far unused).

The equation has two stationary solutions, namely, $x_{st0} = 0$ and $x_{st1} = K$. The former is unstable: Even from the tiniest initial state, the population will grow until the carrying capacity is exactly exhausted. The time-dependent function $x(t)$, which obeys the differential equation, is a monotonically growing function whose graph is an S-shaped curve. This time-dependent function can be written as

$$x(t) = Kx(0) \exp(rt)/\{K - x(0) [1 - \exp(rt)]\}$$

This differential equation is one of the simplest nonlinear ordinary differential equations.

THE LOTKA-VOLTERRA EQUATION

Another well-known system of nonlinear differential equations is the so-called Lotka-Volterra equation, which describes the interaction between predators and prey. It can also be applied to the interaction between a human population (predator) and its natural resources (prey). Here, the relative growth of the prey is a sum of a (positive) constant and a negative term that is proportional to the size of the predator population, whereas the relative growth of the predator population is a sum of a (negative) constant and a positive term that is proportional to the size of the prey population. In other words, in the absence of the predator population the prey would grow infinitely, whereas in the absence of the prey, the predator population would die out.

$$\dot{x} = x (a - by)$$
$$\dot{y} = y (-c + dx)$$

This system of differential equations does not have a closed solution, but it has a number of interesting features that show up no matter how detailed the model is for the interaction between predators and prey: The solution for this system of differential equations is a periodic function with constant amplitude that depends on the initial condition. There is only one stationary state of the system, which is defined by $y = a/b$ (this leads to $\dot{x} = 0$) and $x = c/d$ (this leads to $\dot{y} = 0$); thus if both hold, then no change will happen to the state of the system. Otherwise the populations increase and decrease periodically without ever dying out.

PARTIAL DIFFERENTIAL EQUATIONS

In most applications of differential equations and their systems, the parameter variable will be time, as in the examples above. But it is also possible to treat changes both in time and space with the help of a special type of differential equation, namely, *partial differential equations*. They define the change of the value of some attribute at some point in space and time—for instance, the expected change K of the continuously modeled and measured attitude X of a person that has the value x at time t, where this change will be different for different x and perhaps also for different t—in terms of this point in time and space. Thus,

$$K(x, t) = dx/dt = \partial V(x, t)/\partial x$$

For an application, see the next paragraph. Partial differential equations are seldom used in the social sciences because, typically, continuous properties of individual human beings—if they exist at all in the focus of interest of social scientists and economists—are difficult to measure, and even more difficult to measure within time intervals that are short enough to estimate any parameters of functions such as K and V in the above equation.

STOCHASTIC DIFFERENTIAL EQUATIONS

Stochastic influences can also be inserted into the formulation of differential equations. The simplest case is the so-called Langevin equation, which describes the motion of a system in its state space when there is both a potential whose gradient it follows and some stochastic influence that prevents the system from following the gradient of this potential in a precise manner. This type of description can, for instance, be used to describe the attitudes of voters during an election campaign. Each voter's attitude can be defined (and measured) in a continuous attitude space. Their motions through this attitude space (say, from left to right; see, e.g., Downs 1957, p. 117) are determined by a "potential" that is determined either by some parties that "attract" voters toward their own positions in the same attitude space or by the "political climate" defined by the frequency distribution over the attitude space. In the latter case, voters would give up their attitude if it is shared by only a few and change it into an attitude that is more frequent. Thus they follow a gradient toward more frequent attitudes; but while moving through the attitude space, they would also perform random changes in their attitudes, thus not obeying exactly the overall political climate. And by changing individual attitudes, the overall "climate" or potential is changed. The movement could be described as follows:

$$\dot{q}(t) = -\gamma \partial V(q, t)/\partial q + \varepsilon_t$$

where

$$V(q, t) = -\ln f(q, t)$$

and $f(q, t)$ is the frequency distributions of voters over the attitude space at time t (V would be a polynomial up to some even order in q). One would typically find voters more or less normally distributed at the beginning of an election campaign, but the process described here would explain why and how polarization—a bimodal or multimodal frequency distribution—could occur toward the election date (Troitzsch 1990).

SEE ALSO *Comparative Dynamics; Cumulative Causation; Difference Equations; Phase Diagrams; System Analysis; Taylor, Lance*

BIBLIOGRAPHY

Downs, Anthony. 1957. *An Economic Theory of Democracy.* Boston: Addison-Wesley.

Lotka, Alfred J. 1925. *Elements of Physical Biology.* Baltimore, MD: Williams & Wilkins.

Richardson, Lewis Fry. 1960. *Arms and Insecurity. A Mathematical Study of the Causes and Origins of War.* Pittsburgh, PA: Boxwood.

Troitzsch, Klaus G. 1990. Self-Organization in Social Systems. In *Computer Aided Sociological Research,* eds. Johannes Gladitz and Klaus G. Troitzsch, 353–377. Berlin: Akademie-Verlag.

Verhulst, Pierre-François. 1847. Deuxième mémoire sur la loi d'accroissement de la population. *Nouveaux mémoires de l'Academie Royale des Sciences et Belles-Lettres de Bruxelles* 20: 1–32.

Volterra, Vito. 1926. Variazioni e fluttuazioni del numero d'individui in specie animali conviventi. *Atti della Accademia Nazional dei Lincei* 6 (2): 31–113.

Klaus G. Troitzsch

DIGITAL DIVIDE

The *digital divide* has been conceived as the lack of access to information and communication technologies among underrepresented ethnic minorities, those of lower socioeconomic levels, and people living in rural locales. Several studies have characterized these disparities along dimensions of gender (Kvasny 2003), age (Loges and Jung 2001), race (Hoffman 1999, Kvasny 2003, Payton 2001), geographical location (Sipior et al. 2004), and educational resource characteristics (NTIA 2000, Payton 2001, Kvasny and Payton 2005). Karen Mossberger and Caroline Tolbert (2003) have found that African Americans are less likely to have access to information and communication technologies and the skills to use such technologies, even when controlling for other factors, such as income and education. Similar findings have been documented for Hispanic and Native Americans. Despite these foundations of physical access, the digital divide concept is not limited to a binary taxonomy of access versus nonaccess, or the typical classification of "have" and "have not." In fact, the digital divide warrants a broader definition—one that is inclusive of social, economic, and technology-use attributes—which can capture the notion of digital equity. This concept rests on critical issues of how individuals can use information provided by these technologies and what strategic skills are desirable to prosper in the competitive environment of today's global information age.

WHAT IS DIGITAL EQUITY?

Digital equity raises issues of social justice and can be defined as a trend toward equal access to information and communication technologies among society's citizens. Even more, digital equity enables individuals to gain knowledge and skills to use technological tools, computers, and the Internet (i.e., behavioral outcomes). The National Institute for Community Innovations reports that:

> According to recent research by the National Center for Educational Statistics, 98% of schools and 77% of instructional rooms have computers and are connected to the Internet. But many classrooms and important educational projects are not connected, and these educators are deprived of excellent Internet-based resources. Most important, even though a school or classroom may be connected, the technology may not [be] used by students—leaving many young people technology-illiterate, without key skills they need to succeed in today's job market. (National Institute for Community Innovations 2005)

Similarly, Austan Goolsbee and Jonathan Guryan reported that California's public schools were funded by nearly $937 million for a program known as E-Rate (education rate) during the 1998 to 2000 school years, of which a substantial portion provided Internet access and technologies. This program noticeably closed the digital divide for Internet access between wealthy and poor California schools. If one assesses effectiveness in terms of access, the California E-Rate initiative has been successful. Goolsbee and Guryan note, however, that despite this accomplishment, Internet access did little in the way of improving student performance; they conclude that "the Internet itself … seems unlikely to be a silver bullet for solving the problems of America's public schools" (2006, p. 65).

OTHER CONSIDERATIONS

In its 2003 fiscal budget, the administration of President George W. Bush reduced funding for community-based technology-related programs and training initiatives by $100 million, as shown in Figure 1.

Much of this funding previously supported underrepresented minorities, children, and rural programs. While the digital divide is an immediate and direct effect of the eradication of these training initiatives, the more dire consequences rest in the lack of social justice produced by such digital inequities. Evidence of these outcomes has been documented by the National Telecommunications and Information Administration (NTIA) report "A Nation Online: How Americans Are Expanding Their Use of the Internet" (2002). The NTIA reports that individuals benefit from being prepared with technology skills, and 57 percent of employed Americans over the age of twenty-five use a computer in the workplace. By 2010 jobs in science, technology, engineering, and mathematics

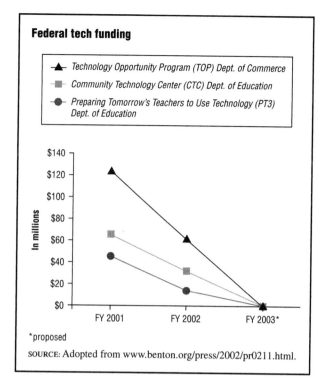

Federal tech funding

▲ *Technology Opportunity Program (TOP) Dept. of Commerce*

■ *Community Technology Center (CTC) Dept. of Education*

● *Preparing Tomorrow's Teachers to Use Technology (PT3) Dept. of Education*

*proposed

SOURCE: Adopted from www.benton.org/press/2002/pr0211.html.

Figure 1

are expected to increase by 67 percent according to the U.S. Department of Labor as reported in the 2002 CyberEducation Report by the American Electronics Association. In addition, the costs associated with broadband access to the Internet heighten digital exclusion and often preclude minority, low-income, rural, and undereducated populations from access to the social justice associated with social, community, economic, and education capital foundations.

Unlike other forms of communication media (e.g., radio, television, and printed materials), the Internet is distinctive because of its integration among diverse communication modalities, such as broadcasting, reciprocal interaction, group discussion, person-machine interaction, and reference research (DiMaggio et al. 2001). The digital equity principle examines how Internet access is used, and evidence supports the argument that parity is achievable when all populations gain the knowledge and skills to impact social inclusion—thereby stimulating social justice. The most noteworthy form of inclusion would necessitate equalities (therefore reducing or eliminating disparities) in education, health care, and economic and financial systems.

The digital divide or inequity issue is not limited to the United States. According to statistics from the World Summit on the Information Society, a comparison of Internet access and use in eight industrialized nations (Canada, France, Germany, Italy, Japan, Russia, the United Kingdom, and the United States) compared to the rest of the world indicates that: (1) In 2004 fewer than three out of every one hundred Africans used the Internet, compared with an average of one out of every two inhabitants of the industrialized countries; (2) the eight industrialized countries are home to just 15 percent of the world's population but almost 50 percent of the world's total Internet users; and (3) there are more than eight times as many Internet users in the United States than on the entire African continent. Sundeep Sahay and Chrisanthi Avgerou concluded that information and communication technologies are key to the development of poorer nations and offer the "potential for turning around uncompetitive industries and dysfunctional public administration, and for providing unprecedented opportunities for the information-intensive social services, such as health and education" (2002, p. 73).

SEE ALSO *Cyberspace; Inequality, Political; Internet; Property Rights; Property Rights, Intellectual*

BIBLIOGRAPHY

American Electronic Association. 2002. CyberEducation, U.S. Education, and the High-Technology Industry: A National and State-by-State Overview. http://www.aeanet.org/publications/idmk_CyEd2002_brochure.asp.

Benton Foundation Press Release. 2002. Bush Abandons National Strategy to Bridge the Digital Divide. http://www.benton.org/press/2002/pr0211.html.

DiMaggio, Paul, Eszter Hargittai, W. Russell Neuman, and John P. Robinson. 2001. Social Implications of the Internet. *Annual Review of Sociology* 27 (1): 307–336.

Goolsbee, Austan, and Jonathan Guryan. 2006. World Wide Wonder? *Education Next* 6 (1): 61–65. http://www.educationnext.org/20061/60.html.

Hoffman, Donna L., and Thomas P. Novak. 1998. Bridging the Racial Divide on the Internet. *Science* 280 (5362): 390–391.

Kvasny, Lynette. 2003. Liberation or Domination: Understanding the Digital Divide from the Standpoint of the "Other." In *Proceedings of the Information Resources Management Association (IRMA) Conference*, ed. Mehdi Khosrow-Pour. Hershey, PA: Idea Group.

Kvasny, Lynette, and Fay Cobb Payton. 2005. Minorities and the Digital Divide. In *Encyclopedia of Information Science and Technology*, ed. Mehdi Khosrow-Pour, 1955–1959. Hershey, PA: Idea Group.

Loges, William E., and Joo-Young Jung. 2001. Exploring the Digital Divide: Internet Connectedness and Age. *Communication Research* 28 (4): 536–562.

Mossberger, Karen, and Caroline Tolbert. 2003. Race, Place, and Information Technology. Telecommunications Policy Research Conference: Programs and Papers Archive. http://tprc.org/papers/2003/184/raceplace4.pdf.

National Institute for Community Innovations. 2005. The Digital Equity Toolkit. http://nici-mc2.org/de_toolkit/.

National Telecommunications and Information Administration. 2000. Falling Through the Net: Toward Digital Inclusion. http://www.ntia.doc.gov/ntiahome/fttn00/contents00.html.

National Telecommunications and Information Administration. 2002. A Nation Online: How Americans Are Expanding Their Use of the Internet. http://www.ntia.doc.gov/ntiahome/dn/nationonline_020502.htm.

Payton, Fay Cobb. 2003. Rethinking the Digital Divide. *Communications of the ACM* 46 (6): 89–91.

Sahay, Sundeep, and Chrisanthi Avgerou, eds. 2002. Letter from the Guest Editors Sundeep Sahay and Chrisanthi Avgerou. Special Issue: Information and Communication Technologies in Developing Countries. *Information Society* 18 (2): 73–76. http://www.indiana.edu/~tisj/readers/full-text/18-2%20Sahey.html.

Sipior, Janice C., Burke T. Ward, Linda Volonino, and Joanna Z. Marzec. 2004. A Community Initiative that Diminished the Digital Divide. *Communications of the Association for Information Systems* 13, Art. 5 (January): 29–56.

World Summit on the Information Society. 2006. What's the State of ICT Access around the World. http://www.itu.int/wsis/tunis/newsroom/stats/.

Fay Cobb Payton

DILEMMA, PRISONER'S

SEE *Prisoner's Dilemma.*

DIOP, CHEIKH ANTA
1923–1986

Cheikh Anta Diop was the most daring African cultural-nationalist historian, scientist, and nonapologetic Egyptologist of the twentieth century. His scholarship on the reclaiming of black civilization produced an immense body of knowledge on ancient Egyptian civilization. His argument that ancient Egypt was essentially Negroid and that the origins of Hellenic civilization were to be found in black Africa challenged the prevailing Eurocentric view of the world.

The implications of Diop's thought should be contextualized within the European imperialist dictum and black resistance movements of the time. He grew up in Senegal when France was consolidating its colonial rule in Africa, and he lived through the consequences of increasing neocolonialism, economic reforms, and militarization in Africa. Born in a Muslim family on December 29, 1923, in Caytu, a small village near the town of Diourbel, Senegal, Diop attended the local Koranic school before enrolling in a French colonial school. In 1945 his interest in science and philosophy was consolidated when he

earned his baccalaureate in mathematics and philosophy in Dakar, Senegal. Diop left Senegal for France in 1946. He pursued graduate studies in France, and elected courses in science while studying philosophy under Gaston Bachelard (1884–1962) at the Sorbonne in Paris, where he earned a degree in philosophy in 1948. In 1950 Diop was awarded a certificate in general chemistry and another in applied chemistry. He studied nuclear physics at the nuclear chemistry laboratory of the Collège de France under the supervision of Frédéric Joliot-Curie (1900–1958) and at the Institut Pierre and Marie Curie. On January 9, 1960, Diop successfully defended his doctoral dissertation: "L'Afrique noire précoloniale et l'unité culturelle de l'Afrique noire" (Precolonial Black Africa and the Cultural Unity of Black Africa).

Back in Senegal, Diop continued his studies on culture, history, and linguistics. He also became involved in politics and established an opposition party, the Rassemblement National Démocratique (National Democratic Rally), having earlier served as secretary-general of the students' unit of the Rassemblement Démocratique Africain. Appointed assistant with teaching duties at the Institut Fondamental d'Afrique Noire of the University of Dakar, he became director of the university's radiocarbon laboratory. In 1981 Abdou Diouf, president of Senegal from 1981 to 2000, appointed Diop professor in the department of history. Diop passed away in Dakar on February 7, 1986. The university and the street in front of it were later named after him.

Diop received a number of awards, including the prestigious African World Festival of Arts and Culture Prize for scholars who had "exerted the greatest influence on African peoples in the 20th century," which he won jointly with W. E. B. Du Bois (1868–1963) in 1966 (a posthumous award for Du Bois). Diop was also awarded the Gold Medal for African scientific research and the African Grand Prize of Merit from the National University of Zaire in 1980.

The journal and publishing house *Présence Africaine*, founded by Alioune Diop (1910–1980) in 1947 in Paris, published most of Cheikh Anta Diop's classic works. These two were not related, but they were both from the Lebu ethnic group that speaks the Wolof language. Diop's important publications include: *Nations nègres et culture* (Negro Nations and Culture, 1955); *L'unité culturelle de l'Afrique noire* (The Cultural Unity of Black Africa, 1959); *Antériorité des civilisations nègres: Mythe ou realité* (The African Origin of Civilization: Myth or Reality, 1967); *Physique nucléaire et chronologie absolue* (Nuclear Physics and Absolute Chronology, 1974); and *Les fondements économiques et culturels d'un état fédéral d'Afrique noire* (The Economic and Cultural Foundations of a Federated State of Black Africa, 1974). In 1981, he published *Civilisation ou barbarie: Anthropologie sans complaisance* (Civilization or Barbarism: Anthropology without Complacency), a masterpiece on ancient Kemet (Egypt) and its influence on the Greek and Roman worlds. In 1991 this title was translated and published as *Civilization or Barbarism: An Authentic Anthropology.*

Diop took Africa seriously, and set it against the artificiality of colonialism. He was never a Marxist or a Pan-Africanist like Ghanaian statesman Kwame Nkrumah (1909–1972), but a nationalist who emphasized the value of historical consciousness as an ideological foundation for building black federalism. His views on development included Africa's acquisition of nuclear capabilities, industrialization, self-determination, and self-reliance.

Married to a white French woman (Marie-Louise) who was an important supporter of his scholarship, Diop abhorred racism. He was also critical of sexism, which he considered a product of foreign influences in Africa. He was, however, accused of being reductionist or essentialist because he insisted on a corrective scholarship. He never argued that black Africans were monolithic and genetically superior to other races. But based on his research on the Nile Valley region and West Africa, he concluded that the ancient Egyptians were bioculturally black. Diop was convinced that the history of Africa would remain in suspension and could not be written correctly until African historians connected it to the history of ancient Egypt. However, despite cultural similarities and historical connections between various layers of African civilizations from the ancient period to the present, Diop did not prove how the study of Kemet semantics could be effectively used to examine the importance of the orality of African traditions. It is unclear how the particularities of other African civilizations fit into Diop's grand paradigm.

Diop's views have been revisited in various forms through the rise of Pan-African discourse in institutions of research and higher learning in Africa and among the African diaspora, especially in Brazil, the United States, and France. Furthermore, the promotion of scholarship on the African renaissance, both as a political concept articulated by well-known African political figures and the African Union and as an analytical and intellectual tool used by scholars to understand Africa, has also contributed to the revisitation of Diop. Because of the serious and degrading socioeconomic and political conditions that paralyzed most African institutions and societies and demotivated researchers during and after the cold war, there has been an intellectual movement to investigate Diop's sources, hypotheses, and arguments as part of a broader search for African solutions to global malaise. For instance, the promotion of indigenous knowledge systems as a new area of study in some African universities and research centers was inspired by Diop's claims concerning

the role of culture, history, linguistics, and science in socioeconomic and political progress. In some parts of the African diaspora, this movement has led, contrary to Diop's intellectual convictions, to the development of a cult of personality. Some have also begun to view as religious or mystical Diop's teachings on the role of science in finding truth and the utilization of these truths as the basis for social progress. Diop himself, however, attempted in his works to separate sentiment and emotion from scientific logic, principles, and objectivity.

In his final book, *Civilisation ou barbarie*, which is considered his magnum opus, Diop expanded on, clarified, and synthesized his arguments from *L'Afrique noire pré-coloniale* (Precolonial Black Africa, 1960) and *Antériorité des civilisations nègres: Mythe ou réalité* (The African Origin of Civilization: Myth or Reality, 1967). He emphasized the primacy of African culture by proving that ancient Egypt was a black society both in its historicity and in its cultural achievements, later claimed by Indo-Aryan cultures. He strongly denounced the falsification of modern history as a major part of an agenda that has slowed world progress. Furthermore, he argued (more like an ethicist than a scientist) that humanity must break definitively from racism, genocide, and slavery and that such efforts should form the ultimate mission of the world in order to build a global civilization and avoid falling into barbarism. Diop believed in the need for a new ethics that could take into account scientific knowledge, which uniquely differentiates "modern" humans from "primitive" people. For Diop, science is a liberating, moralizing, and progress-oriented force; scientific studies on the centrality of the historicity of Africa and its contributions could humanize the world.

There are disagreements among scholars about how specifically Diop's thought has inspired generations of African Americans, both academics and community leaders, and their institutions. Certainly his intellectual impact on them cannot be denied. For Diop, learning the true history of Africa, and of the world for that matter, is essentially a scientific endeavor. In most of his works, he insisted that such a science requires first the utilization of objective methods through which empirical facts can be tested. This position may not distinguish him from other scientists, but the establishment of Africa as the birthplace of the human family is a unique knowledge that has been used differently by various cultures and peoples. For instance, one of the epistemological bases of his disagreement with Senegalese president Léopold Sédar Senghor (1906–2001), a cofounder of the Négritude movement and a member of the French Academy, was Diop's view that Senghor was making historical claims about black cultures on the basis of speculation, imagination, and sentiment and not on scientific grounds. Diop tried to make clear distinctions between science and belief systems or ideology. For Diop, ideology played an important role only in instrumentalizing science. He believed that the use of truth could make the world better. Diop's science can be used to actualize a worldview, an ideological position of humanizing the world. His perspectives tended to privilege social applications of science.

Diop's thought inspired two main groups of American Afrocentrists: those who used Afrocentricity as an interdisciplinary research method with a focus on African history and culture in the academia, and those who used Diop's racial centrality as an ideology of social reconstruction in the struggle for change in society at large. In the academia, Diop's work was consolidated with the expansion of black, Afro American, or Africana studies in the United States, where African Americans had been searching for an African cultural identity. However, with the rise of neo-integrationism in the United States and its tendency, with the support of opportunistic black scholars, to weaken "ethnicity" or "race," Diop's quest for *Negroism* has been marginalized and even trivialized in some institutions. In major American research universities, for instance, as they attempt to meet the rising demand for multiculturalism and diversity, his scholarship is perceived as advancing particularism and separatism. Clearly, these new perspectives are ideological, rather than scientific, constructs. Thus they are strongly supported and promoted by neoconservative university and college administrators with the collaboration of some African American and African academics. Diop's scholarship embodies a defensive epistemology, rejects a myopic determinism, and emphasizes the black cultural renaissance.

Based on Diop's impressive multidisciplinary training, his research, and his philosophical claims on pluralistic methodologies, he is known as an anthropologist, Egyptologist, historian, linguist, mathematician, and physicist. However, his all-embracing disciplinary approach produced, at best, eclectic and binary analytical and intellectual perspectives (black-based paradigms versus white-based paradigms). These perspectives are difficult to assess clearly in terms of their effective collective quality and their impact on the study of specific African cultures and histories, especially those that developed independently of or parallel to the ancient Egyptian civilization. Diop has been much criticized for being a jack-of-all-trades and a master of none. His generalizations about African languages and their connection to ancient Egyptian languages through Wolof, a Senegalese language, were essentially deductive, imaginative, and ahistorical. However, despite controversial hypotheses and conclusions associated with his interdisciplinary methodologies, Diop produced an important and unified referential body of knowledge on Egypto-centrism. His thought is philosophically complex and intellectually challenging, and it embodies an interactive methodological inquiry. Diop's

work cannot be fully translated into a single mode of thinking and doing, as reflected in certain affirmative dimensions of much-simplified American Afrocentricity.

BIBLIOGRAPHY

Alexander, E. Curtis, ed. 1984. *Cheikh Anta Diop: An African Scientist, an Axiomatic Overview of his Teachings and Thoughts.* Pan African Internationalist Handbook: Book 1. New York: ECA.

Diagne, Pathé. 1997. *Cheikh Anta Diop et l'Afrique dans l'histoire du monde.* Dakar, Senegal: Sankoré; Paris: Harmattan.

Hommage à Cheikh Anta Diop. 1989. 1–2. Paris: Présence Africaine.

Tukumbi Lumumba-Kasongo

DIPLOMACY

Diplomacy is often simply referred to as the dialogue among nations, but it is more precisely a dialogue among agents of nations, or diplomats. The word *diplomacy* originated from *diploma*, which in early modern Europe was the letter of credence that certified an ambassador's power to negotiate and serve as the direct representative or plenipotentiary of the sovereign.

DEFINING DIPLOMACY

Diplomacy is a central concept in the study of international relations, although scholars often disagree about its function. There is a general distinction in the social science literature between diplomacy as foreign policy, and diplomacy as the process of negotiation and deliberation that promotes peace and cooperation among nations. Diplomacy as foreign policy is the expressed desire of nations to use words before force. It is the default mode of operation for liberal states, and it is often the aim among nonliberal states to engage in diplomacy if they seek acceptance in international politics. Among early political scientists, the word *diplomacy* was used interchangeably with *international relations*. In the twenty-first century diplomacy often takes the form of membership in international organizations such as the United Nations (UN), the North Atlantic Treaty Organization (NATO), and the World Trade Organization (WTO).

However, diplomacy as simply foreign policy captures only a superficial element of the workings of international relations. Diplomacy encompasses a great number of international activities that do not include processes of cooperation. As José Calvet de Magalhães points out in *The Pure Concept of Diplomacy* (1988), states can engage in unilateral contact such as propaganda, espionage, and political or economic intervention. They can also engage in violent contact such as threat, deterrence, and economic war. Thus, the definition of diplomacy as a dialogue among nations is very broad.

Diplomacy as a process of negotiation and deliberation highlights the fact that the "art of diplomacy" is a skill that certain individuals, called diplomats, possess. Thus, diplomacy is defined specifically as an act of negotiation among accredited persons, not nations as a whole. Social scientific approaches that regard nations as unitary actors ignore the important subtleties of the art of negotiation that can often make or break efforts to reach compromise. Diplomats are people with individual and collective agency who interact over time and who are the products of a rich historical tradition of norms, negotiation, and representation. In political science there are two main approaches to understanding the work of diplomats or the process of diplomacy. One is that negotiations are conducted as hard-bargaining scenarios, and the second is that shared norms among diplomats can result in persuasion and informal methods of compromise.

THE STUDY OF DIPLOMACY

The first approach, bargaining theory, predicts that diplomats are important to outcomes of international cooperation because they reduce "transaction costs" in negotiations among nations. Transaction costs consist of the expense and inefficiency that would be involved in international cooperation if statespeople, as nonexpert negotiators, were to conduct all foreign policy on their own. Robert Putnam (1988) is well known for his argument about two-level games among diplomats. In his model level 1 is the negotiation phase, where diplomats bargain at the international table. Level 2 consists of the ratification stage in which there are separate discussions within each group of constituents about whether to ratify the agreement. For Putnam, there is a "win-set" that represents all the possible level 1 agreements that would "satisfy" level 2 constituencies. The size of the win-set depends on the distribution of power, preferences, and possible coalitions among level 1 constituents.

Many scholars argue that bargaining theory tends to be overdeterministic and advances a snapshot view. The methodology of comparing initial state preferences to final outcomes misses the critical processes that occur in-between. By ignoring factors such as relationships among negotiators, professional background, expertise, and shared normative frameworks, bargaining theorists pass up explanatory power.

The second approach argues that persuasion and informal methods of reaching compromise occur because diplomats come to share norms as they interact over time. For example, who the diplomats are, whether they have interacted on prior occasions, what kind of training they have received, how they were selected, their skill level, and so on are all important. In effect, diplomats cultivate relationships with one another throughout their careers, giving them a fundamental basis of interaction or shared understandings about the way international relations should work. Naturally, relationship building is often strongest among diplomats who work in international organizations. Thus, they are more likely to reach cooperative outcomes through persuasion and informal means than hard-bargaining approaches would anticipate. Of course, the power and resources of each state have some bearing on the leverage diplomats have in negotiation, but outcomes still rest on the abilities of individual diplomats and on their dynamic as a collective. Robert Jervis argues in *Perception and Misperception in International Politics* (1976) that perceptions of power, not actual power, are the key to any form of international relations whether in war or peace. Diplomats may often contribute to such perceptions.

Relative power among nations may play a role in determining whether or not state leaders decide to try to cooperate, but persuasion is to a significant extent out of the grasp of power. The ability to persuade is often in the hands of the diplomats. This was evident in the mammoth efforts of Secretary of State Colin Powell in 2002–2003 to sell the policies of the Bush administration—often relying more on the perception of his own independence and public respect to bring some credibility to a policy that was otherwise resisted. This occurred perhaps most notably in the UN Security Council debates over the possibility of going to war in Iraq, where some distancing by Powell made him more credible in the assurances he gave.

Despite the many ways in which diplomacy may smooth the interaction among nations, either through hard bargaining or persuasion, diplomacy does not always pay off. A compromise solution may seem continuously out of reach, such as in the relationships between Israel and the Palestinians, India and Pakistan, and nations such as Iran and North Korea with the rest of the world. Sometimes historical, religious, cultural, and political differences within nations may be so strong that even diplomacy may have a hard time providing a solution.

SEE ALSO *Cooperation; International Relations; North Atlantic Treaty Organization; Putnam, Robert; United Nations*

BIBLIOGRAPHY

Cross, Mai'a K. Davis. 2006. The European Corps: Diplomats and International Cooperation in Western Europe. In *The Diplomatic Corps and International Society*, ed. Paul Sharp and Geoffrey Wiseman. New York: Palgrave Macmillan.

Jervis, Robert. 1976. *Perception and Misperception in International Politics.* Princeton, NJ: Princeton University Press.

Magalhães, José Calvet de. 1988. *The Pure Concept of Diplomacy.* Trans. Bernardo Futscher Pereira. Westport, CT: Greenwood Press.

Putnam, Robert. 1988. Diplomacy and Domestic Politics: The Logic of Two-Level Games. *International Organization* 42 (3): 427–460.

Watson, Adam. 1982. *Diplomacy.* London: Eyre Methuen.

Mai'a K. Davis Cross

DIRECT ACTION

Direct action is a method and a theory of confronting objectionable practices and/or effecting social change using readily available means. Such action is usually contrasted with indirect forms of social and political participation such as voting. Protest demonstrations, mass rallies, strikes, boycotts, workplace occupations, and riots constitute examples of such action.

The first mention of the term is in the realm of labor struggles. In his book *Direct Action* (1920), William Mellor defined direct action as "the use of some form of economic power for the securing of ends desired by those who possess that power" (p. 15). Mellor considered direct action a tool of both employers and workers. Accordingly, he included within his definition lockouts as well as strikes. Since the late twentieth century, however, direct action has come to be increasingly associated with challenges to established societal practices and institutions by marginalized groups.

The power of direct action depends largely on its contentiousness, or the extent to which it bypasses or violates the routine conflict resolution procedures of a political system. Whereas such action can be used by recognized actors employing well-established means of claim making, substantial short-term political and social change more often emerges from the congruence of newly self-identified political actors with innovative forms of claim making. Most campaigns for social change—notably those seeking to expand the suffrage, protect civil rights, and improve working and living conditions—employ direct action repertoires.

Direct action outside of the political process is usually juxtaposed to institutionalized, routine, and/or regularized forms of social and political participation. Accordingly, one of the most commonly drawn distinctions is whether such action is carried out in a peaceful or forceful manner. Violent direct action, it is often assumed, is more contentious than nonviolent direct action because the former exhibits a high threshold of social transaction costs. Nonviolent direct action, on the other hand, has proved effective in highly repressive settings due to its unpredictability and transformative power.

Nonviolent direct action has been developed into a theory of civil disobedience by civil movements around the world. Pioneered by the American author Henry David Thoreau in his 1849 essay *Civil Disobedience*, it encompasses the active refusal to obey the laws of a government or an occupying power without resorting to physical violence. It has been used effectively by nonviolent resistance movements in the fight for independence in India, in South Africa in the fight against apartheid, and by the civil rights movement in the United States.

The mechanisms that make direct action contentious are then complex. First, there are social actors who are limited in the forms of action that are available to them, and expressions of discontent that are strictly bound to specific social or economic groups. Secondly, the political opportunities that countries make available and the resources that citizens bring to bear on this form of politics vary greatly around the world.

As of 2005, more than half of the world's nations held regular multiparty elections, more than at any time in history. As societies democratize, political opportunities increase, making direct action more routine. With the spread of democratization, some have argued, the protest demonstration has become a modular form of direct action available to multiple groups.

SEE ALSO *Civil Disobedience*

BIBLIOGRAPHY

Bond, Douglas, J., Craig Jenkins, Charles L. Taylor, and Kurt Schock. 1997. Mapping Mass Political Conflict and Civil Society: Issues and Prospects for the Automated Development of Event Data. *The Journal of Conflict Resolution* 41 (4): 553–579.

Carter, April. 1971. *Direct Action and Liberal Democracy.* New York: Harper.

Mellor, William. 1920. *Direct Action.* London: L. Parsons.

Sharp, Gene. 1973. *The Politics of Nonviolent Action.* Boston: Porter Sargent.

Tarrow, Sidney G. 1994. *Power in Movement: Social Movements, Collective Action, and Politics.* Cambridge, U.K.: Cambridge University Press.

José A. Alemán

DIRIGISTE

The counterpart to the economic doctrine of laissez-faire, *dirigisme* refers to an economic system dominated by state control of the market economy. Technically, the concept does not refer to the centrally planned economies of the former Soviet bloc, but to basically capitalistic economies that have extensive regulations and controls throughout that impact production and consumption. Many of the controls are justified because they curb productive inefficiencies, others because they correct market inequities, and still others because they protect consumers from faulty products or their own faulty decisions. In short, dirigisme describes an economic system in which the government is omnipresent and assumed to be omnipotent.

Most modern economies operate to some degree dirigistically. Government regulation and control are a significant part of most economies throughout the world today. But a significant amount of evidence has been amassed that demonstrates that economic freedom rather than government control is positively correlated with economic growth (Gwartney and Lawson 2006). In this work motivated by Milton Friedman's *Capitalism and Freedom* (1962) and *Free to Choose* (1980), economic freedom in a country is determined on the basis of an analysis of the security of private property and the freedom of contract, the tax burden, the inflation rate, the extent of regulation, and the prevailing policies toward foreign trade. When property rights are weak, taxes are high, inflation is ramped, regulation is extensive, and protectionism rather than free trade defines the policy space, the economic freedom score will be low. See Figure 1.

A key issue to remember in debating the role of government in an economic system is to distinguish between scale and scope. Much of the debate over "big government" focuses on the issue of scale—government spending as a percentage of gross domestic product. But in debating the impact of dirigisme, it may be more appropriate to focus on the issue of scope—the extent of activities the public sector attempts to control in economic decision making. A "big government" that permits a wide range of economic freedom would be less cumbersome on economic life than a "small government" that tries to control prices in every sector. The lack of economic freedom, not the size of government, causes the decline in economic growth in nations. See Figure 2.

In many ways, these various indices of economic freedom and the empirical relationship to the economic performance of countries is capturing Adam Smith's wisdom with the modern tools of economic analysis. As Smith put it in the notebooks that were the basis of *An Inquiry into the Nature and Causes of the Wealth of Nations*:

> Little else is requisite to carry a state to the highest degree of opulence from the lowest barbarism, but peace, easy taxes, and a tolerable administration of justice; all the rest being brought about by the natural course of things. All governments which thwart this natural course, which force

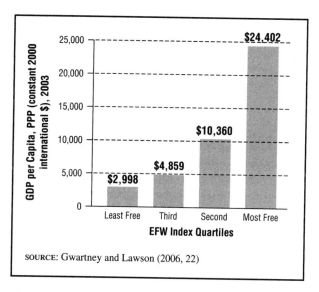

SOURCE: Gwartney and Lawson (2006, 22)

Figure 1

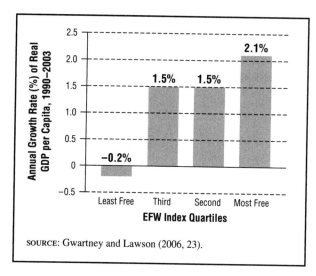

SOURCE: Gwartney and Lawson (2006, 23).

Figure 2

things into another channel or which endeavor to arrest this progress of society at a particular point, are unnatural, and to support themselves are obliged to be oppressive and tyrannical. (Smith 1776, p. xliii)

Thus, the proper scope of government in relationship to the economy is a vital question to address in assessing *dirigisme* as an economic policy regime.

This is not to say that questions of scale do not matter—they clearly do. James Buchanan, who was awarded the Nobel Prize in 1986, would often ask his students whether a fly that grew to nine times its current size could still fly. He was raising the question of "dimensions" to get to the question of "fiscal dimension"—could a government grow to nine times its current size and still function? But Buchanan also raised questions concerning the scope of government.

In *The Limits of Liberty* (1975) he put the puzzle of political economy in the following manner. He first divided the activities of the state by functions: the protective state, the productive state, and the redistributive state. The protective state refers to the government provision of law and order domestically and defense against international aggression. The productive state refers to either the production or provision of certain public goods that are essential to the development of a prosperous social order. The redistributive state refers to those set of government activities that attempt to reallocate resources from unfavored groups to those groups that are more in favor. Buchanan's puzzle is in how to empower the protective and productive state without unleashing the redistributive state. This is a question of constitutionally curbing the scope of governmental activities so that the positive-sum games of economic processes are not undermined by the zero-sum and negative-sum games of redistributive politics.

Dirigisme, in contrast, rejects as old-fashioned any concern among economists with questions of either the scale or scope of government. Instead of curbing government, the social philosophic mindset is to enlist the state to curb the excesses of the profit motive and individual myopia. In French political and economic history dirigisme is associated with Charles de Gaulle and was represented as an alternative to the Soviet model of a command economy and the U.S. model of a laissez-faire economy. When François Mitterrand came to power in 1981 he promised to move the French economy further in the socialist direction by nationalizing firms and banks, but by the mid-1980s he was forced to reverse this policy path due to declining economic performance of the French economy, and dirigisme was rejected (though the remnants of the past policies were certainly not eliminated).

The doctrine of state control of the economy runs into problems of a theoretical and empirical nature. First, empirically, as mentioned above, economic freedom is positively correlated with economic growth, whereas economic control is correlated with economic stagnation. Economic controls thwart innovation, distort the pattern of resource use, and frustrate consumers by offering them a choice of expensive but low-quality products and altogether eliminating from the market the goods they want to secure. Second, the empirical reality of productive inefficiency and consumer frustration follows directly from the persistent and consistent application of the economic way of thinking to questions of the operation of dirigisme.

There are five problems with government attempts to control a market economy:

1. incentive incompatibility—where government controls ask individuals to act in ways that violate their self-interest;

2. distortions in the structure of prices—where government controls result in price signals that lead to malcoordination of economic activities;

3. time inconsistency—where government action at time T1 is inconsistent with the government action required at T2;

4. dynamic instability—where government action results in consequences that are unacceptable from the point of view of the policy maker and thus require adjustment to either more extensive controls or abandonment of the policy altogether; and

5. rent seeking and capture by special interests—where the very existence of government action sets in motion a zero-sum game of privilege-seeking by special interests to cause the government to rule in their favor.

According to arguments 1 through 4, government controls result in unintended consequences; according to argument 5, the undesirable consequences are the result of the logic of concentrated benefits and dispersed costs. These unintended consequences are undesirable because they are wealth-destroying rather than wealth-creating. Dirigisme is an unworkable public policy philosophy.

SEE ALSO *Economics of Control; Laissez-faire; Liberalization, Trade; Market Economy; Markets; Planning; Privatization; Regulation; State Enterprise; Statism*

BIBLIOGRAPHY

Buchanan, James M. 1975. *The Limits of Liberty: Between Anarchy and Leviathan.* Chicago: University of Chicago Press.

Friedman, Milton. 1962. *Capitalism and Freedom.* Chicago: University of Chicago Press.

Friedman, Milton, and Rose Friedman. 1980. *Free to Choose.* New York: Harcourt Brace Jovanovich.

Gwartney, James, and Robert Lawson (with William Easterly). 2006. *Economic Freedom of the World: 2006 Annual Report.* Vancouver, Canada: Fraser Institute.

Smith, Adam. 1776. *An Inquiry into the Nature and Causes of the Wealth of Nations.* Chicago: University of Chicago Press, 1976.

Peter Boettke

DIRTY FLOAT

Dirty float is a term used in international economics to describe a specific policy of a country's monetary authority with respect to control over movements in the value of the nation's currency within the foreign-exchange market. Specifically, a dirty float, also known as a managed float, is a type of exchange-rate regime, or policy, in which the government or the central bank of the country occasionally intervenes in the foreign-exchange market in order to affect the exchange rate. The term is coined as a counterpart to the clean, or free, float, under which the government never intervenes in the foreign-exchange market. Both clean and dirty floats represent the floating exchange-rate regime, under which the government does not commit to maintain a specific level of the exchange rate, as is the case with a fixed exchange-rate regime.

Under dirty float, a country maintains an independent monetary policy that allows its central bank to achieve a balance between inflation and growth. At the same time, occasional interventions in the foreign-exchange market allow the government or the central bank to avoid large swings in the exchange rates that might destabilize the economy. Countries that have a floating exchange-rate regime have to decide on the goals of their monetary policy and whether they want to engage in inflation targeting, as opposed to exchange-rate targeting, which is the case with a fixed exchange-rate regime.

Most economists consider the dirty float to be inferior to the clean float and believe that the exchange rate should be determined by the markets, while other tools of monetary policy, such as interest rates, should be used to assure the price stability.

Empirical and theoretical work suggests that when clean float is not an option, then dirty float is preferable for the developing countries, as compared to a fixed exchange-rate regime. Theoretical reasons for the superiority of a dirty float over a fixed exhange-rate regime include independence of monetary policy and freedom from currency crises. Empirical analysis also shows that countries that have more flexible exchange-rate regimes experience better economic growth on average.

International organizations such as the International Monetary Fund recommend that developing countries adopt a floating exchange-rate regime in combination with inflation targeting. As a result, the dirty float has been a dominant exchange-rate regime in the world since the beginning of the century.

Most of the countries that claim that their exchange-rate regime is floating, rather than fixed, actually engage in dirty float. For this reason, economic researchers do not simply rely on the official statement of the exchange-rate policy, or de jure classification, but rather use de facto classifications they construct based on actual volatility of the exchange rates. Most commonly used classification is constructed by Carmen Reinhart and Kenneth Rogoff in their 2004 article "The Modern History of Exchange Rate Arrangements: A Reinterpretation," based on their study of official and black market exchange rates.

The United States has had a floating exchange-rate regime since the collapse of the Bretton-Woods system in August 1971. Until 2000, the United States has had to maintain a dirty float regime. Nevertheless, the U.S. Treasury, which is in charge of the exchange-rate policy in the United States, has not intervened in the foreign-exchange market since September 2000. Thus, since 2000, the exchange-rate policy in the United States has been a clean, or free, float.

SEE ALSO *Exchange Rates; Policy, Monetary*

BIBLIOGRAPHY

Levy-Yeyati, Eduardo, and Federico Sturzenegger. 2005. Classifying Exchange Rate Regimes: Deeds vs. Words. *European Economic Review* 49 (6): 1603–1635.

Reinhart, Carmen M., and Kenneth S. Rogoff. 2004. The Modern History of Exchange Rate Arrangements: A Reinterpretation. *Quarterly Journal of Economics* 119 (1): 1–48.

Galina Hale

DISABILITY

Disability, and what it means to be a disabled person, is socially, culturally, and historically created. Disability studies, and associated disability research, is a relatively recent and burgeoning arena within the social sciences. This entry shall first summarize the shift in understandings by contrasting the individual and social models of disability—a model being a set of assumptions about how an event or process operates. The entry then explores the implications of this shift in disability research and policy. Finally, the entry looks toward future possibilities in establishing the full participatory citizenship of disabled people.

DISABILITY MODELS

Within every society there are competing models of disability, with some being more dominant than others at different times. The most dominant model of disability is the *individual model*, which is based upon the assumption that the difficulties disabled people experience are a direct result of their individual physical, sensory, or intellectual impairments (Oliver and Sapey 2006). Thus, the blind person who falls down a hole in the pavement does so because he or she cannot see it, and the person with a motor impairment fails to get into a building because of his or her inability to walk. Problems are thus viewed as residing *within* the individual. The individual model of disability is deeply ingrained and "taken as given" in the medical, psychological, and sociological literature. Even in the literature on the sociology of health and illness, disability, as disabled people define it, is basically ignored (Barnes and Mercer 1996).

The *medical model* can be regarded as a subcategory of the overarching individual model of disability, where disability is conceived as part of the disease process, as abnormality, and as individual tragedy—something that happens to unfortunate individuals on a more or less random basis. Treatment, in turn, is based upon the idea that the problem resides within the individual and must be overcome by the individual's own efforts (French 2004). Disabled people have, for example, been critical of the countless hours they have spent attempting to learn to walk or talk at the expense of their education and leisure (Oliver 1996).

None of these arguments implies that considering the medical or individual needs of disabled individuals is wrong; the argument is that the individual model of disability has tended to view disability *only* in those terms, focusing almost exclusively on attempts to modify people's impairments and return them or approximate them to "normal." The effect of the physical, attitudinal, and social environment on disabled people has been ignored or regarded as relatively fixed, which has maintained the status quo and kept disabled people in their disadvantaged state within society (Oliver and Sapey 2006).

The *social model* of disability is often referred to as the "barriers approach," where disability is viewed not in terms of the individual's impairment, but in terms of environmental, structural, and attitudinal barriers that impinge upon the lives of disabled people and that have the potential to impede their inclusion and progress in many areas of life, including employment, education, and leisure, unless the barriers are minimized or removed (Oliver 1996). These barriers include inaccessible education or lack of education, inaccessible information and communication systems, inaccessible working environments, inadequate or lacking disability benefits, discriminatory health and social-care services, and inaccessible transport, housing, public buildings, and amenities (Swain et al. 2004). The social model of disability also encompasses the *tragedy model* in all its manifestations, such as the devaluation of disabled people through negative images in the media, including films, television, and newspapers (Darke 2004).

The social model of disability locates disability not within the individual disabled person, but within society.

Thus the person who uses a wheelchair is not disabled by paralysis but by building design, lack of lifts, rigid work practices, and the attitudes and behavior of others. Similarly, the visually impaired person is not disabled by lack of sight, but by lack of reading materials in Braille, cluttered pavements, and stereotypical ideas about blindness. The social model takes a holistic approach in that specific problems experienced by disabled people are explained in terms of the totality of disabling environments and cultures (Oliver 2004).

The social model of disability has arisen from the thinking and writings of disabled people themselves, and particularly from the disabled people's movement. The disabled people's movement comprises organizations of disabled people in which disabled people are in positions of control.

GLOBAL ATTITUDES TOWARD DISABILITY

The experiences of disabled people in the Western world gave birth to the social model of disability. It is an expression of commonality and resistance to the dominant individual, medical, and tragedy models. To look globally, however, raises a possibly more complex and controversial picture. On one hand is the social and historical construction of disability. To be impaired and disabled in China, in Afghanistan, in Zambia, or in the United States—in the high-income "developed" or minority world and the low-income "developing" or majority world—addresses widely differing experiences and encompasses different meanings. Perhaps not surprisingly, the picture is complex, including both cultural diversity and commonalities (Flood 2005; Sheldon 2005). Provision for disabled people also varies greatly from country to country. Most countries in the majority world, for instance, do not have a welfare state.

Though attitudes toward disability are generally universally negative, there are cultural differences (Ingstad and Reynolds Whyte 1995). First are the ways in which the body and physical characteristics are given value and meaning. Western biomedical definitions of impairment are not universal, and perceptions of the body and mind vary across cultures and also change over time (Hughes 2002). Religion and the messages various religious doctrines convey about disability are also significant (Ingstad and Reynolds Whyte 1995), as is language and the notion that key concepts may not easily translate into other languages and cultures (Stone 1999b).

Notwithstanding the importance of cultural differences, subtle and not so subtle, it can be argued that commonality is an overriding picture. Commonality is engendered particularly by multideprivation, predominantly through common experiences of poverty. Disabled people are the poorest of the poor in all countries, in terms of relative poverty in the developed world and in terms of absolute poverty in the developing world (Stone 1999a).

The establishment and growth of an international disabled people's movement, particularly through the Disabled Peoples' International (DPI), is in part at least an expression and realization of such commonality. As of 2007 DPI represented approximately 130 national assemblies, many of which, in turn, represent thousands of disabled individuals with all manner of impairments, including people with intellectual impairment. In 1992 DPI acknowledged that it was a human rights organization and that its membership was individually and collectively committed to global justice for disabled people. DPI is also committed to ensuring that the voice of disabled people is heard in the development of all policies and programs that directly affect them, a commitment expressed in the DPI slogan, Nothing About Us Without Us. As a result, DPI has had considerable influence in formulating the United Nations World Programme of Action Concerning Disabled Persons (1983) and the United Nations Standard Rules on Equalization of Opportunities for Persons with Disabilities (1993).

In 1992 DPI joined other international disability organizations to set up an international information network on disability and human rights with the objective of supporting disabled people's actions at the grassroots to implement those rights. This network, Disability Awareness in Action, published a monthly newsletter, the *Disability Tribune*, from 1992 to 2005 and produces numerous resource kits on issues of particular concern, such as organization building, consultation and influence, campaigning, and working with the media (Hurst 2005).

DISABILITY RESEARCH AND SOCIAL POLICY

Turning to research, estimates of the number of disabled people are problematic given the variations in definitions of *disability*, both nationally and internationally, and the wide variety of associated impairments (Swain and French 2004). Estimates suggest that there are around 500 million disabled people in the world population. The majority, around 80 percent, of disabled people live in the developing world, the main causes of impairment being poverty, inadequate sanitation, malnutrition and a poor water supply, and more recently AIDS. Furthermore, statistics from European countries suggest that the percentage of the population that is disabled increases with age, particularly for certain disabilities such as visual impairment and hearing loss. Figures concerning comparative numbers of people in employment and education show that people with impairments are among the most disadvantaged groups around the world (Giddens 2006).

Such statistics are clearly important for disabled people, their supporters, service providers, and policymakers in establishing mandates for change. The development of the social model, however, has underpinned critiques of research, challenging who controls and produces research, priorities in funding, and ultimately the establishment of full citizenship for disabled people (Barnes 2004). Again, the central argument is that the individual model has dominated research. Negative impacts have also come from global genetic advances and assessments of disabled people's quality of life, as well as multinational pharmaceutical companies' hold over research, patenting, and genetic advances; the invisibility of disabled people from mainstream activity and information; and the silence of disabled people's voices in the corridors of power and change (Hurst 2003). Statistics, whether valid or reliable, relating to the numbers of disabled people provide no information about the availability of accessible houses, transport, or so-called public buildings. Such counting of heads can carry the connotation that it is disabled individuals who create the "problem," rather than the disabling society. The social model has fueled arguments for a different methodological approach to researching disability issues, an approach that is informed by the social model and in which the production of research is controlled by disabled people. Associated developments in social science research are generally subsumed under the umbrella term *emancipatory research* (Barnes 2004).

In terms of social policy, the international shift driven by the social model is evident in the establishment of rights-based policy, both civil and human. By 2007 antidiscriminatory legislation had been enacted in at least forty UN member states. There are, however, significant differences in these legislative frameworks, and general critiques focus on the lack of clear and effective enforcement mechanisms, with terms such as *reasonable adjustment* providing broad grounds for noncompliance—that is, antidiscriminatory legislation that allows for and legalizes discrimination against disabled people. Furthermore, the social model should not be simplistically equated with what has come to be referred to as the rights-based model. The social model encompasses and informs broader mandates for social change in realizing social justice for disabled people.

One broader front for social change has been developed under the banner of *independent living* (Barnes and Mercer 2006). This concept, as defined by disabled people themselves, is founded on four basic assumptions:

1. All human beings are of equal worth, regardless of the nature, complexity, or severity of their impairments.

2. Everyone, regardless of the nature, complexity, or severity of their impairments, has the capacity to

make choices in controlling their lifestyles and should be supported in making such choices.

3. Disabled people have the right to exercise control over their lives.

4. Disabled people have the right to participate fully in all areas—economic, political, and cultural—of mainstream community living on an equal basis with their nondisabled peers.

The independent-living movement began through the establishment of *centers for independent living* (CILs), which are self-help organizations for disabled people that are run and controlled by disabled people themselves. There are now CILs or similar organizations providing support for disabled people and their families in many countries around the world. Furthermore, the idea of independent living, as conceived by disabled people, has had a notable impact on disability policy globally. Disabled people and organizations of disabled people have increasingly become involved in policymaking at local, regional, national, and international levels (Barnes and Mercer 2006).

Turning finally to the possible directions for disability policy and social science research, the goal remains essentially the same: the creation of a society in which all disabled people are able to participate as equal citizens. Under the umbrella of independent living, this includes equal access to mainstream education, paid employment, transport, "public" buildings, housing, leisure, and health- and social-care services. *Mainstreaming* is a key concept. The mainstreaming of disability issues within policy agendas addresses the marginalization of the needs and rights of disabled people and their treatment as "special" cases. This presents fundamental challenges to policymaking in realizing the prerogatives of flexibility, the expertise of disabled people, and the recognition that "one size does not fit all." Mainstreaming also requires the breaking down of the physical, social, communicative, and economic barriers that prevent disabled people from exercising their rights and participating in policymaking.

The creation of participative citizenship will involve the strengthening and enforcement of legislation and procedures to ensure that disability and independent-living issues are fully integrated into policymaking at all levels: international, national, regional, and local. This includes the enactment of binding and intractable antidiscrimination legislation with effective enforcement and compliance requirements. The economic and management implications include the financing of organizations of disabled people, including CILs, and research controlled by disabled people, particularly organizations of disabled people and their representatives.

There are, furthermore, democratic and participatory possibilities afforded by the Internet and other technological developments. These technologies have opened up opportunities for dialogic, or participative rather than representative, democracy. The Internet allows a greater diversity of voices to be heard and has the potential to be profoundly democratizing. The danger is the possibility of the further marginalization of the "unconnected," the disabled people who are the poorest of the poor, for whom survival is the political perspective and for whom sophisticated technology is not available. It is also the case that new technologies are developed within disabling societies and are not available to many disabled people unless adaptations are made that are often expensive (Goggin and Newell 2003).

Overall, paramount to the evolving direction is the emerging voices of disabled people in controlling decision-making processes across policy and research that shapes day-to-day lifestyles, opportunities, and choices. It is an ongoing struggle for a truly equitable and inclusive society with justice and full participative citizenship for all.

SEE ALSO *Civil Rights; Human Rights; Social Exclusion*

BIBLIOGRAPHY

Barnes, Colin. 2004. Reflections on Doing Emancipatory Disability Research. In *Disabling Barriers—Enabling Environments*, ed. John Swain, Sally French, Colin Barnes, and Carol Thomas, 47–53. 2nd ed. London: Sage.

Barnes, Colin, and Geoffrey Mercer, eds. 1996. *Exploring the Divide: Illness and Disability.* Leeds, U.K.: Disability Press.

Barnes, Colin, and Geoffrey Mercer. 1997. *Doing Disability Research.* Leeds, U.K.: Disability Press.

Barnes, Colin, and Geoffrey Mercer. 2006. *Independent Futures: Creating User-led Disability Services in a Disabling Society.* Bristol, U.K.: Policy Press.

Darke, Paul Anthony. 2004. The Changing Face of Representations of Disability in the Media. In *Disabling Barriers—Enabling Environments*, ed. John Swain, Sally French, Colin Barnes, and Carol Thomas, 100–105. 2nd ed. London: Sage.

Flood, Tara. 2005. "Food" or "Thought"? The Social Model and the Majority World. In *The Social Model of Disability: Europe and the Majority World*, ed. Colin Barnes and Geoffrey Mercer, 180–192. Leeds, U.K.: Disability Press.

French, Sally. 2004. Enabling Relationships in Therapy Practice. In *Enabling Relationships in Health and Social Care*, ed. John Swain, Jim Clark, Karen Parry, et al., 95–108. Oxford, U.K.: Butterworth-Heinemann.

Giddens, Anthony. 2006. *Sociology.* 5th ed. Cambridge, U.K.: Polity.

Goggin, Gerard, and Christopher Newell. 2003. *Digital Disability: The Social Construction of Disability in New Media.* London: Rowman and Littlefield.

Hughes, Bill. 2002. Disability and the Body. In *Disability Studies Today*, ed. Colin Barnes, Mike Oliver, and Len Barton, 58–76. Cambridge, U.K.: Polity.

Hurst, Rachel. 2003. Conclusion: Enabling or Disabling Globalization. In *Controversial Issues in a Disabling Society*, ed. John Swain, Sally French, and Colin Cameron, 161–170. Buckingham, U.K.: Open University Press.

Hurst, Rachel. 2005. Disabled People's International: Europe and the Social Model of Disability. In *The Social Model of Disability: Europe and the Majority World*, ed. Colin Barnes and Geoffrey Mercer, 65–79. Leeds, U.K.: Disability Press.

Ingstad, Benedicte, and Susan Reynolds Whyte. 1995. *Disability and Culture*. Berkeley: University of California Press.

Oliver, Michael. 1996. *Understanding Disability: From Theory to Practice*. London: Macmillan.

Oliver, Michael. 2004. If I Had a Hammer: The Social Model in Action. In *Disabling Barriers—Enabling Environments*, ed. John Swain, Sally French, Colin Barnes, and Carol Thomas, 7–12. 2nd ed. London: Sage.

Oliver, Michael, and Bob Sapey. 2006. *Social Work with Disabled People*. 3rd ed. Basingstoke, U.K.: Macmillan.

Sheldon, Alison. 2005. One World, One People, One Struggle? Towards the Global Implementation of the Social Model of Disability. In *The Social Model of Disability: Europe and the Majority World*, ed. Colin Barnes and Geoffrey Mercer, 115–130. Leeds, U.K.: Disability Press.

Stone Emma. 1999a. *Disability and Development: Learning from Action and Research on Disability in the Majority World*. Leeds, U.K.: Disability Press.

Stone Emma 1999b. Modern Slogan, Ancient Script: Impairment and Disability in the Chinese Language. In *Disability Discourse*, ed. Marian Corker and Sally French, 136–147. Buckingham, U.K.: Open University Press.

Swain, John, and Sally French. 2004. Researching Together: A Participatory Approach. In *Physiotherapy: A Psychosocial Approach*, ed. Sally French and Julius Sim, 317–331. 3rd ed. Oxford, U.K.: Elsevier.

Swain John, Sally French, Colin Barnes, and Carol Thomas, eds. 2004. *Disabling Barriers—Enabling Environments*. 2nd ed. London: Sage.

John Swain
Sally French

DISARMAMENT

The *Oxford English Dictionary* defines *disarmament* as the action of disarming: "the reduction of an army or navy to the customary peace footing." Encompassing the meaning inherent in its root, *disarm*, "to deprive of arms, to take the arms or weapons from, to deprive of munitions of war or means of defense, to dismantle (a city, a ship, etc.)," disarmament refers to armaments and includes any measure by which their existence is reduced or eliminated.

TYPOLOGY

Extending far back in history, the experience of disarmament presents a varied typology. Often a unilateral obligation imposed on the loser by the winner of a conflict (e.g., on Prussia by Napoleon Bonaparte, on France in 1814 by the United Kingdom, or Germany by the Versailles Treaty in 1919), disarmament has also been a reciprocal obligation (e.g., the naval agreement between France and the United Kingdom on October 27, 1787, or the Anglo-American treaty of April 28, 1817, limiting armaments on the Great Lakes and Lake Champlain). Moreover, disarmament phenomena encompass unilateral disarmaments undertaken by states for philosophical, budgetary, strategic, or other reasons (e.g., Costa Rica, the U.S. unilateral destruction of biological stockpiles in 1969, or the Soviet Union's unilateral reduction of forces decided on in 1988).

Disarmament in the context of a peace process following internal or international conflict has specific features. It is part of peace agreements between governments and guerillas in Africa and Latin America (e.g., between the government of El Salvador and the Farabundo Marti National Liberation) and in the Northern Ireland peace process (Irish Republican Army disarmament ended in September 2005), leading to the disarmament of nongovernmental armed groups. Finally, disarmament within the framework of peace enforcement operations (e.g., Security Council Resolution 687 of April 3, 1991, concerning Iraq) is distinct from disarmament through negotiations, even if there is some overlap in the mechanics of weapons inspection and disposal.

Compliance verification is a common challenge in all cases. The main instruments of verification are United Nations (UN) inspectors (in peace enforcement), international or bilateral commissions (in peace agreements), and verification procedures set up by international treaties. Regrettably, some disarmament treaties do not include any supervisory mechanisms.

HISTORICAL AND LEGAL DEVELOPMENT

Disarmament as a general goal came into focus with the Hague Peace Conferences in 1899 and 1907. The resulting rules for hostilities and the means and methods of land warfare included prohibitions against the use of certain kinds of weapons. Although a resolution adopted in 1907 agreed on the desirability of studying a reduction of military charges, the conferences failed to agree on any limitation or reduction of possession of armaments.

General aspirations for disarmament returned after World War I as part of plans for international peace and security. The Versailles Treaty limited Germany, but it was also seen as a first measure toward general disarmament. The fourth point of President Woodrow Wilson's message

(January 8, 1918) proposed a reduction of national armaments to limits compatible with national security and the implementation of international obligations imposed by joint action. The main organs of the League of Nations were charged with drafting plans for the general reduction of national armaments, which was to be the main instrument for the realization of peace and security. "Qualitative disarmament" was to make universal the prohibition of armaments forbidden to the vanquished powers while leaving defensive power untouched (McKnight 1983, pp. 17–20). By 1930 a draft disarmament treaty was circulated to governments for consideration, but most of the politicians at the World Disarmament Conference, which opened on February 2, 1932, believed disarmament impossible and accepted the use of force as an instrument for settling international controversies.

In the twenty-first century disarmament is linked to the principle, established in article 2 of the Charter of the United Nations, denying states the threat or the use of force. Many authors argue that the UN Charter puts less emphasis on disarmament than did the League of Nations. Under the Charter the maintenance of international peace and security is based on collective security and the right of self-defense recognized in article 51, both of which require armed forces (Kalshoven 1985, pp. 198–199). In addition, there is no general rule denying or limiting the right of states to have armed forces and hence acquire and develop armaments (International Court of Justice 1996). By contrast, the Charter charges the General Assembly to consider the general principles governing disarmament and the regulation of armaments (article 11), while the Security Council is responsible for formulating plans for the establishment of a system for the regulation of armaments (article 26).

Cold war tensions prevented any progress toward those goals, although agreement seemed near in 1954, with the Anglo-French Memorandum based on a previous U.S. document titled "Essential Principles for a Disarmament Program," and in 1961, after the U.S.-Soviet Joint Statement of Agreed Principles—the McCloy-Zorin Principles—on general and complete disarmament. Those major failures and growing impatience with the lack of progress on disarmament gave impetus to a new concept: arms control.

In the post–cold war 1990s the world witnessed a new impetus for disarmament, with the approval of the Chemical Weapons Convention, the indefinite prorogation of the Treaty on the Nonproliferation of Nuclear Weapons (NPT), and the beginning of negotiations for new treaties (the Comprehensive Nuclear Test Ban Treaty [CTBT] or the Fissile Material Cutoff Treaty). Nevertheless, the trend of world military expenditures has been rising since 1998, accelerating to an annual average increase of around 6 percent in real terms from 2002 through 2004 (the United States accounts for 47 percent of world military expenditures and is the main representative of this trend). Additionally, no new disarmament measure has been approved and some older ones have been abandoned (e.g., the Treaty on the Limitation of Antiballistic Missile Systems [ABM]).

CONCEPTUAL DELIMITATION

Conceptually, the distinction between disarmament and arms control is troublesome. Some authors use the terms *disarmament* (Myrdal 1976; Kalshoven 1985; Lysén 1990) or *arms control* (Brennan 1961; Schelling and Halperin 1985) to cover all the rules and measures related to the development, production, and deployment of armaments. Nonetheless, most writers recognize a distinction, but disagree on where to draw the line on the continuum from complete reductions to measures restraining the testing, manufacture, possession, or deployment of specific types of weapon. Broad consensus assigns to the term *disarmament* the elimination or reduction of one or more categories of weapons and other measures limiting the acquisition, possession, or deployment of one or more categories of weapons. The Biological Weapons Convention, the Chemical Weapons Convention, and some of the U.S.-Soviet bilateral treaties (e.g., ABM and Strategic Arms Limitation Talks I and II) fall into the category, as does the Treaty on Conventional Armed Forces in Europe, which stands out as the major example of an international treaty reducing conventional armament. As well, the Outer Space Treaty, the Sea-Bed Treaty, the Antarctic Treaty, the Tlatelolco Treaty (for Latin America), and the Rarotonga Treaty (for the South Pacific Ocean) protect specific areas from deployment of certain weapons, while the NPT recognizes only five states as legal nuclear powers and prevents nuclear proliferation. Additionally, measures that prevent or hinder weapons development (e.g., the Partial Test Ban Treaty, the Comprehensive Test Ban Treaty, which is not in force, or the Cutoff Treaty, which is under negotiations in the Conference of Disarmament in Geneva) are more often considered a form of arms control.

SEE ALSO *Arms Control and Arms Race; Weaponry, Nuclear*

BIBLIOGRAPHY

Anthony, Ian, and Adam Daniel Rotfeld, eds. 2001. *A Future Arms Control Agenda: Proceedings of Nobel Symposium 118, 1999.* New York: Oxford University Press.

Boutros-Ghali, Boutros. 1993. *New Dimensions of Arms Regulation and Disarmament in the Post–Cold War Era: Report of the Secretary-General.* New York: United Nations.

Brennan, Donald G. 1961. *Arms Control, Disarmament, and National Security.* New York: G. Braziller.

Burns, Richard Dean, ed. 1993. *Encyclopedia of Arms Control and Disarmament.* 3 vols. New York: Maxwell Macmillan International.

Clark, Grenville, and Louis B. Sohn. 1966. *World Peace through World Law: Two Alternative Plans.* Cambridge, MA: Harvard University Press.

Dahlitz, Julie, and Detlev Dicke, eds. 1991. *The International Law of Arms Control and Disarmament: Proceedings of the Symposium, Geneva, 28 February–2 March 1991.* New York: United Nations.

Department of Political and Security Council Affairs, United Nations Center for Disarmament. 1977. *The United Nations Disarmament Yearbook.* New York: United Nations.

Fürst, Andreas, Voiker Heise, and Steven E. Miller. 1992. *Europe and Naval Arms Control in the Gorbachev Era.* New York: Oxford University Press.

Hallenbeck, Ralph A., and David E. Shaver. 1991. *On Disarmament: The Role of Conventional Arms Control in National Security Strategy.* New York: Praeger.

International Court of Justice. 1996. *Advisory Opinion on the Legality of the Threat or Use of Nuclear Weapons.* July 8, 1996: 226.

Kalshoven, Frits. 1985. Arms, Armaments, and International Law. *Recueil des Cours* 191: 183–342.

Kasto, Jalil. 1998. *International Peace and Disarmament.* Kingston, U.K.: PDC.

Lysén, Göran. 1990. *The International Regulation of Armaments: The Law of Disarmament.* Uppsala, Sweden: Iustus.

McKnight, Allan. 1983. *The Forgotten Treaties: A Practical Plan for World Disarmament.* Melbourne: Law Council of Australia.

Myrdal, Alva. 1976. *The Game of Disarmament: How the United States and Russia Run the Arms Race.* New York: Pantheon Books.

Schelling, Thomas C., and Morton H. Halperin. 1985. *Strategy and Arms Control.* Washington, DC: Pergamon-Brassey's.

Stockholm International Peace Research Institute. 2005. *SIPRI Yearbook: Armaments, Disarmament, and International Security.* Stockholm: Almquist and Wiksell.

Sur, Serge, ed. 1992. *Disarmament and Limitation of Armaments: Unilateral Measures and Policies.* New York: United Nations.

Milagros Alvarez-Verdugo

DISASTER MANAGEMENT

Throughout human history, lives have been cut short by disasters. This term refers to a broad range of events that vary in speed of onset, duration, magnitude, cause, and other characteristics. But always there is both human suffering and disruption of normal community functioning.

Placement of the term *management* next to this category of extreme events implies a belief that some measure of control, maybe prevention, is possible. This is a relatively new idea that remains poorly understood and highly controversial. Understanding this concept requires exploration of four subtopics: (1) types of disasters, (2) social vulnerability trends, (3) social system consequences, and (4) planning and management policy.

TYPES OF DISASTERS

In August 2005 many throughout the world watched on television as thousands of American citizens suffered for days following the destruction caused by Hurricane Katrina. Despite evacuation orders from local and state officials, more than 1,300 people perished. Most deaths resulted from flooding in the New Orleans area after portions of the levee system failed. Not since the terrorist attacks of September 11, 2001, had the world witnessed such disaster-caused suffering within the United States. Elsewhere, of course, the scope of disasters has been far worse. Examples include the earthquakes in Indonesia on May 27, 2006, that killed over five thousand people and the massive tsunami on December 26, 2004, that struck coastal areas along the Indian Ocean in such far-apart places as Thailand, Sri Lanka, and India. The 2004 tsunami alone killed at least 280,000 people. These contrasts hint at the many types of disasters, commonly divided into three categories: (1) natural, (2) technological, and (3) conflict-related.

Natural Disasters Natural disasters include both a wide range of extreme weather-related events and those resulting from geophysical forces, such as earthquakes (Mileti 1999). Extreme weather events include hurricanes like Katrina, which are known as "typhoons in the western North Pacific and cyclonic storms or tropical cyclones in other areas" (World Meteorological Organization 2005, p. 1). The most deadly hurricane to hit the United States struck Galveston, Texas, on September 8, 1900. Estimates of the death toll from this hurricane vary, but at least six thousand people died. In 1992 Hurricane Andrew caused property damage in Florida and Louisiana that totaled about $30 billion. Andrew held the record until Katrina, which had loss estimates as high as $200 billion (Select Bipartisan Committee 2006).

Tornadoes, another type of extreme weather event, occur throughout the United States, especially in the Midwest. The Great Tri-State Tornado of 1925 left 695 people dead in Missouri, Illinois, and Indiana; it was the largest tornado-related death toll as of 2006. Although less deadly, flood disasters cause more property damage than any other type of weather-related event (Mileti 1999, pp. 72–82). The deadliest flood within the United States occurred in Johnstown, Pennsylvania, in 1889 when over two thousand people died. Other weather-related disasters result from drought, extreme heat or cold, fog, hail, blizzards, avalanches, lightning, and wildfires.

Geophysical disasters, such as earthquakes and volcanoes, have also occurred in the United States. For example, the 1906 earthquake in San Francisco left 503 people dead. While only 61 people died in the Northridge quake that shook the Los Angeles area in 1994, a new record in earthquake-related property loss was reached: $30 billion. These losses pale, however, when compared to earthquake-related losses experienced worldwide in such places as China in 1927 (200,000 killed); Armenia in 1998 (25,000 killed); and India in 2001 (20,000 killed).

In 1868 Hilo, Hawaii, was devastated by massive ocean waves originating from earthquakes in Peru and Chile. Similarly, the 1964 Anchorage earthquake produced tsunamis that struck Valdez, Alaska, and Crescent City, California. Records of volcano-related deaths have been kept since the time of the eruption of Mount Vesuvius in Italy in 79 CE, when approximately twenty thousand people died in Pompeii. In 1902, for example, on the island of Martinique in the Caribbean, approximately forty thousand people died when the city of Saint Pierre was destroyed after Mount Pelée erupted. Less deadly volcano disasters have occurred with regularity, including the 1980 eruption of Mount Saint Helens in Washington state, which killed sixty people.

Finally, epidemics of disease constitute a major risk. Although mass immunization programs have curtailed diseases such as diphtheria from which many died before the early twentieth century, a future pandemic could kill thousands, maybe millions. The 1918 influenza outbreak probably started in Haskill County, Kansas, and rapidly spread worldwide, in part because of troop movements during World War I (1914–1918). Approximately 100,000,000 people died from the flu during this pandemic, far more even than died from the infamous Black Death plague of the Middle Ages (Barry 2005).

Technological Disasters Technological disasters reflect a wide range of events stemming from transportation, building, and energy-production failures. For example, airplane and ship failures are illustrated by such disasters as the 1999 Egypt Air crash near Nantucket Island, Massachusetts (217 killed), and the sinking of the *Titanic* in 1912 (1,503 killed). Structural fires, like that which broke out in the Iroquois Theater in Chicago in 1903 (602 dead), and building collapses are another dimension of this category. Energy-production disasters include such events as the explosion and fire that occurred in Texas City, Texas, in 1947, which killed 516 people and injured more than three thousand. Such events pale, however,

next to the thousands killed when a gas leak caused a massive explosion at the Union Carbide plant in Bhopal, India, in 1984, or the Chernobyl nuclear plant disaster in Ukraine in 1986. Experts have estimated that the Chernobyl disaster caused some ten thousand cancer cases within nearby communities and approximately five thousand deaths (Segerståhl 1991).

Conflict Disasters Conflict disasters include wars both among and within nations. The American Civil War (1861–1865), for example, resulted in the deaths of over 500,000 troops. American military casualties during World War II (1939–1945) are estimated at just over 400,000. And these numbers do not include civilian losses, or in the case of World War II, losses of both types from other countries.

Increasingly, however, violence by nonstate militants has become a concern. Using violence toward noncombatants as a political strategy, terrorists have precipitated increased efforts at civil protection. The use of commercial airliners as weapons on September 11, 2001, resulted in over three thousand deaths at the World Trade Center in New York, the Pentagon near Washington, D.C., and a field near Shanksville, Pennsylvania. Increased attacks on "soft targets" such as subways, as occurred in London in July 2005, and hotels, as in Amman, Jordan, in November 2005, illustrate another form of increased vulnerability. Should weapons of mass destruction, such as nuclear bombs, become available to terrorist groups, the destructive potential increases greatly. Finally, civil disorder may erupt within a society when heightened feelings of deprivation and disenfranchisement are ignited by critical incidents, as occurred in Paris and London in 2006 when students and young workers protested new laws regulating employment termination.

SOCIAL VULNERABILITY TRENDS

Human populations are becoming more vulnerable to disasters, especially those of catastrophic scope, for many reasons. In past centuries, people believed disasters were caused by forces outside of human control. Floods, volcanoes, and other natural disasters were labeled "acts of God" and were interpreted as punishment or disfavor. Russell Dynes (2000) has proposed that a naturalistic or "modern" interpretation of disaster events first occurred in 1755 following a major earthquake in Lisbon, Portugal. This earthquake killed at least ten thousand people, although some estimates place the toll as high as seventy thousand. Civil authorities led efforts to rebuild the city and gradually increased their authority over the church in political matters. This shift led to alternative thinking about attribution for disasters. Although not universally accepted even today, "naturalistic" interpretations reflecting Enlightenment philosophy paved the way for new approaches to disaster management. Unfortunately, numerous trends are acting in concert to place more and more humans at risk despite accelerated efforts at management. Among these are population changes, increased reliance on technology, and climate change.

As the world population increases, there are more potential disaster victims. Beyond larger numbers, however, more people are moving into areas of high risk. For example, the coasts of Florida and Texas have witnessed explosive growth since the mid-1970s. In addition, increases in the numbers of elderly and poor, of homes led by single mothers, and of people living in mobile homes add a further dimension to America's social vulnerability. Mobile homes, for example, provide affordable housing to millions, but offer minimal protection during violent storms, especially tornadoes. Not only are more people living in areas that are wind, flood, or avalanche prone, the structures within which many dwell offer inadequate protection. In poorer countries, the use of stone and tile building materials that collapse during earthquakes is a parallel problem.

Climate change, which has been documented in numerous ways, will be reflected in future disasters. For example, increased heat retention by miles of pavement and high-rise structures is related to new storm patterns, and residential and commercial construction is expanding into geographic areas already known to be flood or tornado prone. Moreover, while annual rainfall has remained stable, there is an increased frequency of intense downpours, which cause localized flooding and traffic accidents. Forecasts for a rising sea level and warmer ocean temperatures imply similar pattern change for hurricanes.

These vulnerability trends are exacerbated by shifts in social, economic, and political patterns, such as the globalization of the economy and an increase in feelings of deprivation that reflect long-standing patterns of inequality and social injustice. There is no single trend that contributes to increased vulnerability; rather, it is the cumulative effects of a series of both social and physical forces that result in higher risk levels. These risks are not distributed uniformly, but are skewed, with the poor, elderly, and ethnic minorities at higher risk.

SOCIAL SYSTEM CONSEQUENCES

Disasters have important consequences for social systems. Smaller systems, such as families, may experience short-term oscillations. For example, divorce rates and marriage rates generally drop in the first few months following a disaster (Cohn and Cole 2002). However, after a six-month spike downward and then upward, trend lines smooth out; that is, some put off marriage for a few months, and then join others who were planning to marry

at a later date—hence, a drop, then an increase, followed by a continuation of the prior trend line. Some studies have documented that there is a longer delay in the divorce pattern. Disasters appear to cause some to remain married, at least temporarily, and to drop their plans for divorce. Within these microsystems, however, some changes are permanent. For example, studies have documented that many disaster victims, especially those helped by kin during recovery, report closer kin ties years later. After a disaster, relatives may interact more frequently, and people maintain closer links to both kin and friendship groups, although participation in voluntary associations decreases somewhat. The sole exception is religious organizations, which show slight increases. Hence, after disasters, microsystems reflect tighter links to kin, friends, and religious organizations (Drabek 1986).

Macrosystems, such as communities and societies, experience disaster consequences of at least four types. First, there is an acceleration of preexisting trends. Following the 1964 Anchorage earthquake, for example, William Anderson (1970) documented that numerous changes planned within organizations prior to the earthquake were implemented more rapidly. In another case, social stratification was widening in the Miami area prior to Hurricane Andrew. After the hurricane, Walter Peacock and colleagues (1997) documented acceleration of this trend.

A second consequence of disasters for macrosystems is that disaster preparedness and prevention efforts are increased. Newer, enhanced warning systems may be implemented, as are flood protection measures, for example. Unfortunately, as noted above, these actions rarely take into account the forces that are placing more people at risk, so the net gain may be minimal.

Third, various scholars, including Pitirim Sorokin (1889–1968) and Karl Marx (1818–1883), have proposed that some disasters deflect social, economic, and political developments. For example, the conflicts that developed between business interests, government programs, and upper-class elites during the reconstruction following the 1972 earthquake in Managua, Nicaragua, may have led to the collapse of the Somoza regime in 1979. Other scholars, including Jared Diamond (2005), reject such single-factor explanations and include disasters within a multifactor framework that more convincingly accounts for such changes as total societal collapse. Such collapses occurred on Easter Island around the mid-1800s and among the Anasazi in southwestern Colorado and northern New Mexico about 1300 (Diamond 2005, pp. 112, 154).

The fourth consequence of disasters for macrosystems is policy change. Consistent with Anderson's findings, however, these often reflect policy initiatives that were in process prior to the event. For example, T. Joseph Scanlon and John Handmer (2001) documented the impact on gun-law reform in Australia of a 1996 massacre in Port Arthur in which a lone gunman killed thirty-five people. Reform proposals had been advanced in Australia earlier, but had never been adopted. One year after the massacre, however, reform legislation was implemented. Similarly, in the United States in the years before 2001, several commissions had recommended the establishment of a department of homeland security and other terrorist prevention policy changes. Following the attacks of September 11, 2001, some of these proposals were adopted. Despite serious failures in the official response to the attacks, including a lack of multiagency communication, additional reform proposals remained controversial years later (National Commission on Terrorist Attacks 2004).

PLANNING AND MANAGEMENT POLICY

Following numerous large-scale disasters during the 1960s, state and local governments exerted pressure on the U.S. Congress for reorganization. As various types of disaster events occurred, different federal agencies created event-specific programs for recovery and mitigation in response to floods, earthquakes, hurricanes, and other disasters. These programs evolved over time and paralleled the coterminous development of programs designed to protect civilian populations in the event of an enemy attack. In 1979 President Jimmy Carter established the Federal Emergency Management Agency (FEMA). This agency was to provide a single point of federal contact for state and local governments and other entities, including nongovernmental agencies like the American Red Cross. FEMA also was to be the lead agency within the federal bureaucracy for coordination of all disaster activities, regardless of the type. This all-hazard agency was to be operative across the entire life cycle of all disaster events, with responsibility for coordinating mitigation and preventive actions (e.g., flood-zone mapping), preparedness, response, and recovery. The first line of response remained with local and state governments, but when events created demands that overran their resources, they could request FEMA assistance. A regularized process, as opposed to the ad hoc arrangements of the past, was established through a presidential declaration when conditions warranted (Drabek and Hoetmer 1991).

During the response to Hurricane Andrew in 1992, President George H. W. Bush was severely criticized for FEMA's slow and inadequate response. His successor, President Bill Clinton, placed a priority on strengthening FEMA, and eventually elevated the agency directorship to cabinet-level status. Recruitment and training promoted professionalism within FEMA and within state and local emergency management agencies. FEMA staff facilitated these enhanced state and local capabilities by emphasizing researched-based principles, including the view that disaster planning is a process, not a product, and that disaster plans must be prepared by representatives from the agencies that will implement them. In addition, colleges across the United States established new degree programs in emergency management (Drabek 2004).

Following the 9/11 attacks, FEMA was transferred into the newly created Department of Homeland Security. Despite continuity in name, many FEMA programs experienced reduced funding as terrorist-related program priorities were implemented. During and following the response to Hurricane Katrina, FEMA was criticized severely. While various congressional investigations pointed out failures within state and local government agencies, FEMA was hit hardest, especially in the public perception, and numerous difficult policy issues were raised by the post-Katrina reviews. Among these was whether or not FEMA should be abolished and its functions reassigned within various units of the Department of Homeland Security. Others proposed that FEMA should be upgraded and made into a stand-alone agency independent of the Department of Homeland Security. Many who testified before congressional committees voiced concerns about intergovernmental partnerships, specifically the degree of autonomy and flexibility of state and local emergency management agencies. The degree to which the emergency management function should be conceptualized within a common standardized system became the operative policy question. Many expressed concern that terrorism preparedness had been pushed into high priority, while focus diminished on other types of disasters. Finally, the role of the military in disaster response was revisited.

Consideration of all of these policy matters will be deflected by future disaster events, whatever they may be. When they occur, policymakers will be pressed to demonstrate why they did not do more to prepare. Thus, disaster policy will continue to evolve and reflect both specific events and public perception of the threats believed to be the most harmful.

SEE ALSO *Natural Disasters; September 11, 2001; Shocks*

BIBLIOGRAPHY

Anderson, William A. 1970. Disaster and Organizational Change in Anchorage. In *The Great Alaska Earthquake of 1964: Human Ecology*, ed. Committee on the Alaska Earthquake of the National Research Council, 96–115. Washington, DC: National Academy of Sciences.

Barry, John M. 2005. *The Great Influenza: The Epic Story of the Deadliest Plague in History*. New York: Penguin.

Diamond, Jared. 2005. *Collapse: How Societies Choose to Fail or Succeed*. New York: Viking.

Drabek, Thomas E. 1986. *Human System Responses to Disaster: An Inventory of Sociological Findings*. New York: Springer-Verlag.

Drabek, Thomas E. 2004. *Social Dimensions of Disaster.* 2nd ed. Emmitsburg, MD: Emergency Management Institute, FEMA.

Drabek, Thomas E., and Gerard J. Hoetmer, eds. 1991. *Emergency Management: Principles and Practice for Local Government.* Washington, DC: International City Management Association.

Dynes, Russell R. 2000. The Dialogue between Voltaire and Rousseau on the Lisbon Earthquake: The Emergence of a Social Science View. *International Journal of Mass Emergencies and Disasters* 18: 97–115.

Mileti, Dennis S. 1999. *Disasters by Design: A Reassessment of Natural Hazards in the United States.* Washington, DC: Joseph Henry Press.

National Commission on Terrorist Attacks upon the United States. 2004. *The 9/11 Commission Report: Final Report of the National Commission on Terrorist Attacks upon the United States.* New York: Norton. http://www.9-11commission. gov/report/index.htm.

Peacock, Walter Gillis, Betty Hearn Morrow, and Hugh Gladwin, eds. 1997. *Hurricane Andrew: Ethnicity, Gender, and the Sociology of Disasters.* London: Routledge.

Scanlon, T. Joseph, and John Handmer. 2001. The Halifax Explosion and the Port Arthur Massacre: Testing Samuel Henry Prince's Ideas. *International Journal of Mass Emergencies and Disasters* 19: 181–208.

Segerståhl, Boris, ed. 1991. *Chernobyl: A Policy Response Study.* New York: Springer-Verlag.

Select Bipartisan Committee to Investigate the Preparation for and Response to Hurricane Katrina, U.S. House of Representatives. 2006. *A Failure of Initiative: Final Report of the Select Bipartisan Committee to Investigate the Preparation for and Response to Hurricane Katrina.* Washington, DC: U.S. Government Printing Office. http://katrina.house.gov/ full_katrina_report.htm.

World Meteorological Organization. 2005. *Fact Sheet: Tropical Cyclone Names.* Geneva, Switzerland: World Meteorological Organization.

Thomas E. Drabek

DISASTERS

SEE *Disaster Management; Natural Disasters.*

DISCIPLINE

SEE *Corporal Punishment.*

DISCONTINUITY THEORIES

SEE *Stages of Development.*

DISCOUNTED PRESENT VALUE

Discounted present value is a concept in economics and finance that refers to a method of measuring the value of payments or utility that will be received in the future. Most people would agree that receiving $1,000 today is better than receiving $1,000 in a year, because $1,000 today can be used for consumption or investment. This feature is referred to as time value of money—a given amount of money today is better than the same amount of money in the future. Discounted present value allows one to calculate exactly how much better, most commonly using the interest rate as an input in a discount factor, the amount by which future payments are reduced in order to be comparable to current payments.

There are two ways to think about discounted present value—transferring money from the future to the present via borrowing or transferring money from the present to the future via lending. In both cases the interest rate at which one can borrow or lend is a crucial part of the formula.

Suppose a firm is scheduled to receive a payment of $1,000 in a year. To understand how much this payment is worth to the firm today, we can calculate how much the firm can borrow today against that payment:

$$x \cdot (1 + i) = 1000,$$

where i is the interest rate. Then, $x = 1000/(1 + i)$. The factor $1/(1 + i)$ by which we multiply the future payment is called a discount factor.

If the payment is scheduled to arrive in two years instead, we can use a two-step approach. Assuming the interest rate is the same for two years, a year from today the value of the payment will be $1000/(1 + i)$, which today is worth

$$(1000/(1 + i)) \cdot 1/(1 + i) = 1000/(1 + i)^2.$$

Thus, for discounting the payments far in the future the compound interest rate is used.

To calculate the discounted present value (DPV) of a stream of future payments, one has to discount each payment appropriately and then add them up. If we denote the payment in each future year by y_t, where t is the year, then:

$$\text{DPV} =$$

$$y_1/(1 + i) + y_2/(1 + i)^2 + y_3/(1 + i)^3 + \ldots + y_T/(1 + i)^T = \Sigma_t^T y_t/(1 + i)^t$$

The formula above makes a set of assumptions that are important for the result: (1) interest accrues and is compounded annually; (2) the interest rate is constant over time; (3) the payments occur for T years, starting one year from today. Altering each of these assumptions would lead to different results. To properly calculate the discounted present value of future payments, one also has to use the most appropriate interest rate in calculations.

In addition, individuals might be simply impatient and prefer to receive their utility today instead of waiting for the future payment, even if interest will accrue. This impatience is measured with the individual discount factor, which can be multiplied by the market discount factor described above to measure the discounted present value of future utility in terms of today's utility.

The concept of discounted present value is commonly used in all areas of finance, including decisions individuals commonly make—taking a mortgage credit for purchase of a house, financing the purchase of the car, and the like. Every firm uses the discounted present value of their future cash flow to assess the value of their projects. Investors use discounted present value to estimate the return on their investment. Lawyers use discounted present value in lawsuits to calculate the value of settlement in cases when damage to a client's health deprives him or her of future income.

SEE ALSO *Finance; Interest Rates; Loans; Time Orientation; Time Preference; Utility Function*

BIBLIOGRAPHY

Brealey, Richard A., Stewart C. Myers, and Franklin Allen. 2006. *Principles of Corporate Finance*, 8th ed. New York: McGraw-Hill/Irwin.

Galina Hale

DISCOUNTING
SEE *Time Preference.*

DISCOURAGED UNEMPLOYMENT
SEE *Discouraged Workers.*

DISCOURAGED WORKERS

Discouraged workers are persons who, discouraged about their prospects of finding work, have given up their job searches and are therefore no longer officially counted as unemployed.

The Bureau of Labor Statistics (BLS) of the U.S. Department of Labor defines discouraged workers as those who report that they want a job but did not look for work in the past four weeks because they believe that no work is available in their line of work or area; they have previously not been able to find work; or they lack the necessary education, skills, or experience, or employers consider them too young or too old, and so on.

In 1994 the BLS added two further criteria to the definition. To be counted as a discouraged worker, persons must have looked for a job within the past year (or since their last job, if they worked during the year) and must indicate that they were available to start work during the prior week if a job had been offered. These changes were an outgrowth of suggestions made in the 1979 report of the National Commission on Employment and Unemployment Statistics (the Levitan Commission), which criticized the definition then in use as too subjective and too arbitrary. The commission recommended a measure based on clear evidence of prior job search and of availability for work. The tightened definition cut the number of discouraged workers from a range of 1.1 to 1.2 million throughout 1993 to 541,000 in the first quarter of 1994 (the latter figure is available only on a not-seasonally-adjusted basis).

Discouraged workers are excluded from the ranks of the unemployed because the BLS counts as unemployed only those jobless workers who have actively looked for work within the past four weeks or who have been laid off from a job to which they expect to be recalled. Recognizing, however, that an argument can be made for counting discouraged workers as unemployed, the BLS publishes as an alternative to the official unemployment rate each month a rate that includes discouraged workers. Thus, when the BLS reported that that the official unemployment rate was 4.8 percent in July 2006, it also noted that adding the 428,000 discouraged workers to both the unemployed and the labor force raised the rate to 5.0 percent.

The number of discouraged workers rises when the economy weakens and falls when the economy improves. For example, the number rose from 1,109,000 to 1,793,000 during the recession that lasted from the third quarter of 1981 to the fourth quarter of 1982, and it then dropped to 813,000 by the next economic peak, in the third quarter of 1990. As a result, the changes that occur in the official unemployment rate, which excludes discouraged workers, understate the worsening of the labor market that occurs in bad times and the improvement that occurs in good times.

The definition of discouraged workers differs among countries. In Canada, for example, discouraged workers must have looked for work within the past six months, rather than within the past year. A BLS study warns that international comparisons of the number of discouraged workers "should be viewed with caution because the methods and the questions asked vary from country to country" (Sorrentino 1993, p. 15).

SEE ALSO *Labor Force Participation; Underemployment; Unemployment*

BIBLIOGRAPHY

Castillo, Monica D. 1998. Persons Outside the Labor Force Who Want a Job. *Monthly Labor Review* 121 (July): 34–42.

Sorrentino, Constance. 1993. International Comparisons of Unemployment Indicators. *Monthly Labor Review* 116 (March): 3–24.

Edward I. Steinberg

DISCOURSE

A sentence is a systematic arrangement of words. A discourse is a systematic arrangement of sentences. The domain of discourse includes various genres—such as narrative, epic, journalistic, or poetic—and thematic fields, from the actuarial to the zoological. It includes register—high and low, technical and vernacular, polite, allegorical and literal, and so on—and modes, from the written to the oral, and from monological to conversational. It also includes the dimension of style, as well as diverse functional orders, including referential, heuristic, imperative, and connotative.

So encompassing a category might seem to be of dubious analytical rigor. But perhaps precisely because it is such a hodgepodge, discourse confronts the analyst not merely with the formal dimensions of language, but also with the diverse conditions of its production and use. It serves as a sociocultural tool kit, whose astonishing multiplicity of instruments can be deployed to characterize the world, from one context to another, and to realize a great variety of other ends. An analytical engagement with discourse has come to define sociolinguistics (see Goffman 1981; Romaine 2000; Trudgill 1974), the ethnography of communication (Gumperz and Hymes 1986; Saville-Troike 1982) and more specialized pursuits such as ethnopoetics (Sammons and Sherzer 2000) and metapragmatics (Lucy 1993). The chief philosophical predecessors of this engagement were Ludwig Wittgenstein's treatment of "language games" in his *Philosophical Investigations* (1953) and John Austin's treatment of speech acts, or "performatives," such as promising or pronouncing a couple to be wed in *How to Do Things with Words* (1962).

Since the later 1960s, however, the analysis of discourse has ceased to be the province of linguists and linguistic anthropologists alone. It has instead emerged as one of the leading preoccupations of social thought, and

of cultural studies more broadly (see Howarth 2000; Mills 2004). That it has done so is closely related to the increasing contemporary saliency of two other topics that are often regarded as hallmarks of the post-structuralist turn in social and cultural critique. One of these centers on the variable historicity of the many collective systems in which human beings take part, or of which they are a part (Attridge, Bennington, and Young 1987). The other centers on the ways in which, and the extent to which, such systems are implicated in the reproduction of economic and political domination. Well before the post-structuralist turn, however, the Marxist political theorist Antonio Gramsci (1891–1937) set an influential, if partial, precedent in conceiving of the trajectory of the dynamics of language, history, and power as unfolding in the contest between the prevailing or "hegemonic" ideologies of a ruling class and the counterhegemonic ideologies of the class destined to succeed them. Several decades later, the structuralist Marxist Louis Althusser (1918–1990) supplemented Gramsci's schema with the still-current postulate that bourgeois ideology is, at base, a discursive apparatus through which persons of authority "interpellate" and, in so doing, subject other persons to authority (Althusser 1971, p. 170–178).

At once post-structuralist and post-Marxist, Michel Foucault's (1926–1984) oeuvre is the source of the conception of discourse most widespread today. For Foucault, discourse is always contestable, always "tactically polyvalent," though by no means is it always the tactical weapon of one or another economically defined class. Discourse bears authority by definition. Its domain is not equivalent to that of opinion in general. Nor does its authority necessarily rest on the hegemony of the material interests that it may serve. The proper measure of discursive authority is, for Foucault, the always somewhat conventional measure of what constitutes knowledge. Knowledge is not, per se, a kind of power. Discourse approached without reference to the material practices it serves and informs can yield no more than a purely speculative analysis of domination. Just so, Foucault's research into the establishment of the mental asylum, the prison, and sexology reveals that those discourses of life, labor, and language that, since the early nineteenth century, have been recognized as "human sciences" have provided the rationale for the imposition of entirely material apparatuses of anthropological classification, compartmentalization, and confinement. Yet Foucault's diagnosis of such discourses of "subjectivation" affords no hope of radical liberation (Foucault 1998, pp. 459–460). As Althusser seems also to have believed, human beings have nothing else to be but discursively articulated and discursively "interpellated" subjects. They might still strive to render the terms of their subjectivation more accommodating and less absolute.

SEE ALSO *Althusser, Louis; Foucault, Michel*

BIBLIOGRAPHY

Althusser, Louis. 1971. *Lenin and Philosophy and Other Essays.* Trans. Ben Brewster. London: New Left Books.

Attridge, Derek, Geoff Bennington, and Robert Young, eds. 1987. *Post-structuralism and the Question of History.* New York: Cambridge University Press.

Austin, John L. 1962. *How to Do Things with Words.* Cambridge, MA: Harvard University Press.

Foucault, Michel. 1965. *Madness and Civilization: A History of Insanity in the Age of Reason.* Trans. Richard Howard. New York: Pantheon.

Foucault, Michel. 1970. *The Order of Things: An Archaeology of the Human Sciences.* Trans. Alan Sheridan. London: Tavistock.

Foucault, Michel. 1972. *The Archaeology of Knowledge.* Trans. A. M. Sheridan Smith. London: Tavistock.

Foucault, Michel. 1977. *Discipline and Punish: The Birth of the Prison.* Translated by Alan Sheridan. New York: Pantheon.

Foucault, Michel. 1978. *An Introduction.* Vol. 1 of *The History of Sexuality.* Trans. Robert Hurley. New York: Pantheon.

Foucault, Michel. 1985. *The Use of Pleasure.* Vol. 2 of *The History of Sexuality.* Translated by Robert Hurley. New York: Pantheon.

Foucault, Michel. 1998. Foucalt. In *Essential Works of Michel Foucault,* Volume 2: Aesthetics, Method, and Epistemology, pp. 459–63. New York: The New Press.

Goffman, Erving. 1981. *Forms of Talk.* Philadelphia: University of Pennsylvania Press.

Gramsci, Antonio. 1971. *Selections from the Prison Notebooks of Antonio Gramsci.* Ed., trans. Quentin Hoare and Geoffrey Nowell Smith. New York: International Publishers. (Orig. pub. 1929–1935).

Gumperz, John J., and Dell Hymes, eds. 1986. *Directions in Sociolinguistics: The Ethnography of Communication.* New York: Blackwell.

Howarth, David. 2000. *Discourse.* Philadelphia: Open University Press.

Lucy, John A., ed. 1993. *Reflexive Language: Reported Speech and Metapragmatics.* Cambridge, U.K.: Cambridge University Press.

Mills, Sara. 1997. *Discourse.* London: Routledge.

Romaine, Suzanne. 2000. *Language in Society: An Introduction to Sociolinguistics,* 2nd ed. Oxford: Oxford University Press.

Sammons, Kay, and Joel Sherzer, eds. 2000. *Translating Native Latin American Verbal Art: Ethnopoetics and the Ethnography of Speaking.* Washington, DC: Smithsonian Institute Press.

Saville-Troike, Muriel. 1982. *The Ethnography of Communication: An Introduction.* Oxford: Blackwell.

Trudgill, Peter. 1974. *Sociolinguistics: An Introduction.* Harmondsworth, U.K.: Penguin.

Wittgenstein, Ludwig. 1953. *Philosophical Investigations.* Translated by G. E. M. Anscombe. London: Basil Blackwell and Mott.

James D. Faubion

DISCRIMINANT VALIDITY
SEE *Validity, Statistical.*

DISCRIMINATION

The online version of the *American Heritage Dictionary of the English Language* (2000) defines *discrimination* as, "Treatment or consideration based on class or category rather than individual merit; partiality or prejudice." Discrimination is a broad and multidimensional concept that covers all acts of preferring one thing, person, or situation over another (Block and Walker 1982, p. 6). In this broad sense, discriminatory behavior can occur within many economic or social activities of daily life. For example, the preference of a high school basketball coach for a taller player over a shorter one in selecting a team or an employer paying an African American worker less than a white worker for the same work would both fall under the heading of discrimination. While the latter act carries an unambiguously negative connotation, few people would consider the former act to be malevolent. Thus, discriminatory behavior does not always imply injustice or prejudice. While understanding this distinction is important, a more relevant discussion of discrimination should emphasize the types of discriminatory acts that are socially and economically unjust, the type of acts that have caused the word *discrimination* to gain an unambiguously negative meaning. Denying or restricting equal opportunity in housing, education, and employment to members of a certain demographic group, such as African Americans, women, or other minority groups, constitutes an act of discrimination that violates common notions of social and economic justice and points to a need for policy intervention.

LABOR-MARKET DISCRIMINATION

One of the most common forms of discrimination, *labor-market discrimination* refers to differential treatment of workers within the labor market. It occurs when individual workers with identical productivity characteristics are treated differently with respect to hiring, occupational access, promotion, wage rate, or working conditions because of the demographic groups to which they belong.

Taste for Discrimination Gary Becker, the 1992 Nobel Prize recipient in economics, laid the groundwork for the mainstream economic approach to the analysis of discrimination in *The Economics of Discrimination* (1957). Becker's theory of discrimination represents an example of the neoclassical economics approach. He introduces the concept of *taste for discrimination* to translate the notion of discrimination into the language of economics. According to Becker:

> If an individual has a "taste for discrimination," he must act as if he were willing to pay something, either directly or in the form of reduced income, to be associated with some persons instead of others. When actual discrimination occurs, he must, in fact, either pay or forfeit income for this privilege. This simple way of looking at the matter gets at the essence of prejudice and discrimination. (Becker 1957, p. 14)

Employer Discrimination In cases of employer discrimination, employers with a taste for discrimination act as if employing, for example, African American workers imposes psychological costs that they are willing to pay. The measure of their willingness to pay can be translated into monetary terms by the *discrimination coefficient*. To illustrate, suppose that the costs to an employer of employing an African American worker and a white worker are W_{aa} and W_w, respectively. If the employer possesses a taste for discrimination against the African American worker, he will act as if the actual cost were $W_{aa}(1 + d)$, where d, a positive number, is the discrimination coefficient. The prejudiced employer will be indifferent when choosing between a white worker and an African American worker when the cost of hiring each worker is, to him, equal—that is, $W_w = W_{aa}(1 + d)$. A clear implication is that the African American worker will be hired by the discriminating employer only if his wage rate is below that of a white worker. More precisely, the African American worker will only be hired if his wage rate is less than that of a white worker by at least the amount of the discrimination coefficient.

Employee Discrimination The source of discrimination may also be the prejudice of fellow employees. For instance, white workers may possess discriminatory preferences against African American workers and avoid situations where they have to work alongside them. The extent of employee prejudice can be monetized by the discrimination coefficient, using an analogy parallel to employer discrimination. A white worker who is offered a wage W_w for a job will act as if this wage rate is only $W_w(1 - d)$, where d is the white worker's discrimination coefficient. The white worker will agree to work with African Americans only if he or she is paid a premium equal to $W_w d$.

Customer Discrimination Another source of discrimination in the labor market results from the prejudice of customers. For example, white customers may prefer to be served by white workers, which would reduce the demand for goods and services sold or served by African American workers. More formally, suppose the actual price of a good or a service is p. Then a white customer would act as if the price of this good or service were $p(1 + d)$ when faced with an African American worker. One of the implications of customer discrimination is that it would result in a segregated workforce within a firm, with white workers being placed in positions with high customer contact and African Americans working in positions with minimal customer interaction.

Predictions of Becker's Theory One of the predictions of Becker's theory is that the labor market will become completely segregated over time. This prediction can be illustrated using employee discrimination. In the presence of employee discrimination, nondiscriminating and profit-maximizing employers would never choose to hire both white and African American workers because employers want to avoid paying a premium to white workers. Instead, they would hire only African American workers who offer the same productivity as whites at a lower wage.

Another prediction of Becker's theory is that discrimination cannot persist in the long run in a competitive market where firms can enter and exit freely. This is because free entry by nondiscriminating employers will force discriminating employers out of the market. For example, nondiscriminating employers will hire equally productive African American workers at a wage that is lower than that offered to white workers. Nondiscriminating firms thus have a cost advantage over discriminating firms, and the forces of competition would drive the discriminating firms out of business. As more nondiscriminating firms enter the market, the demand for minority workers will rise, which will gradually erode the wage differentials between different groups of workers. Therefore, Becker's theory suggests that policies aimed at lessening or eliminating barriers to competition in the market place should help reduce discrimination and wage differentials.

Economists have widely tested the predictions made by Becker's model. For example, Orley Ashenfelter and Timothy Hannan (1986), using data from the banking sector, showed that the share of women employed in a firm is negatively related to the extent of competition in a geographical area. Another study by Judith Hellerstein, David Neumark, and Kenneth Troske (2002) found that, among plants with high levels of market power, those that employ more women are more profitable than those employing fewer women; no such relationship was found for plants with low levels of market power. These findings are consistent with Becker's prediction that discrimination can exist in situations where firms possess market power.

Although Becker's analysis of discrimination has found wide support among economists, criticism has been raised about the predictions of the theory. For example, it has been pointed out that, despite the model's predictions, competitive market forces have not eliminated discrimination, and wage disparities between different demographic groups have not completely disappeared (Darity and Mason 1998). Others have shown that the prediction of a segregated market does not accord with today's real world; furthermore, more segregated workforces tend to generate more wage inequality, not less (Mason 1999). There is also evidence of skin-tone differences in wages among underrepresented minorities (Mason 2004). Finally, several studies find that market competition does not decrease the degree of discrimination practiced within a sector, as predicted by Becker (Coleman 2004; Agesa and Hamilton 2004). Alternative theories of discrimination have been proposed to provide explanations for these issues.

Statistical Discrimination Discriminatory behavior can also occur because employers have limited information about the productivity characteristics of potential employees. Therefore, employers' hiring decisions may rely on average group characteristics based on factors such as race and gender. As a result, individuals with identical productivity characteristics will have different labor-market outcomes because of the average quality of the group to which they belong. Judging individuals on the basis of their average group characteristics is referred to as *statistical discrimination.*

For example, suppose an employer has to choose between a male and female job applicant. Assume further that the observable personal characteristics of these two applicants, such as age, years of education, previous work experience, test scores, and recommendation letters, are identical and that both of them performed equally well at the job interview. An employer, having to make a hiring decision between the two applicants, may decide to offer the job to the male applicant based on the employer's belief that female workers are more likely to quit their jobs than their male counterparts because women are likely to engage in childrearing. The employer makes a decision using statistics about the average group characteristics of the applicants. It is important to note that the statistical information used by the employer may or may not be accurate. In this example, whether or not women *actually* have higher quit rates than men is not relevant to the hiring outcome. While the behavior of some employers engaging in statistical discrimination could be rooted in prejudice, it is also possible that these actions are based purely on nonmalicious grounds. Statistical discrimination can result from decisions that may be correct, profitable, and rational on average.

Statistical discrimination helps explain how racial and gender differences between workers of equal productivity can exist in the labor market. It also explains how discrimination can persist over time. Unlike Becker's taste-for-discrimination model, the employer does not suffer monetarily from practicing statistical discrimination. On the contrary, the discriminating employer can benefit from this behavior by minimizing hiring costs. Therefore, there is no compelling reason for discrimination, and wage differentials between males and females or African Americans and whites tend to disappear in the long run in the presence of statistical discrimination.

While much of the focus on statistical discrimination concerns the labor market, such practices can be observed in different sectors of society as well. One nonmarket example of statistical discrimination is the observed racial differentials in policing patterns. John Knowles, Nicola Persico, and Petra Todd (2001) found that police search vehicles driven by African American motorists for illegal drugs and other contraband far more frequently than those of white motorists. If the motive behind this police behavior is the belief that African Americans are more likely to commit the types of traffic violations that police use as pretexts for vehicle searches, this type of behavior is an example of statistical discrimination.

However, William Darity and Patrick Mason (1998, p. 83) argue that statistical discrimination cannot be a plausible explanation for long-lasting discrimination. They assert that employers should realize that their beliefs are incorrect if average group differences are perceived but not real. If, on the other hand, these differences are real, then employers should develop methods to measure future performance accurately rather than engaging in discriminatory behavior, especially in a world with strict antidiscrimination laws.

NONCOMPETITIVE MODELS OF LABOR-MARKET DISCRIMINATION

The models of discrimination discussed above assume that firms operate in competitive markets. However, discriminatory motives can also be drawn from circumstances in which employers possess some degree of market power in wage determination. Alternative explanations of discrimination have been offered for these circumstances.

One of these alternative explanations is *occupational crowding*. The occupational crowding model of discrimination, advanced by Barbara Bergmann (1971), hypothesizes that labor-market disparities between African American workers and white workers (or males and females) are not due to a "taste for discrimination" by employers, but rather to a deliberate policy of segregating African American workers (or females) into lower-paid occupations. Crowding these groups into low-paying occupations and limiting their access to other occupations reduces their marginal productivity in comparison with that of white (or male) workers. At the same time, the exclusion of minorities from high-paying jobs pushes up the wages of whites, including those who might earn lower wages in the absence of discrimination.

However, profit-maximizing motives should induce some firms to start replacing higher-paid white (or male) workers with equally productive but cheaper African American (or female) workers. This process would eventually eliminate wage disparities between the two groups. In this case, the observed wage disparities can be explained by the presence of noncompetitive forces, such as barriers to worker mobility between occupations.

An alternative explanation of discrimination in the context of a noncompetitive market was developed by the British economist Joan Robinson (1933). Robinson argued that in a monopsonistic market (a labor market with a single employer), profits can be increased by discriminating against some workers if the labor supply elasticity (responsiveness to wages) of African American (or female) workers is less than that of white (or male) workers. Although this model offers a plausible explanation for monopsonistic markets, its applicability is limited because these types of markets are relatively rare.

Another explanation for discrimination was put forth by radical economist Michael Reich (1981). Reich criticized the neoclassical approach to discrimination on several grounds and offered an alternative explanation based on *class conflict*. According to Reich, a firm's output and profitability depend not only on the amount of labor hired, but also on the level of collective action or bargaining power among workers within the firm. He further argued that bargaining power is a function of the wage and employment disparities between African Americans and other workers in the firm. Therefore, discriminatory practices, such as paying equally productive African American workers less than white workers or denying employment to African Americans, generates animosity in the work force, which reduces the bargaining power of workers. As a result of the workers' weakened bargaining power, employers are able earn more profits. Unlike Becker's model, a competitive employer is a direct beneficiary of discrimination in Reich's model.

Another economist, William Darity (1989), criticized Reich's emphasis on the employer in the creation of class conflict and argued that racism among the white working class was not necessarily due to collusive behavior by capitalists, but rather to collective racist action by white workers. According to Darity, in a hierarchical society where occupations are stratified so that some occupations are preferred over others, discrimination occurs as members of different ethnic cultures fight over preferred occupations. One prediction of this explanation is that discrimination cannot be eliminated through government interventions like affirmative action that redistribute occupational positions; it can only be rooted out by eliminating the social hierarchy, because it is the main source of ethnic conflict that results in discrimination.

Patrick Mason (1999) showed that if workers face differential conditions of labor supply, if employers are able to limit the power of labor coalitions, and if racial identity is an important factor in job competition among workers, then competitive profit-maximizing firms may persistently discriminate in their labor-market decisions.

MEASURING LABOR-MARKET DISCRIMINATION

Although it is relatively easy to detect discrimination, it is much more difficult to measure it. The difficulty arises from the fact that not all the disparity between, say, the wages of African Americans and whites is due to labor-market discrimination. These two groups may also differ in their productive characteristics because of pre–labor market discrimination (for example, African Americans receiving less and lower-quality education due to educational discrimination). Then, the disparity must be due in part to differences in the productivity characteristics between the groups. It is important to account for all of these productivity characteristics in order to obtain an unbiased estimate of the true measure of discrimination. After accounting for productivity characteristics, the residual in disparity would then represent a measure of discrimination.

CONCLUSION

Discrimination, whether it occurs in the form of denying employment, housing, or education to members of a particular group, places countless burdens on its victims and on society as a whole. These burdens are both economical and social. By provoking hostility between different groups, discrimination may undermine social harmony, leading to such undesirable social consequences as increased rates of crime. Discrimination also has adverse economic consequences because the earnings of those who face discrimination will be depressed and their career paths will suffer. As a result, the rate of poverty will increase among these groups. The negative consequences of poverty on education, health, crime, and the overall economy will further increase the costs of discrimination for society. Furthermore, many of these negative effects are likely to persist over generations. Thus, discrimination will not only place a cost on its current victims, it will also punish future generations, even if these future generations live in a society without discrimination.

Although the discussion above focuses on discrimination based on race or gender, discriminatory behaviors can and do target all minority groups, including the elderly, teenagers, the disabled, homosexuals, ethnic groups such as Hispanics, and members of certain religions such as Jews and Muslims.

SEE ALSO *Discrimination, Racial; Discrimination, Statistical; Discrimination, Taste for; Discrimination, Wage; Discrimination, Wage, by Age; Discrimination, Wage, by Gender; Discrimination, Wage, by Occupation; Discrimination, Wage, by Race*

BIBLIOGRAPHY

Agesa, Jacqueline, and Darrick Hamilton. 2004. Competition and Wage Discrimination: The Effects of Interindustry Concentration and Import Penetration. *Social Science Quarterly* 85 (1): 121–135.

The American Heritage Dictionary of the English Language. 2000. 4th ed. Boston: Houghton Mifflin. www.bartleby.com/61/.

Ashenfelter, Orley, and Timothy Hannan. 1986. Sex Discrimination and Product Market Competition: The Case of the Banking Industry. *Quarterly Journal of Economics* 101: 149–174.

Becker, Gary S. 1957. *The Economics of Discrimination.* Chicago: University of Chicago Press.

Bergmann, Barbara. 1971. The Effect on White Incomes of Discrimination in Employment. *Journal of Political Economy* 79 (2): 294–313.

Block, Walter E., and Michael A. Walker. 1982. The Plight of the Minority. In *Discrimination, Affirmative Action, and Equal Opportunity: An Economic and Social Perspective*, eds. Walter E. Block and Michael A. Walker, 6. Vancouver, BC: Fraser Institute.

Coleman, Major G. 2004. Racial Discrimination in the Workplace: Does Market Structure Make a Difference? *Industrial Relations* 43 (3): 660–689.

Darity, William, Jr. 1989. What's Left of the Economic Theory of Discrimination? In *The Question of Discrimination: Racial Inequality in the U.S. Labor Market*, eds. Steven Shulman and William Darity Jr., 335–374. Middletown, VT: Wesleyan University Press.

Darity, William, Jr., and Patrick L. Mason. 1998. Evidence on Discrimination in Employment: Codes of Color, Codes of Gender. *Journal of Economic Perspectives* 12 (2): 63–90.

Hellerstein, Judith K., David Neumark, and Kenneth R. Troske. 2002. Market Forces and Sex Discrimination. *Journal of Human Resources* 37 (2): 353–380.

Knowles, John, Nicola Persico, and Petra Todd. 2001. Racial Bias in Motor Vehicle Searches: Theory and Evidence. *Journal of Political Economy* 109 (1): 203–229

Mason, Patrick L. 1999. Male Interracial Wage Differentials: Competing Explanations. *Cambridge Journal of Economics* 23: 1–39.

Mason, Patrick L. 2004. Annual Income, Hourly Wages, and Identity among Mexican Americans and Other Latinos. *Industrial Relations* 43 (4): 817–834.

Reich, Michael. 1981. *Racial Inequality: A Political-Economic Analysis.* Princeton, NJ: Princeton University Press.

Robinson, Joan. 1933. *Economics of Imperfect Competition.* London: Macmillan.

Erdal Tekin

DISCRIMINATION, PRICE

Price discrimination is a widely used marketing tactic. It is present when two or more identical units of the same products or services are sold at different prices, either to the same buyer or to different buyers. It is more often observed in sales to end-use buyers (consumers) than in intermediate-goods markets (where the buyer is a manufacturer, wholesaler, or retailer); this is because in many countries price discrimination in intermediate-goods markets is considered to be an "unfair" practice by antitrust authorities. Price discrimination is also known as "flexible pricing" or "targeted pricing." Since they sound neutral, these alternative names are often used by the business community. Whatever it is called, however, price discrimination is nothing but a marketing technique used by a seller to generate higher profits by taking advantage of differences in consumers' "willingness to pay" (i.e., a maximum amount that each buyer is ready to pay).

Typical examples of price discrimination include student discounts for motion pictures and quantity discounts in shopping malls. Other than these obvious examples, however, judgment is often required in deciding whether or not a particular pricing practice should be classified as price discrimination. For instance, a difference in the total price of a delivery is usually not considered to be price discrimination if it simply reflects a difference in transportation costs. Goods sold at different places at different dates give different utility, and they are therefore considered to be, to some extent, different goods. A less trivial example is a pricing practice for tiered classes in airplanes. This may be seen as product differentiation if one emphasizes that passengers in different classes actually enjoy differentiated goods (e.g., spacing, meals). In this case, however, the main part of the good is the flight itself, and it may be that the carrier simply wants to engage in price discrimination. The apparent product differentiation might therefore be of secondary importance. A similar practice is found in the way publishers sell a book. Many books are initially sold in hardcover editions, with a less expensive paperback edition being published at a later time.

To discriminate in pricing, firms must obviously have some control over the price that buyers face. This situation occurs when market competition does not drive the price down to a level at which a firm (i.e., a seller) considers exiting from the market because buyers are somehow "stuck" with particular sellers, either because it is too costly to look into all of the other alternatives, or because the number of firms in the market is so small that competition is not fierce. In addition, the cost of immediate resale among consumers must be impossible; otherwise some consumers will be better off buying the good at a lower price from other consumers (this behavior is called arbitrage).

A common taxonomy of price discrimination, contrived by Arthur C. Pigou in 1920, is based on how a firm sorts buyers, each of whom potentially has a different value of willingness to pay (i.e., a different maximum amount that each buyer is ready to pay). In first-degree price discrimination (also known as perfect price discrimination), a firm captures the entire amount of each buyer's willingness to pay. In reality, however, this type of price discrimination is rarely observed, because the firm needs to know exactly what each buyer's willingness to pay is, and this requirement is difficult to meet. Yet sellers may still have some idea of how many buyers there are for each particular level of willingness to pay. In second-degree price discrimination, a firm, by utilizing information on buyer preference, offers various pricing options, letting each consumer self-select into a different pricing schedule (e.g., quantity discounts or the aforementioned bookselling options). In third-degree price discrimination, the seller uses observable signals (e.g., age, occupation, location, time of use) to categorize buyers into different segments, and each segment is given a constant price per unit.

However, the boundary between second- and third-degree price discrimination is not absolute. For example, with price skimming (or behavior-based price discrimination), in which a firm offers different prices depending on a buyer's history of past purchases and other behaviors (e.g., how often he or she has visited the firm's Web site), a buyer usually faces a constant price for each product, while a different buyer may pay a higher or lower price depending on his or her behavioral history. Thus, price skimming does not fall within the three main types of price discrimination. Advances in information processing technology, such as the widespread use of the Internet, have made this type of price discrimination possible.

Firms are usually happy with discriminatory pricing as long as it does not make price competition too fierce. Since firms extract more of a buyer's willingness to pay by price discrimination, a question arises as to whether buyers are always worse off than they would be with uniform pricing (when a seller offers an identical price to every buyer). Economists do not have a definite answer to this question. One instance of third-degree price discrimination that could benefit buyers as a whole, or in which

every buyer could be better off, is when firms sell a good to consumers who would not purchase it under uniform pricing. In addition, as Takanori Adachi (2005) points out, with goods such as information or communications, where "network effects" are prevalent (that is, as more people buy the good, their willingness-to-pay increases), price discrimination has greater potential to improve consumer welfare. This is because a firm utilizes price discrimination to create more gains from the network effects, which can also benefit the buyers more than the amount a firm extracts from consumers' willingness to pay. In studies combining formal modeling and data analysis, Eugenio J. Miravete (2002), Phillip Leslie (2004), and others have scrutinized the welfare effects of price discrimination. Miravete studied optional calling plans (a variant of quantity discounts) in the telephone service industry, and he concluded that the experimental introduction of optional calling plans might have harmed not only consumers, but also the telephone service company. Leslie investigated the welfare effects of both second- and third-degree price discrimination in the world of musical theater. He found that price discrimination increased a producer's profits by 5 percent, while the loss in consumer welfare was negligible. As these studies show, there seems to be no general answer as to whether discriminatory pricing per se harms the buyer, and the question must therefore be considered on a case-by-case basis.

SEE ALSO *Competition, Imperfect; Discrimination; Discrimination, Wage; Monopoly; Price Setting and Price Taking*

BIBLIOGRAPHY

Adachi, Takanori. 2005. Third-Degree Price Discrimination, Consumption Externalities, and Social Welfare. *Economica* 72 (285): 171–178.

Leslie, Phillip. 2004. Price Discrimination in Broadway Theater. *RAND Journal of Economics* 35 (3): 520–541.

Miravete, Eugenio J. 2002. Estimating Demand for Local Telephone Service with Asymmetric Information and Optional Calling Plans. *Review of Economic Studies* 69 (4): 943–971.

Pigou, Arthur C. 1920. *The Economics of Welfare.* London: Macmillan.

Takanori Adachi

DISCRIMINATION, RACIAL

The word *discrimination* is derived from the word Latin "discriminare" translated as to "distinguish between." Racial discrimination, as a commonly accepted construct, is conceptualized as distinguishing in an unequal or less favorable manner an individual or institution by another individual, institution, or other entity with power to influence outcomes based on the perceived race, nationality, ethnicity, or national origin of the victim. It can occur as an overt action or in a subtler, covert manner.

OVERT AND INDIRECT DISCRIMINATION

Overt racial discrimination occurs when there is an illegal and direct link between an individual's perceived race, nationality, ethnicity, or national origin, or an organization's perceived characteristics and composition, and a particular negative outcome or pervasive disadvantage. Notably, the conceptualization of overt racial discrimination emphasizes the inappropriate reliance on fallible perceptions of another person's race or ethnicity as an estimate of their more general characteristics, skills, abilities, or worth. Consistent with the historical use of the word *race*, contemporary racial discrimination occurs when external characteristics such as skin tone are used as a mechanism for negative appraisal or social or political classification (Goodman 2000). Appropriately or not, race is commonly used to distinguish groups of people according to their ancestry and a more or less distinctive combination of physical characteristics. *Ethnicity*, a term that includes biological, behavioral, and cultural characteristics, is commonly used to describe groups of people with a common history, ancestry, and belief system. Because terms of categorization such as *race* and *ethnicity* are used to quickly appraise and then give meaning to individuals in our environments, they are also principle agents for overt overestimates of knowledge about an individual, group, or organization, and may facilitate inappropriate judgments and social outcomes.

Indirect racial discrimination has existed throughout the history of mankind but has only recently come to the attention of social and medical researchers. The essence of indirect racial discrimination is that a structure or policy that was designed without specific attention to race or ethnicity results in disadvantage and or detriment to a particular group of people based on race or ethnicity. One example is a policy that for security purposes prohibits a particular type of uniform, dress, or head dressing that is the normal uniform, dress, or head dressing of a particular group of individuals of similar racial composition or ethnic heritage. Other examples include the forced participation of school-aged children in a particular celebratory custom or ritual that is incongruent with the religious beliefs or customs of a particular racial or ethnic group of people.

These examples highlight several important factors about overt and indirect racism. The first is that in the context of the multifactoral dimensions of humanity and the multiple characteristics that unite and distinguish individuals (e.g., age, gender, socioeconomic status, etc.), it is sometimes difficult to prove that a single characteristic such as race is the basis of a negative appraisal or outcome. Secondly, inherent in the construct of racial discrimination is the presence of a power differential such that benefits or gains are withheld from deserving or entitled individuals or entities. In the absence of a power differential or a negative consequence, racial discrimination cannot exist.

Based on the complex definitions of race and ethnicity, racial discrimination is sometimes difficult to identify. For example, the existence of racial discrimination is not dependent on the volition of the perpetrator; it can exist even when the (accidental) perpetrator's intentions were honorable. Additionally, in some cases the negative impact on or consequences to a victim may be difficult to identify.

Racial discrimination can occur as a single event or as a more systemic and engrained intentional or unintentional policy. In cases where there is an established pattern of inequity based on race, ethnicity, or culture perpetrated by a definable individual, overt racial discrimination is usually easier to prove, but when it is a single occurrence at issue, or the perpetrator is a system or institution, discrimination may be difficult to document and prove.

CONSEQUENCES OF DISCRIMINATION

Recent evidence presented in the *American Journal of Public Health* indicated that people who experience daily discrimination may be more susceptible to a variety of health problems, including cardiovascular and pulmonary disease and chronic pains (2006). This study was notable because it was the first to explore such issues in a sample of 2,100 Asian Americans, a population traditionally thought to be insulated from negative discriminatory experiences. Similar evidence predicted poor mental health outcomes in black and Latino immigrants who were subject to racial discrimination (Gee et al. 2006). Gary Bennett and colleagues (2005) found that minorities who perceived greater amounts of racial or ethnic harassment were more likely to use tobacco daily, and ultimately may manifest greater risk of tobacco-related morbidity and mortality.

Title VII of the Civil Rights Act of 1964 was passed to protect an individual's right to employment without negative consequence or discrimination as a function of his or her race, color, national origin, sex, or religion. Title VII applies only to employers with more than fifteen employees. Current laws and regulations prohibit racial discrimination that results in differences in recruiting, hiring, determination of salary and fringe benefits, training, work assignments, promotions, transfers, disciplinary actions, firings, and retaliation. Yet, the workplace remains one of the most fertile settings for claims of racial discrimination. Each year from 1997 to 2006, more than 26,000 race-based discrimination charges were filed in the United States (U.S. Equal Employment Opportunity Commission 2007).

SOCIAL AND ECONOMIC EXPLANATIONS

Beyond individual level explanations, economic models have been posited for many years to explain inequity and racial discrimination. For example, Milton Friedman, a Nobel laureate and professor who was often referred to as the "economist's economist," was a strong advocate of personal liberty and freedom. Among his many lifetime achievements and controversial theories were ending mandatory licensing of doctors as well as ending social security as an unfair and unsustainable system exemplary of governmental intervention in a free market economy.

In a manner consistent with his previous writings, Friedman also indicated that market racial discrimination and market competition were antithetical. More specifically, that social and political freedom was maximized and racial equality was best achieved by minimizing the interventional and regulatory role of the government, and that free markets and their associated economic forces would facilitate a state of equilibrium and fairness to all who participated (Friedman and Rose 1962).

Certainly, not all social scientists and economists agreed with Friedman. From a sociological and spatial perspective, many argued that there was a positive relationship between the size of a racial minority and discrimination. More specifically, that market competition encouraged racial discrimination. As the relative size of a racial or ethnic minority group increases, motives for the majority racial population to discriminate against the minority population may also increase toward the reduction of market racial competition and reducing threats to the loss of jobs and other essential scarce resources (Blalock 1967).

The relationship between the size of the minority population and the magnitude of discrimination is imperfect, at best. For example, the more effective the discriminatory economic practices against minorities, the less threat there is to perceived or real resources and, consequentially, the less need for discriminatory practices. In contrast, ineffective discriminatory practices promote the use of additional or more potent attempts to regulate racial competition and preserve resources of the majority. Adjustments to the marketplace mobility and economic growth of minority and majority populations is designed

to preserve majority resources, particularly in the upper echelons of status, while maintaining incentives for the minority racial populations to remain engaged in such a limited and punitive system (Reich 1981).

The compelling logic of this socioeconomic model of discrimination is that the more prominent minorities are in a labor force equally accessible to majority and minority populations, the worse their ultimate economic position at the hands of the majority. Secondly, that a ceiling of economic achievement and mobility will be imposed and maintained by the majority population to preserve economic status and resources as a function of the degree to which minority racial populations are perceived as threatening. Lastly and particularly, for example, in the U.S. market, discriminatory practices against minorities will most likely persist due to the increasingly large number of minorities in the workplace and their perceived threat to the economic existence and stability of the majority unless there are regulatory and other governmental remedies.

OTHER FORMS OF RACIAL DISCRIMINATION

There are several marketplace and non-marketplace forms of racial discrimination. For example, statistical discrimination is unfair or unequal treatment of a racial group because of stereotypes or generalized estimates of group behavior or assumptions about an individual within a group based on the "average" estimated behavior for that group (i.e., greater interest rates for home mortgages for African Americans due to perceptions of greater risk of loan default). Customer discrimination refers to the process by which the racial composition of customers of a direct-public-contact business influences the race of who is hired as an employee. Although customer discrimination occurs in businesses that serve white and black customers, this practice appears to result in some reduction in overall labor demand and wages for blacks (Holzer and Ihlanfeldt 1998).

Social discrimination is the process by which non-meritorious judgments are made and differential treatment is given based on estimates of lower social status or lower social class of an individual secondary to their race or ethnicity. Governmental discrimination, like any other form of racial discrimination, is committed by governmental personnel or in a government setting against an individual based on their race or ethnicity. This can be manifest as direct actions against an individual or as policies that negatively effect groups of individuals. The difficulty of defining and then distinguishing racial discrimination from other concepts such as "preference" or "choice" is highlighted by non-market forms of private discrimination. An individual, based on previous experiences, social norms, or preferences can decide to exclusively pursue or exclude members of a group for mate selection. When is preference for a race elevated to the level of racial discrimination? Is this form of private discrimination harmful? Who gains and, if anyone, who is disadvantaged by such actions? Answers to these types of questions are as varied as the individuals who attempt to answer them.

CONCLUSION

In the context of a growing list of psychological and physical morbidities associated with racial discrimination, and what appears to be consistent numbers of claims of discriminatory acts each year, there remains a robust interest in factors that influence equity of processes and outcomes. Some theories suggest that racial discrimination is pathological and is to be remedied with policies and regulations. Others suggest that marketplace factors should produce a form of equality and that there is no role for government in facilitating equality of process or outcomes. Independent of theoretical orientations for resolving racial discrimination, its economic, social, interpersonal, psychological, and physiological consequences are not in question nor is the degree to which it demoralizes its victims.

SEE ALSO *African Americans; Civil Rights; Civil Rights Movement, U.S.; Colorism; Discrimination; Discrimination, Statistical; Discrimination, Taste for; Discrimination, Wage; Discrimination, Wage, by Age; Discrimination, Wage, by Gender; Discrimination, Wage, by Occupation; Discrimination, Wage, by Race; Disease; Ethnicity; Inequality, Racial; Latinos; Mental Health; Mental Illness; Prejudice; Race; Race-Blind Policies; Race-Conscious Policies; Racism; Stereotypes*

BIBLIOGRAPHY

Bennett, Gary G., Marcellus M. Merritt, Christopher L. Edwards, and John J. Sollers III. 2003. Perceived Racism and Affective Responses to Ambiguous Interpersonal Interactions among African American Men. *American Behavioral Scientist* 47 (7): 963–976.

Blalock, H. M., Jr. 1967. *Toward a Theory of Minority Group Relations.* New York: Wiley.

Friedman, M., and D. Rose. 1962. *Capitalism and Freedom.* Chicago: University of Chicago Press.

Holzer, H. J., and K. R. Ihlanfeldt. 1998. Customer Discrimination and Employment Outcomes for Minority Workers. *Quarterly Journal of Economics* 113 (3): 835–867.

Krieger, Nancy, Pamela D. Waterman, Cathy Hartman, et al. 2006. Social Hazards on the Job: Workplace Abuse, Sexual Harassment, and Racial Discrimination—A Study of Black, Latino, and White Low-Income Women and Men Workers in the United States. *International Journal of Health Services* 36 (1): 51–85.

Merritt, Marcellus M., Gary G. Bennett, Redford B. Williams, et al. 2006. Perceived Racism and Cardiovascular Reactivity and Recovery to Personally Relevant Stress. *Health Psychology* 25 (3): 364–369.

Reich, M. 1981. *Racial Inequality: A Political-Economic Analysis.* Princeton, NJ: Princeton University Press.

Ryan, Albert M., Gilbert C. Gee, and David F. Laflamme. 2006. The Association between Self-Reported Discrimination, Physical Health, and Blood Pressure: Findings from African Americans, Black Immigrants, and Latino Immigrants in New Hampshire. *Journal of Health Care for the Poor and Underserved* 17 (2 Suppl): 116–132.

Terrell, Francis, Aletha R. Miller, Kenneth Foster, and C. Edward Watkins Jr. 2006. Racial Discrimination-Induced Anger and Alcohol Use among Black Adolescents. *Adolescence* 41 (163): 485–492.

Tigges, L. M., and D. M. Tootle. 1993. Underemployment and Racial Competition in Local Labor Markets. *Sociological Quarterly* 34 (2): 279–298.

U.S. Equal Employment Opportunity Commission. 2007. Race-Based Charges FY 1997–FY2006. http://www.eeoc.gov/stats/race.html.

Wadsworth, Emma, Kamaldeep Dhillon, Christine Shaw, et al. 2007. Racial Discrimination, Ethnicity and Work Stress. *Occupational Medicine* 57 (1): 18–24.

Christopher L. Edwards

DISCRIMINATION, STATISTICAL

Received economic theory of the firm admits only one motive: profit maximization. The received theory of the market is that it is most efficient when operating unconstrained. If this is so, hiring policies should seek to assemble the most efficient workforce, disregarding irrelevant factors, which cause loss due to the failure to employ the most competent available workers. (This assumes choice between candidates; namely, some unemployment. But the minimal level, often called *friction unemployment,* should suffice.) Despite the received theory, discrimination is rampant in recruitment against women and members of minority groups (Bertrand and Mullainathan 2004). By the theory of the firm, entrepreneurs should prefer the more productive workers over the better qualified ones, but they do not. (Even ignorance suffices to insure this; see Altonji and Plerret 1997.) This is amenable to statistical tests that may be viewed as empirical tests of the received theory. Also, it signifies discrimination being a burden on the economy. It looks as if data easily refute the received theory. It is possible to save it from refutation by two different claims. First, the perpetrator of discrimination is not the employers but, say, the employee organizations (the incumbent hypothesis). If so, then the theory is not refuted because it is inapplicable, as the (employment) market is not quite free. Advocates of received theory will not admit this defense; they will not suggest that the theory is inapplicable, at least not in the West. If the theory is applicable and is correct, then discrimination is profitable after all, even if it is disguised (Sattinger 1998). If one does not take the theory on faith, it is necessary to learn how discrimination can be profitable.

This problem concerns both the theory of the firm and the theory of the market. First, how does employment discrimination raise profits? Second, does the market mechanism operate optimally without the aid of antidiscrimination legislation? Since, admittedly, employment discrimination is clearly detrimental to the economy, the question is: Will it disappear faster with or without the aid of legislation? By the received market-mechanism theory, legislation against employment discrimination is harmful. Evidence suggests that at times this is so and at times not (Loury 1981; Neumark and Stock 1999). Hence the received theory of the market needs adjustment to allow for some government intervention. (This is scarcely news, since even the most ardent defenders of received theory do not oppose systematic monetary interventions, not to mention fiscal ones.) Does the same hold for the received theory of the firm?

Possibly, discrimination has a cost, and it should be considered a part of entrepreneurs' preference. Their preferences thus become a part of the theory of consumers' preference (Swinton 1977). This is a serious deviation from received theory that takes the theory of consumers' preferences as no more than a theoretical nicety, since the market tends to aggregate demand only (Agassi 1992). The option left for the effort to rescue the received theory of the firm, then, is to explain how discrimination incurs no loss.

One explanation holds that discrimination is economically advantageous because it pleases community leaders, especially in underdeveloped countries where it is socially obligatory. This explanation interests students of business public relations and voluntary organizations such as the United Nations Volunteers and others who attempt to improve matters. Economists tend to ignore this view, since obviously not all countries maintain free markets. This is regrettable, since market freedom is a matter of degree. Economists tend to declare deviations of the market from received economic theory insignificant, praise the market for the advantages of modern liberal society, and blame deviations from it for the disadvantages. According to a second explanation, discrimination is due to employers who cling to refuted views as prejudices. This explanation does not help received economic theory that deems the market mechanism the best means for

eliminating inefficient entrepreneurs through competition. A third explanation holds that the advantage of discrimination is in its reduction of the cost of hiring, since members of the preferred groups keep their jobs for longer periods. Such advantages are called *statistical discrimination*. Not surprisingly, this view of discrimination is pivotal (Collinson et al. 1990), and so it deserves attention. Is the hypothesis true that discrimination is advantageous?

Before examining the hypothesis we should ask the following questions: (1) Does it rescue the theory? (2) Does it suggest that the market mechanism still is the best way to overcome discrimination through recruitment? (3) Does it suggest leaving matters to the market mechanism anyway?

The theory allows for statistical discrimination only if it is cost effective. If so, then reducing the influence of discrimination on workers' turnover should reduce it. Even then, allowing for statistical discrimination cannot be the best strategy, because reducing it by legislation is an improvement, even from the strictly economic viewpoint. Defenders of the received theory are familiar with such criticism, and do not deny it: certain legislations may outdo the market mechanism, but these are too costly and their advantages are temporary at best. In the long run, the market mechanism is the most efficient means for tackling social evils. This response is a reading of received theory as promising social benefits only in the long run.

To this view, John Maynard Keynes (1883–1946) responded with his memorable adage: in the long run we are all dead. This means that we cannot test this version in a lifetime. Moreover, the evils we are facing are pressing, and the promises of received theory are postponed and doubtful. This is still under debate, however, especially since statistical discrimination is less pressing than the massive unemployment that troubled Keynes. The central question then is: Is the statistical discrimination hypothesis true? We do not know. Is it at least testable? If not, should we give the market mechanism the benefit of the doubt or should we fight discrimination or wait for the market to do it? Waiting is questionable, since pockets of poverty and related ills are stagnant, and, notoriously, many social factors hardly benefit from the economy, which adds to the stagnation. Instances for this are understandable but intolerably self-reinforcing: the disposition of the police to seek criminals within the groups in which crime prevails, persistent poor education, underage pregnancy, and the absence of intergenerational mobility where it is needed most. The self-reinforcing of socioeconomic patterns ensures social stability at the cost of retaining various social evils, employment discrimination included.

The opinion that the market mechanism is the best means for the eradication of social ills is questionable.

Opposing laws against discrimination requires particularly strong arguments. Arguing that such legislation is ineffective will not do: many laws are ineffective yet we still want them on the books. The paradigm case is the proscription of statutory rape by minors. The argument against the proscription of discrimination is therefore understandably philosophical. In principle, advocates of the market mechanism theory approve only of laws that are essential for the maintenance of the market. Thus, they approve of imposing the honoring of contracts, but not truth in advertising: the market can live with false advertisements and the market mechanism will eliminate them, they say. Even if we accept this kind of argument, advocates of the market mechanism theory cannot show that the market tolerates no social ills that are too objectionable. As discrimination is both objectionable and a burden on the market, and since laws against it are no burden on any social group, the theory of statistical discrimination is *a priori* too feeble—apart from its dependence on many questionable assumptions. Which is not to say that we need not test these assumptions: they may be interesting for other ends, especially as means of insight into the costs—economic and other—of social stability. As Karl Popper (1902–1994) suggested more than half a century ago, however advisable it is to rely on the market mechanism when it works, the view that it always works well is a metaphysical dogma. This squares with his proposal to replace the demand for social stability with the demand for democratic controls.

SEE ALSO *Discrimination; Discrimination, Racial; Discrimination, Taste for; Discrimination, Wage; Discrimination, Wage, by Age; Discrimination, Wage, by Gender; Discrimination, Wage, by Occupation; Discrimination, Wage, by Race; Distribution, Normal; Expectations; Information, Asymmetric; Probability Distributions; Risk; Uncertainty*

BIBLIOGRAPHY

Agassi, Joseph. 1992. Beyond the Static Theory of Tastes as Exogenous. *Methodology and Science* 25: 99–118.

Agassi, Judith Buber. 1992. Review of David L. Collinson, David Knights, and Margaret Collinson: *Managing to Discriminate. Organization Studies* 13 (3): 472–475.

Altonji, Joseph G., and Charles R. Plerret. 1997. Employer Learning and Statistical Discrimination. U.S. Department of Labor. http://www.bls.gov/ore/pdf/nl970020.pdf.

Arrow, Kenneth. 1973. The Theory of Discrimination. In *Discrimination in Labor Markets*, eds. Orley Ashenfelter and Albert Rhees, 3–33. Princeton, NJ: Princeton University Press.

Bertrand, Marianne, and Sendhil Mullainathan. 2004. Are Emily and Greg More Employable than Lakisha and Jamal? A Field Experiment on Labor Market Discrimination. *American Economic Review* 94: 991–1013

Collinson, David L., David Knights, and Margaret Collinson. 1990. *Managing to Discriminate.* London and New York: Routledge.

Darity, William A., and Patrick L. Mason, 1998. Evidence on Discrimination in Employment: Codes of Color, Codes of Gender. *The Journal of Economic Perspectives* 12: 63–90.

Loury, Glenn C. 1981. Is Equal Opportunity Enough? *American Economic Review* 71: 122–126.

Neumark, David, and Wendy A. Stock. 1999. Age Discrimination Laws and Labor Market Efficiency. *Journal of Political Economy* 107: 1081–1125.

Popper, Karl R. 1945. *The Open Society and Its Enemies.* London: Routledge.

Sattinger, Michael. 1998. Statistical Discrimination with Employment Criteria. *International Economic Review* 39: 205–237.

Swinton, David H. 1977. Racial Discrimination: A Labor Force Competition Theory of Discrimination in the Labor Market. *American Economic Review* 67: 400–404.

Joseph Agassi

DISCRIMINATION, TASTE FOR

A person (an employer, coworker, or consumer) is said to have a *taste for discrimination* if he or she would pay to maintain social or psychological distance from members of a particular group. A related concept, *nepotism*, is used to describe a sacrifice of income to maintain proximity to members of a particular group. A taste for discrimination is, in this analysis, no different from having a taste (preference) or distaste for any market commodity. This approach to discrimination was first articulated in *The Economics of Discrimination* by economist Gary Becker. Since publication of this pioneering work in 1957, Becker's analysis has become the dominant theory of discrimination within mainstream economics.

Becker claimed that the motivations behind discriminatory tastes were the province of sociologists and psychologists. His stated objective was to focus solely on the economic consequences of discriminatory preferences translated into economic behavior. He explicitly considered, however, the motivations to be nonpecuniary. According to Becker, one actually discriminates, as opposed to merely having a taste for discrimination, when one forfeits income in order to indulge this preference. The employer who hires desirable workers pays relatively higher wages and is content to do so. Costs of production increase and therefore diminish profits. Conversely, a nondiscriminating employer—should one exist—will hire the workers with the lowest market wages if they are no less productive than members of the desired group.

According to Becker, uninhibited market forces should punish discriminators whose businesses are less profitable. If the industry is not competitive, however, employer discrimination may be able to persist for a longer time.

Customer discrimination, in contrast, is not subject to the same market discipline. So long as the customer is satisfied with paying to indulge his or her taste, the status quo can continue. Employees' taste for discrimination manifests as a desire for higher wages to compensate for working alongside the undesired group. To avoid such costs, employers can segregate jobs.

The assumption that discrimination is not profitable has important policy implications. Mainstream economists have utilized Becker's model to argue that market competition undermines discriminatory practices, and therefore antidiscrimination regulations are unnecessary. Persistent wage differentials are deemed to be due to productivity differences alone, rather than discrimination. In a 1998 review of empirical research in the *Journal of Economic Perspectives*, however, William Darity Jr. and Patrick Mason note that multiple methodologies have revealed ongoing discrimination. Similarly, Francine Blau and Lawrence Kahn (2000), in the same journal, summarize a range of studies on the gender pay gap and find ongoing evidence of discrimination despite women's increased acquisition of human capital.

Theories that blur the boundaries between in-market and premarket discrimination, as well as those in which market power is viewed as a normal result of competitive processes, better explain why wage differentials can persist and be profitable, according to Darity and Mason. The core assumption of Becker's model is that the preference to associate (or not associate) with people with specific ascriptive characteristics is exogenously given. Nonpecuniary motivations imply a lack of economic incentives to discriminate. This assumption has long troubled political economists focusing on institutionalized discrimination (D'Amico 1987). For political economists, discrimination is endogenous to economic processes (Mason 1995; Shulman 1996). First, employers benefit from discrimination via *class struggle effects*: by perpetuating divisions among social groups, discrimination "divides and conquers" the workforce by limiting worker organization. Second, *exclusion effects* or *job competition effects* imply that members of dominant groups who get preferential access to labor market queues have economic incentives to maintain these hierarchies.

Research by anthropologists, psychologists, and other social scientists indicates that race-ethnicity, sex-gender, and other social categories do not have intrinsic meaning apart from specific social contexts. The process of forming such identities is therefore complex. Treating discrimination as a "taste" presumes that the meanings of such ascriptive characteristics are generated outside of economic processes rather than examining how racial (or gender) identities become "productive property" (Darity et al. 2006, p. 302). Members of privileged groups develop property rights in their racial and gender identities, according to a game-theoretic model developed by Darity, Mason, and James Stewart (2006). In their model, as well as in the historical examples they cite, taking on a racialized identity, as opposed to an individualist mindset, garners concrete benefits. Such identities provide access to income and wealth for group members, making them intransigent over time. Their conception of identity contrasts with the primarily ideological and cultural depiction of identity in George Akerlof and Rachel Kranton (2000); their model discounts the prevalence of discrimination by emphasizing the voluntary choices made by women and others to eschew occupations and economic activities associated with dominant groups.

According to Deborah Figart and Ellen Mutari (2005), Becker's focus on preferences for social distance draws upon the prevailing discourse about racial segregation in the 1950s United States, but it is not a universal theory of discrimination. Impersonal entities such as corporations, for example, do not have a desire for distance. Other forms of discrimination defined out of the scope of Becker's analysis, including *wage discrimination* and *statistical discrimination*, have complex but different dynamics. In fact, forms of discrimination may evolve in response to changes in the political economy (see Darity and Mason 1998; Blau and Kahn 2000). Taste for discrimination, therefore, is at best a partial explanation of labor market practices.

SEE ALSO *Discrimination; Discrimination, Racial; Discrimination, Statistical; Discrimination, Wage; Discrimination, Wage, by Age; Discrimination, Wage, by Gender; Discrimination, Wage, by Occupation; Discrimination, Wage, by Race*

BIBLIOGRAPHY

Akerlof, George, and Rachel Kranton. 2000. Economics and Identity. *Quarterly Journal of Economics* 115 (3): 715–753.

Becker, Gary S. [1957] 1971. *The Economics of Discrimination.* 2nd ed. Chicago: University of Chicago Press.

Blau, Francine D., and Lawrence M. Kahn. 2000. Gender Differences in Pay. *Journal of Economic Perspectives* 14 (4): 75–99.

D'Amico, Thomas F. 1987. The Conceit of Labor Market Discrimination. *American Economic Review* 77 (2): 310–315.

Darity, William A., Jr., and Patrick L. Mason. 1998. Evidence on Discrimination in Employment: Codes of Color, Codes of Gender. *Journal of Economic Perspectives* 12 (2): 63–90.

Darity, William A., Jr., Patrick L. Mason, and James B. Stewart. 2006. The Economics of Identity: The Origin and

Persistence of Racial Identity Norms. *Journal of Economic Behavior & Organization* 60 (3): 283–305.

Figart, Deborah M., and Ellen Mutari. 2005. Rereading Becker: Contextualizing the Development of Discrimination Theory. *Journal of Economic Issues* 39 (2): 475–483.

Mason, Patrick L. 1995. Race, Competition, and Differential Wages. *Cambridge Journal of Economics* 19 (4): 545–567.

Shulman, Steven. 1996. The Political Economy of Labor Market Discrimination: A Classroom-Friendly Presentation of the Theory. *Review of Black Political Economy* 24 (4): 47–64.

Ellen Mutari
Deborah M. Figart

DISCRIMINATION, WAGE

Wage discrimination occurs when, due to the operation of the labor market, similar workers receive different wages on the basis of race, sex, ethnicity, age, sexual orientation, or other ascribed characteristic not directly related to productivity. Workers subject to wage discrimination may earn lower wages in a given job, be assigned to low-wage jobs within firms, or employed in low-wage firms.

Not all wage differentials are discriminatory. If more group A than group B workers are willing to work in dangerous but highly paid jobs, on average, As may earn more than Bs do. But provided that wages are based on the nature of the job and not group membership, the wage differential need not reflect wage discrimination. Similarly, if As are paid less because they are less skilled, there is no wage discrimination unless their lower skills reflect their expectation that their skills will not be rewarded.

MEASURING WAGE DISCRIMINATION

We rarely measure worker productivity directly and, therefore, we cannot test whether equally productive workers earn different wages based on their group membership. Instead, we ask whether apparently similar workers of different races, sex, etc., receive different wages. The difficulty with this approach is determining the dimensions along which workers should be similar. For example, suppose we compared men and women with undergraduate degrees in biology and found that women have lower wages. Suppose we also found that for those of this group that are teachers, wages are similar for such men and women. We might conclude that many women choose to be teachers, perhaps in order to be with their children after school and during vacations. Women (and men) with these preferences accept lower wages, so there is no

wage discrimination. However, perhaps women face significant wage discrimination in jobs outside teaching, so that those who do not teach are the very talented or lucky few who find high-wage jobs outside teaching. In this case, we miss the wage discrimination by comparing men and women in the same occupation.

Moreover, if firms discriminate by offering low wages to, for example, African Americans, individuals offered these low wages may respond by not working, and we will only observe wages for those African Americans employed at good wages by nondiscriminating firms. Ignoring individuals who are not working underestimates the black-white wage differential and thus the extent of wage discrimination.

Estimates of the degree of wage discrimination, and even its existence, depend critically on the factors for which we control. There are large earnings differentials between men and women, blacks and whites, and non-Hispanic whites and Hispanics if we take no other factors into account. Skin-shade studies have found that darker Hispanics and African Americans are paid less than Hispanics and Africans with lighter complexions. Controlling for cognitive test scores in high school eliminates much of the difference between black and white men, but a significant difference reappears if we also control for years of education. Differences in the earnings of black and white (employed) women are modest, but are much larger if we take account of the potential earnings of nonworkers. Much of the Hispanic–non-Hispanic wage differential can be "accounted for" by education and by knowledge of English. Career interruptions are important in "explaining" female–male wage differentials.

THEORY

In his pioneering work *The Economics of Discrimination* (1971), Gary Becker argued that labor market competition will eliminate wage discrimination. If, for example, blacks are paid less than are equally productive whites, unprejudiced employers will hire blacks and make more profit than do employers who hire whites. Nondiscriminating firms will expand, hire more blacks, and drive some discriminating firms out of business. The process continues until black and white wages are equalized. Some discriminating firms that hire only white workers may survive, but there will be no wage discrimination. Similarly, if workers discriminate by requiring a premium to work with blacks, they will be employed in segregated firms, but wages will not depend on group membership.

This conclusion must be tempered somewhat if customers are prejudiced. In this case, blacks will work in jobs where race is invisible and, if there are enough such jobs, receive the same wages as comparable whites.

However, in areas such as professional sports, where workers have highly specialized skills and race is clearly visible, wage discrimination may persist.

If labor markets operate less smoothly than the competitive model implies, through a variety of mechanisms they can exacerbate, not eliminate, the effect of prejudice. For example, firms that announce high wages to attract many applicants may deter black applicants who anticipate losing out to white applicants. Instead, blacks may apply to low-wage jobs in order to avoid competition with whites. Wage discrimination may also persist if workers and firms act collectively and wages are governed by bargaining. Workers may coalesce to exclude those who are "different," and firms may pay lower wages to those with less bargaining power.

Other models also permit persistent wage discrimination. In social distance models, interactions between heterogeneous groups are costly. The market minimizes such interactions and thus encourages segregation, but complete segregation is impossible. Members of subordinate groups must either adopt the dominant group's norms of behavior and social interaction or accept lower wages.

Social distance and the absence of shared networks may also reduce the ability of employers to evaluate potential employees from other groups. In this case, employers may engage in statistical discrimination, whereby they rely more on group membership and less on information about the particular individual. Such workers have less incentive to make unobservable investments in themselves (e.g., work hard in school) and thus will earn less than do observably similar workers whom employers evaluate individually. However, they may also have an incentive to make more observable investments (e.g., years of schooling). Similar mechanisms apply when statistical discrimination reflects self-confirming stereotypes rather than social distance.

POLICY

In the United States the Equal Pay Act of 1963 outlawed payment of different wages for the same job on the basis of race, but this had little effect because most wage discrimination probably arises through workers holding different jobs and working in different firms. The 1964 Civil Rights Act forbade employment discrimination based on race, ethnicity, sex, or religion, and Executive Order 11246 required federal contractors to take affirmative action to ensure that they did not discriminate on the basis of race. Over time, the scope of civil rights legislation in the United States has been extended so that it covers, in various degrees, age, disability, and sexual orientation, as well as race, ethnicity, sex, and religion. Many countries have similar laws. Although most analysts believe that these policies reduced wage discrimination against African

Americans, women, and other groups, the extent of the effect is hotly debated.

SEE ALSO *Discrimination; Discrimination, Racial; Discrimination, Statistical; Discrimination, Taste for; Discrimination, Wage, by Age; Discrimination, Wage, by Gender; Discrimination, Wage, by Occupation; Discrimination, Wage, by Race*

BIBLIOGRAPHY

Altonji, Joseph G., and Rebecca M. Blank. 1999. Race and Gender in the Labor Market. In *Handbook of Labor Economics*, Vol. 3C, ed. Orley Ashenfelter and David Card, 3143–3259. Amsterdam, New York, and Oxford: Elsevier, North-Holland.

Becker, Gary. 1971. *The Economics of Discrimination.* Chicago: University of Chicago Press.

Lang, Kevin. 2007. *Poverty and Discrimination.* Princeton, NJ: Princeton University Press.

Kevin Lang

DISCRIMINATION, WAGE, BY AGE

The differential treatment of a group based solely on the grounds of chronological age is known as *age discrimination*. Unlike race and gender, age is immediately and strongly tied to experience and future job tenure. In addition, a worker can age while still in the same job, whereas changing one's group is unlikely for women and racial and ethnic minorities. Problems of age discrimination are important from a policy standpoint because many older people are able to work longer than was the case with previous generations. Many also wish to work longer, while some may not have saved adequately for retirement. A number of plans to fix Social Security budgetary problems require continued work at older ages.

Employers can discriminate by age across several areas: wages, promotions, hiring, firing and layoffs, and forced retirement. On average, older workers make more money than younger workers because age is highly correlated with both general labor-market work experience and tenure (or longevity of employment) at a particular employer, and experienced workers generally make more money than inexperienced workers. It is difficult to disentangle the effects of age from experience. Older workers may be less likely than younger workers to accept employment at lower wages because they are used to being paid higher wages based on their experience. Promotion probability is also related to experience. Older workers are less likely to be hired or fired than younger workers, but they are often removed through retirement packages.

Not much is known about group differences in age discrimination. Some studies have found that women are affected by age discrimination at an earlier age than men, but others have found no difference between genders in this regard. Even less is known about differences in age discrimination by race. Group characteristics of the person doing the potential discrimination, such as age, race, and gender, among others, also determine the presence and extent of discrimination.

There are a number of reasons that employers could discriminate against older workers. Employers may irrationally dislike older workers, employees may dislike working with older workers, or consumers may dislike buying products and services provided by older workers. This irrational dislike is also known as *animus* or *taste-based* discrimination. Although Gary Becker's models of taste-based discrimination in a competitive market for race and gender can be used to model age discrimination, they are limited by the correlation of age and returns to experience in most jobs in the real world, and by the fact that workers age while employed. No evidence has been found for taste-based discrimination against older workers.

Employers could also discriminate against older workers because of incorrect stereotypes, and because, on average, older workers may be less productive or more expensive than younger workers, causing employers to be reluctant to hire them when there are screening costs. This type of differential treatment is termed *statistical discrimination*. When asked why other companies may be reluctant to employ older workers, human resources managers cite shorter career potential; lack of energy, flexibility, or adaptability; higher costs for benefits and salary; more health problems, leading to more absences; knowledge and skills obsolescence; a need to promote younger workers; suspicions that an older worker might leave his or her current job to retire; and fear of discrimination lawsuits. Many of these reasons support either the incorrect stereotypes hypothesis or the statistical discrimination hypothesis.

Age discrimination against workers over the age of forty is prohibited by the Age Discrimination in Employment Act (ADEA) of 1967/68, which prohibits discrimination in advertisement, hiring, promotions, and firing, except in cases where there is a Bona Fide Occupational Qualification (BFOQ). A BFOQ is allowed if the job requires a member of a certain group to perform it. For example, in a movie, the studio would be allowed to advertise for and hire a young white woman to fill the part of a young white woman. With age, BFOQs are sometimes allowed for safety reasons even if a percentage of older workers would be able to safely perform the job tasks. Examples of BFOQ for safety reasons include mandatory retirement for airline pilots and minimum hiring age for bus drivers and air traffic controllers.

SEE ALSO *Discrimination; Discrimination, Racial; Discrimination, Statistical; Discrimination, Taste for; Discrimination, Wage; Discrimination, Wage, by Gender; Discrimination, Wage, by Occupation; Discrimination, Wage, by Race*

BIBLIOGRAPHY

Crew, James C. 1984. Age Stereotypes as a Function of Race. *The Academy of Management Journal* 27 (2): 431–435.

Diamond, Peter A., and Jerry A. Hausman. 1984. The Retirement and Unemployment Behavior of Older Men. In *Retirement and Economic Behavior*, ed. Henry J. Aaron. Washington, DC: Brookings Institution.

Duncan, Colin, and Wendy Loretto. 2004. Never the Right Age? Gender and Age-Based Discrimination in Employment. *Gender, Work & Organization* 11 (1): 95–115.

Kite, Mary E., and Lisa Smith Wagner. 2002. Attitudes Toward Older Adults. In *Ageism: Stereotyping and Prejudice Against Older Persons*, ed. Todd D. Nelson. Cambridge, MA: MIT Press.

Lahey, Joanna N. 2005. *Age, Women, and Hiring: An Experimental Study*. National Bureau of Economic Research (NBER) Working Paper No. 11435. Cambridge, MA: NBER.

Nelson, Todd D. 2002. *Ageism: Stereotyping and Prejudice Against Older Persons*. Cambridge, MA: MIT Press.

Neumark, David. 2001. *Age Discrimination Legislation in the United States*. National Bureau of Economic Research (NBER) Working Paper No. 8152. Cambridge, MA: NBER

Rhine, Shirley H. 1984. *Managing Older Workers: Company Policies and Attitudes: A Research Report from the Conference Board*. New York: The Conference Board.

Joanna N. Lahey

DISCRIMINATION, WAGE, BY GENDER

Gender wage discrimination occurs when employers pay women lower wages than identically qualified male workers. Whether such employers are acting on their own preferences or those of their firm's owners, managers, employees, or customers, the unequal treatment of women violates norms of equity and considerations of market efficiency and is the subject of policy research and debate in most industrial countries.

Theorists populate the demand side of labor markets with employers who must choose whom to hire and how much to pay them relative to the value of their productivity. Assuming that firm owners and their agents are economically rational and that they must accommodate the wishes of all firm constituents, paying qualified women a wage that is less than their productivity's worth while paying men the value of their productivity must optimize profits. Thus Gary Becker (1971) argues that an employer's choice to discriminate against a particular group can be economically rational but can persist only under noncompetitive product market conditions.

The larger the number of firms competing with a discriminatory employer for male workers, the higher the premium in pay men can garner. However, the larger the number of firms competing with an employer for customers in its product market, the more difficult it is for an individual employer to maintain its discriminatory behavior: competitors who are more willing to hire women (and pay them better than the discriminatory firm) will have lower labor costs and the ability to charge lower prices in the product market. Though the theory is compelling to many, the notion that product market competition (as opposed to antidiscrimination labor market policy) reduces wage discrimination has not been proven empirically and fails to explain the persistence of wage discrimination by gender.

As pointed out by Becker (1998), economists view the supply side of labor markets as populated by workers who choose to equip themselves in specific ways for the jobs available to them. Because average worker characteristics differ by gender, women's choices about education, training, working hours, and number and length of job interruptions (along with socialization by teachers and parents) are often blamed in part for women's overrepresentation in some fields and scarcity in others. The larger the share of women among the unemployed in a particular market, the greater the need for women to compete for scarcer opportunities—offering their services for lower wages and benefits than would otherwise be necessary.

Barbara Bergmann (1986) has shown that if the discriminatory barriers were removed, women's wages would rise relative to the wages of men. Scholars debate the extent to which discriminatory employer practices versus women's own choices bar women's access to jobs in some markets and crowd them into others. This is not a particularly productive policy debate, however. It sidesteps the most relevant policy questions: How do we reduce the ability of gender norms, employers, and markets individually and collectively to limit women's participation in specific occupations? How do we prevent employers from paying qualified women less than their male counterparts when they do choose the same industries, occupations, hours, and other labor market characteristics (a problem convincingly documented in Blau et al. 2001).

Gender wage discrimination persists as women are systematically denied access to jobs in particular markets.

Scholars such as Kenneth Arrow (1973) attribute persistent labor market discrimination to statistical discrimination—employers ranking and paying individual applicants according to average gender group attributes rather than individual ability and productivity. Statistical discrimination is sometimes deemed economically rational because information about individual worker productivity is costly and difficult to attain. Such discrimination persists because gender norms and stereotypes are powerful and because firms' discriminatory practices are difficult to detect and prove. As explained by Lisa Saunders and William Darity Jr. (2003), wage discrimination by gender is further complicated by the fact that the degree of gender wage gaps differs according to the race, age, sexual orientation, and other identity markers of the female or male groups under consideration. The maintenance of social stratification on the basis of multiple identities insures lower wages for a significant share of workers than would otherwise attain more (see Darity et al. 2006). This is especially problematic for workers in competitive firms and more onerous under conditions of globalization. It is also problematic for families that increasingly depend upon women's earnings for their immediate and intergenerational economic security. It could be argued that a more effective policy approach to wage discrimination by gender would assert a definition of discrimination that acknowledges the complex ways it actually manifests in labor markets, a perspective on the roles played by structural changes in the global economy, and a rigorous analysis of wage inequality's effects on inequality in wealth.

SEE ALSO *Arrow, Kenneth J.; Becker, Gary; Crowding Hypothesis; Discrimination; Discrimination, Racial; Discrimination, Statistical; Discrimination, Taste for; Discrimination, Wage; Discrimination, Wage, by Age; Discrimination, Wage, by Occupation; Discrimination, Wage, by Race; Economics, Stratification; Gender Gap; Inequality, Gender; Labor Market; Stratification*

BIBLIOGRAPHY

Arrow, Kenneth. 1973. The Theory of Discrimination. In *Discrimination in Labor Markets*, eds. Orley Ashenfelter and Albert Rees, 3–33. Princeton, NJ: Princeton University Press.

Becker, Gary S. 1971. *The Economics of Discrimination*. 2nd ed. Chicago: University of Chicago Press.

Becker, Gary S. 1993. *Human Capital: A Theoretical and Empirical Analysis, with Special Reference to Education*. 3rd ed. Chicago: University of Chicago Press.

Bergmann, Barbara. 1986. *The Economic Emergence of Women*. New York: Basic Books.

Blau, Francine D., Marianne A. Ferber, and Anne E. Winkler. 2001. *The Economics of Women, Men, and Work*. 4th ed. Upper Saddle River, NJ: Prentice Hall.

Darity, William, Jr., James Stewart, and Patrick L. Mason. 2006. The Economics of Identity: The Origin and Persistence of

Racial Norms. *Journal of Economic Behavior and Organizations* 60 (3): 283–305.

Saunders, Lisa, and William Darity Jr. 2003. Feminist Theory and Racial Inequality. In *Feminist Economics Today: Beyond Economic Man*, eds. Marianne A. Ferber and Julie A. Nelson, 101–114. Chicago: University of Chicago Press.

Lisa Saunders

DISCRIMINATION, WAGE, BY OCCUPATION

Wage discrimination refers to paying women, minorities, or other culturally subordinate individuals lower wages than comparably skilled men, whites, or other privileged groups. This can happen when women or minorities are hired or promoted into lower-paying jobs, or when they are paid less for performing the same work in the same workplace.

In general, past research has found that wage discrimination increases with the rank of the job. Thus, the term *rank segregation* is sometimes used to indicate that job segregation by status is associated with job desirability. Most common have been analyses that demonstrate race and sex wage gaps after controlling for legitimate measures of individual productivity, such as education, experience, or job skills. These studies typically find that most wage inequality is produced by job segregation, though in some contexts there may be additional discrimination in wage setting within jobs. The more desirable the job, the more likely it has within-job wage discrimination and the more likely that women and minorities are excluded from the job.

Employment discrimination and job segregation are the product of a series of well-recognized selection and evaluation mechanisms, such as prejudice, cognitive bias, statistical discrimination, social closure around desirable employment opportunities, and network-based recruitment. These mechanisms tend to be mutually reinforcing and lead to status expectations about the appropriateness of different types of people for different jobs, as well as to expectations as to the value of those jobs to the employer. Bias in evaluation processes, which in turn may lead to between- or within-job wage inequalities, can result from self-conscious prejudice, but it is often produced by subtle social psychological processes of cognitive bias, stereotyping, and in-group preferences. Employers, like everyone else, tend to use preexisting cultural categories such as sex or race to organize and interpret information. These cognitive processes can lead to more favorable evaluations and outcomes for high status individuals (males, majority race) and lower evaluations for others (women, minorities). The theory of statistical discrimination points out that employers are more likely to discriminate when jobs have more responsibility, longer periods of training, or simply pay more, because the cost of hiring an unqualified worker rises in these situations. Economists tend to describe this process in terms of explicit cost-benefit calculations. Sociologists and psychologists see this as a more subtle social psychological process of cognitive bias and stereotyping.

The term *social closure* refers to discrimination around the preservation of group privilege. Social closure processes are consistent with the discriminatory mechanisms already outlined—prejudice, cognitive bias, and statistical discrimination. They are not merely conditioned by individual psychology or the profit motive, however, but also by both social accountability to one's status group and the elaboration of cultural stories that explain and justify status-based inequalities. Because social networks tend to be formed around friendship and family ties, employee recruitment procedures that rely on professional or current workforces will also tend to produce social closure-based opportunity hoarding.

Discrimination and job segregation can be moderated by organizational practices that reduce the influence of personal biases or social expectations. Recent research suggests that control systems that hold managers accountable for equal opportunity outcomes are more effective than those that target unconscious bias processes.

SEE ALSO *Discrimination; Discrimination, Racial; Discrimination, Statistical; Discrimination, Taste for; Discrimination, Wage; Discrimination, Wage, by Age; Discrimination, Wage, by Gender; Discrimination, Wage, by Race*

BIBLIOGRAPHY

Fiske, Susan T. 1998. Stereotyping, Prejudice, and Discrimination. In *Handbook of Social Psychology*, ed. Daniel T. Gilbert, Susan T. Fiske, and Gardner Lindzey, 357–411. New York: McGraw Hill.

Kalev, Alexandra, Frank Dobbin, and Erin Kelly. 2006. Best Practices or Best Guesses? Assessing the Efficacy of Corporate Affirmative Action and Diversity Policies. *American Sociological Review* 71 (4): 589–617.

Mason, Patrick. 1999. Male Interracial Wage Differentials: Competing Explanations. *Cambridge Journal of Economics* 23 (3): 1-39.

Ridgeway, Cecilia. 1997. Interaction and the Conservation of Gender Inequality: Considering Employment. *American Sociological Review* 62 (2): 218–235.

Royster, Deirdre. 2003. *Race and the Invisible Hand: How White Networks Exclude Black Men from Blue-Collar Jobs*. Berkeley: University of California Press.

Tomaskovic-Devey, Donald. 1993. *Gender and Racial Inequality at Work: The Sources and Consequences of Job Segregation*. Ithaca, NY: ILR Press.

Tomaskovic-Devey, Donald, Melvin Thomas, and Kecia Johnson. 2005. Race and the Accumulation of Human Capital across the Career: A Theoretical Model and Fixed Effects Application. *American Journal of Sociology* 111: 58–89.

Donald Tomaskovic-Devey

DISCRIMINATION, WAGE, BY RACE

Wage discrimination involves differential market wage payments for otherwise identical persons. Wage discrimination may occur because of prejudice (statistical discrimination), bigotry and nepotism (animus toward other-group persons and favoritism toward on-group persons), or because it enhances profitability (racism). An early work by Francis Y. Edgeworth in 1922 considered equal work for equal pay by sex, matching the marginal utility of the employer with the marginal disutility of the employee. This concept was accepted with some reservations and adjustments. Equal work means that the worker is indifferent between two tasks, and equal pay means that wage is equal to the marginal product of labor.

Gunnar Myrdal discussed animosity of whites against blacks in the United States from the point of view of the cumulative methodology where increased prejudices caused more discrimination and less employment, worsening both standards of living and health conditions for blacks. Discrimination causes a cumulative degradation of blacks' standard of living, education, health, morals, and social conditions.

Gary Becker's preference theory of discrimination advanced a coefficient of discrimination, d_i, measured under free competition. Assuming away differences in capital, the employer's utility function depends on profits, and the types of workers—whites and blacks. If workers are equally productive, then discrimination enters through the tastes and preferences of the employer. An employer is willing to pay a higher wage, $\pi(1 + d_i)$ to exclude someone from employment. An employee is willing to accept a lower wage, $\pi_j^*(1 - d_j)$, to avoid working near to someone. A consumer is willing to pay a higher price, $p(1 + d_k)$ not to be served by someone. The result is a kinked demand curve for labor if we plot the ratio of the wages of blacks to whites, women to men, young to old, or unskilled to skilled against the person discriminated against. When the ratio is unity, no discrimination happens, $d_i = 0$, and the demand curve is flat. The kink occurs where the wage ratio starts to fall from unity, indicating that the discrimination coefficient, d_i is becoming larger. At equilibrium, the downward sloping part of the demand

curve cuts a normal supply curve that measures more labor offered as the wage ratio increases. One implication of equilibrium is that since minority workers offer the same productivity at lower wages, a discriminating employer will have to pay higher wages to others.

Phelps advanced a statistical discrimination model to explain why, for instance, insurance companies price auto insurance higher for teenage males than females. Companies use the average behavior of the group and not individual characteristics in pricing their policies. Another popular model is Barbara Bergmann's expansion and articulation of the crowding hypothesis. The productivity of minorities who are crowded into certain occupations may depend on group effort and having minorities in a group can be perceived as a hindrance to social interaction, lowering productivity and causing wages to fall. An index of occupational segregation showing by how much mobility between occupations is necessary to equalize wages has been declining over time. Other models consider different market structures.

William A. Darity Jr. and Rhonda Williams argue that governmental actions that allow free occupational choice is not sufficient to eliminate discrimination due to cultural barriers that create imperfect markets. Darity found that research studies on discrimination lack a unified methodology and that some studies that subscribe to the positive methodology find discrimination antithetical to perfect markets. However, Patrick L. Mason has presented a theoretical model and empirical analysis showing that racial wage and occupational discrimination may enhance the profitability of firms and protect dominant group workers from competition in the more desirable occupations. The theoretical analysis by Darity and Williams and Mason is constructed on the notion that racial discrimination is sustained by racism among employers and racial animus among workers. Moreover, in their discussion of the economics of identity, Darity, Mason, and Stewart show that the persistence of racial group identities, that is, the origins of the tastes for discrimination, may be found in the material incentives associated with inter-group antagonism and intra-group altruism.

Since the mid-1970s, government statistics for the United States have indicated that the wage ratio for blacks to whites has been stable indicating a large earning gap. The unemployment rate for blacks is about twice that of whites, but results are similar when comparing unemployment rates for white and black males against the rates for white and black women. For the same timeframe, the index of gender segregation (male vs. female) fell by approximately 16 percent from a high of approximately 68 percent in 1973, indicating that women have made considerable entry into professional occupations. The index for previous age discrimination confirming racial segregation (black vs. white) shows the same trend, falling from 37 to 24 percent for women and from 37 to 26 percent for men.

SEE ALSO *Discrimination; Discrimination, Racial; Discrimination, Statistical; Discrimination, Taste for; Discrimination, Wage; Discrimination, Wage, by Age; Discrimination, Wage, by Gender; Discrimination, Wage, by Occupation*

BIBLIOGRAPHY

Allport, Gordon W. 1958. *The Nature of Prejudice.* New York: Doubleday Anchor Books.

Altonji, Joseph G., and Thomas A. Dunn. 2000. An Intergenerational Model of Wages, Hours, and Earnings. *Journal of Human Resources* 35 (2): 221–258.

Altonji, Joseph G., Ulrich Doraszelski, and Lewis Segal. 2000. Black/White Differences in Wealth. *Economic Perspectives* 24 (1): 38–50.

Arrow, Kenneth J. 1985. *Collected Papers of Kenneth J. Arrow: Applied Economics.* Vol. 6. Cambridge, MA: The Belknap Press of Harvard University Press.

Becker, Gary S. 1957. *The Economics of Discrimination: An Economic View of Racial Discrimination.* 2nd ed. Chicago: University of Chicago Press.

Bergmann, Barbara. 1971. The Effect of White Income on Discrimination in Employment. *Journal of Political Economy* 79: 294–313.

Blau, Francine, and John W. Graham. 1990. Black-White Differences in Wealth and Asset Composition. *Quarterly Journal of Economics* 105 (2): 321–339.

Darity, William A., Jr. 1984. *Labor Economics: Modern Views.* Boston: Kluwer-Nijhoff Publishing.

Darity, William A., Jr., and Jessica Gordon Nembhard. 2000. Racial and Ethnic Economic Inequality: The International Record. *American Economic Review* 90: 308–311.

Darity, William A., Jr., and Patrick L. Mason. 1998. Evidence on Discrimination in Employment: Codes of Color, Codes of Gender. *Journal of Economic Perspectives* 12: 63–90.

Darity, William A., Jr., and Rhonda M. Williams. 1985. Peddlers Forever? Culture, Competition, and Discrimination. *American Economic Review* 256–261.

Darity, William A., Jr., James B. Stewart, and Patrick L. Mason. 1999. Male Interracial Wage Differentials: Competing Explanations. *Cambridge Journal of Economics* 23 (May): 1–39.

Darity, William A., Jr., James B. Stewart, and Patrick L. Mason. 2006. The Economics of Identity: The Origin and Persistence of Racial Norms. *Journal of Economic Behavior and Organizations* 60 (3): 283–305.

Edgeworth, Francis Y. 1922. Equal Pay to Men and Women for Equal Work. *The Economic Journal* 32 (128): 431–457.

Mason, Patrick L. 1995. Race, Competition and Differential Wages. *Cambridge Journal of Economics* 19 (4): 545–568.

Myrdal, Gunnar. 1944. *An American Dilemma.* New York: Harper.

Phelps, Edmund. 1972. The Statistical Theory of Racism and Sexism. *American Economic Review* (September): 659–661.

Schelling, Thomas. 1969. Models of Segregation. *American Economic Review, Papers and Proceedings* 59 (2): 488–493.

Lall Ramrattan
Michael Szenberg

DISEASE

Stedman's Online Medical Dictionary defines disease as an interruption, cessation, or disorder of body function, system, or organ; or a morbid entity characterized usually by at least two of these criteria: recognized etiologic agent(s), identifiable group of signs and symptoms, or consistent anatomic alterations. The *International Classification of Disease, 9th Revision, Clinical Modification* (ICD-9-CM) is one of the main texts used in the United States to identify, categorize, and diagnose disease. The *Diagnostic and Statistical Manual of Mental Disorders,* 4th edition (DSM-IV), is used to define and diagnosis mental disorders. While these sources are used in common medical practice, it is not completely clear in the philosophy of science what truly defines the diseases and disorders that these texts classify. Some have argued that there is not a simple definition of disease. Within the philosophy of medicine and bioethics, there is not only disagreement about what a disease is but whether or not *disease* can be defined or whether it is necessary to have a fixed definition in order to provide care.

NATURALISM AND NOMINILISM

A simplistic yet prevailing conception of what disease is can be viewed from the lens of "naturalism" or "nominilism." Viewed from a naturalistic point of view, disease is a real thing that can be quantified, observed, or described using the language of natural science. To the naturalist, a disease can be discovered in nature, is not invented by social convention, and is not dependent on contextual circumstance. The true naturalist views disease as value free and objective. Disease from a naturalist point of view, according to the philosopher Christopher Boorse, causes interruptions in the ability to "perform typical physiological functioning with at least typical efficiency" (Kovacs 1998, p. 31). This point of view, however, has been critiqued because "typical physiology" and "typical efficiency" cannot be objectively described, nor are they value-free terms (i.e., what is meant by "typical"?).

The nominalist point, on the other hand, views disease not as something essential in nature but rather as a description of socially constructed conditions. As stated by Lester King in 1954, the point of view that "disease is the aggregate of those conditions, which, judged by the prevailing culture, are deemed painful, or disabling, and which, at the same time, deviate from either the statistical norm or from some idealized status" would fit within this nominalist point of view (King 1954, p. 197). Historically a purely naturalistic view of disease as a germ or lesion has given way to a view of disease that appeals more to a nominilist point of view. Ailments that fall within modern medical health care, such as depression or hypertension, challenge a naturalistic point of view because these conditions appeal to socially defined criteria by which one would be in need of professional care or qualify for some sort of intervention.

DISEASE, ILLNESS, SICKNESS, AND HEALTH

In discussing the concept of disease, attention has been brought to how terms such as disease, illness, or sickness relate. Oftentimes these concepts have been used interchangeably. However, philosophers argue that separating the concepts may be useful. Disease is distinguished from illness in that disease is the subject matter of the medical practitioner and scientific medicine. Illness, on the other hand, explains what the person is experiencing. Sickness is what is attributed by society to individuals who conceive of themselves as ill and whom medical professions identify as having a disease. Each of these concepts justifies action. Medical professionals are charged with identifying disease, discovering diseases, and treating persons with such conditions. Persons who are ill are charged with describing the subjective experience of their condition to others who may be able to help. Society is responsible for determining the rights and duties of a person who is ill and/or diseased. Thus conceptualizing disease as separate from illness and sickness can be useful in bringing into perspective the varying roles of the medical practitioner, the individual, and society when negative bodily conditions or states occur.

The concept of disease is also often discussed as it relates to health. That is, to understand what disease is, one must know what health is. The common language conception of health is simply the absence of disease or the negation of being at ease (i.e., dis-ease). A person who is healthy does not have a disease, and a person with a disease is not healthy. However, this simplistic model may not be applicable in all circumstances. For example, a person diagnosed with hypochondriasis certainly is suffering, but the individual does not have any general medical condition that can account for his or her feeling of illness. There are also instances when one feels healthy but may have a serious condition that places the individual at risk

for a disease (e.g., a person with hypercholesterolemia or obesity may develop coronary artery disease).

The holistic approach extends the more simple approach to defining health not just as the absence of disease but as a state of complete physical, mental, and social well-being. The holistic model has been adopted and promoted by the World Health Organization. The holistic model would imply that one could meet the condition of not having a specific disease but still may not be healthy. Within the holistic model, eliminating disease from the body is not primary, but rather, health is primary. However, some have argued that a holistic program of health care with the goal of insuring complete physical, mental, and social well-being is not feasible; especially in developing countries, where there are limited resources available for the provision of care.

The model most familiar to Western medicine is the medical model of disease. The medical model suggests that disease is not just absence of health (as defined by the simplified model), but disease can be identified by some set of standard methods, such as a medical examination, laboratory tests, or correspondence with a set of symptoms. Thus within the medical model a person could potentially not have an identified pathophysiological disease but could still be labeled as having a disease as a result of having a set of symptoms and being deemed not healthy through the process of a medical examination.

CONTROVERSIES IN DEFINING CONDITIONS AS DISEASE

Within modern medicine there are many controversies over what conditions can be properly defined as diseases. One such debate in the general medicine and public health has to do with whether or not obesity can be labeled a disease. George A. Bray, an internationally recognized researcher in the area of obesity and diabetes, has argued that obesity meets the criteria to be labeled a disease. However, other researchers have argued that caution should be taken when labeling obesity as a disease as it may not be appropriate to put it on par with other more serious life-threatening conditions. Those that argue obesity should not be considered a disease suggest that there are no real signs or symptoms of obesity apart from excess adiposity. However, this is circular because excess adiposity is the definition of obesity. Also, while obesity does cause impairment in functioning for some people, there are many people who are obese who have no diminished impairment in functioning. Those who argue that obesity is a disease equate it with other diseases, such as depression. Bray states that obesity involves "deranged neural circuitry responding inappropriately to a toxic environment" (Bray 2004, p. 34).

Another long-standing debate in the medical discipline of psychiatry is whether or not certain psychological conditions can be labeled a disease. A mainstream view of modern practice in psychiatry is that certain psychological conditions rise to the level of an illness when there is a clinically relevant disruption in functioning and distress. The DMS-IV distinguishes a mental pathological condition from a milder form by establishing clinically significant criterion. As stated in the DSM-IV, the condition must cause "clinically significant distress or impairment in social, occupational, or other important areas of functioning" (DSM-IV 1994, p. 7). The determination of significance is a clinical judgment made through the process of a clinical interview with the patient and sometimes with third parties, such as a patient's family. Further, a mental disorder is often distinguished from a condition that arises as a direct physiological consequence of a general medical condition. For example, disorientation or hallucinations due to a brain tumor or stroke would not be considered a psychiatric condition.

Notably the explanation of aberrant behaviors or mental conditions has changed over the centuries. In past centuries aberrant behaviors and mental disorders were explained as the result of "spirits" or "sins." With the birth of psychoanalysis, mental conditions were explained as primarily resulting from poor child rearing or the inability of an individual to meet developmental milestones marking social and moral development. However, early twenty-first-century psychiatric practice tends to explain many psychiatric conditions as the result of disruptions in neural circuitry in the brain resulting from a combination of genetic and environmental determinates.

This change in perception of psychiatric conditions is argued to be due to an increasing scientific knowledge about potential causes and treatments. However, the psychiatrist Thomas Szasz has been a prominent critic of this traditional point of view. Szasz argues that mental disorders, as mainstream psychiatry has conceptualized, are not diseases of the brain and that it is inappropriate to call abnormal behaviors and psychological states "diseases." A crux of difference between these two points of view has to do with the way disease is defined—that is, as a "lesion" of the body or as a social construction or metaphor.

SOCIAL DYNAMICS OF DISEASE AND HEALTH INEQUALITIES

Regardless of how disease is defined, it is widely recognized that the spread of disease and the preponderance of health are linked to social factors. For instance, density and frequency of contact among individuals can influence disease outbreak. Dense social contact in urban environments may lead to a rapid spread of certain infectious diseases. Understanding the social networks and dynamics of these environments is a key strategy for developing targeted vaccinations and treatments.

Disease and health are also influenced by social and economic conditions in society. For example, in the early twenty-first century in the United States, Type 2 diabetes mellitus is more common among African American men than their Caucasian counterparts. However, a 2007 study by Margaret Humphreys and colleagues found rates of diabetes among African American men living circa 1900 to be much lower than Caucasian men at that time. Studies looking at coronary heart disease patterns have also reported prevalence shifts whereby the risk of the disease was historically more prevalent in higher socioeconomic classes and now is more prevalent in lower socioeconomic classes (Kunst et al., 1999; Marmot, Adelstein, Robinson, and Rose, 1978; Rose and Marmot, 1981). These studies highlight the fact that disease patterns as well as the social distribution of risk factors for disease can vary by type of disease, time period, and geographic region.

As disease and health are viewed as socially determined, the search for social conditions that gives rise to diseases has become a growing part of medical and public health science. Medical practice in the past centuries was focused primarily on identifying pathophysiological and biological roots for disease and had largely ignored the social contributions to disease. Correspondingly treatments and interventions for disease management have been one-to-one efforts. However, a growing awareness that societal-level phenomena play a large role in health and disease has prompted the medical community to explore some of the broader social and economic forces that influence disease and risk. As such the approach to disease management is also shifting from primarily individual-level one-to-one efforts to include environmental and policy-level interventions designed to address health.

Finding a clear definition of disease and health is not purely a philosophical matter. Conditions that carry the label of disease have practical and political implications. Society responds by directing resources, and individuals with a certain disease are relinquished from certain social responsibilities. However, what counts as disease is often difficult to determine. In some cases it might appear that a certain condition has pathophysiological roots and causes (e.g., germ or lesion) that can be discovered and treated. However, it may be discovered that there are broader social and economic conditions that allow for certain pathophysiological conditions to arise. What then is the disease? Is it the germ or the social condition? The answer that society provides becomes one of the defining features by which health care resources are allocated.

SEE ALSO *Alzheimer's Disease; Dementia; Depression, Psychological; Ethno-epidemiological Methodology;*

Functionings; Human Rights; Hypertension; Madness; Malnutrition; Medicine; Mental Illness; Obesity; Poverty; Psychoanalytic Theory; Public Health; World Health Organization

BIBLIOGRAPHY

American Psychiatric Association. 1994. *Diagnostic and Statistical Manual of Mental Disorders.* 4th ed. Washington, DC: Author.

Boorse, Christopher. 1977. Health as a Theoretical Concept. *Philosophy of Science* 44: 542–573.

Bray, George A. 2004. Obesity Is a Chronic, Relapsing Neurochemical Disease. *International Journal of Obesity and Related Metabolic Disorders* 28 (1): 34–38.

Bray, George A. 2006. Obesity: The Disease. *Journal of Medicinal Chemistry* 49 (14): 4001–4007.

Centers for Disease Control and Prevention. 2006. National Diabetes Surveillance System. http://www.cdc.gov/diabetes/statistics/.

Eubank, Stephen, Hansan Guclu, V. S. Anil Kumar, et al. 2004. Modeling Disease Outbreaks in Realistic Urban Social Networks. *Nature* 429 (6988): 180–184.

Heshka, Stanley, and David B Allison. 2001. Is Obesity a Disease? *International Journal of Obesity and Related Metabolic Disorders* 25 (10): 1401–1404.

Hofmann, Bjorn. 2001. Complexity of the Concept of Disease as Shown through Rival Theoretical Frameworks. *Theoretical Medicine and Bioethics* 22 (3): 211–236.

Hofmann, Bjorn. 2002. On the Triad: Disease, Illness, and Sickness. *Journal of Medicine and Philosophy* 27 (6): 651–673.

Hofmann, Bjorn. 2005. Simplified Models of the Relationship between Health and Disease. *Theoretical Medicine and Bioethics* 26 (5): 355–377.

Hofmann, Bjorn M., and Harald M. Eriksen. 2001. The Concept of Disease: Ethical Challenges and Relevance to Dentistry and Dental Education. *European Journal of Dental Education* 5 (1): 2–11.

Humphreys, Margaret, Philip Costanzo, Kerry L. Haynie, et al. Racial Disparities in Diabetes a Century Ago: Evidence from the Pension Files of the U.S. Civil War Veterans. *Social Science and Medicine* 64 (8): 1766–1775.

King, Lester S. 1954. What Is Disease? *Philosophy of Science* 21: 193–203.

Kottow, Michael H. 2002. The Rationale of Value-Laden Medicine. *Journal of Evaluation in Clinical Practice* 8 (1): 77–84.

Kovacs, Jozsef. 1998. The Concept of Health and Disease. *Medical Health Care and Philosophy* 1 (1): 31–39.

Kunst, Anton E., Feikje Groenhof, Otto Andersen, et al. 1999. Occupational Class and Ischemic Heart Disease Mortality in the United States and 11 European Countries. *American Journal of Public Health* 89 (1): 47–53.

Rose, Geoffrey, and Michael Marmot. 1981. Social Class and Coronary Heart Disease. *British Heart Journal* 45 (1): 13–19.

Szasz, Thomas. 1974. *The Myth of Mental Illness: Foundations of a Theory of Personal Conduct.* New York: Harper and Row.

Szasz, Thomas. 1998. Parity for Mental Illness, Disparity for the Mental Patient. *Lancet* 352 (9135): 1213–1215.

Szasz, Thomas. 1998. What Counts as Disease? Rationales and Rationalizations for Treatment. *Forsch Komplementarmed* 5 (S1): 40–46.

Twaddle, Andrew. 1994. Disease, Illness, and Sickness Revisited. In *Disease, Illness, and Sickness: Three Central Concepts in the Theory of Health,* eds. Andrew Twaddle and L. Nordenfelt, vol. 18, pp. 1–18. Linkoping, Sweden: Studies on Health and Society.

Vagero, Denny, and Mall Leinsalu. 2005. Health Inequalities and Social Dynamics in Europe. *British Medical Journal* 331 (7510): 186–187.

World Health Organization. 1992. *Basic Documents.* Geneva: World Health Organization.

Bernard F. Fuemmeler

DISEQUILIBRIUM ECONOMICS

SEE *Barro-Grossman Model; Economics, New Keynesian; Patinkin, Don.*

DISGUST

SEE *Sanitation.*

DISNEY, WALT
1901–1966

Walter Elias Disney and his brother Roy established the Walt Disney Company in the late 1920s to produce short animations. The company's first synchronized-sound cartoon, *Steamboat Willie* (1928), featured Mickey Mouse, a character that became one of the best-known icons in the world. In the wake of the nineteenth-century transformation of the oral tradition of fairy tales into a literary tradition by the Brothers Grimm, Hans Christian Andersen, and others, Disney, in the early decades of the twentieth century, employed technological advances to turn literary fairy tales into animations. The first feature-length animation, *Snow White and the Seven Dwarfs* (1937), paved the way for the Disney brand of family-oriented celluloid fantasies targeting children as their primary audience.

A 1941 strike by Disney animators seeking more recognition, along with economic hard times, crippled the company, but World War II (1939–1945) reenergized the Disney Company through government commissions. *The Three Caballeros* (1944) was made at the behest of Nelson Rockefeller's Office of the Coordinator of Inter-American

Affairs to promote "Good Neighborliness" between North America and Latin America. The conservative Disney also served as a Federal Bureau of Investigation (FBI) agent from 1940 to his death in 1966. The public image of "Uncle Walt" with a gentle smile and with roots in rural small-town America is the result of mythmaking, which masks Walt Disney's traumatic childhood and distrustful personality. Disney's vendetta against striking employees of his studio in the 1940s betrays not only a suspicious and controlling character but an anticommunist obsession. His hidden career as a secret informant in the last two decades of his life gives a perverse twist to the family entertainment Disney has come to symbolize.

The Disney television show went on the air in 1954. Theme parks proved to be far more successful than animations and live-action films and television. Disneyland in Anaheim, California, opened in 1955, followed by Disney World in Orlando, Florida, in 1971. Tokyo saw the Japanese version of Disneyland in 1983, France in 1992, and Hong Kong in 2005. Having languished after Walt Disney's death, the Disney Company resurged under Michael Eisner in the 1980s. Disney has now grown into a global business conglomerate of film studio, television network, cable company, magazine, merchandise bearing various Disney logos, theme parks and resorts, and other ventures, with revenues totaling over $25 billion around the turn of the century. Disney also works through the Touchstone label, Miramax Films, Buena Vista International, and other business entities to produce and distribute less family-oriented shows.

With its increasing monopoly of media and entertainment, Disney has given rise to the phenomenon of *Disneyfication*, that is, trivialization and sanitization. The key to the success of the "Magic Kingdom" is indeed carefully controlled, heavily edited images of childhood innocence and fun. Yet what appears to the child to be happy tunes and carefree joy often veils sexist, racist, ageist, and neo-imperialist reality. From Sleeping Beauty to the Little Mermaid to Mulan, every Disney female lead embodies idealized Euro-American beauty in facial features, balletic physique, and youth-culture obsessions. These Disney females, including the sword-wielding Mulan, ultimately derive their meaning in life through male characters. The blatant racism in the happy plantation African Americans in *The Song of the South* (1946) and the slant-eyed, bucktoothed, pidgin-speaking Siamese cats in *Lady and the Tramp* (1955) and *The Aristocats* (1970) has gone underground, occasionally resurfacing in, for example, the cruel, hand-chopping Arabs in *Aladdin* (1992) and the stereotypical, "multicultural" duo of "kung fu" Mulan and her familiar, the blabbering Mushu dubbed by Eddie Murphy.

Theme parks best exemplify the Disney culture of control. The enclosed environment of these sites separates visitors from the outside world, encouraging consumption in the guise of family fun. Main Street U.S.A. at Disneyland is, of course, a shopping mall. Various adventures at Disneyland are centrally themed to formulate a narrative and to shape consumer perception. Even Disney employees with smiling faces are trained in "performative labor": they are not so much working as role-playing; they are cast members in the Disney discourse of happiness.

Any critique of Disneyfication faces the challenge that animated fantasy is customarily regarded as devoid of ideology, notwithstanding the fact that the racial, gender, national, and capitalist undertones of Disney have repeatedly been the subject of study. Adults' nostalgia for childlike simplicity and pleasure further leads to an acquiescence to Disney's ahistorical and apolitical universe. Assuredly, growing up anywhere in the world, one is invariably nurtured on Disney's breast milk of superior quality in terms of ingenuity and craftsmanship. To contend that consumers have been fed with something aesthetically refined but culturally suspect is likely to provoke vigorous opposition. Yet the 1995 defeat of the proposed 3,000-acre Disney theme park in Virginia's Civil War battlegrounds signals the potential of grassroots resistance to corporate greed and expansionism. With the shadows of the omnivorous, lawsuit-happy Disney Company looming over the twenty-first century, new battles will be fought far away from Virginia. Globalization has brought Disney to every corner of the world. In the company of giants such as McDonald's, Nike, Coca-Cola, and Microsoft, Disney's transnational operations will continue to perpetuate Americanization globally, but it remains a severely constricted vision of America, one enjoyed principally by middle-class visitors to Disney World and passive consumers of Disney culture.

SEE ALSO *Children; Culture; Racism; Sexism*

BIBLIOGRAPHY

Bell, Elizabeth, Lynda Haas, and Laura Sells, eds. 1995. *From Mouse to Mermaid: The Politics of Film, Gender, and Culture.* Bloomington: Indiana University Press.

Giroux, Henry A. 1999. *The Mouse that Roared: Disney and the End of Innocence.* Lanham, MD: Rowman & Littlefield.

Smoodin, Eric, ed. 1994. *Disney Discourse: Producing the Magic Kingdom.* New York: Routledge.

Sheng-mei Ma

DISPERSION

SEE *Variation.*

DISPROPORTIONALITY THEORY

SEE *Accumulation of Capital.*

DISSIDENTS

Dissidents are people who work to alter the established social, political, economic, or cultural system. Because they threaten the established order, dissidents are often subjected to official repression and punishment. Still, dissidents have been major contributors to social, political, economic, and cultural change.

Although dissidents have varied foci, the term most commonly refers to political dissidents. Political dissidents do not simply oppose a particular political leader or group of leaders; rather, political dissidents seek to change the existing political *system*. Political dissidents have been most prominent in authoritarian polities. In particular, the term has been applied to public opponents of communist rule. In this context, the earliest clear official use of the term was in the 1965 trial of writers Andrei Sinyavsky (1925–1997) and Yuri Daniel (1925–1988) in the former Soviet Union; in this case, the ruling authorities used the English word *dissident* to suggest that the defendants were under foreign influence (and therefore treasonous).

Political dissidents in communist polities have employed primarily nonviolent methods of dissent. Most commonly, dissidents in communist polities have used pseudonyms to write critical political tracts that circulate underground domestically and are smuggled abroad to be published for a wider readership. Noted examples include Andrei Sakharov (1921–1989) and Alexander Solzhenitsyn (in the former Soviet Union), Václav Havel (in Czechoslovakia, now the Czech Republic), and Wei Jingsheng (in China). Dissidents in communist polities also have formed informal discussion groups and formal dissident organizations. For instance, from 1980 to 1981 labor activist Lech Walesa led Poland's dissident Solidarity Free Trade Union, and in 1998 Chinese dissidents Wang Youcai and Xu Wenli founded a domestic opposition political party, the China Democracy Party. In addition, dissidents in communist polities have engaged in public protest actions, such as hunger strikes and street marches. Some of the most well-known protests occurred in 1989; in Eastern Europe that year, massive public demonstrations, such as those in the former Czechoslovakia, ultimately led to the fall of communism, while in China, widespread popular demonstrations were crushed ruthlessly.

Political dissidents have been prominent in noncommunist authoritarian polities as well, especially in Central and South America, Africa, and Southeast Asia. These dissidents employ many of the same nonviolent forms of dissent found in communist polities. Noted individuals of this sort include Aung San Suu Kyi of Myanmar (formerly Burma) and Francis Seow of Singapore. In addition, dissidents in noncommunist authoritarian polities sometimes have led military struggles seeking to overturn the ruling order. Because dissidents typically lack military resources comparable to those of the ruling authorities, dissident groups that use violent means to pursue their goals commonly employ guerilla war tactics. A prominent example is the South African guerilla insurgency against the apartheid system from the 1940s to early 1990s. Another notable case is the Sendero Luminoso (Shining Path) Maoist guerilla movement in Peru, which was most active from the 1960s to 1980s.

In democracies, criticism of leading politicians and policies is commonplace, but opposition to the democratic *system* is more rare. Still, even in democratic polities, critics of politicians and policies at times have been labeled dissidents and punished for treason against the established order. The most noted instances have occurred in the United States against individuals and groups who publicly opposed existing policies toward the working class and racial minorities. For example, in 1919 and 1920 roughly ten thousand members of labor organizations and socialist-communist groups were arrested in the Palmer Raids, directed by Alexander Mitchell Palmer (1872–1936), the U.S. attorney general. Similarly, in the late 1940s to mid-1950s, hundreds of left-leaning individuals were investigated or blacklisted from certain types of employment. Further, during the civil rights movement of the 1950s and 1960s, many prominent opponents of race-based segregation and political exclusion were arrested and physically harmed by ruling authorities.

Because dissidents challenge established authorities, they often receive harsh treatment. The most common form of official repression is imprisonment, often for extremely lengthy periods. South African antiapartheid leader Nelson Mandela, for example, was jailed for twenty-seven years. Still, many imprisoned dissidents continue to write critical tracts even while behind bars; further, many succeed in smuggling out their texts, or preserve them for later publication. Other typical forms of punishment include blacklisting from employment opportunities, placement under house arrest, continual official surveillance, tax investigations, and forced exile. On occasion, ruling authorities also tacitly encourage paramilitary groups to physically harm or even kill dissidents.

Given these risks, few dare to engage in dissent. Those who do often exhibit an unusual psychological profile, characterized by an unrelenting commitment to ideals and a profound stoicism toward the loss of personal security. At the same time, many turn to dissent only after experiencing what they feel are undeserved limitations on their own social, economic, or political status.

Indeed, despite the harsh punishment meted out to most dissidents, some ultimately succeed in transforming the established order, and even rise to prominent positions in the newly established system. For example, oft-harassed American civil rights activist Thurgood Marshall (1908–1993) later served on the U.S. Supreme Court. Similarly, once-imprisoned political dissidents Lech Walesa, Václav Havel, and Nelson Mandela were elected to their nation's highest political office after democratic political rule was achieved.

SEE ALSO *Passive Resistance; Protest*

BIBLIOGRAPHY

Buruma, Ian. 2002. *Bad Elements: Chinese Rebels from Los Angeles to Beijing.* London: Weidenfeld & Nicolson.

Hamilton, Neil. 2002. *Rebels and Renegades: A Chronology of Social and Political Dissent in the United States.* London: Routledge.

Horvath, Robert. 2005. *The Legacy of Soviet Dissent: Dissidents, Democratisation, and Radical Nationalism in Russia.* London: Routledge.

Teresa Wright

DISTINCTIONS, SOCIAL AND CULTURAL

Over the past forty years, there has been a surge of academic inquiry into the relationship between cultural practices and social stratification. In particular, scholars have explored how distinctions drawn between members of varying social strata with respect to lifestyle, preferences, habits, and consumption practices contribute to unequal access to economic and social rewards. This article reviews key works addressing the role of cultural demarcations in the persistence of class inequality, highlights major debates within the field, and suggests potentially fruitful directions for future research.

DISTINCTIONS AND CLASS CLOSURE

Through his concept of *social closure*, classical social theorist Max Weber (1958) described how social distinctions play a crucial role in the production of systems of power. According to Weber, advantaged groups within societies establish and retain social dominance through monopolizing, or "closing," access to valued resources and opportunities at the expense of other members of the community.

In order to facilitate such exclusion, privileged groups tend to adopt one or more "badges" of social standing so that group membership is readily perceptible, and the distribution of resources can be restricted within group lines.

Building upon Weber's work, Thorstein Veblen and Norbert Elias explored techniques used specifically by economic classes to distinguish themselves from the less affluent masses. In *Theory of the Leisure Class* (1899), Veblen described how the wealthy use material boundaries—specifically, the *conspicuous consumption* of costly consumer goods and services—to outwardly demonstrate their superior standing. Conversely, Elias's *The Civilizing Process* (1978) documents the development of elaborate behavioral codes and etiquette rituals established by elites in premodern Europe to signal membership in the more cultivated classes.

CULTURE AS CAPITAL: THE WORK OF PIERRE BOURDIEU

However, it is the work of French theorist Pierre Bourdieu that has been the most influential in shaping contemporary sociological understandings of the relationship between cultural practices and social stratification. Expanding upon Weber's, Veblen's, and Elias's earlier insights, Bourdieu argues in *Distinction* (1984) that cultural boundaries play a vital role in the reproduction of class inequalities.

According to Bourdieu, differences in material conditions result in different modes of interpreting and experiencing the social world. In particular, the institutions of family and schooling transmit class-specific values to younger generations. As a result of their upbringings, individuals develop goals, attitudes, knowledge, preferences, tastes, codes of appropriate conduct, and consumption practices consistent with their class position, the constellation of which Bourdieu refers to as *cultural capital*. Due to their restricted standard of living, for example, the lower classes develop cultural preferences and practices consistent with their subsistence and survival needs; members of these classes emphasize functionality and usefulness over more ethereal qualities such as aesthetic or intellectual value. Upper-class values, on the other hand, are characterized by their *distance from necessity*, or their removal from the immediate concerns of present-day life. In contrast to the "base" or "vulgar" tastes of the working classes, they emphasize complexity and form over use-value. An important component of upper-class cultural capital is that it is difficult to acquire and exclusive in nature; because the pursuit of these cultural practices and forms of understanding tend to require dedication of significant economic, mental, educational, and/or temporal resources, they are a luxury available only to those who have risen to a certain level of economic comfort. To illustrate the divide between low and high cultural tastes, Bourdieu uses the example of food preferences. Specifically, he argues that lower classes gravitate toward foods that economically satisfy basic nutritional requirements, whereas higher classes cultivate more sophisticated palettes and value features such as presentation and distinctiveness of flavor. Using survey data from his native France, Bourdieu documents similar patterns in preferences for artistic genres, tastes in fashion, and participation in leisure activities.

According to Bourdieu, such seemingly benign differences in culture serve to reproduce existing class relations in two ways. First, shared norms and values foster common aspirations among members of a social class. Consequently, individuals gravitate toward class-appropriate social relations and occupations. Second, culture is used to actively exclude members of lower classes from positions of prestige. Although all social groups possess cultural resources, only the cultural capital of the dominant classes is rewarded in society at large. Key gate-keeping institutions, most notably the educational system, privilege upper-class, or "dominant" styles of thought and behavior, channeling their possessors into positions of power and economic success, while barring lower-class individuals from avenues of mobility. Through such processes of exclusion, elites consolidate their own power and pass on economic privilege to their kin. Consequently, in Bourdieu's model, culture serves to reproduce and even mask systems of economic domination.

CRITIQUES OF BOURDIEU

Throughout the 1980s, Bourdieu's writings, and in particular his concept of cultural capital, sparked a tremendous volume of empirical work in cultural sociology, the sociology of education, and cultural studies. Yet, after an initial surge of scholarship, researchers began in the early 1990s to highlight potential shortcomings of Bourdieu's theory of class reproduction. Specifically, Bourdieu came under fire for (1) overemphasizing the role of early childhood experiences in determining class outcomes (Aschaffenburg and Mass 1997); (2) overestimating the importance of high culture to members of privileged strata, while underestimating the importance of moral, socioeconomic, and racial boundaries (Erickson 1996; Lamont 1992; Peterson and Kern 1996); and (3) failing to account for national and other contextual variations in the content of class boundaries (Lamont 1992). Moreover, the utility of the term cultural capital has been criticized for grouping together too many conceptually distinct variables (Lamont and Lareau 1988) as well as for its inability to reliably predict academic success (Kingston 2001). Finally, given the increasingly fragmented nature of social class and reported declines in class identification in postindus-

trial societies, a few more controversial scholars have questioned the very existence of class, let alone class cultures (Kingston 2000; Grusky and Weeden 2002).

SYMBOLIC BOUNDARIES: CURRENT AND FUTURE DIRECTIONS

In light of such critiques, many scholars shifted away from discussions of cultural capital and focused instead on *symbolic boundaries*, or conceptual distinctions made by actors to make sense of their social world. Drawing heavily on the work of classical theorists such as Émile Durkheim and more recently the work of cultural sociologist Michèle Lamont, this burgeoning literature explores the lines people draw between "us" and "them," particularly when evaluating the worth of others (Lamont and Molnar 2002). Although current studies tend to focus on investigating the context of symbolic boundaries and how they vary by context, the field of culture and inequality could benefit from future research examining how people actively *draw upon* these conceptual categories of worth in their educational, occupational, and social lives, particularly in the context of microsocial interaction.

SEE ALSO *Aesthetics; Bourdieu, Pierre; Class; Cultural Studies; Culture*

BIBLIOGRAPHY

Aschaffenburg, Karen, and Ineke Mass. 1997. Cultural and Educational Careers: The Dynamics of Social Reproduction. *American Sociological Review* 62 (4): 573–587.

Bourdieu, Pierre. 1984. *Distinction: A Social Critique of the Judgement of Taste.* Trans. Richard Nice. Cambridge, MA: Harvard University Press.

DiMaggio, Paul, and John Mohr. 1985. Cultural Capital, Educational Attainment, and Marital Selection. *American Journal of Sociology* 90 (6): 1231–1261.

Durkheim, Émile. 1965. *Elementary Forms of Religious Life.* Trans. Karen E. Fields. New York: Free Press.

Elias, Norbert. 1978. *The Civilizing Process.* Trans. Edmund Jephcott. New York: Urizen Books.

Erickson, Bonnie H. 1996. Culture, Class, and Connections. *American Journal of Sociology* 102 (1): 217–251.

Grusky, David, and Kim Weeden. 2002. Decomposition without Death: A Research Agenda for the New Class Analysis. *Acta Sociologica* 45 (3): 203–218.

Kingston, Paul W. 2000. *The Classless Society.* Stanford, CA: Stanford University Press.

Kingston, Paul W. 2001. The Unfulfilled Promise of Cultural Capital Theory. *Sociology of Education* 74 (4): 88–99.

Lamont, Michèle. 1992. *Money, Morals, and Manners: The Culture of the French and American Upper-Middle Class.* Chicago: University of Chicago Press.

Lamont, Michèle, and Annette Lareau. 1988. Cultural Capital: Allusions, Gaps, and Glissandos in Recent Theoretical Developments. *Sociological Theory* 6 (2): 153–168.

Lamont, Michèle, and Virag Molnar. 2002. The Study of Boundaries in the Social Sciences. *Annual Review of Sociology* 28 (1): 167–195.

Peterson, Richard A., and Roger M. Kern. 1996. Changing Highbrow Taste: From Snob to Omnivore. *American Sociological Review* 61 (5): 900–907.

Veblen, Thorstein. 1899. *The Theory of the Leisure Class: An Economic Study in the Evolution of Institutions.* New York: Modern Library.

Weber, Max. 1958. Class, Status, and Party. In *From Max Weber: Essays in Sociology*, eds. and trans. H. H. Gerth and C. Wright Mills, 180–195. Oxford: Oxford University Press.

Lauren A. Rivera

DISTORTIONS

A central precept in economics is that prices set in perfectly competitive markets provide clear signals of the value the economy places on items. In a competitive market, the value to a consumer of the last pizza sold should equal the value of the resources used in its production. An economic distortion occurs when some market intervention creates a wedge between the value of resources used in the production of that pizza and the value to consumers of consuming it. In the presence of distortions, opportunities exist to make someone better off without making anyone else worse off. This is known as a *Pareto improvement*.

Distortions arise for several reasons. First, companies may erect entry barriers, thereby creating market power. A monopoly is an extreme example of such market power. Firms with market power can sell goods at a price exceeding their marginal cost of production.

Second, the production or consumption of some commodity may have some positive or negative impact on other parts of the economy not transmitted through market prices. Such impacts are called *externalities*. A coal-fired electric utility emitting sulfur dioxide as a by-product of electricity generation creates a negative externality. In general, an unregulated economy produces too many goods with negative externalities and too few goods with positive externalities.

Third, buyers and sellers in a market may have asymmetric information about the good in question. Used-car markets are a good example. Sellers have better information about the quality of their car than do buyers. Since buyers will logically assume that owners of high-quality cars will tend to hold on to them while owners of low-quality cars will tend to sell them, a large share of the cars in the used-car market will be low-quality. Thus buyers will lower their bid for a used car. This will lead to fewer high-quality cars being sold. In the limit, this can lead to a collapse of the market, leaving both buyers and sellers worse off. This is an example of adverse selection, where the pool of items offered in a market are not representative of the typical items in existence.

Finally, government policies, intentionally or unintentionally, may create distortions. Most governments rely on income or consumption taxes to raise revenue for important government programs. Income taxes distort labor supply and savings decisions, while consumption taxes distort labor supply and consumption decisions.

Whether governments should intervene to correct distortions depends on a number of factors. Taxes on pollution set equal to the social marginal damages of pollution, for example, are generally viewed by economists as welfare enhancing. Many countries regulate monopolies or actively intervene in markets to promote competition. It may be, however, that in some cases interventions create more harm than good, in which case it may be preferable to live with the distortion. In other cases, distortions may be a necessary by-product of a desired social aim. Any redistribution through the tax system, for example, will create some degree of distortion, thereby illustrating the classic trade-off between efficiency and equity.

When facing multiple distortions, no clear prescription exists for the optimal ordering of eliminating distortions. Moreover, the first-best prescription for a given distortion may no longer hold in the presence of distortions elsewhere in the economy. This is the classic problem of the second best identified by Richard G. Lipsey and Kelvin Lancaster (1956–1957). Environmental policy provides an example of this phenomenon. In the absence of any other distortions, a first-best solution to the presence of pollution is to set a tax on pollution equal to social marginal damages. When taxes create distortions in capital and labor markets, however, this first-best prescription no longer holds. Instead, the optimal tax on pollution in most circumstances falls short of social marginal damages.

SEE ALSO *Dirigiste; Externality; Frictions; Information, Asymmetric; Liberalization, Trade; Monopoly; Monopsony; Neoliberalism; Pareto Optimum; Price vs. Quantity Adjustment; Prices; Theory of Second Best; Washington Consensus*

BIBLIOGRAPHY

Auerbach, Alan, and James Hines. 2002. *Handbook of Public Economics*, Vol. 3: *Taxation and Economic Efficiency*. Amsterdam: North-Holland.

Fullerton, Don, and Gilbert E. Metcalf. 1998. Environmental Taxes and the Double-Dividend Hypothesis: Did You Really Expect Something for Nothing? *Chicago-Kent Law Review* 73 (1): 221–256.

Lipsey, Richard G., and Kelvin Lancaster. 1956–1957. The General Theory of Second Best. *Review of Economic Studies* 24 (1): 11–32.

Rosen, Harvey S. 2004. *Public Finance.* 7th ed. New York: McGraw-Hill/Irwin.

Gilbert E. Metcalf

DISTRIBUTED LAGS

SEE *Lags, Distributed.*

DISTRIBUTION, BETA

SEE *Probability Distributions.*

DISTRIBUTION, CAUCHY

SEE *Probability Distributions.*

DISTRIBUTION, EXPONENTIAL

SEE *Probability Distributions.*

DISTRIBUTION, GAMMA

SEE *Probability Distributions.*

DISTRIBUTION, GAUSSIAN

SEE *Distribution, Normal.*

DISTRIBUTION, LAPLACE

SEE *Probability Distributions.*

DISTRIBUTION, LOGISTIC

SEE *Probability Distributions.*

DISTRIBUTION, LOGNORMAL

SEE *Probability Distributions.*

DISTRIBUTION, NORMAL

The normal distribution is the single most important distribution in the social sciences. It is described by the bell-shaped curve defined by the probability density function

$$f(X) = \frac{1}{\sigma\sqrt{2\pi}}\ \exp\left(-\frac{(X-\mu)^2}{2\sigma^2}\right)$$

where exp is the exponential function, μ the *mean* of the distribution, σ the *standard deviation*, and σ^2 the *variance*. As a matter of convenience, this distribution is often expressed as $X \sim N(\mu, \sigma^2)$. If $X \sim N(0, 1)$ so that $\mu = 0$ and $\sigma^2 = 1$, the outcome is the *standard normal distribution*. The resulting curve is shown in Figure 1, where the horizontal axis indicates values of X in terms of positive and negative integer values of the standard deviation. The curve's shape is typical of normally distributed variables, even when they have different means and variances.

The normal distribution has two significant features. First, the curve is perfectly symmetrical about the mean of the distribution. As a result, the distribution mean is identical to the two alternative measures of *central tendency*, namely, the *mode* (the most frequent value of X) and the *median* (the middle value of X). Second, the mathematical function provides the basis for specifying the number of observations that should fall within select portions of the curve. In particular, approximately 68.3 percent of the

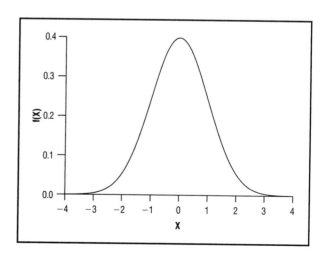

Figure 1. The Standard Normal Distribution.

observations will likely fall within one standard deviation of the mean. In the case of the standard normal deviation, this would indicate that more than two-thirds of the observations would have a value between −1 and +1. Moreover, about 95.4 percent of the observations would fall within two standard deviations above and below the mean, and about 99.7 percent would fall within three standard deviations below and above the mean. Hence, relatively fewer observations are expected in the upper and lower tails of the distribution; the more extreme the departure from the mean the lower the score's probability of occurrence.

HISTORY

The normal distribution was first associated with errors of measurement. In the latter half of the seventeenth century Galileo Galilei (1564–1642) noticed that the errors in astronomical observations were not totally random. Instead, not only did small errors outnumber large errors, but also the errors tended to be symmetrically distributed around a central value. In the first decade of the nineteenth century the mathematicians Adrien-Marie Legendre (1752–1833) and Carl Friedrich Gauss (1777–1855) worked out the precise mathematical formula, and Gauss demonstrated that this curve provided a close fit to the empirical distribution of observational errors. Gauss also derived the statistical method of *least squares* from the assumption that errors were normally distributed.

However, the normal distribution also appeared in other mathematical contexts. In the early eighteenth century Abraham de Moivre (1667–1754) showed that certain *binomial distributions* could be approximated by the same general curve. In fact, the normal curve is the limiting case for a binomial when events have a fifty-fifty chance of occurring and when the number of trials goes to infinity. A commonplace illustration is the distribution of coin tosses. In the early nineteenth century Pierre-Simon Laplace (1749–1827), when working on the *central limit theorem*, showed that the distribution of sample means tends to be normally distributed: The larger the number of samples, the closer is the fit to normality—a result that holds regardless of whatever the population distribution might be. Even if the scores in the population are highly skewed, the distribution of sample means will tend toward the normal curve.

Despite the fact that many mathematicians contributed to the emergence of the concept, it is Gauss whose name became most strongly linked with the discovery. As a consequence, the eponymic term *Gaussian* is often used instead of "normal" or "bell-shaped."

APPLICATIONS

Although the normal distribution was first applied to the description of measurement errors, scientists later began to realize that it also described variation in human phenomena independent of errors of measurement. In 1835 Adolphe Quetelet (1796–1874) applied the normal distribution to many physical attributes, such as height, and in 1869 Francis Galton (1822–1911) extended the same distribution to cover individual differences in ability. The latter application is seen in those psychometric instruments in which test scores are actually defined according to the normal distribution. For instance, the IQ scores on most intelligence tests are assigned in terms of a person's position in the distribution. Thus, under the assumption that IQ has a mean of 100 and a standard deviation of 15, a score of 130 would place the individual in the upper 2 percent of the population in intellectual ability.

Indeed, the concept of the normal distribution has become so universal that it now provides the basis of almost all parametric statistical methods. For example, multiple regression analysis and the analysis of variance both assume that the errors of prediction, or residuals, are normally distributed with a mean of zero and a uniform variance. More sophisticated methods such as canonical correlation, discriminant analysis, and multivariate analysis of variance all require a more complex assumption, namely, *multivariate normality*. This means that the joint distribution of the variables is normally distributed. In the special case of *bivariate normality*, this assumption signifies that the joint distribution will approximate the shape of a three-dimensional bell. To the extent that the normality assumption is violated, the population inferences associated with these statistical methods will become approximate rather than exact.

Given the prominent place of the normal distribution in the social sciences, it is essential to recognize that not all human attributes or behavioral events are normally distributed. For example, many phenomena display extremely skewed distributions with long upper tails. Examples include the distributions of annual income across households, the box-office performance of feature films, the output of journal articles by scientists, and the number of violent acts committed by male teenagers. Sometimes these departures from normality can be rectified using an appropriate data transformation. For instance, a *lognormal* distribution becomes normal after a logarithmic transformation. Yet many important variables cannot be normalized in this way. In such cases, researchers may use statistics based on the specific nonnormal distribution or else employ various nonparametric or distribution-free methods. Furthermore, it is likely that the causal processes that generate normal distributions are intrinsically different from those that generate nonnormal distributions. As an example, the former tend to emerge when multiple causal processes are additive, whereas the latter tend to appear when those processes are multiplicative.

BIBLIOGRAPHY

Patel, Jagdish K., and Campbell B. Read. 1982. *Handbook of the Normal Distribution.* 2nd ed. New York: Marcel Dekker.

Yang, Hongwei. 2007. Normal Curve. In *Encyclopedia of Measurement and Statistics,* vol. 2, ed. Neil J. Salkind, 690–695. Thousand Oaks, CA: Sage.

Dean Keith Simonton

DISTRIBUTION, PARETO

SEE *Probability Distributions.*

DISTRIBUTION, POISSON

The Poisson distribution (named after Siméon Denis Poisson, 1781–1840) is used to describe certain events in time or in space. It is derived from the binomial distribution with the extension that time (or space) is thought to be continuous instead of discrete. In the case of discrete time (binomial distribution), let the probability that a certain event occurs during one period of length 1 be a constant p; then the number of events $Z \in \{0, 1, 2, ...\}$

happening during a certain number n of such periods is binomially distributed with parameters n and p. No event influences any other event—that is, the events are mutually independent. If the length of the period is decreased to Δt, and if we are still interested in the number of events happening during a time span of length n, then this time span consists of $n/\Delta t$ periods within each of which the event probability is $p\Delta t$. For $\Delta t \to 0$ and $np = \lambda$, the formula for the binomial distribution

$$P(Z = k) = f_Z(k) = \binom{n}{k} p^k (1 - p)^{n-k}$$

is transformed into the formula of the Poisson distribution

$$P(Z = k) = f_Z(k) = \exp(-\lambda) = \frac{\lambda^k}{k!}.$$

The difference between the two distributions is shown in two graphs drawn from a sample of 25,000 simulated random events:

Random variables X_t form a Poisson process if the following conditions hold: The probability that exactly one event occurs during a time span of length Δt is proportional to the length of the time span; the probability that more than one event occurs during this time span is negligible; and the number of events occurring in disjoint time intervals are mutually independent. X_s is the number of events that occurred from $t = 0$ until $t = s$. The increments $(X_t - X_s)$ follow the Poisson distribution.

The Poisson distribution is also called a "distribution of rare events," because for a fixed λ and a large n the probability of the individual event occurring per time unit is, of course, small. An important application of the

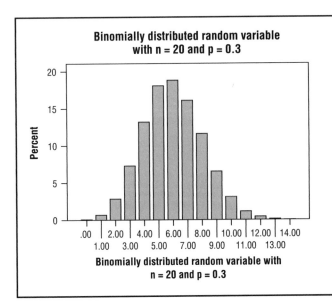

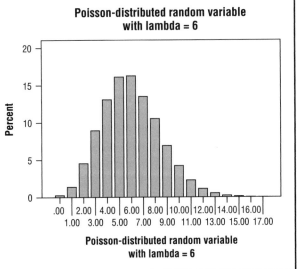

Poisson distribution and of the Poisson process (a stochastic process whose random increments are Poisson distributed) is queuing theory; in this case, the number of new customers arriving during a fixed period is the random increment. The parameter λ of the Poisson distribution is called "intensity" and yields the expected value of customers arriving per time unit in this example.

Another example is the number of accidents that occur in a certain area during a given period. The distribution of this number will also follow the Poisson distribution. If one compares the number of car accidents with passengers killed with and without a seat belt, one has to compare the parameters of the two Poisson distributions and would find out whether using seat belts had a significant influence on the number of deadly accidents.

Given the conditions under which events are Poisson distributed, one could argue that customers arriving at an airport often arrive in pairs or even larger groups—which would violate the applicability of the model to real-world scenarios. Another obvious violation is due to the fact that the arrival intensities at airports (or in emergency units) are not the same over the entire day or the week, such that the model can be applied only to selected times spans during which the arrival intensities are more or less constant over a considerable period of time. Physical processes such as the decay of radioactive material are less prone to violations of this kind than processes where humans are involved; but even here—at least with the help of computer simulation—intensities that vary over time can be successfully modelled.

SEE ALSO *Central Tendencies, Measures of; Distribution, Normal; Distribution, Uniform; Variables, Random*

BIBLIOGRAPHY

Hoel, Paul G. 1984. *Introduction to Mathematical Statistics.* 5th ed. Hoboken, NJ: Wiley.

Poisson, Siméon D. [1837] 2003. *Récherches sur la probabilité des jugements en matière criminelle et en matière civile.* Paris: Editions Jacques Gabay.

Klaus G. Troitzsch

DISTRIBUTION, UNIFORM

Uniform distribution is the probability distribution in which the probability is uniform for all intervals of the same length. The definition of the continuous uniform distribution function contains two parameters, a and b, which are the minimum and maximum values, respectively, that can occur in the set of numbers characterized

by the distribution. The probability of any number in the interval (a, b) is $1/(b - a)$, and 0 outside that interval, as illustrated in Figure 1. Whether a and b are included in the interval does not matter to the integral, and in practice are sometimes included and sometimes not. The distribution is also known as rectangular distribution, because of its rectangular shape. As in all probability density functions, the area under the curve is 1. The standard uniform distribution is the special case where a is 0 and b is 1, so that the distribution takes the form of a square of height 1. In a probability distribution, the area of the curve under any interval represents the probability that a number described by the distribution occurs in that interval. For the standard uniform distribution, the probability of seeing a number in the interval $(0, 0.5)$ would be the same as the probability of seeing a number in the interval $(0.5, 1)$, and both would be 50 percent. In the discrete form of the uniform distribution, the probability of occurrence of all values in a finite set is equal. For example, if the set of possible values were 0 and 1, then there would be a 50 percent chance for 0 and a 50 percent chance for 1; or a 50 percent chance for getting heads and a 50 percent chance of getting tails on a fair coin.

Uniformly distributed phenomena are rare in the social world, because uniform probability implies randomness, and the social world is characterized by pattern, or the lack of randomness. However, social scientists still find use for the uniform distribution; in fact, it is the second-most used distribution after the normal distribution. The most popular use of the uniform distribution is to find the random variates of other probability distributions, such as the normal distribution. A random variate of a distribution is a number chosen randomly out of the set of numbers with likelihoods characterized by the distribution. A uniform normal variate input to an inverse cumulative probability function of any distribution will generate a random variate of that distribution. Random variates are important in Monte Carlo simulation studies, where the distribution of an outcome is estimated by taking many samples in many simulation runs. Ironically,

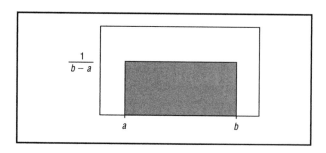

Figure 1. The Continuous Uniform Distribution

truly random variates of any distribution cannot be computed, because truly random numbers cannot be expressed in an equation by definition. Therefore, pseudorandom numbers are accepted, usually created by modulo arithmetic, which have many of the statistical properties of random numbers but repeat themselves at some point. True random numbers are normal in the sense that, for each k, all subsequences of the binary (or decimal, or other) expansion of length k have equal probability, but pseudorandom numbers fail on this requirement for some k.

$$P(x) = \begin{cases} 0 & \text{for } x < a \\ \dfrac{1}{b-a} & \text{for } a \le x \le b \\ 0 & \text{for } x > b \end{cases}$$

Social scientists also use the uniform distribution to represent lack of knowledge. For example, in a simulation where a distribution is not known, uniform random variates are often used. Naturally, the uniform random variate will incorrectly represent the underlying distribution. However, the uniform distribution also represents independence. The random variates of any distribution incorrectly represent dependencies on the random variates of other modeled distributions. A random variate is only a good model when the measure represents phenomena that are independent of the other phenomena being represented. True independence is as rare as true randomness in the social world. A simple illustration of the problem with using the uniform distribution to represent the lack of knowledge is Bertrand's paradox. In Bertrand's paradox, a cube is hidden in a box with a side that has an unknown length, say between 3 and 5 centimeters. Using modulo arithmetic can then generate random numbers between 3 and 5 centimeters, and take their average in multiple runs of 4 centimeters to estimate the side length. Random numbers could also be generated for all the possible surface areas, between 54 and 150 square centimeters, and all the possible volumes, between 27 and 125 cubic centimeters. However, if those possible measures are averaged as well, then an impossible cube emerges with a length of 4 centimeters, a surface area of 102 square centimeters, and a volume of 76 cubic centimeters.

SEE ALSO *Distribution, Normal; Distribution, Poisson; Frequency Distributions; Monte Carlo Experiments; Probability; Variables, Random*

BIBLIOGRAPHY

Chaitin, Gregory. 1975. Randomness and Mathematical Proof. *Scientific American* 232 (5): 47–52.

Clarke, Michael. 2002. *Paradoxes from A to Z.* London: Routledge.

Jaynes, Edwin Thompson. 1973. *The Well-Posed Problem.* Foundations of Physics, vol. 3, pp. 477–493.

Jaynes, Edwin Thompson. 2003. *Probability Theory: The Logic of Science.* Cambridge University Press, 2003.

Deborah Vakas Duong

DISTRIBUTION, WEIBULL

SEE *Probability Distributions.*

DIVERSITY

Diversity, one of the buzzwords of the early twenty-first century, has become a concept that has multiple meanings to different groups of people. Although dictionaries usually define diversity by using terms like "variety," "difference," or "dissimilarity," social scientists usually talk about diversity in at least four different ways.

1. *Counting diversity* refers to empirically enumerating differences within a given population. Using this definition, social scientists take a particular population and simply count the members according to specific criteria, often including race, gender, and ethnicity. In addition, it is possible to take a particular unit within a society like a school, workplace, or government and compare its race, ethnic, or gender distribution to that of the general population. Often, suspicious questions are raised the farther the diversity of a subunit differs from that of the larger population.

2. *Culture diversity* refers to the importance of understanding and appreciating the cultural differences between race, ethnic, and gender groups. Since members of one culture often view others in relationship to their own standards, social scientists using the culture diversity definition would argue that it is important to show that differences do not have to be evaluated along a good-bad or moral-immoral scale. With greater tolerance and understanding, the argument goes, different cultural groups can coexist with one another in the same society.

3. *Good-for-business diversity* refers to the belief that businesses will be more profitable and government agencies and not-for-profit corporations will be more efficient with diverse labor forces. According to this approach, members of particular cultural groups are more effective than non-group members in dealing with their own groups so it is in the interests of organizations to diversify workers and managers.

4. *Conflict diversity* refers to understanding how different groups exist in a hierarchy of inequality in terms of power, privilege, and wealth. According to this definition,

dominant groups oppress subordinate groups in many societies and it is important for social scientists to understand the nature of this oppression in order to help attain a more egalitarian society.

In the real world, these four approaches often overlap. However, people using different approaches often ask different types of questions. One can see how this works by examining a hypothetical city in the United States that is having difficulty between the local police department and the black and Hispanic population.

A social scientist with a counting diversity perspective might compare the black and Hispanic distribution in the police department with the distribution in the city. Typically, blacks and Hispanics would be underrepresented in the police department and even more highly underrepresented at the upper levels of the department.

A culture diversity scholar, on the other hand, would be more concerned with how the police understand the black and Hispanic communities since this also affects their actions. Do the predominantly white police interpret certain types of speech and clothing as threatening when it is simply part of the black and Hispanic subculture? Do they act in ways that inadvertently disrespect members of the community, thus causing even more tension? Being more sensitive to black and Hispanic cultural values might make the job of the police easier.

The good-for-business perspective would argue that the police would be more effective if they had more black and Hispanic officers who would be more likely to be familiar with the culture of those communities. In addition, members of the community might not be so hostile if the police were seen as some of their own.

Finally, culture conflict social scientists would argue that the police represent the interests of the dominant group: wealthy, white men in business and politics. The police represent the property rights of the dominant group and enforce the laws that they have enacted. Black and Hispanic police officers enforce the same unfair laws as their white colleagues, although they may do it more humanely. The goal is not just to have a more representative and culturally sensitive police force. The goal is to change the laws in order to have a more equitable society.

Concerns about diversity, however it is defined, also intersect with policies like affirmative action. Employment-based affirmative action is based on comparing the racial distribution of employees in a given workplace with the racial distribution of the pool of workers who are qualified for a specific job. This is counting diversity. In the United States, employers with $50,000 in federal contracts and fifty or more employees are required to make a "good faith effort" to achieve a representative labor force; that is, they must try. Formal hiring quotas, where employers are legally obligated to hire a certain percentage of underrepresented

workers, are more difficult to justify. In India, on the other hand, these hiring quotas are used much more extensively.

In higher education, both counting diversity and a version of culture diversity are involved. According to the 2003 *Grutter* and *Gratz* decisions of the U.S. Supreme Court, affirmative action in college admissions is constitutional because it is in the educational interests of all students to be exposed to a diversity of views on campus. Racial diversity is one way to enhance the diversity of views. However, strict numerical comparisons and formulas cannot be used. Instead, "holistic" assessments of each candidate must take place in order to achieve an undefined "critical mass" of each student group. Since white and Asian students are overrepresented in American higher education, these critical mass guidelines refer mainly to underrepresented minorities like blacks, Hispanics, and Native Americans. A good-for-business perspective is also involved since the court noted that law schools and, to a lesser extent, all of higher education train future leaders who should be selected from all racial groups.

Neither affirmative action in employment nor in higher education reflects the conflict diversity perspective since the role and structure of higher education and the economy is not questioned. The relative power of workers and their bosses/managers is not addressed. The purpose of higher education is not addressed. All that is addressed is the racial characteristics of those who occupy various positions. When reading an article about diversity, it is critical to understand which approach the author is using.

BIBLIOGRAPHY

Anderson, Margaret L., and Patricia Hill Collins. 2007. *Race, Class and Gender: An Anthology*. 6th ed. Belmont, CA: Thomson Wadsworth.

Ore, Tracy E. 2006. *The Social Construction of Difference and Inequality: Race, Class, Gender and Sexuality*. 3rd ed. Boston: McGraw-Hill.

Pincus, Fred L. 2006. *Understanding Diversity: An Introduction to Class, Race, Gender, and Sexual Orientation*. Boulder, CO: Lynne Rienner.

Rosenblum, Karen E., and Toni-Michelle C. Travis. 2006. *The Meaning of Difference: American Constructions of Race, Sex and Gender, Social Class and Sexual Orientation*. 4th ed. Boston: McGraw-Hill.

Fred L. Pincus

DIVESTITURE

Countries that employ economic sanctions have a number of economic instruments with which they may induce compliance by their targets. Among these is disinvestment or divestiture, in which they shed their capital holdings within the target state. When sanctioning states divest, they effectively seek to reverse the benefits of foreign direct investment (FDI) flows into the target state. Whereas FDI increases states' productive capital stock by funding factories and infrastructure, disinvestment seeks a liquidation of this capital stock. Although divestiture has rarely been used (because, to be effective, the sanctioning state must have previously invested heavily in the target country), when the conditions favor this policy tool, it can be particularly effective.

Perhaps ironically, the short-term effects of divestiture may actually benefit the target country. Because factories and infrastructure are typically immobile, they must be sold in-place, generally to entrepreneurs within the target state and often at fire-sale prices. Thus, in the short term divestiture does little to reduce target states' capital stock; it simply transfers ownership of immobile capital assets from foreign to target state stakeholders.

While the short-term effects of disinvestment may be negative, its long-term effects can prove especially damaging to the target country. This is not only because disinvestment chills future FDI inflows but also because foreign management and technology are mobile and these are generally withdrawn after divestiture. Without access to foreign technology, spare parts, and management skills, in the long run the divested capital stock will eventually run down and become far less productive, becoming a drain on target-state entrepreneurs and increasing their calls for an end to the policies deemed offensive by the divesting state(s).

A notable past case of divestment was undertaken against apartheid South Africa under the context of the Reverend Leon Sullivan's voluntary code of conduct that pressured (mostly U.S.) businesses to liquidate their South African holdings during the 1980s. In the short term South African entrepreneurs were able to acquire a set of highly productive assets at low prices and the black employees of these enterprises often suffered under their new management (Barber 1982). In the long term, however, the lack of foreign capital, technology, and management expertise began to tell on the divested industries, increasing South African entrepreneurs' calls for an end to apartheid. Their pressure was one of the keys to the eventual demise of apartheid (Major and McGann 2005).

More recently, a number of universities and religious organizations, such as the Presbyterian Church (USA), have called for a similar disinvestment campaign against Israel for its continued occupation of Gaza and the West Bank. If U.S. companies could be pressured into disinvesting, it could prove damaging to the Israeli economy: in 2003, the United States' FDI position in Israel equaled 5.62 percent of Israeli gross domestic product. Although Israeli entrepreneurs could be expected to reap a bonanza in the short term, should disinvestment proceed, cutting this crucial link between Israel and U.S. technology, managerial skills, and best practices, it could seriously hobble the Israeli economy in the long run.

In cases in which a sanctioning state has substantial FDI holdings in the target state, and where it is patient enough to ride out the negative, short-term effects of disinvestment, divestiture can be an effective nonviolent policy tool to persuade another nation against engaging in unsavory activities.

SEE ALSO *Apartheid*

BIBLIOGRAPHY

Barber, James. 1982. Economic Interdependence, Sanctions, and Alternatives to Sanctions. In *Chatham House Papers*, ed. James Barber, Jesmond Blumfield, and Christopher H. Hill. London: Royal Institute of International Affairs.

Major, Solomon, and Anthony McGann. 2005. Caught in the Crossfire: "Innocent Bystanders" as Optimal Targets of Economic Sanction. *Journal of Conflict Resolution* 49 (3): 337–359.

Solomon Major

DIVINE RIGHT

The belief that a community's earthly protector has a unique, authority-conferring relationship with the divine has existed in virtually all forms of one-person rule throughout human history. The concept of the "divine right of kings" was developed as a formal theory of legitimacy in the period following the Middle Ages in Europe. It states that God directly authorized the rule of a Christian monarch for life by creating him (or her) as the hereditary heir to the throne. This not only sanctifies and clarifies the often disruptive process of succession, but it also puts the monarch beyond human accountability and enjoins all believers to obey unhesitatingly, thereby ending the recurring instability in Europe caused by divided loyalties between the people's political and spiritual leaders. It was initially propounded against rival claims of authority by feudal lords as much as the pope, thereby serving to strengthen the burgeoning nationalism of the fifteenth and sixteenth centuries. In the seventeenth century, the French bishop Jacques-Bénigne Bossuet (and various English theorists before him) argued for divine right in the face of emerging theories of legitimacy based on the consent of the ruled. In the midst of the reign of Louis

XIV (the "Sun King"), France's greatest exemplar and proponent of divine right, the Glorious Revolution of 1688 put the doctrine largely to rest in England, where it was replaced with a democratically based, limited constitutionalism that revolutionized the practice and acceptance of authority.

Whereas the implied infallibility of God's deputy in the European model tended to have distinctly absolutist implications, the conditionality in the Chinese conception of a "Mandate of Heaven" served to preserve as well as destroy dynasties of various lengths after it was first formulated during the Zhou dynasty (1050–256 BCE). This Chinese variation of divine right is based on the idea that heaven protects human welfare by establishing rulers whose mandate is to be wise and just. If they fail in this, the mandate is passed on as evidenced by their physical overthrow. Originally an outgrowth of pagan ethics and cosmology, it was blended with Confucian principles and Buddhism in such a way as to emphasize the virtues of moderation and reserve on the Emperor's part, rather than power and splendor. By the late sixth century, Buddhism, Confucianism, and other key elements of Chinese culture began to take hold in Japan. A century later, using terms such as "Mandate of Heaven," Emperor Temmu and his consort and successor Jitô established the image of the emperor (*Tenno*) as a descendant of the sun goddess Amaterasu and ruler of "all under heaven." Since then, the *Tenno* has been seen as a bridge between heaven and earth, with duties to Heaven as well as to the people. To this distinction was soon added that of "Servant of the Buddha," and the *Tenno* served in this leading religious role until the end of the nineteenth century. For much of Japanese history, the *Tenno* has served as the religious and cultural leader, lending official sanction to the policies and authority of a largely independent and better-armed political ruler. Throughout history, the prevalence of tenets comparable to divine right around the world suggests that the belief that worldly authority and divine providence coincide is more than simply a convenient premise for establishing authority, but instead speaks to a fundamental human longing.

SEE ALSO *Monarchy*

BIBLIOGRAPHY

Figgis, John Neville. 1914. *The Divine Right of Kings*, 2nd ed. Cambridge, U.K.: Cambridge University Press

Loewe, Michael. 1966. *Imperial China*. New York: Praeger.

Piggott, Joan R. 1997. *The Emergence of Japanese Kingship*. Stanford, CA: Stanford University Press.

William J. G. Bewick

DIVISIA MONETARY INDEX

Aggregation theory and index-number theory have been used to generate official governmental data since the 1920s. One exception still exists. The monetary quantity aggregates and interest rate aggregates supplied by many central banks are not based on index-number or aggregation theory, but rather are the simple unweighted sums of the component quantities and averages of interest rates. The predictable consequence has been induced instability of money demand and supply functions, and a series of "puzzles" in the resulting applied literature. Without coherence between data aggregation formulas and the models within which aggregates are embedded, stable structure can appear to be unstable. This phenomenon has been called the *Barnett critique* by Alec Chrystal and Ronald MacDonald (1994). In contrast, the Divisia monetary aggregates, originated by William A. Barnett (1980), are derived directly from economic index-number theory and are now available from some central banks.

Statistical index-number theory provides indexes that are computable directly from quantity and price data, without estimation of unknown parameters. For decades, the link between statistical index number theory and microeconomic aggregation theory was weaker for aggregating over monetary assets than for aggregating over other goods and asset quantities. Once monetary assets began yielding interest, monetary assets became imperfect substitutes for each other, and the "price" of monetary-asset services was no longer clearly defined. That problem was solved by Barnett, who derived the formula for the user cost of demanded monetary services. Barnett's results on that user cost set the stage for introducing index number theory into monetary economics.

Let $m_t = (m_{1t}, m_{2t}, ..., m_{nt})'$ be the vector of real balances of monetary assets during period t, let $r_t = (r_{1t}, r_{2t}, ..., r_{nt})'$ be the vector of nominal holding-period yields for monetary assets during period t, and let R_t be the yield on the benchmark asset during period t. The benchmark asset is defined to be a pure investment that provides no services other than its yield, so that the asset is held solely to accumulate wealth. Let $\pi_t = (\pi_{1t}, \pi_{2t}, ..., \pi_{nt})'$ be the vector of monetary-asset real user costs, with $\pi_{it} = \dfrac{R_t - r_{it}}{1 + R_t}$.

The user cost formula measures the foregone interest, which is the opportunity cost, of holding a unit of monetary asset i.

In economic aggregation theory, there exists an exact aggregator function over quantities. Let that aggregator function over monetary assets be u, so that the exact monetary aggregate, M_t, is $M_t = u(m_t^*)$. Statistical index-number theory enables us to track M_t exactly, without estimating the unknown function, u.

In continuous time, the exact monetary aggregate, $M_t = u(m_t^*)$, can be tracked exactly by the Divisia index, which solves the differential equation $\frac{d \log M_t}{dt} = \sum_i s_{it} \frac{d \log m_{it}^*}{dt}$, where $s_{it} = \frac{\pi_{it} m_{it}^*}{y_t}$ is the ith asset's share in expenditure on the total portfolio's service flow. The dual user cost price aggregate, $\Pi_t = \Pi(\pi_t)$, can be tracked exactly by the Divisia price index, which solves the differential equation $\frac{d \log \Pi_t}{dt} = \sum_i s_{it} \frac{d \log \pi_{it}}{dt}$.

In continuous time, the Divisia index, under conventional neoclassical assumptions, is exact. In discrete time, the Törnqvist approximation is: $\log M_t - \log M_{t-1} = \sum_i \bar{s}_{it} (\log m_{it}^* - \log m_{i,t-1}^*)$, where $\bar{s}_{it} = \frac{1}{2}(s_{it} + s_{i,t-1})$.

The user cost aggregate, Π_t, then can be computed directly from Fisher's factor reversal formula, $\Pi_t M_t = \pi_t' m_t$.

The formula for Divisia monetary aggregation has been extended to risk aversion and to multilateral (international) aggregation within a common currency area, with particular reference to the concerns of the European Central Bank. Many of those extensions have been collected together in Barnett and Apostolos Serletis (2000).

SEE ALSO *Monetary Theory; Money*

BIBLIOGRAPHY

Barnett, William A. 1980. Economic Monetary Aggregates: An Application of Aggregation and Index Number Theory. *Journal of Econometrics* 14 (1): 11–48. Reprinted in William A. Barnett and Apostolos Serletis, eds. 2000. *The Theory of Monetary Aggregation*, 11–48. Amsterdam: North Holland.

Barnett, William A., and Apostolos Serletis, eds. 2000. *The Theory of Monetary Aggregation*. Amsterdam: North Holland.

Chrystal, Alec, and Ronald MacDonald. 1994. Empirical Evidence on the Recent Behaviour and Usefulness of Simple-Sum and Weighted Measures of the Money Stock. *Federal Reserve Bank of St. Louis Review* 76 (2): 73–109.

William A. Barnett

DIVISION OF LABOR

The phrase *division of labor* can justifiably be used to indicate any form of work specialization, such as the division of labor between men and women; and yet, ever since Adam Smith's *The Wealth of Nations* (1776), it has come to refer to the division of tasks within an industrial process. Smith saw the division of labor within the industrial process as enormously efficient and illustrated his argument by the now hallowed example of the pin factory. A competent pinmaker, we are told, could not make more than twenty pins a day, whereas, upon dividing the tasks into eighteen operations, such as drawing, cutting, grinding, and so on, ten men can make over 48,000 pins in a day. On an average, therefore, each individual's productivity is increased 240-fold. The example is especially interesting because the productivity increase involves *no* change in technique—it is purely a case of applying existing knowledge more efficiently. The only limit to such productivity lies in the ability to sell the additional output, hence Smith also tells us "That the division of labour is limited by the extent of the market" (1776).

We are emphatically told in chapter 1, Book I, of the *Wealth of Nations* that the division of labor is the most important reason for greater production and is the primary force leading to prosperity:

> The greatest improvement in the productive powers of labour, and the greater part of the skill, dexterity and judgement with which it is anywhere directed, or applied, seems to have been the effects of the division of labour. (p. 13)

> It is the great multiplication of the production of all the different arts, in consequence of the division of labour, which occasions, in a well-governed society, that universal opulence which extends itself to the lowest ranks of the people. (p. 22)

Three reasons are given why a concentration of effort upon a single task increases efficiency. First, the skill of individual workers is much improved by specialization; secondly, workers save time and effort involved in having to switch from one operation to another; and finally, the division of labor facilitates the invention of machinery. The three reasons are most applicable only in manufacturing and Smith notes that agriculture is not suited to the division of labor, with the implication that one is not to expect much growth in that sector.

The rhetorical force of Adam Smith's presentation has to be separated from its economic analysis. All individuals have identical capacities in Smith's presentation and he ignored the traditional view of the division of labor as permitting individuals to perform those tasks that were most suitable to them. Dugald Stewart, Smith's successor at Edinburgh, criticized each of Smith's three reasons. Stewart grants that a workman gains in dexterity by concentrating on one task, but the efficiency gains thus obtained he considers to be quite limited (Stewart 1855, vol. 8, p. 315). Secondly, while it was perfectly true that a worker saves time by not having to change jobs, such gains are of small magnitude. If, then, the division of labor is to explain the productivity of labor, it must be by its influence upon the invention of machinery (p. 319).

Stewart now made two very significant innovations. First, his analysis of production focused on breaking production processes down into a series of simple tasks, as simple tasks are the ones that are most easily mechanically duplicated; gains in time and dexterity followed as a corollary of this attempt at simplification. Secondly, the entrepreneur and not the worker is put at the center of the stage. Stewart doubted that workers themselves would engage in the invention of labor-saving machinery, as Smith had conjectured they would, because the effect of such improvements indeed might even lead to his being unemployed. It is the capitalist who is driven by the lure of profits to continually improve his machinery. E. G. Wakefield later elaborated upon this far-reaching criticism by insisting that every successful division of labor must be accompanied by a plan for its subsequent combination. Coordination was prior to, and critical for, the successful division of labor. Smith's one-sided emphasis Wakefield found to be "not only very deficient but also full of error" (Smith [1776] 1840, p. 33).

Later generations have made the division of labor the paramount principle underlying profitable international trade. The international division of labor is a feature that Smith himself laid little stress upon and the argument about its centrality is based on a misinterpretation. The phrase *division of labor* can be used for any activity where there is some element of specialization. When used in the context of international trade, to suggest that trade between two countries is beneficial in allowing two countries to specialize, what is being referred to is, however, not at all the same phenomenon that occurs in the pin factory. The gains here typically arise from the *different endowments* of the two countries, not from the subdivision of tasks within a unified process.

From the scholarly point of view it must be regretted that Smith (1) neglected the fairly extensive British tradition—Petty, Maxwell, and Harris, to name a few—of viewing the division of labor as *a* factor in productivity, and (2) failed to acknowledge his debt to the *Encyclopedie* (see Kindleberger 1976, p. 1). Not only does the example of pinmaking appear to have been taken from the French *Encyclopedie*, the three advantages of the division of labor are also distinctly stated there as well. (This point is distinctly noted by Edwin Cannan, editor of the fifth edition of the *Wealth of Nations*, and subsequently by Roy Campbell and Andrew Skinner, editors of the 1976 edition.) When Adam Smith and Adam Ferguson fell out in the 1760s and 1770s, Smith appears to have accused Ferguson of plagiarism—to which charge Ferguson justifiably replied that he had only dipped into the same French source as Smith (Hamowy 1968).

Charles Babbage (1791–1871) and, independently, the Italian economist Melchiorre Gioja (1767–1829) elaborated on Stewart's insight that work could be matched to individual abilities: "The master manufacturer, by dividing the work to be performed into different processes each requiring different degrees of skill and force, can purchase exactly that precise quantity necessary for each process" (Babbage 1832, pp. 137–138). (Babbage also claims that needlemaking is more illustrative of the division of labor than pinmaking.) Andrew Ure considered the same issue through the employer's eyes and noted how important subdivision is to the social control of industry. The function of science is to mechanize every "difficult" process so as to reduce the bargaining power of skilled workers (Ure 1835, p. 19). Wherever a process requires particular dexterity and steadiness of hand, it should be withdrawn as soon as possible from the "cunning" workman, who is prone to many kinds of irregularities, and entrusted to a specific mechanism, so self-regulating that a child could supervise it. Babbage, Gioja, and Ure foreshadow the twentieth century views of F. W. Taylor and Henry Ford, who wanted to replace worker initiative with rules and assembly lines. With Ford and Taylor, and their associated production philosophies *Taylorism* and *Fordism*, the view of the worker as robot was virtually complete. It appeared that efficiency requires a dehumanized work environment. Yet labor disputes and poor production quality, quite apparent to all by the 1980s, suggest to many that traditional Taylorism and Fordism are at an end. The latest step has been to globalize the division of labor by shipping out unskilled work to low-wage countries, a process that has the added advantage of removing the alienated worker from view.

Ensconced within the *Wealth of Nations*, however, was a potent message about alienation. After having extolled the division of labor in Book I, in Book V Smith emphasized the way in which the division of labor turned human beings into mechanical morons: "The man whose whole life is spent in performing a few simple operations … has no occasion to exert his understanding, or to exercise his invention…. He naturally loses, therefore, the habit of such exertion, and generally becomes as stupid and ignorant as it is possible for a human creature to become" (p. 781). This acquired stupidity makes the ordinary worker an indifferent family man and a poor citizen. Because of this considerable danger to civil society, Smith went against his usual principles and urged the state to become involved in providing primary education. The suggestion that primary education would suffice to save the worker from an alienated, almost disembodied, existence drew Karl Marx's acid remark that Smith had sought to cure the major ill of industrialism with a "homeopathic dose." It is rumored that Smith was indebted to Rousseau for the "alienating insight," but, be that as it may, Smith is properly considered parent of the major stem of modern labor relations and stepfather to the opposition. The dominance of Taylorism as the ideology of work in the 1930s caused a reaction that is exemplified by Elton Mayo's insistence that human relations in the workplace are crucial to maintaining productivity.

The casual treatment of the worker's welfare in the American workplace is to be contrasted with the considerable care taken in the molding of engineers. William Wickendon wrote that educational leaders of the 1920s saw the college as being like a factory and urged that colleges must take raw material and "turn out a product which is saleable," with the significant implication that "the type of curriculum is in the last analysis not set by the college but by the employer of the college graduate" (as quoted in Noble 1984, p. 46). The most effective spokesman for engineering education, William Wickenden emphasized teamwork, rather than individualism. The new "engineer for industry" was urged to be a good subordinate. One notes that these are the very complex of attitudes that America had to "relearn" from Japan in the 1970s and 1980s!

The social approach to technology looks at Fordism as the primary source of misleading insights. In turn, Fordism arose from glorifying the productivity of the pin factory. In order for large capital expenditures to take place, both corporation and state need to be socially stable. Yet such social stability is difficult to arrange under modern conditions, unless one pays attention to the worker's welfare. The full message of the division of labor is a complex one and far too much has been lost by focusing upon the making of pins.

In addition, the effect of the division of labor was to fix attention on one simple operation, whereas the improvement of machinery required knowledge of a great variety of operations. The "popular" view of technological progress sees it as occurring outside the control or guidance of the worker, who has the challenge of adjusting himself to the technology at hand. And yet, one has to remember that perhaps as much as 40 percent of the technological improvements that occurred in the textile industry during the Industrial Revolution have no assigned source. These were all improvements that occurred as workers made small, "invisible" improvements whose aggregate effect was quite noticeable. Of course, there are no rules for obtaining such invisible changes, but we can be sure they will happen if we possess a literate, inquisitive, and enterprising labor force. The creation and sustenance of such a labor force is a social process and it makes the successful implementation of any technology policy the result of investment in building up the requisite social foundations. The modern history of labor use has scarcely proceeded along these lines, however (see Rashid 1997 for a historical review).

The appropriateness of the Fordist model has also been called into question by new alternatives to mass production, such as the Just In Time (JIT) production (also called "flexible specialization") adopted in Japan. The smallness of readily available markets in Japan meant that firms needed to adapt their production strategies. Instead of mass-producing at low costs, they now had to produce relatively small quantities of high quality goods at affordable prices. This was a considerable challenge, requiring product innovation as well as cost minimization.

JIT manufacturing also required further changes in the philosophy of production, best exemplified by the automobile industry. Automobiles are discrete products—as opposed to dimensional products, which are sold by volume or weight. Resetting machinery for discrete products takes time; to reduce the costs associated with machine resetting, workers needed to have several skills. Because quality control became essential to every step of the production process, and because even research and development needed to be discussed factory-wide, unskilled workers with minimal initiative or independence, so appropriate to Fordism, became a liability. While JIT manufacturing requires intelligent, cooperative employees, there is, of course—just as in any other system—nothing to prevent these employees from being overworked.

SEE ALSO *Change, Technological; Productivity; Smith, Adam; Taylorism*

BIBLIOGRAPHY

Babbage, Charles. 1832. *On the Economy of Machinery and Manufactures.* London: C. Knight.

Cooper, Arnold, and Timothy Folta. 1999. Entrepreneurship and High Technology Clusters. In *The Blackwell Handbook of Entrepreneurship*, eds. Donald L. Sexton and Hans Landström, 348–367. Oxford: Blackwell.

Easterlin, Richard A. 1981. Why Isn't the Whole World Developed? *Journal of Economic History* 41 (1): 1–19.

Fransman, Martin. 1986. The Shaping of Technical Change. In *Technology, Innovation, and Change*, ed. Brian Elliot, 7–16. Edinburgh: University of Edinburgh.

Freeman, Christopher, John Clark, and Luc Soete. 1982. *Unemployment and Technical Innovation: A Study of Long Waves and Economic Development.* London: Frances Pinter.

Hamowy, Ronald. 1968. Adam Smith, Adam Ferguson, and the Division of Labour. *Economica* 35 (139): 249–259.

Kindleberger, Charles P. 1976. The Historical Background. Adam Smith and the Industrial Revolution. In *The Market and the State: Essays in Honor of Adam Smith*, eds. Thomas Wilson and Andrew S. Skinner, 1–25. Oxford: Clarendon.

Mayo, Elton. 1933. *The Human Problems of an Industrial Civilization.* New York: Macmillan.

Noble, David F. 1984. *Forces of Production: A Social History of Industrial Automation.* New York: Knopf.

Rashid, Salim. 1997. *The Myth of Adam Smith.* Cheltenham, U.K.: Edward Elgar.

Rosenberg, Nathan. 1970. Economic Development and the Transfer of Technology: Some Historical Perspectives. *Technology and Culture* 11 (4): 550–575.

Smith, Adam. [1776] 1840. *An Inquiry into the Nature and Causes of the Wealth of Nations,* ed. E. G. Wakefield. London: Charles Knight.

Smith, Adam. [1776] 1976. *An Introduction to the Nature and Causes of the Wealth of Nations,* eds. Roy H. Campbell and Andrew S. Skinner. Oxford: Clarendon Press.

Stewart, Dugald. 1855. *Lectures on Political Economy.* Vol. 8–9 of the *Collected Works of Dugald Stewart,* ed. Sir William Hamilton. Edinburgh: T. Constable, 1854–1860.

Ure, Andrew. 1835. *The Philosophy of Manufactures; or, An Exposition of the Scientific, Moral, and Commercial Economy of the Factory System of Great Britain.* London: C. Knight.

Salim Rashid

DIVORCE AND SEPARATION

Divorce and separation are legal actions that affect the civil marriage contract. In the United States, marriage, separation, annulment, and divorce are regulated individually by the states, although some federal benefits are available only to those who are legally married. In most cases, the person filing for the divorce or separation must be a resident for at least ninety days in the jurisdiction where the legal action is filed. Divorce is the formal dissolution of a marriage. Separation formalizes an agreement between a married couple who live apart. Some states and countries require some period of legal separation before divorce. For divorce and separation, the legal agreement may decide child custody, support, and visitation, division of assets and marital property, debt, marital home possession, and in cases of abuse, a protection order.

Separation does not end the marriage. People may choose separation over divorce for a variety of reasons, including religious or financial grounds; for the sake of the children; to retain health care, military, or tax benefits; or to live apart to assess if divorce is the best option. A separation agreement can be converted to a divorce decree.

Marriage annulment is a legal procedure declaring that the marriage never existed. The grounds for an annulment vary by state, but may apply to marriages involving underage partners (with the age varying by state), blood relatives with relationships closer than first cousins, or the absence of mental or physical capacity to consent to marriage. Other grounds for marriage annulment include intoxication, duress, refusal of intercourse, impotence,

and bigamy. Most annulled marriages are brief. In the case of longer marriages the court divides the property of the parties and can determine rights and obligations related to the marital children. Children from an annulled marriage are legitimate. The history of marriage annulment dates back to Henry VIII (1491–1547), who had four of his six marriages annulled.

In the Catholic Church a member who wants to remarry after a divorce or to marry a divorced non-Catholic must have the prior marriage nullified. This is a religious rather than a legal process.

In the United States the trend since the 1960s has been toward no-fault divorces with joint legal custody of children. This contrasts with the former, adversarial process in which one person must prove a "fault" such as adultery, cruelty, desertion, habitual drunkenness, or insanity. Under no-fault laws the court must find irreconcilable differences or that the couple lived apart for a designated period of time. Critics blame no-fault divorce for the increasing divorce rate. In 1997, Louisiana was the first state to adopt "covenant marriages," by which couples must enter into premarital counseling, and in the event that they eventually separate, undergo mandatory marital counseling, then wait two years after separation or provide proof of fault before divorcing.

In Canada the federal government sets divorce law that applies equally across provinces. No-fault divorce was adopted in 1986, allowing divorce for couples who have been separated for one year. In England marriage can be terminated by a "dissolution of marriage" or a "nullification," the equivalent of an annulment in the United States.

In the United States only Massachusetts currently allows same-sex marriages. Canada has also recognized civil marriage between same sex partners. Many same-sex couples from other states travel to marry in Massachusetts, and the legal systems in their home states must determine how to deal with those relationships if the couples want to dissolve them, and what rights and responsibilities couples have upon dissolution, including custody and visitation rights for children born or adopted during the relationships. Similar challenges face states that grant to same-sex couples domestic partnerships, which outline the legal rights and responsibilities of those relationships but do not recognize them as marriages. In 1986 Congress adopted the Defense of Marriage Act (DOMA), which stated that no state has to recognize a marriage between persons of the same sex, even if the marriage was concluded or recognized in another state. In addition, the federal government may not recognize same-sex or polygamous marriages for any purpose, even if concluded or recognized by one of the states.

In the United States the divorce laws of the state the couple resides in, not the state they were married in, govern the dissolution; this is similar in many other countries. International divorces, in which the couple married in one country and then moved to another, face special difficulties. In addition, some countries that have religiously based governments, including Islamic and Jewish states, require religious divorces; others, including Japan and Taiwan, require only a registry office divorce, and only one spouse needs to file the paper. There are also "quickie" divorces in places such as the Dominican Republic, where there is little or no residence requirement.

DEMOGRAPHICS

Divorce rates have been rising in the United States, South Korea, and the nations of the European Union; Japan has the lowest rate. Divorce rates rose slowly from the 1860s to about 1919. There were more dramatic increases after both world wars, followed by a decrease and then a relatively stable divorce rate from 1950 to the mid-1960s. After a dramatic increase between the late 1960s through the mid-1970s, partially due to the introduction of no-fault divorces and economic prosperity, divorce rates in the United States declined, and this decline continues today. The divorce rate was 4.7 per thousand married women fifteen and older from 1990 to 1993, decreasing to 4.0 in 2001. In 2005 in the United States there were 7.5 new marriages for every 3.6 divorces per 1,000 people (Baca Zinn and Eitzen 2005).

In the United States, between 40 and 52 percent of all first marriages end in divorce, whereas in Europe the rate is one in three or four. Approximately 17 percent of married couples are separated at some time. In any given year, between 2 and 4 percent of marriages are granted legal separations. One in five marriages ends in divorce or separation in the first five years, one in three in the first ten years, and more than two-fifths within fifteen years. In the United States divorce rate is higher for remarried white women, whereas for African American women the rate is the same for once-wed or remarried women. In general, the divorce rate is lowest for white and Latino couples, and more than twice as high for African Americans.

A curvilinear relationship exists between income and divorce. Women in very low- and very high-income marriages have higher rates of divorce. Wives with higher education and husbands with higher income are less likely to divorce. Black and white couples who attend religious services together are less likely to divorce (Park 2004).

Age at first marriage is a strong predictor of marital stability. Almost 60 percent of those who marry at or before the age of eighteen dissolve their marriages within fifteen years. A factor accounting for both younger marriages and higher divorce rates is premarital pregnancy and birth. The presence of children also affects the likelihood of divorce. Childless couples divorce at a higher rate than those with children. And there is a curvilinear relationship between number of children and divorce: Divorce rates decrease as families have more children, up to four; those with more than four children are more likely to divorce than those without children. Families with children under three years old are less likely to divorce than those with children over fifteen.

Divorce is more common among those who lived together before marriage. About 40 percent of couples who lived together premaritally divorced after ten years of marriage, compared to 31 percent of those who did not live together.

Religion influences divorce. Twenty-four percent of all adults will experience a divorce over the course of their lifetime. The highest rate is for Jews (30%). Baptists have the highest rate among Christians (29%)—even those who identify themselves as "born again" have a higher than average divorce rate (27%). Protestants and Mormons have a rate of 25 percent, whereas Catholics have a rate of 21 percent (Baca Zinn and Eitzen 2005).

IMPLICATIONS OF DIVORCE AND SEPARATION FOR FAMILIES

Ex-husbands generally experience an increased standard of living after divorce. They are most often the primary wage earners in the family, and after divorce more of their income stays with them. They have more money and leisure time available to them. About 85 percent of men do not seek primary physical custody of their children, so they have greater freedom for dating, furthering their education, travel, hobbies, and sexual relationships. After divorce, males often have difficulty maintaining a routine for eating, sleeping, shopping, cooking, and cleaning. They see their children relatively rarely, and thus experience isolation. The difficulty of adjusting to divorce results in higher rates of illness and death for men.

Typically, women experience a dramatic decline in their standard of living after a divorce—to about half what their living standard had been before divorce, or about half that of divorced men. To improve their situations, divorced women often rely on several sources of wealth, including alimony, which is awarded to 15 percent of divorced women. Equitable division of marital property assumes that men and women are equal at the time of divorce, but awarding primary residences to women assumes that they are able to pay the mortgages, an assumption that disadvantages women who work in the home or those who make low wages. Two-thirds of divorced mothers are awarded child support, but in at least 60 percent of the cases fathers are late with payments or do not pay at all. Women may also experience isolation and over-extension due to their child care, household, and wage-earning responsibilities.

Women also may benefit from divorce. Like men, they experience an increase in freedom, albeit freedom mediated by child and household responsibilities. Domestic violence lessens, and as the divorce rate rises there is a decrease in both suicide and murder rates of women. However, women in separated couples are the group at the greatest risk of assault and murder by intimates.

At various times in history conservative social critics have argued that divorce contributes to a negative decline in the American family, and that the lack of a male role model for children of divorce has a negative effect, and can lead to crime and delinquency. But research indicates that children are resilient in coping with a divorce, and that three out of four kids become healthy and competent adults. The large majority of children in divorced families do not experience severe or long-term problems. For those children in abusive families, the quality of family life may increase.

Girls seem to fare better than boys (Seltzer 1994). Antisocial behavior on the part of children in divorced families is related to lack of parental control rather than the divorce itself. Family size, too, influences children's well-being after divorce—the larger the family, the greater the stress on single parents, which may negatively affect children. Race also affects children's experience of divorce. African American children are more likely to be economically disadvantaged in society and may experience more detrimental effects of divorce.

Parental contact also affects children. Parents with higher socioeconomic status are more likely to have joint legal custody of their children, and so those fathers are more likely to spend time with their children. Contact with both parents helps children adjust favorably to divorce. Children fare better when parents live in the same geographic region, which facilitates visitation.

The economic status of the family importantly predicts the problems families and children face. Children in fatherless families are more likely to drop out of school, use drugs, and engage in delinquent behavior, but the underlying cause is not divorce, but poverty (Kimmel 2004).

Economic security needs to compensate for the drop in the standard of living for divorced families. This could include policies such as a living wage for all workers to counter the low wages that divorced women find themselves confined in. There should also be a safety net providing job training and societal assistance to women and children after a divorce. This assistance could take the form of job training, public employment, quality day care assistance, adequate diet support and medical care. All would reduce the stress on children and families experiencing divorce.

SEE ALSO *Children; Family Functioning; Family Structure; Marriage; Marriage, Same-Sex; Mental Illness; Poverty; Religion; Stress*

BIBLIOGRAPHY

Ahrons, Constance. 2007. Introduction to the Special Issue on Divorce and Its Aftermath. *Family Process* 46 (1): 3–8.

Amato, Paul, and Danielle D. DeBoer. 2001. The Transmission of Marital Instability across Generations. *Journal of Marriage and the Family* 63: 1038–1051.

Baca Zinn, Maxine, and D. Stanley Eitzen. 2005. *Diversity in Families.* 7th ed. Boston: Allyn and Bacon.

Bachman, R., and L. E. Saltzman. 1995. Violence Against Women: Estimates from the Redesigned National Crime Victimization Survey. U.S. Dept. of Justice, Bureau of Justice Statistics. http://www.ojp.usdoj.gov/bjs/pub/ascii/femvied.txt

Coltrane, Scott, and Michele Adams. 2003. The Social Construction of the Divorce "Problem": Morality, Child Victims, and the Politics of Gender. *Family Relations* 52 (4): 363.

Coontz, Stephanie. 2007. The Origins of Modern Divorce. *Quarterly Journal of Economics* 46 (1): 7–17.

Georgetown Journal of Gender and the Law. 2001. *Annual Review of Gender and Sexuality Law.* Vol. 2 Num. 2.

Kimmel, Michael S. 2004. *The Gendered Society.* 2nd ed. New York: Oxford University Press.

Meckler, Laura. 2003. Want a Stable Marriage? Be Rich, Religious, over 20. *Associated Press*, July 25.

Morley, Jeremy. 2004. International Family Law. *New York Law Journal*, November 24.

Parke, Mary. 2003. Are Married Parents Really Better for Children? Couples and Marriage Research and Policy Brief. The Center for Law and Social Policy. http://www.clasp.org/publications/marriage_brief3_annotated.pdf.

Seltzer, Judith A. 1994. Consequences of Marital Dissolution for Children. *Annual Review of Sociology* 20: 235–266.

Stevenson, Betsey, and Justin Wolfers. 2006. Bargaining in the Shadow of the Law: Divorce Laws and Family Distress. *Quarterly Journal of Economics* 121(1): 267–288.

Pat Murphy

DIXIECRATS

Dixiecrats (a combination of "Dixie," referring to the Old South of the Confederacy, and "Democrats"), formally known as the States' Rights Democratic Party, were a splinter party formed by Southern Democrats in 1948 to oppose President Harry S. Truman's civil rights program. The term has also been used to refer to racially conservative Southern Democrats since then. With South Carolina

Governor J. Strom Thurmond leading the ticket, Dixiecrats carried four states but failed to stop Truman's reelection. The core Dixiecrat ideologies of "states' rights" and white supremacy have their roots in the antebellum South and still reverberate in the partisan alignment in the United States in the early twenty-first century.

The Democratic National Convention in 1948 approved a strong civil rights plank despite firm opposition from Southern delegates:

> We again state our belief that the racial and religious minorities must have the right to live, the right to work, the right to vote, the full and equal protection of the laws, on the basis of equality with all citizens guaranteed by the Constitution.…We call upon Congress to [act] in guaranteeing these basic and fundamental rights: (1) the right of full and equal political participation, (2) the right of equal opportunity in employment, (3) the right of security of person, (4) and the right of equal treatment in the service and defense of our nation. (Key 1984, p. 335)

In his fiery convention speech supporting this language, then-Minneapolis Mayor and Senate candidate (and future vice president and Democratic presidential nominee) Hubert H. Humphrey (1911–1978) did not mince words:

> To those who say … that we are rushing this issue of civil rights, I say to them we are 172 years late! To those who say … that this civil-rights program is an infringement on states' rights, I say this: the time has arrived in America for the Democratic Party to get out of the shadow of state's rights and walk forthrightly into the bright sunshine of human rights! (History News Network 2002)

In apparent response, thirty-five delegates from Mississippi and Alabama walked out of the convention, but the walkout had actually been planned for months.

On July 17, just days after the walkout, party leaders from Mississippi, Alabama, and South Carolina met in Birmingham, Alabama. They formed the States' Rights Democratic Party, nominated Thurmond for president and Governor Fielding Wright (1895–1956) of Mississippi for vice president, and issued a "declaration of principles" stating their opposition to "the elimination of segregation, the repeal of miscegenation statutes, the control of private employment by federal bureaucrats called for by the misnamed civil rights program" (Frederickson 2001, p. 240).

In an effort to reach out to the non-Southern Republican members of the Conservative Coalition forged in the 1930s to oppose President Franklin D. Roosevelt's more ambitious New Deal programs,

Thurmond's campaign rhetoric focused largely on states' rights and limited government, leading some conservatives more than fifty years later to claim that these were the true bases of the Dixiecrat movement. This view, however, is naive at best: white supremacy was the party's raison d'être and driving force. As Thurmond thundered to the Birmingham meeting, "There's not enough troops in the Army to force the southern people to break down segregation and admit the Negro race into our theaters, into our swimming pools, into schools and into our homes" (Frederickson 2001, p. 242). The party's platform explicitly supported racial segregation and opposed all efforts to end it as "utterly destructive of the social, economic and political life of the Southern people." Local appeals for votes were also perfectly clear in their intentions—an official sample ballot from the Mississippi State Democratic Party declared:

> A vote for the Truman electors is a direct order to our Congressmen and Senators from Mississippi to vote for passage of Truman's so-called civil-rights program in the next Congress. This means the vicious FEPC [Fair Employment Practices Committee]—anti-poll tax—anti-lynching and anti-segregation proposals will become the law of the land and our way of life in the South will be gone forever. (Mississippi Historical Society, undated)

In the end, the Dixiecrats carried the four states in which they were the official Democratic ticket and received one electoral vote from a "faithless" Tennessee elector. The ticket received 1,169,134 votes in total, 55 percent of which were from the four states they carried, and 99 percent of which were from Southern or border states. Even in the South, they received only 20 percent of the vote, while nationwide, they received only 2.4 percent. Thurmond and Wright received thirty-nine electoral votes, but that was not nearly sufficient to deny Truman his majority. Despite the loss, Dixiecrats remained strong enough in the Congress to block meaningful civil rights laws until the 1960s.

ORIGIN OF THE DIXIECRAT MOVEMENT

The historical roots of the Dixiecrat movement go deep into U.S. history—the Dixiecrat core ideologies of "states' rights" and white supremacy have their roots in the antebellum South and the political philosophy of John Calhoun (1782–1850). The Civil War and Reconstruction cemented these philosophies in the South with the region becoming the one-party "Solid South" after Reconstruction. From 1880 through 1924, with very few exceptions, Southern and border states voted reliably Democratic for president; local and state offices were similarly dominated by Democrats. Meanwhile, African Americans, where they could vote, were loyal Republicans, based on the same Civil War alignment. Through the 1930s, both parties kept racial issues out of electoral politics, although cases on segregation and voting rights were playing out in the courts.

The first major break in the Solid South occurred in 1928 when several southern states (excluding the four later carried by Thurmond) went for Herbert Hoover, because of the Democratic nomination of New York Governor Al Smith—a big city Northern Catholic and a "wet" to boot. In *Southern Politics* (1984), however, V. O. Key showed that voting patterns of "Hoovercrats" in 1928 were the precise opposite of Dixiecrats in 1948. These states all returned to the fold throughout the New Deal era.

Issues of racial justice returned to the political stage in the 1940s, beginning with A. Philip Randolph's (1889–1979) March on Washington movement (1941), which resulted in Roosevelt's 1941 Executive Order 8802 establishing the Fair Employment Practices Committee (FEPC) and banning employment discrimination by defense contractors. The publication of Gunnar Myrdal's *An American Dilemma* in 1944 made American racism an international embarrassment and forced mainstream political and intellectual leaders to reluctantly reexamine racial issues. During the Roosevelt era, African Americans shifted to the Democratic Party as well because of Roosevelt's progressive social policies, becoming key components of the party's electoral coalition by the 1940s.

World War II (1939–1945) created the bitter irony of African American troops fighting and dying overseas to fight Adolf Hitler's racist ideology only to return home to Jim Crow. (The importance of this as a grassroots catalyst of the civil rights movement of the 1950s and 1960s is often overlooked.) The irony was not lost on Truman, who in 1947 began moving toward a civil rights program. This included a strongly worded speech to the National Association for the Advancement of Colored People in June, the publication of the report of his Committee on Civil Rights in October (which recommended the steps that were later included in the 1948 Democratic Party platform), and Truman's strong endorsement of the report in his January 1948 State of the Union speech. With fair warning, the Southern Democratic maneuvering to fight Truman and his policies thus began several months before the convention.

After Truman, with Republicans beginning to make incursions into Southern electoral politics, Democrats played down racial issues to avoid another revolt. Meanwhile, Republicans became publicly associated with civil rights, with *Brown v. Board of Education* (1954), President Dwight D. Eisenhower's forced integration of Little Rock public schools (1957), and the civil rights acts of 1957 and 1960, passed despite Senate filibusters by the conservative "boll weevil" Southern Democrats. Thus, issues other than race dominated the elections of 1952, 1956, and 1960. In contrast to 1928, the Solid South provided Democratic nominee Adlai Stevenson's only electoral votes, including all four Dixiecrat states in 1952.

With the 1964 election, the Democratic Party decisively donned the mantle of civil rights party, while the Republicans backed off. Democrats passed the stronger Civil Rights Act of 1964 (over another filibuster) and President Lyndon Johnson advocated passionately for a new voting rights act with federal enforcement; Republican candidate Barry Goldwater opposed these measures on the grounds of states' rights and limited government. While Goldwater himself was not overtly segregationist, he was not unaware of what a states' rights agenda meant in the South of the 1960s. Thus, it was no coincidence that in Johnson's landslide election the only states Goldwater carried, other than his home state of Arizona, were the four Dixiecrat states plus Georgia. Thurmond (now a senator) switched parties, leading a gradual movement of Dixiecrats to the Republican Party, and bringing their issues with them.

The shift in the parties' platforms was clearly perceived by the voters as well. The 1960 National Election Study survey showed that roughly equal percentages of Americans believed that either Democrats or Republicans were the party most likely to follow civil rights policies, with 70 percent of respondents perceiving "no difference" on school segregation and 62 percent finding no difference on policies of the FEPC. In the 1964 study, most respondents chose the Democrats as the party most likely to follow civil rights policies (50.2% on school segregation and 54.3% on employment practices), while only a small minority (6.1% on school segregation and 6.5% on employment practices) picked the Republicans.

In 1968, with Democratic Party support for civil rights now personified by nominee Humphrey, Alabama Governor George Wallace (1919–1998) attempted to revive the Dixiecrat movement through his American Independent Party. Simultaneously, Republican candidate Richard Nixon's (1913–1994) campaign adopted a "Southern Strategy" designed to split apart once and for all the New Deal coalition that had included African Americans, urban ethnic Catholics and other blue-collar workers, and white Southerners. Both Nixon and Wallace campaigned on "law and order," benefiting from a white backlash against recent race riots, while Wallace added the familiar focus on states' rights and integration. Wallace carried five Southern states, including three of the Dixiecrat states, and won forty-six electoral votes—not enough to deny Nixon the election, despite the very close popular vote. Wallace's national appeal was far stronger than Thurmond's; he received 13.5 percent of the vote nationally, including at least 10 percent in a number of states outside the South.

INFLUENCE OF DIXIECRATS CONTINUES

The Southern Strategy contributed to a period of sustained Republican success at the presidential level, with Republicans winning seven of ten elections through 2004. Nevertheless, the long-awaited Republican realignment failed to materialize; Democrats controlled the House of Representatives until 1994 and the Senate for all but six of those years, due in part to the presence in both the House and the Senate of substantial numbers of Southern Democrats. Conservative white Southern voters split their tickets between conservative Democrats at the local and state level, while voting Republican at the national level, creating a "split-level realignment." While overtly racist rhetoric was not a factor during this period, many social scientists found new forms of "symbolic racism," or "coded racism" in such issues as welfare, crime, cities, and immigration that appealed to white voters' underlying racial resentments. Others have noted the finding that most white voters express a belief in broad principles of racial equality, but oppose specific policies designed to address them.

In the early 1990s many conservative Southern Democrats retired, while others were defeated, leading to the Republican takeover of the Congress in 1994, with Southerners holding all of the top leadership posts in both houses. Ironically, a number of white Democratic incumbents were defeated because the creation of "majority-minority" districts removed loyal Democratic African American voters from their districts.

The electoral sea change of 1994 concluded the process begun with the convention walkout forty-six years earlier—the switch of southern conservative white Democrats to the Republican Party. From the 1950s when there were essentially no Southern Republicans in Congress to the 1980s when the Democrats led slightly, to the 1990s when Southern Democrats became an endangered species—Republicans began to hold the vast majority of Southern congressional seats. It is a testament to the power of party identification as a lifetime psychological attachment that it took the death or retirement of the pre–civil rights generation—both in government and in the electorate—to accomplish this.

Along with the shift of Dixiecrats to the Republican Party, this period also saw the death of the boll weevils' opposites, Northern liberal "gypsy moth" Republicans. While this species was never as important as its Southern counterpart, they combined to require bipartisan coalitions for all major legislation as recently as the early 1990s. Also because of a combination of retirements and electoral losses (the 2006 elections left Christopher Shays the sole Republican House member in all of the twenty-two seats of New England), the North in 2007 was even more dominated by Democrats than the South was by Republicans, with party loyalty (and party polarization) in congressional voting at historical highs in both parties. This state of affairs, with its intense ideological and regional polarizations, may be the Dixiecrats' most enduring legacy of all.

In an odd footnote to Dixiecrat history, in December 2002, incoming Senate Majority Leader Trent Lott, a Republican from Mississippi, was forced to step down from his leadership post after making a statement at Thurmond's 100th birthday party that seemed to endorse the Dixiecrat platform of 1948: "I want to say this about my state: When Strom Thurmond ran for president we voted for him. We're proud of it. And if the rest of the country had followed our lead we wouldn't have had all these problems over all these years, either" (Edsall 2002, p. A06). Following Lott's reelection in 2006 and the Democratic takeovers, Lott was voted minority whip, making him the number-two Republican leader in the Senate.

SEE ALSO *Civil Rights Movement, U.S.; Democratic Party, U.S.; Desegregation; Jim Crow; Johnson, Lyndon B.; Key, V. O., Jr.; Minorities; New Deal, The; Nixon, Richard M.; Republican Party; Roosevelt, Franklin D.; Segregation; Southern Strategy; Thurmond, Strom; Truman, Harry S.*

BIBLIOGRAPHY

Edsall, Thomas B. 2002. Lott Decried for Part of Salute to Thurmond: GOP Senate Leader Hails Colleague's Run As Segregationist. *Washington Post*, December 7: A06.

Frederickson, Kari. 2001. *The Dixiecrat Revolt and the End of the Solid South.* Chapel Hill: University of North Carolina Press.

History News Network. 2002. The Speech by Hubert Humphrey that Helped Trigger Strom Thurmond's Candidacy for President in 1948. December 16. George Mason University. http://hnn.us/articles/1165.html.

Key, V. O., Jr., with Alexander Heard. 1984. *Southern Politics in State and Nation.* Rev. ed. Knoxville: University of Tennessee Press.

Mississippi Historical Society. (undated). This is the Official Democratic Ticket in Mississippi. Mississippi History Now. http://mshistory.k12.ms.us/features/feature7/ms_demo_ballot.html.

Rae, Nicol C. 1994. *Southern Democrats.* New York: Oxford University Press.

Joel David Bloom

DJILAS, MILOVAN

SEE *New Class, The.*

DNA

SEE *Genomics.*

DOBZHANSKY, THEODOSIUS
1900–1975

Theodosius Dobzhansky, born in the town of Nemirov in the Ukraine on January 25, 1900, was one of the most influential biologists of the twentieth century. He is generally regarded as the pioneer of evolutionary genetics, a field established in the 1930s that sought to integrate Darwinian selection theory with Mendelian genetics. Much of this work was summarized in Dobzhansky's magnum opus, *Genetics and the Origin of Species,* published in 1937. It was so influential and widely read that it is regarded as the first "textbook" of evolutionary biology in the twentieth century.

The only child of Sophia Voinarsky and Grigory Dobrzhansky, a high-school mathematics teacher, Dobzhansky early on manifested an interest in natural history and collected insects and especially butterflies in the area of Kiev. He attended the University of Kiev and graduated in 1921 with a major in biology. He subsequently accepted a position on the faculty of agriculture at the Polytechnic Institute of Kiev, where, through the influence of plant geneticist Gregory Levitsky, Dobzhansky's interests shifted from the systematics of insects like the ladybird beetle (the *Coccinelidae*) to the newer areas of genetics. Levitsky was part of a wider scientific movement in the Soviet Union that included such individuals as Nikolai Ivanovich Vavilov (1887–1943) and Sergei Chetverikov (1880–1959). These scientists were following efforts in American genetics to understand the mechanism of Mendelian heredity through model organisms, such as the fruit fly (*Drosophila sp.*). In 1924 Dobzhansky moved to Leningrad (Saint Petersburg), where he became a lecturer in genetics under the wing of Yuri Filipchenko and where he continued to study genetics by turning to basic laboratory studies of *Drosophila melanogaster*. At this time, he married a coworker in genetics, Natalie (or "Natasha") Sivertsev, who was to be his lifelong companion and coworker; they had one daughter, Sophie.

In 1927 Dobzhansky accepted a fellowship from the Rockefeller Foundation to study genetics with the American leader in the area, Thomas Hunt Morgan (1866–1945), and his group of fly geneticists at Columbia University, a group that included A. H. Sturtevant (1891–1970), Calvin Bridges (1889–1938), and H. J. Muller (1890–1967). While working as an assistant to Morgan, Dobzhansky learned of the latest techniques and insights into understanding the cytogenetics of the fruit fly. In 1928 Dobzhansky moved to the California Institute of Technology with Morgan and subsequently became assistant professor of genetics in 1929.

Dobzhansky's most notable breakthrough was made in 1933 when he started working with the geographically diverse *Drosophila pseudoobscura*. He also began to combine the laboratory methods common to the Morgan group with his interests in systematics and biogeography, which reflected his earlier Russian training. His research into the evolutionary history of this complex group of flies was aided by his novel use of the giant salivary or *polytene* chromosome, which permitted the reconstruction of the phylogenetic history of the model organism. This research formed the backbone of what became known as the genetics of natural populations (GNP) series, a set of studies published as papers and monographs that explored the range of species, races, and varieties of this group of flies and that sought to understand the process of speciation in genetic terms. It also informed Dobzhansky's 1937 book, his increasing independence from Morgan's fly group, and his interaction with American mathematical theorist Sewall Wright (1889–1988).

By the late 1930s Dobzhansky was recognized as one of the central figures in the "new" or "modern" synthesis of evolution that integrated Darwinian selection theory and natural history with laboratory methods and insights gleaned from Mendelian genetics. Dobzhansky increasingly drew younger workers to him, and developed an international reputation for being a "charismatic" mentor.

In 1940 he accepted a position at Columbia University, where he continued his research on *Drosophila*. In the 1950s his interests took a more global direction when he traveled to South America to study the speciation patterns in tropical *Drosophila*. In 1962 he moved yet again to Rockefeller University, where he remained until his retirement in 1970.

Dobzhansky's interests were broad and included the application of genetics to evolution and to the understanding of human beings. He wrote extensively, especially in his later years, on subjects with anthropological and philosophical themes. His synthesis of evolution and cultural anthropology appeared in 1962 under the title *Mankind Evolving*. In 1967 he revealed his lifelong interest in the existential aspects of evolution and in traditional religious concerns in *The Biology of Ultimate Concern*.

Becoming one of the most famous Soviet émigrés in the United States, Dobzhansky closely monitored the progress of science in the Soviet Union and was especially active in campaigning against biologist Trofim Lysenko (1898–1976) and his destructive policies against Soviet genetics. Despite his feeling a strong connection to his first home, Dobzhansky was never allowed to return there.

Following his retirement, Dobzhansky moved to the University of California in Davis, where he continued to supervise an active group of geneticists. He died there on December 18, 1975, after a long battle with leukemia. Although he was closely associated with the newer evolutionary biology of the twentieth century, he remained fundamentally religious and was an active member of the Russian Orthodox Church.

SEE ALSO *Racial Classification*

BIBLIOGRAPHY

Adams, Mark B. 1994. *The Evolution of Theodosius Dobzhansky: Essays on His Life and Thought in Russia and America.* Princeton, NJ: Princeton University Press.

Ayala, Francisco J. 1985. Theodosius Dobzhansky. *Biographical Memoirs National Academy of Sciences* 55: 163–213.

Levene, Howard, Lee Ehrman, and Rollin Richmond. 1970. Theodosius Dobzhansky Up to Now. In *Essays in Evolution and Genetics in Honor of Theodosius Dobzhansky*, eds. Max K. Hecht and William C. Steere, 1–41. New York: Appleton-Century Crofts.

Levine, Louis, ed. 1995. *Genetics of Natural Populations: The Continuing Importance of Theodosius Dobzhansky.* New York: Columbia University Press.

Lewontin, R. C., John A. Moore, William B. Provine, and Bruce Wallace, eds. 1981. *Dobzhansky's Genetics of Natural Populations I-XLIII.* New York: Columbia University Press.

Vassiliki Betty Smocovitis

DOCUMENTARY STUDIES

Documentary studies constitute an important approach in social science research. Because institutions are keen on keeping a record on their actions, documentary sources form the basis for understanding institutional behaviors. In using documentary sources, researchers are able to develop classification schemes or taxonomies to clarify societal actions and individual choices. Documentary sources are often used in conjunction with other data collection methods, such as interviews, surveys, and site observations.

Documentary studies are well suited to examine the functions and operation of how government works. In the United States the separation of powers creates a functional division of responsibilities among the three branches of government. Constitutional studies clearly rely on court decisions, judicial reviews, and lower court opinions. Students of legislative decisions can focus on congressional debate, hearings, and actions. Presidential scholars can review volumes of White House papers and archival records (such as tapes of conversations between the president and his staff).

Governmental documents enable social scientists to understand decisions made at critical stages of the policy process. Documents from governmental sources provide policy objectives, options, and the rationale behind the chosen policy options. Analysis on the content of legislative proposals from initiation through committee hearings and the final votes on the floor have yielded theoretically rich perspectives. Theodore Lowi's (1972) comparative analysis on the content of and actions on several federal legislations led to his argument that the nature of the legislation or policy determines political interrelationship among key actors. Policies that allocate jobs and contracts to congressional districts tend to receive broad political support, whereas legislations that aim at redistributing resources to the needy population are politically polarized.

Federalism in the United States tends to complicate documentary analysis, because many governmental decisions are dispersed across states and cities, and contextual variations tend to challenge research efforts to generalize the findings from a few study sites. At the same time, local variations offer an opportunity for experimentation. Researchers of urban reform are keen on analyzing mayors' state-of-the-city speeches as well as city council minutes and voting outcomes. In public education, there are fifty state systems that define their own academic standards, and more than 14,000 locally elected school boards that govern their schools. Studies on school governance have drawn on school board minutes, collective-bargaining agreements, administrative guidelines, financial audits, and evaluation reports. In the context of intergovernmental relations, the literature on policy implementation pays particular attention to the goals of legislation, the definition of eligibility, and the extent to which the intended services and benefits are delivered to the targeted populations (Pressman and Wildavsky 1973). Studies of the federal implementation of education policy have relied on audit findings to identify if state and local agencies are meeting the federal program expectations (Wong 1990).

As the boundary between government and civil society changes, researchers are likely to pay more attention to a broader range of documentary sources. A study of congressional hearings suggests the rise of citizen-based action groups in shaping the direction of the government's role in social welfare since the postmaterialist era of the 1960s (Berry 1999). Using local newspapers as an information source, one study analyzed two major newspapers in one large city to examine editorial support for mayoral control of public schools (Wong and Jain 1999). Further, human conditions can be depicted through the making of, the study of, and the use of documentary films. This type of documentary work is carried out at the Center for Documentary Studies at Duke University and at the Southern Oral History Project at the University of North Carolina at Chapel Hill.

Documentary studies are likely to continue to play a prominent role in social science research. There has been a rapid proliferation and democratization of documentary sources as the World Wide Web has become more accessible to the public. Public-opinion polls, news articles, congressional hearings, and state audits of agencies, schools' performance, and for-profit organizations' performance, just to name a few, are now easily accessible through the World Wide Web. Archaeological sites and artifacts are often scanned into digitalized format for research purposes. The Internet search engine Google and some of the world's major university libraries formed a partnership to convert their entire collections into electronic formats that will be widely accessible. Traditional barriers to access, such as transportation cost, will no longer impede documentary research, both domestically and globally.

Finally, the politics of documentary analysis must be taken into consideration. Documents come from many sources, including public-regarding and interest-based organizations. More often than not, documentary sources, especially secondary analyses conducted by think tanks, reflect a certain bias. Too often, students overlook the need to cross-validate the content of the documents. Furthermore, for students who are interested in in-depth research, there is still a need to navigate the labor-intensive process of obtaining permission to use certain documentary sources from governmental agencies.

SEE ALSO *Film Industry; Narratives*

BIBLIOGRAPHY

Berry, Jeffrey. 1999. *The New Liberalism*. Washington, DC: Brookings Institution Press.

Lowi, Theodore. 1972. Four Systems of Policy, Politics, and Choice. *Public Administration Review*, 298–310.

Pressman, Jeffrey, and Aaron Wildavsky. 1973. *Implementation*. Berkeley: University of California Press.

Wong, Kenneth K. 1990. *City Choices: Education and Housing*. Albany: State University of New York Press.

Wong, Kenneth, and Pushpam Jain. 1999. Newspapers as Policy Actors in Urban School Systems: The Chicago Story. *Urban Affairs Review* 35 (2): 210–246.

Kenneth K. Wong

DOLL STUDY
SEE *Clark, Kenneth B.*

DOMESDAY BOOK
SEE *Census.*

DOMINANT STRATEGY
SEE *Zero-sum Game.*

DOMINO THEORY

The domino theory was articulated by President Dwight D. Eisenhower in an April 7, 1954, news conference in which he worried that if communism remained unchecked, the free world might endure "the 'falling domino' principle. [In that case] you have a row of dominoes set up, you knock over the first one, and what will happen to the last one is the certainty that it will go over very quickly. So you have the beginning of a disintegration [of democratic countries] that would have profound influences" (Eisenhower 1954, p. 382). According to that principle, a change in one country will "spill over," setting in motion the political transformation of an entire region.

GEORGRAPHIC AND POLITICAL ORIGINS

Of particular concern to American leaders at that time was the ongoing crisis in southeastern Asia, where the loss of Vietnam could be expected to lead to eventual Communist domination of Thailand, Indonesia, and perhaps New Zealand and Australia (Gaddis 1982). The application of the domino theory, however, was not limited to southeastern Asia. The growing momentum of communism and the falling of dominoes animated national security debates over American policies toward Western Europe and Latin America as well. After the Eisenhower administration, the Democratic administrations of John F. Kennedy and Lyndon Johnson continued to believe that setbacks in southeastern Asia in general and Vietnam in particular would have dire consequences.

Fears of dominoes falling were based primarily on two mutually reinforcing concerns. The first was that if the United States failed to support an ally against Communist agitation, Communist movements in neighboring countries and their Soviet and Chinese sponsors would be emboldened. Communist success would breed success, and failure to stem the tide early would push countries out of the American orbit, with disastrous long-term consequences. Second, that perception of threat was amplified by concerns that the inability of an American-sponsored government to suppress domestic insurgents or outside provocateurs would signal that the United States could not be counted on as a reliable alliance partner. In that case the insecurities of allied countries and the demonstrated inability or unwillingness of the United States to help overcome them would lead countries to pull away from the United States. On both counts American decision makers feared that seemingly small reverses in peripheral countries ultimately would lead to a massive redistribution of cold war power as country after country fell to Communist pressure.

Although the rhetoric of falling dominoes most often was used to articulate the dangers from the unchecked spread of Soviet expansion, some noted that dominoes might be induced to fall the other way as well. Soon after the end of the World War II (1939–1945) conservatives in the Truman administration advocated "rolling back" Soviet advances in Europe. Although the lexicon of falling dominoes had not been coined yet, the basic logic was the same: It was hoped that American successes would demonstrate the power of the West and the poverty of the Soviet alternative. If that policy was successful, it was hoped that it might set into motion a counterdomino effect in which European Soviet-styled authoritarian regimes were felled by a mix of domestic and Western pressure. The Soviets' continued de facto and then de jure domination of Central and Eastern Europe frustrated those early reactionary impulses to roll back the postwar status quo. Thereafter, the world's dominoes were seen as leaning against the United States from the 1950s through the 1970s.

THE REAGAN AND SECOND BUSH ADMINISTRATIONS

Despite the absence of a positive theory of a Communist rollback for much of the cold war, the idea did not die. After the collapse of détente in the late 1970s, many conservatives called for the Reagan administration to roll back communism in Europe and especially in Latin America. The intellectual basis for American overt and covert involvement in a number of military conflicts in the region, notably the 1983 invasion of Communist-held Grenada, indicated continued support for the concepts found in domino theory. Specifically, it was believed that American weakness in Latin America would lead to further Communist advances, whereas American successes not only would reverse that process but perhaps would lead to conditions in which established Communist regimes might be rolled back and ultimately expelled from Latin America. Again, the key point was the belief that

success breeds success and that small and even tangential victories early can have a snowball effect: Communist successes would increase the support for and allure of that centrally planned and authoritarian model, whereas American successes would reverse the trend and create conditions under which free markets and democracy could flourish.

The end of the cold war did not spell the end of the domino theory. In the first decade of the twenty-first century the Bush administration used the domino theory to motivate and justify its policies in the Middle East and the war on terror. The Bush White House feared that successes by Islamist groups such as Al-Qaeda threatened Western-friendly states and provided a recruiting tool for those opposed to American interests in that region. On the one hand, American and Western successes in routing those elements and spreading democracy throughout the Middle East would set in motion a liberalizing and democratizing dynamic that would bring peace and stability to an unsettled region. On the other hand, if the Islamisists' attacks on friendly governments and Western interests went unchecked, it would catalyze a counter-Western and counterdemocratic movement. According to the logic of the domino theory, the early victors in that struggle would prove their worthiness to be emulated and draw further recruits and converts to their cause; the losers would see their losses compounded as the struggle continued.

Again, the key assumption was that success creates a self-sustaining momentum that will lead to the domination of the region by one side or the other. Implicitly or explicitly that logic was given scholarly support by many "offensive" realists, such as William Wohlforth, who argued in 1999 that American willingness to serve as a leader and a supporter of democracy and free markets will lead to a pax Americana: a new era of American dominance and peace and cooperation.

CRITICISMS

The fact that the logic of domino theory has proved enduring does not mean that it is without critics. "Defensive" realists such as Kenneth Waltz (1998) and Christopher Layne (1993) argue that the success of a country holds within it the seeds of failure. They claim that as a country becomes more powerful, it threatens the sovereignty and autonomy of its neighbors, increasing their willingness to resist further expansion. Rather than going from strength to strength, aggressive countries encourage others to unite against them, and thus early successes make future expansion less rather than more likely.

According to the logic of balancing, early Communist success in southeastern Asia made countries such as Thailand and Japan more likely to support the

United States and pushed them farther from the Communist camp. Likewise, successes by Islamists are likely to drive states into closer cooperation with the United States out of fear that they could be next. At the same time, American activities in the region, such as the invasion and occupation of Afghanistan and Iraq, are likely to drive those governments away as they become increasingly wary of American power and influence. The defensive realist analysis thus turns the domino theory on its head. If it is correct, it should serve as both a comfort to American decision makers combating Islamists in the Middle East and a warning to those who would use American hegemony to launch a program of liberalization and democratization abroad.

SEE ALSO *Al-Qaeda; Cold War; Communism; Democratization; Eisenhower, Dwight D.; Fundamentalism, Islamic; Iraq-U.S. War; Johnson, Lyndon B.; Kennedy, John F.; Strategic Behavior; Vietnam War; Waltz, Kenneth*

BIBLIOGRAPHY

Eisenhower, Dwight D. 1954. *Public Papers of President Dwight D. Eisenhower.* Washington, DC: Office of the Federal Register, National Archives and Records Administration.

Gaddis, John L. 1982. *Strategies of Containment: A Critical Appraisal of Postwar American National Security Policy.* New York: Oxford University Press.

Layne, Christopher. 1993. The Unipolar Illusion: Why New Great Powers Will Rise. *International Security* 17 (4): 5–51.

Waltz, Kenneth N. 1998. The Emerging Structure of International Politics. *International Security* 18 (2): 44–79.

Wohlforth, William. 1999. Stability in a Unipolar World. *International Security* 24 (1): 5–41.

Solomon Major

DOPAMINE

Dopamine is a neurotransmitter that serves as a chemical messenger in the nervous system and permits individual nerve fibers (neurons) to communicate with each other. The dopamine neurotransmitter belongs to the class of compounds known as monoamines, and more specifically to a subclass of chemicals called catecholamines. Dopamine can act either as an inhibitory mechanism or an excitatory mechanism in the nervous system, depending on the location of dopamine neurons, and the receiving characteristics of the next neuron in the chain.

Dopamine activation has long been associated with increased motor output (i.e., increased physical activity) (Wise 2004). Hence, it is not surprising that dopamine depletion is associated with a variety of movement disorders, such as Parkinson's disease. Characterized by tremors, muscle rigidity, and lack of fine motor skills, Parkinson's is caused by a degeneration of dopamine projection fibers originating in a brain region called the substantia nigra. The fact that the administration of a substance (L-DOPA) that increases dopamine synthesis in this brain region is the primary approach to treating Parkinsonism underscores the importance of dopamine in the regulation of motor control and movement.

Changes in dopamine activity also are linked to the expression of certain psychological disorders, such as schizophrenia. Schizophrenia is characterized by shifting, illogical thought patterns, delusional thought processes, and hallucinations. The dopamine hypothesis of schizophrenia suggests that higher than normal levels of dopamine in the midbrain region of patients suffering from schizophrenia produce a biochemical imperative to engage in disordered behavior. Consistent with this position, the most commonly prescribed, and arguably the most effective, drug therapies for schizophrenia are dopamine receptor blockers. A compound labeled chlorpromazine (trade name Thorazine) is especially effective in reducing the symptoms of schizophrenia, and such dopamine antagonists when continued after treatment substantially lessen the chances for relapse compared to cases in which patients stop taking the drug.

There is evidence that blockade of dopamine transmission is associated with the devaluation of incentive systems, perhaps by affecting memory consolidation (Robbins and Everitt 2006). For instance, it is known that stamping-in of stimulus-response associations is blunted under conditions of reduced dopamine activity. Even once a behavior is learned, evidence shows that the ability to retrieve previously acquired information is reduced. Although the precise mechanisms responsible for these challenges to associative processes is not clear, it is clear that reward-seeking is diminished when dopamine systems are compromised.

There is a large literature that shows that a variety of rewarding events elevate the levels of dopamine in pleasure pathways of the brain. There are three major systems that are rich in dopamine fibers: the nigrostriatal system, the mesolimbic system, and the mesocortical system. Of the three, the pathway that has received the most attention from investigators of reward systems is the mesolimbic pathway. The dopamine projection neurons of the mesolimbic system originate in the ventral tegmental area of the midbrain and terminate in several forebrain regions, most importantly the nucleus accumbens. At one time it was believed that the nucleus accumbens constituted "reward central" and any events or substances that increased dopamine activity in this region served as rewards (Wise and Bozarth 1987). It is now known that other pathways and neurotransmitters are involved in defining reward properties, but the scientific community still maintains that elevated levels of dopamine in the nucleus accumbens contribute prominently to the rewarding effects associated with a variety of motivational processes, including the sex drive and hunger (Berridge and Robinson 1998).

Although dopamine plays a role in mediating a broad array of reinforcing (reward) activities, the topic that has been studied most is the modulatory role played by dopamine in determining the rewarding effects of psychoactive drugs. While dopamine is important for drugs such as heroin, marijuana, and alcohol, it does not appear to be crucial with respect to determining the reward value of these types of drugs. It is certain, however, that dopamine is the major neurotransmitter involved in defining the potency and addiction potential of psycho-stimulants such as cocaine and amphetamine. With respect to cocaine, the drug blocks the action of the dopamine transporter (DAT) in the nucleus accumbens. DAT is the reuptake chemical in the synaptic cleft (space between neurons where neurotransmitters are released) that moves dopamine back inside the releasing neuron and restores dopamine levels. When DAT is blocked by cocaine, dopamine remains in the cleft and continues to stimulate the postsynaptic neuron, thus producing euphoria. Amphetamine operates similarly to block dopamine reuptake, but also increases the frequency and amount of dopamine release.

SEE ALSO *Happiness; Needs; Neuroscience; Psychology; Schizophrenia; Wants*

BIBLIOGRAPHY

Berridge, K. C., and T. E. Robinson. 1998. What Is the Role of Dopamine in Reward: Hedonic Impact, Reward Learning, or Incentive Salience? *Brain Research Review* 28 (3): 309–369.

Robbins, T. W., and B. J. Everitt. 2006. A Role for Mesencephalic Dopamine in Activation: Commentary on Berridge (2006). *Psychopharmacology* 191 (3): 433–437.

Wise, Roy A. 2004. Dopamine, Learning, and Motivation. *Nature Reviews in Neuroscience* 5 (6): 483–494.

Wise, Roy A., and Michael A. Bozarth. 1987. A Psychomotor Stimulant Theory of Addiction. *Psychological Review* 94 (4): 469–492.

Jack Nation

DORNBUSCH-FISCHER-SAMUELSON MODEL

The Dornbusch-Fischer-Samuelson (DFS) model of international trade was introduced into the economics literature by three Massachusetts Institute of Technology (MIT) pro-

fessors in 1977. The model extends the widely accepted theory of comparative advantage of classical economist David Ricardo (1772–1823) to a conceptually infinite number of commodities, and the model integrates money and payments into what essentially had been a barter model. From DFS, greater understanding can be gleaned of the determinants of international trade patterns.

The model assumes the traditional classical framework of two trading countries and of labor being the sole factor of production. Suppose the countries are A and B. Country A exports any good where the wage rate for A's workers (WA) multiplied by the labor time needed to produce a unit of the good (LA) is less than the wage rate for B's workers (WB) multiplied by the labor time needed to produce a unit of that good in B (LB); that is, A exports any good where WA · LA < WB · LB. Country A imports goods where WA · LA > WB · LB. Expressed alternatively, country A will export goods where (WA/WB) < (LB/LA) and import goods for which (WA/WB) > (LB/LA), and, in DFS, a continuum of goods is specified in descending order of (LB/LA). (It is assumed for simplicity in this discussion that there are no transport costs and that the exchange rate is fixed at one unit of A's currency = one unit of B's currency.) Thus, if the wage ratio (WA/WB) is given, an examination of labor times can determine which goods in the continuum will be exported from A to B and which from B to A.

But what determines the wage ratio? As noted above, (WA/WB) would, when compared with the (LB/LA) ratios, determine the trade pattern; however, the trade pattern itself would also determine (WA/WB). For example, if the trade pattern is such that most of the different goods are exported from A to B and few goods are exported from B to A, then, in essence, there is strong demand for A's goods (and therefore for A's labor) and a trade surplus for country A. This demand for A's labor will bid up WA relative to WB. As WA rises, some goods previously exported from A to B [because (WA/WB) < (LB/LA) for those goods] will no longer be exported but will be imported by A because (WA/WB) has increased.

With this interaction of the trade pattern and wage rates, an equilibrium trading pattern is established. Equilibrium occurs with balanced trade (exports = imports for each country) and, for the borderline good in the continuum between the goods exported by A and those exported by B, (WA/WB) = (LB/LA). All goods where (WA/WB) < (LB/LA)—the goods with higher (LB/LA) ratios—will be A's exports. All goods for which (WA/WB) > (LB/LA)—the goods with the lower (LB/LA) ratios—will be B's exports. The original DFS article then introduced transportation costs, nontraded goods, and exchange rate and other considerations, but the major contribution was this simultaneous determination of relative wage rates and the trading pattern.

From this equilibrium position, the impact of changes in various economic elements can be analyzed. For example, suppose that all consumers turn their tastes relatively away from *A*'s goods and toward *B*'s goods. The new demand for *B*'s goods will increase the wage rate in *B* relative to the wage rate in *A*, a change that will cause some of *B*'s export goods to become *A*'s export goods. At the new equilibrium, balanced trade will be restored, country *B* will be exporting fewer different goods than originally, and *B*'s wages will have risen relative to *A*'s.

Consider next the perhaps surprising consequences of a uniform productivity increase in all of country *A*'s industries. With this productivity increase, LA (labor time needed for one unit of output) falls in each of *A*'s industries, and there will be a greater number of different goods exported from *A* to *B* than previously [because (LB/LA) will now be greater than (WA/WB) for some goods for which (LB/LA) was formerly less than (WA/WB)]. However, with more demand for *A*'s goods, (WA/WB) will rise and some of the new exports from *A* will revert back to being imports from *B*. In the model, though, the end result is that, on net, the number of different goods exported from *A* has increased and (WA/WB) has risen. Real income has increased in *A*, as its wages have gone up while the cost of producing its goods has gone down. Importantly, though, real income in country *B* also has risen. Even though *B*'s wage has declined relative to *A*'s wage, *B*'s absolute income has risen because the productivity increase has made *B*'s imports from *A* less expensive. Hence, a significant lesson from DFS is that productivity improvements under competition get transmitted across country borders—there is no absolute gain by one country and corresponding absolute loss for the other country.

The original DFS model has formed the basis for a number of extensions. Rudiger Dornbusch, Stanley Fischer, and Paul Samuelson themselves (1980) later incorporated a second factor (capital) into the model in a Heckscher-Ohlin framework and produced further conclusions. (*Heckscher-Ohlin* [or alternatively, *Heckscher-Ohlin-Samuelson*] refers to a standard trade model based on relative factor endowments of countries and relative factor intensities in the production of commodities.) The DFS model also has been extended, among much other research, in its Ricardian formulation to more than two countries in growth and customs union contexts (Wilson 1980; Appleyard at al. 1989) and into a multicountry framework, combined with monopolistic competition and econometric work, in its Heckscher-Ohlin formulation (Romalis 2004). A considerable amount of empirical work over the years has supported the relationship between labor productivity/costs and trade patterns pre-

dicted by the classical economists and DFS, a comprehensive example being Wendy Carlyn, Andrew Glyn, and John Van Reenen (2001). Criticisms of the model can be directed toward the realism of its assumptions of perfect competition and of smooth adjustment to technological change and other disturbances.

SEE ALSO *Absolute and Comparative Advantage; Heckscher-Ohlin-Samuelson Model; Rybczynski Theorem; Stolper-Samuelson Theorem; Trade*

BIBLIOGRAPHY

Appleyard, Dennis R., Patrick J. Conway, and Alfred J. Field Jr. 1989. The Effects of Customs Unions on the Pattern and Terms of Trade in a Ricardian Model with a Continuum of Goods. *Journal of International Economics* 27 (1/2): 147–164.

Carlyn, Wendy, Andrew Glyn, and John Van Reenen. 2001. Export Market Performance of OECD Countries: An Empirical Examination of the Role of Cost Competitiveness. *Economic Journal* 111 (468): 128–162.

Dornbusch, Rudiger, Stanley Fischer, and Paul A. Samuelson. 1977. Comparative Advantage, Trade, and Payments in a Ricardian Model with a Continuum of Goods. *American Economic Review* 67 (5): 823–839.

Dornbusch, Rudiger, Stanley Fischer, and Paul A. Samuelson. 1980. Heckscher-Ohlin Trade Theory with a Continuum of Goods. *Quarterly Journal of Economics* 95 (2): 203–224.

Romalis, John. 2004. Factor Proportions and the Structure of Commodity Trade. *American Economic Review* 94 (1): 67–97.

Wilson, Charles A. 1980. On the General Structure of Ricardian Models with a Continuum of Goods: Applications to Growth, Tariff Theory, and Technical Change. *Econometrica* 48 (7): 1675–1702.

Dennis R. Appleyard

DOUBLE CONSCIOUSNESS

SEE *Veil, in African-American Culture.*

DOUGLAS, MARY

SEE *Sanitation.*

DOUGLASS, FREDERICK
1818–1895

Born into chattel slavery on February 14, 1818, in Tuckahoe on the eastern shores of Maryland, Frederick Augustus Washington Bailey, later known as Frederick

Douglass, created in his time and for future generations one of the most remarkable personalities in American history. As a public figure, Douglass rose through the brutalities of slavery to become at the time of his death on February 20, 1895, the most famous black American in the world and black America's foremost intellectual voice.

Douglass's preeminence in American history is gleaned from his direct contacts with the antebellum abolitionist leadership of William Lloyd Garrison (1805–1879), the suffragist leadership of Susan B. Anthony (1820–1906) and Elizabeth Cady Stanton (1815–1902), the militancy of John Brown (1800–1859) and Martin Delany (1812–1885), his meetings with U.S. presidents from Abraham Lincoln (1809–1865) to James Garfield (1831–1881), and his government assignments as U.S. representative to the Dominican Republic and Haiti. However, there is a private side, of which too little is made, to Douglass's determination to engage the forces of evil, as he saw them, and to form alliances only when it was necessary for him to be heard by more people, read by more citizens, or at times, to present himself to another country, as he did on several occasions on his visits to the British Isles.

Douglass escaped from slavery in 1838. As his biographers have noted, in 1841 the former slave joined the Massachusetts Anti-Slavery Society under the leadership of Garrison, then leader of the radical wing of abolitionism and editor of the successful abolitionist newspaper, the *Liberator*. Douglass clearly modeled some of his behavior on Garrison. Both recognized the fiery spirit in each other, and both were orators connected by a passion to eliminate slavery. Through Garrison's group, Douglass earned money as a speaker, widened his circle of abolitionist acquaintances, and traveled to new places. The most compelling event in 1845 from an abolitionist's perspective was the publication of Douglass's first autobiography, *Narrative of the Life of Frederick Douglass, an American Slave, Written by Himself*. Garrison, in fact, wrote the preface. Douglass later wrote *My Bondage and My Freedom* (1855), and in 1881 he published *Life and Times of Frederick Douglass*, his final autobiography.

The *Narrative* made Douglass famous and started a long and distinguished career for this brave man, prolific writer, and articulate democratic voice. In page after page, he details the painful and violent experiences slaves faced as they were raped, murdered, bought, and sold away from their families. Douglass not only named the murdered, he named the murderers who went unpunished as well, thus providing graphic proof that no law protected slaves against these crimes. Furthermore, his writing critiqued the structure of authority by slicing through the rhetoric of the state to expose slaveholders, especially those professing religious faith, in their role as personal agents in a system of slavery allowed to exist simultaneously with the ideals of a free republic. The *Narrative* established him as a reliable and serious source for presenting any of the issues of his day requiring instruction and correction, most of them related to slavery.

By 1847, as the editor of the second black-owned newspaper in the United States, the *North Star*, Douglass had found that the uses of history enabled him to move back and forth between his private and public worlds. Douglass's use of history permitted him to speak about the signs of the times; it served, furthermore, to help him to judge civilization's behaviors for failing to subject the nation's moral faults to critical reflection. In this way, Douglass used history to critique reason. For him, the realities of slavery placed the present and the future of the United States in an untenable position: The country could not survive if it remained both slave and free. The purpose of Douglass's legacy to America and to the world is to uphold the principle of freedom as an inalienable human right.

Although supportive of each other, Douglass and Garrison split over the issue of the Constitution as a document that supported the institution of slavery. As early as 1851, the relationship between the two became strained as Douglass, having studied the debate over the Constitution, rejected Garrison's position that the Constitution was proslavery, whereas Douglass gradually saw the document as having the potential to eradicate slavery. Biographers have portrayed the breakup in Freudian terms as Douglass's rejection of Garrison as a father figure and his search for his own identity. It is also important to note that freedom for Douglass encompassed a deep, multilayered view of the self that had more to do with being "self-made" than with being a collaborator. His understanding of the Constitution, ultimately, had less to do with what Garrison asserted than with what Douglass realized through his own complex social and historical understanding of the place of all humankind, black and white, male and female, in a democratic social order.

Having been a slave, Douglass instinctively understood the political rights of women. Their demand for equal citizenship and the right to vote found him using his considerable oratorical gifts and intellect on their behalf. As one of the few men to attend the 1848 convention on the rights of women in Seneca Falls, New York, the editor of the *North Star* added to the masthead of the paper his now-famous conviction, formed at this political gathering: Right is of no sex; truth is of no color; God is the father of us all and we are all brethren. He understood that the criticisms leveled against women in their pursuit of freedom against male supremacy were the very same arguments used against the freeing of slaves. While his dedication to women's political rights never wavered,

Douglass did not always support the feminist leadership of Anthony and Stanton. They all supported civil war, but differed on other questions; for example, Douglass supported the Fifteenth Amendment giving black men the right to vote. Anthony and Stanton did not support this amendment because it did not offer the same rights to women.

In 1882 Frederick Douglass, now sixty-four-years old and known as the "sage of Anacostia" after the Washington, D.C., neighborhood where he lived, buried Anna Murray Douglass, his wife of forty-five years, who had long suffered from rheumatism. It was a considerable shock to the world when in 1884 he married Helen Pitts, forty-six, a white woman from a New York abolitionist family with deep roots in radical politics. The interracial marriage eliminated any distinction between private and public worlds: It clashed with social norms. Most whites and blacks, particularly members of the couple's own families, looked upon the marriage as a violation, and neither family fully embraced them. Nevertheless, Douglass and Pitts lived happily and traveled to the great cities of Europe and to Egypt. After his death, and in the face of opposition from his children, she lectured and secured donations to preserve Cedar Hill, their home in Anacostia. The couple is buried in the family plot in Mount Hope Cemetery in Rochester, New York.

SEE ALSO *Slavery*

BIBLIOGRAPHY

McFeely, William. 1991. *Frederick Douglass*. New York: Norton.

Quarles, Benjamin. [1948] 1968. *Frederick Douglass*. New York: Atheneum.

C. James Trotman

DOWN SYNDROME
SEE *Race and Psychology.*

DOWNS, ANTHONY
SEE *Spatial Theory.*

DOWRY AND BRIDE PRICE

Bride price and *dowry* are terms that refer to payments made at the time of marriage in many cultures, primarily in Asia and Africa. Bride price is typically paid by the groom or the groom's family to the bride's family. Dowry is typically paid by the bride's family to the bride or to the wedded couple. Thus bride price and dowry are not necessarily the converse of each other. However, in the twentieth century, dowry payments in South Asia have increasingly been demanded by and paid to the groom's family (and not just to the bride or the wedded couple). This suggests a usage of the term dowry to mean a *groom price*, the reverse of a bride price. Bride price and dowry need not be mutually exclusive, and marriage transfers in both directions can occur simultaneously. A complex set of norms may then govern the nature and the magnitude of payments in either direction.

PREVALENCE

Historically, the payment of bride price has been a more common occurrence than that of dowry. Only 3 percent of the cultures listed in Murdock's *Ethnographic Atlas* (1967) demonstrate the practice of dowry payments, whereas 66 percent follow a norm of bride price. Dowries were common in the Near East, Europe, East Asia, South Asia, and some parts of the Americas. Although the custom of dowry payment has disappeared in most regions in the West, it remains widespread in South Asia. Bride prices were known to have prevailed extensively in Africa and also in areas of mainland, South, and East Asia, and North and South America.

Both dowry and bride price regimes were present in South Asia in the early part of the twentieth century; in the second half of the century, dowry amounts were inflated, including a switch from bride price to dowry in many areas where the former practice was dominant.

CHARACTERISTICS OF MARRIAGE PAYMENTS

The payment of bride price can take several forms. *Bride price* or *bride wealth* is typically a transfer in the form of livestock, goods, or money from the groom (or his family) to the bride's kinsmen. *Bride service* refers to a transfer in the form of labor or other services rendered by the groom to the bride's family. Both these forms of payment can be substantial in magnitude. In contrast, a *token bride price* is usually a small symbolic payment made by the groom's family to the bride's. Finally, *woman exchange* refers to the transfer of a sister or other female relative of the groom to the bride's family in exchange for the bride.

A *dowry* or *groom price* is a payment made from the bride's family to the bride, the groom, the wedded couple, or the groom's family. It may consist of movable property such as money, ornaments, clothing, household goods, or cattle. In some cases land is also provided as a part of the payment.

The norms associated with marriage payments can be complex and vary largely across societies. These norms govern issues such as when the marriage payment is to be made and to whom, to what use the marriage payment may be put, and who inherits the payment in case of death or dissolution of the marriage. In some regions of South India, for example, a bride price is paid by the groom's parents to the bride's but must then be spent on the bride's dowry. The payment may subsequently be claimed by the bride's family, but only upon the death of the bride. In some African societies, on the other hand, the bride price received for a woman may be used to obtain a wife for her brother. But such a transaction is often regarded as a debt owed to the sister, and to repay it the brother must offer his daughter in marriage to her son.

FACTORS BEHIND MARRIAGE PAYMENTS

Many hypotheses have been put forward to explain the occurrence of bride price and dowry. One theory links marriage payments to the rights of inheritance held by women and explains dowry as a premortem bequest made to daughters. Another hypothesis links marriage payments to the economic value of women. Brides command a positive worth—a bride price—in areas where women make valuable contributions to agricultural work or other economic activity. In regions where women do not make an economic contribution, they constitute an economic liability and hence bring a dowry. A third hypothesis argues that marriage payments are "prices" that clear the marriage market—that is, these prices equate the demand for and supply of brides and grooms. Therefore, when grooms are relatively scarce brides pay dowries, and when brides are scarce grooms offer a bride price.

Other theories link the existence of different types of marriage payments to the laws governing marital and social ties (kinship structures). For example, bride price has been observed very often in societies with general polygyny (polygyny practiced by the general populace and not just the rich), whereas dowry almost always occurs in monogamous societies. Marriage payments have also been linked to norms of hypergamy—whereby brides are expected to marry into a higher caste or social group—and hypogamy—whereby brides are expected to marry into a lower caste or social group.

These and other explanations of marriage payments proposed by social scientists are not mutually exclusive, and more than one factor could contribute to the determination of marriage payments in any society. Moreover, because the combination of factors leading to dowry or bride price may be very different, the disappearance of one type of payment over time does not necessitate the appearance of the other.

DOWRY INFLATION AND THE MARRIAGE SQUEEZE IN INDIA

India witnessed a real inflation in dowries in the latter half of the twentieth century. Incidents of violence against brides who were unable to pay the dowries demanded of them (bride burning and dowry deaths) also became increasingly commonplace during this time, despite the passage of the Dowry Prohibition Act (1961), which made the payment of dowries illegal.

The phenomenon of the Indian dowry inflation appears especially perplexing given that the widespread practices of female infanticide and female feticide contributed to a highly masculine sex ratio in India throughout the twentieth century. It seems puzzling, therefore, that scarce women in India should have to pay increasingly higher prices for grooms. However, the nature of marriage payments is determined not by the overall sex ratio of the population, but the ratio of "marriageable" men and women. It is possible that this ratio is skewed in favor of women—leading to a positive price of grooms (i.e., dowry)—even when the overall sex ratio is skewed in favor of men.

The *marriage squeeze hypothesis* uses the idea of differential marriageable age of men and women to argue that population growth (which occurred in India in the 1930s) explains dowry inflation. The argument runs as follows: High rates of population growth lead to younger cohorts outnumbering older cohorts in the population. When older men marry younger women, this leads to an excess supply of marriageable women—or a marriage squeeze against women—causing the price of grooms to be bid up.

The norm of *caste hypergamy*, practiced in some regions of India, has also been invoked to explain the Indian dowry inflation. According to this norm, women must marry into a higher social class and hence pay a higher price for the more "desirable" groom. Alternative explanations of the dowry inflation point to *Sanskritization* (emulation, by lower castes, of the higher-caste practice of paying dowry), the changing economic value of women, and changing social structures in India during this time.

SEE ALSO *Caste; Caste, Anthropology of; Family; Marriage*

BIBLIOGRAPHY

Becker, Gary. 1991. *A Treatise on the Family*. Enl. ed. Cambridge, MA: Harvard University Press.

Botticini, Maristella, and Aloysius Siow. 2003. "Why Dowries?" *American Economic Review* 93 (4): 1385–1398.

Goody, Jack, and S. J. Tambiah. 1973. *Bridewealth and Dowry*. Cambridge, U.K.: Cambridge University Press.

Kuper, Adam. 1982. *Wives for Cattle: Bridewealth and Marriage in Southern Africa*. London and Boston: Routledge & Kegan Paul.

Murdock, George Peter. 1967. *Ethnographic Atlas*. Pittsburgh, PA: University of Pittsburgh Press.

Rao, Vijayendra. 1993. "The Rising Price of Husbands: A Hedonic Analysis of Dowry Increases in Rural India." *Journal of Political Economy* 101 (4): 666–677.

Sudeshna Maitra

DRAFT

SEE *Selective Service.*

DRAKE, ST. CLAIR
1911–1990

John Gibbs St. Clair Drake was a University of Chicago–trained social anthropologist. He was born on January 2, 1911, in Suffolk, Virginia, to an African American schoolteacher mother and a Barbadian-born father who was a Baptist preacher and an international organizer for Marcus Garvey's Universal Negro Improvement Association.

After spending much of his youth in Pittsburgh, Pennsylvania, and Staunton, Virginia, Drake attended Hampton Institute (now Hampton University), graduating with a BS in biology in 1931. After graduation he spent a year in an experimental, nondegree program at Pendle Hill Quaker Graduate Center in Wallingford, Pennsylvania. The next three years he taught biology and English at Christiansburg Normal and Industrial Institute, a Quaker boarding school for blacks in western Virginia. In 1935 his former mentor at Hampton, Allison Davis, invited him to join his interracial team of anthropologists investigating racial caste and social class in Natchez, Mississippi. That project resulted in *Deep South: A Social Anthropological Study of Caste and Class* (Davis, Gardner, and Gardner 1941).

In 1937 Drake began graduate studies at the University of Chicago, where he worked with Lloyd Warner, Robert Redfield, and Fred Eggan. Drake's participation in a Works Projects Administration project in Chicago led to his collaboration with Horace Cayton, a sociology graduate student. Together they wrote the classic *Black Metropolis: A Study of Negro Life in a Northern City* (1945). The Chicago research project was also the basis for "Churches and Voluntary Associations Among Negroes in Chicago" (1940), a memorandum prepared for Gunnar Myrdal, commissioned by the Carnegie Foundation to produce *An American Dilemma: The Negro Problem and Modern Democracy* (1944).

In 1947 he conducted his dissertation research in Cardiff, Wales, where he studied a community made up of African seamen and their Welsh families. Drake examined the forms of social action that arose in response to British racial and colonial domination (Drake 1954). While in Britain he befriended Kwame Nkrumah (1909–1972) and other leaders of the African independence movement.

In 1946 Drake began a twenty-three-year tenure at Roosevelt University. Between 1954 and 1965 he pursued applied research interests during summers and two leaves. In 1954 and 1955 he collaborated with his wife, the sociologist Elizabeth Johns Drake (1915–1996), in a Ford Foundation–funded study of mass media in Ghana. From 1958 to 1961 he served as head of the Department of Sociology at the University of Ghana. He also directed research on the tensions between the postcolonial elite and traditional authorities, and on Tema, a modern port city built to stimulate Ghana's economic development. The new city was populated by resettling villagers from traditional lands, and Drake's analysis of that contested process was both critical and understanding of the government's policy. During his Africa years, he advised Nkrumah and helped train Peace Corps volunteers, sensitizing them to the cultural and political factors likely to affect their work.

After Ghana's 1966 military coup, Drake's scholarly focus shifted to problems in the African diaspora: urban unrest and race relations in the United States; cultural retention, reinterpretation, and syncretism in the Caribbean; patterns of coping and resistance in the African diaspora; and the intellectual history of blacks in anthropology and in black studies. In 1969 he moved to Stanford University to direct its African and Afro-American Studies Program. After retiring in 1976, he produced the two-volume *Black Folk Here and There: An Essay in History and Anthropology* (1987, 1990), in the tradition of W. E. B. Du Bois's *Black Folk Then and Now* (1939). In this his last major work, Drake examined the cultural and intellectual history of antiblack prejudice in the precolonial Old World diaspora and the colonial diaspora that formed within the plantation societies of the New World. He presented a symbolic and textual analysis along with an intellectual history and sociology of the knowledge on the status of sub-Saharan Africans in ancient Egypt and the wider Nile River Valley, the Islamic and Judaic Middle East, Mediterranean Europe, and northern European Christendom. He explained the major shifts during the sixteenth century that led to the emergence of racial slavery. In this book, along with a series of seminal essays, he presented a paradigm for studying the African diaspora.

Influenced by black vindicationism, pan-Africanism, the Quakers, and Depression-era socialists and communists, Drake was an activist intellectual. He organized sharecroppers and tenant farmers in Mississippi and unemployed workers in Chicago. He campaigned against the University of Chicago's urban renewal policy in the 1950s, and advised members of the Student Nonviolent Coordinating Committee (SNCC) in the 1960s. He was also a founder of the American Society for African Culture and the American Negro Leadership Conference on Africa. He died on June 14, 1990.

SEE ALSO *African American Studies; Metropolis; Park School, The; Park, Robert E.; Politics, Urban; Race*

BIBLIOGRAPHY

PRIMARY WORKS

Drake, St. Clair. 1940. *Churches and Voluntary Associations Among Negroes in Chicago.* Chicago: Works Projects Administration.

Drake, St. Clair. 1954. Value Systems, Social Structure, and Race Relations in the British Isles. PhD diss., University of Chicago.

Drake, St. Clair. 1966. *Race Relations in a Time of Rapid Social Change.* New York: National Federation of Settlements.

Drake, St. Clair. 1987. *Black Folks Here and There: An Essay in History and Anthropology.* Vol. 1. Los Angeles: Center for Afro-American Studies, University of California at Los Angeles.

Drake, St. Clair. 1990. *Black Folk Here and There: An Essay in History and Anthropology.* Vol. 2. Los Angeles: Center for Afro-American Studies, University of California at Los Angeles.

Drake, St. Clair, and Horace Cayton. 1945. *Black Metropolis: A Study of Negro Life in a Northern City.* New York: Harcourt Brace.

SECONDARY WORKS

Baber, Willie L. 1999. St. Clair Drake: Scholar and Activist. In *African-American Pioneers in Anthropology,* ed. Ira E. Harrison and Faye V. Harrison, 191–212. Urbana: University of Illinois Press.

Bond, George Clement. 1988. A Social Portrait of John Gibbs St. Clair Drake: An American Anthropologist. *American Ethnologist* 15 (4): 762–781.

Davis, Allison Davis, Burleigh B. Gardner, and Mary R. Gardner. 1941. *Deep South: A Social Anthropological Study of Caste and Class.* Chicago: University of Chicago Press.

Du Bois, W. E. B. 1939. *Black Folk Then and Now: An Essay in the History and Sociology of the Negro Race.* New York: Octagon.

Harrison, Faye V. 1992. The Du Boisian Legacy in Anthropology. *Critique of Anthropology* 12 (3): 239–260.

Myrdal, Gunnar. 1994. *An American Dilemma: The Negro Problem and Modern Democracy.* New York: Harper and Brothers.

Faye V. Harrison

DRAVIDIANS

The Dravidians were the majority population across the Indian subcontinent before the second millennium. The evidence of early Dravidians comes from studying the Indo-Aryan culture, languages, and findings at many mounds, the preeminent of which are Mohenjodaro in Punjab and Harappa in Larkana District in Sind. The sources indicate an early Indian civilization with developments parallel to those of Mesopotamia and Sumeria. Excavations from the 1920s found craftsmanship that defines the Indus (or Harappa) culture of 5,000 years ago. The presence of spears, bows, and cattle suggests society's transition from a matriarchate to a patriarchate state. For transactions they used seals as coins, some of which depict a prototype of the god Shiva.

Dravidians had an advanced city culture more ancient than the Aryans, who, as Indian legends tell and some dispute, invaded India from central Asia in several waves around 1500 BCE. The *Rig Veda*, an ancient Hindu scripture, records the destruction of Harappa, then called *Hariyopiyah* (5.27.5). In particular, the Aryan invaders targeted for extinction the Dasyus tribe, who were dark-skinned—a Dravidian feature. Yet another view indicates that the Harappa culture was already disintegrating when the Aryans arrived, perhaps due to natural causes such as a flood.

Among the jungle tribes in the Indus Valley were the Bhils, Kols, Santals, Kukis, Todas, and Oraos, some of which were Dravidians. One theory is that the Dravidians escaped into the hills after the first Aryan invasion, making the hills the safe ground for the Dravidians. The Aryans, being familiar with farming and cattle breeding, had the incentive to clear the lowlands in cooperation with the Dravidians. Thus, savannas and fens were transformed into rice fields. In this civilization building, the Aryans contributed knowledge of horse-power, iron, and the distinct Sanskrit language to the Harappan oxen-force, copper, and the difficult to define Dravidian language.

The link between the Harappan language and the Dravidians is controversial. One theory holds that the Harappans used a sign language that is not alphabet-based, as in Sanskrit, whereas others maintain that the Harappan language is close to the Dravidian language. The proto-Dravidian language was placed at the scene of the Harappan culture. The prominent language groups of the Dravidians today are Brahue in the north, Gonds in north and central India, Kannadigan in Karnataka and Maharastra, Malayali in Kerala, Tamil in the South, and Telugu in Andhra Pradesh. Inscriptions at Harappan sites suggest a resemblance to the old Tamil that is spoken by Dravidians in southern India today. Geneticists are now exploring relatedness among speakers of over 20 different language groups associated with the Dravidians.

SEE ALSO *Anthropology; Anthropology, Linguistic; Archaeology; Aryans; Caste, Anthropology of*

BIBLIOGRAPHY

Allchin, Bridget, and Raymond Allchin. 1982. *The Rise of Civilization in India and Pakistan.* Cambridge, U.K.: Cambridge University Press.

Bose, Abinash Chandra. 1954. *The Call of the Vedas.* Bombay: Bharatiya Vidya Bhavan.

Crooke, William. 1899. The Hill Tribes of the Central Indian Hills. *Journal of the Anthropological Institute of Great Britain and Ireland* 28 (3/4): 220–248.

Griffith, Ralph T. H., trans. [1889] 1976. *The Hymns of the Rig Veda*, ed. J. L. Shastri. Delhi: Motilal Banarsidass.

Krishnamurth, Bhadriraju. 2003. *The Dravidian Language.* Cambridge, U.K.: Cambridge University Press.

Slater, Gilbert. 1924. *The Dravidian Element in Indian Culture.* London: Earnets Benn.

Wheeler, Mortimer. 1962. *Indus Civilization.* Suppl. vol. of *The Cambridge History of India*. 2nd ed. Cambridge, U.K.: Cambridge University Press.

Lall Ramrattan
Michael Szenberg

DREAMING

Dreaming is an episodic activity of the sleeping mind during which spontaneous sensory experiences occur that are perceived at the time as if real. Although dreaming is common, occurring in all humans, the dreams themselves are unique, based on each person's own memory bank of images, a residue of their particular life experiences. The meaning and purpose of dreaming has been a source of speculation over the course of history. It was not until 1900, when Sigmund Freud (1856–1939) published *The Interpretation of Dreams*, that there was a comprehensive theory that placed dreams as centrally important for the understanding of waking behavior. This theory formed the basis of the psychoanalytic treatment method, which relied on patients' recall of and associations to their dreams.

Dream interpretation dominated the practice of psychiatry for the next fifty years. The key to their understanding rested on Freud's model of the mind as operating on three different levels—the conscious, preconscious, and unconscious—with all three influencing waking behavior. The conscious mind is what is in awareness in the moment; the preconscious consists of mental representations that, although not in immediate awareness, can

be brought to consciousness voluntarily; the unconscious material, while not accessible by an act of will, is a major source of dream scenarios. The unconscious contains the remains of early childhood experiences related to learning to control basic impulses (particularly those of sex and aggression) and to express these only in a socially appropriate fashion. These powerful instinctual drives remain active throughout life and cause anxiety if they threaten to become conscious. They are controlled during waking by defenses, the learned ways of keeping them out of consciousness. These defenses are weakened during sleep, when the danger of a breakthrough into action, which would cause internal guilt or external punishment, is reduced due to our inability to act while sleeping.

Freud believed that dreams allow the mind to hallucinate the fulfillment of these prohibited impulses safely, without the risk of consequences. Because the risk, though lowered, is not completely absent during sleep, and to ensure that the sleeper is not shocked into wakefulness, dreams express these wishes in disguised forms. Thus, dreams require some expert interpretation to decode their true meaning. Freud distinguished the dream story, called the *manifest* dream, from its underlying or *latent* meaning, which refers to the unfulfilled instinctual wishes. The latent meanings can only be expressed symbolically to allow their safe gratification. The interpretation of dreams thus became the basis for understanding patients who came for help with emotional problems of overcontrol or undercontrol of their impulse-related behavior.

A challenge to this view followed the discovery in the 1950s of the close association of rapid eye movement (REM) sleep and the experience of dreaming. By monitoring the brain waves, eye movements, and muscle tone of persons observed while sleeping in a laboratory, three to five episodes of REM sleep could be identified each night. If the sleeper were then awakened at these times and asked to report what he or she had just been experiencing, 85 percent of the time the sleeper would describe a dream. The regularity of REM sleep, occurring approximately every ninety minutes, allowed a more complete sampling of dreaming than had ever before been available. Many people have no recall of their dreams, and even those with good recall rarely remember more than one per night. The sleep laboratory technique opened the door to studies of the continuity of a theme from first dream to last, and of the relation of the dream content to some waking, emotion-arousing stimuli, such as a frightening or sexually arousing movie, or an experimentally induced change in a basic need, such as thirst by depriving sleepers of water beforehand. For the most part, these studies showed that dreams are difficult to influence and more often follow their own agenda.

The finding that REM sleep is turned on periodically, starting at the primitive brain structure called the *pons*, further challenged Freud's view. Dreams could not have any inherent meaning if they spring from the nonthinking pons. The activation-synthesis hypothesis of dreaming, proposed in 1977 by J. Allan Hobson and Robert McCarley, explained the apparent (manifest) meaning of a dream as an afterthought, most likely resulting from associations to the sensory images, which are accidental, triggered by the activation of a brain pathway that flows upward from the pons to the visual association areas of the cortex. These images are then linked into a dream story under the influence of the ongoing emotional concerns of the dreamer. In this way dreams are given meaning in the same way as are waking stimuli, when what we see is colored by the present state of our needs and interests. This theory robbed dreams of any special meaning and had a generally dampening effect on dream research for the next twenty years.

The resurgence of interest in dreaming is partly due to the development of sleep disorder centers, which attract patients with dream disorders, such as the repetitive nightmares of those suffering from posttraumatic stress disorder. The resurgence of interest is also partly a result of the development of more sophisticated technology. Brain imaging methods allow a closer look into the areas of the brain activated when REM sleep is ongoing. Using this technology, differences between those areas that are more active in REM sleep than in non-REM sleep or waking confirm that during REM the brain is more intensely active in areas related to instinctual behaviors (hypothalamus and basal forebrain), the emotional areas (limbic and paralimbic), and the visual association areas of the cortex. Activity is lessened during REM in the areas associated with the executive functions: thinking and judgment (the prefrontal cortex).

Brain imaging studies are looking into differences between REM sleep in normal persons and in those with various psychiatric diagnoses. This method has illuminated the abnormality of REM sleep of those suffering from major depression. These patients, when most symptomatic, have increased REM sleep but greatly reduced recall of any dreaming. Their imaging studies show more activity in the emotional areas (limbic and paralimbic) than do nondepressed persons, and heightened activity in the executive cortex. Perhaps these patients are flooded with negative emotion but are overcontrolled in its expression. In Freud's terms, the dream function has failed to allow gratification of unconscious wishes. Without dreams these patients would be difficult to treat psychoanalytically and require another approach.

SEE ALSO *Psychoanalytic Theory; Psychotherapy*

BIBLIOGRAPHY

Dement, William, and Nathaniel Kleitman. 1957. The Relation of Eye Movements During Sleep to Dream Activity: An Objective Method for the Study of Dreaming. *Journal of Experimental Psychology* 53: 339–346.

Freud, Sigmund. [1900] 1955. *The Interpretation of Dreams.* New York: Basic Books.

Hobson, J. Allan, and Robert McCarley. 1977. The Brain as a Dream-State Generator: An Activation-Synthesis Hypothesis of the Dream Process. *American Journal of Psychiatry* 134: 1335–1348.

Mellman, Thomas, and Wilfred Pigeon. 2005. Dreams and Nightmares in Posttraumatic Stress Disorder. In *Principles and Practice of Sleep Medicine*, 4th ed., eds. Meir Kryger, Thomas Roth, and William Dement, 573–578. Philadelphia: Elsevier.

Nofzinger, Eric. 2005. Neuroimaging and Sleep Medicine. *Sleep Medicine Reviews* 9 (3):157–172.

Rosalind D. Cartwright

DRED SCOTT V. SANFORD

Dred Scott v. Sanford (1857) was a major U.S. Supreme Court case dealing with the status of slaves in the United States. In trying to understand the *Dred Scott* decision today, it is important to point out that African Americans and white Americans see the society in which they live very differently. Contemporary studies by sociologists of race and ethnicity, using public opinion data, continue to show significant racial gaps in the perceptions of racism as an issue. For example, a 2005 Gallup pole indicated that 57 percent of African Americans believed that "black-white relations will always be a problem," but only 45 percent of whites agreed. Furthermore, this racial gap has increased rather than decreased since the 1960s. These data are important in relation to the *Dred Scott* decision and its legacy because they suggest that white Americans and African Americans view this continuing legacy differently. Though the case was decided in the mid-nineteenth century, the *Dred Scott* decision is not irrelevant in contemporary race relations in the United States.

Dred Scott (d. 1858) was a slave who sued his owner for freedom in 1847 based on the fact that during the period in which she owned him she had moved him from state to state, passing through the "free states" of Illinois and Wisconsin. The case was in the court system for a decade before it finally reached the U.S. Supreme Court in 1857. Five of the justices who decided this case were from slave-holding families. Chief Justice Roger B. Taney (1777–1864), speaking for the Court in 1857, wrote that:

They [slaves] had for more than a century before been regarded as beings of an inferior order, and altogether unfit to associate with the white race, either in social or political relations; and so far inferior that they had no rights which the white man was bound to respect; and that the negro might justly and lawfully be reduced to slavery for his benefit. He was bought and sold, and treated as an ordinary article of merchandise and traffic whenever a profit could be made by it.

There were four main judicial outcomes from this case. First, this ruling established that slaves were to be enslaved for life: They could not purchase or sue for their freedom, even if they had lived for periods of time in "free states." Second, this case codified a long-standing belief that slavery was solidly grounded on the "fact" that people of African descent were not fully human. In fact, in another part of this case, the Supreme Court ruled that for taxation and voting purposes slaves constituted only three-fifths of a human life. Though the intent of this ruling was to deny slaveholders power (by devaluing their human property), the ideological outcome was twofold: (1) It served to reinforce the devaluing of people of African descent (slaves) as a fraction of a person; and (2) it reinforced the practice in which people of African descent were held as chattel, no different from cattle— that is, slaves could legally be held as property and their value could be debated and assigned. Third, people of African ancestry, slave or free, could not become citizens of the United States and could not sue in federal court. Fourth, the denial of citizenship prohibited slaves from entering into legal contracts. The implications of this decision set in place barriers that included prohibitions on purchasing land (which is critical to the establishment of wealth), as well as prohibitions against family formation based on civil contracts, namely marriage and adoption, and finally voting.

Interpreted sociologically, *Dred Scott* is a negative legal decision that had continuing legacies for African American civil society. The *Dred Scott* decision was wrong in 1857, and in response to the pounding of the abolitionist movement, the decision was effectively overturned through the implementation of the "Reconstruction Amendments," the Thirteenth, Fourteenth, and Fifteenth Amendments to the U.S. Constitution. These historic developments eventually opened the opportunity structure for African Americans, even if only slightly.

The impact of the *Dred Scott* decision is twofold. First, the section of the decision that ruled that African Americans are less than fully human set the ideological tone for 150 years of discrimination, from Jim Crow–style segregation to the continued and documented discrimination that African Americans face in education, employment, and housing (Bajaj and Nixon 2006; Bonilla-Silva

2006). The systematic and brutal segregation and discrimination by whites of African Americans would not have been so widespread and long-lasting if white Americans believed African Americans were fully human and similar to themselves.

Second, the *Dred Scott* ruling concluded that African Americans had no rights worthy of recognition by whites, specifically the rights associated with citizenship and accorded to all other Americans. This set off a series of voter disenfranchisement laws in the decades following the decision, especially in the South, that were designed to deny African Americans the right to vote. Florida, for example, enacted such a law in 1868 (Earls and Mukamal 2006; Shofner 2001).

Debates about the long-term effects of the *Dred Scott* decision are contentious. Bruce Sacerdote (2005) argues that the descendants of slaves "caught up" to those of free blacks within two generations, at least in terms of schooling and literacy. In contrast, William Darity, Jason Dietrich, and David Guilkey (2001) document the direct economic effects of Jim Crow segregation into the 1980s and 1990s. This debate is similar to another contentious issue in the United States: affirmative action. Some scholars argue that affirmative action policies have leveled the playing field between whites and African Americans, whereas others suggest it will be many years before affirmative action will have accomplished its goal.

Such empirical evidence indicates that the *Dred Scott* decision (1) provided support for long-standing beliefs in the racial inferiority of African Americans that were commonly held by white Americans, and (2) laid the foundation for a series of disenfranchisement laws that prohibited African Americans from taking advantage of one of their citizenship rights—the right to vote.

SEE ALSO *Jim Crow; Racism; Separate-but-Equal; Slavery; Supreme Court, U.S.; White Supremacy*

BIBLIOGRAPHY

Bajaj, Vikas, and Ron Nixon. 2006. For Minorities, Signs of Trouble in Foreclosures. *New York Times*, February 22.

Bonilla-Silva, Eduardo. 2006. *Racism without Racists: Color-Blind Racism and the Persistence of Racial Inequality in the United States.* 2nd ed. Lanham, MD: Rowman & Littlefield.

Darity, William, Jr., Jason Dietrich, and David K. Guilkey. 2001. Persistent Advantage or Disadvantage? Evidence in Support of the Intergenerational Drag Hypothesis. *American Journal of Economics and Sociology* 60: 435–470.

Dred Scott, Plaintiff in Error, v. John F. A. Sanford. 1857. Vol. 60 U.S. 393; 15 L. Ed. 691; 1856 U.S. Lexis 472; 19 How 393. http://www.law.cornell.edu/supct/html/historics/USSC_CR_0060_0393_ZS.html.

Earls, Anita, and Debbie A. Mukamal. 2006. All Sentences Are Life Sentences: Post-prison Sanctions and Barriers to Re-

entry. Breakout session. Conference on Race, Class, Gender,
and Ethnicity. From Georgia to Guantánamo: Understanding
America's Incarceration Addiction and Its Effects on
Communities. February 18, University of North Carolina
School of Law, Chapel Hill. http://www.unc.edu/crcge/
archives/2006/sections.shtml.

Hear the Issues. Americans On: Race Relations in the United
States. http://www.heartheissues.com/americanson-
racerelations-g.html.

Sacerdote, Bruce. 2005. Slavery and the Intergenerational
Transmission of Human Capital. *Review of Economics and
Statistics* 87: 217–234.

Shofner, Jerrell H. 2001. Expert Report on *Johnson v. Bush*. Vol.
00-CV-3542: U.S. District Court, Southern District of
Florida.

Angela Hattery
Earl Smith

DROUGHT

Drought is a feature of climate that is defined as a period
of below-average rainfall sufficiently long and intense to
result in serious environmental and socioeconomic
stresses, such as crop failures and water shortages, in the
affected area. Droughts can occur in any climatic region,
but their characteristics vary considerably among regions.
What droughts in all climatic regions have in common is
their gradual onset, which—in contrast to other natural
hazards—makes their beginning and end difficult to identify. Defined primarily as natural phenomena, droughts
have not received much attention in the social sciences.
Only since the 1990s, with the increasing appreciation of
the linkages between the environment and society, have
droughts begun to be viewed as an issue of interest also for
the social sciences.

Drought is caused by the sinking motion of air in a
high-pressure cell, which results in decreasing relative
humidity of the air and little or no precipitation. Most climatic regions are temporarily under the influence of high
pressure; droughts occur only when atmospheric circulation patterns that cause the high pressure persist or recur
persistently over an unusually long period of time.
Because of the global nature of atmospheric circulation,
explanations for anomalous circulation patterns extend far
beyond the drought-affected area. Thus global patterns of
atmospheric pressure systems and sea surface temperatures
have been invoked to explain the occurrence of periodically recurring drought events in some parts of the globe.
Most prominent among those global patterns is the El
Niño Southern Oscillation (ENSO), a coupled ocean-
atmosphere anomaly that originates in the Pacific basin
but has repercussions on the climatic conditions in areas

as far apart as southern Africa, India, and Brazil.
Anthropogenic processes that lead to changes in land
cover, such as deforestation and overgrazing, affect local-
scale moisture recycling and can induce local reductions in
rainfall. Although simulation models have shown the possibility of substantial reductions in rainfall resulting from
land-cover change, anthropogenic disturbances large
enough to explain more than local-scale reductions in
rainfall have not been observed.

TYPES OF DROUGHT

The effects of drought on environment, economy, and
society are manifold. In order of the increasing severity
and scope of their impacts, four types of drought are commonly distinguished: A *meteorological drought* manifests
itself in a shortfall of precipitation or changes in precipitation intensity and timing, possibly aggravated by other
climatic factors, such as high temperatures and winds.
Risks associated with this type of drought include wildfire
hazard and reduced water infiltration into the soil. If the
drought persists long enough to result in significant soil
water deficits and plant water stress, it crosses the threshold into an *agricultural drought*. Lower crop yields and
quality, as well as increased soil erosion and dust emission,
are possible impacts expected from this type of drought.

Because various crops differ in their water demand, a
farmer's choice of crop type can either buffer or exacerbate
the effects of an agricultural drought. A drought is classified as a *hydrological drought* once the precipitation shortfall affects surface and subsurface water supplies.
Hydrological droughts usually lag behind the occurrence
of meteorological droughts because of the time needed for
precipitation deficits to reach the surface and groundwa-
ter levels of the water cycle. Their impacts, which consequently are also out of phase with those of a
meteorological and agricultural drought, include reduced
stream flow, below-normal reservoir and lake levels, loss of
wetlands, and declining water quality. Although climate is
the primary factor of a hydrological drought, humans
contribute to its effects by changes in land and water use,
such as urbanization and the construction of dams.
Finally, a *socioeconomic drought* occurs when the supply of
economic goods and services, including water, forage,
food, and hydroelectric power, can no longer be met for
drought-related causes. Farmers and ranchers, who
depend on agricultural and pasture productivity, are the
first to suffer losses. Then follow industries depending on
agricultural production. As a result, consumers may have
to pay more for their food and other weather-sensitive
products and services.

The socioeconomic effects of a drought vary not only
in proportion to the severity of the climatological event
but also depending on the vulnerability of the affected

population. Monetary costs arise for any economy hit by drought, such as to cover for lost crops, crop insurance payouts, and fire damage; but only in the most vulnerable populations of the developing world are drought effects—food insecurity, famine, health problems, and loss of life and livelihoods—often paired with economic, social, and political difficulties. Subsistence farmers and pastoralists in particular suffer from crop and livestock losses, as well as from increased food prices. Droughts force many of them to migrate from rural to urban areas, increasing pressure on resources there.

COPING WITH DROUGHT

Scientists and decision-makers have devised a number of ways to deal with drought, which can be grouped into drought monitoring, forecasting, and mitigation. Meteorologists around the world carefully monitor meteorological and hydrological variables (precipitation patterns, soil moisture, stream flow) over time to determine the onset and end of a drought. Satellite remote sensing technology has contributed immensely to quantitative monitoring over large geographic areas. Understanding the complex physical aspects leading to droughts is a prerequisite for making increasingly reliable and credible drought predictions. Empirical studies have shown that drought results from a complex interplay of different climatological factors, which makes forecasting difficult. In the tropics, where scientists have made significant advances in understanding the climate system, the potential for seasonal drought predictions is promising, particularly with respect to droughts related to ENSO. Multiyear droughts as well as droughts outside the tropics still cannot be predicted with a level of accuracy that is without risk for the users of those predictions. Knowing the frequency, duration, and spatial extent of past droughts, however, helps in determining the likelihood and potential severity of future droughts.

In addition to the assessment of meteorological processes, drought mitigation also requires an understanding of the vulnerabilities of different population groups to drought. Mitigation tools range from early warning systems, which monitor both meteorological conditions and vulnerable populations (e.g., the Famine Early Warning Systems Network, operating in Africa, Central America, and Afghanistan), to various forms of weather-related crop insurance schemes (e.g., in the United States and Australia among others), emergency water supply augmentation (e.g., tapping new water resources), and water demand reduction (e.g., by means of economic incentives for water conservation, improvement of water use efficiencies, breeding for drought tolerance, diversification to less weather-dependent economic activities, and public

water conservation awareness programs). As droughts are expected to become more frequent and more extreme with global warming, it is imperative to improve drought mitigation efforts and increase future drought preparedness.

MAJOR DROUGHT EVENTS

Major drought events in modern history include:

- China, 1877–1878: Provinces across northern China were depopulated as grain stocks ran out as a result of severe droughts. Millions of people perished from starvation.

- Soviet Union, 1921–1922: A fierce drought hit the Ukraine and Volga regions. The death toll reached almost five million people, more than the total number of casualties in World War I (1914–1918).

- United States, 1930s: The Dust Bowl drought, which ravaged the American and Canadian Great Plains in the 1930s, is considered one of the major droughts of the twentieth century. Coinciding with the Great Depression, it had major impacts on the United States and Canada, including a mass migration from the Great Plains to the western coast in search of better living conditions.

- West Africa, 1970s: The West African Sahel region experienced droughts of unprecedented spatial extent and duration, which created a famine that killed a million people and affected the livelihoods of more than fifty million. The great Sahelian droughts were also blamed for widespread environmental degradation of this dryland region.

- Ethiopia, 1984–1985: A severe drought, exacerbated by the government's censorship of news of the emerging crisis, brought about famine and forced millions to leave their homes, triggering the world's worst refugee crisis to date.

In 2005 Australia experienced a major drought coupled with above-average temperatures, with the southern agricultural areas particularly hard hit. In 2006 drought conditions prevailed across much of Europe—for Spain the most serious drought in more than a century—and caused water shortages for agricultural and tourism sectors. At the same time, China faced its worst drought in fifty years, with crop failures and deaths of cattle causing huge economic losses.

SEE ALSO *Agricultural Industry; Disaster Management; Famine; Food; Human Ecology; Irrigation; Natural Disasters; Water Resources*

BIBLIOGRAPHY

Glantz, Michael H., ed. 1987. *Drought and Hunger in Africa: Denying Famine a Future.* Cambridge, U.K., and New York: Cambridge University Press.

Glantz, Michael H., ed. 1994. *Drought Follows the Plow: Cultivating Marginal Areas.* Cambridge, U.K., and New York: Cambridge University Press.

Kogan, Felix. 1997. Global Drought Watch from Space. *Bulletin of the American Meteorological Society* 78 (4): 621–636.

National Drought Mitigation Center. University of Nebraska–Lincoln. http://www.drought.unl.edu.

Vogt, Jürgen V., and Francesca Somma, eds. 2000. *Drought and Drought Mitigation in Europe.* Dordrecht and Boston: Kluwer Academic Publishers.

Wilhite, Donald A., ed. 2000. *Drought: A Global Assessment.* London and New York: Routledge.

Wilhite, Donald A., ed. 2005. *Drought and Water Crises: Science, Technology, and Management Issues.* Boca Raton: Taylor and Francis.

Stefanie M. Herrmann

DRUCKER, PETER
1909–2005

Peter F. Drucker was a writer, management consultant, and university professor. He was born in Vienna, Austria, on November 19, 1909. After receiving his doctorate in public and international law from Frankfurt University in Germany, he worked as an economist and journalist in London. He moved to the United States in 1937.

Drucker published his first book, *The End of Economic Man*, in 1939. In it, he describes the causes for the rise of fascism, including the failure of established institutions that led to its emergence. He joined the faculty of New York University's Graduate Business School as a professor of management in 1950. From 1971 until his death, he was Clarke Professor of Social Science and Management at Claremont Graduate University in Claremont, California.

Drucker authored thirty-six major books during his lifetime. Eighteen of these deal primarily with management, including the landmark books *Concept of the Corporation* (1946), *The Practice of Management* (1954), *The Effective Executive* (1967), *Management: Tasks, Responsibilities, Practices* (1974), *Innovation and Entrepreneurship* (1985), and *Managing the Non-Profit Organization* (1990). Fifteen of his books are devoted primarily to society, economics, and politics; two are novels; and one is a collection of quasi-autobiographical essays. His last two books were *The Daily Drucker* (2004) and *The Effective Executive in Action* (2005). He also authored numerous articles that appeared in a vast array of publications, including the *Harvard Business Review*, the *Wall Street Journal*, and the *Economist*.

Drucker consulted with dozens of organizations and executives around the world, ranging from the world's largest corporations, such as General Motors and the General Electric Company, to entrepreneurial startups and various government and nonprofit agencies, such as the American Red Cross, Girl Scouts of the USA, and the Salvation Army. He devoted extensive time during the last two decades of his life to helping professionalize the management of large and small social-sector and nonprofit organizations. He wrote and spoke frequently of the need to revitalize and transform governmental organizations, and he advocated privatizing the delivery of government goods and services as much as possible.

Drucker's most significant contribution was to codify management as both a discipline and a practice—he is widely recognized as the "father of modern management." His second major accomplishment was to develop "innovation and entrepreneurship" as a systematic discipline and practice for the purpose of managing change in all of the institutions of society. This accomplishment was a continuation of his work in support of what he called "a functioning society."

Drucker referred to himself as a "social ecologist." Social ecology, he wrote, requires a "rigorous method of looking, identifying, and testing" for changes that are in the process of emerging in society (Drucker 1992, p. 62). Thus, a social ecologist tries to identify and define new developments that are occurring or that have already occurred. These developments, or discontinuities, appear gradually and may not be noticeable until they cause major impacts on society and its institutions. Drucker's ability to identify and define new developments in the twentieth century was legendary, and it can be seen in almost all of his works.

Drucker first identified the emergence of knowledge work, the knowledge worker, and the knowledge society in his 1959 book *Landmarks of Tomorrow*. He identified an event that was very important to society—the shift from manual work to knowledge work in developed economies. He believed that organizations and executives needed to prepare themselves to manage and exploit this shift for the good of society and its citizens. He tracked the emergence of knowledge work for a half-century, tracking its emergence from a trickle to a major force in developed societies. He described this major force in his 1993 work *Post-Capitalist Society*.

A fair amount of the methodology Drucker used as a social ecologist is contained in *Innovation and Entrepreneurship*. This book "shows how one systematically looks to the changes in society, in demographics, in meaning, in science and technology, as opportunities to make the future" (Drucker and Maciariello 2004, p. 4).

Valid criticisms of Drucker's work have to do with his frequent use (or abuse) of data. With the exception of demographic data, Drucker often used data to make a larger point, for which the precision he specified was unnecessary. In addition, throughout his work, he generally under-referenced the works of other authors.

Critics have also argued that Drucker's management is "utopian," that it relies on an unrealistically positive view of human nature, human potentialities, and organizational potential. While Drucker knew of the human proclivity toward corruption—perhaps better than his critics, having seen firsthand the rise of Hitler and the rise of German anti-Semitism (see *The End of Economic Man*)—he chose to focus primarily on the more noble aspirations of human beings. Peter Drucker died of natural causes on November 11, 2005, in Claremont, California.

SEE ALSO *Entrepreneurship; Information, Economics of; Knowledge Society; Management; Management Science*

BIBLIOGRAPHY

Beatty, Jack. 1998. *The World According to Peter Drucker*. New York: Free Press.

Drucker, Peter F. 1992. Reflections of a Social Ecologist. *Society* 29 (4): 57–64.

Drucker, Peter F., and Joseph A. Maciariello. 2004. *The Daily Drucker*. New York: HarperCollins.

Edersheim, Elizabeth Haas. 2007. *The Definitive Drucker*. New York: McGraw-Hill.

Flaherty, John E. 1999. *Shaping the Managerial Mind*. San Francisco: Jossey-Bass.

Maciariello, Joseph A. 2006. Peter F. Drucker on Executive Leadership and Effectiveness. *The Leader of The Future 2*, eds. Frances Hesselbein and Marshall Goldsmith, pp. 3–27. San Francisco: Jossey-Bass.

Joseph A. Maciariello

DRUG TRAFFIC

Drug trafficking (or distribution) refers to the production, selling, transportation, and illegal import of unlawful controlled substances such as marijuana, cocaine, heroin, methamphetamine, MDMA (ecstasy), LSD, and a variety of other "club drugs," such as GHB and Rohypnol typically associated with the young adult "rave" dance-party scene. Trafficking laws, and punishments for their violation, vary according to drug type, the quantity seized, the location of the distribution (e.g., drug-free school zones), and whether minors were sold to or targeted. Drug traf-

ficking laws can implicate a single individual or syndicates involving broad rings of people participating in organized illegal drug activity.

Drug trafficking and trafficking networks take many different forms that are specific to the type of drug involved, the geographic origin of the drug, the risk of detection by law enforcement, the level of competition for consumers in the marketplace, and the people to whom the drugs are being sold or distributed. In addition, recent studies have shown that the nature of drug trafficking and drug markets is affected by society's perception of the particular drug and the types of people trafficking in the drug, often independent of how serious the drug is deemed by lawmakers (Mohamed and Fritsvold 2006).

Trafficking is the direct result of a political decision to criminalize particular substances that are in demand among members of a society. The illegal drug market in the United States has established itself as one of the most profitable in the world. Americans are the world's largest consumers of cocaine, and they rank among the top consumers of other drugs, such as heroin, marijuana, and methamphetamine (CIA 2006). According to the U.S. Department of Health and Human Services (HHS), nearly 20 million Americans aged twelve or older were current illicit drug users in 2004, meaning they had used an illegal drug at least once in the previous last month. The HHS also reports that marijuana is the most commonly used illicit drug among Americans. In 2002, for example, the drug was used either alone or in combination with another illegal drug by 75 percent of current illicit drug users.

This high demand for drugs (in spite of their illegality) and the lure of profits are two of the primary reasons people knowingly enter into the drug trade. In the upper echelons of the international drug trade, political ambitions and influence are also motivating factors. However, for many people, particularly those at the cultivation and harvesting end of drug trafficking pipelines, the drug trade is merely a means of survival. For example, peasant farmers in Peru, Colombia, Bolivia, and Ecuador have been driven from traditional crops like coffee to coca cultivation, the plant from which cocaine is manufactured. For many of these peasants, coca is the only marketable crop they can produce to sustain their already meager lifestyles—a sustenance that amounts to about $750 to the grower for every 500 kilograms of coca leaves produced (Inciardi 2002).

DRUG TRAFFICKING: A MULTINATIONAL PHENOMENON

Most of the illicit street drugs consumed in the United States come from plants that are cultivated in the less developed nations of Latin America, Southwest Asia, and

Southeast Asia. Usually, when the plants reach maturity, they are harvested and go through a local refinement process that prepares them for trafficking to U.S. street drug markets. For example, most of the marijuana consumed in the United States originates in Mexico. As already discussed, the coca leaf from which cocaine is derived is primarily grown in the South American nations of Colombia, Bolivia, and Peru. The opium poppy, from which heroin originates, is grown in the Southwestern Asian nations of Afghanistan and Pakistan, the Southeastern nations of Myanmar and Laos, increasingly in Columbia and Mexico, and in a handful of other nations around the globe.

It is no coincidence that these less developed countries are the primary sources of the raw materials used to supply America's illicit drug habits. Aside from being geographically conducive to opium poppy, coca, or marijuana cultivation, most of these nations have been overlooked by the global economy and resort to or tolerate drug trafficking as a means to gain an economic foothold through the estimated $400 billion a year international drug market. "As a consequence, whole nation-states—Bolivia, Colombia, Laos, Malaysia, Mexico, Pakistan, Peru, Puerto Rico, Thailand, and Turkey—depend upon opium, coca, and hemp production for their agricultural base, and the manufacture of heroin, cocaine, and marijuana is a significant productive sector of the economy" (Chambliss 2001, p. 101). In the relatively small-player South American nation of Guyana, cocaine traffickers earn an estimated $150 million every year, the equivalent of 20 percent of the country's gross domestic product (Hutchinson-Jafar 2006).

For other participants in international drug trafficking, contempt for what they perceive to be a heavy-handed American foreign policy also plays a role in the funneling of drugs into the United States. The anti-Western Taliban regime in Afghanistan was believed to be largely funded by opium poppy cultivation. In the 1970s, Carlos Lehder Rivas emerged as a power broker in the notorious Medellin Cartel in Colombia. Lehder was known for being intensely anti-American, and he saw cocaine smuggling into the United States as a move toward political independence for his native Colombia (Inciardi 2002). In 2005, Evo Morales, the head of a federation of Bolivian coca leaf *campesinos* (simple farmers) who banded together to oppose U.S.-backed coca eradication programs, was elected president of the country. While Morales insists "I am not a drug trafficker" (BBC 2005), the vast majority of coca harvested in Bolivia and other Andean nations is not used for traditional cultural practices. Rather, the bulk of this coca is refined into cocaine for sale on the black market in the United States and elsewhere, and cocaine exports have historically provided Bolivia with more income than all of its other exports combined (Chambliss 2001).

Currently, the U.S.-Mexico border is the primary point of entry for cocaine shipments being smuggled into the United States, and approximately 65 percent of the cocaine smuggled into the nation crosses its southwestern border. But, before this cocaine reaches Mexico, it has typically made stops in several other countries whose drug traffickers play key roles in bringing cocaine to market. After the coca leaf is refined into coca paste, typically in remote locations somewhat close to where the coca is harvested, it works its way through Amazonia (the river valley and rain forest region covering 2.5 million square miles of South America) to Colombia, where it is refined into powder cocaine. From Colombia, the cocaine travels by air and sea through the Caribbean, Central America, Cuba, and Mexico on to the United States (Inciardi 2002).

DRUG TRAFFICKING AND CRIME

On the international level, drug production, largely fueled by U.S. demand, has brought about the establishment of criminal syndicates that organize their law-breaking activities around drugs and jeopardize political stability in drug-producing nations. "The concentration of economic and paramilitary resources in the hands of outlaw trafficking 'cartels' has presented a serious challenge to governmental authority" (Smith 1992, p. 1). In many cases, drug traffickers resort to violence and other criminal activities to intimidate opponents, including law enforcement, and to protect and expand their market share. However, according to some experts, the claims of the strong-arm cartels have been somewhat overstated. With regard to Colombian cocaine cartels, Guy Gugliotta notes that the murder and intimidation of small drug traffickers and other dissenters by large traffickers in the late 1970s and early 1980s was largely mythological. While there was undoubtedly a great deal of violence perpetrated by these cartels, proprietary leverage was their greatest asset. "The large traffickers' success as a cartel was probably due to a more mundane factor—the members controlled cocaine's infrastructure . . . [and] had established vertically integrated processing networks that could move cocaine by the hundred-weight" (Gugliotta 1992, p. 112).

Nonetheless, for a variety of reasons, most of which stem from the illegality of illicit drugs, crime and violence are mainstays of the drug economy. Increased pressure by U.S. drug enforcement agencies and increased cooperation from international governments in the fight against drug distribution have driven traffickers to search for new smuggling routes into the United States. Many of these new routes, particularly those used to smuggle cocaine and marijuana, are in the Caribbean and contribute to increases in crime, violence, and political corruption in the region. In 2005, for example, drug-fueled violence drove Jamaica's murder rate to a record high. However, as smuggling routes become more stabilized and drug territory becomes more clearly distributed among those controlling the Caribbean drug trade, levels of crime and violence may level off and decline in the region.

In efforts to avoid the violence, vice, and property crimes associated with drug trafficking, several nations (and a few U.S. cities) have adopted formal or informal drug decriminalization policies, with some success. Chambliss found that a de facto drug decriminalization policy in Seattle, Washington, reduced crimes associated with drugs, particularly murder and other crimes of violence. One of the primary reasons for this reduction was decreased competition among black-market sellers, who typically employ violent measures to protect their drug dealing territory. The Netherlands, Spain, Denmark, Switzerland, Austria, and Italy have also experimented with formal or de facto drug decriminalization policies. These nations have found that crimes committed by addicts attempting to support their drug habits have declined, while other public health problems, such as HIV transmission, have decreased as well (Chambliss 2001). However, because of the enormous profits to be gained by high-level distributors from the supply of drugs, and because of the lack of viable economic opportunities for participants at the lower levels of the drug trade, illegal drug trafficking and the ills that come with it are likely to remain mainstays of modern society.

SEE ALSO *Borders; Crime and Criminology; Drugs of Abuse*

BIBLIOGRAPHY

BBC News. 2005. Profile: Evo Morales—Aymara Indian Evo Morales Has Become in Recent Years Both a Key and Controversial Figure in Bolivian Politics. December 14. http://news.bbc.co.uk/1/hi/world/americas/3203752.stm.

Central Intelligence Agency (CIA). 2006. World Fact Book: Field Listing—Illicit Drugs. http://www.cia.gov/cia/publications/factbook/fields/2086.html.

Chambliss, William J. 2001. *Power, Politics, and Crime*. Boulder, CO: Westview Press.

Drug Enforcement Administration (DEA). 2004. Briefs and Background: Drug Trafficking in the United States. http://www.usdoj.gov/dea/concern/drug_trafficking.html.

Gugliotta, Guy. 1992. The Colombian Cartels and How to Stop Them. In *Drug Policy in the Americas*, ed. Peter H. Smith. Boulder, CO: Westview Press.

Hutchinson-Jafar, Linda. 2006. Drug Violence Afflicts Caribbean Countries. Reuters, March 30.

Inciardi, James A. 2002. *The War on Drugs III: The Continuing Saga of the Mysteries and Miseries of Intoxication, Addiction, Crime, and Public Policy*. Boston, MA: Allyn and Bacon.

Mohamed, A. Rafik, and Erik D. Fritsvold. 2006. Damn, It Feels Good to Be a Gangsta: The Social Organization of the Illicit Drug Trade Servicing a Private College Campus. *Deviant Behavior* 27 (1): 97–125.

Smith, Peter H. 1992. The Political Economy of Drugs: Conceptual Issues and Policy Options. In *Drug Policy in the Americas*, ed. Peter H. Smith. Boulder, CO: Westview Press.

United States Department of Health and Human Services, Substance Abuse and Mental Health Services Administration. 2004. National Survey on Drug Use and Health: National Findings. http://www.drugabusestatistics.samhsa.gov.

United States Department of State, Bureau of International Narcotics and Law Enforcement Affairs. 2000. *International Narcotics Control Strategy Report*. Washington, DC: United States State Department. http://www.state.gov/p/inl/rls/nrcrpt/.

A. Rafik Mohamed

DRUGS

SEE *Drugs of Abuse.*

DRUGS OF ABUSE

Drugs of abuse are commonly classified by their pharmacological and behavioral effects into six categories: (1) opiate analgesics, (2) stimulants, (3) depressants, (4) hallucinogens, (5) inhalants, and (6) anabolic steroids. Most of these drugs mimic endogenous neurotransmitters that are naturally present in the human body and regulate certain processes within the central and peripheral nervous systems. Because the quantity of drugs consumed by abusers typically far exceeds the level that naturally occurs in the body, the effects on neurons can range from subtle changes associated with tolerance (i.e., reduced sensitivity) to cell damage or cell death.

Dependence liability refers to the risk that repetitive use of a drug will lead to physical or psychological dependence, also known as addiction. Alcohol and tobacco have by far the highest rates of documented physical dependence in the United States (see table 1). Moreover they have high dependence liabilities: Roughly one-third of individuals who repeatedly smoke tobacco will develop nicotine dependence, and approximately 15 percent of those who repeatedly drink alcohol will become alcoholic. These dependence liabilities are comparable to or exceed those of cocaine, stimulants, and heroin. Although it has been asserted that cannabis is not addictive, Alan Budney and John Hughes pointed out in a 2006 article that nearly one in ten people who smoke marijuana will come to satisfy diagnostic criteria for dependence, including compulsive usage and withdrawal symptoms of mild to moderate severity.

Dependence Liability of Drugs of Abuse in the United States		
Drug	Proportion of U.S. population with a history of dependence	Proportion of abusers who became dependent
Tobacco	24%	32%
Alcohol	14%	15%
Cannabis	4%	9%
Cocaine	3%	17%
Stimulants	2%	11%
Heroin	<1%	23%
Other opiates	<1%	8%
Hallucinogens	<1%	5%
Benzodiazepines	1%	9%
Inhalants	<1%	4%

SOURCE: Anthony, Warner, and Kessler 1994 (figures rounded to the nearest whole-number percent).

OPIATE ANALGESICS

Opiates are drugs derived from the opium poppy plant that have analgesic and sedative qualities commonly used to treat pain. Examples include opium, heroin, and morphine. Synthetic analogs of these drugs, which are called opioids, have been created in the laboratory. Examples include methadone, hydrocodone, and oxycodone. The short-term psychoactive effects of opioids involve euphoria, drowsiness, and impaired motor and cognitive functioning. Because opiates and opioids also inhibit activity in brain regions that regulate basic functions such as respiration, they can precipitate death by suffocation. The risks increase dramatically when these drugs are combined with alcohol or other depressants. All opiates and opioids have a high potential for abuse and dependence, which increase with higher potency of the drug and more efficient routes of administration, such as injection or smoking. Injection practices also carry additional health risks from communicable diseases such as HIV/AIDS and hepatitis.

STIMULANTS

Stimulants such as amphetamines increase the activity of one or more of the monoamine neurotransmitters (dopamine, norepinephrine, and serotonin). Activation of the dopamine system is primarily responsible for the euphoric effects, or "rush," of stimulants. Stimulants also enhance mood, promote wakefulness, increase respiration and blood pressure, and decrease appetite. Chronic abuse of stimulants can severely damage nerve cells and cause an array of psychiatric disturbances, including psychosis and paranoia, as well as motor disturbances, including tics.

Methamphetamine, sometimes known as "ice" or "crank," is the product of a "street" modification of amphetamine using over-the-counter decongestants. It has an even greater stimulant effect on the dopamine sys-

tem. In addition some of the precursor chemicals and solvents used to manufacture methamphetamine can be highly toxic and flammable, leading to serious safety risks from inhalation and potential explosions or fires. Methamphetamine can be taken orally, intranasally, intravenously, or by smoking. Abuse of methamphetamine has been associated with serious physical dependence and severe health consequences, including nervousness and agitation, tactile hallucinations, and paranoid psychosis, of which hallucinations and delusions may be refractory to treatment.

"Designer" stimulants such as "ecstasy" (methylenedioxymethamphetamine, or MDMA) have potent effects on norepinephrine and serotonin in addition to dopamine. This elicits psychedelic or hallucinogenic reactions in addition to euphoria. Because norepinephrine affects the autonomic system, it can also precipitate rapid heart rate, increased blood pressure, and an elevated risk of cardiovascular events. MDMA intoxication enhances the pleasure of tactility, and users often seek physical contact with others. This may be observed at MDMA parties, or "raves," where users may dance closely or aggressively with each other. Withdrawal from MDMA can precipitate disturbances in mood, insomnia, fatigue, and depression. Similar to methamphetamine, MDMA abuse can cause chronic damage to the brain.

Cocaine is a potent and highly addictive stimulant that can be snorted or injected. Cooking sodium bicarbonate (i.e., baking soda) with cocaine enables it to be smoked in the crystallized form of "crack," which delivers a more potent yet shorter-lived high that may last only a few minutes. This rapid cycle of acute intoxication and withdrawal (or "crash") has the potential to elicit sustained binge patterns and severe addiction to the drug. In addition to the health risks typically associated with stimulant abuse, the chemical properties of cocaine—such as its acidity and its typical intranasal method of delivery—can cause damage to nasal and sinus tissue.

DEPRESSANTS

Depressants represent a broad class of drugs that include anxiolytics, hypnotics, and sedatives. The most commonly abused depressant is alcohol. Benzodiazepines, which act on the inhibitory neurotransmitter GABA, are the second most commonly abused depressant and among the most commonly prescribed medications. Benzodiazepines prescribed for anxiety are called anxiolytics, while those prescribed for insomnia are called hypnotics. They have a wide therapeutic profile, covering the spectrum of sedation from minor tranquilizers to preoperative anesthetics. Acute side effects can range from mild memory loss to anterograde amnesia for new events occurring while intoxicated. The anterograde amnesia may be worsened when the drug is combined with alcohol. Few deaths have been attributed to benzodiazepine ingestion alone. It has been suggested that long-term use might cause permanent impairment of motor and cognitive functioning. But despite being in use for over forty years, its long-term effects are still uncertain.

Barbiturates are an older class of depressants that were prescribed similarly for anxiety and sedation. They were associated with serious side effects and had a relatively narrow therapeutic profile. Any mixture of barbiturates with alcohol has the potential to precipitate seizures, a severe withdrawal syndrome, or death. As a result their use has been almost totally usurped by benzodiazepines, and they are now prescribed only rarely for the treatment of convulsions or refractory migraine headaches.

HALLUCINOGENS

Most hallucinogens exist naturally in certain plants (e.g., mescaline and peyote). Others, such as LSD (lysergic acid diethylamide), are synthesized from ergot, a mold that grows on rye and other grains. Hallucinogens cause sensory or perceptual alterations that can be visual, auditory, tactile, olfactory (smell), or gustatory (taste). They can also cause thought disturbances, such as grandiose or paranoid thinking, and can lead to feelings of irrational pleasure or panic. Intense panic can lead to bizarre or dangerous behavior and have long-lasting psychiatric repercussions similar to those of post-traumatic stress disorder (PTSD). Hallucinogens act primarily on the serotonin system, which, like MDMA, can elicit psychotic-like experiences.

Cannabis, or marijuana, is the most widely used illegal drug in the United States. Cannabis contains delta-9-tetrahydrolcannabinol (THC), a psychoactive chemical that binds to naturally occurring cannabinoid receptors in several brain regions, including the hippocampus. The precise mechanism of action of THC is unclear. According to the FDA, cannabis has no legitimate medical usage; however, a synthetic analog of THC called dronabinol may be used medicinally as an appetite stimulant, to reduce nausea and pain, or to reduce intraocular pressure in glaucoma patients. Cannabis is typically smoked, but it can also be cooked and eaten with high-fat foods. Many users report feelings of euphoria, relaxation, and perceptions of heightened awareness, whereas others report mild to moderate levels of anxiety and paranoia. Long-term side effects of chronic use of cannabis may include reductions in sperm motility, increased estrogen levels, and decreased high-density ("good") cholesterol. Although an "amotivational syndrome" characterized by impaired ambition and substandard productivity has been anecdotally attributed to long-term cannabis use, the existence of this syndrome has not been scientifically established. No deaths have been reliably attributed to cannabis ingestion, apart from vehicular or other accidents stemming from impaired judgment or motor coordination.

ANABOLIC STEROIDS

Anabolic-androgenic steroids (AAS) are synthetic forms of the primary male sex hormone, testosterone. The major consumers of illegally obtained AAS are bodybuilders and athletes, who seek their anabolic properties for athletic or aesthetic gains while also attempting to minimize their androgenic properties, which elicit most of the unwanted side effects. The dangers of AAS are clearly documented, even when they are used according to prescription standards. Documented adverse physical risks include permanent liver injury, increased blood pressure and risk of stroke, acne, hair loss, and sudden cardiac death. Males may experience testicular atrophy and the development of female sex characteristics such as breast enlargement. Female users may develop masculine characteristics such as facial hair and voice deepening as well as menstrual irregularities and clitoral enlargement. The psychiatric effects of AAS abuse can be unpredictable and range from elevated mood to sudden and irrational aggressiveness. Upon cessation of AAS, particularly after sustained high doses, users may experience depression and withdrawal, lowered energy, decreased libido, and a precipitous loss of muscle mass. All AAS carry a risk of physical and psychological dependence.

INHALANTS

Inhalant abuse, or "huffing," involves the deliberate intake of fumes from solvents (e.g., paint thinner) or aerosol gases used as propellants (called "whippets"). Inhalant intoxication may appear similar to alcohol intoxication, but the subjective effects are reported to be more anesthetic than those of alcohol. Solvent inhalants are cor-

U.S. Drug Enforcement Administration Schedule of Controlled Substances

Schedule	Examples	Abuse potential and prescription practices
I	Heroin, cannabis, LSD.	Illicit.
II	High-potency opioid analgesics (e.g., oxycodone),high-potency stimulants (e.g., methylphenidate or Ritalin).	High abuse potential.Rx must be handwritten, no refills permitted.
III	Low-potency opioid preparations (e.g., codeine cough suppressant), anabolic steroids.	Moderate abuse potential.Verbal Rx's permitted, 5 refills permitted up to 6 months.
IV	Most prescription sedatives and sleep aids (e.g., benzodiazepines, Ambien).	Low to moderate abuse potential. Verbal Rx's permitted, 5 refills permitted up to 6 months.

SOURCE: United States Controlled Substances Act, 21 U.S.C. § 802 *et seq.*

Table 2: U.S. Drug Enforcement Administration Schedule of Controlled Substances

rosive to tissue and extremely dangerous to inhale in concentrated forms. All huffing temporarily deprives the brain of oxygen, and anoxia is a risk to all inhalant abusers. Inhalant abuse can cause severe adverse health effects, including damage to the heart, lungs, liver, and kidneys. Inhalant abuse can also lead to acute amnesia, stroke, coma, and death.

LAW ENFORCEMENT EFFORTS

In the United States the Drug Enforcement Administration (DEA) "schedules" drugs according to whether they have (1) a legitimate medical usage and (2) a potential liability for abuse or dependence. Similar scheduling mechanisms are employed by many other countries as well. If the U.S. Food and Drug Administration (FDA) determines that a drug of abuse has no legitimate medical usage, then it is classified as Schedule I by the DEA. Drugs with legitimate medical uses are classified into Schedules II through IV, depending on their abuse potential (see table 2). The schedule has important implications for prescription practices, including permissible refills and the need for handwritten, as opposed to verbal, prescription orders. Issues of toxicity and side-effect profiles do not influence scheduling by the DEA, but they do influence the FDA's approval of medications for specific conditions, based upon a balancing of each medication's risks versus benefits.

Tobacco and alcohol each have a moderate to high abuse potential and no legitimate medical usage (not to mention high mortality and morbidity risks), yet they are neither regulated by the FDA nor scheduled by the DEA. Instead, largely for policy reasons, they are regulated by the U.S. Bureau of Alcohol, Tobacco, and Firearms (ATF) with regard to such matters as licensing and regulation of sales.

DEMOGRAPHIC USE PATTERNS

In 2005 rates of substance abuse or dependence in the United States varied to some degree by racial or ethnic group. However, they did not vary across the most populous demographics of Caucasians, African Americans, and Hispanics (see table below).

Despite similar use-prevalence patterns, Hispanics in the United States are imprisoned at more than twice the rate of Caucasians for drug-related offenses, while African

Rates of Substance Abuse and Dependence in the U.S. by Racial and Ethnic Census Category

Racial/Ethnic Group	Percentage
American Indians/Alaskan Natives	21.0%
Pacific Islanders	11.0%
Caucasians	9.4%
Hispanics	9.3%
African-Americans	8.5%
Two or more races	10.9%

SOURCE: Office of Applied Studies 2006.

Americans are imprisoned at nearly four times the rate of Caucasians (Bureau of Justice Statistics 2006). These apparent discrepancies might be attributable to differential law enforcement practices. For instance, police might focus greater attention on minority communities, or prosecutors might offer minority defendants fewer opportunities for plea bargains or diversionary programs. In addition sentencing guidelines could contribute to unintended disparate impacts on minority groups. For example, there is some indication that crack-cocaine may be used relatively more frequently among African American individuals in urban environments, whereas methamphetamine may be used more frequently among Caucasians in rural environments. Higher penalties can attach in the United States to the crack form of cocaine, as compared to its powder form, and this might account in part for higher incarceration rates among African Americans. With newer laws being enacted to stem the rising tide of methamphetamine abuse, changes might also be seen in demographic patterns among arrestees and inmates. More research is required to gain a better understanding of this important issue and to plan for effective corrective actions.

SEE ALSO *Hallucinogens; Psychotropic Drugs*

BIBLIOGRAPHY

Anthony, J. C., L. A. Warner, and R. C. Kessler. 1994. Comparative Epidemiology of Dependence on Tobacco, Alcohol, Controlled Substances, and Inhalants: Basic Findings from the National Comorbidity Study. *Experimental and Clinical Psychopharmacology* 2: 244–268.

Booth, Brenda M., Carl Leukefekd, Russel Falck, and Robert G. Carlson. 2006. Correlates of Rural Methamphetamine and Cocaine Users: Results from a Multi-State Community Study. *Journal of Studies on Alcohol* 67 (4): 493–501.

Budney, Alan J., and John R. Hughes. 2006. The Cannabis Withdrawal Syndrome. *Current Opinions in Psychiatry* 19 (3): 233–238.

Bureau of Justice Statistics. 2006. *Prisoners in 2004*. Washington, DC: U.S. Department of Justice.

Dawkins, Marvin P., and Mary M. Williams. 1997. Substance Abuse in Rural African-American Populations. In *Rural Substance Abuse: State of Knowledge and Issues*, eds. Elizabeth B. Robertson et al., 484–487. National Institute on Drug Abuse Research Monograph 168. Rockville, MD: U.S. Department of Health and Human Services, National Institutes of Health, National Institute on Drug Abuse.

Substance Abuse and Mental Health Services Administration (SAMSHA). 2006. *Results from the 2005 National Survey on Drug Use and Health*. Washington, DC: SAMSHA, Office of Applied Studies. http://www.oas.samsha.gov.

Douglas B. Marlowe
Nicholas S. Patapis

DUAL ECONOMY

In the mid-twentieth century, theoretical modeling of economic growth was dominated by single-sector models, such as that of the Nobel Prize winner Robert Solow. Other analysts, however, felt that economies should be characterized as having multiple sectors, which they stylized into dual-economy models. Foremost among the early dual-economy modelers were two other Nobel Prize winners, W. Arthur Lewis and Simon Kuznets. The dual economy models posited an economically "advanced" sector and an economically "backward" sector. These have alternatively been called capitalist and subsistence, formal and informal, modern and traditional, industry and agriculture, urban and rural, primary and secondary, and good-jobs and bad-jobs sectors.

For both Lewis and Kuznets, the two sectors differed in terms of the goods produced, the nature of the growth process, and conditions in labor markets. Lewis specified a capitalist sector that produced industrial goods and a subsistence sector that produced agricultural goods, services, and commercial activities. Kuznets distinguished an agricultural sector from all others, primarily the industrial sector. For Lewis, capital accumulation took place in the capitalist sector only, and he viewed this sector as the engine of growth. For Kuznets, the essence of modern economic growth was the gradual shift of production from lower-income to higher-income sectors. For both Lewis and Kuznets, the advanced sector offered higher real wages than the backward sector did.

This coexistence of high-wage and low-wage sectors is the defining feature of labor-market dualism, the generalization of which is labor market segmentation. Besides real wages being higher in the good–jobs sector, dualism and segmentation require that access to this sector be restricted, in the sense that not all who want to work there are able to do so. As summarized by Michael Wachter, the dual labor-market model advances four hypotheses:

> First, it is useful to dichotomize the economy into a primary and a secondary sector. Second, the wage and employment mechanisms in the secondary sector are distinct from those in the primary sector. Third, economic mobility between these two sectors is sharply limited, and hence workers in the secondary sector are essentially trapped there. Finally, the secondary sector is marked by pervasive underemployment because workers who could be trained for skilled jobs at no more than the usual cost are confined to unskilled jobs. (1974, p. 639)

Some of the subsequent writings on labor-market dualism adopted human capital theory, as developed in the Nobel Prize–winning work of T. W. Schultz and Gary Becker and the work of Jacob Mincer. Human capital theory maintains that workers with more education and training have higher skills, which the labor market rewards. Thus, it is not enough for labor-market dualism that workers in one sector earn systematically more than those in another; it must also be true that workers with the same skills do better in one sector than in another. Ample research has demonstrated empirical evidence that wages are systematically higher for observationally equivalent workers in some economic sectors than in others: non-agriculture versus agriculture, urban versus rural, formal versus informal, and so on. Many observers take this as evidence of labor-market dualism, though some dismiss it as merely indicating the existence of unmeasured skills and abilities.

What the works reviewed thus far have in common is that all available workers are employed either in the advanced sector or in the backward sector. Thus, unemployment is absent in these models. Later models, such as that of John Harris and Michael Todaro, specified two types of employment (industrial and agricultural) plus unemployment.

One feature that could not be ignored by labor market modelers was the duality within the urban economy, with some jobs being desirable and others being deemed quite miserable to have. This observation led to the development of a model with three types of employment: an urban formal sector, an urban informal sector, and a rural agricultural sector—plus unemployment (Fields 1975).

More recently, one more need has become apparent. This is to give due recognition to the fundamental duality to be found within the informal sector. On the one hand, the informal sector has free-entry activities such as street vending and small-scale services that enable those who do such work to eke out a meager existence. Individuals who engage in such enterprises do so because it is better for them than being unemployed. On the other hand, the informal sector also has restricted-entry activities that people who could be working formally choose to take up instead, such as leaving a formal sector auto repair shop to set up one's own backyard operation or moving from a formal sector restaurant to operate one's own noodle stand. Some current segmented labor-market models include both the "free entry" part of the informal sector and the "upper tier" of the informal sector.

In the 2000s, dual-economy and multisector models dominate both academic research and applied policy work. Analysts routinely utilize models with many economic sectors and many labor markets. The sectors, at a minimum, include industry and agriculture, while other sectors, such as commerce and services, may also play a role. As for the labor market, workers might be employed (be it in wage employment or self-employment) in one of four sectors: the formal sector, the free-entry part of the

urban informal sector, the upper tier of the urban informal sector, and rural agriculture. They might also be unemployed. Models assuming that the economy has only a single sector or that all employed workers earn the same amount seem hopelessly unrealistic.

SEE ALSO *Harris-Todaro Model; Labor Market Segmentation*

BIBLIOGRAPHY

Becker, Gary S. 1964. *Human Capital: A Theoretical and Empirical Analysis.* New York: Columbia University Press for the National Bureau of Economic Research.

Fields, Gary S. 1975. Rural-Urban Migration, Urban Unemployment and Underemployment, and Job Search Activity in LDC's. *Journal of Development Economics* 2 (2): 165–188.

Harris, John, and Michael Todaro. 1970. Migration, Unemployment, and Development: A Two Sector Analysis. *American Economic Review* 60 (1): 126–142.

Kuznets, Simon. 1955. Economic Growth and Income Inequality. *American Economic Review* 45 (1): 1–28.

Lewis, W. Arthur. 1954. Economic Development with Unlimited Supplies of Labour. *Manchester School* 22: 139–191.

Schultz, T. W. 1961. Investment in Human Capital. *American Economic Review* 1 (2): 1–17.

Wachter, Michael. 1974. Primary and Secondary Labor Markets: A Critique of the Dual Approach. *Brookings Papers on Economic Activity* 3: 637–680.

Gary S. Fields

DUALISM
SEE *Functionalism.*

DU BOIS, W. E. B.
1868–1963

William Edward Burghardt Du Bois was a leading public intellectual whose extensive body of research, social analysis, and cultural critique helped to establish the foundations for the social sciences, the study of race relations, and Africana studies in the United States. Widely recognized as a historian and sociologist, he also engaged anthropological discourse on race during the era of Franz Boas (1858–1942) (Baker 1998; Harrison 1992). His influence on African American anthropologists W. Allison Davis (1902–1983), St. Clair Drake (1911–1990), and Irene Diggs (1906–1998), who studied with both him and Fernando Ortiz (1881–1969), is particularly significant. Beyond his work in the social sciences, his immense interdisciplinary breadth encompassed autobiography, philosophy, journalism, and creative writing. In his two earliest novels, *The Quest of the Silver Fleece* (1911) and *Dark Princess: A Romance* (1928), he explored important political and economic themes, situating them in the context of romance and dramatic psychosocial plots featuring female protagonists in complex settings. Novels represented one of the many genres in which Du Bois expressed his evolving vision of the possibilities of antiracist and anticolonial agency.

Du Bois was born on February 23, 1868, in Great Barrington, Massachusetts. In 1884 he graduated as the valedictorian of his high school class. In 1885 he went to Nashville, Tennessee, to attend the historically black Fisk College (now University). During his summers in Tennessee, he taught in segregated rural schools. That experience gave him a close look at the poverty and racial discrimination that African Americans faced in the South. It also exposed him to their dynamically expressive cultural life. Memories from that period inspired some of his later writings, namely, *The Souls of Black Folk* (1903). After three years, he graduated from Fisk with a BA. With a scholarship, he continued his studies at Harvard, where he was classified as a junior because of the presumed inferiority of his education at Fisk. He studied with philosophers William James (1842–1910) and George Santayana (1863–1952), and with economist Frank William Taussig (1859–1940), completing his bachelor's degree in philosophy cum laude in 1890. He remained at Harvard for graduate training in history and political science, earning his MA and PhD in 1891 and 1895, respectively. Historian Albert Bushnell Hart (1854–1943) encouraged his research on the transatlantic slave trade.

Financed by a Slater Fund Fellowship, Du Bois spent 1892 to 1894 at the Friedrich-Wilhelm III Universität at Berlin, known also as the University of Berlin, where he concentrated in history and political economy, and developed a scientific approach to the study of social problems. He took courses from political theorist Rudolph von Gneist (1816–1895) and economist Adolph Wagner (1835–1917). He also attended lectures by Max Weber (1864–1920), whose temporary lectureship at Berlin coincided with Du Bois's second year there. The most significant aspect of his graduate studies in Germany was his training in economics and sociology under the tutelage of Gustav von Schmoller (1838–1917), the leader of the "younger German historical school" that revealed economics' interrelations with the other social sciences. This school of thought also questioned theories of universal laws, emphasizing that economic behaviors were contingent upon historical, social, and cultural contexts. Schmoller's methodology valorized the use of induction to

accumulate historical and descriptive facts. In his view, "the goal of social science was the systematic, causal explanation of social phenomena" (Green and Driver 1978, p. 6). He also believed that methodologically rigorous social scientific research "could be used as a guide to formulate social policy" (p. 6). This empirical approach strongly influenced Du Bois's early career as a social scientist who applied sociological techniques to study the problems presented by "the color line."

Du Bois's experiences in Europe expanded his thinking considerably. He realized that the racial discrimination he had encountered in the United States was not universal and that racism's scope was larger than the problems in the United States. American racism, colonial oppression in Africa and Asia, and Europe's political-economic development were all components of the same set of interrelated problems. Du Bois also gained greater exposure to Marxism and socialist analysis from attending meetings of the Social Democratic Party. The maturation of thinking that began to emerge in Germany was reflected many years later in *Color and Democracy: Colonies and Peace* (1945) and, even before that, in *Black Reconstruction* (1935). In the latter book, he innovatively used Marxist categories and "anticipated" Gramscian and poststructural approaches to hegemony and discourse in his analysis of the socioeconomic, political, and ideological conditions that prevailed in the U.S. South after the Civil War (1861–1865) (Nonini 1992). Contrary to the Dunning school's notion that freed blacks were incapable of exercising the rights of citizenship, Du Bois posited that African Americans played a major role in building democracy after emancipation. He further argued that the racism and ambivalent allegiance of poor whites to the white elite could be attributed to a public psychological wage. These ideas were controversial but seminal in influencing later generations of scholars, such as those who study the social construction of whiteness (e.g., Roediger 1991).

Although he intended to complete his doctorate in economics in Germany, Du Bois had to return to the United States. Despite Schmoller's and Wagner's strong support for his exemption from the doctoral program's four-semester rule, a professor of chemistry was adamant against it. However, even more of an obstacle was the paternalistic Slater Fund. It refused to renew his fellowship for only one more semester because of the higher priority it gave to channeling African Americans into elementary and industrial education. Du Bois was urged to "devote [his] talent and learning to the good of the colored race" (Lewis 1993, p. 146). A comparative study of the household economies and quality of life among German peasants and rural African Americans in Tennessee was not viewed as a suitable goal for an educated black person.

The following year, while teaching at the African Methodist Episcopal Church–affiliated Wilberforce University in Ohio, he earned his PhD from Harvard's Department of History and Government, becoming the first African American to earn a doctorate from that university. His dissertation, *The Suppression of the African Slave Trade to the United States of America, 1638–1870*, was published as the first volume in the Harvard Historical Studies series (1896). Representing a "new historiography of interpretation," the dissertation provided thorough documentation for the argument that due to "an interregional bargain [between the North and South] sealed by profits," the United States continued to participate in the slave trade after it was internationally abolished in 1807 to 1808 (Lewis 1993, pp. 156, 160). Despite federal and state laws codifying suppression, a clandestine nonenforcement persisted for half a century.

In 1896 Du Bois assumed a temporary position as "assistant instructor" at the University of Pennsylvania, which created a position beneath its lowest rank to accommodate hiring a Negro. Du Bois's charge was to conduct research on the cause of urban problems in the predominantly African American seventh ward of Philadelphia. The city's "reforming elites" had commissioned the research, which Du Bois conducted over fifteen months, collecting survey and demographic data, and conducting interviews with five thousand people (Lewis 1993, p. 180). The result was *The Philadelphia Negro: A Social Study* (1899), an exemplary treatise that was the first large-scale empirical study in U.S. sociology and the first scientific investigation of African Americans (Green and Driver 1978, p. 113; Lester 1971, p. 26). Given many of the project's substantive concerns as well as the centrality of participant observation, *The Philadelphia Negro* may also be placed in the context of the history of urban anthropology (Harrison 1992). In a social and intellectual climate dominated by social Darwinism, Du Bois's analysis demonstrated that the problems of poverty and crime were not caused by innate black inferiority. They were instead symptoms of institutionalized racial inequality. Although his empirical results challenged conventional thinking, his elitist disposition, nonetheless, led him to play into the moralizing judgments of his patrons. Despite the intellectual and public policy significance of this research, Du Bois was not retained in either a temporary or permanent position at the University of Pennsylvania, where white classmates of lower rank became full professors (Du Bois 1968, p. 199).

After Philadelphia, Atlanta University appointed Du Bois professor of economics and history with the responsibility of directing the Sociological Laboratory and the Atlanta University Conference. The latter was a series of annual conferences to report the results of the laboratory's research on the impact of urban problems on black Americans. The emphasis, especially during the earlier years, was on the collection of factual evidence on social conditions rather than on social reform, which was believed to be possible only after ignorance was countered by knowledge. The goal of the research was the "careful search for truth" that would offer an empirical alternative to the speculative theories and "vindictive ignorance" of much of the social science of that time (Green and Driver 1978, p. 14). Du Bois published the results of this research program in the monograph series that made up the Atlanta University Publications (1896–1914). The studies addressed a wide range of issues: health and physique, housing, black businesses, education, artisans, the black church, crime, economic cooperation, the family, morals, and manners. In *Health and Physique of the Negro American* (1906), for example, Du Bois offered a critique of early physical anthropology's biological determinism and scientific racism. Using craniometric and public health data, he documented the adverse effects of social conditions on the black body.

Du Bois's tenure at Atlanta University ended in 1910 when he shifted his focus from that of a detached social scientist to an activist, following "the path of sociology as an inseparable part of social reform" (Green and Driver 1978, p. 20). Convinced at this point that knowledge and truth were insufficient for promoting social change, he became editor of the newly established NAACP's magazine, *The Crisis*. This transition into the life of an activist intellectual followed his antiracist activism of three years earlier in cofounding the Niagara Movement, which had a short life. Du Bois served as *Crisis* editor until 1934, when friction over his editorial independence from the NAACP's executive secretary, Walter F. White (1893–1955), and board led him to resign. During the twenty-four years of his editorship, he became the most influential black public intellectual in the United States, educating the public on the plight of African Americans and others in the African world, articulating a vision for civil and human rights and black empowerment (one that was often more radical than that of the NAACP), and providing an outlet for talented young writers and scholars.

A prolific scholar, Du Bois published across a wide interdisciplinary terrain. His most widely read book was *The Souls of Black Folk*, a collection of essays, some autobiographical, written in a compellingly lyrical, poetic style. Positing that the color line was the problem of the twentieth century, the book redefined the meanings of black identity and lived experience, illuminating the dilemmas of double consciousness as well as the enhanced social vision that could potentially emerge from it. The book also offered a poignant view of the South, including an examination of everyday life in the Black Belt and the limits of Booker T. Washington's (1856–1915) accommodationist stance. *Souls* is also invaluable for its "pioneering excursion into the sociology of music" (Lewis 1993, p. 286), religion, education, and politics.

In 1934 Du Bois began his second tenure at Atlanta University, serving as head of the Department of Economics and Sociology. During this phase, he focused his scholarship on comparison and synthesis informed by his commitment to social action and politicization within an international context. Among his publications were *Black Reconstruction* (1935) and *Black Folk Then and Now: An Essay in the History and Sociology of the Negro Race* (1939)—an expansion of *The Negro* (1915). He also started to work on the *Encyclopedia Africana*, which he had initially envisioned early in the century. He established *Phylon*, a journal devoted to critical studies of race and culture, and in the early 1940s he worked to revive the Atlanta University Conference. The conference held in 1943 featured a number of prominent black and white sociologists, including E. Franklin Frazier (1894–1962), Charles S. Johnson (1893–1956), Howard W. Odum (1884–1954), and Edgar T. Thompson (1900–1989).

Despite his success, the university administration, wary of his radicalism, forced Du Bois to retire. He accepted an offer from the NAACP to serve as its director of special research, a position he held for only four years. He sought to revitalize the Pan-Africanist movement, help define international human rights standards for the newly established United Nations, and examine the global scope of racism. His radical anticolonial views, however, were not consistent with the NAACP's policies. After his second tenure with the NAACP, Du Bois went on to leadership positions with the Council on African Affairs and the Peace Information Center, which led him to become involved in controversial international affairs related to the cold war. His participation in the leftist peace movement and his travels to the Soviet Union and China during the 1940s and 1950s were viewed as "un-American" as McCarthyist anticommunism held sway. In 1951 Du Bois was indicted on charges of being an unregistered agent of a foreign principal. Although acquitted of the crime, the prosecution stigmatized Du Bois, alienating him even further from the mainstream civil rights leadership.

Du Bois devoted much of his life to building international networks and deepening anticolonial convictions among activist intellectuals from Africa and the African diaspora. He organized a series of Pan-African Congresses over the first half of the twentieth century. In the last years of his life, he accepted an invitation from Prime Minister Kwame Nkrumah (1909–1972) to work on the *Encyclopedia Africana* with support from the government of postcolonial Ghana. Du Bois moved to Accra and became a Ghanaian citizen. His encyclopedia unfinished, he died on August 27, 1963, the day before the historic March on Washington.

SEE ALSO *African American Studies; Anticolonial Movements; Boas, Franz; Drake, St. Clair; Frazier, E. Franklin; Garvey, Marcus; Gramsci, Antonio; Hurston, Zora Neale; James, William; Marxism; Marxism, Black; National Association for the Advancement of Colored People (NAACP); Nkrumah, Kwame; Ortiz, Fernando; Pan-African Congresses; Pan-Africanism; Poststructuralism; Reconstruction Era (U.S.); Slave Trade; Slavery Industry; Social Science; Veil, in African American Culture; White, Walter*

BIBLIOGRAPHY

PRIMARY SOURCES

Du Bois, W. E. B. 1896. *The Suppression of the African Slave Trade to the United States of America, 1638–1870.* New York: Longmans, Green.

Du Bois, W. E. B. [1899] 1967. *The Philadelphia Negro: A Social Study.* New York: Schocken.

Du Bois, W. E. B. [1903] 1990. *The Souls of Black Folk: Essays and Sketches.* New York: Vintage.

Du Bois, W. E. B., ed. 1906. *Health and Physique of the Negro American.* Atlanta University Study, no. 11. Atlanta, GA: Atlanta University Press.

Du Bois, W. E. B. [1911] 2004. *The Quest of the Silver Fleece.* New York: Harlem Moon.

Du Bois, W. E. B. [1915] 1970. *The Negro.* New York: Oxford University Press.

Du Bois, W. E. B. [1928] 1995. *Dark Princess: A Romance.* Jackson: University Press of Mississippi.

Du Bois, W. E. B. [1935] 1992. *Black Reconstruction in America, 1860–1880.* New York: Atheneum.

Du Bois, W. E. B. [1939] 1970. *Black Folk Then and Now: An Essay in the History and Sociology of the Negro Race.* New York: Octagon.

Du Bois, W. E. B. 1945. *Color and Democracy: Colonies and Peace.* New York: Harcourt, Brace.

Du Bois, W. E. B. 1968. *The Autobiography of W. E. B. Du Bois: A Soliloquy on Viewing My Life from the Last Decade of Its First Century.* New York: International Publishers.

SECONDARY SOURCES

Baker, Lee D. 1998. *From Savage to Negro: Anthropology and the Construction of Race, 1896–1954.* Berkeley: University of California Press.

Green, Dan S., and Edwin D. Driver, eds. 1978. *W. E. B. Du Bois on Sociology and the Black Community.* Chicago: University of Chicago Press.

Harrison, Faye V. 1992. The Du Boisian Legacy in Anthropology. *Critique of Anthropology* 12 (3): 239–258.

Lester, Julius, ed. 1971. *The Seventh Son: The Thought and Writings of W. E. B. Du Bois.* New York: Vintage.

Lewis, David L. 1993. *W. E. B. Du Bois: Biography of a Race, 1868–1919.* New York: Holt.

Lewis, David L. 2000. *W. E. B. Du Bois: The Fight for Equality and the American Century, 1919–1963.* New York: Holt.

Nonini, Donald. 1992. Du Bois and Radical Theory and Practice. *Critique of Anthropology* 12 (3): 293–318.

Roediger, David R. 1991. *The Wages of Whiteness: Race and the Making of the American Working Class.* New York: Verso.

Faye V. Harrison

DUE PROCESS

The term *due process* refers to the guaranteed rights that ensure that an individual cannot be deprived of "life, liberty, or property, without due process of law." This provision, as it applies to the U.S. federal government, is found in the Fifth Amendment to the U.S. Constitution. It is also found in the Fourteenth Amendment, where it constrains the actions of the states. The notion of due process arises from the premise that law should be fair, predictable, and transparent. Perhaps more importantly, a guarantee of due process ensures that whenever the sovereign or government interacts with an individual, it is bound by the law from both a substantive and procedural perspective.

The Bill of Rights (the first ten amendments to the U.S. Constitution) initially only acted as a constraint on the actions of the federal or national government. Once the Fourteenth Amendment was enacted after the Civil War, the U.S. Supreme Court utilized the due process clause to incrementally apply those constraints to the state governments. Through the process known as "incorporation," the due process clause served as the conduit to apply the Bill of Rights to the relationship between individuals and the state governments.

The Court did not apply all the governmental restrictions of the Bill of Rights at once, however. Rather, over time, the Court incorporated more discreet rights using a progressively broader configuration of the due process clause. For instance, in *Mapp v. Ohio* (1961), the Court ruled that the Fourth Amendment prohibited states from introducing illegally obtained evidence during criminal prosecutions. This "exclusionary rule"—which holds that improperly obtained evidence must be excluded from the prosecution's case—supported and gave weight to a line of previous cases that prohibited unreasonable searches and dictated the need for "probable cause" before a search warrant could be issued. The Fifth Amendment prohibitions on double jeopardy or compelled self-incriminating testimony were also held to apply to state actions. In *Miranda v. Arizona* (1966), the Court determined that the right to an attorney contained in the Sixth Amendment and the right against self-incrimination contained in the Fifth Amendment were so important that the police must affirmatively advise suspects of those rights before questioning a detained suspect.

The notion of due process is not limited by the text of the Bill of Rights. Although the Court has incorporated many specific provisions of the rights contained in the Constitution, it has embraced a broader notion of due process that suggests an independent constraint on governmental procedures that are not particularly derived from constitutional text apart from the due process clauses. For instance, in *Rochin v. California* (1952) the Court held that shocking behavior can violate procedural due process even if no specific text of the Constitution is at issue (in this case, the police forcibly pumped out a suspect's stomach to recover drugs he had swallowed upon their entry). Fundamental notions of decency and fair process are thus intrinsic aspects of due process.

Although most questions about due process are concerned with procedural due process—the process or procedure at issue—on occasion the Court has considered substantive aspects of due process. In *Skinner v. Oklahoma* (1942), the Court used a substantive due process analysis as the basis for overturning a criminal statute in Oklahoma that provided for the sterilization of some three-time felony offenders but not others. There is a debate as to whether the right to privacy found in the emanations and penumbras of the Bill of Rights, as found in *Griswold v. Connecticut* (1965) and *Roe v. Wade* (1973) is grounded in substantive due process. In *Griswold* the Court found that a right to privacy prohibited Connecticut from outlawing birth control for married couples, and in *Roe* the Court recognized the right of women to obtain an abortion before the third trimester of pregnancy.

The foundational expectation of due process means that government bodies, agencies, and actors must provide some set review before depriving an individual of life, liberty, or property, broadly defined. The required process may take the form of administrative hearings, appellate procedures, or some other forum to hear and oppose the prospective governmental action. Since the time of the Magna Carta in England, due process has meant a fundamental demand that the government follow the appropriate law. The concept, as well as the fundamental transparency and fairness it implies, holds in both international legal regimes and any constitutionally grounded government.

SEE ALSO *Civil Liberties; Civil Rights; Constitution, U.S.; Supreme Court, U.S.*

BIBLIOGRAPHY

Hensley, Thomas R., Christopher E. Smith, and Joyce A. Baugh. 1997. *The Changing Supreme Court, Constitutional Rights and Liberties.* Minneapolis, MN: West Publishing.

Orth, John V. 2003. *Due Process of Law: A Brief History.* Lawrence: University Press of Kansas.

Schwartz, Bernard. 1993. *A History of the Supreme Court.* New York: Oxford University Press.

Charles Anthony Smith

DUMMY VARIABLE TRAP

SEE *Econometrics.*

DUMPING, PRODUCT

Product dumping is selling exports at a price that is less than "normal value." The traditional definition of *dumping* is selling exports to buyers in a foreign country at a price that is less than the price that is charged to comparable domestic buyers (or to buyers in other foreign-country markets). A second, alternative definition, adopted starting in the 1970s, is selling exports to buyers in a foreign country at a price that is less than the average cost of producing the product (including allocation of fixed costs and profit).

Why would an exporting firm be dumping (according to one or the other of these definitions)? There are different reasons. A firm may be engaged in predatory dumping, planning to drive out other competitors and then raise its price once it has achieved monopoly power. A decline in market demand can drive the market price to a level that is below full average cost. A firm with substantial production or inventory of a product that is perishable or going out of fashion may optimally set a price that is below its full average cost. A firm may be introducing its product into a new foreign market, and to encourage initial sales it may set a low price. A firm with market power may be using geographic price discrimination, charging a higher price in its home market (where the price elasticity of demand is lower) and a lower price in the foreign market (where the demand elasticity is higher).

The rules of the World Trade Organization permit the importing country's government to impose an antidumping duty if the government follows a process that finds that dumping is occurring and that the dumping is causing injury to domestic import-competing firms. The antidumping duty is intended to force the price of the imported product back up to its normal value.

For the well-being of the importing country (and the world overall), the process of imposing antidumping duties has two major shortcomings. First, the process does not require the government to consider possible benefits to other groups in the country (for instance, domestic consumers of low-priced imports). Second, the process is subject to political manipulation and bias. Import-competing producers can exert substantial pressure for favorable rulings. There is leeway in how a government body makes comparisons of prices in different national markets or measures full average costs of foreign producers. For instance, the U.S. Department of Commerce finds that dumping has occurred in more than 90 percent of the cases that it examines. But Brink Lindsey and Dan Ikenson (2002) examined a sample of cases in depth and concluded that in over half of them there was no dumping or much less than the Department of Commerce had determined. It appears that antidumping policy often is used not to combat unfair exporting policies that harm the importing country, but rather to provide new protection for domestic firms against competitive imports, with the typical inefficiency losses to national (and world) well-being.

Up to the late 1980s, only three countries (the United States, Canada, and Australia) and the European Union actively used antidumping policies. Since then, more countries have adopted antidumping laws (at least ninety-five countries as of 2005). According to data compiled by the World Trade Organization, the importing countries that initiated the most cases during the 2000–2006 period are India, the United States, China, Argentina, and Turkey, as well as the European Union. During this period, China is the exporting country whose firms were most often found to be dumping. Other exporting countries whose firms were often found to be dumping include Korea, Taiwan, Japan, and the United States.

SEE ALSO *Beggar-Thy-Neighbor; Competition; Exports; Imports; Predatory Pricing; Trade; World Trade Organization*

BIBLIOGRAPHY

Lindsey, Brink, and Dan Ikenson. 2002. Antidumping 101: The Devilish Details of "Unfair Trade" Law. Cato Institute Trade Policy Analysis no. 20. http://www.freetrade.org/node/43.

Pugel, Thomas A. 2007. Pushing Exports. In *International Economics.* 13th ed. 209–237. New York: McGraw-Hill Irwin.

World Trade Organization. Anti-dumping. http://www.wto.org/english/tratop_e/adp_e/adp_e.htm.

Thomas A. Pugel

DUNCAN, OTIS DUDLEY
1921–2004

One of sociology's most influential practitioners, Otis Dudley Duncan was instrumental in transforming mainstream American sociology into a quantitatively based empirical social science in the second half of the twentieth century. His key scholarly contributions include the introduction of path analysis to sociology, the measurement of occupational socioeconomic standing with an index (Duncan Socioeconomic Index), the study of intergenerational occupational mobility, the spatial analysis of residential patterns, the application and advancement of loglinear models and Rasch models for categorical social science data, and a landmark treatise on social measurement (Duncan 1984).

Duncan's best-known work is a 1967 book coauthored with the late Peter Blau, *The American Occupational Structure.* Based on quantitative analyses of the first large national survey of social mobility in the United States, the book elegantly depicts the process by which parents transmit their social standing to their children, particularly through affecting the children's education. The book's impact went far beyond its analyses of occupational mobility. Using survey data and statistical techniques, it showed how an important sociological topic could be analyzed effectively and rigorously with appropriate quantitative methods. The work helped inspire a new generation of sociologists to follow suit and pursue quantitative sociology. Today, a worldwide community of sociologists studying the transmission of social standing from one generation to the next still works on elaborating the Blau-Duncan model to include such additional factors as cognitive ability, race, and social context.

Duncan introduced path analysis to social science. A path diagram and a corresponding path model describe a set of equations summarizing complex scientific ideas in terms of statistical relationships. Path analysis was first invented by Sewell Wright, a biologist and evolutionary theorist. Duncan discovered Wright's method of path analysis by chance and then applied it to sociology. Together with Arthur Goldberger, an econometrician, he showed that path analysis models were closely related to the simultaneous equation models of economics and the confirmatory factor analysis of psychology. These three different ways of analyzing certain kinds of data can be viewed within a single general framework called *structural equation models.* Later in his career, Duncan concentrated his methodological interests on loglinear models and Rasch models for categorical data.

In his last book, *Notes on Social Measurement, Historical and Critical* (1984), Duncan shifted his attention to social measurement and presented his general philosophy of social science. Tracing the historical development of social measurement from Ancient Greece to the present, Duncan identified the difficulties of quantitative analyses in the social sciences, in which variability is the norm rather than the exception. Partly in response to his own critics, Duncan also presented himself as a fierce critic of aspects of the quantitative approach—something

that he had helped launch as a new standard for social science. This change in Duncan's methodological thinking can be traced to his realization that population heterogeneity renders statistical analyses of social science data essentially descriptive rather than causal. Indeed, avoidance of drawing law-like causal statements from statistical analyses became the hallmark of the intellectual tradition in quantitative sociology that is associated with Duncan. He was openly disdainful of the search for supposedly universal laws of society that would mimic those of physical science. The central tenet in Duncan's new paradigm for quantitative sociology is the primacy of empirical reality.

Duncan was born on December 2, 1921, in Nocona, Texas, and grew up in Stillwater, Oklahoma. He completed a BA at Louisiana State University in 1941, and an MA at the University of Minnesota in 1942. He then served three years in the U.S. Army during World War II (1939–1945) before completing his PhD in sociology at the University of Chicago in 1949. He was on the faculty in the departments of sociology at Pennsylvania State University, the University of Wisconsin, the University of Chicago, the University of Michigan, the University of Arizona, and the University of California, Santa Barbara, from which he retired in 1987.

Duncan was elected to membership in the National Academy of Sciences, the American Academy of Arts and Sciences, and the American Philosophical Society. He was also awarded honorary degrees by the University of Chicago, the University of Wisconsin, and the University of Arizona. He was president of the Population Association of America from 1968 to 1969.

SEE ALSO *Blau, Peter M.; Demography; Occupational Status; Social Status*

BIBLIOGRAPHY

Blau, Peter M., and Otis Dudley Duncan. 1967. *The American Occupational Structure.* New York: Wiley & Sons.

Duncan, Otis Dudley. 1984. *Notes on Social Measurement, Historical and Critical.* New York: Russell Sage Foundation.

Xie, Yu. Otis Dudley Duncan's Legacy: The Demographic Approach to Quantitative Reasoning in Social Science. http://www.yuxie.com.

Yu Xie

DURATION MODELS

Duration models are used to describe the amount of time that elapses until a given event, or the length of time spent in a given state. Duration models have been used to examine many phenomena, including labor-market outcomes, by modeling the length of time spent in unemployment; industry consolidation, by modeling time elapsed until a firm is acquired by another firm; criminal recidivism, by modeling time elapsed until conviction for a criminal offense for persons released from prison; and the viability of medical procedures, by modeling time until death, relapse, or recurrence after surgery.

Duration models share a duality relationship with count-data models. In count-data models, one models the number of occurrences of some event within a specified interval of time. If, for example, counts of some event are distributed Poisson, then the intervals between events can be shown to have an exponential distribution. One can model either counts over a time interval, or the intervals between the events comprising the counts. Duration models are often used in situations where only one interval is observed for each agent, as in the case of unemployment spells or the lives of firms.

In many cases, data on durations are censored. Suppose one collects data on durations in a given state by conducting surveys at calendar times t_A and t_B. Figure 1 illustrates four possibilities. At time t_A, agent 1 has not yet entered the state of interest, but by time t_B, he has entered and exited the state at times between t_A and t_B. Hence if the survey at time t_B asks the right questions, it will be possible for the researcher to observe this agent's time in the spell completely. Agent 2 enters the state of interest prior to the time of the first survey, and exits prior to the time of the second survey; again, if the right questions are asked, it will be possible for the researcher to observe this agent's complete duration as well. In some cases, however, depending on how the first survey is conducted, agent 2's time of entry into the state may be unobserved, in which case this agent's duration will be left-censored; all the researcher would know in this case is that the agent was already in the state of interest at time t_A, and the time of exit before time t_B. Agents 3 and 4 remain in the given state until after the time of the second survey; for these agents, the researcher can know only that they remained in the state of interest at time t_B and were still waiting to exit. Observations for these agents are right-censored; in addition, if the entry time for agent 3 is unknown, the observation for this agent will be both left- and right-censored.

The *maximum likelihood method* is often used to estimate duration models after specifying a distribution function

$$F(t) = \Pr(T \le t)$$

for the random variable T describing the length of time spent in a state. Because durations are necessarily non-negative, one must specify a one-sided distribution for T; examples include the exponential, Weibull, Gompertz, and log-normal distributions. The distribution function

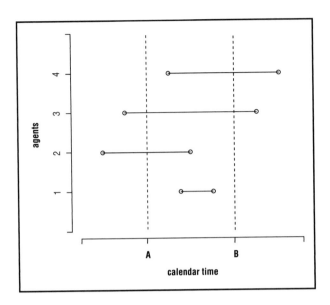

Figure 1

$F(t)$ implies a density function $f(t) = dF(t)$, a survivor function $S(t) = 1 - F(t)$ which gives the probability of remaining in the state up to time t, and a hazard function

$$\lambda(t) = f(t)/S(t) = \lim_{h \to 0} \frac{\Pr(t \le T < t + h \mid T \ge t)}{h}$$

giving the *rate* at which exits occur at time t. The goal of researchers is often to estimate the marginal effects of various covariates on the hazard rate.

John Kalbfleisch and Ross Prentice (2002), Tony Lancaster (1990), and Colin Cameron and Pravin Trivedi (2005) give extensive details on specification, censoring in, and estimation of duration models, as well as examples of applications.

SEE ALSO *Censoring, Left and Right; Maximum Likelihood Regression; Regression Analysis; Variables, Random*

BIBLIOGRAPHY

Cameron, A. Colin, and Pravin K. Trivedi. 2005. *Microeconometrics: Methods and Applications*. Cambridge, U.K., and New York: Cambridge University Press.

Kalbleisch, John D., and Ross L. Prentice. 2002. *The Statistical Analysis of Failure Time Data*. 2nd ed. Hoboken, NJ: J. Wiley.

Lancaster, Tony. 1990. *The Econometric Analysis of Transition Data*. Cambridge, U.K., and New York: Cambridge University Press.

Paul W. Wilson

DURKHEIM, ÉMILE
1858–1917

Émile Durkheim, the son of a rabbi from Eastern France, has long been recognized as a founding figure in modern sociology following his attempt to establish the subject as a respected scientific discipline in the academic world. Durkheim defined the subject matter of sociology as separate not only from that of natural sciences such as biology but also from other social sciences such as psychology and economics, which also studied the activities of the individual as a member of a group. Durkheim's seminal contribution to the establishment of sociology centered upon his founding of the journal *L'Année sociologique* in 1896, which addressed a whole range of issues including the economy, crime, law, and punishment. Journal entries on these and other topics allowed Durkheim to have an important influence in sociology and other social science disciplines.

Durkheim also advanced knowledge of the ideas of society, morality, and religion. One claim open to debate is that Durkheim was a social realist. This led him to challenge the assumption made by earlier Enlightenment philosophers that society was only a subjective and artificial entity because it was not part of nature. Instead, Durkheim argued that one should see society as an objective or observable reality that could be studied scientifically using empirical methods. To become scientific, sociology must study *social facts*. In *Rules of Sociological Method* (1895) Durkheim defined social facts as those emergent properties and realities of a collectivity which could not be reduced to the actions and motives of individuals, and that individuals were shaped and constrained by their external social environments. It was because social facts existed in their own right independently of individuals that Durkheim viewed society as a *sui generis* reality, which was subject to processes that could be understood only with reference to other social forces. Examples of social facts include language, religion, the economy, and law. These facts were real and should be studied as things. This meant that social phenomena could be known through observation which in turn made them capable of being analyzed as rigorously as objects or events in nature. Durkheim's conceptualization of society was nevertheless criticized for being ambiguous. In *Émile Durkheim: His Life and Work* (1973) Steven Lukes noted that Durkheim used the term *society* in various senses to mean the association of individuals, cultural transmission, socially prescribed obligations, system of rules, symbolic representations, or a national entity such as "French society." In 1894 Gabriel Tarde challenged Durkheim's notion of social facts, suggesting that they could not exist in their own right independently of individuals because social phenomena were transmitted from individual to individual.

Closely linked to the idea of society was Durkheim's original theory of morality. Here the obligation to act in accordance with moral rules came from society not nature, as earlier Enlightenment philosophers had supposed. Durkheim consequently saw morality as a collective social fact. Rules of moral conduct existed outside individuals and transcended personal likes and dislikes by being directed towards others in line with society's ideals and values concerning the common good. Observable laws and sanctions were imposed by society to prevent deviations from its moral rules. The scholar J. M. A. Darlu nevertheless objected, arguing in 1906 that Durkheim's interpretation of morality prevented him from addressing the individual's capacity for reason and their scope for rebellion against an existing set of collectively agreed moral rules. Furthermore, other scholars often allege that Durkheim's theory of morality—and indeed his sociology more generally—led him to ignore the phenomenon of social conflict. Marxist critics such as Tom Bottomore build upon this point when arguing that Durkheim placed an exaggerated emphasis on social order at the expense of paying adequate attention to social change. Anthony Giddens challenged the validity of this criticism when noting Durkheim's deep concern with the turmoil affecting European societies in his own day. This concern was expressed through Durkheim's conceptualization of the interests of the individual in conflict with those of society as a whole.

Durkheim's understanding of society and morality were inextricably bound up with his sociological theory of religion, which advanced knowledge by challenging the ideas of traditional theology. In *The Elementary Forms of Religious Life* (1912), Durkheim saw religion as the source of everything social. Central to Durkheim's definition of religion was the idea of the *sacred*. Sacred objects included symbolic things as diverse as a cross, flags, owls, or stones, all of which could be seen as extraordinary and set apart from the ordinary or *profane* things in everyday life. Beliefs and practices such as religious rituals also existed in relation to sacred things. Beliefs and practices generated the idea of moral community which in turn brought us back to the idea of sacred things. The sacred, beliefs and practices, and moral community, as the three basic elements of religion, were important because they bound individuals to the social group. Theological ideas about God and the supernatural were, however, missing from Durkheim's definition of religion. Religion was not simply an individual's communion with God. It was above all a form of collective life, and a way for the faithful, in their relationships with the sacred, to understand their connections with one another in society.

Durkheim's theory of religion has been criticized on a number of grounds. W. D. Wallis argued that religion was not essentially social and that the sociological viewpoint was only one among many. Contrary to Durkheim's own view, it was necessary to include the concept of the supernatural into a definition of religion. In the 1990s critics such as Fernando Uricoechea claimed that Durkheim took the idea of the sacred for granted and did not account for its genesis or source. Stjepan Meštrović further suggested that there has been a failure in contemporary Western societies to renew shared moral values. This has led agreement about what is sacred to become splintered into a myriad of competing meanings. This last criticism nevertheless overstates the diminution of the sacred. Meštrović's criticism, argued Jonathan Fish, was weakened through its failure to engage with Durkheim's important insights on the recurrent nature of sacralizing and resacralizing tendencies as an enduring feature of social life.

Durkheim's status as a founder of modern sociology was also linked up with his original theories of the division of labor, collective consciousness, and anomie in modern Western society. As societies industrialized, urbanized, and became more complex, specialized institutions concerned with government, industry, business, and education arose each with their own particular functions. A complex *division of labor* based on occupational specialization, diversification, and cooperation accompanied the emergence of these specialized institutions where people performed different work activities or occupational roles in society in line with their respective talents. Durkheim advanced sociological knowledge by rejecting the French philosopher Auguste Comte's earlier view of the division of labor. Instead of seeing this division as a negative force which eroded the sense of community between people, Durkheim viewed it in more positive terms as a potential source of social cohesion capable of binding individuals together through the performance of their specialized and yet interdependent work roles.

It was through the performance of these interconnected work roles that human beings could express their individuality. Individuality here referred to a person's singular capacity for thinking and acting. Individuality was part of modern society's *collective consciousness*. Collective consciousness referred to a body of ideas, attitudes, beliefs, and practices shared by all members of a society and which determined the relations of individuals to one another and society. A cult of the individual, which promoted the dignity and sacredness of the human person, emerged in support of this common belief in individuality. The problem in Durkheim's own day was that the division of labor and shared belief in individuality were unable to establish strong social bonds between people because they were centered upon maximizing self-interest. The pursuit of selfish interests and desires also did much to produce the problem of *anomie*. In *The Division of Labor* (1893) and *Suicide* (1897), Durkheim referred to anomie as a situation of normlessness in which the norms

or rules that regulated people's lives did not function properly. When the norms and rules which kept people's goals, expectations, and desires within achievable limits broke down, people began to pursue unattainable levels of pleasure and excitement which led them to feel uncertain about goals and values. The feelings of persistent unhappiness and disillusionment caused by such uncertainty also led to a rise in the suicide rate.

Durkheim's conception of the social origins of morality also provided a useful backdrop for introducing moral individualism as a solution to the problem of anomie. Durkheim's writings on this subject were of sociological importance because they challenged the nineteenth-century ideas of Jean-Marie Guyau who positively supported the idea of anomie, and a future society where fixed moral frameworks, norms, and rules would not exist. The concept of moral individualism, which was fully developed in Durkheim's work *Individualism and the Intellectuals* (1898), remained the direct opposite of egoistic individualism. Whereas egoistic individualism was concerned with purely private, selfish interests, moral individualism, by contrast, stressed the importance of individual rights as a basis for creating genuinely new social bonds and common or shared identities across Western industrial societies. This transcendence of selfish interests would allow the moral ideal of individualism to attach individuals to society as never before by inspiring strong feelings of collective devotion. These feelings would in turn allow the common belief in individuality to generate strong social bonds which relieved individual uncertainties about values thereby solving the problem of anomie.

Durkheim's proposed solution to anomie in the form of moral individualism also challenged the rise of orthodox or economistic forms of socialism, which attempted to solve this and other social problems in nineteenth-century Western societies by advocating a redistribution of wealth through centralized state control of the economy. Durkheim believed that these forms of socialism did not provide an adequate program for social reconstruction as the problem of anomie was neither class based nor did it have economic roots and therefore could not be solved by economic measures. The social problems facing modern society, which arose because industrialization, commercialization, and urbanization occurred too rapidly, were perceived by Durkheim as moral issues which required forms of moral authority capable of uniting individuals irrespective of their class position. Durkheim's belief that socialism was primarily concerned with economic regulation has been challenged by Giddens when suggesting that this view merely forced socialist theories into a conceptual niche which he had prepared for them.

Problems in democracy were also highlighted in Durkheim's writings. One major problem identified by

Durkheim concerned isolated individuals who made electoral choices on purely selfish grounds rather than through informed and considered opinions about current political issues. In the 1902 preface to *The Division of Labor*, Durkheim argued that this problem could be overcome through the reemergence of occupational groups or associations comprised of people who performed the same specialized work roles. These small and yet diverse functional groups would be bound together through modern society's wider collective belief in individuality. Occupational groups would stand between the individual and the democratic state through their internal election of delegates to an elected chamber. Local representatives of the occupational group would then democratically elect other delegates to national government. This procedure removed the problem of unreflective and selfish patterns of voting by only requiring average citizens to vote on internal matters within their occupational experience. Durkheim believed that this two-tier electoral system would facilitate the Western democratic state's reflection and effective promotion of informed opinion on the need for moral individualism in the future. Yet, as editor Robert Bellah pointed out in *Émile Durkheim on Morality and Society* (1973), this subordination of particular interests to the general interest has not occurred. Western society has not seen the revival of associational life that Durkheim originally hoped for.

Durkheim also addressed problems in education throughout his work. In *Moral Education* (1898–1899), Durkheim labeled as outdated traditional theological teachings of key elements in moral education such as the need for discipline and group attachment, following Catholicism's failure to adjust to the growth of individuality through occupational specialization in modern society. Durkheim's solution to this problem was to support a purely secular education for school children based upon the principles of science and reason. Secular education was needed if the historical link between moral education and mythical, transcendent forces was to be broken and the social reality behind moral rules brought to the fore. Durkheim hoped that the secular teaching of discipline and group attachment would over time enable moral individualism, and its pursuit of a genuine type of collective self-understanding, to replace traditional religion at the center of collective consciousness in modern Western society. Durkheim's belief in the ascendancy of secular education over traditional theological teachings has not, however, been realized in Western societies at the end of the twentieth-century. Ernest Wallwork noted that theologians have not only responded in a creative way to the intellectual challenges posed by sociology, they have found new ways of using traditional language to speak meaningfully of the human condition in this world. Although Durkheim's prediction has not yet been realized it may be premature, argued Fish, to rule out the possibility that his secular vision might come to fruition sometime in the future.

SEE ALSO *Morality; Suicide*

BIBLIOGRAPHY

PRIMARY WORKS

Durkheim, Émile. [1893] 1964. *The Division of Labor in Society*. Trans. George Simpson. Glencoe, IL: The Free Press.

Durkheim, Émile. [1895] 1938. *Rules of Sociological Method*. Trans. Sarah A. Solovay and John H. Mueller. Chicago: Chicago University Press.

Durkheim, Émile. [1897] 1970. *Suicide: A Study in Sociology*. Trans. John A. Spaulding and George Simpson. London: Routledge.

Durkheim, Émile. [1898] 1969. Individualism and the Intellectuals. In *Émile Durkheim: Critical Assessments*. Vol. 4. Trans. Steven Lukes and ed. Peter Hamilton. London: Routledge.

Durkheim, Émile. [1898–1899] 1961. *Moral Education: A Study in the Theory and Application of the Sociology of Education*. Trans. Everett K. Wilson and Herman Schnurer. New York: The Free Press.

Durkheim, Émile. [1912] 1995. *The Elementary Forms of Religious Life*. Trans. and with an Introduction by Karen E. Fields. New York: The Free Press.

SECONDARY WORKS

Bellah, Robert. 1973. Introduction. In *Émile Durkheim on Morality and Society*, ed. Robert Bellah, ix–lv. Chicago: University of Chicago Press.

Bottomore, Tom. 1981. A Marxist Consideration of Durkheim. *Social Forces* 59 (3): 902–917.

Fish, Jonathan S. 2005. *Defending the Durkheimian Tradition: Religion, Emotion and Morality*. Aldershot, U.K.: Ashgate Publishing.

Giddens, Anthony. 1978. *Durkheim*. Glasgow: Fontana/Collins.

Lukes, Steven. 1973. *Émile Durkheim: His Life and Work*. London: Allen Lane.

Meštrović, Stjepan. 1997. *Postemotional Society*. London: Sage.

Uricoechea, Fernando. 1992. Durkheim's Conception of the Religious Life: A Critique. *Archives de Sciences Sociales des Religions* 37 (79): 155–166.

Wallis, W. D. 1914. Durkheim's View of Religion. *Journal of Religious Psychology* 7: 252–267.

Wallwork, Ernest. 1972. *Durkheim, Morality and Milieu*. Cambridge, MA: Harvard University Press.

Jonathan S. Fish

DUTCH DISEASE

The term *Dutch disease* refers to the adverse effects on manufacturing industries that took place in the Netherlands with the natural gas discoveries of the 1970s and the process of real currency appreciation that followed. Similar "illnesses" affected several oil-exporting countries following the oil price shocks of the 1970s, providing further motivation to a growing literature on the subject. In this literature a natural resource boom comes close to being a curse because specialization in natural resource intensive goods can be harmful to long-term growth.

Indeed, the development of a natural resource intensive export sector can crowd out the manufacturing sector through a number of mechanisms. First, the expansion of the natural resource sector raises labor demand in this sector, thus increasing the wage in manufacturing and reducing its profitability. The profitability squeeze in manufacturing slows down capital accumulation and growth. Second, the increase in natural resource rents generates a higher demand for nontradable goods (the spending effect in Corden 1984), which leads to a higher relative price of nontradables and thus to real currency appreciation. The higher demand for and prices of nontradables leads to a reallocation of labor away from manufacturing and into services. Third, the fall in profitability in manufacturing (especially if the nontradable sector produces inputs for manufacturing) will cause capital to move into the nontradable goods sector and the resource intensive sector. This is indirect deindustrialization because it results from the real currency appreciation caused by the spending effect and depends on its strength (see Corden 1984; Corden and Neary 1982). Finally, the increase in land endowment or in the prices of the natural resource will create an increase in the profitability of capital invested in the resource intensive sector, causing capital to move away from manufacturing and into the resource intensive sector. This resource movement is labeled "direct deindustrialization" because it is independent of real currency appreciation.

The contraction of manufacturing through each of these mechanisms may make a country worse off in the long run because manufacturing industries are those with the most externalities and rapid technical progress (Matsuyama 1992). This may happen even if the resource boom is temporary. Temporary resource booms can lead to a long-term loss of competitiveness and a lower level of per capita income than would have been the case in the absence of the resource boom (Krugman 1987).

SEE ALSO *Imports; Inflation; Stagflation*

BIBLIOGRAPHY

Corden, W. Max. 1984. Booming Sector and Dutch Disease Economics: Survey and Consolidation. *Oxford Economic Papers* 36 (3): 359–380.

Corden, W. Max, and J. Peter Neary. 1982. Booming Sector and Deindustrialization in a Small Open Economy. *Economic Journal* 92: 825–848.

Krugman, P. R. 1987. The Narrow Band, the Dutch Disease, and the Competitive Consequences of Mrs. Thatcher. *Journal of Development Economics* 27: 41–55.

Matsuyama, K. 1992. Agricultural Productivity, Comparative Advantage, and Economic Growth. *Journal of Economic Theory* 58: 317–334.

Jaime Ros

DUVALIERS, THE

The rule of François "Papa Doc" Duvalier (1907–1971), president of Haiti from 1957 to 1971, was marked by autocracy and violence. He passed on his position to his son, Jean-Claude "Baby Doc" Duvalier (b. 1951), who moderated the violence of the regime but tolerated gross corruption. Jean-Claude was overthrown by a popular uprising in 1986.

When François Duvalier was born, Haiti was dominated by an elite of mixed racial origins, called in Haitian Creole *mulat*. The black majority suffered under discrimination and was often excluded from education, jobs, and public places. Duvalier was black, the child of one of Haiti's very small black middle class. He managed to go to college and became a physician, and was the director of a successful program to eradicate yaws, a dangerous communicable disease that was common in Haiti's countryside. From the country people he worked with, he came to appreciate Haiti's traditional folktales and religion, and he became a practitioner of Haitian *vaudou*. He also was a leading member of Haiti's Ethnographic Society, where he came in contact with Jean Price-Mars, one of the most important figures in the philosophical movement of *noirisme*, or black consciousness. François and Simone Duvalier married in 1939 and had three children, two daughters and a son, Jean-Claude.

Duvalier became involved in politics, supporting the *noiriste* political leader Dumarsais Estimé (1900–1953). When Estimé became president in 1946, Duvalier became minister of health. When Estimé was overthrown in 1950, Duvalier went into hiding. During this period, he became friendly with junior officers in the military. When the military permitted elections in 1956, Duvalier ran, and was successful thanks to his military allies. After a chaotic election process that saw three heads of state inaugurated in less than a year, Duvalier finally took office in 1957. At first he governed with the support of the military, but he formed a private militia, the Volunteers for National Security (VSN), also known as the *tontons macoutes*. With the support of the VSN, Duvalier dismissed the military high command and brought the Haitian armed forces under civilian control. He used his militia to extend his control over all aspects of Haitian society, ruthlessly killing or exiling political opponents. Many of the Haitian ruling class, both *mulat* commercial elites and darker-skinned military men, were his victims. Duvalier also had opponents outside the country, most notably the Kennedy administration in the United States, but in the end the United States gave him grudging support in response to his unwavering opposition to communism. In 1964 he declared himself president for life. Duvalier did open up opportunities for some blacks to rise in Haitian society, but he brooked no dissent, and there was no semblance of democracy in Haiti.

When Duvalier died in 1971 his son, Jean-Claude, then just nineteen years old, succeeded him. At first, Jean-Claude was happy to be a figurehead while his mother and his father's old advisers ran the country for him. But in 1974 he married Michele Bennet, a light-skinned divorcée several years his senior, whose father had been in prison for financial irregularities under François Duvalier. Michele enjoyed the privileges of rank, including a lavish wedding and regular shopping trips to Paris, but she also craved power for her husband and for her own family. There was a power struggle between the old Duvalierists and the supporters of Jean-Claude and Michele that ended with the retirement of Simone and many of the old hard-liners. Jean-Claude made some ineffective political reforms, and stole huge amounts of money from the Haitian state and foreign development programs. In 1983 Pope John Paul II visited the country and told the president and the Haitian people that "something needs to change here." Priests and Catholic lay workers, motivated by liberation theology, began to work against the government. A street protest in Gonaives in 1985 turned violent, and VSN gunmen killed a dozen students. Protests broke out across the country, reacting to news carried on the Catholic Church radio station, Radio Soleil. Under pressure from the U.S. government and his own military, Duvalier agreed to step down, and he fled the country on February 7, 1986. He took with him billions of dollars of stolen money.

A transitional military government took power and promised to hold elections, but instead Haiti plunged into political chaos from which it is now only beginning to emerge. Jean-Claude and Michele lived together in exile in France for some time, plotting his return to power and fomenting disorder, but they divorced in 2000. She got most of the remaining money and remains active in Haitian politics, while he lives in modest circumstances.

SEE ALSO *Coup d'Etat; Dictatorship; Vodou*

BIBLIOGRAPHY

Diederich, Bernard, and Al Burt. 2005. *Papa Doc and the Tontons Macoutes.* 2nd ed. New York: Markus Weiner.

Greene, Graham. [1966] 1991. *The Comedians.* New York: Penguin Classics.

Stewart R. King

DUVERGER'S LAW
SEE *Political Parties.*

E

EAST INDIA COMPANY

SEE *Opium Wars.*

EAST INDIAN DIASPORA

Indian indentured migration was a distinctively mid-nineteenth-century British labor-reallocation policy. It was predicated on and institutionalized a racial division of labor across the globe. While men and women from throughout British India were recruited during the scheme's seven decades of operation (1836–1917), the majority were came from what are now the states of Bihar, Bengal, Uttar Pradesh, and Tamil Nadu. This policy played a significant, if under-appreciated, role in the emergence and crystallization of nationalist, nativist, and anticolonial discourses and movements, not only in India from the turn of the twentieth century on, but also in the other colonies to which men and women from the Indian subcontinent (whether under indentures or not) migrated and settled. The discursive contexts in which government-supervised indentured migration emerged was criticized, regulated, defended, and finally abolished also frame subsequent migration streams. Further, they continue to haunt the relations among the descendents of these various migrants, the Indian government, and those proliferating and polarizing transnational cultural and political economies characteristic of the early twenty-first century.

Migration around, to, through, and from the Indian subcontinent has been a characteristic and defining feature of the region's recorded pasts. It was augmented and expanded in the colonial period by the migration and settlement of laborers, soldiers, and bureaucrats from British India to British enterprises in Burma, the Malay peninsula, and Ceylon. However, the streams currently referred to as the "Indian diaspora" are commonly understood as those that began with the mid-nineteenth-century policy of assisted indentured labor migration; that proliferated in the migrations of traders and merchants, missionaries, and teachers to serve communities of settled indentured migrants (in Uganda, for example); and that expanded in separate, but not unrelated, individual and voluntary emigrations to north America, Australia and New Zealand, and Britain and Europe. One such migration in the late nineteenth and early twentieth centuries was that of Punjabi men to the west coast of Canada and the United States (peaking from the 1890s through World War I [1914–1918]). Some of these migrants married and started families and farms with Mexican women, who were themselves participants in yet another labor emigration stream.

Another, more extended and extensively studied stream of the Indian diaspora comprises the skilled and unskilled workers and students that since the 1960s have migrated to jobs and schools in primarily Anglophone countries in the "Global North." A further subset of the diaspora includes relocations (voluntary or under duress) of earlier migrants' descendents. These individuals have moved from newly independent nations and former British colonies like Kenya, Tanzania, Uganda (from which they were expelled in 1972), Fiji, or the Caribbean to the United Kingdom, Canada, Australia, and the United States. Another substantial overseas migration stream from India during the last thirty years has been that of both skilled and unskilled wage workers on short-term contracts to the oil-rich Gulf States.

Insofar as they do not result in permanent settlement or communities, the short-term migration of skilled and unskilled workers are not considered part of the Indian diaspora, either in the vocabulary of the Indian government (wherein they are designated "Non-Resident Indians," or NRIs), or in the scholarly and popular literature on diaspora—their financial contributions to families in India notwithstanding. To distinguish these and other temporary migrants from those permanently settled overseas (sometimes for a generation or more), the government of India has coined the term "Persons of Indian Origin," or "PIOs."

Indentured migration from British India was a strategy (variously successful) to preserve the individual, industrial, and imperial wealth and power flowing from the highly protectionist plantation mode of sugar production in the British West Indies. While never uncontested by critics in the West Indies, Britain, or India, Indian indentured migration and the sugar plantation economy it sustained were deemed sufficiently successful to be introduced to Fiji in 1879. Indeed, in the decades before its abolition by the Indian government in 1917, indentured migration was extended to new industrial enterprises, most notably the construction and operation of railroads in the British colonies in eastern and southern Africa, where migrant and sojourning merchant communities with kinship and business ties in western India had flourished for several centuries.

Almost from its inception, the system of indentured migration was cast by detractors in India, in the labor-importing colonies and in metropolitan Britain as a "new system of slavery" (as Colonial Secretary Russell put it in a communication to Governor Henry Light on February 15, 1840). It was distinguished only nominally from the hereditary servitude it replaced. Charges of deception and coercion in recruitment in India, and of highly exploitative conditions at colonial work sites generated innumerable exposés in the antislavery press, scores of government inquiries and investigations, and ongoing efforts to devise protocols to govern the recruitment, transportation, employment, living conditions, and repatriation (or permanent residence) of indentured workers and their descendents.

Of particular concern to critics and apologists alike was the status of women among the indentured migrants, of whom a stipulated proportion (40%) was mandated by the government of India in each importing colony's annual recruitment and allotment, despite the varied objections of employers, recruiters, and critics throughout the empire. Contemporaries and subsequent generations of observers have generally agreed that, whether inden-

tured migration unconscionably exploited or positively benefited those who migrated under its aegis, the system helped to further institutionalize and reify categories of race, nation and division of labor, not only in broad strokes across the British Empire (and, indeed, the globe, since French and Dutch colonies also imported Indian indentured labor), but also among the various and varied populations of individual importing colonies.

Indentured migrants from British India, together with their descendents, were identified and categorized as "Indian." Thus, men and women who may have been accustomed to identifying themselves and others according to locally significant affiliations—such as clan, lineage, village, religious practice, or language—found themselves cast as "Indian" en route to plantations (and other work sites) in the Caribbean, Africa, or the Indian and Pacific Oceans, where they would be distinguished from others encountered and cast as "African," "Fijian," "European," "Chinese." In the Caribbean colonies, for example, Indian migrants and their descendents were cast as docile, industrious, and thrifty wage laborers, in stark contrast to emancipated creole populations and their descendents, whose alleged inability or refusal to engage in plantation labor for wages provoked employers' turn to India. That this strategy was subsidized by the colonial and imperial states did not go unnoticed by workers and critics in the sugar colonies, India, or the metropole, who charged, variously, that imported Indian labor was depressing plantation wages and forcing African-creole people out of that sector, or that it amounted to a deliberate policy of racial-national "divide and rule" on the part of employers and the state alike.

In the Fiji islands, which were brought under British protection in 1874, the bureaucratized system of Indian indentured labor recruitment and administration enabled the British government to assure Fijian chiefs that native Fijians' exclusive rights, privileges, and identity as owners and custodians of the land would not be compromised by the introduction of plantation agriculture. The land to be brought under cultivation would be leased (and never sold) to sugar companies, and the labor would be imported (the skilled from Britain, and the unskilled—nearly 61,000 men and women between 1879 and 1917—from India).

In the Caribbean, Fiji, and indeed everywhere Indian indentured migration proceeded, large and complex bodies of legislation regulating indentured workers and Indian migrants' personal mobility (pass laws), personal relations (stipulations recognizing as legal only those marriages performed before a magistrate or a Christian clergyman) and community organizations proliferated, further institutionalizing and normalizing indentured migrants and their communities, and separating them from others.

In addition, from the 1880s on, missionaries representing various reformist strains of Hindu and Muslim practice in India began to circulate and proselytize among the growing Indian indentured and immigrant communities in Fiji, the Caribbean and the Indian Ocean colonies, facilitating the spread of news of India to dispersed migrants, and news of the migrants to India. Together with the emergence of a specifically nationalist critique of British rule in India, this further contributed to the ongoing production and consolidation of an "Indian" identity among indentured migrants and their growing communities.

However, particularities and differences among indentured migrants (religious and linguistic ones, for example, based on where, when and how they were recruited) did not disappear en route to the importing colonies, where Hindu and Muslim immigrants pursued their separate faiths and practices in their articulated but distinctive communities. In addition, caste—and assumptions about the significance of caste and religion (as well as region of birth) to recruits' value as plantation laborers—exercised the imagination of critics, supporters, and administrators of the system, whose observations and assessments comprise the definitive official archive on Indian indentured migration. Some employers instructed their recruitment agents in India to avoid or pursue recruits of particular castes. In 1919, an observer writing in the *Journal of the Royal Agricultural and Commercial Society of British Guiana* observed that "Excepting ex-policemen, ex-soldiers, Brahmins, Chatris, Rajputs, Barbers, Dhobis, Nats, Banias, Fakirs, Punjabis, and coolies of any of the non-agricultural castes, all other castes are recruited and have been sent to the Colonies" (Rodway, 1919).

The data generated in the recruitment process (and preserved in the records of Indian government agencies mandated to regulate indentured emigration, which was restricted to the ports of Calcutta and Madras) have similarly attracted considerable scholarly and popular attention. These data, about which even some contemporaries were skeptical, along with data from importing colonies, indicate that the majority of indentured emigrants who left from Madras (the major port for migration to colonial Ceylon, Fiji, Malaya, Natal and Burma) were from the Tamil-speaking, eastern districts of the Presidency, while the majority of emigrants embarking from Calcutta were from what are now Bihar, Uttar Pradesh, and eastern Bengal (with some recruits from Punjab and farther east also recruited and embarked from Calcutta). The most exhaustive and critical study of these data was conducted by Sir George Grierson in 1883. His "Report on Colonial Emigration from the Bengal Presidency" suggests strongly that throughout the Bengal Presidency there was considerable awareness of what indentured migration would entail. He noted, "About caste, the people have invented a curious theory regarding ship-board life, which shows the adaptability of native customs," in which they likened the pollutions (dietary and other) encountered on the passage from India to those encountered en route to the temple of Jagannath, a popular destination for Hindu pilgrims. He was told that "a man can eat anything on board-ship. A ship is like the temple of Jagannath, where there are not caste restrictions."

The legal, social, and political discriminations faced by indentured migrants in other British colonies, along with the real and perceived extension of handicaps and prejudice to non-indentured overseas Indian communities, provoked intense and sustained outrage and political organization both in these colonies and in India. In South Africa, for example, members of Indian merchant communities who had settled in Natal hired Mohandas K. Gandhi to represent them in their ongoing disputes with the government between 1893 and 1914. Gandhi continued to play a role here—working on the Colour Bar and Class Areas Reservation bills of 1925 and 1926, for example—long after his return to India, despite lukewarm support from Indian nationalists focused on the struggle for self-determination at home. Those Indians in the subcontinent denied access to employment in the highest echelons of the Indian civil service and army because they were not European found it galling that, through indentured migration, "Indian" came to be associated throughout the world with unskilled and low-wage labor.

In 1912, Gopal Krishna Gokhale, an Indian nationalist leader and member of the Legislative Council (for Bombay), proposed legislation abolishing indentured emigration from India. He argued, "Wherever the system exists, there the Indians are only known as coolies, no matter what their position might be.... [T]here are disabilities enough in all conscience attaching to our position in this country, ... why must this additional brand be put upon our brow before the rest of the civilised world?" (Government of India, Legislative Proceedings, March 4, 1912). The association was an important factor in the strategies and rhetoric leading to abolition of the migration scheme.

The equation of Indians with cheap labor continued to frame intra-imperial resistance to extending to India the self-rule and sovereignty accorded all the white settler colonies, even after abolition of indentureship in 1917. At the 1923 Imperial Conference held in London, for example, Prime Minister Mackenzie King of Canada argued that for his government "the problem is not a racial one; it is purely ... economic." He attributed Indians' limited citizenship rights to the electoral clout of organized labor, which was fearful of Indians' perceived willingness to work for wages lower than those acceptable to European-descended Canadians, and to the politics of constitutional federalism. Referring to the legal disabilities faced by Indians in South Africa, Prime Minister Jan Smuts explained that they were merely means toward ensuring that the culture and values brought to southern Africa by European settlers in the nineteenth century continue to flourish in his country. In his comments at the Imperial Conference, he explained that white South Africans "are not there to foster Indian civilisation, they are there to foster Western civilization" (Smuts, 1988).

The implications of indentured migration's role in the racialization or nationalization of labor through the empire extended through anticolonial struggles, independence, and beyond. In Trinidad, for example, a racialized division of labor and residential segregation (with Indian-Trinidadians predominating in rural areas and agricultural occupations, and African-Trinidadians in urban and manufacturing ones) led to political divisions between the two most numerous population groups that persisted well past independence in 1962. In British Guiana in 1957, divisions in the People's Progressive Party (PPP) between African and Indo-Guyanese members and interests (each constituting nearly 40% of the population) led Linden Forbes Sampson Burnham to establish the predominantly African Guyanese People's National Party (PNC). This left the PPP, led by Cheddi Jagan, primarily Indo-Guyanese. Exacerbated by Anglo-American antipathy toward Jagan's unapologetically socialist sympathies, the racially charged political divisions were accompanied by ongoing civil unrest and violence that well lasted past independence in 1966, when a government headed by Burnham and his party took office. Indeed, these divisions were still in play after Jagan was elected president in 1992.

The pattern is evident in Fiji, as well, where a military coup in 1987, led by Colonel Sitiveni Rabuka (the army is almost exclusively ethnic Fijian), produced a new constitution (in 1992) that banned Indo-Fijians from holding the post of prime minister and ensured that more than half of all Parliamentary seats were held by native Fijians. These provisions were revised in 1997, however, and Mahendra Chaudhry of the Fiji Labour Party was swept into office as the first Indo-Fijian prime minister in 1999. But a second coup, under the leadership of ethnic Fijian George Speight, toppled the newly-elected government in May 2000. Speight explained that for ethnic Fijians like himself, "it's not so much a hate of the Indians but a fear of our host culture and everything unique about ourselves being eroded to the extent that it could be lost" (Mercer, 2000).

The 2000 coup precipitated a wave of anti-Indian violence and accelerated Indo-Fijian emigration to Australia, New Zealand, Canada, the United States, and the United Kingdom, where (together with emigrants and refugees from Trinidad, Guyana, Tanzania, Uganda, the nations of South Asia, and elsewhere) they contribute to growing and increasingly heterogeneous Indian, Caribbean, African, and other minority communities. As "Paki-bashing" in Britain in the 1970s and 1980s, the "dot-busting" (attacks on women with *bindis* on their foreheads) in the United States in the 1990s, and the targeted violence following the 9/11 attacks in 2001 all testify, these migrants—along with those directly from the subcontinent—often encounter hostility from already-settled citizenries and populations, whether native-born or immigrant.

The impact of these multiple and varied migrations is evident in every aspect of the economies, politics, and social and cultural histories and productions of the nations in which migrants from India have settled, as well as in the subcontinent itself. The Vishwa Hindu Parishad (VHP, or World Hindu Council, founded in 1964) has successfully tapped resources in the diaspora (through such media as the VHP of America) for funds and political lobbying to advance the aim of establishing India as a Hindu state. The VHP is closely linked historically and organizationally to the Hindu nationalist Rashtriya Swayamsevak Sangh (RSS, or National Volunteers' Union), founded in 1925, and to the Bharatiya Janata Party (BJP, or Indian People's Party), formed in 1980. This alliance led a coalition government (the National Democratic Alliance) from 1998 to 2004. The VHP has also been associated with the 1992 destruction of a sixteenth-century Muslim mosque in Ayodhya (allegedly built on the site of the birthplace of Rama, an important aspect of the Hindu god Vishnu), and with the spiral of anti-Muslim violence and political unrest this act precipitated, both at that time and in Gujarat in 2002.

On the cultural front, the post-independence Indian film industry, based in Bombay, has emerged as an important and dynamic common ground for Indians both in India and abroad. The popular cultures projected through cinema (and ancillary industries like television, music, and dance) have been increasingly inflected by and attentive to diasporic viewers. Judging from the sheer volume of sites devoted to a vast array of aspects of South Asian, Indian, and diasporic identities and interests, the Internet has proved a generative space for forging community and delineating differences among those with ancestral and affective ties to India.

In the United States, passage of the 1965 Immigration Act facilitated the immigration from South Asia of professional and technical workers (as well as students seeking professional and advanced postgraduate degrees). Many of these individuals became naturalized citizens of the United States, where they and their children have been cast as "model minorities" who demonstrate the promise of American citizenship. Since the mid-1970s, patterns have shifted again, with family reunification rather than employer preference accounting for a growing proportion of immigrants from South Asian countries. This has also led to a decline in the proportion of highly skilled and professional and technical workers among those emigrating.

In India, in the meantime, the Citizenship Act of 1955 conclusively precluded the possibility that emigrants settled overseas, whether born in India themselves or born overseas to Indian citizens, could be citizens both of their countries of domicile and of India. Instead, the act reserved to the Indian government the right to extend Indian citizenship to citizens of Commonwealth countries and the Republic of Ireland on "a basis of reciprocity" and agreement between itself and the governments in question. However, in 2004, after decades of lobbying, some PIOs who may have forfeited Indian citizenship when they became naturalized citizens (or second-generation PIOs, born overseas) were permitted to pursue a partial restitution of Indian citizenship. While it withholds the right to vote, the amendment permitting "dual citizenship" promulgated in 2004 substantially facilitates financial investments and property ownership in India by eligible PIOs, in part through the Ministry of Overseas Indian Affairs (MOIA), which was formed expressly to administer to the PIO population. While the government of India estimates that emigrants from "territories that are currently within the borders of the Republic of India" numbers over 20 million people, only emigrants to sixteen countries—none of which was involved in Indian indentured migration—are eligible for dual citizenship.

BIBLIOGRAPHY

Bates, Crispin, ed. 2001. *Community, Empire and Migration. South Asians in Diaspora.* London: Palgrave Publishers.

Breman, Jan. 1989. *Taming the Coolie Beast: Plantation Society and the Colonial Order in Southeast Asia.* Delhi: Oxford University Press.

Carter, Marina. 1995. *Servants, Sirdars, and Settlers: Indians in Mauritius, 1834–1874.* New York: Oxford University Press.

Carter, Marina, and Khal Torabully. 2002. *Coolitude: An Anthology of the Indian Labour Diaspora.* London: Anthem South Asian Studies.

Clarke, Colin G., Ceri Peach, and Steven Vertovec, eds. 1990. *South Asians Overseas: Migration and Ethnicity.* New York: Cambridge University Press.

Daniel, E. Valentine, Henry Bernstein, and Tom Brass, eds. 1992. *Plantations, Proletarians, and Peasants in Colonial Asia.* London: Frank Cass.

Kale, Madhavi. 1998. *Fragments of Empire: Capital, Slavery, and Indian Indentured Labor Migration in the British Caribbean.* Philadelphia: University of Pennsylvania Press.

Kelly, John D. 1991. *A Politics of Virtue: Hinduism, Sexuality, and Countercolonial Discourse in Fiji.* Chicago: University of Chicago Press.

Kelly, John D., and Martha Kaplan. 2001. *Represented Communities: Fiji and World Decolonization.* Chicago: University of Chicago Press.

Khan, Aisha. 2004. *Callaloo Nation: Metaphors of Race and Religious Identity among South Asians in Trinidad.* Durham, NC: Duke University Press.

Lal, Brij V. 1983. *Girmitiyas: The Origins of the Fiji Indians.* Canberra, Australia: Journal of Pacific History.

Lal, Brij V., ed. 2004. *Bittersweet: The Indo-Fijian Experience.* Canberra, Australia: Pandanus Books.

Laurence, K. O. 1994. *A Question of Labour: Indentured Immigration into Trinidad and British Guiana 1875–1917.* Kingston, Jamaica: Ian Randle.

Leonard, Karen Isaksen. 1992. *Making Ethnic Choices: California's Punjabi Mexican Americans.* Philadelphia: Temple University Press.

Look-Lai, Walton. 1993. *Indentured Labor, Caribbean Sugar: Chinese and Indian Migrants to the British West Indies, 1838–1918.* Baltimore, MD: Johns Hopkins University Press.

Mercer, Phil. 2000. Future Bleak for Fiji's Indians. BBC News, July 12. http://news.bbc.co.uk/2/hi/asia-pacific/830926.stm.

Oxford University Press Transnational Communities Programme. 2001. Paper Given to the Conference on Transnational Migration: Comparative Perspectives. Oxford: Oxford University Press.

Parekh, Bhiku C., Gurharpal Singh, and Steven Vertovec, eds. 2003. *Culture and Economy in the Indian Diaspora.* London: Routledge.

Prashad, Vijay. 2000. *The Karma of Brown Folk.* Minneapolis: University of Minnesota Press.

Rodway, James. 1919. Labour and Colonisation. *Timheri: Journal of the Royal Agricultural and Commercial Society of British Guiana.* Special Colonisation Issue, VI, 3rd series (September): 20-42.

Smuts, J. C. 1923. Summary of Proceedings, Imperial Conference, 1923, London, 1 October–8 November, 1923 (Cmd. 1988, Appendices, volume V, *Speeches Regarding the Position of Indians in Other Parts of the Empire*).

Tinker, Hugh. 1974. *A New System of Slavery: The Export of Indian Labour Overseas, 1830–1920.* New York: Oxford University Press.

Tinker, Hugh. 1977. *The Banyan Tree: Overseas Emigrants from India, Pakistan, and Bangladesh.* New York: Oxford University Press.

Van der Veer, Peter, ed. 1995. *Nation and Migration: The Politics of Space in the South Asian Diaspora.* Philadelphia: University of Pennsylvania Press.

Vertovec, Steven, ed. 1991. *Aspects of the South Asian Diaspora.* Delhi: Oxford University Press.

Vertovec, Steven. 2000. *The Hindu Diaspora: Comparative Patterns.* London: Routledge.

Vertovec, Steven, and Ceri Peach, eds. 1997. *Islam in Europe: The Politics of Religion and Community.* New York: St. Martin's Press.

Madhavi Kale

EAST INDIES

The East Indies cover a wide geographical expanse in South and Southeast Asia ranging from the Indian subcontinent to the Malay Archipelago, described as the world's largest island group. Initially referring to India, these colonial demarcations of territory later comprised more than thirteen thousand islands located across the Indian and Pacific Oceans between mainland Southeast Asia and Australia. Coveted for their rich natural resources, including rubber, spices, cotton, and indigo, and their strategic location as important trading centers along the spice routes, the East Indies were colonized by Europe in the seventeenth century after the initial exploratory missions of the Portuguese and Spanish, and especially after the founding of various European trading companies. These companies carved out zones of influence named after the particular colonizing power they represented, such as the British East Indies (India and Malaysia), the Dutch East Indies (Indonesia), and the Spanish East Indies (Philippines).

Christopher Columbus's (1451–1506) miscalculation of westward navigation routes from Spain to Asia brought him to the New World instead of India. To avoid confusion with the "original" Indies (i.e., India), the terms *East Indies* and *West Indies* were applied by Europeans to highlight territorial distinctions between Indians from the East (Asia) and the West (the Americas). These territorial designations became racial designations to distinguish East Indians from their West Indian counterparts, thereby authenticating the centrality of Europe and its power to arbitrarily classify and homogenize entire populations from the non-Western world.

East Indian also became a marker of diasporic identity in North America to designate Indians from India and to avoid further confusion with indigenous Native American or First Nation peoples also known as *Indians* due to Columbus's navigational errors. Consequently, East Indians had to be distinguished from American Indians even though the former did not necessarily identify with the appellation East Indian on account of its specific ethnic connotations in India and the political realities of decolonization. In the postcolonial period, the blanket characterization of East Indians as colonized subjects inhabiting the East Indies became invalid with the establishment of sovereign states. The term consequently misrepresented diasporic Indians who preferred to self-identify as South Asians instead.

In India, the term *East Indian* refers to a specific ethnic minority from the western Konkan coast that settled in and around the area of Bombay (Mumbai) during the period of Portuguese rule in India. They were Christianized by the Portuguese and called *Bombay Portuguese* to distinguish them from Goans migrating to Bombay from the former Portuguese territory Goa. They

may have adopted the name *East Indian* under British rule to show their allegiance to the British. It is therefore misleading to label all Indians from India as East Indians because of this constituency's historical and cultural specificity in India.

In addition, the label *East Indian* added another polemic in the West Indies, where it designated people of South Asian origin in the Caribbean. These East Indian-West Indians further exemplified the ruptures created by colonial history and its random demarcation of boundaries through misleading nomenclature.

SEE ALSO *Caribbean, The*

BIBLIOGRAPHY

Selvon, Sam. 1987. Three Into One Can't Go: East Indian, Trinidadian, West Indian. In *India in the Caribbean*, eds. David Dabydeen and Brinsley Samaroo, 13–24. London: Hansib.

Van Kley, Edwin and Donald F. Lach, eds. 1993. *A Century of Advance: South Asia*. Vol. 3, Book 2 of *Asia in the Making of Europe*. Chicago: University of Chicago Press.

Brinda J. Mehta

EASTERLIN PARADOX

SEE *Happiness.*

EASTERN BAND OF THE CHEROKEES

SEE *Cherokees.*

EASTON, DAVID
1917–

David Easton has been one of the most prominent and influential political scientists in the post–World War II (1939–1945) period. He was one of the leading scholars at the heart of the behavioral revolution that sought to develop a unified empirical theory of political science to replace the traditional study of politics. Easton has also been the leading proponent of the application of systems theory to the study of politics.

Easton received his B.A. and M.A. from the University of Toronto, and his PhD from Harvard University in 1947. From 1947 to 1984, he taught at the University of Chicago, being named the Andrew MacLeish distinguished service professor in 1955. In 1984 he moved to the University of California at Irvine, where he is distinguished research professor of political science. He has served as vice president of the American Academy of Arts and Sciences (1985–1986) and as president of the American Political Science Association (APSA) from 1968 to 1969. His 1969 presidential address is perhaps the single most influential such address delivered by an APSA president. He has also been a fellow at the Center for Advanced Study in the Behavioral Sciences at Stanford University (1957–1958), and from 1971 to 1980 Easton was the Sir Edward Peacock professor of political science at Queen's University in Kingston, Ontario.

Easton's first major work was *The Political System: An Inquiry into the State of Political Science* (1953). There he analyzed the state of political science, which he argued had become dominated by a combination of constitutional legalism and the history of ideas that tended to lapse into antiquarian historicism. As such, in comparison to other sciences, political science was theoretically moribund. Easton argued that in order for political science to become scientifically mature, it needed to internalize scientific principles and methods and focus on the empirically observable behavior of political actors. Toward that end he proposed the adoption of systems theory as the foundation for the behavioral paradigm, and much of his subsequent work (Easton 1965a, 1965b) was directed at developing systems theory in detail. By the late 1960s, the behavioral paradigm, if not systems theory per se, had become the hegemonic paradigm in American political science. Easton went on to develop a version of structural theory to augment the framework provided by systems analysis. During that same period, another dimension of his work, one that too often goes unnoticed, is his extensive empirical research on the political socialization of children (Easton and Dennis 1969).

In his 1969 APSA presidential address, Easton called for a "post-behavioral revolution," a term misunderstood by some critics and proponents of behavioralism alike. Easton's vision was that the scientific procedures of social science should be brought to bear on the social and political problems facing the United States, problems whose severity could not be ignored. More recently, Easton (1997) has argued that political science has become increasingly fragmented, in part because of misunderstandings surrounding postbehavioralism that have led to an abandonment of scientific principles. Despite this fragmentation, Easton claims that the resilience of the scientific foundations of political science can provide the basis for what he calls neobehavioralism, a union of behavioralism and rational choice theory. Neobehavioralism would provide the unified science of politics to which both empiricists and rational choice theorists aspire.

Whether David Easton's recent neobehavioralist vision will have the same impact on political science as his earlier work is yet to be determined. But his contributions to and impact on the discipline of political science since the mid-twentieth century continue to be substantial and widely recognized.

SEE ALSO *American Political Science Association; Democracy; Political Science*

BIBLIOGRAPHY

Easton, David. 1953. *The Political System: An Inquiry into the State of Political Science.* New York: Knopf.

Easton, David. 1965a. *A Framework for Political Analysis.* Englewood Cliffs, NJ: Prentice Hall.

Easton, David. 1965b. *A Systems Analysis of Political Life.* New York: Wiley.

Easton, David, ed. 1966. *Varieties of Political Theory.* Englewood Cliffs, NJ: Prentice Hall.

Easton, David. 1969. The New Revolution in Political Science. *American Political Science Review* 63: 1051–1061.

Easton, David. 1990. *The Analysis of Political Structure.* New York: Routledge.

Easton, David. 1997. The Future of the Postbehavioral Phase in Political Science. In *Contemporary Empirical Political Theory,* ed. Kristen Renwick Monroe, 13–46. Berkeley: University of California Press.

Easton, David, and Jack Dennis. 1969. *Children in the Political System: Origins of Political Legitimacy*. New York: McGraw-Hill.

Easton, David, John G. Gunnell, and Luigi Graziano, eds. 1991. *The Development of Political Science: A Comparative Survey.* New York: Routledge.

Easton, David, John G. Gunnell, and Michael B. Stein, eds. 1995. *Regime and Discipline: Democracy and the Development of Political Science.* Ann Arbor: University of Michigan Press.

Easton, David, and Corinne S. Schelling, eds. 1991. *Divided Knowledge: Across Disciplines, Across Cultures.* Newbury Park, CA: Sage.

Monroe, Kristen Renwick, ed. 1997. *Contemporary Empirical Political Theory*. Berkeley: University of California Press.

Michael T. Gibbons

ECLA/ECLAC

SEE *Economic Commission for Latin America and the Caribbean.*

ECOLOGICAL SYSTEMS THEORY

SEE *Developmental Psychology.*

ECONOMETRIC DECOMPOSITION

Ronald Oaxaca (1973) and Alan Blinder (1973) introduced a statistical tool that enables social scientists to identify the ability of a particular observable characteristic to explain the difference in the outcomes of two groups (e.g., the black-white wage gap). The tool, known as a *decomposition*, provides an estimate of the contribution of discrimination to the difference in the outcomes of the two groups. Prior to Oaxaca and Blinder's innovation, researchers were only able to identify collective contribution of all observable differences in the characteristics of two groups. The decomposition has become a required tool in many social science disciplines. It is used to explain pay differences between men and women, public and private sector workers, union and nonunion workers. Most recently, the decomposition has been applied to explaining pay differences between older and younger workers, people with disabilities and those without disabilities, and the pay disadvantage that gays, lesbians, and bisexuals experience (see, for example, Rodgers 2005, Badgett 2006, Baldwin and Johnson 2006, and Adams and Neumark 2006).

Since Oaxaca and Blinder's seminal work, numerous extensions have been developed. Using the white-black wage gap as the example, this entry summarizes the technique's major extensions and limitations.

THE BASIC DECOMPOSITION

Oaxaca (1973) combines log-earnings function estimates for blacks and whites and standardizes the error term to construct the following expression:

$$D_t = \bar{y}_{wt} - \bar{y}_{bt} = \Delta X_t \beta_t + X_{bt}(\beta_{wt} - \beta_{bt}) + \sigma_t \Delta \theta_t + (\sigma_{wt} - \sigma_{bt})\theta_{bt} \quad (1),$$

where the D_t denotes the total log earnings differential. On the right-hand side, the first term is the explained gap (the portion explained by differences in measured characteristics). The second term is the residual gap (the portion attributed to differences in rates of compensation to the characteristics). The remaining two terms are generally ignored, as the decomposition is usually done at the means; otherwise, the sum of the last three terms is considered the residual gap. The residual gap is interpreted as the contribution of discrimination and characteristics that have been excluded from the model. These characteristics both predict wages and are correlated with race.

Interpreting the residual gap as discrimination requires that the model contain all of the factors that predict wages. Otherwise, discrimination's estimated contribution is biased. Little theoretical guidance exists on the selection of the characteristics that should be included. For example, some researchers control for racial differences in occupational outcomes. Yet these outcomes are influenced by discrimination. Another major issue is that the choice of weights is arbitrary. This is a problem when the weights differ across groups, generating a range of decompositions. Some efforts have attempted to utilize economic theory to provide guidance on the weight's choice (see, for example, Cotton 1988 and Neumark 1988). In practice, researchers either present results assuming different weighting structures, or present their preferred specification and say in a note that the results are not sensitive to choice of weights.

DECOMPOSING CHANGES OVER TIME AND ACROSS GROUPS

An extension developed by Chinhui Juhn, Kevin Murphy, and Brooks Pierce (1991) is to decompose time series changes in the wage gap into four components. For example, a narrowing or widening in the white-black wage gap from year t to t', can be written as

$$D_{t'} - D_t = (\Delta X_{t'} - \Delta X_t)\beta_t + \Delta X_{t'}(\beta_{t'} - \beta_t) + (\Delta \theta_{t'} - \Delta \theta_t)\sigma_t + \Delta \theta_{t'}(\sigma_{t'} - \sigma_t) \quad (2).$$

The change in the actual wage gap is decomposed into (1) changes in measured characteristics holding the coefficients or prices fixed; (2) changes in prices holding characteristics fixed; (3) the contribution of shifts in central tendency or the movement of the average black in the white distribution; and (4) the contribution of shifts in spread, or changes in the variance of wages (see Juhn, Murphy, and Pierce 1991 for a detailed description of how these components are constructed). Term 3 measures changes in the position of blacks in the white residual wage distribution due to changes in unmeasured racial-specific factors (e.g., discrimination). Term 4 measures changes in residual white inequality, the wage disadvantage for having a position below the mean in the white residual wage distribution. Even this decomposition contains the index number problem. Similar decompositions can be constructed using different base years or by substituting the estimated white prices with the black prices. In practice, researchers use the average across all years as the base to avoid possible extremes within any given year.

Wing Seun (1997) identifies another potential limitation to this decomposition. The procedure generates biased results if wage inequality (Term 3) and the percentile ranks (Term 4) are not independent of one another. As wage inequality expands, the term that measures the contribution of unobservable prices increases while the term capturing movements in the position of blacks falls. This problem is greatest at the tails of the distribution. As inequality rises, the tails become fatter, artificially moving blacks up in the white distribution. The bias will be larger at the lowest percentiles because of the skewed shape of wage distributions, but bias could be present at segments of the distribution where mass points exist. Mass points are wages that are common to a significant portion of the population.

William Rodgers III (2005) constructs distribution-specific approaches to address this potential bias. His extension of the Juhn, Murphy, and Pierce residual wage procedure (1991) starts with estimating a log wage equation for year *t* using only whites. He then uses the estimated coefficients to construct white and black residual distributions. With these distributions, Rodgers finds the white residual wage that equals the median black wage. This location is denoted as the *qth* quantile. Now using the year *t'* white residual distribution, Rodgers finds the white residual that corresponds to the *qth* quantile. This residual is interpreted as the predicted year *t'* black wage residual, assuming that the median black's initial year *t* position is preserved. The actual change, predicted change, and the ratio of the two are then constructed. This local approach can be performed at any quantile of the wage distribution, breaking the correlation between wage inequality and percentile rank.

DECOMPOSING OUTCOMES WITHIN SPECIFIC GROUPS

At first glance, decomposing within group differences seems like a trivial exercise, but Oaxaca and Michael Ransom (1999) show that applying the typical wage decomposition techniques within groups leads to unidentified estimates. Lack of identification occurs because one cannot identify the separate contributions of the dummy variables that are included in the model. It is only possible to identify the relative effects of the dummy variable on the gap. The size of the residual wage gap depends on the omitted reference group chosen by the researcher (see Oaxaca and Ransom 1999 for a detailed description of this econometric problem).

For example, a decomposition of the racial wage gap in the *jth* occupation can be written as:

$$\overline{y}_j^b - \overline{y}_j^w = (\hat{\beta}_j^b - \hat{\beta}_j^w) + (\hat{\alpha}^b - \hat{\alpha}^w) + \\ \overline{X}_j^b(\hat{\theta}^b - \hat{\theta}^w) + (\overline{X}_j^b - \overline{X}_j^w)\hat{\theta}^w \quad (3),$$

where the first three terms on the right-hand side measure occupation *j*'s unexplained racial gap. The last term is the predicted racial gap due to observable racial differences in characteristics.

The typical approach defines the unexplained portion of the wage gap as:

$$\hat{g}_j = (\hat{\beta}_j^b - \hat{\beta}_j^w) + (\hat{\alpha}^b - \hat{\alpha}^w) \quad (4).$$

The expression represents for occupation *j* racial differences in the coefficients after removing the adjusted wage

difference between the average black and white in the excluded occupation (the difference in each regression's constants). The $\hat{\beta}_j$s denote race-specific coefficients on the *jth* occupation dummy variables in each black and white log wage equation. The $\hat{\alpha}$s are the constants from each black and white log wage equation.

The black-white wage gap for the *jth* occupation is not identified because it depends on the selection of the omitted reference group of any dummy variable contained in the regression. The estimates of the $\hat{\beta}$s, the coefficients on the predictor variables (e.g., education, potential experience, industry), and the $\hat{\alpha}$s, the intercepts are not robust to choice of the omitted reference group. The $\hat{\alpha}$s will change when different omitted groups are specified.

To achieve identification, William Horrace and Oaxaca (2001) construct three estimators. One of the estimators is written as follows:

$$\widehat{\Phi}_j = (\hat{\beta}_j^b - \hat{\beta}_j^w) + (\hat{\alpha}^b - \hat{\alpha}^w) + \overline{X}_j^b(\hat{\theta}^b - \hat{\theta}^w) \quad (5),$$

where the $\hat{\beta}$s and $\hat{\alpha}$s are defined as earlier. The term x_j^{-b} denotes the average characteristics of African Americans in occupation *j* and $(\hat{\theta}^b - \hat{\theta}^w)$ denotes the difference between the black and white coefficients on the characteristics of blacks and whites. This estimator avoids the identification problem because the changes in the coefficients $(\hat{\theta}^b - \hat{\theta}^w)$ offset any changes in the intercepts $(\hat{\alpha}^b - \hat{\alpha}^w)$. One potential drawback to this estimator is that the predicated racial wage gap varies with the average characteristics of black workers in each occupation (x_j^{-b}). In order to deal with this potential problem, Horrace and Oaxaca use the means of blacks across all occupations.

Horrace and Oaxaca's third estimator provides information about the significance of the ordered occupation wage gaps. The relative wage gap in the *jth* occupation can be written as:

$$\hat{\gamma}_j = \max_{n=1,\ldots,J}\hat{g}_n - \hat{g}_j = \max_{n=1,\ldots,J}\hat{\delta}_n - \hat{\delta}_j \quad (6).$$

Horrace and Oaxaca take advantage of the fact that $\hat{\gamma}_j \geq 0$ and create the normalization $e_{-\gamma} \in [0,1]$. This normalization expresses the wage gaps as a percentage of the largest normalized wage gap (1.0). The estimator removes racial differences for all the excluded reference groups for all dummy variables $(\hat{\alpha}^b - \hat{\alpha}^w)$ and the omitted occupation. The standard errors on the differences between the wage gaps are used to determine whether these differences are statistically significant and whether or not the order statistic has any statistical meaning.

SEE ALSO *Discrimination*

BIBLIOGRAPHY

Adams, Scott, and David Neumark. 2006. Age Discrimination in U.S. Labor Markets: A Review of the Evidence. In *Handbook on the Economics of Discrimination*, ed. William M. Rodgers III, 187–214. Northampton, MA: Edgar Elgar.

Badgett, M.V. Lee. 2006. Discrimination Based on Sexual Orientation: A Review of the Literature. In *Handbook on the Economics of Discrimination*, ed. William M. Rodgers III, 161–186. Northampton, MA: Edgar Elgar.

Baldwin, Marjorie L., and William G. Johnson. 2006. A Critical Review of Studies of Discrimination Against Workers with Disabilities. In *Handbook on the Economics of Discrimination*, ed. William M. Rodgers III, 119–160. Northampton, MA: Edgar Elgar.

Blau, Francine, and Andrea H. Beller. 1992. Black-White Earnings Over the 1970s and 1980s: Gender Differences in Trends. *Review of Economics and Statistics* 74 (2): 276–286.

Blinder, Alan. 1973. Wage Discrimination: Reduced Form and Structural Estimates. *Journal of Human Resources* 8 (4): 436–455.

Cotton, Jeremiah. 1988. On the Decomposition of Wage Differentials. *Review of Economics and Statistics* 70 (2): 236–243.

Horrace, William, and Ronald Oaxaca. 2001. Inter-Industry Wage Differentials and the Gender Wage Gap: An Identification Problem. *Industrial and Labor Relations Review* 54: 611–618.

Juhn, Chinhui, Kevin Murphy, and Brooks Pierce. 1991. Accounting for the Slowdown in Black-White Wage Convergence. In *Workers and Their Wages: Changing Patterns in the United States*, ed. Marvin Kosters, 107–143. Washington, DC: American Enterprise Institute Press.

Neumark, David. 1988. Employers Discriminatory Behavior and the Estimation of Wage Discrimination. *Journal of Human Resources* 23 (3): 279–295.

Oaxaca, Ronald. 1973. Male-Female Wage Differentials in Urban Labor Markets. *International Economic Review* 14 (3): 693–709.

Oaxaca, Ronald, and Michael Ransom. 1999. Identification in Detailed Wage Decompositions. *Review of Economics and Statistics* 81 (1): 154–157.

Rodgers, William M., III. 2005. Male White-Black Wage Gaps, 1979–1994: A Distributional Analysis. *Southern Economic Journal* 72 (4): 773–793.

Rodgers, William M., III. 2006. *Handbook on the Economics of Discrimination*. Northampton, MA: Edgar Elgar.

Seun, Wing. 1997. Decomposing Wage Residuals: Unmeasured Skill or Statistical Artifact? *Journal of Labor Economics* 15 (3, part 1): 555–566.

William M. Rodgers III

ECONOMETRIC SOCIETY

SEE *Schumpeter, Joseph Alois.*

ECONOMETRICS

Econometrics is a branch of economics that confronts economic models with data. The "metrics" in "econometrics" suggests measurements. As Lawrence Klein (1974, p. 1) pointed out, measurement alone describes only the theoretical side of econometrics. Its empirical side deals with data and the estimation of relationships. Econometricians construct models, gather data, consider alternative specifications, and make forecasts or decisions based on econometric models (Granger 1999, p. 62). Many textbooks do econometrics rather than define it, mainly because it is not all science, for it requires a "set of assumptions which are both sufficiently specific and sufficiently realistic" (Malinvaud 1966, p. 514). As with any empirical discipline, econometric model building may not precede data analysis. One may be amused to find that econometrics can be used to answer the question "Which came first: the chicken or the egg?" by the use of causality testing (Thurman and Fisher 1988). Sometimes econometricians use "a minimum of assistance from theoretical conceptions or hypotheses regarding the nature of the economic process by which the variables studied are generated" (Koopmans 1970, p. 113). Other times, econometric models such as in time-series analysis use clearly defined approaches such as identification, estimation, and diagnostics.

The tradition for introductory econometrics is to start with a single equation emanating from economic theory and knowledge of how to fit the theory to a sample of data. For example, on the economic side, econometricians have some a priori notions of the demand schedule such as the law of demand, implying that more will be bought as the price falls. This is enough of a hypothesis to allow statistical testing. The econometrician needs to confront this demand hypothesis with a sample of data, which is either time-series or cross-section.

The econometrician's best friend is randomness. One way to appreciate randomness is to assume that the econometrician wants to explain how prices vary with the quantity sold in the form of a linear single equation model $P_t = a + bQ_t + \varepsilon_t$, where P is price, Q is quantity, a, b are coefficients to be estimated, t is time, and ε is an error term. The error term is the main random mechanism in this model. It is normally distributed with a zero mean and a constant variance, independence of the independent variables, and uncorrelated for different sets of observations. Besides the assumptions, the error term makes the dependent variable probabilistic, clarifying that a statistical test may not be based on the independent variables, which are not stochastic. Another requirement of randomness is that the observations should be kept sequentially in time in order to detect whether the errors are related serially, which is called "serial" or "autocorrelation" of the error terms. This is measured by the Durbin-Watson statistic, ideally equal to 2. Other preliminary diagnostic tests would require the t-statistics of the coefficients to be approximately 2 or greater, and the adjusted R-square should be in the 90 percent range. The test of a good econometric model "… should emphasize the quality of the output of the model rather than merely the apparent quality of the model" (Granger 1999, p. 62).

Besides single equations, econometricians study systems of equations models. A system of equations is necessary to capture interrelations or feedbacks among economic variables. In microeconomics, the demand and supply curves and their equality are thought of as a model to study market conditions such as equilibrium, excess demand, or excess supply. In macroeconomics, the Keynesian consumption and investment functions and a national income identity are required to study full employment and full production. A system of equations is usually solved or reduced to a single equation for forecasting purposes, which requires variables to be classified either as given (exogenous), such as the money supply and tax rates, or as variables determined by structural equations within the system (endogenous), such as prices and quantities. When the value of a variable is not in doubt at the current time, perhaps because we are relying on its previous values, then the variable is classified as predetermined. Structural equations are required in order to estimate the coefficients, whereas identity equations are required to sum up definitional terms such as that gross national product is the sum of consumption and investments. The Keynesian system of equations requires that planned savings must be equal to planned investment, which is referred to as an *ex ante* condition, as opposed to an *ex post* condition, where the variables are equal from an accounting perspective. The reduced form of the model can be used for policy purposes as instrument-versus-target models as suggested by Jan Tinbergen (1952) for the attainment of social welfare goals as suggested by Henri Theil (1961), or to simulate probable outcomes.

A system of equation models has peculiarities on both the model and the estimation sides. On the modeling side, the main difficulties reside with identification and reflection problems. Briefly stated, the identification problem requires that enough information be present in the model to make each equation represent a definite economic relation such as supply or demand. The reflection problem is concerned with getting a unique group data in order to explain individual behavior. Depending on the results of

the identification problem, appropriate techniques for establishing a system of equations are available, such as ordinary least square (OLS), and three-stage least squares (3SLQ).

Some pitfalls are common to both single and systems of equations. Multicollinearity occurs when the independent variables are related, such as when one variable measures activity for a day and another variable measures the same activity for a week, requiring that one is seven times the other. A dummy variable trap occurs when binary variables such as for the treatment of sex, seasonality, or shocks all add up to a column of ones.

Expectations can be treated in both single and systems of equations. An expected variable may be present in the model, which requires one to specify, before estimation, how expectations are formed. One method calls for an adaptive mechanism to correct for past errors. The most recent method of rational expectation models requires the econometrician to adjust the expected value of the variable for all the information that is available. For instance, if one's average commuting distance to work is 10 minutes, and one hears on the news that a traffic jam has occurred, an adjustment must be made to the average time for the forecast of the arrival time to be rational. Econometricians are trying to build large-scale rational expectation models to rival standard models such as the Wharton Econometric model, the Data Resource model, or the Federal Reserve Board U.S. model, but such achievements are not in sight as yet.

SEE ALSO *Bayesian Econometrics; Causality; Classical Statistical Analysis; Expectations; Heteroskedasticity; Klein, Lawrence; Koopmans, Tjalling; Least Squares, Ordinary; Matrix Algebra; Models and Modeling; Multicollinearity; Random Samples; Regression; Regression Analysis; Residuals; Statistics; Structural Equation Models; Tinbergen, Jan*

BIBLIOGRAPHY

Granger, Clive W. J. 1999. *Empirical Modeling in Economics: Specification and Evaluation.* London: Cambridge University Press.

Klein, Lawrence R. 1974. *A Textbook of Econometrics.* 2nd ed. Englewood Cliffs, NJ: Prentice Hall.

Koopmans, Tjalling C. 1970. *Scientific Papers of Tjalling C. Koopmans.* Vol. 1. New York: Springer-Verlag.

Malinvaud, Edmond. 1966. *Statistical Methods of Econometrics.* Amsterdam: North-Holland.

Thiel, Henri. 1961. *Economic Forecasts and Policy.* 2nd ed. Amsterdam: North-Holland.

Thurman, Walter N., and Mark E. Fisher. 1988. Chicken, Eggs, and Causality, or Which Came First? *American Journal of Agricultural Economics* (May): 237–238.

Tinbergen, Jan. 1952. *On the Theory of Economic Policy.* Amsterdam: North-Holland.

Lall Ramrattan
Michael Szenberg

ECONOMIC COMMISSION FOR LATIN AMERICA AND THE CARIBBEAN (ECLAC)

The Economic Commission for Latin America (ECLA) was founded in 1948 by the United Nations Economic and Social Council. It was given the task of facilitating development and strengthening economic ties within the region and between the Latin American countries and the rest of the world. The main venues for promoting these goals have been seminars, the funding and broad dissemination of developmental research and policy options, and the compilation of an ongoing and comprehensive database on region-wide and individual-country economic performance.

The name of the commission was officially changed to the Economic Commission for Latin America and the Caribbean (ECLAC) in 1984, when the Caribbean subregion was added to its mandate. One of the United Nations' five regional commissions, ECLAC is also frequently referred to by its Spanish acronym, CEPAL (Comisión Económica para América Latina). Headquartered in Santiago, Chile, it also maintains subregional offices in Bogotá, Brasilia, Buenos Aires, Mexico City, Montevideo, and Port-of-Spain.

THE STRUCTURALIST PARADIGM

During its first fifteen years of existence, ECLA was directed by the Argentine economist Raúl Prebisch, who had authored a highly influential work titled *The Economic Development of Latin America and its Principal Problems* (published in English by ECLA in 1950). Frequently referred to as the "structuralist manifesto," Prebisch's work addressed the growing gap between the core of wealthy industrialized countries that dominated the world economy and the much larger group of poor, underdeveloped countries that sat on the global periphery. For Prebisch, this asymmetrical relationship between rich and poor countries in the global economy was due to the very structures of trade and technological adaptation that distinguished these two groups of countries, as well as to the self-perpetuating nature of the relationship between North and South.

Prebisch and his ECLA colleagues argued that the phenomenon of chronic underdevelopment within Latin America was due to the predominant reliance of countries within the region on exporting primary commodities to the United States and western Europe. In turn, Latin America was highly dependent on these northern industrial trading partners for the import of manufactured and technology-intensive goods. Over the first half of the twentieth century, commodity-exporting countries in the South were plagued by price volatility, demand fluctuation, and periodic natural disasters that adversely affected their ability to export. At the same time, the northern industrial countries were experiencing a steady upward price for the manufacturing goods they were exporting to Latin America, as technological innovation and labor productivity rendered this group of countries ever more competitive.

Throughout the 1960s, ECLA analysts defined this tendency for Latin America to pay increasingly more for imports from industrial countries and to earn less for primary exports as a problem of unequal exchange. Although subsequent economic analyses have shown these particular ECLA claims concerning unequal exchange between North and South to be exaggerated, this diagnosis stands as the overriding theoretical contribution made by ECLA. Given the heavy weight afforded by ECLA to these structural bottlenecks, a major policy prescription was to restructure the region's terms of trade with the North by laying down a viable and competitive industrial base.

The heyday of Latin American import substitution industrialization, whereby countries such as Argentina, Brazil, Chile, Mexico, and Peru raised tariffs on industrial imports and offered generous state subsidies to spur domestic manufacturing production, coincided with the ECLA paradigm up through the 1970s. However, ECLA's main contribution was more the diagnosis of the underlying causes of underdevelopment and less the actual policies for rectifying it. In its early years, for example, ECLA was quite prescient in identifying such causal factors as the pattern of oligopolistic ownership within industrial-country markets and an adverse shift in the international division of labor, both of which worked against the ability of the developing countries to catch up with the North. But, in the end, the kinds of industrial policies that were pursued to counter these barriers and the specific sectors targeted for success were more a matter of domestic politics and policy choices within countries in the region.

ECLAC: A RESPONSE TO CHANGING THE TIMES

By the 1980s it would have been difficult for even the most sympathetic ECLAC analyst to put a positive spin on Latin America's efforts to industrialize via import substitution during the post–World War II era. With the advent of the 1982 Latin debt crisis and the plummeting of growth across the region, the shortcomings of this model were all too apparent. Over time, government-sponsored subsidies and high industrial tariffs had spawned powerful urban coalitions across sectors that succeeded in sustaining the import-substitution model despite its obvious failure to promote productivity, growth, and higher living standards across Latin America. As fiscal and exchange-rate policies favored urban manufacturers over rural producers, the agricultural sector languished, and resource-rich countries like Argentina, Mexico, and Peru could only meet domestic needs by importing food.

As import substitution collapsed under the weight of the debt crisis, ECLAC's emphasis shifted in the 1980s. The agency concerned itself with macroeconomic recovery and the kinds of social policies that would do the most to cushion Latin America's poor from the impacts of a decade-long recession. With the widespread structural reforms and restoration of growth that finally occurred in the early 1990s, ECLAC became an important advocate for greater technological adaptation and the need for enhancing competitiveness in the region. Interestingly, ECLAC's earlier misgivings concerning the role of free trade and comparative advantage in the development process were eclipsed as the agency became a tripartite partner, along with the Inter-American Development Bank and the Organization of American States (OAS), in promoting the negotiation of a Free Trade Area of the Americas that would include all thirty-four democratically elected countries in the region.

ECLAC'S INTERNATIONAL SWAY

While the original analyses conducted by ECLAC at its inception were specific to Latin America, the academic literature on other developing countries in Asia and Africa has clearly borrowed and been enriched by the ECLAC paradigm. From the application of theories of unequal exchange to the structuralist critique of industrial-bloc dominance of international commodity and labor markets, ECLAC has left an indelible print on the fields of development economics and area studies.

SEE ALSO *Import Substitution; Macroeconomics, Structuralist; Prebisch, Raúl; Prebisch-Singer Hypothesis; Taylor, Lance*

BIBLIOGRAPHY

Love, Joseph L. 2005. The Rise and Decline of Economic Structuralism in Latin America. *Latin American Research Review* 40 (3): 100–125.

Prebisch, Raúl. 1950. *The Economic Development of Latin America and its Principal Problems.* New York: United Nations Economic Commission for Latin America.

Sikkink, Kathryn A. 1991. *Ideas and Institutions: Developmentalism in Brazil and Argentina.* Ithaca, NY: Cornell University Press.

Taylor, Alan M. 1998. On the Costs of Inward-Looking Development: Price Distortions, Growth, and Divergence in Latin America. *Journal of Economic History* 58 (1): 1–8.

Carol Wise

ECONOMIC CRISES

An economic crisis is typically defined as "a turning point for the worst." It refers to a period when "good times" turn quickly into "bad times," when economic agents panic, leading to economic dislocation. The dislocation is the crisis—for instance, from the upper turning point of the business cycle to its immediate aftermath, until people's expectations improve.

The history of crisis theory has a long and distinguished pedigree, ranging from Marxist economics, business-cycle analysis, and social and political analysis (Clarke 1994). There are various types of economic crises, ranging from cyclical crises to structural crises of the long wave and financial crises. These crises are interrelated with other types of crises, such as legitimization crises and, indeed, personal crises.

This entry will begin by discussing economic crises associated with business cycles. Cycles undergo upswing when economic growth, investment, and consumption are growing at respectable rates. Such cycles take various forms, as Joseph Schumpeter (1883–1950) pointed out, but if we take the typical eight-to-eleven year (Juglar) cycle as an example, factors start to negatively impact on growth as the upswing slows down. These factors variously include speculative bubbles, which eventually bust; higher costs of production, such as real wages, materials and oil, interest rates, and rent; and inadequate demand impinging on the process.

These myriad factors reduce the rate of profit before the upper turning point of the cycle. Eventually, this declining profit rate impacts on investment as businesses realize that underlying profitability has declined, and they react by reducing the rate of accumulation. Consumers, in turn, usually reduce the rate of consumption expenditure. This decline in demand then transmits into an economic crisis at the upper turning point of the cycle, leading to declining confidence, a deteriorating business environment, lower consumer confidence, and a degree of overreaction in the markets. This overreaction is a critical element of the crisis, as people often panic, selling their stock and reducing business activity. Such overreaction occurred, for instance, in the early phases of the (Juglar) recessions of 1974 to 1975, 1982 to 1983, 1990 to 1993 (1997 to 1998 in Asia), and 2000 to 2002 throughout much of the world.

Typically, the economic crisis also leads to or is associated with a financial crisis (especially during long-wave downswings). Martin Wolfson (1994) has shown that during the early phases of recession, the (U.S.) economy undergoes a financial crisis as the declining profitability, confidence, and animal spirits lead to a massive devaluation of capital and banking assets, causing consumers and businesses to withdraw such assets from financial institutions (and sell them off) and effectively engaging in a run on the banking and financial systems. Financial crises tend to moderate as lender-of-last-resort facilities are utilized to rescue the system from negative chains of bankruptcy, as Hyman Minsky (1919–1996) recognized. The crisis thus encompasses the early months of a recession, including financial crisis.

Crises are usually reserved for the most protracted periods of uncertainty, instability, and panic. Some analysts may extend the short-cycle crisis to the remaining months or years of recession, but this view may be problematic because, after a while, expectations tend to improve, leading to a recovery in the cycle. Slowly, investment and consumption demand pick up as bubble crashes moderate along with costs of production and perceptions.

Karl Marx (1861–1863) differentiated between the potential for crises and the necessity of crises. The potential for crises emanates from money and credit, which enable buying and selling to be separated, leading to realization problems. The goods may be "exchanged" before the payment of "money," due to the existence of trade credit, promissory notes, IOUs, credit cards, and so forth. The market enables potential circulation crises to emerge through supply-demand coordination failures as the final payment of money fails to materialize due to insufficient demand and over-indebtedness.

The necessity for crises, according to Marx, lay in "the very nature of capital." The clash between competition and monopoly, for instance, leads to innovation, which starts rounds of productive investment, imitation, and gradually excess competition and low profits, leading to crisis. The conflict between capital and labor during cycle upswings may variously lead to a diminished reserve army of labor, high wages, and low productivity, and thus low profits and economic crisis. The conflict between industry and finance will periodically lead to speculative bubbles rising and crashing, and thus to economic crisis. Marx saw these contradictions of capitalism as necessarily leading to crises, which *may* perform the useful functions

of flushing out unproductive capitals and providing the basis for renewed accumulation after a period of crisis (Mattick 1981), except in the severest types of crisis.

The possibility of severe crises is associated with problems of: (1) debt deflation, (2) insufficient demand, and (3) structural crises of capitalism. Debt deflation, according to Irving Fisher (1867–1947), is endogenously generated through a series of interrelated processes. Innovation that is financed largely by debt in an environment of endogenous money often leads to speculative excess and euphoria, resulting in the liquidation of debt, greater uncertainty, declining velocity of money, falling prices, depression, and disarray. The psychology of business is important to this process; debt deflation occurred, for instance, during crises and panics in the United States in 1837, 1873, 1893, and circa 1929, in Japan from 1990 to 2003, and so forth. Fisher saw debt deflation as counter to laissez-faire and caused by the paradox of "over-indebtedness [being] so great as to depress prices faster than liquidation, [while] the mass effort to get out of debt sinks us more deeply into debt" (Fisher 1933, p. 350). He saw policy efforts toward reflation, consistent with the New Deal in the United States, as being potentially able to tackle such problems.

This is linked to the crisis theories of John Maynard Keynes (1883–1946) and Michal Kalecki (1899–1970), both of whom saw deficiency of demand as the principal momentum underlying the trend toward economic crises. For Keynes (1936), capitalism is inherently unstable because uncertainty emanates from investment in capital assets with a prospective yield linked to future prospects, knowledge of which is close to zero. In such an environment, investment is usually determined by the prevailing business climate, which generates waves of upward and downward accumulation through history. These cycles and waves of investment variously generate overproduction as the euphoria of upswing expands prospective yield (minus supply price) beyond fundamentals, with downswings manifesting in insufficient aggregate demand linked to stock market crashes, deep recessions, and depressions. Such instability leads to periods of moderate economic crises during the short cycles and more intense crises during the longer-wave downswings.

Kalecki (1971) was able to demonstrate technically how insufficient demand generates such crises from the investment-consumption dynamics of capitalism. For instance, in a simple model, "capitals get what they spend" and "workers spend what they get." Profit, the critical variable affecting growth, depends upon the propensity to invest, which is affected by uncertainty. Uncertainty, however, is endemic in the system as a result of deep capital projects and speculative tendencies. The severity of crises, therefore, ultimately depends upon the intensity of this uncertainty, and the extent to which overproduction leads eventually to insufficient aggregate demand and instability.

Structural crises, the deepest and most prolonged form of crisis, are linked to long waves of development and relative demise (O'Hara 2006). Long-wave upswing typically occurs when institutions and technology are developed, leading to twenty or thirty years of higher than average growth without major financial crises or deep recessions. This approximates the era of the bourgeois revolutions in France and the United States; the Industrial Revolution of the late 1700s and early 1800s; the American and Australian gold rushes along with the "age of capital" of the 1850s to early 1870s; the period of industrial consolidation and business expansion of the late 1890s to 1910s; the postwar boom of the 1950s to early 1970s (O'Connor 1984); and possibly the age of the Internet, biotechnology, and sustainable energy during the second and third decades (at least) of the twenty-first century.

However, as institutions undergo demise and technologies mature, long-wave downswings occur for twenty or thirty years. These are the structural crises of capitalism, when profit rates, growth, investment, and (usually) standards of living for the masses have stalled. Hence the long periods when cyclical recessions and financial crises are deeper than usual: 1820 to 1850, 1875 to 1895, 1920 to 1945, and 1973 to the early 2000s. These structural, accumulation crises are long periods of above-average uncertainty, when the business outlook is generally negative (although short-cycle booms can be quite buoyant before the periodic crash). They also tend to lead to legitimization problems for many vested interests, including governments, businesses, institutions, and individuals. Personal crises tend to escalate during these times, along with social dislocation. Lender-of-last-resort facilities and big *productive* governments are quite likely needed to moderate such crises through raising the floor of cycles and reducing instability.

There is room for a better understanding of economic crises. More studies are needed to comprehend the early stages of recession; the linkages between economic and financial crises; and the relationship between business-cycle crises, debt deflation, insufficient demand, and structural crises of capitalism. There is also a need for further research on ways of moderating these crises and how the crises themselves may (in certain circumstances) be useful to clear the way for change and development.

SEE ALSO *Bubbles; Business Cycles, Empirical Literature; Capitalism; Depression, Economic; Economics, Keynesian; Economics, Post Keynesian; Financial Instability Hypothesis; Great Depression; Long Waves;* *Marx, Karl; Panics; Recession; Schumpeter, Joseph Alois; Underconsumption; Wage and Price Controls*

BIBLIOGRAPHY

Clarke, Simon. 1994. *Marx's Theory of Crisis.* New York: St. Martin's Press.

Fisher, Irving. 1933. The Debt Deflation Theory of Great Depressions. *Econometrica* 1 (4): 337–357.

Kalecki, Michal. 1971. *Selected Essays on the Dynamics of the Capitalist Economy 1933–1970.* Cambridge, U.K.: Cambridge University Press.

Keynes, John Maynard. 1936. *The General Theory of Employment, Interest, and Money.* London: Macmillan.

Marx, Karl. 1861–1863. Ricardo's Theory of Accumulation and a Critique of It (The Very Nature of Capital Leads to Crises). In *Theories of Surplus Value,* Vol. 2, 470–546. Moscow: Progress Publishers.

Mattick, Paul. 1981. *Economic Crisis and Crisis Theory.* Trans. Paul Mattick Jr. London: Merlin.

Minsky, Hyman. 1995. Longer Waves in Financial Relations: Financial Factors in the More Severe Depressions II. *Journal of Economic Issues* 29 (1): 83–96.

O'Connor, James. 1984. *Accumulation Crisis.* London: Blackwell.

O'Hara, Phillip Anthony. 2006. *Growth and Development in the Global Political Economy: Social Structures of Accumulation and Modes of Regulation.* London and New York: Routledge.

Schumpeter, Joseph. [1939] 1982. *Business Cycles: A Theoretical, Historical, and Statistical Analysis of the Capitalist Process.* 2 vols. Philadelphia: Porcupine.

Wolfson, Martin H. 1994. *Financial Crises: Understanding the Postwar U.S. Experience.* 2nd ed. Armonk, NY: Sharpe.

Phillip Anthony O'Hara

ECONOMIC FORECASTING

SEE *Autoregressive Models.*

ECONOMIC GROWTH

The improvement of a society's living conditions is a complex process whose study has been at the very origins of economics. This process is called *economic growth*. In Western civilization, the first attempts to comprehend the mechanism of growth are recent, dating back to the end of the Renaissance only. We owe them to Giovanni Botero (1540–1617), Maximilien de Béthune, Duc de Sully (1560–1641), and Josiah Child (1630–1699). Why not earlier? Because the Middle Ages were doomed by endless conflicts and plagues; in the fourteenth century alone, more than one-third of the European population was wiped out by the great plague. It would have taken a bold thinker to even entertain the idea of development. As the French historian Pierre Gaxotte (1895–1982) wrote: "The man of the Middle Ages does not know of time and numbers" (1951, p. 237).

It is not surprising therefore that we owe to Arab civilization the first known comprehensive explanation of the fundamental causes of economic growth. They were given in a masterly way by Ibn Khaldūn (1332–1406) in his *Muqaddimah: An Introduction to History* (1377). Ibn Khaldūn's objectives went beyond explaining economic growth; he gave himself the formidable task to unveil the causes of the rise and decline of civilizations. The British historian Arnold Toynbee (1889–1975) commented about Ibn Khaldūn's magnum opus that "in the Prolegomena to his *Universal History* he has conceived and formulated a philosophy of history which is undoubtedly the greatest work of its kind that has even been created by any mind in any time or place" (Toynbee 1935, Vol. III, p. 322).

Western civilization would have to wait four centuries to see the independent blossoming of very similar ideas in Adam Smith's (1723–1790) *Inquiry into the Nature and Causes of the Wealth of Nations* (1776). Today, economic theory has vindicated the conjectures made by these major thinkers, as will be discussed in the last section of this entry. Before that, the entry will explain how growth is measured, what the process of economic growth is, and how optimal growth can be achieved.

MEASURING ECONOMIC GROWTH

The standard, international measure of economic growth is the increase in *real income per person* (the increase is a percentage rate per year). By *income* is meant *national income*; this concept is derived from the gross domestic product (GDP), which is closely related to the measure of economic activity.

There are three conceivable approaches to measuring society's economic activity. The result of this activity can be considered in terms of the amount of goods and services that society manages to put at its disposal within a given time span (e.g., one year). Broadly speaking, it is customary to distinguish *consumption* goods and services (produced for their own sake, these will not be transformed at a later stage, and are not used for manufacturing other goods or services) from *investment* goods. Examples of the latter are equipment, factories, and transportation infrastructure, which will be used for production in coming years. The investment goods will be added to the capital stock in existence; along with technological progress, they will play a major role in the growth process. *Exports* are added to consumption and investment, since

they also reflect society's activity. Naturally, consumption, investment, and even some exports include various amounts of imports; these are finally deducted in order to achieve a first measure of GDP from an expenditure point of view.

A second, equivalent, way to measure economic activity is to count the contribution of each sector of the economy (e.g., agriculture, industry, and services). Since the production of one sector (e.g., aluminum) may be used in another sector (automobiles), double counting must be avoided. For that purpose, only the net production of each sector is taken into consideration, in the form of its added value, equal to its total production less all purchases to other sectors. The sum of the added values of all sectors is then equal to GDP viewed from the production perspective.

Finally, it is clear that the only source that can be used to remunerate the production factors (labor and capital) is the value-added of each sector. In the third approach to measuring GDP, all categories of income are counted: labor income, capital income (interest and rentals paid by firms), and profits. Income used in measuring the growth of an economy is real net national income, determined as follows. First, the yearly depreciation of capital is deducted from the gross domestic product to obtain the *net domestic product*. We then add all capital and labor income received from abroad by residents, and deduce payments of capital and labor income made abroad to nonresidents. We thus obtain the *net national product*.

Two further corrections are needed to obtain the income distributed to society: First, we deduct all indirect taxes (paid by firms) and add subsidies (received by individuals and firms). The result is called *national income*. Finally, we are less interested in national income than in its purchasing power. To that effect, statisticians attempt to measure the average relative price increase of the various pieces of GDP from the expenditure side, and they deflate the yearly national income by that amount. For instance, supposing they estimate that prices have increased from year t to $t + 1$ by 10 percent; they will divide the year's ($t + 1$) national income by 1.1 to obtain real national income with reference to year t as a base.

THE SIGNIFICANCE OF INCOME PER PERSON AS A MEASURE OF WELFARE

How much can we rely on income per person to gauge a society's standard of living and its progress? This type of measure shows defects that may be detrimental to its significance. Indeed, many expenses are counted in GDP (as well as in national income), although they should not be if we are interested in measuring society's welfare. For example, all expenditures forced upon individuals should be excluded from the measure. These include all public expenses made by authoritarian regimes that would not have received the population's approval through parliamentarian representation. Also included in this category are public expenditures made in countries where democracy is weak. In such countries, for example, the level of military expenditure is often far above what the country would require for pure defense purposes. These unwanted public expenses replace those that the population would have chosen, namely, expenditure for health and education.

We also count in GDP and national income a number of expenses that individuals may choose of their own free will, but which are also sometimes forced upon them by unwanted circumstances. Security expenses—*security* taken in its largest meaning—is an example. Those expenses are considerably higher today than they were decades ago, and of course have nothing to do with well-being. Think also of expenses resulting from accidents, disease, or epidemics. Each of the above has two negative effects upon society's welfare. First, society suffers directly from these circumstances and events. Second, those expenditures replace the goods and services that society could have enjoyed instead. No account is taken of working conditions in the measurement of national income. In particular, no account is taken of forced labor, particularly the labor forced upon women and children.

Furthermore, no equity measure appears in national accounts. This entry defines *equity* as the ability for society to reward each individual according to his or her own qualities and effort, and at the same time protect those hurt by fate.

Finally, national income does not account for damage done to the environment, and more generally to the biosphere. Inasmuch as depreciation of capital is deducted from GDP to obtain, after other adjustments, national income, we should also deduct the cost of the damage to the biosphere due to economic activity.

Despite these reservations, income per person remains a reliable gauge of society's welfare. If not an absolute measure, it is an adequate relative measure, since one can still make international comparisons based upon it. The fundamental reason is that the level of income in any country is intimately linked to its level of democracy. If one establishes a list of countries ranked according to their level of democracy, and set it beside another list on the basis of real income per person, there would be a great similarity in both lists. Economic growth has steadily accompanied societies that have—however slowly—managed to protect the individual and have abided by the principle of equality of opportunity. A third ranking of countries according to their welfare would be very similar because democracy is highly correlated to welfare. This is

the reason why it is reasonable to measure welfare by income per person, imperfect as that index may be.

THE GROWTH PROCESS

The growth process has been well understood for at least two centuries, and can be described as follows. At the beginning of some time period—for instance, year t—any given country has a capital stock K_t at its disposal, and a workforce L_t, which may be proportional to the population. This workforce enjoys a degree of technological knowledge inherited from the past, just as the stock of capital has been accumulated in the past. During year t, society makes use of those resources to turn out a product referred to earlier as the GDP. Part of the GDP is used to replace the capital stock K_t, inherited at time t, which has depreciated during that year. Subtracting depreciation gives the net domestic product, which can be divided into two parts: By far the largest is consumption (perhaps 85%); the rest is net investment, which is equipment that will be added to increase the capital stock at the beginning of year $t + 1$. In the same time span, the labor force may have increased from L_t to L_{t+1}, and technological advances may have been made, carrying the technological capabilities to a new level. This enables society to acquire a higher net domestic product in period $t + 1$.

It is clear that the resulting increase in income will depend both on the size of net investment made in year t and on the possible technological advances that the labor force may have made. Two fundamental questions now may be asked. Under what conditions will income per person increase? In other words, under what conditions will the economy grow? And if growth is to be observed, can we expect growth to continue indefinitely? The answers to these questions require a quantitative description of the economy and the building of a model of the growth process. This requires making hypotheses on the functioning of the economy, on society's behavior, and on population growth.

First, the functioning is described by a *production function* linking capital K_t, labor L_t, and technological progress to production Y_t (which is considered equal to income) at any time t. This relationship can be written as the three-variable production function $Y = F(K, L, t)$, where F is homogeneous of degree one in K and L. This hypothesis means that if at any point in time t, K and L are multiplied by λ, then Y is also multiplied by λ: We have $\lambda Y = F(\lambda K, \lambda L, t)$. For instance, if $\lambda = 1.1$, it means that if K and L both increase by 10 percent, then Y also increases by 10 percent. A common, simple example of such a function is the Wicksell-Cobb-Douglas function proposed by the Swedish economist Knut Wicksell (1851–1926) at the turn of the nineteenth century: $Y = K^\alpha L^{1-\alpha} e^{gt}$. The function is homogenous of degree one, and technological progress is taken into account in the exponential term e^{gt}, where g is $(1/Y)\partial Y/\partial t$, the rate of growth of income when K and L are constant (e.g., $g = 1.5$ percent per year).

A second hypothesis reflects the behavior of society with regard to saving and investment; one possibility is to posit that society saves and invests a fraction s of its income (e.g., $s = 0.1$ or 10 percent). Investment I being the rate of increase of capital, we then have $I = dK/dt = sY = sF(K, L, t)$.

Finally, the last hypothesis is about the growth of the population (considered as the labor force). The growth rate of the population is supposed to be constant and equal to n (e.g., $n = 1\%$ per year). Equivalently, it means that $L_t = L_0 e^{nt}$.

With these three hypotheses, we have a complete, albeit simple, model of the growth process. Observe that the rate of increase of capital, $I = dK/dt$, is a linear function of income, $Y_t = F(K_t, L_t, t)$, and the stock of capital K_t is driven by the differential equation,

$$I = \frac{dK}{dt} = sF(K_t, L_t, t). \qquad (1)$$

In the example above, we would have

$$\frac{dK}{dt} = sK^{\alpha}(L_0 e^{nt})^{\alpha} e^{gt}. \qquad (2)$$

Equation (2) is a Bernoulli equation that can be easily solved, leading to a trajectory of capital $K(K_0, t)$ which depends on the initial value of capital K_0 at some point of time $t = t_0$. In turn, this capital time path can be plugged into the production function $Y = F(K, L, t)$ to yield the time path of Y, as well as the evolution of income per person, $y = Y/L$, our variable of foremost importance.

In fact, a general, qualitative picture of the evolution of the economy can be drawn by making clever use of a fundamental property of the production function, as Robert Solow did in "A Contribution to the Theory of Economic Growth" (1956). Observe that if λ is replaced by $1/L$ in $\lambda Y = F(\lambda K, \lambda L, t)$, then $y = Y/L = F(K/L, 1, t)$, which depends now solely upon the capital-labor ratio r and time. Suppose for the time being that there is no technological progress; then $y = f(r)$, and income per person is simply a function of r. This function is always increasing, if $Y = F(K,L)$ and $Y/L = f(r)$, $Y = Lf(r) = Lf(K/L)$, $\partial Y/\partial K = Lf'(r)(1/L) = f'(r)$. Assuming that the marginal productivity of capital $\partial Y/\partial K$ is positive leads to $f'(r) > 0$. This result is of central importance, because it means that the evolution of income per person is driven by the evolution of the capital labor ratio. Thus, the qualitative evolution of $r = K/L$ will enable us to reach conclusions as to the evolution of income per person, and to answer the second question we asked at the beginning of

this section. This can be achieved for very broad families of the production functions, without resolving the differential equation (1), nor knowing the exact mathematical specification of $F(K, L, t)$.

Consider the rate of increase of $r(t)$. Denoting $\dot{K} = dK/dt$ and $\dot{L} = dL/dt$, it is

$$\dot{r} = \frac{dr}{dt} = \frac{d}{dt}\frac{K_t}{L_t} = \frac{\dot{K}L - K\dot{L}}{L^2} = \frac{\dot{K}}{L} - \frac{K}{L}\frac{\dot{L}}{L} = \frac{\dot{K}}{L} - nr.$$

Since $\dot{K} = I = sY$, we have finally,

$$\dot{r} = sy - nr \qquad (3)$$

which is the fundamental equation of positive economic growth. It has an immediate economic interpretation: The rate of increase of the capital-labor ratio is the difference between investment per person ($sY/L = sy$) and the investment per person that is necessary to maintain the capital-labor ratio constant (nr); indeed, if L grows at rate n, and if K is to grow at the same rate ($\dot{K}/K = n$), then $\dot{K}(= I)$ must be nK, and investment per person $\dot{K}/L$ must be $nK/L = nr$. It is obvious that r will increase ($\dot{r} > 0$) if and only if investment per person (sy) is higher than the investment per person necessary to maintain r constant (nr). Now equation (3) is a differential equation in r, but it does not need to be solved in order to infer the evolution of the economy and its ultimate outcome. Only a picture—a phase diagram—is required. We can simply draw the curve $sy = sf(r)$ and the ray nr, and consider the difference, $\dot{r} = sy - nr$, which will be the rate of increase of $\dot{r}$. This is done in Figure 1.

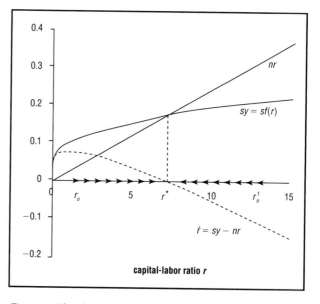

Figure 1: The phase diagram of the growth process.

Suppose that, initially, the capital-labor ratio is r_0. We can immediately see that $\dot{r}$ is positive at that point; therefore r will increase, and income per person will increase as well. This process will drive r toward its equilibrium value r^*, where $\dot{r} = 0$, and therefore r stays constant. (Whether r^* will be reached or not cannot be inferred from the simple reading of the phase diagram. Solving the corresponding differential equation is required; it can then be shown that r^* is reached asymptotically only—that is, when t tends to infinity.) On the other hand, if the initial value r_0 is above r^*, then $\dot{r} < 0$; r will decrease toward r^*. If the marginal productivity of capital $\partial F / \partial F = f'(r)$ diminishes in such a way that the curve $sf(r)$ intersects the ray nr, then the economy will tend toward a fixed, equilibrium point $(r^*, f(r^*)) = (r^*, y^*)$. Therefore, income per person is bound to tend toward the limit y^*.

Two circumstances, however, may arise in which this phenomenon will not occur and income per person is not bounded. The first possibility is that the curve $sf(r)$, concave as it may be, will not intersect the ray nr. Such a possibility may arise if the elasticity of substitution between capital and labor is sufficiently high (the elasticity of substitution measures the ease by which capital may be substituted with labor to achieve a given level of output when the price of labor increases relative to the rental rate of capital (on this concept, see La Grandville 2007b). Then, the curve $sf(r)$ tends asymptotically toward a ray with a slope equal to or larger than n. If that is so, there will be no intersection between $sf(r)$ and nr; $\dot{r}$ will always be positive, and r will always grow.

The second circumstance that may lead to permanent growth is the very existence of technological progress. Indeed, suppose that $f(r)$ is multiplied, as in our previous example, by e^{gt}. It means that in Figure 1 the curve $f(r)$ is constantly shifted upward by the mere force of technological progress. It implies that even if, in a first phase, capital labor is decreasing, it will ultimately increase, carrying with it an increase in income per person.

From a methodological point of view, economic growth is first described by a dynamic model that captures the motion of the economy; such models typically generate one, or a set, of differential equation(s). The next fundamental questions are: If we are confident in the validity of such models, can we determine a trajectory of the economy that would be optimal compared to other possible time paths? And how is optimality to be defined?

OPTIMAL GROWTH

Suppose that we are able to infer the future trajectory of an economy from the solution of the model described above. An infinity of choices are offered to society, in the sense that society can choose an infinitely large number of savings investment ratios s, and to each of those corre-

sponds a given future time path for the economy. Which is to be chosen? What would be an optimality criterion for society? A natural answer could come from what was discussed above: Society does not accumulate capital for its own sake, but it does care for the consumption goods and services that capital can provide in the future. So a logical aim for society would be to determine a time path K_t that would maximize the sum of consumption flows to be received in the future, with an important proviso: A consumption flow received in thirty years is to be valued less than the same flow received much sooner. Accordingly, such future consumption flows have to be discounted, and a discount rate that would reflect society's rate of preference for the present must be defined. Furthermore, following Frank Ramsey's (1903–1930) opening treatment of the subject in 1928, it was proposed that consumption flows C_t should be transformed into utility flows through some concave, increasing, utility function $U(C_t)$. Thus, for about three-quarters of a century, the problem of optimal growth was defined as follows: find a trajectory K_t that would maximize the integral

$$\int_0^\infty U(C_t) e^{-it} dt$$

subject to the constraint

$$C_t = F(K_t, L_t, t) - \dot{K}_t$$

which is equivalent to maximize

$$I = \int_0^\infty U\left[F(K_t, L_t, t) - \dot{K}_t\right] e^{-it} dt. \qquad (4)$$

This fundamental problem of optimal growth belongs to the calculus of variations, an extension of differential and integral calculus. Differential calculus deals, among many other things, with the optimization of functions, that is, relations between one or several variables and a number. The integral in (4) does not have that characteristic; rather, (4) is a relation between a whole function (K_t, for t between 0 and ∞) and a number (I). Such a relationship has been given a special name: a *functional*. The calculus dealing with functionals is the *calculus of variations* because the increase of a variable in differential calculus is now replaced by the variation of a whole function. This branch of mathematics was born when Johan Bernoulli (1667–1748) submitted in 1698 to his fellow mathematicians the problem of finding the curve joining points A to B such that a bead sliding along the curve would reach B in minimum time. The problem was solved by Bernoulli himself, his brother Jacob (1654–1705), and also by Gottfried Wilhelm Leibniz (1646–1716), Isaac Newton (1642–1727), and Guillaume de l'Hôspital (1661–1704), each using different methods. A general method of solving variational problems however had to wait for the genius of Leonhard Euler (1707–1783), who in 1744 showed that if a functional $\int_a^b G(K_t, \dot{K}_t, t) dt$ is to be maximized, a first-order condition is that it satisfies the differential equation

$$\frac{\partial G}{\partial K_t}(K_t, \dot{K}, t) - \frac{d}{dt}\frac{\partial G}{\partial \dot{K}}(K_t, \dot{K}_t, t) = 0 \qquad (5)$$

Equation (5) is generally a second-order, nonlinear differential equation. Its second-order character comes from the fact that the second term on the left-hand side of (5) is the total derivative of $G_{\dot{K}}(K, \dot{K}, t)$ with respect to t, which will generate a term depending on K, $\dot{K}$, and t, $G_{K\dot{K}}$, multiplying $\ddot{K}_t$.

Applied to the problem of optimal growth, the Euler equation yields,

$$i(t) = F'_{K_t}(K_t, L_t, t) + \dot{U}'_c/U'_c. \qquad (6)$$

The Euler equation (6) unfortunately is seldom solvable analytically, and this is precisely the case here. Only numerical analysis is available to determine the optimal trajectory K^*_t, from which optimal investment $I^*_t = \dot{K}^*_t$, income $Y^* = F(K^*_t, L_t, t)$, and finally savings rate $s^*_t = I^*_t/Y^*_t$ can be deduced. The difficulty of solving the problem numerically led economists to keep it in the realm of theory. The problem with this situation is that short shrift was given to the fact that each time some numbers were obtained, the strangest results appeared in the form of an exceedingly high "optimal" initial savings rate, often on the order of 40 percent.

With the invention of efficient computing software, it became possible to undertake a much more systematic examination of the problem of optimal growth. It was found that the culprit was the introduction of an arbitrary utility function, $U(C)$ (La Grandville 2007a). When the objective functional is more simply the sum (the integral) of the discounted consumption flows, then two remarkable consequences emerge: First, the Euler equation is no longer a differential equation solvable only by numerical methods, but an algebraic equation from which the optimal trajectories K^*_t, I^*_t, and s^*_t can be derived in analytic form. Second—and more importantly—the optimal savings rate now has reasonable, reachable values.

THE FUNDAMENTAL FACTORS OF ECONOMIC GROWTH

As mentioned above, Ibn Khaldūn provided the fundamental factors of economic growth. These are not set at random, but follow a logical order, one implying the other.

Demographic Growth and Technological Progress Ibn Khaldūn's idea is that a larger population enhances the division of labor. This view of demographic growth was rediscovered four centuries later by Adam Smith in his *Wealth of Nations*. In addition, the enhancement of division of labor that accompanies technological progress improves the chances that an individual, by concentrating on a specific task, will find ways to innovate.

The Search for Individual Profit The search for individual profit is a factor of growth that is far from obvious. According to Ibn Khaldūn: "Civilization and its well-being as well as business prosperity depend on productivity and people's efforts in all direction in their own interest and profit" (Ibn Khaldūn [1377] 1958, p. 104). Those words were later echoed by Smith:

> Every individual is continually exerting himself to find out the most advantageous employment for whatever capital he can command. It is his own advantage, indeed, and not that of the society, which he has in view. But the study of his own advantage naturally, or rather necessarily, leads him to prefer that employment which is most advantageous to the society.... He generally, indeed, neither intends to promote the public interest, nor knows how much he is promoting it.... He intends only his own gain, and he is in this, as in many other cases, led by an invisible hand to promote an end which was no part of his intention. (Smith [1776] 1977, pp. 398–400)

It is of fundamental importance that neither Ibn Khaldūn nor Smith defended the idea of using any means to make a profit. Quite on the contrary, both sternly condemned the abuse of dominant positions and monopoly power. But if profits can be made by inventing new processes or new products, how is it possible that such profits might be to the advantage of society as a whole? In addition, a further step was taken by Smith, for whom the optimum employment of capital by an individual would result in a maximum advantage for society.

Ibn Khaldūn's and Smith's conjecture can be illustrated and formally demonstrated. A first illustration is based upon the outcome of introducing technological progress. It can be shown that if innovations reduce marginal production costs, society's surplus will always increase, although ultimately some firms may see their profit diminish. Enhanced productivity (to quote Ibn Khaldūn) will induce firms to produce more, thereby increasing competition among them and forcing prices down. The lower prices and increased quantity will benefit consumers. Consumer surplus will increase in such a way that it will always more than compensate for any reduction in surplus suffered by producers. A striking example is the spectacular growth of China since the late 1970s, a growth process never witnessed at any other place or time. Its origin can be pinpointed to the suppression of the popular communes by Deng Xiaoping (1904–1997) in 1978. When farmers were allowed to increase production on private lots beyond the quota they were required to remit to cooperatives, they generated enormous surpluses for consumers and for themselves alike. Savings and investments increased on a large scale, setting in motion the growth process described in the beginning of this article. Clearly, the aim of farmers was to make a profit, but this benefited the entire Chinese economy, even though such a result had not been their intention (on this and for a formal proof of Smith's conjecture, see La Grandville 2007b).

Private Property The fourth factor of economic growth enunciated by Ibn Khaldūn is the principle of private property. Ibn Khaldūn lists three major transgressions to that principle. The first is slavery, condemned by Ibn Khaldūn who, to the best of our knowledge, was the first thinker to denounce what he considered "one of the greatest injustices and one which contributes most to the destruction of civilization" (Ibn Khaldūn [1377] 1958, pp. 108–109).

The second transgression against private property is private and public monopolies and, more generally, the infringement of competitive markets. (It is striking that Ibn Khaldūn also described the very system that would be implemented in many countries in the coming centuries, whereby farmers would be compelled to sell their product to a central authority that would market it at monopoly prices.)

The third transgression is excessive taxation, which destroys the desire to set up firms, and ultimately the very income that is supposed to be taxed.

The Soundness of Political and Legal Institutions In his *Introduction to History*, Ibn Khaldūn stressed the fundamental, necessary role that institutions play in the growth process. One of his aims was to warn his contemporaries of the dangers that lurked for their civilization if they did not manage to maintain a political system that would protect the individual. He tells us that he was not able to elaborate a better system of government than that embodied in a famous letter sent in 822 by Tahir, one of the generals of the king of Egypt, to his son Abdallah, which Ibn Khaldūn quotes in full. Here is one of its most significant messages:

> Consider it your most important task to take personal charge of the affairs of [your] officials and to protect your subjects by looking after their needs and providing for their requirements.... Do not be greedy. Let the treasures and riches you gather and hoard up be piety, the fear of God, justice, the improvement of your subjects, the cultivation of their country, the supervision of their affairs, the

protection of the mass of them, and support of the unfortunates. You should know that property, once it is gathered and stored in treasuries, does not bear fruit, but if it is invested in the welfare of the subjects and used for giving them what is due to them and to prevent them from need, then it grows and thrives. The common people prosper.... Devote yourself to looking after the affairs of the poor and indigent, those who are not able to bring before you complaints about injustices they have suffered, and other lowly persons who do not know that they may ask for their rights. Inquire about these people in all secrecy, and put good men from among your subjects in charge of them. Command them to report to you their needs and conditions, so that you will be able to look into the measures through which God might improve their affairs. Have regard also for people who have suffered accidents, and for their widows and orphans. Give them stipends from the treasury, following the example of the Commander of the Faithful.... Set up houses for muslims who are ill, shelter them, [appoint] attendants in these houses who will handle them kindly, and [appoint] physicians who will treat their diseases. Comply with their desires so long as it does not lead to waste in the treasury. (Ibn Khaldūn [1377] 1958, pp. 143–153)

Prosperity, for Ibn Khaldūn, thus implies as a necessary condition the protection of the individual and at the same time a social policy that corresponds very closely to the equity principle defined above.

CONCLUSION

William Letwin, in his introduction to the *Wealth of Nations*, described Adam Smith's message thus: "Far from being a hymn in praise of anarchic greed, the *Wealth of Nations* is a reasoned argument for justice, order, liberty and prudent plenty" (Smith [1776] 1977, p. xxii). One could not better characterize the *Muqaddimah* by Ibn Khaldūn. The similarity of those two messages, from different civilizations and four centuries apart, prompts us to beg the question of the convergence of ideas and values among civilizations. Economic growth does require the factors enunciated by Ibn Khaldūn; it also requires peace. Ibn Khaldūn spent a good part of his life trying to negotiate peace treaties on all shores of the Mediterranean. For his part, Smith denounced wars and the financing of wars as the greatest deterrent of economic growth. In Western civilization, one of the most fundamental values is the principle of defensive war, which probably originated in the writings of Augustine of Hippo (354–430 CE). Shared by Ibn Khaldūn and Smith, did this idea appear elsewhere? Indeed, they were preceded by the Chinese philosopher Mo-Tzu (c. 470–391 BCE) (Watson 1967).

Mo-Tzu tried—in vain—to advocate this idea, which he based upon another fundamental principle: that of equality of individuals and states. This latter principle would take more than two thousand years to be slowly implemented in state constitutions, and even longer in social behavior.

Nevertheless, the last millennia definitely witnessed a convergence of ideas and values among civilizations, and such is the reason why we may hope that societies will ultimately achieve economic growth for all.

SEE ALSO *Business Cycles, Real; Business Cycles, Theories; Democratization; Development; Development Economics; Golden Rule in Growth Models; Ibn Khaldūn; Immiserizing Growth; Neoclassical Growth Model; Optimal Growth; Productivity; Property, Private; Saving Rate; Slavery; Smith, Adam; Solow Residual, The; Solow, Robert M.*

BIBLIOGRAPHY

Botero, Giovanni. [1589] 1956. *The Reason of State.* Trans. P. J. and D. P. Waley. London: Routledge and Kegan Paul.

Botero, Giovanni. [1598] 1956. *The Greatness of Cities.* Trans. Robert Peterson. London: Routledge and Kegan Paul.

Child, Josiah. 1668. *Brief Observations Concerning Trade, and Interests of Money.* London: Calvert.

Economic Growth Resources. Maintained by Jonathan Temple; hosted by the University of Bristol. http://www.bris.ac.uk/Depts/Economics/Growth/.

Elsgolc, Lev E. 1961. *Calculus of Variations.* London: Pergamon.

Gaxotte, Pierre. 1951. *Histoire des Français.* Paris: Flammarion.

Ibn Khaldūn. [1377] 1958. *The Muqaddimah: An Introduction to History.* Trans. Franz Rosenthal. London: Routledge and Kegan Paul.

La Grandville, Olivier de. 2007a. The 1956 Contribution to Economic Growth Theory by Robert Solow: a Major Landmark and Some of its Undiscovered Riches. *Oxford Review of Economic Policy* 23 (Spring 2007): 15–24.

La Grandville, Olivier de. 2007b. *Economic Growth: A Unified Approach.* With two special contributions by Robert M. Solow. Cambridge University Press, forthcoming.

Serra, Antonio. 1613. *Breve trattato delle cause che possono far abbondare li regni d'oso e argento dove non sono miniere.* Naples, Italy: Lazzaro Scorriggio.

Smith, Adam. [1776] 1977. *An Inquiry into the Nature and Causes of the Wealth of Nations.* New York: Dent.

Solow, Robert M. 1956. A Contribution to the Theory of Economic Growth. *Quarterly Journal of Economics* 70 (1): 65–94.

Sully, Maximilien de Béthune, Duc de. 1634. *Mémoires des sages et royales économies.* Paris: Courbé.

Toynbee, Arnold J. 1935. *A Study of History.* Vol. III. 2nd ed. London and New York: Oxford University Press.

Watson, Burton, trans. and ed. 1967. *Basic Writings of Mo Tzu, Hsün Tzu, and Han Fei Tzu.* New York: Columbia University Press.

Olivier de La Grandville

ECONOMIC HISTORY

SEE *Cliometrics.*

ECONOMIC METHODOLOGY

Economic methodology is concerned with how economic knowledge is pursued. It covers a range of issues: Can we establish rules for good economic analysis, and if so what are they? If we cannot establish rules, are there principles for guidance? What principles do economists use in practice? How are we to understand the evolution of the discipline? How separate is economics from other social sciences, and to what extent should economic methodology be discussed independently of the methodology of other social sciences?

The term *methodology* is often used incorrectly, to refer to methods. Methodologists use the term to refer to the approach taken to building knowledge (and the status of that knowledge), which provides among other things the basis for choosing methods. Some also draw the distinction between *Methodology* and *methodology*, the former being prescriptive (setting rules) and the latter descriptive (providing an account of methodology in practice). We will see that the balance has shifted over the last few decades from Methodology to methodology (see further Sheila Dow's introductory *Economic Methodology* [2002], and D. Wade Hands's more specialized *Reflection without Rules* [2001]).

Economic methodology is now a large specialist field in its own right. Before the 1980s, it was examined from a philosophical perspective only by a limited number of texts, drawing directly from the philosophy of science, or was discussed in the context of historical discussions of past methodological disputes. When it was discussed, as in the introductions to textbooks, it tended to be associated with a positivist philosophy of science, with an emphasis on testing theory against objective facts, and a distinction of positive from normative statements. Indeed, this was the approach taken by Milton Friedman (1953) in what for a long time was the most famous piece of methodological writing in economics. Friedman argued that the purpose of theory was to predict, regardless of the realism or otherwise of assumptions; theory was thus simply "instrumental." This sparked heated debates with those (ranging from Samuelson to Kaldor) who saw the primary purpose of theory to be explanation, and thus considered the realism of assumptions to be important. Indeed, Friedman had drawn distinctions too sharply: In order to predict, there has to be some understanding of causal mechanisms, along with the capacity this provides to adapt theories to changing economic structures. Thus theory content is still important. Nonetheless, the boldness of Friedman's challenge forced dissenters to formulate their methodological positions more explicitly.

Beginning with the publication in 1980 of Mark Blaug's authoritative *The Methodology of Economics*, there has been a tremendous increase in interest in economic methodology, which led to the setting up of the International Network for Economic Methodology, with its *Journal of Economic Methodology* and Web site www.econmethodology.org—which in turn have generated even more interest and activity, among both specialist methodologists and practitioners. The growth in the field also no doubt reflects a need to understand debates in economics at a deeper, foundational, level. The wide range of topics now covered by economic methodology is evident from the *Handbook of Economic Methodology* (1998).

Blaug's text appeared at a time when new developments in the philosophy of science had challenged the whole idea of establishing a single set of independent rules for good practice (monism). Blaug called on economics to build on Karl Popper's idea that, even if we cannot be certain that we have identified a true explanation, we can at least be certain of identifying a false explanation, if the evidence contradicts the theory (falsificationism). While Popper had advocated exposing all elements of theory to empirical testing, he made an exception for the axioms of rational individual behavior from which mainstream economic theory was built. These axioms specified the basis for individual choice, which in turn was the basis for the optimal allocation of scarce resources. They were necessary for setting economic theory up as a deductive logical structure, generating hypotheses that could be tested against empirical evidence (the methodology presented for many decades in introductory economics textbooks).

In the tradition of seeing methodology as prescribing good practice, Blaug drew attention to how economists' practice fell short of Popper's principles, due to a reliance (if at all) on evidence that confirmed theory—namely, verificationism. Indeed, such an approach was supported by the priority given by many to explanation over prediction. But in the meantime a divide had grown between pure theory, which was not generally tested, and applied economics, which had little impact on theory. Other methodologists shifted attention to understanding why this was so, drawing on the philosophy of science of Thomas Kuhn. In the absence of any absolute rules for good scientific practice, Kuhn had analyzed science in terms of activity within scientific communities, each of which has its own methodology and understanding of reality. Because of the latter state of affairs, we cannot think in terms of an independent set of "facts" against which theory is tested in any absolute sense.

Kuhn's ideas encouraged the development of what came to be known as *constructivism*, based on the idea of knowledge being "constructed," rather than established by facts. This development encompassed postmodernism (the denial of any general knowledge), rhetoric (the focus on techniques of persuasion other than methodological principle), and the sociology of scientific knowledge (the sociological study of scientific communities). Within constructivism, "Methodology" has no role, only "methodology" as a descriptive device. A high proportion of methodological work now falls into this category.

Kuhn had also encouraged the legitimation of a range of heterodox schools of thought, which proceeded to define themselves in terms of methodological differences from the mainstream. The differences started from a rejection of the whole idea of founding theory on axioms of rational choice (or indeed any deterministic account of behavior), as such axioms did not mesh with heterodox understandings of reality. Methodological awareness is thus wider spread in heterodox economics, playing a more central role in debate. Current leading topics focus at the levels of reality and of mode of thought, that is, below the methodological level: Is reality an open system (and what does that mean), and does such a system require an open system of knowledge, and what does that imply for methodology? Should there be a plurality of methodologies, and should methodology be pluralist (employing many methods)? How far does realism allow us to specify methodological principles after all? The realism debates have moved well beyond the old debates about the extent to which assumptions should be realistic.

In the meantime, there have been new developments in mainstream economics that require methodological discussion. Experimental and survey evidence contradicting the rationality assumptions, for example, is now encouraging theoretical change. Nevertheless the change is in the direction of a more complex account of rational individual choice, maintaining the traditional logical structure of mainstream theory, with its methodology of deducing arguments by logic from axioms, to be tested against facts. Within the mainstream, economics continues to be defined by this methodology, which requires fully specified individual behavior.

Current methodological discussion is thus both diverse and wide-ranging. Much of it is "micro" in the sense of examining particular developments in economics in methodological terms. At the "macro" level, it is concerned much less with principles to guide practice and much more with principles by which to understand the discipline.

SEE ALSO *Economics; Methodology*

BIBLIOGRAPHY

Blaug, Mark. 1980. *The Methodology of Economics, or, How Economists Explain.* 2nd ed. Cambridge, U.K.: Cambridge University Press, 1992.

Davis, John B., D. Wade Hands, and Uskali Mäki, eds. 1998. *The Handbook of Economic Methodology.* Cheltenham, U.K.: Edward Elgar.

Dow, Sheila C. 2002. *Economic Methodology: An Inquiry.* Oxford: Oxford University Press.

Friedman, Milton. 1953. The Methodology of Positive Economics. In his *Essays in Positive Economics*, 3–43. Chicago: University of Chicago Press.

Hands, D. Wade. 2001. *Reflection without Rules: Economic Methodology and Contemporary Science Theory.* Cambridge, U.K.: Cambridge University Press.

Sheila C. Dow

ECONOMIC MODEL

Economic models may be seen as intermediate between theories and the world, and are accordingly differently understood depending on how one sees their relationships to each. Models are specifically economic models when they address forms of social interaction involving prices and other money magnitudes. Daniel Hausman (1992) takes models to be either trivially true or neither true nor false, and thus to constitute conceptual explorations of theories. His emphasis is on theoretical models, not on empirical models, and thus on how models enable us to investigate theoretical concepts. In contrast, Ronald Giere (1988) sees science as a cognitive process, and is concerned with how models help us learn about the world. He sees the relationship between models and the world as one of similarity (though not of isomorphism). This allows models to be both somehow "true" of the world and yet at the same time not be expected to fully reflect the structure of the world.

Models may be defined, then, as instruments of investigation that allow us to concentrate on relationships of special interest, whether in theory or in the world or in combination of the two (see Morgan and Morrison 1999). That they focus attention on aspects of the world implies that they should not be taken as complete explanations, but as particular ways of examining those aspects. Within this framework, several different approaches to Giere's similarity idea have been suggested. Models have been taken to be idealizations or approximations that provide "realistic" though partial representations of the world. Models can also be seen to be like analogies and metaphors in that they exhibit similarities between different domains or systems. Another view is that models are like stories told to explain how theories may be interpreted or how theories relate to the world.

There are a number of misconceptions about the nature of economic models. While economic models are often seen to be sets of highly formal statements, there is nothing in the concept of an economic model that requires formal representation. Indeed, whether formal models or qualitative ones are preferred depends on the subject matter being modeled. Another widespread belief is that models are essentially instruments for making predictions about the future. But models have many different uses. There are theoretical models, simulation models, policy models, econometric models, measurement models, experiment models, formal models, accounting models, and so forth, all of which are constructed for different, often highly specific, purposes. Further, even good models designed expressly for making predictions can fail to produce reliable predictions in changing environments. Thus, because economic models have both limited and usually quite specific purposes, it is important to avoid uncritical use of the information they generate. Models are instruments for all kinds of investigation, and our investigations of the world are fallible, partial, and subject to revision.

SEE ALSO *Macrofoundations; Maximization; Microfoundations; Minimization; Models and Modeling; Multisector Models; Optimizing Behavior; Two-Sector Models*

BIBLIOGRAPHY

Giere, Ronald. 1988. *Explaining Science: A Cognitive Approach.* Chicago: University of Chicago Press.

Hausman, Daniel. 1992. *The Inexact and Separate Science of Economics.* Cambridge, U.K.: Cambridge University Press.

Morgan, Mary, and Margaret Morrison. 1999. *Models as Mediators: Perspectives on Natural and Social Science.* Cambridge, U.K.: Cambridge University Press.

John B. Davis

ECONOMIC PSYCHOLOGY

The field of economic psychology explores how economics impinges on the psychology of both individuals and groups, as well as how people both individually and collectively affect the economy. This transactional interplay between society at both the micro level and the more macro level of sociocultural institutions suggests that traffic between the two is not just possible but should be welcomed as a new field of study. The study of economic psychology originated in the late nineteenth century, with contributions from the French social scientist Gabriel Tarde and the American sociologist Thorstein Veblen.

The early ambitions of individuals like Tarde and Veblen to challenge the very foundations of economics have become more modest, and one of the legacies of their critique of economics has been the establishment of psychological considerations as important in economic theory and research. The field of economic psychology is populated by a small but vigorous intellectual community in its own right. The assumptions of rationality that underpin "homo economicus" have been effectively challenged, and the cognitive biases that influence decision-making and are part of human nature are now well known in all branches of social science.

Today, marketing students are taught about the social-emotional meaning of brands and how consumption practices are driven by considerations of social identity. The economist Richard Thaler points out that money, which is said by economists to be "fungible" (i.e., one sort of money is equivalent to any other), is in fact subject to mental accounting, meaning that money is viewed differently in different contexts. For example, money received as regular income is put in a different category than money from a windfall. Fungibility is not just a simplifying assumption. It does not do justice to the ways people manage their economic affairs in the real world. People have a concept of money that is situated and context-dependent.

Economic psychology is also interested in economic behavior in different cultural and historical contexts. So economic socialization, or how children learn the ways of their own economic world, has become a thriving part of economic psychology. The developmental changes that occur as children grow up mean that any theory of their economic decision-making is inevitably dependent on their level of psychological development. In household economics, economic psychologists have been exploring money management within the family. The psychologist Carole Burgoyne has argued that the styles that families and couples adopt to negotiate their finances can reflect deep-rooted tensions and reveal significant aspects of their relationships that would be otherwise difficult to access.

There are other areas of research and scholarship apart from economics and psychology that impinge on and influence economic psychology. Behavioral economics, for example, attempts to blend together economics and psychology, though in the main it is limited to the examination of psychological aspects of decision-making and the improvement of economics by placing it on a more realistic psychological foundation. Economic sociology, on the other hand, is firmly rooted in the sociological approach to the study of society. Here, the concepts and epistemology of sociological enquiry are applied to

economic institutions. The field of economic psychology will remain valid and important as long as the cross-fertilization between economic and psychological theories and practices is mutually respected, and as long as there is a will to synthesize from debates and disputes.

SEE ALSO *Child Development; Choice in Economics; Choice in Psychology; Conspicuous Consumption; Economics, Behavioral; Happiness; Money; Permanent Income Hypothesis; Relative Income Hypothesis; Sociology; Sociology, Economic*

BIBLIOGRAPHY

Earl, Peter E., and Simon Kemp, eds. 1999. *The Elgar Companion to Consumer Research and Economic Psychology.* Cheltenham, U.K.: Edward Elgar.

Webley, Paul, et al., eds. 2001. *The Economic Psychology of Everyday Life.* Hove, U.K.: Psychology Press.

Brian Young

ECONOMIC RHETORIC

The expression *economic rhetoric* refers to the practice and study of the communication process of economic ideas, both in oral and written form. It conveys the notion of economics as a particular type of social discourse, one that uses analogies, appeals to authority, arguments by transitivity, and other rhetorical devices to persuade its audience.

The rhetorical nature of economics is the focus of a research program that began in the early 1980s, generating a significant amount of research, still ongoing, and eliciting much controversy. The pioneer authors were D. N. McCloskey and Arjo Klamer, who, moved by their dissatisfaction with conventional economic methodology, decided to investigate the scientific culture of economics.

Klamer conducted a series of interviews with eleven prominent economists from different schools of thought, asking them about their intellectual trajectory and the circumstances in which they came to elaborate their well-known models. He claims that theoretical disputes within economics are not settled by the accumulation of empirical evidence. Instead, Klamer suggests that a more promising interpretation of these disagreements should focus on their rhetorical aspects, the ongoing conversation through which economists everywhere try to persuade their audiences.

McCloskey also criticizes traditional epistemology. Under the influence of postmodernism and neopragmatism, she holds that the prevailing methodological approach is rooted in modernism, which views science as axiomatic and mathematical. Although the progressive mathematization of contemporary economics allowed certain questions to be formulated with greater clarity, it involved major costs, one of them being a widespread tendency to confuse statistical significance with economic significance. McCloskey acknowledges that the change in language brought some transparency to economic arguments, but she claims that it hindered the dialogue with other humanistic disciplines and led economists to subscribe to a positivist methodology. She argues that economists should pay attention to their rhetoric, in order to gain a new self-consciousness of their conversation practices.

At the heart of the debate raised by the rhetorical turn in the history of economics lies a tension that has existed since the ancient Greeks and is not yet settled. It stems from the two potentially conflicting meanings that the word *rhetoric* acquires, as form and as substance, as mere ornament to speech and as a set of arguments directed at an audience. While some Sophist philosophers stressed the ornamental aspect of rhetoric, thus helping to give the concept the pejorative meaning of "mere rhetoric," Aristotle legitimated it as a rational procedure, intimately connected to logic and dialectic. During the twentieth century, the rehabilitation of the Aristotelian tradition expressed the need for a better understanding of how a persuasive discourse works to influence its intended readers.

Still, the pejorative and dismissive meaning of rhetoric as empty speech persists. The rhetorical turn in economics was unable to give a satisfactory answer to its critics, who accused it of neglecting the truth-seeking nature of scientific inquiry. Yet it drew attention to the argumentative aspect of economics, highlighting the importance of rhetorical analysis as a research tool, to be used to show how texts conceived in a given social context create meaning, construct knowledge, and elicit action. By paying attention to their rhetoric, economists can improve the quality of their discourse.

SEE ALSO *Aristotle; Economics; Epistemology; Mathematical Economics; Persuasion; Philosophy; Rhetoric*

BIBLIOGRAPHY

Klamer, Arjo. 2007. *Speaking of Economics: How to Get in the Conversation.* London: Routledge.

McCloskey, D. N. 1994. *Knowledge and Persuasion in Economics.* New York: Cambridge University Press.

Ana Maria Bianchi

ECONOMIC SOCIOLOGY

SEE *Sociology, Economic.*

ECONOMICS

The theory of the division of labor is at least two and a half millennia old. The practice of the division of labor undoubtedly has a much longer history. Both the theory and the practice stress that joint activity is more productive compared with individual or isolated activity, and both apply to different spheres of work: work within a factory or group and work among firms (e.g., between factories). The division of labor is therefore a principal mode of coordination for all such disparate but connected activity.

The theory of the division of labor has different facets to it, in that it applies to both physical labor and intellectual labor. As an object of study and a tool of analysis, it is at the foundation of substantially all of economics. Moreover, the practice of economics itself makes use of, and thus reflects, the division of labor. This, perhaps more than any other factor, explains the importance of economics.

The combination of human psychology and the division of labor also help explain two major features of human behavior: selective perception and status emulation. Each of the major skill groups (or crafts or trades) that work more or less together to produce a pin, a truck, or a house tends to think that its contribution is the most valuable. Individuals acquire their status based on how they perform in their own domain of work, and they seek to emulate those already successful in that domain. The same is true in economics insofar as it too is erected upon the principle of the division of labor. It is no accident that the division of labor, selective perception, and status emulation were also among the major themes of Adam Smith's *Wealth of Nations* (1776).

DIVISION OF LABOR IN ECONOMICS

The division of labor within economics takes place along a number of axes, with their respective spheres interacting in a recursive manner. The existence of a multiplicity of practices on each axis is due both to the multifaceted nature of the economy and its study (economics) and to the different positions or standpoints that economists can take. Each such standpoint, and its correlative body of practice, is accompanied by selective perception and status emulation, for the practitioner of each type laud its attributes and pursues success defined in its terms.

One axis is that of the criteria by which economists produce knowledge. One of these criteria is deduction, which, when correctly practiced, produces conclusions that are valid, given the premises and the system of logic, but necessarily true. Another is induction, which produces conclusions that may or may not be true, depending on the entirety of practice. This is the field of epistemology, or methodology, which is also practiced along twin axes in another respect. Given the variety of credentials that a proposition may have, two uses of those credentials may be made: The prescriptive use postulates that one and only one set of credentials produces acceptable knowledge, while the credentialist use affirms that every proposition has its own set of credentials and that the individual is free to accept or reject it. These modes of use tend to be at the heart of competing practices, each yielding status emulation.

A second axis has to do with the fundamental substantive paradigms that tend to govern all work in economics. This axis constitutes the ontology of economics. Among the different paradigmatic possibilities are the fundamental theories of a surplus; constrained maximization (maximization subject to constraints, such as cost or legal prohibitions or requirements); productivity or exploitation; culture; and the attainment of a level of welfare and the structure of its distribution. Paradigms are among the most important elements in the social construction of economics.

A third axis concerns the fundamental problem of economics. Among the multiplicity of contenders for this designation are: the organization and control of the economic system, the efficient (or optimum) allocation of resources, economic growth, maximization of welfare, distribution of income (and wealth), and the ordinary business of life in terms of earning a living.

A fourth axis, somewhat related to the third, concerns the organization and control of the economic system itself. A central focus here is the institution of private property, while institutions such as the market, the development of the division of labor itself, and the system of social control are also relevant. One composite approach is that of the "market plus framework," in which markets exist on the basis of the framework of social controls. The identity of the framework tends to be reduced to legal and moral rules, inclusive of custom, education, religion, and various forms or sources of law. In this model, markets are not given, they are socially constructed by the interactions of the institutions that form and operate through them. At the very least, markets—and indeed the economic system itself—depend upon the legal foundations of those in control of the state (or those who create the laws of property, contract, tort, etc.) and the strategic behavior of firms and other economic agents.

ECONOMIC THEORY

The conventional assumptions of economic theory, in its static form, have tended to include (1) perfect competition and perfect knowledge (and therefore perfect foresight); (2) given and unchanging technology, resources, tastes, population, and structure of rights; and (3) individual agents that operate independent of each other, that are mobile, and that calculate rationally in order to maximize

the satisfaction (or utility) derivable from their real incomes. One or more of these assumptions can be modified, thereby engendering an array of further possibilities, such as a variety of noncompetitive conditions, imperfect information, asymmetrical information, interdependent tastes, changes in the distribution and content of rights, behavior that is less than maximizing, and changes in technology, resources, tastes, and population. Such modifications may or may not add realism, but they do tend to introduce dynamic elements.

The conduct of economics, like that of any intellectual discipline, inevitably involves some type of abstraction, such as the reduction of the number of variables in a model down to the ones deemed most important. This makes the enterprise more manageable. That being the case, economics involves both the study of actual economies and the analysis of conceptual, abstract economies. Closely related is the research protocol stipulating epistemological credentials. At one end of a spectrum is the capacity to produce unique determinate optimal equilibrium results; at the other, to produce an array of possibilities at the conditions governing their realization.

APPROACHES TO ECONOMICS

The history of economics is very much a story of schools of thought. There have been multiple schools of thought, together constituting a heterogeneous discipline, and each school has itself been heterogeneous. This heterogeneity is the result of a combination of a multifaceted economy and different positions or standpoints from which the economy can be studied. There is nothing about the economy or the training of economists that requires that one and only one variable, point of entry, or perspective be used. Accordingly, in every period in the history of the field there has been more than one school of economic thought. A particular school may endeavor to cover the entirety of economics, or it may examine only one or more parts thereof. Economics as a whole is itself further heterogeneous, and because each school typically can be formulated differently, each school is itself heterogeneous. All of this comes under the heading of "theoretical pluralism," which differs from the ontological or paradigmatic pluralism and the epistemological or methodological pluralism described above. And all of these approaches can be rendered further complex and heterogenous by introducing normative premises of one kind or another, such as accepting existing institutions or the status quo distributions of income and wealth.

Theoretical pluralism also takes another form. Every topic in economics is characterized by particular theories. Consider the following: competition, equilibrium, business cycles, income distribution, consumption, supply of money, commodity demand, capital, investment, the entrepreneur, optimization, money, interest rates, imperialism, economic growth, supply of labor, technology, externalities, incidence of taxation, the origin of the division of labor, and the economic role of government. Each has multiple theories, even multiple groups of theories, that attempt to describe or explain the object of their respective author's attention.

FROM CLASSICALISM TO MARGINALISM

Several questions come to mind when considering why a school of economic thought arises and flowers. The rise of marginal utility economics in the 1870s is a suggestive case in point. "Marginal utility" is the change in utility associated with a change in consumption level. The term also refers to a utilitarian-calculus approach to economic analysis and decision-making. "Classical economics" refers to a group of economic thinkers who wrote after Adam Smith. The school commences with Thomas Robert Malthus, and David Ricardo and also consists of John R. McCoulloch, William Nassau Senior, and James Bill. The approach was largely finished with the work of John Stuart Mill and John Elliott Cairnes.

Among the factors that explain its existence are the following: (1) the deficiencies of classical economics, including its neglect of psychological valuation as an important demand-side aspect of value theory, its focus on economic classes and labor theory (including cost-of-production theory), and its perceived weaknesses as a defense of capitalism; (2) the logical continuation of earlier writings on utility analysis; (3) the growth of static and positivistic theory (laws of the coexistence of variables) challenging Hegelian and other historical theory (the laws of the succession of variables)—or of the study of being rather than becoming; (4) a reaction to Marxism's emphasis on exploitation and the transient character of capitalism as part of an attack on socialist theory in general; and (5) the emergence of academic economics and its tendency to deal with trivia unsuitable for reformers. Academic economics included the use of mathematics, which was attractive insofar as it enabled economics to resemble physics, and because it effectuated a reduction of variables to the neoclassical model of demand and supply.

Among these varied explanations for the rise of the marginal utility approach, one finds ironic incongruities, such as positivism's emphasis on the objective analysis of confirmable materials rather than metaphysical, unconfirmable general theories of history, and the marginal utility school's criticism that classicism's broad conclusions were based on a small structure of knowledge wrapped up in a few theorems. Both of these positions were in conflict

with key features of the marginal utility school's subjectivism.

MAINSTREAM ECONOMICS

There has also been a more or less amorphous mainstream of economics, yielding a combination of schools, some more or less orthodox and others more or less heterodox. The mainstream has run from the classical economics of Adam Smith (1723–1790), David Ricardo (1772–1823) and Thomas Robert Malthus (1766–1834), through the early versions of neoclassical economics formulated by Carl Menger (1840–1921) and Alfred Marshall (1842–1924), to the modern formulation by a group led by Paul A. Samuelson (b. 1915). Differences within each school (and between schools) arose along the different axes identified above. These differences were often identified in terms of a school's central problem or focus. The mainstream changed from a grand macroeconomic story of production, growth, and distribution to an equally imposing story of subjectively acting individual economic units and their interaction in markets, along with the resultant allocation of resources. Under the name of "neoclassical economics," the mainstream developed a variety of technical identifications of its central problem, many of them mutually reinforcing, such as the mechanics of utility, the operation of the price system, the working of the free enterprise system, the operation of pure markets, the mechanics of the pure theory of choice, constrained maximization decision making, the allocation of resources, and the mechanics of welfare. Schools of economic thought have tended to define themselves in terms of a central problem; the two most common have been explaining how people make their living and explaining how the economy is organized and controlled. Because the assumptions that characterized the core of mainstream neoclassicism could be changed, a further variety of subschools emerged within general neoclassicism. Varieties of theories of noncompetitive conditions, uncertainty, changing tastes, rights, institutions, ideology, technology, and population developed, each offering a more or less distinctively different picture of the economy.

Among the alternatives to the mainstream has been "institutional economics." The central problem here is literally the organization and control of the economy, though with several different foci. One focus was the legal foundations of the economic system; another was the system of cultural beliefs by which people organized and instituted their economic relations, and with which they explained those relations to themselves. Common to both foci was power. The key figures of institutional economics have been Thorstein Veblen (1857–1929), Walton Hamilton (1881–1958), John R. Commons (1862–1945), and John Kenneth Galbraith (1908–2006).

KEYNESIAN ECONOMICS

In the middle third of the twentieth century, nurtured in part by reactions to the Great Depression, the focus of macroeconomics changed from growth in classical terms and the allocation of resources to the determination of the level of income. The key figure of the new macroeconomics was John Maynard Keynes (1883–1946), who argued that classical doctrines to the contrary notwithstanding, the level of income, resulting from factors governing the level of aggregate spending, was not necessarily at the full employment level. This was important not just because variations in spending were involved in the business cycle and in unemployment, but also because so many people depended on employment for their livelihood. In time, Samuelson combined neoclassical microeconomic price and resource-allocation theory with Keynesian macroeconomic income-determination theory to produce the "neoclassical synthesis."

Thus, in combination with the further differentiating sources outlined above, one could practice economics in numerous different ways. Indeed, it could be argued that neoclassicism, or the neoclassical synthesis, was no longer the undifferentiated hegemon atop the mainstream, and today there are countless variations and combinations of treatments of topics that make up economics. This is true of all of the numerous topics that have had different but useful approaches formulated for them. Macroeconomics, for example, has had a variety of interpretations of what Keynes said and what he intended to say, plus a variety of post-Keynesian theories, not to mention new classical, real, new Keynesian, and other business-cycle theories. Microeconomics has a variety of treatments of how prices and resource allocation are determined; macroeconomics has a variety of treatments of the causes of instability; and both have in common a variety of treatments of uncertainty.

The foregoing does not exhaust the variety of ways in which economists do economics. Some economists study the performance of economic agents as if the agents were engaged in some type of cooperative or noncooperative game. That form of economics was instrumental in developing the strategy of mutual assured destruction (MAD) by the United States and the Soviet Union during the cold war, a strategy which worked to prevent World War III despite its seeming barbarous quality, mainly because the two sides thought more alike than not. Economists who do game theory are among the hordes who practice mathematical economics, a research language and mode of analysis that has been increasingly dominant since the 1960s. Other economists (and psychologists working on economic problems), have enriched the meaning of "rationality" and its attendant motivational attributes. Much of the work of economists is devoted to the descrip-

tion, explanation, and interpretation of what the economy is all about—as should be evident from what has been written above. Many economists self-consciously work at constructing or applying the normative, subjective, and ideological justification for market economies; many others work at its critique. Indeed, it has been said that much of the history of economics has been driven by attempts to influence the distributions of income, wealth, and opportunity in society, as well as by the control and use of government as a political means to economic ends. Which brings this discussion to such combined fields as economic sociology, law and economics, economic anthropology, economic psychology, economic history, and the history of economic thought—fields that are rich in and of themselves.

SEE ALSO *Austrian Economics; Austro-Marxism; Capitalism; Capitalism, Managerial; Chicago School; Competition; Economics, Classical; Economics, Institutional; Economics, Islamic; Economics, Keynesian; Economics, Neoclassical; Economics, Neo-Ricardian; Economics, New Classical; Economics, New Keynesian; Economics, Post Keynesian; Institutionalism; Libertarianism; Macroeconomics; Marginalism; Market Economy; Marx, Karl; Microeconomics; Smith, Adam; Stockholm School*

BIBLIOGRAPHY

Colander, David C., Richard P. F. Holt, and J. Barkley Rosser. 2004. *The Changing Face of Economics: Conversations with Cutting-Edge Economists.* Ann Arbor: University of Michigan Press.

Ingrao, Bruna, and Giorgio Israel. 1990. *The Invisible Hand: Economic Equilibrium in the History of Science.* Cambridge, MA: MIT Press.

Medema, Steven G., and Warren J. Samuels, eds. 1996. *Foundations of Research in Economics: How Do Economists Do Economics?* Brookfield, VT: Edward Elgar.

Shackle, George L. S. 1967. *The Years of High Theory: Invention and Tradition in Economic Thought 1926–1939.* New York: Cambridge University Press.

Weintraub, E. Roy. 2002. *How Economics Became a Mathematical Science.* Durham, NC: Duke University Press.

Warren J. Samuels

ECONOMICS, BEHAVIORAL

Underlying behavioral economics and distinguishing it from contemporary (neoclassical) economics is the presumption that the realism of behavioral and institutional assumptions matter substantively to the modeling of the economic agent (Simon 1959, 1978, 1987). In contemporary economic theory (e.g., Friedman 1953), assumptions are of little analytical consequence as long as the model's predictions are correct. In behavioral economics, the realism of assumptions affects the accuracy of models' predictions. It also helps distinguish between spurious correlations and actual cause-and-effect relationships between independent and dependant variables. Even when "as if" neoclassical behavioral assumptions yield correct predictions, if alternative, more realistic assumptions also generate accurate predictions, abiding by the former spawns false and therefore unscientific causal results. However, behavioral economics does not dispute the notion of abstraction and simplicity in model building; it questions models built upon unrealistic simplifying assumptions. When theory and evidence conflict, one includes in one's search for modeling deficiencies misspecified assumptions, unlike in conventional analysis that focuses largely on missing variables and questioning the validity of the evidence itself (Reder 1982).

Unlike behavioral economics, economic theory typically plays a marginal role in economic psychology. The latter focuses upon applying psychological tools to economic questions and generating evidence that might underlie behavioral assumption of economic agency. It also examines the psychological motivation for economic behavior (Lewis, Webley, and Furnham 1995).

Contemporary behavioral economics is often associated with the contributions of Hebert Simon and, more recently, Daniel Kahneman and Amos Tversky (Kahneman and Tversky 1979; Tversky and Kahneman 1981), all of whom are Nobel Prize Laureates. Thus far, George Katona's earlier pioneering contributions (1951, 1975) revising the psychological assumptions of consumer behavior in economic theory have gone largely unnoticed. Connected with Simon, Kahneman, Tversky, and their colleagues and associates are the presentation of new theories that either supplement or revise neoclassical micro and macro theories (Altman 2006; Camerer, Lowenstein, and Rabin 2003; Cyert and March 1963; Frank 1988; Shiller 1993; Thaler 1992; Williamson 1975).

Simon introduced the concepts of *bounded rationality* and *satisficing*, integrating into economic theory the reality of the cognitive limitations of individuals in terms of computational ability and knowledge acquisition that can only be realized at a cost. Rational individuals adopt behavioral procedures designed to limit such costs that differ descriptively and normatively from the conventional economic standard. Satisficing is the rational alternative to optimizing in a world of bounded rationality. In this case, it is possible for the firm's output and profit and the individual's utility to be less than they would be in

a world with no limits to human cognitive abilities. Neoclassical norms are no longer optimal or descriptively accurate. Simon also emphasized the importance of recognizing the importance of power relationships, conflicts, fairness, altruism, and institutions for modeling economic agency—variables that are given little space in conventional theory. Individuals might be maximizing their own well-being at the expense of others or society at large; utility might be enhanced at the expense of material wealth (Kahneman, Knetsch, Thaler 1986). Kahneman and Tversky developed prospect theory based on their experiments as an alternative to expected subjective utility theory, where individuals weigh losses more than gains and evaluate their utility in terms of relative positioning. Wealth maximization is not the end game in their descriptive modeling framework. Perspectives developed here have given rise to the revealing ultimatum and dictator game experiments wherein individuals make material sacrifices in the name of fairness (Güth 1995).

Independent of the work of Simon and more contemporary behavioral economists, Harvey Leibenstein (1957, 1966, 1979) developed the concepts of efficiency wages and x-efficiency theory (see Frantz 1997, for details). Based on the evidence, he assumes that effort inputs into the process of production are variable, not fixed at some maximum, as is assumed in conventional theory. Therefore, costs need not be minimized nor output maximized. Effort maximizing remains the ideal for wealth maximization or x-efficiency to be achieved. However, for this to transpire, appropriate market conditions and in-firm incentive environments (often far removed from neoclassical norms) must be developed. The efficiency wage and x-efficiency literature have been extended, for example in Akerlof (2002), Akerlof and Yellen (1986), Altman (1996), Darity and Goldsmith (1996), Stiglitz (1987), and Tomer (1997).

There are roughly two major perspectives within behavioral economics. The one that follows and extends the work of the psychologists Kahneman and Tversky is especially focused on, demonstrating through experiments the extent to which human behavior deviates from neoclassical norms, where the latter are used as the benchmark for economic rationality. By such standards individuals are found to be largely irrational, but such behavior might possibly be corrected through education or government intervention. Irrationality in behavior as the norm is completely inconsistent with conventional theory, and would be regarded as suboptimal in the realm of production and consumption. Such findings are therefore thought to undermine the legitimacy of much contemporary economic modeling. Conventional theory is assumed to provide an adequate description of how individuals behave, and holds that this behavior is also normatively optimal. Many behavioral economists argue that conventional theory fails as an accurate descriptor of even average human behavior, although it might very well be normatively correct. Vernon Smith (2003, 2005) has challenged many of the empirical findings of such behavioral economists, arguing that the incentive environment of many of their experiments are far removed from what is typically found in the real world of economic life. But Smith and his colleagues have also challenged the modeling assumptions (especially their institutional parameters) of contemporary theory, also using experimental data. Smith finds that human behavior is largely economically rational.

Compatible with Smith's view on behavioral economics is a perspective that builds on the contributions of Simon. Individuals are assumed to be largely rational and intelligent, developing procedures and institutions that best suit their individual needs given the constraints that they face (March 1978; Smith 2003; Todd and Gigerenzer 2003). This approach to human behavior is sometimes referred to as "ecological rationality." Deviations from neoclassical norms are therefore not regarded as expressions of irrationality yielding suboptimal socioeconomic outcomes. Neoclassical procedures might very well yield suboptimal outcomes, but errors in decision making can be corrected through evolutionary processes such as learning.

Behavioral economics enriches conventional theory by introducing modeling variables and parameters that make for more scientific causal and predictive analysis. It does not reject the importance of incentives and opportunity costs in decision making, but it does question wealth maximization as dominating the decision-making process, economic efficiency as the end product of individual decision making, and the extent to which neoclassical behavioral norms should serve as appropriate benchmarks for economic analysis (Altman 2005). This in turn opens the door wide open for reconstructing economic theory, engaging institutional analysis as a partner in model building and inviting public policy analysis to help better understand the constraints and incentive environments under which economic agents make boundedly rational choices.

SEE ALSO *Akerlof, George A.; Behaviorism; Economic Psychology; Economics, Experimental; Economics, Institutional; Economics, Neoclassical; Galbraith, John Kenneth; Maximization; Rationality; Satisficing Behavior; Smith, Vernon L.; Social Psychology; Sociology, Economic; Wages*

BIBLIOGRAPHY

Akerlof, George A. 2002. Behavioral Macroeconomics and Macroeconomic Behavior. *American Economic Review* 92: 411–433.

Akerlof, George A., and Janet L. Yellen, eds. 1986. *Efficiency Wage Models of the Labor Market.* Cambridge, U.K.: Cambridge University Press.

Altman, Morris. 1996. *Human Agency and Material Welfare: Revisions in Microeconomics and Their Implications for Public Policy.* Boston, Dordrecht, and London: Kluwer Academic.

Altman, Morris. 2005. Reconciling Altruistic, Moralistic, and Ethical Behavior with the Rational Economic Agent and Competitive Markets. *Journal of Economic Psychology* 26: 732–757.

Altman, Morris, ed. 2006. *Handbook of Contemporary Behavioral Economics: Foundations and Developments.* Armonk, NY: M. E. Sharpe.

Camerer, Colin F., George Lowenstein, and Matthew Rabin, eds. 2003. *Advances in Behavioral Economics.* Princeton, NJ: Princeton University Press.

Cyert, Richard M., and James C. March. 1963. *A Behavioral Theory of the Firm.* Englewood Cliffs, NJ: Prentice-Hall.

Darity, William, Jr., and Arthur H. Goldsmith. 1996. Social Psychology, Unemployment, and Macroeconomics. *The Journal of Economic Perspectives* 10: 121–140.

Frank, Robert H. 1988. *Passions Within Reason: The Strategic Role of the Emotions.* New York: W. W. Norton.

Frantz, Roger S. 1997. *X-Efficiency Theory, Evidence and Applications* (Topics in Regulatory Economics and Policy 23). Boston, Dordrecht, and London: Kluwer Academic.

Friedman, Milton. 1953. The Methodology of Positive Economics. In *Essays in Positive Economics*, 3–43. Chicago: University of Chicago Press.

Güth, Werner. 1995. On Ultimatum Bargaining Experiments—A Personal Review. *Journal of Economic Behavior and Organization* 27: 329–344.

Kahneman, Daniel, and Amos Tversky. 1979. Prospect Theory: An Analysis of Decision Under Risk. *Econometrica* 47: 263–291.

Kahneman, Daniel, Jack L. Knetsch, and Richard H. Thaler. 1986. Fairness and the Assumptions of Economists. In *Rational Choice: The Contrast Between Economics and Psychology*, eds. Robin M. Hogarth and Marvin W. Reder, 101–116. Chicago and London: University of Chicago Press.

Katona, George. 1951. *Psychological Analysis of Economic Behavior.* New York: McGraw-Hill.

Katona, George. 1975. *Psychological Economics.* New York: Elsevier Scientific.

Leibenstein, Harvey. 1957. *Economic Backwardness and Economic Growth.* New York: J. Wiley and Sons.

Leibenstein, Harvey. 1966. Allocative Efficiency vs. "X-Efficiency." *American Economic Review* 56: 392–415.

Leibenstein, Harvey. 1979. A Branch of Economics Is Missing: Micro-Micro Theory. *Journal of Economic Literature* 17: 477–502.

Lewis, Alan, Paul Webley, and Adrian Furnham. 1995. *The New Economic Mind.* New York: Harvester Wheatsheaf.

March, James G. 1978. Bounded Rationality, Ambiguity, and the Engineering of Choice. *Bell Journal of Economics* 9: 587–608.

Reder, Melvin W. 1982. Chicago Economics: Permanence and Change. *Journal of Economic Literature* 20: 1–38.

Shiller, Robert J. 1993. *Market Volatility.* Cambridge, MA: MIT Press.

Simon, Herbert A. 1959. Theories of Decision Making in Economics and Behavioral Science. *American Economic Review* 49: 252–283.

Simon, Herbert A. 1978. Rationality as a Process and as a Product of Thought. *American Economic Review* 70: 1–16.

Simon, Herbert A. 1987. Behavioral Economics. In *The New Palgrave: A Dictionary of Economics*, eds. John Eatwell, Murray Millgate, and Peter Newman, 221–225. London: Macmillan.

Smith, Vernon L. 2003. Constructivist and Ecological Rationality in Economics. *American Economic Review* 93: 465–508.

Smith, Vernon L. 2005. Behavioral Economics Research and the Foundations of Economics. *Journal of Socio-Economics* 34: 135–150.

Stiglitz, Joseph E. 1987. The Causes and Consequences of the Dependence of Quantity on Price. *Journal of Economic Literature* 25: 1–48.

Thaler, Richard H. 1992. *The Winner's Curse: Paradoxes and Anomalies of Economic Life.* New York: Free Press.

Todd, Peter M., and Gerd Gigerenzer. 2003. Bounding Rationality to the World. *Journal of Economic Psychology* 24: 143–165.

Tomer, J. F. 1997. *The Human Firm: A Socio-Economic Analysis of Its Behavior and Potential in a New Economic Age.* London and New York: Routledge.

Tversky, Amos, and Daniel Kahneman. 1981. The Framing of Decisions and the Psychology of Choice. *Science* 211: 453–458.

Williamson, Oliver E. 1975. *Markets and Hierarchies: Analysis and Antitrust Implications.* New York: Free Press.

Morris Altman

ECONOMICS, CLASSICAL

The term "classical economics" was coined by the German political philosopher and economist Karl Marx, who stated "that by classical Political Economy, I understand that economy which, since the time of W. Petty, has investigated the real relations in bourgeois society" (Marx 1954, p. 85n.). Classical economics included, for example, the physiocrats, the English economist David Ricardo, and partly the Scottish economist Adam Smith; it excluded such authors as Thomas Robert Malthus and Jean-Baptiste Say, whom Marx considered "vulgar economists" dealing with "appearances" only.

Generally, economists and scholars have not adopted Marx's definition of classical economics. According to

other interpreters there was no deep cleavage between earlier and later economists. The continuity thesis was expressed most forcefully by Alfred Marshall around the turn of the eighteenth century and in contemporary times by John R. Hicks and Paul A. Samuelson. Marshall perceived the classical economists as essentially early and somewhat crude demand and supply theorists, with the demand side in its infancy. The received Marshallian interpretation was challenged by Piero Sraffa, first in his introduction to volume I of his edition of Ricardo's works and correspondence (1951), and secondly in his *Production of Commodities by Means of Commodities: Prelude to a Critique of Economic Theory* (1960), in which he reformulated the classical approach to the theory of value and distribution and showed that its analytical structure is fundamentally different from later marginalist (or neoclassical) analysis.

METHOD, SCOPE, AND CONTENT

The classical economists were concerned with the laws governing the emerging capitalist economy, characterized by the stratification of society into three classes of workers, landowners, and the rising capitalists; wage labor as the dominant form of the appropriation of other people's capacity to work; an increasingly sophisticated division of labor within and between firms; the coordination of economic activity via a system of interdependent markets in which transactions are mediated through money; and significant technical, organizational, and institutional change. In short, they were concerned with the production, distribution, and use of wealth of an economic system that was incessantly in motion. How should one analyze such a system? The ingenious device of the classical authors for seeing through the complexities of the modern economy consisted of distinguishing between the "actual" or "market" values of the relevant variables—the distributive rates and prices—and their "normal" or "natural" values. The former were taken to reflect all kinds of influences, many of an accidental or temporary nature, about which no general propositions were possible, whereas the latter were seen to express the persistent, nonaccidental, and nontemporary factors governing the economy, which could be systematically studied.

The method of analysis the classical economists adopted is known as the method of long-period positions of the economy. Any such position is one toward which the system is taken to gravitate as the result of the self-seeking actions of agents, thereby putting into sharp relief the fundamental forces at work. In conditions of free competition, that is, the absence of significant barriers to entry or exit from all markets, the resulting long-period position is characterized by a uniform rate of profits (subject, perhaps, to persistent inter-industry differentials reflecting different levels of risk) and uniform rates of remuneration for each particular kind of primary input. Competitive conditions were taken to engender cost-minimizing behavior of profit-seeking producers.

The determination of the general rate of profits, the rents of land, and the corresponding system of relative prices constitute the analytical core of classical political economy. It was meant to lay the foundation of all other economic analysis, including the investigation of capital accumulation and technical progress; of development and growth; of social transformation and structural change; and of taxation and public debt. The pivotal role of the theory of value and distribution can be inferred from the fact that the latter is typically developed right at the beginning of major classical works.

VALUE AND DISTRIBUTION

The classical concept of production starts from the following interrelated premises. First, human beings cannot create matter, they can only decompose or recompose and move it. Production involves productive consumption, and the real cost of a commodity consists in the commodities necessarily destroyed in the course of its production. This concept of physical real cost, according to Sraffa, differs markedly from later marginalist concepts, with their emphasis on "psychic cost." Second, production consists essentially of a circular flow: Commodities are produced by means of commodities. This idea was advocated by William Petty and Richard Cantillon and was most effectively expressed in François Quesnay's *Tableau économique* (Aspromourgos, 1996). It is in stark contrast with the "Austrian" view of production as a one-way avenue leading from the services of original factors of production to consumption goods. Third, all property incomes—profits and rents—are explained in terms of the social surplus; that is, those quantities of the different commodities that are left over after the necessary means of production used up and the means of subsistence in the support of workers have been deducted from the gross outputs produced during a year. In this conceptualization, the necessary real wages of labor are considered no less indispensable as inputs and thus "agents of production" (James Mill 1826, p. 165) than raw materials, tools, or machines. Fourth, profits, rents, and relative prices are explained essentially in terms of magnitudes that can, in principle, be observed, measured, or calculated. The objectivist orientation of classical economics has received its perhaps strongest articulation in a famous proclamation by William Petty, who, in his *Political Arithmetick*, published in 1690, stressed that he was to express himself exclusively "in Terms of Number, Weight, or Measure" (Petty 1986, p. 244).

The classical economists proceeded essentially in two steps. In a first step they isolated the main factors that

were seen to determine income distribution and the prices supporting that distribution in specified conditions; that is, in a given place and time. The theory of value and distribution was designed to identify in abstracto the dominant factors at work and to analyze their interaction. In a second step, the classical authors turned to an investigation of the causes that, over time, systematically affected the factors at work from within the economic system. This was the realm of the classical analysis of capital accumulation, technical change, economic growth, and socioeconomic development.

The rate of profits is the ratio of two bundles of heterogeneous commodities, the social surplus (exclusive of rent), and the social capital. In order to be able to compare these bundles, a theory of value was needed. With a circular flow the values of commodities can only be determined by means of simultaneous equations, a tool not available to the classical economists. They therefore approached the problem of value and distribution in a roundabout way, typically by first identifying an "ultimate measure of value" by means of which heterogeneous commodities were meant to be rendered commensurable. Several authors, including Smith, Ricardo, and Marx, had reached the conclusion that labor was the sought standard and thus arrived at some version of the labor theory of value. This was understandable in view of the unresolved tension between concepts and tools. However, it is far from clear how these labor values could be ascertained in a circular framework except by solving a system of simultaneous equations. In fact, with the benefit of hindsight, contemporary economists know that the labor theory of value landed the classical approach in an impasse and was one of the reasons for its premature abandonment and the rise to dominance of marginalist theory.

Yet, as Sraffa (1960, p. 6) showed, the classical economists were correct in assuming that a coherent determination of the general rate of profits and prices was possible in terms of the two sets of data on which they based their theory of value:

(1) the system of production in use, described in terms of the methods of production and productive consumption actually employed; and

(2) the real wage rate (or, alternatively, the share of wages).

This can be shown as follows: Let T_i, M_i and F_i designate the inputs of three commodities—tools (t), raw materials (m), and the food of workers (f)—employed as means of production and means of subsistence in industry i ($i = t, m, f$), and T, M and F the total outputs in the three industries. Denoting the value of one unit of commodity i by p_i ($i = t, m, f$), one has the following system of price equations:

$$(T_t p_t + M_t p_m + F_t p_f)(1 + r) = T p_t$$
$$(T_m p_t + M_m p_m + F_m p_f)(1 + r) = M p_m$$
$$(T_f p_t + M_f p_m + F_f p_f)(1 + r) = F p_f$$

Flukes apart, these equations are independent of one another. Fixing a standard of value, for example, $p_f = 1$, provides a fourth equation and no additional unknown, so that the system of equations can be solved for the dependent variables: the general rate of profits and prices. The distribution of the surplus must be determined at the same time and in the same way as are the prices of commodities.

CAPITAL ACCUMULATION AND ECONOMIC DEVELOPMENT

With the rate of profits determined on the basis of data (1) and (2), the classical authors turned to the problem of the accumulation of capital and thus of the growth of the system. They typically assumed that the process of economic expansion was not constrained by an insufficient supply of labor, because the workforce needed was seen to be created endogenously, either via some population mechanism, as in the case of Malthus, or via the labor-displacing effects of machinery, as in the case of Marx's "industrial reserve army of the unemployed" (Marx 1977, p. 600). Ricardo discussed both mechanisms and also analyzed the case in which capital accumulates and the population grows, but there is no technical progress. Due to diminishing returns in agriculture, a rise in differential rents paid on intramarginal lands will, for a given real wage rate, entail a falling rate of profit. (The theory of intensive diminishing returns was later taken up by the marginalist economists who thought that the underlying principle could be generalized from agriculture to all industries and to all factors of production [labor, land, and capital] alike and a theory be elaborated in terms of a single principle only: that of relative scarcity.)

The classical authors also discussed different forms of technical progress. In Adam Smith capital accumulation increases the extent of the market and thus allows for an ever deeper division of labor. This increases labor productivity due to gains of specialization and induced inventions of machinery and thus engenders growing levels of income per capita. Smith's endogenous growth mechanism is a virtuous circle. Other classical authors were somewhat less optimistic. Ricardo, in the chapter on machinery in the *Principles* (1821) contemplated the case of a kind of mechanization that is gross output reducing: While labor productivity rises, total employment and the output-capital ratio (or maximum rate of profits) fall. This case reappears in Marx's discussion of the rising organic composition of capital and, given the share of wages, falling tendency of profitability. In 1967 Richard

Goodwin formalized some of the classical ideas on accumulation and distribution in terms of an adaptation of the predator-prey model developed in the theory of animal populations.

TRADE AND MONEY

The classical economists advocated trade liberalization. According to Smith the specialization pattern of an economy would follow its absolute cost advantages. Via an opening of domestic and foreign markets trade would allow a deeper division of labor and thus enhance productivity growth. Ricardo showed, contrary to Smith, that what really mattered were comparative advantages and not absolute ones. Assume that one of two economies is able to produce all commodities at lower unit costs. Only this economy would export and the other one import. This would, however, engender a specie-flow mechanism with prices in the former economy rising and in the latter one falling. Ricardo's theory of money, a version of the quantity theory, was an integral part of his trade theory. Sooner or later some prices in the latter economy would have fallen below the levels in the first one and thereby reverse the competitive situation. This would relate precisely to those commodities in the production of which the second economy has a comparative advantage.

Since the publication of Sraffa's *Production of Commodities by Means of Commodities* there has been a revival of the classical approach. For a summary account of what has been achieved, see, for example, the work of Heinz D. Kurz and Neri Salvadori.

SEE ALSO *Capitalism; Capitalism, Managerial; Chicago School; Competition; Competition, Marxist; Economics, Institutional; Economics, Islamic; Economics, Keynesian; Economics, Neoclassical; Economics, Neo-Ricardian; Economics, New Classical; Economics, New Keynesian; Economics, Post Keynesian; Institutionalism; Libertarianism; Marginalism; Market Economy; Marx, Karl; Mill, John Stuart; Ricardo, David; Smith, Adam; Stockholm School*

BIBLIOGRAPHY

Aspromourgos, Tony. 1996. *On the Origins of Classical Economics: Distribution and Value from William Petty to Adam Smith.* London and New York: Routledge.

Garegnani, P. 1987. Surplus Approach to Value and Distribution. In *The New Palgrave: A Dictionary of Economics.* Vol. 4, eds. John Eatwell, Murray Milgate, and Peter Newman, 560–574. London: Macmillan.

Goodwin, Richard. 1967. A Growth Cycle. In *Socialism, Capitalism and Economic Growth,* ed. C. Feinstein. Cambridge: U.K.: Cambridge University Press.

Kurz, Heinz D. 2004. The Surplus Interpretation of the Classical Economists. In *A Companion to the History of*

Economic Thought, eds. W. J. Samuels, J. E. Biddle, and J. B. Davis, 167–183.

Kurz, Heinz D., and Neri Salvadori. 1995. *Theory of Production: A Long-Period Analysis.* Cambridge, U.K.: Cambridge University Press.

Kurz, Heinz D., and Neri Salvadori. 1998a. *Understanding "Classical" Economics: Studies in Long-Period Theory.* London: Routledge.

Kurz, Heinz D., and Neri Salvadori, eds. 1998b. *The Elgar Companion to Classical Economics.* 2 vols. Cheltenham, U.K., and Northhampton, MA: Edward Elgar.

Marx, Karl. 1954. *Theories of Surplus Value.* Moscow: Progress Publishers.

Marx, Karl. 1977. *Capital.* Vol. 3. Moscow: Progress Publishers.

Mill, James. 1826. *Elements of Political Economy.* 2nd ed. London: Harry G. Bohn.

Petty, William. 1986. *The Economic Writings of Sir William Petty.* 2 vols. Ed. C. H. Hull. Reprint, New York: Kelley.

Quesnay, François. 1972. *Quesnay's Tableau Economique.* Eds. M. Kuczynski and R. L. Meek. London: Macmillan. (Orig. pub. 1759).

Ricardo, David. 1951–1973. *The Works and Correspondence of David Ricardo.* 11 vols. Ed. Piero Sraffa with the collaboration of M. H. Dobb. Cambridge, U.K.: Cambridge University Press.

Smith, Adam. 1976. *An Inquiry into the Nature and Causes of the Wealth of Nations.* Oxford: Oxford University Press. (Orig. pub. 1776).

Sraffa, Pierro. 1960. *Production of Commodities by Means of Commodities: Prelude to a Critique of Economic Theory.* Cambridge, U.K.: Cambridge University Press.

Heinz D. Kurz

ECONOMICS, DEVELOPMENT

SEE *Development Economics.*

ECONOMICS, EVOLUTIONARY

SEE *Schumpeter, Joseph Alois.*

ECONOMICS, EXPERIMENTAL

For generations economics was a nonlaboratory science. Economists could construct theories and analyze naturally occurring data, but the luxuries of control and replication were elusive. The discipline of experimental economics has challenged and changed this perception. Experimental economics provides for a variety of modes of scientific inquiry through the creation of small-scale but real laboratory economic systems. Most experimental economics research has dealt with microeconomic problems, but there is a growing body of work with a more macroeconomic flavor.

Experimental economics got its start in the 1950s and was fully credentialed when Vernon L. Smith was awarded half of the 2002 Nobel Prize in Economic Science. In the Nobel citation Smith is recognized as the father of experimental economics, in the sense that he "made the most important early contributions, but he also remains a key figure in the field to date." However, as with any scientific advance, there are other pioneering streams that feed into the final river. One universally recognized starting point for experimental economics was the effort by Harvard economist Edward H. Chamberlin (1866–1967) to demonstrate to his students the poor predictive theory of perfectly competitive market models. Chamberlin assigned each student a hypothetical "cost" or "value" and encouraged them to make profitable trades through a random meeting process. Chamberlin's major insight was to argue that if the hypothetical costs and values were valid representations, then supply and demand curves could be computed for the minieconomy. Chamberlin's result was that the markets failed to converge to the perfectly competitive predictions.

A few years later Smith, a young Harvard Ph.D. then on the faculty at Purdue, decided to try an exercise similar to Chamberlin's, but with some critical changes. First, Smith conducted the markets with an institution, the double oral auction, which is an analog of the trading process on the New York Stock Exchange. The double auction has information and price progression features different from the Chamberlin exercise. Second, the markets were repeated. Third (and somewhat later), the individual costs and values were made salient by making real payments to the market participants. Under these conditions the markets converged robustly to the competitive outcomes. The *Journal of Political Economy* published Smith's results in 1962, and experimental economics as it is most widely known today was born. Smith published his major methodology treatise on experimental economics in 1982. As delineated by Smith, the elements of an induced economic environment (essentially the conditions of supply and demand) and of a carefully defined economic institution are the core of any economics experiment. This holds true even when the institutions look less like regular markets and more like voting rules or bargaining processes (Fiorina and Plott 1978). Paired with this, the 1982 article also discussed experimental design conditions sufficient to produce a valid, controlled economics experiment.

Meanwhile, at about the same time as Smith's earliest work, others were making seminal contributions. James W. Friedman (1967), Lawrence E. Fouraker and Sidney Siegel (1963), and Heinz Sauermann and Reinhard Selten (1959) were similarly pioneering, although all were more oriented toward oligopoly and bargaining. Selten in particular continued to pursue experimental research and was a Nobel laureate for his theoretical contributions in the first game theory year of 1994.

When Smith visited the California Institute of Technology (Caltech) in the late 1970s, he met a former Purdue colleague on the Caltech faculty, Charles R. Plott, who had also become a fan of experimental methodology. Smith and Plott began a highly productive collaboration, and Plott also staked out crucial methodological advances for using experimental economics in regulatory and public policy analyses. For example, when the government proposed altering the way that the pricing of inland barge transportation was regulated, Plott and James T. Hong (1982) used experimental markets to evaluate the change. Experimental economics has been used as an evaluative public policy tool in areas as disparate as airport "slot" auctions, markets for pollution permits, water auctions, and antitrust issues. Another 1970s' stream of experimental economics was the work at Texas A&M of Raymond C. Battalio and John H. Kagel (often with Leonard Green 1981) in designing small experimental economics environments for animal economies.

The growth in the number of experimental researchers naturally led to the organization of professional societies; for example, in Germany there is the Society for Experimental Economics Research, and in the United States there is the Economic Science Association. Both sponsor activities with a worldwide audience. A basic undergraduate textbook in the area is available from Douglas D. Davis and Charles A. Holt (1993).

SEE ALSO *Arrow-Debreu Model; Economics; Knowledge, Diffusion of; Microeconomics; Natural Experiments; Nonparametric Regression; Positive Social Science*

BIBLIOGRAPHY

Battalio, Raymond C., Leonard Green, and John H. Kagel. 1981. Income-Leisure Tradeoffs of Animal Workers. *The American Economic Review* 71 (4): 621–632.

Chamberlin, Edward H. 1948. An Experimental Imperfect Market. *Journal of Political Economy* 56 (2): 95–108.

Davis, Douglas D., and Charles A. Holt. 1993. *Experimental Economics*. Princeton, NJ: Princeton University Press.

Fiorina, Morris P., and Charles R. Plott. 1978. Committee Decisions under Majority Rule: An Experimental Study. *The American Political Science Review* 72: 575–598.

Fouraker, Lawrence E., and Sidney Siegel. 1963. *Bargaining Behavior*. New York: McGraw-Hill.

Friedman, James W. 1967. An Experimental Study of Cooperative Duopoly. *Econometrica* 35: 379–397.

Hong, James T., and Charles R. Plott. 1982. Rate Filing Policies for Inland Water Transportation: An Experimental Approach. *Bell Journal of Economics* 13: 1–19.

Sauermann, Heinz, and Reinhard Selten. 1959. Ein Oligopolexperiment. *Zeitschrift für die gesamte Staatswissenschaft* 115: 427–471.

Smith, Vernon L. 1962. An Experimental Study of Competitive Market Behavior. *Journal of Political Economy* 70 (2): 111–137.

Smith, Vernon L. 1982. Microeconomics Systems as an Experimental Science. *American Economic Review* 72 (8): 923–955.

Robert Mark Isaac

ECONOMICS, INSTITUTIONAL

Institutional economists are the leading American heterodox school of economics. They differ from the orthodox neoclassical mainstream in their emphasis on the man-made institutions that help form and operate through the markets created by the institutions. They study individual institutions, culture, actual economies and their institutional foundations, and the mutual impacts of private and public sectors, the domain sometimes called the legal-economic nexus. Neoclassicists tend to emphasize an abstract, idealized economic system and the play of market forces. Institutionalists treat government as important and ubiquitous, like it or not—as part of, rather than exogenous to, the economic system.

Institutionalists seek to develop a body of empirical and theoretical knowledge of the organization, control, operation, and evolution of the economic system, particularly the institutions that produce, together with individual choices, the allocation of resources and the distribution of income. Institutionalists have produced a critique of capitalism and of neoclassicism as its expression and rationalization. Relatively few institutionalists oppose capitalism, but most distinguish between capitalism and a market economy. Many are sympathetic to the evolution of the economic system along lines giving increased effect to the interests of workers. Some call for conscious, activist government planning of varying types, but most seek a truly more competitive economy, a government not dominated by business interests, and laws not catering to the interests of business and upper-income classes.

The principal early institutionalists included the American economists Thorstein Veblen (1857–1929), John R. Commons (1862–1945), Walton Hamilton (1881–1958), Wesley Clair Mitchell (1874–1948),

John Maurice Clark (1884–1963), Robert Lee Hale (1884–1969), and Richard Ely (1854–1943). Veblen's satiric critique of business and consumerism under capitalism—not least his emphasis on status emulation and conspicuous consumption—influenced both the other institutionalists and most economists. All members of the school stressed the allocative and distributional importance of actual institutions. Some, like Mitchell, pioneered the empirical and theoretical study of business cycles in an economy dominated by high finance and a pecuniary culture. Most if not all institutionalists pursued the analysis of the economy as both a cultural system and a system of power. Some followed Commons's complex analysis of the legal foundations of capitalism and studied empirically and theoretically the legal-economic nexus.

Differences of emphasis and interpretation have rendered institutionalism as heterogeneous as any other school of economics. Some institutionalists have been conservative, most quite liberal. In addition to planning versus competition, other conflicts have developed between the followers of Clarence Edwin Ayres (1891–1972) and of John R. Commons over the theory of value appropriate for institutional economics, and the relative importance of deliberative and nondeliberative decision making. All agree, however, that the principal determinant of resource allocation is institutions and not the pure abstract market. Other topics commonly agreed upon as important are evolution, behavior, power, stratification, agency, the creation and structuring of markets, the legal-economic nexus, the role of culture and belief systems, and the corporate system.

The Canadian-born American economist John Kenneth Galbraith (1908–2006) has been for some time the most prominent institutionalist. Institutionalism as a whole has a complex existence: Institutionalists contribute to most fields in economics but tend to be marginalized by the mainstream. Most institutionalists accept, however reluctantly, their heterodox status, and they work hard to improve their position in the world. Several journals are institutionalist in orientation. Institutionalism has developed strongly in Europe.

SEE ALSO *Galbraith, John Kenneth; Veblen, Thorstein*

BIBLIOGRAPHY

Hodgson, Geoffrey M., Warren J. Samuels, and Mark R. Tool, eds. 1994. *Elgar Companion to Institutional and Evolutionary Economics.* 2 vols. Aldershot, U.K.: Edward Elgar.

Rutherford, Malcolm, and Warren J. Samuels, eds. 1997–1998. *Classics in Institutional Economics.* 10 vols. London: Pickering and Chatto.

Warren J. Samuels

ECONOMICS, INTERNATIONAL

International economics is a standard, and perhaps the oldest, field discipline within economics. This discipline involves an analysis of all economic aspects of an international nature, aspects that coincide with the existence of multiple countries and to some extent separated economies. In a historical coincidence, parts of international economics that developed prior to general micro- or macroeconomics deal in a peculiar way with essentially the same phenomena as general economic theory.

International economics addresses such issues as international trade, movements of factors of production between countries, exchange rates, open-economy macroeconomic policy, international monetary institutions, and globalization. All these issues relate to the so-called open economy, a term economists use for an economy of a country that is to some extent separated from the rest of the world (politically, monetarily, or otherwise) but at the same time has economic ties to it. These ties manifest themselves on one hand as flows of physical goods or factors of production and their services, or on the other as flows of money or its substitutes. For broad classification, then, it is possible to divide international economics into two areas of study: international trade and international finance.

INTERNATIONAL TRADE THEORY

Probably the most prominent position within international economics is enjoyed by international trade theory, which seeks to identify the gains from trade between countries; the factors that determine the pattern of specialization; the volume of trade and the terms of trade (i.e., prices); the impact of trade on income distribution; and the impact of the barriers to trade on all of the above. From a practical point of view, however, its goal has always been, as the international economist Edward Leamer remarked, to answer one single question of paramount importance: when, if ever, is it beneficial to put obstacles to the flow of goods between countries?

It is precisely this question that gave rise to early economic speculations and philosophizing, and in that sense international trade theory was an indispensable part of political economy (and later economics) from the very beginning. All the scholars who can be considered among the founding fathers of economics—Richard Cantillon (1680–1734), David Hume (1711–1776), Adam Smith (1723–1790), and David Ricardo (1772–1823)—explicitly addressed this question, and for the most part their answer was negative. The work of these early economists formed the basis of what would be known as the free-trade doctrine and provided the intellectual foundation for the free-trade movement in the nineteenth century. These authors showed that many of the apprehensions surrounding foreign trade (trade deficits and crises) were based on myth.

The theory of comparative advantage made a major contribution to the theory of international trade (and later to general microeconomics). This theory, attributable to Robert Torrens (1780–1864), James Mill (1773–1836), and Ricardo, demonstrated that two countries can engage in trade even when one of the countries can produce all goods more cheaply (because of greater productivity or lower nominal cost).

Although the theory of comparative advantage understood trade to be based on differences in productivity, later theories enriched the perspective by pointing to two other sources of trade. First, trade can also result from differences in resource endowments; in other words, countries can specialize in, and export, products made from resources that are plentiful in that country. This has come to be known as the Heckscher-Ohlin theorem (which became the basis of the Heckscher-Ohlin-Samuelson model, after its authors, Eli Heckscher, Bertil Ohlin, and Paul Samuelson). Second, the source of trade can be the consumers themselves: the difference in their preference. Before this model was developed, much of the trade flows between countries seemed puzzling, as they consist of similar types of products (so-called intra-industry trade), rather than dissimilar products as the theory based on differences in productivity or resource endowment would predict.

Besides sources of trade, international trade theory focuses on the consequences of trade for prices of factors of production, and explains the tendency of trade to bring about their equalization across countries (which became known as the Factor Price Equalization Theorem, developed, independently, by Abba Lerner and Samuelson). Further development of international trade theory incorporated the effects of the economies of scale and market structure (imperfect competition) on all aspects of trade. A special part of the theory is concerned with the alternative to international movements of goods: the movement of labor and capital across borders.

During the twentieth century, the answers offered by international trade theory developed greater precision. Although the theory, as it became increasingly refined, made some theoretical qualifications of the conditions under which free trade is the first best policy, the practical presumption in favor of free-trade policy remains largely unchallenged. Indeed, in opinion surveys of economists the statement "trade barriers reduce general economic welfare" typically draws the greatest consensus.

INTERNATIONAL FINANCE

A corollary to flows of tangible goods, services, and factors of production are financial flows. The openness of an economy, and the existence of "the rest of the world," adds several new dimensions to the discussion of such macroeconomic topics as national product, price level, interest rates, and their interrelations, and government policies aimed at their management. Only the international context gives rise to such frequently discussed issues as balance of payments, exchange rates, international monetary institutions, international aid, borrowing, and indebtedness.

Balance of Payments *Balance of payments* refers to the financial flows between the given economy on one hand and the rest of the world on the other. Understanding the logic of the balance of payments and knowing the determinants and consequences of its various subcomponents, although not a policy goal in itself, is helpful in setting policy goals and formulating policy measures.

Exchange Rate The *exchange rate*, the value of domestic currency with respect to foreign currencies, has a major influence on the balance of payments. The theory of how the exchange rate is determined is therefore central to this part of international economics, which examines the role of export and import demands, differences in interest rates, and expected inflation across countries. One theory, the interest rate parity, points out certain necessary relations between the expected changes in the exchange rate and countries' interest rate differentials. As the rate of return on assets in each country must be equal, lower interest rates in one country as compared to the other will be seen as justifiable only if the currency of this country is expected to gain in value with respect to the currency of the other country. If this were not so, one of the currencies would be seen as more attractive by investors, and their attempt to exploit this opportunity would bring the real rates of return ultimately to equality.

Another theory of exchange rate determination, the theory of Purchasing Power Parity (PPP), stipulates that the exchange rate tends to correspond to the ratio of price levels in the two respective countries (or, in its modern version, that changes in exchange rate correspond to changes in the price level ratios, i.e., inflation rates). If this were not so, prices in the one country would be generally lower than in the other, which would make buying in the first more attractive than in the second. Greater demand for currency of the first country compared to that of the second would cause its value (i.e., its exchange rate) to appreciate, which would tend to eliminate the difference in the attractiveness of buying in the two countries. Only when the exchange rate will equal the ratio of the price levels will there be no difference between the countries, and no tendency for change.

Exchange rates, in their relation to the balance of payments, are also linked to the open-economy output determination. They are related to the national product through two channels. First, the exchange rate is decisive in determining the amount of production demanded by, and thus produced for, buyers in foreign countries. The less valuable the domestic currency vis-à-vis the foreign one, the higher the output the country tends to generate. Second, through the asset market, any level of product corresponds to a particular interest rate, and the interest rate in turn is important in determining the exchange rate. The higher the output, the higher the interest rate and the more valuable the domestic currency. Thus there is likely to be one particular level of exchange rate compatible with a given level of output.

Given the importance of exchange rates as a factor in open-economy macroeconomics, it is no wonder that exchange rates are subject to different degrees of government attention. A country's policy may vary from nonintervention (a "floating" currency) to a fixed exchange rate (a currency "peg"). In the latter case, a government, typically through its central bank, attempts to keep the exchange rate within certain limits. Besides the standard tools of monetary policy (influencing domestic money supply), this is generally achieved through foreign exchange interventions. These are purchases or sales of foreign exchange currency for domestic currency through which the value of domestic currency is decreased (if foreign currency is purchased) or increased (if foreign currency is sold). The feasibility of such management is limited, on one hand by the danger of inflation (if too much domestic currency is swapped for foreign currency), and on the other by limited supplies of foreign currency (a central bank can boost the value of its currency only as long as it has foreign currency at its disposal). Special fixed-rate monetary and exchange rate regimes would include two somewhat similar arrangements: the gold standard and a currency board. The former—historically prevalent internationally but now abandoned for not entirely economic reasons—consists of defining the monetary units of currencies in terms of gold. The currency board, a relatively recent though still not very common phenomenon, replaces gold metal in a currency definition with a foreign exchange. If domestic currency becomes defined as a particular amount of gold or a particular number of units of foreign currency, both money supply and the exchange rate are determined.

If market forces are suppressed altogether and domestic currency cannot be freely exchanged for the foreign one (as assumed so far), the domestic currency is considered nonconvertible. In such cases, the official exchange rate becomes a matter of government fiat and decree, although it is likely to coexist with a much different exchange rate that is likely to develop on a black market.

The policy choice regarding the exchange rate regime has important repercussions for macroeconomic policy. Floating exchange rates allow for greater autonomy in monetary policy and provide insulation from outside monetary shocks and an automatic mechanism for maintaining external balance. This comes, however, at a cost of greater uncertainty about its level and the lack of any disciplining factor for domestic monetary authority. Yet, at the beginning of the twenty-first century, floating exchange rates seem to have prevailed. In an open economy, it is generally considered unfeasible to maintain fixed exchange rates while insisting on autonomous policy.

In some sense, the heritage of fixed exchange rates survives in the theory of optimum currency areas (developed by Robert Mundell). For the countries involved, fixed exchange rates have the same effect on (in)dependence of monetary policy as would the common currency. And just as fixed exchange rates are not always feasible, neither can common currency always be thought of as an improvement. The theory of optimum currency areas recognizes both benefits (lower transaction cost) and costs (loss of policy autonomy and openness to shocks) of monetary integration, and thus makes clear under what conditions such integration is beneficial.

In today's globalized world economy, international economics stands only to gain in importance. However, as borders between countries become increasingly irrelevant and their policies harmonized, international economics may become indistinguishable from conventional economics. After all, if the world were one country, the difference between international and domestic would disappear altogether.

SEE ALSO *Absolute and Comparative Advantage; Cantillon, Richard; Central Banks; Customs Union; Dornbusch-Fischer-Samuelson Model; Economics; Exchange Rates; Free Trade; Heckscher-Ohlin-Samuelson Model; Hume, David; Mundell-Fleming Model; Policy, Monetary; Protectionism; Quotas, Trade; Ricardo, David; Samuelson, Paul A.; Smith, Adam; Tariffs; Trade*

BIBLIOGRAPHY

Bhagwati, Jagdish. 2002. *Free Trade Today*. Princeton, NJ: Princeton University Press.

Irwin, Douglas A. 1996. *Against the Tide: An Intellectual History of Free Trade*. Princeton, NJ: Princeton University Press.

Krugman, Paul R., and Maurice Obstfeld. 2006. *International Economics*. 7th ed. Boston: Addison-Wesley.

Lal, Deepak, and Richard H. Snape, eds. 2001. *Trade, Development, and Political Economy*. Houndmills, Basingstoke, U.K., and New York: Palgrave.

Mikić, Mia. 1998. *International Trade*. New York: St. Martin's.

Obstfeld, Maurice, and Kenneth Rogoff. 1996. *Foundations of International Macroeconomics*. Cambridge, MA: MIT Press.

Dan Stastny

ECONOMICS, ISLAMIC

As part of the Islamization of Knowledge agenda, Islamic economics as a discipline was formally laid down in the First International Conference on Islamic Economics in 1976. The objective was to present the case of Islamic economics (IE) in a language common to financiers, politicians, and economists. Deriving its inspiration from the ideals of Islam, IE studies the interaction of the spiritual and material paradigm, with the ultimate aim of establishing a just and fair socioeconomic system.

The biggest challenge faced by IE has been, and still is, to reconcile the material self-interest with the "ethoreligious" or moral self-interest of agents and the welfare of society as a whole, and to replace interest-based financial institutions with interest-free institutions guided by Shariah, Islamic law, and moral standards. The compatibility between Islam and capitalism is studied by Maxime Rodinson in his book *Islam and Capitalism* (1966). In his work on the textual analysis of Qur'an and other Islamic knowledge sources and the economic history of the Islamic world, Rodinson demonstrates that Muslims never had any trouble reconciling the money-making mechanism under the Islamic framework. In contrast, Bryan S. Turner in *Weber and Islam: A Critical Study* (1974) argues that, for Max Weber, "it was the patrimonial nature of Muslim political institutions which precluded the emergence of capitalist preconditions, namely rational law, a free labor market, autonomous cities, a money economy and a bourgeois class" (Turner [1974] 1998, p. 2). Thus, Turner does not ultimately subscribe to Weber's view of Islam. While posing a different critique from Rodinson's, Turner ascribes a combination of Puritanism and orientalism to Weber that skews the latter's view of the relationship between Islam and capitalistic development. However, the process of reconciliation between IE and other economic systems needs to emerge by implementing just socioeconomic paradigm (Chapra 2003).

IE seeks to devise ways in which economic agents and markets can be directed by moral and social values based on Shariah. Its supporters believe that all economic and business activities should be based on an ethoreligious paradigm, with the sole aim being the welfare of individuals and society as a whole. In many ways, it pursues the same objective as conventional economics, but within religious-based moral codes of Islam.

According to IE, moral codes and principles should regulate economic activities to ensure the elimination of poverty and glaring inequalities in the distribution of wealth and resources. The state should take responsibility for those objectives and utilize Islamic fiscal tools such as *zakat* (the annual 2.5% voluntary tithe to the needy), taxation, equity, loss-profit, and risk sharing to achieve them. Factors of production should be treated on an equity basis, and no predetermined return on capital is allowed. These are the core features of Islamic economics, and are what make it different from its conventional counterpart.

IE provides the means for the material and spiritual growth and welfare of the human race. It reflects the physical and spiritual aspects of life, holding them in a balance so that they supplement and reinforce each other, and if any clash does occur, moral and ethical values reign supreme. Religiously based moral checks on economic and market activities are set up to ensure the true success of both individuals and society. Activities that are in conflict with Islamic spiritual, social, and moral values are prohibited in Islamic economics.

Both the literature on IE and the number of financial institutions based on Islamic principles have increased rapidly in recent years. Many economics journals are allocating space for Islamic economics and finance, and there are some that are dedicated especially to the publication of articles related to Islamic economics and finance, including the *International Journal of Islamic Economics* (London), the *Journal of Islamic Economics* (Jeddah), and the *Islamic Development Bank Journal*. Islamic economics, especially Islamic banking and finance, is taught at universities around the world, including International Islamic University (Malaysia), International Islamic University (Pakistan), the International Centre for Education in Islamic Finance (Malaysia), the London School of Economics, Harvard University, University of Cairo, Monash University, University of Tehran, and numerous universities in Kuwait, United Arab Emirates, Sudan, Malaysia, Indonesia, and Saudi Arabia. Nevertheless, Islamic economics is still a nascent discipline, and a lot of work is being done to put theoretical, empirical, and applied proofs to its claims.

SEE ALSO *Banking; Banking Industry; Development Economics; Ibn Khaldūn; Interest Rates; Islam, Shia and Sunni; Muhammad; Orientalism; Weber, Max*

BIBLIOGRAPHY

Chapra, M. Umer. 2003. *Islam and the Economic Challenge*. Leicester, U.K.: Islamic Foundation.

Rodinson, Maxime. [1966] 1978. *Islam and Capitalism*. English rev. ed. Austin: University of Texas Press.

Turner, Bryan S. [1974] 1998. *Weber and Islam: A Critical Study.* London: Routledge.

M. Ishaq Bhatti

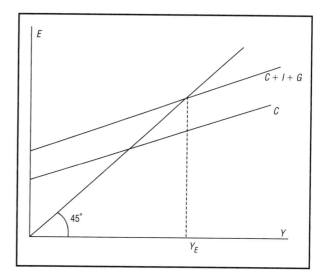

Figure 1

ECONOMICS, KEYNESIAN

Keynesian economics is the approach to macroeconomics that grew out of John Maynard Keynes's work, especially his *The General Theory of Employment, Interest and Money* (1936) written during the Great Depression. Since Keynes's work has been interpreted in different ways and inspired various formulations of macroeconomics, it is defined in a number of different ways, including the approach to macroeconomics in which: aggregate demand plays a major role in determining output and employment; involuntary unemployment can persist; and fiscal and monetary policy can affect the level of output and employment. Keynes himself recognized that he had a number of predecessors, and it has been suggested that major elements of his approach were anticipated by others (most notably, Michal Kalecki).

In *The General Theory* Keynes argued that employment is determined by the aggregate demand for goods, which is in turn determined (in a closed economy) by consumption demand and investment demand. Consumption depends mainly on the level of real income while investment demand depends on the interest rate, which is determined by money supply and the demand for money, and by business expectations. Given expectations and monetary conditions, employment is determined so that output produced is equal to aggregate demand. The level of employment thus determined may be less than the full employment level at which the supply and demand for labor (which depend on the real wage) become equal. He also examined the aggregate supply side of the economy with a given money wage, and a production function relating output to employment, which determined the average price level. Keynes argued that the wages are likely to be rigid downward when unemployment exists because of the concern of workers with their wage relative to that of others: however, even if wages (and hence the price level) fall, it is unlikely to increase the level of aggregate demand in the face of uncertainty and the negative effect of falling prices on the demand for goods by debtors. Keynes therefore recommended expansionary monetary and especially fiscal policy to increase the level of aggregate demand, employment, and output to reduce unemployment.

Keynes's analysis is most simply depicted with the income-expenditure model of Figure 1, in which the axes measure income and output, *Y*, and expenditures or demand, *E*. The line marked *C* is the consumption function that shows the relation between consumption and real income, and the line marked *C* + *I* + *G* is aggregate demand that adds (planned) investment, *I*, and government expenditure, *G*, both assumed to be exogenously given, to it. Equilibrium output, Y_E, is determined where the aggregate expenditure line intersects the 45° line so that output equals expenditure. The level of output determines employment, which may imply unemployment. Fiscal and monetary expansion, by increasing *G* or *I*, can increase output and reduce employment.

Economists such as John Hicks and Franco Modigliani, who were persuaded by Keynes's theory, tried to relate it to pre-Keynesian neoclassical macroeconomic theory in which the economy was generally thought to be at full employment. A series of models, including the IS-LM and later the aggregate demand–aggregate supply (AD-AS) models, were developed to produce what has come to be called the neoclassical synthesis approach to Keynesian economics. This approach, which uses different types of demand and supply curves and equilibrium condition as in neoclassical theory, implies that unemployment can exist, due to wage rigidity, in the short run, but in the medium and long runs, in which the wage is flexible, the economy is at full employment. When unemployment exists, over the medium and longer runs the money wage falls, which reduces the costs of firms and hence the price level, which reduces the nominal demand for money. The resulting excess supply of money is used to increase spending on goods (by what is called the real balance effect), or is lent out, implying a fall in the interest rate and a rise in investment (and possibly consumption) demand. This increase in aggregate demand increases output and employment and takes the economy to full employment. With rigid wages in the short run, however, this mechanism does not work itself out, and unemployment can exist. Expansionary fiscal and monetary policy can increase output in the short run, but only increases the price level in the medium and long runs when the economy is at full employment.

In the 1960s, after most advanced countries experienced low unemployment for long periods (arguably due to the success of Keynesian macroeconomic policies), and inflationary pressures began to mount, alternative approaches to macroeconomics began to emerge. Three of them adopted positions opposed to Keynesian economics and can be briefly discussed to show what it is not. The first, monetarist, approach developed by Milton Friedman in 1968 and others returned to the pre-Keynesian idea of flexible wages in the short run, so that full employment always prevails, but allows changes in aggregate demand to affect the level of output and employment, because of misperceptions about the effects of aggregate demand changes, to make it consistent with the facts regarding business cycles. For instance, when money supply increases, workers find their money wage to be higher, but by not taking into account that the price of goods is higher too, they supply more labor, which leads to an increase in output. In the longer run, as workers revise their price expectation, this expansionary effect disappears. According to this approach, although full employment always prevails due to the flexibility of wages, macro policy has a temporary effect on real variables due to the misperceptions of the workers. The second also maintains the assumption of flexible, labor-market clearing wages, but assumes that economic agents do not make systematic expectational errors as they do in the earlier monetarist approach, and assumes rational expectations. This new classical approach developed by Robert Lucas in 1983 and others points out that with agents having rational expectations in the sense that they use all relevant information about the economy to calculate price expectations, fiscal and monetary policy (apart from tax policy changes that affect the supply of labor) are not effective even in the short run, unless the policies' changes are random and hence unanticipated. The third approach, called the real business cycle approach, continues in this tradition, but explains business cycle fluctuations in terms of technology shocks that affect investment demand and the interest rate and bring about the intertemporal substitution of labor to explain changes in employment.

In addition to real-world phenomena mentioned earlier, Keynesian economics lost ground to these new classical approaches because of its alleged problem in providing proper microfoundations to macroeconomics. The neoclassical synthesis Keynesian approach explained unemployment in terms of wage rigidity, but did not relate the

analysis to optimizing microfoundations. The new Keynesian approach tries to develop Keynesian economics to address this problem. An early branch of this approach merely introduced fixed prices and wages into the standard micro-founded general equilibrium model, examining disequilibrium situations in which actual transactions occurred at the "short" side of the market and the effects of such deviations from market clearing in one market spilled over into other markets. Another branch of the approach responded directly to the monetarist and rational expectations approaches, introducing wage price stickiness (such as staggered or sticky wage adjustment) into models with rational expectations to show that it is complete wage flexibility, rather than the assumption about expectations, that produced the policy ineffectiveness result. A final, and most popular new Keynesian branch, provided optimizing microfoundations to wage, price, and interest rate rigidity. Efficiency wages (which prevent the wage from falling when unemployment exists because of its adverse effect on labor efficiency) and wage bargaining, imperfect competition and the "menu" costs of price changes, and asymmetric information in credit markets have been used to explain these rigidities. Some models, such as those that distinguish the role of insiders and outsiders in the wage determination process, imply that aggregate demand changes can have long-term effects on output due to what are called hysteresis effects. While some new Keynesian models imply involuntary unemployment in equilibrium, others do not, but imply only that aggregate demand policies can have effects on output.

The central feature of both the neoclassical synthesis and new Keynesian approach is the rigidity of wages and prices. While wage rigidity is an important element of Keynes's theory, we have seen that according to Keynes the wage flexibility is no guarantee for full employment. The fact that flexible wages may exacerbate rather than solve unemployment problems has been stressed by another approach to Keynesian economics, called the post-Keynesian approach, which emphasizes the implications of decision-making under uncertainty, monetary institutions, and the effect of income distribution on aggregate demand. According to this approach when the wage and price falls due to the existence of unemployment, the interest rate and real balance effects need not work to increase aggregate demand because an excess supply of money may just lead to a fall in money supply as loans are repaid in a credit money economy with no further effects on the interest rate, because even if the interest rate falls asset holders may wish to hold more money and firms unwilling to increase investment in an uncertain environment, and because falling real wages redistribute income from workers to profit recipients who save a larger proportion of their income. Greater wage flexibility also tends to increase uncertainty in the economy given the importance of wages for both firm costs and profits and household income. These ideas add to Keynes's own discussion on the implications of wage flexibility, and are also corroborated by some optimizing models with a new Keynesian flavor.

Keynesian economics has generally been thought to be valid for short-run macroeconomics, but ignored in the analysis of long-run growth analysis. However, if wage flexibility does not automatically take the economy to full employment or at least the natural level of output consistent with price stability, and governments are unwilling or unable to do the same over the medium run, and if technology responds to aggregate demand and output, Keynesian economics may be relevant for the longer run as well. Post-Keynesians and other heterodox economists have, in fact, followed Joan Robinson and others in applying Keynesian economics to the study of long-run growth.

SEE ALSO *Economics, New Keynesian; Economics, Post Keynesian; Kalecki, Michal; Keynes, John Maynard*

BIBLIOGRAPHY

Clower, Robert. 1965. The Keynesian Counterrevolution: A Theoretical Appraisal. In *The Theory of Interest Rates,* ed. F. Hahn and F. P. R. Brechling. London: Macmillan.

Dutt, Amitava Krishna, and Edward J. Amadeo. 1990. *Keynes's Third Alternative?* Aldershot: Edward Elgar.

Friedman, Milton. 1968. The Role of Monetary Policy. *American Economic Review* (March): 1–17.

Hahn, Frank, and Robert M. Solow. 1995. *A Critical Essay on Modern Economic Theory.* Cambridge, MA: MIT Press.

Hicks, John R. 1937. Mr. Keynes and the Classics. *Econometrica.* 5 (2), 147–159

Kalecki, Michal. 1971. *Selected Essays on the Dynamics of the Capitalist Economy.* Cambridge, U.K.: Cambridge University Press.

Keynes, John Maynard. 1936. *The General Theory of Employment, Interest and Money.* London: Macmillan.

Lucas, Robert E. B. 1973. Some International Evidence on Output-Inflation Tradeoffs. *American Economic Review* 63 (June): 326–334.

Mankiw, N. Gregory, and David Romer, eds. 1991. *New Keynesian Economics.* 2 vols. Cambridge: MA: MIT Press.

Modigliani, Franco. 1944. Liquidity Preference and the Theory of Interest and Money. *Econometrica.* 12 (1):45–88.

Robinson, Joan. 1961. *Essays in the Theory of Economic Growth.* London: Macmillan.

Amitava Krishna Dutt

ECONOMICS, LABOR

The field of labor economics is involved with the study of the labor market, including the determinants of employ-ment, unemployment, and wages. The labor market developed as societies moved from feudal to capitalist processes. The development of capitalism in turn led to powerful capitalist owners and an industrial workforce that was concentrated in factories. Conditions of work became, by present Western standards, dirty, demanding, and dangerous. As a result, workers organized unions and began to demand better pay and working conditions, and they set up political organizations like the Labour Party in the United Kingdom. Over the years, organized labor managed to achieve many of their goals, as legislation was introduced in many countries to provide minimum wages, poverty relief, unemployment benefits, and pensions, and to ensure safe working conditions.

The labor market consists of employers, workers, and a government that provides an institutional and legal framework. The distinctive features of labor as a commodity are: (1) except for a slave society, people can only buy and sell labor services; (2) the quality of the labor services provided depends not only on the innate ability of the workers but also on their attitudes to work, to their fellow workers, and to their employers; (3) most employment contracts last for a fairly long time, so there are not frequent repeat purchases of this "commodity"; (4) there is asymmetric information in the labor market about the "quality" of labor services; and, (5) there is an unequal power relationship in the labor market.

Labor markets are different from other markets. As Arthur Okun points out in *Prices and Quantities* (1981), they are not auction markets that clear instantaneously, but are influenced by "custom and practice." For example, firing is usually based on last in, first out, and seniority is often given special privileges. There are many interrelated labor markets, differentiated by geography, occupation, industry, and often by gender and race. Analyses of segmented labor markets (primary and secondary markets) provide an interesting window into the role of "power" in labor markets, as demonstrated in the work of Peter Doeringer and Michael Piore (1971). Robert Solow, meanwhile, has emphasized the idea that the labor market is a social institution, and that it is therefore important to consider issues of equity and fairness in labor markets (1990). The labor market is different from other markets because the commodity being traded (labor) is capable of reasoned thought. Hence, the way employers treat workers, and the way other workers treat each other, influences their behavior and productivity, as well as wages.

Labor economics was once an interdisciplinary (institutionalist) study that included historical analysis, industrial relations, sociology, and political science. In the early literature, Adam Smith, David Ricardo, and Karl Marx employed versions of the labor theory of value, which states that the determinant of the value of a commodity is the amount of labor embodied in it. Marx pointed to the "exploitation" of labor, believing that workers produced "surplus value." Subsequently, at some point in the post-World War II era, labor economics became a narrow economics subdiscipline in terms of methodology that used neoclassical economic theory (assumptions of maximizing behavior in atomistic, mainly, competitive markets) to analyze various aspects of the labor market, including aspects of employment, unemployment, wages, gender and race discrimination, and immigration. It expanded its boundaries in terms of subject matter, exploring areas of demography, crime, health, marriage, and social relationships ("economics imperialism") under the guidance of the Nobel Prize-winning economist Gary Becker.

Econometric methods have been used on time-series, cross-section, and panel or longitudinal data to study labor economics and the evaluation of government policies on the labor market. Thus, under the influence of another Nobel Prize-winning economist, George Akerlof, modern labor economics has moved full circle—it now studies labor markets in an interdisciplinary framework (although with formal economic models) that includes concepts of psychology, anthropology, industrial relations, and management theory. Modern labor economics has developed new econometric methods to analyze social safety policies by using controlled experiments, "matching" techniques, and panel estimation techniques with fixed and random effects. Since the mid-1990s, labor economics has embraced "experimental economics" methods devised by innovative economists such as Ernst Fehr and Simon Gächter (2000). In these studies, the concepts of fairness, reciprocity, and equity in the labor market are investigated.

The Great Depression of the 1930s led to studies of unemployment, including long-term unemployment, the impact of unemployment on society, and human degradation caused by unemployment. Much work was done to explain the massive rise of unemployment in terms of "rigid wages" (classical economics), and of inadequate aggregate demand (Keynesian economics). The big increase in unemployment following the "oil shocks" of the 1970s led to theories of "stagflation." Subsequently, explanations of unemployment pointed to imperfectly functioning markets, with regulated labor market institutions being blamed. Theories then moved on to using concepts of search in a labor market with imperfect information, as described by Edmund Phelps (1970) and Dale Mortenson and Christopher Pissarides (1999). In these models workers are looking for a job when they receive wage offers which follow a normal distribution; some are good and some are bad. They have to decide whether to accept the offer or reject it. If they reject the offer, they are unable to return to it if the subsequent offers are worse.

The rise of rational expectations led to the concept of the "natural rate of unemployment" (Friedman 1968), and to a Keynesian variant, the non-accelerating inflation rate of unemployment (NAIRU), which was supposed to be constant and immutable. However, econometric work has found this concept to be ill-defined and poorly estimated. More important, it was found that there is "hysteresis" in the behavior of unemployment and in the so-called natural rate. The current rate of unemployment depends on the past evolution of the unemployment rate. Hence the "natural rate" is not a constant to which the unemployment rate will gravitate.

Much has been made about the role of "monopolistic" unions in raising wages above market-clearing wages and causing unemployment. Several studies have compared the differences between the wages of union and nonunion members. In an important book published in 1984, Richard Freeman and James Medoff argued that unions have a positive impact on the functioning of labor markets.

The post-1960s literature on labor economics moved from macroeconomic analyses of labor markets and industry-level studies to the study of microeconomics (on a firm and individual/household level) of the demand and supply of labor. The development of the human capital approach to analyzing the investments of rational maximizing individuals in education and skills, as outlined by Gary Becker in *Human Capital* (1964), led to a better understanding of labor supply. Given that investment in human capital is irreversible, work done in the 1990s treated the acquisition of skills as an "investment option" under uncertainty.

The growth of computer usage, and the subsequent development of large data sets, has led to an explosion of econometric analyses. Most of the research to explain wage rates (or earnings) has used earnings functions. Thus, the logarithm of wages (earnings) was explained by human capital, work experience, and various other control variables. Although most studies have found human capital variables to be significant, the explanatory power of these equations is very low. Yet the role of human capital in explaining economic growth has had important policy implications. Minimum wage policies have been analyzed to see if they have helped the poor and led to a fall in employment. David Card and Alan Kreuger's 1995 critical analysis of the data for the United States suggested that minimum wages had little impact on unemployment. This conclusion led to a huge controversy that has continued into the early twenty-first century. The re-introduction of minimum wages in the United Kingdom in 1998 was found by Alan Manning (using monopsonistic models in 2003) to have had no significant impact on employment.

There have been significant advances in the study of the determinants of labor supply and demand using modern econometric techniques and panel data. In studies of labor supply, individuals are assumed to maximize lifetime utility, subject to given budget and time constraints, where they choose an optimal amount of education, work, and leisure. Tax and welfare policies are studied in this framework and have important implications for the policy analysis of negative income taxes and social security benefits. Labor demand is studied for firms that maximize present values of profits by choosing optimal amounts of labor. Labor is treated by firms as a "quasi-fixed" input, according to Walter Oi (1962), and it is analogous to investing in physical capital goods. Advanced studies suggest that firms choose wages to maximize the efficiency of labor (Akerlof and Yellen 1986), or else choose an appropriate sequence of wages to maximize present values (Lazear 1995).

Labor economics has made significant theoretical and empirical strides in understanding the workings of labor markets. Econometric analyses of various tax, welfare, and active labor-market policies have helped to develop new policies for improving the functioning of the labor market and helping the unemployed and the poorer segments of society. However, there is still much work to be done to truly understand the nature of unemployment and poverty.

SEE ALSO *Demography; Economics, Neoclassical; Employment; Human Capital; Information, Asymmetric; Labor; Labor Demand; Labor Force Participation; Labor Market; Labor Market Segmentation; Labor Supply; Labor Union; Labor, Marginal Product of; Labour Party (Britain); Marginal Productivity; Marx, Karl; Minimum Wage; Ricardo, David; Slavery; Smith, Adam; Solow, Robert M.; Surplus Value; Unemployable; Unemployment; Unemployment Rate; Unions; Wages; Wages, Compensating*

BIBLIOGRAPHY

Akerlof, George A. 1982. Labor Market Contracts as Partial Gift-Exchange. *Quarterly Journal of Economics* 97: 543–569.

Akerlof, George A., and Janet L. Yellen, eds. 1986. *Efficiency Wage Models of the Labor Market*, Cambridge, U.K.: Cambridge University Press.

Ashenfelter, Orley C., and David Card, eds. 1999. *Handbook of Labor Economics*. Vols. 3A, 3B, and 3C. Amsterdam: North Holland.

Ashenfelter, Orley C., and Kevin F. Hallock, eds. 1995. *Labor Economics*. 4 vols. International Library of Critical Writings. Cheltenham, U.K.: Edward Elgar.

Ashenfelter, Orley C., and Richard Layard, eds. 1986. *Handbook of Labor Economics*. Vols. 1 and 2. Amsterdam: North Holland.

Becker, Gary. 1964. *Human Capital*. New York: Columbia University Press.

Becker, Gary. 1976. *The Economic Approach to Human Behavior*. Chicago: University of Chicago Press.

Card, David, and Alan B. Krueger. 1995. *Myth and Measurement: The New Economics of the Minimum Wage*. Princeton, NJ: Princeton University Press.

Doeringer, Peter B., and Michael J. Piore. 1971. *Internal Labor Markets and Manpower Analysis*. Lexington, MA: Heath Lexington Books.

Fehr, Ernst, and Simon Gächter. 2000. Fairness and Retaliation: The Economics of Reciprocity. *Journal of Economic Perspectives* 14 (3): 159–181.

Freeman, Richard, and James L. Medoff. 1984. *What Do Unions Do?* New York: Basic Books.

Friedman, Milton. 1968. The Role of Monetary Policy. *American Economic Review* 58 (1): 1–17.

Junankar, P. N., ed. 2000. *Economics of Unemployment: Causes, Consequences, and Policies*. 4 vols. International Library of Critical Writings. Cheltenham, U.K.: Edward Elgar.

Lazear, Edward P. 1995. *Personnel Economics*. Cambridge, MA: MIT Press.

Manning, Alan. 2003. *Monopsony in Motion: Imperfect Competition in Labor Markets*. Princeton, NJ: Princeton University Press.

Mortensen, Dale T., and Christopher A. Pissarides. 1999. New Developments in Models of Search in the Labor Market. In *Handbook of Labor Economics*. Vol. 3, eds. Orley C. Ashenfelter and David Card. Amsterdam: North Holland.

Okun, Arthur. 1981. *Prices and Quantities: A Macroeconomic Analysis*. Oxford: Basil Blackwell.

Oi, Walter J. 1962. Labor as a Quasi-Fixed Factor. *Journal of Political Economy* 70 (6): 538–555.

Phelps, Edmund S. 1970. *Microeconomic Foundations of Employment and Inflation Theory*. New York: Norton.

Solow, Robert M. 1990. *The Labor Market as a Social Institution*. Oxford: Blackwell.

P. N. Junankar

ECONOMICS, MARXIAN

The term *Marxian economics* refers to economic theory inspired by the work of Karl Marx (1818–1883). The salient feature of this research program is the idea that all societies in order to reproduce themselves require labor that will be used to produce the material requirements of reproduction. In all societies, a particular social class performs more work than that required for its own reproduction and the excess labor is appropriated by the dominant classes through property relations, traditions, the legal system, and also force. Such exploitative relations are quite transparent in precapitalist modes of production (e.g., slavery and feudalism), whereas in capitalism they are embedded in monetary transactions that give the impression of equal and therefore fair exchanges. Marx was the first to argue that in capitalism workers are exploited not because they are not paid their full wage, but because with the full wage they receive workers are able to pay only for the basket of goods required for the reproduction of their capacity to work (their labor power), which is acquired through what is only a portion of their total labor time. The difference between total labor time and that required to reproduce the workers' capacity to work is called *surplus labor time* and its monetary expression, the *surplus value*, is appropriated by the propertied classes (capitalists and landlords) and the state. The wealth accumulated in a society is directly related to the amount of surplus labor time, which is inversely related to the necessary labor time. Furthermore, Marx argued that labor time also regulates the surface phenomena of capitalism, such as the price of commodities. Hence, the law of value—according to which the socially necessary labor time is directly and indirectly embodied in a commodity—is the regulator of the movement of market prices. Prices are the means through which capitalists realize their profits and losses and regulate their behavior accordingly. In Marx, the role of the law of value is analogous to Adam Smith's "invisible hand," for it provides an explanation of how capitalist society reproduces itself and the various scales of its reproduction.

There are many different interpretations of Marx, and this often gives the impression that his work is vague. A careful examination of the history of the socialist movement, the origins of which were inspired to a great extent by Marx himself, shows, however, that those engaged in this movement often ignored Marx's major work, that is, the three volumes of *Capital*. More specifically, during the period of the First International (1864–1876), Marxists paid particular attention to the political or philosophical writings of Marx and Engels (e.g., the *Communist Manifesto* (1848), the *German Ideology* (1845–1846/1932), etc.). Volume I of *Capital* (1867) was not read as much as one would expect, except for the "historical" chapters that refer to the exploitation of workers and their struggles for the reduction of the length of the working day. The other chapters were difficult to comprehend, let alone to use in any direct way for the needs of the workers movement. The Marxists of the Second International (1889–1916) began using volume I of *Capital* and to some extent volume II (published in 1885), which was focused on the mechanisms of reproduction. Their discussions focused on whether Marx's purpose was to demonstrate the possibility of the balanced growth of capitalism, or to reveal capitalism's instability and predict its

inevitable collapse, unless it expanded to incorporate the noncapitalist economies as an additional source of cheap raw materials and a market to dispose of the products. Hence, the foundation for an economic theory of imperialism was developed by a number of radicals. Volume III of *Capital* was published in 1894, but was considered "too scientific," as Rosa Luxemburg (1870–1919) once remarked, and only a few Marxists during the 1930s, notably Henryk Grossmann (1881–1950) and Maurice Dobb (1900–1976), read it attentively. The subsequent Keynesian revolution in economics led many Marxists to "keynesify" the economic theory of *Capital* and "marxify" the economic policy conclusions of Keynesian economics. The idea is that many Marxists of the time abandoned partly or completely the analysis of *Capital* and adopted the Keynesian analysis, and from that they tried to derive radical policy conclusions with regard to the treatment of monopolies and income distribution. More specifically, Paul Sweezy (1910–2004) and also Paul Baran (1910–1964) claimed that Marx's analysis was more appropriate for the conditions of nineteenth-century capitalism, where there were neither monopolies nor a powerful state, than for the current economic situation in which powerful monopolies dominate and together with the state influence economic outcomes. Naturally, many radical economists claimed that once the workers' party seized power it could use the state for its own purposes. In this context, it has been argued that the law of value no longer holds in conditions of monopoly capitalism and also that Marx's laws of motion should be revised because the economy is under the control of monopolies and the state. Notable exceptions to this stream of thought were Paul Mattick (1904–1981) and Ernest Mandel (1923–1995), who in the 1970s and 1980s were what Grossmann and Dobb were in the 1920s and 1930s. That is to say, they were from the very few Marxists who consistently used and expanded the analysis of *Capital* in the conditions of their time.

One might have expected that Marxian economics would flourish during the Soviet era, and it is true that the first decade after the revolution saw the development of theories of medium- and long-term cyclical fluctuations—on the basis of which the technique of material balances was developed. The latter became a tool of national planning and also the starting point for input-output analysis and mathematical economics. Soon, however, Marxism and Marxian economics became dogmatic in the Soviet Union and other East European countries. On the other hand, developments in China, together with student unrest in Europe and the antiwar movement in the United States, sparked a renewed interest in Marxian economics. This time there were systematic efforts to comprehend the totality of Marx's work and in this context volume III of *Capital* was integrated into a single economic theory that seeks "to lay bare the economic law of motion of modern society" (Marx 1867–1894, Vol. I, p. 10). There were a number of efforts, on the one hand, to clarify and expand Marx's theoretical scheme and, on the other, to give it empirical content. Thus we find many studies that test the validity of the law of value with input-output data. Similarly, inter-industry data is used to test the law of the tendential equalization of rates of profit across industries, as well as the long-run fall of the general rate of profit and its connection to long-term fluctuations in the level of economic activity. Other topics of interest include extensions of Marx's work into the areas of international trade, exchange rate determination, the theory of effective demand, the state's redistributive role, and so on. There is no doubt that in recent decades significant progress has been achieved within Marxian economics, creating a theoretical foundation for further, fertile developments.

Even though the renewed interest in Marxian economics started in non-Soviet countries, the demise of the Soviet Union as well as the dissolution of most Communist parties and the weakening of the labor movement in Western countries during the past few decades have all certainly had a negative effect on the development of Marxian economics. On the positive side, though, one may count the demise of doctrinaire Marxism and the emergence of more pluralistic approaches that have brought to the fore important issues such as gender, race, and the environment. In this sense, the rise to preeminence of China (with its strong Marxist tradition), together with the movement against globalization may give new impetus to the Marxian research program worldwide. This research program has always been under attack and, despite its undeniable progress over recent decades, has never really found much support among Western academic economists. In fact, Marxian economics has always been misunderstood and its importance downplayed by mainstream economics; because of its ideological connotations, it has been relegated, at best, to being a mere chapter in the history of economic thought.

In conclusion, Marx's most important contribution to political economy was the distinction between labor and labor power, on the basis of which he was able to present a consistent theory of exploitation as a source of profits. Furthermore, he argued that the pursuit of profit as an end in itself has created the laws of motion of capitalist society that operate independently of people's will. These laws create the objective conditions within which the class struggle and wider political intervention take place. Moreover, Marxian economics integrates macroeconomics (falling rate of profit, reserve army of unemployed) and microeconomics (prices of commodities) through the law of value. Because of this integration, Marxian economics will continue to provide a great deal of fertile ground for

further research, at least as long as current orthodox economic theory maintains the dichotomy of micro- and macroeconomics. Only in the last few decades has there been a systematic effort to base macroeconomic analysis and conclusions on solid microeconomic foundations.

SEE ALSO *Marx, Karl; Marx, Karl: Impact on Economics; Marxism*

BIBLIOGRAPHY

Anderson, Perry. 1976. *Considerations on Western Marxism.* London: New Left Review Books.

Dobb, Maurice. 1937. *Political Economy and Capitalism.* London: Routledge & Keegan Paul.

Marx, Karl. 1867–1894. *Capital.* 3 vols. Moscow: International Publishers.

Shaikh, Anwar. 1981. "The Poverty of Algebra." In *The Value Controversy,* ed. Ian Steedman, 266–300. London: Verso.

Lefteris Tsoulfidis

ECONOMICS, NEOCLASSICAL

Mainstream economics is often characterized as neoclassical economics, usually to distinguish it from classical economics which had its origin in the rationalist era of the eighteenth century and in particular the work of the patriarch of economics, Adam Smith. The early-twentieth-century critic of economics, Thorstein Veblen, is usually credited with creating the term *neoclassical.* The obvious reason for the "neo" was that the economics being taught after 1890 somehow went beyond the economics of Smith. While classical economics was concerned with the broad questions facing nations such as growth and development, neoclassical economics instead focused on the decisions of independent and autonomous individuals who participate in the economy.

There are two fundamental ideas that characterize neoclassical economics: A metaphysical one about what motivates individuals to choose one option rather than another and a methodological one about the essential elements of any neoclassical explanation.

THE METAPHYSICS OF NEOCLASSICAL ECONOMICS

The primary and only behavioral assumption of neoclassical economics is that an individual is motivated to do what is best for him or her. To keep in touch with its eighteenth-century roots, this is commonly stated as: People are rational. While many economists mistakenly see this as a proposition about psychology, in reality it has nothing to do with psychology. A choice (or decision) is rational only if one can state a rational argument that entails the choice at issue. As such, rationality is always an attribute of the argument, not the mind.

Usually, an argument consists of several statements identifying explicit assumptions or reasons that are asserted to be true. These are connected by means of ordinary logic to form a logical structure defined by logical connective words (*and, or, if*) and words formed from the verb "to be." Usual arguments include quantitative relational words (*some, all,* and *at least one*). To be a rational argument, two conditions must be met. Everyone who accepts the truth of all of the assumptions of a logically valid argument must accept the truth of all statements entailed (or predicted) by the argument. The first essential condition involves the term *anyone*. That is, rationality is universal and it is its universality that makes it useful as an explanation of a choice made by an individual. The second essential condition is that each statement entailed by the argument is unique. When the entailed statement represents the one choice an individual makes as in the case of every neoclassical explanation, that choice must be unique. That is, anyone who accepts the truth status of all of the assumptions of the economic theorist's explanation will reach exactly the same conclusion concerning the individual's choice made.

While these conditions of universality and uniqueness likely were taken for granted in the eighteenth-century conception of rationality, neoclassical economics of the late nineteenth century chose to express rationality as maximization (which historians of economic thought call marginalism). The idea of a maximizing choice captures the necessary ingredients of any rational argument. For example, it says that whenever choosing how much to consume of some good, individuals are motivated to maximize their level of satisfaction subject to three things: the limitations of the budget, the going price of the good, and the personal "utility function" (which is the mathematical relation that indicates the quantitative level of satisfaction obtained when consuming each possible total amount of that good). While everyone faces the same price, each individual has a personally specific utility function as well as a specific budget. Thus, a maximizing individual will be said to choose that singular quantity of the good that yields the maximum level of satisfaction. Moreover, the explanation also implies that any individual who has specifically the same utility function, facing the same budget and price will make exactly the same choice. As such then, the maximization explanation fulfills the conditions of a rational explanation as it is both universal and unique. And one can always construct an analogous explanation of the choices made by the producers of the product where their motivation may be assumed to be profit maximization.

THE METHODOLOGY OF INDIVIDUALISM

In neoclassical economics things do not decide, only individuals do. This is called methodological individualism. It means that in neoclassical economics any social event must be explained as being the unintended aggregative consequence of the maximizing decisions and choices made by the independent and autonomous individuals participating in the economy or society. Of course, individuals are constrained by existing institutions and laws but this does not invalidate the neoclassical conception of individualism. Instead, it just says that whatever constrains individuals other than nature-given constraints such as weather and resource endowments must be explained. All institutions and laws are the consequence of decisions made by other individuals and thus can and must be explained in any complete neoclassical explanation.

It is the explicit mathematical analysis of the individual decision maker that primarily distinguishes neoclassical from classical economics and the latter's focus on the nation as a whole. But in principle the end result cannot be different, only the emphasis is different. Whatever the nation is, it is the result of decisions made by all of its constituents both past and present. So, when one explains how each and every individual makes or made their choices, one has explained the whole economy.

The two writers credited with promoting this individualist economics were the Cambridge economist Alfred Marshall and the French economist Léon Walras. Marshall focused on the method of partial equilibrium analysis which recognizes that individuals must take things like prices and product availability as given and do the best they can with the few things they can decide or choose; Walras was instead concerned with general equilibrium analysis for the whole economy and in particular the logical requirements for the determination of a system of prices that would allow all individuals to be maximizing simultaneously. Specifying the necessary mathematical requirements for such a general equilibrium is not trivial and remains a puzzle even in the twenty-first century. While it is always possible to specify assumptions that are sufficient to produce such equilibria, it is another thing to specify assumptions that are necessary.

It is important to note that going beyond the narrow confines of equilibrium analysis, the maximizing individual is still a useful concept even when explaining change or disequilibrium. Specifically, individuals are motivated to change whenever they think they are not maximizing. If the amount of a good an individual would want to buy is not available, that individual could offer to pay a higher price.

Thus change, too, is compatible with methodological individualism. So, with this in mind, even a changing world could be seen to be amenable to neoclassical analysis.

THE POSSIBLE LIMITATIONS OF NEOCLASSICAL ECONOMICS

It is easy to see why anyone would think neoclassical economics could be used to explain every social fact or event. Examples are marriage decisions, career decisions, voting patterns, and so on. A generalized form of neoclassical economics can be found in other social sciences under the name of rational choice theory. The philosopher Karl Popper called it "situational analysis." But critics of neoclassical economics still find it reasonable to doubt the usefulness of such explanations. The primary criticism is based on asking the troublesome question: What must a rational decision maker know in order to make a successful maximizing choice? As Friedrich Hayek in 1937 argued, at minimum, the theorist must identify how the decision makers come to know their choice is the maximizing one. For the most part neoclassical economists have been slow in taking-up Hayek's suggestion. Instead, neoclassical economists have continued by knowingly making conceivably false assumptions about the economy, usually assuming that all participants in the economy are successfully maximizing with all decisions and choices, and on that basis construct social policies concerning tax rates, interest rates, trade policies, and the like. And critics of such policies continue claiming it is unrealistic to assume everyone is capable of such successful behavior.

Such criticism is not new, however. In the early 1940s, critics such as Richard Lester claimed that empirical evidence did not support the assumption that decision makers in manufacturing firms consciously did the intricate calculations needed to maximize profit as required by the calculus of maximization. In response to such criticism, Armen Alchian in a social-Darwinian fashion argued in 1950 that conscious maximization (and hence deliberate calculation) is unnecessary for success. His argument was based on the notion that if the economy is in a long-run equilibrium—that is, not only are all markets cleared but there has been sufficient time for every producer to have made the optimum decision concerning which markets to enter—then every firm is making what neoclassical economists call zero excess profit. Zero excess profit merely means that the price charged for the product just covers all costs including the normal rate of return expected by owners and investors. In such a world, Alchian notes, the only survivors are those firms maximizing profit—whether or not they deliberately set about applying calculus. That is, in a state of long-run equilibrium, the maximum (excess) profit is zero and thus any firm not maximizing cannot cover all costs and hence cannot survive.

The question of the acceptability of knowingly employing false assumptions when forming economic policy has been a continuing object of dispute since 1953 when Milton Friedman made his argument in favor of an instrumentalist methodology in his famous essay. His argument simply said that as long as the theory works when put to practical use as a tool, the truth status of the constituent assumptions does not matter. Since 1953 economists can be divided into two groups: those that agree with Friedman's essay and those that do not. While most methodologists are critical of Friedman's essay or instrumentalism in general, economists who are engaged in practical policy issues are often willing to accept false assumptions as approximations and thus push on with their practical efforts. And as long as the practical uses of such assumptions are seen to yield successful policies, methodologists who demand realism will likely find an audience only among the many critics of neoclassical economics who object to its emphasis of individual maximization as the sole motivation for decision making.

SEE ALSO *Economic Methodology; Economics*

BIBLIOGRAPHY

Agassi, Joseph. 1960. Methodological Individualism. *British Journal of Sociology* 11: 244–270.

Alchian, A. 1950. Uncertainty, Evolution, and Economic Theory. *Journal of Political Economy* 58: 211–221.

Boland, Lawrence. 1979. A Critique of Friedman's Critics. *Journal of Economic Literature* 17: 503–522.

Boland, Lawrence. 1988. Situational Analysis beyond Neoclassical Economics. *Philosophy of the Social Sciences* 28: 515–521. http://www.sfu.ca/~boland.

Boland, Lawrence. 2003. *The Foundations of Economic Method: A Popperian Perspective*. London: Routledge.

Friedman, M. 1953. Methodology of Positive Economics. In *Essays in Positive Economics*, 3–43. Chicago: University of Chicago Press.

Hayek, Friedrich. 1937. Economics and Knowledge. *Economica* 4: 33–54.

Lester, R. 1946. Shortcomings of Marginal Analysis for Wage-Employment Problems. *American Economic Review* 36: 63–82.

Popper, Karl. 1994. *The Myth of the Framework: In Defense of Science and Rationality*. London: Routledge.

Lawrence A. Boland FRSC

ECONOMICS, NEO-RICARDIAN

Neo-Ricardian economics is a school of thought that aims to revive classical economics, which flourished during the eighteenth and nineteenth centuries, by reformulating it analytically and extending its approach to economic theorizing. As discussed below, neo-Ricardians focus on the classical theory of value and distribution originally elaborated by Adam Smith and subsequently amended, reformulated, and systematized by David Ricardo.

The earliest use of the term *neo-Ricardian* can be traced to the eminent neoclassical economist Dennis Holme Robertson. Bob Rowthorn (1974) was the first to identify a school with this term. The contributions of Piero Sraffa—in particular, the editing of and the introduction to Volume I of *The Collected Works and Correspondence of David Ricardo* (1951) and the short but dense book *Production of Commodities by Means of Commodities* (1960)—played a crucial role in the development of the neo-Ricardian or (after him) *Sraffian* approach. Sraffa's objectives, as revealed in a small number of published works and an enormous archive of unpublished manuscripts, were: (1) to revive and clarify the tradition of the classical economists from Adam Smith to David Ricardo, including Karl Marx; (2) to expose the weaknesses besetting the neoclassical theory of value and distribution; (3) to construct a coherent approach to economic theorizing that maintains the classical methodology and perspective.

Neo-Ricardian economics had a prominent position in the literature in the 1960s and early 1970s, during the "Cambridge capital controversy" between neoclassical economists centered mainly at MIT (the "Cambridge" of America) and neo-Ricardian economists at Cambridge University in England (for a detailed account see Harcourt 1972). The central theme of the debates was the questioning of the very notion of aggregate capital as a physical, measurable quantity and of the validity of the neoclassical theory of distribution based on such a concept. Even though the neo-Ricardian critique was correct, following the early 1970s the interest of the profession drifted away from the "paradoxes" of capital theory. By the 1980s, there was little attention to the difficulties inherent in the aggregation of capital in the formulation of economic models. As suggested by Luigi Pasinetti (2000), the suppression of the contradictions in the neoclassical theory of capital is evidence of the Kuhnian mechanism by which a dominant paradigm is defended against apparent anomalies.

In the following years, neo-Ricardian scholars applied increasing effort to building up their approach. A short list of journals that publish their contributions includes *The Cambridge Journal of Economics, The Review of Political Economy, Metroeconomica,* and *Contributions to Political Economy.* Today, neo-Ricardian economics is well grounded, yet still much in need of theoretical development.

The core of the neo-Ricardian approach to value and distribution is the determination of the size of the *social surplus* (Garegnani 1984), that is, what is left of the social product after subtracting the inputs necessary to restart the production cycle (the used-up means of production and subsistence wages). Analysis involves the following independent variables:

1. the set of techniques available to producers;

2. the size and composition of the social product;

3. one of the distributive variables—either the wage rate or the rate of profit;

4. the existing stock of natural resources.

These givens are sufficient to identify the "normal" or "long-period" position of an economy, which corresponds to a set of values for the relevant variables: relative prices (derived by using the cost-minimizing technique, which minimizes the cost of production), the social surplus, and—excluding, for simplicity, land rentals—the other distributive variable, the rate of profit or the wage rate. Under conditions of free competition, the long-period position is characterized by the equalization of the profit rate throughout the economy. The economy does not necessarily settle into a long-run position, due to changing economic circumstances that cause shifts. However, there is a presumption that "current" or "market" values continuously gravitate toward the corresponding natural or normal values. The underlying dynamic process is based on the idea that capital-owners move capital between sectors in search of the highest remuneration (for a review of modern analytical formulations of the gravitational process, see Kubin 1991).

The important features of the above analysis are: (1) deductive reasoning; (2) *objectivism,* that is, the use of data that are directly observable, measurable, or calculable; and (3) the asymmetric treatment of the distributive variables—that is, the treatment of one as an independent variable.

DIFFERENCES BETWEEN NEO-RICARDIAN AND NEOCLASSICAL APPROACHES

The objectivism of neo-Ricardian economics contrasts with neoclassical subjectivism, which allows for variables that are not directly observable within the initial set of data. The neoclassical data set consists of: (1) the set of techniques available to producers; (2) the preferences of consumers; and (3) the initial endowments of individual agents, including all the means of production, both produced (i.e., capital) and non-produced (i.e., land and labor). In neoclassical theory, all factors of production are treated symmetrically in terms of their scarcity. For each of them there are analogous demand and supply functions for their productive services. Equilibrium quantities and prices correspond to the intersection of these functions. This approach requires quantities of labor and capital that are unambiguously measurable and independent of their remunerations.

However, as the Cambridge controversies highlighted, capital cannot be treated in the same way as the other factors of production. In fact, though we may envisage a long-run equilibrium (the neoclassical equivalent of a long-period position) involving different types of labor with different remunerations, an equilibrium with heterogeneous capital goods and many rates of profit cannot exist. The existence of a tendency toward a uniform rate of profit, enforced by free competition, makes the determination of a unique equilibrium impossible if capital is treated in kind. Only after capital is expressed in "value" terms is it possible to construct a coherent aggregate production function (the basic tool of neoclassical macroeconomic analyses) in which all factors of production play the same role and from which demand functions for factor services can be derived through differentiation.

However, a measure of capital in value terms is affected by changes in the rate of profit (and in relative prices) giving rise to the possible occurrence of the phenomena known as reverse capital deepening and reswitching of techniques. The latter can be described taking the simplest case of only two techniques of production α and β with different capital intensities. Suppose that α, which is more profitable at lower rates of profit, is the technique in use. As the profit rate increases, producers may find β more profitable and switch from α to β. However, as the profit rate increases further, α could become the more profitable technique, so producers are induced to switch back to it. Reswitching is a sufficient but not necessary condition for capital reversing (Garegnani 1970). The latter phenomenon is a change in direction (from negative to positive) of the relationship between the capital/labor ratio (or the capital/output ratio) and the profit rate.

The occurrence of capital reversing (and *a fortiori* of reswitching of techniques), which excludes smooth production functions (both at the industry and the economy levels), does not rule out the possibility of constructing more "irregular" but logically coherent technological relationships between capital and the rate of profit (for an application, see Kurz and Salvadori 1995).

NEW LINES OF RESEARCH FOR NEO-RICARDIANISM

A clear weakness of neo-Ricardian economics is the lack of a comprehensive perspective on all the relevant aspects of economic enquiry; much remains to be investigated outside the core theory of value and distribution. Indeed,

some suggest that as yet no well-defined neo-Ricardian school can be identified (see Roncaglia 1991). Tony Aspromourgos (2004) provides a detailed review of current neo-Ricardian developments and research projects, some of which include:

1. The identification of a "Classical" theory of endogenous growth in which different types of technology are taken into account (Kurz and Salvadori 1998)

2. The Sraffa-Keynes synthesis, whereby the social product (or, in its long-period version, its growth rate) is determined by the autonomous components of demand (or their growth rates). This synthesis requires some form of harmonization between effective demand and the notions of normal prices (corresponding to the uniform rate of profit) and normal productive-capacity utilization (Garegnani 1978, 1979, and 1992)

3. An explanation of changes in the composition of demand with a Classical flavor, but employing modern analytical tools (Schefold 1985)

4. A monetary theory of distribution—elaborated by Panico (1988) and Pivetti (1991) following Sraffa's suggestion (*Production of Commodities*, p. 33)—according to which the rate of profit can be determined by the monetary rate of interest, fixed exogenously by the monetary authority

5. The incorporation of renewable and exhaustible resources (Bidard 2004)

SEE ALSO *Cambridge Capital Controversy; Capital; Competition; Economics, Classical; Income Distribution; Kuhn, Thomas; Lakatos, Imre; Long Period; Pasinetti, Luigi; Ricardo, David; Sraffa, Piero; Surplus; Value; Value, Objective*

BIBLIOGRAPHY

Aspromourgos, Tony. 2004. "Sraffian Research Programmes and Unorthodox Economics." *Review of Political Economy* 16 (2): 179–206.

Bidard, Christian. 2004. *Prices, Reproduction, Scarcity.* Cambridge, U.K.: Cambridge University Press.

De Vivo, Giancarlo. 2003. Sraffa's Path to Production of Commodities by Means of Commodities: An Interpretation. *Contributions to Political Economy* 22 (1): 1–25.

Garegnani, Pierangelo. 1970. Heterogeneous Capital: The Production Function and the Theory of Distribution. *Review of Economic Studies* 37 (3): 407–436.

Garegnani, Pierangelo. 1978. Notes on Consumption, Investment, and Effective Demand: I. *Cambridge Journal of Economics* 2 (4): 335–353.

Garegnani, Pierangelo. 1979. Notes on Consumption, Investment, and Effective Demand: II. *Cambridge Journal of Economics* 3 (1): 181–187.

Garegnani, Pierangelo. 1984. Value and Distribution in the Classical Economists and Marx. *Oxford Economic Papers* 36 (2): 291–325.

Garegnani, Pierangelo. 1992. Some Notes for an Analysis of Accumulation. In *Beyond the Steady State: A Revival of Growth Theory*, eds. Joseph Halevi, David Laibman, and Edward J. Nell, 47–71. New York: St Martin's Press.

Harcourt, Geoff C. 1972. *Some Cambridge Controversies in the Theory of Capital.* Cambridge, U.K.: Cambridge University Press.

Kubin, Ingrid. *Market Prices and Natural Prices: A Study in the Theory of the Classical Process of Gravitation.* 1991. Frankfurt: Peter Lang.

Kurz, Heinz D., and Neri Salvadori. 1995. *Theory of Production: A Long-Period Analysis.* Cambridge, U.K.: Cambridge University Press.

Kurz, Heinz D., and Neri Salvadori. 1998. "Endogenous" Growth Models and the "Classical" Tradition. In *Understanding "Classical" Economics: Studies in Long-Period Theory*, eds. Heinz D. Kurz and Neri Salvadori, 66–89. London: Routledge.

Panico, Carlo. 1988. *Interest and Profit in the Theories of Value and Distribution.* London: Macmillan.

Pasinetti, Luigi Lodovico. 2000. Critique of the Neoclassical Theory of Growth and Distribution. *Banca Nazionale del Lavoro Quarterly Review* 53 (215): 383–431.

Pivetti, Massimo. 1991. *An Essay on Money and Distribution.* New York: St. Martin's Press.

Roncaglia, Alessandro. 1991. The Sraffian Schools. *Review of Political Economy* 3 (2): 187–219.

Rowthorn, Robert Eric. 1974. Neo-Classicism, Neo-Ricardianism, and Marxism. *New Left Review* 86 (July/August): 63–87.

Schefold, Bertram. 1985. On Changes in the Composition of Output. *Political Economy: Studies in the Surplus Approach* 1 (2): 105–142.

Sraffa, Piero. 1951. Introduction. In *On the Principles of Political Economy and Taxation*, vol. 1 of *The Collected Works and Correspondence of David Ricardo*, ed. Piero Sraffa, with Maurice H. Dobb, xiii–lxii. Cambridge, U.K.: Cambridge University Press.

Sraffa, Piero. 1960. *Production of Commodities by Means of Commodities: Prelude to a Critique of Economic Theory.* Cambridge, U.K.: Cambridge University Press.

Pasquale Commendatore

ECONOMICS, NEW CLASSICAL

New classical economics takes the view that short-run fluctuations in the aggregate economy—the business cycle—can be understood within an equilibrium frame-work of rational, forward-looking agents, without relying on the presumption that market rigidities or imperfections (such as *sticky prices*), and the consequent disequilibrium adjustment as articulated in John Maynard Keynes's (1883–1946) *General Theory of Employment, Interest, and Money* (1936), are necessary to explain the cyclical behavior of the macroeconomy. New classical economics assumes universal market clearing, rational expectations, an equilibrium or "natural" rate of employment and output, and labor suppliers who respond rationally to intertemporal relative prices. At the same time, it assumes that information about relative prices is costly to obtain and therefore imperfect, which can provide a means for aggregate demand to act as a determinant of real economic activity.

This school of thought is known as the *new* classical economics because it builds on the general equilibrium principles of classical economics to give aggregate demand a causal role in explaining observed correlations among prices, income, employment, and money. Such a role is difficult to find in the writings of the pre-Keynesian classical economists, who tended to view the overall market economy as self-adjusting and aggregate demand as being neutral in its effects on the economy.

New classical economics has its genesis in the work of Nobel laureate Robert E. Lucas Jr. Lucas summarizes the new classical approach and justifies its insistence on explaining business cycles using *equilibrium* models of economic behavior, that is, models that "account for the observed movements in *quantities* … as an optimizing response to observed movements in prices" (1977, p. 14). Elsewhere, Lucas (1980) discusses the new classical view in the historical context of business cycle theory.

Lucas and Leonard Rapping (1969) made the first attempt to explain aggregate employment and wage behavior based on a dynamic theory of competitive labor market equilibrium. The Lucas-Rapping model relies on a precise formulation of households' optimal choices of labor and leisure over time. This approach has since become the foundation for dynamic macroeconomic models.

Because the Lucas-Rapping model rules out disequilibrium adjustment in the labor market, it must account for short-run fluctuations in employment owing to real wage changes, while remaining consistent with the accepted fact that employment is independent of real wages in the long-run. It does so through appeal to the *intertemporal substitution of labor and leisure*—the response of workers to incentives to alter their supply of labor across different periods of time. Suppose that labor suppliers face wages temporarily below their expected normal or long-run levels. Dynamic utility maximization implies that these workers will respond by reducing hours of work today (that is, by increasing the consumption of leisure today), and increasing work in the future, at the expense of future leisure. The response of rational, forward-looking agents to changes in intertemporal relative prices is a cornerstone of new classical economics, and indeed of modern macroeconomics.

Drawing further inspiration from Edmund Phelps et al. (1970), Lucas (1972, 1973) goes on to develop a general equilibrium extension to the Lucas-Rapping partial equilibrium model of the labor market. His primary motivation is to explain the positive empirical correlation of money and output while retaining the "classical" assumptions that consumers and producers respond rationally to relative prices, that all markets clear, and that expectations are *rational*—agents' forecasts of unknown variables relevant for decisions are, on average, unbiased conditional on available information. Taken alone, the classical assumptions suggest a world in which money and nominal aggregate demand are *neutral*, affecting all nominal prices proportionately and therefore leaving relative prices and real activity unaltered. The challenge Lucas faced is therefore one of accounting for monetary nonneutralities while avoiding appeal to nonclassical (Keynesian) frictions.

Lucas meets this challenge by assuming, as suggested by Phelps, that information does not flow freely across markets, so that rational (Lucas-Rapping) producers mistake common money supply shocks with market-specific supply and demand shocks. Ideally, producers base supply decisions on their going market price *relative* to prices in all other markets (as summarized by the price level). However, a lack of current information concerning other prices prevents local producers from knowing with certainty what the overall price level is. An unperceived economy-wide increase in the money stock, which tends to raise demand and prices in all markets, will therefore be perceived by the individual producer as an increase in his or her product's relative price. The producer's rational response in this case is to increase production. Because all producers are similarly confused, the nominal money shock will increase overall output, which would not be the case if information flowed freely.

Lucas's "imperfect-information" model further implies that the extent of producers' confusion regarding the sources of movements in market prices depends on the volatility of economy-wide shocks relative to market-specific shocks. In particular, in economies with high aggregate demand variance, producers are reasonably sure that a change in their market price is caused by an aggregate shock (thus leading the price level, not relative prices, to change) since these shocks are typically large relative to market-specific shocks. In this case, producers will have little incentive to respond to any given aggregate shock by altering production, because they are less likely to be "fooled." Lucas (1973) explicitly tests this implication using cross-country data and finds that countries with relatively high aggregate demand variability respond less to aggregate demand shocks than countries with relatively low aggregate demand variability, a finding consistent with his theory.

The so-called Lucas supply curve, which makes explicit the dependence of output on the difference between the realized and expected price level, is the new classical reformulation of the expectations-augmented Phillips curve of Milton Friedman (1968) and Phelps (1968). The new classical approach is consistent with the *natural rate* hypothesis of Friedman and Phelps—that deviations in output from its natural or full-employment level cannot be sustained without a sustained deviation of actual from expected inflation.

The rational expectations hypothesis, conceived by John Muth (1961) and formalized by Lucas and Edward Prescott (1971), is an essential (though not unique) feature of new classical economics and an important innovation in the study of macroeconomics. It applies the basic principles of rational, economic behavior to forecasting, requiring economic agents to equate their "subjective" probabilities with those "objective" probabilities implied by the model itself. Lucas justifies rational expectations based on the implausibility of systematic forecast errors in the face of the "recurrent character of the [business] cycle" (1977, p. 15). Indeed, rational expectations are now assumed in most macroeconomic models, including ones that do not take market-clearing prices for granted and therefore fall outside the boundaries of new classical economics.

Lucas's work and the new classical economics it has fostered have had a lasting influence on our understanding of the effects of aggregate demand policies, in particular monetary policy, on the economy. One of the most important implications, further developed by Thomas Sargent and Neil Wallace (1975), is the *policy ineffectiveness* proposition. Lucas's canonical new classical model implies that only *unanticipated* shocks to money or aggregate demand can alter incentives; anticipated shocks will be quickly incorporated into all nominal magnitudes, so that relative prices will remain unaltered. Therefore, systematic monetary policies—those manipulations of money and interest rates by the central bank that are anticipated by market participants—can have no hope of influencing income or employment. This implication provides theoretical backbone to Friedman's earlier proposal for a constant money growth rule, while condemning the "fine-tuning" polices of the 1960s and 1970s.

A corollary to the ineffectiveness proposition is that *credible* changes in policy rules can have immediate effects on inflation without much effect on output. Sargent

(1982) shows convincingly that some historical episodes of "big inflations" ended quickly without severe recessions when people fully understood and anticipated permanent anti-inflation reforms.

The consensus view of macroeconomists today is that the imperfect-information theory of new classical economics is not satisfactorily borne out by the data, and is therefore inadequate for understanding business cycles or providing a framework for policy analysis (see, for example, Woodford 2003, p. 6). Nonetheless, its influence continues beyond the now common use of the assumption of rational expectations. *Real business cycle* theories, first formulated by Finn Kydland and Prescott (1982), take up the mantle of equilibrium economics from the new classical paradigm, but emphasize the role of "real" shocks—shocks to preferences and technology—as the sources of aggregate fluctuations as opposed to nominal or monetary shocks. On the other hand, and somewhat ironically, the new classical critique of Keynesian models that they lack theoretical foundations for market and price rigidities has led to a resurgence of such models. The reaction to this critique, *new Keynesian economics*, attempts to explain such rigidities as the outcome of optimizing behavior on the part of rational agents. The papers in N. Gregory Mankiw and David Romer (1991) provide a good summary of some of the early work in this vein.

SEE ALSO *Economics, Classical*

BIBLIOGRAPHY

Friedman, Milton. 1968. The Role of Monetary Policy. *American Economic Review* 58: 1–17.

Keynes, John Maynard. 1936. *The General Theory of Employment, Interest, and Money*. London: Macmillan.

Kydland, Finn E., and Edward C. Prescott. 1982. Time to Build and Aggregate Fluctuations. *Econometrica* 50: 1345–1370.

Lucas, Robert E., Jr. 1972. Expectations and the Neutrality of Money. *Journal of Economic Theory* 4: 103–124.

Lucas, Robert E., Jr. 1973. Some International Evidence of Output/Inflation Tradeoffs. *American Economic Review* 63: 326–334.

Lucas, Robert E., Jr. 1977. Understanding Business Cycles. In *Carnegie-Rochester Conference Series on Public Policy*, Vol. 5, eds. Karl Brunner and Allan H. Meltzer, 7–29. Amsterdam, NY: North-Holland.

Lucas, Robert E., Jr. 1980. Methods and Problems in Business Cycle Theory. *Journal of Money, Credit, and Banking* 12: 696–715.

Lucas, Robert E., Jr., and Edward C. Prescott. 1971. Investment Under Uncertainty. *Econometrica* 39: 659–681.

Lucas, Robert E., Jr., and Leonard Rapping. 1969. Real Wages, Employment, and Inflation. *Journal of Political Economy* 77: 721–754.

Mankiw, N. Gregory, and David Romer, eds. 1991. *New Keynesian Economics*. 2 vols. Cambridge, MA: MIT Press.

Muth, John F. 1961. Rational Expectations and the Theory of Price Movements. *Econometrica* 29: 315–335.

Phelps, Edmund S. 1968. Money-Wage Dynamics and Labor Market Equilibrium. *Journal of Political Economy* 76: 678–711.

Phelps, Edmund S., et al. 1970. *Microeconomic Foundations of Employment and Inflation Theory*. New York: Norton.

Sargent, Thomas J. 1982. The Ends of Four Big Inflations. In *Inflation: Causes and Effects*, ed. Robert E. Hall, 41–98. Chicago: University of Chicago Press.

Sargent, Thomas J., and Neil Wallace. 1975. "Rational Expectations," the Optimal Monetary Instrument, and the Optimal Money Supply Rule. *Journal of Political Economy* 83: 241–254.

Woodford, Michael. 2003. *Interest and Prices: Foundations of a Theory of Monetary Policy*. Princeton, NJ: Princeton University Press.

William D. Lastrapes

ECONOMICS, NEW KEYNESIAN

The macroeconomic debates on the effectiveness of fiscal and monetary policy have raged for many decades on both sides of the Atlantic. Up to the 1970s many economists and policymakers believed in a short-run Keynesian trade-off between inflation and unemployment (termed a Phillips Curve), so that an expansionary fiscal or monetary policy would at least boost employment and lower unemployment for some time. The accelerator hypothesis popular in the 1970s insisted that extra jobs could only be achieved at the expense of ever-increasing inflation. The critique of econometric policy evaluation put forward by Robert Lucas in 1976 insisted that people cannot be fooled all the time. The subsequent outburst of new classical economics led by Lucas and Thomas Sargent and Neil Wallace killed the popularity of Keynesian economics.

By the end of the 1970s policymakers and economists became skeptical about the possibility of expansionary demand management lowering unemployment. The new classical economists rejected Keynesian theories of aggregate demand with sluggish price and wage formation and insisted on modelling dynamic, competitive general equilibrium models with rigorous micro foundations, rational expectations, and prices and wages adjusting instantaneously to clear all goods and labor markets. Fluctuations thus arise from technology shocks rather than changes in economic policy. This generation of economists works in the spirit of classical economists like Adam Smith, David Hume, David Ricardo, John Stuart Mill, Knut Wicksell,

Irving Fisher, and John Maynard Keynes of *The Treatise of Money* (1930) who all insisted that output is primarily determined by productive capacity.

However, in 1980 Robert Solow (1980) in his Presidential Address to the American Economic Association criticized the new classical school and its Panglossian policy prescriptions for being unrealistic and irrelevant. He missed returns to scale and oligopolistic interdependence, and was unable to accept that all unemployed households are voluntarily unemployed. Involuntary unemployment and non-clearing labor markets needed to be addressed, which, according to Solow, would require an analysis of real and nominal wage and price rigidities, which may well follow from optimizing behavior of agents in the economy during their normal activities. Solow gave a host of reasons why labor markets do not clear immediately (varying from Keynes's idea of case-by-case resistance to wage reductions to trade unions and efficiency wages).

Soon afterward, Oliver Hart, Oliver Blanchard, and Nobu Kiyotaki, and others in Gregory Mankiw and David Romer's *New Keynesian Economics* (1991) explained that aggregate demand externalities in economies with monopolistic competition produces Keynesian multipliers. With small menu costs prices can be rigid and monetary policy has real effects on the economy. In the 2000s Michael Woodford (2003) and Jordi Galí (2003) continued the New Keynesian counter-attack on the new classical orthodoxy. Their objective is to develop dynamic, noncompetitive general equilibrium models with rigorous microfoundations, but where it is costly to adjust prices instantaneously. They obtain a micro-founded, forward-looking New Keynesian Phillips Curve with a short-run trade-off between inflation and unemployment. The main advantage of this approach is that a second-order approximation to a proper micro-founded welfare loss function can be obtained. This leads to the advice that central bankers should not target the actual output gap, but should target the economy as close as possible to the level of output that would prevail under flexible wages and prices.

An important implication is that inflation is forward rather than backward looking. The reason is that prices stay fixed for a while and thus depend on expected future marginal costs and demand conditions. A big difference with the accelerator version of the Phillips Curve is that inflation leads output rather than the other way round. A monetary expansion always expands output, but only generates a lower interest rate if risk aversion is sufficiently high and money growth is not too autocorrelated. The Keynesian liquidity effect is thus not necessarily operative in the New Neoclassical Synthesis. Another insight is that policy makers should target deviations of actual output from the first-best level of output that would prevail in the absence of price and wage rigidity rather than from the de-trended level of output.

The New Keynesian approach cannot explain the quintessential Keynesian features that inflation displays inertia and monetary disinflations are contractionary. Other challenges for the New Keynesian approach are to explain pro-cyclical real wages in the face of demand shocks, allow for inventories, credit constraints, and bankruptcies in explaining the business cycle, model unemployment as a catastrophic event, and allow for psychological features such as downward rigidity of wages and not taking account of the full effects of changes in inflation at low rates of inflation.

Keynesian economics was not popular in the 1970s and 1980s. However, with the advent of New Keynesian economics, Keynes has become a source of inspiration again. Apart from giving more rigorous micro foundations, an important factor is undoubtedly that Keynesian economics is better able to explain the events of the 1970s and the 1980s as well as the recessions of the late twentieth century than the new classical economics. The New Keynesian approach must be able to explain periods of persistent, widespread involuntary unemployment, since otherwise it does not capture quintessential Keynesian features. One cannot rely on people's misperceptions about relative prices or technology shocks alone to explain such periods. Keynes stressed the importance of animal spirits, coordination failures, and the possibility of multiple equilibrium outcomes. Coordination failures and bootstrap equilibria are important, since economies can get stuck in situations of deficient demand and widespread unemployment. Policymakers must then react by boosting confidence in the economy again. Investment by firms is financed by retained profits rather than borrowing, and this together with changes in the functional distribution of income is an important source of macroeconomic fluctuations. However, neither traditional nor New Keynesian Phillips Curves capture real world features that affect firm and bank behavior such as credit constraints, equity constraints, bankruptcies, and other market failures arising from imperfect information as discussed in Joseph Stiglitz and Bruce Greenwald's *Towards a New Paradigm in Monetary Economics* (2003). If allowance is made for these features and the role of financial intermediaries, it follows that the nominal interest rate as well as the real interest rate affects the aggregate demand for goods. Monetary policy is associated with big distortions in allocation and is as much about supervision and regulation as the interest rate.

SEE ALSO *Economics, Keynesian; Economics, New Classical; Economics, Post Keynesian*

BIBLIOGRAPHY

Blanchard, Oliver, and Nobu Kyotaki. 1987. Monopolistic Competition and the Effects of Aggregate Demand. *American Economic Review* 77 (4): 647–666.

Galí, Jordi. 2003. New Perspectives on Monetary Policy, Inflation, and the Business Cycle. In *Advances in Economics and Econometrics*, eds. Matthias Dewatripont, Lars Hansen, and Stephen J. Turnovsky, Vol. VIII, 151–197. Cambridge, U.K.: Cambridge University Press.

Hart, Oliver D. 1982. A Model of Imperfect Competition with Keynesian Features. *Quarterly Journal of Economics* 97: 109–138.

Keynes, John Maynard. 1936. *The General Theory of Employment, Interest, and Money.* New York: Macmillan.

Lucas, Robert E., Jr. 1973. Some International Evidence on Output-Inflation Tradeoffs. *American Economic Review* 63: 326–335.

Lucas, Robert E., Jr. 1976. Econometric Policy Evaluation: A Critique. *Carnegie-Rochester Conference Series on Public Policy* 1: 19–46.

Mankiw, N. Gregory, and David Romer, eds. 1991. *New Keynesian Economics.* Vols. 1 and 2. Cambridge, MA: MIT Press.

Sargent, Thomas J., and Neil Wallace. 1975. "Rational" Expectations, the Optimal Monetary Instrument, and the Optimal Money Supply Rule. *Journal of Political Economy* 83: 241–245.

Solow, Robert M. 1980. On Theories of Unemployment. *The American Economic Review* 70 (1): 1–11.

Stiglitz, Joseph, and Bruce Greenwald. 2003. *Towards a New Paradigm in Monetary Economics.* Raffaele Mattioli Lectures. Cambridge, U.K.: Cambridge University Press.

Woodford, Michael. 2003. *Interest and Prices: Foundations of a Theory of Monetary Policy.* Princeton, NJ: Princeton University Press.

Frederick van der Ploeg

ECONOMICS, NOBEL PRIZE IN

The Bank of Sweden Prize in Economic Sciences in Memory of Alfred Nobel, the founder of the Nobel Prize, was instituted by the Bank of Sweden (the world's oldest central bank) for its three-hundredth anniversary in 1968, sixty-seven years after the first Nobel Prizes were awarded for other fields. Known also as the Nobel Memorial Prize in Economics, and less formally as the Nobel Prize in Economics, it is the only prize granted that was not specified in Alfred Nobel's will. Its addition was justified as a recognition that the use of quantitative methods had made economics a science like physics and chemistry.

The Nobel Prize in Economics is awarded each year for outstanding intellectual contributions to the field of economics. The laureates are chosen by the Royal Swedish Academy of Sciences, from nominations of about one hundred living persons made by qualified nominators each year. Prizewinners receive their award during a ceremony in Stockholm, together with the laureates in the other fields. No more than three people can share the prize for a given year. The names of the nominees can only be published after fifty years.

From 1969, when the first prize was awarded, up to 2006, fifty-eight people have received the Nobel in economics. Economics is the only discipline in which no woman has ever been awarded a Nobel. The United States has dominated the award, with forty laureates, followed by nine laureates from the United Kingdom. The University of Chicago has employed the highest number of laureates in economics, nine up to 2006, followed by Harvard University and U.C. Berkeley, with four laureates each. Out of the thirty-eight prizes awarded up to 2006, seventeen were shared. With an average age of sixty-six at the time of the award, laureates in economics are the oldest to receive the prize—the youngest are in physics, with an average age of fifty-four. The youngest person to receive the prize in economics was Kenneth Arrow, in 1972, at the age of fifty-one; the oldest was Thomas Schelling, in 2005, at the age of eighty-four.

The prize has been awarded to work ranging from theory to empirical application, from macroeconomics to microeconomics, from economic policy to economic history, and from mathematical modeling to psychology. The early awards were focused on acknowledging the past contributions of "giants" such as Paul Samuelson (1970), the father of the modern economic theory; Simon Kuznets (1971), the father of the empirical analysis of economic growth; John Hicks and Kenneth Arrow (1972), pioneering contributors to general economic equilibrium theory and welfare theory; Wassily Leontief (1973), who developed the input-output method and a number of applications to economic problems; and Milton Friedman (1976), whose long list of contributions include consumption analysis, monetary history and theory, and stabilization policy.

The scope of the award has been broadened over the decades, while the work awarded has become more specialized. One could already see these trends in the 1980s, with prizes given for work on the theory of economic growth (Robert Solow, 1987), financial economics (James Tobin, 1981; Franco Modigliani, 1985; Harry Markowitz, Merton Miller, and William Sharpe, 1990), empirical work and econometrics (Lawrence Klein, 1980; Richard Stone, 1984; Trygve Haavelmo, 1989), and eco-

Nobel Laureates in Economics, 1969–2006	
Ragnar Frisch, Jan Tinbergen	1969
Paul A. Samuelson	1970
Simon Kuznets	1971
John R. Hicks, Kenneth J. Arrow	1972
Wassily Leontief	1973
Gunnar Myrdal, Friedrich August von Hayek	1974
Leonid Vitaliyevich Kantorovich, Tjalling C. Koopmans	1975
Milton Friedman	1976
Bertil Ohlin, James E. Meade	1977
Herbert A. Simon	1978
Theodore W. Schultz, Sir Arthur Lewis	1979
Lawrence R. Klein	1980
James Tobin	1981
George J. Stigler	1982
Gerard Debreu	1983
Richard Stone	1984
Franco Modigliani	1985
James M. Buchanan Jr.	1986
Robert M. Solow	1987
Maurice Allais	1988
Trygve Haavelmo	1989
Harry M. Markowitz, Merton H. Miller, William F. Sharpe	1990
Ronald H. Coase	1991
Gary S. Becker	1992
Robert W. Fogel, Douglass C. North	1993
John C. Harsanyi, John F. Nash Jr., Reinhard Selten	1994
Robert E. Lucas Jr.	1995
James A. Mirrlees, William Vickrey	1996
Robert C. Merton, Myron S. Scholes	1997
Amartya Sen	1998
Robert A. Mundell	1999
James J. Heckman, Daniel L. McFadden	2000
George A. Akerlof, A. Michael Spence, Joseph E. Stiglitz	2001
Daniel Kahneman, Vernon L. Smith	2002
Robert F. Engle III, Clive W. J. Granger	2003
Finn E. Kydland, Edward C. Prescott	2004
Robert J. Aumann, Thomas C. Schelling	2005
Edmund S. Phelps	2006

nomic theory (George Stigler, 1982; Gerard Debreu, 1983; James Buchanan, 1986; Maurice Allais, 1988).

These trends have become even more apparent in recent years. Since 1990, the prize has been awarded for contributions that address economic problems with tools and results from fields outside economics, such as mathematics and game theory (John Harsanyi, John Nash and Reinhard Selten, 1994; Robert J. Aumann and Thomas Schelling, 2005), psychology (Daniel Kahneman and Vernon Smith, 2002), and philosophy (Amartya Sen, 1998). It has also been given for contributions that apply economic tools to other fields, such as work that uses microeconomic analysis to explain a wide range of human behavior and interaction (Gary Becker, 1992), and work using economic theory and quantitative methods to explain economic and institutional change in history (Robert Fogel and Douglass North, 1993). It has been awarded for econometrics (James Heckman and Daniel McFadden, 2000; Robert Engle and Clive Granger, 2003), and for broadening and deepening economic theory by incorporating transaction costs and property rights (Ronald Coase, 1991), rational expectations (Robert Lucas, 1995), and asymmetric information (George Akerlof, Michael Spence, and Joseph Stiglitz, 2001). It has also been given for work with direct policy implications, such as that addressing monetary and fiscal policy under different exchange rate regimes (Robert Mundell, 1999) and the intertemporal trade-offs in macroeconomic policy (Phelps 2006), and for contributions that were first criticized as too specialized and limited in scope, but later proved more influential and applicable than most had expected, such as the pricing formula for financial derivatives (Robert Merton and Myron Scholes, 1997).

The Nobel Prize in Economics has been a source of controversy since its introduction. Some have even suggested that the award should be discontinued. Its very name has been questioned, as it was not part of Alfred Nobel's bequest. It has also been argued that the criteria for an award for a social science cannot be as objective as for the other fields, although similar concerns have been raised for the prizes for peace and literature. Indeed, this may explain why it takes much longer to receive the Nobel in Economics after a contribution is made than in any other field—an average of thirty-three years, compared with an average of twelve years for prizes in the hard sciences—which has also been a source of controversy. Finally, some of the recent selections have been criticized for honoring contributions that are too narrowly focused.

The prize has affected both the field of economics itself and the field's impact. It has been argued that the prospect of receiving a Nobel Prize motivates economists to pursue original research ideas. Although there has been no empirical study documenting such an effect, it is consistent with one of the most basic laws in economics that people respond to incentives. The impact that an economist can have on the literature, on economic policy, and on public opinion is substantially enhanced if they can add the title *Nobel Laureate* after their name. Elite universities lose no opportunity to advertise the laureates on their faculty to attract new faculty members and graduate students. Even Hollywood has been inspired by the prestige of the prize, as reflected in the Oscar-winning movie *A Beautiful Mind*, about the life of John Nash.

SEE ALSO *Economics*

BIBLIOGRAPHY

Baffes, John, and Athanasios Vamvakidis. Are You Old Enough for a Nobel Prize? Washington, DC: World Bank and International Monetary Fund. (Forthcoming).

Feldman, Burton. 2000. *The Nobel Prize: A History of Genius, Controversy, and Prestige.* New York: Arcade.

Jones, Benjamin F. 2005. Age and Great Invention. NBER Working Paper 11359. Cambridge, MA: National Bureau of Economic Research.

Nasar, Sylvia. 1998. *A Beautiful Mind: A Biography of John Forbes Nash, Jr., Winner of the Nobel Prize in Economics, 1994.* New York: Touchstone. Reissued as *A Beautiful Mind: The Life of Mathematical Genius and Nobel Laureate John Nash.* New York: Touchstone, 2001.

Nobel Prize Internet Archive. http://www.almaz.com/nobel/.

Nobelprize.org. http://nobelprize.org/index.html.

Shalev, Baruch A. 2002. *One Hundred Years of Nobel Prizes.* Los Angeles: Americas Group.

Weinberg, Bruce A., and David W. Galenson. 2005. Creative Careers: The Life Cycles of Nobel Laureates in Economics. NBER Working Paper 11799. Cambridge, MA: National Bureau of Economic Research.

Athanasios Vamvakidis

ECONOMICS, NON-WALRASIAN

SEE *Barro-Grossman Model; Patinkin, Don.*

ECONOMICS, POST KEYNESIAN

John Maynard Keynes's 1936 book *The General Theory of Employment, Interest, and Money* attempted to overthrow classical theory and revolutionize how economists think about the economy. Economists who build upon Keynes's *General Theory* to analyze the economic problems of the twenty-first-century global economy are called Post Keynesians. Keynes's "principle of effective demand" (1936, chap. 2) declared that the axioms underlying classical theory were not applicable to a money-using, entrepreneurial economic system. Consequently, the mainstream theory's "teaching is misleading and disastrous if we attempt to apply it to the facts of experience" (Keynes 1936, p. 3). To develop an economic theory applicable to a monetary economy, Keynes suggested rejecting three basic axioms of classical economics (1936, p. 16).

Unfortunately, the axioms that Keynes suggested for rejection are still part of the foundation of twenty-first-century mainstream economic theory. Post Keynesians have thrown out the three axioms that Keynes suggested rejecting in *The General Theory.* The rejected axioms are the ergodic axiom, the gross-substitution axiom, and the neutral-money axiom, which are explained below. Only if these axioms are rejected can a model be developed that has the following characteristics:

- Money matters in the long and short run, that is, changes in the money supply can affect decisions that determine the level of employment and real economic output.

- As the economic system moves from an irrevocable past to an uncertain future, decision makers recognize that they make important, costly decisions in uncertain conditions where reliable, rational calculations regarding the future are impossible.

- People and organizations enter into monetary contracts. These money contracts are a human institution developed to efficiently organize time-consuming production and exchange processes. The money-wage contract is the most ubiquitous of these contracts.

- Unemployment, rather than full employment, is a common laissez-faire situation in a market-oriented, monetary production economy.

The ergodic axiom postulates that all future events are actuarially certain, that is, that the future can be accurately forecasted from an analysis of existing market data. Consequently, this axiom implies that income earned at any employment level is entirely spent either on produced goods for today's consumption or on buying investment goods that will be used to produce goods for the (known) future consumption of today's savers. In other words, orthodox theory assumes that all income is always immediately spent on producibles, so there is never a lack of effective demand for things that industry can produce at full employment. The proportion of income that households save does not affect total (aggregate) demand for producibles; it affects only the composition of demand (and production) between consumption and investment goods. Thus, saving creates jobs in the capital-goods-producing industries just as much as consumption spending creates jobs in the consumer-goods-producing industries. Post Keynesian theory rejects the ergodic axiom.

In Post Keynesian theory, however, people recognize that the future is uncertain (nonergodic) and cannot be reliably predicted. Consequently, people decide on how much of current income is spent on consumer goods and how much is not spent on consumption goods but is instead saved by purchasing various liquid assets.

Liquid assets are time-machine vehicles that savers use to store and transport savings to an indefinite future date or dates. Unlike savers in the classical system who can reliably predict their economic future, real-world savers do not know exactly what they will buy, and what contractual obligations they will incur, at any specific future date. As long as money discharges all contractual obligations and monetary contracts are used to organize production and exchange activities, the possession of money (and liquid assets that have small carrying costs and can be easily resold for money) means that holding one savings in the form of liquid assets gives savers the ability to demand products whenever they desire in the uncertain future and/or to meet a future unforeseen contractual commitment. Liquid assets are savers' security blankets, protecting them from possible hard times. As Nobel Price winner John Hicks has stated, income recipients know that they "do not know just what will happen in the future" (1977, p. vii).

Keynes (1936, chap. 17) argued that money (and all liquid assets) have two essential properties. First, money does not grow on trees, and hence labor cannot be hired to harvest money trees when income earners reduce consumption to save more in the form of money or liquid assets. Accordingly, the decision to consume rather than to save is a choice between an employment-inducing demand and a non-employment-inducing demand. When savings increase at the expense of the demand for producibles, sales and employment decline. Second, liquid asset prices will increase as new savings increase the demand for such assets. Because of high carrying and high resale costs, producible durables are not gross substitutes for liquid assets, contrary to the classical gross-substitution axiom where the latter assumes anything is a good substitute for anything else. Post Keynesians reject the gross substitution axiom as applicable to assets that savers use to store their savings. Consequently, higher liquid-asset prices do not divert this savings demand for liquid assets to a demand for producibles whose relative price has declined. (If producibles were gross substitutes for liquid assets and if savings increase the relative price of liquid nonproducible assets, then the gross substitution axiom implies that savers would be induced to substitute the lower relative priced producibles as a place for their savings. Thus savings would create a simultaneous demand for the durable producibles and there would never be a lack of effective demand for the products of industry.)

In the real world, investment spending on producible durables is constrained solely by entrepreneurs' expectations of profits. If the future is uncertain, these expecta-

tions depend on "animal spirits" rather than on a reliable calculation of future profit income (Keynes 1936, p. 161). In an economy where money is created by banks, if entrepreneurs borrow from banks to finance the production of working capital goods, the resulting increases in the quantity of money will be associated with increasing employment and output. In contrast, the classical neutral-money axiom implies that, for example, if the money supply increases as people borrow more from banks, this change in the money quantity cannot affect the level of employment or output.

Post Keynesians reject the classical neutral-money axiom when they argue that changes in the money supply due to borrowing from banks to finance the production of investment goods affect the level of employment and output in both the short run and the long run.

SEE ALSO *Economics, Neoclassical; Economics, New Classical*

BIBLIOGRAPHY

Davidson, Paul. 1994. *Post Keynesian Macroeconomic Theory: A Foundation for Successful Economic Policies for the Twenty-First Century.* Cheltenham, U.K.: Elgar Publishing.

Hicks, John R. 1977. *Economic Perspectives.* Oxford: Clarendon Press.

Keynes, John Maynard. 1936. *The General Theory of Employment, Interest, and Money.* New York: Harcourt, Brace.

Paul Davidson

ECONOMICS, PUBLIC

Public economics is often defined as the economic study of the public sector. Contemporary public economics draws from two traditions, public finance and public choice. The older public finance tradition of economists such as Arthur Pigou and Richard Musgrave views government as essentially benevolent. The roles of government are, first, to raise funds and provide basic public goods, such as national defense; second, to correct market failure, namely the failure of markets to achieve efficiency in the presence of externalities, public goods, and imperfect information; and third, to improve equity. Equity is viewed primarily in terms of income distribution, and so more equity is generally associated with less inequality in the distribution of income.

Unlike many other areas of mainstream economics, much of the public finance literature is explicitly normative. For example, optimal tax theory prescribes how governments should raise revenue so as to achieve both equity and efficiency. The American Economic Association's

Journal of Economic Literature classification system reflects the public finance tradition, categorizing the subfields of public economics as "structure and scope of government; taxation, subsidies and revenues; fiscal policies and behaviour of economic agents; publicly provided goods; national government expenditures and related policies; national budget, deficit and debt; state and local government; intergovernmental relations" (American Economics Association 2006, pp. 1157–1158).

The public choice tradition, associated with the economist James Buchanan, sees government as a collection of rational, self-interested agents. These agents trade and exchange in the public sector, just as firms and consumers do in private markets. Central concerns of public choice include the behavior of bureaucracies and the design of political institutions, including constitutional rules. Although public choice is an avowedly positive research program, it has normative implications. For example, a positive statement that bureaucrats attempt to maximize the size of their budgets thereby extracting all benefits from government activity has implications for how large governments should be. Public choice has had a major influence on current political science research, and this intersection between economics and politics is frequently referred to as political economy.

In the twenty-first century the borders between public economics and other areas of economics have blurred, as has the division between the public finance and public choice traditions. Since government impacts all aspects of the economy, economists in other fields also study the public sector. For example, labor economists study the effects of taxation and income support programs on labor supply, environmental economists study the problem of externalities, and so on. In the later part of the twentieth century the size of government in industrialized countries stabilized or shrank, while economists became aware that governments, like markets, could fail. Public economists began to study nongovernmental forms of collective action, for example, the private provision of public goods. The central insight of public choice, that politicians and bureaucrats are rational—and not necessarily benevolent—agents, became widely accepted. The *Journal of Public Economic Theory* describes the scope of contemporary public economic research in its mission statement: "public goods, local public goods, club economies, externalities, taxation, growth, public choice, social and public decision making, voting, market failure, regulation, project evaluation, equity, and political systems" ("Aims and Scope"). Public economics is no longer simply the economics of the public sector.

SEE ALSO *Decision-making; Externality; Government; Political System; Public Choice Theory; Public Goods;* *Public Sector; Public Utilities; Regulation; State Enterprise; Taxation; Voting*

BIBLIOGRAPHY

American Economics Association. 2006. Journal of Economic Literature Classification System. *Journal of Economic Literature* 44 (4): 1157–1158. http://www.aeaweb.org/journal/jel_class_system.html#h.

Atkinson, Anthony B., and Joseph E. Stiglitz. 1980. *Lectures on Public Economics.* New York: McGraw-Hill.

Auerbach, Alan J., and Martin Feldstein, eds. 1985–2002. *Handbook of Public Economics.* 4 vols. Amsterdam: North-Holland.

Buchanan, James M., and Gordon Tullock. 1962. *The Calculus of Consent: Logical Foundations of Constitutional Democracy.* Ann Arbor: University of Michigan Press.

Diamond, Peter A., and James A. Mirrlees. 1971. Optimal Taxation and Public Production I: Production Efficiency. *American Economic Review* 61 (1): 8–27.

Journal of Public Economic Theory. 2006. Aims and Scope. http://www2.warwick.ac.uk/fac/soc/economics/staff/faculty/wooders/apet/mission/.

Musgrave, Richard Abel. 1959. *The Theory of Public Finance: A Study in Public Economy.* New York: McGraw-Hill.

Samuelson, Paul. 1954. The Pure Theory of Public Expenditure. *Review of Economics and Statistics* 36 (4): 387–389.

Frances Woolley

ECONOMICS, SRAFFIAN

SEE *Economics, Neo-Ricardian.*

ECONOMICS, STRATIFICATION

Stratification economics is an emergent subfield of economics that uses the concept of social stratification as a point of departure for examining structural and intentional processes that generate hierarchy and economic inequality among groups whose members are defined by one or more characteristic or attribute. *Social stratification* typically refers to the hierarchical arrangement of social classes, castes, and strata within a society. Stratification economics analyzes the social processes influencing the nature and reproduction of stratification not only within, but also across, different societies. Within stratification economics, special attention is directed to the role of racial and caste distinctions and similar group affiliations in producing and perpetuating income and wealth inequality.

Stratification economics treats group identities as produced forms of individual and collective property with both income and wealth-generating characteristics. In addition, these groups' supply and demand are responsive to changes in production costs and budget constraints. Cooperative economic and noneconomic behaviors are treated as normal outcomes of individuals' propensity to engage in own-group altruism and other-group antagonism. Theoretical stratification-economics models predict that a person's reward for cooperative behavior increases with the mean wealth of the person's group, so that income and wealth inequality strengthen incentives to engage in cooperative behavior.

Within stratification economics, an individual has constrained choices among various identities, such as racial classification and nationality, which establish the foundations for intergroup conflict. For example, powerful groups often attempt to create property rights that facilitate the exclusion and exploitation of nonmembers and provide privileged access to private and public goods for members of the dominant group. Such rights are maintained by social custom, history, law, and other means. Ascriptive markers such as skin color serve as signals to dominant interests to vary the intensity of discrimination targeted at particular subordinate individuals and groups. For example, during the era of slavery in the United States, lighter-skinned blacks were often afforded more privileges than their darker-skinned counterparts, while still encountering discrimination.

Theoretical stratification economics challenge conventional wisdom about the dynamics of intergroup inequality. Stratification economists argue, for example, that intergroup conflict in both economic and noneconomic settings is an endogenous characteristic of the social space, rather than an exogenous contaminant of market allocation processes and individual decision-making. Reductions in intergroup equality and income will not automatically lead to the erosion of traditional patterns of collective identification if the expected returns to additional investments in group identity are unequal across groups. Movement toward more egalitarian intergroup distributions of wealth must therefore be a major element in any earnest attempt to reduce intergroup conflict, because inequities are institutionalized through processes that enable the transfer of material resources across generations.

Stratification economics is supported by studies of mechanisms perpetuating domination in various countries including white privilege in the United States and throughout the Americas, high-caste Hindu privilege in India, and Protestant privilege in Northern Ireland. Studies of economic discrimination targeting particular subgroups in various market societies, including African Americans in the United States, the Buraku in Japan, East and West Indians in Britain, and blacks in Canada, also provide useful insights for stratification economists.

As stratification economics evolves, it is likely to pose increasingly robust challenges to schools of thought that emphasize group-based deficits in personal responsibility and cultural practices as the primary sources of persisting intergroup economic inequality.

BIBLIOGRAPHY

Akerlof, George and Rachel Kranton. 2000. Economics and Identity. *Quarterly Journal of Economics* 115 (3): 715–753.

Darity, William, Jr. 2005. Stratification Economics: The Role of Intergroup Inequality. *Journal of Economics and Finance* 29 (2): 144–153.

Darity, William, Jr. and Ashwini Deshpande. 2000. Tracing the Divide: Intergroup Disparity Across Countries. *Eastern Economic Journal* 26 (1): 75–86.

Darity, William, Jr. and Patrick Mason. 1998. Evidence on Discrimination in Employment: Codes of Color, Codes of Gender. *Journal of Economic Perspectives* 12 (2): 63–90.

Darity, William A., Jr., Patrick L. Mason, and James B. Stewart. 2006. The Economics of Identity: The Origin and Persistence of Racial Identity Norms. *Journal of Economic Behavior & Organization* 60 (3): 283–305.

Harris, Cheryl. 1993. Whiteness as Property. *Harvard Law Review* 106 (8): 1709–1791.

McAdams, Richard. 1995. Cooperation and Conflict: The Economics of Group Status Production and Race Discrimination. *Harvard Law Review* 108: 1005–1084.

James B. Stewart

ECONOMICS, WELFARE

SEE *Welfare Economics.*

ECONOMICS OF CONTROL

The *economics of control*, perhaps best represented by Abba Lerner's (1903–1982) 1944 book of that title, based on his 1943 doctoral dissertation for the London School of Economics, is a halfway-house policy approach to capitalist economies between laissez-faire on the one side and socialist economic planning on the other. The economics of control accepts the basic institutional framework of capitalist markets as the organizing principle but recognizes market imperfections, macroeconomic deficiencies, and other problems that require government intervention to improve market outcomes. It was an attempt, in the words of Sidney Ratner (1908–1996), at a "reconciliation of liberalism and socialism in welfare economics" (Ratner 1949, p. 133).

John Maynard Keynes (1883–1946), in a letter written at sea on a voyage to the United States during which he read *The Economics of Control*, wrote to Lerner that the latter had "written two books largely distinct … which you have placed within one cover" (Colander and Landreth 1996, p. 116). The first was dedicated to microeconomic problems analyzed through the neoclassical marginalist approach but infused with a spirit of market socialism that Lerner described as "socialist free enterprise." This work was part of the debate on socialist planning that has often been viewed as dealing with the question of the viability of a socialist economy but really concerned a more specific, technical issue: whether or not neoclassical theory, in particular general equilibrium analysis, was applicable to a planned economy. Friedrich August von Hayek (1899–1992) and the Austrians said no; Lerner, Oskar Lange (1904–1965), and others claimed that it was (Kirzner 1988).

The second "book" covered macroeconomics and Keynesian theory, which included demonstrating the theoretical justifications for employing Lerner's *functional finance* approach. This approach implied strong fiscal and monetary policies for promoting macro goals, such as full employment, price stability, and stable economic growth, not only for their own sake, but also because full employment was seen as a precondition for the relatively smooth workings of the microeconomy. Keynes called this "second of the two books which you have placed within one cover … very original and grand stuff," adding:

> I shall have to try when I get back [to England, from his trip to the United States] to hold a seminar for the heads of the Treasury on Functional Finance. It will be hard going—I think I shall ask them to let me hold a seminar for their sons instead, agreeing beforehand that, if I can convince the boys, they will take it from me that it is so! (Colander and Landreth 1996, pp. 116–117)

Keynes does not trust that the heads of the Treasury can understand, because, as Lerner often noted, "Functional Finance is seen to run counter to economic principles" (Lerner 1951, p. 142). Functional finance, or Keynesian economics taken to its furthest logical conclusions (causing David Colander to ask, "Was Keynes a Keynesian or a Lernerian?" [1984]), was, in its application to unemployment, Lerner admitted, "topsy-turvy economics": "But this is no objection at all. Topsy-turvy economics is just what is appropriate for an economy that is suffering from unemployment. An economy suffering from unemployment is an upside-down economy for

which *only* a topsy-turvy economic theory is of any use" (Lerner 1951, pp. 142–143).

By an "upside-down economy," Lerner means an economy in which strongly held traditional economic principles, such as those regarding thrift and the economical use of scarce resources, do not hold. Lerner noted that when there is unemployment, efficiency becomes inefficient: "an increase in efficiency in any particular productive process does not result in any increase in efficiency in the economy as a whole. … The savings due to greater technical efficiency merely go to waste in more unemployment" (Lerner 1951, pp. 143–144). Likewise when there is unemployment, a country has to suffer over its trade balance, because it must worry about rising unemployment stemming from an increase in the value of its imports over the value of exports. Since "the input of the foreign trade industry consists of the effort involved in the manufacture of our exports" and "the output of our foreign trade industry consists of the imports which it yields to us for our use," exports are a cost and imports are a benefit (Lerner 1951, p. 321). Thus when a nation attempts to cure its unemployment problems by reducing its trade deficit, it is promoting costs and restricting benefits.

Other supporters of the economics of control went beyond what they viewed as Lerner's approach, made up as it was between neoclassical welfare economics on the one side and traditional Keynesian fiscal and monetary policies on the other. Adolph Lowe (1893–1995) made the distinction between *primary* and *secondary* controls (Lowe [1965] 1977). Primary controls, or conventional economic policies, take the behavior of the microunits as given, whereas secondary controls, or what Lowe sometimes called *instrumental* controls, seek to shape the behavioral patterns of the microunits themselves, either directly or through creating the structural or environmental contexts that can influence motivations and behaviors (Lowe 1969, p. 33). Examples of the former include a variety of fiscal and monetary policies. The latter would be exemplified by policies that shape expectations (e.g., reducing uncertainty). The line between the two is not always clear, because fiscal and monetary policies can also influence expectations. If business investors know that the state is committed to maintaining a high, stable rate of growth of demand, they will have less uncertainty about future conditions that affect investment and thus output and employment. As Lerner noted, the purpose of taxation is its "effect on the *public* of influencing their economic behavior" (Lerner 1951, p. 131).

SEE ALSO *Economics, Keynesian; Exports; Full Employment; Imports; Keynes, John Maynard; Laissez-faire; Marginalism; Microeconomics; Planning; Policy, Fiscal; Policy, Monetary; Socialism; Socialism, Market; Taxation; Unemployment*

BIBLIOGRAPHY

Colander, David. 1984. Was Keynes a Keynesian or a Lernerian? *Journal of Economic Literature* 22 (4): 1572–1575.

Colander, David C., and Harry Landreth, eds. 1996. *The Coming of Keynesianism to America: Conversations with the Founders of Keynesian Economics.* Cheltenham, U.K.: Elgar.

Kirzner, Israel. 1988. The Economic Calculation Debate: Lessons for Austrians. *Review of Austrian Economics* 2: 1–18.

Lerner, Abba P. 1944. *The Economics of Control: Principles of Welfare Economics.* New York: Macmillan.

Lerner, Abba P. 1951. *The Economics of Employment.* New York: McGraw-Hill.

Lowe, Adolph. [1965] 1977. *On Economic Knowledge: Toward a Science of Political Economics.* Enlarged ed. Armonk, NY: Sharpe.

Lowe, Adolph. 1969. Toward a Science of Political Economics. In *Economic Means and Social Ends: Essays in Political Economics,* ed. Robert Heilbroner, 1–36. Englewood, NJ: Prentice-Hall.

Ratner, Sidney. 1949. Review: *Individualism and Economic Order* by Friedrich A. Hayek. *American Political Science Review* 43 (1): 132–133.

Mathew Forstater

ECONOMIES, TRANSITIONAL

The breakdown of centralized socialism in the Union of Soviet Socialist Republics (USSR), Central and Eastern Europe, and Asia at the end of the twentieth century resulted in the adoption of the market process as a means of organizing the economy. The movement from a centralized socialist economy to an economy based on market relations has been termed *transition* and thus the economies that have adopted this process are called *transitional economies.* In particular, the transition process was associated with an explicit end-state, namely the establishment of a capitalist economic system. Hence, the transition involved, in essence, the introduction of private ownership and restructuring through the privatization of state enterprises; the establishment of market equilibrium through the abolishment of centrally administered commands; the liberalization of economic activity through institutional reform; a change in economic behavior as a result of economic actors adjusting their behavior in line with self-interest and the rules of market exchange; and the reduction of the state to the role of legislator and facilitator of economic activity.

The term *transition* has been criticized as being inadequate, however, because it does not capture all the complications involved during the process. The term implies a linear movement from point A (centralized socialism and disequilibrium) to point B (capitalism and equilibrium). Specifically, because transition implies an end-state, the achievement of that end-state completes the whole process. It can thus be argued that the process is already complete, for the transition economies have in fact established a capitalist economic system and most of the countries of Central and Eastern Europe are members of the European Union. In this view, the term *transitional economy* is obsolete.

It can also be argued, however, that the "transition" process is continuous, and that equilibrium can never be achieved. This has led to the use of terms such as *transformational economy* and *developing economy.* In addition, capitalism comes in many varieties, so the question of what type of capitalism should be the goal complicates the process (Marangos 2004). Some commentators have also questioned the goal of achieving a capitalist economic system, with alternatives such as market socialism being proposed as the most appropriate economic system. China and Vietnam are examples of this type of system. Lastly, an alternative term, "integration-assisted transition," has been introduced by Aristidis Bitzenis and John Marangos (2007), who argued that the goal of transitional economies was the participation in the globalization process and attempting to integrate their economies into the globalized system by opening their borders, liberalizing their markets, and attracting foreign direct investments with the assistance of international financial institutions and multinationals.

The economic program of transition involved four elements. The first was macroeconomic stabilization, which reduced inflation and decreased the debt burden. The second was the liberalization of economic activity, including prices, trade, currency, and convertibility. The third was the reduction of the size of the public sector through privatization and the restructuring of state-owned enterprises. The last element was the establishment of new laws and regulations in areas such as property rights, corporate law, accounting practices, and tax regulation. It is clear, then, that the decision to move to a market-based economy required a total transformation of the economy. Meanwhile, the citizens of these countries were unprepared to face the economic adversity and uncertainty resulting from the free-market process, mainly because they had been protected for so long by the Socialist State.

Although all the countries in transition had more or less the same final goal, the results of their efforts are diverse. This is because different strategies, policies, paths, and conditions ensured a variety of *transition* processes and outcomes (Bitzenis 2007).

BIBLIOGRAPHY

Bitzenis, Aristidis. 2007. Political and Economic Alternatives for the Central and East European Region and China. *Global Business and Economics Review* 9 (1): 101-122.

Bitzenis, Aristidis, and John Marangos. 2007. Globalization and the Integration-Assisted Transition in Central and Eastern Europe Economies. *Journal of Economic Issues* 41 (2): 427–434.

Marangos, John. 2004. *Alternative Economic Models of Transition.* Aldershot, U.K.: Ashgate. Reprinted in paperback in 2007 by Transaction Publishing.

Aristidis Bitzenis
John Marangos

EDGEWORTH, FRANCIS YSIDRO

SEE *Probability Theory; Crowding Hypothesis.*

EDGEWORTH-BOWLEY BOX

SEE *Welfare Economics.*

EDUCATION, INFORMAL

Informal education refers to intentional educational encounters occurring beyond the classroom. Many learning experiences are random and accidental; however, informal education, although it may flow from chance encounters or fortuitous events, embodies an element of premeditation. Certainly informal educators, like their compatriots operating in schools and colleges, consciously set out to promote learning and impart skills. They are teachers and like all teachers will plan, evaluate, and reflect upon their teaching. Clearly some overlap exists with *experiential learning*, since informal educators may also create opportunities for learning. However, the key difference between the two is that informal educators predominately work via the conversation that emerges from reflection on the daily experiences of the individuals and groups rather than the analysis of experiences initiated by the facilitator and educator (see Warner Weil and McGill 1989).

The first text to deliberately employ the term was *Informal Education* (1946) by Josephine Macalister Brew (1904–1957). However, such essentially unstructured edu-cation, characterized by spontaneity and built upon the interplay inherent in dialogue and conversation, clearly has a long history. Possibly predating the formal variety, unstructured education flourished in ancient Athenian society (Jeffs 2001). There it stood apart from rote learning and instruction as the accepted way whereby individuals acquired social skills, an understanding of the arts, and appreciation of matters philosophical and spiritual.

Although it is important to avoid minimizing the commonalties between teaching in the formal and informal sectors, crucial differences do exist. First, informal educators predominately operate via the mediums of conversation and dialogue. Unlike the formal sector, where the curriculum and syllabus mold the educational encounter, here content emerges from conversational encounters. Informal educators consciously engage in conversation with the purpose of fostering learning, intentionally encouraging others to clarify their thinking, formulate their ideas, and articulate learning needs. The objective is to cultivate dialogue that will enable both parties to learn from and better understand each other (Jeffs and Smith 2005).

Second, informal education is based upon a voluntary relationship. Even within such institutions as prisons or schools, where attendance for one party is compulsory, informal educators strive to ensure those engaging with them do so freely.

Third, informal education requires the practitioner to operate where people are. They need to be "around" and "accessible." Therefore they must either work in settings they do not control, such as schools and the "street," or establish sites, such as settlement houses, youth clubs, and community centers, that provide services, programs, or activities that individuals and groups will seek out. For example, those operating in schools work the public spaces, such as hallways and canteens, in ways that enable students and staff to engage them in conversation (see Hazler 1998). In the clubs, community centers, and settlements, informal educators make time between and in activities for users to engage with them (see Hirsch 2005). They also create social spaces in these buildings where conversation will naturally occur. Those operating on the "street" usually target "hot spots" where, for example, young people or the homeless gather. Irrespective of the environment, informal educators draw upon a repertoire of skills to enable them to make contact and develop relationships. This means they must improvise and think for themselves. To be successful, practitioners must, as Brew (1946) stressed, be interesting and trustworthy people with whom others will freely spend time. Also they must be sensitive to the social and cultural environment they operate within if those they work for are to respect their judgment and opinions. Simply being "around" is never enough.

Overall, what distinguishes informal education is not its role and purpose, as generally these approximate those encountered elsewhere. Rather, it is the location and modus operandi of the educator. Although largely associated with youth work, settlement houses, and community work, informal education has noticeably been adopted as a means of intervention by a wide range of agencies since the 1980s (Smith 1988; Jeffs and Smith 1999). Notably health and criminal justice agencies have looked to informal education as a means of reaching groups and individuals resistant to their message. Sadly, the repertoire of skills developed by informal educators is often employed merely to deliver a packaged message, and the underlying commitment to dialogue and shared learning is set aside. This incorporation of elements of formal practice, notably in the United Kingdom and United States, has led to attempts to create an informal education curriculum and undertake the assessment of learning outcomes from "informal education" encounters (see Ord 2004). Unfortunately such accreditation is based on a profound misunderstanding of the informal education process: a naive assumption that because curriculum-led learning is taking place in clubs and centers, it is not formal education. This view overlooks the reality that formal and informal education can operate side by side yet remain discrete entities. Venue is not the defining characteristic; rather, it is whether or not the intervention is curriculum or dialogically led.

In parts of Europe aspects of informal education are frequently designated *social pedagogy*. The two are not synonymous but share many characteristics and historical antecedents.

SEE ALSO *Education, USA; Knowledge*

BIBLIOGRAPHY

Brew, Josephine Macalister. 1946. *Informal Education: Adventures and Reflections.* London: Faber and Faber.

Hazler, Richard J. 1998. *Helping in the Hallways: Advanced Strategies for Enhancing School Relationships.* Thousand Oaks, CA: Corwin.

Hirsch, Barton J. 2005. *A Place to Call Home: After-School Programs for Urban Youth.* Washington, DC: American Psychological Association.

Jeffs, Tony. 2001. First Lessons: Historical Perspectives on Informal Education. In *Principles and Practice of Informal Education: Learning through Life*, ed. Linda Deer Richardson and Mary Wolfe, 34–51. London: Routledge.

Jeffs, Tony, and Mark K. Smith, eds. 1990. *Using Informal Education: An Alternative to Casework, Teaching, and Control?* Philadelphia and Buckingham, U.K.: Open University Press.

Jeffs, Tony, and Mark K. Smith. 1999. Informal Education and Health Promotion. In *Evidenced-Based Health Promotion*, eds. Elizabeth R. Perkins, Ina Simmett, and Linda Wright, 206–215. Chichester, U.K.: Wiley.

Jeffs, Tony, and Mark K. Smith. 2005. *Informal Education: Conversation, Democracy, and Learning.* Nottingham, U.K.: Education Now.

Ord, Jon. 2004. The Youth Work Curriculum and the Transforming Youth Work Agenda. *Youth and Policy* 83: 43–59.

Smith, Mark. 1988. *Developing Youth Work.* Milton Keynes, U.K.: Open University Press.

Warner Weil, Susan, and Ian McGill. 1989. A Framework for Making Sense of Experiential Learning. In *Making Sense of Experiential Learning: Diversity in Theory and Practice*, eds. Susan Warner Weil and Ian McGill, 3–24. Philadelphia: Open University Press.

Tony Jeffs

EDUCATION, RETURNS TO

There is a strong consensus among economists that education is one of the key determinants of people's earnings. According to the human capital theory, education is an investment that increases the market skills and productivity of individuals who undertake it. Consequently, these individuals earn higher wages in the labor market for their higher skills and productivity. While monetary returns to education take the form of higher earnings that people command in the labor market, there may also be nonmonetary returns since higher education is often associated with psychic gains, such as increased respect from others.

Like any other investment decision, investing in human capital through education entails costs that are borne in the short term with the expectation that benefits will be captured in the long term. Since the returns to education will not accrue for some time, the theory predicts that present-oriented individuals are less likely to invest in education than forward-looking individuals and that younger individuals will be more likely to invest than older individuals.

The question of whether returns to education are high enough to justify the costs of additional education is an important question, not only for individuals but also for policymakers. It is often argued that government policies can improve the economic well-being of the poor by subsidizing their education, offering loans for college students, and imposing minimum education requirements.

It is important to make the distinction between the private and social rate of returns to education. The private rate of returns to education is the increase in the earnings from an additional year of education for an individual who makes the investment decision on education, while the social rate of returns to education measures the increase in national income resulting from the same year of education (Borjas 2004). It is often the social rate of returns to education that provides a basis for government programs, such as scholarships and education loans that are aimed at increasing the levels of education of individuals.

Numerous studies suggest that the rate of returns to education in the United States was around 9 percent in the 1990s (Borjas 2004). The rate of returns to education varies from individual to individual due to differences in age, ability, quality and quantity of education, and socioeconomic status. For example, it is often assumed that more able individuals benefit more from an additional year of education. Also, better-quality education is likely to enhance the productivity of individuals by improving cognitive skills, thereby increasing the rate of returns to education. It is also assumed that the rate of returns to education is a decreasing function of the quantity of education. In other words, the additional earnings generated from an extra year of education are likely to be higher for people with low levels of education than for those with high levels of education.

The rate of returns to education may also vary between individuals from different races, ethnicity, or gender due to discrimination. However, the empirical evidence on this is mixed. On the one hand, studies by Pedro Carneiro, James Heckman, and Edward Vytlacil (2003) and Christopher Taber (2001) show that the return to education is greater for more able individuals. On the other hand, Orley Ashenfelter and Cecelia Rouse (1998) find some evidence that the rate of return may be even higher for individuals coming from more disadvantaged backgrounds, and Lisa Barrow and Cecelia Rouse (2005) find that returns are similar for African Americans, Hispanics, and whites. The large disparity in education levels between different racial and ethnic demographic groups is considered to be a major reason for the observed inequality in the distribution of income and wealth in the United States. While increased educational opportunities for minority groups will certainly help narrow these inequalities, they are likely to be most effective only if coupled with policies that are aimed at eliminating the barriers to equal access to education for these groups.

The typical method for estimating the rate of returns to education requires data on the earnings and levels of education of different individuals, along with estimations of the percentage change in earnings associated with an additional year of education. This formulation is often called the *Mincer earning function*, named after Jacob Mincer (1922–2006), one of the pioneers of modern labor economics.

When estimating the rate of returns to education, it is important to adjust for all other differences in individ-

ual characteristics in the data, such as ability, race, ethnicity, gender, and age. A failure to adjust for all these differences will result in bias in the estimated rate of returns to education. However, the empirical difficulty of appropriately accounting for these differences constitutes an important challenge for researchers studying the returns to education. While characteristics such as age, gender, and race are readily available in most data sets, the ability levels of individuals are seldom observed in these data. It may be true that more able individuals are likely to obtain more years of education than others because it is easier for them to do so. Therefore, these individuals are likely to have higher earnings. However, such individuals may also earn more than others simply because they are more productive regardless of their levels of education. In other words, higher-ability individuals may earn higher wages than lower-ability individuals with equal levels of education. Therefore, a study not taking into account the differences in ability across individuals will result in a biased estimate of the rate of returns to education.

The discussion above assumes that education increases individuals' earnings by raising their productivity. An alternative argument is that education can increase earnings even if it does not make individuals more productive. According to this view, education mainly serves as a signal about the qualifications of the workers to potential employers (Arrow 1973; Spence 1973; Stiglitz 1975). Employers, especially in situations where they cannot easily observe the abilities or productivity of workers, may rely on education as a signaling device in their hiring decisions. As far as the private rate of returns to education is considered, it may not matter whether it is the productivity or the signaling model that represents a correct picture of the education and earnings relationship because education is positively linked to earnings under either scenario. However, if the signaling model is the correct link between education and earnings, society will not benefit from increased education. In this case, the social rate of return to education will be zero.

SEE ALSO *Educational Quality; Human Capital*

BIBLIOGRAPHY

Arrow, Kenneth J. 1973. Higher Education as a Filter. *Journal of Public Economics* 2: 193–216.

Ashenfelter, Orley, and Cecilia Rouse. 1998. Income, Schooling, and Ability: Evidence from a New Sample of Twins. *Quarterly Journal of Economics* 113 (1): 253–284.

Barrow, Lisa, and Cecilia E. Rouse. 2005. Do Returns to Schooling Differ by Race and Ethnicity? Federal Reserve Bank of Chicago Working Paper, WP 2005–02.

Borjas, George. 2004. *Labor Economics.* 3rd ed. New York: McGraw-Hill.

Carneiro, Pedro, James J. Heckman, and Edward Vytlacil. 2003. Understanding What Instrumental Variables Estimate: Estimating Marginal and Average Returns to Education. University of Chicago Working Paper.

Spence, Michael A. 1973. Job Market Signaling. *Quarterly Journal of Economics* 87: 355–374.

Stiglitz, Joseph. 1975. The Theory of Screening, Education, and Distribution of Income. *American Economic Review* 65: 283–300.

Taber, Christopher. 2001. The Rising College Premium in the Eighties: Return to College or Return to Unobserved Ability? *Review of Economic Studies* 68 (3): 665–691.

Erdal Tekin

EDUCATION, UNEQUAL

In the social sciences, education is recognized as playing a central role in maintaining and reproducing modern systems of inequality. Hierarchies of race, class, and gender are understood to be reflected in both the content of educational offerings and in the context in which schooling is provided. As such, attempts to address patterns of social inequality have focused on improving educational access and conditions for various populations. In the case of the twentieth-century United States, efforts to equalize access to schooling along lines of race and class have drawn heavily upon the insights of American social scientists, while responding to the demands of both liberal and conservative political constituencies.

Despite residing in communities where they often represented significant parts of the population, blacks and other racialized minorities often possessed little or no ability to control their educational destinies—not in choice of curricula, the hiring and firing of teachers, nor the availability of school facilities or the length of the school term. Long practiced by custom in many localities and written into state constitutions in the decades following the American Civil War, racial segregation in schools was given legal mandate in the U.S. Supreme Court's ruling in *Plessy v. Ferguson* (1896), out of which came the doctrine "separate but equal," which allowed states effectively to separate access to educational resources on the basis of race as long as those provided to each racial group were equal. After some sixty years of state-mandated racial segregation in education, during which blacks and other minority populations lagged behind whites on most indicators of educational progress, the U.S. Supreme Court, heavily influenced by the findings of social scientists, decided unanimously in *Brown v. Board of Education of Topeka, Kansas* (1954) that the practice of segregated schooling was not only unconstitutional but also inherently damaging to children, with dire effects for society as a whole. While the *Brown* decision has generally been viewed as a landmark development in the struggle to dismantle racial inequality in American education and society at large, it was in many ways limited. The court's rulings were unendorsed, loosely defined, and, by some accounts, underfunded as a federal mandate for public schools. Institutionalized resistance by southern states prevented full implementation of the court's rulings until 1968, when schools in the rural South were given a mandate that they must desegregate in order to be in compliance with federal law. Additionally, because of the Court's focus on de jure segregation common in the South, the de facto segregation that had been practiced in the northeastern and midwestern states remained largely intact until the 1970s, when concerns were expressed about the education of minority schoolchildren in such cities as Pasadena, Chicago, San Francisco, and Boston.

The *Brown* ruling and the subsequent reexaminations of the American educational system it inspired called attention to the complex intersections of race and class in American education and their effects on academic achievement. The Elementary and Secondary Education Act of 1965, which provided additional federal monies to schools with a significant proportion of poor or disadvantaged students, grew out of the concerns expressed in *Brown*. Perhaps one of the most influential works of social science research in the immediate post-*Brown* era was James Coleman's *Equality of Educational Opportunity* (1966), sponsored by the U.S. Department of Health, Education, and Welfare and commonly referred to as the Coleman Report. The study's specific purpose was to evaluate indicators of educational opportunity among white and minority students (blacks, Puerto Ricans, Mexican Americans, Asian Americans, and Native Americans) by assessing educational quality in terms of the availability of curricula, school facilities, academic practices, and the academic characteristics of teachers and student bodies in schools. Among Coleman's chief findings were that while persistent and unequal separation by race was found to be detrimental as per the Supreme Court's ruling in *Brown*, it was the combination of the socioeconomic composition of the school, the familial and socioeconomic background of the students, and the nature of their peer groups that accounted for the majority of the differences observed in academic achievement between white and minority schoolchildren. Racial integration alone, Coleman and his associates concluded, could not improve the academic performance of poor minority children.

In a context where explanations for patterns of social inequality favored concepts of "cultural deprivation" among poor and minority communities, the report's widely cited findings proved to be controversial. Commentators recognized that schools in and of themselves were limited in their power to change society at large. Conservative critics of educational reform argued that social science research had justified their resistance to increased educational spending for underachieving populations. They argued that this underachievement was the result of a "cultural mismatch" between schools and targeted populations. Others, such as Jencks et al. (1972), noted that only by addressing the underlying economic causes of race and class inequality could patterns in education be remedied. Ultimately, federal educational policies continued to favor funding compensatory programs such as Head Start and remedies such as busing under the assumption that they would address the twin problems of differentials in academic performance and differential access to educational resources among minority and poor schoolchildren. In addition to encountering resistance from various segments of the population, these programs received mixed reviews of their long-term effectiveness, and the persistence of the gap in educational achievement for much of the 1970s continued to trouble reformers and policymakers. This period witnessed a resurgence of Marxian analyses of education, which focused on the role of schools in maintaining the class structure of capitalist societies. Neo-Marxist works contend that educational systems not only expand in response to economic shifts but also chiefly serve to reproduce a large class of workers by stressing obedience to authority and contentment with one's place in the system. Critiquing this view as a "black box" perspective in which class is assumed to be reproduced through schooling, cultural sociologists such as Willis, Bourdieu, McLeod, and Oakes further elaborated on this work by examining strategies of social reproduction as they take place in everyday school interactions. These include academic sorting, interactions between students and school personnel, interactions among peers, and the general culture of the school.

The 1980s marked what some consider the end of "liberal hegemony" in American education and ushered in the neoconservative turn in educational reform. The publication of *A Nation at Risk*, which cited generally lower rates of performance among American schoolchildren and a persistent achievement gap by race and class as proof the failure of liberal reform, served as a manifesto for conservative reformers. Influenced by the findings of the Coleman Report and other studies that took a dim view of compensatory education, neoconservative reformers sought to remedy race and class achievement gaps through what they described as a focus on "standards and accountability" and an application of market forces to education. Under the administrations of Ronald Reagan and George H. W. Bush, federal support for compensatory educational reforms diminished drastically and school districts were released from court-imposed plans for achieving racial balance without, as Orfield notes, having done so. Rather than continuing to search for solutions for failing schools through expensive government programs, the parents of poor and minority schoolchildren were encouraged to exercise their rights as consumers of public education and to improve their educational prospects by leaving failing schools and choosing those schools (whether public, private, or charter) with demonstrated levels of achievement.

The neoconservative influence in educational reform continued under the Clinton administration, during which the Improving America's Schools Act (Public Law 89-10) was passed. While reauthorizing the Elementary and Secondary Schools Act of 1965, the 1994 act also endorsed the establishment of charter schools as a means of improving teaching and student performance. This pattern of reform greatly expanded under the presidency of George W. Bush in the form of the No Child Left Behind Act (Public Law 107-110). Signed into law by the Bush administration in 2002, NCLB's expressed goal was to close the persistent race and class gap in educational achievement. While supporters of the act pointed to the implementation of much needed standards and timelines for schools to measure progress and make improvements and the ability of parents to choose better schools for their children, critics maintained that the act severely limited the means by which schools can effect those improvements. Rather than increasing the amount of federal support for public education, the act applies strict legislative guidelines for the use of Title I funds that limit curricular innovation in favor of an emphasis on "basic" subjects such as reading and mathematics, a mandate that schools meet state-determined measures of annual yearly progress, and, as a means of assessing student performance, the use of high-stakes standardized testing on which poor and minority students typically score lower. Many schools argue that by imposing a rigid framework and encouraging poor and minority parents to abandon neighborhood schools for better equipped, higher-scoring schools in affluent neighborhoods, the achievement gap will persist by encouraging individual rather than group mobility.

The American educational system's foundations as an unequal system rooted in hierarchies of race and class have both inspired and limited attempts at reform that seek to remedy the long-term effects of these inequalities. Over the course of the twentieth century, social scientific considerations of educational inequality have shifted from a belief that schools are the sources of social difference with the capacity to fundamentally change society to the more critical understanding that schools have powerful effects in society but are limited in their ability to effect change through social engineering. The current body of social science literature on education focuses on the role that schools played in reinforcing and legitimizing hierarchies of race and class through a variety of means, including, but not limited to, curricular choices, school cultures, patterns of organization, and policies governing school funding.

SEE ALSO Brown v. Board of Education, *1954;* Brown v. Board of Education, *1955; Class; Cultural Capital; Desegregation, School; Education, USA; Equal Opportunity; Equality; Hierarchy; Inequality, Racial; Jencks, Christopher; Neoconservatism; Racism; Schooling in the USA; Segregation, School; Stratification*

BIBLIOGRAPHY

Bourdieu, Pierre, and Jean-Claude Passeron. 1990. *Reproduction in Education, Society, and Culture.* Beverly Hills, CA: Sage.

Bowles, Samuel, and Herbert Gintis. 1976. *Schooling in Capitalist America: Educational Reform and the Contradictions of Economic Life.* New York: Basic Books.

Coleman, James, Ernest Q. Campbell, and Carol J. Hobson. 1966. *Equality of Educational Opportunity.* Washington, DC: U.S. Department of Health, Education, and Welfare.

Jencks, Christopher, et al. 1972. *Inequality: A Reassessment of the Effect of Family and Schooling in America.* New York: Basic Books.

McLeod, Jay. 1987. *Ain't No Makin' It: Leveled Aspirations in a Low-Income Neighborhood.* Boulder, CO: Westview Press.

Oakes, Jeannie. 2005. *Keeping Track: How Schools Structure Inequality.* New Haven, CT: Yale University Press.

Orfield, Gary, and Susan Eaton. 1997. *Dismantling Desegregation: The Quiet Reversal of* Brown v. Board of Education. New York: The New Press.

Patterson, James T. 2001. Brown v. Board of Education*: A Civil Rights Milestone and Its Troubled Legacy.* New York and London: Oxford University Press.

Peterson, Paul E., and Martin R. West, eds. 2003. *No Child Left Behind? The Politics and Practice of School Accountability.* Washington, DC: Brookings Institution Press.

United States National Commission on Excellence in Education. 1983. *A Nation at Risk: The Imperative for Educational Reform.* Washington, DC: U.S. Department of Education.

Willis, Paul E. 1981. *Learning to Labor: How Working Class Kids Get Working Class Jobs.* New York: Columbia University Press.

Joseph O. Jewell

EDUCATION, USA

The most universally recognized function of schools is to impart knowledge and skills that will enable the learner to participate successfully in a society's institution (Epps 1995). As early as the 1920s, social policy became directed toward using elementary education to further children's social and emotional adjustment outside of the home. Recognizing that educational training in the early years of human development was essential for enhancing cognitive skills, reinforcing social norms, and preparing youth for participation in the labor market as adults, educational policy in general, and the public school system in particular, aimed to train youth to become productive citizens.

During the early part of the twentieth century, various administrative progressives, philanthropic associations, and civil rights organizations (to a lesser degree) played an integral role in shaping educational opportunities. The chief architects of educational policy were an elite group of white men that consisted of city superintendents, education professors, state and federal officers, leaders in professional organizations (i.e., the National Education Association), and foundation officials (Tyack and Cuban 1995). These men provided the blueprint for an educational institution mandating criteria for schooling, differentiating curricula according to students' career paths, standardizing the structure of schools in order to provide uniform staffing and social and health services, and overseeing the regulation of educational practices. Moreover, the Carnegie and Rockefeller foundations, the General Education Board (which helped to develop black education in the Jim Crow South), and various civil rights organizations (i.e., the National Association for the Advancement of Colored People) provided financial support, developed curriculum, and trained educators with the hopes of creating an equitable educational system. Although the institution of education aimed to provide youth with a solid foundation for the future, the separation of blacks and whites into different and inherently unequal educational institutions created a system that reflected economic and social inequalities.

To the creators of these institutions, educational attainment was considered the panacea for social inequality. However, due to the racial order and quality of schools, blacks lagged behind whites on all indicators of performance. Research providing explanations for these differences was biologically deterministic. Critical studies that addressed educational inequalities and the problem of race/ethnicity coincided with the racial order; variations in performance were attributed to innate differences in cognitive ability.

From the 1920s to the 1950s, the educational opportunities of blacks were shaped by popular discourse characterizing blacks as intellectually inferior. The genetic interpretation of race and research on the inheritability of intelligence influenced the types of learning materials afforded to segregated schools and shaped conclusions about black youth (Anderson 1988). Moreover, Jim Crow education was designed, implemented, and upheld by the state. As a result, for over thirty years, the majority of blacks attended substandard schools, primarily in rural areas or in the South, which often lacked the most basic aids for learning such as textbooks, slates and chalk, desks, had relatively small classes, and were taught by instructors without postsecondary training (Tyack and Cuban 1995).

Some early sociological studies argued that the various components of the educational system were disconnected and that the system could not cure the social ills of society as originally believed. Willard Waller (1932) conceptualized schools as unstable social systems in which different components—administrators, teachers, parents, students, and community groups—all with competing interests, vie for power and authority. Scholars did not address the question of how the convoluted structures of segregated schools further increased social inequality for black students or attempted to understand why a significant proportion of this population remained poor and socially immobile. The first sociologist to conceptualize a theoretical framework that attempted to solve the "race problem" was Robert Park (1950), who examined how ethnic groups acculturate into American society through contact, competition, accommodation, and eventual assimilation. Park's work, however, focused solely on white ethnic groups (i.e., Irish or German immigrants), and the assimilation of blacks and the racial problems that thwarted their progress were not addressed. At the same time, various contemporary empirical studies of educational achievement and motivation reinforced the notion that better performers had higher drives, and implied that racial variations in performance resulted from a lack of motivation on the part of black students.

Not until school segregation was challenged by the landmark case *Brown vs. Board of Education* (1954) was attention given to the detrimental effects of separate and unequal educational institutions on the academic achievement of black students. This case, which desegregated K–12 education, forced empirical studies to look toward structural inequalities as the culprit for disparities in performance, as opposed to lack of motivation or biologically deterministic explanations. Empirical studies provided evidence that racial/ethnic differences in achievement were associated with differences in socioeconomic status (Rosen 1959).

During the 1960s civil unrest, government emphasis on alleviating poverty, and black political mobilization brought new attention to the ways in which inequality undermined educational attainment for blacks. As part of national efforts to alleviate poverty, President Lyndon B. Johnson created Title I programs targeting funds to students from low-income families to prevent poverty from restricting school opportunities and academic achievement. Also, the 1965 civil rights act, executive order 11246, called for vigorous, proactive steps, later termed *affirmative action*, to broaden and increase access to higher education for previously excluded and underrepresented groups (Allen et al. 2002).

In addition to policies mandated to improve educational access and quality, research studies examining racial differences in academic performance received much funding. Among several empirical studies investigating the relationship between inequality and educational attainment, a 1966 report by James S. Coleman was the most influential. It demonstrated that family background had a significant effect on academic achievement and that schools played a role in creating and sustaining student differences in achievement. Moreover, the Moynahan Report (1965) presented a cultural argument for educational inequality that did not rest on IQ differences but on the attitudes, time perspectives, family patterns, and values of the poor. Samuel Bowles and Herbert Gintis (1976) provided further evidence that poor school quality was a predictor of limited economic success and viewed schools as an instrument used by the dominant class to maintain the status quo.

Contrary to earlier studies of educational attainment that emphasized biologically deterministic explanations for performance, educational research in the 1970s and 1980s took a more holistic and liberal approach. Scholars consistently showed that race and ethnicity, along with socioeconomic status, were significant determinants of educational and occupational success; that stratification processes worked differently for students from various backgrounds; and that schools could depress the relationship between background and occupational attainment by providing more equal access to educational resources and training (Hallinan 2000). Much educational research since the 1980s has sought to identify the problems associated with educational inequality and outcomes and has focused on implementing strategies to decrease racial gaps in academic achievement. However, some argue that the approaches employed have actually increased educational disparities rather than alleviating them.

PRESENT-DAY PROBLEMS AND PROSPECTS

Despite various policies aimed at reducing educational inequality, such as the *Brown* decision of 1954, educational opportunity programs created in 1965, and Affirmative Action of 1964, the educational system at the start of the twenty-first century—more than forty years after the civil rights movement began—still remains segregated by socioeconomic status (SES) and race/ethnicity. For students that come from more affluent families with high levels of social capital, the educational system serves to adequately prepare them for competitive jobs in the labor market. Conversely, for students with low SES and limited resources, the educational system has failed to pro-

Percent distribution of students across NAEP mathematics achievement levels, by race/ethnicity and grade: 2003

Level	White, non-Hispanic	Black, non-Hispanic	Hispanic	Asian/Pacific Islander	American Indian/ Alaska Native
4th grade					
Below basic	13	46	38	13	36
At or above basic	87	54	62	87	64
At or above proficient	43	10	16	48	17
8th grade					
Below basic	20	61	52	22	48
At or above basic	80	39	48	78	52
At or above proficient	37	7	12	43	15

SOURCE: U.S. Department of Education, National Center for Education Statistics, National Assessment of Educational Progress (NAEP), 2003 Mathematics Assessments.

Table 1

vide the needed foundation and skills to sustain an adequate lifestyle. Most importantly, minority students—namely, blacks and Hispanics—are overwhelmingly overrepresented in the lower SES category and attending schools that are substandard in terms of instruction, curricula, socialization practices, preparation for the job market, and providing equal access to higher education opportunities.

Disparities in educational achievement are evident in the early years of primary school, where blacks and Hispanics lag behind whites and Asians on several indicators of educational achievement. Table 1 illustrates the percent distribution by race and ethnicity of mathematics achievement levels for a representative sample of students taking the National Assessment of Educational Progress (NAEP) exam in 2003. As can be seen, 46 percent of black and 38 percent of Hispanics performed below the

basic levels of achievement for fourth graders. Moreover, differences in achievement levels worsen as students advance to higher grades (as measured by the performance of eighth graders).

Table 2 illustrates the percent distribution by race and ethnicity of achievement levels on reading comprehension tests for a representative sample of students taking the NAEP in 2003. Results show that 60 percent of blacks and 56 percent of Hispanics are below basic fourth-grade reading levels compared to 25 percent of whites. Although performance in reading improves for blacks and Hispanics by the eighth grade, disparities in performance between racial groups remain constant. Contemporary research examining racial differences in educational achievement in primary and secondary education indicates that the gap continues to widen as students advance to higher educational levels (Steele 1997).

Percent distribution of students across NAEP reading achievement levels, by race/ethnicity and grade: 2003

Level	White, non-Hispanic	Black, non-Hispanic	Hispanic	Asian/Pacific Islander	American Indian/ Alaska Native
4th grade					
Below basic	25	60	56	30	53
At or above basic	75	40	44	70	47
At or above proficient	41	13	15	38	16
8th grade					
Below basic	17	46	44	21	43
At or above basic	83	54	56	79	57
At or above proficient	41	13	15	40	17

SOURCE: U.S. Department of Education, National Center for Education Statistics, National Assessment of Educational Progress (NAEP), 2003 Reading Assessment.

Table 2

The next section examines some of the structural obstacles that limit educational attainment for minority students (i.e., blacks and Hispanics) and may account for racial/ethnic variations in academic performance.

RESIDENTIAL SEGREGATION, INSTITUTIONAL INEQUALITY, AND EDUCATIONAL OPPORTUNITIES

Due to the history of racial stratification in the United States, blacks and whites reside in neighborhoods that are economically, socially, and racially distinct from one another (Jargowsky 1996; Massey and Denton 1996; Massey 2004). Although structural barriers that prohibited residential mobility for minorities have been removed in the post–civil rights era, the historical vestiges of exclusionary practices that were and continue to be pervasive have implications for the racial formation of more recent residential patterns. As a result, minority integration into diverse neighborhoods has been slow to non-existent. Research has shown that blacks remain the most segregated racial group (Massey and Denton 1992), even when factors such as neighborhood preferences (Farley et al 1978; Zubrinsky and Bobo 1996), racial attitudes and stereotyping, and preferred educational level of neighbors (Benabou 1992; Cutler and Glaeser 1997) are taken into account. Residential patterns for Hispanic families are very similar to those of blacks.

Residential segregation is a mechanism that has historically perpetuated systemic inequality and is mainly responsible for inequality in primary and secondary education. Two-thirds of urban blacks live under conditions of high segregation and two-thirds attend minority-dominant public schools (Massey 2006). Considerable research documents the disadvantaged conditions experienced by blacks in segregated schools, such as limited spending on students and curricula, and a lack of qualified teachers (Anderson and Byrne 2004). Since American schools are funded by local property taxes, the wealthiest districts spend as much as three times per-pupil compared to the most economically disadvantaged districts (Condron and Roscigno 2003). Although schools that are located in lower-SES communities may receive additional funds from federal Title I programs, these schools normally spend a sizeable majority of their budgets on repairs, maintenance, and structural improvement of school buildings. Compared to low-SES segregated schools that primarily educate black and Hispanic students, high-SES schools that are predominantly white spend more on instructional materials and provide higher pay for teachers. As a result, low performing students are less likely to get placed into vocational tracks, are better prepared for postsecondary education, and receive the skills necessary to acquire competitive jobs. Consequently, for minority students that attend public schools in residentially segregated neighborhoods, institutional quality has negative implications for educational outcomes. Teachers' expectations are lower, and minority students are more likely to be placed in lower tracks (vocational vs. honors/college preparatory) by their instructors, more likely to have lower reading and math scores compared to the national average, and are less likely to attend four-year colleges and universities (Oaks and Guiton 1995; Allen et al. 2001; Dinwiddie and Allen 2003). Recent sociological research has shown that improved education (as a result of money spent on curricula, the hiring of qualified teachers, and providing access to resources) is a strong predictor of academic achievement, which contradicts culturally deterministic theories that claim minorities do not value education (e.g., the popular "acting white assumption").

School districts and the federal government have recognized that public schools provide different levels of educational preparation for their students. Therefore, in an effort to provide options, various voucher systems and school-choice policies have given parents the opportunity to take advantage of schools that are known to better educate children (i.e., magnet and charter schools). Magnet-school programs allow public school students to leave their neighborhood schools to attend specialized institutions that offer unique curriculums. Thirty-four percent of the nation's school districts have magnet-school programs, making magnet-school choice one of the most widely used forms of school choice in the country (Saporito 2003). However, students must qualify based on test scores, grades, behavior, and other criteria that are evaluated by teachers from their neighborhood schools. A problem with magnet schools and the voucher system is that there are many more applicants than openings and school districts are prohibited from taking race or ethnicity into account when deciding which students to admit.

CURRENT POLICY ADDRESSING EDUCATIONAL INEQUALITY

Educational reforms have been the preferred methods of addressing educational inequalities (Tyack and Cuban 1995). One contemporary approach that has received much criticism is No Child Left Behind (NCLB), President George W. Bush's effort to renew the Elementary and Secondary Education Act of 1965. The NCLB law requires yearly standardized testing of students from kindergarten to eighth grade in reading, language, and math and holds schools accountable for meeting state and district goals. It also requires schools that have historically underperformed and receive federal Title I funds to submit progress reports yearly. In addition, NCLB provides students who attend low-performing schools the choice of transferring to a different public school in their district or a charter school if their public school fails to meet district or federal educational mandates.

Although the main objective of NCLB is to improve educational quality through test-based accountability and to provide students flexibility in terms of educational choice, it has presented more problems than solutions. For example, NCLB does not address the issue of institutional inequality that contributes to student underperformance. Moreover, as a result of the pressure to improve student test scores, curricula have become centered around enhancing test-taking skills instead of learning acquisition. Another problem with a system of accountability based on test score performance is that questions asked on standardized tests are racially and culturally biased. This places an already vulnerable student population at risk of underperforming, because the educational experiences of black and Hispanic students vastly differ from those of white and Asian students from more affluent schools (Steele 1992; Horn 2005). Standardized tests are good measures of the skills obtained from schooling, so if lower-SES students are less likely to receive adequate levels of instruction compared to their more privileged peers, it should come as no surprise that the majority of low-SES students have trouble meeting federal, state, and district expectations.

Achievement on standardized tests is used to determine advancement to the next grade, high school graduation, and admission to college. In most states, students attending public schools are required to take high school exit exams in order to receive their diplomas. For example, the California High School Exit Examination, enacted as state law in 2006, was designed to ensure that all high school graduates have received an adequate foundation in English-language arts and mathematics, based on state standards. According to the California Department of Education (2006), by the end of eleventh grade white students had the highest pass rate on the English-language arts portion of the exam at 96 percent, and Hispanic and black students had the lowest at 83 percent. Also, by the end of eleventh grade Asian students had the highest passing rate in mathematics at 97 percent and African American students had the lowest at 76 percent. Test outcomes from this diverse state suggest that exit exams can increase the drop-out rate and limit degree attainment for minority students. Results also provide an indication of how marginalized students will perform nationally once other states implement exit exams as a main criteria for graduation.

Preparation for high school exit exams and earned grades are directly associated with performance on the Scholastic Aptitude Test (SAT) used for postsecondary admission. National mean SAT scores disaggregated by race and ethnicity show disparities in verbal and math

Percent of people aged 18 to 24 who completed four or more years of high school in 1993–2004, by race									
	White			**Black**			**Hispanic**		
Year	**Both**	**M**	**F**	**Both**	**M**	**F**	**Both**	**M**	**F**
2004	82.0	81.0	85.4	77.4	72.4	81.8	65.6	60.3	71.8
2003	83.3	80.5	86.1	76.8	73.9	79.5	65.1	60.9	69.9
2002	82.0	79.4	84.7	77.5	73.5	81.0	62.6	57.7	68.6
2001	81.2	78.5	83.9	77.0	70.8	82.4	62.0	56.1	68.6
2000	82.4	80.1	84.7	77.0	73.7	79.9	59.6	54.0	65.7
1999	81.7	79.6	83.9	76.1	73.9	77.9	58.8	54.9	63.0
1998	81.6	78.8	84.5	73.4	67.5	78.4	58.5	54.3	66.0
1997	82.7	80.6	84.8	74.7	71.4	77.5	62.0	58.9	65.7
1996	82.3	80.8	83.9	75.3	71.3	78.7	57.5	54.8	60.6
1995	81.9	80.2	83.7	76.9	75.1	78.4	58.6	58.0	59.6
1994	82.6	80.7	84.6	77.0	73.7	80.0	56.6	53.8	59.8
1993	83.4	81.5	85.2	74.8	72.8	76.7	65.6	60.3	71.8

SOURCE: U.S. Census Bureau 2006.

Table 3

scores. Most recent data from 2002 show that white and Asian students had the top scores at 1060 and 1070, respectively, whereas Hispanics averaged 903 and blacks were at the bottom at 857 (College Board 2002). Racial and ethnic variation in grades parallels that of test scores. Most recent national data reporting mean grade-point averages (GPA) for high school twelfth graders indicates that blacks are the lowest at 2.63 compared to 2.80 for Hispanics, 3.01 for whites, and 3.20 for Asian/Pacific Islanders (U.S. Department of Education 2000). Many contend the underrepresentation of minorities in colleges and universities is a direct result of low GPA and SAT scores, poor preparation for college-level work, and limited access to postsecondary education.

THE SPILL-OVER EFFECT: DISPARITIES IN HIGHER EDUCATION AND LABOR MARKET PARTICIPATION

The differing school environments that condition disparities in educational attainment for minorities have implications for the persistence of inequality that has consequential and enduring effects on higher education and labor market participation. Individuals with higher education degrees are more likely to have better paying positions, job security, and wealth compared to individuals with low levels of schooling (Mare 1995). Table 3 shows the percent distribution of white, black, and Hispanic students between the ages of eighteen and twenty-four who completed high school between 1993 and 2004. As can be seen, the distribution of high school diplomas varies: Whites had the highest graduation rate at 82 percent, Hispanics had substantially the lowest at 71

Percent of people aged 18–24 who enrolled in college in 1993–2004, by race

Year	White			Black			Hispanic		
	Both	M	F	Both	M	F	Both	M	F
2004	41.7	38.4	—	31.8	26.5	36.6	24.7	21.7	29.4
2003	41.6	38.5	44.5	32.3	28.2	36.0	23.5	18.3	24.4
2002	40.9	38.9	42.8	31.9	26.3	36.9	19.9	16.2	25.5
2001	39.3	37.1	41.4	31.2	26.4	35.4	21.1	17.3	25.4
2000	38.7	36.2	41.3	30.5	25.1	35.2	21.7	18.5	21.8
1999	39.4	38.3	40.6	30.4	28.9	31.6	18.7	15.8	24.9
1998	40.6	39.4	41.9	29.8	26.1	32.9	20.4	16.4	26.1
1997	40.6	39.3	41.9	29.8	25.4	33.7	22.4	19.2	24.0
1996	39.5	38.3	40.6	27.4	25.7	28.8	20.1	16.5	22.9
1995	37.9	37.0	38.8	27.5	26.0	28.7	20.7	18.7	21.5
1994	38.1	37.0	39.2	27.7	25.6	29.5	18.8	16.5	23.6
1993	36.8	36.6	37.1	24.5	22.8	26.1	21.6	19.8	—

SOURCE: U.S. Census Bureau 2006.

Table 4

persist to college directly after high school. This finding is significant considering that blacks are 12.3 and Hispanics are 12.5 percent of the U.S. population, respectively (U.S. Census 2002).

For minority students who do pursue university degrees, their educational experiences, grades and graduation rates are much lower compared to white and Asian students. In fact, once in college minority students receive grades that are on average half a letter below those of their white classmates (Steele 1992). Racism, financial constraints, lack of preparation for college-level work, few opportunity programs on campus that would help facilitate the adjustment to rigorous academic work for minority students, and slower time to degree rates are among the factors that explain college outcomes for minority students. Research has shown that minority students experience additional constraints that can negatively affect academic achievement.

For example, in a study of college students attending selective colleges and universities, Camille Charles, Gniesha Dinwiddie, and Douglas Massey (2004) found that for high-achieving black and Hispanic students from residentially segregated neighborhoods, college-related, economic and family social stress negatively produced a drop in academic performance and levels of satisfaction with college. Although minority students work hard academically to attend and succeed in college, there are additional stressors and constraints that substantially and negatively impede their educational progression.

Failure to obtain a high school diploma or college degree has direct implications on earning potential for minority youth who go directly into the labor market. Table 5 illustrates mean yearly earnings of workers eighteen years and older between the years of 1993 and 2003,

percent, and blacks were in between at 81 percent. Although the data is not disaggregated by geographic region, gross disparities in high school degree attainment are apparent. To show the negative effects of differentials in high school completion for postsecondary education, Table 4 illustrates the percent distribution by race of high school graduates between the ages of eighteen and twenty-four who enrolled in colleges and universities between 1993 and 2004. Comparing enrollment rates for 2004, for example, the table illustrates that 41 percent of whites, 31 percent of blacks, and 24 percent of Hispanics were enrolled at postsecondary institutions. What is most astonishing about these results is that the majority of blacks (69 percent) and Hispanics (76 percent) did not

Mean earnings of workers 18 years or older, by level of educational attainment

Year	White			African American/Black			Hispanic		
	None	H.S.	B.A.	None	H.S.	B.A.	None	H.S.	B.A.
2003	19,110	28,708	52,259	16,201	23,777	42,968	18,349	23,472	43,676
2002	19,264	28,145	52,479	16,516	22,823	42,285	18,981	24,163	40,949
2001	19,120	27,700	51,631	17,248	21,743	40,165	18,334	22,866	40,586
2000	18,285	26,444	50,969	15,201	21,789	41,513	17,156	22,009	44,661
1999	16,623	25,270	46,894	13,569	20,991	37,422	16,106	20,704	36,212
1998	16,474	24,409	44,852	13,672	19,236	36,373	15,832	20,978	35,014
1997	16,596	23,618	41,439	13,185	18,980	32,062	15,069	19,558	33,465
1996	15,358	22,782	38,936	13,110	18,722	31,955	13,287	18,528	32,955
1995	14,234	22,154	37,711	12,956	17,072	29,666	13,068	18,333	30,602
1994	13,941	20,911	37,996	12,705	16,446	30,938	13,733	17,323	29,165
1993	13,171	19,918	35,846	11,065	16,122	29,953	11,852	16,591	30,359

SOURCE: U.S. Census Bureau, Current Population Survey.

Table 5

differentiated by level of educational attainment. The data illustrate that in 1993 mean earnings for blacks and Hispanics were similar for individuals without a high school diploma. It is not until 2003 that blacks without a high school diploma have the lowest mean earnings per year, compared to Hispanics and whites without a diploma. If we look at earnings for individuals with high school diplomas in 1993, blacks and Hispanics have similar earnings; blacks and Hispanics, however, made roughly $3,000 less than whites with the same level of educational attainment. On the other side, for those with college degrees, whites made $5,000 more on average compared to minorities in 1993. Moreover, in 2003 disparities in mean earnings by level of educational attainment are more pervasive. Whites with bachelor degrees, on average, made $10,000 more than minorities with bachelor degrees. Although minorities on average earn less than whites with similar working experience and degree attainment, having a college degree substantially increases earning potential for everyone, particularly blacks and Hispanics.

CONCLUSION

The adverse effects of inequality have long-term implications for educational opportunities and earning potential, particularly for racial/ethnic minorities. Returning to the original question of whether education improves life chances or reinforces social inequality, from the evidence provided it is apparent that educational disadvantages experienced by racial/ethnic groups have snowball effects. Most importantly, laws such as NCLB, school voucher policies, the increase in the use of standardized testing as indictors of determinants for persistence, and various school accountability mechanisms are very limited in scope. For example, NCLB is not intended to produce equal segregated schools, but to fix a macro problem with micro methodologies. Moreover, the impact of residential segregation on primary, secondary, and postsecondary educational outcomes speaks volumes about the strong negative influence of systemic racism, which has effects that endure long after minority students have left the educational system.

As the demographics of the United States change, educational policy will need to take a more progressive approach to alleviating racial/ethnic disparities in educational outcomes. At the present time, the Hispanic population is growing and is fast becoming more segregated compared to blacks. Moreover, due to the failure of social policy in taking an active role in desegregating the public educational system, public schools are becoming "resegregated" (Orfield 1999), where gaps in achievement are once again widening, and classrooms are still overwhelmingly racially homogenous. Overall, the institutional inequalities that condition racial/ethnic variations in educational outcomes must first receive more attention if the federal government and policymakers are to deliver what they promise.

SEE ALSO *Education, Unequal; Educational Quality; Honor Rolls; Mobility; Schooling in the USA; Tracking in Schools*

BIBLIOGRAPHY

Allen, Walter R., Marguerite Bonous-Hammarth, and Robert Teranishi. 2001. *Stony the Road We Trod: African American Access and Success in California Higher Education.* Los Angeles: CHOICES Project, University of California, Los Angeles.

Allen, Walter R., Robert Teranishi, Gniesha Dinwiddie, and Gloria Gonzalez. 2002. Knocking at Freedom's Door: Race, Equity, and Affirmative Action in U.S. Higher Education. *Journal of Public Health Policy* 23 (4): 440–452.

Anderson, James D. 1988. *The Education of Blacks in the South, 1860–1935.* Chapel Hill: University of North Carolina Press.

Anderson, James D., and Dara N. Byrne. 2004. *The Unfinished Agenda of* Brown v. Board of Education. New York: Wiley.

Bowles, Samuel, and Herbert Gintis. 1976. *Schooling in Capitalist America: Educational Reform and the Contradictions of Economic Life.* New York: Basic Books.

California Department of Education. 2006. *2005–2006 California High School Exit Examination (CAHSEE): Summary of Results.* http://www.cde.ca.gov/ta/tg/hs.

Charles, Camille Z., Gniesha Dinwiddie, and Douglas S. Massey. 2004. The Continuing Consequences of Segregation: Family Stress and College Academic Performance. *Social Science Quarterly* 85 (5): 1353–1373.

Coleman, James S. 1968. The Concept of Equality of Educational Opportunity. *Harvard Educational Review* 38 (1): 7–22.

College Board. 2002. *Profile of College Bound Seniors National Report.* National Education Statistics and Other Equity Indicators. http://www.maec.org/natstats.html.

Condron, Dennis J., and Vincent J. Roscigno. 2003. Disparities Within: Unequal Spending and Achievement in an Urban School District. *Sociology of Education* 76 (1): 18–36.

Cutler, David M., and Edward L. Glaeser. 1997. Are Ghettos Good or Bad? *Quarterly Journal of Economics* 112 (3): 827–872.

Dinwiddie, Gniesha, and Walter Allen. 2003. Two Steps Forward, Three Steps Back: Campus Climate, Gender, and African American Representation in Higher Education. In *Surmounting All Odds: Education, Opportunity, and Society in the New Millennium,* eds. Carol Camp Yeakey and Ronald D. Henderson, 563–594. Greenwich, CT: Information Age Publishing.

Epps, Edgar G. 1995. Race, Class, and Educational Opportunity: Trends in the Sociology of Education. *Sociological Forum* 10 (4): 593–608.

Farley, Reynolds, Howard Schuman, Suzanne Bianchi, Diane Colasanto, and Shirley Hatchett. 1978. Chocolate City,

Vanilla Suburbs: Will the Trend toward Racially Separate Communities Continue? *Social Science Research* 7 (4): 319–344.

Hallinan, Maureen, T. 2000. On the Linkages between Sociology of Race and Ethnicity and Sociology of Education. In *Handbook of the Sociology of Education*, ed. Maureen T. Hallinan, 65–84. New York: Plenum Publishers.

Horn, Catherine. 2005. Standardized Assessments and the Flow of Students into the College Admission Pool. *Education Policy* 19 (2): 331–348.

Jargowsky, Paul A. 1996. Take the Money and Run: Economic Segregation in U.S. Metropolitan Areas. *American Sociological Review* 61 (6): 984–998.

Mare, Robert D. 1995. Changes in Educational Attainment and School Enrollment. In *State of the Union: America in the 1990s*, vol. 2, ed. Reynolds Farley, 155–213. New York: Russell Sage Foundation.

Massey, Douglas S. 2006. Social Background and Academic Performance Differentials: White and Minority Students at Selective Colleges. *American Law and Economics Review* 8 (2): 390–409.

Massey, Douglas S., and Nancy A. Denton. 1993. *American Apartheid: Segregation and the Making of the Underclass*. Cambridge, MA: Harvard University Press.

Moynahan, Daniel. 1965. *The Negro Family: The Case for National Action*. Washington, DC: Office of Policy Planning and Research, United States Department of Labor.

Oaks, Jeannie, and Gretchen Guiton. 1995. Matchmaking: The Dynamics of High School Tracking Decisions. *American Educational Research Journal* 32 (1): 3–33.

Orfield, Gary, and John T. Yun. 1999. *Resegregation in American Schools*. Cambridge, MA: Civil Rights Project, Harvard University.

Park, Robert E. 1950. *Race and Culture*. Glencoe, IL: Free Press.

Perkins, Robert, et al. 2004. *The High School Transcript Study: A Decade of Change in Curricula and Achievement, 1990–2000*. Washington, DC: National Center for Education Statistics, United States Department of Education, Institute of Education Sciences.

Saporito, Salvatore. 2003. Private Choices, Public Consequences: Magnet School Choice and Segregation by Race and Poverty. *Social Problems* 50 (2): 181–203.

Steele, Claude M. 1992. Race and the Schooling of Black Americans. *Atlantic Monthly* April: 68–78.

Steele, Claude M. 1997. A Threat in the Air: How Stereotypes Shape the Intellectual Test Performance of African Americans. *Journal of Personality and Social Psychology* 69 (5): 797–811.

Tyack, David, and Larry Cuban. 1995. *Tinkering toward Utopia: A Century of Public School Reform*. Cambridge, MA: Harvard University Press.

United States Census Bureau. *Census 2000 Summary File*. http://www.census.gov.

United States Census Bureau. *Current Population Survey: Educational Attainment in the United States, 2006*. http://www.census.gov/population/www/socdemo/educattn.html.

Waller, Willard. 1932. *The Sociology of Teaching*. New York: John Wiley & Sons.

Zubrinsky, Camille L., and Lawrence Bobo. 1996. Prismatic Metropolis: Race and Residential Segregation in the City of Angels. *Social Science Research* 24 (4): 335–374.

Gniesha Y. Dinwiddie

EDUCATION FOR ALL HANDICAPPED CHILDREN ACT (1968)

SEE *Mental Retardation.*

EDUCATIONAL QUALITY

Education often yields higher earnings, opens career opportunities, improves health, widens social circles, and increases political activity. Although education can play a central role in the economic development of a society, there is no consensus about measuring quality, nor even assurance that more effort will necessarily yield positive results.

Counts of inputs like teachers and classrooms or, more broadly, spending per student, have been used to challenge school segregation and unequal school financing. Measures of outputs, however, are necessary for judging effectiveness. More years of schooling is a simple measure of output that is effective as long as the skills developed have value. When time spent in school builds pointless skills, years of schooling is a poor measure of educational quality. Indeed, there comes a point at which further schooling is not worth its cost, and that point differs among students, reflects the character of the schooling, and depends on the opportunities for people with different kinds of schooling.

A better measure of output, then, is the gain in earnings over a lifetime due to education. Because each person can have only one level of education and lifetime earnings, estimating the gains from added education involves comparing averages for otherwise similar people with different levels of education well after graduation.

The average gain in earnings from a baseline level of education to a higher level can be summarized as a financial flow. Consider an amount in a mutual fund before the education begins (earning interest at market rates) that would pay out the gain in earnings due to better education each year over a lifetime with the balance in the fund dropping to zero when the person retires. The initial amount needed in such a fund is called the *present value* of the gain in earnings from the added education. The student's cost of the schooling is the present value of any tuition, transportation, and, for older students, earnings foregone to attend school. When the present value of the added earnings exceeds the present value of the cost of the schooling, the expenditure on education increases wealth. This is a benchmark for educational quality. The higher the present value net of cost, the higher the quality of education. Just as financial capital yields future payoffs, education creates human capital with its own future payoff.

Measuring quality as the gain in earnings often means that, compared to white males, women and underrepresented minorities have higher returns. Education can narrow the gap in earnings from wide differentials with low education to smaller gaps with more education. A larger gain often means a higher financial return for women and minorities than for white males.

Since 1980, the return to education has been high in the United States, about a 10 percent increase in earnings for each added year of schooling with the implication that the schooling is of good quality. The gains arose primarily because the earnings of workers with only a high school education or less have fallen remarkably.

Looking beyond gains in earnings, many students add the value of improved health, more effective participation in politics, and personal fulfillment as additional dimensions of benefit. In addition to developing skills, education identifies talents that allow a better match of individuals to opportunities. A better match may yield both higher earnings and more personal fulfillment. It is difficult to distinguish the degree to which measured gains in earnings from education reflect learning versus simply identifying talent.

Educational gains extend beyond the individual student. Less-educated workers are more productive when working with more-educated workers. For this reason, each of us is affected by the educational achievement of other people's children. Voters and taxpayers, even those without children, often support expenditures on education to promote the general welfare.

Education may, however, be wasteful when the goal is only to gain relative position. When a second-rank student applies more effort to top the first, the first responds with more effort to retain place. The result can be that every student down the hierarchy gets more education to gain place, but when all do so, the rank order and pattern of earnings are unchanged. An educational system that promotes hierarchy to the exclusion of other goals will be enervating for all.

Measuring quality as the financial value of education involves using information from many people observed years after the completion of their education. Such measures are of limited value in judging the details of educational services. Analysts turn to tests to measure educational performance that is specific to school and class size, teacher characteristics, peer students in the classroom, and attendance. Each affects test scores. The increase in test score this year over last year measures a student's gain in knowledge during a school year. The difference in test score is a measure of the value added during the school year, an indicator of educational quality. The analysis, however, must account statistically for other influences like native talent and family background to isolate the effect of the school. Because some attributes of schools are not subject to management's control, an analyst may seek to isolate features of the school that the school can control from those it cannot. For example, a school may have little influence on student turnover as families migrate.

Moreover, test scores are limited measures of educational quality. Standardized tests ask the same questions (or questions calibrated to have the same expected pattern of results) each time they are given. Many such tests have a limited scope, often aimed at judging the performance of average students. Some tests do a poor job of measuring gains among students who learned this year's material the previous year. They also do a poor job of measuring gains among students who are far below average. Test scores support insightful analysis of educational quality in carefully devised statistical studies, but they are not foolproof.

Standardized tests are particularly problematic when used as the basis of incentive systems for schools. Such systems rarely attempt to control for sources of differences in test scores that are beyond the control of the school. Schools may systematically game the tests. Drilling students on the specific items on the test may cause test scores to rise as learning falls. Rewarding schools on the basis of average test scores will focus a school's attention on the middle students, with less attention given to others. A focus on tests also diminishes educational outcomes that are not monitored by tests.

Standardized tests play a pivotal role in efforts to privatize the provision of elementary and secondary education. Private operators might have sharper incentives to provide more quality for a given expenditure per student through contracts, charters, or by scholarship and vouchers. The performance of independent operators receiving public funds may be judged unevenly, however, when other factors that influence test scores are not taken into account. Whether private operators yield consistently better performance when other attributes of students are accounted for remains controversial.

Clever teachers and effective principals turn their students' curiosity into discovery. Quality schools engage students, promote community, develop abstract thinking skills, and raise aspirations. Students develop talents they did not know they had and acquire valued skills. Physical, social, and visual skills grow with mathematical, language, and problem-solving skills. Quality schools are grounded in the lives of their students and challenge them on many levels. Social science can inform judgments about quality but cannot provide formulae that substitute for insightful leadership.

SEE ALSO *Cultural Capital; Human Capital; Skill; Social Capital*

BIBLIOGRAPHY

Akerlof, George A., and Rachel E. Kranton. 2002. Identity and Schooling: Some Lessons for the Economics of Education. *Journal of Economic Literature* 40 (4): 1167–1201.

Donovan, M. Susan, John D. Bransford, and James W. Pellegrino, eds. 1999. *How People Learn: Bridging Research and Practice.* Washington, DC: National Academy Press.

Krueger, Alan B., and Mikael Lindahl. 2001. Education for Growth: Why and for Whom? *Journal of Economic Literature* 29 (4): 1101–1136.

Wolf, Alison. 2002. *Does Education Matter? Myths about Education and Economic Growth.* London: Penguin.

Malcolm Getz

EFFICIENCY VS. EQUITY
SEE *Distortions.*

EFFICIENT BARGAINING HYPOTHESIS
SEE *Labor Union.*

EFFICIENT MARKET HYPOTHESIS

The efficient market hypothesis (EMH) holds that financial markets make efficient use of available information so that traders cannot base profitable trading strategies on available information. Such information will already be incorporated in asset prices, because when traders take advantage of profitable arbitrage opportunities, their trading changes the prices of assets, and thus public information cannot be used to outperform the market. The weak form of EMH holds that all past prices of an asset are fully

reflected in its current market prices, so that charting and technical analysis of stock price movements cannot provide an abnormal profit. The semistrong form of EMH views asset prices as incorporating all publicly available information, so that fundamental analysis of a company's business prospects, based on its reports and on published news and analysis, will not yield an excess return. According to the strong form of EMH, prices of securities fully reflect all public and private information, so that even insider trading does not achieve excess profits (see Fama 1970).

Although some earlier observers had the concept of market efficiency due to arbitrage (at least in the weak form of EMH and arguably in the semistrong form), notably Jules Regnault (d. 1866) (see Franck Jovanovic in Poitras 2006–2007, vol. 1), the mathematical implications were first set out with regard to the prices of options on French government bonds by the probability theorist Louis Bachelier (1870–1946) in his 1900 dissertation *Théorie de la spéculation* (translated in Cootner 1964). By analogy to fair bets in games of chance, Bachelier showed that the absence of unexploited arbitrage opportunities implies that changes in asset prices are unpredictable, so that in efficient markets asset prices follow a random walk (in discrete time) or Brownian motion (in continuous time), stochastic processes that Bachelier characterized five years before Albert Einstein (1879–1955) independently formalized Brownian motion for gas particles.

Although Bachelier's thesis was published sixty years before John Muth proposed the rational expectations hypothesis, Bachelier assumed that speculators had what Muth would call rational expectations: Their expectations of prices were correct except for completely unpredictable, random errors. Disillusioned with the failure of stock market forecasting services to predict the crash of 1929, Alfred Cowles III (1891–1984) compiled evidence (1933) that the forecasters did no better than random portfolios would have done, so that the fees paid by their subscribers were wasted—although Cowles (1944) later changed his mind, accepting that one unnamed forecaster (apparently William Peter Hamilton's [1867–1929] version of the Dow theory) had outperformed the market more often than could be attributed to chance. Cowles questioned why anyone who could actually predict the movement of stock prices would sell the prediction for a fee instead of making a fortune by trading on his or her own account. In 1934 Holbrook Working (1895–1985) showed that, for there to be no unexploited possibilities for profitable arbitrage, commodity prices must follow a random walk. Despite Cowles's role as founder of the Cowles Commission for Research in Economics and Working's influence on the Food Research Institute at Stanford University, the early research on efficient markets had little influence until the late 1950s (see Cootner 1964; Fama 1970; Poitras 2006–2007, vol. 2).

In 1958 Franco Modigliani (1918–2003) and Merton Miller (1923–2000) used the no-arbitrage principle to argue that firms cannot increase their market value by altering how their financial structure is divided between debt and equity, because if a firm could do so, then individual investors could make arbitrage profits by analogous portfolio changes between shares and bonds (see Miller et al. 1988). The Modigliani-Miller proposition abstracted from any differences in tax treatment of different financial structures and from the asymmetry that corporations have limited liability but individual investors do not.

As influentially expounded by Eugene Fama (1970) and Burton Malkiel ([1973] 1999), the weak form of EMH implies that the only way to profit from charting and technical analysis of stock price movements is by selling worthless forecasts to the gullible, and the semistrong form implies that investors should just invest in broad market averages, avoiding the costs of active portfolio management and security analysis. These ideas were anathema to the forecasters and managers whose livelihood they threatened, to successful investors who were told their above-average risk-adjusted returns were due to luck rather than skill, and to the widely held hope that there is some expert or formula that, for a thousand dollars, will tell one how to make a million. Nonetheless, the weak and semistrong forms of EMH became increasingly accepted and contributed to the growth of index funds.

The strong form of EMH, implying the failure of laws against insider trading, was advanced more tentatively even by firm believers in the weak and semistrong forms. However, the current status of the efficient market hypothesis is unsettled (see the debate between Malkiel and Shiller 2003). Financial markets cannot be more than approximately efficient, because perfect information efficiency would leave no incentive for professionals to discover the information that is incorporated in prices. Andrew Lo and Craig MacKinlay (1999) find evidence of serial correlation in stock price movements, contrary to the weak form of EMH. Robert Shiller (1989, 2005) presents evidence of excess volatility of asset prices, which move not just because of random shocks and rational expectations of underlying fundamentals but also because of what John Maynard Keynes (1883–1946) called "animal spirits" and Alan Greenspan termed "irrational exuberance," as during the Internet bubble of the late 1990s. Defending the EMH against advocates of behavioral finance, Burton Malkiel argues that speculative bubbles can be identified only in retrospect and that "whatever patterns or irrationalities in the pricing of individual stocks that have been discovered in a search of historical

experience are unlikely to persist and will not provide investors with a method to obtain extraordinary returns. If any $100 bills are lying around the stock exchanges of the world, they will not be there for long" (Malkiel and Shiller 2003, p. 80).

SEE ALSO *Arbitrage and Arbitrageurs; Bubbles; Equity Markets; Expectations, Implicit; Expectations, Rational; Finance; Financial Markets; Gambling; Information, Economics of; Interest Rates; Modigliani-Miller Theorem; Random Walk; Risk; Speculation; Stationary Process; Stock Exchanges; Stock Exchanges in Developing Countries*

BIBLIOGRAPHY

Cootner, Paul, ed. 1964. *The Random Character of Stock Market Prices.* Cambridge, MA: MIT Press.

Cowles, Alfred, III. 1933. Can Stock Market Forecasters Forecast? *Econometrica* 1 (4): 309–324.

Cowles, Alfred, III. 1944. Stock Marketing Forecasting. *Econometrica* 12 (3): 206–214.

Fama, Eugene. 1970. Efficient Capital Markets: A Review of Theory and Empirical Work. *Journal of Finance* 25 (2): 383–417.

Lo, Andrew W., and A. Craig MacKinlay. 1999. *A Non-Random Walk down Wall Street.* Princeton, NJ: Princeton University Press.

Malkiel, Burton G. [1973] 1999. *A Random Walk down Wall Street.* 7th ed. New York: Norton.

Malkiel, Burton G., and Robert J. Shiller. 2003. Symposium: Financial Market Efficiency. *Journal of Economic Perspectives* 17 (1): 59–104.

Miller, Merton H., Joseph E. Stiglitz, Stephen A. Ross, Sudipto Bhattacharya, and Franco Modigliani. 1988. Symposium: The Modigliani-Miller Propositions after Thirty Years. *Journal of Economic Perspectives* 2 (4): 99–158.

Poitras, Geoffrey, ed. 2006–2007. *Pioneers of Financial Economics.* 2 vols. Cheltenham, U.K., and Northampton, MA: Elgar.

Shiller, Robert J. 1989. *Market Volatility.* Cambridge, MA: MIT Press.

Shiller, Robert J. 2005. *Irrational Exuberance.* 2nd ed. Princeton, NJ: Princeton University Press.

Working, Holbrook. 1934. A Random Difference Series for Use in the Analysis of Time Series. *Journal of the American Statistical Association* 29 (1): 11–24.

Robert W. Dimand

EFFORT-SHAPE NOTATION

SEE *Dance.*

EGALITARIANISM

Egalitarianism is a political ideology centered on the belief in human equality. As a basic concept, equality by itself refers only to a relation, such as "less than" or "greater than," rather than a quality or essence. To judge two things equal, we must also specify the relevant qualities they have in common. Therefore, egalitarianism is the belief that all humans share an essence or quality that makes them equal. Although all egalitarians believe in equality, they often differ in their understanding of the qualities all humans share.

Every form of egalitarianism is cosmopolitan and inclusive. Those who see only the members of their own group as equal are not egalitarian. Because egalitarianism is always based on a theory of *universal* human commonality and because such universal human qualities are difficult to define, their essence is often unspecified by egalitarian thinkers. Nonetheless, anyone who believes all humans are equal must also believe all humans have some kind of essence or quality in common, because without commonality there can be no equality.

All theories of universal human commonality fall into one of two categories. Either the essentially human qualities come from the laws of nature, or those qualities are transcendent or spiritual. Theories of a universal human nature belong to the first category, whereas the belief in a transcendent spark of essential human dignity belongs to the second. In European and North American thought, the egalitarianism of nature is descended from ancient Greek ideas about the invariable, underlying patterns that govern all things. These patterns are understood as scientific laws, and human nature in this view is universal and relatively invariable. Transcendent or supernatural ideas of human equality developed from the traditions of monotheism, according to which a supernatural creator gave to all humans a spark of the divine essence. According to this view, all humans share the power of self-creativity, the ability to define their own nature.

Hence these two kinds of egalitarianism are at odds with each other on the question of human malleability. In the egalitarianism of human nature, the natural qualities shared by everyone vary only within a limited range, whereas in the egalitarianism of self-creativity, all humans share the power to define their own essence. Therefore the egalitarianism of nature tends to be more conservative, and the egalitarianism of self-creativity is usually more liberal or progressive.

Although the egalitarianism of human nature is seen as too limited by those in the tradition of self-creativity, historically it led to ideas of natural rights that inspired revolutions. The U.S. Declaration of Independence begins by asserting the natural rights of life, liberty, and the pursuit of happiness, which in turn were based on John Locke's ideas of human nature. In this view, the forces of nature provide humans with fixed wants and the power of labor to fulfill them. Equality is the common freedom to pursue our given wants with our natural powers. All humans have the same nature and therefore the same rights.

In the nineteenth century the egalitarianism of human nature increasingly came to be seen as inauthentic by those who saw freedom as the ability to transcend such limits. The equality of natural powers led to inequalities of social outcomes, which economic theories of human nature seemed to excuse. In the alternative view, to achieve true equality we must first eliminate the inherited constraints of the past. According to the newer egalitarianism of self-creativity, the Lockean theory of human nature is a mere social construct used by the rich to justify their privileges. True equality instead requires the ability to make society anew. For egalitarians such as Karl Marx, labor is not just a natural force but also, more importantly, the power of human self-existence, which the rich had alienated from the poor in a way that robbed them of their essential humanity. Only when the workers of the world were reunited in the self-creative circle of production and consumption would true equality be achieved.

In the early twenty-first century the two dominant versions of egalitarianism continue to compete in the politics of Western societies. Almost everyone is an egalitarian of some sort, but equality continues to be understood in different ways. In the egalitarianism of human nature, governments should provide fairness of competition and opportunity, but success depends on natural talent and effort. In the egalitarianism of self-creativity, politics is itself a mode of social self-definition, and equal participation in self-government is both a means and an end of equality. The politics of all democracies contain some mixture of these competing beliefs.

SEE ALSO *Alienation; Creativity; Democracy; Equal Opportunity; Equality; Happiness; Humanism; Labor; Liberty; Locke, John; Meritocracy; Naturalism; Philosophy*

BIBLIOGRAPHY

Cohen, Gerry A. 1995. *Self-ownership, Freedom, and Equality.* Cambridge, U.K.: Cambridge University Press.

Nagel, Thomas. *Equality and Partiality.* New York: Oxford University Press.

Raz, Joseph. 1986. Equality. In *The Morality of Freedom*, 217–244. Oxford: Clarendon.

Boris DeWiel

EGO
SEE *Psychoanalytic Theory.*

EGO-INVOLVEMENT
SEE *Social Judgment Theory.*

EHRENREICH, BARBARA
SEE *Managerial Class; New Class, The.*

EHRENREICH, JOHN
SEE *Managerial Class; New Class, The.*

EIGENVALUE
SEE *Eigen-Values and Eigen-Vectors, Perron-Frobenius Theorem: Economic Applications.*

EIGEN-VALUES AND EIGEN-VECTORS, PERRON-FROBENIUS THEOREM: ECONOMIC APPLICATIONS

Production prices, proportionate growth, maximum rate of profit and growth, and Italian economist Piero Sraffa's standard commodity can be easily presented and analyzed by referring to the Perron-Frobenius theorem, which needs mathematical definitions concerning eigen-values and eigen-vectors.

EIGEN-VALUES, EIGEN-VECTORS OF A SQUARE MATRIX

Given a square matrix A composed of real numbers α_{ij}, consider the vector x such that $Ax = \alpha x$. Obviously the vector $x = 0$ satisfies the equality $Ax = \alpha x$ for any real number α. The aim is to determine the non-zero vectors x and the real numbers α such that $Ax = \alpha x$.

Consider a square matrix of order k. If there exists a real number α and a non-zero vector x such that $Ax = \alpha x$,

α is said to be an eigen-value of A and x is an eigen-vector corresponding to α.

Determination of the Eigen-Values of A Any eigen-value α of A is such that there exists a non-zero vector x which satisfies $Ax = \alpha x = \alpha I x$ where I is the identity matrix of the same order k as the square matrix A. Thus any eigen-value α of A satisfies $(A - \alpha I)x = 0$. Since $A - \alpha I$ is a non-zero matrix and since x is a non-zero vector, we must have $|A - \alpha I| = 0$, (recalling that $|A - \alpha I|$ is the determinant of the square matrix $[A - \alpha I]$), i.e., α is a solution of the equation of the kth degree $|A - \alpha I| = 0$, since the square matrix $[A - \alpha I]$ is of order k.

The equation $|A - \alpha I| = 0$ is called the *characteristic equation* of matrix A and has at most k real solutions. If the characteristic equation has no real solution, matrix A has neither real eigen-values nor eigen-vectors with real components.

Determination of the Eigen Vectors of A If the real number $\bar\alpha$ is a solution of the characteristic equation $|A - \alpha I| = 0$ of the square matrix A, $\bar\alpha$ is an eigen-value of A. Any non-zero eigen-vector x of A associated with $\bar\alpha$ satisfies the matrix equation $Ax = \bar\alpha x = \bar\alpha I x$ or $(A - \bar\alpha I)x = 0$. This equation represents in fact a system of k homogeneous linear equations with k unknowns, i.e., the components $x_1, x_2, \ldots, x_k$ of the eigen-vector x. Since $|A - \bar\alpha I| = 0$, the rank of matrix $A - \bar\alpha I$ is at most equal to $k - 1$. One can then distinguish the following cases:

- Rank $(A - \bar\alpha I) = k - 1$: one of the components, say x_1, can be arbitrarily chosen and the $k - 1$ others are uniquely determined by the value chosen for x_1. The eigen-vector x is thus *uniquely determined up to the multiplication by scalars.*

- Rank $(A - \bar\alpha I) \leq k - 2$: p components ($p \geq 2$), say $x_1, x_2, \ldots, x_p$, can be arbitrarily chosen and the $k - p$ others are determined by $x_1, x_2, \ldots, x_p$. One can then have p linearly *independent* eigen-vectors corresponding to the *same* eigen-value $\bar\alpha$.

Only one eigen-vector x (up to the multiplication by scalars) corresponds to the real eigen-value $\bar\alpha$ when $\bar\alpha$ is a simple root of the characteristic equation. But when the eigen-value $\bar\alpha$ is a multiple root of order p of the characteristic equation, then:

- either *one* eigen-vector x (up to the multiplication by scalars) is associated with $\bar\alpha$; in this case $\bar\alpha$ is said to be a *semi-simple* eigen-value;

- or *several linearly independent* eigen-vectors correspond to $\bar\alpha$.

One can also determine a vector y such that $yA = \alpha y$. Call *y the eigen-vector on the left* of A associated with the eigen-value α. The vector x such that $Ax = \alpha x$ is then *the eigen-vector on the right* of A associated with α.

One can determine the eigen-values and the eigen-vectors of the matrix:

$$A = \begin{bmatrix} \dfrac{1}{2} & \dfrac{4}{15} & \dfrac{1}{8} \\ \dfrac{5}{18} & \dfrac{5}{18} & \dfrac{5}{16} \\ \dfrac{2}{9} & \dfrac{4}{45} & \dfrac{5}{12} \end{bmatrix}.$$

The eigen-values α of matrix A are the solutions of a third degree equation $|A - \alpha I| = 0$ which can be written $-\alpha^3 + (43/36)\alpha^2 - \tfrac{1}{3}\alpha + (35/1296) = -(\alpha - \tfrac{5}{6})(\alpha - 7/36)(\alpha - \tfrac{1}{6}) = 0$. Thus A has three eigen-values $\tfrac{5}{6}$, 7/36 and $\tfrac{1}{6}$, which are the simple roots of the characteristic equation.

One can determine an eigen-vector on the right p and an eigen-vector on left q of matrix A associated with the highest eigen-value α.

An eigen-value on the right $p = \begin{bmatrix} p_1 \\ p_2 \\ p_3 \end{bmatrix}$ of A associated with the eigen-value $\alpha = \tfrac{5}{6}$ satisfies the matrix equation $(A - \tfrac{5}{6}I)p = 0$, and its components $p_1, p_2,$ and p_3 are solutions of a system of homogeneous equations which is an undetermined system of rank 2. If one gives to p_1, the value 11, one has $p_2 = 10$ and $p_3 = 8$; i.e. $p = \begin{bmatrix} 11 \\ 10 \\ 8 \end{bmatrix}$ is an eigen-vector on the right of A associated with $\alpha = \tfrac{5}{6}$ and any vector $\begin{bmatrix} 11\mu \\ 10\mu \\ 8\mu \end{bmatrix}$ where μ is any scalar, is also an eigen-vector on the right associated with $\alpha = \tfrac{5}{6}$.

Similarly, an eigen-vector on the left $q = (q_1, q_2, q_3)$ of A associated with the eigen-value $\alpha = \tfrac{5}{6}$ satisfies the matrix equation $q(A - \tfrac{5}{6}I) = 0$ and its components $q_1, q_2,$ and q_3 are solutions of a system of homogeneous equations which is an undetermined system of rank 2. If one assumes $q_1 = 1$, we have $q_2 = \tfrac{2}{3}$ and $q_3 = \tfrac{3}{4}$, so $q = (1, \tfrac{2}{3}, \tfrac{3}{4})$ is an eigen-vector on the left of A associated with $\alpha = \tfrac{5}{6}$ and any vector $q = (\mu, \tfrac{2}{3}\mu, \tfrac{3}{4}\mu)$, where μ is any scalar, is also an eigen-vector on the left associated with $\alpha = \tfrac{5}{6}$.

PERRON-FROBENIUS THEOREM FOR INDECOMPOSABLE SEMI-POSITIVE MATRIX

Different kinds of matrices can be distinguished by using permutation. A permutation of a square matrix A is the square matrix $\bar{A}$ obtained by the permutation of the rows of A combined with the same permutation of the columns.

Indecomposable Matrix A square matrix is said to be *decomposable* or *reducible* if there exists a permutation $\bar{A}$ of A: $\bar{A} = \begin{bmatrix} A_1^1 & 0 \\ A_2^1 & A_2^2 \end{bmatrix}$ where A_1^1 and A_2^2 are square matrices.

$\bar{A}$ is said to be a *quasi-triangular* matrix, i.e. containing only zeros at the intersection of the first rows and its last columns.

When a square matrix is not decomposable, it is said to be *indecomposable* or *irreducible*.

Matrices with Nonnegative Elements A is said to be *nonnegative* when $\alpha_{ij} \geq 0$ for any i and any j.

A is said to be *semi-positive* when $\alpha_{ij} \geq 0$ for any i and any j and $A \neq 0$.

A is said to be *positive* when $\alpha_{ij} > 0$ for any i and any j.

Perron-Frobenius Theorem Any indecomposable semi-positive square matrix A possesses a positive eigen-value αA and a positive eigen-vector x corresponding to $\alpha(A)$. The positive number $\alpha(A)$ is a simple root of the characteristic equation $|A - \alpha I| = 0$ and is the only eigen-value of matrix A with a positive eigen-vector. The absolute values of the $k - 1$ other eigen-values of matrix A are not greater than $\alpha(A)$.

The positive eigen-value $\alpha(A)$ (or equivalently α^*) of the indecomposable non-negative square matrix with an associated eigen-vector $x > 0$ is called the dominant eigen-value of matrix A.

PERRON-FROBENIUS THEOREM AND ITS ECONOMIC APPLICATIONS

Profit Rate and Production Prices with "Advanced Wage" Assumption Consider a square input-output system with quite standard assumptions except one: one shall assume that "wages are consisting of the necessary subsistence of the workers and thus entering the system on the same footing as the fuel for the engines or the feed for the cattle" (such is the assumption made by Sraffa in *Production of Commodities by Means of Commodities* [1960, p. 9]). In such a simplified case, which corresponds to classical ecomomists' and the German political philosopher Karl Marx's assumption of "advanced wage," one can interpret the preceding matrix equation $Ap = \alpha p$ in the following way. When $\alpha < 1$ (which appears in all productive systems generally considered), one can write $\alpha = 1/(1 + R)$ with $R > 0$ and one gets: $p = (1 + R)Ap$. There appears, with uniform positive profit rate R, a vector positive system p; each element of vector p, say p_j, represents the "cost of production" of each commodity, since it takes into account not only materials used in the production of the commodity considered but also wages paid to workers. However, since we consider here an indecomposable production it is better to resort to the denomination of "production prices" and not "costs."

In matrix notation:

$$Ap(1 + R) = p \Leftrightarrow Ap = \frac{1}{1 + R}p = \alpha p$$

which means that p is the eigen-vector corresponding to the eigen-value $1/(1 + R)$. In this way, one determines simultaneously the dominant eigen-value α of A (i.e., the rate of profit R) and the corresponding eigen-vector p (i.e., the $[k - 1]$ relative prices) are necessarily positive from the Perron-Frobenius theorem.

Note that in the preceding example, one gets $\alpha = \frac{5}{6}$ and consequently $R = 20\%$ with $p = \begin{bmatrix} 11\mu \\ 10\mu \\ 8\mu \end{bmatrix}$ which means that one determines in such a case the uniform rate of profit and the whole *structure* of prices, or exchange rates. One must note that this allows determination of price structure, not exact level, since μ is any scalar. (Money quantitative theory may be used to find price level but this is quite another problem and there exist many other possibilities.)

Profit Rate, Production Prices with Wages Paid "Post Factum" Whereas classics assumed wages to be advanced by the capitalist, another assumption is that wages are paid as a share of the annual product, *post factum* according to Sraffa's terminology. In such a case, quantities of commodities necessary for workers' subsistence no longer appear in the technology matrix. The quantity of labor employed in each industry (with labor of uniform quality) must now be entered explicitly. In such a case, and getting back to the preceding example, the production price system must now be written $(1 + r)Ap + wL = p$, with w as a scalar for wages paid to workers and L a column vector representing labor needs for production of each commodity. In the particular limit case of $w = 0$, one comes back to the preceding case so $R = \frac{1 - \alpha}{\alpha}$ represents the "maximum rate of profit" determined by the dominant eigen-value of matrix A.

Price-Movements and Sraffa's "Standard Commodity" Consider the preceding system $(1 + r)Ap + wL = p$. Obviously, prices cannot stay unchanged when distribution varies. But, the study of the price-movements that

accompany a change in distribution is complicated by the necessity of having to express the price of one commodity in terms of another that is arbitrarily chosen as standard. For instance, when one studies the variations of price p_j when distribution changes, and one has already chosen (implicitly or explicitly) a peculiar commodity price p_i for "numeraire" or "standard," it is impossible to determine if the change in p_j/p_i arises from the variation of the commodity which is measured or from those of the measuring standard.

This problem of an "invariable standard" has already been considered by the English economist David Ricardo who imagined, in a rather abrupt way and without any justification, that "gold" could be such an invariable standard. The presentation of the modern solution, given by Sraffa, can be given using preceding developments concerning eigen-vectors and eigen-values.

Remember that a particular commodity (i) is produced by using a row vector of intermediate consumption a_i and a quantity l_i of labor. Its price is given, with preceding notations, by equation $p_i = (1 + r)a_ip + l_i$. When distribution changes, p_i will change because of modifications of the value of the different "layers" composing the means of production of the commodity considered; such heterogeneity implies that if we consider the ratio of the value of such a commodity to its means of production, this ratio cannot remain unchanged when distribution changes; this is obvious since $\frac{p_i}{a_ip} = 1 + r + \frac{wl_i}{a_ip}$.

So, such ratio cannot, in general, be invariant to changes in distribution. But does there exist a particular commodity, or a "basket" of commodities, a "composite commodity" $u = (u_1, u_2, \ldots u_k)$ satisfying this condition? If such is the case, the condition should be written $\frac{up}{uAp} = Cste$, where up is the price, or value, of the "composite commodity" and uAp price, or value, of means of production uA is used in the production process of u. And one knows from preceding developments that in the case of semi-positive indecomposable matrix A there exists a unique positive vector q which satisfies this condition since $qA = \alpha q$ with $\alpha = 1/(1 + R)$.

In the preceding example, the "composite commodity" is vector $q = (\mu, \frac{5}{6}\mu, \frac{3}{4}\mu)$ where μ is any scalar.

Such "balanced" commodity would have the same proportions in all its layers. As noted by Sraffa, "It is true that, as wages fall, such a commodity would be no less susceptible than any other to rise or fall in price relative to other individual commodities; but we should know for certain that any such fluctuation would originate exclusively in the peculiarities of production of the commodity which was being compared with it, and not in its own." Such commodity is the standard capable of isolating the price-movements on any other product "so that they could be observed in a vacuum" (1960, p. 18).

PROPORTIONAL GROWTH: DUALITY

Consider a square indecomposable semi-positive matrix, as for instance the preceding example. In such a case, where the dominant eigen-value is $\alpha = \frac{5}{6}$, one can get:

- uniform rate of profit $R = 20\% = \dfrac{1-\alpha}{\alpha}$ and prices of production structure p determined by *right eigen-vector*: $p = (1 + R)Ap$

- uniform growth rate $R = 20\% = \dfrac{1-\alpha}{\alpha}$ and levels of activities structure q determined by *left eigen-vector*: $q = (1 + G)qA$.

Both uniform growth rate and uniform profit rate are determined by maximum matrix eigen-value. Of course, there is no final consumption, since constituents of matrix A take into account labor subsistence needs and all profits are re-invested. Note that, in such case of "proportional growth," Marx's analysis concerning rate of profit is validated: rate of profit R is equal to the ratio of total surplus-value to the value of total advanced capital.

Such model of "proportionate growth" implies some similarity with Hungarian-born mathematician John von Neumann's model. However, the von Neumann model is much more complicated. Among the main differences:

- In the von Neumann model, there is a difference between free goods and economic goods, when in the preceding simplified model all goods considered are economic goods; free goods (such as industrial wastes, superabundant commodities) are explicitly taken into account in the von Neumann model.

- In the von Neumann model, all production processes (activities) are not necessarily used (there occurs a problem of "choice of techniques") when here all processes are used (input-output matrix is square but rectangular in von Neumann).

- In the von Neumann approach there occurs a possibility of joint production: the "cattle breeding" process produces simultaneously meat and wool. Traditional input-output systems are single production processes: one process produces meat, another wool.

- In the von Neumann approach, the uniform growth rate and profit rate are no longer determined by referring to the Perron-Frobenius theorem.

SEE ALSO *Inverse Matrix; Linear Systems; Marx, Karl; Matrix Algebra; Sraffa, Piero; Vectors*

BIBLIOGRAPHY

Abraham-Frois, Gilbert, and Edmond Berrebi. 1979. *Theory of Value, Prices and Accumulation.* Cambridge, U.K.: Cambridge University Press.

Abraham-Frois, Gilbert, and Emeric Lendjel. 2001. Une Première Application du Théorème de Perron-Frobenius à l'économie: l'abbé Potron comme précurseur. *Revue d'Economie Politique* 111 (4): 639–666.

Gale, David. 1960. *The Theory of Linear Economic Models.* New York: McGraw-Hill.

Morishima, Mishio. 1973. *Marx's Economics: A Dual Theory of Value and Growth.* Cambridge, U.K.: Cambridge University Press.

Nikaido, Hukukane. 1987. Perron-Frobenius Theorem. In *The New Palgrave: A Dictionary of Economics*, ed. John Eatwell, Murray Milgate, and Peter Newman, Vol. 3, 849–851. New York: Macmillan.

Ricardo, David. 1951. *On the Principles of Political Economy and Taxation.* Cambridge, U.K.: Cambridge University Press. (Orig. pub. 1821).

Sraffa, Piero. 1960. *Production of Commodities by Means of Commodities.* Cambridge, U.K.: Cambridge University Press.

Von Neumann, John. 1945–1946. A Model of General Equilibrium. *Review of Economic Studies* 13 (I): 1–9

Gilbert Abraham-Frois

EIGENVECTOR

SEE *Eigen-Values and Eigen-Vectors, Perron-Frobenius Theorem: Economic Applications.*

EISENHOWER, DWIGHT D.
1890–1969

Dwight David "Ike" Eisenhower, a five-star general and the thirty-fourth president of the United States, was born in Texas and raised in Abilene, Kansas. He entered the United States Military Academy as a member of the class of 1915, later known as "The Class the Stars Fell On" for the record number of general officers it produced. As a West Point cadet, he was best known for his football skills and disregard for military discipline.

His first assignment was at Fort Sam Houston, Texas, where he met and married Mamie Doud. When the United States entered World War I (1914–1918), Eisenhower expected orders to Europe; instead, he commanded a training base near Gettysburg, Pennsylvania. Certain his lack of combat duty meant the end of his career, his fears were compounded by the rejection of his proposals for the role of tanks in future warfare. Those concerns diminished under the mentorship of Brigadier General Fox Conner, who arranged to have Eisenhower assigned to his staff in Panama. He encouraged and inspired Eisenhower, and ensured his selection to attend the Army's staff college, where Eisenhower graduated first in his class. In the 1930s Eisenhower held key political-military posts under Army Chief of Staff Douglas MacArthur. He chafed at MacArthur's control, and frequently requested reassignment. In 1939 MacArthur finally released Eisenhower for duty with troops.

Two weeks after the Japanese attack on Pearl Harbor, Army Chief of Staff General George Marshall summoned Eisenhower to serve as an Army war planner. Six months later, Eisenhower was selected to command all Allied forces in Europe. At the war's end, Eisenhower was a five-star general, chief of staff of the Army, and an international hero touted as a possible Democratic candidate for president. In 1949 Eisenhower was named president of Columbia University. Despite his lack of academic credentials, he initiated important curriculum changes and established new academic programs. Eisenhower was recalled to active duty in 1950 to serve as Supreme Allied Commander–Europe.

Eisenhower was again urged to run for president in 1952, this time as a Republican challenging isolationist Senator Robert Taft for the GOP nomination. Taft was a strong candidate, but a compromise between those urging fiscal restraint and those promoting internationalist foreign policy resulted in Eisenhower's nomination. The Korean War stalemate, and Eisenhower's campaign promise to "go to Korea," contributed significantly to his victory over Democrat Adlai Stevenson.

The cold war was President Eisenhower's dominant foreign policy challenge. His efforts built a cohesive Allied defense capability in Europe, and his 1954 refusal to commit U.S. troops to support the French in Indochina is still considered one of his wisest decisions. His handling of the Hungarian uprising in 1956 and his use of the Central Intelligence Agency in covert operations were among his less successful policies. Eisenhower's domestic successes included the interstate highway system. Following the Soviet launch of Sputnik, Eisenhower refocused the space program and increased support for math and science education. He used federal troops in Little Rock, Arkansas, to enforce court-ordered school desegregation. Eisenhower would not, however, support a broader, proactive civil rights agenda.

Eisenhower was reelected in 1956 despite concerns about a heart attack suffered a year earlier. His second term was marked by foreign policy disappointments in Cuba, heightened Soviet–U.S. tensions, and charges of corruption against his chief of staff. In his final address as president, he warned against the influence "sought or unsought" by the "military-industrial complex"—an imperative of the cold war with "grave implications." Eisenhower died in 1969 and is buried in Abilene, Kansas, near the small home where he was raised.

SEE ALSO *Cold War; Cuban Revolution; Desegregation; Foreign Policy; Military-Industrial Complex; Nixon, Richard M.; Presidency, The; World War II*

BIBLIOGRAPHY

Ambrose, Stephen. 1983. *Eisenhower: Soldier, General of the Army, President-Elect, 1890–1952.* New York: Simon and Schuster.

Ambrose, Stephen. 1984. *Eisenhower: The President.* New York: Simon and Schuster.

D'Este, Carlo. 2002. *Eisenhower: A Soldier's Life.* New York: Henry Holt.

Greenstein, Fred I. 1994. *The Hidden-Hand Presidency: Eisenhower as Leader.* Baltimore, MD: Johns Hopkins University Press.

Jacobs, Travis Beal. 2001. *Eisenhower at Columbia.* New Brunswick, NJ: Transaction.

Pickett, William B. 2000. *Eisenhower Decides to Run: Presidential Politics and Cold War Strategy.* Chicago: Ivan R. Dee.

Tudda, Chris. 2006. *The Truth Is Our Weapon: The Rhetorical Diplomacy of Dwight D. Eisenhower and John Foster Dulles.* Baton Rouge: Louisiana State University Press.

Jay M. Parker

ELASTICITY

In economics, *elasticity* measures a response of one variable to changes in the other variable. The concept of elasticity can be applied to any two variables, but the most commonly used are price elasticity of demand and elasticity of substitution between factors of production, consumer goods, or bundles of consumption in different periods of time (elasticity of intertemporal substitution).

Elasticity measures the percentage change in variable Y in response to a 1 percent change in variable X. Formally, the elasticity of Y with respect to X is defined as

$$E_{Y,X} = \frac{\text{percentage change in } Y}{\text{percentage change in } X}$$

$$= \frac{\text{change in } Y}{Y} \cdot \frac{X}{\text{change in } X}$$

or, for continuous changes,

$$E_{Y,X} = \frac{dY}{dX} \cdot \frac{X}{Y} = \frac{d \ln Y}{d \ln X}$$

The concept of the price elasticity of demand, which was introduced in 1890 by Alfred Marshall, measures the percentage change in the quantity of a good demanded when the price of this good changes by 1 percent. The demand is elastic if price changes lead to large changes in quantity demanded. The demand is inelastic if the quantity demanded does not respond much to changes in price. If demand is perfectly elastic, even a small increase in price will send the quantity demanded to zero. If demand is perfectly inelastic, the quantity demanded will be constant regardless of the price.

Price elasticity of demand for goods depends on the characteristics of the goods—that is, whether or not they are necessities and whether or not there are close substitutes for these goods. Price elasticity of demand also varies with the time horizon in consideration. For example, demand for gasoline is very inelastic in the short run, because people have to fill up their gas tanks, but in the long run, if prices remain high, people will switch to more gasoline-efficient cars and will demand less gasoline. By the estimates of the Mackinac Center for Public Policy, a 10 percent increase in the price of gasoline will lower the demand for it by 2 percent in the short run (elasticity of –0.2), and by 7 percent in the long run (elasticity of –0.7).

Price elasticity of demand also depends on how narrowly a good is defined. For example, demand for milk in general is quite inelastic, because there are no close substitutes. However, demand for milk of a specific brand is very elastic because there are many close substitutes (i.e., other brands of milk).

The concept of the elasticity of substitution was introduced independently by John Hicks and Joan Robinson in 1932 and 1933, respectively. It is used to measure how easily factors of production can be substituted for one another. For example, how much will the ratio of capital input to labor input in production increase if the ratio of capital cost to labor cost falls by 1 percent? Samuel de Abreu Pessoa, Silvia Matos Pessoa, and Rafael Rob (2005) estimate this elasticity to be 0.7, on average.

The concept of the elasticity of substitution can also be applied to consumption of goods, to measure how relative consumption of two goods is affected by their relative price. Most frequently, the concept of the elasticity of substitution in consumption is used to construct the bas-

kets of consumer goods in economic models and to measure the substitutability of consumption across different time periods—"elasticity of intertemporal substitution." This measures how the ratio of future to current consumption reacts to the change in relative price of consumption tomorrow and consumption today, commonly measured by the interest rate. Elasticity of intertemporal substitution is estimated to be close to zero, indicating that consumers are not sensitive in their intertemporal consumption decisions to the changes in the interest rate.

SEE ALSO *Demand; Hicks, John R.; Marshall, Alfred; Production Function; Robinson, Joan; Substitutability; Time*

BIBLIOGRAPHY

Anderson, Patrick L., Richard D. McLellan, Joseph P. Overton, and Gary L. Wolfram. 1997. Price Elasticity of Demand. Mackinac Center for Public Policy. http://www.mackinac.org/article.aspx?ID=1247.

Hicks, John. 1932. *The Theory of Wages.* London: Macmillan.

Marshall, Alfred. [1890] 1920. *Principles of Economics.* 8th ed. London: Macmillan.

Pessoa, Samuel de Abreu, Silvia Matos Pessoa, and Rafael Rob. 2005. Elasticity of Substitution between Capital and Labor and Its Applications to Growth and Development. PIER Working Paper Archive 05-012, Penn Institute for Economic Research, Department of Economics, University of Pennsylvania.

Robinson, Joan. 1933. *The Economics of Imperfect Competition.* London: Macmillan.

Yogo, Motohiro. 2004. Estimating the Elasticity of Intertemporal Substitution When Instruments Are Weak. *Review of Economics and Statistics* 86 (3): 797–810.

Galina Hale

ELASTICITY OF SUBSTITUTION

SEE *Elasticity; Separability; Production Function; Utility Function.*

ELECTIONS

The Austrian economist Joseph Schumpeter (1883–1950) is well known for portraying competitive elections as the crux of democracy. Since Schumpeter, competitive elections have been depicted as catalysts that spur other aspects of democracy—public participation, governmental transparency, and public debates about policy. Adam Przeworski, in particular, argues that "once political rights are sufficiently extensive to admit conflicting interests, everything else follows, even if effective participation is far from universal" (1991, p. 10). Yet, political scientists and policymakers must be mindful not to equate elections—even free and fair ones—with democracy. Terry Lynn Karl (1986) emphasizes that focusing solely on elections could lead one to overlook where real political power lies. If an external actor—for example, the military or a foreign power—promotes competitive elections only when the results advance that actor's self-interest and rescinds them when they do not, then one could hardly call the polity in question a democracy. Likewise, elections alone are not likely to constrain the temptations of corruption and graft. Rather, elections must operate alongside other democratic institutions—independent media, developed parties, the rule of law, and an active civil society—if they are to yield the codes of conduct associated with representative democracy. Despite these caveats, however, even critics of minimalist definitions of democracy view free and fair elections as necessary, though not sufficient, for democracy.

Although scholars generally agree that elections are necessary democratic institutions, little consensus exists as to what the rules governing elections should look like. For example, majority rule may seem like a logical option because the winner under such a voting system is the candidate or party that enjoys the support of over half of the voters participating in the election. However, Kenneth Arrow (1951) demonstrates that, when three or more candidates or parties compete in an election, it is possible for none of the candidates to enjoy the support of a majority. Just as social choice theorists, like Arrow and Amartya Sen (1970), have considered the normative implications of specific voting rules, other scholars have considered the advantages and disadvantages of different electoral systems.

One of the most important decisions for a new democracy is the selection of the parliamentary electoral system: the rules governing how popular votes are translated into parliamentary seats. Perhaps the most important feature of a parliamentary electoral system is its district magnitude—the number of legislators representing each electoral district. District magnitude is a fundamental feature for differentiating among parliamentary electoral systems. Single-member district systems, like the system used to elect members of the U.S. House of Representatives, are systems where each legislator represents a different district. Since only one seat is allocated from each district, the system's average district magnitude equals one. At the extreme opposing a single-member district system is a proportional representation system where all representatives are elected in a single, nationwide district on the basis of party lists. In these cases, the average district magnitude equals the number of seats in parlia-

ment. A system's average district magnitude is important because it directly influences the degree to which the number of seats that a political party receives is proportional to its share of the popular vote. The higher the district magnitude and the larger the assembly size, the better the fit between the percentage of votes cast for a party and the percentage of seats allocated to it.

Not all proportional representation systems have district magnitudes equal to the number of seats in their parliament, however. Some electoral systems divide the country into several multimember districts—districts that elect two or more legislators—even varying the number of representatives per district. Theoretically, then, the number of possible electoral systems is infinite. Indeed, electoral systems vary in many ways besides their district magnitudes. For example, they differ with regard to the mathematical formula used to allocate district seats. Single-member district systems can distribute each seat on the basis of plurality rule (i.e., the candidate with the most votes wins), majority rule, or preference voting (i.e., allowing voters to rank candidates and then distributing the vote according to those rankings). Likewise, different mathematical formulas are used for allocating parliamentary seats in multimember districts. In addition, some electoral systems require political parties to win a minimum level of support (e.g., a percentage of the vote or a number of district elections) to gain representation in parliament.

Although electoral systems take many forms, the consequences of electoral systems are commonly discussed in terms of their levels of proportionality (Duverger 1954; Rae 1967; Taagepera and Shugart 1989; and Cox 1997). Systems that are more proportional allow smaller parties representing specific societal interests a better chance of representation. However, since more-proportional systems grant more parties seats in parliament, they decrease the likelihood that one party will enjoy a parliamentary majority. Thus, a common criticism leveled against proportional representation systems is that they are more likely to produce coalition governments. Accordingly, proportional representation systems can produce unstable governments, governments in which coalition partners blame one another for policy shortcomings to shirk public accountability, and even governments where the policy influence of small parties outstrips their popular support simply because they emerge as critical to coalition formation. Under proportional representation systems, then, the process of government formation—as opposed to the actual election—can be decisive in determining whether voter preferences are fulfilled or denied.

Less-proportional systems, meanwhile, limit party fragmentation. They undermine the incentives that elites have to form new parties, as well as the incentives that voters have to support new parties. Under single-member district plurality, in particular, one party is more likely to win a majority of seats in parliament. As a result, these systems can prove more responsive to changes in public attitudes: Where candidates need just a plurality of the vote to win elections, a small shift in the distribution of votes can create a significant shift in the distribution of parliamentary seats. Yet majoritarian systems can also frustrate public accountability. In New Zealand, for example, popular dissatisfaction with the two major parties that dominated politics spurred notable third-party voting in the 1970s and 1980s. However, New Zealand's single-member district plurality system also kept third parties out of parliament while overrepresenting the two major parties. As a result, growing distrust of the system fueled a reform movement that ultimately led to a change in the electoral system itself (Denemark 2001).

Electoral systems, then, influence the degree to which elections fulfill different visions of democracy (Powell 2000). Less-proportional systems limit party proliferation while underrepresenting smaller groups in society. While these systems may make it easier for voters to hold policymakers accountable, the range of policymakers is more constrained than under more-proportional systems. More-proportional systems, meanwhile, permit the representation of a broader cross section of the public. However, these systems can make it more difficult for voters to hold policymakers accountable, since policies result from a complex bargaining process among a larger number of political parties in parliament.

Implicit in much of this literature, then, are the consequences that electoral systems have on attitudes toward government and on voter behavior during elections. Of course, extensive research exists on how and why people vote, and much of this literature goes beyond institutional impediments or incentives. For example, Anthony Downs (1957) argues that voters assess the expected costs and benefits associated with different options and choose the one whose policies are likely to net them the greatest gain. While this contention seems straightforward, its underlying logic also makes the act of voting seem paradoxical. If voters make decisions by simply weighing costs and benefits, why do they vote at all? The probability of one vote determining an election's outcome is so small that any expected benefit associated with voting will not outweigh the costs of collecting information, or even going to the polls. Numerous scholars have sought to resolve this paradox within the framework of rational choice (Riker and Ordeshook 1968, Aldrich 1993), while others have chosen to understand voter turnout using social-psychological explanations (Teixeira 1987, Franklin 1996). Of course, when one compares voter turnout across countries, institutional explanations (i.e., the rules of the game) once

again prove significant (Jackman 1987, Blais and Carty 1990).

SEE ALSO *Authority; Campaigning; Democracy; Democracy, Indices of; First-past-the-post; Gerrymandering; Ideology; Political Parties; Voting Patterns; Winner-Take-All Society*

BIBLIOGRAPHY

Aldrich, John. 1993. Rational Choice and Turnout. *American Journal of Political Science* 37 (1): 246–278.

Arrow, Kenneth J. 1951. *Social Choice and Individual Values.* New York: Wiley.

Blais, André, and R. K. Carty. 1990. Does Proportional Representation Foster Voter Turnout. *European Journal of Politics* 18 (1): 167–181.

Cox, Gary W. 1997. *Making Votes Count: Strategic Coordination in the World's Electoral Systems.* New York: Cambridge University Press.

Denemark, David. 2001. Choosing MMP in New Zealand: Explaining the 1993 Electoral Reform. In *Mixed-Member Electoral Systems: The Best of Both Worlds?*, eds. Matthew Soberg Shugart and Martin P. Wattenberg, 70–95. New York: Oxford University Press.

Downs, Anthony. 1957. *An Economic Theory of Democracy.* New York: Harper.

Duverger, Maurice. 1954. *Political Parties: Their Organization and Activity in the Modern State.* Trans. Barbara North and Robert North. New York: Wiley.

Franklin, Mark. 1996. Electoral Participation. In *Comparing Democracies: Elections and Voting in Global Perspective*, eds. Lawrence LeDuc, Richard G. Niemi, and Pippa Norris, 216–235. Thousand Oaks, CA: Sage.

Jackman, Robert W. 1987. Political Institutions and Voter Turnout in the Industrial Democracies. *American Political Science Review* 81: 405–423.

Karl, Terry Lynn. 1986. Imposing Consent: Electoralism vs. Democratization in El Salvador. In *Elections and Democratization in Latin America, 1980–1985*, eds. Paul W. Drake and Eduardo Silva, 9–36. San Diego: Center for Iberian and Latin American Studies, University of California, San Diego.

Powell, G. Bingham. 2000. *Elections as Instruments of Democracy: Majoritarian and Proportional Visions.* New Haven, CT: Yale University Press.

Przeworski, Adam. 1991. *Democracy and the Market: Political and Economic Reforms in Eastern Europe and Latin America.* New York: Cambridge University Press.

Rae, Douglas W. 1967. *The Political Consequences of Electoral Laws.* New Haven, CT: Yale University Press.

Riker, William H., and Peter C. Ordeshook. 1968. A Theory of the Calculus of Voting. *American Political Science Review* 62: 25–42.

Schumpeter, Joseph. 1947. *Capitalism, Socialism, and Democracy.* 2nd ed. New York: Harper.

Sen, Amartya K. 1970. *Collective Choice and Social Welfare.* San Francisco: Holden Day.

Taagepera, Rein, and Matthew Soberg Shugart. 1989. *Seats and Votes: The Effects and Determinants of Electoral Systems.* New Haven, CT: Yale University Press.

Teixeira, Ruy A. 1987. *Why Americans Don't Vote: Turnout Decline in the United States, 1960–1984.* New York: Greenwood.

Bryon J. Moraski

ELECTORAL COLLEGE

Electoral college is the popular name for the system used to elect the president and vice president of the United States. Voters in the United States choose among candidates for these offices in November every four years, but the votes they cast are actually for another office, that of elector. In most states the names of the candidates for elector are not even on the ballot. Those chosen as electors collectively constitute the electoral college, a body that never meets as a group. State delegations of electors meet in early December in their respective state capitols to cast their "electoral votes" for president and vice president. These votes are then counted in early January at a session of Congress. If a majority of the electoral votes for president (at least 270 of a total of 538) is cast for the same person, that person wins the presidency. Likewise, if a majority of the electoral votes for vice president is cast for the same person, that person wins that office.

If no person receives a majority of the electoral votes for president, the selection of the president is placed with the U.S. House of Representatives. If no person receives a majority of votes for vice president, selection for that office is placed with the U.S. Senate. When this "contingent election" procedure is used to select a president, every state delegation in the House has one vote, which may only be cast for one of the top three recipients of electoral votes for that office. The winner must receive the vote from a majority of the states. When the contingent procedure is used to select the vice president, each senator has one vote, and only the top two recipients of electoral votes for that office may be considered. The winner must receive a vote from a majority of the senators.

This framework for electing a president and a vice president is specified in Article II, section 1, of the U.S. Constitution, ratified in 1789. This provision awards each state a number of electors equal to the number of members the state has in Congress, with one elector assigned for each of the state's representatives and senators. Representatives are allotted to the states based on population, with the caveat that every state must receive at least one. Larger states therefore have more electors than smaller states. Every state, however, is allotted the same number of senators, two, regardless of population. This allocation, along with the minimum of one representative for every state, results in smaller states receiving proportionately more electoral votes, per population, than larger states.

Two amendments to the Constitution have directly altered the electoral college system. The Twelfth Amendment, adopted in 1804, separated electoral voting for the president and the vice president. Prior to this amendment each elector had two votes to cast and the person receiving the highest number of votes, provided that number constituted a vote from a majority of the electors, won the presidency. The vice presidency went to the person receiving the second highest number of votes. In the election of 1800 this resulted in the presidential and vice presidential candidates of one party receiving the same number of votes from a majority of the electors, pushing the selection of the president into the House. The Twelfth Amendment was added to preclude this type of result. The other amendment altering the electoral college was the Twenty-Third, adopted in 1961, which allowed voters in the District of Columbia, which is not a state, to choose as many electors as the least populous state, currently three. These electoral votes are cast in Washington, D.C.

Article II, Section 1, leaves the method of choosing electors to the states themselves, through their respective legislatures. Since 1836 all states but one have let the voters make this choice; the exception, South Carolina, switched to popular elections in 1860. Another important change made by states has been the adoption, by all but two states, of the "unit rule" for allocating electors to the candidates. Candidates for elector are vetted by the political parties and pledged to vote for that party's candidates. This unit rule is a winner-take-all provision under which all of a state's electors are awarded to the slate of presidential and vice presidential candidates that received the most votes in that state in November. Congress has specified that the unit rule applies to electors for the District of Columbia as well. Maine and Nebraska award two electoral votes to the slate of candidates winning a statewide plurality of votes, and another electoral vote to the slates winning a plurality within each of their U.S. House districts.

Commentators have described the electoral college as everything from "a brilliant constitutional device" (Ross 2004, p. 9) to "an anti-democratic relic of the eighteenth century" (Edwards 2004, p. 158). Those who defend the electoral college typically assert that it is a fundamental part of the American federal system of government that needs to be maintained, and that it provides more diverse interests, especially those of smaller states, with a voice in the election of the president. Those who find the system antidemocratic argue that the people, not the electors, should determine who is elected. The votes cast in November for president and vice president, which only determine how electoral votes are distributed among sets of candidates, do show which slate of candidates was preferred by the people. With rare exception, the people's choice and the electors' choice are the same. But when the popular vote is close, the unit rule and the fact that electors are not allocated based strictly on population make it possible for the winners of the two votes to be different.

This happened in the 2000 election, when George W. Bush finished second in the popular vote with 47.8 percent, but first in the electoral vote with 50.5 percent. He was labeled by many as the "wrong winner." Presidents and vice presidents chosen under the contingent election procedure likewise need not be the public's choice.

The American public has demonstrated numerous times, in surveys and polls, that they prefer their president and vice president to be their choices, not those of intermediaries. A variety of reforms have been proposed that would accomplish this (see Edwards 2004, pp. 153–157; Bennett 2006, pp. 49–58, 161–178; and Koza et al. 2006).

SEE ALSO *Congress, U.S.; Constitution, U.S.; Democracy, Representative and Participatory; Democratic Party, U.S.; Elections; Presidency, The; Republican Party; Voting*

BIBLIOGRAPHY

Bennett, Robert W. 2006. *Taming the Electoral College.* Stanford, CA: Stanford University Press.

Edwards, George C., III. 2004. *Why the Electoral College Is Bad for America.* New Haven, CT: Yale University Press.

Koza, John R., Barry Fadem, Mark Grueskin, et al. 2006. *Every Vote Equal: A State-Based Plan for Electing the President by National Popular Vote.* Los Altos, CA: National Popular Vote Press.

Ross, Tara. 2004. *Enlightened Democracy: The Case for the Electoral College.* Los Angeles: World Ahead Publishing.

Richard L. Engstrom

ELECTORAL SYSTEMS

An electoral system is a set of institutional formulas producing a collective choice through voting. The main elements of an electoral system are: assembly size or total number of seats; district magnitude or number of seats to be elected in a district; the electoral rule to allocate seats from votes; and the ballot permitting the voter different choices. Different rules and procedures have combined these elements in many ways to produce a variety of electoral systems in the real world.

In late medieval and early modern assembly elections in local communities with homogeneous electorates, relatively simple electoral systems prevailed. A typical system until the nineteenth century was composed of: (1) multimember districts; (2) plurality or majority rule; and (3) an open ballot. Essentially, voters could vote for their preferred individual candidates, and those with the higher numbers of votes were elected. This type of electoral system can produce a consensual individual representation of the community, especially in contexts of high economic and ethnic homogeneity in which it is relatively easy to identify common interests and select collective goods. Such systems have survived at the local level in some countries, and they are still typically used in meetings and assemblies of modern housing condominiums, neighborhood associations, school and university boards, professional organizations, corporation boards, and students' and workers' unions.

However, in contexts of relatively complex and heterogeneous electorates, simple electoral rules create incentives for the coordination of candidacies and voting. Forming a list of candidates, a faction, or, in more modern terms, a *party*, may move voters to vote *en bloc* rather than for individuals weighed separately. In multimember districts using plurality rule, voting en bloc (or the *general ticket*) may produce a party *sweep* or overrepresentation by a single party. Once partisan candidacies and partisan voting emerged in a number of countries by the mid-nineteenth century, some political leaders, activists, and politically motivated scholars began to search for new electoral rules and procedures that could reduce single-party sweeps and exclusionary victories. The two main options were either retaining plurality or majority rule but in smaller *single-member districts*, or retaining multimember districts but using new *proportional representation* rules.

RULES AND PROCEDURES

In a small single-member district, a candidate that would have been defeated by a party sweep in a larger multimember district may be elected. Thus, this type of system tends to produce more varied representation than the old system with voting en bloc. Several *majoritarian* rules can be applied. With simple plurality, the winner is the candidate supported by only a *relative majority*, that is, by a higher number of voters than any other candidate but not requiring any particular number, proportion, or threshold of votes. In practice, this makes it possible for generally binding decisions presumably decided by "majority" to actually be won by only a minority of voters. Plurality rule has traditionally been used in England and the United

Kingdom and in modern times in former British colonies, including the United States, Canada, and India. Plurality-based electoral systems are also called *first-past-the-post* and *winner-takes-all* systems.

With other rules based on the majority principle, if no alternative receives an absolute majority (more than half) of the votes, further rounds of voting are implemented, these rounds either requiring a simple plurality or reducing the choice to the two candidates with the highest numbers of votes in the first round. Such *majority-runoff* systems have traditionally been used in France, among other countries. A variant requires voters to rank all candidates, and includes several counts of votes (instead of several rounds of voting), until a candidate obtains the most preferences, as in the *majority-preferential* electoral system used in Australia (also called *alternative vote* or *instant runoff*).

Proportional representation in multimember districts allocates seats to multiple parties competing in an election on the basis of the votes received. The basic mathematical formulas that make this principle operable were invented in late eighteenth century for apportioning seats in the U.S. House of Representatives among differently populated states. These formulas were reinvented in Europe in late nineteenth century for the allocation of parliamentary seats to political parties with different numbers of votes. A proportional representation formula defines a quota of inhabitants or votes worth a seat. The "simple" quota (as devised by both Alexander Hamilton [1755/57–1804] and Thomas Hare [1806–1891]) is the divisor between the total number of inhabitants or votes and the total number of seats. But it usually requires an additional criterion to allocate some of the seats, most commonly to the *largest remainders* after the quota is used. In contrast, the smaller *highest average* or *distributive number* (as devised by both Thomas Jefferson [1743–1826] and Victor d'Hondt [1841–1901]) is sufficient to allocate all seats. This quota can be calculated after the election by several procedures, including trial and error, a series of divisors, or by lowering the simple quota until it fits.

Different forms of ballots may either force a categorical vote or permit some choice of individual candidates. *Categorical ballots* are used in single-member districts where voters can vote for only one candidate, as well as in multimember districts where voters can vote for only a closed list of candidates or en bloc. In contrast, *open lists* permit voters to select one or several candidates from a party list. With the *double vote*, voters choose both a closed party list and one individual candidate. The *open ballot* permits voters to vote for individual candidates from different parties. The *majority-preferential vote* and the *single-transferable vote* require voters to rank individual candidates.

ELECTORAL SYSTEM CONSEQUENCES

Elections in single-member districts by plurality or majority rule always produce a single absolute winner, who may have the support of only a minority of voters as a first preference. A winner by plurality or by second-round majority might be defeated by a losing candidate by absolute majority if a choice between the two were available. Majoritarian rules may thus induce nonsincere or "strategic" voting that favors the voter's second-best or less-rejected candidate, so as to prevent the victory of a least-preferred one. In contrast, proportional representation electoral systems are more inclusive of several groups. Since most votes count to elect seats, they promote a more sincere revelation of preferences by voters.

In parliamentary elections with multiple single-member districts, plurality rule typically gives overrepresentation to one or two parties at the expense of others and fabricates a single party's absolute majority of seats, thus permitting the formation of a single-party cabinet. In contrast, multiparty parliaments based on proportional representation tend to produce multiparty coalition governments based on a majority of seats and popular votes. In practice, there is a paradox: "majoritarian" electoral systems often create governments with minority electoral support, while proportional representation rules, which were initially devised to include minorities, tend to produce governments with majority electoral support. In plurality-rule electoral systems, a small change in the total number of popular votes can provoke a complete alternation of the party in government. Proportional representation systems, where parties may have opportunities to share power with different partners, produce more policy stability in the long term.

THE CHOICE OF ELECTORAL SYSTEMS

In general, the *Micro-mega rule* applies: the large prefer the small and the small prefer the large. Specifically, dominant and large parties prefer small assemblies and single-member districts that are able to exclude others from competition. In contrast, multiple small parties prefer large assemblies and large districts with proportional representation that can include them. Existing parties tend, thus, to choose electoral systems that are able to crystallize or consolidate the previously existing party configurations and systems.

However, the size of the assembly is a structural variable positively correlated to the country's population and difficult to change dramatically. In large countries, such as Australia, Canada, France, India, the United Kingdom, and the United States, a large assembly can be sufficiently inclusive, even if it is elected in small, single-member districts, due to the territorial variety of the representatives. In small countries, by contrast, the size of the assembly is small and, as a consequence, the development of multiple parties favors more strongly the adoption of inclusive, large multimember districts with proportional representation rules. Proportional representation was first adopted for parliamentary elections in relatively small countries such as Belgium, Denmark, Finland, Netherlands, Norway, Switzerland, and other western European democracies in early twentieth century. In the long term, both the number of countries and the number of democracies in the world increase, while large countries decentralize, leading to an overall decrease in the size of democratic assemblies. This induces the adoption of more inclusive, proportional representation electoral rules.

In addition, the number of parties tends to increase under any electoral system as a consequence of the broadening of suffrage rights, as well as initiatives to politicize new issues and change the public agenda by groups seeking power or new policy decisions. Indeed, plurality rule provides incentives to form only a few viable large candidacies or parties. But coordination fails with relative frequency, due to the costs of information transmission, bargaining, and the implementation of agreements among previously separate organizations. Lack of coordination may produce defeats and no representation for candidates, groups, and parties that have significant support among voters. Parties unable to coordinate themselves into a small number of candidacies to compete successfully under plurality rule tend to choose electoral systems that can reduce the risks of competing, giving all participants greater opportunities to obtain or share power.

There is, thus, a general trend toward proportional representation over time. Nowadays, most democratic countries in the world use electoral systems with proportional representation rules. Likewise, for presidential elections, plurality rule tends to be replaced with second-round majority rules permitting multiparty competition in the first round. Many countries have also introduced a greater element of individual candidate voting. In fact, none of the new democracies established in countries with more than one million inhabitants in the "third wave" of democratization (since 1974) has adopted the old British model of a parliamentary regime with elections in single-member districts by plurality rule.

SEE ALSO *Cleavages; Democracy; Franchise*

BIBLIOGRAPHY

Balinski, Michel L., and H. Peyton Young. 2001. *Fair Representation: Meeting the Ideal of One Man, One Vote.* 2nd ed. Washington, DC: Brookings Institution Press.

Blais, André, and Louis Massicotte. 1997. Electoral Formulas: A Macroscopic Perspective. *European Journal of Political Research* 32: 107–129.

Colomer, Josep M., ed. 2004. *Handbook of Electoral System Choice.* London and New York: Palgrave Macmillan.

Colomer, Josep M. 2005. It's the Parties that Choose Electoral Systems (or Duverger's Laws Upside Down). *Political Studies* 53 (1): 1–21.

Colomer, Josep M. 2006. On the Origins of Electoral Systems and Political Parties. *Electoral Studies* 25 (3).

Cox, Gary W. 1997. *Making Votes Count: Strategic Coordination in the World's Electoral Systems.* New York: Cambridge University Press.

Grofman, Bernard, and Arend Lijphart, eds. 1986. *Electoral Laws and their Political Consequences.* New York: Agathon.

Negretto, Gabriel L. 2006. Choosing How to Choose Presidents. *Journal of Politics* 68 (2): 421–433.

Taagepera, Rein, and Matthew Soberg Shugart. 1989. *Seats and Votes: The Effects and Determinants of Electoral Systems.* New Haven, CT: Yale University Press.

Josep M. Colomer

ELECTRA COMPLEX

SEE *Oedipus Complex; Stages of Development.*

ELITE THEORY

"Classic" elite theories were formulated at the end of the nineteenth century and in the first decades of the twentieth century by Vilfredo Pareto (1848–1923), Gaetano Mosca (1858–1941), and Robert Michels (1876–1936). Subsequent renditions of these theories also carried a strong imprint of Max Weber's ideas, especially concerning the centrality of political power and charismatic leadership.

The classic theorists focused on the inevitability of a group of powerful "elites" in all large-scale societies, offering a radical critique of two competing theoretical-ideological streams of thought: the democratic theory ("government of the people, by the people, for the people" in Lincoln's Gettysburg Address), and the Marxist vision of class conflict leading to revolution and egalitarian socialism. In contrast with both of these ideologies, the elite theories suggested an inescapable division between dominant minorities (variously called "elites," "ruling classes," "political classes," "oligarchies," "aristocracies," etc.) and the dominated majority, or the "masses" (Bottomore, 1993).

Mosca saw this inevitable polarization of power as reflecting a "material, intellectual, or even moral superiority" (1939, p. 50) of ruling minorities, with their small size and organizational skills helping to maintain this position; Pareto anchored elite domination in the talent and psychological dispositions of such groups, combined with the skilled use of force and persuasion; and Michels saw the domination of "oligarchies" as the necessary outcome of large-scale organization. All three agreed that political power, and not property, forms the foundation of social-political hierarchies, and that these hierarchies can neither be reduced to nor deduced from economic class relations. Most importantly, elite theorists insisted that there could be no escape from elite power: revolutions merely mark elite circulation and, as illustrated by the Russian Revolution, do not narrow the power gap between the elites and the masses. Egalitarian political order and participatory democracy are, therefore, ideological dreams. History, observed Pareto, is a graveyard of successive elites or "aristocracies" ([1915] 1963, p. 1430).

Elite theories can also be seen as an intellectual response to the "modern trends" that strengthened the state and have led to the rapid expansion of government bureaucracies, the emergence of bureaucratized mass parties, the concentration of corporate power, the growth of powerful and centralized mass media, and the rise of fascist and communist movements and regimes—all of which have weakened liberal capitalism and dented the hopes for participatory democratization. Mosca, Pareto, Michels, and Weber all saw these trends as a consequence of bureaucratic industrialism. In their view, the increasing complexity of modern society implied progressive bureaucratic organization of all activities and power concentration in the hands of elites, who can effectively manage democratic institutions, accumulate the privileges that power brings, orchestrate mass support, and protect their positions by controlling access to the top. This view of power stratification, combined with the insistence on the universality of elites and treatment of elite characteristics as key explanatory variables, constitutes the most distinctive tenet of classic elite theory.

The second theoretical tenet concerns the capacity of power holders to organize themselves and form cohesive groups. Strong cohesion does not preclude the possibility of temporary intra-elite conflicts and divisions on specific policy questions. However, when it comes to defending common power interests, members of the elite act in unison, and this makes their power irresistible.

The third tenet concerns the linkages between elites and various "social forces," such as social movements, classes, and ethno-racial groups. The classic elite theorists insist that such linkages are an essential condition of elite power, but they are less than clear on precise meaning of such linkages.

The fourth tenet is about access and succession. Entry to the elite ranks depends on acquiring certain rare attributes (e.g., wealth, prestige, education), and it is carefully controlled—directly and indirectly—by elite incumbents. Elites control recruitment of their successors through institutional "gatekeepers" (e.g., corporate hierarchies, political party machines) as well as through elite "selectorates" operating at each level of hierarchical promotion. One outcome of these selective practices is a biased social composition; another is a persistence of elite outlooks, even at times of rapid social mobility and elite circulation, that is, replacement of elite members.

The final tenet highlights the way in which elites typically exercise their power. All elite theorists converge on a view of "engineered" elite domination through persuasion and manipulation, occasionally backed by force. Democratic elections have a symbolic character and are an important tool for the orderly circulation of elite personnel, but they seldom alter elite structure.

The post–World War II (1939–1945) students of elites played down the cohesion of elites and questioned the classic theorists' skepticism as to the prospects for democratization. In the seminal formulation of Joseph Schumpeter (1954), elites are an essential ingredient of modern democracy, which implies a regular electoral competition for political leadership. This idea was followed up by Robert Dahl (1971), Giovanni Sartori (1981) and many other "plural," "demo-," and "neo-" elite theorists. It was backed by empirical studies of modern elites (summarized by Robert Putnam in 1976), especially in advanced democracies, that revealed complex networks of competing and collaborating elite groups, rather than cohesive minorities. The key question was whether elites (mainly in the United States) formed a cohesive and unassailable "power elite" or more open, competitive, and responsive "plural" or "strategic" elite groups. The results of these studies, however, were inconclusive, largely because any picture of power distribution depends on the way power is defined and measured. Those who identified power holders by their reputation and incumbency in top organizational positions produced a picture of cohesive "establishments" and "power elites." In contrast, those who defined elites as key decision makers produced a picture of "plural" elites, that is, competing elite groups.

Contemporary elite theorists, especially those studying postcommunist transformations, transcend these debates, incorporate elites into broader power and stratification schemes, acknowledge the complexity of power sources and structures, and analyze elites as important "crafters" and "sustainers" of democratic regimes. Perhaps the best-known theoretical syntheses of the class and elite visions of the power structure were undertaken by Wlodzimierz Wesolowski and Eva Etzioni-Halevi, who both saw elites and classes as being linked. In this view, elites enter into alliances (via "coupling") with major classes and other "social forces." As mentioned above, elites are defined in political terms as the most powerful minorities, while classes are defined in economic terms as owners or workers. The relations between elite and regime types of power (including postcommunist regimes and established liberal democracies) have been explored by John Higley and his collaborators (e.g., Field and Higley 1980; Higley and Pakulski 1995; Higley and Burton 2006), who have focused on two elite characteristics—structural integration and value/normative consensus—as key determinants of political stability and democratic character of regimes. Only consensually united elites—that is, elites characterized by inclusiveness and open access (wide integration), as well as strong and widely shared agreement about the norms of political behavior ("rules of the game")—can sustain stable liberal democracies. Elites united by ideological formulas (e.g., the Chinese) operate stable but undemocratic regimes, while disunited elites accompany—and perpetuate—unstable regimes.

SEE ALSO *Class; Class Conflict; Communism; Democracy; Marx, Karl; Michels, Robert; Mills, C. Wright; Power, Political*

BIBLIOGRAPHY

Bottomore, Tom. 1993. *Elites and Society.* 2nd ed. London: Routledge.

Dahl, Robert A. 1971. *Polyarchy: Participation and Opposition.* New Haven, CT: Yale University Press.

Domhoff, William. 1967. *Who Rules America?* Englewood Cliffs, NJ: Prentice-Hall.

Etzioni-Halevi, Eva. 1993. *The Elite Connection: Problems and Potential of Western Democracy.* Cambridge, MA: Polity Press.

Field, G. Lowell, and John Higley. 1980. *Elitism.* London: Routledge.

Higley, John, and Michael Burton. 2006. *Elite Foundations of Liberal Democracy.* Lanham, MD: Rowman and Littlefield.

Higley, John, and Jan Pakulski. 1995. Elites and Democratic Transitions in Eastern Europe. *Australian Journal of Political Science* 30 (2): 32–54.

Higley, John, Jan Pakulski, and Wlodzimierz Wesolowski, eds. 1998. *Postcommunist Elites and Democracy in Eastern Europe.* New York: St. Martin's.

Keller, Suzanne. 1963. *Beyond the Ruling Class: Strategic Elites in Modern Society.* New York: Random House.

Mills, C. Wright. 1956. *The Power Elite.* Oxford: Oxford University Press.

Mosca, Gaetano. 1939. *The Power Elite.* Oxford: Oxford University Press.

Pareto, Vilfredo. [1915] 1963. *A Treatise on General Sociology.* New York: Dover.

Putnam, Robert. 1976. *The Ruling Class.* New York: McGraw-Hill.

Sartori, Giovanni. 1987. *The Theory of Democracy Revisited.* Chatham, NJ: Chatham House.

Schumpeter, Joseph. 1943. *Capitalism, Socialism, and Democracy.* London: Allen and Unwin.

Wesolowski, Wlodzimierz. 1977. *Classes, Strata, and Power.* London: Routledge and Kegan Paul.

Jan Pakulski

ELITES

The term *elites* refers to a small number of actors who are situated atop key social structures and exercise significant influence over social and political change. Much of the power of elites stems from their economic resources, their privileged access to institutions of power, and their ability to exercise moral or intellectual persuasion. At the same time, however, elites embody the values and represent the interests of particular groups in society. This can limit their autonomy, complicate efforts to cooperate with each other, and narrow the support they elicit from the public. It is this contradictory aspect of elites—simultaneously empowered and constrained by their positions as leaders in society—that defines their role in the political system.

While traditional notions of elites have typically focused on members of an aristocracy (or oligarchy), whose positions were based on claims to hereditary title and wealth, elites today comprise key figures across various sectors of society. In and around government, they include political leaders within the executive and legislative branches of government, those in command of the bureaucracy and military, and leading representatives of organized interests in society (such as labor unions or corporate lobbying groups). Within the economy, elites reside at the pinnacle of finance, banking, and production. In the cultural sphere, elites include major patrons of the arts, cultural icons (including pop culture), writers, academics, religious leaders, and prominent figures within the mass media. Most recently, transnational elites have arisen within emergent supranational institutions, such as corporate actors in the World Economic Forum, technocrats working in the United Nations system, and the heads of international nongovernmental organizations.

EVOLUTION OF THE TERM

Although the idea of elites can be traced back to the writings of Aristotle and Plato, the term *elites* was first used in modern social science by the Italian economists Vilfredo

Pareto (1902–1903) and Gaetano Mosca (1939) in the early twentieth century. In contrast to class theories, in which the sources of societal power inhered in institutions of property and class relations in society, early elite theories saw power concentrated among a minority of the population who were able to rule over the rest of the population with little accountability to them. As a result, elites were often conceptualized as "ruling elites," by virtue of their authority over the masses. As critics noted, however, the origins of elite power were underspecified. It was not clear, for example, if elites were inevitable products of modern organization, or if their position was contingent on their ability to control vital resources in society and mobilize the public.

In 1915, in his book *Political Parties*, the German sociologist Robert Michels introduced the "iron law of oligarchy." Michels contended that the existence of elites sprang from an inherent tendency of all complex organizations to delegate authority to a ruling clique of leaders (who often take on interests of their own). Accordingly, even the most radical organizations will develop a self-interested elite. In a prominent 1956 study of the United States, C. Wright Mills proposed that elite power was defined by its institutional origins. Mills argued that the place of a "power elite" was maintained by their positions in government, the military, and major corporations, which enabled them to command the organized hierarchies of modern society. While these and other works of the time, including Joseph Schumpeter's 1954 "competitive elitist" account of democracy, demonstrated the importance of the organizational bases of elite power, the origins of elites are more socially contingent on factors such as patronage and factionalism, leadership, and social structure than on institutional structure. Nonetheless, this classic work has heavily influenced elite studies, particularly scholars studying intra-elite political struggles within East bloc countries (through work termed "Kremlinology").

Distinguishing themselves from these classical theorists, scholars since the 1960s have begun to differentiate elites and recognize their diverse roles. Major works, such as Suzanne Keller's *Beyond the Ruling Class* (1963), have traced elites' sociological origins, examined their varied social functions, and engaged in empirical studies of a range of actors at the apex of almost any area of human activity. In contrast to classical approaches, these authors have highlighted ways in which elites conveyed societal claims upon the state. While this opened new avenues of research, their tendency to rely on the social profile of elites (such as age, education and occupation, and region or country of birth) at times produced inaccurate predictions of elite behavior. Though influential in shaping latent political attitudes, empirical research has shown that background characteristics are mediated by personal beliefs and values. As scholars

such as Robert D. Putnam (1976) have concluded, the attitudes and political styles of elites do affect political outcomes, but behavioral patterns must be placed in a context of elite linkages to different social strata.

There has also been considerable cross-national variation in the openness of elites. In many societies, the elite manipulation of political patronage and the organization of political parties have perpetuated elites' positions. In some countries, however, government programs have been designed to desegregate elites (though the success of these programs has been limited). As Richard L. Zweigenhaft and G. William Domhoff demonstrated in *Diversity in the Power Elite* (1998), affirmative action initiatives within the United States have led to some openness along racial, gender, and class lines. However, they also showed that minorities and women absorbed into the elite often minimize their differences and, paradoxically, strengthen the existing system. Thus, government reforms (in the United States and elsewhere) seeking to enhance the diversity of elites have not produced the expected or hoped for results.

ELITES AND THE POLITICAL SYSTEM

As suggested in foundational studies of elites, the importance of elites to the political system is heavily affected by struggles within ruling cliques and by elites' relationships to social structures. Although elites influence the political system in numerous ways, the focus here will be on their effects on political regimes and democracy, the politics of state development, and incidences of violent conflict.

The nature of competition and compromise among ruling elites carry major implications for democracy. Although pluralist theory suggests that the dispersion of power in democratic systems across interest groups and institutions leaves elites in charge of different sectors of democratic politics, elites have a coordinated effect in mobilizing public opinion and ushering in political change. In *The Nature and Origins of Mass Opinion* (1992), John Zaller describes how, even in established democracies, elites attempt to construct a political world through messages delivered via media outlets to the mass public. In nondemocratic regimes, concentrations of power within ruling circles means that stability and prospects for political change hinge on the skill and engineering of elites, who can negotiate compromises between competing factions. Indeed, it has been long held that elite failures to rise above societal divisions can contribute to the rise of extremist politics, as typified by the rise of Nazism in interwar Germany. As Dankwart A. Rustow (1970) and more recently John Higley and Michael Burton (1989) have argued, democratic elites must not only establish a language of compromise across factions, but also accept the boundaries of political competition, and become habituated to the rules of the game. Recent studies, however, have shown that extremist popular mobilization can coexist with elite negotiations, and that the success of democratic transition depends not on moderation per se, but on elite calculations and projections of whether the forces of political change—moderate or extremist—will threaten their interests after they cede power (Bermeo 1997).

In addition to power struggles within ruling circles, the struggle between rulers and local elites has been crucial in centuries-long efforts to complement states' juridical sovereignty with empirical statehood. As much of western European history attests, nobles, magnates, and landlords (among others), supported by property holdings and large armies, posed substantial challenges to the centralization of state power. Initially, future sovereign rulers were little more than members of the elite, as illustrated by Perry Anderson's reprint of the famous oath of allegiance among Spanish nobility: "We who are as good as you swear to you who are no better than we to accept you as our king and sovereign lord, provided you observe all our liberties and laws; but if not, not." (Anderson 1974, p. 65) Such diffuse systems of authority under local societal elites are also found in many "weak states" in contemporary Asia, Africa, and post-Communist Eurasia. Both historically and today, therefore, the emergence of effective state infrastructures depends on whether mixtures of coercion and patronage dispensed by rulers convince entrenched elites to cede political authority.

A final realm of politics in which elites play a critical role is violent conflict within society. In particular, intra-elite politics and elite-mass linkages reside at the center of civil wars, and elite power-sharing models have been applied across a diversity of contexts. Among the most well-known is Arend Lijphart's "consociational" model (1977), which claims that a coalition of elites, drawn from the conflicting sides, can mitigate violence through a system of elite consensus built on mutual veto power, proportional allocation of offices, and granting each group partial autonomy. The success of such negotiated pacts has been variable, deterring violence in the Netherlands and in post-apartheid South Africa but failing to prevent an explosion of intra-state conflicts in the immediate post–cold war period. Ultimately, the prevention or cessation of violence is causally related to how elites interact with one another and how effectively they channel societal claims through political institutions.

SEE ALSO *Aristocracy; Campaigning; Elections; Elitism; Power; Power Elite; Public Opinion*

BIBLIOGRAPHY

Anderson, Perry. 1974. *Lineages of the Absolutist State*. London: Verso.

Aron, Raymond. 1950. Social Structure and the Ruling Class. *British Journal of Sociology* 1 (1): 1–16, 126–143.

Bermeo, Nancy. 1997. Myths of Moderation: Confrontation and Conflict during Democratic Transitions. *Comparative Politics.* 29 (3): 305–322.

Bottomore, Thomas B. 1964. *Elites and Society*. London: C.A. Watts.

Higley, John, and Michael G. Burton. 1989. The Elite Variable in Democratic Transitions and Breakdowns. *American Sociological Review* 54 (1): 17–32.

Keller, Suzanne. 1963. *Beyond the Ruling Class: Strategic Elites in Modern Society*. New York: Random House.

Lijphart, Arend. 1977. *Democracy in Plural Societies: A Comparative Exploration*. New Haven, CT: Yale University Press.

Michels, Robert. 1915. *Political Parties: A Sociological Study of the Oligarchical Tendencies of Modern Democracies*. Trans. Eden and Cedar Paul. New Brunswick, NJ: Transaction Publishers, 1999.

Mills, C. Wright. 1956. *The Power Elite*. New York: Oxford University Press.

Mosca, Gaetano. 1939. *The Ruling Class*. Trans. Hannah D. Kahn. New York: McGraw-Hill. Originally published as *Elementi di scienza politica* (1896).

Pareto, Vilfredo. 1902–1903. *Les systemes socialistes*. 2 vols. Paris: Giard.

Putnam, Robert D. 1976. *The Comparative Study of Political Elites*. Englewood Cliffs, NJ: Prentice-Hall.

Rustow, Dankwart A. 1970. Transitions to Democracy: Toward a Dynamic Model. *Comparative Politics* 2 (3): 337–363.

Schumpeter, Joseph. 1942. *Capitalism, Socialism, and Democracy*. London: Harper & Brothers.

Zaller, John. 1992. *The Nature and Origins of Mass Opinion*. Cambridge, U.K.: Cambridge University Press.

Zweigenhaft, Richard L., and G. William Domhoff. 1998. *Diversity in the Power Elite: Have Women and Minorities Reached the Top?* New Haven, CT: Yale University Press.

Lawrence P. Markowitz

ELITISM

Elitism refers to the belief that leadership positions within a society, or in government more specifically, should be held by those possessing the highest levels of education, wealth, and social status. According to elitism, a select subgroup should make or influence decisions for the whole society. Overall, elitism as an ideology advocates that select citizens are best fit to govern.

First noted in Western philosophy by Socrates (c. 470–399 BCE), who described the good society as one headed by philosopher kings, elitism is distrustful of the masses and is in clear opposition to egalitarian or pluralistic principles. Contradicting democratic theory, elitism contends that the capacity to effectively control a dynamic and multifaceted political arena is absent in the average citizen and should be reserved only for a limited few. Thus elitism defers to those individuals whose backgrounds and experiences are believed to make them superior. Depending on the society in question, superiority can be based on perceived intellectual aptitude, skin color, or other factors. Most commonly, characteristics of the elite include educational achievement, family background, and economic affluence. In some societies ethnic heritage, religious affiliation, or gender are the basis of a classification system that distinguishes the elite from the nonelite. In sum, elitism can be defined as an asymmetrical relationship in which a select few, who are considered superior, exercise control over the many, who are considered inferior.

In practice, elites pervade most societal institutions in industrialized Western democratic nations, according to Jack C. Plano and Milton Greenberg (1997). Elites may wield significant influence in such specific arenas as commerce, the military, and government operations. Sociology and political science scholarship has analyzed the role of elites in decision-making processes in various institutional settings. A seminal work by the sociologist C. Wright Mills (1916–1962), *The Power Elite* (1956), argues that a single elite, rather than a variety of competing groups, makes key decisions for the nation as a whole. The governing elite includes political leaders, corporate leaders, and military leaders.

Due to its advocacy of the virtues of the select over the "commoners," elitism as a normative theory often comes under fire for its antidemocratic tendencies. Critics argue that elitism leads to corruption, greed, intolerance, racism, and other undesirable social outcomes. Many political reform movements have been defined by their desires to eliminate elitist political structures. The historian Richard Hofstadter (1916–1970), in his book *The Age of Reform*, gives as an example of antielitism the late nineteenth-century populist movement in the United States. The populists, he argues, believed in the "people versus the interest, the public versus the plutocrats, the toiling multitude versus the money power—in various phases this central antagonism was expressed" (1955, p. 65).

SEE ALSO *Aristocracy; Corporatism; Elites; Hierarchy; Inequality, Wealth; Leadership; Meritocracy; Mills, C. Wright; Populism; Power Elite; Stratification*

BIBLIOGRAPHY

Hofstadter, Richard. 1955. *The Age of Reform: From Bryan to F. D. R.* New York: Vintage.

Plano, Jack C., and Milton Greenberg, eds. 1997. *The American Political Dictionary.* 10th ed. New York: Harcourt Brace.

Beth A. Rosenson
H. E. Schmeisser

ELLIS, ALBERT

SEE *Psychotherapy.*

ELLIS ISLAND

When people today refer to Ellis Island, they generally invoke its legacy in the national saga of immigration to America, standing with the Statue of Liberty in New York Harbor as a beacon of opportunity for the world's dispossessed. However, the building of a federal facility at the site of an old naval arsenal on Ellis Island in 1892 grew out of the newly established federal authority to regulate and restrict immigration.

Before federal processing was institutionalized at Ellis Island, states had the right to set the criteria for the suitability of immigrants, with an interest in recruiting labor and excluding potential wards of the state. Two-thirds of the migrants to the United States between 1786 and 1892 came through New York City, and after 1855 immigration processing, including medical exams, customs inspection, and name registration, took place at Castle Garden in lower Manhattan, where social reformers set up voluntary services to help immigrants find work and housing. Similar immigration stations were located in Boston, Baltimore, and Galveston.

With the emergence of a national economy and a national transportation system in the years following the Civil War (1861–1865), immigration fell increasingly under federal scrutiny, and the federal government passed laws to restrict the entry of immigrants thought to be undesirable. Early efforts restricted the entry of prostitutes, convicts, incapacitated people, and contract labor. The most important exception to general practices of open immigration was Chinese exclusion, codified in federal law as the Chinese Exclusion Act of 1882, establishing the prerogative of the federal government to raise restrictive barriers against specific national groups and to mark them as permanently foreign, aliens without rights. Between 1880 and 1900, the pace of immigration to the United States increased dramatically, with nine million immigrants arriving in these years. Laborers from England, Ireland, Germany, and the Scandinavian countries were now joined by new arrivals from Italy, Austria-Hungary, Russia, Canada, Greece, Syria, the West Indies,

Mexico, and Japan. Nativist concerns about the new immigrants led to escalating pressures for a federal immigration policy.

The new federal immigration station that opened in 1892 on Ellis Island was a key component of the new federal immigration policy, which set standards for minimum health and competency, regulated the process of inspection and deportation for overseas immigration, and delegated enforcement to a superintendent of immigration and an Office of Immigration, located within the Department of the Treasury, later Commerce, and then Labor, until 1940, when the Immigration Service was transferred to the Department of Justice. Ellis Island was the entry point for twelve million people, about three-fourths of the migrants who entered the United States between 1892 and 1924. On its busiest day, April 17, 1907, Ellis Island officials processed 11,747 immigrants. Other federal immigrant processing stations were established at Boston, Philadelphia, Baltimore, and at Angel Island in San Francisco Bay.

Many European immigrant accounts of their experience at Ellis Island emphasized the hopefulness of arrival and the often confusing and sometimes frightening aspects of inspection. Steerage passengers entering New York Harbor boarded ferries for Ellis Island (American-born passengers and those travelling first and second class were examined on board ship). After being tagged with their number from the ship's official listing, immigrants walked into the baggage room where they were encouraged to check their belongings. Then they moved up the steps to the second-floor registry room in the Great Hall, where they were evaluated by medical inspectors looking for contagious diseases and physical disabilities, and by legal inspectors checking that names, birthplaces, ages, and occupations matched ship registries and ascertaining that immigrants were not likely to become wards of the state. Stories from prior travelers helped immigrants rehearse answers for the inspectors, and provided strategies for passing through successfully, for example, discretely passing the same twenty-five dollars from immigrant to immigrant to preempt the requirement for proving self-support. A literacy test for immigrants over fourteen was administered after 1917.

The shipping lines had to bear the cost of returning "excluded aliens" to their point of departure. Most newcomers, 80 percent or more, passed through the process successfully; detention for the remaining 20 percent, for legal or medical reasons, lasted in most cases less than two weeks. Although most of the patients held in medical detention recovered and were able to complete the immigration process, between 1900 and 1954, over 3,500 people, including 1,400 children, died on Ellis Island. Historians have calculated that despite a growing number of excludable categories, only about 2 percent of Ellis Island migrants failed to gain entry. In comparison, Chinese immigrants trying to gain entry through Angel Island by making use of the very few exceptions provided by the Chinese exclusion laws faced much more rigorous interrogation and isolation, and much lengthier detentions.

Ellis Island's functions changed dramatically with the passage of immigration restriction in the 1920s, ending the era of open European immigration. Combined pressures for exclusion proposed by white Anglo-Saxon Protestant restrictionist groups, reinforced by theories of scientific racism spurred by World War I (1914–1918) rhetoric of "100 percent Americanism," the Red Scare's linking of foreigners with radicalism, and the labor movement's fears of rising unemployment, resulted in the passage of the Quota Act in 1921 and the Johnson-Reed Act in 1924. The Quota Act limited the total number of immigrants who could enter the United States and required that immigrants bring passports. The Johnson-Reed Act did not limit immigration from the Western Hemisphere, but it reduced the total number of entering immigrants, and most significantly, established national-origins quotas to favor northern and western European immigrants, who received 82 percent of the annual total quota allotted. The Johnson-Reed Act also expanded the category of illegal aliens, reaffirming the principle of Chinese exclusion and barring Japanese and other immigrants from the "Asiatic Zone," defined in 1917 as stretching from Afghanistan to the Pacific, on the legal grounds of their exclusion from citizenship.

By the 1920s, Ellis Island officials were processing far fewer arrivals and were no longer providing medical or mental exams or housing immigrants who were ill, since the passport and visa requirements relocated many aspects of verification and inspection from Ellis Island back to the country of origin. During the 1930s, nearly as many people left as entered the United States, and Ellis Island officials processed some immigrants returning to Europe. During World War I, Ellis Island became a temporary detention center for "enemy aliens," and in 1919 radicals rounded up by Attorney General A. Mitchell Palmer (1872–1936) and housed incommunicado prior to deportation included the Russian anarchist activists Emma Goldman (1869–1940) and Alexander Berkman (1870–1936). Ellis Island was increasingly used for detention and deportation of "aliens." By the 1930s, the people detained on the island were undocumented immigrants without passports or visas, foreign-born criminals awaiting deportation, and sick merchant mariners receiving treatment at the hospital.

During World War II (1939–1945), "enemy aliens" were again held on the island. After 1950, immigrants suspected of being communists were denied entry or detained awaiting deportation, including the West Indian Marxist writer C. L. R. James (1901–1989) in 1952. Despite the needs of the many refugees created during World War II, the restrictive immigration laws kept the numbers of European immigrants very small. Ellis Island was finally abandoned by the Immigration and Naturalization Service in 1954 and classified as surplus property. President Dwight D. Eisenhower's (1890–1969) General Services Administration tried unsuccessfully to sell Ellis Island and its buildings to the highest bidder in 1956. President Lyndon B. Johnson (1908–1973), who traveled to the Statue of Liberty to sign immigration reform in 1965, granted landmark status to Ellis Island as part of the Statue of Liberty National Monument within the jurisdiction of the National Park Service. New interest in historic preservation and in European-heritage ethnicity generated popular and public support for the restoration and reopening of Ellis Island as an immigration museum in 1990.

SEE ALSO *Immigrants, European; Immigrants, New York City*

BIBLIOGRAPHY

Chermayeff, Ivan, Fred Wasserman, and Mary J. Shapiro. 1991. *Ellis Island: An Illustrated History of the Immigrant Experience.* New York: Macmillan.

Moreno, Barry. *Encyclopedia of Ellis Island.* 2004. Westport, CT: Greenwood.

Ngai, Mai M. 2004. *Impossible Subjects: Illegal Aliens and the Making of Modern America.* Princeton, NJ: Princeton University Press.

Smith, Judith E. 1992. Celebrating Immigration History at Ellis Island. *American Quarterly* 44: 82–100.

Yans-McLaughlin, Virginia, and Marjorie Lightman. 1997. *Ellis Island and the Peopling of America: The Official Guide.* New York: New Press.

Judith E. Smith

EMOTION

Over the last three decades, the sociology of emotions has developed a number of distinct theoretical and research programs (for recent reviews, see: Turner and Stets 2005, 2007; Stets and Turner 2006). While there is considerable overlap among some perspectives on emotions in sociology, they can be roughly grouped into six basic approaches: (1) dramaturgical and cultural, (2) ritual, (3) symbolic interactionist, (4) exchange, (5) structural, and (6) evolutionary.

Dramaturgical and cultural approaches all draw upon the early insights of Goffman (1967), who argued that human interaction is very much like a performance on a stage. Like all stage performances, there is a script—in this case written by cultural ideologies and norms of a society—with actors engaging in strategic performances as they interpret the script and use props to make a dramatic presentation of self to an audience. Hochschild (1983) was the first to adopt elements of this metaphor by analyzing how the cultural script, social structure, and audience expectations force individuals to manage emotions that they do not feel. As a consequence, individuals must engage in "emotion work" that is inherently alienating. Other researchers have stressed how individuals use cultural scripts as a cover for more strategic performances in games of micropolitics and microeconomics (Clark 1997).

Ritual approaches draw from Durkheim's analysis of "collective effervescence" and emphasize that when individuals are co-present, the dynamics that ensue can build up positive and negative emotional energy that, ultimately, is the energy driving the formation, reproduction, and change of social structures and culture (Collins 2004). When initial greeting rituals arouse mild positive sentiments, subsequent talk and body language become rhythmically synchronized, leading to emotional entrainment and heightened emotions that increase social solidarity, which, in turn, is represented with group symbols. When these processes fail, negative emotional energy is aroused, thereby lowering solidarity.

Symbolic interactionist approaches all emphasize the central place of self in arousing emotions (Stryker 2004; Burke 1991). When self is verified by others, positive emotions ensue, whereas when self is not confirmed, negative emotions are aroused. Self is seen as a cybernetic control system in which individuals seek to maintain consistency among cognitions about self, behavior, situation, and other; discrepancies between any of these cognitions lead to negative emotional arousal that serves as the motivation to change the self presented, behaviors, definitions of the situation, or assessments of others (Heise 1979). Psychoanalytic variants of symbolic interactionism emphasize that individuals often protect self through the activation of defense mechanisms, which push the negative emotions, such as shame, below the level of consciousness (Scheff 1988). Once repressed, the emotions are transmuted into new kinds of more intense negative emotions (Turner 2002).

Exchange approaches view social interaction as the reciprocal flow of resources. Individuals seek to gain a profit in all exchanges by assessing whether or not their rewards exceed costs and investments. When individuals see that their and others' shares of resources are proportionate to respective costs and investments, they experience positive emotions; and when they do not, negative emotions are aroused (Lawler 2001). People always compare their receipt of resources to cultural standards of justice. When actual shares of resources meet standards of what constitutes a "just share," positive emotions are experienced; when shares do not correspond to perceptions of a "just" share, negative emotions are aroused (Homans 1974; Jasso 1980). The positive emotions in profitable exchanges become yet another resource to be exchanged and lead individuals to make suboptimal commitments (or less than maximum payoffs) to social relations that increase solidarity (Lawler and Yoon, 1996).

Structural approaches see interaction as revolving around the distribution of power and prestige, with individuals having expectations for how much power or prestige they can claim in a situation (Kemper 1978; Ridgeway and Johnson 1990). When these expectations are realized, positive emotions ensue, but when there is competition for status and/or prestige or when a person does not receive anticipated prestige or power, negative emotional arousal among some actors will ensue. Moreover, once the distribution of power and prestige is established, expectations operate to sustain this distribution, and the emotions generated become yet another expectation state.

Evolutionary approaches seek to outline the selection pressures that operated on humans' hominid ancestors to produce the neurological structures responsible for emotional arousal (Wentworth and Yardly 1994; Turner 2000; Hammond 2004). Although these approaches vary in terms of how much they see biology as determining specific emotional responses, they all emphasize that the human brain was rewired under intense selection pressures to produce a wider palate of emotions, which enhanced the fitness of humans' ancestors by increasing bonds of social solidarity.

As is evident, then, the sociology of emotions has grown enormously from its tentative beginnings in the 1970s. There is a broad set of approaches, each with a coherent body of theory and most with active research programs testing and extending these theories. The sociology of emotions is now the leading edge of sociological social psychology and microsociology in general.

SEE ALSO *Emotion and Affect; Psychosomatics, Social*

BIBLIOGRAPHY

Burke, Peter J. 1991. Identity Processes and Social Stress. *American Sociological Review* 56 (6): 836–849.

Clark, Candace. 1997. *Misery and Company: Sympathy in Everyday Life.* Chicago: University of Chicago Press.

Collins, Randall. 2004. *Interaction Ritual Chains.* Princeton, NJ: Princeton University Press.

Goffman, Erving. 1967. *Interaction Ritual: Essays in Face-to-Face Behavior.* Garden City, NY: Anchor Books.

Hammond, Michael. 2004. The Enhancement Imperative and Group Dynamics in the Emergence of Religion and Ascriptive Inequality. In *Theory and Research on Human Emotions*, Advances in Group Processes 21, ed. Jonathan H. Turner, 167–188. New York: Plenum.

Heise, David R. 1979. *Understanding Events: Affect and the Construction of Social Action.* Cambridge, U.K.: Cambridge University Press.

Hochschild, Arlie Russell. 1983. *The Managed Heart: Commercialization of Human Feeling.* Berkeley: University of California Press.

Homans, George C. 1974. *Social Behavior: Its Elementary Forms.* 2nd ed. New York: Harcourt Brace and World.

Jasso, Guillermina. 1980. A New Theory of Distributive Justice. *American Sociological Review* 45 (1): 3–32.

Kemper, Theodore D. 1978. *A Social Interactional Theory of Emotions.* New York: John Wiley.

Lawler, Edward J. 2001. An Affect Theory of Social Exchange. *American Journal of Sociology* 107 (2): 321–352.

Lawler, Edward J., and Jeongkoo Yoon. 1996. Commitment in Exchange Relations: Test of a Theory of Relational Cohesion. *American Sociological Review* 61 (1): 89–108.

Ridgeway, Cecilia L., and Cathryn Johnson. 1990. What Is the Relationship between Socioemotional Behavior and Status in Task Groups? *American Journal of Sociology* 95 (5): 1189–1212.

Scheff, Thomas. 1988. Shame and Conformity: The Deference-Emotion System. *American Sociological Review* 53 (3): 395–406.

Stets, Jan E., and Jonathan H. Turner, eds. 2006. *Handbook of the Sociology of Emotions.* New York: Springer.

Stryker, Sheldon. 2004. Integrating Emotion into Identity Theory. In *Theory and Research on Human Emotions*, Advances in Group Processes 21, ed. Jonathan H. Turner, 1–23. New York: Plenum.

Turner, Jonathan H. 2000. *On the Origins of Human Emotions: A Sociological Inquiry into the Evolution of Human Affect.* Stanford, CA: Stanford University Press.

Turner, Jonathan H. 2002. *Face to Face: Toward a Sociological Theory of Interpersonal Behavior.* Stanford, CA: Stanford University Press.

Turner, Jonathan H., and Jan E. Stets. 2005. *The Sociology of Emotions.* New York: Cambridge University Press.

Turner, Jonathan H., and Jan E. Stets. 2006. Sociological Theories of Human Emotions. *Annual Review of Sociology* 32, 25–52.

Wentworth, William M., and D. Yardley. 1994. Deep Sociality: A Bioevolutionary Perspective on the Sociology of Human Emotions. In *Social Perspectives on Emotion*, eds. David D. Franks, William M. Wentworth and John Ryan, 21–55. Greenwich, CT: JAI Press.

Jonathan H. Turner

EMOTION AND AFFECT

Emotions are central to one's personal and social life, and they have been an important topic in psychology throughout history. The terms *mood* and *emotion* are often used interchangeably to refer to certain aspects of affect. But while there are similarities, mood and emotion are fundamentally different. For example, emotions appear to have a particular cause and are short-lived. They are psychological experiences that involve the interplay of cognitive, physiological, and expressive behavior. In contrast, psychologists define *affect* as an individual's externally displayed mood. Typically people feel some level of positive affect and some level of negative affect in their daily life.

CATEGORIES AND TYPES OF EMOTION

Although psychologists and philosophers have discussed emotions for years, debates continue about what constitutes an emotion and how different emotional experiences should be classified. In 1990 Andrew Otrony and Terence Turner summarized a list of the basic emotions that had been compiled by a wide variety of researchers. In general nearly everybody who postulates basic emotions includes anger, happiness, sadness, and fear. In addition there are two main approaches in proposing basic emotions. The biological view suggests that emotions can be understood in terms of their evolutionary origin and significance and that this knowledge can contribute to understanding the function of emotions. The psychological view suggests that there might be some small, basic set of emotions on which all others are built. Basic emotion classification has been useful in explaining how emotions evolve and exist in all cultures.

Another way to classify emotions involves whether they are discrete categories or continuous dimensions. Categorical models focus on a number of discrete emotions (e.g., basic emotions). In contrast, dimensional models typically focus on varying levels of self-reported feelings on a particular dimension varying from positive to negative. Categorical and dimensional models are often discussed separately, but they are not necessarily incompatible. For example, the discrete emotion of happiness corresponds with high activation and pleasantness (positive valence), whereas the discrete emotion of sadness corresponds to low activation and low pleasantness (negative valence). Researchers can employ both models of categorizations, or they can advantage one over the other.

THEORIES ON EMOTION AND AFFECT

Historically the James-Lange theory was independently proposed by William James and Carl Lange in the 1880s. Together they argued that emotion is the perception of physiological changes in the body. For example, a person experiences fear because he or she perceives physiological changes, such as an increase in heart rate and breathing, muscle tension, and sweat gland activity. In 1927 Walter Cannon and Philip Bard criticized this theory, suggesting that an individual experiences an emotional event first, after which more information is collected through one's senses. This additional information is sent through the nervous system to the brain, where a message is sent to the cortex, thereby producing a specific emotion, and to the hypothalamus, which controls the body's responses, such as crying or laughing.

In 1962 Stanley Schachter and Jerome Singer proposed that there were two factors that determine different emotions: the physical changes in a person's body in response to an event or stimulus and the interpretation that the person gives to those changes. An important assumption in the Schachter-Singer view is that once an emotional feeling has been produced, that particular feeling can cause specific actions. There has also been considerable theoretical and empirical work attempting to identify specific cognitive dimensions that shape the emotional response. In 1990 Richard Lazarus and Craig Smith described a specific appraisal model detailing the specific cognitive evaluations that are associated with (and hypothesized to be causally antecedent to) the experience of a number of distinct emotions.

Although these and many other emotion theorists have postulated and tested their ideas, there are many aspects of emotion that are still untested and undiscovered. New advances in neuroscience will allow researchers to observe physiological characteristics that are more objective compared to cognitive appraisals. A number of noninvasive techniques have been developed to measure physiological responses, such as heart rate reactivity, skin conductance, and cortisol levels with greater accuracy. Researchers can also study an individual's response to emotional stimuli and record the individual's expression of emotion. Concurrent measures of physiological, cognitive, and expressive behaviors of emotion allow researchers to study emotions in a more complete and dynamic way.

RELATIONS TO DEVELOPMENTAL OUTCOMES

The experience of emotions has significant psychological and physiological effects. How people interpret their experience motivates and guides their actions and specific behaviors. Emotions convey to others what the individual is feeling, and they may also help regulate social interactions. Several studies have demonstrated that children's understanding of emotions, awareness of emotional states, and emotion regulation are associated with children's socio-emotional competence and coping skills. Social competence in turn is associated with positive development in areas such as peer acceptance, school achievement, and emotional well-being. Nancy Eisenberg has suggested that sympathy (concern for others based on the apprehension of another's state) and empathy (an emotional reaction elicited by and congruent with another's state) stimulate the development of internalized moral principles reflecting concern for other people's welfare. Indeed in a 1999 study Eisenberg and colleagues found a relation between sympathy and empathy and prosocial behavior.

Some research indicates that an inability to express and interpret emotions in socially appropriate ways may lead to maladaptive behaviors, such as aggression and social withdrawal. For example, even though anger can serve to regulate interpersonal behavior, it comes to be regulated in an interpersonal context through socialization. The individual has to learn when and how to express anger in culturally acceptable ways. Problems in emotion regulation and the expression of anger are implicated with failures in social interaction (see Lemerise and Dodge 1993), while difficulty in the regulation of anger is further reflected in psychopathology (see Dodge and Garber 1991). Thus the ability to modulate and express emotions is associated with a variety of maladaptive and adaptive developmental outcomes.

SEE ALSO *Behavior, Self-Constrained; Emotion; Emotion Regulation; Empathy; James, William; Schachter, Stanley*

BIBLIOGRAPHY

Cannon, Walter B. 1927. The James-Lange Theory of Emotion: A Critical Examination and an Alternative Theory. *American Journal of Psychology* 39: 106–124.

Dodge, Kenneth A., and Judy Garber. 1991. Domains of Emotion Regulation. In *The Development of Emotion Regulation and Dysregulation*, eds. Judy Garber and Kenneth A. Dodge, 3–11. New York: Cambridge University Press.

Eisenberg, Nancy, Amanda Cumberland, and Tracy L. Spinard. 1998. Parental Socialization of Emotion. *Psychological Inquiry* 9 (4): 241–273.

Eisenberg, Nancy, I. K. Guthrie, B. C. Murphy, et al. 1999. Consistency and Development of Prosocial Dispositions: A Longitudinal Study. *Child Development* 70 (6): 1360–1370.

Ekman, Paul. 1999. Basic Emotions. In *Handbook of Cognition and Emotion*, ed. Tim Dalgleish and Mick J. Power, 45–60. Chichester, U.K.: Wiley.

James, William. 1884. What Is an Emotion? *Mind* 9: 188–205.

Lazarus, Richard S. 1966. *Psychological Stress and the Coping Process.* New York: McGraw-Hill.

Lemerise, Elizabeth, and Kenneth A. Dodge. 1993. The Development of Anger and Hostile Interactions. In *The*

Handbook of Emotions, eds. Michael Lewis and Jeannette M. Haviland, 537–544. New York: Guilford.

Ortony, A., and T. J. Turner. 1990. What's Basic about Basic Emotions? *Psychological Review* 97 (3): 315–331.

Schachter, Stanley, and Jerome Singer. 1962. Cognitive, Social, and Physiological Determinants of Emotional State. *Psychological Review* 69: 379–399.

Smith, Craig A., and Richard S. Lazarus. 1990. Emotion and Adaptation. In *Handbook of Personality: Theory and Research*, ed. Lawrence A. Pervin, 609–637. New York: Guilford.

Pa Her

EMOTION REGULATION

The study of emotion regulation is a burgeoning subfield within the modern social sciences. It explores how individuals influence the emotions they have, as well as when and how they experience and express their emotions. Whereas an *emotion* refers to a brief response to an internal or external event, *emotion regulation* is the process by which individuals influence the intensity, duration, valence, or manifestation of that response. Some researchers argue that all emotions are inherently regulated, so that emotion need not be distinguished from emotion regulation.

Emotion regulation is distinct from *coping*, insofar as coping focuses primarily on decreasing a negative emotional experience. Emotion regulation, in contrast, can include increasing or decreasing both positive and negative emotions. Emotion regulation may be conscious or unconscious, it may reflect controlled or automatic cognitive processes, it may occur at multiple time points in the course of an emotional response, and it may exert a multiprong effect on numerous facets of emotion (i.e., subjective experience, behavioral expression, physiological response).

Early interest in the field of emotion regulation can be traced back to Freudian psychoanalytic perspectives on unconscious anxiety regulation, as well as to the early stress and coping literature. Contemporary perspectives now rely heavily on James Gross's process model of emotion regulation (1998), in which he distinguishes between *antecedent-focused* strategies, which occur before an emotion is generated, and *response-focused* strategies, which are aimed at altering an already existing emotion by increasing or decreasing the experience, outward behavior (such as by suppressing), or physiological response. Antecedent-focused strategies include situation selection, situation modification, attentional deployment, and cognitive change (i.e., reappraisal). Situation selection refers to either approaching or avoiding specific places, people, or objects in order to alter their emotional impact. Attentional deployment is used to alter a specific aspect of a situation by focusing one's attention toward it. Cognitive change has gained increasing attention in cognitive therapies as a means to alter a person's emotional response upstream by changing the way one thinks about a given situation. Response-focused strategies include any act that influences one's ongoing experience of behavioral or physiological emotion response. An example includes behavioral suppression, or the dampening of one's outward displays of emotion (such as trying to constrain facial expressions of happiness).

ADAPTIVE AND MALADAPTIVE EMOTION REGULATION STRATEGIES

Researchers have begun to examine whether some types of emotion regulation strategies are more adaptive than others. Initial evidence demonstrates that reappraisal is an adaptive strategy associated with improved social functioning, positive emotion, and well-being. Suppression, by contrast, is a maladaptive strategy associated with elevated levels of negative affect and decreased positive affect. The chronic use of maladaptive strategies is thought to represent a core mechanism underlying numerous clinical disorders, ranging from binge eating and schizophrenia to bipolar disorder and generalized anxiety. In a 2004 paper, Ann Kring and Kelly Werner highlight two ways in which clinical disorders might represent difficulties regulating strong feelings; namely, through either *emotion dysregulation*, which involves the inappropriate use of otherwise intact regulatory processes, and *problems in emotion regulation*, involving an absence or deficit of basic regulatory processes. Whereas emotion dysregulation might involve an individual who is able to reappraise but simply does not implement his or her skills in the appropriate context, problems in emotion regulation refers to profound deficit in the requisite skills of reappraisal. Additional research is needed to examine the ways different clinical disorders represent such impairments, and whether such difficulties are transdiagnostic.

EMOTION REGULATION AND DEVELOPMENT

Developmental psychologists have given extensive treatment to the study of emotion regulation in infancy. Temperamental differences in emotion regulation have suggested that children have innate differences in the threshold to elicit positive or negative emotions as well as differences in the capacity to self-soothe, an important regulatory strategy. Emotion regulation is learned early in life largely by external agents such as caregivers. Joseph Campos, Carl Frankel, and Linda Camras argue that the infant and caregiver represent a "coregulatory system," and that early in development the parents' expressive behaviors serve as powerful regulators of a child's current emotional state. Children often synchronize and coordinate the expressions of their caregivers as a means to learn how to appropriately express feelings in given contexts. However, as the infant develops, he or she becomes increasingly less reliant on the caregiver and more independent in the initiation and control over regulating his or her feelings. With further age advancement, research across the lifespan suggests people also become more effective in regulating their own feelings as they age.

SEE ALSO *Behavior, Self-Constrained; Coping; Emotion and Affect; Freud, Sigmund*

BIBLIOGRAPHY

Campos, Joseph J., Carl B. Frankel, and Linda Camras. 2004. On the Nature of Emotion Regulation. *Child Development* 75 (2): 377–394.

Gross, James J. 1998. The Emerging Field of Emotion Regulation: An Integrative Approach. *Review of General Psychology* 2: 271–299.

Kring, Ann M., and Kelly H. Werner. 2004. Emotion Regulation in Psychopathology. In *The Regulation of Emotion*, eds. Pierre Philippot and Robert S. Feldman, 359–385. Mahwah, NJ: L. Erlbaum.

June Gruber

EMOTIONAL INTELLIGENCE

SEE *Intelligence, Social; Multiple Intelligences Theory.*

EMOTIONS, PSYCHOLOGY OF

SEE *Emotion and Affect.*

EMPATHY

Although definitions of empathy vary, the word is frequently defined as a vicarious emotional reaction based on the apprehension or comprehension of another's emotional state or condition. Inherent in this definition is that this reaction is identical or very similar to what the other person is feeling or would be expected to feel in the situation. Indeed, empathy may often be the origin of other related emotional reactions. In many situations, for example, empathy is likely to turn into either sympathy or personal distress. Sympathy is an emotional reaction based on the apprehension of another's emotional state or condition that involves feelings of compassion, sorrow, or concern for another person, rather than feeling merely the same emotion as the other individual. Sympathy is believed to involve an "other" orientation and the motivation to assist the other person, whereas empathy by itself does not. However, empathy may also turn into personal distress—an aversive, self-focused emotional reaction (such as anxiety or discomfort) to another's emotional state or condition. Personal distress is associated with a focus on "self," with a desire to make the self, not the other person, feel better. Sympathy, on the other hand, tends to be related to other-oriented altruistic behavior, particularly when it is not easy to escape from the need or distress of the other person, or from social sanctions for not helping. Moreover, inducing adults to feel sympathy for a stigmatized group improves attitudes toward the group as a whole.

Empathy and sympathy appear to increase with age in childhood, but they may stabilize by mid- to late adolescence. Sympathy is not only related to engaging in prosocial behaviors such as helping and sharing, it is also correlated with high levels of social competence, low aggression in children, and measures of psychological adjustment. Females tend to score higher in sympathy and empathy than males, especially if the measure is self-reported or other-reported. Girls tend to display more concerned behaviors than boys, but there is no gender difference in males' and females' physiological reactions to empathy-inducing stimuli. Thus, males and females may respond similarly to empathy-inducing stimuli but interpret or react differently to them (Eisenberg and Fabes, 1998).

Empathy appears to have a biological basis. Identical twins, for example, tend to be more alike in empathy and sympathy than are fraternal twins. However, the familial and larger social environment appears to affect individual differences in empathy and sympathy. People tend to be more empathic or sympathetic if they are securely attached to their mother and if their parents are sympathetic, supportive, and warm in their parenting. In addition, parental expression of positive emotion in the family, parental discussion of emotion, and parental use of reasoning that emphasizes the effects of children's behavior on others (and helps them to take the perspective of another) have been associated with the development of sympathy (and often empathy) in children. The expression of hostile negative emotions (e.g., anger) in the home has been associated with low levels of sympathy in children, but this association may not hold by adolescence.

Finally, because self-regulation is associated with being sympathetic, parenting practices that foster the regulation of emotion and behavior appear to promote the development of sympathy.

SEE ALSO *Altruism and Prosocial Behavior; Emotion; Perspective-taking; Role Theory*

BIBLIOGRAPHY

Batson, C. Daniel. 1991. *The Altruism Question: Toward a Social-Psychological Answer.* Hillsdale, NJ: L. Erlbaum.

Davis, Mark H. 1994. *Empathy: A Social Psychological Approach.* Madison, WI: Brown & Benchmark.

Eisenberg, Nancy, and Richard A. Fabes. 1998. Prosocial Development. In *Social, Emotional, and Personality Development.* Vol. 3 of *Handbook of Child Psychology,* 5th ed., eds. William Damon (series ed.) and Nancy Eisenberg (vol. ed), 701–778. New York: John Wiley.

Nancy Eisenberg

EMPIRE

Empire, imperial, and *imperialism* are terms with complex and contested histories: one is even tempted to think of them as *essentially* contested concepts in the philosophers' sense. In the political discourse of the twentieth century's second half, they were well-nigh always used pejoratively. Almost nobody, and no state, was willing to adopt them as self-descriptions. The idea of empire has often been associated, sometimes in emotive or polemical style, with particularly aggressive, coercive, expansionist, hierarchical, and indeed racist forms of power. Such associations have been yet more widely perceived in relation to *imperialism,* a term whose uses have tended to be more monolithically pejorative than have those of *empire.*

THEORIES AND POLEMICS

The concept of empire has also tended, at least until recently, to be far more widely employed and debated among humanities scholars—especially, and naturally enough, historians—than by social scientists. Few among the latter have explicitly or elaborately theorized the concept of empire. In the early twenty-first century, however, there were some signs of a change in these patterns, especially amidst widespread and often heated debate over the idea of a new American "empire."

The relative dearth of theoretical elaboration thus coexisted with a remarkable effervescence of controversy and (especially, perhaps, since the 1980s) with influences coming from numerous academic disciplines, milieus, and indeed theoretical traditions. Empire, its aftermaths, and its enduring significance have not only been the concerns of historians and political or international relations analysts. In recent years, they have become major preoccupations among cultural and literary critics and theorists. In some other fields too—political theory, economics and development studies, anthropology, human geography, and more—they have generated a rapidly growing and often highly contentious literature. There has, however, been a relative lack, still, of interaction between political, economic, and strategic studies of global power on the one hand, and work by literary and cultural studies scholars interested in the cultures and discourses of imperialism on the other. These spheres of research have operated largely in an atmosphere of mutual indifference or even antagonism, and although here too a growing body of recent work seeks to close the gaps, they remain wide.

Diversity, imprecision, and ideological inflection have inevitably followed from that background. The terms *empire* and *imperialism* have at times been used to refer to all forms of relation between more powerful states or societies and less powerful ones. They have also, even beyond these loose boundaries, often been employed in academic discourse in a great range of vaguely allusive, metaphorical, or polemical ways. They have additionally been intertwined with several other, mostly newer but equally contentious words: especially *colonialism*, and latterly *neocolonialism*, *globalization*, and others. A great range of compound terms has also been thrown into the stew at different times and places: *informal empire, subimperialism, cultural imperialism, internal colonialism, postcolonialism*, and many more.

DEFINITIONS

More substantive attempts at definition have centered around the notion of an empire as a large political body that rules over territories outside its original borders. It has a central power or core territory—whose inhabitants usually continue to form the dominant ethnic or national group in the entire system—and an extensive periphery of dominated areas. In most cases, the periphery has been acquired by conquest. But in earlier imperial systems, expansion sometimes came about by such means as the intermarriage of ruling families from previously separate states. And in some modern instances, the ruling elites of the peripheral territory may have chosen willingly to be brought under the control of the imperial center. Some scholars have argued that empire necessarily involves political sovereignty or direct control by core over peripheries; but others, probably more, have used the term also for informal control, influence, or hegemony. A world, or parts of it, dominated by empires is often explicitly or implicitly contrasted to one of nation-states; especially in terms of a (usually implied) narrative of twentieth-century

global history in which the former is seen as having been replaced by the latter, involving the extension of an originally European nation-state model across the globe. However, whilst some analysts have seen the concept of empire as distinct from or even the antithesis to that of the state, others identify it rather as a particular *form* of state.

Empires, then, are composite entities, formed out of previously separate units. Diversity—ethnic, national, cultural, often religious—is thus of their essence. But that cannot be a diversity of equals. If there is no relation of inequality and domination between *core* and *periphery*, then the system is not truly an empire but a federation or perhaps a *commonwealth*. Both the British Empire in its last stages and the post-Soviet Russian federation used the latter term for themselves, indicating the claim that they were no longer imperial systems but free associations of equals.

The relationship between the concepts of empire and imperialism on the one hand, and colony and colonialism on the other, have been particularly fraught with ambiguity. Early usages of the latter mainly associated it with the physical transfer of large settler populations to new places: often, but not always, associated with the political conquest of such places and with the settlers attaining a position of dominance over (or even exterminating) indigenous peoples. More recently, some scholars have distinguished between imperialism and colonialism by way of seeing the former as an attitude or policy advocating territorial expansion, whilst the latter is the practice of domination or overrule. Most often, however, the distinction drawn (albeit not always explicitly) is that colonialism is used to mean situations of direct control or the exercise of sovereignty by one people or country over another, whilst the concepts of empire and imperialism are more encompassing and embrace also less direct or formal forms of domination.

ETYMOLOGIES AND HISTORIES

The word *empire* comes from the Latin *imperium*, for which the closest modern English equivalent would perhaps be *sovereignty*, or simply *rule*. For the Romans, an *emperor* was originally a victorious general, later a supreme magistrate—though the military overtones of the title never disappeared. *Imperium* also came, both in the Roman era and later in Christian Europe—which derived so much of its political language and thought from Roman precedents—to have three further connotations. All these have continued to shape thinking about empire. First was size. Empire came to mean rule over extensive, far-flung territories, far beyond the original "homeland" of the rulers. Although some quite small entities have, historically, described themselves as empires, in most modern usages the term is reserved for very large political units.

Second was the notion of *absolute* sovereignty, acknowledging no overlord or rival claimant to power. When Henry VIII (1491–1547) of England had his realm proclaimed an "empire" in the 1530s, the aim was to assert that he owed no allegiance to, and would tolerate no interference from, either the papacy or any secular power. Third was an aspiration to universality. Christian (and, in a distinct but related idiom, Islamic) empire was in principle boundless, as the Roman imperium to which it was partial heir had claimed to be.

An empire is therefore, by a minimalist or semiconsensual definition, a large, composite, multiethnic or multinational political unit, usually created by conquest, and divided between a dominant center and subordinate, sometimes far distant, peripheries. Core and periphery are usually geographically separate, clearly bounded places. In modern seaborne empires, they might indeed be thousands of miles apart. In other cases, though, the geographical lines between them might be blurred. They might even inhabit the same physical spaces: ideas like *internal colonialism* were developed to try and explain such situations.

Imperialism is generally used to mean the actions and attitudes that create or uphold such big political units—but also, often, less direct kinds of control or domination by one people or country over others. Terms like *cultural* or *economic imperialism* are often used to describe some of these less formal sorts of domination: but such labels are invariably contentious. So too is the concept of *informal empire,* which has nonetheless been very influential and widely used to describe varied forms of dominance without formal sovereignty or direct political control, as with Britain's nineteenth-century hegemony in Chile and Iran, or the more recent role of the United States in much of Central America.

Even formal empire, however, typically involved some combination of direct and indirect rule. The central power has ultimate sovereignty, and exercises some direct control, especially over military force and money-raising powers, in all parts of its domain. But there has usually been some kind of "colonial" or "provincial" government in each of the empire's major parts, with subordinate but not insignificant devolved powers of its own. These authorities may be headed by men sent out from the dominant center. But their leaders, and certainly their more junior administrators or enforcers, may also be drawn from the ranks (usually from the preconquest ruling orders) of the dominated people. In many empires, ancient and modern, there was a general tendency over time for imperial rulers to devolve ever more power to such groups. In the long run, of course, this might lead to the gradual breakup of the empire itself. But many historians argue that the key to understanding empire lies in the bargains struck between the imperial center and local "collaborators." No empire could last for long if it depended entirely on naked power exerted from the center outward. Local intermediaries might enjoy much autonomy within their own spheres, and command considerable wealth, power, and status, in return for delivering their people's obedience, financial tribute, and military services to the center. This is so also in a different sense where (unlike the British or indeed any modern European-imperial case) the ruling elites of empires were themselves ethnically diverse, as with the later Roman Empire or the Ottoman Empire.

The emphasis on intermediaries, collaborators, bargains, and decentralization should not be pushed too far. Empire was also often, indeed perhaps typically, established and maintained by violence. Sometimes extreme violence: some historians say that most episodes of genocide and mass murder in world history have been associated with empire building. This includes the Nazi Holocaust, which is increasingly analyzed as part of an "empire-building" project. More generally, the idea of empire in modern history has also usually been associated with European, white rule over non-Europeans, with "racial" hierarchies and racist beliefs. Some analysts, again, build this association into their very definitions of empire.

One other aspect of debates over the historical salience and transformative force of European (especially British) expansion has been especially vigorous. Should colonial rule be viewed primarily in terms of modernization or of archaism? The notion of *colonial modernity*—even colonialism *as* modernity—has been widely invoked, especially among recent cultural historians of empire. The idea of colonialism as a modernizing, state-building, centralizing, developmentalist, and secularizing force has been deployed too by those urging a positive appraisal both of the British imperial record and of American "empire" today. Yet on the other hand, some historians stress instead the traditionalist and even archaizing features of British imperial ideology.

VARIATIONS AND SIMILARITIES

Empires have, rather obviously, taken a wide variety of forms across history. Even where empires, especially imperial ideologies, display close family resemblances, this has sometimes reflected conscious imitation more than structural congruity. Some scholars, indeed, urge a definitive abandonment of the singular term *empire*—which tends, even when its users are stressing and tracing differences, to imply that these are variations on a single essence—and propose a mandatory pluralization of the terms *empires* and *imperialisms.* Yet most see, at least, broad similarities as well as some fundamental subcategories among empires. Perhaps the most basic and important of the latter is the division between those that grew by expansion overland, extending directly outward from original frontiers, and those that were created by sea power, spanning the oceans and even the entire globe. The first, land-based form of empire is by far the older and the more historically ubiquitous. Land empires were created by Asians, Africans, and pre-Columbian Americans as well as Europeans. The second, mainly European form, however, has been the most powerful and dynamic in the modern world—roughly the last five hundred years. It in turn is often analyzed as having two main forms: settlement and nonsettlement colonies. The former category includes those places where large numbers of Europeans moved and remained. In some—notably, most of the Americas and Australasia—they became the vast majority. In others, like Algeria, South Africa, and more precariously in Kenya or Zimbabwe, European settlers became dominant minorities. The nonsettler colonies, embracing most of Africa and South and Southeast Asia, were considerably more numerous and far more disparate in nature.

The character and continuing consequences of empire thus remain intensely contentious. At the peak of their strength in the first half of the twentieth century, European colonial powers, plus their offshoot the United States, ruled well over 80 percent of the world's land and effectively controlled all the oceans too. That direct physical dominance mainly came to an end, with remarkable rapidity, between the end of World War II (1939–1945) and the 1960s. But its effects remain indubitably important, both for formerly colonized and for ex-imperial peoples. And a wide range of critics—especially socialists and third world nationalists, but also such disparate currents as contemporary antiglobalization protesters and militant Islamists—argue that the twenty-first-century world witnesses not just the continuing consequences of old-style European colonialism, but a new kind of global empire headed by the United States and its allies. For some such critics, indeed, *empire* is now effectively a simple synonym for American foreign policy. In a slightly less polemical vein, scholarly argument has proliferated over the existence, character, and importance of continuities or parallels between the formal colonialism of the nineteenth and twentieth centuries and the global politics of the twenty-first.

SEE ALSO *Colonialism; Decolonization; Holy Roman Empire; Imperialism; Ottoman Empire*

BIBLIOGRAPHY

Abernethy, David B. 2000. *The Dynamics of Global Dominance: European Overseas Empires, 1415–1980.* New Haven, CT: Yale University Press.

Alcock, Susan E., et al., eds. 2001. *Empires: Perspectives from Archaeology and History.* Cambridge, U.K.: Cambridge University Press.

Cooper, Frederick. 2005. *Colonialism in Question: Theory, Knowledge, History.* Berkeley: University of California Press.

Doyle, Michael W. 1986. *Empires.* Ithaca, NY: Cornell University Press.

Fieldhouse, D. K. 1999. *The West and the Third World: Trade, Colonialism, Dependence, and Development.* Oxford: Blackwell.

Lieven, Dominic. 2000. *Empire: The Russian Empire and Its Rivals.* London: Murray.

Louis, William Roger, ed. 1998–1999. *The Oxford History of the British Empire.* Oxford: Oxford University Press.

Maier, Charles S. 2006. *Among Empires: American Ascendancy and Its Predecessors.* Cambridge, MA: Harvard University Press.

Osterhammel, Jürgen. 1997. *Colonialism: A Theoretical Overview.* Princeton, NJ: Wiener.

Pagden, Anthony. 2001. *Peoples and Empires: A Short History of European Migration, Exploration, and Conquest, from Greece to the Present.* London: Weidenfeld and Nicolson.

Said, Edward W. 1993. *Culture and Imperialism.* London: Chatto and Windus.

Young, Robert J. C. 2001. *Postcolonialism: An Historical Introduction.* Oxford: Blackwell.

Stephen Howe

EMPIRICISM

Empiricism can be traced back to Aristotle's dictum, "there is nothing in the intellect that is not first in the senses," although Aristotle himself is not usually regarded as an empiricist in the modern sense. The theoretical foundations of modern philosophical empiricism are found in the works of John Locke, George Berkeley, and David Hume, and in the nineteenth-century philosopher William James. These philosophers inquired about the limits and scope of the human mind, and argued that experience itself is the primary source of all knowledge. Empiricism is thus a theory of knowledge that highlights the importance of experience. The term *experience* can be defined minimally, as in terms of the senses, or expanded to include all forms of consciousness.

Locke's project in his *Essay Concerning Human Understanding* (1690) was to set out "to enquire into the origin, certainty, and extent of human knowledge" (Locke 1975, p. 43). Locke argued that knowledge is restricted to ideas generated by objects that one experiences through the senses (ideas of sensation) or by reflection upon our mental operations on those ideas (ideas of reflection). In this complex sense, knowledge and human understanding in general (including unscientific beliefs such as justice) originate in experience, as the origin of all ideas is in experience, which involves two logical levels, sensation and reflection. Each person's mind can be thought of as initially a blank tablet (tabula rasa) first written upon by the sensations of experience (ideas of sensation), which can then be manipulated in various ways, the ideas of which—the ideas of reflection—being the second level of experience.

Berkeley argued in both *Principles* (1710) and *Dialogues* (1713) against the actual existence of matter, and claimed in his dictum "to be is to be perceived" (or to perceive). This means that objects can never be understood independently of their ideas since, for Berkeley, the object and sensation are the same thing. Berkeley maintained that there are only ideas and minds, or the location where ideas occur. Thus a thing is understood as the sum of perceived qualities. Although for Berkeley it is impossible to think of anything except as it related to the mind, both Berkeley and Locke believed that all knowledge about the existence of things and the reality of matter depends on visual and sensory experience.

In his work *Enquiry Concerning Human Understanding* (1784), Hume claimed that human senses allow people to perceive, and these perceptions (made up of impressions and ideas) are the contents of the mind. The original thought itself, according to Hume, is an impression, and an idea is only a copy of an impression. The difference between the two is their vividness, for when one reflects upon these impressions one has ideas of them. Hume's work does not ground impressions to a material world, and argues instead that impressions are internal subjective states that do not provide evidence of an external reality.

In his metaphysics, James wrote in a tradition that focuses on the process of consciousness based in experience—a "process metaphysics." For James, humans have a continuous development of thought that is based in interpretations of the experiences themselves. In this way, human consciousness consists of experienced relations (a "stream of thought"), which are themselves experienced (affectively and effectively), as one both transforms and is transformed by these experiences. Indeed, James's radical empiricism is pluralistic in that it allows for different points of view—different "givennesses"—of reality. Because James allowed for individual perspectives of experience, it follows that one's epistemologies themselves are informed by one's experiences. Absolute unity of reality, for James, is "ever not quite," as "fact" is based on experience, and the multiple experiences of experience itself. Thus there is no objective truth, as Jamesian truth is experientially cognized at the level of subjective/individual perception.

The empirical tradition runs counter to rationalist philosophy, which poses that knowledge can be derived through the exercise of reason alone, and in terms of a person's rational power. All of the aforementioned philosophers wrote in a tradition that opposes the rationalist view, represented most notably by the French mathematician and philosopher René Descartes, that humans enter the world with innate ideas built into the mind itself. Instead, these philosophers argue that persons must rely on experience itself to inform knowledge claims.

RESEARCH AND EMPIRICAL METHODS

Within the social sciences, empiricism describes research methods that depend on the collection of facts and observations, some of which require verification, counting, and measuring. Although a researcher may use empirical methods, it does not follow that he or she is a philosophical empiricist, and does not make one an empiricist per se. There are thus many forms of empirical research methods.

Auguste Comte, a sociologist and philosopher, held that knowledge of the world arises from observation, and conceived of positivism as a method of study based on the strict use of the scientific method. He asserted that authentic knowledge (or all true knowledge) is scientific knowledge that is objective, predictable, and has logical structures. Logical positivism (or logical/rational empiricism) combines positivism with a verifiability criterion for meaningfulness. For logical positivists, all knowledge should be based on logical inference, justification, and verifiability through experience or observation. Meaningful statements fall into two categories for the logical positivist, a priori analytic knowledge (necessary truths that are knowable prior to experience; for example, all circles are round) and a posteriori synthetic knowledge (or contingent knowledge that is verified by sensory experience; for example, it is raining outside). Quantitative methodology is a kind of scientific empiricism and refers to the compilation and analysis of numerical data, which for the social scientist is empirical in nature since it can be tested and verified (validated or falsified) by empirical observation. Moreover, quantitative methodology is positivistic since it relies on scientific and systematic observation and experiment, and can be thought of as the scientific approach to the study of sociocultural life.

Nonetheless, although social scientists do not ask underlying metaphysical questions about the actual existence of objects, they are indeed concerned with the experience of social objects and phenomena. For example, the first professor of sociology, Émile Durkheim, in his book *The Rules of Sociological Method* (1938), enshrined this idea with his conceptualization of a "social fact," which is as objective as facts are in the natural sciences.

For Thomas Kuhn, empirical methods are capable of elucidating and eradicating problems within paradigms during periods of "normal science." Interestingly, Kuhn shows how this "science" is reflective of one's theoretical connectedness to a specific paradigm itself, and is not the reflection of any truth-claims to knowledge.

Social constructivism is a philosophical theory of knowledge that states that knowledge itself is contingent upon social experience, context, convention, and human perception. Some examples of socially constructed knowledge are gender (feminine and masculine), sexuality, and racial categories. This theory of knowledge does not necessarily reflect any external "transcendent" metaphysical reality, and is instead based on a socially constructed reality as opposed to an ontological reality. However, the notion of experience is still important for a constructivist, as experiences between and among individuals differs within and outside of varying contexts, thereby allowing for different "realities," some of which are based in oppression (for example, women, minorities, and homosexuals).

Empirical methods have been used to study race, gender, sexuality, and religion, among a plethora of other social phenomena such as crime, deviance, attitudes, and beliefs.

Considering race, there has been much research done in social science regarding migration, connections with class, connections to skin color, social surveys of self-image and self-regard among ethnic minorities, and measuring prejudice in terms of scales of social and ethnic "distance." Additional quantitative studies concerning race have focused on social inequality, institutional racism, patterns of interaction and segregation, genocide, social standing, poverty, and assimilation of dominant culture patterns.

Gender has been studied in the social sciences through the analysis of images of women in media and culture. These empirical studies of symbols and images range from studies of archaeological statues of goddesses to contemporary studies of how women are portrayed in film or advertisements. Discrepancies in gender stratification and sexism can be analyzed from a quantitative approach, as can the important issue of violence against women. Additionally, empirical studies of gender also inform analyses of family relations, employment patterns, and distribution of wealth, education trends, and politics.

Using empirical methods to study sexuality, social scientists focus on topics such as sexual orientation, contraception, prostitution, gender identity, and attraction. Additional research can also be found on teen pregnancy, fertility, pornography, activist movements, sexual violence, sex education, and queer studies. One of the most

important works in this area is *The Archaeology of Knowledge* (1972) by Michel Foucault.

Religion has also been analyzed empirically in terms of socioeconomic status, the family, marriage patterns, social class, family violence, cohabitation, political affiliation, church attendance, opinions about religious matters, as well as feelings, beliefs, and behaviors pertaining to religion as measured by social surveys. This is especially evident in the work of Rodney Stark, but began as early as 1904 in Max Weber's seminal work *The Protestant Ethic and the Spirit of Capitalism.*

Louis Althusser critiqued empiricism as a methodological stance and argued against the empirical process of knowledge, claiming that theoretical discourse is a "production," making empiricism itself ideological and dogmatic, and therefore not scientific. According to Althusser, "facts" of theoretical discourse are tied to theoretical practice, making knowledge itself a form of discourse.

SEE ALSO *Kuhn, Thomas; Methodology; Methods, Research; Positivism; Revolutions, Scientific*

BIBLIOGRAPHY

Althusser, Louis. 1971. Ideology and Ideological State Apparatuses: Notes Toward an Investigation. In *Lenin and Philosophy and Other Essays.* Trans. Ben Brewster. New York: Monthly Review Press.

Berkeley, George. 1988. *Principles of Human Knowledge/Three Dialogues between Hylas and Philonius.* Ed. Roger Woolhouse. Amherst, NY: Prometheus Books. (Orig. pub. 1710).

Curd, Martin, and J. A. Cover. 1998. *Philosophy of Science: The Central Issues.* New York: W. W. Norton.

Durkheim, Émile. 1982. *The Rules of Sociological Method.* 8th ed. Trans. Sarah A. Solovay and John H. Mueller. New York: The Free Press.

Foucault, Michel. 1972. *The Archaeology of Knowledge and the Discourse on Language.* Trans. A. M. Sheridan Smith. New York: Pantheon Books.

Hume, David. 1999. *An Enquiry Concerning Human Understanding.* Ed. Tom L. Beauchamp. New York: Oxford University Press. (Orig. pub. 1748).

James, William. 1977. *The Writings of William James: A Comprehensive Edition.* Ed. John J. McDermott. Chicago: University of Chicago Press.

Locke, John. 1975. *An Essay Concerning Human Understanding.* Ed. Peter H. Nidditch. Oxford: Oxford University Press. (Orig. pub. 1690).

Locke, John. 1995. *An Essay Concerning Human Understanding.* Ed. Roger Woolhouse. Amherst, NY: Prometheus Books. (Orig. pub. 1690).

Mills, C. Wright. 1967. *The Social Construction of Reality.* New York: Oxford University Press.

Weber, Max. 1992. *The Protestant Ethic and the Spirit of Capitalism.* Trans. Talcott Parsons. New York: Routledge.

Ryan Ashley Caldwell

EMPLOYMENT

Employment measures the number of employees in a country, region, or sector. Employees are generally defined as persons on payrolls, that is people who are compensated for the work they perform. Depending on the particular definition, this may or may not include self-employed people, also called proprietors, who work for themselves. Along with unemployment, employment (including proprietors) constitutes the labor force. Including people working without pay, for example housewives, volunteers, and sometimes armed forces, one obtains the workforce. Finally, all the population capable of working constitutes the manpower.

MEASUREMENT

Measurement of employment is quite diverse across countries, which makes cross-country comparisons difficult. There can be variations in definitions, coverage, data collection methods, information sources, and estimation methods. For example, the United States publishes employment data from two different sources. The National Current Employment Statistics (the so-called establishment survey) from the Bureau of Labor Statistics does not cover agriculture, hunting, forestry, fishing, the armed forces, and private household services. Sick leaves, paid holidays, and employees on strike (but not the whole period) are counted. The Current Population survey (the so-called household survey), also from the Bureau of Labor Statistics, covers the civilian population sixteen years of age and older in all sectors, except armed forces. It counts as employees those who "(1) did any work at all as paid employees, worked in their own business or profession or on their own farm, or worked fifteen hours or more as unpaid workers in a family-operated enterprise; and (2) all those who did not work but had jobs or businesses from which they were temporarily absent due to illness, bad weather, vacation, childcare problems, labor dispute, maternity or paternity leave, or other family or personal obligations, whether or not they were paid by their employers for the time off and whether or not they were seeking other jobs."

Intertemporal comparisons of employment are more reliable, although they can also be subject to changes in definition or coverage. For example, the introduction of child labor laws and mandatory schooling has increased the minimum age considered for employment statistics.

Most frequently, employment data is based on surveys, sometimes complemented by various techniques to increase precision or interpolate between data points. Employment may also be inferred from data provided by trade unions, trade associations, social security administration, or other government agencies.

LONG-TERM TRENDS

The sectoral composition of employment has changed considerably in human history. Because under a strict definition of employment self-employment is not considered, a labor market with an explicit exchange of work for payment evolved sometime during the last millennium, after both the introduction of money and the existence of surplus labor in agriculture. This surplus labor made the specialization of tasks possible, in particular for various manufacturing trades. Once production expands beyond the abilities of a family, external labor needs to be hired and a labor market is born. The extent of this labor market has been very limited, however, for a long time, in particular as slavery and servitude are not considered to be employment. It is the Industrial Revolution that allowed a significant take-off of employment, through the creation of factories where proprietors constituted a very small minority of workers and the preceding second agricultural revolution that created significant excess labor on farms. Even in the twenty-first century, employment measures typically exclude agriculture, as the latter is still considered to be largely the domain of proprietors.

In all industrialized economies, employment has thereafter gradually shifted toward services, which now typically constitute a larger share of employment than manufacturing. Employment also requires better skilled workers and has an ever-increasing share of female employees. Better skills are required to operate or monitor more sophisticated machinery, to provide more elaborate services, or to use computers. The increased female involvement in employment can be traced back to two main factors: (1) the emancipation of women breaking the traditional role of the housewife, along the decline of the wage gap with men; and (2) significant improvements in technology used in housekeeping (such as washing machines and vacuum cleaners) that made it possible to pursue paid work outside of the house.

One source of considerable controversy is whether technological progress has a positive impact on employment or not. As was the case with the Industrial Revolution, rapid technological progress can lead to a massive sectoral reallocation of employment, which does not necessarily mean a reduction in employment. For example, while the introduction of the steam engine rendered horses obsolete for most of their original tasks, such obsolescence is more difficult to reach for humans, given their versatility and their ability to adapt. But this still happens, in particular for workers close to retirement. On a more microeconomic level, technological progress simultaneously destroys and creates jobs. In this context, several kinds of technological progress can be identified, depending on how they alter the aggregate capital/labor ratio in the production progress; it is labor augmenting if progress reduces this ratio, labor saving otherwise, or nonbiased if it leaves the ratio unchanged. Over the long term, the capital/labor ratio has increased steadily, both through capital accumulation and through a reduction in the work hours. The labor income share, however, does not exhibit any particular trend and there is no conclusive relationship between the unemployment rate and various measures of the growth rate.

The last two decades of the twentieth century witnessed another important development: globalization. The wage pressure from developing or emerging countries influenced employment, in particular for low skill jobs in manufacturing, but also increasingly for higher skilled positions in services. There is, however, no agreement among scholars whether this impact has been significant at the macroeconomic level (it certainly was in some sectors of the economy), and whether it has been negative at all. Indeed, while some jobs were "exported," the availability of intermediate goods at lower prices increased the productivity of some sectors that then expanded. It is, however, clear that lower skilled workers face reduced employment opportunities, a phenomenon that started even before globalization accelerated.

INFORMAL EMPLOYMENT

One important distinction in the labor market is between formal and informal employment. There are many definitions of informal employment, the most common being employment that escapes taxation and regulation, and thus is not protected by the government: Various social programs do not apply to informal workers, such as unemployment insurance, social security, some labor laws (in particular the enforcement of contracts), or invalidity and accident coverage by the government. Informal employment is much more widespread in developing economies, where social programs are less common and tax authorities have less control. Yet informal employment is still present in developing economies; for instance in 2000 Friedrich Schneider and Dominik H. Enste estimated informal employment to reach around 10 percent of employment in the United States, higher in other countries, typically those with higher labor income tax rates or inefficient taxation.

As the informal sector escapes regulation, it is generally viewed that it should be limited. In many cases, however, it is a response to overregulation or corruption.

Workers may migrate between formal and informal sectors as opportunities arise, the informal sector often being regarded as a stepping-stone in which skills are learned before being hired in the formal sector. Accordingly, wages are lower in the informal sector. Informal firms are typically family based and small, have low productivity, and have very low capital intensity. Workers are hired on a casual basis on arrangements of short duration.

CHILD LABOR

One aspect of labor markets, especially in developing economies, is child labor. One commonly defines child labor as the participation of school-aged children on a regular basis in the labor force in order to earn a living for themselves (street children) or to supplement household income. The International Labour Organization (ILO) divides child labor into three categories: (1) labor that is performed by a child who is under the minimum age specified for that kind of work defined by national legislation, and that is likely to impede the child's education and full development; (2) labor that jeopardizes the physical, mental, or moral well-being of a child, either because of its nature or because of the conditions in which it is carried out, known as hazardous work; (3) the unconditional worst forms of child labor, which are internationally defined as slavery, trafficking, debt bondage and other forms of forced labor, forced recruitment of children for use in armed conflict, prostitution and pornography, and illicit activities.

The national laws of most industrialized countries abolished child labor by the end of the nineteenth century. However, in 2000 Douglas Kruse and Douglas Mahony estimated that several hundred thousand children work illegally in the United States. Worldwide, the ILO estimated (with considerable uncertainty) that 218 million, or 16 percent of children aged five to eleven were working in 2004, 126 million in hazardous work.

The ILO pushes very hard to eliminate child labor where it is the most prevalent, in developing countries. While the strategy is generally to have governments ratify conventions and implement child labor laws, those methods are often insufficient. As long as schools are sufficiently effective in providing education (not a given), parents are very aware of the high returns to education. Yet they often send their children to work because their contribution is needed to sustain household income. As the children do not get an education, their income as adults will be too low to allow their offspring to go to school. Breaking these vicious circles is the key to eliminating child labor, as the implementation of child labor laws in North America or Europe has shown.

BUSINESS CYCLES

All economies are subject to fluctuations and one important aspect of business cycles is the systematic changes in employment. Indeed, in most cycles and most economies, employment and gross domestic product (GDP) evolve in tune: GDP and the total number of hours worked typically reach their peaks or troughs at the same time and fluctuate about as much. Employment, however, tends to fluctuate (in percentage terms) less than GDP and tends to lag the movements of GDP by a few months. While these regularities can be observed across all economies, there are some striking differences. For example, fluctuations in total hours worked in some economies tend to happen on the intensive margin (hours per worker) rather than on the extensive margin (employment). In other words, there are more changes in overtime or undertime than hiring and firing. This is true for several European economies, but not for the United States, primarily because of the influence of labor laws, labor market traditions, and unions.

There are also clear patterns through the business cycles in terms of hiring and firing. Plant level studies have revealed that most of the fluctuations in employment can be explained by job destructions: These are high in a recession and low in booms. Job creations are, however, much more stable through the business cycle. It is also generally observed that employment fluctuates significantly more for less educated workers.

POLICY

Many government policies affect employment, and it is impossible to review them all. One can distinguish between those that have an impact on the average level of employment, and those that try to mitigate employment fluctuations. Whenever policy is involved, some welfare criterion needs to be established if one is to determine whether policies are good or bad. In this respect, psychologists consider that it is good for people to be employed, as this improves their self-esteem. Sociologists would consider the negative impact on one's standing in society due to unemployment. Employment of women is considered to be a necessary part of their empowerment. Economists consider the fact that people would not necessarily want to work: They appreciate leisure more than work, and one symptom of this is that they are paid to work, instead of paying for this privilege. However, employment is a way to obtain the income necessary for consumption and savings. There are also various frictions on the labor market, such as the transaction costs and the difficult matching process between vacancies and unemployed workers, which make full employment unattainable. Thus, high employment is preferable, but not at any cost. However, child employment should be reduced to a minimum.

Also, given that households generally do not like fluctuations in income, as they imply fluctuations in consumption, policies that stabilize employment are considered preferable, as long as they do not reduce average employment too much.

Employment is influenced indirectly but sometimes significantly by various policies, such as provisions of the tax code. For example, high or increasing marginal tax rates are known to discourage the participation of spouses on the labor market. The so-called marriage penalty in some tax codes—whereby the incomes of two spouses are added to determine the tax rate instead of considering the incomes separately—has the same effect.

Employment policy is enacted to improve working conditions or facilitate the employment opportunities of some workers. Those categorized as active employment policies include job placement agencies, labor market training, and subsidized employment. Passive policies include unemployment insurance and early retirement programs. Scholars, including David Grubb and John Martin, debate the effectiveness of these policies, in particular in light of their costs, which lead to an indirect discouragement of employment through higher tax rates. Or a generous unemployment insurance system may also encourage unemployed workers to reject job offers in the search of better matches, thereby lowering employment and increasing the costs to fill vacancies.

Labor laws are put in place to prevent abuses and to organize the labor market. They may also have perverse effects on employment. For example, laws putting restrictions or making it more difficult to lay off workers may prevent them from being hired in the first place, especially in sectors where employment would exhibit stronger fluctuations or where workers may have private information about their qualifications. Finally, generous minimum wage laws are generally thought to have adverse effects on employment, as some employers would not open vacancies if wages have to be higher. While there is controversy in the literature about this, the employment effects of minimum wages may simply be small.

This discussion may give the impression that any intervention in the labor market has harmful effects. Labor markets have particular characteristics that make government intervention necessary, but without excess as negative indirect effects may outweigh positive direct effects. The right to unionize is enforced to counter the monopoly power that employers have in a very fragmented labor market. But too much union power leads to excessive negotiation power for employees, and then to high wages that prevent the hiring of additional workers.

Stabilization of employment through the business cycle is generally viewed through the lens of avoiding fluctuations in unemployment. Monetary policy has a long tradition of playing with the trade-off between (expected) inflation and the unemployment rate, the so-called Phillips curve. Monetary policy has, however, shifted from an active stance in the Keynesian tradition to a more passive stance seeking to stabilize inflation at rather low levels. It has been recognized that monetary policy can do little about (un)employment due to large delays and uncertainty about the impacts.

Fiscal policy has and is still being used for stabilization purposes in some countries, but again the tendency is toward a hands-off approach. Where it is applied, it is through public works programs, temporary tax breaks directed to firms to encourage hiring or to prevent layoffs, or income tax breaks to encourage consumption and economic activity in general. Again, such policies are not generally viewed to be advisable as delays in implementation or effectiveness are typically longer than a recession. However, they have a certain political appeal.

SEE ALSO *Beveridge Curve; Blue Collar and White Collar; Business Cycles, Empirical Literature; Business Cycles, Political; Business Cycles, Real; Business Cycles, Theories; Child Labor; Economics; Economics, Keynesian; Economics, Labor; Employment, White Collar; Informal Economy; Labor; Labor, Marginal Product of; Labor, Surplus: Conventional Economics; Labor, Surplus: Marxist and Radical Economics; Labor Demand; Labor Force Participation; Labor Law; Labor Market; Labor Supply; Labor Union; Leisure; Macroeconomics; Misery Index; Monetarism; Okun's Law; Phillips Curve; Self-Employment; Skill; Sociology; Unemployable; Unemployment; Unemployment Rate; Unions; Wages; Work; Work Day; Work Week; Working Class; Working Day, Length of; Workplace Relations*

BIBLIOGRAPHY

Bean, Charles, and Christopher Pissarides. 1993. Unemployment, Consumption and Growth. *European Economic Review* 37: 837–854.

Daveri, Francesco, and Guido Tabellini. 2000. Unemployment, Growth and Taxation in Industrialized Countries. *Economic Policy* (April): 49–104.

Davis, Steven J., John C. Haltiwanger, and Scott Schuh. 1998. *Job Creation and Destruction.* Cambridge, MA: MIT Press.

Greenwood, Jeremy, Ananth Seshadri, and Mehmet Yorukoglu. 2005. Engines of Liberation. *Review of Economic Studies* 72 (1): 109–133.

Grubb, David, and John Martin. 2001. What Works and for Whom: A Review of OECD Countries' Experiences with Active Labor Market Policies. *Swedish Economic Policy Review* 8: 9–56.

International Labor Organization. 2006. *The End of Child Labor: Within Reach.* Geneva: Author.

Kennan, John. 1995. The Elusive Effects of Minimum Wages. *Journal of Economic Literature* 33 (4): 1950–1965.

Kruse, Douglas, and Douglas Mahony. 2000. Illegal Child Labor in the United States: Prevalence and Characteristics. *Industrial and Labor Relations Review* 54 (1): 17–40.

Lazear, Edward. 1990. Job Security Provisions and Employment. *Quarterly Journal of Economics* 105: 699–725.

Nardinelli, Clark. 1990. *Child Labor and the Industrial Revolution.* Bloomington: Indiana University Press.

Phillips, Alban W. 1958. The Relation between Unemployment and the Rate of Change of Money Wage in the United Kingdom, 1861–1957. *Economica* 25: 283–299.

Schneider, Friedrich, and Dominik H. Enste. 2000. Shadow Economies: Size, Causes, and Consequences. *Journal of Economic Literature* 38 (1): 77–114.

Christian Zimmermann

EMPLOYMENT, WHITE COLLAR

The concept of "white-collar" employment has been deeply embedded in ordinary language since the early twentieth century, denoting those who work in offices and apart from the dirtier "blue-collar" world of manual or physical labor. Historically, when the large majority of work was of the latter type and large corporations were just beginning to expand the ranks of office workers, the "white collar" symbolized new opportunities for upward mobility. Over time, however, an increasing economic complexity has created new categories and blurred the original lines, so that the term has gradually lost usefulness as an analytic concept. In 2006, the U.S. Bureau of Labor Statistics declared that "the white collar and blue collar series are no longer useful categories and will be discontinued in 2007" in compiling its Employment Cost Index data.

For most of the twentieth century, white-collar employees were united by some perquisites that distinguished them in practice from blue-collar workers. For one thing, they were treated as nonproduction overhead and were, therefore, protected to a considerable extent from efforts to control production costs. White-collar workers were also paid salaries, rather than wages, and they generally enjoyed a high degree of job security. When layoffs were needed in production downturns, it was generally those on the factory floor who were let go.

White-collar employment grew substantially during the twentieth century, primarily at the expense of farm and manual workers. According to the Bureau of the Census data, white-collar workers increased from 17.6 percent of total employment in 1900 to 59.9 percent in

2002 (analyzed and reported by the Department for Professional Employees 2003, p. 5). But this general statement obscures many crucial distinctions.

CONCEPTUAL AND DEFINITIONAL INCONSISTENCIES

Even in its early usage, "white-collar" was less than coherent conceptually, covering at least three radically different types of workers. Clerical occupations were largely female, low-status, and low-wage; managers and professionals, on the other hand, were largely male and high in status and pay. A third piece of the white-collar picture was comprised of professionals, who themselves changed dramatically in status from largely independent workers in the early part of the twentieth century to primarily working for corporations at the end. There was practically no mobility among these three categories, and their wages varied widely. As unionization advanced in mid-century, for example, clerical workers were paid less than blue-collar workers, but managers and professionals were paid more.

This conceptual inconsistency has grown even more marked and complex with the growth of services and knowledge work. Beneath the seemingly precise counts in various surveys lie important dissimilarities in definitions. For example, most analysts believe there has been a significant growth in service work since the early 1900s, though they disagree on how to define it. Service work is, in some sense, different from the production of "things," which defines blue-collar work, but service workers are not necessarily white-collar. Building maintenance, for example, is certainly "manual" in nature, but it is not considered "office work."

The Census data calculate that about 14 percent of the U.S. workforce is in services, though an independent analysis by Marc Uri Porat in 1977 put the percentage at 30 percent, without counting "information workers." This is just one indication of the inconsistencies in the field.

Many analysts argue that a large economic discontinuity has occurred with the growth of "knowledge work" as a key part of the economy. There have been many attempts to count knowledge workers, starting with Fritz Machlup's pioneering 1962 study. The estimates continue to vary rather widely, depending on what assumptions are made, but it is clear that adding this category produces a radically different view from that based on "collar." For instance, a recent study by Edward Wolff estimates that 15 percent of the workforce in 2000 were knowledge workers (producing new knowledge), 44 percent were data workers, 14 percent were service workers, and 24 percent were goods producers.

Percentages of workforce by "Collar" categories

	White-collar	Blue-collar	Other
Management occupations	4.6		
Business and financial operations occupations	4.2		
Computer and mathematical occupations	2.3		
Architecture and engineering occupations	1.8		
Life, physical, and social science occupations	0.9		
Community and social services occupations			1.3
Legal occupations	0.8		
Education, training, and library occupations	6.2		
Arts, design, entertainment, sports, and media occupations	1.3		
Health-care practitioners and technical occupations	5.0		
Health-care support occupations			2.6
Protective service occupations			2.3
Personal care and service occupations			2.4
Sales and related occupations	10.7		
Office and administrative support occupations	17.5		
Farming, fishing, and forestry occupations			0.3
Food preparation and serving-related occupations		8.3	
Building and grounds cleaning and maintenance occupations		3.3	
Construction and extraction occupations		4.9	
Installation, maintenance, and repair occupations		4.1	
Production occupations		7.9	
Transportation and material moving occupations		7.4	
Total	55.3%	35.9%	8.9%

SOURCE: Analysis based on May 2005 estimates from Occupational Employment Statistics (OES) Survey of the U.S. Bureau of Labor Statistics. http:/stat.bls.gov/oes/home.htm.

Table 1

KEY THEORETICAL TREATMENTS

Theoretical treatments of white-collar work have struggled to identify consistent patterns, hampered in part by the diversity of definitions. One of the most famous, C. Wright Mills's *White Collar*, focused on administrative staff in large corporations in the late 1940s. Mills found that these workers were caught in a psychology of "prestige striving," with no independent basis of identity, and he predicted they would remain a weak and confused force socially and politically. Marxist treatments, such as that of Nicos Poulantzas, have also often suggested that white-collar workers lack a clear class identity and can potentially be drawn to either side of the primary class divide. Some, however, have identified distinct and independent forms of white-collar consciousness: Barbara and John Ehrenreich sketched a new "professional-managerial class"; Robert Merton sketched a "bureaucratic personality" based on "strong sentiments which entail devotion to one's duties, a keen sense of the limitations of one's authority and competence, and methodical performance of routine activities"; and Olivier Zunz suggests that middle managers and professionals in America have adopted a distinctive "rational" ethic. Scholars of Nazi Germany, meanwhile, have suggested that white-collar workers provided a reactionary base for Hitler's rise (Kocka 1980).

RECENT DEVELOPMENTS: PRODUCTIVITY, UNIONIZATION, AND SECURITY

The growth of white-collar occupations has posed a new problem for economic analysts: The productivity of these workers is very hard to measure. There was deep concern in the 1980s about the slowdown of productivity growth, especially in the white-collar and technical ranks. However, this concern was accompanied by a debate about whether the slowdown was real or merely an artifact of measurement failure. Steven Roach, the chief economist at the investment bank Morgan Stanley, suggests that "it may well be that white-collar productivity improvements are simply much harder to come by than blue-collar ones" (Roach 1998).

A good deal of attention has been paid to the potential for unionization of this sector. Many scholars and practitioners have assumed that white-collar workers are resistant to unionism because of their identification with management, and for the first half of the twentieth century their unionization rate was apparently very low. In some countries, such as Sweden, however, white-collar employees (including managers) have formed strong unions of their own; and since the 1950s there has been a substantial growth of white-collar unionism in the United States as well—especially among professionals such as teachers and nurses.

Among the most dramatic and important developments since the 1970s has been the breaking of the widely recognized "psychological contract" of loyalty and job security between corporations and their white-collar forces. Beginning with the 1974 recession, and accelerating greatly in the 1980s, corporate managers began to explicitly consider middle managers as a focus of potential

cost saving. This was in part a rational response to the growing weight of white-collar labor costs, but it was also linked to a broader ideological shift that downplayed the value of stability and security and emphasized instead values of entrepreneurship and individual risk taking. Though economists have found only modest evidence of real changes in white-collar employment tenures, there has been strong documentation (e.g., Leinberger & Tucker 1991, Heckscher 1995, Cappelli 1999, and Newman 1998) of a sharp shift in "mindset" among managers and technical staffs. There is now a mix of fear and anger at the loss of security and enthusiasm for new opportunities, though this mindset has not yet settled into a consistent attitude toward the widespread changes these workers are facing.

SEE ALSO *Blue Collar and White Collar; Employment; Management; Mills, C. Wright; Occupational Status; Self-Employment*

BIBLIOGRAPHY

Cappelli, Peter. 1999. *The New Deal at Work.* Boston: Harvard Business School Press.

Department for Professional Employees, AFL-CIO. 2003. *Current Statistics on White Collar Employees.* Washington, DC: AFL-CIO.

Ehrenreich, Barbara, and John Ehrenreich. 1979. The Professional Managerial Class. In *Between Labor and Capital,* ed. P. Walker, 5–45. Boston: South End Press.

Heckscher, Charles. 1995. *White-Collar Blues: Management Loyalties in an Age of Corporate Restructuring.* New York: Basic Books.

Kocka, Jürgen. 1980. *White-Collar Workers in America, 1890–1940: A Social-Political History in International Perspective.* London: Sage.

Leinberger, Paul, and Bruce Tucker. 1991. *The New Individualists: The Generation after the Organization Man.* New York: HarperCollins.

Machlup, Fritz. 1962. *Production and Distribution of Knowledge in the United States.* Princeton, NJ: Princeton University Press.

Merton, Robert K. 1940. Bureaucratic Structure and Personality. *Social Forces* 18 (4): 560–568.

Meyer, G. J. 1995. *Executive Blues: Down and Out in Corporate America.* New York: Franklin Square Press.

Mills, C. Wright. 1951. *White Collar: The American Middle Classes.* New York: Oxford University Press.

Morton, John D. 1987. BLS Prepares to Broaden Scope of Its White-Collar Pay Survey. *Monthly Labor Review* 110 (3): 3–7. http://www.bls.gov/opub/mlr/1987/03/art1exc.htm.

Newman, Katherine S. 1988. *Falling From Grace: The Experience of Downward Mobility in the American Middle Class.* New York: Free Press.

Porat, Marc Uri. 1977. *The Information Economy: Definition and Measurement.* Vol. 1. Washington, DC: U.S. Dept. of Commerce, Office of Telecommunications.

Poulantzas, Nicos. 1973. On Social Classes. *New Left Review* 78 (March– April): 27–54.

Prandy, K., A. Stewart, and R. M. Blackburn. 1983. *White-Collar Unionism.* London: Macmillan.

Roach, Stephen S. 1998. Is Information Technology Creating a Productivity Boom? *Issues in Science and Technology Online,* Summer. http://www.issues.org/14.4/roach.htm.

Sturmthal, Adolf, ed. 1966. *White-Collar Trade Unions: Contemporary Developments in Industrialized Societies.* Urbana: University of Illinois Press.

Tomasko, Robert M. 1987. *Downsizing: Reshaping the Corporation for the Future.* New York: Amacom.

U.S. Bureau of Labor Statistics (BLS). 2006. *Change Has Come to the ECI.* Washington, DC: BLS. http://www.bls.gov/ncs/ect/sp/ecsm0001.htm.

U.S. Census Bureau. *American Factfinder.* www.census.gov.

Wolff, Edward N. 2005. The Growth of Information Workers. *Communications of the ACM* 48 (10).

Wright, Erik Olin, and Bill Martin. 1987. The Transformation of the American Class Structure, 1960–1980. *American Journal of Sociology* 93 (1): 1–29.

Zunz, Olivier. 1990. *Making America Corporate, 1870–1920.* Chicago: University of Chicago Press.

Charles Heckscher

ENCLOSURE MOVEMENT

SEE *Primitive Accumulation.*

ENDOGENOUS PREFERENCES

Preferences are endogenous when they are determined by, and may change as a result of, other factors. Preference endogeneity appears as an issue, for example, in explaining behavior driven by altruistic, reciprocal, or envious preferences, conformity to social norms, and the effect of persuasive advertising. Although it may appear obvious to noneconomists that preferences change and that economists should account for them, standard neoclassical economic theory takes preferences as exogenous. There is no doubt that apparent evidence for unstable preferences can be explained by suitable ad hoc assumptions embedded into stable, and exogenous, utility functions. Nevertheless, it is questionable whether ad hoc assumptions can be held as serious competitors to more psychologically realistic views of preferences as subject to change.

But endogenous preferences are unattractive to many economists for understandable reasons: (1) neoclassical economic theory assumes utility maximization of a stable utility function, and the risk of allowing the utility function to change is to be able to explain everything by suitable tinkering, and thus explain nothing; (2) endogenous preferences typically imply a loss of parsimony in the economic model, a loss accepted as essential by some (e.g., Bowles 1998) but not by most; and (3) endogenous preferences also make welfare analysis more difficult since normally welfare is measured in terms of utility, and if the utility function changes as a result of a policy change, the metric on the basis of which welfare is measured also changes. A partial solution to problem three is to show that a policy change is better, or worse, according to the preferences held both before and after the policy change. Problems one and two might be answered by good theory and evidence combined.

There is clear evidence for the instability and endogeneity of preferences in specific setups. For example, when decision makers repeatedly face a new situation, such as a market in the experimental laboratory, a learning process takes place where agents shape their preferences in interaction with the market setup. Gary Becker and Kevin Murphy (1993) reviewed the ten U.S. companies with the largest ratio of advertising expenditures to sales, and noted that many of the products the companies produced—such as chewing gum, beer, or cola—conveyed no or very little information. Among others, Samuel Bowles (1998) and Daniel Zizzo (2003) reviewed a variety of evidence on the endogeneity of altruistic, reciprocal, and envious preferences.

The status of theories of endogenous preferences is, however, less satisfactory. Institutional economics accounts, such as Wilfred Dolfsma (2002), are interesting but generic. Behavioral economics models do little more than arbitrarily postulate certain endogenous relationships. Evolutionary game-theoretical models of altruistic, reciprocal, and envious preferences abound (e.g., Bowles 1998), but they typically involve zero-rational agents (where a modicum of rationality could make a difference) and are liable to criticism as evolutionary just-so stories. Artificial-intelligence approaches (based on neural network or hybrid modeling) may help and may be testable against data, but have so far been mostly neglected.

SEE ALSO *Lexicographic Preferences; Preferences; Preferences, Interdependent*

BIBLIOGRAPHY

Becker, Gary S., and Kevin M. Murphy. 1993. A Simple Theory of Advertising as a Good or Bad. *Quarterly Journal of Economics* 108 (4): 941–964.

Bowles, Samuel. 1998. Endogenous Preferences: The Cultural Consequences of Markets and Other Economic Institutions. *Journal of Economic Literature* 36 (1): 75–111.

Dolfsma, Wilfred. 2002. Mediated Preferences: How Institutions Affect Consumption. *Journal of Economic Issues* 36 (2): 449–457.

Zizzo, Daniel J. 2003. Empirical Evidence on Interdependent Preferences: Nature or Nurture? *Cambridge Journal of Economics* 27 (6): 867–880.

Daniel John Zizzo

ENDOGENOUS VARIABLES

SEE *Variables, Predetermined.*

ENERGY

The broadest definition of energy is the ability to do work. Human societies tap into various forms of energy, including chemical energy in biomass, natural gas, coal, and petroleum; nuclear energy in uranium; gravitational energy captured in hydroelectric plants; wind energy; and solar energy. Energy is usually measured in British thermal units (BTUs). A BTU is defined as the amount of heat energy that will raise the temperature of one pound of water by one degree Fahrenheit. In 2005 the world economy obtained about 40 percent of its nonsolar energy from petroleum, about 23 percent each from natural gas and coal, 8 percent total from hydroelectric, wind, and thermal sources, and about 6 percent from nuclear. Most of this energy is used in the industrialized world, although the most rapid growth in energy use is occurring in the industrializing world, especially China. The largest use of energy by far is for industrial production and transportation.

Energy has been a crucial factor in human cultural evolution. The evolution of increasingly complex human societies was driven by the capacity to harness energy. Harnessing energy may have also played a key role in our biological evolution. The large human brain, unique even among primates, has enormous energy requirements. The human brain represents about 2.5 percent of body weight and accounts for about 22 percent of resting metabolic needs. This large energy requirement was met by a much higher proportion of protein in the diet of early humans and the use of fire to predigest meat. The use of fire played a role in the anatomical development of our species—larger brains and shorter guts—and paved the way for further advances in technological and cultural evolution.

Beginning about 10,000 years ago, early agricultural technology harnessed flows of solar energy in the forms of animal-muscle power, water, and wind. With the widespread use of wood for fuel, humans began to tap into stocks of solar energy rather than flows. The use of stocks of energy made it possible to capture ever larger amounts of energy per capita with smaller amounts of effort. Wood, wind, and water power fueled the industrial revolution, which began in the early eighteenth century. In the nineteenth century, ancient solar energy, fossil hydrocarbons in the form of coal, rapidly became the fuel of choice. During the twentieth century, petroleum and natural gas replaced coal as the dominant fuel. Each step in the history of energy use has been characterized by a dominant fuel type that is increasingly flexible and substitutable.

Since our industrial economy depends so heavily on fossil fuels, an obvious question is, "Are we running out of it?" Most economists answer this question with an emphatic "No!" As energy becomes scarce, its price will increase, calling forth substitutes, increasing conservation efforts, and encouraging more exploration for new supplies. Economists point out that past warnings of impending shortages have proved to be greatly exaggerated. Critics of the economic argument counter that the inverse relationship between energy supply and energy demand may be trivially true, but this does not mean that the increasing scarcity of an essential resource like petroleum can be easily accommodated. The economic argument also ignores the geopolitical consequences of the waning of the petroleum age.

A useful supplement to the price-based analysis of economists is the concept of energy return on investment (EROI). This is a measure of how many units of energy can be obtained from a unit of energy invested. If the EROI is less than one, it makes no sense to tap that energy source, no matter how high the price.

Although the world uses many types of energy, none of them have the flexibility and high EROI of petroleum. Of paramount concern is when world petroleum production will peak and start to decline. Most predictions of when worldwide oil production will peak are based on variations of a model developed by the geophysicist M. King Hubbert in the 1950s. He created a mathematical model of the pattern of petroleum exhaustion assuming that the total amount of petroleum extracted over time would follow a bell-shaped pattern called a logistic curve. Past experience for individual oil fields shows that once peak production is reached, production tends to fall quite rapidly. A number of petroleum experts argue that technological advances in the past decade or so have extended the peak of the Hubbert curve for specific oil fields, but this has made exhaustion more rapid after the peak occurs. Since oil is limited, policies promoting technology to make more energy available today mean that less will be there in the future.

Estimates of when world oil production will peak run from 2005 (production has already peaked) to 2030, with most predictions clustering around the years 2010–2012. Predicted consequences of declining oil production range from catastrophic scenarios as agricultural and industrial outputs plummet, to relatively mild scenarios as the world's economies endure inflation and temporary economic hardships to adjust, to the rosy scenarios of free-market fundamentalists who claim that markets will quickly call forth substitutes and conservation that overcome the scarcity of any particular fuel type.

It is impossible to predict how the world's economies will adjust to the end of the fossil-fuel age. So far energy policies in the developed and developing worlds have shown little concern for the limited amount of fossil fuels. What happens in the future depends on how much developing economies (especially China) grow and how energy-dependent they become. Also of concern is how the rest of the world will react to the growing concentration of petroleum reserves in politically volatile areas and to the increasingly ominous effects of global climate change.

SEE ALSO *Energy Sector; Solar Energy*

BIBLIOGRAPHY

Hall, Charles, Pradeep Tharakan, John Hallock, et al. 2003. Hydrocarbons and the Evolution of Human Culture. *Nature* 426: 318–322.

Simmons, Matthew. Various speeches. http://www.simmonsco-intl.com/research.aspx?Type=msspeeches. A good overview of the evidence for and negative consequences of the oil peak.

Tainter, Joseph. 1988. *The Collapse of Complex Societies.* Cambridge, U.K.: Cambridge University Press.

John M. Gowdy

ENERGY INDUSTRY

The *energy industry* has evolved with the industrialization of the world economy and rising consumer incomes. Many sources of energy have been important in human history, including dung, timber, and whale oil. The modern energy industry, however, is focused primarily on coal, crude oil, natural gas, and electricity.

COMPOSITION OF GLOBAL ENERGY CONSUMPTION

As reported in the *BP Statistical Review of World Energy*, in 2005 oil accounted for 36.4 percent of total world energy consumption, followed by coal at 27.8 percent, natural gas at 23.5 percent, hydroelectricity at 6.4 percent,

and nuclear energy at 5.9 percent. The composition of energy consumption differs remarkably across regions due to the relative costs of consuming differing energy sources, as determined by the relative abundance of domestic energy supplies and the stringency of environmental regulation. In North America oil accounts for 40.4 percent of total energy consumption, followed by natural gas at 24.9 percent, coal at 21.9 percent, nuclear energy at 7.5 percent, and hydroelectricity at 5.3 percent. This differs substantially from the composition of total energy consumption in the Asia-Pacific region, for example, where coal is the major energy source accounting for 48.1 percent, followed by oil at 32.6 percent, natural gas at 10.7 percent, hydroelectricity at 4.9 percent, and nuclear energy at 3.6 percent. China and India account for 79 percent of all coal consumption in the Asia-Pacific region and 44 percent of total world coal consumption.

CRUDE OIL MARKETS

Crude oil has evolved from an industry controlled by a small number of vertically integrated companies in which there were few market-based transactions to an industry in which crude oil is a commodity traded on organized exchanges—such as the New York Mercantile Exchange futures contract, which began trading in 1983—as well as on over-the-counter spot markets (Verleger 1982). The distinguishing feature of the crude oil market since 1973 is the resource cartel known as OPEC, the Organization of Petroleum Exporting Countries. The large oil price increases of 1973 and 1979 are generally attributed to the exercise of market power by OPEC, though there are several alternative hypotheses about OPEC's behavior (Gately 1984). James M. Griffin (1985) and Clifton T. Jones (1990) provide direct empirical evidence on OPEC behavior. Their empirical analyses suggest that OPEC engaged in cartel behavior during periods of rising as well as falling prices. The empirical evidence is also consistent with competitive behavior on the part of non-OPEC producers of crude oil.

OPEN ACCESS ENERGY TRANSMISSION

The recent restructuring of natural gas and electricity industries around the world is based on the separation of the energy commodity from its transmission. These energy industries had been organized as natural monopolies in which a single regulated firm provided service to all customers. Under this organization, merchant transporters purchased energy upstream and resold it downstream. The move toward a system based on a property right in transportation has allowed for multiple owners and promoted a more competitive organization of these energy markets. Through use of transportation rights and contracts nearly any organizational structure can be created for pipelines and electricity transmission, including all the historical forms of merchant carriage, common carriage, contract carriage, and vertical integration.

When a property right in transportation is issued, for example by a pipeline, the pipeline becomes a supplier of transportation rights rather than a supplier of transportation. The holders of the rights are the ones who supply transportation and this supply is allocated through the market (De Vany and Walls 1994c; Smith et al. 1988). Property rights in transportation capacity have decentralized control, permitting users to acquire transportation interests through purchase or by contract.

NATURAL GAS

Before open access gas transmission there was no competitive market for natural gas (Smith et al. 1988; Teece 1990; De Vany and Walls 1994a; Michaels 1993). Regulators organized the industry as separated monopolies. Transportation and gas were bundled together and buyers and sellers did not have direct access to one another. As a result, gas purchases were made under long-term contract (Mulherin 1986a; Mulherin 1986b). These regulatory policies balkanized the natural gas industry and disconnected the pipeline grid. Even though, over time, a vast grid of pipelines developed to serve users, its competitive power was nullified because the grid was disconnected and gas flows were fixed.

As a result of open access transmission, much pipeline capacity has been reallocated from the pipelines to their customers. In the U.S. interstate gas market, control of transportation has been decentralized, with 1,400 local distributors holding transportation rights on twenty-one major interstate pipelines (Bradley 1991). Open access transmission brought forth new markets where none had existed; over fifty gas spot markets now exist at scattered points throughout the pipeline grid (De Vany and Walls 1994c) and they have been extremely successful in disciplining prices and allocating natural gas (De Vany and Walls 1994b; De Vany and Walls 1996).

ELECTRIC POWER INDUSTRY RESTRUCTURING

The electricity industry in the United States—and in many other countries around the world—is in the midst of fundamental change as a result of regulatory reform aimed at restructuring the industry, in order to introduce and increase the intensity of competition in wholesale and retail markets. Contrary to the situation in a number of other countries, in the United States restructuring efforts have been hampered by divided regulatory jurisdictions. (See, for example, the discussion in Brennan [2003] for legal and economic perspectives on the roles of different

levels of government in a federation.) The federal government has jurisdiction over wholesale electricity sales and movement because electricity at the wholesale level crosses state borders and therefore qualifies as interstate commerce. (In addition to interstate trade, there is substantial Canada–U.S. trade in electricity that adds another level of institutional complexity. See Feldberg and Jenkins [2003] for a brief legal and institutional analysis of this issue.) Retail markets, on the other hand, are under individual states' jurisdiction. This historical fact has led to a patchwork of different rules and regulations governing electricity markets.

Currently, according to a 2002 U.S. General Accounting Office report, twenty-four states and the District of Columbia have enacted legislation or issued regulatory orders to open their retail markets to competition. However, of these, seven states have either delayed or suspended implementation of restructuring and the remaining twenty-six states have not yet taken any steps to introduce competition at the retail level. The result of this divided jurisdiction and diverse approaches to restructuring has been the introduction of a great deal of regulatory uncertainty into the market. This uncertainty is having an impact on the development of new generation facilities.

POWER PLANT INVESTMENT

One key feature of restructuring has been a move away from centralized planning of new generating capacity and transmission upgrades by unities and state-level public utilities commissions. Instead, a decentralized process of development and investment decisions—largely by nonutility companies—is evolving. The development plans of these companies are not subject to approval by public utilities commissions nor are they coordinated by a central body. Because the development process can be long, regulatory and market conditions may change considerably, causing developers to reassess the relative merits of each of their projects during development, in response to both volatile energy prices and long and uncertain state and federal approval processes.

Power plant investment is higher in states that have restructured electricity markets than in states that have taken no restructuring actions (Walls, Rusco, and Ludwigson, in press). Development is also more prevalent in areas of the country with a robust wholesale market infrastructure. Ownership of new power plants also differs across states, with non-utility companies accounting for the bulk of new power plants in states taking restructuring actions, while utilities still have a strong or dominant role in new development in states that have not restructured at all. States' decisions to implement retail competition result in more investment in new power plants.

NUCLEAR POWER

In 2005 there were 440 operating nuclear power plants in thirty-one countries and these accounted for 16 percent of the world's electricity supply (World Nuclear Association 2005). However, with few exceptions, there has been no new construction of nuclear power plants in the restructured electricity markets. Nuclear power plants have been plagued by problems of public acceptance and waste disposal. There are also important regulatory and financial issues that act as disincentives to the development of nuclear generating plants in liberalized power markets. Nuclear power plants are unattractive to for-profit electricity generation companies due to the extremely large up-front cost associated with nuclear construction and the large correlation between electricity prices and fossil fuel prices. Merchant power producers are interested in locking in the spread between input and output prices. When power prices fall, fuel input prices also fall for conventional fossil-fueled power plants. However, nuclear plants are extremely unprofitable under this scenario, leading to the decision of most private investors to not choose nuclear power units (Roques et al. 2006).

ENERGY AND THE MACROECONOMY

James Hamilton (1983) presented the first systematic analysis of the effects of oil price shocks on the macroeconomy. His research suggested that the two large price increases in crude oil in the 1970s had a significant real economic impact, lowering economic growth in the United States. However, subsequent empirical analysis has found that this relationship may in fact be asymmetric; Knut Anton Mork (1989) found that shocks increasing oil prices were associated with lower economic growth, but that oil price reductions has no impact on real economic activity. More recent analysis that includes the oil price shocks associated with the Iraqi invasion of Kuwait find that the relationship between energy and macroeconomic activity is very weak, even allowing for asymmetries (Hooker 2002; Barsky and Kilian 2004).

ENERGY AND LABOR

Working conditions and salaries in the energy industries largely reflect the overall labor market conditions for any particular time period and geographic location under consideration. However, one notable difference between the energy industry and most manufacturing or service industries is the requirement that a combination of technical and blue-collar workers be physically present at the specific location where energy resources are extracted from the earth. In the United States—home to most of the world's multinational energy companies and to a large pool of skilled and unskilled labor—this historically led to the formation of communities in the locations where energy supplies were discovered. In other countries where large multinational energy companies operate—such as Nigeria and Russia—a combination of domestic blue-collar migrant workers and expatriate technical workers are employed in energy extraction.

SEE ALSO *Energy; Industry; Petroleum Industry; Solar Energy*

BIBLIOGRAPHY

Barsky, Robert B., and Lutz Kilian. 2004. Oil and the Macroeconomy since the 1970s. *Journal of Economic Perspectives* 18 (4): 115–134.

BP. 2006. *BP Statistical Review of World Energy: June 2006.* London: BP p.l.c.

Bradley, Robert L., Jr. 1991. *Reconsidering the Natural Gas Act.* Issue Paper no. 5. Houston: Southern Regulatory Policy Institute.

Brennan, Timothy J. 2003. Provincial and Federal Roles in Facilitating Electricity Competition: Legal and Economic Perspectives. In *Regional Transmission Organizations: Restructuring Electricity Transmission in Canada*, ed. W. David Walls, 20–40. Calgary, Canada: Van Horne Institute.

De Vany, Arthur S., and W. David Walls. 1994a. Natural Gas Industry Transformation, Competitive Institutions, and the Role of Regulation: Lessons from Open Access in U.S. Natural Gas Markets. *Energy Policy* 22 (9): 755–763.

De Vany, Arthur S., and W. David Walls. 1994b. Network Connectivity and Price Convergence: Gas Pipeline Deregulation. *Research in Transportation Economics* 3: 1–36.

De Vany, Arthur S., and W. David Walls. 1994c. Open Access and the Emergence of a Competitive Natural Gas Market. *Contemporary Economic Policy* 12 (2): 77–96.

De Vany, Arthur S., and W. David Walls. 1996. The Law of One Price in a Network: Arbitrage and Price Dynamics in Natural Gas City Gate Markets. *Journal of Regional Science* 36 (4): 555–570.

Feldberg, Peter, and Michelle Jenkins. 2003. Reciprocity, Regional Transmission Organizations, and Standard Market Design: Some Implications for Canadian Participation in North American Wholesale Electricity Trade. In *Regional Transmission Organizations: Restructuring Electricity Transmission in Canada*, ed. W. David Walls, 60–75. Calgary, Canada: Van Horne Institute.

Gately, Dermot. 1984. A Ten-Year Retrospective: OPEC and the World Oil Markets. *Journal of Economic Literature* 22 (3): 1100–1114.

Griffin, James M. 1985. OPEC Behavior: A Test of Alternative Hypotheses. *American Economic Review* 75 (5): 954–963.

Hamilton, James. 1983. Oil and the Macroeconomy since World War II. *Journal of Political Economy* 91 (2): 228–248.

Hooker, Mark A. 2002. Are Oil Shocks Inflationary? Asymmetric and Nonlinear Specifications versus Change in Regime. *Journal of Money, Credit, and Banking* 34 (2): 540–561.

Jones, Clifton T. 1990. OPEC Behavior under Falling Prices: Implications for Cartel Stability. *Energy Journal* 11 (3): 117–129.

Michaels, Robert J. 1993. The New Age of Natural Gas: How Regulators Brought Competition. *Regulation* 16 (1): 68–79.

Mork, Knut Anton. 1989. Oil and the Macroeconomy When Prices Go Up and Down: An Extension of Hamilton's Results. *Journal of Political Economy* 97 (3): 740–744.

Mulherin, J. Harold. 1986a. Complexity in Long Term Natural Gas Contracts: An Analysis of Natural Gas Contractual Provisions. *Journal of Law and Economic Organization* 2: 105–117.

Mulherin, J. Harold. 1986b. Specialized Assets, Governmental Regulation, and Organizational Structure in the Natural Gas Industry. *Journal of Institutional and Theoretical Economics* 142: 528–541.

Roques, Fabien A., William J. Nuttall, David M. Newbery, et al. 2006. Nuclear Power: A Hedge against Uncertain Gas and Carbon Prices? *Energy Journal* 27 (4): 1–23.

Smith, Rodney T., Arthur S. De Vany, and Robert J. Michaels. 1988. An Open Access Rights System for Natural Gas Pipelines. In *Interstate Natural Gas Pipeline Rate Design Studies*, 88–162. Washington, DC: Natural Gas Supply Association.

Teece, David J. 1990. Structure and Organization of the Natural Gas Industry: Differences between the United States and the Federal Republic of Germany and Implications for the Carrier Status of Pipelines. *Energy Journal* 11 (3): 1–36.

U.S. General Accounting Office. 2002. *Lessons Learned from Electricity Restructuring: Transition to Competitive Markets Underway, but Full Benefits Will Take Time and Effort to Achieve*. Technical Report GAO-03-271. Washington, DC: U.S. General Accounting Office.

Verleger, Philip K., Jr. 1982. The Evolution of Oil as a Commodity. In *Energy: Markets and Regulation: Essays in Honor of M. A. Adelman*, eds. Richard L. Gordon, Henry D. Jacoby, and Martin B. Zimmerman, 161–186. Cambridge, MA: MIT Press.

Walls, W. David, Frank W. Rusco, and Jon Ludwigson. 2007. Power Plant Investment in Restructured Markets. *ENERGY–The International Journal* 32 (8): 1403–1413.

World Nuclear Association. 2005. Plans for New Reactors Worldwide. http://www.world-nuclear.org/info/inf17.html.

W. David Walls

ENERGY SECTOR

Twentieth-century affluence in the industrialized countries relied on the highly concentrated energy found in fossil fuels, especially easily accessible oil. Steep increases in the productivity of workers resulted in economic growth and rising household incomes, which transformed the experience of everyday life. In particular, automobile-dependent suburbs spread, and increasingly larger living spaces became filled with electrified appliances of all descriptions.

The industrialized countries, with less than 20 percent of the world's population, still use more than 60 percent of all primary energy. However, most future growth in production and consumption will take place in developing countries with huge populations eager to emulate lifestyles of the affluent. A pressing question is how future demand for energy can be accommodated.

With most commercial energy long provided by fossil fuels, networks of facilities for prospecting, extracting, refining, and distributing are well established. But the richest oil reserves are being depleted, and alternatives to fossil fuels—nuclear power and various forms of renewable energy—pose a variety of challenges requiring substantial investments in research and infrastructure. Such investments will be forthcoming only when alternatives such as nuclear power have long-term prospects for social acceptability, which is necessary for profitability.

Since energy is required for all aspects of production and consumption, a sharp increase in its price can have a substantial dampening effect on the entire economy. The experience of the oil embargo by the Organization of Petroleum Exporting Countries (OPEC) and sharp increases in oil prices in the 1970s demonstrated the vulnerability of even the most powerful oil-importing countries and their susceptibility to panic, inflation, and recession. Some of the incremental wealth amassed by oil exporters ended up as loans to developing countries (in part to pay for oil) that they were unable to reimburse. Such a sequence of events could easily be repeated.

The history of human use of fuels and minerals has been a race between the exhaustion of the richest deposits, which bids up the price, and the development of powerful new technologies that lower the costs by exploiting lower-quality resources or obtaining more work per unit of raw-energy input. Temporarily higher prices for oil could stimulate massive investments in research and infrastructure to expand the long-term supply of energy from unconventional sources. However, the costs and risks, including those associated with the inevitable environmental impacts, may be extremely high. In parallel with the search for new sources of supply, the effective demand for energy services needs to be substantially reduced by changes in the energy-intensive lifestyles made possible by cheap oil.

Lifestyle decisions about housing, mobility, and diet have the most impact on household demand for energy. The affluent have come to require diets rich in animal products, foods transported long distances, large housing spaces with year-round temperature controls, personal cars for trips to work and shopping, and air travel for recreation. It remains to be seen if a marked shift in lifestyles can be achieved voluntarily, either as a response to crisis or in search of what has been called a "new American dream." One hopes that the race to build consumer societies in developing countries can be based on more sustainable lifestyles. While engineering research and corporate research and development focus on new technologies for enhancing energy supply and improving efficiency, social scientists face the double challenge of developing credible scenarios involving sustainable lifestyles and evaluating possible ways to achieve those scenarios.

SEE ALSO *Energy; Energy Industry; Natural Resources, Nonrenewable; Petroleum Industry; Solar Energy*

BIBLIOGRAPHY

Smil, Vaclav. 2000. Energy in the Twentieth Century: Resources, Conversions, Costs, Uses, and Consequences. *Annual Review of Energy and the Environment* 25: 21–51.

Faye Duchin

ENGELS, FREDERICK
SEE *Poverty, Urban.*

ENGERMAN, STANLEY
1936–

Stanley L. Engerman, the John H. Munroe Professor of Economics and History at the University of Rochester, was born in New York City on March 14, 1936. Engerman, who received BS and MBA degrees from New York University and a PhD in economics from Johns Hopkins University, is a pioneer and major figure in the branch of economic history called "new economic history" or "cliometrics." *Cliometrics*, a term that marries the muse of history—Clio—to the statistical analysis of data, emerged in the 1960s to become a central approach in addressing historical questions.

Engerman is best known for his work on slavery, especially his research with Robert Fogel on the U.S. South. Their two-volume book *Time on the Cross*, published in 1974, revolutionized the historical interpretation of the slave system. By combining the wealth of information that they collected from slave plantations and other sources and employing the techniques of the new economic history, Fogel and Engerman overturned accepted views.

Engerman and Fogel argued that economic incentives of owners and slaves were central to the way slavery functioned. They found that by the approach of the Civil War in 1860, the system had never been stronger economically. Slaves were selling at record high prices, and slave owners enjoyed substantial profits, especially on the larger plantations. Engerman and Fogel showed that, although violence or the threat of violence was part of the life of a slave, positive incentives in the form of better material conditions and even cash payments led to a slave labor force that was highly motivated. Through the statistical analysis of farm data, they also showed that productivity levels were higher than on free farms, especially so on plantations, where cotton was produced using gang labor. Their main conclusions were criticized at first but are now widely accepted.

Engerman's study of slavery has extended to the Caribbean and other parts of the world, where his emphasis has been on the process by which the slaves ultimately gained their freedom. Engerman has often been at the epicenter of the debates about slavery and emancipation; in his presidential address to the Economic History Association in 1985, he summarized some of these debates. Engerman points out that whereas the colonies of mainland North America were settled largely by Europeans, the rest of the Americas received many more immigrants from Africa, who were forced there by an active slave trade. Engerman has helped describe the slave economies, which by the middle of the nineteenth century were producing much of the world's sugar, cotton, coffee, and tobacco. He has also explored the transition of these economies to free labor. Unlike in the United States, which ended slavery through a bloody Civil War, slave emancipation in the rest of the Americas was largely peaceful. Engerman again highlights the importance of economic incentives, showing that, in contrast to what happened in the United States, slave owners in the British colonies received cash compensation for their emancipated slaves. As well, former slaves were required to work for a period of time under regulated conditions, further reducing the cost of emancipation to the owners and easing the transition to free labor.

In the late twentieth century Engerman's work helped get to the heart of economic growth. During the nineteenth and twentieth centuries the economies of the United States and Canada were among the most successful in terms of total output and output per person, whereas other parts of the Americas fell far behind. Yet in 1800 the Caribbean and other regions based on slavery had been among the world's wealthiest, indeed much wealthier than the free Americas that later did so well. Working mainly with Kenneth Sokoloff, Engerman has argued that although the slave system could generate high levels of output and large profits for slave owners, the extreme levels of inequality led to institutions that could not sustain growth once slavery was abolished. Most importantly, inequality discouraged the flowering of democracy and the establishment of an effective schooling system.

The archetypal inductive scholar, Engerman has been adviser to generations of students and colleagues. In *Slavery in the Development of the Americas* (2004), an edited volume based on the papers of a conference held in Engerman's honor, David Eltis wrote that "his office (with its triple layer of books lining the walls) and home have functioned as a crossroads and clearing house for nearly four decades, not just for new ideas, but also for scholars seeking intellectual assistance and commentary" (Eltis, Lewis, and Sokoloff 2004, p. viii). Engerman has served on numerous editorial boards and edited more than fifteen books, many of which have been highly influential, particularly *The Reinterpretation of American Economic History* (1971), coedited with Robert Fogel; *Long-Term Factors in American Economic Growth* (1986), with Robert Gallman; *A Historical Guide to World Slavery* (1998), with Seymour Drescher; and the three-volume *Cambridge Economic History of the United States* (1996, 2000), coedited with Robert Gallman.

Engerman also has published more than one hundred articles in leading academic journals and edited volumes. Most of these deal with issues associated with slavery, but his work has spanned areas as diverse as fiscal policy, education, international trade, population and migration, industrial development, and the long-run process of economic growth. In addition to being a former president of the Economic History Association, Engerman is a Distinguished Fellow of the American Economic Association.

SEE ALSO *Caribbean, The; Cliometrics; Economic Growth; Fogel, Robert; Inequality, Political; Inequality, Racial; Plantation; Slavery;* Time on the Cross; *U.S. Civil War*

BIBLIOGRAPHY

Davis, Lance, and Stanley Engerman. 2006. *Naval Blockades in Peace and War: An Economic History since 1750.* New York: Cambridge University Press.

Drescher, Seymour, and Stanley Engerman, eds. 1998. *A Historical Guide to World Slavery.* New York: Oxford University Press.

Eltis, David, Frank Lewis, and Kenneth Sokoloff. 2004. *Slavery in the Development of the Americas.* New York: Cambridge University Press.

Engerman, Stanley. 1986. Slavery and Emancipation in Comparative Perspective: A Look at Some Recent Debates. *Journal of Economic History* 46 (June): 317–339.

Engerman, Stanley, and Robert E. Gallman, eds. 1986. *Long-Term Factors in American Economic Growth.* Chicago: University of Chicago Press.

Engerman, Stanley, and Robert E. Gallman, eds. 1996, 2000. *Cambridge Economic History of the United States.* 3 vols. New York: Cambridge University Press.

Engerman, Stanley, and Kenneth Sokoloff. 2005. Colonialism, Inequality, and Long-Run Paths of Development. National Bureau of Economic Research Working Paper 11057.

Fogel, Robert W., and Stanley Engerman, eds. 1971. *The Reinterpretation of American Economic History.* New York: Harper and Row.

Fogel, Robert W., and Stanley Engerman. 1974. *Time on the Cross: The Economics of American Negro Slavery.* 2 vols. Boston: Little, Brown.

Fogel, Robert W., and Stanley Engerman, eds. 1992. *Without Consent or Contract: Technical Papers on Slavery.* 2 vols. New York: Norton.

Frank D. Lewis

ENGINEERING

Engineering is a body of complex knowledge and a sophisticated art. Because it incorporates mathematical and physical sciences in its applications and designs, it is often mentioned together with science. Engineers, however, deal with the operation of things and apply scientific methods to understand and solve problems, whereas scientists focus on the discovery of knowledge. The traditional role of engineering is to apply natural laws in order to meet the practical needs of society. The scope of engineering is broad, ranging from designing a paper clip, to building space shuttles for space missions, to inspecting the Eiffel Tower.

Engineering is of great importance to modern societies. Participation in engineering, however, is closely linked to gender and race. Historically, engineering, like other intellectual endeavors, was considered a white male domain. Women and racial minorities were virtually absent from the development of engineering as a profession, but not because there were no females or minorities with technical knowledge and expertise. Many female and black inventors remained unrecognized because of economic, legal, and political barriers. Cultural assumptions about the "proper" roles of women and minorities and discriminatory practices, both individual and institutional, discouraged and restricted creative activities among women and minorities. This traditional negating of the intellectual achievements and abilities of women and minorities had a long-term adverse impact on female and minority participation in and contribution to engineering.

Engineering education and employment has become more inclusive, due to a variety of progressive reforms, such as the Civil Rights Act (1964), Title IX of the Education Amendments (1972), and affirmative action programs. Furthermore, industrialization and development in defense and information technology industries have created a rising demand for technical workers. As a result, employers turn to nontraditional workers—women, minorities, and immigrants—as an additional source of skilled labor.

The notion that there is a male culture of engineering has been invoked to account for existing gender disparities in the engineering profession. Due to gender role socialization, women tend to lack "tinkering" experience in childhood. This deficit in technical skills presents challenges for female college students in predominantly male fields such as engineering. It has been suggested that the masculine nature of technological work and male dominance in the workplace have made it difficult for female engineers to fit in. The dearth of women in engineering fields in turn helps perpetuate the male culture of engineering.

Prior to 1880, engineering practice in the United States was primarily a private, independent endeavor, but since then it has become institutionalized and professionalized. By contrast, in Britain engineering is still considered a craft-based occupation rather than an elite profession. A traditional emphasis on apprenticeship as the means to obtain practical skills and experience sets British engineers apart from their American counterparts, who undergo formal training in engineering science. In Britain, neither the government nor the private sector has a significant role in the development and expansion of engineering education. It has been argued that the focus on training through apprenticeship limits the development of science-based high-tech industry, and that the "craft" model is responsible for Britain's economic decline. The British engineering population can be categorized into three groups: chartered engineers, technical engineers, and technicians. Unlike autonomous managers, British engineers who perform non-manual technical work enjoy a marginal status in the organizational structure. They organize themselves by unions instead of opting for professional structuring. As a result, engineers in Britain occupy a relatively low social status compared to their European and American counterparts.

Unlike the British, the French rely on elite engineering schools to produce their technical experts. French engineers put a premium on theoretical knowledge. They tend to identify themselves more with high-status management than with low-status technical staff and, as with their American counterparts, they are expected to join the ranks of management. Having formal training in mathematics and science prepares them for their managerial careers. The French engineering workforce is highly stratified, based on divisions among academic institutions and among employers. The same can be said about the German engineering community. However, instead of concentrating on abstract knowledge and basic research, the training of engineers in Germany has incorporated practical training into engineering science. German engineers have played a key role in the nation's industrialization. The vast majority of them are employed by the state and industry.

Engineering in the United States is not a homegrown product. The American engineering profession began to take shape after European engineering practices were introduced into the United States. The government, industry, and academic institutions have collectively shaped the professionalization and internationalization of engineering. Professional engineering in the United States evolved as a synthesis of the British "craft" system, with its focus on the practical and empirical; the French "school" system, with its emphasis on formal and theoretical training; and, later, the German "estate" model, with its orientation toward research. During the nineteenth century, most American engineers were trained on-the-job or through apprenticeship in a machine shop. The British "craft" method became the training system for many American civil and mechanical engineers. Others received formal training at military academies, such as the United States Military Academy at West Point. Gradually, civilian engineering schools replaced military academies as the principal training ground for engineers. After the passage of the Morrill Act by Congress in 1862, civilian engineering schools became the principal producers of engineers. Under this act, the federal government offered land grants to states for the establishment of schools or college programs in engineering. Many academic institutions took advantage of these land grants and began to offer courses in engineering. As the professionalization of engineering took shape, new engineering fields began emerging in the late nineteenth century. Meanwhile, the influence of business and industry on formal engineering training became increasingly stronger. Besides land, a lot of resources are required to set up an engineering school, including expensive laboratory equipment. Through their financial backing of engineering schools and to a lesser extent the training of engineers at their own company schools, business and industry have exerted direct, strong, and enduring influence over engineering curricula as well as the supply of engineers. As a result, the private sector has become a major sponsor and beneficiary of university engineering schools. Although universities have assumed the role of educating engineers, the private sector has maintained its control over engineering education by offering critical financial backing to engineering programs across the country, new and old.

Economic integration and expanding free trade have made engineering a complex global endeavor transcending national boundaries. With the advent of information technology and advanced telecommunications, transnational projects involving engineers from different cultures are not uncommon. Collaborations in research and development between engineers and scientists from diverse backgrounds are also routine. Engineers can be found in both public and private sectors, and enjoy enormous influence in business and industry.

Engineering is manifested in many facets of our lives. At the end of the twentieth century, the integration of engineering with disciplines such as mathematics, cognitive science, and artificial intelligence resulted in the creation of computer science and information science programs at universities. Many medical applications—such as robotics, artificial organs, radiology, and ultrasound—are the culmination of research pairing engineering and other disciplines.

Because technical competence is so critical for business and industry, engineers have become very much part of the modern system of *technocracy*, or rule by experts. "Engineer-inventors" believe that they can offer technical, logical, and practical solutions to social problems and, eventually, facilitate social progress. Indeed, no one can deny that technological developments have transformed the structure of society and changed our work and lifestyles. Very few people have any real knowledge of the planning, design, and evaluation associated with the creation and maintenance of utilities, buildings and other structures, machines and equipment, and a host of commercial products. But for many people, a world without automobiles, computers, and mobile phones would be unthinkable. Like managers, engineers are trusted by employers to perform sophisticated tasks with little or no supervision. For these reasons, engineers, who enjoy relatively high prestige in many countries, have been called the "production arm," "trusted workers," and "symbolic analysts."

Technological inventions and innovations have served diverse economic, cultural, and political purposes. On the one hand, in democratic societies technology can be a constructive tool used to foster positive social change. On the other hand, it can also be a destructive force, used by a ruling class to preserve domination and control over the masses. Thus, despite the universal applications of engineering designs, engineering is never truly value-neutral.

SEE ALSO *Division of Labor; Machinery; Smith, Adam; Technocracy; Technocrat; Technological Progress,*

Economic Growth; Technological Progress, Skill Bias; Veblen, Thorstein

BIBLIOGRAPHY

Downey, Gary Lee, and Juan C. Lucena. 1995. Engineering Studies. In *Handbook of Science and Technology Studies*, eds. Sheila Jasanoff, Gerald E. Markle, James C. Petersen, and Trevor J. Pinch, 167–188. Thousand Oaks, CA: Sage Publications.

Layton, Edwin T., Jr. 1986. *The Revolt of the Engineers: Social Responsibility and the American Engineering Profession.* 2nd ed. Baltimore, MD: Johns Hopkins University Press.

McIlwee, Judith S., and J. Gregg Robinson. 1992. *Women in Engineering: Gender, Power, and Workplace Culture.* Albany: State University of New York Press.

Meiksins, Peter, and Chris Smith. 1996. *Engineering Labour: Technical Workers in Comparative Perspective.* London and New York: Verso.

Nye, Mary Jo, ed. 2003. *The Modern Physical and Mathematical Sciences.* Vol. 5 of *The Cambridge History of Science.* Cambridge, U.K., and New York: Cambridge University Press.

Stabile, Donald R. 1986. Veblen and the Political Economy of the Engineer: The Radical Thinker and Engineering Leaders Came to Technocratic Ideas at the Same Time. *American Journal of Economics and Sociology* 45 (1): 41–52.

Stabile, Donald R. 1987. Veblen and the Political Economy of Technocracy: The Herald of Technological Revolution Developed an Ideology of "Scientific" Collectivism. *American Journal of Economics and Sociology* 46 (1): 35–48.

Stanley, Autumn. 1995. *Mothers and Daughters of Invention: Notes for a Revised History of Technology.* New Brunswick, NJ: Rutgers University Press.

Tang, Joyce. 2000. *Doing Engineering: The Career Attainment and Mobility of Caucasian, Black, and Asian-American Engineers.* Lanham, MD: Rowman & Littlefield.

Whalley, Peter. 1986. *The Social Production of Technical Work: The Case of British Engineers.* Albany: State University of New York Press.

Wharton, David E. 1992. *A Struggle Worthy of Note: The Engineering and Technological Education of Black Americans.* Westport, CT: Greenwood Press.

Joyce Tang

ENLIGHTENMENT

"It was the common presupposition of all thinkers of the Enlightenment that the being of man is implied in and subordinated to the being of nature and that it must accordingly be explained by the same universal laws" (vol. 5, p. 548). So wrote Ernst Cassirer (1874–1945) in the entry on "Enlightenment" in the original *Encyclopedia of the Social Sciences* (1931). To the Dutch philosopher

Baruch Spinoza (1632–1677), Cassirer attributed the idea that the "stirrings and movements of the will on which the world of man is founded are subject to rules just as universal as the movements within the world of physical bodies. There is a mechanics of human inclinations and urges…. This analogy was emphasized so severely by the philosophy of the Enlightenment that it became finally a complete logical identity" (vol. 5, p. 548).

A generation later Hayden White wrote, "It follows that the Enlightenment was altogether misguided in its attempt to construct a science of human nature on the basis of a study of physical nature: understanding cultural phenomena, which are creations of man alone, in terms of incompletely understood natural principles is doomed from the start" (White 1968, vol. 16, p. 314). This passage appeared in the entry on "Giambattista Vico" in the first edition of the *International Encyclopedia of the Social Sciences* (1968), published in an age in which the Enlightenment had fallen on such hard times that it did not even rate a separate entry in that *Encyclopedia*. The inclusion of the present entry in this second edition is indicative of the rising fortune of the Enlightenment not only in its own right but also with respect to the social sciences specifically.

From the 1970s to the 1990s, there were several attempts to place the origins of the social sciences in the eighteenth century. Yet, although the term *la science sociale* was first used around the time of the French Revolution (1789–1799), a consensus has emerged that, whatever was invented by eighteenth-century social theorists, it was not modern social science. When the editor of *History of the Human Sciences* devoted an issue (6 [1] 1993) of that journal to the Enlightenment origins of the social sciences, he received a set of articles that called that very premise into question. Christopher Fox wrote that "we cannot visit the eighteenth century with a modern campus map" (Fox et al. 1995, pp. 3–4). Claude Blanckaert asserted that to name the Comte de Buffon (1707–1788) as the founder of modern anthropology is really to say that Buffon is the earliest author read by modern anthropologists. Roger Smith contended that it is no longer tenable to trace modern disciplines like sociology, psychology, anthropology, and economics back to Enlightenment precursors, as was the practice in many histories of the disciplines throughout the twentieth century. With the expansion of the eighteenth-century canon since the 1970s, historians of the social sciences have found that the configurations of eighteenth-century science, politics, and social theory were much more complicated than indicated by the tidy narratives of Enlightenment and revolution that characterized much of twentieth-century scholarship.

It was against those narratives of individual liberty, limited government, and toleration of religious practice that continental historians in the mid-twentieth century set up an alternative narrative of Enlightenment social science: one that emphasized efficiency in government, technical bureaucracy, and the assimilation of populations into a centrally administered territorial nation-state, all of which converged for one purpose—domination.

Max Horkheimer (1895–1973) wondered how the liberal project of the Enlightenment could have culminated in the authoritarian regimes, death camps, and armed conflict of the twentieth century. Where Vico saw the project of a mathematical, laws-based social science as doomed from the start, Horkheimer found that, in historical terms, that project was only too successful. As enlightened science played out in the nineteenth and twentieth centuries, all particulars came to be understood as mere representatives of universals. All qualities were reduced to quantities, and all things ultimately became identical, including people. The Enlightenment, wrote Horkheimer, represented the triumph of oppressive equality. Quantitative methods became so pervasive that the human and natural sciences, initially intended to eradicate irrational appeals to myth, magic, and religion, became mythic in their own right.

Under the old regime, domination was clearly visible in political and ecclesiastical hierarchies and in the dogmas by which they were legitimized. The Enlightenment produced new forms of domination that were even more insidious because they were not only vindicated by critical reason but were also applied by reason itself. Michel Foucault (1926–1984) characterized every victory of enlightenment as a step further into the darkness of domination. Biology and medicine exposed to light the hidden recesses of the body in search of life, but found only disease and death. Psychology penetrated the rational mind only to discover irrationality and insanity. Prisoners were freed from dungeons only to be captured all the more securely in the light that flooded Jeremy Bentham's (1748–1832) Panopticon prison, and, not only for criminals, the entire world became a prison that subjected the individual to every form of manipulation and control. Language itself was appropriated by reason (and later by positivism), so that every attempt to resist enlightenment only served the cause of enlightenment. Theory was rendered irrelevant. Critique, once the hallmark of the Enlightenment, came to be dismissed as mere belief or ideology, or worse, as art. In place of the human spirit and critical inquiry was the commodification of all things—science and language as well as material culture—and Horkheimer proposed a theorem that the pliability of the masses increased as the quantity of commodities offered to them increased. Even the individual's own self became alienated and objectified through technologies of psychology.

Against the poststructuralist attack on the Enlightenment, several studies have highlighted the intellectual and social network of the international republic of letters that enabled individuals and texts to cross national boundaries and find common ground in ideologies of republicanism, universal human rights, toleration of beliefs and practices, and freedom of thought, all of which went under the heading of "cosmopolitanism."

Despite the reservations of Europeans regarding the legacy of their own supposed Enlightenment, the traditional narrative of Enlightenment liberalism has been appropriated by social theorists in regions briefly (although brutally) colonized and dominated by the European states in the nineteenth and twentieth century. "Post-colonial scholarship is committed, almost by definition," wrote Dipesh Chakrabarty, "to engaging the universals—such as the abstract figure of the human or that of Reason—that were forged in eighteenth-century Europe and that underlie the human sciences" (2000, p. 5). He finds that although it is inadequate, the European narrative of Enlightenment and technological advancement is indispensable to understanding the history and future of "developing" nations. But this was precisely the point made by the poststructuralists: that cosmopolitanism, like all universal systems, was artificially homogenizing. Responding to Immanuel Kant's (1724–1804) "history of pure reason" at the end of the *Critique of Pure Reason* (1781), Johann Gottfried Herder (1744–1803) wrote a *Metacritique* (1798) that argued that there was no such thing as "pure" reason. There was only particular reason. That is, there were no universal ideas or truths, no world soul into which all particular souls were tapped. There were only particular, unique, historical communities, and these were easily extinguished by totalizing systems like universal reason and imperialism of all sorts, whether ancient Roman or modern European. Universal reason was a chimera, perpetual peace a pipe dream.

It was not merely the case that the party of humanity, as Peter Gay called the two dozen or so philosophes who comprised the twentieth-century canon of eighteenth-century thought, was shouted down by counter-enlightened conservatives and reactionaries. The tendency toward mass democracy and domination, both physical and psychological, was never a sinister plot of imposters. It was built into the very Enlightenment itself—built, that is, into cosmopolitanism, universal reason, and the instrumental reason aimed at reforming the inefficiencies and abuses of old regime society.

Writing on the twentieth-century culture industry, Theodor Adorno (1903–1969) augmented Horkheimer's penetrating critique of the technological society by showing that even the objects of individual choice were instruments of homogenizing conformity. Production technology, hailed in the eighteenth and nineteenth century as the means by which Europe could finally cultivate the land and meet its needs efficiently so that the individual could cultivate himself or herself, was transformed into the economic logic of standardization and mass consumption. One city, with its gleaming skyscrapers, was essentially the same as the next. Older houses outside the city center decayed into slums, while new suburban houses were thrown up quickly and cheaply, as if designed to be discarded in a short while like empty food cans. Suburban housing projects were intended to perpetuate the rational-critical individual as an independent unit in a small hygienic dwelling, but in fact they made the individual all the more subservient to the absolute power of capitalism. Adorno took the development from telephone to radio as indicative. The telephone was liberal: it allowed the person to play the role of subject. The radio was democratic: it turned all participants into listeners, authoritatively subjecting them to broadcast programs that were all exactly the same. Other mass spectacles performed the same function, including popular music, cinema, and sports, to say nothing of television. Focus groups and market research, employing the techniques of propaganda, ensured that something was provided for all so that none might escape. Even improvisational jazz was a perfected technique that homogenized all particulars into a universal jargon of style, a style that, in Friedrich Nietzsche's (1844–1900) terms, was "a system of non-culture, to which one might even concede a certain 'unity of style' if it really made any sense to speak of stylized barbarity" (Nietzche 1917, p. 187; Horkheimer and Adorno 1972, p. 128).

Deeply implicated in the movement from liberal Enlightenment to mass deception were the social sciences. Adorno characterized that movement as an inexorable trend built into the Enlightenment itself. But social scientists themselves worried about their own role in social engineering and manipulation.

Both the modernist view of Enlightenment liberalism as an alternative to twentieth-century totalitarianism and the postmodernist view of the Enlightenment as the source of that same totalitarianism depended on selective readings of eighteenth-century social theorists. In fact, few in the eighteenth century were as sanguine about the power of light and reason as they were made out to be in the twentieth century. Edmund Burke (1729–1797) worried about a world in which power became gentle, obedience became liberal, and all shades of life were harmonized, blandly assimilated, and dissolved. Justus Möser (1720–1794) asserted that the civil administrator who hoped to reduce everything to an academic theory or a few rules paved the road to despotism and lost the wealth of variety. Whether in local administration or global ethnology, particularist sentiments like these were echoed across the continent by social theorists such as Louis François Jauffret (1770–1840), Aubin Louis Millin (1759–1818), Joseph-Marie Degérando (1772–1842), Johann Jakob Moser (1701–1785), Ludwig Timotheus Spittler (1752–1810), Christoph Meiners (1747–1810), Johann Georg Hamann (1730–1788), and of course Herder. Historical scholarship since the mid-1970s has also celebrated the variety of eighteenth-century social thought in counter-Enlightenment, radical Enlightenment, Enlightenment in national context, and so forth. Just as social science cannot be taken as monolithic, neither can the Enlightenment.

BIBLIOGRAPFHY

Baker, Keith M. 1964. The Early History of the Term "Social Science." *Annals of Science* 20 (3): 211–226.

Blanckaert, Claude, ed. 1999. *L'histoire des sciences de l'homme.* Paris: L'Harmattan.

Burke, Edmund. [1790] 1968. *Reflections on the Revolution in France.* Harmondsworth, U.K.: Penguin.

Cassirer, Ernst. 1930–1935. Enlightenment. In *Encyclopedia of the Social Sciences.* Vol. 5 (1931), 547–552. New York: Macmillan.

Chakrabarty, Dipesh. 2000. *Provincializing Europe: Postcolonial Thought and Historical Difference.* Princeton, NJ: Princeton University Press.

Foucault, Michel. [1966] 1970. *The Order of Things: An Archaeology of the Human Sciences.* New York: Vintage.

Fox, Christopher, Roy Porter, and Robert Wokler, eds. 1995. *Inventing Human Science: Eighteenth-Century Domains.* Berkeley: University of California Press.

Gusdorf, Georges. 1966–1988. *Les Sciences humaines et la pensée occidentale.* 15 vols. Paris: Payot.

Horkheimer, Max, and Theodor Adorno. [1944] 1972. *Dialectic of Enlightenment.* Trans. John Cumming. New York: Continuum.

Möser, Justus. 1943–1990. *Sämtliche Werke.* 14 vols. Oldenburg, Germany: Stalling.

Nietzsche, Friedrich. [1873] 1917. "Unzeitgemässe Betrachtengun." In *Werke,* Vol. 1. Leipzig, Germany: Kröner.

Schmidt, James, ed. 1997. *What Is Enlightenment? Eighteenth-Century Answers and Twentieth-Century Questions.* Berkeley: University of California Press.

Smith, Roger. 1997. *Norton History of the Human Sciences.* New York: Norton.

White, Hayden. Vico, Giambattista. 1968. In *International Encyclopedia of the Social Sciences,* ed. David L. Sills. New York: Macmillan, Vol. 16, pp. 313–316.

Michael C. Carhart

ENTERPRISE

An enterprise is a business venture initiated by an entrepreneur, the person who assumes the organization, management, and risks of a business enterprise. Entre-preneurship is considered a factor of production that involves human resources, most commonly performing the functions of raising capital; organizing, managing, and assembling other factors of production; and undertaking business decisions. It involves a combination of initiative, foresight, and willingness to take the risks and undertake the new ventures required to establish a successful business.

The term *entrepreneur* (and consequently *enterprise*) appears to have been introduced by the Irish banker and economist Richard Cantillon (c. 1680–1734). The term was popularized as a result of John Stuart Mill's classic work, *Principles of Political Economy* (1848). To the classical economist of the late eighteenth century, the term described an employer, in the character of one person, who assumed the risk and management of an enterprise. In practice, entrepreneurs were not differentiated from capitalists until the nineteenth century, when their function developed into that of coordinators of processes necessary to large-scale industry and trade. At that point, much like today, the entrepreneur was involved in the management of the enterprise, in contrast to the ordinary capitalist, who merely owned an enterprise and might choose not to take any part in the day-to-day operation. Henry Ford is an example of the rising class of entrepreneurial manufacturers in the twentieth century in the United States of America. However, the entrepreneur's functions and importance have declined with the growth of the corporation.

Nevertheless, the term *entrepreneur* had disappeared from the economics literature by the end of the nineteenth century. This was due to the fact that economists began to use the simplifying assumption that all individuals in an economy have perfect information. Under this assumption, there is no reason for an entrepreneur, or an enterprise, to exist. If individuals have perfect information, they will all make the same assessments of alternative economic activities. More recently, however, economists have increasingly removed this unrealistic assumption of perfect information, allowing once again for the presence of entrepreneurship in the literature. In addition, entrepreneurship has been added as the fourth production factor, after labor, capital, and natural resources.

Almost any business or organization can be called an enterprise, and an enterprise can be either private or public in nature. A private enterprise is a business organization especially directed toward profit and generating personal wealth for the owners. In other words, the owners and operators of a private business have as their main objective the generation of a financial return in exchange for their expense in time, energy, innovation, skills, and money. The private enterprise is the main institution of market capitalism, and as the price mechanism is a co-

coordinating instrument, the entrepreneur performs a coordinating function. *Free enterprise*, which is the result of free markets, is another term used to denote market capitalism. Indeed, the terms *enterprise, company, corporation,* and *organization* are often used synonymously.

A firm is a unit that employs factors of production to produce goods and services. A firm is a commercial partnership comprising a collection of individuals grouped together for economic gain, especially when unincorporated. It is represented by the name or designation under which a company transacts business. The term became popularized in Ronald Coase's 1937 article, "The Nature of the Firm." Operating within a market involves some costs, but by establishing a firm and the authority to direct resources, certain costs are reduced. As Coase states, "When the direction of resources (within the limits of a contract) becomes dependent on the buyer in this way, that relationship which I term a 'firm' may be obtained" (Coase 1937, p. 392).

In an article published in 1972 in *American Economic Review*, Armen Alchian and Harold Demsetz defined a firm as a contractual structure subject to continuous renegotiation with the central agent, or the firm's owner and employer. Thus, a firm is a hierarchical organization attempting to make profits. There are various types of firms, such as: (1) a sole trader or sole proprietorship, in which there is only one owner of the firm with unlimited liability; (2) a partnership, in which there are two or more partners who own, control, and finance the firm and have unlimited liability; (3) a private limited company (Ltd.) or corporation, in which a limited number of shares are issued and the firm is owned by shareholders who have limited liability. In the latter case, these corporations are legal entities, and the firms or corporations owned by the shareholders are treated by law as an artificial person.

By the latter half of the nineteenth century, corporations increased substantially, displacing other forms of enterprises. The control of industrial production thus became the responsibility of corporate finance, resulting in what the Norwegian-American economist Thorstein Veblen (1857–1929) called "absentee ownership." Often, however, shareholding ownership is so widely dispersed that the majority of shareholders reluctantly experience the separation of ownership from control. That is, control can be maintained by a minority interest with access to corporate finance: "ownership continually becomes more dispersed; the power formerly joined to it becomes increasingly concentrated; and the corporate system is thereby more securely established" (Berle and Means 1933, p. 9). According to Veblen, absentee ownership has grave consequences for the structure of the society, because "law and politics … serve the needs of the absen-

tee owners at the cost of the underlying population" (Veblen 1923, p. 6).

When an enterprise has operations in more than one country, this enterprise is named a *multinational enterprise* (MNE), a *multinational corporation* (MNC), or a *transnational corporation* (TNC). Such a firm engages in foreign direct investment (FDI) and owns or controls income-generating assets or value-adding activities in more than one country. A multinational enterprise can participate in the economic activities of a foreign country through five general means of involvement: (1) trading (importing or exporting, and incorporate transfers); (2) foreign direct investment (such as joint ventures, wholly owned subsidiaries, green-field FDI, brown-field FDI, acquisition [the firm can have a "majority" or "stake" interest], merger and acquisition, or privatization); (3) indirect (portfolio) investment; (4) agreements that do not involve money transfer from the part of the foreign partner (e.g. licensing agreement, franchising, turnkey projects, or management contracts), and (5) collaboration or strategic alliance with another enterprise in order to cope with pressures of intense global competition and increasingly complex and rapid technological development.

The United Nations and the governments of most developing nations use the term *transnational*, rather than *multinational*, to describe an enterprise that has operations in more than one country. The United Nations' specialized agency, the United Nations Conference on Trade and Development (UNCTAD), for example, employs the following definition: "Transnational corporations comprise parent enterprises and their foreign affiliates: a parent enterprise is defined as one that controls assets of another entity or entities in a country or countries other than its home country, usually by owning a capital stake. An equity capital stake of at least 10 percent is normally considered as a threshold for the control of assets in this context." Actually, this 10 percent rule has been accepted by the International Monetary Fund (IMF) and the Organisation for Economic Co-operation and Development (OECD), thus identifying this to be the minimum equity stake for an investment to qualify as foreign direct investment and not a portfolio investment.

SEE ALSO *Business; Capitalism, State; Corporations; Entrepreneurship; Mill, John Stuart; State Enterprise; Veblen, Thorstein*

BIBLIOGRAPHY

Alchian, Armen A., and Harold Demsetz. 1972. Production, Information Costs, and Economic Organization. *American Economic Review* 62 (5): 777–795.

Berle, Adolf A., Jr., and Gardiner C. Means. 1933. *The Modern Corporation and Private Property.* New York: Macmillan.

Coase, Ronald. H. 1937. The Nature of the Firm. *Economica* 4 (16): 386–405.

International Monetary Fund, and Organisation for Economic Co-operation and Development. 1999. Report on the Survey of Implementation of Methodological Standards for Direct Investment. Paris: OECD, Directorate for Financial, Fiscal and Enterprise Affairs (DAFFE). http://www.oecd.org/dataoecd/40/45/2752183.pdf.

Mill, John Stuart. 1848. *Principles of Political Economy.* New York: D. Appleton.

Veblen, Thorstein. 1923. *Absentee Ownership and Business Enterprise in Recent Times: The Case of America.* New York: B. W. Huebsch.

Aristidis Bitzenis
John Marangos

ENTERTAINMENT INDUSTRY

Entertainment as an industry—in the United States alone—is responsible each year for $150 billion in expenditures and some 120 billion hours of consumed time (Vogel 1998, p. xvii). Entertainment as an economic sector consists of diverse products and services including motion pictures, television, music, broadcasting, print media, toys, gaming, gambling, sports, and fine arts.

ECONOMIC DEVELOPMENT AND THE DEMAND FOR LEISURE

Leisure time has been a determining factor in the development of recreation and entertainment as an industry. Entertainment has grown as an industry in step with increased income and time available for leisure and recreation. Economic development, often quantified in terms of productivity or output per person-hour, has enabled goods and services to be produced with fewer labor inputs. The growth of the entertainment industries has been directly related to the development of a modern economy and rising economic productivity, though precise estimation of the demand for leisure is a thorny task (Owen 1971). An important issue in the development of entertainment as an industry is the rising productivity of workers, and in particular the ways in which technical progress has increased worker productivity. Progress in technology, in addition to creating the demand for entertainment products and services, has also led to the creation of much of the dominant forms of contemporary entertainment.

INDUSTRY OVERVIEW

Substantial production in the creative industries takes place within the U.S. economy and creative products are a major U.S. export. Motion pictures, home video and television programming, music and sound recordings, books, video games, and software are collectively one of the largest and fastest-growing economic sectors, responsible for about 6 percent of total U.S. gross domestic product per annum (Motion Picture Association of America 2006a). Multinational entertainment/media conglomerates such as Vivendi, Sony, and AOL/Time Warner are increasingly becoming dominant in this sector, with operations that permit substantial economies across the line of entertainment products. The process often begins with a literary work of fiction, which is then made into a movie exhibited in cinemas and later on syndicated and network television domestically and abroad, and finally released on home video. Characters and other elements from the movie can be developed into a line of toys cross-promoted with fast food, and further developed into a video game or board game, and perhaps even featured in a line of clothing.

In the motion-picture industry, the sector of entertainment with the highest profile, domestic (U.S. and Canadian) box-office receipts accounted for about $9 billion, while worldwide box-office revenue was over $23 billion for 2005 (Motion Picture Association of America 2006b). The international market now yields more revenue than the North American market and it is also the source of revenue growth for the motion-picture industry, though success in the international market is largely conditional on success in the North American market. The dominance of Hollywood films in worldwide box-office revenue gives rise to claims of cultural imperialism, though major Hollywood studios in fact design films for distribution in the worldwide market even though the films are screened in North America first. While international box-office revenues have been rising, the major sources of new revenues for the motion-picture industry have been from home video and digital versatile disc (DVD) sales, and from merchandising arrangements such as toys, video games, clothing lines, and other products that are tied to successful motion pictures.

While Hollywood films dominate worldwide box-office revenue, the American film industry does not dominate worldwide production. The Mumbai-based Indian film industry—commonly known as Bollywood because it is the "Hollywood of Bombay" (the former name of present-day Mumbai)—produces more motion pictures each year than any other country. Throughout the 1980s about 250 individual film production companies completed an annual average of about 700 feature films per year with the encouragement of official government policy requiring commercial movie theaters to screen at least one Indian film per show (Gomery 1996). In 2003 the Indian film industry produced 877 feature-length films and 1,177 short films (Central Board of Film

Certification 2006); this contrasts with the 459 new films released in the United States during 2003 (Motion Picture Association of America 2006b).

The music industry consists primarily of the sales of prerecorded music—albums distributed on compact disc and audiocassettes, and singles distributed on compact disc. Music videos are also sold as product in traditional formats. Music is also available in alternate digital formats—including MP3, OGG, and WAV—through Internet retailers. The authorized digital distribution of music content has been overshadowed by unauthorized distribution, both free and for profit, though academic research on this issue is much less clear than one would glean from journalistic reports (as is discussed in more detail below).

Gambling in the United States is popularly associated with the cities of Atlantic City, New Jersey, and Las Vegas, Nevada, which are responsible for 9 and 21 percent, respectively, of the 2005 U.S. annual gambling revenues of about $53 billion (PricewaterhouseCoopers 2005). Native American casino-operators account for over 40 percent of gambling revenues. While the United States is a large gambling market, accounting for over 60 percent of worldwide gambling revenues, substantial new growth in gambling revenues is occurring in international markets, especially in the former Portuguese colony of Macao, which began granting licenses to new casinos a few years after being returned to Chinese sovereignty in 1999. While gambling revenues in aggregate make the United States the largest market, the character of North American gambling is quite different from Asian gambling markets. For example, in horse track gambling the average total amount bet on a race day at a North American track is on the order of $100,000, whereas at Hong Kong tracks and Japanese tracks a day's bets are on the order of $200 million to $300 million, respectively (Busche and Walls 2000).

Expansion of casino gambling opportunities in Asia, with new casinos in Macao and proposed casinos in Japan, Thailand, Singapore, and Taiwan, together with recent changes in British gambling taxation and online gambling opportunities, make prospects favorable for the expansion of international gambling markets (Paton et al. 2002).

IMPORTANT CHARACTERISTICS OF ENTERTAINMENT MARKETS

The entertainment industries differ in important ways from traditional manufacturing and service industries. Richard Caves (2000) enumerates seven ways in which the creative industries—including fine arts, music, and motion pictures—differ distinctly from what he terms the humdrum industries:

1. Neither producers nor consumers know the demand for product until after it is revealed. Creative products and services are "experience goods" and there is symmetric ignorance of information, not an informational asymmetry.

2. The creative talents producing the product care about the creative output explicitly, in addition to their pecuniary compensation in production.

3. The creators engage in joint multiplicative production with an array of diverse inputs in which all inputs are essential, because there is less substitutability than in other production processes.

4. Entertainment products are horizontally differentiated products. Each product is unique and must be experienced before demand is known.

5. Products are vertically differentiated by the quality of the inputs used in production. Furthermore, inputs of different quality levels may be combined—for example, a B-list screenplay and an A-list actor.

6. Profitability depends on temporal coordination and prompt realization of revenues once assets are sunk. Delays may occur once assets have been committed to production.

7. Creative products are durable and this leads to issues regarding rents, collection and monitoring of royalties, warehousing, and retrieval.

The seven features identified by Richard Caves are essential in understanding the markets for entertainment products both qualitatively and quantitatively (Walls 2005). Additionally, the demand for entertainment has two properties that are deserving of our particular attention. The first is that consumption of entertainment requires the time of the consumer. The second is that the demand for entertainment is not fixed in advance of the product being produced; instead, it is discovered by the consumers after the product has been consumed. We will discuss these properties of entertainment demand briefly.

The time-cost element is important in understanding the demand for entertainment, because consumption of entertainment necessarily implies customer-supplied inputs; recognizing this explicitly is essential if we are to understand the functioning of demand and supply in this market. Perhaps the best illustration of this point, in a more general context, is the seminal paper by Arthur De Vany and Thomas Saving (1983). De Vany and Saving demonstrate that when all else is equal, consumption cost is lower for a product that requires less time to consume. Of course, price can be adjusted and this implies a trade-off between time-cost and the monetary price. In the entertainment industry, this may also involve substitution across alternative media for a similar product. For example, reading an 800-page book may involve a substantial element of time, but a consumer may substitute a video-cassette or DVD film version of the book to be viewed on a computer or television monitor, or a compact disc or audiocassette version of the book to be listened to while at home, at work, or while commuting. All of these alternative means of consumption involve tradeoffs in which the time-cost of consumption varies greatly and may be of primary importance in consumption decisions.

The demand for entertainment products is not fixed in advance, but is discovered by consumers as they consume many entertainment products. Understanding this aspect of demand is essential if one is to make sense of many of the entertainment industry's unique business practices. When movie audiences see a movie they like, they make a discovery and tell their friends about it. This and other information is transmitted to other consumers and demand develops dynamically as the audience sequentially discovers which movies it likes. Supply adapts to revealed demand through flexible exhibition contracts and other business practices that permit the increasing returns in film demand to be realized. For example, early viewers of a motion picture may substantially affect the choices of other potential viewers. This type of behavior is known in the social sciences as, variously, *herding, contagion, network effects, bandwagons, path-dependence, momentum,* and *information cascades* (Arthur 1994; Banerjee 1992; Bikhchandani et al. 1992). The particular algebraic models of this behavior differ in the mathematical details, but they are all dynamical processes: Demand depends on revealed demand. As a result of this sequential demand process, initial advantages in movie attendance can lead to extreme differences in outcomes when demand has recursive feedback. De Vany and Walls (1996) showed that box-office revenues have a contagion-like property where the week-to-week change in demand is stochastically dependent on previous demand. A big opening of a bad movie can cause consumption to evaporate. But a big opening of a good movie can lead to an avalanche of attendance. Demand for movies, music, fashion, and other entertainment products and services are characterized by extreme uncertainty due to the nature of dynamical demand.

THE CHALLENGE OF PIRACY

The most substantial challenge facing the entertainment industry is intellectual property piracy, largely due to the easily copyable digital format of many entertainment products. Infringement of copyrights and other forms of intellectual property is a large and growing problem around the world and it is of particular importance for the entertainment industry. The Motion Picture Association

of America estimates that losses due to piracy exceed $3 billion annually in potential worldwide revenue (Motion Picture Association of America 2005). The intellectual capital of the S&P 500 companies is worth 3.4 trillion U.S. dollars (Bowers 2001), so it follows that even a small percentage infringement on such a large base generates enormous absolute losses to property rights holders. Peggy E. Chaudhry and Michael G. Walsh (1996) provide an overview of trends in counterfeiting in the international marketplace, including a consideration of the legal framework that governs the protection against piracy and a review of different anticounterfeiting strategies.

Piracy of entertainment products can take many forms. These range from illegal copying and distribution of videocassettes and optical media (CD-ROM, VCD, and DVD) to Internet piracy, which can involve commerce and the sharing of digital content. Unauthorized signal transmission and theatrical performances are other types of movie and music piracy. Music and movie piracy are either commercial sale of physical media or the sharing of videocassettes, optical media, and digital content over the Internet.

For most entertainment products the pirate good is identical to the authentic article, except for the packaging and after-sale support. For example, music CDs will be an exact digital copy of the authentic product, but liner notes and lyrics will either be missing or will contain numerous, and often humorous, typographical errors. Many entertainment companies use copy-protection technologies, including the Content Scrambling System for DVDs, dedicated DSL set-top boxes, digital encryption encoding of satellite signals, and Macrovision for videocassettes. The use of antipiracy technologies raises the cost of engaging in piracy, as Sougata Poddar (2003) had modeled analytically. Despite efforts to increase the cost of piracy, however, in practice it is not too difficult even for a computer hobbyist to work around the latest antipiracy technologies (Perry 2005). Even the copy-protection technologies employed in computer software—including online authentication—are quickly rendered obsolete by digital pirates (Harvey and Walls 2006).

Copy-protection technologies, whether effective or not, are aimed primarily at preventing retail products from becoming a source of pirate supply. But the source of pirate movies is often not a retail copy but instead is an insider copy, such as the advance copies used for screening and marketing purposes (Byers et al. 2003). Other copies are made from handheld video camera recordings of motion picture films off of a theater screen. While the quality may be low, the latest movies are also readily available over internet-based file-sharing networks, such as BitTorrent (Kwok 2004). This contrasts with music piracy, in which high-quality copies of songs and entire albums are available either freely through file-sharing networks, such as those available with the Kazaa program, or available for purchase through for-profit retailers such as allofmp3.com.

Many factors are associated with piracy (Limayem et al. 1999), and according to Seung Kyoon Shin et al. (2004) sociological factors may in fact be more important than some economic factors. Most studies suggest that the level of piracy is systematically related to the level of income. Income reflects a person's average cost of time and the demand for quality. Patrick J. Harvey and W. David Walls (2003) examined the demand for pirate software in a laboratory study and found that the demand for counterfeit goods decreased as the expected penalty for consuming the illicit goods increased. Income may be correlated with other infrastructure that provides alternative means of consuming the product. All of these factors would be expected to decrease the demand for pirate products as income rises. As average income rises, the supply of pirate products would also be expected to decrease due to the availability of more attractive opportunities for employment than pirating. There is, however, no unambiguous prediction of the equilibrium effect of income changes on piracy.

In a forthcoming article, the present author empirically examines the rate of motion-picture piracy across a sample of twenty-six countries and finds that the level of piracy is explained by the level of income, the cost of enforcing property rights, the level of collectivism present in a country's social institutions, and the level of Internet usage. Conclusions about the behavioral aspects of piracy are more certain than piracy's actual impact on the entertainment industry revenues, however: Felix Oberholzer-Gee and Koleman Strumpf (2004) found that Internet music piracy had no negative effect on legitimate music sales; on the contrary, their study found that piracy may even boost sales of some types of music, contradicting the music industry's assertion that the illegal downloading of music online is causing revenues to fall. In contrast, Rafael Rob and Joel Waldfogel (2006) found that the U.S. music industry lost one fifth of a sale for each album downloaded from the Internet. There is no definitive answer to the question of whether or not piracy has a net negative effect on consumer demand in the entertainment industry.

SEE ALSO *Film Industry; Gambling; Industry; Music; Recording Industry; Sports Industry; Television*

BIBLIOGRAPHY

Arthur, W. Brian. 1994. *Increasing Returns and Path Dependence in the Economy.* Ann Arbor: University of Michigan Press.

Banerjee, Abhijit V. 1992. A Simple Model of Herd Behavior. *Quarterly Journal of Economics* 107 (3): 797–817.

Bikhchandani, Sushil, David Hirshleifer, and Ivo Welch. 1992. A Theory of Fads, Fashion, Custom, and Cultural Change as Informational Cascades. *Journal of Political Economy* 100 (5): 992–1026.

Bowers, Barbara. 2001. Minding the Store. *Best's Review* 102 (7): 93–97.

Busche, Kelly, and W. David Walls. 2000. Decision Costs and Betting Market Efficiency. *Rationality and Society* 12 (4): 477–492.

Byers, Simon, Lorrie Cranor, Dave Korman, et al. 2003. Analysis of Security Vulnerabilities in the Movie Production and Distribution Process. In *Proceedings of the 2003 ACM Workshop on Digital Rights Management*, ed. Moti Yung, 1–12. New York: ACM Press.

Caves, Richard E. 2000. *Creative Industries: Contracts between Art and Commerce.* Cambridge, MA: Harvard University Press.

Central Board of Film Certification, Government of India. 2006. Statistics. http://www.cbfcindia.tn.nic.in/statistics.htm.

Chaudhry, Peggy E., and Michael G. Walsh. 1996. An Assessment of the Impact of Counterfeiting in International Markets: The Piracy Paradox Persists. *Columbia Journal of World Business* 31 (3): 34–48.

De Vany, Arthur S., and Thomas R. Saving. 1983. The Economics of Quality. *Journal of Political Economy* 91 (6): 979–1000.

De Vany, Arthur S., and W. David Walls. 1996. Bose-Einstein Dynamics and Adaptive Contracting in the Motion Picture Industry. *Economic Journal* 106 (439): 1493–1514.

Gomery, Douglas. 1996. The New Hollywood. In *The Oxford History of World Cinema*, ed. Geoffrey Nowell-Smith, 475–482. Oxford: Oxford University Press.

Harvey, Patrick J., and W. David Walls. 2003. Laboratory Markets in Counterfeit Goods: Hong Kong versus Las Vegas. *Applied Economics Letters* 10 (14–15): 883–887.

Harvey, Patrick J., and W. David Walls. 2006. Digital Pirates in Practice: Analysis of Market Transactions in Hong Kong's Pirate Software Arcades. *International Journal of Management* 23 (2): 207–214.

Kwok, Sai Ho. 2004. File Sharing Activities over BT Networks: Pirated Movies. *Computers in Entertainment* 2 (2): 11.

Limayem, Moez, Mohamed Khalifa, and Wynne W. Chin. 1999. Factors Motivating Software Piracy: A Longitudinal Study. In *ICIS 1999: Proceedings of the Twentieth International Conference on Information Systems*, eds. Prabuddha De and Janice I. DeGross, 124–131. Atlanta, GA: Association for Information Systems.

Motion Picture Association of America. 2005. Anti-Piracy Home Page. http://www.mpaa.org/piracy.asp.

Motion Picture Association of America. 2006a. Economies. http://www.mpaa.org/piracy_Economies.asp.

Motion Picture Association of America. 2006b. 2005 Theatrical Market Statistics Report. http://www.mpaa.org/researchstatistics.asp.

Oberholzer-Gee, Felix, and Koleman Strumpf. 2004. The Effect of File Sharing on Record Sales. Harvard Business School working paper.

http://www.unc.edu/~cigar/papers/FileSharing_March2004.pdf.

Owen, John D. 1971. The Demand for Leisure. *Journal of Political Economy* 79 (1): 56–76.

Paton, David, Donald S. Siegel, and Leighton Vaughan Williams. 2002. A Policy Response to the E-Commerce Revolution: The Case of Betting Taxation in the U.K. *Economic Journal* 112 (480): F296–F314.

Perry, Tekla S. 2005. DVD Copy Protection: Take 2. *IEEE Spectrum* 42 (1): 38–39.

Poddar, Sougata. 2003. On Software Piracy When Piracy Is Costly. Working paper 03/09. Singapore: Economics Department, National University of Singapore.

PricewaterhouseCoopers. 2005. *Global Entertainment and Media Outlook: 2005–2009.* New York: PricewaterhouseCoopers LLP.

Rob, Rafael, and Joel Waldfogel. 2006. Piracy on the High C's: Music Downloading, Sales Displacement, and Social Welfare in a Sample of College Students. *Journal of Law and Economics* 49 (1): 29–62.

Shin, Seung Kyoon, Ram D. Gopal, G. Lawrence Sanders, and Andrew B. Whinston. 2004. Global Software Piracy Revisited: Beyond Economics? *Communications of the ACM* 47 (1): 103–107.

Vogel, Harold L. 1998. *Entertainment Industry Economics: A Guide for Financial Analysis.* 4th ed. New York: Cambridge University Press.

Walls, W. David. 2005. Modeling Movie Success When "Nobody Knows Anything": Conditional Stable-Distribution Analysis of Film Returns. *Journal of Cultural Economics* 29 (3): 177–190.

W. D. Walls

ENTREPRENEURSHIP

The concept of entrepreneurship and the portrayal of the entrepreneur as leading economic figure, even cultural hero, derive from both the evident nature of the market system and the projected self-image of middle-class business leaders. As with any such concept, its meaning depends on the larger model of which it is a part and its more or less precise relationships to other key figures. Defining the entrepreneur or entrepreneurship deals with a term whose meaning is highly variable in use, and generates serious questions.

The term *capitalist* could refer to all business people, or to only the suppliers of capital, with the others as managers—the promotional, organizational, and operational decision makers—and with the entrepreneur performing a particular function or role, transcending the others. Even that array of possibilities is rendered further complicated by formulations that treat the entrepreneur as either (1) an active promoter or agent of change; or (2) a passive responder to market signals and to change; and either (1) a creator or (2) finder of opportunities.

A troublesome question is whether entrepreneurship refers (1) to a particular function(s) or (2) to persons. If the answer is persons and not function(s) per se, then the correlative question is whether it refers to a particular group of persons or to an aspect of the behavior of all persons. Some individuals may well undertake more and/or more specialized entrepreneurship. But all individuals undertake one or more of the functions of entrepreneurship that can enter the definition of the term—even if it is a matter of reacting to price and other signals in a creative way.

Further difficulties arise when one tries to distinguish the certain behavior(s) or qualities that constitute entrepreneurship, requiring that one identify what makes any activity or quality "entrepreneurial." But that effort is a part of the larger and vexing question of the definition of entrepreneur(ship), say, one that does not equate entrepreneurs with business managers as organizers and decision makers.

Two further, interrelated questions are, first, whether the meaning and defense of capitalism involves a system dominated by capitalists and/or entrepreneurs, or a market system of economic agents without such domination, that is, whether capitalism or market economy is the more systemic term; and, second, whether some kind of entrepreneur(ship) has the critical role in all economic systems, i.e., whether only one generic economic system exists and therefore actual economies differ principally in the identity and institutional setting of entrepreneurship.

Several considerations almost invariably enter discussions of entrepreneurship. One consideration is that the entrepreneur is achievement oriented, manifesting the type A personality and always seeking success. The second consideration is that the substantive meaning of achievement is a matter of culture. In market economies, especially capitalist ones, success is achieved through rising in large, important organizational structures, acquisition of wealth, and similar iconic honors. The third consideration concerns the entrepreneur serving as a driving force in the economy, whatever the specifics of its organization and structure. One consideration that often but by no means always enters discussion is the relation of business and governmental entrepreneurs. This relation may take the form of a competition over the use of resources; movement among key leadership positions in private and public sectors; another involves the tendency of entrepreneurs to act up to, if not even beyond, the limits imposed by law.

Definitions typically turn on the incorporation of functions. One definition, centering on coordination, can be close to that of manager or decision maker within the firm; alternatively the usage may turn on the contribution that individual entrepreneurship makes to coordination that is systemic, that is, going beyond the firm to the economic system. In either case, the key element is capability in participating in institutionalized decision making processes specializing in the making of policy.

A second function often ensconced within a definition is that of adventurer, the role of formulating a vision and acting upon it. At its most dramatic, this definition tends to make capitalism a civilized game of power in monetary form. This entrepreneur is not content with finding niches or paths not seen by others, and therefore goes beyond finding to creating them themselves. One definition centers on the heroic role itself. This definition recognizes entrepreneurship as a system-specific honorific channel of achievement motivation and/or a designation of such achievement.

Other definitions that incorporate functions are the management of risk or, more properly, uncertainty; the marshalling, management or analysis, and application of information; serving as the adjudicator of conflicting interests within and between firms; and the identification if not creation of opportunities. Some definitions may combine functions, such as innovation under uncertainty and asymmetrical information. Not all definitions apply equally well to both entrepreneurial function and their application to specific individuals.

The concept of the entrepreneur, whether it be understood to pertain to a class of person or an aspect of all agents' activity or one function or another, is related to other concepts as well. Innovation can result from entrepreneurial activities in in-house or external research and development generating new technology. Both market structure and the form of competition are both influenced by entrepreneurial activity along technological, strategic, and political lines, and influence the form, direction, and mode of entrepreneurial activity. Although much economic theorizing is static, the introduction of entrepreneurship both opens up a wider range of efficient results and multiple paths of economic growth, and the possibility of multiple efficient results and economic-growth paths amenable to entrepreneurial activity. The realm of entrepreneurship is, moreover, transformed by Canadian-American economist John Kenneth Galbraith's concept of a new industrial state in which corporate and general economic decision making are expanded from the top levels of corporate managements and a mix of government-business antagonism and quid pro quo relationships to decision making lower down in the corporation, in technological and educational elements, and to a system of more or less joint planning for economic stability. In Galbraith's conception, the entrepreneur is less heroic but no less important a figure.

Finally, attention should be given to Italian economist Vilfredo Pareto's theory of the circulation of elites

and what may or may not be its modern formulation, the market for corporate control and therein competition between entrepreneurs. An alternative formulation juxtaposes individuals with power to competitive forces.

SEE ALSO *Capitalism, State; Enterprise; Socialism; State, The*

BIBLIOGRAPHY

Barreto, Humberto. 1989. *The Entrepreneur in Microeconomic Theory.* New York: Routledge.

Casson, Mark. 2003. *The Entrepreneur.* 2nd ed. Northampton, MA: Edward Elgar.

Galbraith, John Kenneth. 1967. *The New Industrial State.* Boston: Houghton Mifflin.

Kalantaridis, Christos. 2004. *Understanding the Entrepreneur: An Institutionalist Perspective.* Burlington, VT: Ashgate.

Kirzner, Israel M. 1973. *Competition and Entrepreneurship.* Chicago: University of Chicago Press.

Kirzner, Israel M. 1985. *Discovery and the Capitalist Process.* Chicago: University of Chicago Press.

Klapp, Merrie Gilbert. 1987. *The Sovereign Entrepreneur: Oil Policies in Advanced and Less Developed Capitalist Countries.* Ithaca, NY: Cornell University Press.

McClelland, David C. 1961. *The Achieving Society.* Princeton, NJ: Van Nostrand.

McIntosh, Wayne V. 1997. *Judicial Entrepreneurship.* Westport, CT: Greenwood Press.

Witt, Ulrich. 2003. *The Evolving Economy.* Northampton, MA: Edward Elgar.

Warren J. Samuels

ENVIRONMENTAL ECONOMICS

SEE *Resource Economics.*

ENVIRONMENTAL IMPACT ASSESSMENT

An environmental impact assessment (EIA) is a planning tool that provides decision makers with an understanding of the potential effects that human actions, especially technological ones, may have on the environment. By understanding the potential environmental effects of an action, policymakers can choose which should proceed and which should not. Governments from around the world perform environmental impact assessments at the national, state or provincial, and local levels. The underlying assumption of all environmental impact assessments is that all human activity has the potential to affect the environment, and that knowledge concerning the environmental impact of a major decision will improve that decision. As part of an EIA, planners try to find the ways and the means to reduce the adverse impacts of the project and to shape projects to suit the local environment. EIAs can produce both environmental and economic benefits, such as reducing the costs and time needed for project implementation and design, avoiding treatment and clean-up costs, and alerting planners to any potential clashes with laws and regulations.

The original and probably best-known form of the EIA is the environmental impact statement (EIS) used by the U.S. government. The National Environmental Policy Act of 1969 (NEPA) mandates that an EIS must accompany every major federal action or nonfederal action with significant federal involvement within the United States. The precise definition of "major" and "significant" has been very contentious and has resulted in considerable litigation. The NEPA ensures that U.S. agencies give environmental factors the same consideration as any other factors in decision making.

Since 1970 dozens of other nations have established their own versions of an EIA, partly on their own and partly in response to the call of a number of international meetings. In particular, the seventeenth principle of the Rio Declaration on Environment and Development (1992) is devoted to the creation of processes for environmental impact assessments by governments around the world.

THE ENVIRONMENTAL IMPACT STATEMENT PROCESS

Most environmental impact assessments follow a process similar to the one mandated for the EIS, in which a lead agency collects and assimilates all the environmental information required for the EIS (Sullivan 2003). The first step in the process is to determine whether a complete EIS is required. When there is likely to be little impact, the lead agency can write an environmental assessment (EA), which is much simpler. In the late 1980s agencies annually prepared only 450 complete environmental impact statements, compared to an average of 15,000 environmental assessments (Gilpin 1995).

The first element of the actual EIS is scoping, where the lead agency identifies key issues and concerns of interested parties. A notice of the intent to conduct an EIS is published in the Federal Register and is sent to all potentially interested parties. Usually, the agency releases a draft environmental impact statement (DEIS) for comment. After interested parties and the general public have had the opportunity to comment on the draft, the agency releases the final environmental impact statement (FEIS).

In some instances, usually as the result of litigation or the availability of new information, the agency later releases a supplemental environmental impact statement (SEIS). Once all the protests are resolved the agency issues a record of decision, which is its final action prior to implementation.

The Council on Environmental Quality (CEQ), also mandated by the NEPA, sets the regulations that outline the format for the actual EIS. They mandate that an EIS should contain the impact of the proposed action, any adverse environmental effects that cannot be avoided, any possible alternatives to the proposed action, and any irreversible commitments of resources that the action would require if it were implemented. All mitigation measures to address identified harms must also be included in the EIS. Throughout the EIS process, the public must have opportunities for participation (Sullivan 2003). In 1994 President Bill Clinton issued an executive order adding environmental justice issues to the EIS process.

PROBLEMS WITH ENVIRONMENTAL IMPACT ASSESSMENTS

One of the problems with environmental impact assessments is that in many cases, after the factors have been analyzed, there is little to force the actors to change their decisions. Once the EIA is complete, the action can go forward regardless of any negative environmental consequences. In the case of the EIS, the NEPA provides no enforcement provisions, though various court decisions have held that an EIS must be done and that it should be used to inform decision makers of potential environmental problems. However, at present nothing requires planners to change their decisions based on an EIS's findings, nor is there any penalty for ignoring an EIS. In the early 1970s groups trying to stop an action used EISes to initiate numerous lawsuits. At the end of the 1970s the U.S. Supreme Court in *Vermont Yankee v. NRDC* (1978) reversed two district court decisions remanding the NRC for not addressing environmental issues adequately in their EIS. This decision limited the ability of district courts to reverse agency decisions (Vig and Kraft 2000). By the end of the 1980s the federal courts consistently declined to hear lawsuits on environmental issues if the EISes were properly done. According to the courts, planners may elect to include or exclude EIS findings from their projects, and if they choose to ignore it, others have a right to bring pressure on them. The CEQ cannot stop an action, but it can delay it by requesting further reassessment.

Another problem with the creation of EIAs springs from the uncertainty surrounding some situations. Uncertainty may come from a lack of scientific understanding of an issue or from the nature of the information required. The issues may be extremely complex, or may deal with timescales that create potential problems for understanding the issue. For example, the proposed nuclear waste facility at Yucca Mountain, Nevada requires the consideration of environmental changes at the site over a 10,000-year period. The Yucca Mountain case also provides an example of another problem—the quality of the information used in creating an EIS. It was discovered that the researchers doing the assessment at Yucca Mountain manufactured some of the information they used for the EIS; a subsequent government study ruled that even though the data was suspect, the overall decision based on it was sound (Department of Energy 2006). For some governments around the world, the lack of resources and skilled personnel create problems for producing a quality EIA.

This is not to say that identifying environmental issues has no effect on the decision-making process. A number of studies have shown that EISes force greater environmental awareness and more careful planning by federal agencies (Vig and Kraft 2000). The very fact that the information exists means it plays a role. The EIS is circulated among state, local, and federal agencies and the public. Because of this circulation, the EIS can become an early warning system for environmental groups, alerting them of potential issues for their consideration (Rosenbaum 2005). The identification of potential problems has motivated public support against actions and led to rethinking of initial plans. Having the information is better than not having information, even though it may not be used.

SEE ALSO *Decision-making; Disaster Management; Love Canal; Planning; Pollution; Resource Economics; Resources; Uncertainty*

BIBLIOGRAPHY

Department of Energy. 2006. Evaluation of Technical Impact on the Yucca Mountain Project Technical Basis Resulting from Issues Raised by Emails of Former Project Participants. DOE/RW-0583 QA:N/A, April.

Gilpin, Alan. 1995. *Environmental Impact Assessment (EIA): Cutting Edge for the Twenty-First Century.* Cambridge, U.K.: Cambridge University Press.

Rosenbaum, Walter A. 2005. *Environmental Politics and Policy.* 6th ed. Washington, DC: CQ Press.

Sullivan, Thomas F. P. 2003. *Environmental Law Handbook.* 17th ed. Rockville, MD: ABS Consulting Government Institutes.

Vig, Norman J., and Michael E. Kraft. 2000. *Environmental Policy.* 4th ed. Washington, DC: CQ Press.

Franz Foltz

ENVIRONMENTAL KUZNETS CURVES

Casual observation suggests that cities in newly industrialized countries such as Bangkok, Beijing, Calcutta, and Mexico City are more polluted today than they were twenty to thirty years ago, while cities in older industrial countries such as New York, Tokyo, and London are cleaner than they were twenty to thirty years ago. This apparent paradox raises the question of whether higher income levels result in a better or worse environment. The environmental Kuznets curve (EKC) hypothesis proposes that there is an inverted U-shaped relationship between various indicators of environmental degradation and income per capita. This became known as the environmental Kuznets curve because of its similarity with the shape of the income-inequality relationship discovered earlier by Russian-American economist Simon Kuznets.

THE EKC AND ENVIRONMENTAL DEGRADATION

This relationship was discovered by Gene Grossman and Alan Kreuger in the early 1990s. They found that at low levels of per-capita income, concentrations of sulphur-dioxide, suspended particulate matter, and water pollutants increase as income increases. However, once per-capita income reaches a particular threshold, concentrations of these pollutants decrease as income continues to rise.

The emissions studied by Grossman and Kreuger have local or own-country pollution effects and relatively low abatement costs. Global pollutants such as greenhouse gases represent a second important type of environmental degradation. A 1995 study by Douglas Holtz-Eakin and Thomas Selden examined emissions of carbon dioxide, which is a global pollutant. Their analysis reveals that the emissions continue to rise with income, a finding that is not consistent with the EKC.

Deforestation is a third important type of environmental degradation. Economic development is generally expected to reduce a nation's agricultural sector and increase its industrial sector. Such development is also associated with the use of modern agricultural technology, which reduces land requirements. Logging and the demand for wood as an energy source is likely to grow as a country develops, but this demand may wane as industrialization takes over.

In their 1994 study, Maureen Cropper and Charles Griffiths examined the EKC shape for deforestation. The overall result was a hump-shaped relation between per-capita income and deforestation. The income at which the rates of deforestation peak is very high. Although it is reassuring that the rates of deforestation level off at suffi-

Graphical representation of the intuition behind the environmental Kuznets curve

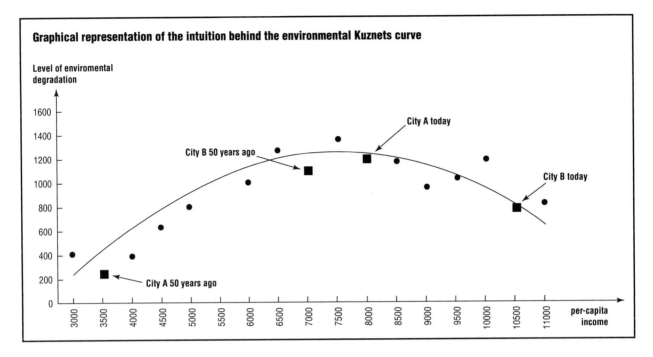

Figure 1

ciently high per-capita income levels, the major damage to the environment occurs before these income levels are reached.

FACTORS AFFECTING THE INCOME-ENVIRONMENT RELATIONSHIP

Having looked at three varieties of environmental degradation, it is necessary to recognize that the environmental quality is the outcome of the interplay of emissions and abatement (or depletion and regeneration in the case of renewable resources). The income-environment relationship captured by simple regression exercises cannot distinguish between the demand side and supply side forces that drive this relation. Income acts as a surrogate for a variety of underlying influences. Grossman and Kreuger provide an intuitive explanation of these influences, as outlined below.

The Scale of the Economic Activity A larger scale of economic activity per unit of area, all else being equal, results in increased levels of resource use and waste generation. Here, income acts as an indicator of economic activity, encouraging a positive relation between environmental degradation and income.

The Composition of the Economic Activity Different sectors of the economy have differential pollution and resource use intensities. Industry, especially manufactur-

ing, tends to be more pollution intensive than either agriculture or services. The share of industry in a nation's gross domestic product (GDP) first rises with economic growth and then declines as the country moves from the preindustrial to the postindustrial stage of development. This influence encourages an inverted U-shaped relationship between environmental pollution and income level.

The Technique Effect At low income levels, people are more concerned with their food and other material needs and less concerned with environmental quality. At higher income levels, people begin to demand higher levels of environmental quality to go with their increased prosperity. On the supply side, low incomes mean that countries and individuals cannot afford much expenditure on pollution abatement, even if the demand were there. Economic growth not only creates the demand for improved environmental quality, it also makes resources available to supply it, resulting in cleaner technologies. Stripped of the scale and composition effects, the technique effect predicts that environmental degradation would decline as per capita income increases.

The sum of all these effects defines the observed income-environment relationship. For example, in the case of global pollutants, the technique effect is weak because a disciplining of domestic production would not benefit domestic consumers, who therefore do not demand cleaner techniques of production. For economies that experience growth later than the developed economies, it is possible that they will continue to produce industrial goods not only for their own use, but also for their trading partners. In these economies, the composition effect that is relevant for developed nations that have moved beyond the industrial phase does not apply. This reduces the possibility of a decrease in environmental degradation at higher incomes. Hence, more than the actual shape of the EKC, it is the lessons learned from analyzing it that are important in understanding the relation between per capita income and environmental degradation.

BIBLIOGRAPHY

Cropper, Maureen, and Charles Griffiths. 1994. The Interaction of Population Growth and Environmental Quality. *American Economic Review* 84 (2): 250–254.

Grossman, Gene M., and Alan B. Krueger. 1991. *Environmental Impacts of a North American Free Trade Agreement.* National Bureau of Economic Research (NBER) Working Paper No. 3914. Cambridge, MA: NBER.

Holtz-Eakin, Douglas, and Thomas M. Selden. 1992. *Stoking the Fires? CO_2 Emissions and Economic Growth.* National Bureau of Economic Research (NBER) Working Paper No. 4248. Cambridge, MA: NBER.

Bidisha Lahiri

EPIDEMICS

SEE *Morbidity and Mortality.*

EPIDEMIOLOGICAL TRANSITION THEORY

SEE *Morbidity and Mortality.*

EPIDEMIOLOGY

SEE *Ethno-epidemiological Methodology.*

EPISTEMOLOGY

Any systematic exposition of the grounds of and means to knowledge constitutes an epistemology. Standard epistemologies of mathematics find such grounds in axiomatic self-evidence and means in methods of proof. Epistemologies of the natural sciences additionally underscore methods of experimental verification. Emerging in

the shadow of the natural sciences, the social sciences have since their inception been the province of a stubborn epistemological divide. On the one side are those who insist that the natural sciences offer the only valid model of the attainment of knowledge about the empirical world and that the social sciences should thus strive to emulate their methodological precedent. On the other side are those who insist that human actions and creations are different in kind from the events and objects to which natural scientists attend and require methods of approach and comprehension entirely their own. Strictly speaking, these alternatives are incompatible; no perfect compromise is possible.

Emerging clearly in the middle of the nineteenth century, the divide at issue rests in distinct philosophical precedents and traditions of scholarship. On the side of a unified science is Auguste Comte's "positivism," which casts society as the final and most complex object to become available to the senses in the course of the evolution of human cognition and amenable, if not precisely to experimental manipulation, then to controlled comparative inquiry rigorous enough to yield knowledge in its wake. Comte's *Course of Positive Philosophy* (1830–1842) inaugurates what he coined "sociology" as a science every bit as natural as its predecessors, but clearly reflects both the rationalism of René Descartes and the empiricism of Etienne Bonnot de Condillac. Comte's most influential epistemological heir is Émile Durkheim, who takes particular pains to distinguish the empirical domain of psychology from that of sociology in his late nineteenth-century work. The former encompasses at once what is common to all human beings and what is idiosyncratic to one or another of them. The latter, encompassing what marks human beings as members of specific collectivities, is the proper domain of "social facts" available to the senses first of all as the experience of externally imposed obligation or coercion. It yields the classic definition of society as a "normative order." It permits two basic modes of inquiry, both of which might be put into the service of controlled comparison. One of these pursues a sampling of particular cases substantial enough to reveal patterning variables and their statistical co-variations. Another seeks to extract from perhaps only a single case a model of the system of which it is representative or expresses the limit. The first is the mode of statistical and quantitative inquiry not only in sociology but across all the social sciences. The second is the mode of model-theoretic inquiry—whether rigorously algebraic, as in much of contemporary economics, or largely qualitative, as in Durkheim's own *Elementary Forms of the Religious Life* (1912).

On the side of the divide itself is Wilhelm Dilthey's programmatic distinction between the natural sciences and what he termed the *Geisteswissenschaften*, sciences of "spirit" or "mind" or "human sciences." The latter category includes all of the disciplines that make up the social sciences, but its cardinal focus is the discipline of historical inquiry and what would come by the late nineteenth century to be known as cultural anthropology. The human sciences do not in Dilthey's typology produce "knowledge" but instead produce "understanding." The latter is a mode of knowing grounded of necessity in self-reflection because the objectifications of spirit or mind—human actions and artifacts—that constitute its investigative terrain are precisely the objectifications of such psychic states as intentions, beliefs, values and sentiments. The human scientist understands any such objectification not in determining its efficient cause but in interpreting its always particular "meaning" or "significance" in light of the broader historical or cultural context in which it is embedded. Dilthey's work follows the founder of biblical hermeneutics, Friedrich Schleiermacher, in presuming that the process of interpretation rests essentially in the interpreter's capacity imaginatively and empathetically to enter into the lives of others. He derived his thoroughgoing separation of the physical from the experiential world from Immanuel Kant's similarly thorough separation of the objective from the subjective in his three *Critiques*, published in 1781, 1788, and 1790. In his appropriation of Kant at least, Dilthey is at one with his only slightly later contemporary, Max Weber.

Weber is well known for his address of the "problem of objectivity" in the human sciences. He recognized that particular evaluative commitments do and even should influence the content of the questions that the human scientist poses. He insisted that the scientist's research, properly conducted, should and can produce nothing else but facts. His resolution still has its adherents, but the problem of objectivity itself long predates him and lasts beyond him. In its general form, it is the result of the reflective recognition that beliefs and evaluative orientations are generally conditioned by or contingent upon their historical, cultural and social context; hence, for example, Thorstein Veblen's observation that distinct fractions of the dominant classes are drawn to those intellectual pursuits that are most intimately concerned with the practical bases of their dominance. Prima facie, the same should broadly be true of beliefs about and evaluative orientations toward the historical, the cultural and the social themselves. This does not entail that the latter beliefs and orientations are wrong-headed, but it does point to the need for an account of how and when and why a researcher is right to suppose that they are enduringly true or valid. Thus construed, the problem of objectivity has inspired three general responses. One is Comte's own: a progressivist rendering of cognitive and moral evolution positing that modern society has become disburdened of the sources of the errors and confusions that clouded the mental and moral landscapes of societies less developed.

Though no longer with a positivist inflection, a similar evolutionism has a central place in Jürgen Habermas' much more recent efforts to reestablish the foundations of a critical social theory. A second response emerges in the later Marxist tradition, in which the problem of objectivity gains intensity with the presumption that the prevailing ideas of every class-divided society are ideological distortions that serve not truth but the reproduction of the dominant class.

Though with many variations, it seeks in social institutions or psychosocial circumstances those factors that permit certain individuals to become detached from their classes of origin and so think outside of the boundaries that would otherwise constrict their judgment. In a classic contribution to what is thus a "sociology of knowledge," Karl Mannheim's work sees such factors in the coalescence of the secular, liberal university in late eighteenth- and early nineteenth-century Europe. Louis Althusser's work focuses instead on the conjunctures of politico-economic structure and personal circumstance in which an investigator's exercise of experiment and critique effect an "epistemic break" from the ideology in which his thinking had previously been mired. Though once again with many variations, a third response might be called pragmatic. The philosophical resources it taps include Kant and Ludwig Wittgenstein. From Weber to anthropologist Clifford Geertz and social theorist Niklas Luhmann, its proponents regard proper intellectual labor in the human sciences as having its end in heuristic and diagnostic constructions and interventions that, whatever their contingencies or motivations, facilitate clarity, communication and translation. Hardly a return to positivism, this response nevertheless highlights the analytical service of an intellectual device of steadily increasing saliency in the epistemological toolkit of the natural sciences themselves: the model.

BIBLIOGRAPHY

Althusser, Louis. [1965] 1969. *For Marx*. Trans. Ben Brewster. New York: Pantheon Books.

Comte, Auguste. [1830–1842] 1896. *The Positive Philosophy of Auguste Comte*. Trans. Harriet Martineau. London: G. Bell & Sons.

Condillac, Etienne Bonnot de. [1746] 2001. *Essay on the Origin of Human Knowledge*. Trans. and ed. Hans Aarsleff. New York: Cambridge University Press.

Descartes, René. [1637] 1993. *Discourse on Method; and Meditations on First Philosophy*. Trans. Donald A. Cress. Indianapolis: Hackett.

Dilthey, Wilhelm. [1883] 1989. *Introduction to the Human Sciences: Selected Works*. Vol. 1. Ed. Rudolf A. Makkreel and Frithjof Rodi. Princeton, NJ: Princeton University Press.

Durkheim, Émile. [1895] 1982. *Rules of Sociological Method.* Ed. Steven Lukes and trans. W. D. Halls. New York: The Free Press.

Durkheim, Émile. [1912] 1995. *The Elementary Forms of the Religious Life.* Trans. Karen E. Fields. New York: The Free Press.

Geertz, Clifford. 1973. Thick Description: Toward an Interpretive Theory of Culture. In *The Interpretation of Cultures,* 3–30. New York: Basic Books.

Geertz, Clifford. 1980. From the Native's Point of View: On the Nature of Anthropological Understanding. In *Local Knowledge: Further Essays in Interpretive Anthropology,* 55–70. New York: Basic Books.

Habermas, Jürgen. 1984. *Reason and the Rationalization of Society* Vol. 1 of *The Theory of Communicative Action.* Trans. Thomas McCarthy. Boston: Beacon Press.

Habermas, Jürgen. 1987. *Lifeworld and System: A Critique of Functionalist Reason.* Vol. 2 of *The Theory of Communicative Action.* Trans. Thomas McCarthy. Boston: Beacon Press.

Kant, Immanuel. [1781] 1978. *Immanuel Kant's Critique of Pure Reason.* Trans. Norman Kemp-Smith. London: Macmillan.

Kant, Immanuel. [1788] 2002. *Critique of Practical Reason.* Trans. Werner S. Pluhar. Indianapolis: Hackett Publishing Company.

Kant, Immanuel. [1790] 1987. *Critique of Judgment.* Trans. Werner S. Pluhar. Indianapolis: Hackett Publishing Company.

Luhmann, Niklas. 1998. *Observations on Modernity.* Trans. William Whobry. Stanford, CA: Stanford University Press.

Mannheim, Karl. [1929] 1948. *Ideology and Utopia: An Introduction to the Sociology of Knowledge.* Trans. Louis Wirth and Edward Shils. London: Routledge & Kegan Paul.

Schleiermacher, Friedrich. [1799] 1988. *On Religion: Speeches to Its Cultured Survivors.* Trans. Richard Crouter. Cambridge, U.K.: Cambridge University Press.

Veblen, Thorstein. 1919. *The Place of Science in Modern Civilization and Other Essays.* New York: B. W. Heubsch.

Weber, Max. [1905] 1975. *Roscher and Knies: The Logical Problems of Historical Economics.* Trans. Guy Oakes. New York: The Free Press.

Weber, Max. [1919] 1946. Science as a Vocation. In *From Max Weber: Essays in Sociology,* eds. Hans Gerth and C. Wright Mills, 129–156. New York: Oxford University Press.

Weber, Max. 1949. *The Methodology of the Social Sciences.* Trans. Edward Shils and Henry Finch. Glencoe, IL: The Free Press.

Wittgenstein, Ludwig. 1953. *Philosophical Investigations.* Trans. G. E. M. Anscombe. New York: Macmillan.

James D. Faubion

EQUAL EMPLOYMENT OPPORTUNITY COMMISSION

SEE *Integration.*

EQUAL OPPORTUNITY

The term *equal opportunity* refers to the absence of discrimination based on involuntary personal attributes, such as sex, racial or ethnic origin, religion or belief, disability, age, or sexual orientation. The concept of equality of opportunity identifies equality with open and fair competition for scarce resources but does not challenge an inequalitarian distribution of resources within society. This has sparked disagreement in political and theoretical struggles over what constitutes a "just society."

FORMAL EQUALITY OF OPPORTUNITY

The notion of formal equality of opportunity requires that positions, offices, and admissions in society are open to all applicants and that formal procedures are used to select candidates based on qualifications deemed relevant to successful performance in a position or program. Individual abilities and ambition are valued as criteria while factors derived from group identities assigned by birth or social class, such as race, family, caste, religion, are excluded. Equality of opportunity carries with it the promise of upward social and economic mobility due to the removal of legally protected rights and privileges for particular classes or groups. Equality of opportunity emphasizes procedural and legal means of providing equal access to social goods, in contrast to alternative approaches to equality; for example, equality of outcomes, equality of resources, and democratic equality.

Equality of opportunity assumes that it is unfair if factors beyond the control of an individual significantly shape a person's chances in life. Formal equality of opportunity can be justified as an enhancement of individual life chances as well as a means for maximizing the well-being of society. Proponents of equality of opportunity associate it with a meritocratic system in which the most talented and ambitious are the most rewarded regardless of socioeconomic background.

LIMITATIONS OF FORMAL EQUALITY OF OPPORTUNITY

A central challenge to the very concept of formal equality of opportunity is that it does not take into consideration how circumstances beyond the control of an individual influence the ability to compete for scarce resources. In the case of standardized tests to evaluate a student's educational and professional potential, such as the Scholastic Aptitude Test (SAT) in the United States, formal equality of opportunity requires students to take the test under the same conditions and use the final test score as a measure to evaluate students' performance. It thereby disregards the access some students have to more economic and educational resources to prepare for these test than others. By asserting neutrality toward all students, the test indirectly reinforces preexisting social inequalities.

A narrow perception of equality of opportunity is not inherently incompatible with profiling or statistical discrimination, which uses group characteristics such as gender, ethnicity, or age as a proxy for productivity in hiring and promotion. Profiling occurs when statistical trends are used to justify associating negative attributes with members of a group, such as a high crime rate, or risks associated with a particular phase in the life course like having children. These group characteristics are used as indicators for current and future productivity, thereby compromising the notion of equality that calls for an evaluation of each applicant on its own merits.

Equality of opportunity has historically been confined to the public sphere, neglecting the sources of inequality identified with areas traditionally held as private, such as family, marriage, and religion. Opening up all sectors of employment to women, for example, does not offer them equal opportunity for advancement when employers deny them (paid) pregnancy leave. While all workers may be subject to identical rules, women are disproportionately adversely affected. Formal equality of opportunity does not seek to change the social, economic, and cultural forces that structure the division of labor along gender, race, and class lines. Rather than resolving the question of equality, a larger degree of formal equality often reveals the impact of socioeconomic inequality within society.

SUBSTANTIVE EQUALITY OF OPPORTUNITY

Substantive equality of opportunity takes the broader social situation into consideration in determining criteria for qualification and performance. The appropriate means for achieving substantive equality of opportunity are often controversial. One possibility for achieving substantive equality of opportunity is affirmative action. The challenges of affirmative action in theory and practice are illustrated in the reform of the admissions system of the Indian Institutes of Technologies (IITs), French elite universities, and higher education in the United States.

Indian Institutes of Technology were founded in 1951 and became a leading institution in professional training in India. Entrance is based on a standardized test without consideration of socioeconomic status and is granted to approximately 2 percent of the applicants. Despite the formal neutrality of the test, the vast majority of students admitted come from the urban middle class with access to good schools and the resources to attend costly preparatory courses. To further substantive equality of opportunity IITs were required to reserve 22.5 percent

of seats for students of historically disadvantaged schedule castes and tribes in 1973. Reserved seats were awarded to candidates scoring at least 66 percent of the score of the lowest admitted applicant in the general test or to candidates successfully completing a one-year preparatory course. Despite these lower admission standards not all reserved seats are filled pointing to the challenge of opening elite educational institutions to low-income students without further counterbalancing vast power and wealth disparities in Indian society (Murali 2003).

France's elite universities also use highly competitive standardized exams for admission. The vast majority of students performing well on these tests have attended very selective preparatory schools that rarely admit working class or immigrant students. In 2001 Sciences Po, one of these universities, began a special entrance program that admits a limited number of students from designated zones in impoverished suburbs. Relying on geographic criteria rather than socioeconomic status or ethnicity, the program does not directly challenge "republican values" that hold the French republic to be indivisible and all citizens to share equally in a common civic culture. While in practice the program admits many first- and second-generation immigrants from Morocco and Algeria their ethnicity is not officially taken into consideration, thereby avoiding discrimination between citizens or delineating the separate communities within France.

In the United States President Lyndon Johnson introduced affirmative action as a method of redressing the legacy of racial discrimination in 1965. Affirmative action programs in education and training were brought before the Supreme Court in the 1970s. In *Bakke v. Regents of the University of California* (1978) the Supreme Court struck down a medical school's affirmative action program that set aside sixteen seats for consideration by a separate admissions committee but the court upheld the legality of affirmative action per se. In 2003 the Supreme Court upheld affirmative action in higher education ruling that race can be one of many factors considered for college admission (*Gratz v. Bollinger* and *Grutter v. Bollinger* [2003]). Affirmative is no longer justified on the basis of redressing past oppressions and injustice but in terms of a "compelling state interest" in diversity at all levels of society.

These three examples show that substantive equality can be furthered through very different affirmative action programs posing different kinds of challenges. India relies on reserved seats while the United States dismissed such quotas as unconstitutional. The United States uses race as one of many factors in evaluating an application while France dismisses affirmative action based on socioeconomic and ethnic status as running counter to its republican values. France, while not having a formal affirmative action policy in higher education, is currently experimenting with geographically based programs. The political struggle over substantive equality of opportunity is inseparable from the normative question, what makes institutions legitimate? As Xavier Brunschvicg, the Science Po's director of communication explains: "We believe, here, that we are creating the elite of French society. But in order for these elites to be accepted, they have to be legitimate. Reproduction is not legitimate. We need to diversify to be legitimate, to help the egalité des chances [equality of opportunity] along" (Conley 2003). Pursuing substantive equality of opportunity redresses many of the limitations of formal equality, but it cannot resolve the question of why so many must compete for so little.

JUSTICE AND EQUALITY OF OPPORTUNITY

Is equality of opportunity the most basic formulation of equality, or merely one type of equality among others? In his theory of justice as "fairness," John Rawls argues that equality of opportunity must be combined with a redistribution of social goods. Rawls incorporates both formal and substantive forms of equality of opportunity into his theory of a just society through his second principle of justice, which holds that "Social and economic inequalities are to be arranged so that they are both (a) to the greatest benefit of the least advantaged [the "difference principle"] and (b) attached to offices and positions open to all under conditions of fair equality of opportunity" (Rawls 1971, p. 83). Rawls argues that even without formal barriers to equality, those with greater social and natural advantages, for example intelligence and strength, will get a disproportionate percentage of social goods like income and positions. These advantages are beyond an individual's control and thus the unequal outcomes are unjust.

Rawls's theory of fair equality of opportunity requires that resources be redistributed across social classes. In order to give every individual the same opportunity to cultivate his or her abilities and pursue his or her ambitions, the state must provide additional resources, for example bilingual education or health care, when individual families are unable to provide them. No amount of substantive equality of opportunity, however, will eliminate all socioeconomic and natural inequality. Consequently, Rawls argues that equal opportunity requires the addition of the "difference principle." By restricting the unequal distribution of goods to the benefit of the least advantaged, the difference principle requires that the rewards gained from individual talents benefit society as a whole and not solely the individual who possesses them.

In contrast to Rawls, there are many who question whether equality of opportunity is compatible with alternative conceptions of equality. John Schaar criticizes the idea that equality of opportunity is a basic definition of equality because it "really only defends the equal right to become unequal by competing against one's fellows" (Schaar 1967, p. 241). He rejects the supposed neutrality of equality of opportunity and emphasizes its underlying individualistic competitive ethic. As Schaar contends, equality of opportunity reinforces particular social values to the exclusion of others and rewards only those with talents that conform to these values.

Robert Nozick (1974) embraces this individualistic competitive ethic in his libertarian approach and argues that the equality of opportunity Rawls endorses is undermined by the difference principle. Nozick's "entitlement theory" insists that only the process by which goods are acquired is relevant for a just distribution. He thus rules out redistributive approaches to equality like Rawls's that consider equality of outcome as well as procedures.

Michael Walzer (1983) concurs with Schaar as well as many communitarians that there is no single, universal standard for what constitutes an egalitarian society. Equality of opportunity is one principle of just distribution among others, each of which expresses a particular set of social values. These alternative conceptions are not necessarily compatible and compete for priority within a particular society. Walzer argues for a "complex equality" approach that maintains a plurality of distributive principles in light of the diverse range of social goods and actors in any society.

Feminist theorists question Rawls's basic assumption, shared by many in equality of opportunity debates, that equality must be based on qualities that are shared by all and that certain kinds of difference (such as sex, race, sexual orientation, and religion) should not be taken into consideration. Universal standards like Rawls's theory of justice often assume values and characteristics that are drawn from more privileged members of society. Susan Okin (1989) shows how Rawls's theory of justice depends on the family, but does not sufficiently address whether relationships within the family are equal. Iris Young (1990) argues that forms of inequality are not limited to material resources, such as wealth, income, and positions that can be redistributed among members of society. Evaluating equality of opportunity also requires an analysis of the particular social structures (i.e., decision-making procedures, the division of labor, and culture) in which opportunities can be realized.

The debate over equality of opportunity opens onto core political and theoretical questions, including the delineation of public and private domains, individual versus group identity, and the possibility of impartial standards. At stake in this debate are shared concerns with legitimating and transforming political institutions, negotiating competing social values, and cultivating practices of social justice.

SEE ALSO *Egalitarianism; Equality*

BIBLIOGRAPHY

Alexander, John M. 2003. *Inequality, Poverty, and Affirmative Action: Contemporary Trends in India.* Paper prepared for the WIDER conference Inequality, Poverty, and Human Well-Being, May 30–31, 2003. Helsinki, Finland.

Altbach, Philip. 1993. The Dilemma of Change in Indian Higher Education. *Higher Education* 26 (1): 3–20.

Bakke v. Regents of the University of California, 438 U.S. 265 (1978).

Cohen, G. A. 1999. Socialism and Equality of Opportunity. In *Political Thought*, eds. Michael Rosen and Jonathan Wolff, 354–358. Oxford: Oxford University Press,

Conley, Marjorie. 2003. Sciences Po: An Elite Institution's Introspection on its Power, Position, and Worth in French Society. http://journalism.nyu.edu/portfolio/conley/sciencespo.html.

Dworkin, Ronald. 1981. What is Equality? Part 2: Equality of Resources. *Philosophy & Public Affairs* 10: 283–345.

Economist. 2002. A Question of Colour, a Matter of Faith. *Economist* 365, November 16.

Fishkin, James S. 1993. *Justice, Equal Opportunity, and the Family.* New Haven, CT: Yale University Press.

Galston, William. 1986. Equality of Opportunity and Liberal Theory. In *Justice and Equality Here and Now*, ed. Frank S.Lucash, 89–107. Ithaca, NY: Cornell University Press.

Gratz v. Bollinger, 539 U.S. 244 (2003).

Grutter v. Bollinger, 539 U.S. 306 (2003).

Hirschmann, Nancy J. 2003. *The Subject of Liberty: Toward a Feminist Theory of Freedom.* Princeton, NJ: Princeton University Press.

Jacobs, Lesley A. 2004. *Pursuing Equal Opportunities.* Cambridge, U.K.: Cambridge University Press.

Murali, Kanta. 2003. The IIT Story: Issues and Concerns. http://www.flonnet.com/fl2003/stories/20030214007506500.htm.

Nozick, Robert. 1974. *Anarchy, State, and Utopia.* New York: Basic Books.

Okin, Susan. 1989. *Justice, Gender, and the Family.* New York: Basic Books.

Pateman, Carole. 1993. Feminist Critiques of the Public/Private Dichotomy. *Public and Private in Social Life*, eds. Stanley Benn and Gerald Gaus. London: Croom Helm.

Rawls, John. 1971. *A Theory of Justice.* Cambridge, MA: Belknap Press.

Sandel, Michael. 1998. *Liberalism and the Limits of Justice.* 2nd ed. Cambridge, MA: Cambridge University Press.

Schaar, John H. 1967. Equality of Opportunity, and Beyond. In *Equality: Nomos IX*, eds. Roland Pennock and John Chapman, 137–147. New York: Atherton Press.

Scott, Joan. 1988. Deconstructing Equality-versus-Difference: Or, the Uses of Poststructuralist Theory for Feminism. *Feminist Studies* 14 (1): 32–50.

Sen, Amartya. 1992. *Inequality Reexamined.* Cambridge, MA: Harvard University Press.

Smith, Craig. 2005. Elite French Schools Block the Poor's Path to Power. *New York Times*, December 18.

Tawney, Richard H.1964. *Equality.* 4th ed. New York: Barnes & Noble.

Walzer, Michael. 1983. *Spheres of Justice. A Defense of Pluralism and Equality.* Oxford: Martin Robinson.

Young, Iris. 1990. *Justice and the Politics of Difference.* Princeton, NJ: Princeton University Press.

Nicole Richardt
Torrey Shanks

EQUAL PROTECTION

Equal protection as a legal concept is the idea that individuals should be treated in the same manner as other individuals in similar circumstances. The Equal Protection Clause of the Fourteenth Amendment to the U.S. Constitution provides that "no state shall … deny to any person within its jurisdiction the equal protection of the laws." According to the U.S. Supreme Court, the Due Process Clause of the Fifth Amendment also has an "equal protection component," protecting against arbitrary or unreasonable discrimination by the federal government.

Adopted during the five years following the Civil War, the Thirteenth, Fourteenth, and Fifteenth Amendments abolished slavery, extended U.S. citizenship to slaves and descendants of former slaves, ensured the right to vote regardless of race, and gave Congress the power to enforce these guarantees through legislation. In that context, the Fourteenth Amendment's Equal Protection Clause was intended to provide equal rights for blacks, and that was the view taken by the U.S. Supreme Court in the first case in which the clause was invoked. According to the Court in the *Slaughterhouse Cases* (1873), the purpose of the Equal Protection Clause was to protect "Negroes as a class" from discrimination "on account of their race."

In subsequent decisions, however, the U.S. Supreme Court limited both the scope and the substance of the Constitution's equal protection guarantee. In the *Civil Rights Cases* (1883), the Court ruled that Congress's authority to enforce the Fourteenth Amendment applied only to government actors, not private individuals. Thus, Congress could not use its enforcement power to prohibit racial discrimination in places such as hotels, restaurants, and theaters. And in *Plessy v. Ferguson* (1897), the Court held that state laws requiring "equal but separate" facilities for blacks and whites did not violate the Equal Protection Clause, because the Fourteenth Amendment guaranteed political equality but not social equality. According to the *Plessy* Court, denying blacks the right to serve on juries deprived them of equal protection of the laws, but maintaining dual school systems for black and white students did not. With these decisions, the Supreme Court gave constitutional sanction to racial segregation in education, transportation, public accommodations, employment, and housing.

The *Plessy* Court cited the maintenance of dual school systems as an example of a policy that was consistent with the separate but equal doctrine. It is noteworthy, then, that it was in a case involving segregated schools that the Court later overturned *Plessy v. Ferguson* and its approach to equal protection. The Supreme Court's decision in *Brown v. Board of Education* (1954) was the culmination of a twenty-year litigation campaign led by the National Association for the Advancement of Colored People to eradicate the separate but equal doctrine in public education. Throughout the 1930s and 1940s the NAACP had brought cases to the Court, seeking to enforce equality between schools for black and white students. By 1954, in the cases that comprised *Brown v. Board of Education*, the organization was poised to challenge segregated education itself, and the Supreme Court was prepared to agree. In *Brown*, the Court ruled that "in the field of public education, the doctrine of separate but equal has no place. Separate educational facilities are inherently unequal."

The *Brown* Court explicitly limited its rejection of segregation to public education, but the decision gave momentum to the nascent civil rights movement that would highlight racial inequality in the United States and motivate political change. One of the early events of the movement was the Montgomery bus boycott of 1955 and 1956. The boycott ended when, in *Gayle v. Browder* (1956), the U.S. Supreme Court struck down the ordinance requiring segregated seating on city buses as a violation of equal protection of the laws. In other decisions, the Court rejected segregation in public facilities such as courthouses, parks, beaches, and golf courses.

Because the Fifth and Fourteenth Amendments did not prohibit discrimination by private actors, segregation persisted in interstate transportation, public accommodations, employment, and housing. But in *Boynton v. Virginia* (1960), the Supreme Court ruled that Congress could use its power to regulate interstate commerce to bar discrimination in interstate transportation, and with the Civil Rights Act of 1964, Congress used the commerce power to prohibit discrimination in public accommodations and employment as well. Spurred by the sit-ins of

the early 1960s, in which nearly 75,000 demonstrators were involved, the passage of Title II of the Civil Rights Act guaranteed equal access to restaurants, hotels, and places of entertainment that operated in or affected interstate commerce. Title VII, as the Supreme Court interpreted it in *Griggs v. Duke Power Company* (1971), proscribed "not only overt discrimination" in employment, but also employment policies that were "fair in form but discriminatory in practice." Four years later, Congress passed Title VIII of the Civil Rights Act of 1968. Known as the Fair Housing Act, the law forbade discrimination in the sale, rental, and financing of housing.

Although the Supreme Court initially ruled that the Equal Protection Clause of the Fourteenth Amendment was intended to guarantee equal rights for blacks, the Court later adopted an expansive interpretation of the "persons" to whom equal protection was guaranteed by the clause, even recognizing corporations as persons. But after 1938, discriminatory treatment by the government based on race would be more difficult to justify than other types of discrimination. Following on Justice Harlan Stone's famous footnote in *United States v. Carolene Products* (1938) in which he suggested that "prejudice against discrete and insular minorities" called for "more searching judicial inquiry," the Supreme Court developed a three-tier approach to equal protection claims. In this approach, government classifications based on race are "suspect" classifications to which "strict scrutiny" must be applied. Strict scrutiny requires government to prove that making distinctions based on race is the least restrictive means available to achieve a compelling interest. Since 1976, sex-based classifications have been identified as "quasi-suspect" and entitled to intermediate or heightened judicial scrutiny. Under "intermediate scrutiny," a policy that categorizes individuals based on sex must be substantially related to an important government interest. Regarding all other bases for discrimination, the Court requires that the discrimination be reasonably related to a legitimate governmental objective.

SEE ALSO *Affirmative Action;* Brown v. Board of Education, *1954;* Brown v. Board of Education, *1955; Civil Rights; Civil Rights Movement, U.S.; Constitution, U.S.; Desegregation; Reconstruction Era (U.S.); Segregation; Separate-but-Equal; Supreme Court, U.S.*

BIBLIOGRAPHY

Abraham, Henry J., and Barbara A. Perry. 2003. *Freedom and the Court: Civil Rights and Liberties in the United States.* 8th ed. Lawrence: University Press of Kansas.

Baer, Judith A. 1983. *Equality Under the Constitution: Reclaiming the Fourteenth Amendment.* Ithaca, NY: Cornell University Press.

McWhirter, Darien A. 1995. *Equal Protection.* Phoenix, AZ: Oryx Press.

Malia Reddick

EQUAL RIGHTS AMENDMENT

SEE *National Organization for Women.*

EQUALITY

Equality is a highly complex concept, there being as many forms of equality as there are ways of comparing the conditions of human existence. Equality can refer to numerous features of human life, which is why the term is usually preceded by an adjective that specifies which one is captured, such as social equality, legal equality, political equality, formal equality, or racial equality, to mention but a few. This entry will focus on the more important variants.

THE STRUGGLE FOR EQUALITY

There is, firstly, political or legal equality, which is concerned with the right to vote, to stand for office, and to be treated equally before the law, irrespective of gender, race, religion, age, disability, social background, or other such features. In medieval times, rulers took it for granted that hierarchy is natural or inevitable and that a few are entitled to privileges denied to the many. One of the achievements of the Enlightenment in the eighteenth century was the acknowledgement that all human beings have equal moral worth by virtue of a shared human essence. The Declaration of Independence ("All men are created equal") and the Declaration of the Rights of Man and Citizen ("Men are born and remain free and equal in rights") enshrined this principle in the national constitutions of the United States and France, respectively.

Numerous privileges of rank and order that had survived from feudal times were abolished in the following centuries: Slavery was done away with, universal suffrage was introduced, public offices were opened up to competition, and racial segregation was replaced with racial integration. Not everyone has been content with these achievements, however, and many today demand further changes, particularly with regard to race relations, gender equality in the workplace, and the rights of the disabled.

While the struggles over legal and political equality continue, the academic discourse in the social sciences has been concerned more with another type of equality, namely, that of substantive equality.

SUBSTANTIVE EQUALITY

Political thinkers started to question the worth of the principle of political or legal equality, given that, if left on its own, it merely grants each person an equal right to eat in an expensive restaurant—in the sense that no one is excluded on the grounds of race, gender, or religion—but entirely fails to address individuals' capacity to exercise that right, that is, their money. If wealth or some other measure of welfare is a prerequisite for exercising rights to equal treatment in other spheres, the question arises as to how social goods should be distributed. Once this normative issue is settled within political philosophy, the related practical question in public policy becomes imminent as to whether, how, and to what extent liberal democracies should ensure a level of substantive equality.

While many issues surrounding this question remain contentious, others are now regarded as relatively uncontroversial. Figure 1 depicts some of the more important debates carried out in political philosophy in recent decades. Once substantive equality is agreed upon as an aim worth pursuing, it is necessary to specify if equality is seen as an instrumental or intrinsic ideal. A wide consensus in favor of the latter has emerged, which states that equality is a good thing because of its implications for values other than equality itself, such as greater individual choice, personal autonomy, or the capacity to exercise rights. Hence, the desirability of a more equal distribution is due, not to the fact that it is more equal but that it is expected to promote that other value. Inequality can therefore be acceptable, provided a so-called Pareto improvement is achieved so that at least one person has been made better off without making anyone else worse off.

On the next level, the concept of equality requires a further distinction between individual features that result from voluntary choices and those that are a product of social and natural circumstances. The majority of egalitarian philosophers claim that it is unfair if, to employ a term coined by John Rawls (1921–2002), "morally arbitrary factors" differentially influence the course of people's lives, and that redistribution is justified as a way of neutralizing them (1971). The fundamental aim of equality should be to compensate people for undeserved bad luck, for aspects of their situations for which they are not responsible. As Ronald Dworkin states (2000), there is a moral warrant to level the inequalities in the distribution of social goods that are generated by differing endowments, while leaving intact those inequalities generated by differential effort,

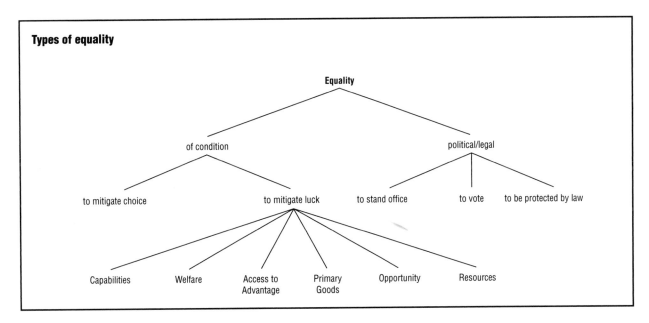

Types of equality

Equality
- of condition
  - to mitigate choice
  - to mitigate luck
    - Capabilities
    - Welfare
    - Access to Advantage
    - Primary Goods
    - Opportunity
    - Resources
- political/legal
  - to stand office
  - to vote
  - to be protected by law

Figure 1

planning, and risk taking. No one deserves their genetic endowments or other accidents of birth, such as who their parents are and where they were born. The advantages that flow from those blessed with such fortunes must not be retained exclusively by them.

This is the stage where the traces of consensus in political philosophy end, as much work in the discipline has been dedicated unsuccessfully to the subsequent question as to what it is that is to be equalized. The aim has been to establish the appropriate standard of interpersonal comparison, or "currency" of egalitarian justice. Several suggestions have been made. Rawls proposes what he calls "primary goods": income, wealth, opportunity, and the bases of self respect. Nobel laureate Armatya Sen concentrates on "capabilities" to choose between various "functionings" that a person is able to realize in his or her life. Further accounts are G. A. Cohen's "access to advantage" and Dworkin's "resources."

The diversity of these proposals shows how difficult it is to assess the features of an individual's conditions that are to be rendered equal: They all have different causes and require compensation in a different way. Should we follow proposals that ensure an equal end-state outcome? Or should we guarantee equality achieved at some initial point in time, irrespective of what level of equality is achieved thereafter?

While the debate in political philosophy is ongoing, substantive equality is a more imminent concern for political practice, where policymakers in liberal democracies face pressures from their electorates if they fail to take measures that ensure equal life prospects to some degree.

Historically, the welfare state has been the vehicle through which governments have sought to address the problem. Social and economic security has been provided to the state's population by means of pensions, social security benefits, free health care, and so forth. However, increasing pressures of globalization toward the end of the twentieth century compelled welfare states to subject their public expenditures to much more stringent economic scrutiny. Public spending and taxes were cut and responsibility for welfare was reassigned from the state to the individual. States have done so to varying degrees, however, and the measurable levels of equality today differ markedly as a result.

MEASURING EQUALITY

When complex social phenomena are condensed into a single measure, criticism is bound to arise. Even so, the most common statistical index in the social sciences to measure substantive equality within a society is the so-called Gini-coefficient, named after the Italian statistician Corrado Gini (1884–1965). The Gini-coefficient (Figure 2) varies between the limits of 0 (perfect equality) and 1 (perfect inequality) and is best captured visually with the help of a diagram that measures the percentage share of the population on the x axis and the percentage income distribution on the y axis. The coefficient represents the geometrical divergence of the so-called Lorenz curve, which measures the *actual* percentage income distribution, from a line with a 45-degree angle, which represents perfect equality, in the sense that everyone is equally

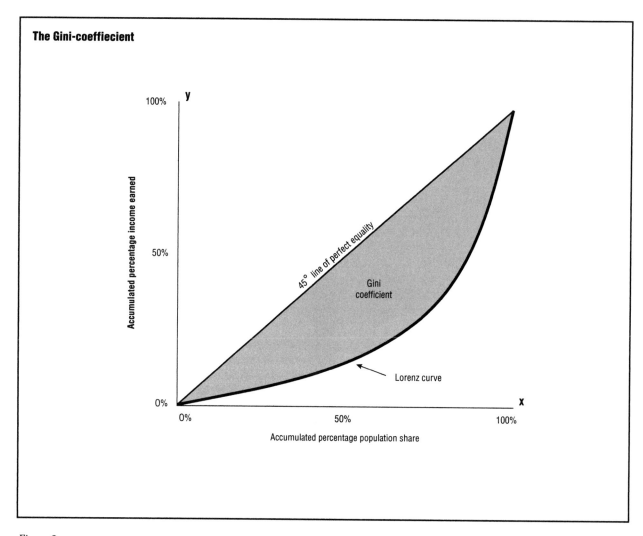

The Gini-coeffiecient

Figure 2

wealthy. The closer the Lorenz curve is to the diagonal line, the smaller the shaded area beneath that line, and the smaller the resultant Gini-coefficient, the more equal is the society's income distribution.

During the 1980s and 1990s, some advanced industrial nations experienced significant shifts in this coefficient, most notably the United Kingdom and the United States, where the neoliberal economic policies introduced by the governments of the day brought about notable increases in income inequality. As statistics produced by the United Nations show (UNDP 2005), in the United Kingdom the Gini-coefficient rose from 0.25 in 1979 to 0.35 in 2000, while the United States saw an increase from 0.36 to 0.43 over the same period. By comparison, countries with more extensive welfare state arrangements, such as most Scandinavian countries, have experienced only minor changes and continue to record Gini-coefficients of between 0.24 and 0.26. On the other end of the

spectrum, states such as Brazil, Mexico, and, increasingly, China report the highest income inequality, with coefficients of between 0.47 and 0.60.

BIBLIOGRAPHY

Dworkin, Ronald. 2000. *Sovereign Virtue: The Theory and Practice of Equality.* Cambridge, MA.: Harvard University Press.

Esping-Andersen, Gøsta. 1990. *Three Worlds of Welfare Capitalism.* Cambridge, U.K.: Polity.

Nozick, Robert. 1974. *Anarchy, State, and Utopia.* New York: Basic Books.

Rawls, John. 1971. *A Theory of Justice.* Cambridge, MA: Belknap.

United Nations Development Program. 2005. Human Development Report 2005: *International Cooperation at a Crossroads: Aid, Trade, and Security in an Unequal World.* New

York: UNDP. http://hdr.undp.org/reports/global/2005/. See especially Table 15.

Williams, Andrew, and Matthew Clayton, eds. 2000. *The Ideal of Equality*. New York: Palgrave MacMillan.

Dirk Haubrich

EQUALITY OF EDUCATIONAL OPPORTUNITY

SEE *Education, Unequal.*

EQUALITY OF OPPORTUNITY

SEE *Equal Opportunity.*

EQUI-FINALITY

SEE *Multifinality.*

EQUILIBRIUM, GENERAL

SEE *General Equilibrium.*

EQUILIBRIUM, PARTIAL

SEE *Partial Equilibrium.*

EQUILIBRIUM, PUNCTUATED

SEE *Punctuated Equilibrium.*

EQUILIBRIUM IN ECONOMICS

The concept of an economy in equilibrium is pervasive in modern economics. The modern neoclassical concept has been a central tenet of economics since the late nineteenth century when economists began importing notions from physics and mechanics. The idea imported from physics is that claiming an economy is in a state of equilibrium implies forces exist that would correct any accidental deviation from that state of equilibrium. As such, equilibrium is a dynamic concept as it involves constant corrective movement, movement that is always in the direction of restoring an equilibrium state whenever perturbed by frequent, possibly random, deviations. An equilibrium can be dynamic in another sense, such as when it represents a persistent pattern even though the objects that form the pattern may be in constant movement. The obvious physics example is the solar system with the planets in constant movement but in predictable and stable patterns. Similarly, one can think of an entire economy in a "stationary state" with constant flows of goods and services that year by year maintain a stationary equilibrium pattern (i.e., no growth or decay).

The classical school of the early nineteenth century advanced a notion of an equilibrium that was invested mostly in the static outcome of exhausting all possibilities of improvement. Typical examples were the improvements realized by an individual firm's progressive division of labor or by a firm's choice to switch industries to one where the rate of return on investment capital is higher. The individual firm was said to be in equilibrium only when its production process cannot be further divided. Industries in an economy were said to be in equilibrium only when all firms in all industries are earning exactly the same rate of return and hence there would be no possibility of gain by switching industries. In both cases, the state of equilibrium depends on whether the firm knows of any possibility of improvement. It is always possible that the necessary condition for equilibrium—such as the uniform rate of return—is not actually fulfilled because firms are either unaware of any possibility of improvement or are in some way constrained from moving to a more profitable industry (as would have been the case in the eighteenth century when the king granted a profitable monopoly to one producer).

For the most part, given the diverse history of the concept, economists and economics textbooks seem confused about just what equilibrium means. Is it a static balance such as when a market's supply equals demand? Or is it a singular state of affairs in a dynamic system that explains how the balance was obtained? A balance can be static but an equilibrium is always a dynamical concept. When modern economists say that an economy is in equilibrium they seem to be saying only that the operative forces in the economy are in balance as there is rarely anything said about the explicit dynamics needed to restore or obtain the equilibrium.

In the case of a market where supply and demand are in balance, what is most important is that there can be only one going price: the one price that clears the market and thus the one price at which it is possible for every participant to be maximizing. And while the classical economists were interested in a state of affairs where there would no longer be a reason to change as there is no possibility of gain, the primary purpose for the neoclassicals' assumption of a state of equilibrium is to obtain the state of affairs where everyone is knowingly maximizing. It is primarily the mathematics of universal maximization that characterizes modern economic theory since the late 1930s.

EQUILIBRIUM AS A PROBLEM FOR MATHEMATICAL ANALYSIS

The beginning of neoclassical attempts to incorporate explicit equilibrium concepts in economics in the late nineteenth century was coupled with the attempts to make economics a mathematical science like physics. The main methodological question was whether one could build a mathematical model of a whole economy consisting of many independent decision makers guided by prices determined in various markets such that the model would imply the existence of a unique set of prices (one price for each good or service transacted in the economy). One of the first economists to attempt this in the nineteenth century was the French economist Léon Walras. His approach was to represent all participants in the economy (producers or consumers of goods and services) with their objective functions (i.e., their respective utility or production functions), which represent what they wish to maximize. Each individual was simply assumed to be a maximizer such that Walras could deduce the necessary calculus conditions for each individual to be maximizing. For each individual, these conditions are in the form of equations, one for each and every good or service. Obviously this involves a huge number of equations in a real economy but this is a mathematics problem so the number does not matter. Together these conditions amount to a system of simultaneous equations and the task is to find a means of specifying the objective functions to assure the logical existence of the unique set of prices that would allow all individuals to be maximizing. Walras thought that the existence of such a set of equilibrium prices was assured whenever the number of equations equaled the number of unknowns (the prices and the quantities of all good and services transacted). He was in error about this and for many decades mathematical economists would try to create more mathematically sophisticated models that would assuredly entail equilibrium prices and quantities. The first success was not obtained until the 1930s.

It was also realized that proving the existence of a set of equilibrium prices is not enough. Model builders always face two methodological problems. First, if the equilibrium model is to explain why prices are what they are, it must also explain why they are not what they are not. If the model entailed more than one set of possible equilibrium prices, one of those sets may fit the observable prices but since the other sets are also entailed, the question is begged as to why the observed set existed and not one of the other sets. In other words, a model with multiple equilibria is an incomplete explanation of observable prices. Second, even if the model entails a unique set of equilibrium prices, not only must that set be unique but it must be stable. That is, if for any reason the equilibrium is upset (i.e., one or more of the prices deviate from the equilibrium values) will the system return to a state of equilibrium? Any possibility of multiple equilibria aggravates this problem, too. Much of the mathematical work of the 1950s and 1960s was devoted to solving both the existence problem and the stability problem. From a mathematical point of view, many models were provided that were indeed logically sufficient to solve these two problems. But critics would be quick to point out that too often the assumptions made to construct these models were unrealistic.

EQUILIBRIUM MODELS AS A MODE OF EXPLANATION

Leaving aside the mathematical economist who is more interested in the mathematics of equilibrium models than the economy those models are designed to explain, the problems of stability and existence must be dealt with if those models are ever to be a satisfactory explanation or even a useful guide for economic policy. This is particularly so if the equilibrium model is to be used to explain prices. While claiming that the observed price of a good or service is what it is because it is an equilibrium price—that is, it is at a value that allows its market to clear (i.e., allows demand to equal supply)—the explanation is not complete unless one can also explain the how or why the price was adjusted to that equilibrium value.

Any adjustment or change in the price is a decision made by an individual who is not maximizing at the current price. So, if one assumes all demand curves are negatively sloped and supply curves are positively sloped, then for someone to be motivated to change the price it must not be at the one value necessary for market equilibrium. In particular, either the price is above the value necessary for equilibrium and thus some supplier is unable to sell the amount necessary for profit maximization or it is below that equilibrium value and at least one demander is unable to buy enough to maximize utility. Kenneth Arrow raised this issue in a 1959 article "Towards a Theory of

Price Adjustment," where he recognized that textbook theory presumes that all decision makers are in effect small fish in a big pond. That is, all textbook decision makers are price takers because they are too small to have an effect on the going price. But, if the market is in disequilibrium and everyone is a price taker, who changes the price and why? Since textbook economics has maximization as the only behavioral assumption, Arrow said that how much someone changes the price is a decision that must be explained as a maximizing choice. Interestingly, textbooks have an explanation for someone who chooses the price but it is in the chapter about the monopoly producer. While this might be seen as a means of completing the explanation of the price, it creates a contradictory situation. One would have one theory for when the market clears (everyone is a price-taking maximizer) and a different theory for the disequilibrium price adjustment. As every equilibrium model must deal with the dynamics needed to assure stability, it means that both theories must be true at the same time but they are contradictory. This is a very unsatisfactory situation for anyone wishing to use an equilibrium model to explain the one going price, one that clears the market so all participants can be maximizing.

EQUILIBRIUM ATTAINMENT VERSUS THE EQUILIBRIUM PROCESS

Critics of equilibrium model building complain that devoting so much effort to mathematically proving the existence of a possible equilibrium misses the policy point of market equilibrium theory. The primary virtue of a market system as the basis of social organization is not the mathematical properties of a state of equilibrium but the fact that a stable market will always give the correct information to would-be market participants whenever the equilibrium has not yet been reached. A rising price indicates to producers to supply more and to consumers to demand less. But critics also claim the time required to make adjustments to achieve an equilibrium may exceed the time allowed before consumer tastes or technology changes.

In order to recognize an equilibrium process, a model must include an explanation of how the equilibrium is achieved and how long it would take to reach it. Without such recognition, the notion of a market being in a state of equilibrium adds nothing beyond the behavioral assumption of universal maximization. This is so because the assumption of utility maximization is used to explain the individual consumer's demand decision at any given price and the assumption of profit maximization for the individual producer's supply decision at that price. Thus if everyone is maximizing at the going price, that price must

be the one that clears the market (i.e., the one where demand equals supply)—no other price is logically possible.

SEE ALSO *General Equilibrium; Nash Equilibrium; Partial Equilibrium*

BIBLIOGRAPHY

Arrow, Kenneth. 1959. Towards a Theory of Price Adjustment. In *Allocation of Economic Resources*, ed. Moses Abramovitz. Stanford, CA: Stanford University Press.

Boland, Lawrence. 1986. *Methodology for a New Microeconomics: The Critical Foundations.* London: Allen & Unwin. http://www.sfu.ca/~boland.

Boland, Lawrence. 1989. *The Methodology of Economic Model Building: Methodology after Samuelson.* London: Routledge. http://www.sfu.ca/~boland.

Hahn, Frank. 1973. *On the Notion of Equilibrium in Economics.* Cambridge, U.K.: Cambridge University Press.

Mirowski, Philip. 1989. *More Heat than Light: Economics as Social Physics, Physics as Nature's Economics.* Cambridge, U.K.: Cambridge University Press.

Wald, Abraham. [1936] 1951. On Some Systems of Equations of Mathematical Economics. *Econometrica* 19: 368–403.

Lawrence A. Boland FRSC

EQUILIBRIUM IN PSYCHOLOGY

The concept of equilibrium plays an important role in diverse domains of psychology. At a basic physiological level, an organism strives to regulate drives and to maintain homeostasis—that is, physiological equilibrium. On an emotional level, people work to balance the dictates of competing desires and instincts. At a more cognitive and social level, people strive to reconcile discrepancies among different types of thought, behavior, and attitude. The existence of competing drives, conflicts, and inconsistencies leads to the need to restore equilibrium when a system is out of balance.

Because of the diversity of meanings of *equilibrium*, psychologists use the term in ways and in contexts that may vary substantially. For instance, the regulatory drives associated with hunger and thirst bear little resemblance to the experience of holding two mutually inconsistent attitudes that must be reconciled. The glue that binds them is the need to maintain a balance. It is this basic need that gives the construct of equilibrium its central role in explaining human and nonhuman behavior at multiple levels.

EQUILIBRIUM IN PSYCHODYNAMIC THEORY

Beginning with Sigmund Freud's psychodynamic theory, and continuing with that theory's intellectual descendants, equilibrium has played a central role in descriptions of the emotional landscape. At a basic level, Freud postulated that the three components that underlie personality—the id, ego, and superego—exist in dynamic tension, requiring a constant attempt to achieve or retain equilibrium.

The id reflects an unconscious set of instinctive drives solely oriented toward self-gratification. When a need is unmet, the individual is driven to reduce the tension it causes. According to Freud, the id has no contact with reality; its primary process is to form merely an image of the object that will satisfy its drive. At some point, the person needs a reality-based reduction of the drive, not simply an image. The ego was seen to develop from the id to provide an actual reality-based drive-reduction, the so-called secondary process. Freud theorized that this id-ego combination dominates a person's behavior until social awareness leads to emergence of the superego, which recognizes that some behaviors are inappropriate. At that point, the superego needs to be factored into the equation for equilibrium.

The individual must develop equilibrium by maintaining a balance between the need to reduce drives and the need to recognize the realities of behavior within a societal or familial context. When people achieve equilibrium, the forces of the id, ego, and superego are in balance. With disequilibrium, anxiety arises. With realistic anxiety, the rationality of the ego can help resolve the anxiety. With neurotic or moral anxiety, however, the tension caused by the imbalance can lead to the emergence of defense mechanisms that help relieve the anxiety. Freud also speculated that dreaming can help a person resolve anxieties caused by tension between id, ego, and superego.

Subsequent psychodynamic theorists (e.g., Loevinger 1976) have responded to some of the limitations of Freud's theory by shifting the emphasis from id to ego. The goal, however, remains largely the same: to characterize the way people balance basic desires and realities as they adjust to the world around them. Another shift in psychodynamic theories moved from largely internal sources of potential disequilibrium to social sources (Adler 1964; Erikson 1974).

A further psychodynamic theory that features some overlap with Freudian ideas is Carl Jung's analytical psychology. It specifies that one of two attitudes, introversion or extraversion, dominates a person. Two additional sets of dichotomies are important as well: thinking versus feeling—both rational processes—and sensing versus intuiting, which are not rational. People are predisposed, according to the theory, toward one element of each dichotomous pair. The commonly used, but controversial, Myers-Briggs Type Inventory is based on Jung's theory.

The details of these psychodynamic theories differ, sometimes greatly, but each theory, at its base, postulates that people must resolve a series of conflicts as they progress through life. Most of the theories posit that normal sexual or social development requires that people successfully navigate through stages of development, bringing their underlying instincts and motivations into equilibrium.

EQUILIBRIUM IN HUMANISTIC THEORY

The humanistic psychologists took a very different approach to understanding people, their motivations, and their behaviors. Whereas the psychodynamic theories rely greatly on unconscious drives and instincts and have a negative cast (i.e., people are always working to resolve crises in order to restore equilibrium), the humanists suggest that people are aware of their motives and are predisposed to full functioning or self-actualization, and that problems arise only when the normal state of equilibrium is breached.

Carl Rogers (1961) speculated that if people are accepted unconditionally, they will develop positive self-regard. On the other hand, if acceptance by oneself or by others is dependent on particular behaviors, people will have difficulty accepting themselves unconditionally. Consequently, their path to self-actualization will be interrupted. According to this framework, disequilibrium occurs when there is a mismatch between people's views of their real self and their ideal self. Such a mismatch prevents self-actualization.

Therapies to remedy such disequilibrium focus on one's own insight into the problem. Rogers's client-centered therapy relies on the therapist's acceptance of and empathy with the clients, who are responsible for resolving their problems. Another humanistic approach, Gestalt therapy, also relies on insight, but the therapist is more directive and may confront the client in order to resolve important issues, so the client can regain equilibrium.

EQUILIBRIUM IN SOCIAL AND COGNITIVE THEORY

The developmental theory of Jean Piaget relies on the concept of equilibrium in that it maintains that as children become more cognitively sophisticated, they recognize the inconsistency between what they already know and new information they encounter.

Piaget developed the notion of *equilibration*, which relates to a person's attempt to balance psychological schemas with the new information that he or she processes. During the process of equilibration, children assimilate new information and new ways of thinking, and then accommodate that new information by changing their psychological schema.

An alternate developmental viewpoint conceived by Lev Vygotsky (1978) postulates that the source of disequilibrium is external. In this view, the disequilibrium that moves children from one stage of development to another is based on social interaction. Vygotsky suggested that differences across cultures affect what children learn and how they learn it. That is, a teacher or parent can elevate children's cognitive complexity beyond the level the children have attained on their own by appropriate help during a learning session. In contrast, Piagetian theories of how children move to new levels of cognitive sophistication are focused on internal processes.

Outside the realm of developmental psychology, social and cognitive psychologists have described the role of equilibrium in social interaction. For instance, Fritz Heider speculated that people embrace new information that is consistent with what they already know and reject incompatible information because of the need to retain balanced cognitive schemas. For example, research has shown that when people engage in a behavior that is inconsistent with a stated attitude, they experience what is known as *cognitive dissonance* and will often change the attitude to be consistent with the behavior. There are, however, circumstances in which people are able to maintain inconsistent attitudes and behaviors.

EQUILIBRIUM IN PHYSIOLOGICAL THEORY

The body regulates itself in many dimensions simultaneously, each achieving its own balance. Such regulation involves drives such as hunger, thirst, sex, sleep, and others. An early behavioral psychologist, Clark Hull, developed a drive theory that used regulatory mechanisms to predict and explain the emergence of behavior.

According to Hull, an organism rests when in a state of equilibrium. When a drive, like hunger or thirst, develops, the organism is motivated to alleviate this disequilibrium by engaging in appropriate behavior regarding that drive. The act of eating to reduce hunger or drinking to reduce thirst is known as *drive-satisfying behavior*. Hull developed a complex mathematical theory to characterize the emergence of behavior. The theoretical shortcomings of his concepts led to modifications of the model, however. Contemporary psychologists now employ theories based on the concept of *optimum-level*. In this framework, the body is viewed as having an optimal level of arousal that differs from one person or animal to another and that differs in varied settings. When arousal is either too high or too low for comfort, the organism engages in behaviors to return the arousal level to the optimal level.

EQUILIBRIUM IN SENSATION AND PERCEPTION

Animals are quite proficient at maintaining appropriate posture, or equilibrium, due to structures in the inner ear that very rapidly provide information to the eyes and to the muscles that regulate balance. The structures responsible for appropriate posture include the three semicircular canals in the inner ear that provide feedback regarding rotational movement of the head and two otolith organs that register linear movement. The canals contain fluids that move when the head moves, creating neural signals about the movement. The otoliths contain calcium carbonate crystals that stimulate neurons when an organism moves.

These five structures send information to the muscles, allowing maintenance of balance even during complex movement. When the structures send information to the eyes, accurate visual tracking of the environment during even rapid head movements is made possible.

SEE ALSO *Child Development; Chomsky, Noam; Cognitive Dissonance; Developmental Psychology; Festinger, Leon; Freud, Sigmund; Gestalt Psychology; Hull, Clark; Jung, Carl; Neuroscience; Piaget, Jean; Psychology; Self-Actualization; Self-Esteem; Social Statics*

BIBLIOGRAPHY

Adler, Alfred. [1938] 1964. *Social Interest: A Challenge to Mankind.* New York: Capricorn Books.

Erikson, Erik H. 1974. *Dimensions of a New Identity.* New York: Norton.

Loevinger, Jane. 1976. *Ego Development: Conceptions and Theories.* San Francisco: Jossey-Bass.

Rogers, Carl R. 1961. *On Becoming a Person: A Therapist's View of Psychotherapy.* Boston: Houghton Mifflin.

Vygotsky, L. S. 1978. *Mind in Society: The Development of Higher Psychological Processes,* eds. Michael Cole et al. Cambridge, MA: Harvard University Press.

Bernard C. Beins

EQUIPOSSIBILITY

SEE *Probability Theory.*

EQUITY MARKETS

Firms that want to raise capital have a choice between attracting debt or equity. The main difference between these financing forms is that debt holders have a contract that states that their claims must be paid in full before the firm can make payments to equity holders. Equity holders are entitled to the rest of the company after the debt holders are paid off. Therefore equity is often referred to as a residual claim. Equity markets, also known as stock markets, are markets where different types of equity are traded. The most common forms of equity are common stocks and preferred stocks. The term *common stock* is reserved for stock that does not have a special preference in either dividend payments or in bankruptcy. Preferred stock has preference over common stock in dividends and/or bankruptcy.

Equity markets are generally divided into primary and secondary markets. The primary market is where the securities are first offered to the general public. This takes place in the form of a so-called Initial Public Offering (IPO). There is abundant evidence that IPOs are underpriced. This means that the offer price of the shares is, on average, lower than the market price at the end of the first trading day. In 2003 Jay Ritter overviewed evidence on underpricing for thirty-eight countries and found that the average first day returns vary between 5.4 percent for Denmark and 256.9 percent for China. The average first day returns for the United States were 18.4 percent. After the initial public offering, shares can be traded in public secondary markets. These markets can either be organized as an exchange or as an over-the-counter market. An exchange is a physical location where buyers and sellers come together to buy and sell securities. In an over-the-counter (OTC) market buyers and sellers can transact without meeting at a physical place.

The first trading in shares started in 1602 with the formation of the Dutch East Indies Company in Amsterdam. According to Geoffrey Poitras's *Security Analysis and Investment Strategy* (2005), the trading of stocks in the United States goes back to 1792 when twenty-one individual brokers and three firms signed the so-called Buttonwood Agreement. In the end this arrangement evolved into the New York Stock Exchange (NYSE), a title that was introduced in 1863. Over time equity markets have expanded enormously. In 1974 the market capitalization of the combined world equity markets was less than $1 trillion. According to *Focus*, the monthly overview of the World Federation of Exchanges, this total grew to $43.9 trillion at the end of June 2006. At that time, the largest stock exchange in the world, the earlier mentioned NYSE, had a market capitalization of $13.9 trillion and counted 2,205 listed companies. The second-largest exchange, the Tokyo Stock Exchange, had a market capitalization of $4.5 trillion that was accounted for by 2,377 companies. The third-largest exchange in terms of market capitalization is the National Association of Securities Dealers Automated Quotation system (NAS-

DAQ) with a market capitalization of $3.5 trillion. This is an automated quotation system that operates in the United States. Even though its market capitalization is much smaller than that of the NYSE, it has a larger number of listed companies (3,161) than the NYSE. This also illustrates the move from traditional exchanges to automated quotation systems.

Another source of equity is private equity. This is equity that is not traded in public markets. Categories of private equity include venture capital and equity for companies that are in a restructuring process. Private equity funds offer opportunities to invest large sums of money into this type of equity.

In the context of the internationalization of equity markets, firms are often cross-listed on different stock exchanges. Since the United States is the world largest capital market, a large number of firms want to list their equities there. However, this also means that the firms have to submit themselves to the very strict U.S. financial disclosure requirements. In order to avoid these requirements many firms use American Depositary Receipts (ADRs). With an ADR the firm deposits a number of its own shares with a bank in the United States. The bank then issues an ADR; this is a security with a claim on the dividends and other cash flows of the shares that are deposited with the bank. Another internationalization trend that deserves mentioning is the fact that stock markets in emerging economies have become more important. There is a large growth in equity markets in Asia (e.g., Korea and Hong Kong) as well as in Eastern Europe (e.g., Poland and Slovenia). In a number of emerging markets stocks are divided into A and B shares. In such cases the B shares have no or less voting rights than the A shares. Foreigners are then restricted to holding the B shares in order to prevent them from taking control over the firm.

SEE ALSO *Capital; Expectations; Financial Instability Hypothesis; Financial Markets; Hedging; Initial Public Offering (IPO); Liquidity Premium; Stock Exchanges; Stock Exchanges in Developing Countries; Wealth*

BIBLIOGRAPHY

Poitras, Geoffrey. 2005. *Security Analysis and Investment Strategy.* Malden, MA: Blackwell.

Ritter, Jay R. 2003. Investment Banking and Security Issuance. In *Handbook of the Economics of Finance*, eds. George M. Constantinides, Milton Harris, and Rene M. Stulz, 253–304. Amsterdam: Elsevier North-Holland.

Chris Veld

ERIKSON, ERIK
1902–1994

Erik Homburger Erikson was born on June 15, 1902, in Frankfurt, Germany. He died on May 12, 1994, in Massachusetts. As a young man, he restlessly traveled through Europe, attending art schools and subsequently teaching art and history in Vienna. Beginning in the late 1920s, while teaching children, he was trained by Anna Freud (1895–1982) as a child psychoanalyst at the Vienna Psychoanalytic Institute. There he met his future wife Joan Serson. In 1933 they immigrated to the United States, where he was offered a teaching position at Harvard Medical School. While teaching, Erikson maintained a private practice in child psychoanalysis. He later held teaching positions at the University of California at Berkeley, Yale University, the San Francisco Psychoanalytic Institute, the Austen Riggs Center in Stockbridge, Massachusetts, and the Center for Advanced Studies of the Behavioral Sciences in Stanford, California, finally returning to Harvard, where he completed his career (Coles 1970).

Erikson invigorated and expanded psychoanalytic theory with concepts he drew from Freud, biology, observations of children from several cultures, and self-observations that emerged from his psychoanalysis. As a clinician and theorist, his central contributions to human development research were to understand and illuminate, not to collect data, regarding both psychopathology and normal growth and development in varied cultural and historical contexts. Among his most important contributions was his *eight-stage lifespan* approach to personality development, elaborated in *Childhood and Society* (1950). Another was his introduction of the concept of *identity crisis*, described in *Identity: Youth and Crisis* (1968) and exemplified in *Young Man Luther* (1958). His focus on adolescence and identity crises may have been shaped in part by his own early life stressors, youthful wanderings, and lack of direction (Friedman 1999). His Danish appearance (tall, blond, blue-eyed), inherited from his unknown biological father, contrasted sharply with that of his Jewish mother and his stepfather. His Jewish peers often taunted him at school. He terminated his formal education at the age of eighteen and began his lifetime of travel and questioning. One of his best-known books that exemplifies the individual struggle with justice and reconciliation in a social and historical context is *Gandhi's Truth* (1969), for which Erikson won a Pulitzer Prize in 1970.

The underpinning for Erikson's theory of eight stages of psychosocial (ego) personality development is the biological epigenetic principle. With the proper sequence and rate of development, each stage reaches its time of greatest salience as a healthy individual becomes ready to benefit from experiences provided by significant others relevant to the particular stage crisis. The ego, the central focus of Erikson's theory, regulates and resolves the tensions between the individual's psyche and society's expectations with the goal of a predominance of the syntonic end of the continuum, such as more trust than mistrust. Each stage builds on the preceding stages and prepares one for subsequent stages. The society is initially defined as the mother figure and expands at each stage until it encompasses humankind. Providing an optimistic view of human growth and development, Erikson described the outcome of each stage as modifiable, thus affording the opportunity for growth but also weakness, based on later life experiences. The positive resolution of each stage resulted in a virtue—for trust, for example, the corresponding virtue would be hope. The eight psychosocial stages with their virtues are:

> Stage 1: Trust versus mistrust (first year) virtue: hope.
>
> Stage 2: Autonomy versus doubt/shame (one to two years) virtue: will.
>
> Stage 3: Initiative versus guilt (two to four years) virtue: purpose.
>
> Stage 4: Industry/mastery versus inferiority (five years to puberty) virtue: confidence.
>
> Stage 5: Identity versus role confusion/identity diffusion (adolescence) virtue: fidelity.
>
> Stage 6: Intimacy versus isolation (early adulthood) virtue: love.
>
> Stage 7: Generativity versus self-absorption (young and middle adulthood) virtue: care.
>
> Stage 8: Integrity versus despair (later adulthood) virtue: wisdom.

After her husband's death, Joan Serson Erikson proposed a ninth stage, old age, focused on the effort not to lose one's "indomitable core" (Davidson Films 1995).

Because Erikson's writings were at times complex and evocative, interpretation of his theory for application to research has resulted in vigorous debate. Nevertheless, all of the personality components have been studied. Identity, a major task of adolescence, has been empirically investigated the most extensively (Kroger 2007; Marcia, Waterman, Matteson, et al. 1993). The concepts of identity and identity crisis have had a major impact on the fields of psychology, sociology, literature, and history, being applied to career, ethnicity, race, sexuality, ideologies, diasporas, and so forth.

Erikson's lifework continues to be described as one of the most important contributions to the understanding of normal personality development across the lifespan. He is identified as a major factor in the framework and expansion of ego psychology. Erikson was among the first great theorists to place extensive responsibilities on the widening circle of significant others in the context of culture and history for the healthy growth of the individual.

SEE ALSO *Adolescent Psychology; Freud, Sigmund; Identity Crisis; Justice; Maturation; Personality; Psychoanalytic Theory; Psychology; Stages of Development*

BIBLIOGRAPHY

Coles, Robert. 1970. *Erik H. Erikson: The Growth of His Work.* Boston: Little, Brown.

Davidson Films. 1995. *On Old Age II: A Conversation with Joan Erikson at 92.* Davis, CA: Author.

Friedman, Lawrence J. 1999. *Identity's Architect: A Biography of Erik H. Erikson.* New York: Scribner.

Kroger, Jane. 2007. *Identity Development: Adolescence through Adulthood.* 2nd ed. Thousand Oaks, CA: Sage.

Marcia, James E., Alan S. Waterman, David R. Matteson, et al. 1993. *Ego Identity: A Handbook for Psychosocial Research.* New York: Springer-Verlag.

Sally L. Archer

EROTICISM

Although there is no accepted definition of *eroticism*, it is understood in this entry to describe the focus of an individual's sexual arousal pattern. It differs from *erotica* (the story, picture, or other media), which depicts and appeals to someone's eroticism. A different perspective defines eroticism as a component of sexuality involving a focus on pleasure and the heightening of arousal for its own sake (Kleinplatz 1996).

It is said that anything can be and everything has been eroticized. The subject of an eroticism can be specific or general, stable or fluid over time, and necessary, preferred, or irrelevant for a satisfactory sexual response. The intensity and importance of an eroticism can and does change over time. Sometimes those changes are substantive, sometimes minimal. Eroticisms are idiosyncratic; what one person finds extremely erotic is only somewhat arousing to the next, neutral to another, boring to someone else, and disgusting to the last person. Having an eroticism does not imply necessarily an interest in acting it out; fantasy can be sufficient. Sexual interests may affect each other; an interest in feet, for example, can lead to an interest in shoes. Additionally, a shoe eroticism may be expressed differently depending on sexual orientation (e.g., work boots for a homosexual man and high heels for a heterosexual man).

Every society attempts to restrict the sexual behavior of its members, even though they are usually unsuccessful. The control methods include making the act (or even a depiction of the act) a crime, immoral, a violation of religious teachings, or pathognomonic of an illness. Individuals who flout the societal mores are subject to imprisonment, shunning, eternal damnation, medical or surgical interventions, involuntary hospitalization, and civil penalties. Individuals have been imprisoned or disowned and have lost jobs, inheritances, security clearances, custody of their children, their standing in the community, and their marriages for violating these mores. This can involve admitting an interest in, promoting acceptance of, distributing or creating depictions of, or engaging in the proscribed acts.

Societal attempts to control an eroticism often include trying to censor the erotica, now labeled as indecent or obscene, that depict that eroticism. What legally constitutes obscenity continues to be debated extensively; it varies from society to society, within each society, and changes over time. What was once accepted can become proscribed and what was proscribed can become accepted.

A basic and unanswered question is how specific eroticisms develop and how many different developmental mechanisms exist. Other important social science questions include: What is the importance of having eroticisms? Why does every society try to control eroticisms and fail? How can eroticisms be changed or influenced? What is the relationship between sexual orientation and eroticism? How do the eroticisms of men and women differ?

There is great debate among both professionals and the public concerning the effect of exposure to sexually explicit material on one's eroticism or sexual behavior. We know eroticisms can evolve or change over time, but psychotherapy has been ineffective in directing those changes purposefully. Although controversial, it is improbable that exposure to erotica has any significant or lasting effect on one's sexual interests, or they would be easy to change. It is more probable that exposure allows individuals to recognize the nature of their own eroticism. Additionally, there is great concern about the effects of erotica on minors. Some believe that the material will provoke the minor to engage in the depicted sexual activity or incorporate it into a new eroticism; others suggest that lack of exposure stymies sex rehearsal play, which eventuates in adult sexual dysfunction or other sexual concerns.

Although rare, there are people who have no eroticism. These individuals often present with inhibited sexual desire, arousal difficulties, indifference to, or avoidance of sex. Nevertheless, on further evaluation they are quite capable of a "normal" sexual response; they just have nothing upon which to focus sexually.

Recognition of one's eroticisms enhances an individual's sex life, can enrich a couple's sex interactions, helps individuals connect with others who share their eroticisms, and promotes a feeling of completeness as a person.

BIBLIOGRAPHY

Kleinplatz, Peggy J. 1996. The Erotic Encounter. *Journal of Humanistic Psychology* 36 (3): 105–123.

Charles Moser

ERROR, SPECIFICATION

SEE *Specification Error.*

ERROR-CORRECTION MECHANISMS

Consider an econometric model of a dynamic relationship between a variable y_t and explanatory variables $x_1, \ldots, x_{kt}$, taking the form

$$
\begin{aligned}
y_t = \beta_0 & \\
& + \beta_{11}x_{1t} + \cdots + \beta_{1k}x_{kt} \\
& + \beta_{21}x_{1,\,t-1} + \cdots + \beta_{2k}x_{k,\,t-1} \\
& + \beta_3 y_{t-1} + u_t
\end{aligned} \tag{1}
$$

where u_t is a random error term. An alternative representation of this model is

$$
\begin{aligned}
\Delta y_t = \gamma_0 & \\
& + \Delta\gamma_{11}\Delta x_{1t} + \cdots + \gamma_{1k}\Delta x_{kt} \\
& + \gamma_2 (y_{t-1} - \delta_1 x_{1,\,t-1} - \cdots - \delta_k x_{k,\,t-1}) + u_t
\end{aligned} \tag{2}
$$

where $\Delta y_t = y_t - y_{t-1}$ and $\Delta x_{it} = x_{it} - x_{i,\,t-1}$ for $i = 1, \ldots, k$, and the relationships between the coefficients are $\gamma_0 = \beta_0$, $\gamma_{1i} = \beta_{1i}$, $\gamma_2 = \beta_3 - 1$, and $\delta_i = (\beta_{1i} + \beta_{2i})/(1 - \beta_3)$. Equation (1) is sometimes called the autoregressive distributed lag (ARDL) representation, while (2) is the error correction mechanism (ECM) representation. Generalizations to higher orders of lag are easily obtained. The ECM representation has the attractive features of representing an economic agent's decision in terms of a rule-of-thumb response to current changes, according to parameters γ_1, and corrections to deviations from a desired long-run equilibrium relation with parameters δ_i. For this reason the acronym ECM is sometimes taken to stand for equilibrium correction mechanism. Equation has the disadvantage of being nonlinear in parameters, so

that estimation and inference are less straightforward than in the case of equation.

The ECM form was first proposed by Denis Sargan (1924–1996) for a model of wages and prices (Sargan 1964). It was subsequently popularized by the work of David Hendry and others in the context of modeling applications in macroeconomics, such as the consumption function and the demand for money. The seminal contribution is J. E. H. Davidson, D. F. Hendry, F. Srba, and J. S. Yeo (1978), commonly referred to in the literature as DHSY.

The approach later acquired special prominence due to the work of Clive W. J. Granger, who independently explored the implications of modeling economic time series as integrated (I(1)) processes; in other words, processes generated as the partial sums of stationary, weakly dependent increments. (A random walk is a simple example.) This type of model, also called a stochastic trend model, describes many series observed in economics and finance. If in the driving processes $x_1, \ldots, x_{kt}$ are I(1), and $\gamma_2 < 0$, then $y_t \sim \text{I}(1)$ also, but

$$
z_t = y_t - \delta_1 x_{1t} - \cdots - \delta_k x_{kt} \tag{3}
$$

is I(0) (i.e., a stationary, weakly dependent process). The variables are then said to be cointegrated and z_t is called the cointegrating residual. Cointegration (i.e., combining the twin modeling concepts of stochastic trend representations for economic series and cointegrated relations characterizing long-run interactions over the economic cycle) has been a profoundly influential idea in macroeconomics, earning Robert F. Engle and Granger (1987) the Nobel Prize for economics in 2003.

In practice, such models are often generalized to a system of dynamic equations, explaining several variables in terms of a common set of cointegrating relations. In reduced form the resulting models are called vector error correction models (VECMs) or reduced rank vector autoregressions (VARs). Following the work of Søren Johansen, a closed VECM for an m-vector of variables x_t is commonly represented in matrix notation as

$$
\begin{aligned}
\Delta x_t = & \\
& \Gamma_0 + \Gamma_1 \Delta x_{t-1} + \cdots + \Gamma_k \Delta x_{t-k} + \alpha\beta' x_{t-1} + u_t \\
& (m \times 1)
\end{aligned} \tag{4}
$$

where $z_t = \beta' x_t$ ($s \times 1$) is the vector of cointegrating residuals. The rank of the $m \times s$ matrices β and α is called the cointegrating rank of the system. In a cointegrated system the inequalities $0 < s < m$ must hold. The Granger representation theorem states that a linear dynamic model generates cointegrating relations if and only if it has a VECM representation.

SEE ALSO *Cointegration; Lags, Distributed; Least Squares, Two-Stage*

BIBLIOGRAPHY

Davidson, J. E. H., D. F. Hendry, F. Srba, and J. S. Yeo. 1978. Econometric Modelling of the Aggregate Time-Series Relationship between Consumers' Expenditure and Income in the United Kingdom. *Economic Journal* 88: 661–692.

Engle, Robert F., and Clive W. J. Granger. 1987. Cointegration and Error Correction: Representation, Estimation, and Testing. *Econometrica* 55 (2): 251–276.

Johansen, Søren. 1988. Statistical Analysis of Cointegrating Vectors. *Journal of Economic Dynamics and Control* 12: 231–254.

Nelson, Charles R., and Charles I. Plosser. 1982. Trends and Random Walks in Macroeconomic Time Series: Some Evidence and Implications. *Journal of Monetary Economics* 10: 139–162.

Sargan, J. D. 1964. Wages and Prices in the United Kingdom: A Study in Econometric Methodology (with Discussion). In *Econometric Analysis for National Economic Planning*. Vol. 16 of *Colston Papers*, eds. Peter Edward Hart, Gordon Mills, and John King Whitaker, 25–63. London: Butterworth.

James Davidson

ERROR TERM, IN REGRESSION

SEE *Generalized Least Squares.*

ERROR TERMS

SEE *Residuals.*

ERRORS, STANDARD

Reports of the values of sample statistics (e.g., means, or regression coefficients) are often accompanied by reports of the "estimated standard error." A statistic is simply an index or description of some characteristic of the distribution of scores on a variable in a sample. The "standard error" associated with the statistic is an index of how much one might expect the value of the statistic to vary from one sample to another. The estimated standard error of a sample statistic is used to provide information about the reliability or likely accuracy of the sample statistic as an estimate of the population parameter.

For example, the 1,514 adults responding to the *General Social Survey* (National Opinion Research Center

2006) for 1991 reported that their average age was 45.63 years. Along with this statistic, a "standard error" of .458 was reported. This suggests that if we were to draw another sample (of the same size, using the same methods) and to calculate the mean age again, we might expect the result to differ by about .458 years from that in our first sample.

DEFINITION

Formally, the *standard error* of a statistic is the standard deviation of the sampling distribution of that statistic. Most texts in estimation theory in statistics contain detailed elaborations (e.g., Kmenta 1986, chapter 6). Some elaboration in less formal terms, however, may be helpful.

When we select a probability sample of cases from a population, collect data, and calculate the value of some statistic (e.g., the mean score on the variable age), we are using the sample statistic to estimate the mean of the whole population (the population parameter). If we were to draw additional samples and calculate the mean each time, we would expect the values of these sample means to vary because different cases will be included in each sample. The random variation of the value of a statistic from one sample to another is termed the *sampling variability* of the statistic.

Imagine that we collected the values of a statistic from a very large number of independent samples from the same population, and arrayed these values in a distribution. This distribution of the values of a statistic from repeated samples is termed the *sampling distribution* of that statistic. The statistic (e.g., average age) will sometimes be somewhat lower than the average of all samples, and sometimes higher. We can summarize how much any one sample is likely to differ from the average of all samples by calculating the standard deviation of sampling distribution. This value is the standard error; it is the average amount by which the value of the statistic in any one sample differs from the average value of the statistic across all possible samples.

USES OF THE STANDARD ERROR

The estimated standard error of a statistic has two primary uses. First, the standard error is used to construct confidence intervals; second, the standard error is used to conduct hypothesis tests for "statistical significance."

In the example above, the mean age of persons in the sample was 45.63 years. The estimated standard error of this statistic was .458 years. Most observers would conclude that our estimate of the population age is fairly accurate—that is, if we drew another sample, it would be expected to differ very little from the current one. On average, the differences between samples will be less than one-half year of age (.458 years).

It has been proven that the sampling distribution of sample means has a normal or Gaussian shape. Because this is true, we can describe the reliability of the sample estimate with a confidence interval. In the case of our example, the "95 percent confidence interval" is equal to the value of the sample statistic (45.63) plus or minus 1.96*.458 (the standard error). That is: 95 percent of all possible samples will report a value of the mean age between 44.73 years and 46.52 years. Confidence intervals are a common way of summarizing the reliability of inferences about population parameters on the basis of sample statistics. Large standard errors indicate low reliability (wide confidence intervals); small standard errors indicate high reliability (narrow confidence intervals).

Standard errors are also used in the process of "hypothesis testing" to determine "statistical significance." In hypothesis testing, we propose a "null" hypothesis about the true value of a population parameter (e.g., a mean). We then calculate a "test statistic" that is used to determine how likely the sample result actually observed is, if the null hypothesis is true. Test statistics usually take the general form of: ((value observed in sample − value proposed by the null hypothesis) / standard error). Our decision about whether a sample result is likely, assuming that the null hypothesis is true, is based on the size of the observed difference of the sample from the hypothesis relative to sampling variability—summarized by the standard error.

ESTIMATING STANDARD ERRORS

Most reports will show the "standard error" as "estimated" (even if they do not use this terminology, the values reported for the standard errors are probably estimates). When we conduct a study, we usually collect information from only one sample. To directly calculate the sampling distribution and standard error, we would need to collect all possible samples. Hence, we rarely know the actual value of the standard error—it is itself an estimate.

Statistical theory and research has provided a number of standard formulae for estimates of standard errors for many commonly used statistics (e.g., means, proportions, many measures of association). These formulae use the information from a single sample to estimate the standard error. For example, the common estimator of the standard error of a sample mean is the sample standard deviation divided by the square root of the sample size. When computer programs calculate and print standard errors, calculate confidence intervals, and perform hypothesis tests, they are usually relying on these standard formulae.

The standard formulae, however, assume that the observed sample is a simple random one. If this is not the case, the estimates may be wrong. If the actual sampling methodology used involves clustering, estimated standard errors by the standard formulae may be too small. Consequently, we may reach incorrect conclusions that our estimates are more reliable than they actually are, or that null hypotheses may be rejected when they should not be. If the sampling methodology actually used involves stratification, estimated standard errors by the standard formulae may be too small. Consequently, we may think our point estimates of population parameters are less reliable than they actually are; we may fail to reject null hypotheses that are, in fact, false.

Where probability sampling designs are not simple random, there are several alternative approaches to estimating standard errors. For some complex survey designs, more complex formulae are available, as, for example, in the statistical packages Stata (Stata Corporation 2006) and Sudaan (Research Triangle Institute 2006). In other cases, "bootstrap" and "jackknife" methods may be used (Efron and Tibshirani 1993).

Bootstrap methods draw large numbers of samples of size N from the current sample, but with replacement. Bootstrap samples are the same size as the original sample, but contain "duplicate" observations. For each of a very large number of samples (1,000 to 10,000), the statistic of interest is calculated. These estimates are then used to construct the sampling distribution, from which the standard error is estimated. Large sample sizes are required for bootstrap methods.

Jackknife estimators divide the current sample into many random samples that are smaller than the full sample, but are drawn without replacement. Large numbers of samples are selected, and the statistic of interest is calculated for each sample. This then allows the calculation of the sampling distribution and the estimated standard error.

SEE ALSO *Logistic Regression; Methods, Quantitative*

BIBLIOGRAPHY

Efron, Bradley, and Robert J. Tibshirani. 1993. *An Introduction to the Bootstrap*. Monographs on Statistics and Applied Probability, no. 57. London: Chapman and Hall.

Kmenta, Jan. 1986. *Elements of Econometrics*. 2nd ed. New York: Macmillan.

National Opinion Research Center. 2006. General Social Survey Home Page. http://www.norc.org/projects/gensoc.asp.

Research Triangle Institute. 2006. Sudaan Home Page. http://www.rti.org/sudaan.

Stata Corporation. 2006. Stata Home Page. http://www.stata.com.

Robert Hanneman

ERRORS IN VARIABLES

SEE *Measurement Error.*

ESKIMOS

SEE *Inuit.*

ESSENTIALISM

Essentialism is the idea that members of certain categories have an underlying, unchanging property or attribute (essence) that determines identity and causes outward behavior and appearance. An essentialist account of gender, for example, holds that differences between males and females are determined by fixed, inherent features of those individuals. The doctrine of essentialism is widespread in practice, underlying many approaches (both historical and current) in the biological sciences, the social sciences, and cultural studies. Essentialist ideas underlie much lay skepticism toward biological evolution; such ideas saturate discussions of race and gender as well as of ethnicity and nationality. In gender studies, essentialism has been important as a focus of criticism and, less often, as an explanatory strategy (e.g., the notion of a "gay gene").

TYPES OF ESSENTIALISM

Essentialism may be divided into three types: sortal, causal, and ideal. The *sortal essence* is the set of defining characteristics that all and only members of a category share. This notion of essence is captured in Aristotle's distinction between essential and accidental properties. For example, on this view the essence of a mother would be the property of having given birth to a person (rather than an accidental property, such as baking cookies). In effect, this characterization is a restatement of the classical view of concepts: Meaning (or identity) is supplied by a set of necessary and sufficient features that determine whether an entity does or does not belong in a category. However, the viability of this account has been called into question by psychological research on human concepts. The *causal essence* is the entity or quality that causes other category-typical properties to emerge and be sustained, and that confers identity. The causal essence is used to explain the observable properties of category members. Whereas the sortal essence could apply to any entity, the causal essence applies only to entities for which inherent, hidden properties determine observable qualities. For example, the

causal essence of water may be something like H_2O, which is responsible for various observable properties that water has. Thus, the cluster of properties "odorless, tasteless, and colorless" is not a causal essence of water, despite being true of all members of the category, because the properties have no direct causal force on other properties.

The *ideal essence* has no actual instantiation in the world. For example, on this view the essence of "justice" is some abstract quality that is imperfectly realized in real-world instances of people performing just deeds. None of these just deeds perfectly embodies "justice," but each reflects some aspect of it. Plato's cave allegory (in *The Republic*), in which what we see of the world are mere shadows of what is real and true, exemplifies this view. The ideal essence thus contrasts with both the sortal and the causal essences. There are relatively little empirical data available on ideal essences in human reasoning.

CRITICISMS OF ESSENTIALISM

Essentialism is often implicit. Theorists rarely self-identify as essentialist; more often, a position is characterized as "essentialist" by others, typically as a form of criticism. Essentialist indications include a cluster of separable ideas—for example, treating properties as genetically rather than socially determined, assuming that properties are immutable, or assuming that a category captures a wealth of nonobvious properties, thereby having the potential to generate many novel inferences (e.g., Arthur R. Jensen's arguments in his 1969 article regarding racial differences in IQ). Any of these assumptions could be considered evidence for an essentialist framework.

In the social sciences, essentialist accounts are highly controversial. Essentialist accounts of race, ethnicity, or gender have been criticized for reducing complex, historically contingent effects to fixed and inherent properties of individuals. Anti-essentialist accounts emphasize the importance of social context, environmental factors, and structural factors (including economics and class). Such accounts are often grouped together under the heading *social* (or *cultural* or *discursive*) *constructionism*; as Laura Lee Downs noted in her 1993 article, at their best they provide detailed accounts of the social reproduction of gender, ethnic, and racial categories, and at their worst slide into voluntarism. An important analytic strategy, put forward by Fredrik Barth in 1969 and Judith Irvine and Susan Gal in 2000, has been to eschew an account of the categories of social groups in favor of examining the social and cultural conditions by which they are differentiated.

Racial categories illustrate the perils and shortcomings of essentialism. Although race is often essentialized, anthropologists and biologists widely agree that race has no essence. The superficial physical dimensions along which people vary (such as skin color or hair texture) do not map neatly onto racial groupings. Observable human differences also do not form correlated feature clusters. Skin color is not predictive of "deep" causal features (such as gene frequencies for anything other than skin color). There is no gene for race as it is commonly understood.

Culture frequently serves as a stand-in for *race* in sortal essentialist frameworks, as it did in South Africa under the apartheid regime. The doctrine of ethnic primordialism (that ethnicities are ancient and natural) was a popular explanatory device in the 1950s and 1960s to account for apparent ethnic and regional fissures in the developing world. It returned after the fall of the Berlin wall to account for the instability of former socialist republics, most dramatically in Yugoslavia, and remains a powerful force in international relations despite the availability of nuanced, nonessentialist explanatory accounts.

Essentialism is also criticized for its political and social costs, in particular for encouraging and justifying stereotyping of social categories (including race, gender, and sexual orientation), and perpetuating the assumption that artificial distinctions (such as caste or class) are natural, inevitable, and fixed. Nonetheless, some feminists and minorities appropriate essentialism for their own group(s)—at least temporarily—for political purposes. *Strategic essentialism*, Gayatri Spivak's term from her 1985 study, can devolve into an embrace of essentialism, with the argument that essential differences are deserving of celebration. Other theorists, while recognizing many of the problems of essentialism characterized above, have proposed that at least some tenets of essentialism (e.g., that categories may have an underlying basis) are rooted in real-world structure.

However, criticisms of essentialism extend to biological species as well. In the case of biological species, essentialism implies that each species is fixed and immutable, thus leading Ernst Mayr to note, "It took more than two thousand years for biology, under the influence of Darwin, to escape the paralyzing grip of essentialism" (1982, p. 87). An additional concern, for biological as well as social categories, is that essentialism assumes that the essence is a property of each individual organism. In contrast, according to evolutionary theory, species cannot be characterized in terms of properties of individual members but rather in terms of properties of the population. Elliott Sober (1994) distinguishes between "constituent definitions" (in which groups are defined in terms of characteristics of the individual organisms that make up the group) and "population thinking" (in which groups need to be understood in terms of characteristics of the larger group; e.g., interbreeding populations, in the case of species). Sober suggests there is no essence for biological species—let alone groupings of people, such as races—at a surface level or even at a genetic level.

PSYCHOLOGICAL ESSENTIALISM

Some psychologists, such as Susan A. Gelman in her 2003 book and Douglas Medin in his 1989 article, have proposed that (causal) essentialism is a cognitive bias (*psychological essentialism*) found cross-culturally and even in early childhood, with important implications for a range of human behaviors and judgments: category-based inductive inferences, judgments of constancy over time, and stereotyping. Psychological essentialism requires no specialized knowledge, as people may possess what Medin calls an "essence placeholder" for a category, without knowing what the essence is. Preschool children expect category members to share nonobvious similarities, even in the face of obvious dissimilarities. For example, on learning that an atypical exemplar is a member of a category (e.g., that a penguin is a bird), children and adults draw inferences from typical instances that they apply to the atypical member (e.g., they infer that penguins build nests, like other birds). Young children judge nonvisible internal parts to be especially crucial to the identity and functioning of an item. Children also treat category membership as stable and unchanging over transformations such as costumes, growth, metamorphosis, or changing environmental conditions. Therefore, essentialism as a theoretical construct may emerge from fundamental psychological predispositions.

SEE ALSO *Blackness; Cultural Studies; Darwin, Charles; Gender; Groups; Identity; Intergroup Relations; Meaning; Race; Sexual Orientation, Determinants of; Sexual Orientation, Social and Economic Consequences; Social Science; Stereotypes; Whiteness*

BIBLIOGRAPHY

Aristotle. 1924. *Metaphysics.* Oxford, U.K.: Clarendon.

Barth, Fredrik, ed. 1969. *Ethnic Groups and Boundaries: The Social Organization of Culture Difference.* Boston: Little Brown.

Downs, Laura Lee. 1993. If "Woman" Is Just an Empty Category, Then Why Am I Afraid to Walk Alone at Night? *Comparative Studies in Society and History* 35: 414–437.

Gelman, Susan A. 2003. *The Essential Child: Origins of Essentialism in Everyday Thought.* Oxford, U.K., and New York: Oxford University Press.

Irvine, Judith, and Susan Gal. 2000. Language Ideology and Linguistic Differentiation. In *Regimes of Language: Ideologies, Polities, and Identities,* ed. Paul V. Kroskrity, 35–83. Santa Fe, NM: School of American Research Press.

Jensen, Arthur R. 1969. How Much Can We Boost I.Q. and Scholastic Achievement? *Harvard Educational Review* 33: 1–123.

Mayr, Ernst. 1982. *The Growth of Biological Thought: Diversity, Evolution, and Inheritance.* Cambridge, MA: Belknap.

Medin, Douglas. 1989. Concepts and Conceptual Structure. *American Psychologist* 44: 1469–1481.

Sober, Elliott. 1994. *From a Biological Point of View: Essays in Evolutionary Philosophy.* Cambridge, U.K., and New York: Cambridge University Press.

Spivak, Gayatri. 1985. Subaltern Studies: Deconstructing Historiography. In *Subaltern Studies: Writings on South Asian History and Society* IV, ed. Ranajit Guha, 330–363. Delhi: Oxford University Press.

Strevens, Michael. 2000. The Essentialist Aspect of Naive Theories. *Cognition* 74: 149–175.

Templeton, Alan R. 1998. Human Races: A Genetic and Evolutionary Perspective. *American Anthropologist* 100: 632–650.

Susan A. Gelman
Bruce Mannheim

ETHICS

Ethics in the social sciences can be best understood by distinguishing normative ethics from metaethics. Normative ethics derives from the practical purpose of guiding how we ought to live and inquires into the proper guidelines of conduct for a responsible human being. Metaethics asks what ethics is, how it can be distinguished from other forms of human practice, and where it finds its proper place. Twentieth-century social science was dominated by normative ethical questions: questions about what ethical guidelines a professional social scientist should adopt. Normative ethics dominated the discussion because social scientists generally took the model of professional ethics—institutionalized in the codes of conduct and peer review committees of associations of (among others) legal or medical practitioners—for granted. This preoccupation with professionalist models reduced social scientists' interest in metaethics and thus their capacity to understand what ethics is. Since the 1970s, however, processes of "deprofessionalization" or "horizontalization" have reduced the independence of professional practitioners, giving rise to new forms of institutionalizing ethics and increasing the demand and opportunity for metaethical reflection.

In the context of the rise of the welfare state's demand for expertise, sociologists, in particular, propounded a folk ideology of professionalism, and its model of ethics—of safeguarding the quality of professional service by codes of conduct administered, in the case of conflict, by a committee of peers—was adopted by social scientists from the 1950s onward. Two famous cases in social psychology—one in which religious informants seemed misinformed about researchers' own beliefs (Smith 1957), and another where experimental subjects appeared to be put under intolerable stress (Milgram 1964)—became paradigmatic in sensitizing many social scientists to the possible abuse

of people researched. In addition, anthropologists and sociologists were worried by the use of research for U.S. counterinsurgency operations in Latin America and Southeast Asia, and made the interests of people researched paramount in their first ethical codes. This resulted in guidelines of conduct that focused predominantly on the responsibility to avoid doing unnecessary harm to research subjects—by the experimental situation itself, by secret or clandestine research, or by insufficiently protecting the research subjects' privacy. When institutionalized by social scientific associations around 1970, such codes and committees were primarily seen as a prerogative of professionals, whose expertise allowed them to speak for or interpret the interests of "clients." This assumption of professional autonomy remains dominant today in many ways. Most social scientists think that an ethical code is a necessary and self-evident element of their profession, despite the fact that they managed without codes for half a century or more.

In society at large, however, professional autonomy decreased by changing practices of professional control. In the field of ethics, this was particularly manifested by the increasing insistence on the right to "informed consent" of people researched, adopted from the medical profession since the mid-1960s. If "informed consent" already "horizontalized" the professional expert's relationship to some of his audiences, the increasing employment of social scientists outside the university system since the late 1970s forced them to be more explicitly responsible to private employers and sponsors as well. While some protested this dual loss of professional autonomy, others embraced the new ethics of accountability to sponsors and people researched—although neither group always knew how "accountability" was tied to the spread of neoliberal market models and auditing techniques throughout the academic world.

These developments implied new institutionalizations of ethical practice: From the 1980s onward, codes of conduct and "good practice" mushroomed, but now increasingly produced by universities or funding agencies rather than professional associations. These institutions' internal review boards introduced ethical audits, for example, at the level of the grant application, thus increasing the possibility of external control of practitioners by ethical codification (while previously, codes were aimed at safeguarding the practitioners' professional autonomy). Meanwhile, professional social science associations reduced their involvement in ethical arbitration (partly because, unlike the medical or legal professions, they could not effectively sanction violations of their codes) and fell back more insistently on the role of the ethical code in professional public relations and education. Surprisingly, such pleas for an education in ethics often focus on teaching by codes rather than by the more appropriate—because more practice-oriented—casebook method.

This crisis of the professional model exacerbated existing problems with normative ethics, and especially with ethical codification. In the professional model, the ethical code presupposes a community of scholars who hold each other accountable to its guidelines, but this Enlightenment conception of social contract breaks down once infractions of these guidelines cannot be sanctioned. Moreover, when the membership of such communities is not exclusive, practitioners may find themselves subject to the rules of a multiplicity of organizations (including, of course, ordinary citizens' duties)—a situation in which most members of social scientific associations find themselves. The adoption of codes of conduct by universities and funding bodies is criticized for merely increasing the means of such institutions' internal control, while falling short of achieving its actual goal: improving academic practice. This gives rise to the metaethical question of whether one can speak of an administrative fetishization of ethical codes, and whether this distracts from academic ethical awareness, so that ethical codes reduce rather than promote ethical practice (Bauman 1993). The answer to this question is not unequivocal: the codification of good practice may be a necessary instrument to sensitize practitioners to the possibility of doing harm (there is, for example, surprisingly little agreement on the ethics of research into human genetics). Once a code is in place, however, it can perform some of the less desirable functions mentioned above.

Other recent metaethical reflections radically broaden social scientific ethics, if only because they do not restrict themselves to normative ethics and the do's and don'ts of the research relationship. Inspired by philosophers such as Michel Foucault (1926–1984) or Charles Taylor, social scientists increasingly discuss ethics as the way in which people constitute themselves—and others—as subjects, by not just considering what it is "right to do" but, more broadly, striving after "what it is good to be" (Taylor 1989, p. 3). In this way, ethics is recognized as part of the everyday technologies of the self, and therefore as a topic of social scientific study in its own right, claiming a place next to and in comparison with law, politics, or economics (among other things) in understanding human behavior. Thus, sociologists of culture can be seen to study ethics when discussing, for example, the Protestant or the romantic ethic.

The comparative study of ethics, started by the Finnish anthropologist and philosopher Edward Westermarck (1862–1939) around 1900 and only feebly followed up by anthropologists in the 1950s and 1960s, may be revived. Such studies also open up spaces for alternative models of ethics: sociocultural anthropologists and archaeologists, for example, have explored a model of open-ended ethical negotiation (Meskell and Pels 2005)—an ethics as necessary for the research relationship as it is for human behavior in general. Such explorations can also question the implicit distinction between fact and value that still often keeps the teaching of research methodology apart from the teaching of research ethics, impoverishing social science education in the process. It seems obvious that only the latter move—toward a full integration of ethics and methodology—can lead to a truly ethical social scientific practice, in which students are made aware of the situational, case-bound ethics of research from the moment they start their first training.

BIBLIOGRAPHY

Bauman, Zygmunt. 1993. *Postmodern Ethics*. Cambridge, MA: Blackwell.

Meskell, Lyn, and Peter Pels, eds. 2005. *Embedding Ethics*. New York and London: Berg.

Milgram, Stanley. 1964. Issues in the Study of Obedience: A Reply to Baumrind. *American Psychologist* 19: 848–852.

Smith, M. Brewster. 1957. Of Prophecy and Privacy: *When Prophecy Fails*, by L. Festinger, H. W. Riecken, and S. Schachter. *Contemporary Psychology* 2 (4): 89–92.

Taylor, Charles. 1989. *Sources of the Self: The Making of the Modern Identity*. Cambridge, U.K.: Cambridge University Press.

Peter Pels

ETHICS, BUSINESS

When discussing the subject of business ethics, points of view range from those who believe that ethics in business is one of the most pressing issues if companies are to ensure creditability and trust to the cynic who is of the view that the term *business ethics* is an oxymoron, a contradiction in terms, and that the concepts of *ethics* and *business* are inherently incompatible. In the early twenty-first century, the general public, fueled by the general media, is quick to seize upon ethical wrongdoing by both small and large companies and is anxious to spotlight ethical violations. In doing so, demands are also increasing for greater levels of accountability in business. The reality, therefore, is that the term *ethics*—the expectation of appropriate behavior—and *business*—the current mercantile environment—cannot be separated as one experiences increasing expectation of higher standards of ethical behavior in organizations.

FACTORS PROMOTING ETHICAL AWARENESS

The factors promoting ethical awareness in both business organizations and business education programs are varied. Societal expectations and tolerance of what constitutes appropriate business conduct have also broadened. For example, companies such as Nike and Reebok have had to fend off criticisms of sweatshop practices in their off-shore contract manufacturing facilities by posting their factory labor audits on the Fair Labor Association (FLA) Web site. Both consumer and shareholder attitudes toward an organization and its ethical profile are increasingly impacting on purchasing decisions and investment strategy. Examples are the consumer boycotts, as historically experienced by Nestlé, and also the growing popularity of ethical investment funds. Undoubtedly, media attention has been instrumental in highlighting ethical misdemeanors. The popular press has been littered with high-profile cases such as Enron, WorldCom, Parmalat, and Adelphi Communications, as well as the audit companies who appear to have been complicit in their oversight of the financial practices of those organizations. The potential cost of ethical violations is also a motivating factor for organizations to reassess their stance. Companies such as Ford, for example, have been subject to significant compensation claims in relation to endangering consumer welfare as a result of faulty tires used on the Ford Explorer.

Ethical violations, when made public, can have a damning effect on publicly listed companies, as supported by the efficient market hypothesis, which maintains that markets are very efficient in interpreting data and arriving at equilibrium prices. Share prices reflect publicly available information, and it appears that any unethical conduct that is discovered and publicized impacts the corporation and shareholders by ultimately lowering the value of a company's shares for an appreciable period of time. Similarly, for unlisted companies it is assumed that when an ethical violation is made known it will erode the trust of consumers and will ultimately be reflected in diminished sales.

The relationship between ethical behavior and company performance is intriguing. More than ninety-five empirical studies have examined the effect of the relationship between ethics and corporate social responsibility on financial performance, with the outcomes being both positive and negative. Positive relationships prevailed but it is not entirely clear whether increased ethical activity leads to increased performance or, alternatively, whether higher performance provided firms with additional resources that they could devote to social and ethical activities. Furthermore, there are varying levels of ethical engagement by organizations. The first level is one of self-protection; that is, ethical behavior is promoted in order to avoid criminal liability or additional costs. The next level is reputational awareness and the associated benefits that accrue to the organization. The final level is when an organization has an interest in being ethical because it believes it is, in fact, the right thing to do; it is the way the company does business.

MORALITY AND ETHICS

While it is tempting to think of business entities as the primary moral agent, business organizations are, in fact, commonly comprised of a number of individuals making decisions that may have an ethical dimension. These ethical dimensions could relate to environmental and social considerations, such as pollution; stakeholder interactions, for example, product liability; competitive dealings, for example, price collusion; employer obligations, for example, employee safety; or personal behavior, for example, conflict of interest, so it is important to realize that the ethical performance of an organization is a reflection of the individual behavior of its employees. What guides this behavior? Essentially, morality relates to principles of right and wrong and is comprised of numerous moral norms or standards. These moral expectations have a number of sources such as family, society, church, education, training, and even one's organization or employment. This is the intellectual base one frequently refers to when faced with an ethical dilemma (the head part). Ethics is the discipline of dealing with moral duty and obligation and might be described as the practice of morality (the actual behavior part). Business ethics is, therefore, the practice of morality as it applies to business behavior.

There is extensive scholarly debate on whether moral principles apply universally, or whether ethical judgments are relative to their context. The ethical relativists assert that there is no consistency of beliefs because moral principles are relative to individual persons and cultures, so moral standards will differ between individuals, groups, circumstances, and across time. The absolutists, however, contend that there are common moral standards upon which ethical reasoning rests and that, despite variations in ethical behavior, individuals are rooted in common moral standards. In support of the absolutists, it has been suggested that because the purpose of morality is to help make social cooperation possible, moral principles are universally necessary for that to occur.

As one witnesses the differing ethical behavior being exhibited in companies it has been suggested that there are varying levels of moral development. According to Lawrence Kohlberg's well-established stages of moral development, there are six stages of moral development that can be summarized into three levels: the preconventional level is one at which individuals are motivated by a childlike avoidance of punishment, obedience to authority, fear, and self-interest. At the conventional level, individuals are motivated by loyalty to a group or professional norms. At the highest level, postconventional, individuals have a wide view of what is right and wrong and of those who might be affected by their decisions. An individual operating at this level has broad ethical principles in place and his or her decisions are based not on the current norms of the group or standards of society, but on personal conscience grounded in these principles.

THE RESEARCH LITERATURE

Historically the literature on business ethics has been anchored in normative philosophy and can be seen to be broadly delineated into three areas: prescriptive/hortatory literature, which attempts to sermonize and instruct the business community and education in raising ethical standards; descriptive/positive literature, which is characterized by extensive empirical research into, for example, ethical attitudes of students and business personnel; and meta ethical/analytical literature, which investigates meaning and justification relating to the corporate and individual decision-making process. Naturally, the field of business ethics is readily evolving. The colloquy on business ethics is being extended with the lexicon broadening and being claimed by related terminologies such as corporate social responsibility, stakeholder management, corporate governance, sustainability, and corporate citizenship.

SEE ALSO *Corruption; Efficient Market Hypothesis; Hypothesis and Hypothesis Testing; Information, Economics of; Lying; Morality*

BIBLIOGRAPHY

Bowie, N. 2004. Relativism and the Moral Obligations of Multinational Corporations. In *Ethical Theory and Business*, eds. Tom L. Beauchamp and Norman E. Bowie, 538–544. Englewood Cliffs, NJ: Pearson Prentice Hall.

Kohlberg, L. 1969. Stage and Sequence: The Cognitive Development Approach to Socialisation. In *Handbook of Socialization Theory and Research*, ed. D.A. Goslin, 347–380. New York: Rand McNally.

Trevino, Linda K., and Katherine A. Nelson. 2004. *Managing Business Ethics: Straight Talk About How to Do it Right.* 3rd ed. Hoboken, NJ: John Wiley & Sons.

Gael M. McDonald

ETHICS IN EXPERIMENTATION

Experimentation in the social sciences, by its very nature, requires researchers to manipulate and control key aspects of the social setting so as to determine what effect, if any, these manipulations have on the people in that setting. Such studies, although unmatched in terms of their scientific yield, nonetheless raise questions of ethics: Do researchers have the moral right to conduct experiments on their fellow human beings? What practices are unacceptable and what procedures are allowable? Can standards be established to safeguard the rights of participants?

ETHICAL CONTROVERSIES AND HUMAN RESEARCH

Historically, ethical concern for the rights and well-being of participants in social science research emerged in the context of a heightened public scrutiny of all forms of research with human participants. This scrutiny resulted from the public debate surrounding a series of research projects dating back to the mid-1930s. As early as 1932, physicians in the United States, with sponsorship by the Public Health Service, began a study on the effects of untreated syphilis. This project, commonly known as the Tuskegee syphilis study, continued until 1973, even though penicillin was accepted as an effective cure for this disease in the 1940s. During World War II (1939–1945), German physicians conducted a series of appalling medical experiments in concentration camps, in which prisoners were routinely used to test the effectiveness of various procedures, with fatal results. From 1944 to 1974, U.S. researchers studied the effects of radiation poisoning by injecting people with plutonium without their consent. In the late 1950s, a drug manufacturer paid physicians to administer the drug thalidomide to patients, who were not warned that the drug was an experimental one not yet approved for general use. The drug caused birth defects when taken by pregnant women (Dunn and Chadwick 2002).

These studies raised fundamental questions about the rights of individuals and the ethical responsibilities of investigators. Physicians have long been bound by the oath of "do no harm," yet all these projects violated this principle of beneficence. Investigators denied participants basic freedoms of choice and self-determination, and they acted unjustly when they selected subjects based on prejudice and antipathy. The horrific German medical studies singled out for study Jews held illegally in Nazi concentration camps, and the Tuskegee syphilis study used disadvantaged, rural black men. These studies exploited people who society is duty-bound to protect.

Although social science research was considered relatively risk-free in comparison to these biomedical studies, Yale psychologist Stanley Milgram's 1963 study of obedience suggested that behavioral studies could also harm participants in significant ways. Milgram recruited volunteers from the local community to take part in what they thought was a study of learning. The volunteers were ordered by the experimenter to give increasingly powerful and painful electric shocks to another participant whenever he made mistakes. The other participant was, in reality, a member of the research staff who deliberately made errors during the procedure. He did not actually receive any shocks, but he feigned pain and eventually begged to be released. Milgram, by using this elaborate procedure, discovered that the majority of the people he studied obeyed the experimenter's orders, and many experienced extreme distress during the procedure. He reported that fourteen of the forty original participants were seized by fits of nervous laughter, and three displayed "full-blown, uncontrollable seizures" (Milgram 1963, p. 375).

STANDARDS AND SAFEGUARDS

Public inquiry into these cases of scientific malfeasance resulted in the promulgation of codes of conduct for experimentation with human participants. The tribunal that judged the German doctors developed the Nuremberg Code, which stresses the importance of voluntary consent, the scientific value of the procedure, and the minimization of physical and mental suffering. In 1964 the World Medical Association issued the Declaration of Helsinki to clarify the ethical boundaries between therapeutic and nontherapeutic research. The U.S. Congress, in 1974, mandated the formation of the National Commission for the Protection of Human Subjects, and this commission crafted a set of guidelines commonly called the Belmont Report. This report stresses the need for consent, the protection of vulnerable populations, and the fair treatment of all participants. Professional associations, including the American Medical Association and the American Psychological Association, have also promulgated standards of ethics for investigators, and censure those members who violate their standards.

These standards of conduct for experimental research with human participants all recognize the substantial benefits of scientific research, but require that these benefits be weighed against the risk the research creates for participants. Possible risks include invasion of participants' right to privacy, physically or psychologically harming participants, subjecting participants to public embarrassment or legal sanction, and wasting their time and money. Ethicists also suggest that the use of deception by researchers, although necessary in order to gain valid data about their spontaneous reactions to social stimuli, may engender distrust and contribute to the dehumanization of research participants. Although these risks are offset, in part, by specific benefits for participants (such as monetary payment, educational gains, increased self-understanding, and self-approbation for having helped further scientific research), the key benefits are the contribution

of the work to society and scientific knowledge. When risks to subjects are too great, researchers must use low-risk alternatives, such as nonexperimental procedures or simulations.

Ethical guidelines also require that participants be fully informed about the procedures and their risks, and that their understanding of these risks be documented in some way. In most laboratory experiments, the researcher provides participants with a brief but accurate description of their duties in the research and then gives them a choice to participate or not. This practice is known as *informed consent*, and it serves to remind subjects that they can terminate their participation in the study at any time if they choose to do so. In cases where the possibility of harm is negligible, then the requirement for consent can be waived, as it also would be when documentation of consent will harm participants by making them identifiable. If individuals are unable to provide full consent, because their autonomy as individuals is limited, then they must be afforded special protections. Children, for example, cannot fully understand or provide consent, and their parents' consent is required. Similarly, institutionalized individuals, such as prisoners, can only take part in research if they are completely uncoerced and if the risks posed by the study are minimal.

Most researchers also fully clarify the hypotheses once the study is over. This phase of the research process is typically known as *debriefing*, and it involves reviewing the hypotheses with participants, answering any questions, and removing any harmful effects of the experience. Such a debriefing phase is particularly critical when the investigator did not provide the participants with a full disclosure of the purposes of the study during the consent process—as is often the case when participants are deceived about the study's actual hypotheses or when research is conducted in a naturalistic field setting. Researchers are also enjoined to establish and follow data and safety monitoring procedures. The well-being of their participants must be monitored at all times, and if any unforeseen negative consequences of the study arise, the researcher must intervene and minimize those risks. The data generated by the research process must also be safeguarded, particularly when the research deals with sensitive, personal topics or the disclosure of the participants' responses would subject them to legal prosecution or social harm.

In many research settings, investigators must also submit their research plans to impartial reviewers before they carry out their research. Often referred to as *institutional review boards* (IRBs), these panels ensure that researchers are complying with required standards for research involving human participants, including the required elements of informed consent, protection of privacy, and minimization of all risks. Such panels would be responsible for reviewing, for example, deception studies: those research projects in which the participants are not informed of the actual purposes of the study in advance. Researchers request a waiver of the usual requirement for complete and accurate informed consent only in rare cases when they feel that participants would respond differently if they were fully informed of the study's purposes, and when they can provide clear evidence that the study will not harm participants in any way.

ETHICS AND SCIENCE

Social scientists, as members of the scientific community, strive to expand the knowledge of human behavior and apply that understanding for the enrichment of society and its members. But social scientists, as members of the larger social community, are also bound by norms that define what actions are considered moral and what actions are considered immoral. Researchers, in their quest for knowledge, cannot sacrifice the welfare of their participants in the name of maximizing the power of their research designs. The ethics guidelines that have emerged ensure that researchers' studies will be both scientifically valid and ethically acceptable.

SEE ALSO *Bioethics; Experiments, Human; Institutional Review Board; Milgram, Stanley; Tuskegee Syphilis Study*

BIBLIOGRAPHY

Dunn, Cynthia M., and Gary Chadwick. 2002. *Protecting Study Volunteers in Research: A Manuel for Investigative Sites.* 2nd ed. Boston: CenterWatch.

Milgram, Stanley. 1963. Behavioral Study of Obedience. *Journal of Abnormal and Social Psychology* 67 (4): 371–378.

Donelson R. Forsyth